HANDBOOK TO
THE CHURCH HYMNARY
With Supplement

HANDBOOK TO
THE CHURCH HYMNARY
With Supplement

EDITED BY

The Rev. Professor JAMES MOFFATT
D.D., D.LITT., LL.D.

AND

The Rev. MILLAR PATRICK
D.D.

OXFORD UNIVERSITY PRESS
LONDON : HUMPHREY MILFORD
1935

OXFORD
UNIVERSITY PRESS
AMEN HOUSE, E.C. 4
London Edinburgh Glasgow
New York Toronto Melbourne
Capetown Bombay Calcutta
Madras Shanghai
HUMPHREY MILFORD
PUBLISHER TO THE
UNIVERSITY

CONTENTS

v

PRINCIPAL AUTHORITIES CONSULTED

Julian, *Dictionary of Hymnology* (Revised Edition, 1915).

Zahn, Johannes, *Die Melodien der deutschen Evangelischen Kirchenlieder* (6 vols., 1889–93).

Bäumker, Wilhelm, *Das Katholische Deutsche Kirchenlied in seinen Singweisen* (3 vols., 1883–91).

Douen, O., *Clément Marot et le Psautier Huguenot* (2 vols., 1878–9).

Grove, *Dictionary of Music* (1905).

Fétis, *Biographie Universelle des Musiciens* (1860–5).

Brown and Stratton, *British Musical Biography* (1897).

Hymns Ancient and Modern, Historical Edition (1909).

Bumpus, John S., *History of English Cathedral Music*.

Dictionary of National Biography,

Eitner, R., *Biographisch-Bibliographisches Quellen-Lexicon Musiker und Musikgelehrten* (1900).

Love, James, *Scottish Church Music* (1891).

Cowan and Love, *The Music of the Church Hymnary* (1901).

Lightwood, James T., *Hymn Tunes and their Story* (1905).

The Musical Times.

PREFACE

THE object of this Handbook is to explain, as far as is possible and needful, the words and music of every hymn in *The Church Hymnary*. All that you require is a copy of the *Hymnary* itself.

But, before opening the *Hymnary*, glance at the device upon the cover. While the hymns themselves are drawn from many churches, in a truly catholic spirit, the emblem on the cover is designed to recall the symbols of the various Presbyterian churches which have co-operated in the preparation of the book. The outer ring, or oval aureole, represents the Church, the Bride of Christ, and the motto, 'Nec tamen consumebatur', is the historical comment upon the Burning Bush as the symbol of Presbyterianism. The Cross of St. Andrew, the patron saint of Scotland, is often employed also, like the Burning Bush, as an emblem of Churches within the Presbyterian Communion and Alliance. The Dove with the Olive Branch, symbolizing the spread of the gospel of peace, was the emblem of the former United Presbyterian Church of Scotland, whilst the Dove over the open Bible is the symbol belonging to the Presbyterian Church of Wales, the Dove being a representation of the Holy Spirit. The Presbyterian Church of England continues to employ the Burning Bush with the open Bible, and in the Irish Presbyterian Church the Burning Bush has 'ardens sed virens' as its motto. The stars at the top of the device are the Stars of the Southern Cross, symbolizing the Churches south of the equator.

So much for the outside of the *Hymnary*. Open it for any hymn which you may desire to study, and you have only to turn to its number in this Handbook; then, should you desire fuller information about the author or the composer, pass on to the Biographical and Historical Notes. The indexes will offer you further aid in choosing or in tracking hymns. In this way you discover what you may need to know about the time when a hymn was written or a tune composed, about its author, or about the origin of the words or the music in some cases, perhaps a little also about the use of the hymn in the work of the Church or in the lives of individual Christians. You may miss some pretty stories in this connexion, but this omission is deliberate. A vast amount of mythology has grown up round some well-known hymns. Tales have been circulated which have no foundation in fact, and these pious fancies have been ruthlessly swept away from the pages of this book. We have taken some pains to verify the traditional matter in the case of words and music, and although there are gaps in the history of some writers and of some hymns, what is presented here is on the whole reliable. If there is less than you may expect occasionally, at least there is nothing more than what rests on what appears to us to be fairly certain evidence. In some cases research has failed to add almost anything to what has been already ascertained. Much still remains obscure and uncertain, especially with regard to some of the medieval hymns and melodies. But we hope that our inquiries have provided secure ground for such statements as we have ventured to make.

The pages of the Handbook will help to explain and to some extent justify the procedure of the Revision Committee in dealing with the texts before them. If the form of a tune is unfamiliar, or if the wording of a hymn is not that to which you have been accustomed, the notes will indicate why the alteration has been made, or at any rate they will show candidly what the alterations are. We have thus sought to meet the demands of the hymnologist or of the expert musician, who requires some details about the technical structure of the *Hymnary*.

But we have also had in mind those who do not possess any book of reference, and the ordinary person who, in the pulpit or in the class-room, desires to use the *Hymnary* intelligently, as well as the individual Christian who seeks devotional aid. He may be interested in the ways by which a given hymn has reached its present form, for example. Probably he will admit after reading the account of such hymns as, say, 140 or 156 or 196 or 312 or 413 or 533, that some alterations in the original text are justified ; furthermore, the notes on such hymns as 4 and 61 and 511 will enable him to sing them with more intelligence. 'I will sing with the spirit', says the Apostle, 'and I will sing with the understanding also.' It is indeed possible to sing a hymn without knowing or caring very much who wrote it, or how it ever came into the use of the Church. There are moods and moments when such knowledge is irrelevant, as the soul worships God with words and music which it can make instinctively its own expression of devotion. But such knowledge often adds to our appreciation, and thereby to our spiritual profit. And it is especially the function of preachers and teachers from time to time to convey this knowledge to their congregations and classes. Thus, to take one instance, I have made a Calendar of the *Hymnary*, to be used along with the rest of the notes, so that upon almost any day of the year it will be possible to find something relevant to a hymn or hymns. Many hymns, of course, fall naturally into the sections appropriate to the Church's Year; but there are a large number of other hymns which should be recalled on certain days. A hymn gains by its associations. If these are present to the mind of the worshipper, he will be likely to sing it with some quickened sense of its message and meaning, as he realizes that the words or the music have come through Christian lives already, and perhaps that they have touched the very day on which he chances to be singing it. The Calendar is intended to aid preachers and teachers in recalling such associations, and thus imparting vividness and depth to common worship.

We are indebted naturally to our predecessors in hymnology and musical history, notably to works like Mr. James Love's *Scottish Church Music* and Canon Julian's *Dictionary of Hymnology*. Personally I have found great help in an annotated edition of Canon Julian's standard volume, which belonged to the Rev. James Mearns, his collaborator, as well as in the Mearns Collection of home and foreign hymnological works, now in the library of the United Free Church College, Glasgow. Our general debt to such works has been acknowledged incidentally in the course of the Handbook. But Mr.

Mearns's corrections and additions in that volume have proved specially valuable.

The task of preparing this Handbook was entrusted by the Hymnary Revision Committee to a sub-committee, who divided up the work as follows. The biographies of authors were prepared in the first instance by the Rev. Thomas Marjoribanks, B.D., and the Rev. Millar Patrick, D.D. ; those of composers were written by Dr. Patrick. Mr. Marjoribanks compiled the Index of Texts. The material for the notes upon the words of the hymns was gathered by the Rev. W. T. Cairns, M.A., and myself. Mr. William Cowan, who was joint author of *The Music of the Church Hymnary* (1901), has contributed, after revision, the relevant annotations on tunes given in that book, and has also written notes on the musical material which is new to the *Hymnary* in the present edition. The Index of Subjects is the work of the Rev. G. Wauchope Stewart, D.D.; he and Dr. Millar Patrick have also written the Introduction. Dr. Millar Patrick was convener of this sub-committee, and in issuing the Handbook to the public the rest of us desire to say emphatically that it owes more than any one can realize to his keen and competent care.

JAMES MOFFATT.

INTRODUCTION

1. THE HYMNS

HYMNODY in the Presbyterian Churches had a very late beginning. The Church which Luther founded had been singing hymns for a century or two before those that followed the leadership of Calvin admitted them to their worship. The reaction against the practices of the Roman Church was less extreme in Luther's mind than in that of the French reformer. He was a musician himself, an accomplished amateur, with a passionate love for much of the music of the cultus whose errors drove him into separation, and, with a just eclecticism, he was eager to preserve as much of it as would answer his purposes. He found in existence also a large body of vernacular hymns which had sprung from the heart of the people and proved their power to express their faith and emotion in worship. The task he set himself, therefore, was, on the basis of this material to build a new type of congregational hymn which would give the people a voice in the new liberty of worship into which he was leading them. With the hymns he gave them on their lips, the German people sang themselves into the Reformation.

Calvin, on the other hand, was no musician. It is true that he was alive to the value of singing as an instrument of worship. He had no sympathy with the Zwinglian inclination to outlaw it from all use in public services; he recognized too well its mysterious power to move the soul, and counted it one of God's highest gifts for the refreshment of the spirit of man. It is to his honour also that he took with him from Paris to Geneva the distinguished musician, Louis Bourgeois, to whom the Consistory entrusted the task of providing tunes for the metrical Psalter then gradually being brought into existence. But he was essentially puritanical in his ideals of worship. He saw no way of redeeming the hymnody of the Church from whose errors he was revolting; there was nothing, he thought, to be done with it but to discard it altogether. Founding on a saying of his master Augustine, that we have nothing worthy to sing to God but what we have received from Him, he held that the Psalms were the only vehicle of praise that rose to the level of what the worship of God required. One New Testament paraphrase also he permitted, and a metrical version of the Ten Commandments, but it is a measure of his extraordinary ascendancy over the Churches that looked to him as their teacher, that, accepting his axiom that the Psalms are the fittest medium of worship-song, they restricted their praise to these throughout many generations.

There was much to be said for this position, of course. The hymnody which he found in use was one of the most potent means of disseminating error. Possibly the quickest way to get rid of the error was to jettison entirely the songs that published it. We may fully assent also to his view that the Psalms are 'an anatomy of all the parts of the soul, for no one can feel a movement of the spirit which is not reflected in this mirror'. And we recognize that not the least of the services he rendered to the Churches that followed him was that of laying down the principle that their materials of praise should be in strict accord with the Scriptures. An examination of the hymn-books of Communions that have not applied this standard deepens our feeling of indebtedness to the great man who so firmly schooled his followers in the observance of it. It will be long before the Reformed Churches consent—and they will have forgotten much that was most salutary in their tradition before they do it—to admit into use in their worship anything that in its substance or its spirit is not in full harmony with the teaching of Holy Writ.

But this gain was purchased at a heavy price. The Psalms, after all, belong to a dispensation which Christianity fulfilled, and in fulfilling, partly abrogated. The ideas in many of them our Lord made obsolete; the temper in some is quite definitely unchristian; there are whole psalms, and there are portions of others, which Christian lips should never utter in the presence of God. Grant that the portions of them which can be used as the fit expression of Christian worship are often unsurpassed for beauty and dignity and fullness of spiritual content, and that these portions will always form the most precious part of the Church's praise; they are yet not adequate to express the thought and feeling of souls that are walking in the light of Christ. It seems extraordinary now that the Reformed Churches should so long have been content, as Watts put it, to pray and preach in Christ's name, but to sing in terms of the Law, and above all to be inhibited entirely from using the name of Christ in their worship-song. Religion could not fail to suffer from such an unnatural restriction. Notoriously, it did suffer. The severity of thought and austerity of life which long characterized the Churches of this order were undoubtedly traceable in part at least to the compulsion laid upon the people to praise God only in terms of pre-Christian categories of thought. The discovery was early made in the Christian era that popular religion is moulded largely by the ideas enshrined in its hymns. Sermons often fly over the people's heads; prayers uttered in their name often fail to carry their hearts and even their intelligence with them; but their songs sink into the memory, colour their thought, and fashion their theology, much more than any deliberate instruction. And if the Churches which followed Calvin's leading emerged slowly into the breadth of Christian thought and the catholicity of spirit which are their honourable marks to-day, this must be definitely put down in no small measure to the saturation of the minds of their people, throughout many generations, with the theology of the Old Testament, imbibed from childhood through their only medium of praise.

Not until the close of the eighteenth century did Presbyterianism begin to throw off this restriction and assert its liberty to Christianize its song. And not until the middle of the nineteenth century was well past, was the battle for this liberty really won. Since then, however, the progress has been rapid, and with the publication of the present book, the Presbyterian Churches of the British commonwealth (that of Canada alone excepted), for the first time acting in concert, serve themselves heirs to their full inheritance from all the ages of Christian song.

A collection like this may be claimed to be a mirror of Christian history. There are few centuries—only the tenth, the eleventh, and the fourteenth—that are not represented. But a century is a purely artificial division of time. Thus the eighteenth in English history really begins, not in 1700, but in 1689. If the division be made according to periods rather, there is none that does not make its characteristic contribution to this book. It is necessary only to cite such illustrious historic names as, say, Clement of Alexandria, St. Ambrose, St. Gregory the Great, St. Patrick, St. Columba, Abélard, St. Thomas Aquinas, St. Francis of Assisi, Luther, Gerhardt, Wesley, Keble, Newman, to call up in each case the entire historic scene in which each played his part in the shaping of the Church's history. Every great quickening of the Church's life, every fierce conflict through which it has passed, every new momentum it has received, has left its legacy of song for the enrichment of subsequent ages. To know the circumstances out of which all the hymns contained in this book sprang would be to see spread before us a complete conspectus of the history of the Church.

It follows that the collection is in the best sense catholic. Many of the greatest of its hymns were sectarian in their origin. Some were composed as party battle-cries. Others were written by men who passionately unchurched hosts of their Christian brethren, and denied them a right to any but the uncovenanted mercies of God. But these circumstances of their birth are now forgotten, except by those who are curious enough to search out their origin. Who that feels his own heart fired and exalted by the noble passion of his hymns now thinks of Scheffler as the acrid controversialist his contemporaries saw in him? Who that sings 'Rock of Ages' remembers that it was written in the white heat of a doctrinal quarrel, to proclaim a particular view of the Atonement in opposition to that which another school of hymn-writers, with equal emphasis, held? Who takes out of 'Praise to the Holiest in the height' the doctrine of the Eucharist which its author intended it to express? Or who cares that Faber's hymns were designed to furnish English-speaking Romanists with a counter-force to the hymns which had sung Protestant doctrine into the hearts of the British people? It is all gain that each hymn is lifted clean out of the narrow matrix of its origin, and in its own undimmed radiance set in the coronal of praise which is used by the Church in the crowning of its King.

It follows, again, that a book like this illustrates the unity of the Church, underlying all its differences. Most branches of the Church Universal have some representation here. The early Greek and Latin Churches furnish treasures of great price. Out of the monasteries of primitive times and those of the Middle Ages hymns come that give to the faith once for all delivered to the saints some of the most perfect of its expressions. The Church of Luther contributes some of the greatest of all hymns. If the gift of the Reformed Church of Germany is slender, its quality is high. The Church of the Huguenots bequeathes us its battle-song, as well as the incomparable music of many of its psalms. The Church of England of last century produced a galaxy of hymn-writers whose names will shine as stars of magnitude so long as the English tongue is used in worship-song. If the Roman Church of this modern age has much to give us also, the fact has to be noted that all its singers from whom we draw learned their song in the Church of the Reformation. Newman, Caswall, Faber, Henry Collins, Matthew Bridges, to name a few, took the singing impulse with them from the Church which they forsook. Romanism nowadays produces no catholic hymns. The reason is that it seeks its inspiration elsewhere than in the sure truth of Holy Scripture; it uses dogmas and a dialect that are foreign to the rest of Christendom : the Church Universal cannot sing what bears so deeply stamped upon it the sign-manual of a sect. Of the nonconforming Churches there is a notable representation. It is not to be forgotten that the father of the modern hymn was the Congregationalist, Isaac Watts; or that though Charles Wesley never left the Church of England, it was under the impulse of an essentially non-conforming movement, which his brother John carries to its logical conclusion, that his genius found the glorious voice that set the whole Church singing. The Baptist

Church is represented, and the Moravian, and the Catholic Apostolic. The Quakers make their contribution. The Sandemanians (Glasites) are not absent. Even Unitarianism gives us some of the best-loved of our Christian songs. And Plymouth Brethrenism is here, in its founder and arch-priest, John Nelson Darby, in Edward Denny, and Albert Midlane, and James George Deck. If the contribution of Presbyterianism is not impressively large, it is of impressive value. The name of Horatius Bonar alone would rank it high. Nor must it be forgotten that the young Churches in the mission-lands of the East begin to contribute rills to the great stream of the Church's song. Narayan Vaman Tilak's 'One who is all unfit to count' fills us with expectation of what the East will give us when more of its Christian singers have found their voice.

This catholicity of its range makes the collection a rich manual of devotion. When this book was in preparation, members of liturgical Communions expressed some surprise at the importance attached to it and the eagerness of debate with which, when its contents were tentatively submitted, its merits and demerits were discussed. But to the Presbyterian, the hymn-book, with the Psalter, occupies the place of a liturgy. It gives him the only means he has of letting his voice be heard in the offices of public worship. It has need, therefore, to contain prayers as well as praises, and to afford utterance for every phase of Christian thought and feeling that claims expression in the Church's offering of its devotion to God. Moreover, next to the Bible, it is to many people their chief manual of private devotion. Multitudes have no other. It gives language to their thoughts and aids their worship. Comprehensiveness, therefore, is essential. This is one justification of the inclusion of many intensely individualistic hymns. Purists would summarily exclude them. But the loss would not be light. Bishop Wordsworth may say, 'The pronouns *I* and *my* are rarely found in any ancient hymn. But in modern hymns the individual often detaches himself from the body of the faithful and in a spirit of sentimental selfishness obtrudes his own feelings concerning himself.' But to restrict our selection to hymns of the objective order, which do undoubtedly best befit communal worship, would not only deprive us of many of the dearest of the Psalms, including the 23rd; it would withdraw from the Church's use many hymns —such as 'Jesus, Lover of my soul,' 'Abide with me,' 'Sun of my soul,' 'Lead, kindly Light'—which the instinct of Christendom has grappled to its heart. Many hymns that are individualistic in expression utter universal feelings, and doubtless do it better because their sentiments are intensely personalized. But in any case, the fact that to the Presbyterian, the hymn-book serves many of the purposes of the Breviary to the Roman Catholic and *The Book of Common Prayer* to the Anglican, makes it imperative that all the elements of devotion, public and private, should find expression here.

There is abundance of material in the *Hymnary*, therefore, to enrich the mind and nourish the piety of the individuals and the Churches that will use it. After a generation, probably, it will cease to satisfy. Revision will again be called for. Experience will disclose what is of permanent value and what may be discarded without loss. But it is safe to say that a very large proportion of what is included has the quality of enduring life in it, and will continue to give a voice to the faith and hope and love of the faithful people of our Presbyterian Churches, not for one generation only, but for many that are to come.

MILLAR PATRICK.

2. THE MUSIC

During the course of its history the Christian Church has accumulated a rich store of musical treasure; and in the present edition of *The Church Hymnary* an attempt has been made to take more advantage than was done in the original book of the resources at our disposal. Under the various hymns full information is supplied as to the origin and composition of the tunes. Here it is proposed to take a comprehensive survey, and to indicate briefly the characteristics of the various periods and types of music represented in the tunes.

First in point of time come the plainsong melodies. The number of these is not large; but it is proper that there should be some representation of this, the oldest type of Church music. The chief characteristics of plainsong are its use of the old ecclesiastical modes and its freedom of rhythm. In these old modes the semitones in the scale do not fall at the same points as they do in the major and minor modes, which are the only two with which we are familiar at the present day. Consequently, melodies in these old modes fall upon our ears with a certain uncouthness, which is, indeed, part of their charm. That these old modes were not the exclusive property of the Church is shown by the fact that some of them still linger on in some of our folk-tunes. When the tune *Veni Immanuel* was first brought into use in our congregations by its introduction in the original edition of *The Church Hymnary*, one was surprised to find how readily they accommodated themselves to the flattened seventh in the penultimate note. Possibly it was owing to the comparative familiarity of this progression at the end of some of our older folk-tunes. Among the few plainsong melodies introduced into the present book, there is none that is likely to cause serious difficulty through the strangeness of the modal idiom.

The other outstanding feature of plainsong is the freedom of its rhythm. Originally it was intended to be sung to various parts of the liturgy. As these were in prose, it naturally took the form of a chant in which the rhythm of the music was entirely subservient to that of the text. This is the form which it assumes in Gregorian Chant. Examples of such chants will be found in the settings of the Canticles to the Gregorian Tones (Hymns 714–16, 718). In the plainsong hymn-tune the freedom of the rhythm of the music is not quite so unrestricted as in the Gregorian Chant. To this two different and seemingly opposite causes contributed. In the first place one type of plainsong melody which evolved, the sequence, was due to sheer delight in the music without any consideration for words at all. It originated in the practice of elaborating the final note of the melody in certain chants into a florid melisma. Hence arose a group of melodies without any words to them at all, though later words were supplied for them; and naturally these melodies assumed a certain rhythmic form in their own right, so to speak. The other cause that contributed to the restriction of the freedom of the plainsong melody was, not its development apart from the text, but its association with words which were cast in metrical form. In course of time metrical hymns had come into vogue in worship in addition to the old prose texts round which Gregorian Chant grew up. Naturally the music which was designed to accompany these hymns acquired a more definite form than that which had been a mere accompaniment to a prose text. But if, for these reasons, the plainsong hymn-melody has acquired a certain rhythmic form of its own, it must be understood that subject to this modification it still retains a great measure of the plasticity that characterizes Gregorian Chant. Any attempt to measure it out into bars of equal length is to be deprecated. The melody still remains entirely subservient to the text; and while in the present *Church Hymnary* the music is printed in minims—it having been considered unadvisable to adopt the old system of notation—it must be understood that this does not mean that the tune is to be sung in strict time or with notes of equal length.

It is a moot point whether the plainsong melodies were originally of simple syllabic character. In the earliest forms in which they have been preserved they show a considerable amount of elaboration, certain syllables being spread out over more or less intricate melismatic windings. Contrary to what one would expect, it is usually the weak syllables in the line that are thus elaborated in the melody. There can be no doubt that the Latin text seems to suit plainsong much better than an English version. But it would be a great loss were these plainsong melodies to be allowed to fall into desuetude because the Latin words are no longer in use; and it is good that they should retain a place in our hymnals, even though the substitution of an English version be an offence to the purist. To assist those who have not a musical edition in their hands, the device has been adopted in the 'words only' editions of the present *Hymnary* of indicating by dots over the syllables how many notes are to be sung to each syllable.

For the most part the plainsong melodies in the *Church Hymnary* are assigned to hymns with which they have been traditionally associated. In some cases this traditional association, though long established, does not go back to the original setting of the tune. Thus the *Veni Creator* (182) belonged originally to an Easter hymn of St. Ambrose, *Hic est dies verus Dei*, and the tune which became associated with *Jesu dulcis memoria* (421) was originally that of a Christmas hymn, *Christe Redemptor omnium*.

Plainsong was originally sung in unison without any accompaniment; and it must be confessed that the addition of harmony in any form seems alien to its character. If it is to be accompanied at all, then the harmony should be strictly modal, and the accompaniment should be kept so subdued as in no way to hamper the freedom of the singers or detract from the predominance of the melody.

We may regard the French Church tunes of the sixteenth and seventeenth centuries, of which a considerable number are included in the book, as a development of plainsong. The elaborate melisma of the old Church song is now reduced to the regularity of measured music. Like plainsong these French tunes are sung in unison; and while they do not demand the complete rhythmic freedom of plainsong, they should be taken with a good swing. They are admirably suited for congregational singing. As examples we may cite *Deus Tuorum militum* (356) and *St. Venantius* (142).

With the Reformation a new type of music came into being. Its primary purpose was to provide for the congregation taking an active part in the praise. Both Luther and Calvin were keenly alive to the value of song for advancing the cause which they had at heart. But they had different ideas as to what kind of music was becoming in Church worship; and the consequence was that the stream of praise that was let loose through their instrumentality flowed in widely different channels in Germany and in Geneva. Let us look first at the course of events in Germany.

As Luther had given the German people the Bible in their own tongue, so he resolved to set before them the great truths of the evangelical faith in songs which would go home to their hearts and which they could thrill with their own feelings. 'I wish,' he said, 'after the example of the Prophets and Ancient Fathers of the Church, to make German psalms for the people, that is to say, sacred hymns, so that the Word of God may dwell among them by means of song also.' He had none of Calvin's scruples about admitting into Church worship songs of praise which were not directly taken from the Bible. He wrote many hymns himself, and enlisted the services of his friends to assist him in the work. The consequence was that from the date of the Reformation the floodgates were opened in Germany for the outpouring of a volume of praise for which those countries which were under the Calvinistic ban had to wait till a much later period. For the music he drew upon any source that he found serviceable. Some of the tunes were adaptations of old Church melodies, some were taken from secular sources, some were original. At first the melodies were worked up into motets for use in the service; but after the publication of a collection of sacred songs by Osiander in 1586 with the melody transferred from the tenor to the treble, the participation of the congregation was secured. The German chorale tunes are admirably suited for congregational singing. They are always solemn and dignified, with a massive strength about them that has a most impressive effect. *The Church Hymnary* is greatly enriched by the examples that have been included. Some of them are already familiar; but the number in the present volume has been greatly increased. In many cases where the translation of a German hymn has been introduced, the proper tune is provided for it. Such, for instance, is the case with 'All my hope on God is founded' (448), 'Deck thyself, my soul, with gladness' (324), and 'Praise to the Lord' (22). We all know how dear these chorale tunes were to the heart of Bach, and how he delighted to deck them out in the richest and most moving harmonies. Many of his beautiful settings have likewise been included.

In Geneva the case was different. Calvin would not permit anything but the Psalms of David to be used as sacred songs in Church. He was fortunate in having as the Cantor of his church at Geneva Louis Bourgeois, a musician of sterling ability. The nucleus of the Psalm-Book which gradually came into use in the Genevan Church was a small collection of psalms with tunes which Calvin compiled in 1539 in Strasburg. The tunes in this book were mainly of German origin. Of these two are included in the present *Hymnary*, Nos. 217 and 342. Calvin brought this Strasburg collection with him to Geneva, and at various dates the number of Psalms was increased, till in 1562 the book was completed. Bourgeois came to Geneva in 1541, and till his departure in 1557 worked at the music of the Psalter. By that time the number of tunes in the book had increased from twenty, the number in the original Strasburg collection, to eighty-five. He retained three of the Strasburg tunes in their original form, others he altered; the remainder of the eighty-five were composed or adapted by himself. They are all of the highest quality, and it is greatly to the enrichment of the *Hymnary* that a place has been found for several examples of so excellent a type of tune.

At the time of the Reformation many refugees from England and Scotland found a home in Switzerland. These took back with them the practice of psalm-singing; and during the succeeding century various Psalters appeared in England and Scotland, the music of which has been drawn upon to supply some of the tunes introduced in the *Hymnary*. Among the most important of these Psalters from a musical point of view may be mentioned Este's of 1592, Ravenscroft's of 1621, and the Scottish Psalters of 1564, 1615, and 1635. The tunes taken from these Psalters are of two kinds, Proper and Common. Originally it had been the practice for each Psalm to have a tune of its own, which had no designation save the number of the Psalm with which it was associated. Some of the old Psalters, notably the 1564 Scottish Psalter, had a considerable variety of metres, as had been the case in the Genevan Psalters; and these required tunes of corresponding form. The tunes which were identified with particular Psalms came to be known as Proper tunes. But in course of time when the number of Psalms included in the Psalter exceeded the number of available tunes, the practice came in of regarding certain tunes as Common, i.e. not identifying them with any particular Psalms but using them for any Psalms in the corresponding metre. To distinguish them it became customary to call them by local names. Whether these names may be regarded as affording any evidence of the origin of the tunes in question is a doubtful point. Of these Proper and Common tunes from the old Psalters a considerable number appear in the present *Hymnary*. Most of the Common tunes introduced are familiar to us by name at any rate, as they still hold a place in our Psalters. But a good many of them have been allowed to fall into disuse, and it is to be hoped that their inclusion in the *Hymnary* may rescue them from the oblivion into which they appeared to be in danger of falling. The Proper tunes had in many cases been almost completely lost sight of; and while it is the case that some of them are rather dry and uninteresting, there are others which are excellent and which it is believed may still find a place in the repertory of our congregations. Some of the best of these are included in *The Church Hymnary*.

One Psalter which was never published, Archbishop Parker's, privately printed in 1560, is of special musical interest because of nine tunes it contains by Tallis, eight of them composed in the first eight modes. Some of these have been in general use in our congregations, the tune known as 'Tallis' (353) and the familiar Canon (291). But three of the others, the First (433), Third (559), and Fifth (250) Mode Melodies are included in the present edition for the first time; and though they may take some time to win the favour of those whose taste has been nurtured on more piquant fare, there can be no doubt as to their chasteness and beauty.

With the gradual removal of the ban upon the employment of 'human' hymns in England, freer scope was given to the power of the musician; and a great volume of hymn-tunes has accumulated of varying character and excellence. The earliest hymn-book published was George Wither's *Hymnes and Songs of the Church* (1623). It is of special interest musically as it contained a number of tunes by Orlando Gibbons. Several of these have been included in the present *Hymnary*. Not quite so austere as the Tallis Melodies, they are yet solemn and dignified in character, some of them with rhythmical features which add greatly to their charm. In the early part of the eighteenth century a new type of hymn-tune began to appear. Jeremiah Clark was the pioneer, and in his tunes we note a greater warmth of feeling symptomatic of the direction in which the hymn-tune was to develop. In his case the balance is admirably preserved between emotional appeal and artistic restraint, and his tunes are among the best examples of the English type of hymn-tune. The number of tunes characteristic of this period included in the *Hymnary* is not very large, but they are mostly excellent in character. Dr. Croft, Henry Carey, and later Samuel Howard may be cited as representative names. During the course of the eighteenth century the English hymn-tune degenerated sadly in character. A catchy and florid type of tune came into fashion; vain repetitions were freely indulged in to make the words fit the music; popularity was aimed at no matter at what sacrifice of dignity and propriety; secular melodies were caught up from the street and the theatre and pressed into the service of the Church. No doubt this practice of utilizing secular music for sacred purposes may occasionally be employed with excellent results. It had been used with success by Luther, and some of the finest German chorale tunes were originally associated with secular words. It has been used, we believe without offence, in such modern hymn-books as *The English Hymnal*, where many English traditional melodies have been happily wedded to sacred words. And it is employed in the present *Hymnary*, in which the folk-music of various nations has been freely utilized to supply tunes which our congregations may find it a delight to sing. But it all depends on the nature of the tunes so utilized. Some, like 'Innsbruck' (284) or Hassler's 'Mein Gmüt ist mir verwirret' (107), have such inherent beauty and dignity that, whatever their origin, we feel as though the soul of the music had at last found its true body in the sacred text; others are so essentially vulgar and tawdry that when we find them associated with solemn words we feel inclined to exclaim

> Immane quantum discrepat; impium
> Lenite clamorem.

Of the florid type of hymn-tune characteristic of this period there are fortunately not many examples in the present *Hymnary*.

During the nineteenth century an earnest endeavour was made by many musicians to provide a worthier type of English hymn-tune. There are many names deserving of grateful recognition on the part of the Church. The two Wesleys, Dr. Gauntlett, Dr. Monk, the musical editor of *Hymns Ancient and Modern*, Henry Smart, Dr. Dykes, Sir Hubert Parry, Sir John Stainer, musical editor of the first *Church Hymnary* —these are a few of the outstanding names, and many examples of their work will be found in the present edition of the *Hymnary*. They were followed by a crowd of minor composers whose work is largely represented in the hymn-books of the Victorian era. Speaking generally we may say that the type of hymn-tune that came into vogue in the latter half of the nineteenth century is somewhat lacking in breadth and robustness. The influence of Spohr, Mendelssohn, and Gounod is strongly marked. The tunes are too often of a weak and sentimental character, depending for their appeal not on bold and clearly outlined curves of melody or on strong and forceful rhythms, but on chromatic harmonies which are apt to cloy and become loathsome in their own deliciousness. A much robuster and healthier spirit is shown in our present day composers, such as Dr. Vaughan Williams, Sir Walford Davies, and Mr. Martin Shaw. Some of the tunes by them and other recent writers are likely to prove among the most popular in the book.

The number of Welsh tunes in the *Hymnary* is considerable, and these should prove not the least attractive feature in the music. Some are traditional melodies, others are compositions of a group of men whose names, though for the most part little known in other departments of music, deserve honourable recognition for the contribution they have made to hymnody. In the Church life of Wales the Gymanfa Ganu or Psalmody Festival plays an important part; and it has done much to foster community singing and to stimulate the production of fine tunes. The secret of its success lies in the fact that it is regarded as something more than a musical performance. It is a religious service in which the united congregations rejoice to pour forth their feelings in song. It is gratifying to find religious fervour expressing itself in music so excellent in character. The vogue that a certain type of cheap and vulgar tune gained in some recent revivals has led to the belief that this is the only kind of music suitable for mission services. But these Welsh Psalmody Festivals teach us otherwise. From the descriptions one receives of them there can be no doubt of the religious fervour that pervades such gatherings. Yet it finds expression and stimulus not in the 'lean and flashy songs' which are so often associated with the mission service, but in music of a robust and edifying character. It is to be hoped that some of these Welsh tunes, which have proved themselves so powerful in their appeal in the community which gave them birth, will establish themselves in favour in the wider circle to which they are now made known. Many of them are in the minor mode, and this may tell against their immediate popularity. In some quarters there is a prejudice against minor tunes. It were a pity if any such bias were allowed to stand in the way of the introduction of these Welsh tunes into our Church praise. Let them be given a fair trial, and I do not doubt that the grave sweet melody of such tunes as 'Aberystwyth' (414) and 'Moab' (572) will soon secure for them a warm place in the heart of our congregations. Among the Welsh contributions to the *Hymnary* it is right that special mention should be made of the tunes by the musical editor of the new edition, Professor Evans, many of which exhibit in a marked degree the characteristics which make the Welsh hymn-tune such a valuable accession to our congregational praise.

In addition to the tunes specially composed for use in church, the *Hymnary* contains a number of traditional melodies which have been pressed into the service of religion. The propriety of thus utilizing secular melodies for sacred purposes is a point upon which there may be difference of opinion. In defence it may be urged that it secures tunes which have the true elements of popularity in them. We wish the people to sing, but they sometimes find that the kind of music which those who profess to be authorities prescribe as becoming makes no appeal to them. But here in their traditional melodies we have music that is the natural and spontaneous expression of popular feeling, music which the people themselves made for themselves, and which thereby brings with it the guarantee of that popular appeal which the professional musician sometimes strives in vain to secure. Further, in thus utilizing secular melodies for religious purposes we are pursuing a policy which has long obtained in the Church, and which has been attended with excellent results. It is a plausible conjecture that some of the superscriptions of the Psalms, e.g. Ps. 9 'upon Muthlabben' (of which the meaning is uncertain), Ps. 22 'upon Aijeleth Shahar' ('the hind of the morning'), Ps. 57 'Al-taschith' ('destroy not'), refer to songs to the tunes of which the Psalms are directed to be sung. Some of the noblest of our Church tunes have been so derived. A learned authority is of opinion that 'the oldest Catholic Church music was transplanted into the Church from the pagan streets' (Gevaert). Acting upon the principle that 'the devil does not need all the good tunes for himself', Luther seized upon whatever secular tunes he thought suitable, and turned them to sacred uses. Some of his best known hymns, e.g. 'Nun freut euch' (211), and 'Vom Himmel hoch' (56), were written to popular airs. In Scotland the Wedderburns did the like, e.g. in their translation of the last-named hymn, 'ane sang of the Birth of Christ with the tune of Baw lulalaw'. Many of the beautiful airs in Petri's *Piae Cantiones* (Greifswald, 1582), e.g. *Corde natus* (60), bear plain evidence of being tunes of the people, and one at least of them, the spring carol 'Tempus adest floridum', has come to have an almost international vogue as 'Good King Wenceslas'. We have already seen that some of the most beautiful of the German chorale tunes, such as 'Innsbruck' (284) and the 'Passion Chorale' (107), were originally associated with secular words. But 'only the shameless curiosity that characterizes our boasted historical sense can rejoice at these discoveries. The musician does not trouble himself about them, and forgets them as soon as they are told to him; for they tell him no more than what he already knew by instinct—that all true and deeply felt music, whether secular or sacred, has its home on the heights where art and religion dwell. Happy are the chorales of whose origin nothing is known!' (Schweitzer).

In British hymn-books this vein had been more rarely worked till the publication of *The English Hymnal*, when Dr. Vaughan Williams, himself one of the principal collectors of folk-songs, brought out of his note-books a large number of beautiful traditional melodies. In their selection from these and other folk-tunes the Committee have exercised a certain discretion. They have been careful to choose melodies that are really worthy, such as do not bear on their face unmistakable evidence of having been designed for ignoble use. Our aim is different from that of the Reformers. They were concerned not merely to have tunes serviceable for their purpose, but to transform the secular songs whose melodies they borrowed 'into Christian and moral songs, for the abolishing in course of time of the bad and vexatious practice of singing idle and shameful songs in the streets, in fields, and at home, by substituting for them good, sacred, honest words',—to quote the title of a collection of such transformed songs published at Frankfurt in 1571. But we desire not to impose a sacred text on melodies which are still in vogue with secular words, but to utilize such as are no longer in general use, and which do not bring with them the strong secular associations that clung to them in their original setting. Where this association was strong, so that the introduction of a tune would almost inevitably have recalled the secular words, the Committee have refrained from using it, even though it seemed otherwise suitable. For instance, they have not made use of any Scottish melody, declining to follow Heber, who wrote 'Brightest and best of the sons of the morning' to 'Wandering Willie', beautiful as the tune is and closely fitting the rhythm of the words. Nor have they taken 'John Brown's body', which, in a sense, is the 'proper' tune to 'Mine eyes have seen the glory' (155), or the German drinking-song 'Crambambuli' to 'When mothers of Salem' (659). On the other hand, the Irish traditional airs, of which in many cases the words are lost beyond all hope of recall except the first line which has survived as a title, have been freely drawn upon; and the beautiful Welsh and Gaelic airs speak for themselves, and bring a noble contribution to the strength and beauty which are in God's sanctuary. It is hoped that the folk-tunes which have been included may prove themselves fitted for the sacred use to which they are now applied, and that in their new setting they may find a secure place in the Church praise of the people from whose heart they have sprung.

G. WAUCHOPE STEWART.

3. THE STORY OF THE REVISION

The first *Church Hymnary* was published in 1898. The Committee that prepared it represented four Churches—the Church of Scotland, the Free Church of Scotland, the United Presbyterian Church, and the Presbyterian Church in Ireland. Two years later, the Free and United Presbyterian Churches joined forces in the United Free Church of Scotland. No authoritative account of the preparation of the book has ever been published, but it is known that the task was not an easy one. For one thing, the state of ecclesiastical politics in Scotland at that time made the entire cordiality that prevailed in the later Committee difficult; and for another, the new book was to supersede not one, but three others, which had all legitimate claims on the loyalty of those who were accustomed to use them. Difficulties notwithstanding, the book which was produced leapt at once into a wide popularity, and it retains much affection still.

The lapse of a generation, however, stales even the best of hymn-books, and in the early twenties of this century the demand for revision became urgent. In the interval there had been a great advance in general musical culture, and several almost epoch-making new books had appeared, bringing into use so much fine ancient and modern music that the late-Victorian *Hymnary* came to seem very much out of date. The General Assemblies were not all equally ready to recognize this, but in 1922 all three gave the necessary sanction, and their respective Praise Committees selected their representatives for the Revision Committee and gave them authority to proceed.

This Committee had been but a few months at work when the Presbyterian Church of Wales and the Presbyterian Church of England asked leave to co-operate. The *Hymnal* of the former was older than the *Hymnary*, and though *Church Praise*, the book in use in the latter, had been revised in 1905–7, it was recognized that a further revision would be necessary before many years more elapsed. In these circumstances the ideal of a common book for all the hymn-

using Presbyterian Churches of the United Kingdom attracted many minds in both Churches, and that ideal was
rendered still more attractive by the readiness of the Presbyterian Churches of all the Dominions except Canada to
co-operate also. The Presbyterian Church of England,
indeed, stipulated that its collaboration should be tentative
and provisional. A strong minority entertained a preference
for a revision of their own book; the right was therefore
retained to withdraw from the collaboration if the draft of
the revised *Hymnary*, when produced, should fail to satisfy
their Assembly. As the event turned out, however, there was
no withdrawal; the solidarity of the Churches, hesitatingly
begun, was in the end firmly and happily established.

The final constitution of the Revision Committee was as
follows:

MEMBERS OF COMMITTEE.

Church of Scotland.

Rev. G. Wauchope Stewart,
    D.D., Haddington.
,, R. Sangster Kemp, D.D.,
    Deer.
,, L. Maclean Watt, D.D.,
    Glasgow.
,, D. J. Moir Porteous, B.D.,
    Port Glasgow.
,, J. M. Hunter, B.D., Ab-
    botshall.
,, G. W. Mackay, D.D., Killin.

Rev. Ninian Hill, Edinburgh.
,, Thomas Marjoribanks,
    B.D., Colinton.
,, J. Hutchison Cockburn,
    B.D., Dunblane.
,, James Coullie, B.D., Pen-
    caitland.
,, Alexander Smart, M.A.,
    Broughty Ferry.[1]
Mr. J. A. Cairns, L.L.B.,
    S.S.C., Glasgow.[2]

[1] *Vice* Rev. R. Harvie Smith, deceased (1926); *vice* Col. J. A. Hope,
deceased (1925).
[2] *Vice* Rev. Alexander Galloway, B.D., deceased (1926).

United Free Church of Scotland.

Rev. Professor James Moffatt,
    D.Litt., D.D., Glasgow.
,, J. R. Fleming, D.D., Edin-
    burgh.
,, Millar Patrick, D.D., Edin-
    burgh.
,, W. T. Cairns, M.A., Edin-
    burgh.

Rev. G. S. Stewart, M.A., Edin-
    burgh.
,, Arch. C. Craig, M.C.,
    M.A., Glasgow.[1]
,, Joseph Hibbs, M.A., Kil-
    marnock.
,, John Young, B.D., Green-
    ock.

[1] *Vice* Rev. J. G. Goold, M.A., deceased (1923).

United Free Church of Scotland—continued.

Rev. A. K. Walton, M.A., Glasgow.[1]

,, Alexander Chisholm, M.A., A.T.C.L., Alloa.[2]

Mr. William Cowan, Edinburgh.

,, W. M. Page, S.S.C., Edinburgh.

[1] *Vice* the late Rev. John Tainsh, resigned (1924).

[2] *Vice* Rev. J. R. Cameron, D.Phil., resigned (1925); *vice* Rev. John A. Hutton, D.D., resigned (1923).

Presbyterian Church in Ireland.

Rev. Professor J. Ernest Davey, B.D., Belfast.

,, James Salters, M.A., Newtownards.

Rev. W. P. Hall, M.A., Ballysillan.

Professor R. A. S. Macalister, Litt.D., LL.D., F.S.A., A.R.C.O., Dublin.

Presbyterian Church of England.

Rev. R. C. Gillie, M.A., D.C.L., London.

,, W. King H. Macdonald, M.A., Glanton.

,, Nichol Grieve, M.A., Liverpool.[1]

Rev. David Anderson, B.A., Cardiff.[2]

Mr. George Angus, Tynemouth.

,, James Shaw, London.[3]

[1] *Vice* Rev. J. S. Hastie, B.D., resigned (1925).

[2] Substitute for Rev. J. D. M. Rorke, M.A.

[3] *Vice* Mr. T. N. Philip, resigned (1924).

Presbyterian Church of Wales.

Rev. Sydney O. Morgan, B.A., B.D., Hoylake.

,, Richard Jones, M.A., Llandinam.[1]

Professor David Evans, Mus.D. (Oxon.), Cardiff.

Mr. A. O. Roberts, Liverpool.

Substitutes—

Mr. J. Morgan Lloyd, Mus.B. (Dublin), Barry.

,, A. P. Morgan, Builth Wells.

[1] *Vice* Rev. T. C. Jones, Penarth, deceased (1925).

CO-OPTED MEMBERS.

Societies of Organists.

Edinburgh—Mr. J. S. Anderson, Mus.B. (Oxon.), F.R.C.O.

Glasgow—Mr. T. C. L. Pritchard, M.A., Mus.B. (Dublin), F.R.C.O.

Aberdeen—Mr. John M. Nisbet.

Ulster—Mr. William Curran.

English Organist.

Mr. R. F. Jarman, Mus.B. (Dunelm), F.R.C.O., Sunderland.

Correspondents of Colonial Presbyterian Churches.

Australia—Rev. R. Scott West, D.D., Sydney.

New Zealand—Rev. James H. Mackenzie, Wellington.

South Africa—Rev. E. Macmillan, M.A., Pretoria.

Represented on the Committee by Rev. J. R. Fleming, D.D., and Rev. Ninian Hill.

The Conveners of the Praise Committees of the three Churches which initiated the work were appointed joint chairmen—the Rev. James Coullie, who, however, soon gave place to the Rev. G. Wauchope Stewart, D.D.; Mr. William Cowan; and the Rev. James Salters. A most fortunate choice of Secretary was made in the appointment of Mr. W. M. Page. His knowledge, enthusiasm, forethought, and executive ability incalculably facilitated and shortened the labours of the Committee.

The first task to be undertaken was to decide which hymns in the existing *Hymnary* should be retained in the new one, and which should be discarded. This proved surprisingly difficult. About the rejection of few hymns was there anything like unanimity. Few were there so poor as not to have any defender. Custom, of course, dulls the edge of the critical faculty. Judgement tends to be very lenient to the faults of hymns endeared by many associations. It was found also that hymns which some had tested and proved to have value were by others who had never tried them held in light esteem. A single flaw—an offending verse or phrase—might lead to a hymn's rejection. Faber's 'My God, how wonderful Thou art' is an instance. Again and again it was set aside because of the image of its concluding verse, in spite of the most earnest urging of its merit in other respects; and it was salved from the débris of the discarded only at one of the final reconsiderations, and then only on the understanding that a more acceptable closing verse should be found. Sometimes the Committee registered the most curious variations of judgement. A hymn which in one survey would be approved by a decisive majority would in a later one be as decisively cast out. The opposite also would happen: persuasions which on one occasion would fail to move the Committee would at a later stage find it more complaisant and would prevail.

An endeavour was made to lay down principles to govern the choice, but invariably they were found easier to postulate than to keep. At an early stage, for example, the decision was come to that no hymns for children of primary-school age should be included, on the ground that the commission given by the Assemblies was to prepare a book for congregational use and that to make it possible for congregations to be called upon to sing baby-hymns was to risk the ridiculous. This rule, however, foundered on the rock of 'Jesus loves me', one distinguished member of the Committee making so impassioned an appeal for the inclusion of that hymn that the Committee capitulated. This opened the door to further concessions of the same kind, with the result that in the end there was quite a group of hymns of this order, and these had to be segregated in a section by themselves as to be used, not in church, but only in home or school. In this case, as in others, doubtless second thoughts were best.

The sifting of the contents of the old book having been completed, the Committee next addressed itself to the task of selecting new hymns. An enormous task this proved to be. The literature of hymnody is of vast proportions; the number even of new books issued since the original *Hymnary* appeared is very great. There was relief, it is true, in the fact that many hymns are common to practically all the books in the English language, but even with that deduction the examination of the available material was very laborious. Members of Committee submitted lists of new hymns that seemed to them worthy of consideration; suggestions came also from various quarters outside; and from these, lists were compiled in which about 1,300 hymns were enumerated for the Committee's valuation. Here again the most remarkable divergences of judgement appeared. Every member of Committee sustained numerous disappointments. These were invariably accepted with entire good humour, sometimes with jocular lamentations that the majority should exhibit so determined an antipathy to genuine poetry. In the result, some hymns of a quality that entitled them to a place undoubtedly slipped through the meshes of the Committee's choice; every member could draw up his own list of illustrations. Equally, every one could set out an array of hymns whose inclusion he would regard as a blemish on the book. But on the whole, when an estimate is taken of the risks inherent in any process of selection by a Committee of almost forty members, the errors either of inclusion or of exclusion must be accounted surprisingly few.

The most critical stage of this part of the proceedings arrived when the co-operating Committees submitted their lists of hymns to which the Churches they represented attached special value, and for which admission was requested rather for that reason than because of any intrinsic merit. Taking its courage in both hands, however, the Committee executed what seemed to it impartial judgement. Admission was given to a few of the hymns which had special claims apart from their own merit, but the guillotine fell ruthlessly on the rest.

At an early stage a Text Sub-Committee was appointed. The function of this Committee really was that of literary editorship. The text of every hymn had to be considered and compared wherever possible with the original. The rule was laid down that unless for good reasons to the contrary the author's version should in each case be adhered to, and changes in some familiar hymns are accounted for in this way. But such a rule is impossible of uniform application. There are many instances in which alterations in the author's text are necessary; in some they have become so thoroughly established in general use that to make a fetish of conformity to the original would merely provoke resentment without securing any compensating advantage. The Committee itself altered texts only with the most reluctant and sparing hand, and all changes of any importance received the sanction of the full Committee. Many hymns also are improved by abbreviation, provided that their continuity and completeness are not impaired. It was part of this Sub-Committee's task to judge what verses in hymns that were too long for singing throughout should be telescoped or omitted. Two hymns of which it was felt that nothing should be sacrificed were divided into two parts, each making a separate hymn, and numerous instances will be found in which judicious compression has enhanced a hymn's suitability for congregational use. The distribution of the hymns under their appropriate sections, the arrangement of their order, the suggestion of captions to facilitate reference, and, not least, the settlement of the punctuation, were among the duties of this Committee.

When the selection was finally made and the text adjusted, the book was printed in draft and submitted to the Assemblies. In some of the co-operating Churches it was submitted to Presbyteries also, every member receiving a copy. Each Assembly instructed its Praise Committee to receive suggestions, and, if it approved them, to pass them on to the Revision Committee, which in its turn was given power to adjudicate upon them, to select the music, and in due time to issue the completed book.

Many criticisms were submitted. In most cases they cancelled each other. Only in a few instances was there anything like a consensus of opinion such as to induce the Committee to waive its own judgement and accept the requisition of the Churches. In all, twenty-six hymns from the old *Hymnary*, omitted in the draft, were restored; six of the proposed new hymns were rejected; and nine new hymns were added. The Committee felt that it had been quite salutary that their work should have had to run the gauntlet of such widespread criticism. Interest was created; much useful suggestion was received; and the net result of the process was an assurance that in the main their work was approved by the Churches in whose behalf it was done.

The selection of the music was remitted to a Sub-Committee, along with whom a panel of organists acted in an advisory and consultative capacity. At a later stage the preparation of the music for the press passed through the hands of a Sub-Committee consisting of these musical experts, with Dr. Evans as chairman and musical editor-in-chief.

The selection of music was guided by the following principles: (1) that in the case of the Common, Long, and Short Metres, every effort should be made to retain the old Psalm Tunes which are in danger of being forgotten; and (2) that, as far as possible, each hymn should have its 'proper' tune.

When the selection of words was completed, lists of all the hymns, classified according to their metres, were put into the hands of the General Committee, with the names of the tunes to which they had been set in all the representative hymn-books of Great Britain and Ireland.

Some hymns have 'proper' tunes. No person of normal mentality could think of singing, say, 'The Church's one foundation' to any tune but 'Aurelia', though, as a matter of fact, that tune was originally composed for 'Jerusalem the Golden'—any more than a Scotsman would dream of singing any tune but 'French' to 'I to the hills will lift mine eyes'. But the diversity of usage and of taste in regard to a very large number of hymns is so great that, in some instances, as many as eight or ten different tunes, set to a single hymn, were noted in the lists submitted. The Sub-Committee therefore went very carefully over these lists, selecting the tune or tunes most suitable, in their judgement, for each hymn, in many cases voting on each tune, and finally submitting the results of their deliberations to the General Committee. By the latter this work was all reviewed in minute detail, further voted upon, and accepted, rejected, or remitted back for further consideration. The results were all gone over by the small Committee of musical experts, who had also taken part in both the earlier stages of the work, and their verdicts and suggestions were recorded and reported to the General Committee. In some instances they reported that tunes selected by the General Committee were musically unworthy of inclusion. Their advice was usually taken, though occasionally usage prevailed over the admitted soundness of their opinion.

A large mass of original music in manuscript was submitted to the Experts' Committee—more than 300 tunes in all—and sifted by them. A considerable number of these tunes were set to words which were already supplied with music so well known that only in exceptional cases was it possible to use them. Of those that were judged worthy of further consideration, copies were lithographed and circulated, together with tunes found in books not readily accessible, such as Roman Catholic hymn-books, College or Public School collections and supplements, old Scottish Psalters, and Welsh and Continental hymn-books. Some eighty of the original tunes, and sixty of the latter class, were thus submitted. All the original tunes were presented anonymously, and were voted upon and accepted or rejected on their merits. Of the whole number, original and selected, fifty-five were accepted. At least fifty modern hymn-books were examined, besides collections of tunes so varied as Wesley's *European Psalmist*, Woodward's *Songs of Syon*, *The Bristol Tune Book*, Livingston's *The Scottish Psalter of 1635;* a great array of German Chorale books, French, Hungarian, Scandinavian, and American collections, the *Journals of the Folk Song Society*, reprints of old music, and various private compilations, were passed under review; and it may confidently be claimed that of the thousands, literally, of tunes which one or more of the Committee saw and reported upon, few possessing any merit can have escaped notice. All the members were keen; several of them developed those famous characteristics of the book-hunter, 'the scent of a slow-hound and the snap of a bull-dog'; and tune-hunting, with some, passed from being a pursuit into a positive mania.

Both the Musical Sub-Committee and the General Committee represented all varieties of opinion and musical taste. Some sections had a marked proclivity for minor tunes; others said that the Churches they represented would tolerate these only if they were given a major tune in addition in every case. For some, the tunes of the 1635 Scottish Psalter, the 'Songs' of Orlando Gibbons, and the Chorales in the superb settings of Bach, were the absolute standard;

while the taste of others was more eclectic. Discussion was keen and voting often close. Every member of the Committee had many experiences of being in a minority, but in spite of defeats would fight on with undiscourageable good humour for the tunes he had faith in, and often not unsuccessfully, for some tunes repeatedly rejected were successful only on an eighth or ninth attempt.

But both Committees and the individual members had one aim only—an ardent desire to make the book as good as they possibly could make it. Even after all their endeavours mistakes and misfits will doubtless be discovered, and may even obtrude themselves. But as a result of their entering into the abundant labours of others, and profiting by the example and even by the mistakes of their predecessors, the Committee honestly felt that their arduous and delightful work was not in vain in the effort to provide a worthy manual of praise for the Churches that honoured them with their trust.

In 1925 a Sub-Committee was appointed to prepare a Handbook for simultaneous issue with the *Hymnary*, containing historical information about its contents. The result of their labours, which entailed an enormous amount of inquiry and research, appears in the present volume.

The preparation of the *Hymnary* occupied the Committee for four and a half years. In all, they had fifty-four whole-day meetings; the Music Sub-Committee had twenty-three further whole-day meetings, and the other Sub-Committees had numerous and often prolonged meetings as well. To attend these, several members had to travel very long distances by land and sea. As every meeting involved a great deal of private preparation beforehand on the part of every member, the finished result represents a vast amount of continuous labour on the part of otherwise busy men. Without exception, however, they brought enthusiasm to the task, and their eagerness in the common interest made the work an unalloyed delight. As time went on, the intimacy of the members became close, and their fellowship, the harmony of which was never in the faintest degree interrupted, will remain with them all as a cherished memory.

The work had brought home to them in a very practical way the essential unity in faith and order of the Churches represented, and they parted with good assurance that the book they had prepared would in the future stand as a symbol of that unity, and exercise a powerful influence in bringing together in closer fellowship and co-operation the Churches in which it will be used in private and public worship throughout the United Kingdom and the Britains beyond the seas.

NOTES ON THE WORDS AND MUSIC
OF THE HYMNS IN ORDER

1 HOLY, HOLY, HOLY, LORD GOD ALMIGHTY

This 'splendid metrical paraphrase of Rev. iv. 8–11' (Julian) was composed when Heber was vicar of Hodnet (1807–23), but it was not published till after his death, in *A Selection of Psalms and Hymns for the Parish Church of Banbury* (3rd ed., 1826). It was a favourite of Tennyson ('Of hymns I like Heber's "Holy, holy, holy," better than most, and it is in a fine metre too') and was sung at his funeral service in Westminster Abbey on April 12, 1892.

In the autograph copy, which is preserved in the British Museum, the second verse has

and ever art to be.

As this is the first of the eight hymns by Heber in *The Church Hymnary*, it is well to recollect that he designed them to be sung 'between the Nicene Creed and the sermon' in Anglican worship; in composing them he claimed that 'no fulsome or indecorous language has been adopted, no erotic addresses to Him whom no unclean lips can approach, no allegory, ill-understood and worse applied'.

The tune NICAEA was composed for it by Dr. J. B. Dykes, and appeared in *Hymns Ancient and Modern* (1861). The name was appropriate, for the hymn celebrates the doctrine of the Trinity as first expressed officially in the Nicene Creed (Hymn 725).

2 ROUND THE LORD IN GLORY SEATED

From Mant's *Ancient Hymns* (1837), published when he was bishop of Down and Dromore. The original hymn consisted of four eight-line stanzas; here as usual the first four lines of stanza 3 and the last four lines of stanza 4 are omitted. In verse 3 'conspire', which is sometimes altered to 'unite', is used in its older sense of 'agree together'. The hymn originally opened thus:

Bright the vision that delighted
Once the sight of Judah's seer;
Sweet the countless tongues united
To entrance the prophet's ear.

This explains the sense of 'conspire', and suggests the basis of the hymn in Isaiah vi. 1–3.

The only other contribution by Bishop Mant to the *Hymnary* is in the translation of Hymn 99. His hymn beginning 'For all Thy saints, O Lord', which was in the former edition of *The Church Hymnary* (338), is now omitted.

James Langran's tune DEERHURST is from *Psalms and Hymns adapted to the Services of the Church of England, with accompanying tunes, selected and revised by John Foster* (1863). This hymn-book, which had appeared without music in 1836, was edited by the Rev. W. J. Hall, and was commonly known as the Mitre Hymn-Book, from the figure of a mitre which appeared on the boards. The 1863 edition is a cut-leaved book, and the tune DEERHURST is referred to the hymns 'Lord of heaven and earth and ocean' and 'May the grace of Christ our Saviour'. It was composed in 1862, and at a Choral Festival in Peterborough Cathedral was set to the hymn 'Hark the sound of holy voices'.

The second tune SANCTUS was published by John Richards in *Hymns and Tunes of the Presbyterian Church of Wales*, 1900.

3 WE PRAISE, WE WORSHIP THEE, O GOD

This is an anonymous version of the first part of the *Te Deum* (Hymn 718), as found originally in Gell's *Collection of Psalms and Hymns* (Derby, 1825). Ver. 5 is commonly added to it. The original form read in ver. 1 (line 1) 'the eternal Father', in ver. 2 (lines 3 and 4)

> The heavens and all the powers on high
> With raptures constantly do cry,

in ver. 4 (line 3) 'Prophets enraptured' instead of 'Prophets and martyrs', and in ver. 5 (line 1)

> Triune Jehovah, God on high,

with 'Creator, Saviour, Comforter' in line 4.

Jeremiah Clark's tune BROCKHAM (CONFIDENCE) first appeared in *The Divine Companion; or, David's Harp new Tun'd . . .* (second edition, 1709, published by Henry Playford).

4 O TRINITY, O BLESSÈD LIGHT

By the ninth century, the Latin original of this vesper hymn had been attributed to St. Ambrose of Milan; but it had no place in the services of the Milan Church, and is probably an anonymous early Latin composition. It has been repeatedly translated into English. The present version belongs to a group of nineteen hymns which appeared in an English *Primer or Office of the Blessed Virgin Mary* (1619): they were described as 'a new translation done by one most skilful in English poetry', and evidently this was believed to be the distinguished poet Drummond of Hawthornden by the editors of the folio edition of his works in 1711, where they are for the first time printed as his compositions. The internal and external evidence is not quite decisive. Professor Kastner thinks that 'the somewhat colourless language of the hymns is the strongest argument against their ascription to Drummond, though it must be admitted that, on the whole, the evidence is in his favour' (*The Poetical Works of William Drummond of Hawthornden*, vol. ii, p. 417, 1913).

The Latin doxology underlying verse 3 was added to the original hymn in two stanzas.

2

'Most principal' in ver. 1 is a literal rendering of the Latin adjective 'principalis', whose meaning might be better conveyed by 'royal' or ' true source of all'; 'princely' or 'primal' is the idea. In ver. 2 'our glory' is an echo of Psalm xvi. 9, 'my heart is glad, and my glory rejoiceth', 'glory' being an equivalent for 'soul'.

O LUX BEATA is the proper plain-song melody, which has been universally associated with this hymn.

AETERNA CHRISTI MUNERA is a Rouen Church melody (*English Hymnal*, 151). During the sixteenth and seventeenth centuries there came into use, throughout the churches and cathedrals of several dioceses in France, a number of tunes in measured form, taking the place of the older unmeasured plain-song melodies. These tunes were in many cases founded on the plain-song melody and, in others, on favourite secular airs; but the original sources of the individual tunes have not been ascertained. This note applies also to the following tunes—78, 142, 188, 280, 356, 524, 554, 636.

5 FATHER OF HEAVEN, WHOSE LOVE PROFOUND

Contributed to a Staffordshire *Selection of Psalms and Hymns for Public and Private Use* (Uttoxeter, 1805), by E. Cooper, the rector of Yoxall, who republished it in his small *Selection of Psalms and Hymns* (Lichfield, 1811).

The melody of DAS LEIDEN DES HERRN has been associated in Germany with the hymn 'Da Jesus in den Garten ging,' but it is not known in what book it first appeared.

RIVAULX was composed by Dr. Dykes for this hymn in *A Hymnal for use in the English Church, with accompanying tunes* (1866), edited by the Hon. and Rev. J. Grey.

6 O KING OF KINGS, BEFORE WHOSE THRONE

John Quarles, who like his father Francis took the royalist side in the Civil War and fought for King Charles, wrote *Divine Meditations upon several subjects . . . with several Divine Ejaculations* (1655). The present hymn is an adaptation of one of these 'Divine Ejaculations' by Rev. Thomas Darling, in his *Hymns for the Church of England* (ed. 1887).

LEICESTER, John Bishop's tune, is from *A Sett of New Psalm Tunes in Four Parts by John Bishop, Organist of the College at Winton* (about 1700), where it was called BEDFORD and set to Psalm 112.

7 GLORY BE TO GOD THE FATHER

According to his son, H. N. Bonar (in *Hymns by Horatius Bonar*, 1904, 1908), this hymn, together with Hymn 255, was 'written specially' for the English Presbyterian Church's *Psalms and Hymns for Divine Worship* (1867), though both appeared in the author's third series of *Hymns of Faith and Hope* (1866), when Dr. Bonar was minister of the Free Church at Kelso. The present hymn was set to

Henry Smart's tune REGENT SQUARE in the English Presbyterian volume, the tune being named from Regent Square Church, the cathedral of English Presbyterianism in London, of which Dr. Hamilton, the editor of the book, was then minister.

8 THERE IS A BOOK, WHO RUNS MAY READ

Keble's original poem, for Septuagesima Sunday in *The Christian Year*, was written in 1819 on the text of Romans i. 20 ('The invisible things of him from the creation of the world are clearly seen, being understood by the things that are made'), and contained four stanzas between the present third and fourth, and another between the present fifth and sixth. 'The dew of heaven', in ver. 4, is an allusion to Psalm lxviii. 9. The chapter read on Septuagesima Sunday is Genesis i.

The tune ST. FLAVIAN is from the *English Psalter* of 1562 (see under Biographical Notes, &c). The present is the first half, with slight alterations, of the tune of Psalm 132: the complete tune is as follows:

9 O WORSHIP THE KING ALL-GLORIOUS ABOVE

A free and felicitous version of Ps. civ, published in Bickersteth's *Christian Psalmody* (1833), the year before Sir Robert Grant became governor of Bombay; then in his own posthumous *Sacred Poems* (1839). 'The' is usually added in ver. 2 (line 3) for metrical reasons. In *Christian Psalmody* ver. 1 (line 2) runs, ' O gratefully sing his unchangeable love', ver. 3 (line 4) reads 'a girdle' (not 'a mantle'), and ver. 6 begins, 'O Lord of all might, how boundless thy love!'

HANOVER is from *A Supplement to the New Version of Psalms by Dr. Brady and Mr. Tate, &c. The Sixth edition, corrected and much enlarged* (1708), where it is set to the version of Psalm 67 beginning 'Our God bless us all with mercy and love.' It is without a name, and is headed 'A New Tune to the 149th Psalm of the New Version, and the 104th Psalm of the Old.' No composers' names are given. It is generally believed that Dr. Croft was concerned in the production of the above book, but the evidence in support of his being the composer of the present tune is not entirely conclusive. In collections issued at the end of the eighteenth and beginning of the nineteenth centuries it is frequently attributed to Handel; but as Handel did not come to England till 1710, it is almost impossible that a hymn tune by him should have been published in an English collection in 1708. Further, the tune is found in many collections published during Handel's residence in England, and in none of them is he mentioned as composer: while in Riley's *Parochial Music Corrected* (published in 1762, within three years of Handel's death) the tune is headed 'Hanover tune, the author not known'. In the collection of tunes called *The People's Music Book* (edited by J. Turle and E. Taylor in 1844), the tune is called 'Old 104th', and has Handel's name attached to it; but in the Index it is credited to Dr. Croft, and the following note added:—'This Tune has been ascertained to be the composition of Dr. Croft, by satisfactory evidence, since the page in which it is contained was printed.'

10 THE SPACIOUS FIRMAMENT ON HIGH

At the close of a paper (see on Hymn 26) in *The Spectator* for Aug. 23, 1712, Addison observes that as Psalm xix. 1–3 'furnishes very noble matter for an ode, the reader may see it wrought into the following one'. Then he prints these lines, which are, as Lord Selborne declared, 'a very perfect and finished composition, taking rank among the best hymns in the English language. . . . If it be not poetry, I do not know what is; and to prove that it is song, and soul-stirring song too, it is only necessary to hear it, as I often have, heartily sung to an appropriate tune.'

Such a tune is FIRMAMENT, composed by Sir H. Walford Davies for the hymn and published in *The Fellowship Hymn Book Supplement* (1920) with the name 'Laudare Domine'.

11 LET US WITH A GLADSOME MIND

A selection from the twenty-four stanzas of the original, a paraphrase of Psalm cxxxvi; it is one of Milton's youthful translations done 'at fifteen years old', i.e. when he was a schoolboy at St. Paul's. Some slight alterations of the original text have been generally introduced, in order to adapt it for congregational singing. Thus, the last stanza as Milton wrote it runs,

> Let us therefore warble forth
> His mighty majesty and worth.

Among the stanzas omitted are the original third and the original last verse, as follows ;

> O let us His praises tell,
> That doth the wrathful tyrants quell.

> That His mansion hath on high,
> Above the reach of mortal eye.

The first tune HARTS is from *Sixteen Hymns as they are Sung at the*

Right Honorable the Countess of Huntingdon's Chapel in Bath. Set to Music by Benjn. Milgrove (1769?). It is No. 15 in that collection, and is set as under to the hymn 'Brethren, let us join to bless', with the addition of a 'Hallelujah', which has now been dropped.

A note at the beginning of the book says, 'The Men that sing the Air must rest where 'tis written the Women to sing this part alone, and begin where the word Altogether is written.'

John Fawcett's tune MELLING is from *A New Set of Sacred Music* (?1830).

12 IMMORTAL, INVISIBLE, GOD ONLY WISE

From Dr. W. C. Smith's *Hymns of Christ and the Christian Life* (1867). Written on 1 Timothy i. 17: 'Now unto the King eternal, immortal, and invisible, the only wise God.' To complete the rhythm, 'and' has been added before 'silent' in ver. 2 (line 1), and in the second line of the same verse 'wanting' replaces 'striving', while (line 3) 'high' has been inserted after 'mountains', and in the fourth line 'goodness' replaces 'mercy'. In ver. 3 (line 1) 'to' has been added before 'both', and in the second line 'the' before 'true'; the last two lines of this verse originally ran,

> Thy blossom and flourish only are we,
> To wither and perish—but nought changeth Thee.

The fourth stanza of the original has been omitted, and the present fourth verse is made up from the opening couplets of the fifth and sixth stanzas as Dr. Smith wrote them.

JOANNA is a Welsh air, probably founded on a folk-song melody sung to a ballad about the beginning of the nineteenth century.

13 ALL CREATURES OF OUR GOD AND KING

This thrilling improvization upon the theme of Psalm cxlv is the Rev. W. H. Draper's rhymed version or free paraphrase of the famous Sun Song or Song About Creatures (*Cantico di fratre sole, laude della creature*) which St. Francis of Assisi wrote in Italian during the fierce heat of the summer of 1225. He lay prostrate and depressed by blindness at San Damiano, unable to endure any light on his weak eyes, and 'incidentally plagued by a swarm of field-mice who probably had their home in the straw walls of the hut, and who eventually ran over his face, so that he had no peace by day or night. And yet it was precisely in this wretched sickness that he composed his wonderful masterpiece' (Jorgensen, *St. Francis of Assisi*, 308–9). Full details are accessible in the *Speculum Perfectionis* (chapters 100, 101, 120, and 123.)

LASST UNS ERFREUEN in the *Geistliche Kirchengesäng* (Cologne, 1623) is a tune set to an Easter hymn beginning, 'Lasst uns erfreuen herzlich sehr'. Compare with 'Psalm 36 (68)', Hymn 217.

14 THE STRAIN UPRAISE OF JOY AND PRAISE

This is Dr. Neale's version, in his *Mediaeval Hymns* (second edition, 1863) of an anonymous Latin hymn which comes from the monastery of St. Gall in Switzerland, where, on its first appearance in 1507, it is credited to Balbulus Notker, an earlier (840–912) member of the monastery, probably because Notker introduced this new type of hymn, technically called 'Sequence'. The 'a' at the end of 'Alleluia' was musically prolonged and embroidered, under Byzantine influences, during the eighth century; then in northern France words were set to these notes, and at St. Gall this practice became popular, under Notker, who composed rhythmical 'proses', which were sung before the reading of the Gospel for the day. Hence perhaps their name, 'Sequences'. The present hymn is a specimen of this class. It was originally written for a secular melody called 'Puella turbata' (the troubled maiden).

Troyte's chant (about 1850), from *Forty-Eight Hymn Tunes for Hymns in the Salisbury Hymnbook* (1860), is an adaptation of a chant by Dr. William Hayes.

15 LET ALL THE WORLD IN EVERY CORNER SING

As in *The Temple* (number 21), published in 1633, the year after Herbert's death—except that the refrain is repeated at the beginning of the second stanza. This hymn and the other one in our collection (514) from George Herbert show how his verses answered to the prayer 'that we shew forth Thy praise, not only with our lips, but in our lives'. The manuscript of *The Temple* poems was handed by Herbert on his death-bed to his executor, with the humble request that he would ask Mr. Nicholas Ferrar to read it, 'and then, if he can think it may turn to the advantage of any dejected soul, let it be made public'.

Basil Harwood's tune LUCKINGTON (*The Oxford Hymnbook*, 1908) was composed for this hymn. So was Professor Macalister's ST. DARERCA, written for the present edition of *The Church Hymnary*.

16 PRAISE THE LORD, HIS GLORIES SHOW

A version of Psalm cl. from Lyte's *The Spirit of the Psalms* (1834), where it appeared as two eight-line stanzas. No fewer than six hymns from this collection are in *The Church Hymnary*. Lyte had a humble ambition like Ken's (see on Hymn 256), which he put into these lines:

> Might verse of mine inspire
> One virtuous aim, one high resolve impart—
> Light in one drooping soul a hallowed fire,
> Or bind one broken heart,
>
> Death would be sweeter then,
> More calm my slumber 'neath the silent sod,
> Might I thus live to bless my fellowmen,
> Or glorify my God.

LLANFAIR, by Robert Williams, is named BETHEL in the composer's MS. book, and dated July 14, 1817. It appeared in J. Parry's collection, *Peroriaeth Hyfryd* (1837), harmonized by John Roberts, Henllan.

17 FOR THE BEAUTY OF THE EARTH

The original form of Mr. Pierpoint's hymn as it appeared in Rev. Orby Shipley's *Lyra Eucharistica* (second edition, 1864), omitting the three last stanzas. The change of 'brain's delight' to 'mind's delight' in ver. 3 (line 2) was sanctioned by the author's representatives.

Mr. Arthur's tune LUCERNA LAUDONIAE was specially written for this hymn, and for the present collection.

18 ALL THINGS BRIGHT AND BEAUTIFUL

From Mrs. Alexander's poem in her *Hymns for little Children* (1848). She wrote the book before her marriage, when she was in her twenty-fifth year. In Keble's preface to it, he claimed that her hymns would 'win a high place in the estimation of all who know how to value true poetry and primitive devotion'—a forecast which has been amply fulfilled. Five hymns in our collection are taken from this volume (i. e. 18, 69, 105, 591, 663); several are written to illustrate the Apostles' Creed (see on 69), the present being a comment on 'Maker of heaven and earth' (Hymn 724). The third stanza, which ran as follows, is omitted:

> The rich man in his castle,
>   The poor man at his gate:
> God made them high or lowly,
>   And ordered their estate.

Sir John Stainer's tune GOD IN NATURE (*The Westminster Abbey Hymnbook*, 1897) was composed for this hymn.

Sir F. A. G. Ouseley's ALL THINGS BRIGHT is printed as arranged by the composer for *The Children's Hymnbook* (1881).

19 O LORD OF HEAVEN AND EARTH AND SEA

From Dr. Wordsworth's *Holy Year* (third edition, 1863), where it is an offertory hymn in nine stanzas. The compilers print here the first six. Originally the last line of the first three verses was

> Giver of all.

Hymns 126, 268, and 484 are from the same collection. When this hymn was included in *Hymns Ancient and Modern*, Dr. Wordsworth agreed to alter the third line of the fourth verse from

> And e'en that gift Thou didst outrun

to

> And freely with that blessèd One.

The first tune, ES IST KEIN TAG, is from *Geistliche Seelenfreud* (Ulm, 1692); the editor of this work was J. D. Mejer (or, Mayer), and the melody is marked as his own composition.

ALMSGIVING was composed by Dr. Dykes for this hymn in *The Holy Year, by Charles Wordsworth, D.D., with appropriate tunes, edited by W. H. Monk* (1865).

20 GOD, WHO MADE THE EARTH

Written by Mrs. Rhodes for the Whitsuntide (1870) Festival of the Sheffield Sunday School Union.

BEECHWOOD was composed by Josiah Booth for this hymn, and published in *The Congregational Sunday School Hymnal* (1891).

21 PRAISE, MY SOUL, THE KING OF HEAVEN

A complete and exact form of the hymn as first published in Lyte's *Spirit of the Psalms* (1834). It is a free paraphrase of Psalm ciii.

Sir John Goss composed PRAISE, MY SOUL for this hymn. The tune appeared in *The Supplemental Hymn and Tune Book, compiled by the Rev. R. Brown-Borthwick. Third edition, with new Appendix* (1869), where it is given both as here with the varied arrangement of the several verses, and also in four-part vocal harmony, the latter setting being in key E.

22 PRAISE TO THE LORD, THE ALMIGHTY, THE KING OF CREATION.

A free paraphrase of Psalms ciii and cl, written at Düsseldorf and first published in Joachim Neander's *Glaub- und Liebesübung* (Bremen, 1680). The translation is by Miss Winkworth, who wrote, in ver. 2, 'Shelters thee under His wings, yea so gently', and 'desires' for 'hearts' wishes', and in ver. 3 'here' for 'shall'.

The earliest form of the melody of LOBE DEN HERREN is in the *Stralsund Gesangbuch* (1665), where it is set to the hymn 'Hast du denn, Liebster'. In 1680 it was set to this hymn by Neander, to which it has been attached ever since. Later German books show many variations in the form of the melody, but the present is that adopted in *The Chorale Book for England* (1863), for which Miss Winkworth's version was prepared.

23 SING TO THE LORD A JOYFUL SONG

First issued in Dr. Monsell's *Hymns of Love and Praise for the Church's Year* (1863), when he was vicar of Egham; then in his *Parish Hymnal* (1873). It is based on Psalm cxlv. 1–2. One verse is omitted:

> For life below, with all its bliss,
> And for that life, more pure and high,
> That inner life, which over this
> Shall ever shine, and never die.

Dr. Percy Buck's tune GONFALON ROYAL is set, in *The Public School Hymnbook* (1919) to 'Lord of all being, throned afar' (Hymn 24 below).

24 LORD OF ALL BEING, THRONED AFAR

First printed in *The Atlantic Monthly* (December, 1859) at the end of Dr. Holmes's *Professor at the Breakfast Table*, with this introduction, 'Peace to all such as may have been vexed in spirit by any utterance these pages may have repeated! They will doubtless forget for the moment the difference in the hues of truth we look at through our human prisms, and join in singing (inwardly) this hymn to the source of the light we all need to lead us, and the warmth which alone can make us all brothers.'

Mr. W. H. Gladstone's tune OMBERSLEY is from *The Hymnary* (Novello, 1872), where it is set to 'Jesus shall reign where'er the sun'.

25 THE LORD IS KING! LIFT UP THY VOICE

From Mr. Conder's *Star in the East* (1824), omitting two stanzas.

Mr. J. W. Elliott's tune CHURCH TRIUMPHANT is from *Church Hymns with Tunes* (1874), where it is set to three different hymns; but he stated that it was originally composed, not for any of these, but for a hymn beginning, 'Again the Lord's own day is here.'

26 WHEN ALL THY MERCIES, O MY GOD

Stanzas 1, 2, 5, 6, 8, 10, and 11 of the original thirteen as published by Addison in *The Spectator* for Aug. 9, 1712, with the promise that he would 'from time to time publish' more pieces of this kind. One of these is Hymn 10. The two hymns gained circulation in the Churches by a curious side-wind; they were among the hymns added by the University printers about 1818 to Tate and Brady's version of the Psalms. In *The Scottish Paraphrases* they were also two out of the five 'Hymns' appended; one of the three others was Hymn 116.

Horsley's tune BELGRAVE appeared in *National Psalmody. . . . A Collection of Tunes . . .The Music harmonized, arranged, and adapted by B. Jacob* (1817). It is marked in the Index as a new composition, and set to Psalm xvi. 5: 'My lot is fallen in that blest land.'

27 MY GOD, HOW WONDERFUL THOU ART

The original, in Faber's *Jesus and Mary* (1849) had nine stanzas; the third is the sixth verse in the present arrangement. In ver. 5 (line 2) Faber wrote 'half so mild'.

James Turle's tune WESTMINSTER appeared, under the name of BIRMINGHAM, in *The Psalmist: A Collection of Psalm and Hymn Tunes . . . edited by Vincent Novello* (Part II, 1836), a collection which was issued in four parts, each containing a hundred hymns, between 1835 and 1844.

28 A GLADSOME HYMN OF PRAISE WE SING

Written in 1876 for the Sunday School Anniversary of Mr. Blatchford's Church at Lewins Mead, Bristol.

DEGANWY, by Benjamin Williams, is in *Supplement to Tunes, Chants, and Anthems*, edited by D. Jenkins (1894). This tune bears a close resemblance to a folk-melody, 'The Rat-Catcher's Daughter.'

29 NOW THANK WE ALL OUR GOD

Martin Rinkart's German original was a paraphrase of Ecclus. l. 22–4, composed about 1630; it first appeared in *Jesu Herz-büchlein* (Leipzig, 1636). The first two verses were composed as a grace after meat, to be sung by the author's household; the third verse was added as a doxology. The hymn is the German 'Te Deum', sung on all national occasions of thanksgiving, but there is no foundation for the tradition which connects its origin with the Peace of Westphalia (1648) at the close of the Thirty Years War. The translation is from Miss Winkworth's *Lyra Germanica* (1858).

NUN DANKET is from Johann Crüger's famous collection, *Praxis Pietatis Melica*, of which no fewer than fifty or sixty editions were issued, dating from the middle of the seventeenth to the middle of the eighteenth century. Of the first two editions no copies have survived, but a single copy (wanting title-page) has been preserved of what is, on good grounds, believed to be the third edition, issued in 1648. The present melody is found in this book, but it may have appeared in one or both of the earlier editions. It is set to the hymn 'Nun danket alle Gott', of which the present hymn is a translation, as follows:

With slight variation, the hymn and tune are found in almost all German collections down to the present day. The arrangement here is substantially that by Mendelssohn in his *Lobgesang*, the harmony being reduced from six parts to four.

30 THOUGH TROUBLES ASSAIL, AND DANGERS AFFRIGHT

Written in February, 1775, and first published two years later in *The Gospel Magazine* with the title 'Jehovah-Jireh. The Lord will provide' (Genesis xxii. 14). Newton's autobiography, as vivid a piece of writing as anything in Defoe, is the most illuminating comment on this hymn. Of its eight verses in the original text, the following are too characteristic of the writer's robust piety to be omitted:

> We may, like the ships,
>   By tempests be tossed
> On perilous deeps,
>   But cannot be lost;

Though Satan enrages
  The wind and the tide,
The promise engages,
  'The Lord will provide'

When life sinks apace,
  And death is in view,
The word of His grace
  Shall comfort us through;
No fearing or doubting
  With Christ on our side,
We hope to die shouting,—
  'The Lord will provide'.

The third verse refers to Hebrews xi. 8: 'By faith Abraham, when he was called . . . went out, not knowing whither he went.'

The tune OLD 104TH is from *Ravenscroft's Psalter* (q.v.) of 1621, where it is set to Psalm 104. In the earlier psalters this psalm is set to a tune from the Anglo-Genevan Psalter (1561). The accents and rhythm are exceedingly bad, and this may have induced Ravenscroft to discard it and substitute the present tune, which may be his own composition.

31 GOD MOVES IN A MYSTERIOUS WAY

This profound hymn of Cowper's appeared anonymously in Newton's *Twenty-six Letters on Religious Subjects; to which are added Hymns, &c.* (1774); then in the *Olney Hymns*, signed 'C'. Its original title was 'Light shining out of Darkness', but there is no basis for the popular legend that the hymn was written after he had been mercifully prevented from committing suicide in October 1773, when suffering from religious melancholia. In one manuscript copy of the hymn, ver. 5 (line 4) runs: 'But wait to smell the flower'.

The first tune COLESHILL is not an original tune, but is really a modified form of the tune 'Dundee'. In the first edition of William Barton's *Book of Psalms in Metre* (1644) there is found a tune headed 'London long tune, proper for solemn ditties, and used everywhere'. The music is full of evident misprints, but the tune bears close resemblance to 'Coleshill'.

According to H. E. Dibdin (*Standard Psalm Tune Book*, 1851), the tune appears under the name 'Mepsell' in Edmund Ireland's *Tunes of the Psalms in Two Parts* (York, 1699), thus:

In Ireland's *The Most Useful Tunes of the Psalms* (1713) it is named 'Hull Tune', the melody being as follows:

So far as has been yet ascertained, the earliest appearance of the tune in its present form is in *The Psalms of David in Metre. Newly Translated. With Amendments. By William Barton, M.A. And Set to the best Psalm Tunes, in Two Parts, viz. Treble and Bass. . . .* By Thomas Smith (Dublin, 1706). The tune is here printed as follows, and called 'Dublin Tune', the bass given being at the end of the volume:

The curious misplacement of the bars is common to all the tunes in the book.

The name 'Coleshill' is attached to the tune in *A Collection of Psalm Tunes in Four Parts. Fitted to the Old or New Versions* (London, 1711). It is here set to Psalm 116, the melody being as follows:

So far as has been discovered, its earliest appearance in Scotland is in Thomas Moore's *Psalm Singer's Delightful Pocket Companion* (Glasgow, 1762), where the melody is accompanied with the note, 'Sing Dundee Bass and Counter to this Tune.'

The second tune ST. DAVID is from *Ravenscroft's Psalter* of 1621, where it is set to Psalms 43 and 95, the arrangement of the tune

14

being by Ravenscroft himself. In the Index it is under the heading 'Welsh Tunes'. The melody is as follows:

In John Playford's *Psalms and Hymns* (1671), the melody appears exactly in the above form, but in his *Whole Book of Psalms* (1677) it is found in its *present* form.

32 PRAISE TO THE HOLIEST IN THE HEIGHT

From Newman's poem, *The Dream of Gerontius* (dated 'January, 1865'). Here as usual the first stanza is repeated at the close, for purposes of worship. Sung at Mr. Gladstone's funeral on May 28, 1898, it having been one of his favourite hymns; 'during the last weeks of his life we all heard that "Rock of Ages" was in his judgment the grandest of hymns, and that "Praise to the Holiest" was constantly on his lips' (Canon Scott Holland in *The Household of Faith*, p. 41).

RICHMOND appeared in *Carmina Christo* (1792), which was edited by the Rev. Thomas Haweis and contained original hymns by him. It was set to 'O Thou from whom all goodness flows', and in its original form the tune has a florid repeat of the third line.

GERONTIUS, from *Hymns Ancient and Modern* (Appendix, 1868), was composed by Dr. Dykes for the hymn.

33 GOD IS LOVE: HIS MERCY BRIGHTENS

From Sir John Bowring's *Hymns*, which were published in the year (1825) when he became editor of *The Westminster Review*.

SUSSEX, a traditional English melody (from *The English Hymnal*, 1906) arranged by R. Vaughan Williams.

34 PRAISE YE JEHOVAH, PRAISE THE LORD MOST HOLY

A free version of Psalm cxlix, composed by Lady Cockburn-Campbell at Exeter, Dec. 24–7, 1838.

BELHAVEN was composed by Mr. Pritchard for this collection.

35 PRAISE THE LORD! YE HEAVENS, ADORE HIM

The author is unknown. The hymn is first found, pasted on a leaflet, in *Psalms, Hymns, and Anthems of the Foundling Hospital* (London, 1798), and headed 'Hymn from Psalm cxlviii, Haydn'.

LAUS DEO is from *Church Hymn Tunes, ancient and modern, for the several seasons of the Christian Year . . . selected, composed, and edited by Richard Redhead* (1853).

36 ETERNAL LIGHT! ETERNAL LIGHT!

According to Dr. Binney (writing in 1866), 'this hymn was written about forty years ago, and was set to music and published by Power of the Strand, on behalf of some charitable object to which the profits went'. It was composed at Newport (Isle of Wight) where Binney was then minister, one evening, after sundown.

The tune NEWCASTLE was composed on Sept. 16, 1876, by H. K. Morley, and set to this hymn in *The London Tunebook, A Companion to all Hymnals now in use* (edited by Edwin Moss, 1877).

37 ABOVE THE CLEAR BLUE SKY

From *Hymns of the Church, Mostly Primitive* (1841), which Mr. Chandler published when he was vicar of Witley. In ver. 4 (line 4) the original had, 'Shall lift'.

Dr. Hopkins composed CHILDREN'S VOICES for this hymn (*Church Hymns with Tunes*, 1874).

38 SONGS OF PRAISE THE ANGELS SANG

Based on St. Luke ii. 13, 14; indeed, the title in Montgomery's *Christian Psalmist and Original Hymns* is, 'Glory to God in the highest'. In the original the last two lines of the first verse are:

> When Jehovah's work begun,
> When He spake and it was done.

It appeared first in the 8th edition of Thomas Cotterill's valuable *Selection of Psalms and Hymns*. The allusion in the first verse is to Job xxxviii. 7 ('The morning stars sang together, and all the sons of God shouted for joy').

MONKLAND. This tune appeared in *Hymn Tunes of the United Brethren* (edited by John Less, Manchester, 1824), where the composer's name is not given. When it appeared in *Hymns Ancient and Modern* (1861), it was 'arranged by J. Wilkes', who was organist at Monkland, where Sir Henry Baker was vicar.

CULBACH comes from *Heilige Seelenlust, Oder Geistliche Hirtenlieder . . . von Johann Angelo Silesio und von Herren Georgio Josepho mit aussbundig Melodeyen geziert* (Breslau, 1657). See Biographical Notes under Scheffler and Joseph. The present tune is set to the hymn beginning, 'Ach wann kommt die Zeit heran'. The majority of the melodies are believed to be compositions of Joseph, but a few, of which this is one, are noted as 'To a well-known melody'.

39 YE HOLY ANGELS BRIGHT

The germ of this hymn lies in 'A Psalm of Praise to the tune of Psalm cxlviii', which Richard Baxter appended to *The Poor Man's*

Family Book, the preface to which is dated Aug. 26, 1672. The hymn contains sixteen cheerful stanzas, the first two being these:

> Ye holy angels bright,
>> Which stand before God's throne,
> And dwell in glorious light,
>> Praise ye the Lord, each one!
>>> You there so nigh,
> Fitter than we
> Dark sinners be,
>> For things so high.

> You blessèd souls at rest,
>> Who see your Saviour's face,
> Whose glory, ev'n the least,
>> Is far above our grace,
>>> God's praises sound
> As in His sight
> With sweet delight,
>> You do abound.

These have been drawn upon for the first two verses of the present hymn, but nothing in Baxter's original answers to the third and fourth. The re-shaping of the hymn was done mainly by R. R. Chope, in whose *Hymnal* (1858) it appears, as well as in the S.P.C.K. *Church Hymns* (1871).

The tune CROFT'S 136th is from the same source as 'Brockham' (see on Hymn 3), where it is headed, 'A Psalm Set by Mr. William Crofts. Psalm cxxxvi.' The melody in the original is as follows:

40 HARK, THE GLAD SOUND! THE SAVIOUR COMES

The original of this hymn was composed by Doddridge on Dec. 28, 1735. It was revised twice, in 1745 and 1781, for the *Translations and Paraphrases of the Church of Scotland*, the second and final revision being the work of William Cameron (q.v.). Doddridge acknowledged that his 4th stanza contained reminiscences of Pope's *Messiah*, e.g. of the lines

> He from thick films shall purge the visual ray,
> And on the sightless eyeballs pour the day.

But the hymn has originality and force of its own, as a paraphrase of St. Luke iv. 18 f. (Isaiah lxi. 1 f.). It is as though 'the poet had been present in the Nazareth synagogue when Jesus read the prophet's words about Himself, and the poet had taken down those words from His mouth and made them into a song' (Dr. L. F. Benson).

Thomas Clark's CREDITON is from *A Second Set of Psalm Tunes adapted to the use of Country Choirs* (*c.* 1810), where it is set to the new version of Psalm viii ('O Thou to whom all creatures bow').

41 ALL MY HEART THIS NIGHT REJOICES

A selection (verses 1, 7, 8, and 15) from Paul Gerhardt's original in fifteen verses, which first appeared in Crüger's *Praxis Pietatis Melica* (Berlin, 1653). The translation as in *Lyra Germanica*, though Miss Winkworth originally wrote 'Heedfully my Lord I'll cherish' in ver. 4, and in *The Chorale Book for England* altered the line to 'Thee, dear Lord, with heed I'll cherish'. The lilt of the German carol, which Miss Winkworth has not unsuccessfully preserved, may be felt by reading the first stanza:

> Fröhlich soll mein Herze springen
> Dieser Zeit,
> Da vor Freud
> Alle Engel singen.
> Hört, hört, wie mit vollen Chören
> Alle Luft
> Laute ruft:
> Christus ist geboren!

The note of personal religion distinguishes the German carols always; for German Christmas poetry more than for that of any other nation, 'the birth of Christ in the individual soul, not merely the redemption of man in general, is a central idea' (C. A. Miles, *Christmas in Ritual and Tradition*, p. 76).

The tune BONN is from *Geistliche Andacht-Lieder Herrn Paul Gerhardt . . . gesetzt von J. G. Ebeling* (Berlin, 1666, 1667), where it is set to Gerhardt's hymn, 'Warum sollt ich mich denn grämen'.

42 WHILE HUMBLE SHEPHERDS WATCHED THEIR FLOCKS

In the Earl of Oxford's *Fifty Years of Parliament* (vol. ii, p. 219) the list of Poets Laureate contains this entry: 'Nahum Tate. A butt of Pope and Swift. Mainly remembered for his Christmas carol, "While Shepherds watched their flocks".'

The original hymn (on St. Luke ii. 8–15) appeared in the 1703 *Supplement* to the *New Version of the Psalms of David* by Tate and

Brady. Like Hymn 40, it was revised and improved for the Paraphrases of the Church of Scotland. In the original the first stanza was

> While Shepherds watched their flocks by night,
>> All seated on the ground,
> The angel of the Lord came down,
>> And glory shone around:

also the last two lines of verse 6 were

>> Good-will henceforth from heaven to men
>> Begin, and never cease.

In verse 2 the Scottish revisers further altered Tate's 'mighty dread' to 'sudden dread'.

In *Church Hymns with Tunes* (1874) EVANGEL is set to this hymn and called 'An Old Carol'. But it seems to be founded on a setting composed by G. W. Fink (in 1842) of the song by M. Claudius beginning 'War einst ein Riese Goliath'. The melody of this song is as follows:

43 IN THE FIELD WITH THEIR FLOCKS ABIDING

Written in 1871 for a concert at Harrow, where F. W. Farrar had been for some years an assistant master.

The tune, like the words, is reproduced from Farmer's *Christ and His Soldiers: A Sacred Oratorio* (1878).

44 LITTLE CHILDREN, WAKE AND LISTEN

This hymn is printed as it appeared anonymously in Williamson's *Children's Manual* (1876), except that the last line of ver. 2 replaces the original

> Howe'er sad our lot may be.

CHARTRES is one of a number of carols sung in the church of Notre Dame, Chartres, during the Christmas season. The air is found in a collection of *Ancient Christmas Carols*, edited by Edmund Sedding in 1860. See Duncan, *The Story of the Carol*, p. 98, for original form.

45 THE FIRST NOWELL THE ANGEL DID SAY

'Nowell' is from the French Noël, which is commonly identified with the Provençal Nadal, i.e. the Latin Natalis or Birthday. It came to mean, as here, a song of the Birthday, or 'News' (as if from

'Novellare'), and such carols became popular in France during the fifteenth century. A carol 'may perhaps be defined as a religious song less formal and solemn than the ordinary Church hymn—an expression of popular and often naïve devotional feeling, a thing intended to be sung outside rather than within church walls' (C. A. Miles, *Christmas in Ritual and Tradition*, p. 47). In England carols rise in the fifteenth century, and like the ballads they are generally anonymous. The present song, a West of England piece, is printed in W. Sandys's *Christmas Carols* (1833), where its form, however, is slightly different. Thus the second line of the first verse is

> Was to three poor Shepherds,

and the editor points out that some traditions made them four in number. Three stanzas are omitted.

The tune is from Sandys's book. It is said to be a popular carol air in the West of England.

46 HARK, THE HERALD ANGELS SING

From Charles Wesley's *Hymns and Sacred Poems* (1739), the first two lines and the refrain as in G. Whitefield's *Collection* (1755). The original hymn had no refrain, and was composed of ten four-line stanzas, of which the first six are here printed; it also ran, in the last couplet of ver. 1,

> Universal Nature say,
> Christ the Lord is born to-day,

in the last couplet of ver. 2,

> Pleased as man with men to appear,
> Jesus our Immanuel here,

and in ver. 3 (line 1), 'heavenly' instead of 'heaven-born', with 'and' instead of 'lo' in the third line.

BETHLEHEM is from Mendelssohn's *Festgesang for Male Chorus and Orchestra*, composed for and first performed at the festival held at Leipzig in June 1840 to celebrate the invention of printing. The tune is adapted from the chorus No. 2 of that work. When Dr. W. H. Cummings was organist at Waltham Abbey it struck him that this chorus would be a suitable setting for the hymn 'Hark, the herald angels sing'. He copied out the parts, and had the tune sung by the choir at Waltham Abbey. Finding that it was received with favour, he published the adaptation in 1856, and it soon found its way into many hymn books, the first of these being the Rev. R. R. Chope's *Congregational Hymn and Tune Book* (1857), where the tune is called ST. VINCENT.

It is curious that some years previous to the publication of Dr. Cummings's adaptation, Mendelssohn in writing to his English publishers on the subject of an English translation of the Festgesang, said: 'I must repeat the wish I already expressed in my letter to Mr. Bartholomew. I think there ought to be other words to No. 2. If the right ones are hit at, I am sure that piece will be liked very much by the singers and the hearers, but it will *never* do to sacred words. There must be a national and merry subject found out, something to which the soldier-like and buxom motion of the piece has some re-lation, and the words must express something gay and popular as the music tries to do it.'

47 IT CAME UPON THE MIDNIGHT CLEAR

This hymn, written by Mr. Sears when he was a Unitarian minister at Wayland, Massachusetts, appeared in *The Christian Register* for December 1850. Mr. Sears wrote to Bishop Bickersteth, 'Though I was educated in the Unitarian denomination, I believe and preach the Divinity of Christ.'

NOEL appeared in *Church Hymns with Tunes* (1874). Sir Arthur Sullivan, the editor, received from a friend the melody of the first four lines; he altered it slightly, harmonized it, and composed the second half of the tune, setting it to the present hymn.

48 O LITTLE TOWN OF BETHLEHEM

Written by Dr. Phillips Brooks for his Sunday School at Holy Trinity Church, Philadelphia, in 1868, after he had visited Bethlehem in 1866.

CHRISTMAS CAROL, from *Worship Song* (1905), was composed for this hymn by Sir Walford Davies.

So was VILLAGE, which Dr. Stocks published in *Repton School: Hymns for Use in Chapel* (1924).

49 STILL THE NIGHT, HOLY THE NIGHT

This favourite song was first published in the *Leipziger Gesangbuch* (1838), but it had been composed in 1818 and was first sung on Christmas eve of that year in the church of Oberndorf near Salzburg, where Mohr was assistant-priest. It was sung to the well-known air, composed the same day by Franz Gruber, a musical friend of Mohr. As the organ had become useless, Mohr sang the melody in the tenor, accompanying himself on a guitar, while the composer sang the bass. A choir of girls from the village joined in the melody, repeating the last two lines of each verse.

The translation is based on Stopford Brooke's version (in his *Christian Hymns*, 1881) which has been considerably altered in order to render it more faithful to the original.

Both Mohr's hymn and Gruber's tune became popular before they were printed, owing to their being sung by wandering Tyrolese singers.

50 IN THE BLEAK MIDWINTER

As printed in her collected *Poems*, this is marked as having been composed by Miss Rossetti 'before 1872'. For purposes of musical rhythm, the compilers have ventured to alter 'only His mother' to 'His mother only' in the third verse. One stanza has been omitted.

Gustav Holst's tune CRANHAM was written for the hymn, and appears in *The English Hymnal*.

51 SEE IN YONDER MANGER LOW

Slightly altered from a longer poem in Edward Caswall's *Masque of Mary* (1858).

Sir John Goss wrote HUMILITY for this hymn. It appeared in *Christmas Carols, New and Old*, edited by the Rev. H. R. Bramley and J. Stainer (second series, 1870).

52 LOVE CAME DOWN AT CHRISTMAS

Another (see 50) of Miss Rossetti's exquisite lyrics. From her *Verses* (1893).

In the Petrie Collection of Irish Melodies, GARTAN is said to be a hymn tune popular in Co. Donegal. It has been harmonized by Dr. Evans.

53 CHILD IN THE MANGER

Mr. Lachlan Macbean of Kirkcaldy has kindly supplied the following information about this hymn and its tune: 'The verses have been chosen from a longer, beautiful hymn by Mary MacDougall, who in the earlier decades of the nineteenth century was a widely recognized poetess in the island of Mull. This hymn she named "The Child of Agh", i.e. of Happiness, Good Fortune, Power, or Wonder.

'The tune BUNESSAN was noted down by Alexander Fraser from the singing of a wandering Highland singer. Its bold movements are in keeping with the freedom shown in Gaelic song.' It is printed from *Songs and Hymns of the Gael* (ed. L. Macbean, 1888).

54 CHRISTIANS, AWAKE, SALUTE THE HAPPY MORN

From a longer poem or carol written for his daughter Dolly about 1749. Like Hymn 456, it proves that Dr. Byrom, as Palgrave claims (in *The Treasury of Sacred Song*), 'was one of the many men of strong feeling in whom faith burned "like a hidden flame" throughout the eighteenth century.' Both hymns are from his posthumous *Miscellaneous Poems* (1773, 1814).

In Byrom's notebook there is this entry: 'Christmas, 1750. The singing men and boys with Mr. Wainwright came here and sang " Christians awake".' STOCKPORT is said to have been first sung in Stockport parish church on the day this entry was made, but it was not published till ten years later, in Ashworth's *Collection* (*c.* 1760). Subsequently it appeared in Wainwright's own *Collection of Psalm Tunes* (1766).

55 O COME ALL YE FAITHFUL

No manuscript copies of the original Latin go back earlier than the middle of the eighteenth century, and these are English. The French evidence is slightly later, but the hymn may have been composed in France about 1700. It was sung later in the chapel of the Portuguese Embassy in London.

The first form is that composed in 1841 by Canon Oakeley, who translated it for his congregation at Margaret Street Chapel, London; this version appeared in Murray's *Hymnal* (1852).

The second form is from W. Mercer's *Church Psalter and Hymn-book* (1854), but 'Now' has been substituted for 'Late' in the second last line.

The origin of the tune ADESTE FIDELES is equally obscure. It has been stated that the music was composed either by John Reading, who was organist of Winchester College, and died in 1692, or by another English musician of the same name, who was a pupil of Dr. John Blow, and died in 1764. This assertion seems to rest solely on the authority of Vincent Novello. In a collection published by him in 1843, entitled *Home Music, the Congregational and Chorister's Psalm and Hymn Book, &c.*, the music appears arranged as a psalm tune, set to Psalm 106. It is headed 'Air by Reading, 1680', and the following note is appended: 'This piece obtained its name of "The Portuguese Hymn" from the accidental circumstance of the Duke of Leeds, who was a director of the Concert of Ancient Music, many years since (about the year 1785), having heard the hymn first performed at the Portuguese Chapel, and who, supposing it to be peculiar to the service in Portugal, introduced the melody at the Ancient Concerts, giving it the title of "The Portuguese Hymn", by which appellation this very favourite and popular tune has ever since been distinguished; but it is by no means confined to the choir of the Portuguese Chapel, being the regular Christmas hymn, "Adeste Fideles", that is sung in every Catholic chapel throughout England.' As Novello was for many years organist of the Portuguese Chapel, this note may be taken as giving a correct account of how the tune received the name of 'The Portuguese Hymn'. Novello's statement as to the composer of the music is, however, a different matter. Nothing in the least resembling the music of 'Adeste Fideles' has been found either in any of the second John Reading's published works, or in two manuscript volumes in his autograph long in the possession of Dr. W. H. Cummings. As to the claim of the older John Reading, the organist of Winchester, no evidence whatever has been produced in its favour.

So far as has yet been ascertained, the earliest book in which the music appears in print is a small volume entitled *An Essay on the Church Plain Chant* (London: Printed and published by J. P. Coghlan, in Duke Street, Grosvenor Square. MDCCLXXXII). The book is in three parts, and the 'Adeste Fideles', with its music, is in the second of these, which is headed 'Part Second, containing several Anthems, Litanies, Proses, and Hymns, as they are sung in the Public Chapels at London'. In his 'Advertisement' to the public, Coghlan, the publisher, says, 'It is necessary to observe that the Third Part, or Supplement to this work, was not compiled by the Gentleman who did the other Two Parts.' It seems highly probable that the 'Gentleman' so referred to was Samuel Webbe, senior, for nearly all the pieces in the second part of the volume (including the 'Adeste Fideles' and the tune now known as 'Melcombe') appear again in Webbe's *Collection of Motetts or Antiphons* (1792), and several of them have his name appended to them there as composer.

Although the *Essay on the Church Plain Chant* is at present the earliest book known to contain the 'Adeste Fideles', it is found in manuscripts of older date. One of the earliest of these yet discovered is a volume preserved at Stonyhurst College, Lancashire, dated 1751. It is the work of John Francis Wade, who seems to have employed himself in writing out music for use in Roman Catholic families and institutions. The 'Adeste Fideles' is given in four stanzas, with the music repeated to each, and is headed 'In Nativitate Domini Hymnus'.

The conclusion seems to be that the hymn and tune came into use together, in the services of the Roman Church, during the first part of the eighteenth century; that they were in circulation in manuscript for some time before they appeared in print, but that nothing definite can as yet be stated as to the author of either words or music.

56 FROM HEAVEN ABOVE TO EARTH I COME

A selection from the delightful carol of fifteen verses which Luther wrote for his small son Hans at a Christmas Eve festival. It was published in Klug's *Gesangbuch* (Wittenberg, 1535). Luther had a man dressed as an angel to sing the first three verses; the children responded with the fourth and following. The first verse was based upon a popular song 'I come from lands afar', to the tune of which the hymn was originally sung; but, owing to its secular associations, this melody was finally abandoned in favour of the present tune, which Luther himself composed in 1539.

The translation is in Miss Winkworth's *Lyra Germanica*. A vigorous Scottish version was composed by John Wedderburn of Dundee, who took refuge in Wittenberg about 1539; it is published in the *Gude and Godlie Ballatis*, where we find, for example, this equivalent of ver. 5:

> And war the warld ten tymes sa wyde,
> Cled ouir with golde and stanis of pryde,
> Unworthie were it zit to thee,
> Under thy feit ane stule to be!

This, modernized, would run:

> And were the world ten times as wide,
> Clad o'er with gold and stones of pride,
> Unworthy were it yet for Thee,
> Under Thy feet a stool to be!

Geistliche Lieder (Leipzig, 1539) contains VOM HIMMEL HOCH. The present setting is Bach's in his *Christmas Oratorio*.

57 THE RACE THAT LONG IN DARKNESS PINED

Dr. Watts had also written a hymn on Isaiah ix. 2–8, but this paraphrase was composed by Dr. John Morison independently. It is printed as it appeared in the 1781 edition of *The Scottish Paraphrases*.

The tune TIVERTON is from *A Selection of Psalm and Hymn Tunes, from the best authors, in three and four parts: adapted principally to Dr. Watts's Hymns and Psalms, and to Dr. Rippon's Selection of Hymns, by John Rippon, D.D. (c. 1795).* The composer's name is given as '— Grigg', without any Christian name. His identification with the Rev. Joseph Grigg, the hymn-writer, is purely conjectural.

58 GOOD CHRISTIAN MEN, REJOICE

A carol by Dr. J. M. Neale, contributed to *Christmas Carols, New and Old* (edited by Rev. H. R. Bramley). See above, on 51.

The tune IN DULCI JUBILO appears in Klug's *Gesangbuch* (Wittenberg, 1535), where it is set to a hymn consisting of a mixture of Latin and German, beginning 'In dulci jubilo nun singet und seid froh'. Both hymn and melody are probably much earlier than the above date. See Duncan's *The Story of the Carol*, p. 61, for original form.

59 GOD AND FATHER, WE ADORE THEE

This hymn is founded on a verse attributed to John Nelson Darby, the founder of Plymouth Brethrenism. The verse appears in William Blair Neatby's *History of the Plymouth Brethren* (1901), the bulk of which was issued as a series of articles in *The British Weekly*; it was sent by a critic of these articles and appeared in that paper on Jan. 17, 1901. When the drafting Committee of the Presbyterian Church of England were engaged on *Church Praise*, they asked Dr. Falconer to write a Christmas hymn with some reference to 'the family idea', or to the forbears who are much in people's minds at this season. He took this verse as a starting-point, altering 'Christ' to 'Son' in the second line. Verse 6 is also a modification of Darby's verse; otherwise the hymn is Falconer's.

Samuel Smith's tune NEWTON FERNS is from a *Selection of Psalm and Hymn Tunes*, issued privately by the composer in 1865.

60 OF THE FATHER'S LOVE BEGOTTEN

The Latin original is a cento of eight verses from a longer hymn in the *Cathemerinon* (ix) of the Spanish poet Prudentius (348–413). His idea is that 'at every hour of the day should a believer be mindful of Christ who is the Alpha and Omega, the beginning and the end. Prudentius therefore praises Him as the creator of all things, as the everlasting Son of the Father's love begotten' (A. S. Walpole, *Early Latin Hymns*, p. 123). The fifth verse represents a doxology which was added, though not by Prudentius, to his hymn. Dr. J. M. Neale's version was altered and adapted by Sir H. W. Baker for *Hymns Ancient and Modern* (original edition), and this current form is reproduced here, with the omission of four stanzas.

In *The Hymnal Noted* (part ii, 1856) the melody of CORDE NATUS is given as 'from a MS. at Wolfenbuettel of the thirteenth century', but this statement has never been verified. The air was in use during the thirteenth century to the words 'Divinum mysterium', and probably Mr. Helmore, the editor of *The Hymnal Noted*, took it from Petri's *Piae Cantiones* (Greifswald, 1582). Both he and the original editors of *Hymns Ancient and Modern* misread, at some points, the melody in the *Piae Cantiones*. The present is the correct form, which was adopted in the new edition of *Hymns Ancient and Modern* (1904).

61 RING OUT, YE CRYSTAL SPHERES

From the *Ode on the Nativity*, which Milton began upon Christmas Day, 1629, when he was still at Cambridge University. Hallam calls this Ode 'perhaps the finest in the English language'. The ringing music is the song of the angels heard by the shepherds who 'sat simply chatting in a rustic row'. Suddenly

> The helmèd cherubim
> And sworded seraphim
Are seen in glittering ranks with wings displayed.

They chant

> Such music (as 'tis said)
> Before was never made,
> But when of old the Sons of Morning sung,
> While the Creator great
> His constellations set
And the well-balanced World on hinges hung.

Then follow the verses of this hymn, in which Milton is appealing for the song of the angels to be heard once more on earth. He was acquainted with the new Copernican astronomy, but preferred the Ptolemaic as being more poetical. According to it, the ten spheres (which he makes 'nine' here) revolved round the earth in concentric circles, carrying with them the sun and moon and the planets, and producing music as they went.

In verse 1 'consort' is used in our modern sense of 'concert'.

Dr. Ross composed CARILLON for the present collection.

62 'JESUS!' NAME OF WONDROUS LOVE

From *Psalms and Hymns* (1854), composed by Dr. How himself and Rev. T. B. Morrell on St. Matthew i. 21: 'thou shalt call his name Jesus: for he shall save his people from their sins'.

PSALM 136 (LOUEZ DIEU) is the tune set to this psalm in the complete French Psalter of 1562.

NOMEN DOMINI was harmonized by Sir John Stainer for the former *Church Hymnary*, from a melody in *Ein Gesangbuch der Brueder in Behemen und Merherrn* (Nuremberg, 1544: preface by Johann Horn), where it is set to 'O liebster Herr Jesu Christ'.

63 AS WITH GLADNESS MEN OF OLD

Composed by Mr. Dix during an illness in 1860, and first published in *Hymns of Love and Joy* (1861). The text as in *Hymns Ancient and Modern*, approved by the author, who had originally written in verse 2

> To that lowly manger-bed

and

> Him Whom,

and in verse 3

> At that manger.

The changes were made because the wise men come to a house (St. Matthew ii. 11), not to a stable.

The tune DIX appeared originally in *Stimmen aus dem Reiche Gottes . . . herausgegeben von Conrad Kocher* (Stuttgart, 1838), where Kocher set his melody to the hymn ' Treuer Heiland, wir sind hier'.

64 BRIGHTEST AND BEST OF THE SONS OF THE MORNING

First published by Heber in *The Christian Observer* (November 1811), when he was vicar of Hodnet. Zachary Macaulay, Lord Macaulay's father, was editor of the journal.

The tune SPRINGFIELD is from *The Comprehensive Tune Book,*

edited by H. J. Gauntlett (1846–51), where it is named 'Stowell', and is in 7 7 7 7 metre, as follows:

The present form of the tune appeared, without composer's name, in Maurice's *Choral Harmony* (1854).

EPIPHANY was contributed by the Rev. J. F. Thrupp to Turle's *Psalms and Hymns for Public Worship* (1863), where it was set to this hymn.

LIEBSTER IMMANUEL is from *Himmels-Lust und Welt-Unlust* (Jena, 1679), which contains the oldest form of the melody. Later German books show considerable variations. The present form is mainly Bach's, in his Church Cantata on this Chorale.

65 ANGELS FROM THE REALMS OF GLORY

The original form of Montgomery's hymn, as it appeared first, on Dec. 24, 1811, in *The Sheffield Iris*, a newspaper on whose staff he was then employed. The first verse repeats the allusions to the song of angels at creation which occurs in Montgomery's other hymn of praise (Hymn 38 above). Ver. 4 echoes the words of Malachi iii. 1: 'the Lord, whom ye seek, shall suddenly come to his temple'.

Dr. Randall published LEWES about 1774 on a separate sheet, set to the hymn 'Mighty God, while angels bless Thee'.

LLANDINAM, by Thomas Williams, appears in D. Jenkins's *Tunes, Chants, and Anthems* (1883), and is there stated to be from *The National Psalmist*, by Hafrenydd.

66 FROM THE EASTERN MOUNTAINS

Written in 1873 and published by Prebendary Thring in his *Hymns and Sacred Lyrics* (1874). The last stanza is omitted, and slight alterations have been made in ver. 4, for the sake of euphony. The text on which the hymn is based is St. Matthew ii. 2: 'We have seen His star in the east and are come to worship Him.'

COLYTON, in *The Children's Hymnbook* (edited by Mrs. Carey Brock, 1881), was composed by Dr. W. H. Monk for this hymn.

67 THOU DIDST LEAVE THY THRONE

Privately printed in 1864 for the choir and school-children of St. Mark's Church, Brighton. Here reproduced as in Miss Elliott's

Chimes for Daily Service (1880), except that she wrote ' cedar' instead of 'forest' in ver. 3 (line 3), and 'Lord' instead of 'O Lord' in ver. 4 (line 1). The text for the hymn was St. Luke ii. 7: 'there was no room for them in the inn'.

MARGARET, by the Rev. T. R. Matthews, is from *Children's Hymns and Tunes* (1876).

68 THERE CAME A LITTLE CHILD TO EARTH

First printed by Miss Elliott in *Matty's Missionary Box* (1856), then revised for her *Chimes for Daily Service*.

NADOLIG has been specially composed by Mr. J. M. Lloyd for this hymn, as CHILDREN'S SONG was composed for it by Mr. Walton in the former edition of *The Church Hymnary*.

69 ONCE IN ROYAL DAVID'S CITY

From Mrs. Alexander's *Hymns for Little Children* (1848). Like Hymns 105 and 591, it was written on a clause of the Apostles' Creed (Hymn 724), i.e. on 'Who was conceived by the Holy Ghost, born of the Virgin Mary'.

Dr. Gauntlett originally wrote IRBY for this hymn, to be sung by voices in unison, with harmonized accompaniment. It appeared in *Hymns for Little Children. . . . Set to music with piano accompaniment, by H. J. Gauntlett* (1858).

70 COME, PRAISE YOUR LORD AND SAVIOUR.

This hymn was first published in *Children's Hymns* (S.P.C.K., 1873), under Dr. How's name.

GOSTERWOOD (*The English Hymnal*, 1906), as arranged by Dr. Vaughan Williams from a folk-song entitled 'The brisk young lively lad'. The air seems to have been known at one time in the Isle of Man as a carol tune.

71 I LOVE TO HEAR THE STORY

Mrs. Miller composed this hymn in less than a quarter of an hour one afternoon. It appeared in *The Little Corporal* (Chicago, 1867). a magazine which she edited.

The tune ANGEL'S STORY was composed for it by Dr. A. H. Mann, and appeared in *The Methodist Sunday School Hymnbook* (1881).

72 WE SAW THEE NOT WHEN THOU DIDST COME

A free version, by Rev. J. H. Gurney (in his *Psalms and Hymns*, 1851, prepared for St. Mary's, Marylebone, of which he was rector), of an earlier hymn on the same lines by Mrs. Anne Richter, which appeared in *Songs from the Valley* (Kirkby Lonsdale, 1834). The authoress, Miss Anne Rigby, married the Rev. W. H. Richter. 'Successive alterations', says Mr. Gurney, ' have left nothing of the original composition remaining but the first four words and the repeated words'.

Sir John Stainer wrote CREDO for this hymn, and it appeared in *Hymns Ancient and Modern* (1875).

73 WHO IS THIS, SO WEAK AND HELPLESS

First published by Dr. How in the supplement (1867) to his *Psalms and Hymns* (see on 62); then revised by him for *Church Hymns* (1871).

Mr. Lloyd's tune HENRYD, appeared first in *Aberth Moliant* (1873).

74 O SING A SONG OF BETHLEHEM

Contributed to *The School Hymnal* (Philadelphia), which Dr. Benson edited for the American Presbyterian Church in 1899.

The melody of KINGSFOLD, arranged by Miss L. E. Broadwood from a folk-song entitled 'The Red Barn'. From *The English Hymnal* (1906), where it is set, however, to 'I heard the voice of Jesus say' (Hymn 410 below).

75 YE FAIR GREEN HILLS OF GALILEE

Contributed by Dr. E. R. Conder to the *Congregational Church Hymnal* of 1887.

Sullivan's tune SAINTS OF GOD, from *Church Hymns with Tunes* (1874), was written, as the title suggests, for 'The saints of God, their conflict past' (Hymn 219 below).

76 BEHOLD A LITTLE CHILD

This hymn, like 70, was first published in *Children's Hymns* (S.P.C.K., 1873), under Dr. How's name.

LOVE UNKNOWN was contributed by Mr. Ireland to *Songs of Praise* (1925), where it was set to 'My song is love unknown'.

The original source of WESLEY, to which the hymn is set in *The English Hymnal*, cannot be traced.

77 WHO IS HE, IN YONDER STALL

This hymn is printed as it appeared in *The Dove: A Collection of Music for Day and Sunday Schools* (Chicago, 1866), except that 'He who' in ver. 7 is changed to 'He that'. The authorship is not quite certain, but probabilities point to B. R. Hanby (see G. F. Root's *Story of a Musical Life*, p. 142). In the 1875 edition of *Chapel Gems*, which Root and Hanby edited, it is marked B. R. H. This means that he wrote the tune, but there is no indication in the book of any authorship of words. Still, no other author has ever been suggested, and Hanby's name may be provisionally associated with the hymn, words as well as music.

78 ON JORDAN'S BANK THE BAPTIST'S CRY

One of Coffin's Latin hymns in his *Hymni Sacri* (Paris, 1736), freely translated in Chandler's *Hymns of the Primitive Church* (1837), so freely indeed that the close of the 4th verse, though excellent in itself, misses the thought of the original Latin:

> aegris salutarem manum
> extende; prostratos leva;
> ostende vultum; jam suus
> mundo reflorescet decor.

Chandler prepared his volume 'in order that the psalms might be supplemented by hymns, which, though unauthorized (like all the rest) by the Church of the day, had at any rate the authority of the older Church and were consonant with the sources of the Prayer Book' (Dr. W. H. Frere).

SOLEMNIS HAEC FESTIVITAS is one of the French melodies referred to in the note on Hymn 4 (second tune).

79 FORTY DAYS AND FORTY NIGHTS

Apart from the omission of the last stanza, this represents the Rev. Francis Pott's version (in his *Hymns Fitted to the Order of Common Prayer*, 1861) of nine stanzas which were originally contributed by the Rev. G. H. Smyttan to *The Penny Post* for March 1856.

AUS DER TIEFE (HEINLEIN) in the *Nürnbergisches Gesangbuch* (1676?), 1677, is set to the hymn 'Aus der Tiefe rufe ich'. There the melody has the initials M. H. attached to it, and Zahn conjectures that these may stand for Martin Herbst. But the tune was occasionally attributed to Paul Heinlein; hence its alternative name.

80 IT FELL UPON A SUMMER DAY

From Dr. Stopford Brooke's *Christian Hymns* (1881).

In *A Students' Hymnal* (University of Wales, 1923), CHILDHOOD is the tune written for this hymn.

81 GOD WHO HATH MADE THE DAISIES

From *The Children's Choir*, which Dr. Paxton Hood himself edited in 1870. Like hymns 80, 82, and 658 it is based on St. Matthew xix. 13–15.

Mr. J. S. Anderson has arranged ES IST EIN ROS' ENTSPRUNGEN for this hymn. The air, a traditional carol-melody of the Rhineland, is to be found in the *Alte Catholische Geistliche Kirchengesang* (Cologne, 1599).

82 I THINK, WHEN I READ THAT SWEET STORY OF OLD

The words and the music are knit together. Mrs. Luke wrote the hymn in 1841 to suit a Greek air SALAMIS, which had caught her fancy. She informed the late Dr. John Brownlie that she had to go one day on some missionary business to the little town of Wellington, five miles from Taunton, in a stage coach. It was a beautiful spring morning, it was an hour's ride, and there was no other inside passenger. On the back of an old envelope I wrote in pencil the first two of the verses now so well known, in order to teach the tune to the village school supported by my stepmother, and which it was my privilege to visit. The third verse was added afterwards to make it a missionary hymn.' They were printed in *The Sunday School Teacher's Magazine*, at the end of the volume for 1841.

83 FIERCE RAGED THE TEMPEST O'ER THE DEEP

Composed by Prebendary Thring in 1861 and published in R. R. Chope's *Congregational Hymn and Tune Book* (1862); based on St. Mark iv. 39 ('And he arose, and rebuked the wind, and said unto the sea, Peace, be still').

The tune ST. AËLRED was written for it by Dr. Dykes, and in this book the last line was in common time, and ended in minor, thus—

It was altered to the present form by the composer when included in *Hymns Ancient and Modern Appendix* (1868).

84 FIERCE WAS THE WILD BILLOW

No Greek original has been ever found for this hymn, which Dr. Neale published in his *Hymns of the Eastern Church* (1862). Like 83, it is based on St. Mark iv. 39. Neale imagined it was composed by St. Anatolius of Constantinople, but the only hymn-writer of that name in the Greek Church lived in the eighth century, not in the fifth.

It was set to SILAS in *The Hymnary* (Novello, 1872).

85 WHEN THE LORD OF LOVE WAS HERE

From Dr. Stopford Brooke's *Christian Hymns* (1881).

SALVATOR was composed by M. B. Foster for this hymn in *Worship Song* (edited by W. Garrett Horder in 1905).

86 THINE ARM, O LORD, IN DAYS OF OLD

Written in 1864 by Dr. Plumptre for use in the Chapel of King's College Hospital, London.

The tune ST. MATTHEW appeared in *A supplement to the New Version of Psalms by Dr. Brady and Mr. Tate . . . The Sixth Edition, corrected and much enlarged . . .* (1708), under its present name, and was marked in the Index as a new tune. It was set to Psalm 33, in two parts, treble and bass, as follows:

The above publication contains no composers' names, but it is generally believed that Dr. Croft was concerned in its production, and that 'St. Matthew' is his composition. From the middle of the eighteenth century his name is invariably attached to it in all the collections in which composers' names are found.

87 WHAT GRACE, O LORD, AND BEAUTY SHONE

From Sir Edward Denny's *Selection of Hymns* (1839), where it is entitled '*The Forgiving One*, Psalm xlv. 2'.

The tune ST. BERNARD is from *Neues . . . Kirchen und Hauss Gesang der . . . Tochter Sion. . .* (Cologne 1741), where in its original form it is set to one of the hymns in praise of the Virgin Mary, the melody being as follows:

In *Heil- und Hülfs-Mittel zum thätigen Christenthum* (1767) the melody appears in the following form:

This is also found in *Cantica Spiritualia* (vol. ii, Munich, 1847). The present tune has probably been arranged from the last-named book, and seems to have first appeared in *Easy Hymn Tunes with the words in full, adapted for Catholic Schools, &c.* (1851). The tune is set to the hymn 'Jesus, the very thought of Thee', and is headed 'Hymn of St. Bernard'. The adaptation was possibly made by J. Richardson, and the tune has been attributed to him in several collections.

88 O MASTER, IT IS GOOD TO BE

A Transfiguration hymn; the original in six stanzas was published by Dean Stanley in *Macmillan's Magazine* for April 1870.

The tune WER DA WONET, in the St. Gall *Gesangbuch* of 1863, is arranged, with considerable alterations, from a melody in Michael Vehe's *Neu Gesangbuchlin* (Leipzig, 1537), where it is set to a metrical version of Psalm xci.

89 O WONDROUS TYPE! O VISION FAIR

An anonymous fifteenth-century Latin hymn, as rendered by Dr. Neale in his *Hymnal Noted*, and revised in *Hymns Ancient and Modern* (1861). Three verses are omitted, two of which refer to the presence of Moses and Elijah at the Transfiguration; the Latin is

> res memoranda saeculis,
> hic cum tribus discipulis,
> cum Moyse et Helia
> grata promit eloquia.
>
> assistunt testes gratiae
> legis, atque prophetiae;
> de nube testimonium
> sonat Patris ad Filium.

DAS WALT' GOTT VATER as arranged and harmonized by J. S. Bach in his *Choralgesänge*, from an air in the second volume of the *Musikalische Kirch- und Hauss- Ergötzlichkeit* (Leipzig, 1713, edited by Daniel Vetter).

90 LORD, AS TO THY DEAR CROSS WE FLEE

From Mr. Gurney's *Lutterworth Collection of Hymns* (1838), published when he was curate of Lutterworth.

The tune ST. FRANCES was composed by Mr. Löhr for the hymn 'Now that the daylight dies away' in *The Chorale Book*, compiled by H. W. Bemrose and arranged by W. Adlington (1861).

91 ALL GLORY, LAUD, AND HONOUR

The Latin original is a cento from the long processional hymn for Palm Sunday in the medieval Church, a hymn commonly attributed to St. Theodulph, bishop of Orleans, who had been imprisoned (from 818 onwards) at Angers by the emperor Louis on a charge of conspiracy. The version is by Dr. Neale, in his *Hymnal Noted*, but in the form revised for *Hymns Ancient and Modern* (new edition). He notes that 'another verse was usually sung, till the seventeenth century, at the pious quaintness of which we can scarcely avoid a smile:

> Be Thou, O Lord, the rider,
>   And we the little ass;
> That to God's holy city
>   Together we may pass.'

The scriptures behind the hymn are Psalms xxiv. 7–10 and cxviii. 25–6, St. Matthew xxi. 1–17 and St. Luke xix. 37–8.

The tune ST. THEODULPH comes from *Ein andächtiges Gebet . . . so wol ein tröstlicher Gesang, darinnen ein frommes Herz dieser Welt Valet gibet, &c.*, Leipzig, 1615), a small tract of six leaves containing the hymn by Herberger, 'Valet will ich dir geben', and two melodies set to it by Melchior Teschner. Both are arranged for five voices. The present is the second of the two, and is as follows:

Later German books exhibit various slight changes in the melody. The substitution of C for A at the eleventh note is found in the Gotha Cantional, 1648.

92 RIDE ON! RIDE ON IN MAJESTY

In the original, first published in Heber's posthumous *Hymns* (1827), the third line of the first verse was,

> Thy humble beast pursues his road.

The alteration was made in F. H. Murray's *Hymnal for use in the Church of England* (1852).

It is said that when Heber received the manuscript of Milman's hymn for a collection of Church Hymns in which he hoped to include contributions by the best living poets, he exclaimed enthusiastically, ' A few more such hymns and I shall neither need nor wait for the aid of Scott and Southey.'

The first tune CRASSELIUS (WINCHESTER NEW) comes from *Musicalisch Hand-Buch der Geistlichen Melodien à Cant. et Bass* (Hamburg, 1690), where the following form of the melody is set to the hymn ' Wer nur den lieben Gott lässt walten':

In Moore's *Psalm-Singer's Delightful Pocket Companion*, Glasgow (1762), the tune appears in the following form, and is named 'Winchester':

Professor Macalister's OBER AMMERGAU is an adaptation of the music accompanying the entry into Jerusalem in the Passion-Play at Oberammergau.

93 HOSANNA, LOUD HOSANNA

From Miss Threlfall's volume of poems, *Sunshine and Shadow* (1873); in verse 3 (line 3) 'whilst' has been altered to ' while'.

In the *Vollständige Sammlung der gewohnlichen Melodien zum Mainzer Gesangbuche . . . von Xavier Ludwig Hartig* (Mainz, *circa* 1833), the melody of ELLACOMBE is set to the hymn ' Der du im heiligen Sakrament'. It is there dated 1700, but Dr. Bäumker states that Hartwig is very incorrect as to the sources of tunes, and he does not believe that the present melody is older than the beginning of the nineteenth century.

94 WEEP NOT FOR HIM WHO ONWARD BEARS

Based on St. Luke xxiii. 28: 'Weep not for me'. It is from Mr. Pollock's original six stanzas as first printed in *The Gospeller* (1870).

CROWLE is an anonymous tune, which first appears in *A Book of Psalmody &c. by James Green* (fifth edition, 1724). How much earlier the tune is, it is not possible to say.

95 MY LORD, MY MASTER, AT THY FEET ADORING

This happens to be the only hymn in our collection which is taken directly from the French—from *Les Cantiques spirituels de Saint Sulpice* (1765). But Bridaine's hymn appeared first at Montpellier in 1748. The text here is that of Mr. Pollock's version (1887), as in *Hymns Ancient and Modern*, and its faithfulness may be judged by a comparison with the second verse of the original:

Judas vous livre aux Juifs dans sa fureur extrême;
Peut-il à cet excès, le traître, vous haïr?
Comme lui, mille fois je dis que je vous aime,
Et je ne rougis point, ingrat, de vous trahir!

The tune PSALM 110 (L'OMNIPOTENT) was composed or adapted by L. Bourgeois for the psalm in the French Psalter of 1551, replacing the melody formerly used for it. In the Scottish Psalter of 1564 it was set, with some alterations, to a version of the psalm by John Craig. Its present form is in accordance with the original.

96 O COME AND MOURN WITH ME AWHILE

From Faber's longer poem in twelve stanzas, as published in his *Jesus and Mary* (1849). Some alterations have been made in the original text, which has in ver. 1 (line 2)

See, Mary calls us to her side,

and (line 3)

O come and let us with her mourn,

also 'Love' for 'Lord' in the last line of every verse, except in the fourth, which reads

And Love Himself is crucified,

and in the sixth, which runs

For Love Himself is crucified.

Dr. Dykes composed ST. CROSS for this hymn in *Hymns Ancient and Modern* (1861).

97 O WORD OF PITY, FOR OUR PARDON PLEADING

Miss Greenaway's hymn appeared first in the 1904 edition of *Hymns Ancient and Modern*.

The tune PSALM 80 has not been traced earlier than the complete edition of the *Scottish Psalter* in 1564, where it is set to Robert Pont's version of that psalm. It may therefore be of Scottish origin. The present adaptation has been made by Mr. J. S. Anderson.

98 LORD, WHEN THY KINGDOM COMES, REMEMBER ME

Written by Dr. Maclagan for the revised edition of *Hymns Ancient and Modern* (1875); the text as altered and authorized in the new edition of 1904.

At the end of *The Psalms of David, by Robert Goodridge* (1684), there are seven tunes in two parts, melody and bass, 'to which all the psalms may be sung as directed'. The present tune CONGLETON is set to Psalm lxvii, and has appended to it the name of 'Mr. Michael Wise'.

99 AT THE CROSS, HER STATION KEEPING

The Latin original, based on St. John xix. 26, 27, is a longer poem in rhyme; thus the first stanza runs

> stabat mater dolorosa
> iuxta crucem lacrimosa,
> dum pendebat filius;
> cuius animam gementem,
> contristatam et dolentem,
> pertransivit gladius.

It is a thirteenth-century production, and hymnologists are still divided upon the question of its authorship. Pope Innocent III (1161–1216) was credited with it, in the eighteenth century, and the claims of Jacopo dei Benedetti, an eccentric lay brother of the Franciscan order (*d.* 1306) have also been urged. In his critical study in Julian's *Dictionary* (p. 1082) Mr. Mearns concludes that it is very doubtful 'if Jacopone wrote any Latin hymns'; indeed he 'does not seem to have been capable of writing such a poem as the *Stabat mater dolorosa*'. Probably it was an anonymous hymn, first used in private prayer-books. However, it rises clear above all such uncertainties. As Dr. Schaff claims, it 'is the most pathetic, as the "Dies Irae" is the most sublime, hymn of the middle ages. . . . The soft, sad melody of the verse is untranslatable.' Yet numerous attempts have been made to render it into English. The present version is the work of several hands; the first two lines of the first stanza, and the first three of the second, are practically Caswall's (in his *Hymns and Poems*), and the remainder of the hymn is drawn mainly from Bishop Mant's version as altered in F. H. Murray's *Hymnal* (1852) and other collections.

When Sir Walter Scott lay dying at Abbotsford, 'his mind, though hopelessly obscured, appeared,' Lockhart says, 'when there was any symptom of consciousness, to be dwelling, with rare exceptions, on serious and solemn things . . . Commonly, whatever we could follow him in was a fragment of the Bible (especially the Prophecies of Isaiah, and the Book of Job)—or some petition in the Litany—or a verse of some psalm (in the old Scotch metrical version) —or of some of the magnificent hymns of the Romish ritual. . . . We very often heard distinctly the cadence of the *Dies Irae*; and I think the very last stanza that we could make out, was the first of a still greater favourite:

> Stabat Mater dolorosa,
> Juxta crucem lachrymosa,
> Dum pendebat Filius.'

The hymn has been wedded to the music of the tune STABAT MATER in several books and manuscripts of the eighteenth century. It goes back to the form in the *Mainz Gesangbuch* of 1661, which is as follows:

Sta - bat ma - ter do - lo - ro - sa   Jux - ta cru - cem la - cry - mo - sa,

Dum pen - de - bat fi - li - us,   Dum pen - de - bat fi - li - us.

100 THRONED UPON THE AWFUL TREE

Canon Ellerton's hymn, written in 1875, appeared first in *Hymns Ancient and Modern* of that year.

The tune ARFON is a Welsh air, arranged by the Rev. Hugh Davies from a folk-song melody.

101 HIS ARE THE THOUSAND SPARKLING RILLS

Written by Mrs. Alexander in 1875.

The tune ISLEWORTH, by Dr. Samuel Howard, is from *Melodies of the Psalms of David according to the version by Christopher Smart,* where it is set to the version of Psalm vi.

102 O PERFECT LIFE OF LOVE

Written by Sir H. W. Baker in 1875 and first published in the revised edition of *Hymns Ancient and Modern* that year. It is one of the most adequate hymns in this section, for form and spirit; the deep feeling of the lines is expressed with artistic self-restraint, and the effect deepens as verse follows verse to the climax.

NEWLAND is from *The Congregational Psalmist* (1858), which was edited by Dr. Henry Allon and Dr. Gauntlett himself.

SOUTHWELL is set to Psalm xlv in Damon's *Psalmes of David* (1579), and is called by this name in Ravenscroft's book (1621). Originally the melody was in the Dorian mode, and had C♯ in line 3.

103 AND NOW, BELOVÈD LORD, THY SOUL RESIGN-ING

Written by Mrs. Alderson in 1868 at the request of her brother, the Rev. J. B. Dykes. Two stanzas are omitted. In the original, verse 3 (after 'yieldest') ran thus,

ere its ending
Purged from sin's awful and accursèd load,
The conflict o'er,

and in ver. 4 (line 3) 'Thine' has been substituted for 'Those'.

In the *Allgemeines Choralbuch* (Leipzig, 1819), J. G. Schicht's tune ZU MEINEM HERRN is set to a German metrical version of Psalm cx.

104 BY THE CROSS OF JESUS STANDING

From the third series of Dr. Bonar's *Hymns of Faith and Hope* (1866). One stanza is omitted:

> Here the holy, happy greeting,
> Here the calm and joyful meeting,
>   God with man in glad accord;
> Love that cross to us is telling,
> Darkness, doubt, and fear dispelling,
>   Love in Jesus Christ our Lord.

Probably the earliest appearance of SHILOH in Scotland is in a *Collection of Psalms and Hymn Tunes* by Henry Boyd (Glasgow, 1793); it is found in many later Scottish collections. The present arrangement is by Mr. J. S. Anderson.

105 THERE IS A GREEN HILL FAR AWAY

Another of Mrs. Alexander's *Hymns for Little Children* (1848), composed to illustrate 'Suffered under Pontius Pilate, was crucified, dead, and buried' (Hymn 724). See on Hymn 69.

HORSLEY is the third tune in *Twenty-Four Psalm Tunes and Eight Chants, composed by William Horsley* (1844), where, however, it has no name.

106 WHEN I SURVEY THE WONDROUS CROSS

The original form, in Watts's *Hymns and Spiritual Songs* (1707), read in ver. 1 (line 2) 'Where the young Prince', and in ver. 4 (line 2) 'That were a present'; the fourth stanza of the original is omitted, i.e.

> His dying crimson, like a robe,
> Spreads o'er His Body on the Tree;
> Then am I dead to all the globe,
> And all the globe is dead to me.

The original title of this great hymn is: 'Crucifixion to the World by the Cross of Christ. Gal. vi. 14.' Matthew Arnold thought it the finest hymn in the English language. He heard it sung after sermon in Sefton Park Presbyterian Church, Liverpool, on the last Sunday of his life, and was overheard repeating the third verse shortly before his sudden death on April 15, 1888.

This is the first of sixteen hymns by Watts in the *Hymnary*. 'The English Independents, as represented by Dr. Watts, have a just claim', says Lord Selborne, 'to be considered the real founders of modern English hymnody . . . As long as pure nervous English, unaffected fervour, strong simplicity, and liquid yet manly sweetness are admitted to be characteristics of a good hymn, works such as these must command admiration.'

ROCKINGHAM (COMMUNION) is from *The Psalms of David for the Use of Parish Churches. The Music Selected, Adapted, and Composed by Edward Miller, Mus. Doc.* (1790), where it occurs seven times. It is headed 'Part of the melody taken from a hymn tune', and is named 'Rockingham'. This name has been generally retained in English books. Dr. Miller may have adapted the tune from one named 'Tunbridge', which is found in a *Supplement to Psalmody in Miniature* published by A. Williams about 1780. In Scotland it seems to have appeared first in the collections edited by R. A. Smith and John Wilson. It is there attached to Paraphrase xxxv, and called 'Communion', doubtless from the fact that this paraphrase is almost invariably sung on Communion occasions. In both these books the third note of the melody in the second line is flattened, but this reading has now been universally dropped in favour of the original.

107 O SACRED HEAD, SORE WOUNDED

The original medieval hymn, sometimes attributed to St. Bernard of Clairvaux, was probably the work of Arnulf von Loewen (1200–1250). The Latin was rendered into German, and this version, entitled 'To the suffering Face of Jesus Christ', is ascribed to Paul Gerhardt (*Praxis Pietatis Melica*, 1656). The original is a long hymn in seven parts on the suffering Saviour, the verses beginning ' Salve caput cruentatum' being the seventh section. 'This classical hymn has shown an imperishable vitality in passing from the Latin into the German, and from the German into the English, and proclaiming in these tongues . . . with equal effect the dying love of our Saviour, and our boundless indebtedness to Him' (Schaff). The closing verse has been associated specially with the death-bed of many eminent Germans. Thus it was sung in Tamil by the native assistants of C. F. Schwartz, as he died at Tanjore on Feb. 13, 1798. Ritschl, it is true, in his *History of Pietism* criticized the undue stress laid by the hymn on the physical sufferings of our Lord; yet on his death-bed (March 20, 1889) he asked for the closing verse to be repeated to him.

The present version is based on Dr. J. W. Alexander's rendering in his book, *The Breaking Crucible, and other Translations* (New York, 1861). It appears in several forms, one of which, as in C. D. Cleveland's *Lyra Sacra Americana* (1861), has nothing corresponding to the second verse, and presents a slightly different text of the other stanzas; e.g. ver. 1 runs:

> O sacred Head, now wounded,
>   With grief and shame weigh'd down,
> O sacred Brow, surrounded
>   With thorns, thine only crown!

Once on a throne of glory,
  Adorn'd with light divine,
Now all despised and gory,
  I joy to call Thee mine.

The tune PASSION CHORALE is from *Lustgarten Neuer Teutscher Gesäng . . . Componirt durch Hanns Leo Hassler von Nürmberg* (1601), where it is set to a secular song beginning 'Mein Gmüt ist mir verwirret', as follows:

In *Harmoniae Sacrae* (Görlitz, 1613) it is set to the hymn 'Herzlich thut mich verlangen', and in later books it is generally associated with 'O Haupt voll Blut und Wunden', of which the present hymn is a free translation. Bach used the chorale five times in his *St. Matthew Passion*. The form of the melody used by him is that adopted here, and the harmony is also mainly his.

108 SING, MY TONGUE, HOW GLORIOUS BATTLE

This Latin hymn is ascribed to Venantius Fortunatus, and tradition associates its composition with Nov. 19, 569, when the poet is supposed to have celebrated the success of his patroness, Queen Radegundis, in securing, among other sacred relics, a fragment of the true Cross. She deposited this precious trophy in the convent which she had founded, and over which she presided, at Poitiers, and Fortunatus on this solemn occasion wrote his famous poem.

The present version renders four of the original ten stanzas, together with a doxology which was occasionally added to the poet's verses, when they passed into Church use. Mr. A. W. Wotherspoon kindly furnishes this account of the version. 'In preparing *The Scottish Mission Hymnbook*, the Committee of the Church of Scotland had before it a collection of some hundred hymns made (and printed) for an important mission-week carried through in Aberdeen under Professor Cooper. I was one of the missioners, and some things of mine were among these hundred hymns. The Committee took a few of them for the first draft of the new book. When we went over those that formed the draft, Dr. Mair was interested in the translation of the hymn of Fortunatus, and as they knew by that time that it was mine, he and I were asked to revise it together—with the Latin, of course. His suggested changes were all to the good. Those which I remember gave the first two lines of the second verse, the "patient" before "body" in the third verse, and he greatly improved the doxology. We liked Neale's "Faithful Cross, &c." in verse 4 too well to change it. They gave me a large share in the editing and all the arranging of the book, and so I gave myself the pleasure of coupling Dr. Mair's name with mine as translators. He was surprised when he saw that I had done so, but it pleased him.'

PANGE LINGUA is the proper plain-song melody of the hymn.

ARDUDWY is a tune by John Roberts from *Llyfr Tonau Cynulleid-faol (Ychwanegiad)*, 1870.

109 WE SING THE PRAISE OF HIM WHO DIED

The original form, in Mr. Kelly's *Hymns* (Dublin, 1815) ended
'Tis all that sinners want below,
'Tis all that angels know above.

He altered it himself, in later editions.

The tune WALTON is from *Sacred Melodies from Haydn, Mozart, and Beethoven, adapted to the best English Poets, and appropriated to the use of the British Church, by William Gardiner* (vol. ii, 1815), where it is headed 'Subject from Beethoven', but the original has not been discovered in any of that composer's works. In his *Music and Friends* (1838), Gardiner gives some information as to the source of his Sacred Melodies, and states regarding the present one that it 'is somewhere in the works of Beethoven, but where I cannot now point out'.

110 AND CAN IT BE THAT I SHOULD GAIN

Written at 'Little Britain', London, in May 1738, and published the same year in *Psalms and Hymns*. One of the greatest and most characteristic of Charles Wesley's hymns, in which the incidents of his conversion are clearly portrayed.

Under date of 23 May, Charles Wesley writes in his Journal: 'At nine I began a hymn on my conversion but was persuaded to break off for fear of pride. . . . I prayed Christ to stand by me and finished the hymn. It is not unusual with the enemy to preach humility when speaking will endanger his kingdom or do honour to Christ. Least of all would he have us tell what things God has done for our souls: so tenderly does he guard us from pride. But God has showed me He can defend me from it while speaking for Him.' Two days afterwards John Wesley was able to say 'I believe', and went to his brother Charles's room. He tells us, 'We sung the hymn with great joy.' It is difficult to determine whether it was this hymn or another written at the same time, viz. 'Where shall my wondering soul begin?' that was then sung, but it was certainly one of them.

The tune ISRAEL was composed by Sir George C. Martin for 'Come, O Thou traveller unknown', as the name indicates, in the former edition of *The Church Hymnary* (1898).

111 O SAVIOUR, WHERE SHALL GUILTY MAN

From Maurice's *Choral Hymnbook* (1861). In ver. 2 (line 3) Mrs. May wrote 'yield to Satan's power'. The first verse appeared in a tune-book called Maurice's *Choral Harmony* (1858).

Mr. W. H. Gladstone originally composed HAMMERSMITH for 'Eternal Light' (Hymn 36).

112 DARK THE DAY ON CALVARY'S CROSS

Like 402, this hymn, composed by Dr. MacLean Watt, appears for the first time here.

In Freylinghausen's *Neues Gesangbuch* (1719) PRESSBURG is set to Gerhardt's hymn, 'Nicht so traurig, nicht so sehr'.

113 IN THE CROSS OF CHRIST I GLORY

Another (see on 33) of Sir John Bowring's *Hymns* (1825). It was based on Gal. vi. 14. When he died, on Nov. 23, 1872, the words 'In the Cross of Christ I glory' were placed on his tombstone.

C. F. Witt's tune STUTTGART is from *Psalmodia sacra, oder, Andächtige und schöne Gesänge* (Gotha, 1715) where it is set to the hymn, 'Sollt es gleich bisweilen scheinen'.

114 BY JESUS' GRAVE, ON EITHER HAND

From Dr. Gregory Smith's *Hymnbook for the Services of the Church and for Private Reading* (1855). The compilers insert this hymn, as it is almost alone in commemorating the Saturday evening between Good Friday and Easter Sunday.

The tune O MENSCH SIEH is from the Bohemian Brethren's *Gesangbuch* (1566), but in the form adopted by *The English Hymnal* (1906). The rhythm is much altered from the original.

115 'WELCOME, HAPPY MORNING!'—AGE TO AGE SHALL SAY

Canon Ellerton's exultant hymn is a free paraphrase (originally published in Borthwick's *Supplementary Hymn and Tune Book*, 1869) of some couplets from a long Latin poem by Fortunatus (see on Hymn 108) on the Resurrection, beginning

> Salve festa dies toto venerabilis aevo,
> qua Deus infernum vicit et astra tenet.

The poem, addressed to his friend Felix the bishop of Nantes, was composed before A.D. 582; 'in it he dwells with much poetical force and with deep religious feeling upon the beauty of spring, which has come in her gayest attire to greet her risen Lord. He endows nature with a soul, much as a modern poet might. No writer has with truer insight and keener observation pourtrayed her outburst of rejoicing after the winter of her discontent than Fortunatus has done in this poem. Each verse brings a fresh trait, a new point of beauty and of exultation, and all this rejoicing is brought into connexion with the resurrection of Christ' (A. S. Walpole, *Early Latin Hymns*, pp. 181, 182).

Writing to his friend, the Rev. Godfrey Thring, Canon Ellerton observes that Cranmer, in a letter to Henry VIII (Oct. 7, 1544), mentions that he had tried to translate this favourite church hymn *Festa Dies*; 'it would appear from this letter that this was the first Church hymn ever translated from Latin directly into English'.

There is a version by Canon Lacey in *The Altar Hymnal* (1884), which begins:

> Hail! Festal Day, to endless ages known,
> When Christ, o'er death victorious, gained His throne.
> Now, with the Lord of new and heavenly birth,
> His gifts return to grace the springing earth.

Sir Arthur Sullivan's tune FORTUNATUS (*The Hymnary*, 1872) was composed for this hymn, as its title indicates.

116 BLEST MORNING, WHOSE FIRST DAWNING RAYS

This version, by an unknown hand in *The Scottish Paraphrases* (1781), has altered and decidedly improved the original five stanzas by Watts (*Hymns*, 1707), which began,

> Blest morning, whose young dawning rays
>   Beheld our rising God;
> That saw Him triumph o'er the dust,

read (ver. 2),

> In the cold prison of a tomb
>   The dead Redeemer lay,

and went on (ver. 3),

> Hell and the grave unite their force
>   To hold our God in vain;
> The sleeping Conqueror arose,

closing ver. 4 (first couplet) thus,

> These sacred hours we pay,

with 'triumph' for 'triumphs' in the last line.

Dr. Howard's tune LANCASTER is called 'St. Clement's Tune' in *Parochial Harmony: consisting of a Collection of Psalm Tunes in three and four parts &c., by William Riley* (1762), where it is set to Psalm i.

117 ON WINGS OF LIVING LIGHT

Dr. How's hymn appeared in the S.P.C.K. *Children's Hymns* (1873).

WATERSTOCK appeared in *Parochial Psalmody: A Collection of Ancient and Modern Tunes. . . . The whole arranged with an accompaniment for the Organ or Pianoforte by John Goss, organist of Chelsea New Church* (1826). There it is set to Psalm cxxxvi.

118 CHRIST THE LORD IS RISEN TO-DAY

The original form of Wesley's hymn (*Hymns and Sacred Poems*, 1739), in eleven four-lined stanzas, read in ver. 2 (line 7)

> Dying once, He all doth save.

The change to the present text was made by Madan in his *Psalms and Hymns* (1760).

Sir George Elvey's tune ST. GEORGE'S, WINDSOR, appeared in *A Selection of Psalm and Hymn Tunes, edited and arranged by E. H. Thorne.... Adapted to Psalms and Hymns compiled by the Rev. T. B. Morrell and the Rev. W. W. How* (1858), where it was set to the hymn 'Hark! the song of Jubilee' (Hymn 389 below).

119 JESUS CHRIST IS RISEN TO-DAY

This anonymous hymn is printed as in Arnold's *Complete Psalmodist* (7th ed., 1779), except that 'praises' has been changed into 'praise' (ver. 2, line 1). The last verse was added by Charles Wesley. The germ of the hymn was three stanzas contributed to a small anonymous collection called *Lyra Davidica* in 1708, but only the first of these was used in the later version. In Heber's posthumous *Hymns* (1827), where it is ascribed by mistake to Heber, the form is slightly different. Thus ver. 1 runs

> Jesus Christ is risen to-day,
> Our triumphant holiday!
> Who so lately on the cross
> Suffer'd to redeem our loss;

and ver. 3 runs:

> For the pains which He endured
> Our salvation have secured.
> Now He reigns above the sky,
> Where the angels ever cry.

It is there followed by an original Easter hymn of Heber which deserves to be rescued from oblivion. The first three verses are:

> God is gone up with a merry noise
>   Of saints that sing on high,
> With His own right hand and His holy arm
>   He hath won the victory.
>
> Now empty are the courts of Death,
>   And crush'd thy sting, Despair;
> And roses bloom in the desert tomb,
>   For Jesus hath been there!
>
> And He hath tam'd the strength of Hell,
>   And dragg'd him through the sky,
> And captive behind His chariot wheel,
>   He hath bound captivity.

Notes on Words and Music

EASTER HYMN is from *Lyra Davidica, or a Collection of Divine Songs and Hymns, partly New Composed, partly Translated from the High German and Latin Hymns; and set to easy and pleasant Tunes* (1708). The hymn and tune appear as under, headed 'The Resurrection'—

For LLANFAIR see Hymn 16.

120 THE LORD IS RISEN INDEED

From the seven stanzas of the original in Mr. Kelly's *Collection of Psalms and Hymns* (1802). The text is St. Luke xxiv. 34: 'The Lord is risen indeed'. The tone of it resembles that of Heber's hymn first quoted.

OLD 134TH (ST. MICHAEL) is an adaptation of the following tune in the French Psalter of 1551, composed or arranged by L. Bourgeois for Marot's version of Psalm ci:

In the 1561 edition of the *Anglo-Genevan Psalter*, the tune appears as under, set to Psalm cxxxiv:

Possibly the fourth and fifth notes here are due to a misprint, as those of the original (G instead of B flat) are restored in all other editions. With the exception of these two notes, the above form of the melody is retained in all the editions of the *Scottish Psalter*, but those of the *English Psalter* show some variations. In all of these the third line is the same as at present, while line 4 is found in two forms. The earlier editions from 1562 have

but from 1577 the form adopted in nearly all editions is

The present form of the tune, and also the name 'St. Michael', by which it is usually known in England, are probably due to Dr. Crotch.

QUINTA in *A Students' Hymnal* (University of Wales, 1923) (see 80) was composed for 'O Lord our God, arise' (Hymn 376 below).

121 JESUS LIVES! THY TERRORS NOW

This 'Easter hymn' appeared in Gellert's *Geistliche Oden und Lieder* (Leipzig, 1757); Miss Cox's version in her *Hymns from the German* (1841) followed the original six-line form, but the present four-line form of her translation (first in Rorison's *Hymns and Anthems*, 1851) became very popular, owing largely to the tune ST. ALBINUS, although it misses the note of triumphant faith in the last line of each verse in Gellert's poem ('Dies ist meine Zuversicht'). The text prefixed is Rom. viii. 11.

Miss Cox agreed to the present form of the first two lines, and also to the addition of the 'Hallelujah'.

CHRIST IST ERSTANDEN. The hymn beginning with these words was in use in Germany as an Easter hymn at an early period, being referred to in manuscripts of the thirteenth century. It was probably sung to the present melody, but the earliest appearance of the latter in print seems to be in Weisse's *Ein Neu Gesangbuchlen* (1531). In subsequent German books it appears with many alterations. The refrain at the close of each verse is in some books 'Alleluia' and in others 'Kyrie eleison'. This melody is said to occupy the same place in German music as 'Sumer is icumen in' does in English.

ST. ALBINUS is from *The Church Hymn and Tune Book* (1852), edited by W. J. Blew and Dr. Gauntlett himself. It was composed for an Easter hymn, 'Angels to our jubilee'.

122 THE STRIFE IS O'ER, THE BATTLE DONE

This translation of the anonymous medieval hymn which appears first in the Jesuit *Symphonia Sirenum* (Cologne, 1695), was made by Mr. Pott about 1859, and included in his *Hymns Fitted to the Order of Common Prayer* (1861); then it was revised for *Hymns Ancient and Modern*.

VICTORY is an adaptation from the 'Gloria Patri' of the 'Magnificat Tertii Toni', contained in the work entitled 'Magnificat Octo Tonorum', published by Palestrina in 1591. The present arrangement was made by Dr. W. H. Monk for this hymn, and appeared in *Hymns Ancient and Modern* (1861).

123 THE DAY OF RESURRECTION

This Greek hymn for Easter, composed by John of Damascus, was translated by Dr. Neale very freely in his *Hymns of the Eastern Church*. His version opened,

> 'Tis the day of resurrection,

and read in ver. 3 (lines 5 and 6)

> Invisible and visible
> Their notes let all things blend.

The present form of the translation as in *Hymns Ancient and Modern*.

The reference in ver. 2 is to St. Matthew xxviii. 9: 'Jesus met them, saying, All hail.'

LANCASHIRE was composed about 1836 by Henry Smart for 'From Greenland's icy mountains'; it appeared in *Psalms and Hymns for Divine Worship* (1867).

124 O SONS AND DAUGHTERS, LET US SING

This hymn, by a Minorite friar at Paris, called Jean Tisserand (*d.* 1494), has been traced to a booklet published in France between 1518 and 1536, where it consists of 9 stanzas. Three were eventually added, i.e. the Latin originals of verses 4, 5, and 8 in our version, which corresponds to the earlier form of Dr. Neale's renderings (in *Mediaeval Hymns* and *Hymnal Noted*) as modified in *Hymns Ancient and Modern*. The English translation therefore reproduces six of Tisserand's stanzas and the three subsequently incorporated in his poem. See Dr. W. H. Grattan Flood's article in *Musical Opinion* (1916), pp. 445, 446.

The melody of O FILII ET FILIAE is found in slightly varying forms in books of the eighteenth century, including La Feillée's *Méthode*

Nouvelle pour apprendre . . . les règles du Plain Chant. In a German Jesuit collection published in 1671, entitled *Nord-Sterns Führers zur Seeligkeit,* a German translation of the Latin hymn is given with the melody, as follows:

The present form of the tune is slightly modified from that found in *An Essay on the Church Plain Chant* (1782), and Webbe's *Collection of Motetts* (1792).

125 OUR LORD CHRIST HATH ARISEN

First published in the Irish *Church Hymnal* (1873), when Dr. Plunket was bishop of Meath. In *Lyra Hibernica Sacra,* the last line of ver. 2 begins, 'The grave cannot scare us.' The alteration was made by the editors of the present collection.

KIRN was composed by Mr. Prentice Taylor for this hymn in the present collection.

126 HALLELUJAH, HALLELUJAH!

Bishop Wordsworth's hymn, as first published in *The Holy Year* (1862), had five stanzas.

Sir Arthur Sullivan composed LUX EOI for 'Hark! a thrilling voice is calling', in the second edition of *Hymns for the Church of England with proper Tunes*; but that book not having been published till 1875, the actual first appearance in print of the tune was in *Church Hymns* (1874).

127 JESUS, LORD, REDEEMER

Mr. Kirkland's hymn appeared in the revised edition (1907) of *Church Praise.*

Dr. Evans composed KIRKLAND for the words in this collection.

128 OUR LORD IS RISEN FROM THE DEAD

From the Wesleys' *Collection of Psalms and Hymns* (1743).

CANTATE DOMINO was composed for Hymn 23 by Sir Joseph Barnby. It is from *The Hymnary* (1872).

129 HE IS GONE—BEYOND THE SKIES!

A selection from the original seven stanzas in *Macmillan's Magazine* (1862), which were written about 1859, as Dean Stanley explained, 'at the request of a friend whose children had complained to him that there was no suitable hymn for Ascension Day'. In the author's copy, which he presented to Dr. Schaff, 'shall' in the last line was 'may'. The text is Acts i. 9.

In the nineteenth edition (1678) of *Praxis Pietatis Melica*, this tune ALLE MENSCHEN MÜSSEN STERBEN appears anonymously, but it appears in the twenty-fourth edition (1690) with the initials J. H., which are known to stand for Jacob Hintze. The tune has been frequently attributed to J. Rosenmüller. This mistake seems to have arisen from the fact that the above hymn, 'Alle Menschen', &c., was written for the funeral of a Leipzig merchant in 1652, and was printed with music by Rosenmüller. This music, however, is totally different from the present tune. The present arrangement is by J. S. Bach in his *Choralgesänge*.

130 THE GOLDEN GATES ARE LIFTED UP

From Mrs. Alexander's *Hymns Descriptive and Devotional* (1858). PRAETORIUS is from *Harmonicae Hymnorum scholae Gorlicensis* (Görlitz, 1599). It appeared later in M. Praetorius's *Musae Sionae* (Part VI, 1609), and was supposed therefore to have been written by him. Hence its name.

131 THE HEAD THAT ONCE WAS CROWNED WITH THORNS

From Mr. Kelly's *Hymns* (5th edition, 1820), based on Hebrews ii. 10.

The tune ST. MAGNUS (NOTTINGHAM) appeared in *The Divine Companion: or David's Harp new tun'd. Being a Choice Collection of New and Easy Psalms, Hymns, and Anthems . . . the second edition* (1709). There it is anonymous, but the three preceding tunes are said to be by 'Mr. Jer. Clark', and in W. Riley's *Parochial Harmony* (1762) the tune bears its present name and is assigned to Clark. In Gawthorn's *Harmonia Perfecta* (1730) it is called NOTTINGHAM.

132 THE LORD ASCENDETH UP ON HIGH

Mr. Russell's hymn in *The English Hymnal* is marked 'by A. T. Russell and others', and has been rearranged and altered there, to suit the melody 'Nun Freut Euch'. (See note on 211.)

In the *Allgemeines Choralbuch* which Schicht edited in 1819 (Leipzig), his tune ASCENDIT DEUS was set to the words 'So hoff ich denn mit festem Mut.'

133 GOLDEN HARPS ARE SOUNDING

Written by Miss Havergal in December 1871. 'When visiting at Perry Bar she walked to the boys' schoolroom, and being very tired she leant against the playground wall while Mr. Snepp went in. Returning in ten minutes, he found her scribbling on an old envelope, and at his request she handed him the hymn just pencilled' (*Memorials of F. R. Havergal*, pp. 136, 137). It is an Ascension Song based on Ephesians iv. 8.

Her tune HERMAS appeared in *Havergal's Psalmody* (1871).

134 LOOK, YE SAINTS! THE SIGHT IS GLORIOUS

From the third edition (1809) of Mr. Kelly's *Hymns*.

TRIUMPH is from the same source as 'St. Albinus' (121), but it received its present name in *The Congregational Psalmist* (1858) of which Dr. Gauntlett was musical editor.

135 REJOICE, THE LORD IS KING

The sixth stanza of the original, in Wesley's *Hymns for our Lord's Resurrection* (1746), has been omitted.

This hymn and 427 were among the three Wesley hymns for which Handel composed tunes, his tune for the present hymn being GOPSAL —so named from Gopsal House near Ashby-de-la-Zouche, where his friend Charles Jennens, the composer of the libretto for *The Messiah*, resided.

The tune DARWALL was composed for the new version of Psalm cxlviii in *Williams's New Universal Psalmodist* (1770). The Rev. Henry Parr, in his *Church of England Psalmody*, states that the Rev. John Darwall 'composed Tunes in two parts to the whole 150 psalms, the autograph of which is now in the possession of his grandson, the Rev. Leicester Darwall'.

136 CROWN HIM WITH MANY CROWNS

The original, in six stanzas, appeared in Matthew Bridges's *Hymns of the Heart* (2nd edition, 1851) and in his *Passion of Jesus* (1852), under the text, Revelation xix. 12. The present form of the hymn is arranged from a recast of Bridges's verses in *Church Hymns* and in Prebendary Thring's *Church of England Hymnbook* (1880); the former had, in ver. 3 (line 3), 'Those' instead of 'Rich'.

Sir George Elvey's DIADEMATA was composed for this hymn in *Hymns Ancient and Modern* (Appendix, 1868).

137 BLEST BE THE EVERLASTING GOD

This paraphrase of 1 Peter i. 3–5 was originally written by Isaac Watts and published in his *Hymns* (1707), from which it was taken over unchanged into *The Scottish Paraphrases* of 1745 and 1751.

But in the final edition of 1781 the Church of Scotland omitted one stanza (the third) and altered the following one from

> There's an inheritance divine
> Reserv'd against that day;
> 'Tis incorrupted, undefil'd,
> And cannot waste away.

The improvements are attributed to William Cameron.

BISHOPTHORPE cannot be traced earlier than *The Psalms of David for the use of Parish Churches. The Music Selected, Adapted, and Composed by Edward Miller, Mus. Doc.* (1790). There the tune is named as at present, and assigned to Jeremiah Clark. It may be an adaptation by Dr. Miller.

138 ALLELUIA! SING TO JESUS

From Mr. Dix's *Altar-Songs* (1867), omitting one stanza, which links it to the Sacrament of the Lord's Supper. The title was 'Redemption by the Precious Blood'; the hymn echoes Rev. v. 9 ('Thou hast redeemed us to God by thy blood out of every nation').

ALLELUIA was composed by Dr. S. S. Wesley for this hymn in *Hymns Ancient and Modern* (Appendix, 1868).

139 ALL HAIL, THE POWER OF JESUS' NAME

This is a selection from the original eight stanzas which were first printed anonymously in *The Gospel Magazine* for April 1780. Even when Perronet issued his *Occasional Verses*, in which he included it, he did not reveal his authorship directly; the one indication is in some acrostic verses which disclose his name.

In the original text, the 3rd line of ver. 2 ran,

> Extol the stem-of-Jesse's Rod

and ver. 5 had 'tribe . . . tongue' in the 1st line, followed by

> That bound creation's call,
> Now shout in universal song
> The crownèd Lord of all.

These changes, together with the addition of the last verse, occur partly in Dr. J. Rippon's *Selection of Hymns from the Best Authors* (1787), though Dr. Rippon still kept (ver. 3)

> Ye chosen seed of Israel's race,
> A remnant weak and small,

and began ver. 5 thus:

> Let every kindred, every tribe,
> On this terrestrial ball.

MILES LANE was printed in *The Gospel Magazine* (November 1779) with one verse of the hymn, but without author's or composer's name. Shortly afterwards the tune appeared in the Rev. Stephen

Addington's *Collection*, under the name 'Miles's Lane', Shrubsole being named as the composer.

LADYWELL was composed for the hymn in *The Public School Hymnbook* (1919). Mr. W. H. Ferguson, being one of the editors, inserted it there as 'Anonymous'.

140 WHERE HIGH THE HEAVENLY TEMPLE STANDS

This most impressive paraphrase of Heb. iv. 14–16 differs from the hymn which is printed by Logan in his *Poems* (1781) in several details; 'Guardian' replaces 'patron' (ver. 1), 'their surety' replaces 'in mercy' (ver. 2), 'his mighty plan' is an improvement upon 'his plan of grace' in ver. 2 (line 3), 'The Saviour and the Friend of man' is substituted for 'The Guardian God of human race' in the next line, and in ver. 4 'His tears, His agonies, and cries' is put for 'His tears and agonies and cries'. The original hymn was probably composed by Michael Bruce, that 'youth of real genius' (Southey).

SOLDAU is from *Geystliche gesangk Buchleyn. Wittenberg* (1524); edited by Johann Walther. There it is set to Luther's hymn, 'Nun bitten wir den heiligen Geist', as follows:

The melody may be from a pre-Reformation source, and adapted by Walther.

The present form of the tune appeared in Dibdin's *Standard Psalm Tune Book* (1851).

141 IMMORTAL LOVE, FOR EVER FULL

A cento arranged from Whittier's poem 'Our Master', which appeared on Aug. 16, 1867, in the Boston *Congregationalist*.

Mr. Anderson's tune FINGAL appeared first in *The Scottish Hymnal* (1885), where it was set to 'I am not worthy, Holy Lord'.

142 STRONG SON OF GOD, IMMORTAL LOVE

The first stanzas (written in 1849) of Tennyson's *In Memoriam* (printed in May 1850). In his *Commentary* on the poem (pp. 80 f.) Professor A. C. Bradley points out that 'immortal Love is addressed as the Son, or revelation, of God'; 'thou art just' implies that it would have been unjust either 'to make him merely that he might die' or 'to make him such that he thinks himself immortal when he is really not so'; 'as before' means 'before the growth of knowledge disturbed' the union of mind and soul; in the last two lines, to 'bear thy light' (i.e. the light of knowledge) is opposed to the idea of the vain or conceited worlds imagining proudly that this intellectual knowledge was their own. One stanza (the second) is omitted.

ST. VENANTIUS, a Rouen Church melody (as in *The English Hymnal*), is one of the tunes referred to under Hymn 4.

143. O LOVE DIVINE! THAT STOOPED TO SHARE

Dr. Holmes printed these lines in *The Professor at the Breakfast Table* (1859), but they were written in 1849.

O AMOR QUAM EXSTATICUS, as in *The Oxford Hymnbook* (1908). It is said to be an old French melody, but its source has not yet been traced. The Latin title is the first line of a hymn by Thomas à Kempis.

144 AND DIDST THOU LOVE THE RACE THAT LOVED NOT THEE?

A selection from Miss Ingelow's longer hymn in her *Poems* (1863).

TEMPLE BRYAN was composed by Professor Macalister for this hymn, and for the present collection.

145 ONE THERE IS, ABOVE ALL OTHERS

Newton's hymn, as it appeared in the *Olney Hymns* (1779), had six stanzas, and was based on the text, 'There is a Friend that sticketh closer than a brother' (Proverbs xviii. 24). One of the verses omitted is:

> Men, when raised to lofty stations,
> Often know their friends no more;
> Slight and scorn their poor relations,
> Though they valued them before;
> But our Saviour always owns
> These whom he redeem'd with groans.

GODESBERG is from Heinrich Albert's *Fünfter Theil der Arien oder Melodeyen* (Königsberg, 1642). There it is set to the hymn 'Gott des Himmels und der Erden', the melody being exactly as in the present form of the tune.

146 O SON OF MAN, OUR HERO STRONG AND TENDER

See under Mr. Fletcher's name, in the Biographical Notes.

Dr. Evans wrote CHARTERHOUSE for this hymn.

147 THOU WHO DIDST STOOP BELOW

First published in *The Christian Examiner* (1827), when Mrs. Miles was a girl of twenty. One verse is omitted. In verse 3 'rudest' is sometimes printed for 'earth's fierce', and the opening lines of ver. 4 run,

> E'en through the awful gloom
> That hovers o'er the tomb.

ELVEY was originally called 'Windsor Castle', in *Choral Harmony, with Supplement : A Collection of Tunes in short score for four voices. . . . By the Rev. Peter Maurice, D.D.* (1858).

148 THERE IS NO SORROW, LORD, TOO LIGHT

Mrs. Crewdson's hymn, in her volume called *A Little While, and other Poems* (Manchester, 1864) opened

> There 's not a grief, however light,
> Too light for sympathy,
> There 's not a care, however slight,
> Too slight to bring to Thee;

in ver. 2 (line 3) she wrote

> For He who bore,

and ver. 4 began

> Life's woes without.

The alterations, together with some other slight improvements, were made by Dr. B. H. Kennedy.

WALSALL comes from *A Choice Collection of Psalm Tunes by W. Anchors* (*c.* 1721). There is no authority for attributing it to Henry Purcell.

149 O COME, O COME, IMMANUEL

By the ninth century the Roman Church had adopted the custom of singing the Greater Antiphons or short anthem-verses at Vespers from Dec. 17 onwards; they were sung before or after the Magnificat.

Five of them are reproduced in this hymn, each being a short verse beginning with 'O'. The Latin original, which is supposed to date from about the twelfth century, was found in the *Psalteriolum Cant. Catholicarum* (7th edition, 1710), and Dr. Neale's version of it is reproduced as in *Hymns Ancient and Modern*, where however ver. 2 is placed last, its Latin original being

> veni, veni, Adonai,
> qui populo in Sinai
> legem dedisti vertice
> in majestate gloriae:
>> gaude, gaude; Immanuel
>> nascetur pro te, Israel.

The tune VENI IMMANUEL, as in *The Hymnal Noted* (Part II, 1856), where the melody is said to be 'From a French Missal in the National Library, Lisbon'. These Missals have all been examined by the Rev.

W. Hilton of the English College, Lisbon, but this melody is not to be found in them. In all probability it is not a genuine medieval melody, but has been made up of a number of plain-song phrases, most of these being found in settings of the Kyrie. The tune in its present form cannot be traced to an earlier source than *The Hymnal Noted*, and the likelihood is therefore that the adaptation was made for that book to suit Dr. Neale's translation.

150 COME, THOU LONG-EXPECTED JESUS

Originally two eight-line stanzas in Wesley's *Hymns for the Nativity of our Lord* (1744).

ST. NICOLAS, by R. Redhead, appears first in *Church Hymn Tunes for the Several Seasons of the Christian Year* (second series, 1859).

151 THE LORD WILL COME AND NOT BE SLOW

A cento from Milton's paraphrases of Psalms lxxxii (fourth stanza), lxxxv (first three stanzas), and lxxxvi (fifth and sixth stanzas).

PSALM 107 was an air composed or adapted by L. Bourgeois for this psalm in the *French Psalter* (1543, 1544); in the *Scottish Psalter* of 1564 it was altered to suit W. Kethe's metrical version of the same psalm. The present form is as in *The English Hymnal*.

152 THY KINGDOM COME, O GOD

From Mr. Hensley's *Hymns for the Minor Sundays* (1867), where ver. 3 (line 3) had 'Oppression, lust, and crime'.

Dr. Hayne's ST. CECILIA appeared in *The Merton Tune Book: A Collection of Hymn Tunes used in the Church of St. John Baptist, Oxford, Compiled by the Rev. H. W. Sargent, M.A. Edited and Arranged by the Rev. L. G. Hayne* (Oxford, 1863). There it was composed for what is 553 in the present *Church Hymnary*.

153 'THY KINGDOM COME!'—ON BENDED KNEE

Written by Mr. Hosmer on June 12, 1891, for the Commencement of the Meadville Theological School, Pennsylvania.

IRISH appears first in *A Collection of Hymns and Sacred Poems* (Dublin, 1749), among the 'Tunes adapted to the foregoing Hymns' at the end of the volume. It is without a name, and seems to have received the name 'Irish' in Ashworth's collection, published about 1760.

154 HAIL TO THE LORD'S ANOINTED

Written by Montgomery in 1821 for the Christmas worship of a Moravian settlement, perhaps at Fulneck in Yorkshire; his father was a Moravian minister. It was recited by the author on April 14, 1822, at a missionary meeting in Pitt Street Wesleyan Chapel, Liverpool, and the chairman, Dr. Adam Clarke, the famous Bible commentator, was so impressed that he printed it in his notes upon the seventy-second psalm, of which it is a flowing paraphrase.

The text as in his *Original Hymns* (1853); three stanzas have been omitted. 'For' is sometimes altered into 'To' in ver. 7 (line 1), as in Hymn 388 (where see note).

CRÜGER as arranged by W. H. Monk for *Hymns Ancient and Modern* (1861). It appeared originally in J. Crüger's *Neues vollkómlicher Gesangbuch* (Berlin, 1640), but the melody has often been altered in German books since then.

155 MINE EYES HAVE SEEN THE GLORY OF THE COMING OF THE LORD

Written in 1861 at the outbreak of the American Civil War. Mrs. Howe, on a visit to Washington, heard the Union troops singing 'John Brown's Body'. James Freeman Clarke suggested that she should compose new words for the melody; 'You ought to write some new words to go with that tune.' 'I will,' she said, and the words of the hymn came to her that night; she jotted them down before daybreak. They were first published in *The Atlantic Monthly* for February, 1862.

Here printed in the form followed by *Hymns of the Kingdom*, where, however, 'fatal' in ver. 1 is 'fateful'. In Mrs. Howe's poem, as printed in *The Treasury of American Sacred Song*, there is a second verse which is here omitted, and nothing corresponding to the fourth verse of our hymn, which has been added to Mrs. Howe's original.

VISION, by Sir Walford Davies, was composed for this hymn, and appeared in *In Hoc Signo* (Hymns of War and Peace, 1915).

BATTLE SONG, by Martin Shaw, was also written for it, at the request of *The Church Times*, and published in their monthly magazine *The Treasury* (December 1915).

156 YE SERVANTS OF THE LORD

From a posthumous edition (1755) of Doddridge's *Hymns*. It was entitled, 'The active Christian'; in ver. 5 it had 'favourite' instead of 'faithful', but to substitute the latter adjective is, as Dean Alford remarked, 'more a matter of duty than of choice'.

For the tune, see Hymn 120.

157 THOU ART COMING, O MY SAVIOUR

'It was on Advent Sunday, Dec. 2, 1873, I first saw clearly the blessedness of true consecration' (F. R. Havergal). This was the first hymn she wrote afterwards. It appeared in *Under the Surface* (1876).

BEVERLEY, by W. H. Monk, was composed for it in *Hymns Ancient and Modern* (revised edition, 1875).

158 WHEN HE COMETH, WHEN HE COMETH

First published in *The Red Bird* (Chicago, 1866), then in Sankey's *Sacred Songs and Solos*. Suggested by the words of Malachi iii. 17: 'They shall be mine, saith the Lord of hosts, in that day when I make up my jewels.'

The tune WHEN HE COMETH was composed for the hymn in *Our Song Birds* (1866). So was NESTA, which appeared in the Supplement (1894) to *Tunes, Chants, and Anthems, edited by D. Jenkins.*

159 LORD OF MERCY AND OF MIGHT

The second stanza of Heber's original, first published in *The Christian Observer* (1811), has been omitted.

ST. HILD, by W. Ellis, was originally written, as in *The Public School Hymnbook* (1919), for 'Holy Father, cheer our way'. It is named after St. Hild's Training College, Durham, where the composer was music master.

160 LO! HE COMES, WITH CLOUDS DESCENDING

The first, second, and fourth verses of this hymn, which has been called "The English "Dies Irae" ' (Schaff), go back to Charles Wesley's form (1758), the third to Cennick's (in the fifth edition of his *Collection of Sacred Hymns*, 1752), as rearranged by Martin Madan (*Collection of Psalms and Hymns*, 1760), whose poem had six stanzas of which the third and fifth are here omitted. In ver. 3 (line 3) Cennick wrote

> All his people, once despisèd,

and in ver. 3 (line 6)

> Now the promised Kingdom 's come!

The last two lines of ver. 4 are from Cennick; Wesley had written

> Jah, Jehovah,
> Everlasting God, came down.

In Heber's posthumous *Hymns*, where it is by mistake assigned to Heber, the last line of ver. 1 is

> Christ is come to earth again.

There has been much discussion about HELMSLEY. It is attributed to Thomas Olivers who is said to have adapted it from a tune he had heard whistled in the street. In Wesley's *Select Hymns* (second edition, 1765) it appears in the following form:

In Martin Madan's *Collection* (1769) it is found in practically the same form as the present.

161 THAT DAY OF WRATH, THAT DREADFUL DAY

Sir Walter Scott's version of the 'Dies Irae' is from *The Lay of the Last Minstrel* (1805), at the end of the sixth canto. Mr. Gladstone, speaking at Hawarden on Feb. 3, 1866, said, 'I know nothing more sublime in the writings of Sir Walter Scott—certainly I know nothing so sublime in any portion of the sacred poetry of modern times, I mean of the present century, as the "Hymn for the Dead", extending only to twelve lines, which he embodied in *The Lay of the Last Minstrel*.' See note on Hymn 99.

The translation reproduces only a very small part of the Latin original which, in its various forms, contains between fifty and sixty lines. Tradition, in this case upon adequate evidence, ascribes it to Thomas of Celano, who on Feb. 25, 1229 had completed his famous biography of St. Francis of Assisi. But, though composed in the thirteenth century, it did not come into vogue until the sixteenth to any great extent. Since then the hymn, in its original Latin or in some translation, has continued to impress both individuals and congregations; thus the last tender lines of the following extract were often on the lips of Dr. Johnson

> Recordare, Jesu pie,
> Quod sum causa tuae viae;
> Ne me perdas illa die!
>
> Quaerens me sedisti lassus,
> Redemisti crucem passus:
> Tantus labor non sit cassus!

The last three lines are inscribed on the tombstone of Dean Church in Whatley churchyard.

In Goethe's *Faust* the strains of the hymn harrow the conscience of Margaret as she worships in the cathedral. In Mr. C. F. S. Warren's monograph on *The Authorship, Text, and History of the Hymn Dies Irae* (reissued in 1902) nearly 250 versions of the hymn in English are chronicled.

Sir Walter's poem was included in the posthumous *Hymns Written and Adapted to the Weekly Church Service of the Year*, which Heber's widow published in 1827. The 'adapting', by Heber or some other hand, turned the last line of ver. 1 into

> Whom shall he trust that dreadful day?

And the third line of ver. 3 became

> Be Thou, Oh Christ! the sinner's stay.

LLEF is from *Gemau Mawl* (edited by D. Jenkins, 1890).

162 WAKE, AWAKE! FOR NIGHT IS FLYING

Miss Winkworth's translation, in her *Lyra Germanica* (2nd series), of this famous hymn composed by Dr. Nicolai in 1596 or 1597 during the appalling plague. His manse overlooked the churchyard, where there were sometimes as many as thirty funerals a day. 'I wrote out my meditations, found myself, thank God, wonderfully well, comforted in heart, joyful in spirit, and truly content; gave my manuscripts the name of "A Mirror of Joy", to leave behind me the token of my peaceful, joyous departure, or to comfort other sufferers whom He should also visit with the pestilence.' The hymn was entitled, 'Of the Voice at midnight and the wise Virgins who meet their Heavenly Bridegroom: Matthew xxv.' In ver. 2 Miss Winkworth wrote,

> Oh come, Thou blessèd Lord,
> O Jesus, Son of God.

Nicolai is also believed to have written the tune, WACHET AUF, which appears in *Frewden Spiegel des ewigen Lebens . . . durch Phillippum Nicolai* (Franckfurt am Mayn, 1599). The following is the melody as it is in the above book:

Owing, possibly, to misprints, there are some false rhythms in the above. To correct these Zahn suggests that the note at (1) should be a dotted semibreve, the rest at (2) should be omitted, and the note at (3) should be a semibreve. The present arrangement, both as to melody and harmony, is substantially that adopted by Mendelssohn in *St. Paul*.

163 CHRIST IS COMING! LET CREATION

From Dr. Macduff's *Altar Stones* (1853), published when he was minister of St. Madoes, Perthshire. He based it upon Rev. xxii. 20: 'He which testifieth these things saith, Surely I come quickly. Amen. Even so, come, Lord Jesus.'

Joachim Neander's tune, in his *Glaub- und Liebesübung . . .*

(Bremen, 1680), is set to the hymn 'Unser Herrscher, unser König', as follows:

164 TO THE NAME OF OUR SALVATION

The Latin original cannot be traced earlier than the fifteenth century, when it probably originated in Germany. The author is unknown. Dr. Neale's rendering (in his *Mediaeval Hymns*, 1851), which has an extra stanza, was altered thus for the first edition of *Hymns Ancient and Modern*.

ORIEL is from *Cantica Sacra in usum Studiosæ juventutis. Collegit et edidit J. Michael Hauber . . . Cantui Chorali accommodavit vocem organi Casparus Ett, Regiæ Ecclesiæ aulicæ ad S. Michael Monac. organoedus* (Monachii, 1840). There it is set in four parts to the hymn 'Pange lingua gloriosi'. It is not quite certain whether the tune was entirely composed by Ett, or only arranged by him; but it has not been traced to any earlier source. In *Easy Music for Church Choirs* (Part III, 1853), Ett is named as the composer.

165 JOIN ALL THE GLORIOUS NAMES

A selection from the original twelve stanzas in Watts's *Hymns and Spiritual Songs* (1709), printed exactly as Watts wrote them, except that ' before' replaces 'beneath' in the last line of the fourth verse. Watts called the hymn 'The same as the 148th psalm'.

It is doubtful whether WARSAW is by Thomas Clark of Canterbury. In Holdsworth's edition of *Chetham's Psalmody* (1832) the composer's name is merely given as 'Clark'.

166 O FOR A THOUSAND TONGUES, TO SING

A selection from the original eighteen stanzas in Wesley's *Hymns and Sacred Poems* (1740), where it was entitled 'For the Anniversary Day of One's Conversion'. It was composed on the first anniversary of his great spiritual change (see on Hymn 110), Sunday, May 21, 1738. The suggestion of it doubtless came from a remark made by Peter Böhler, the Moravian missionary to whom he owed that change: 'had I a thousand tongues I would praise Him with them all.' Since John Wesley's arrangement in *The Wesleyan Hymnbook* (1780), the first stanza of the original has been generally put last, as here, and Wesley wrote in the second line

My dear Redeemer's praise.

SOUTHWARK appears in *The Actes of the Apostles, translated into*

Englyshe Metre, and dedicated to the Kynges moste excellent Maiestye, by Christopher Tye, Doctor in Musyke, and one of the Gentylmen of hys graces moste honourable Chappell, wyth notes to eche chapter, to synge and also to play upon the Lute, very necessarye for studentes after theyr studye, to fyle theyr wyttes, and also for all Christians that cannot synge, to reade the good and Godlye storyes of the lyves of Christ hys Apostles (1553). This quaint work, of which the above is the full title, contains a metrical version of the first fourteen chapters of the Acts of the Apostles, each chapter having set to it a tune in four parts. The present is the first half of the tune set to chap. viii, thus:

The death of Steven did Saule com-fort Who did a - gre with them

That wold have slayne the god - lye sort Then at Je - ru - sa - lem.

167 WHEN MORNING GILDS THE SKIES

The German original is an anonymous hymn which appears variously in the *Katholisches Gesangbuch* (1828) and Von Ditfurth's *Fränkische Volkslieder* (1858). The present text is a cento from Caswall's rendering, which was first printed in Rev. Henry Formby's *Catholic Hymns* (1854), and in an enlarged form in his own *Hymns and Poems* (second edition, 1873), where ver. 2 begins

> The sacred minster bell,
> It peals o'er hill and dell

and ver. 6 ends with 'ages on'. This was one of Canon Liddon's favourite hymns; it was sung at his funeral on Sept. 16, 1890.

The tune PSALM 3 was composed or arranged by L. Bourgeois for the *French Psalter* in 1551, replacing an earlier melody. In the *Anglo-Genevan Psalter* (1561) it was set, with a slight change, to Kethe's version of Psalm cxxii. The psalm and tune were adopted in the complete *English Psalter* of 1562 and in the *Scottish Psalter* of 1564.

Sir Joseph Barnby's tune LAUDES DOMINI was composed for this hymn in *Hymns Ancient and Modern* (Appendix, 1868). In his *Original Tunes* published in 1869, the composer altered the last two bars as follows:

This alteration, however, has not been adopted in other collections.

168 YE SERVANTS OF GOD, YOUR MASTER PROCLAIM

Wesley's original, in *Hymns for Times of Trouble and Persecution* (1744), had six stanzas, and read in ver. 3 (line 3) 'Our Jesus' praises', and in ver. 4 (line 2) 'and wisdom' instead of 'all wisdom'. The first of the two stanzas omitted between verses 1 and 2 ran thus:

> The waves of the sea have lift up their voice,
> Sore troubled that we in Jesus rejoice;
> The floods they are roaring, but Jesus is here;
> While we are adoring, He always is near.

LAUDATE DOMINUM, by Sir Hubert Parry, was published in *Hymns Ancient and Modern* (Second Supplement).

HOUGHTON, by Dr. Gauntlett, was composed for 'O worship the King' in *The Congregational Psalmist* (Part III, 1861).

169 BLESSING AND HONOUR AND GLORY AND POWER

A cento from Dr. Bonar's hymn, 'The Song of the Lamb' in the third series of *Hymns of Faith and Hope* (1866), which had eight stanzas, and began with the present second verse. The last stanza of the original is the first of our cento.

TRISAGION, by Henry Smart, appeared first in *Hymns Ancient and Modern* (Appendix, 1868). It was written for the hymn 'Stars of the morning, so gloriously bright.'

170 SWEETER SOUNDS THAN MUSIC KNOWS

A 'Christmas' hymn contributed by Newton to the *Olney Hymns* (1779).

LÜBECK, in *Geistreiches Gesang-Buch . . . von Johann Anastasio Freylinghausen* (Halle, 1704), was originally set to the hymn 'Gott sei Dank in aller Welt', as follows:

BONN (FESTUS) is abridged greatly from its original form in the same book, where it was set to 'O du Hüter Israel'.

171 LIGHT OF THE WORLD! FOR EVER, EVER SHINING

From Dr. Bonar's *Hymns of Faith and Hope* (second series, 1861); three verses of the original are omitted.

Dr. Mann's tune WILTON was composed for this hymn in the first edition of *The Church Hymnary* (1898).

172 O LIGHT, WHOSE BEAMS ILLUMINE ALL

Written in May 1864, and published by Dr. Plumptre in his *Lazarus and Other Poems* (1864).

SURREY is among some 'entirely new' pieces at the end of John Church's *Introduction to Psalmody* (1723), where it is headed, 'Psalm the 23rd, Paraphrased by Mr. Addison, set to Musick by Mr. Henry Carey'. Addison's paraphrase was the beautiful 'The Lord my pasture shall prepare'.

173 THOU ART THE WAY: TO THEE ALONE

From Bishop Doane's *Songs by the Way* (1824); based on St. John xiv. 6: 'I am the way, the truth, and the life'.

ST. JAMES comes from *Select Psalms and Hymns for the Use of the Parish Church and Tabernacle of St. James's, Westminster* (1697).

174 REST OF THE WEARY

From Dr. Monsell's *Hymns of Love and Praise*. In ver. 3 (line 2) 'I'll' has been changed to 'I'.

THEODORA was the tune composed for this hymn in *The Congregational Psalmist* (edited by Dr. Henry Allon. Second Appendix, 1875). But it had been written some time previously for the use of the choir of the Parish Church, Ashford, where Mr. Legge was organist.

FORTUNE is adapted, as in *The English Hymnal*, from the melody of an old English song entitled 'Fortune my foe'. In the sixteenth and seventeenth centuries a number of ballads are marked to be sung to the tune of 'Fortune my foe'.

175 COME, LET US JOIN OUR CHEERFUL SONGS

The fourth verse of Watts's hymn (*Hymns and Spiritual Songs*, 1707) is omitted. The hymn was headed 'Christ Jesus, the Lamb of God, worshipped by all the creation, Rev. v. 11–13'.

HEBDOMADAL, Bishop Strong's tune, is set, in *The Oxford Hymnbook* (1908), to 'Praise to the Holiest in the height'.

176 O JESUS, EVER PRESENT

From Mr. Tuttiett's *Germs of Thought on the Sunday Services* (1864).

KOMM, SEELE was originally set, in *Geistliche Lieder* (Hamburg, 1681), to the hymn, 'Komm, Seele, Jesu Leiden'.

177 COME, CHILDREN, JOIN TO SING

The original hymn, in Mr. Bateman's *Sacred Melodies* (1843), had five stanzas.

The origin of the tune MADRID is obscure. So far as has been ascertained, its earliest appearance as a hymn tune was in a publication under the following title, 'The Spanish Hymn, arranged and composed for the Concerts of the Musical Fund Society of Philadelphia, by Benjamin Carr. The Air from an ancient Spanish Melody. Printed from the condensed score of the Society, and presented to the Composer as a tribute of respect and regard by some of the members, his friends. Philadelphia, 1826.' The preface to the publication states that the music was performed on Dec. 29, 1824.

Under the name 'Spanish Chant', the tune appears in *A Collection of Metrical Versions, &c., by M. Burgoyne* (London, 1827).

178 IN THE NAME OF JESUS

Miss Noel's original hymn had seven stanzas, of which 2 and 4 are here omitted. It was a processional hymn for Ascension Day, contributed to her book called *The Name of Jesus, and other Poems* (1870 edition). The text for the hymn was Philippians ii. 9, 10: 'God hath given Him a name which is above every name, that at the name of Jesus every knee should bow.' When the R. V. pedantically changed 'at' into 'in', the authoress desired that her hymn should open thus, instead of with 'at', as she had originally written.

CUDDESDON, by W. H. Ferguson, was composed for this hymn, in *The Public School Hymnbook*. So was EVELYNS, by W. H. Monk, in *Hymns Ancient and Modern* (1875).

179 CHRIST IS THE WORLD'S REDEEMER

The second part of the hymn from which Hymn 475 is taken. Both are printed in Duncan Macgregor's *S. Columba* (1898), where however, line 7 of verse 3 runs

'Whence He had ne'er departed'.

This was the medieval way of asserting the full divinity of Jesus; it recurs, for example, in the well-known hymn of Thomas Aquinas ('Verbum supernum prodiens, Nec Patris linquens dexteram'). But it has an awkward sound, and the compilers here ventured to substitute

In glorious dominion,

in order to prevent any misconception. The original Latin was:

Christus cum deo sederat,
ubi nunquam defuerat.

MOVILLE has been adapted from a traditional Irish melody in the Petrie-Stanford Collection.

180 OUR BLEST REDEEMER, ERE HE BREATHED

Six out of the seven stanzas in the original form of Miss Auber's hymn, as it appeared in her *Spirit of the Psalms* (1829); she is said to have written it on a pane of glass in a window of her house at Hoddesdon, Herts., but the story is no more than a pleasant myth.

ESSEX, by Gustav Holst, was composed for this hymn, in *The Public School Hymn-book* (1919). So was ST. CUTHBERT, by Dr. Dykes, in *Hymns Ancient and Modern* (1861).

181 WHEN GOD OF OLD CAME DOWN FROM HEAVEN

Four stanzas (2, 5, 8, and 10) are here omitted from Keble's Whit-Sunday poem, as it appeared in *The Christian Year* (1827) under the text of Acts ii. 2–4.

The tune WINCHESTER is from *The Whole Booke of Psalmes with their wonted Tunes, as they are song in churches, composed into foure parts . . . Compiled by sondry authors* (London, Thomas Est, 1592). There it is set to Psalm lxxxiv, the name of G. Kirby being attached to it, meaning that the *arrangement* is by him. In the editions of this book issued in 1594, 1604, and 1611 the tune does not appear, Psalm lxxxiv being set to the tune known as 'Old Common Tune'; but in Ravenscroft (1621) and Playford (1671 and 1677) that Psalm is again set to WINCHESTER. The name of the tune appears first in Ravenscroft.

The tune seems to be partly adapted from the second half of the melody set to chap. viii in C. Tye's *Actes of the Apostles*, which is as follows:

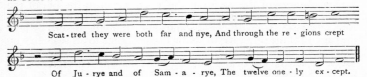

Scat-tred they were both far and nye, And through the re-gions crept
Of Ju-rye and of Sam-a-rye, The twelve one-ly ex-cept.

The second last note is shown by the harmony to be a misprint for E. The first half of this melody is the tune SOUTHWARK (see above, on Hymn 166).

182 COME, HOLY GHOST, OUR SOULS INSPIRE
184 CREATOR SPIRIT! BY WHOSE AID

The *Veni Creator Spiritus*, of which these are two versions, is a Latin hymn which cannot be traced earlier than the ninth century. There are some threads of evidence that seem to connect it with Rabanus Maurus (776–856), archbishop of Mainz; but its origin and authorship form one of the numerous enigmas in medieval hymnology.

182 is from Cosin's *Collection of Private Devotions in the Practice of the Ancient Church*, published in 1627 when he was still rector of Brancepeth. 'For this book', says Canon Ellerton, 'John Cosin translated the *Veni Creator*, not intending it to be sung in church, but said privately every morning at nine o'clock, in commemoration of the hour when God the Holy Ghost came down upon the Church. . . . He was one of the revisers of the Prayer Book in 1661–2, and thus

it came to pass that his version of the *Veni Creator* was inserted in the Ordination Service.'

184 is Dryden's version, from which fifteen lines have been omitted between lines 4 and 5 of ver. 3. It was adapted for congregational use by John Wesley in his *Psalms and Hymns* (1738). The two lines immediately before line 5 of ver. 3 in the omitted material are characteristically strong:

> Make us eternal truths receive,
> And practise all that we believe.

In a note upon lines 1 and 2 of ver. 2 Mr. W. D. Christie (Globe edition of *Dryden's Poetical Works*) observes that 'there is a pronunciation in Scotland of *glebe* as *glibe*, which may help to explain this rhyme of *light* and *Paraclete*'. In Heber's posthumous *Hymns*, indeed, where it is printed under Dryden's name, Paraclete is spelt 'Paraclite'. This form of the hymn has 'expectant mind' in ver. 1 (line 3), 'Plenteous in grace' (ver. 3, line 1), 'rule' instead of 'power' (ver. 3, line 4), and 'Eternal Comforter' in the last line. The same collection reproduces Cosin's version in an altered form; thus 'the darkness of our blinded sight' (ver. 2, line 4), and 'This, this may be our endless song' (ver. 4, line 4).

One instance of the vogue of this great hymn in the life of the Middle Ages may be cited. When the French Crusaders sailed on Aug. 28, 1248, from Roche-de-Marseille, Joinville describes how the captain of the ship carrying King Louis, 'called to his seamen who stood at the prow, and said, "Are you ready?" And they answered, "Aye, sir, let the clerks and priests come forward!" As soon as these had come forward, he called to them, "Sing, for God's sake!" And they with one voice chanted the *Veni Creator Spiritus*. Then he cried to his seamen, 'Unfurl the sails, for God's sake!' and they did so; in a short space the wind filled our sails and had borne us out of sight of land.'

The melody of VENI CREATOR (182) has been associated with the hymn ever since it came into use in the Church services.

ATTWOOD was published in separate form: 'Come Holy Ghost, a Hymn for Four Voices . . . composed by Thomas Attwood, organist of St. Paul's Cathedral' (1831).

This tune was written by Attwood at the request of the Bishop of London (Dr. Blomfield) for an Ordination Service at St. Paul's on Trinity Sunday, 1831. He had but two days in which to do it, and put the finishing touches to it while driving from his home in Norwood on the morning of that Sunday. For the full story see Bumpus's *History of English Cathedral Music*, ii. 407.

183 SPIRIT DIVINE, ATTEND OUR PRAYERS

Dr. Reed's hymn is taken from *The Evangelical Magazine* (June 1829) and *The Hymnbook* of 1842. It was sung by instruction of the London Board of Congregational Ministers (issued on Feb. 10, 1829) at the services of 'Solemn Prayer and Humiliation in the Eastern district of the metropolis' on Good Friday of that year, services designed 'to promote, by the divine blessing, a revival of religion in the British churches'. One of Reed's characteristic sayings was, 'We never rise to the highest, nor are our moralities safe, till we can say, "of Him, and through Him, and to Him are all things".'

ABERGELE, by J. A. Lloyd, comes from *Aberth Moliant* (1873).

185 SPIRIT OF GOD, THAT MOVED OF OLD

The original text of Mrs. Alexander's hymn, as in the S.P.C.K. *Hymns* (1852), except that 'make' has been altered into 'keep' in ver. 3 (line 3).

For the tune see Hymn 140.

186 COME, THOU HOLY PARACLETE

This thirteenth-century Latin hymn has been claimed for Pope Innocent III (1161-1216) and also for his contemporary, Stephen Langton (archbishop of Canterbury), but the authorship cannot be definitely determined. It is 'the loveliest of all the hymns in the whole circle of Latin sacred poetry', according to Trench, 'composed by one who had been acquainted with many sorrows and also with many consolations'.

Dr. Neale's version was first printed in his *Hymnal Noted*. In ver. 8 (line 3) 'Strengthen' has been changed to 'straighten'; the Latin of the verse is

> Flecte quod est rigidum,
> Fove quod est languidum,
> Rege quod est devium.

ST. PHILIP, by W. H. Monk, as in *Hymns Ancient and Modern* (1861), was composed for this hymn.

The second tune, VENI SANCTE SPIRITUS, is anonymous in *An Essay on the Church Plain Chant* (1782), but in the *Collection of Motetts or Antiphons* (1792) it is marked 'published by permission of Mr. Webbe'.

187 GRACIOUS SPIRIT, DWELL WITH ME

Omitting the 4th and 5th stanzas of the original in Lynch's *Rivulet* (1855). See on Hymn 354, and biographical note.

The earliest appearance of CASSEL seems to be in the *Erbaulicher Musicalischer ChristenSchatz* (Basle, 1745), compiled by Johann Thommen. But it had been used already in the churches of the Bohemian Brethren.

Notes on Words and Music

188 COME, GRACIOUS SPIRIT, HEAVENLY DOVE

The original hymn in seven stanzas, as it appeared in Browne's *Hymns and Spiritual Songs* (1720) was altered and improved in Ash and Evans's Bristol *Collection* of 1769 and in later hymn-books. The hymn, as Browne wrote it, was in the first person singular, and began, 'Come, holy Spirit'. The last verse is due to W. Mercer's *Church Psalter and Hymnbook* (1864 edition).

VERBUM SUPERNUM, as in *The English Hymnal* (1906), is one of the French tunes referred to under Hymn 4.

Mr. Matthews composed LUDBOROUGH, he explains, 'on May 5, 1846, the day before I left home to go to a tutorship. Whilst my mother and sister were packing up my clothes, &c., I composed it to the hymn beginning, "From every stormy wind that blows".' But it was not published till 1874, in *Church Hymns*.

189 HOLY SPIRIT, HEAR US

Mr. Parker's hymn appeared first in *The School Hymnal* (1880) and *The Children's Book of Praise* (1881).

ERNSTEIN, by J. F. Swift, was composed for the hymn, 'Summer suns are glowing', in *The Methodist Sunday School Tune Book* (1881).

190 COME, HOLY SPIRIT, COME

Three stanzas from Hart's original hymn (in his *Hymns Composed on Various Subjects*, 1759) are here omitted.

FRANCONIA is from *Harmonischer Lieder-Schatz, oder Allgemeines Evangelisches Choral-Buch . . . gestellet von Johann Balthasar König* (1738), where the melody, as under, is set to the hymn 'Was ist, das mich betrübt?'

The present tune was arranged from this by the Rev. W. H. Havergal, and published in his *Old Church Psalmody* (1847).

DOLE is from *Llyfr Tonau Cynulleidfaol, Ail-Attodiad* (1890).

191 COME DOWN, O LOVE DIVINE

This is a cento from the original eight stanzas as published in Bianco da Siena's *Laudi Spirituali* (Lucca ed., 1851). The translation appeared in Dr. Littledale's *People's Hymnal* (1867). 'The Italian

Laudi Spirituali', says Dr. W. H. Frere, ' grew up with the Franciscan movement as a style of vernacular hymnody . . . Jacopone da Todi represents the earliest period of them, i.e. the thirteenth century: Bianco da Siena represents the end of the fourteenth, and his *Laudi* more than Jacopone's hold a place in the later collections.'

DOWN AMPNEY, composed by R. Vaughan Williams for this hymn, in *The English Hymnal*, is named after his birth-place.

192 SPIRIT OF GRACE, THOU LIGHT OF LIFE

The German original appeared in Tersteegen's *Geistliches Blumengärtlein* (1745). Mrs. Bevan's rendering, in her *Songs of Eternal Life* (1858), reproduces the spirit rather than the letter of the original eight stanzas. Like Hymn 148, it was partly improved by Dr. B. H. Kennedy, in his *Hymnologica Christiana* (1863). The present form of the text is as in Dr. John Hunter's *Hymns of Faith and Life* (1896). The third verse echoes the language of Isaiah xxxv. 1 and l. 3.

LLANSAMLET comes from *Moliant Cenedl* (1920).

193 HOLY SPIRIT, TRUTH DIVINE

Contributed by Mr. Longfellow to the Unitarian *Hymns of the Spirit* (1864), of which he was an editor. Ver. 6 alludes to Numbers xxi. 17.

BUCKLAND, by L. G. Hayne, is from *The Merton Tune Book* (1863).

194 BREATHE ON ME, BREATH OF GOD

First published by Dr. Hatch in a privately printed pamphlet called *Between Doubt and Prayer* (1878), where ver. 3 (line 2) read
Blend all my soul with Thine.

VENI SPIRITUS was the tune composed by Sir John Stainer for this hymn in the first edition of *The Church Hymnary* (1898).

WIRKSWORTH appeared in *A Book of Psalmody containing Variety of Tunes for all the Common Metres of the Psalms in the Old and New Versions, and others for Particular Measures . . . all set in Four Parts, within such a compass as will most naturally suit the voices in Country Churches, yet may be sung in Three or Two without any Disallowances. By John Chetham* (1718). Here the tunes are not named, and no composers are given. The present tune is set to Psalm l, as follows:

In the third edition, 1724, of the same book, the last line is altered to

The present form of the tune is found in *A Book of Psalm Tunes with variety of Anthems in Four Parts. . . . By James Green* (Fifth edition, 1724).

195 SPIRIT OF GOD, DESCEND UPON MY HEART

From Dr. Croly's *Psalms and Hymns for Public Worship* (1854). Based on Galatians v. 25: 'If we live in the Spirit, let us also walk in the Spirit.'

SONG 22 appeared in *The Hymnes and Songs of the Church, by George Wither* (1623). The poet obtained from the King a patent authorizing the issue of his book bound up with the Psalter, i.e. the Old Version of the Psalms; but the Company of Stationers offered strenuous and successful opposition, and in this form Wither's book never passed into circulation. It contained a number of tunes, in two parts, treble and bass, by Orlando Gibbons. This one was set to a paraphrase of Hezekiah's Prayer in Isaiah xxxvii, and hence is in some collections named 'Hezekiah'.

196 COME, HOLY GHOST, OUR HEARTS INSPIRE

Wesley's hymn, entitled 'Before reading Holy Scripture', appeared in his *Hymns and Sacred Poems* (1740). Two slight changes have been made in the text; 'Thy' is altered to 'Thine' in ver. 1 (line 2), and in ver. 3 (line 1) 'prolific' has been dropped in favour of 'celestial'. This second alteration was made by John Wesley in 1780.

ST. COLUMBA (ERIN), from *The Church Hymnal* (authorized by the Irish Episcopal Church, 1874), is one of the traditional Irish melodies collected by Dr. George Petrie (1855). It is said in his collection to be the melody of a hymn sung at the dedication of a chapel.

197 THE SPIRIT BREATHES UPON THE WORD

The original form of Cowper's poem, as in the *Olney Hymns* (1779).

CASTLEFORD comes from *Sacred Harmony (being an entire new set of Psalm Tunes), by B. Clifford* (Leeds). Here printed as arranged by Dr. S. S. Wesley in *The European Psalmist* (1872).

198 O WORD OF GOD INCARNATE

Dr. How's hymn appeared in the supplement (1867) to Morrell and How's *Psalms and Hymns*. In ver. 3 (line 8) 'guide' has been changed to 'guides'.

CHEBAR, by Henry Smart, appeared in *The Song of Praise; or, Psalm and Hymn Tunes, collected and arranged by Victoria Evans-Freke* (1876).

199 LORD, THY WORD ABIDETH

Written by Sir H. W. Baker for *Hymns Ancient and Modern* (1861).

The tune RAVENSHAW, in *Ein Neu Gesengbuchlen* (1531), the earliest German hymn-book of the Bohemian Brethren (edited by Michael Weisse), is set to the hymn 'Menschenkind, merk eben', as follows:

The melody is of pre-Reformation origin, and was associated with the Latin hymn beginning 'Ave Hierarchia, coelestis et pia'. The present arrangement by Dr. Monk appeared in *Hymns Ancient and Modern* (1861).

200 TO THEE, O GOD, WE RENDER THANKS

Prebendary Thring's hymn was based on 2 Tim. iii. 16 and 2 Peter i. 21. It was written in 1880 and published that year in *The Church of England Hymnal*, which he edited.

ROTHLEY was composed by Sir John Goss for ' Our blest Redeemer, ere He breathed'. It appeared in *The Hymnary* (1872).

201 LAMP OF OUR FEET, WHEREBY WE TRACE

Five out of the eleven stanzas first published by Barton in *The Reliquary* (1836). He was then employed in a bank at Woodbridge, Suffolk. The original had, in ver. 5 (line 1)

And we, if we aright would learn,

and in line 3 ' Must to' instead of ' And to'.

ELVET, by Dr. Dykes, comes from *The Congregational Hymn and Tune Book, edited by the Rev. R. R. Chope* (1862).

202 BREAK THOU THE BREAD OF LIFE

Miss Lathbury's very popular hymn was originally composed in 1880 for the Chautauqua Literary and Scientific Circle.

ALL SOULS, by J. Yoakley, is from *The English Hymnal* (1906). For CONGLETON see under Hymn 98.

203 LOOK UPON US, BLESSÈD LORD

The German original (from *Altdorffisches Gesang-Büchlein*) was written in 1663, when Clausnitzer was a minister at Weiden; it was intended to be sung by the congregation before the Scripture Lesson.

The third verse contains an echo of the Nicene Creed (Hymn 725), viz. 'God of God, Light of Light, begotten not made', as the Creed was recited in the Liturgy.

The present translation by Professor Macalister appears for the first time.

LIEBSTER JESU (DESSAU) comes from the *Neue geistliche auf die Sonntage durchs gantze Jahr gerichtete Andachten* . . . (Mühlhausen, 1664).

In this collection the original form of Ahle's melody appears as under, set to the hymn 'Ja, er ists, das Heil der Welt'.

Later German collections contain the same melody with numerous variations, set to the hymn by Clausnitzer of which the present is a translation. The present form of the tune is that adopted by J. S. Bach in his *Choralgesänge*.

204 HOLY FATHER, THOU HAST GIVEN

First published in *The Presbyterian Hymnal* (1876) of the United Presbyterian Church. Dr. Bruce's motto for the hymn was, 'The entrance of Thy words giveth light.'

The tune, appropriately called ILLUMINATIO, by Sir G. J. Elvey, appeared in *The Chenies Tune Book, specially adapted to the Book of Common Praise* (Dedicated to the Rev. the Rt. Hon. Lord Wriothesley Russell, Rector of Chenies, with affectionate respect by his Daughter. Edited by E. G. Cocks), the preface of which is dated Dec. 1885. There, however, the tune is called 'Cephas', and is marked 'Composed expressly for this work'. It is not referred to any particular hymn, but was probably written for 'Rock of Ages'.

205 THE CHURCH'S ONE FOUNDATION

Written by Mr. Stone in 1866, out of admiration for the opposition shown by Bishop Gray of Capetown to Bishop Colenso's teaching (see ver. 3). The text as revised for the Appendix to *Hymns Ancient and Modern* (1868). It was one of a set of hymns on the Apostles' Creed (Hymn 724), to illustrate 'I believe in the Holy Catholic Church'.

AURELIA, in *A Selection of Psalms and Hymns arranged for the Public Services of the Church of England, edited by the Rev. Charles Kemble and S. S. Wesley* (1864), was originally composed for the hymn 'Jerusalem the golden'. Probably the first time it is set to 'The Church's one foundation' is in the *Appendix to Hymns Ancient and Modern* (1868); it is now universally associated with that hymn.

206 GLORIOUS THINGS OF THEE ARE SPOKEN

Newton's hymn is really based on Psalm lxxxvii, although it was entitled 'Zion, or the City of God, Isaiah xxxiii. 20, 21'. The fourth stanza of the original (in the *Olney Hymns*) has been omitted, although the first four lines of it have been added to the first four lines of the original third stanza, in order to make up the present third verse. The present form of the hymn, as in *Hymns Ancient and Modern* (1875), has proved most acceptable.

Joseph Haydn's air, AUSTRIAN HYMN, was composed for the national hymn by Hauschka, 'Gott erhalte Franz den Kaiser', and first performed on the Emperor's birthday, Feb. 12, 1797. The composer afterwards used the melody as the subject of one of the movements of his String Quartet, No. 77.

207 CHRIST IS MADE THE SURE FOUNDATION

Four stanzas out of five which were published by Dr. Neale in his *Hymnal Noted*, as freely altered for *Hymns Ancient and Modern* (1861). The lines are a version of the second part of a Latin hymn, 'rugged but fine' (Trench), which was in use by the ninth century. The third and fourth verses indicate the vogue of the hymn at the dedication of churches. The first verse echoes Ephesians ii. 20,21.

TANTUM ERGO SACRAMENTUM is one of the *Chants Ordinaires de l'Office Divin* (Paris, 1881); it is certainly much older than this, but its source has not been discovered.

208 JESUS, WITH THY CHURCH ABIDE

One of Mr. Pollock's litanies (see on 399), reprinted from the previous edition of *The Church Hymnary*, with the omission of four stanzas.

Georg Joseph's tune HELFER MEINER ARMEN SEELE is from the same source as 'Culbach' (38). The melody here as adapted in *The English Hymnal*.

209 CITY OF GOD, HOW BROAD AND FAR

From *Hymns of the Spirit* (1864), written when Mr. Johnson was minister of a Free Church at Lynn, Massachusetts.

For the tune see under Hymn 32.

210 I LOVE THY KINGDOM, LORD

In 1800, Dr. Dwight, President of Yale, published his revision of *The Psalms of David &c., by Isaac Watts*, a task he had been requested to carry out. This, with the omission of two stanzas, is his version of part of Psalm cxxxvii.

ST. AUDOËN was set to this hymn by Sir Robert Stewart, in *The Church Hymnal* (authorized by the Church of Ireland, 1874).

211 WE COME UNTO OUR FATHERS' GOD

From his *Golden Chain of Praise* (1869). Mr. Gill writes: 'The birthday of this hymn, Nov. 22, 1868 (St. Cecilia's Day), was almost the most delightful day of my life. Its production employed the whole day and was a prolonged rapture.' The hymn is based on the first verse of the ninetieth psalm. It 'was inspired', the author explains, 'by a lively delight in my Puritan and Presbyterian forefathers of East Worcestershire. Descended from a Moravian martyr and an ejected minister, I rejoice not a little in the godly Protestant stock from which I spring. A staff handed down from him, and inscribed with the date 1692, was in my hand when I began the hymn.'

The following three stanzas, from the middle of the hymn, have been omitted:

> Unto Thy people we belong,
> Elect, redeemed, renewèd:
> We join the blessed pilgrim throng
> With Thine own strength enduèd:
> Our hands their tasks divine essay,
> Our feet pursue the heavenly way
> Their steadfast feet pursuèd.

> The cleaving sins that brought them low
> Are still our souls oppressing;
> The tears that from their eyes did flow
> Fall fast our shame confessing;
> As with Thee, Lord, prevailed their cry,
> So our strong prayer ascends on high
> And bringeth down Thy blessing.

> Their precious things on us bestowed
> The same dear Lord discover:
> The joy wherewith their souls o'erflowed
> Makes our glad hearts run over;
> Their fire of love in us doth burn,
> As yearned their hearts, our hearts do yearn
> After the Heavenly Lover.

The tune NUN FREUT EUCH is from *Geistliche Lieder* (Wittenberg, 1535), where it was set to the hymn, 'Nun freut euch lieben Christengemein'. This hymn by Luther appeared first in 1523 or 1524, but was then set to a different tune. The present tune came into use in England to the words, 'Great God, what do I see and hear?' It was popularly known as Luther's Hymn, though there is no evidence that it was his composition.

Dr. Ebenezer Prout composed LAUS SEMPITERNA for the hymn, in *The Congregational Church Hymnal* (1887).

212 FOR THE MIGHT OF THINE ARM WE BLESS THEE

Mr. Silvester Horne wrote this hymn to be used at Whitefield's Tabernacle, London; it was suggested by Mrs. Hemans's 'Hymn of the Vaudois Mountaineers' which begins,

For the strength of the hills we bless Thee.

The first collection in which it appeared was *The Fellowship Hymn-book* (1909).

CORMAC is a traditional Irish melody, in the *Feis Ceoil Collection of Irish Music*. It is said to be the melody of an Irish song beginning, 'Down by the salley gardens', the first three lines of which W. B. Yeats has extended in his poem with this title (*Poems*, 1912).

213 FATHER OF ALL, FROM LAND AND SEA

A selection from Dr. Wordsworth's longer hymn which he wrote for the Church Congress at Nottingham in October 1871.

OLDBRIDGE, by R. N. Quaile, from *The English Hymnal*; but it was originally composed for the hymn, 'The radiant morn has passed away'.

214 THROUGH THE NIGHT OF DOUBT AND SORROW

The Danish original was composed by Professor B. S. Ingemann. The present hymn is a cento from Baring-Gould's version in *The People's Hymnal* (1867), as improved in *Hymns Ancient and Modern* (1875).

The tune ST. OSWALD, by Dr. Dykes, appeared in *A Manual of Psalm and Hymn Tunes used in the Parish Church of St. Michael, Houghton-le-Spring* (edited by the Hon. and Rev. J. Grey, 1857), where it was set to the hymn 'Praise the Lord! ye heavens, adore Him', and named 'St. Bernard'. In *Hymns Ancient and Modern* (Revised edition, 1875) the tune is named 'St. Oswald', and is set to the present hymn.

MARCHING, by Martin Shaw, was composed for this hymn; it appeared in *Additional Tunes and settings in use at St. Mary's, Primrose Hill* (1915).

215 THY HAND, O GOD, HAS GUIDED

Dr. Plumptre's hymn is taken from the supplement (1889) to *Hymns Ancient and Modern*. Two stanzas are omitted.

Dr. Basil Harwood's THORNBURY was composed for this hymn; it is from the second supplement (1916) to the old edition of *Hymns Ancient and Modern*.

216 LORD OF OUR LIFE, AND GOD OF OUR SALVATION

A 'Sapphic ode: for spiritual and temporal peace' by von Löwenstern, in *Geistliche Kirchen und Haus-Musik* (Breslau, 1644), very freely paraphrased by Philip Pusey in 1834; his version appeared in

A. R. Reinagle's *Psalm and Hymn Tunes* (Oxford, 1840). 'It refers to the state of the Church, that is to say, of the Church of England in 1834—assailed from without, enfeebled and distracted within, but on the eve of a great awakening' (letter of Philip Pusey to his brother Dr. E. B. Pusey). The original hymn also reflected a disturbed situation, viz. the troubles and terrors of the Thirty Years War.

One stanza is omitted, and two slight alterations have been made in ver. 4, which originally read 'till backward they are driven', and 'on earth or, after'.

CLOISTERS was composed by Sir Joseph Barnby for this hymn, in *Hymns Ancient and Modern* (Appendix, 1868).

Johann Crüger's tune HERZLIEBSTER JESU is from his *Gesangbuch* (Berlin, 1640). In Crüger's original the opening phrase is

It is so given in *The Oxford Hymn Book*, but the present form is in most later German books, and is that adopted by J. S. Bach.

217 FEAR NOT, THOU FAITHFUL CHRISTIAN FLOCK

The German original, of which the first verse here, and the first verse alone, is an echo, dates from the period of the Thirty Years War, and may have been actually sung on the field of Lützen, where Gustavus Adolphus the Protestant champion was killed, on Nov. 6, 1632. It was printed as early as 1632 in Leipzig as the 'Kingly Swan-Song', and was possibly composed by Altenburg, a good musician and pastor at Erfurt.

This version from *The Yattendon Hymnal* is an independent improvization rather than a translation.

The tune PSALM 36 (68) is a melody probably by Matthäus Greiter. Set to words written by him, it appears in several books for church use published at Strasburg early in the sixteenth century. It is found in the early *French Psalter* issued at Strasburg in 1539 and is retained for Psalm xxxvi in all succeeding editions of the *French Psalter*. In the complete psalter of 1562 it is, in addition, set to the version of Psalm lxviii by Beza, beginning 'Que dieu se monstre seulement', which became known as the battle song of the Huguenots. In the *Anglo-Genevan Psalter* (1561) it is set to Kethe's version of Psalm cxiii, and psalm and tune were included in the complete English and Scottish Psalters of 1562 and 1564. It was known in England as 'Old 113th', and is frequently found in an abbreviated form. A striking instance of its use by the Huguenots is cited by Lord Ernle in *The Psalms in Human Life*, chap. vii.

218 FOR THOSE WE LOVE WITHIN THE VEIL

Written for a funeral service at Mr. Charter Piggott's church in Streatham, and published in *Congregational School Worship*, of which he was one of the editors.

The tune ST. KENTIGERN was composed for this hymn in the present edition of *The Church Hymnary*.

219 THE SAINTS OF GOD! THEIR CONFLICT PAST

'The Rev. W. Ball Wright, who was one of Mr. Maclagan's staff at Newington, remembers his sitting in the vestry on the eve of All Saints, 1871, correcting the proofs of this famous hymn, which was first printed on leaflets for use in St. Mary's Church, Newington' (F. D. How's *W. D. Maclagan*, p. 56).

PSALM 84 (JERVAULX ABBEY) is from the complete *French Psalter* of 1562. The present adaptation was made by Rev. Alexander Galloway for *The Scottish Mission Hymnbook* (1912).

Sir John Stainer's tune REST appeared in *The London Church Choir Association Festival Service* (1873), where, however, it was set to the hymn 'Thou hidden love of God'.

In *Hymns Ancient and Modern* (enlarged edition, 1875), the tune was set, under the composer's sanction, to the present hymn.

220 FOR ALL THE SAINTS WHO FROM THEIR LABOURS REST

Dr. How's original hymn, as published in Earl Nelson's *Hymns for Saints' Days* (1864) had eleven stanzas. The author altered 'Thy saints' to 'the saints' in the first line. One of the stanzas omitted deserves to be quoted:

> 'For the Apostles' glorious company,
> Who, bearing forth the Cross o'er land and sea,
> Shook all the mighty world, we sing to Thee.

SINE NOMINE was composed by Dr. Vaughan Williams for this hymn, in *The English Hymnal*.

221 TEN THOUSAND TIMES TEN THOUSAND

The full form of Dean Alford's hymn, as printed in his *Life* (1872); it was sung at his funeral on Jan. 17, 1871. The first three stanzas were written as early as 1866 (1867); the fourth was added in 1870.

GRESHAM, by Geoffrey Shaw, from the same source as 'Marching' (214), was composed for this hymn.

ALFORD, by Dr. Dykes, was also composed for this hymn, in *Hymns Ancient and Modern* (Revised edition, 1875).

In a letter to Mrs. Dykes on the occasion of the composer's death, Sir Henry Baker says, 'We are going to sing *only his* tunes to every hymn all next Sunday, and the "Dies Irae" after Evensong *for him*; followed by "Ten thousand times ten thousand".'

222 WHO ARE THESE, LIKE STARS APPEARING

Miss Cox's successful version (in her *Hymns from the German*, 1841) of the only hymn Schenck wrote; in the *Frankfurter Gesang-*

buch (1719) it runs to twenty verses. The basis is Rev. vii. 13–17. This hymn was sung at the funeral of Pastor Friedrich von Bodelschwingh, the famous founder of the Colony of Mercy at Bethel, near Bielefeld, Westphalia, on April 4, 1910.

ALL SAINTS comes from the *Geistreiches Gesangbuch* (Darmstadt, 1698), where it is set to 'Zeuch mich, zeuch mich, mit den Armen'. Here it is slightly altered from the original form.

223 HOW BRIGHT THESE GLORIOUS SPIRITS SHINE

This paraphrase of Rev. vii. 13–17 is another composite production. The first and last verses have been altered from a similar hymn by Watts, which was taken over into the 1745 and 1751 editions of *The Scottish Paraphrases*, and finally re-cast in the 1781 edition. Tradition ascribes these finishing touches to William Cameron (see on 483).

ST. ASAPH is from *Sacred Music . . . sung in St. George's Church, Edinburgh, edited by R. A. Smith* (1825). The tune has not been found in an earlier collection than the above. It is there assigned to Giornovichi, but the original has not been discovered among the works of that composer.

The second tune, in *Ravenscroft's Psalter* (1621) is set to Psalms x, xlviii, and cxliii, and called 'Glocester Tune', being classed in the Index among English tunes. A slightly different form of the last line is found in *Playford's Psalter* of 1677, which is adopted in several books. The present form of GLOUCESTER is the original.

224 O WHAT THEIR JOY AND THEIR GLORY MUST BE

One of the hymns written by the great scholar and theologian, Pierre Abelard, for the abbey of the Paraclete at Nogent-sur-Seíne, over which Héloïse presided. It was the hymn for Saturday evening worship. Two stanzas are omitted from this version by Dr. Neale (in *Hymnal Noted*) as partly altered for *Hymns Ancient and Modern*. It is really a version, not a paraphrase, as a comparison of the first stanza with its Latin original will suffice to show:

> O quanta qualia sunt illa sabbata,
> Quae semper celebrat superna curia,
> Quae fessis requies, quae merces fortibus,
> Cum erit omnia Deus in omnibus!

As Dr. W. H. Frere observes, Abelard's hymn 'deserves attention for its origin as well as for its merits. It was a feat that few smaller men would have cared to attempt, to produce a whole hymnal off the reel; but Abelard did this in *Hymnus Paraclitensis*, written for the nunnery of Heloisa' (*Hymns Ancient and Modern, Historical Edition*, p. xxv).

The melody of O QUANTA QUALIA is found in *La Feillée's Méthode du Plain-Chant* (1808), where it is set to the hymn 'Regnator orbis'. But it is probably older than this. It was adapted and set to the present hymn in Helmore's *The Hymnal Noted* (1854).

225 HE WANTS NOT FRIENDS THAT HATH THY LOVE

A cento from Richard Baxter's poem 'The Resolution' (*Poetical Fragments*, 1681). Before 'Saints' in ver. 2 'the' has been added, for the sake of smoothness.

Lampe's tune KENT (Devonshire) in *Hymns on the great festivals and other occasions by Charles Wesley* (1746) is set to the hymn, 'Sinners obey the Gospel word'.

No composer's name is given in the above work, but in the second edition (published in 1753) it is stated that the work may be obtained at 'Mr Lampe's lodging', and a letter of Wesley's refers to 'Mr Lampe's tunes'. This tune appears in Moore's *Psalm Singer's Pocket Companion* (Glasgow, 1756), set to Psalm cxlv.

226 O BLEST

See under John Roberts, in the Biographical Notes.

The tune BRAINT is a Welsh air, from *Llyfr Tonau Cynulleidfaol* (1859).

227 LET SAINTS ON EARTH IN CONCERT SING

The original hymn, in Wesley's *Funeral Hymns* (1759), consisted of five eight-line stanzas, which have been shortened and altered in most hymn-books. Thus the first stanza, as Wesley wrote it, ran:

> Come let us join our friends above
> Who have obtained the prize,
> And on the eagle-wings of love
> To joys celestial rise.
> Let all the saints terrestrial sing
> With those to glory gone;
> For all the servants of our King
> In earth and heaven are one.

The original form of the last two verses was this:

> Ten thousand to their endless home
> This solemn moment fly,
> And we are to the margin come,
> And we expect to die.

> O that we now might grasp our Guide!
> O that the word were given!
> Come, Lord of hosts, the waves divide,
> And land us all in heaven.

Thus a good hymn sometimes needs to be made better.

FRENCH (DUNDEE) is one of the twelve Common Tunes appearing in *The CL Psalmes of David*, &c. (Edinburgh, A. Hart, 1615). Its first appearance in an English Psalter is in Ravenscroft's *Whole Booke of Psalms* (1621), where it is called 'Dundy' and indexed among the 'Scottish Tunes'.

228 FROM ALL THAT DWELL BELOW THE SKIES

A paraphrase of Psalm cxvii, from Watts's *Psalms of David* (1719). The original lacked the Hallelujahs, and had 'by every tongue' in ver. 1 (line 4).

For the tune see Hymn 13.

229 ALL PEOPLE THAT ON EARTH DO DWELL

This classical version of the hundredth psalm appears in 1561 in the *Anglo-Genevan Psalter* and in the Psalter published probably in the same year by John Daye; it was included in the *Scottish Psalter* of 1564 (1565), where it is assigned to William Kethe, who was at Geneva in 1559 and contributed to the Anglo-Genevan version of the Psalter. The historical and metrical evidence, according to Julian, 'is certainly in favour of W. Kethe . . . and decisive against both Sternhold and Hopkins'. The authorship may be therefore considered as fairly certain. As for the text, the *Scottish Psalter* of 1650 changed 'fear' into 'mirth' (in ver. 1) and 'The Lord ye know' into 'Know that the Lord' (in ver. 2), but the early misspelling of 'folck' (folk) as 'flock' (in ver. 2) has persisted. In ver. 4 'For why' means 'because': it gives the reason for the call to praise God in the previous verse.

This version, 'composed by William Kethe, a friend of John Knox and set to the music of Louis Bourgeois, survives all the changes of thought and fashion that the progress of four centuries has witnessed' (Lord Ernle, *The Psalms in Human Life*).

OLD 100TH was composed or adapted by L. Bourgeois for Psalm cxxxiv in the *French Psalter* of 1551. Its original form was as follows:

The first edition of the *Anglo-Genevan Psalter* in 1556 did not contain any version of Psalm c. That by William Kethe, 'All people that on earth do dwell', appeared in an edition printed at Geneva in 1561, containing eighty-seven psalms, and in another printed at London the same year, containing eighty-three psalms. It is an unsettled point which of these two editions was issued first. In both of them the present tune is attached to this psalm, and has ever since remained indissolubly associated with it.

230 BEFORE JEHOVAH'S AWFUL THRONE

This version of the hundredth psalm is a composition of Watts (in his *Psalms of David*, 1719), as altered by John Wesley, who began the hymn with the second verse, which he altered to its present form from

> Nations attend before His throne
> With solemn fear, with sacred joy.

In stanza 5 the original had 'shall stand'.
Watts's first stanza, omitted by Wesley, ran thus:

> Sing to the Lord with joyful voice,
> Let every land His name adore;
> The British isles shall send the noise
> Across the ocean to the shore.

ANDERNACH is found in the *Catholische Geistliche Gesänge* (Andernach, 1608), where it is set to a German version of 'Vexilla regis prodeunt'.

231 ALL LANDS AND PEOPLES, ALL THE EARTH

Another piece from Dr. Stopford Brooke's *Christian Hymns* (1881). In *Church Hymns* (1874) the tune GLORIA IN EXCELSIS, by J. W. Elliott, is set to a hymn for use at the dedication of an organ.

232 WORSHIP THE LORD IN THE BEAUTY OF HOLINESS

From Dr. Monsell's *Parish Hymnal* (1873).
MOREDUN, by Henry Smart, in *The Presbyterian Hymnal* (1877), was composed for this hymn.

233 STAND UP, AND BLESS THE LORD

Written by Montgomery for the anniversary service of the Sheffield Red Hill Wesleyan Sunday School, on March 15, 1824. The text as in his *Christian Psalmist* (1825); one stanza is omitted.
KERRY comes from Jowett's *Parochial Psalmody* (1832).

234 GOD REVEALS HIS PRESENCE

Another (see Hymn 192) hymn from Tersteegen's *Geistliches Blumengärtlein* (1729). This magnificent expression of the spirit of worship, entitled 'Remembrance of the glorious and delightful presence of God', is inadequately reproduced in the English version, which is a patchwork from Foster and Miller's English Moravian *Collection of Hymns* (1789), as revised by W. Mercer in his *Church Psalter and Hymnbook* (1854).

GOTT IST GEGENWÄRTIG (ARNSBERG) appears in *Joachimi Neandri Glaub- und Liebes-übung* (Bremen, 1680), a collection of fifty-six

G 2

hymns by Neander, most of them being provided with tunes. This melody appears as follows:

It is set to the hymn 'Wunderbarer König, Herrscher von uns allen', and is believed on good grounds to have been composed by Neander. In later German collections it is associated with the hymn 'Gott ist gegenwärtig,' of which the present hymn is a translation.

235 PLEASANT ARE THY COURTS ABOVE

From Lyte's *Spirit of the Psalms* (1834), a free paraphrase of Psalm lxxxiv.

Dr. Gilbert's tune MAIDSTONE, from *Songs of Praise, and Ten Other Hymns set to Music, by Walter B. Gilbert* (1862), was composed for the hymn, 'Songs of praise the angels sang'.

236 WE LOVE THE PLACE, O GOD

This is Dean Bullock's hymn, from his *Songs of the Church* (1854), as revised by Sir H. W. Baker for *Hymns Ancient and Modern*. The hymn, based on Psalm xxvi. 8, was composed in 1827 for the dedication of a church at Trinity Bay, Newfoundland, where he was rector. It is interesting to learn that seventy years later, when a new building on the same site was being dedicated, this hymn was once more sung. Sir H. W. Baker took over the first verse, altering only 'other' to 'earthly' in the fourth line; he re-wrote the second, which, as Dean Bullock wrote it, ran thus:

> We love the house of prayer,
>> Wherein Thy servants meet;
> For Thou, O Lord, art there,
>> Thy chosen ones to greet.

The next four verses were omitted, and those now printed (verses 3–5) are Sir Henry's own.

QUAM DILECTA, by H. L. Jenner, was composed for the hymn, in *Hymns Ancient and Modern* (1861).

237 AGAIN THE MORN OF GLADNESS

From the S.P.C.K. *Children's Hymns*, written when Canon Ellerton was rector of Hinstock.

For the tune see Hymn 618.

238 LORD, THIS DAY THY CHILDREN MEET

From Dr. How's *Psalms and Hymns* (1864 edition).

In *The Lowestoft Supplemental Tune book, containing fifty-six Hymn Tunes . . . composed by J. Downing Farrer* (1885), this tune NEW CALABAR is set to the hymn, 'Come, my soul, thy suit prepare'.

239 SWEET IS THE SOLEMN VOICE THAT CALLS

Another hymn from Lyte's *Spirit of the Psalms*, on Psalm cxxii.

Samuel Wesley's tune HIERAPOLIS was written for *The Psalmist: A Collection of Psalms and Hymn Tunes, edited by Vincent Novello* (Part IV, 1842).

240 GOD OF PITY, GOD OF GRACE

Written by Mrs. Morris on Sept. 4, 1857, and published in *The Voice and the Reply* (1858). Stanza 2 was originally stanza 6.

Sir Walter Parratt's HUDDERSFIELD was composed for 'HolyFather, cheer our way', in *The English Hymnal*.

241 COMMAND THY BLESSING FROM ABOVE

Written by Montgomery for the Sheffield Sunday School Union on June 3, 1816. The text as printed in Cotterill's *Selection of Psalms and Hymns* (1819).

EISENACH was first published on a single sheet entitled 'Trost-Liedlein über den seligen Hintritt der Frawen Margariten, des Herrn Caspar Werners . . . Hausfrawen . . . Componirt und Musicirt von Johan-Herman Schein, 1628'. Then it was included in the second edition (1645) of *Cantional oder Gesangbuch Augsburgischer Confession*, edited by Schein.

The hymn for which it was composed is also, as indicated in the above title, by Schein, and begins, 'Machs mit mir, Gott, nach deiner Güt.'

The present arrangement is that used by J. S. Bach in his *St. John Passion* and *Choralgesänge*.

242 BEHOLD US, LORD, A LITTLE SPACE

Written by Canon Ellerton 'for use at mid-day service in a London City Church', and published in *Church Hymns* (1871).

The tune BEDFORD cannot be exactly fixed to any year, the oldest books containing it being unfortunately undated. Probably the earliest of these is *The Divine Musick Scholars Guide, wth the Famous Mr. Tho. Ravenscroft's Psalm Tunes in four parts. . . . Collected and Printed by Francis Timbrell.*' In this volume, the tune is printed twice, first to Psalm xxvii and second to Psalm lxxxiv. The latter is headed 'Bedford tune. By Wm. Wheal.' It is in three parts, Cantus, Medius, and Bassus, the melody being as follows:

As set to Psalm xxvii, it is headed 'Bedford Tune', without name of composer. The melody is the same as above, except in line 3, which reads thus—

The British Museum Catalogue gives '1715?' as the date of Timbrell's book. This is probably too early, but a copy formerly in the possession of Sir John Stainer contains the inscription 'Thomas Bradford ejus liber, 1723'.

In *A Choice Collection of Psalm Tunes, Hymns, and Anthems. . . . Collected and Printed by Michael Broom, Singing Master, Isleworth, Middlesex*, the tune appears again set to Psalm lxxxiv. It is headed 'Bedford Tune, by W. Wale, organist of Bedford, B. of M.', and the melody is the same as in the setting to Psalm xxvii in Timbrell's book. Broom's book is also undated, but a copy in the Euing Library, Glasgow, has the autograph of a former owner and the date 1731. In Matthew Wilkins's *Book of Psalmody* (also undated, but probably issued about 1730) the tune is set to Psalm lxxxiv, the melody being the same as in the setting to that psalm in Timbrell. Mr. Havergal states in his *Old Church Psalmody* that he had found the tune in *The Psalm-Singers' Magazine* (1729). This has not been verified, as no copy of this book can now be discovered. In all the older psalmodies and in most modern books the tune is in triple time. Probably its first appearance in common time is in William Gardiner's *Sacred Melodies* (1812). Here it is set to the hymn 'Our God, our help in ages past', the melody being as follows:

In his *Music and Friends* (published in 1838) Gardiner gives information as to the sources of some of his Sacred Melodies, and says regarding the above: 'This fine old tune was written by Wm. Wheal, organist of Bedford. Originally printed in the key of F and in triple time, I have changed the key to D and written it in common time, a measure that is more stately and better accords with that solemn grandeur in which it is disposed to move.'

243 FATHER, AGAIN IN JESUS' NAME WE MEET

Lady Whitmore's hymn appeared in her small volume of *Family Prayers for Every Day in the Week* (1824); it was based on St. Luke xv. 20.

BONT NEWYDD is from *Llyfr Tonau, Ail Attodiad* (1890).

MAGDA, by Dr. Vaughan Williams, from *Songs of Praise* (1925), was composed for the hymn, 'Saviour again to Thy dear name we raise'.

244 O BE WITH US, GRACIOUS FATHER

Contributed to Dr. Charles Rogers's *Lyra Britannica* (1867), 'a collection of British Hymns printed from the genuine texts, with biographical sketches of the hymn-writers'. The compilers have altered 'whilst' to 'while' in ver. 1, and changed the full stop after 'above' in ver. 4 into a comma; otherwise the text stands as the author composed it, for the 'opening of Sabbath Morning Worship'.

The tune DULCINA is the first half of the melody of an old English song, beginning 'As at noon Dulcina rested'. It is found in a manuscript book of songs in the British Museum, dated between 1615 and 1626. The song is mentioned in Walton's *Compleat Angler* (1653), in the conversation with the milk-woman in Chap. IV. The tune is included in Forbes's *Cantus* (Aberdeen, 1662), with a second half differing entirely from that in the manuscript referred to above.

245 DEAR LORD AND FATHER OF MANKIND

From Whittier's poem, 'The Brewing of Soma' (1872). He argues that people nowadays are still as pagan as the Indian drinkers of Soma who hoped thereby to reach union with the Deity.

> In sensual transports wild as vain
> We brew in many a Christian fane
> The heathen Soma still—

Soma being an intoxicating drink made from a plant of that name. Then follow the verses of this hymn, extolling the quiet spiritual communion of the heart as opposed to any 'soma' of sensuous excitement in worship.

Dr. Monk's tune CAMPFIELDS was composed for this hymn in the first edition of *The Church Hymnary* (1898).

246 DEAR SHEPHERD OF THY PEOPLE, HEAR

Newton's lines were written in 1769 and published in the *Olney Hymns* ten years later. His first, third, and seventh stanzas are omitted, and the fifth is placed last. The fifth (i.e. the present fourth verse) originally began,

The feeling heart, the melting eye.

ELGIN is one of the fifteen Common Tunes in *The Psalms of David &c.* (Edward Raban, Aberdeen, 1625).

BAGINTON is included in S. S. Wesley's *European Psalmist* (1872), but it is not known where the tune first appeared.

247 JESUS, WHERE'ER THY PEOPLE MEET

Cowper wrote this, as Newton wrote the previous hymn, for the opening of 'the great room in the Great House' at Olney, where local prayer-meetings were to be held. The hymn appeared first in the *Olney Hymns.* Here the fifth verse is omitted, with its allusion to Isaiah liv. 2:

Behold! at Thy commanding word
We stretch the curtain and the cord;
Come Thou and fill this wider space,
And help us with a wide increase.

LLANDAF comes from *Moliant Cenedl* (1920).

248 JESUS, STAND AMONG US

Mr. Pennefather, the founder of the Mildmay Conferences, wrote this hymn as it stands, except that in ver. 3 'we'll' has been changed to 'we' and 'the' omitted before 'eternal'. His hymns were published posthumously in his *Original Hymns and Thoughts in Verse* (1873), but many of them, like the present, had been already used at the Conferences.

The MS. of ADSIS, JESU was given by Mrs. Monk, after the composer's death, to Dr. A. H. Mann, musical editor of *The Church of England Hymnal*, and it was published in that work (1895).

249 LIGHT OF THE ANXIOUS HEART

Newman's rendering (originally in *Tracts for the Times*, 1836, n. 75) of a cento in the revised Roman Breviary of 1632; this cento is a free adaptation from the famous medieval hymn 'Jesu dulcis memoria' (see below, on Hymn 422).

SELMA is found in *Sacred Music . . . sung in St. George's Church, Edinburgh, edited by R. A. Smith* (1825). There it is set to Psalm lxvii), and described as an 'Ancient Scottish Melody. Noted in the Island of Arran, and harmonized by Mr. Smith'. It is probable that the tune is really Smith's own composition.

250 ENTER THY COURTS, THOU WORD OF LIFE

Words written by Dr. Robert Bridges for a tune by Tallis; published in *The Yattendon Hymnal* (1899).

The FIFTH MODE MELODY, by Thomas Tallis, occurs in *The whole*

*Psalter translated into English Metre, which contayneth an hundreth
and fifty Psalmes.* This version of the Psalms bears neither date nor
author's name, but it is known to be the work of Matthew Parker,
Archbishop of Canterbury, and was probably printed about 1561. It
contains at the end nine tunes in four parts by Thomas Tallis. Of
the first eight one is in each of the eight ecclesiastical modes, the
ninth tune being that now well known as 'Tallis' (Hymn 353).

251 HUSHED WAS THE EVENING HYMN

These verses on the incident of 1 Samuel iii were published by
Mr. Burns in his *Evening Hymn* (1857), when he was minister of
Hampstead Presbyterian Church, London. See on Hymn 472.

The tune SAMUEL was composed by Sir Arthur Sullivan for this
hymn, in *Church Hymns with tunes* (1874). The original arrangement is for treble voices in unison with organ accompaniment. The
present four-part arrangement was made by the composer for *The
Presbyterian Hymnal* (1877).

252 ANGEL VOICES, EVER SINGING

From Mr. Pott's *Hymns Fitted to the Order of Common Prayer*
(1866).

The tune ANGEL VOICES was written by E. G. Monk for the hymn.
Both were written at the request of the Rev. W. K. Macrorie, afterwards Bishop of Maritzburg, for the opening of an organ at Wingate
Church, Lancashire, in February 1861. The Rev. Francis Pott, author
of the hymn, states that the tune was repeatedly printed in Choral
Festival books and similar publications. It appears in *The Congregational Church Hymnal* (1887) and in the *Supplement to Hymns Ancient
and Modern* (1889), but may have been included in collections of an
earlier date.

253 THIS STONE TO THEE IN FAITH WE LAY

Montgomery's hymn was published in his *Christian Psalmist*
(1825), but had previously appeared for the first time in his paper,
The Sheffield Iris, on Nov. 5, 1822.

Knapp's tune WAREHAM comes from *A Sett of New Psalm Tunes
and Anthems, in Four Parts by William Knapp* (1738), where it is
set to Psalm xxxvi. 5–10, and headed 'For the Holy Sacrament'.
The melody is as follows:

In another publication entitled *New Church Melody . . . by William Knapp* (1754), the tune appears as under, in common time, set to Psalm cxxxix, and called 'Blandford Tune'.

254 ALL THINGS ARE THINE; NO GIFT HAVE WE

Written by Whittier in 1873 for the opening of Plymouth Church, St. Paul's, Minnesota.

HERR JESU CHRIST, as arranged in Bach's *Choralgesänge*, from the Görlitz *Pensum Sacrum* (1648).

255 WHEN THE WEARY, SEEKING REST

From Dr. Bonar's *Hymns of Faith and Hope* (3rd series, 1866); based on 2 Chronicles vi. 29, 30, verses which came into his mind when he was asked to provide a refrain for 'the two lovely lines of Mendelssohn's with which Callcott's tune INTERCESSION ends'. One stanza, the last, is omitted.

The two lines are from the *Elijah*, part of the prayer for rain by the prophet and the people. Dr. Callcott's tune appeared in *Psalms and Hymns for Divine Worship* (1867).

256 AWAKE, MY SOUL

The first three, fifth, sixth, and fourteenth stanzas of Ken's Morning Hymn as revised by him in *A Manual of Prayers For the Use of the Scholars of Winchester College, and All Other Devout Christians* &c. (edition of 1709). Hymn 257 contains the ninth, twelfth, thirteenth, and fourteenth stanzas. At his request the hymn was sung at his burial, on Mar. 21, 1711.

In George Eliot's romance of *Adam Bede* (ch. i), the hero, going home across the fields after a hard, honest day's work in the carpenter's shop, 'broke out into the tune which had all day long been running in his head', i.e. verse 3. On verse 5 ('I wake') Dean Alford (*Contemporary Review*, vol. i, p. 441) notes that it illustrates the truth that 'the very best experimental and spiritual hymns of all ages of the Church have been in the singular, from the fifty-first and twenty-third Psalms downwards'.

The good bishop's modest ambition has been richly fulfilled:

> And should the well-meant songs I leave behind
> With Jesus' lovers an acceptance find,
> 'Twill heighten e'en the joys of Heaven to know
> That in my verse the saints hymn God below.

The tune MORNING HYMN is found in *The Hymns and Psalms used at the Asylum or House of Refuge for Female Orphans. Printed for W. Gawler, Organist to the Asylum* (1789?). There it is set to the present hymn, and headed 'New Tune. Published by permission of Mr. Barthélémon.' The book has no date, but a copy in the possession of Dr. W. H. Cummings has the autograph of a former owner and the date 1789. A previous edition of the work was published in 1785; in this the hymn is set to a different tune. In the *Life* of Barthélémon, by his daughter, it is stated that 'about the year 1780 an acquaintance commenced between Mr. B. and the Rev. Jacob Duché, then chaplain to the Asylum. . . . One immediate consequence of this acquaintance was an application to Mr. B. to compose a hymn tune to "Awake, my soul".'

257 ALL PRAISE TO THEE WHO SAFE HAST KEPT

See on previous hymn.

The arrangement of Hudson's tune ST. OLAVE, by Dr. S. S. Wesley, appeared in *The European Psalmist* (1872).

258 NOW THAT THE DAYLIGHT FILLS THE SKY

Dr. Neale's free version of the Latin text of 260, as in *The Hymnal Noted*.

The tune IAM LUCIS is one of several set to the hymn 'Iam lucis orto sidere', in Guidetti's *Directorium Chori* (first published in 1582). It seems to have been adapted from music in use before that date to some of the short versicles and responses occurring in various Church offices.

259 O TIMELY HAPPY, TIMELY WISE

A selection from the original sixteen stanzas which Keble composed on Sept. 20, 1822, and published in *The Christian Year* (1827). In ver. 5 (line 2) he wrote 'Would furnish'.

James Smetham quotes the third verse in his *Letters* (p. 206) with this remark: 'Don't think it a slur merely on secular things that they must be "new" if they are to please. The sweet poet of the *Christian Year* knew better . . . and don't think that Keble was the first to perceive this, for "His mercies are *new* every morning"' (referring to Lamentations iii. 22, 23).

MELCOMBE is found in *An Essay on the Church Plain Chant*, 1782 (cf. Hymn 55). The tune appears in the second part of the work, set to the words 'O Salutaris hostia', &c., and is headed 'At Exposition, Elevation, or Benediction of the Blessed Sacrament'. No composer's name is attached, but in *A Collection of Motetts*, &c. (1792), it is one of the pieces to which Webbe's name is appended as composer. It appeared as a hymn tune under its present name in vol. ii of R. Harrison's *Sacred Harmony* (published in 1791), and here also Webbe is named as the composer.

260 NOW THAT THE DAYSTAR GLIMMERS BRIGHT

Another (see on Hymn 249) of Newman's translations. In his *Verses on Various Occasions* it is dated 'Littlemore, February, 1842'. The Latin original appears in the French Breviary (Paris) for 1736, but goes back to a much earlier date, although it cannot be placed earlier than the eighth century, when the first (German) manuscripts of it are to be found. It was the hymn for Prime (i.e. First Hour, 7 a.m.) service, and this service was not started till the fifth century, after Ambrose had died.

BRISTOL is set in *Ravenscroft's Psalter* (1621) to Psalms xvi and lxiv; it is there called 'Bristol Tune', and classified among the English tunes.

261 CHRIST, WHOSE GLORY FILLS THE SKIES

From Wesley's *Hymns and Sacred Poems* (1740).

George Eliot uses this hymn in *Adam Bede* (ch. xxxviii), describing how Seth Bede, the young Methodist, on leaving his brother one Sunday morning in February, 'walked leisurely homeward, mentally repeating one of his favourite hymns'. It was this hymn.

The tune PSALM 135 (MINISTRES DE L'ÉTERNEL) is set to this psalm in the complete *French Psalter* of 1562.

262 JESUS, SUN OF RIGHTEOUSNESS

Baron von Rosenroth's hymn, in his *Neuer Helicon* (Nürnberg, 1684), as translated with more spirit than accuracy by Miss Borthwick in her *Hymns from the Land of Luther* (1855).

MORGENGLANZ DER EWIGKEIT is the tune set to the original hymn in Freylinghausen's *Gesangbuch* (Halle, 1704).

263 FATHER, WE PRAISE THEE, NOW THE NIGHT IS OVER

This translation was contributed by Dr. Dearmer to *The English Hymnal* (1906). The Latin original has been ascribed to St. Gregory the Great (540–604), and some scholars still accept the tradition, while others date it in the reign of Charlemagne. Dr. Dearmer's verse happily reproduces the metre of the original, the first stanza of which, e.g., is

> Nocte surgentes vigilemus omnes,
> Semper in psalmis meditemur, atque
> viribus totis Domino canamus
>   dulciter hymnos.

The tune CHRISTE SANCTORUM is drawn from *La Feillée's Méthode du Plain-Chant*.

264 O LORD OF LIFE, THY QUICKENING VOICE

From George Macdonald's *The Disciple, and other Poems* (1860).
EPWORTH is from *The Psalmist : A Collection of Psalm and Hymn Tunes, edited by Vincent Novello* (Part III, 1838). There it is called 'Loughton', and headed 'Charles Wesley. Arr. by S. Wesley.'

265 AT THY FEET, O CHRIST, WE LAY

Dr. Bright's hymn appeared first in *The Monthly Packet* for October 1867.
BARMOUTH was the tune composed for it in *Hymns Ancient and Modern* (Revised edition, 1875). The composer wrote the tune for Dr. W. H. Monk, who called it by this name to commemorate an exciting adventure in which he and Mr. Macfarren had shared; during a holiday at Barmouth they were lost for a day and a night among the Welsh mountains. See Macfarren's *Musical Memories*.

266 HAIL, THOU BRIGHT AND SACRED MORN

Arranged from Mrs. Elliott's contributions to her husband's *Psalms and Hymns for Public, Private, and Social Worship* (1835). First printed in 1833 privately. Three stanzas are omitted.
MORNING was composed by Dr. W. H. Monk for this hymn; it appeared in *The Scottish Hymnal* (1871).

267 THIS IS THE DAY OF LIGHT

Canon Ellerton's hymn is taken from *Hymns for Special Occasions and Festivals* (1867) in Chester Cathedral. One stanza is omitted.
DOMINICA, by Sir H. S. Oakeley, was composed for this hymn, in *Hymns Ancient and Modern* (Revised edition, 1875).
FAREHAM, by Sir John Goss, appeared in *The Hymnary* (1872).

268 O DAY OF REST AND GLADNESS

From Dr. Wordsworth's *Holy Year* (1862), with the omission of two stanzas. In the sixth edition (1872) he wrote in ver. 1 (lines 6 and 8) 'Through ages join'd in tune' and 'the great God Triune'. The hymn is based on Psalm cxviii. 24: 'This is the day which the Lord hath made : we will rejoice and be glad in it.'
BERNO is from *The Church of England Hymnal* (1895). It was composed for this hymn by Dr. A. H. Mann in 1874, but he does not think it was ever published till its appearance in the above book, of which he was musical editor.

269 HAIL, SACRED DAY OF EARTHLY REST

Thring's hymn, composed in 1863, was not originally intended for public worship, but has gained wide popularity since its inclusion in *Hymns Congregational and others* (1866). It had thirteen stanzas, as he wrote it, and was based on Psalm cxviii. 24 ; 'This is

the day which the Lord hath made : we will rejoice and be glad in it.'
Two of the stanzas omitted are:

> The merry throstle, as he sings,
>   The merrier sings to-day,
> The sun shines out from 'mid the clouds
>   With brighter ray,
>
> I join the quiet, thoughtful crowd,
>   That throngs the house of prayer,
> And, kneeling on my knees, I reap
>   A blessing there.

HOLY CROSS, by A. H. Brown, first appeared in *The Congregational Mission Hymnal* (1890).

270 THE DARKNESS NOW IS OVER

From Mrs. Brock's *Children's Hymn Book* (1881), over the initials 'E. T.'

DEVONSHIRE is an English traditional melody (*The English Hymnal*, 1906), arranged by L. E. Broadwood from a North Devon folk-song entitled 'The unquiet grave'.

271 BEFORE THE DAY DRAWS NEAR ITS ENDING

Written by Canon Ellerton on April 22, 1880, for a festival of choirs at Nantwich, and published in the *Nantwich Festival Book* of that year.

SUNSET was composed for this hymn by Dr. Stocks, and comes from the same source as 'Village' (Hymn 48).

GOTTLOB, ES GEHT is a melody found in various forms among German music-books from 1742 onwards. The present form of the melody and the harmony are Bach's, in his *Choralgesänge*.

272 THE SUN IS SINKING FAST

The long-lost Latin original was at last discovered by Rev. James Mearns, who printed it in Julian's *Dictionary* (p. 1704) with the remark that Caswall produced 'a hymn in every way superior to its original'. His version was published in his *Masque of Mary* (1858): it is printed here as in his *Hymns and Poems*, except that the second line of the second verse originally ran, 'In death reclined', although there is nothing corresponding to it in the terse Latin original of verses 2 and 3:

> ut Christus moriens in cruce spiritum
> commendans, patrias tradidit in manus,
>   totam mens mea summo
>   se vult tradere numini.

ST. COLUMBA, from *Hymns Ancient and Modern* (1861), was written for this hymn. It is so named from St. Columba's College, Rathfarnham, of which H. S. Irons was for a time organist.

273 THE SUN DECLINES; O'ER LAND AND SEA

Written by Mr. Walmsley in 1893 and published in his *Sacred Songs for Children of all Ages* (1900).

Sir John Stainer's GLOAMING was composed for the hymn in the first edition of *The Church Hymnary* (1898).

274 AS NOW THE SUN'S DECLINING RAYS

Another Latin hymn by Charles Coffin (see on 78) is the original of this translation. Coffin's verses are in the Paris Revised Breviary of 1736, and were done into English by Mr. Chandler in his *Hymns of the Primitive Church* (1837). The text as in *Hymns Ancient and Modern*. The original opened less happily ;

> And now the sun's declining rays
> Towards the eve descend,
> E'en so our years are sinking down
> To their appointed end.

DURHAM, in *Ravenscroft's Psalter* (1621), is set to Psalms xxviii and lxxvi, and marked as a 'Northern Tune'. It is included among the Common Tunes in the 1635 edition of the *Scottish Psalter*.

BURFORD is set to Psalm xlii (new version) in *A Book of Psalmody, containing Variety of Tunes for all the Common Metres of the Psalms in the Old and New Versions, and others for Particular Measures . . . By John Chetham* (1718). In this book the tunes are without names, and no composers' names are given. But our tune is named 'Burford' in Gawthorn's *Harmonia Perfecta* (1730).

In many modern collections 'Burford' is attributed to Henry Purcell, but there seems to be no evidence for this. Probably the earliest books in which it is so assigned are Cotterill's *Christian Psalmody* (1831) and Novello's *Psalmist* (1835). The tune is found in a very large number of the eighteenth-century psalmodies, and in none is Purcell named as composer.

275 AGAIN, AS EVENING'S SHADOW FALLS.

From Mr. Longfellow's *Vespers* (1859), in the form printed by himself for congregational use.

The tune UFFINGHAM appears in *The Divine Companion, or, David's Harp New tuned*, &c. (1701), under the heading 'An Evening Hymn. Set by Mr. Jer. Clarke', beginning, 'Sleep, downey Sleep, come close mine eyes'.

WOOLMER'S, by Sir F. A. G. Ouseley, appeared in *Hymns Ancient and Modern* (1861).

276 AS DARKER, DARKER FALL AROUND

A selection from the original thirteen stanzas of the so-called 'Hymn of the Calabrian Shepherds', as altered and added to in the Unitarian *Hymns of the Spirit*, 1864. This anonymous poem appeared first in William Young's *Catholic Choralist* (1842).

ST. AMBROSE is dated 1847; it appeared in *Church Psalmody* (1849), edited by Dr. Steggall.

DUNDEE (WINDSOR) is found in *The Booke of the Musicke of M. William Damon, late one of her maiesties Musitions: conteining all the tunes of David's Psalmes, as they are ordinarily soung in the Church: most excellently by him composed into 4 parts* (1591). In this book 'Dundee' appears for the first time in the form of a psalm tune, but it is probable, as has been pointed out by the Rev. H. Parr, that it is an adaptation from one of the tunes (see on 166) in Christopher Tye's *Actes of the Apostles* (1553). The tune in question is that set to chapter iii, the treble being as follows:

The tune is next found in *The Whole Booke of Psalmes with their wonted tunes . . . by Thomas Est* (1592). In a table at the end of this volume the tune is included among 'those tunes newly added in this booke'. It is set to Psalm cxvi, the harmony being by G. Kirby. The melody is as follows:

No name is here attached to the tune, but in three subsequent editions of the same book it is called 'Suffolk Tune'. In *Ravenscroft's Psalter* (1621) it appears four times, and is named 'Windsor or Eaton', being classed in the Index among 'English tunes'. The name 'Windsor' is that by which it has continued to be known in England. The earliest appearance of the tune in Scotland is in the edition of the *Scottish Psalter* printed by A. Hart in 1615. It is printed, as under, among the Common Tunes, and headed 'Dundie Tune'.

277 AT EVEN, WHEN THE SUN WAS SET

The full and original form of Canon Twells's hymn as contributed to *Hymns Ancient and Modern* (1868). But 'ere' was changed to 'when' in the first line, to suit St. Mark i. 32 ('At even, when the sun did set, they brought unto Him all that were diseased', though the author defended his original wording by an appeal to the R. V. of St. Luke iv. 40 ('And when the sun was setting'). In a letter to the Rev. Duncan Campbell, the author of *Hymns and Hymn Makers* (p. 144), he said the hymn was written 'in 1868, at the request of Sir Henry Baker, who said a new evening hymn was wanted for the first edition of *Hymns Ancient and Modern*, and being at that time head master of a large grammar-school—the Godolphin School, Hammersmith—I wrote it one afternoon while the boys were under examination (paper-work), and I was supposed to be seeing "all fair". . . . Copies have been kindly sent to me in Greek, Latin, German, French, Welsh, and Irish. I like to think it may have brought souls nearer Christ, and if so, I heartily thank God for it.'

ANGELUS goes back to *Heilige Seelenlust, oder geistliche Hirten-Lieder . . . von Johann Angelo Silesio, und von Herren Georgio Josepho mit aussbundig schönen Melodeyen geziert . . . Breslau* (1657). But, though this volume has always been cited as the source of the present tune, the first line and half of the second are the only parts of it which are really to be found there. The earliest publication in which the entire tune has been found is *Cantica Spiritualia, oder Auswahl der schönsten geistlichen Lieder älterer Zeit*, &c. (vol. ii, Munich, 1847). Here it appears in its present form, set to the hymn 'Du meiner Seelen güldne Zier'. As the source of hymn and tune the editor of *Cantica Spiritualia* names the 1657 book, of which the title is given above, and also Braun's *Echo Hymnodiæ Cœlestis* (1675). The melody of the hymn 'Du meiner Seelen, &c.' in both of these books is exactly the same, and is as follows:

Dr. W. Bäumker is of opinion that this, the original melody, was arbitrarily altered by the editor of *Cantica Spiritualia*.

278 NOW CHEER OUR HEARTS THIS EVENTIDE

Selnecker's hymn has been frequently translated. This version in *The Yattendon Hymnal* (p. 13) was written to suit Bach's setting of the Proper tune, and freely though finely expands two of the original nine stanzas.

The melody of ACH BLEIB BEI UNS is in *Geistliche Lieder* (Leipzig, 1589); the form here printed is Bach's in his *Choralgesänge*.

279 THE RADIANT MORN HATH PASSED AWAY

Printed as it appeared in Prebendary Thring's *Hymns* (1866), under the heading of 'The Lord shall be thine everlasting Light' (Isaiah lx. 20). The second verse underwent some changes in the author's hands. The present form is that adopted in *The Church of England Hymnal*. The author pointed out that the hymn 'was composed as an afternoon hymn, as in most of the parishes in that part of Somersetshire, in which I lived, the second service was nearly always held in the afternoon, and not in the evening'.

ST. GABRIEL, by Sir F. Ouseley, was composed for this hymn in *Hymns Ancient and Modern* (Appendix, 1868).

280 NOW GOD BE WITH US, FOR THE NIGHT IS CLOSING

Petrus Herbert's hymn was contributed to the *Gesangbuch der Böhmischen Brüder* (1566), which he helped to edit. This is Miss Winkworth's translation, as in *The Chorale-Book for England* (1863), except that 'Protector' replaces her 'O Master' in ver. 2 (line 2), and 'holy thoughts' has been preferred to 'pious thoughts' in ver. 3 (line 1).

The tune DIVA SERVATRIX, from *The English Hymnal*, is one of the French melodies mentioned in the note on Hymn 4.

281 HAIL, GLADDENING LIGHT, OF HIS PURE GLORY POURED

This anonymous Greek hymn is quoted by St. Basil in the fourth century. The Greek Church uses it in the Vesper Service. Keble's rendering appeared first in *The British Magazine* (1834), then in *Lyra Apostolica* (1836). In his edition of the latter work, contributed to Methuen's Library of Devotion, Canon Beeching wrote: 'On the whole, this would undoubtedly rank as a successful translation; but it misses the directness which is so great a charm of the Greek; and I am not sure that the cumbrous relative sentence in the second line, and the restless interpolation of "Holiest of Holies" in the third, does not obscure to the ordinary reader the fact, which should be absolutely luminous, that the hymn is addressed to Christ.' Another version of the Greek hymn is to be found in Longfellow's poem, *The Golden Legend* (1851), and for this version Sir Arthur Sullivan wrote a fine setting.

SEBASTE was composed by Sir John Stainer for the hymn in *Hymns Ancient and Modern* (1875).

282 HOLY FATHER, CHEER OUR WAY

Composed by Mr. Robinson in 1869 for the congregation of St. Paul's, Upper Norwood, London. The original text had 'later', not 'latter', in ver. 2. It was intended to be sung after the third collect in the evening service of the English Prayer Book; 'Lighten our darkness, we beseech Thee, O Lord; and by Thy great mercy deliver us from all perils and dangers of this night; for the love of Thy only Son our Saviour, Jesus Christ.' The text for the hymn was Zechariah xiv. 7, 'At evening time it shall be light.'

CAPETOWN comes from *Vierstimmiges Choralbuch herausgegeben von Dr. F. Filitz* (Berlin, 1847).

283 FATHER, IN HIGH HEAVEN DWELLING

Mr. Rawson's hymn, based on St. Luke xi. 3, 4, was published in *The Leeds Hymnbook* (1853), then in his own *Hymns* (1876).

The tune EVENING HYMN was contributed by William Jackson to *The Bradford Tune Book* (1863).

284 THE DUTEOUS DAY NOW CLOSETH

For the last hundred years Gerhardt's hymn has been a household word in Germany, but, though it appeared in Crüger's *Praxis Pietatis Melica* (1647), it failed to win popularity during the eighteenth century, when it was regarded, in Frederick the Great's words, as 'töricht und dummes Zeug' (silly and stupid trash). It was a special favourite of the poet Schiller. The present rendering by Dr. Bridges, in *The Yattendon Hymnal*, is an extremely free paraphrase; thus the original has nothing corresponding to the third and fourth verses.

The melody of INNSBRUCK has been commonly attributed to Heinrich Isaak. So far as known it first appeared in print in *Ein ausszug guter alter ün newer Teutscher liedlein* (Nürnberg, 1539). It is there set to the song 'Innsbruck ich muss dich lassen' in the following form:

Later the melody was adapted to the hymn 'O Welt ich muss dich lassen', and later still to Gerhardt's hymn 'Nun ruhen alle Wälder'. The melody appears in a large variety of forms in German collections from the above date to the present day. The arrangement here is that adopted by Bach in his *St. Matthew Passion* and elsewhere.

285 SAVIOUR, BREATHE AN EVENING BLESSING

From Mr. Edmeston's *Sacred Lyrics* (1820). He had been reading in Salte's *Travels in Abyssinia* how at night the native Christians' 'short hymn, "Jesus forgive us", stole through the camp'. This suggested his verses.

LUGANO is set to a Kyrie, and headed 'Litany B.V.M.' in *Catholic Hymn Tunes and Litanies, adapted to Latin and English words, edited by J. M. Capes, Esq.* (1849). No information is given as to the source of the melody. The present arrangement and adaptation to this hymn was made by William Shore, and appeared in *The Musical Times* for July 1850.

ZUM FRIEDEN was one of a number of melodies contributed by Bach to *Musicalisches Gesangbuch*, edited by Christian Schemelli (Leipzig, 1736).

286 ABIDE WITH ME; FAST FALLS THE EVENTIDE

Lyte's most famous hymn was composed in 1820, according to the Rev. T. H. Bindley (*Spectator*, Oct. 3, 1925). 'In that year Lyte, as a young clergyman, was staying with the Hores at Pole Hore near Wexford. He went to see an old friend, William Augustus Le Hunte, who lay dying, and who kept repeating the phrase "abide with me". After leaving the bedside Lyte wrote the hymn and gave a copy of it to Sir Francis Le Hunte, William's brother, amongst whose papers it remained when they passed to his nephew the Rev. Francis Le Hunte. No doubt, when Lyte felt his own end approaching, his mind reverted to the lines he had written so many years before, and then it was that they became first popularly known. These details were given to me some years ago by Sir George Ruthven Le Hunte, grandson of William Augustus, and I have recently had them confirmed by members of his family.' The usual tradition is that Lyte first wrote the hymn on the evening of Sept. 4, 1847, after a farewell sermon to his congregation; he was then on the point of leaving for the Continent in bad health. In any case it was not meant to be an evening hymn originally; the outlook is on the closing day of life.

As Lyte wrote it the hymn had eight stanzas, and in some texts verse 5 (line 2) had

Hold then Thy cross.

The present version is the same as in his *Miscellaneous Poems* (1870).

Dr. W. H. Monk composed EVENTIDE for this hymn, in *Hymns Ancient and Modern* (1861).

287 THE DAY IS PAST AND OVER

The Greek original is a cento from anonymous verses used in the Evening Service of the Greek Church; they may date from the sixth or the seventh century. According to Dr. Neale (in his *Hymns of the Eastern Church*) this hymn 'is, to the scattered hamlets of Chios and

Mitylene, what Bishop Ken's evening Hymn is to the villages of our own land'. His text has been altered slightly; the refrain of ver. 3 has been made uniform throughout (i.e. in verses 1 and 2), and 'pray' has been repeated, from ver. 1 (line 3), in the similar lines of verses 2 and 3.

ST. ANATOLIUS was composed by A. H. Brown for this hymn, and published with eight other tunes by the same composer in 1862, under the title, 'The Day is past and over; an Evening Hymn, to which are added a few other hymns'.

288 NOW THE DAY IS OVER

Mr. Baring-Gould's hymn, based on Proverbs iii. 24, was first published, without the doxology, in *The Church Times* for Feb. 16, 1867.

The tune LYNDHURST was given to the Committee who compiled *Church Praise, with Tunes* (1883), by Mr. Alexander Guthrie, after whose residence in Liverpool it is named. Mr. Guthrie states that the daughter of the Russian Consul in Liverpool having 'heard the air somewhere on the Continent, noted it down, and had it harmonized by a musical friend'. When it came into Mr. Guthrie's hands, it was set to the present hymn. The tune had been composed by Mr. F. W. Blunt, a solicitor (London), in 1871, for the hymn 'In the hour of trial'. Mr. Baring-Gould strongly preferred this tune for this hymn, though he wrote EUDOXIA for it. The latter appeared in the Appendix.

EUDOXIA was written for this hymn by Mr. Baring-Gould; it appeared in the Appendix (1868) to *Hymns Ancient and Modern*. Mr. Baring-Gould afterwards said that he wrote the hymn to a tune he wished to popularize for his Mission at Horbury Bridge in 1865. He fancied the melody (EUDOXIA) to be original, of his own, but afterwards discovered it was a reminiscence of a German air he had heard as a child. The German air in question remains unidentified.

289 THE DAY THOU GAVEST, LORD, IS ENDED

The final form of Canon Ellerton's hymn, which was written in 1870 and appeared in *Church Hymns* (S.P.C.K., 1871).

LES COMMANDMENS DE DIEU was composed or adapted by L. Bourgeois, and set in the *French Psalter*, 1549, to the metrical version of the Ten Commandments by Clément Marot. The present form of the melody is, with one slight alteration, that of the original.

RADFORD was composed by S. S. Wesley for this hymn, in *Church Hymns with Tunes* (1874).

So was ST. CLEMENT, by C. C. Scholefield; it also appeared in *Church Hymns with Tunes* (1874).

290 OUR DAY OF PRAISE IS DONE

The final form of Canon Ellerton's hymn, as in the S.P.C.K. *Church Hymns* of 1871; an earlier form was composed in 1867 for the Nantwich Festival of choirs.

Dr. Steggall wrote DAY OF PRAISE for this hymn, in *The Supplemental Hymn and Tune Book, Compiled by Rev. R. Brown-Borthwick* (3rd edition, with new appendix, 1869).

291 ALL PRAISE TO THEE, MY GOD, THIS NIGHT

The text of Bishop Ken's Evening Hymn is also (see on Hymn 256) taken from the 1709 revision.

TALLIS' CANON is the eighth of nine tunes by Tallis in *The Whole Psalter* (see above, on Hymn 250), where it is referred to Psalm lxvii. The melody in the original is the same as at present, except that each line is repeated before the next is introduced. The four-line form appears in Ravenscroft's *Whole Book of Psalms* (1621).

292 SUN OF MY SOUL, THOU SAVIOUR DEAR

From the original poem on Evening, in fourteen stanzas, which appeared in *The Christian Year* (1827). It was composed on Nov. 25, 1820, and based on St. Luke xxiv. 29.

Sir Herbert Oakeley wrote ABENDS for this hymn, in the Irish *Church Hymnal* (1874), and revised the harmony for the first edition of *The Church Hymnary*.

HERR GOTT VATER comes from *Tisch Gesänge* (Breslau, 1615).

HURSLEY is a form of Pascal (413).

293 GOD THAT MADEST EARTH AND HEAVEN

The first verse appeared in Heber's posthumous *Hymns* (1827); the second is Archbishop Whately's free version of the Compline Antiphon ('salva nos, Domine, vigilantes, custodi nos dormientes, ut vigilemus in Christo, et requiescamus in pace'); it was contributed to *Sacred Poetry* (Dublin, 1838).

TEMPLE was composed by Dr. E. J. Hopkins for this hymn, in *The Temple Church Choral Service, edited by E. J. Hopkins* (1867).

294 ERE I SLEEP, FOR EVERY FAVOUR

The full form of Cennick's hymn, as in his *Sacred Hymns for the Children of God* (1741).

THANET is from Jowett's *Parochial Psalmody* (1832); CWM DU appears in *Gemau Mawl*, edited by D. Jenkins (1890).

295 ALMIGHTY GOD, THY WORD IS CAST

From Cawood's six stanzas as first published and edited in T. Cotterill's *Selection of Psalms and Hymns for Public Worship* (8th edition 1819), for use 'After Sermon'. As originally written, it had in ver. 1 (line 3)

Oh may it grow in humble hearts

in ver. 2 (line 3) 'praying souls' instead of 'every heart', in ver. 3 (lines 3 and 4)

But may it in converted minds
Produce the fruits of joy,

and, as a closing verse,

> Great God! come down, and on Thy Word
> Thy mighty power bestow:
> That all who hear the joyful sound
> Thy saving grace may know.

DUNFERMLINE is one of the twelve Common Tunes appearing in *The CL Psalms of David*, &c. (Andro Hart, Edinburgh, 1615). Its first appearance in an English book is in Ravenscroft's *Whole Book of Psalms* (1621), where it is classified in the index among the Scottish tunes.

296 AND NOW THE WANTS ARE TOLD THAT BROUGHT

From Dr. Bright's *Hymns* (1866).

In *Ravenscroft's Psalter* (1621) SALISBURY is set to Psalms xvii and liv as 'Salisbury Tune', and classified as an English tune. The melody is exactly as at present.

297 COME, DEAREST LORD, DESCEND AND DWELL

From Watts's *Hymns and Spiritual Songs* (1709).

WHITEHALL, by Henry Lawes, is set to Psalm viii in the source mentioned at Hymn 456 (first tune).

298 OF THY LOVE SOME GRACIOUS TOKEN

One of the thirty-three contributions by Kelly and some others to the appendix of *A Collection of Psalms and Hymns Extracted from Various Authors* (1802).

HENLLAN was composed by Dr. Evans for this hymn.

299 LORD, DISMISS US WITH THY BLESSING

This hymn is ascribed to Dr. John Fawcett (see on Hymn 490), a Yorkshire Nonconformist minister, by the York *Selection of Psalms and Hymns* (1791), although its earlier appearances, e.g. in the *Supplement to the Shrewsbury Hymnal* (1773), are anonymous. In Dr. Conyers's *Collection of Psalms and Hymns* (3rd edition, 1774) the present sixth line replaces the original

> In this dry and barren place.

In Toplady's *Psalms and Hymns* (1776) the last two lines of the present text replace the original

> Ever faithful
> To the Truth may we be found.

The third stanza is omitted.

The tune HOLYWOOD seems to have come into use in Roman Catholic churches in England about the same period as 'Adeste Fideles', but nothing definite has yet been discovered as to its composer or source. It is found in *An Essay on the Church Plain Chant* (1782), in Webbe's *Collection of Motetts*, &c. (1792), and in the Wade MS. at Stonyhurst College. (See under 'Adeste Fideles', No. 55.) In all of these it is set to the Hymn at Benediction, ' Tantum ergo sacramentum'. The Stonyhurst MS. contains five, and the *Essay* four settings of the same words in addition to the present one. The melody in all the above books is, with very trifling exceptions, the same as in the present version. A slightly different form appeared in Gardiner's *Sacred Melodies* (vol. ii, 1815), where it is headed 'Subject from the Missal Book', and set to the hymn 'Lord, dismiss us with Thy blessing'. The same arrangement and adaptation appeared in *Sacred Harmony for St. George's Church* (Edinburgh, 1820), and this form of the tune, under the names 'Dismission' and 'Augustine', is found in several collections since that date.

300 NOW MAY HE WHO FROM THE DEAD

Newton wrote this (in the *Olney Hymns*) to be sung 'after sermon', basing it on Hebrews xiii. 20–2. The tune KEINE SCHÖNHEIT HAT DIE WELT is from *Heilige Seelenlust oder Geistliche Hirten-Lieder . . . von Johann Angelo Silesio, Und vom Herren Georgio Josepho mit aussbundig schönen Melodeyen geziert . . . Breslau* (1657), where it is set to the hymn by Scheffler, 'Keine Schönheit hat die Welt'.

301 SAVIOUR, AGAIN TO THY DEAR NAME WE RAISE

Canon Ellerton's hymn was written in 1866 for a Choral Festival at Nantwich, Cheshire; then revised and abridged for *Hymns Ancient and Modern* (1868). The last verse was sung at his funeral on June 20, 1893, in Torquay.

ELLERS comes from the same source as 'Day of Praise' (290). It was composed for this hymn, and arranged for voices in unison, with organ accompaniment, the latter being varied in each verse. The present four-part arrangement appeared in the *Appendix to the Bradford Tune Book*, edited by Samuel Smith (1872). The following note is appended: 'The above four-part vocal arrangement has been kindly prepared by the composer, at the request of the editor, specially for this work'. Another four-part arrangement appeared in *Church Hymns* (1874), and in Dr. Allon's *Congregational Psalmist* (1875). In the latter book the arrangement is stated to be by Sir A. Sullivan.

Dr. Dykes wrote PAX DEI for the hymn, in *Hymns Ancient and Modern* (Appendix, 1868).

302 O SAVIOUR, BLESS US ERE WE GO

Written in 1849 and printed in Faber's *Jesus and Mary* (2nd edition, 1852). One stanza is omitted, and 'Sweet Saviour' changed to 'O Saviour'. Faber himself altered 'gone' to 'done' in ver. 2 (line 1), and 'simple' to 'loving' in ver 4 (line 3).

ST. MATTHIAS was composed by W. H. Monk for this hymn, in *Hymns Ancient and Modern* (1861).

For SURREY, see above on Hymn 172.

303 PART IN PEACE: CHRIST'S LIFE WAS PEACE

From a chorus sung by early Christians facing martyrdom, in a dramatic poem called *Vivia Perpetua* (1841). In the last line, 'Brethren, sisters' has been added as usual to Mrs. Adams's verse, in order to adapt the song to congregational purposes.

PAX VOBISCUM has been specially written for the hymn in the present book.

304 LORD JESUS CHRIST, OUR LORD MOST DEAR

Heinrich von Laufenburg's hymn was originally a mother's cradle-song over her child. It dates from 1429 and was translated by Miss Winkworth in her *Christian Singers of Germany*; her rendering was altered to its present form by Rev. Henry White in his *Savoy Hymnary* (1870).

The tune DAS NEUGEBORNE KINDELEIN comes from *Ein schön geistlich Gesangbuch*, which was edited by Melchior Vulpius himself (Jena, 1609). The present arrangement is that by Bach in his Cantata on this chorale.

305 A LITTLE CHILD THE SAVIOUR CAME

Contributed to the Church of Scotland's *Hymns for Public Worship* (1861) by the Rev. William Robertson, minister of Monzievaird parish, Perthshire.

COMMANDMENTS is a tune adapted from the melody already used for Hymn 289.

ST. ALKMUND (INTERCESSION) comes from *Easy Music for Church Choirs* (part III, 1853), which contains music for various parts of the Roman Catholic worship. Neither the source nor the composer of the tune is known. It was included in the Appendix of 1868 to *Hymns Ancient and Modern*.

306 OUR CHILDREN, LORD, IN FAITH AND PRAYER

Part of a baptismal hymn from the author's *Carmina Christo* (2nd edition, 1808), as arranged in J. Nunn's *Psalms and Hymns from the Most Approved Authors* (1817). Haweis was one of the chaplains to Lady Huntingdon, who was keenly interested in church music.

The melody from which the tune MORAVIA is derived seems to have appeared in David Wolder's *New Catechismus Gesangbüchlein* (Hamburg, 1598). Since that date it has been included in many German collections, but with very numerous variations. In J. S.

Bach's *Vierstimmige Choralgesänge* it appears as under, and is referred to the hymn 'Aus meines Herzens Grunde'.

307 BLESSED JESUS, HERE WE STAND

Schmolk's hymn originally appeared in the third edition (1706) of his *Heilige Flammen*, entitled 'Seasonable Reflections of the Sponsors on their way with the child to Baptism'. Six of the seven stanzas were rendered into English by Miss Winkworth in *Lyra Germanica* (second series, 1856), and from her version these four stanzas are taken.

For LIEBSTER JESU see on Hymn 203.

308 O FATHER, THOU WHO HAST CREATED ALL

Composed by a hymnologist who was himself a true poet. Knapp wrote this hymn for the baptism of one of his children : it appeared in the 'Christenlieder' supplement to *Evangelischer Liederschatz* (1841), and was translated by Miss Winkworth in the second series of her *Lyra Germanica*. Her version began,

O Father-heart who hast created all,

and the last three lines of ver. 1, as she composed them, were—

Bend o'er him now with blessing fraught,
And make Thou something out of nought,
O Father-heart.

Sir Arthur Sullivan composed ST. FRANCIS for this hymn, in *Church Hymns with Tunes* (1874).

309 BY COOL SILOAM'S SHADY RILL

As in Heber's *Hymns* (1827); its first form (in *The Christian Observer* for April 1812) was slightly different, beginning

By cool Siloam's shady fountain.

These two stanzas, which lay between verses 2 and 3, are omitted :

By cool Siloam's shady rill
The lily must decay;
The rose that blooms beneath the hill
Must shortly fade away.

And soon, too soon, the wintry hour
Of man's maturer age
Will shake the soul, with sorrow's power,
And stormy passion's rage!

The hymn was entitled 'Christ a pattern for children', and based on St. Luke ii. 40.

BELMONT has been ascribed to Samuel Webbe, to his son Samuel Webbe, jun., and also to Mozart; but there are no sufficient grounds for assigning its composition to any of these. It appears to be an adaptation from a melody in William Gardiner's *Sacred Melodies . . . adapted to the best English Poets* (vol. 1, 1812). This consists of eight lines, and the first half of the melody is as follows:

No name of composer is attached, but in a catalogue appended to his *Music and Friends* (1838) Gardiner cites it as his own composition. The tune appears, practically in its present form, in *A Church Hymn and Tune Book* (1859), where it is said to be harmonized by J. Bentley; in Routledge's *Church and Home Metrical Psalter and Hymnal* (1860), and in other books of about the same date.

310 GRACIOUS SAVIOUR, GENTLE SHEPHERD

The nucleus of this hymn is in some verses of Miss Leeson's *Hymns and Scenes of Childhood* (1842). Keble, in *The Salisbury Hymn-book* (1857), made verse 1 of the present form out of lines written by Miss Leeson, wrote the second and the third verses practically himself, and rewrote the fourth on the basis of Miss Leeson's original.

BRYNTIRION is by A. H. T. Lutteroth, who edited *Chants Chrétiens* (Paris, 1834), where it first appears. In the index he entered his own tunes under 'Heinrich Roth'.

311 MY GOD, AND IS THY TABLE SPREAD?

First published in the posthumous edition of Doddridge's *Hymns* (1755), under the title of 'God's Name profaned, when his Table is treated with contempt. Malachi i. 12. Applied to the Lord's Supper'. Two stanzas are omitted, one being this at the close:

> Revive Thy dying churches, Lord,
> And bid our drooping graces live;
> And more, that energy afford,
> A Saviour's love alone can give.

In the original sequence ver. 4 precedes ver. 3.

BROMLEY, as in *The Yattendon Hymnal*. It is taken from a manuscript in the Foundling Hospital.

312 'TWAS ON THAT NIGHT WHEN DOOMED TO KNOW

This noble paraphrase, like Hymn 400, was composed by Dr. John Morison, and improved by some unknown hands for the 1781 edition of *The Scottish Paraphrases*. Dr. Morison's original version of ver. 1 was:

> 'Twas on that night when doom'd to know
> The eager rage of every foe,
> The Lord of Life embraced a fiend
> In semblance of a courteous friend.

This and some other features of the hymn have suggested the conjecturè that Morison must have used a Latin hymn by Andreas Ellinger (b. 1526), a medical professor at Jena—a hymn translated by the Rev. William Archibald, parish minister of Unst in Shetland (d. 1785). Ellinger's hymn is reproduced in D. J. Maclagan's *Scottish Paraphrases* (1889, p. 107).

For the tune see on Hymn 106.

313 ACCORDING TO THY GRACIOUS WORD

First published in Montgomery's *Christian Psalmist* (1825); two stanzas are omitted here.

The tune BANGOR is from *A Compleat Melody: or, The Harmony of Zion . . . By William Tans'ur* (Preface dated Sept. 29, 1734). There it is set to Psalm xii and headed 'Bangor Tune. Composed in Three Parts. W. T.' It is doubtful whether the tune is an original composition by Tans'ur, or was merely harmonized by him. In some books the tune has appeared in the *Dorian* mode, with no flat in the signature; in the original, however, it is in D minor, as at present. Its popularity as a psalm-tune was very great in Scotland in the eighteenth and early nineteenth centuries. See Burns's *The Ordination*.

BALLERMA is found in *A Selection of Original Sacred Music. . . . Intended to form the sixth Vol. of Steven's Selection of Sacred Music, edited by John Turnbull* (Glasgow, 1833). There it is attributed to R. Simpson, but it seems to be an adaptation from a melody published by F. H. Barthélémon, set to the words of a poem entitled 'Belerma and Durandarte', which appeared in the once famous romance, *The Monk*, by M. G. Lewis.

314 JESUS, TO THY TABLE LED

In *The Canterbury Hymnal*, edited by Canon Baynes himself, this hymn appears under the heading, 'To know the love of Christ, which passeth knowledge' (Ephesians iii. 19), but the second verse, which echoes this text, is omitted:

> While in penitence we kneel,
> Thy sweet Presence let us feel,
> All Thy wondrous Love reveal.

In ver. 3 (line 1) Canon Baynes wrote, 'While on Thy dear Cross we gaze'. The order of the second and third verses has been reversed.

ST. KERRIAN is a melody quoted by Zahn from a Manuscript Book of Chorales, written at Dresden, 1761. There it is set to the hymn 'Da Christus geboren war', as follows:

The present adaptation is by Sir John Stainer, and was published in *The Hymnal Companion* (third edition, 1890), set to this hymn.

Sir Arthur Sullivan's tune LACRYMAE was composed for the hymn 'Lord, in this Thy mercy's day', and appeared first in *The Hymnary* (1872).

315 THOU STANDEST AT THE ALTAR

From *Hymns for the Use of the Churches* (London, 1864; 2nd edition, 1871), compiled by Mr. Eddis himself for the Catholic Apostolic Church.

CARDEN PLACE was composed by Mr. Nisbet for this hymn in the present collection.

316 I AM NOT WORTHY, HOLY LORD

Written by Sir H. W. Baker for the revised edition (1875) of *Hymns Ancient and Modern*, on St. Matthew viii. 8; 'Lord, I am not worthy that thou shouldest come under my roof; but speak the word only'.

LEICESTER, by W. Hurst, was composed for this hymn, in the same edition of *Hymns Ancient and Modern*.

317 AUTHOR OF LIFE DIVINE

From *Hymns on the Lord's Supper* (1745) by John and Charles Wesley; there is no decisive evidence to show which of the brothers composed it.

AUCTOR VITAE, by Sir Walford Davies, was composed for this hymn, in *Hymns Ancient and Modern* (second supplement, 1915).

318 BREAD OF THE WORLD, IN MERCY BROKEN

Heber's hymn appeared in *Hymns Written and Adapted for the Weekly Church Service of the Year* (1827), the year after his death.

PSALM 118 (RENDEZ À DIEU) was composed or adapted by L. Bourgeois for the *French Psalter* (1543, 1544), where it was set to Psalm cxviii. In the *Scottish Psalter* of 1564 it was set to John Craig's version of the same psalm.

319 THEE WE ADORE, O HIDDEN SAVIOUR, THEE

As the Latin original indicates, this hymn of Thomas Aquinas was an expression of private, personal adoration; thus the last stanza runs,

> Iesu, quem velatum nunc aspicio,
> Quando fiet illud quod tam sitio,
> Ut te revelata cernens facie
> Visu sim beatus tuae gloriae.

It has been repeatedly translated. The present version, by Bishop Woodford, was written in 1850, when he was incumbent of St. Mark's, Easton, Bristol. Slight changes have been made in it by hymn-book editors to suit congregational worship; thus the present second line of ver. 1 originally read

> Who in Thy supper with us deign'st to be,

and (in line 3) 'in Thy presence'.

Bishop Woodford's Latin text, following a version in the Paris Breviary, substitutes in ver. 3 'Fountain of Goodness' for 'Pious Pelican': Thomas Aquinas employed the medieval idea that the pelican fed its young, if need be, with its own blood, an idea which made it in those days a frequent symbol of Christ. The translation has shortened the original text. Thus the last two lines of ver. 3 are taken from one of the three verses omitted—

> Plagas sicut Thomas non intueor,
> Deum tamen meum te confiteor;
> Fac me tibi semper magis credere,
> In te spem habere, te diligere.

ADORO TE, the proper plainsong melody of this hymn, has been altered slightly, in order to suit the metre of the translation.

320 AND NOW, O FATHER, MINDFUL OF THE LOVE

From a poem in six stanzas, first published in *The Monthly Packet* (of which Miss C. M. Yonge was editor), October 1873. Dr. Bright's hymn has been warmly praised. 'As long as our Church lives, we shall sing at most sacred hours "And now, O Father", and so his breath will be ever with us, and his memory never willingly let die. It is worth living for to have left behind one such hymn which will be sung by unnumbered generations' (H. Scott Holland in *Personal Studies*, p. 270). 'It is wonderful: it is a poem, and yet it conveys the deepest teaching' (George J. Romanes, *Life*, p. 336).

UNDE ET MEMORES was composed by Dr. Monk for this hymn in the revised edition (1875) of *Hymns Ancient and Modern*.

321 'TILL HE COME'! O LET THE WORDS

Written in 1861, and, like 322, on 1 Corinthians xi. 26. 'This hymn for the Holy Communion presents one aspect of the Lord's Supper which is passed over in many hymnals, "Ye do show forth the Lord's death till He come", and also our Communion with those of whom we say "We bless Thy holy name for all Thy servants departed this life in Thy faith and fear" ' (Note by Bishop Bickersteth in *Annotated Hymnal Companion to the Book of Common Prayer*, 1890).

HINTON-MARTELL ('Ida') is from *Gemau Mawl, Ail-Attodiad*.

322 BY CHRIST REDEEMED, IN CHRIST RESTORED

Mr. Rawson's hymn, written in 1857 for the Baptist *Psalms and Hymns*, had, after ver. 4, this stanza:

> Until the trump of God be heard,
> Until the ancient graves be stirred,
> And with the great commanding word,
> The Lord shall come.

In ver. 3 (line 1) he originally wrote

> His fearful drops of agony,

and later he changed this into

> The streams of His dread agony.

Dr. Wesley composed MEMORIA for the hymn, 'O Lord of heaven and earth and sea', in *The Hymnary* (1872).

323 HERE, O MY LORD, I SEE THEE FACE TO FACE

Written for Dr. Bonar's elder brother, Dr. John James Bonar, Greenock, and read after the Communion in his church, October 1855. The original has ten stanzas. One comes after ver. 5:

> I have no wisdom, save in Him who is
> My Wisdom and my Teacher, both in One;
> No wisdom can I lack while Thou art wise,
> No teaching do I crave save Thine alone.

Two others come between ver. 6 and ver. 7:

> I know that deadly evils compass me,
> Dark perils threaten, yet I would not fear,
> Nor poorly shrink, nor feebly turn to flee;
> Thou, O my Christ, art Buckler, Sword, and Spear.

> But see! the Pillar-Cloud is rising now,
> And moving onward through the desert night;
> It beckons, and I follow; for I know
> It leads me to the heritage of light.

A facsimile of the original draft (considerably altered before publication) may be seen in *Hymns by Horatius Bonar* (p. 233).

James Langran composed ST. AGNES for 'Abide with me', and published it in separate form (1861). Then it appeared in *Psalms and Hymns adapted to the services of the Church of England, with accompanying tunes selected and revised by John Foster* (1863).

324 DECK THYSELF, MY SOUL, WITH GLADNESS

Composed by Franck about the year 1649, and published in *Praxis pietatis melica* (Berlin, 1653). The version, by Miss Winkworth (*Lyra Germanica*, 1858), was rewritten for *The Chorale Book for England* (1863). In many German churches it is the hymn invariably sung at Communion, as an expression of the reverent joy which should accompany the sacrament. It has been rendered into Tamil, and is widely used throughout the churches in Southern India.

Crüger's tune SCHMÜCKE DICH, from his *Geistliche Kirchen-Melodien* (Berlin, 1649), has always been associated with this hymn in Germany.

325 O GOD OF LOVE, TO THEE WE BOW

From *The Fellowship Hymn Book* (1909). Written by Mr. Jenkins for his own wedding.

ERSKINE was composed by W. H. Gladstone for the hymn, 'O Jesus, I would be Thine own'.

326 O FATHER ALL CREATING

Written by Canon Ellerton on Jan. 29, 1876, at the request of the Duke of Westminster, for the marriage of his daughter, Lady Elizabeth Harriet Grosvenor, to the Marquis of Ormonde, on Feb. 2.

For AURELIA see on Hymn 205.

327 O PERFECT LOVE, ALL HUMAN THOUGHT TRANS-CENDING

Written by Mrs. Gurney in a quarter of an hour, one Sunday evening in 1883 at Pull Wyke, Windermere, for the marriage of her sister. It was intended to be sung to Dr. Dykes's tune 'Strength and Stay', but the settings of Sir Joseph Barnby and Lord Crofton have become more popular at fashionable weddings.

O PERFECT LOVE is a tune arranged from the anthem which Sir Joseph Barnby composed for the marriage of the Duke and Duchess of Fife in 1889.

328 SAFELY, SAFELY GATHERED IN

Mrs. Dobree's hymn appeared in *The Children's Hymnbook* which Mrs. Carey Brock edited in 1881.

RAMOTH, by J. B. Calkin, is from the same source as 'Day of Praise' (290). It was composed for the hymn, 'Lord, to Thee alone we turn'.

329 WHEN OUR HEADS ARE BOWED WITH WOE

Milman's hymn as published in Heber's posthumous *Hymns* (1827). Based on the Gospel for the Sixteenth Sunday after Trinity, i.e. the passage in St. Luke vii. 11–17 (The raising of the Widow's Son at Nain).

The refrain of each verse in the original is

Gracious Son of Mary, hear.

It was sung at Professor W. Robertson Smith's funeral on April 4, 1894, at Keig, Aberdeenshire.

ST. DUNSTAN is from Redhead's *Church Hymn Tunes* (1853).

330 NOW THE LABOURER'S TASK IS O'ER

Canon Ellerton wrote this for *Church Hymns* (1871). One stanza is omitted, and another (the original fourth) has been replaced by the present fifth.

REQUIESCAT, by Dr. J. B. Dykes, was written for this hymn, in *Hymns Ancient and Modern* (1875).

HAZEL, by Dr. Basil Harwood, was written for it, in *The Oxford Hymn Book* (1908).

331 O LORD OF LIFE, WHERE'ER THEY BE

Composed by Mr. Hosmer in 1888 for the Easter Service in his own (Unitarian) church at Cleveland, Ohio. In the original 'Hallelujah' is appended to the last verse alone.

The melody of VULPIUS is from the same source as 'Das neugeborne Kindelein' (304).

332 GOD OF THE LIVING, IN WHOSE EYES

Canon Ellerton's hymn was written for *Hymns for Schools and Bible-Classes* (1858); then expanded and altered to its present form in *Hymns Original and Translated* (1867). It was sung at his funeral in Torquay on June 20, 1893. The original text of ver. 4 began:

O Breather into man of breath,
O Holder of the keys of death,
O Giver of the life divine.

COLCHESTER, by S. S. Wesley, was contributed to *The European Psalmist* (1872).

333 POUR OUT THY SPIRIT FROM ON HIGH

Written by Montgomery on Jan. 23, 1833, as a hymn to be sung at a meeting of clergy. The original text accordingly has 'Assembled servants' (ver. 1, line 2), in ver. 2 (line 1) 'we', and in ver. 3 (line 3) and ver. 5 (lines 1 and 2) 'our'.

MAINZER is set to a version of Psalm cvii in *Mainzer's Choruses*, No. 2 (*c.* 1841). In his *Standard Psalmody of Scotland* (1845) it is set to the second version of Psalm cii.

334 O THOU WHO MAKEST SOULS TO SHINE

Mr. Armstrong's hymn appeared first in his own book *The Pastor in his Closet* (1847), and was written when he was vicar of Tidenham, near Chepstow. As in the Appendix to *Hymns Ancient and Modern* (1868), where four or five slight emendations have been made.

ELY, by Bishop Thomas Turton, appears in Turle and Taylor's *Collection of Psalm and Hymn Tunes* (1844), where it is set to the Tate and Brady version of Psalm c. Its original name was 'St. Catherine'.

335 LORD OF THE LIVING HARVEST

First published in Dr. Monsell's *Hymns of Love and Praise* (1866). The second line of ver. 2 originally read

> Send them out, Christ, to be.

COELI ENARRANT, as the title suggests, was composed by Sir Robert Stewart for the hymn 'The heavens declare Thy glory'. It appeared in the Irish *Church Hymnal* (1874).

336 SHINE THOU UPON US, LORD

A hymn for teachers. As first published in Canon Ellerton's *Hymns* (1881), it began,

> Break Thou to us, O Lord,
> The Bread of Life to-day,

and line 7 ran, 'The little ones may learn'.

Revised by the author, as in the text, for *Hymns Ancient and Modern* (1889).

HAWARDEN, by S. S. Wesley, is from *The European Psalmist* (1872).

337 LORD OF LIGHT, WHOSE NAME OUTSHINETH

Mr. Lewis's hymn appears as in *The Congregational Hymnary* (1916). 'This hymn was written to declare that in doing God's will, active co-operation is as much needed as humble resignation. Charlotte Elliott in her hymn, "My God and Father, while I stray", had expressed the latter thought beautifully. My hope was to supplement her hymn as best I could' (Note by the author).

LLANSANNAN is a Welsh melody, from *Aberth Moliant* (1873).

338 LORD, SPEAK TO ME, THAT I MAY SPEAK

Composed by Miss Havergal on April 28, 1872, at Winterdyne, and headed, 'A Worker's Prayer. None of us liveth unto himself' (Romans xiv. 7).

WINSCOTT is from *The European Psalmist* (1872); it was composed for 'Sun of my soul'.

339 O MASTER, LET ME WALK WITH THEE

From three eight-line stanzas in *Sunday Afternoon* for March, 1879, a magazine of which Dr. Gladden was editor; under the title 'Walking with God'.

In the original ver. 1 (line 3) ran,

> Teach me Thy secret: help me bear.

THANKSGIVING, by Dr. J. B. Dykes, is from *A Hymnal for use in the English Church, with a supplement containing additional Tunes* (1866).

340 LOOK FROM THE SPHERE OF ENDLESS DAY

Composed by W. C. Bryant in 1840, for a missionary meeting.

LICHFIELD, by Archbishop Maclagan, was originally called 'Spes Poenitentis', and appeared in *Hymns for Mission Services, by the Compilers of Hymns Ancient and Modern* (1877).

341 SOLDIERS OF THE CROSS, ARISE!

First published by Dr. How in Morrell and How's *Psalms and Hymns* (1864). Here as revised by the author for *Church Hymns* (1871).

The origin of ORIENTIS PARTIBUS is this. In some parts of France, notably at Beauvais, during the Middle Ages, there was celebrated on January 14 a church festival known as the Feast of the Ass. It was intended to commemorate the flight into Egypt. On this occasion a young woman holding a child in her arms was seated on an ass, and after a procession through the streets of the town, the ass with its burden was led into the principal church, and took its stand beside the high altar while mass was celebrated. During the service a hymn was sung, written in a mixture of medieval Latin and old French, of which the first lines were 'Orientis partibus adventavit asinus'. The melody of this hymn has been preserved, and from it the present tune was adapted, and published by R. Redhead in his *Church Hymn Tunes* (1853). M. Félix Clément has traced the melody to a manuscript preserved in the Library of Sens, entitled 'Office de la Circoncision à l'usage de la ville de Sens'. In his *Notice sur les Chants de la Sainte Chapelle* (1852), M. Clément states that this 'Office' is the work of Pierre de Corbeil, Archbishop of Sens, who died in 1222. He further says: 'Among the items composing this office, there is a piece which has been called "Prose of the Ass" ("Prose de l'âne"). Nothing in this piece justifies the opinion that the ass played a burlesque and ridiculous role. The French refrain, and two of the verses cited by MM. Dulaure, Millin, and Michelet, do not exist in the Sens manuscript, which is older by two hundred years than that of Beauvais, which these historians have consulted.

. . . These writers have taken the parody of the Prose for the Prose it-self.' The melody, as quoted by M. Clément, is as follows:

342 BOWED LOW IN SUPPLICATION

First published by Dr. How in *Church Hymns* (1871), with the heading 'For the Parish'. Two stanzas are here omitted.

ST. VICTOR is from *Ancient Hymn Melodies and other Church Tunes, as used at All Saints' Church, Margaret Street. Arranged, Composed, and Harmonized by Richard Redhead, Organist* (1859).

PSALM 130 is the melody of this psalm in *Aulcuns Psaulmes*, printed at Strasburg in 1539, and with slight changes it is set to the same psalm in all subsequent editions of the *French Psalter*. In the earliest *Anglo-Genevan Psalter* it is set to Whittingham's version of that psalm, and is included in the complete English and Scottish Psalters.

343 CHRISTIAN, WORK FOR JESUS

Miss Hasloch's hymn first appeared in *The Congregational Church Hymnal* (1887) in the section, 'Anniversary of a Temperance Society or Band of Hope'. Three stanzas are omitted.

NORTH COATES is from *Congregational Melodies: A Collection of Tunes . . . by the Rev. T. R. Matthews* (1862).

344 RISE UP, O MEN OF GOD!

In *A Students' Hymnal* ('University of Wales', 1923), Dr. Merrill's hymn is altered, in ver. 3 (lines 3 and 4), to

> Her strength shall make your spirit strong,
> Her service make you great.

CARLISLE, by C. Lockhart, was originally set to 'Come, Holy Spirit, come', in the *Lock Hospital Collection, edited by Martin Madan* (second edition 1792).

345 FOUNTAIN OF GOOD, TO OWN THY LOVE

From Doddridge's hymn beginning 'Jesus, my Lord, how rich Thy grace', and headed 'On relieving Christ in the Poor'. Here as re-written by Edward Osler (1798–1863) for Hall's *Mitre Hymn Book* (1836).

ALBANO, by Vincent Novello, is from *Hymns Ancient and Modern* (Appendix, 1868).

346 WE GIVE THEE BUT THINE OWN

Dr. How's hymn was written in 1858 and published in Morrell and How's *Psalms and Hymns* (1864). Next to 'For all the Saints', this is the most extensively used of all Bishop Walsham How's hymns. ' "We give Thee but Thine own" sounds the real humanitarian note to the fatherless and widows. Hymnology is feeble and ineffective when it ignores the humanitarian side of religion' (Dr. George Matheson).

ST. GILES, by J. Montgomerie Bell, was set to this hymn in *The Scottish Hymnal* (1885).

347 HERE, LORD, WE OFFER THEE ALL THAT IS FAIREST

Mr. Blunt's hymn was written in 1879 for a Flower Service on Hospital Sunday (June 15) at St. Luke's, Chelsea. Of this famous church, 'probably the most unspoilt old church in all England', with its chained books and Sir Thomas More's monument, Mr. Blunt was rector for many years.

BLODYN, by A. O. Roberts, comes from *Hymns and Tunes of the Presbyterian Church of Wales* (1900). The name in Welsh means 'flowers'.

348 O THOU, BEFORE WHOSE PRESENCE

Mr. Stone's hymn first appeared in the 1889 Supplement to *Hymns Ancient and Modern*, under the heading 'For Temperance Meetings', with the text, 'The Lord hath done great things for us already' (Psalm cxxvi. 3).

ST. CATHERINE, by R. F. Dale, is from *Twenty-two Original Hymn-Tunes by two Oxford Graduates* (1867).

349 FATHER, WHO ON MAN DOST SHOWER

First published, under the heading 'Societies: Temperance', in *The English Hymnal* (1906), on the editorial committee of which Dr. Dearmer was a leading member.

QUEM PASTORES LAUDAVERE is a fourteenth-century carol, found in many German chorale-books.

350 MAKER OF EARTH AND SEA AND SKY

Miss Lord's hymn, in *A Proposed New Hymnal* (1910) which was compiled by Rev. A. W. Hutton, Rector of St. Mary-le-Bow Church, Cheapside, London, was taken from the *St. Olave's Hymnal* (1898), where its source is given as Timmins and Angell's *Band of Mercy Melodies* (published by the Massachusetts Society for the Prevention of Cruelty to Animals, about 1882).

For the tune, see on Hymn 332.

351 FROM THEE ALL SKILL AND SCIENCE FLOW

This hymn consists of stanzas 3–6 of a hymn beginning 'Accept this building, gracious Lord', written for the laying of the foundation-stone of the Working Men's block of the Queen's Hospital, Birmingham, Dec. 4, 1871, and sung on that occasion by a choir of 1,000 school children. (In Kingsley's 'Poems' it is dated Eversley 1870, and is said to have been sung 'at the opening of the New Wing of the Children's Hospital, Birmingham'). The introductory verses were:

> Accept this building, gracious Lord,
>   No temple though it be;
> We raised it for our suffering kin
>   And so, good Lord, for Thee.
>
> Accept our little gift, and give
>   To all who here may dwell,
> The will and power to do their work,
>   Or bear their sorrows well.

The tune NUN DANKET ALL (GRÄFENBERG) is from the fifth edition of Crüger's *Praxis Pietatis Melica* (Berlin, 1653). The present is the original form of the melody.

352 THOU TO WHOM THE SICK AND DYING

Prebendary Thring's Hospital Hymn was written in 1870, under the text of St. Matthew iv. 24 ('And they brought unto Him all sick people . . . and He healed them'). After being published in Prebendary W. H. Hutton's *Hymns for the Church Services* (1871), it was revised for the author's *Hymns and Sacred Lyrics* (1874). One stanza is omitted.

HIMMEL is from the Irish *Church Hymnal* (1874), where it is attributed to F. H. Himmel. But the actual source of the melody has not been ascertained.

353 FATHER, WHOSE WILL IS LIFE AND GOOD

First published in *A Missionary Hymn Book* (S.P.C.K., 1922).

CULROSS is one of the Common Tunes in *The Psalms of David* (Edinburgh, Hart's heirs, 1634).

TALLIS is the ninth tune by Tallis in Parker's Psalter. See under Hymn 250.

354 DISMISS ME NOT THY SERVICE, LORD

Mr. Lynch's hymn appeared in his *The Rivulet: a Contribution to Sacred Song* (1855), a supplement to *Watts's Hymns* for use in the author's own congregation. The title was chosen by him because 'Christian poetry is indeed a river of the water of life, and to this river my rivulet brings its contribution'. The hymns themselves are described as 'short Christian poems to peruse for stimulus and solace or to sing in family and social communion'.

FAIRFIELD was originally composed by James Turle for the hymn 'Father, I know that all my life'. It appears in *Psalms and Hymns for Divine Worship* (1866).

355 O LORD OF LIFE, AND LOVE, AND POWER

Written by Mrs. Armitage at Waterhead, Oldham, in 1875 for the opening of a new Sunday School. Published in a service of song, called *The Garden of the Lord* (1881).

OLD 81ST, in the English Psalter of 1562, was set to Psalms lxxx and lxxvii, both of these versions appearing for the first time in this edition. In the complete Scottish book printed in 1564, a different version of Psalm lxxxi was inserted and the tune is also different, but Psalm lxxvii is the same as in the English book, and is set to the present tune. There are some points of difference in the tune as printed in the various editions, the chief of these being that it is sometimes in *common* and sometimes in *triple* time.

ST. URSULA, by Frederick Westlake, is taken from *Hymns and Sacred Songs for the Year* (1863).

356 GO, LABOUR ON: SPEND AND BE SPENT

Written by Dr. Bonar in 1836, to encourage his faithful helpers in a Leith mission district. It was printed at Kelso in a small booklet of hymns, and entitled 'Labour for Christ' in *Songs for the Wilderness* (1843).

The tune DEUS TUORUM MILITUM is a Grenoble Church melody, as in *The English Hymnal*. It is one of the tunes referred to under Hymn 4.

357 WORK, FOR THE NIGHT IS COMING

Written in 1854, when Miss Walker was eighteen years old. It appeared in her small volume of poems called *Leaves from the Backwoods* (Montreal, 1861), then in Lowell Mason's *Song Garden* (1864). After her marriage, Mrs. Coghill continued to write verses, which are collected in her *Oak and Maple*. There the authorized text of the hymn shows that the last line in each verse was

> Night, when man's work is done,

and also that the fourth line in every verse has an extra syllable:

> Work 'mid the springing flowers,
> Rest cometh sure and soon,
> Work for the daylight flies.

Mrs. Coghill wrote, 'I am utterly unable to see what advantage there can be in any alteration that has been proposed. I cannot sign, or in any way agree to what I extremely dislike.' But the tyranny of Mason's tune has proved too much alike for the authoress and for the compilers of hymn-books.

Dr. Lowell Mason wrote DILIGENCE for this hymn, in *The Song Garden*.

358 O YE WHO TASTE THAT LOVE IS SWEET

From *Time Flies: a Reading Diary* (1885), under June 21, being the last three verses of a poem of which the first four are:

> O ye, who are not dead, and fit
> Like blasted tree beside the pit
> But for the axe that levels it.
>
> Living show life of love, whereof
> The force wields earth and heaven above:
> Who knows not love begetteth love?
>
> Love poises earth in space, Love rolls
> Wide worlds rejoicing on their poles,
> And girds them round with aureoles.
>
> Love lights the sun, Love through the dark
> Lights the moon's evanescent arc,
> Lights up the star, lights up the spark.

The tune HELENSBURGH was written by Mr. Finlay for this hymn and this collection.

359 SON OF GOD, ETERNAL SAVIOUR

Written at North Holmwood, Surrey (of which Mr. Lowry was then vicar), in 1893. It was entitled 'For Unity', and published in *Goodwill* (February 1894) and in *The Christian Social Union Hymn-book* (1895).

The tune PSALM 42 was composed or adapted by L. Bourgeois for this psalm in the French Psalter (1551). In the Anglo-Genevan Psalter of 1561 the tune is set to Kethe's version of Psalm xxvii, and this was taken over into the complete *Scottish Psalter* of 1564. As the scansion and the rhythm of Kethe's psalm are quite different from that of the French version by Beza, the adaptation is exceedingly bad. Modern books give the tune in a variety of forms.

360 O SON OF GOD, OUR CAPTAIN OF SALVATION

Composed by Canon Ellerton on April 5, 1871, and published in *Church Hymns*, of which he was one of the editors. It was written for St. Barnabas' Day (Acts iv. 36: 'Barnabas, which is, being interpreted, The son of consolation'), and the original form of ver. 5 (line 1) echoed this:

> Thus, Lord, Thy Barnabas in memory keeping.

So did one verse, here omitted:

> Such was Thy Levite, strong in self-oblation
> To cast his all at Thine apostles' feet;
> He whose new name, through every Christian nation,
> From age to age our thankful strains repeat.

PSALM 12 (DONNE SECOURS) was composed or adapted by L. Bourgeois for this psalm in the French Psalter of 1551.

361 DEAR MASTER, WHAT CAN CHILDREN DO?

Miss Matheson's hymn was written for a Harvest Festival, about 1882, with the heading, 'Children as workers for Christ'.

ST. JOSEPH, by J. B. Calkin, was originally, in *The New Mitre Hymnal, adapted to the Services of the Church of England, with accompanying tunes* (1875), set to the hymn, 'My God and Father, while I stray'.

362 THE FIELDS ARE ALL WHITE

This anonymous hymn, based on St. John iv. 35, appeared in *The Book of Praise for Children* (1881), but was probably written about 1875. The second line of ver. 3 originally was

By the pennies we bring,

Mr. Lamb wrote INVERMAY for this hymn, in *The Presbyterian Hymnal for the Young* (1882).

363 THE WISE MAY BRING THEIR LEARNING

This also appeared anonymously in *The Book of Praise for Children* (1881), where ver. 2 (line 7) read 'gifts that ever' (i.e. always).

CHRISTMAS MORN, by Dr. E. J. Hopkins, is from *The Children's Hymnbook* (1881), which was edited by Mrs. Carey Brock.

364 THOU WHOSE ALMIGHTY WORD

Written by Mr. Marriott about 1813, on Genesis i. 3, and printed first in *The Evangelical Magazine* (June, 1825) and then in *The Friendly Visitor* in the following month. The reason of its being printed was that the hymn had been quoted at a meeting of the London Missionary Society on May 12, 1825, and had greatly impressed the audience. The author had died just six weeks before.

MOSCOW comes from *A Collection of Psalm and Hymn Tunes, never published before* (1769. Edited by the Rev. M. Madan), which is known as the 'Lock Collection'. It was composed for the hymn 'Come, Thou almighty King', and headed 'Hymn to the Trinity, set by F. G.'.

In the original the last two lines read as under:

MALVERN is from *The Hallelujah*, edited by J. J. Waite and H. J. Gauntlett in 1849.

365 BEHOLD! THE MOUNTAIN OF THE LORD

The original form of this paraphrase of Isaiah ii. 2–6 appeared n the first edition of *The Scottish Paraphrases*, 1745. It may possibly have been revised, and verse 3 added, by Michael Bruce. Logan published it in his *Poems*, 1781, and it was included the same year in the final edition of the *Paraphrases* with a few alterations; 'above the mountains and the hills' (line 3 of ver. 1) was changed, 'on' was altered to 'from' in ver. 3 (line 1) and 'Zion's' to 'Salem's' (line 3), ver. 4 was improved from

> No strife shall vex Messiah's reign,
> Or mar the peaceful years;
> To ploughshares soon they beat their swords,

and ver. 5 (line 2) replaced

> Their millions slain deplore.

The last verse (line 1) was substituted for

> Come then—O come from every land.

GLASGOW appears in *The Psalm Singer's Pocket Companion, containing great variety of the best English Psalm Tunes. . . . Likewise all the Tunes that are usually sung in most parts of Scotland* (Glasgow, 1756). This was one of the collections edited by Thomas Moore, a publisher of music in Glasgow.

366 GREAT GOD OF ABRAHAM, HEAR OUR PRAYER

Appeared first in Cotterill's well-known *Selection of Psalms and Hymns* (8th edition, 1819).

BABYLON'S STREAMS is first found as a psalm-tune in *Harmonia Perfecta* (1730), a collection edited by Nathaniel Gawthorn. But the melody comes from Campion's *First Booke of Ayres* (1613). It derives its name from the fact that it was set to a metrical version of Psalm cxxxvii, beginning,

> As by the streams of Babilon
> Farre from our native soyle we sat.

367 WHEN ISRAEL, OF THE LORD BELOVED

From *Ivanhoe* (chap. xxxix), sung by Rebecca on the evening of the day of her trial for sorcery at Templestowe. Scott's original has four stanzas of eight lines each, with 'Our foes' and 'our fathers' in ver. 4. After ver. 6 came:

> Our harps we left by Babel's streams,
> The tyrant's jest, the Gentile's scorn;
> No censer round our altar beams,
> And mute our timbrel, trump and horn.
> But Thou hast said, 'The blood of goat,
> The flesh of rams, I will not prize,
> A contrite heart, an humble thought,
> Are Mine accepted sacrifice'.

The first appearance of Rebecca's Song as a hymn is in *Hymns Adapted for the Worship of God, selected and sanctioned by the Synod of*

Relief (1833). This was only six months after Scott's death and fourteen years after the publication of *Ivanhoe*. Comparatively few compilers of hymn-books in those days had any eye for poetry. Therefore honour to whom honour is due.

For the tune see Hymn 333.

368 O THAT THE LORD'S SALVATION

This paraphrase of Psalm xiv. 7 is from Lyte's *The Spirit of the Psalms*. The original second verse which appeared in the former edition of *The Church Hymnary* was:

> How long the Holy City
> Shall heathen feet profane?
> Return, O Lord, in pity,
> Rebuild her walls again.

It is now omitted on account of the British occupation of Jerusalem and Palestine.

The tune CHRISTUS DER IST MEIN LEBEN (=BREMEN) is from *Ein schön geistlich Gesangbuch. . . . Durch Melchiorem Vulpium Cantorem zu Weymar* (Jena, 1609), where the melody appears as under, set to the hymn 'Christus der ist mein Leben'.

The present form of lines 3 and 4 is found in Crüger's *Praxis Pietatis Melica* (edition 1662).

369 ARM OF THE LORD, AWAKE, AWAKE

It is sometimes doubted whether this hymn was written by William Shrubsole, Junr. (1759–1829) or by his father (1729–97). The latter view is upheld in the usually very accurate *Lyra Britannica*, which prints two additional verses, one of which, before ver. 3, is extremely pointed:

> Arm of the Lord, Thy power extend;
> Let Mahomet's imposture end;
> Break papal superstition's chain,
> And the proud scoffer's rage restrain.

The date of this is given as 1780.

TRURO, in *Psalmodia Evangelica: A Collection of Psalms and Hymns in Three Parts for Public Worship, by Thos. Williams* (2 vols., 1790), was set to the hymn 'Now to the Lord a noble song'. The tune has been assigned to Dr. Burney, but there seems to be no evidence in support of this. It is without composer's name in the above collection, while several tunes by Burney have his name duly attached to them.

370 FOR MY SAKE AND THE GOSPEL'S, GO

From *The Church Missionary Hymn-book* (1899). Dr. Bickersteth wrote it to be sung to Sullivan's tune, BISHOPGARTH (as here set), which had been composed for Bishop How's hymn,'O King of kings, whose reign of old', written for the Diamond Jubilee of Queen Victoria in 1897.

371 FROM GREENLAND'S ICY MOUNTAINS

Written to be sung at a service in Wrexham Parish Church on Whit-Sunday 1819, when a Sermon in aid of the Society for the Propagation of the Gospel in Foreign Parts was preached by Dr. Shipley, vicar of the parish and Dean of St. Asaph. On the previous day Dr. Shipley asked his son-in-law Reginald Heber, then vicar of Hodnet, for a hymn suitable to the occasion; and Heber, retiring to a distant corner of the room, began to write. 'In a short time the Dean inquired, "What have you written?" Heber having then composed the first three verses, read them over. "There, there! that will do very well", said the Dean. "No, no, the sense is not complete", replied Heber. Accordingly he added the fourth verse, and, the Dean being inexorable to his repeated request of "Let me add another, oh let me add another", thus completed the hymn.' All was done in twenty minutes. It was Heber's custom to write his hymns to the airs of favourite songs, e.g. 'Brightest and best of the sons of the morning' was sung by him to the well-known and beautiful Scotch air, 'Wandering Willie'. The air chosen by him for 'From Greenland's icy mountains' was the fine but quite incongruous tune, ''Twas when the seas were roaring' (in *The Beggar's Opera*).

Heber's second verse, here omitted, runs:

> What though the spicy breezes
>   Blow soft o'er Java's isle,
> Though every prospect pleases
>   And only man is vile;
> In vain with lavish kindness
>   The gifts of God are strewn,
> The heathen in his blindness
>   Bows down to wood and stone.

This is the form in his posthumous *Hymns* (1827), though Heber originally wrote 'Ceylon's' in the second line, just as he wrote 'the savage' in the seventh.

The tune HEBER was composed by Dr. Lowell Mason in 1824 for this hymn, and published in *The Boston Handel and Haydn Society Collection* (ninth edition, 1829).

TALYLLYN is a Welsh melody, from *Brenhinol Ganiadau Seion*, edited by Owen Williams (1830).

372 HILLS OF THE NORTH, REJOICE!

Mr. Oakley's poem appeared in Bishop T. Valpy French's *Hymns adapted to the Christian Seasons*; it came into common use from its insertion in successive editions of *The Hymnal Companion to the Book of Common Prayer*, from 1870 onward. In *A Students' Hymnal* the last two words are 'with thee', not 'in thee'.

LITTLE CORNARD is from the same source as 'Marching' (214), and was composed for this hymn.

373 FAR ROUND THE WORLD THY CHILDREN SING THEIR SONG

'It appeared originally in my book "The Fascinated Child", but the verses dealing with the peoples of Asia, Africa, and the Islands were added about three years later' (Note by Mr. Basil Mathews).

DUNBLANE CATHEDRAL was composed by Dr. Barnes for this hymn and this collection.

374 ONCE AGAIN, DEAR LORD, WE PRAY

Written by Mrs. Willcox in 1888.

MORNING, by S. S. Wesley, is from *The European Psalmist* (1872).

375 GOD OF HEAVEN, HEAR OUR SINGING

Written by Miss Havergal on Oct. 22, 1869, at Leamington, and published in *Twelve Sacred Songs for Little Singers* (1870).

SEFTON, in *The Burnley Tune Book* (1875), was originally composed by H. A. Crosbie for the hymn, 'Saviour, breathe an evening blessing'.

376 O LORD OUR GOD, ARISE!

First published by Ralph Wardlaw in *A Collection of Hymns for the use of the Tabernacles in Scotland* (1800)—a book largely used by the Scottish Congregationalists in the beginning of last century.

HAMPTON comes from *Psalmody in Miniature*, by Aaron Williams (c. 1770). There, and in a contemporary *Collection of Psalm Tunes in Three Parts . . . by Is. Smith*, it is named 'Durham'. The present is the original form of the melody.

377 WAKE, SPIRIT, WHO IN TIMES NOW OLDEN

First published in *Die Uebung der Gottseligkeit in allerley Geistlichen Liedern* (Halle, 1750): entitled 'For faithful labourers in the Harvest of the Lord, for the blessed spread of the Word to all the world'. The original consists of fourteen stanzas. The present form of the translation is an adaptation by Miss Winkworth of her former version 'Awake, Thou Spirit, who of old', in order that the words might be sung to their proper chorale. Bogatzky's hymn appeared too late for admission into the great hymn-books of the eighteenth century, and it was only after its inclusion in the famous Würtemberg Hymn-book of 1842, ninety-two years after its composition, that it became well known. Since that date it has held its place as one of the greatest, as it was the earliest written, of the purely missionary hymns of the German Church.

The present is its first appearance in a British hymn-book. For the sake of smoothness the compilers have altered the third line of ver. 1 to its present form.

DIR, DIR JEHOVAH is an expansion of 'Crasselius'; it is from the same source as the tunes to 170.

378 LORD, HER WATCH THY CHURCH IS KEEPING

Written at Geneva in 1866, where Mr. Downton was resident English Chaplain, sung at the annual meeting of the Church Missionary Society in that year, and first published in Rev. D. T. Barry's *Psalms and Hymns for the Church, School and Home* (1867).

For the tune see Hymn 2.

379 GOD OF MERCY, GOD OF GRACE

First published in Lyte's *The Spirit of the Psalms* (1834), as a version of Psalm lxvii. In ver. 2 (line 5) he wrote 'tributes'.

ZÜRICH is in the *Weimar Gesangbuch* of 1681. The present form is that found in later German books.

380 GOD IS WORKING HIS PURPOSE OUT

Mr. Ainger composed this hymn at Eton in 1894, dedicating it to Archbishop Benson. It was published in leaflet form, with Miss Kingham's tune 'Benson'. Like 370, it appeared in *The Church Missionary Hymn-book* (1899).

ALVESTON was composed for this hymn, in *The Public School Hymn-book* (1919).

381 LIGHT OF THE LONELY PILGRIM'S HEART

Sir Edward Denny's hymn appeared in *Psalms and Hymns and Spiritual Songs* (Deck's Collection, Plymouth Brethren, 1842). In the author's *Hymns and Poems* (1848) it is entitled 'The heart watching for the morning'. One stanza is omitted.

The tune BROMSGROVE, as originally in *Psalmodia Evangelica, Part II* (1789), was anonymous, and the melody ran as follows:

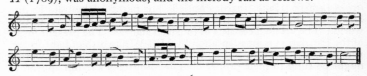

382 SAVIOUR, SPRINKLE MANY NATIONS

Bishop Coxe began this hymn on Good Friday, 1850, in America; it was laid aside and completed next year in the grounds of Magdalen College, Oxford. First published in *Verses for 1851 in Commemoration of the Third Jubilee of the S.P.G.*, a collection in which Bishop Doane's hymn 'Fling out the banner', 383 in the present *Church Hymnary*, also appeared. The insertion of this hymn has been specially desired by missionaries, as the beautiful thought in ver. 2 is very rarely found in any missionary hymn. Accordingly it appears here, despite the faulty exegesis of Isaiah lii. 15 in ver. 1 and some imperfect rhymes in verses 2 and 3.

The tune CONTEMPLATION appeared in '*Lord, how long wilt Thou forget me?' Psalm 13. Music by F. Mendelssohn-Bartholdy*, 1840. It is the music of the Chorale, 'Lord, my God, behold and hear me', No. 2 of that work.

383 FLING OUT THE BANNER! LET IT FLOAT

Published along with 382, but written in Dec. 1848, by Bishop Doane at Riverside, Massachusetts. In the *Treasury of American Sacred Song* the third line of the first stanza runs

> The sun shall light its shining folds,

and a verse (here omitted) is printed, viz.

> Fling out the banner! sin-sick souls
> That sink and perish in the strife,
> Shall touch in faith its radiant hem,
> And spring immortal into life.

CATHCART was composed by Professor Bell for this hymn, in *The English Hymnal* (1906).

384 ONWARD MARCH, ALL-CONQUERING JESUS

From *Gloria in Excelsis, or, Hymns of Praise to God the Lamb* (Carmarthen, 1772). 'Williams's monthly visit to Llangeitho to assist Daniel Rowland gave him the opportunity on many occasions to see the overpowering influence of the latter's ministry on the thousands who went to hear him. Whitefield himself records that he saw twenty thousand people in a state of ecstasy shouting "Gogoniant!" (glory) and "Bendigedig" (Blessed be God). The theme of the hymn suggests such a scene' (Note by Mr. Abraham Morris).

The origin of the tune GWALIA is obscure. It appears in the book known as the *Lock Hospital Collection* (edited by the Rev. Martin Madan, 1769). There it is entitled 'Love Divine' and is set to the hymn 'Love Divine, all love excelling'. In Rev. H. Parr's *Church of England Psalmody* it is included under the same name, and the editor notes that it is 'from a Welsh melody'. The present form is, with very slight exceptions, the same as that in Madan's book. It is therefore uncertain whether it was an original tune in 1769, or an adaptation from an older melody known in Wales. The tune 'Moriah' (435) seems to be another adaptation, with some changes from the same original.

385 LIFT UP YOUR HEADS, YE GATES OF BRASS

Montgomery's hymn appeared in *The Evangelical Magazine* (1843), and, ten years later, in his *Original Hymns*, where it extended to nineteen stanzas, and was entitled 'China Evangelized'. The original in ver. 5 (line 3) read

> To Christ shall Buddhu's votaries bow.

Samuel Stanley's tune WARWICK is marked as a new tune 'never before published', in *Sacred Music . . . An Appendix to Dr. Watts's Psalms and Hymns, by Edward Miller, Mus.Doc.* (1802).

For WINCHESTER see Hymn 181.

386 O SPIRIT OF THE LIVING GOD

Written by Montgomery in 1823, 'to be sung at the Public Meeting of the Auxiliary Missionary Society for the West Riding of Yorkshire, in Salem Chapel, Leeds, June 4, 1823'. It had this stanza after verse 5:

> God from Eternity hath willed
> All flesh shall His salvation see;
> So be the Father's love fulfilled,
> The Saviour's sufferings crowned through Thee.

The tune ST. ANSELM is found in *Easy Music for Church Choirs* (Part III, 1853), where it is set to the hymn 'Jesu Redemptor omnium'. The present arrangement is by the Rev. L. G. Hayne, and appears in *The Merton Tune Book* (1863). It is there said to be an 'ancient melody', but it has not yet been traced to an earlier source than the above.

387 O'ER THOSE GLOOMY HILLS OF DARKNESS

Published, like 384, in *Gloria in Excelsis, or, Hymns of Praise to God the Lamb* (Carmarthen, 1772). The English version is by Williams himself and was translated into Welsh by him. 'The mountains known as the Black Mountain range in Carmarthenshire may be seen from Pantecelyn, the poet's home. To any one who has been there and views the distant scene from the old home it calls forth in one's mind the "gloomy hills of darkness", and it is generally agreed that Williams derived his inspiration from that particular landscape' (Note by Mr. A. Morris).

It is a striking fact that the date of publication, 1772, was just twenty years before the Northamptonshire Association of Baptist

Ministers met at Nottingham, when William Carey preached his famous sermon (from Isaiah liv. 3), 'Expect great things from God: Attempt great things for God'; it was the inauguration of the Foreign Mission Movement in Britain. The hymn has therefore something of a prophetic character.

Originally the hymn had seven stanzas, in the first of which the author wrote 'On a glorious day of grace', and in the third 'May Thy eternal wide dominions'.

For NEANDER see Hymn 163. BLAENCEFN is from *Llyfr Tonau, Ail Attodiad* (1890).

388 JESUS SHALL REIGN WHERE'ER THE SUN

In Watts's *Psalms of David* (1719). This hymn forms the second part of his version of Psalm lxxii, and is headed 'Christ's Kingdom among the Gentiles'. It had between verses 1 and 2, this:

> Behold the islands with their kings,
> And Europe her best tribute brings;
> From north to south the princes meet
> To pay their homage at His feet.

> There Persia glorious to behold,
> There India shines in Eastern gold:
> And barbarous nations at His word
> Submit, and bow, and own their Lord.

Between verses 4 and 5 the following stanza also lay:

> Where He displays His healing power,
> Death and the curse are known no more;
> In Him the tribes of Adam boast
> More blessings than their father lost.

In ver. 5 'peculiar honours' means 'honours belonging to itself'. As the Prayer Book version of the Psalms reads 'Prayer shall be made ever unto Him' (Psalm lxxii. 15), some hymn-books alter 'For' into 'To' in ver. 2 (line 1).

This is the earliest of the great hymns on missions which have appeared in English.

WARRINGTON is by R. Harrison, and appeared in his *Sacred Harmony* (vol. i, 1784), a collection of psalm-tunes.

389 HARK! THE SONG OF JUBILEE

Like 386, this hymn of Montgomery appeared in *The Evangelical Magazine* (1818).

Dr. Gilbert composed THANKSGIVING for the hymn, ' Come, ye thankful people, come ', in *Songs of Praise, and Ten Other Hymns* (1862).

390 COME UNTO ME, YE WEARY

Mr. Dix's hymn was published in *The People's Hymnal*, edited by Dr. R. F. Littledale (1867).

There is some uncertainty about the text, as various changes have been made from time to time and have passed into common use. The original has in ver. 2 (line 1) 'Come unto me, dear children', in ver. 3 (lines 3 and 4):

> O cheering voice of Jesus
> Which comes to aid our strife,

and in ver. 4 (line 3), 'O welcome voice of Jesus'.

COME UNTO ME was composed by Dr. J. B. Dykes for this hymn in *Hymns Ancient and Modern* (1875).

WHITFORD, by J. Ambrose Lloyd, is from *Aberth Moliant* (1873).

391 ART THOU WEARY, ART THOU LANGUID

First published by Dr. Neale in his *Hymns of the Eastern Church* (first edition, 1862) as being a translation from St. Stephen the Sabaite (725–794); but in subsequent editions he admitted that this hymn, and also 'O happy band of pilgrims' (No. 576), contained so little from the Greek that they must be relegated to the Appendix of the Collection. The original of ver. 7 (line 3) was 'Angels, Martyrs, Prophets, Virgins'.

The scenery around the Monastery of Marsaba in which St. Stephen lived is thus described by Colonel Conder. 'A desert indeed, riven by narrow ravines leading to deep gorges, and rising between the stony gullies into narrow ridges of dark brown limestone, capped with gleaming white chalk, full of cone-like hillocks and fantastic peaks. . . . There is no stirring of the grass by the breeze, no rustling of leaves, no murmur of water, no sound of life save the grackle's note or the jackal's cry, re-echoed from the rocks. The sun beats down from a cloudless sky: the white glare of the chalk, the smooth face of the Dead Sea, are broad stretches of colour unbroken by variety. . . . Here really out of the world the solitary hermits sate in the rocky cells which were their tombs; here in the awful prison of the Marsaba Monastery men are still buried, as it were, alive, without future, without hope, without employment, with no comradeship save that of equally embittered lives' (*Palestine*, pp. 36, 37).

STEPHANOS was composed for this hymn, in *Hymns Ancient and Modern* (Appendix, 1868). Harmonized by W. H. Monk.

FRONDEG is from *Moliant Cenedl* (1920).

392 COME, YE SOULS BY SIN AFFLICTED

Mr. Swain's hymn is taken from *Walworth Hymns, by J. Swain, Pastor of the Baptist Church Meeting there* (second edition, 1796). The closing stanza is omitted.

ASHBURTON, by S. S. Wesley, is from Kemble's *Psalms and Hymns* (1864).

393 COME, YE SINNERS, POOR AND WRETCHED

Hart's hymn appeared in *Hymns composed on various subjects* (1759) and was headed 'Come, and welcome, to Jesus Christ'. Two stanzas are omitted. In the course of its use in hymnals it has acquired its present form. Thus 'broken' has replaced 'mangled' in ver. 3.

NEUADD WEN has been previously published in the pages of a magazine.

394 SINNERS JESUS WILL RECEIVE

Mrs. Bevan's excellent version, in her *Songs of Eternal Life* (1858), of Neumeister's popular German hymn, which appeared first in *Evangelischer Nachklang* (Hamburg, 1718); the five verses in our text correspond to verses 1, 3, 5, 6, and 8 of the original. Neumeister composed it as a conclusion to one of his sermons on St. Luke xv. 1. He was a leading opponent of Pietism, but this hymn is in no sense inferior to any of the most fervent Pietistic hymns.

JESU, MEINE ZUVERSICHT is from Crüger's *Praxis Pietatis Melica*. Probably the melody is an adaptation of an air set to the same hymn in Runge's *Geistliche Lieder* (Berlin, 1653).

395 SOULS OF MEN, WHY WILL YE SCATTER

From the thirteen verses of the original in Faber's *Hymns* (1862), with the heading 'Come to Jesus'.

The original order is, verses 1 and 2, followed by

> It is God; His love looks mighty
> But is mightier than it seems!
> 'Tis our Father: and His fondness
> Goes far out beyond our dreams.

verses 3 and 4 follow, then:

> There is welcome for the sinner
> And more graces for the good;
> There is mercy with the Saviour,
> There is healing in His blood.

> There is grace enough for thousands
> Of new worlds as great as this;
> There is room for fresh creations
> In that upper home of bliss.

Ver. 6 follows, and then:

> But we make His love too narrow
> By false limits of our own;
> And we magnify His strictness
> With a zeal He will not own.

Then comes ver. 5, followed by:

> 'Tis not all we owe to Jesus,
>   It is something more than all;
> Greater good because of evil,
>   Larger mercy through the fall.

Verses 7 and 8 close the hymn.

ST. MABYN, by A. H. Brown, appeared in *The Bristol Tune Book* (Second Series, 1876), and was composed in 1868.

OMNI DIE was the tune for a hymn 'Omni die dic Mariae' in the *Gross Catolisch Gesangbuch* (Nuremberg, 1631), compiled by D. G. Corner.

396 THE KING OF GLORY STANDETH

The authoress, then Miss C. L. Smith, contributed this to *Lyra Britannica* (1867), where it was entitled, 'Mighty to Save'. The original, in ver. 3 (lines 1, 2, and 4) had 'His' instead of 'Thy', and, in line 8, 'Him' for 'Thee'. Four stanzas are here omitted.

The tune PEARSALL is from the St. Gall *Katholisches Gesangbuch* (1863). The work contains five settings of hymns for the service of the mass. The present tune is that of the Sanctus in the first setting, the German words beginning 'Singt Heilig, heilig, heilig, ist unser Herr und Gott'. No composers' names are attached to the tunes, but the preface states that this tune was composed by Pearsall, who also harmonized about half of the tunes in the work.

397 O JESUS, THOU ART STANDING

Written by Dr. How in 1867, and published that year in the supplement to *Psalms and Hymns* (by Morrell and How). Based on Rev. iii. 20.

LLANGLOFFAN is a Welsh melody, from *Hymnau a Thônau* (1865).

398 THE LORD IS RICH AND MERCIFUL

Like 187 and 354, from Lynch's *Rivulet* (third edition, 1868), where it is headed 'Have faith in God'.

PETERSHAM, by C. W. Poole, was originally set to 'The roseate hues of early dawn', in *The Congregational Psalmist* (second appendix, 1875).

399 JESUS, WE ARE FAR AWAY

From Mr. Pollock's *Metrical Litanies for Special Services and General use* (1870). For Lent.

Dr. Bunnett's tune AGNES, from *The Hymnal Companion to the Book of Common Prayer* (second edition, 1877), was composed for the hymn, 'Jesu, from Thy throne on high.'

400 COME, LET US TO THE LORD OUR GOD

By the Rev. John Morison, D.D., minister from 1780 to 1798 of the parish of Canisbay, Caithness, in which John O'Groat's House is situated. It is a version of Hosea vi. 1–4, and appears in the form adjusted for *The Scottish Paraphrases* of 1781.

KILMARNOCK appears in *Parochial Psalmody: A New Collection of the Most Approved Psalm Tunes. . . . By J. P. Clarke, Second edition* (1831). This seems to be the earliest collection in which the tune was printed, but it was certainly circulated in manuscript for some time previously. In 1854 the composer issued *Poems and Songs by Neil Dougall, with a Memoir of the Author*. The following passage occurs in the Memoir:—'One day R. A. Smith and the late John Taylor, who was then Precentor in the Middle Parish Church, Greenock, paid him (Dougall) a visit. . . . After some conversation Smith said, "Anything new doing, Mr. Dougall? no scraps to divert us?" Mr. Dougall went to a drawer and brought the first few scraps of paper he could lay his hand on. Smith took up one, and hastily humming it over, said, "A very pretty melody; and what do you call it?" "It 's not christened yet," was the answer; "but do you observe anything peculiar about it?" "I do," said Smith; "it is on the Caledonian scale, the same as 'Morven'. " "Yes; the same as your tune." "No, no; not my tune," said Smith. "Will you oblige me with a copy of your nameless tune?" "With pleasure," said the composer, "and we'll christen't 'Kilmarnock';" and this ended the conference.'

401 O LORD, TURN NOT AWAY THY FACE

One of the 'Songs' appended to the Old Version (Sternhold and Hopkins) of *The Whole Book of Psalms* (Day, 1562); also in the Scottish Psalter (1635), with the title 'The Lamentation of a Sinner'. Only the letter M. is attached to this hymn; it stands almost certainly for John Marckant or Marquaunt, incumbent of Clacton Magna (1559) and Shopland (1563–1568), both in south-east Essex. The 'Song' has eleven verses of which the present hymn is verses 1–3, 9, and 11. It is one of the very earliest English hymns.

ST. MARY is set to the second psalm in *Llyfr y Psalmau, wedi eu cyfieithu, a'i cyfansoddi ar fesur cerdd, yn Gymraeg* (1621), the Welsh Metrical Translation of the Psalms by Archdeacon Prys. There, the second line reads thus—

There is no B flat in the signature, so that the tune is apparently in the Dorian mode, the B in the first line remaining natural. As, however, the music printing in the volume is very faulty it is possible the omission of the flat may be accidental. The tune is found in its present form in Playford's *Book of Psalms* (1677).

402 O THOU, MY JUDGE AND KING

Specially written for *The Church Hymnary* by Dr. MacLean Watt to suit Hugo Nyberg's tune HELSINGFORS, which is taken from *Hengellisiä Lauluja ja Wirsiä*, the revised edition of the Finnish hymn-book (1926).

403 LORD JESUS, THINK ON ME

This is the last of the odes composed by Synesius, the bishop of Cyrene (375–430), whom most readers know from the pages of Kingsley's *Hypatia*. The English version is in Mr. Chatfield's *Songs and Hymns of the Earliest Greek Christian Poets, Bishops, and others* (1876); he observes in a note, 'In translating this ode I have given my spirit more liberty. It may be considered as a paraphrase or amplification, rather than an exact translation of the original.' The first, eighth, and ninth stanzas are omitted.

ST. BRIDE comes from *Parochial Harmony; consisting of a Collection of Psalm Tunes in three and four parts, &c.*, by William Riley (1762), where it is set to the new version of Psalm cxxx, and headed 'St. Bridget's Tune, by Mr. Sam¹. Howard'.

404 LORD, THY MERCY NOW ENTREATING

Contributed to *The Children's Hymn Book* (1881, edited by Mrs. Carey Brock), under the initials A. N. It appeared thus in *The Scottish Hymnal* and in the former *Church Hymnary*, but is now known to have been composed by Miss Sidebotham.

ALICE is a tune from *Hymnau a Thônau* (1897).

405 LORD, IN THIS THY MERCY'S DAY

From 'Image the Twenty-Second', a poem on 'The Day of Days, or the Great Manifestation' in 105 stanzas of three lines each, which Isaac Williams published in his *Baptistery: or, the Way of Eternal Life* (1842). Hymn-books have generally improved the wording here and there; thus ver. 3 (lines 1 and 2) originally ran;

> Supplication on us pour,
> Let us now knock at the door.

The tune HEILIGER GEIST is drawn from *Vollständige Psalmen und geistliche Lieder*. . . . (Bremen, 1639), where the melody appears as under, set to the hymn 'Heil'ger Geist, du Tröster mein.'

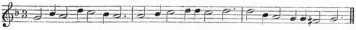

In Crüger's *Gesangbuch* (1640) it is set to the same hymn, but in the following form:

For ST. PHILIP see Hymn 186.

406 ONE WHO IS ALL UNFIT TO COUNT

This hymn has a special interest as being the only hymn in the present book by an Indian Christian. Narayan Vaman Tilak was a distinguished poet, whose hymns and *Metrical Life of Christ* have had great vogue in western India. The translation is to be found in the *Life of Tilak* by J. C. Winslow, and was originally contributed to *The Indian Interpreter* by Dr. Macnicol, missionary of the United Free Church at Poona. Its first appearance in any collection was in *A Missionary Hymn Book* (1922, S.P.C.K.), where another hymn by the same author is printed:

> Prayer to a heart of lowly love
> Opens the gate of heaven above.
> Ah, prayer is God's high dwelling-place
> Wherein His children see His face.
>
> From earth to heaven we build a stair,
> The name by which we call it prayer.
> Prayer is the gracious Father's knee;
> On it the child climbs lovingly.
>
> Love's rain, the Spirit's holy ray,
> And tears of joy are theirs who pray,
> Prayer to a heart of lowly love
> Opens the gate of heaven above.

WIGTOWN is one of the Common Tunes in *The Psalmes of David* (Edinburgh, Hart's heirs, 1635).

407 FROM DEPTHS OF WOE I RAISE TO THEE

One of the greatest hymns of the Reformation, written by Luther in 1523, as a paraphrase of Psalm cxxx. In the 'Table Talk' it is told that when once asked which Psalms were the best of all, Luther replied 'Psalmi Paulini', and being pressed to say which these were, replied 'Psalms 32, 51, 130, and 143'. The hymn appeared first in Johann Walther's *Chorgesangbüchlein* (Wittenberg, 1524). It was sung in the following year (May 9) at the funeral of Luther's friend the Elector Frederick the Wise, in the Schloss-Kirche at Wittenberg, and at Halle in 1546 (Feb. 20), when Luther's own funeral was passing on its way to Wittenberg from Eisleben. It was a special favourite with Luther himself. During the Diet of Augsburg 1530, at a very critical hour for the Reformation cause, when he was living in the Castle at Coburg, one day under the stress of anxiety he fainted. On regaining consciousness he said to his servant, 'Come, let us defy the devil, and praise God by singing the hymn, "Aus tiefer Noth schrei' ich zu Dir."' It was during the same stay at Coburg that Luther wrote the charming letter to his little son Hans, beginning 'I know a fair garden', and also, very probably the greatest of all his hymns, 'Ein' feste Burg' (see Note on Hymn 504).

The translation is in Massie's *Martin Luther's Spiritual Songs* (1854).

ALLEIN GOTT IN DER HÖH SEI EHR (STETTIN) is from *Geistliche Lieder auffs new gebessert und gemehrt . . .* (Leipzig, 1539), where it is set to the hymn 'Allein Gott in der Höh sei Ehr', the version by Nicolaus Decius of the 'Gloria in excelsis', as follows:

The melody is probably an adaptation from a pre-Reformation source.

The present form of the tune is that used by Mendelssohn in *St. Paul*.

408 THERE IS A HOLY SACRIFICE

First appeared anonymously in Cotterill's *Selection* (1819), like 368. In Miss Elliott's book *Hours of Sorrow* it appears along with all the other pieces as her own.

COLWINSTONE was composed by Mr. Morgan Lloyd for this hymn in the present collection.

409 O JESUS, FULL OF PARDONING GRACE

Published in *Hymns and Sacred Poems* (1749). The present hymn is made up of verses 2, 3, and 6 of Wesley's original. The first verse runs,

> Weary of wandering from my God,
>   And now made willing to return,
> I hear, and bow me to the rod:
>   For Thee not without hope I mourn,
> I have an advocate above,
> A Friend before the throne of Love.

Lines 5 and 6 of ver. 3 (2 in the present hymn) are a reminiscence of one of John Wesley's favourite books, Augustine's *Confessions* (i. 5: 'Narrow is the home of my soul: Enlarge it that Thou mayest enter in. It is ruinous; do Thou repair it').

The origin of GIESSEN has not been discovered, but the melody occurs in *The Comprehensive Tune Book* (1851), where it is harmonized by Dr. Gauntlett, and called 'Hoxton'.

410 I HEARD THE VOICE OF JESUS SAY

This hymn, 'so beautiful in its severe simplicity' (Dr. E. H. Bickersteth), was written at Kelso during Dr. Bonar's ministry there, and published in *Hymns Original and Selected* (1846), under the title of 'The Voice from Galilee'.

An extremely interesting facsimile of the page of Dr. Bonar's Notebook, on which the first draft of the hymn is written in pencil, is given in *Hymns by Horatius Bonar* (1904); it has corrections and inter-lineations and quaint marginal sketches, showing the author's manner of work. It was based on St. John i. 16 ('Of His fulness have all we received, and grace for grace').

VOX DILECTI was composed by Dr. J. B. Dykes for this hymn, in *Hymns Ancient and Modern* (Appendix, 1868).

411 JUST AS I AM, WITHOUT ONE PLEA

Written for and published in *The Invalid's Hymn Book* (1841), to which in its various editions Miss Elliott contributed no fewer than 112 hymns. This is headed with the text, 'Him that cometh unto me I will in no wise cast out' (St. John vi. 37). Along with Hymn 539 (below), it may be said to form the best of all Miss Elliott's pieces. 'More than half a century of patient suffering went to the making of her hymns.'

In a very interesting letter written by Edward Quillinan, husband of Dora Wordsworth, the daughter of the poet, to Miss Charlotte Elliott on July 28, 1847, he tells how the hymn had been sent to his wife, then on her death-bed, by her friend Charlotte Oxenden. Dora said 'That is the very thing for me', and continually repeated it during her last days on earth. The letter goes on, 'Mrs. Wordsworth (her mother) has told me that your hymn forms part of her daily solitary prayers. I do not think that Mr. Wordsworth could bear to have it repeated in his presence, but he is not the less sensible of the solace it gave his one and matchless daughter.'

MISERICORDIA, by Henry Smart, is the tune composed for it in *Hymns Ancient and Modern* (1875).

GWYNETH also was composed for it, by John Price (Beulah).

412 NONE OTHER LAMB, NONE OTHER NAME

From Miss Rossetti's *The Face of the Deep* (1892), on Rev. v. 6: 'I beheld, and lo, in the midst of the throne stood a Lamb as it had been slain.'

NONE OTHER LAMB is the tune composed for it by C. J. Ridsdale in *The New Office Hymn Book* (1907).

413 ROCK OF AGES, CLEFT FOR ME

'Every word, every syllable in this really great poem', says Professor Saintsbury, 'has its place and meaning.' 'No other English hymn', says Dr. Julian, 'can be named which has laid so broad and firm a grasp upon the English-speaking world.' It appeared first in *The Gospel Magazine* for March 1776, at the end of an article by Toplady, who was then Editor, with the title 'A remarkable calcula-

tion Introduced here for the sake of the Spiritual Improvements subjoined. Questions and answers relating to the National Debt.' The
original article is designed to show how impossible the payment of
the National Debt is, and the 'Spiritual Improvement' is obvious,
the calculation being made on the basis of how many sins each human
being commits in the day, half-day, hour, minute, and second. The
closing words of this very curious article are '*A living and dying*
PRAYER *for the* HOLIEST BELIEVER *in the World*'. Then follows the
hymn exactly as given here with two exceptions, in ver. 4 'Whilst'
for 'While', and 'When my eye-strings break in death' instead of
the present second line. There seems to be no foundation for the
picturesque story that Toplady composed the hymn while he was
sheltering from a thunderstorm in a great cleft of a lime-stone rock
in Burrington Combe in the Mendips, some twelve years before the
hymn was published. The tradition was first heard of about the year
1850. The idea of our Lord as a Rock was one that always fascinated
Toplady. In a sermon on Isaiah xlii. 11 he says 'Chiefly may they
sing who inhabit Christ the Spiritual Rock of Ages. He is a Rock in
three ways: as a Foundation to support, a Shelter to screen, a Fortress to protect.' In *The Church Quarterly Review* for April, 1920,
there is an article on the use of 'Rock of Ages' as a phrase of religion,
in which it is pointed out that 'though the term was employed as a
recognized title of our Saviour long before Toplady's day, yet there
can be no question that it is his employment of it that has given it
its place in the hearts of English people.'

In the preface to his *Hymns and Carols* (privately printed, 1907)
Mr. A. C. Benson writes: 'To have written words which should come
home to people in moments of high, deep, and passionate emotion,
consecrating, consoling, uplifting . . . there can hardly be anything better worth doing than that. I was present at Mr. Gladstone's funeral
and heard "Rock of Ages" sung, tenderly and softly, by a mighty
congregation, the air gaining volume and majesty, not from loud-
ness and force, but from the gentle grief of a multitude for a very
old and honourable and wearied warrior. All that passed somehow
into the hymn, so that, apart from its own holy and trustful mood,
it was a symbol charged with many remote meanings.'

Liberties have been sometimes taken with the text. Thus Dr.
Rippon's *Selection of Hymns* not only retains 'When my eye-strings
break in death', but alters 'cleft for me' to 'shelter me' (both in ver. 1
and in ver. 4), reads 'Black, I to the fountain fly' (in ver. 3), and 'soar
to worlds unknown' (in ver. 4).

PETRA is from Richard Redhead's *Church Hymn Tunes, Ancient and
Modern* (1853).

PASCAL is found in the *Katholisches Gesangbuch* (Vienna). This
book has no date, but from internal evidence it cannot be earlier than
1774, nor later than 1780, the year of Maria Theresa's death. The
origin of this melody is obscure. So far as at present known, the

above book contains its earliest appearance as a hymn tune. It is set
to the hymn 'Grosser Gott, wir loben dich', as follows:

It is associated with the same hymn in many later German books,
both Catholic and Protestant. Its earliest appearance in a Protestant collection seems to be in Schicht's *Choral-Buch*, published at
Leipsic in 1819. It is there set to the above words in the following
form—

The chorale-book edited by Jakob and Richter in 1873 contains a
setting of the melody ascribed to Peter Ritter, a Mannheim musician
born in 1760. This gave rise to the opinion, which had the support
of the late Dr. Rimbault, that the tune was composed by Ritter; but
it is hardly conceivable that a melody by Ritter could appear in a
book published in Vienna while the composer was still in his teens.
Further, the tune appears in several German books issued during
Ritter's lifetime, and in none of them is he designated as the composer.

The tune seems to have been first set to English words in vol. ii
of the Sequel to Weyman's *Melodia Sacra*, published in Dublin
about 1844. It there appears as a long metre tune called 'Stillorgan'
in the form now known as 'Hursley', and is set to the hymn 'Jesus,
and shall it ever be'. The name 'Hursley' is that of the parish of
which the Rev. J. Keble was vicar, and it was doubtless given to the
tune when it came to be associated with his hymn 'Sun of my soul'.

NICHT SO TRAURIG is from Bach's *Vierstimmige Choralgesänge* (1769).

414 JESUS, LOVER OF MY SOUL

Many stories have arisen as to the origin of this famous hymn.
It has been confidently asserted, for example, that the occasion
of its being written was a sea-bird flying in time of storm to
Wesley, or a dove pursued by a hawk taking refuge in his room, or
his own escape from a threatening mob. Such legends may be dismissed as fancies. It first appeared in *Hymns and Sacred Poems* (1740)
with the title 'In time of Prayer and Temptation'. The epithet in
the opening line was doubtless suggested by the words in Wisdom
xi. 26, 'But Thou sparest all; for they are Thine, O Lord, Thou

lover of souls.' The hymn was not inserted in the official Methodist Hymn-book till 1797, when its author had been dead nine years. In John Wesley's 'Journal' (under the date Sept. 25, 1767) a long notice is inserted about the last illness and death of William New, 'one of the first Methodists in Bristol who always walked as became the Gospel.' On his death-bed 'he desired them that were present to sing, and began "Jesu, lover of my soul".'

Wesley's great antagonist, Toplady, inserted the hymn in his own book *Psalms and Hymns* (1776).

The text as given here is unaltered, with the omission of the original v. 3:

> Wilt Thou not regard my call?
> Wilt Thou not accept my prayer?
> Lo, I sink, I faint, I fall,
> Lo, on Thee I cast my care.
> Reach me out Thy gracious hand,
> While I of Thy strength receive,
> Hoping against hope I stand,
> Dying, and behold I live.'

It is remarkable that in ver. 1, thirty-six out of forty-six words are monosyllables, in ver. 2, thirty-seven out of forty-six, in ver. 3, forty-eight out of fifty-one, and in ver. 4, thirty-six out of forty-five.

Regarding the hymn as an example in literary style, Professor Saintsbury says 'The mere word-music is fingered throughout in the most absolutely adequate manner' (*History of English Prosody*, vol. ii. 531).

Wesley wrote the first word as 'Jesu', his favourite form, as it is the correct form, of the vocative.

When the Rev. Hugh Price Hughes died, on Nov. 17, 1902, it was found that he had given instructions in his will for the words 'Thou, O Christ, art all I want' to be carved on his tombstone.

Liberties have been taken sometimes with the text. Thus, in Dr. Rippon's *Selection of Hymns*, 'raging billows roll' in the third line of ver. 1, 'All in all' begins the second line of ver. 3, and 'Vile' is substituted for 'False' in ver. 3 (line 7). For some account of such variations, see an article in *The Choir* (November, 1918, pp. 206–8).

HOLLINGSIDE was the tune composed for it by Dr. Dykes, in *Hymns Ancient and Modern* (1861). It was so named because Hollingside Cottage was Dr. Dykes's first home in the parish of St. Oswald's, Durham.

ABERYSTWYTH is from *Ail Lyfr Tonau ac Emynau* (Stephens, 1879).

415 MY FAITH LOOKS UP TO THEE

First published in Hastings' *Spiritual Songs for Social Worship* (1831), and entitled 'Self-Consecration'. It was Ray Palmer's first and best hymn, written in 1830 when he was only twenty-one, shortly after leaving Yale College. 'I gave form to what I felt, by writing with little effort, the stanzas. I recollect I wrote them with very tender emotion, and ended the last lines with tears.' Dr. Lowell Mason wrote for it the tune OLIVET with which ever since it has been associated, and said to the author 'Mr Palmer, you may live many years, and do many good things, but I think you will be best known to posterity as the author of "My faith looks up to Thee".'

The second tune DENBIGH is from *Llyfr Tonau Cynulleidfaol*, edited by J. Roberts (1859).

416 COME, O THOU TRAVELLER UNKNOWN

First published in *Hymns and Sacred Poems* (1742), under the title 'Wrestling Jacob'. The subject was a favourite one with Charles Wesley and repeatedly preached on by him. This is undoubtedly the greatest of Wesley's hymns and, as Dean Stanley says (in Ward's *English Poets*, vol. iii, p. 258), is 'not only a hymn, but a philosophical poem . . . filled on the whole with a depth and a pathos which might well excite Watts to say that "it was worth all the verses he himself had written", and induce Montgomery to compare it to the action of a lyrical drama'. The original has fourteen stanzas of which the present arrangement is 1, 2, 8, 9, and 11.

A fortnight after his brother's death John Wesley was preaching at Bolton, and gave out this hymn. As he read the lines:

> My company before is gone,
> And I am left alone with Thee,

he completely broke down, and bursting into tears, sat down in the pulpit and covered his face with his hands, while the whole crowded congregation wept with him. Recovering himself after a little, he went on with the service, which no one who was present ever forgot.

The same verse was quoted by Dean Stanley at the unveiling of the tablet to the Wesleys in Westminster Abbey in 1876, shortly after the death of his wife, Lady Augusta Stanley.

PENIEL (originally named, like the hymn, 'Wrestling Jacob') was composed, as the name suggests, for this hymn, by S. S. Wesley. It is from *The European Psalmist* (1872).

417 HARK, MY SOUL, IT IS THE LORD

Cowper's hymn was first published in Thomas Maxfield's *New Appendix*, 1768. It had been written at Huntingdon some three or four years previously during the period when Cowper enjoyed 'a serenity of soul such as ever attends the gift of lively faith in the all-sufficient atonement, and the sweet sense of mercy and pardon purchased by the blood of Christ' (quoted in Thomas Wright's *Life of Cowper*, p. 150). The motto, in the *Olney Hymns*, is 'John xxi. 16; Lovest thou me?' The original hymn had, in ver. 2, 'wounded' instead of 'bleeding'.

ST. BEES appeared in *The Congregational Hymn and Tune Book*, *edited by the Rev. R. R. Chope* (1862): it was composed by Dr. Dykes for the hymn 'Jesus, name of wondrous love'. Set to the present hymn in *Hymns Ancient and Modern*, Revised edition (1875).

NUN KOMM, DER HEIDEN HEILAND is set to the German version of 'Veni, Redemptor Gentium' in the Wittenberg *Geistliche Gesang-buchlein* of 1524. Probably the tune is an adaptation of the medieval melody set to this Latin hymn. The present form is that adopted by Bach in his Church Cantatas.

418 JESUS, THESE EYES HAVE NEVER SEEN

Written in 1858 at Albany, N.Y., and published in *The Sabbath Hymn-book* that year. It is based on 1 Peter i. 8; 'Whom having not seen ye love.' Dr. Ray Palmer told Dr. S. W. Duffield, the author of *English Hymns*, how he had composed it. He was 'preparing a sermon which had Christ for its special theme. Needing a volume from his closed book-case, he rose and opened the door, when the book appeared first in his hand. At once it occurred to him that in some such way the face of Christ would be unveiled to us: and the thought so filled his heart that he turned to his desk and composed the hymn.' The words of ver. 5 were among the last he was heard to utter on his death-bed.

SOUTHWELL, by H. S. Irons, is from *Hymns Ancient and Modern* (1861).

CLIFTON, by J. C. Clifton, was set to the Tate and Brady version of Psalm xxiv, in *Psalms and Hymns for the Service of the Church . . . arranged by J. B. Sale* (London, 1837).

419 HOW SWEET THE NAME OF JESUS SOUNDS

Contributed by Newton to the *Olney Hymns*, where one stanza was included which is here omitted:

> By Thee my prayers acceptance gain,
>   Although with sin defiled:
> Satan accuses me in vain,
>   And I am owned a child.

The hymn was written on the text of Canticles i. 3: 'Thy name is as ointment poured forth.' Various efforts have been made to alter the first line of the present fourth verse, since many take exception to Jesus being called 'Husband', but Newton was writing with the allegory of the Song of Solomon in his mind. 'Jesus my Saviour, Shepherd, Friend' is perhaps the least violent of the alternatives proposed, but the Committee have decided to leave the line as Newton wrote it.

Newton carried on the slave-trade even after he became a Christian. But a wise word on this anomaly was written by Mr. Dan Crawford in *Back to the Long Grass* (pp. 173, 174). 'You may draw all your distinctions, allow all your extenuations, but finally must face the fact that he it was who penned these ugly words: "I never knew sweeter or more frequent hours of divine communion than in my last two [slave] voyages to Guinea." Fancy the Lord's Table spread across that slave track, then fancy further the conflicting emotions of the same John Newton as arch-slaver and arch-hymn-writer, both the slaving and the hymning in his Christian career. . . . But, after all, good John Newton could shut our mouths in this matter of distracting thoughts at the Lord's Table. For who ever suggests that his hymn ran, "How sweet the name of Newton sounds" ? Does not the memorial command brush aside all such human phantoms in the sweeping, centralizing words: "This do in remembrance of *me*"? and if the supreme Eucharistic privilege be to forget ourselves and remember Christ, then can we surely forget the John Newton who really, after all, did die a beloved bond-servant of Jesus Christ. William Jay saw John just at the end of his life. The mind and tongue of the old preacher were past their business: "my memory is nearly gone," he murmured, "but I remember two things; that I am a great sinner, and that Christ is a great Saviour".'

ST. PETER is from A. R. Reinagle's *Psalm Tunes for the Voice and the Pianoforte* (1830), where it is set to Psalm cxviii. It is named after the church in Oxford of which the composer was organist.

420 JESUS, THOU JOY OF LOVING HEARTS
421 JESUS! THE VERY THOUGHT IS SWEET
422 JESUS, THE VERY THOUGHT OF THEE
423 O JESUS, KING MOST WONDERFUL

These hymns represent short centos from a long Latin hymn of forty-two stanzas from the eleventh century at the latest.

It has been assigned to several authors, but commonly to St. Bernard of Clairvaux (1091-1153), on account of the resemblance between its devotional spirit and his characteristic piety. For this tradition there is no definite evidence, and the researches of Dom Pothier (in the *Revue du Chant Grégorien*, x. 147) have discovered that some eleventh-century manuscripts ascribe the hymn to a Benedictine abbess. Dom Pothier's conclusions are accepted by Dr. W. H. Frere: St. Bernard's claim 'to be reckoned as a hymn-writer has to be set on one side. It is now clear that the long poem from which *Jesu dulcis memoria* and other centos are taken is older than his date, and is, probably, the work of a woman' (*Hymns Ancient and Modern*, Historical edition, p. xxv). In the light of this new evidence, the hymn cannot be described as more than 'attributed to St. Bernard'.

The beautiful poem almost defies translation. In its Latin it has charmed many, including Dr. Livingstone, who used to repeat it to himself as he explored Africa. 'That hymn of St. Bernard, on the name of Christ, although in what might be termed dog-Latin, pleases me so: it rings in my ears as I wander across the wide, wide wilderness.'

Short extracts really give a better impression of the hymn than a complete rendering would, for the quatrains circle round the same theme without developing any thought, and they are unequal in quality. 'The composition, as a whole, lies under the defect of a certain monotony and want of progress' (Trench), and this defect is not felt in a cento of the finer lines. As the two last quatrains are a climax, and as they are only partly reflected in one of the translations (421, ver. 6), they deserve to be quoted here:

> Jesus ad Patrem rediit,
> Coeleste regnum subiit;
> Cor meum a me transiit,
> Post Jesum simul abiit:
>
> Quem prosequamur laudibus,
> Votis, hymnis, et precibus:
> Ut nos donet coelestibus
> Secum perfrui sedibus.

420 JESUS, THOU JOY OF LOVING HEARTS

Dr. Ray Palmer's version, which appeared in *The Sabbath Hymnbook* (Andover, 1858), reproduces a different cento, beginning with the fourth stanza of the original:

> Jesu, dulcedo cordium;
> Fons vivus, lumen mentium,
> Excedens omne gaudium
> Et omne desiderium.

The Latin behind ver. 3 is:

> Qui te gustant, esuriunt:
> Qui bibunt, adhuc sitiunt;
> Desiderare nesciunt
> Nisi Jesum quem diligunt.

MARYTON was composed by Canon Percy Smith for the hymn, 'Sun of my soul,' in *Church Hymns with Tunes* (1874).

JESU DULCIS MEMORIA is set to this Latin hymn in the *Catholische Geistliche Gesänge* (Andernach, 1608).

421 JESUS! THE VERY THOUGHT IS SWEET

This is a selection from the verses by Dr. Neale in his *Hymnal Noted*.

The second, fourth, and fifth verses in the wonderful original are:

> Nil canitur suävius,
> Nil auditur jucundius,
> Nil cogitatur dulcius,
> Quam Jesus Dei filius.
>
> Nec lingua valet dicere,
> Nec littera exprimere,
> Expertus potest credere
> Quid sit Jesum diligere.

Jesus, spes poenitentibus,
Quam pius es petentibus,
Quam bonus te quaerentibus,
Sed quid invenientibus?

CHRISTE, REDEMPTOR OMNIUM has been long associated with this hymn.

422 JESUS, THE VERY THOUGHT OF THEE

Caswall's translation was printed in his *Lyra Catholica* (1849), before he became a Roman Catholic, then in his *Hymns and Poems*. It is taken practically from the same cento as that used by Dr. Neale. In ver. 4 he sanctioned a proposal to alter 'loved ones' to 'lovers'. But, after all, as he said, 'the word "lovers" is not nice'. It certainly brings out the meaning of the original, which is that only those who have some experience of loving Jesus understand what it is. This is expressed in Dr. Neale's version (Hymn 421, ver. 4). But 'loved ones', though it is inaccurate, is sense, and good Christian sense.

ROCHESTER, from *Songs of Praise* (1925), was composed by Mr. Hylton Stewart for the hymn, 'How bright these glorious spirits shine.'

ST. AGNES, DURHAM, was composed by Dr. Dykes for this hymn, in *A Hymnal for use in the English Church, with accompanying tunes* (1866: edited by Hon. and Rev. J. Grey).

423 O JESUS, KING MOST WONDERFUL

This version by Caswall (see on 422) reproduces another cento, which starts with the 9th stanza of the original. His second verse corresponds to the following:

Quando cor nostrum visitas,
Tunc lucet ei veritas,
Mundi vilescit vanitas,
Et intus fervet caritas.

METZLER comes from *Ancient Hymn Melodies and other Church Tunes as used at All Saints' Church, Margaret Street, arranged, composed, and harmonized by Richard Redhead, organist* (Preface dated Easter, 1859).

424 O LOVE THAT WILT NOT LET ME GO

Dr. Matheson's hymn first appeared in *Life and Work* (January 1883), and in the following year was included in *The Scottish Hymnal*, where it was set to 'St. Margaret', specially written for it by Dr. A. L. Peace, the musical editor of that book. Concerning both words and music much controversy has raged—the not unnatural reaction from the enthusiasm with which both were received forty-two years ago. Both have won for themselves a real place in the hearts of multitudes in Scotland and beyond it.

The hymn, the author tells, was written in the Clydeside Manse of Innellan, Argyllshire, on the evening of June 6, 1882. 'It was composed with extreme rapidity: it seemed to me that its construction occupied only a few minutes, and I felt myself rather in the position of one who was being dictated to than of an original artist. I was suffering from extreme mental distress, and the hymn was the fruit of pain.'

As originally written, ver. 3, line 3 runs 'I climb the rainbow through the rain'—an unconventional expression altered by Dr. Matheson to the present text, at the request of *The Scottish Hymnal* committee when the hymn was under its consideration.

Dr. Matheson used to explain that when he wrote 'blossoms red' in the last verse, he was thinking of the blossom that comes out of sacrifice—of the sacrificial life which blossoms by shedding itself. 'White' is the blossom of prosperity, 'red' of self-sacrificing love.

INNELLAN was composed for this hymn in the present collection.

Dr. Peace wrote ST. MARGARET in Brodick Manse, Arran, in 1884. The Committee of *The Scottish Hymnal* (published in 1885) had requested him to compose a tune for this new hymn. 'After reading it over carefully, I wrote the music straight off, and I may say that the ink of the first note was hardly dry when I had finished the tune.'

425 O SAVIOUR, I HAVE NAUGHT TO PLEAD

Written by Mrs. Crewdson shortly before her death, and, like Hymn 148, published posthumously in *A Little While, and other Poems* (1864).

AMOR DEI is in *Oeffentliche Kirchen-Gesänge* (Bremen, 1707), set to the hymn 'Hör, liebe Seel'. The present arrangement of the melody was made by Sir John Stainer for the first edition of *The Church Hymnary* in 1898.

426 O THOU, WHOSE MERCY FOUND ME

These verses are selected from Dr. Monsell's hymn in five eight-line stanzas, beginning 'To Thee O dear, dear Saviour'.

The full text may be found in *The Church Hymnary* (1st edition). The present cento appeared in *The Presbyterian Hymnal* (1876) and was repeated in *Hymns and Tunes of the Presbyterian Church of Wales* (1900).

ST. MARY MAGDALENE is from *The English Hymnal* (1906), and is so named from the church in Taunton of which the composer, H. A. Jeboult, was organist.

427 I LIFT MY HEART TO THEE

Written in October 1871 by C. E. Mudie, the founder of Mudie's Library, and published in his *Stray Leaves*.

BODLONDEB has been already published in a magazine.

428 O LOVE DIVINE, HOW SWEET THOU ART

From Wesley's *Hymns and Sacred Poems* (1749), under the title 'Desiring to love'. It was one of the three hymns (see on 135) which Handel set to music. Three stanzas are omitted after ver. 4. The compilers have altered 'and die' to 'I die' (in ver. 1).

ALLGÜTIGER, MEIN PREISGESANG, is from *Choral-melodien Buch* (Erfurt, 1803), where it is noted as Weimar's composition.

SONG 18, by Orlando Gibbons, is from the same source as Song 22 (see on Hymn 195); it was set to a metrical paraphrase of a passage from the Song of Solomon.

429 NOT WHAT I AM, O LORD, BUT WHAT THOU ART

From Dr. Bonar's *Hymns of Faith and Hope* (2nd series, 1861). Three stanzas are omitted.

DALKEITH, by Thomas Hewlett, is from *The St. Albans Tune Book* (1866).

430 JESUS, MY LORD, MY GOD, MY ALL

Mr. Collins's hymn is taken from *Hymns for Missions* (1854), i.e. three years before the author joined the Church of Rome. The hymn has many echoes of Faber's Corpus Christi hymn (in *Jesus and Mary*, 1849) beginning

> Jesus! my Lord, my God, my all,
> How can I love Thee as I ought?

with the refrain

> Sweet Sacrament! we Thee adore!
> O make us love Thee more and more!

ST. CHRYSOSTOM was composed for this hymn, in *The Hymnary* (1872), of which Sir Joseph Barnby was editor. But it was first printed in *The Musical Times* (December 1871).

431 THEE WILL I LOVE, MY STRENGTH, MY TOWER

From Scheffler's *Heilige Seelenlust* (1657, Breslau). Wesley's translation appeared in *Hymns and Sacred Poems* (1759), and the present hymn is verses 1, 4, 5, and 7. In the original lines 5 and 6 of the first verse are,

> Thee will I love, till the pure fire
> Fills my whole soul with chaste desire.

The final stanza is said to have been repeated by Richard Cobden on his death-bed.

Scheffler's volume, from which both this and 498 are taken, was published after he had joined the Roman Church, but 'his hymns are generally so free from the expression, or even the indirect suggestion, of Roman Catholic doctrine, that it has been supposed they were written before his conversion, though published afterwards. The evangelical Churches of Germany found no difficulty in admitting them to that prominent place in their services which they have ever since retained' (Lord Selborne).

In *Sixteen Psalms . . . set to music for the use of Magdalen College Chapel in Oxford* (about 1774), the melody of NEW 113TH is set to Merrick's version of Psalm cxxxiv.

432 JESUS, THY BOUNDLESS LOVE TO ME

From Crüger's *Praxis* (1653); a poetical rendering by Gerhardt of a prayer, in Arnd's *Paradiesgärtlein* (Magdeburg, 1612), for the realization of the Love of Christ. The original consists of sixteen verses. It was the pleasant custom of the catechumens in the Mark of Brandenburg to sing hymns on their way to church. This hymn was a special favourite and was known among them as the *Postwagen*, because the singing of it greatly lightened and shortened the length of their journey.

Wesley's translation appeared in *Hymns and Sacred Poems* (1739). In his *Plain account of Christian Perfection* Wesley says, 'In the beginning of the year 1738, as I was returning from Savannah, the cry of my heart was

> O grant that nothing in my soul
> May dwell but Thy pure love alone'

—a prayer abundantly answered on the memorable May 24 of that year, when, in the Society Meeting in Aldersgate Street, about a quarter before nine, during the reading of Luther's Preface to the Epistle to the Romans, 'I felt my heart strangely warmed. I felt I did trust in Christ, Christ alone, for Salvation; and an assurance was given me that He had taken away my sins, even *mine*, and saved *me* from the law of sin and death.'

DAVID'S HARP, by Robert King, is set to Miles Smyth's version of Psalm ci in *The Divine Companion: or, David's Harp new tun'd* (2nd edition, 1709).

433 MY GOD, I LOVE THEE; NOT BECAUSE

Caswall's hymn is in his *Lyra Catholica* (1849) and his *Hymns and Poems* (1873). He wrote originally in the last line of the first verse, 'Must burn eternally,' which is a literal rendering of the Latin text:

> O Deus ego amo te,
> Nec amo te ut salves me,
> aut quia non amantes te
> aeterno punis igne.

The Latin underlying the last stanza is:

> Sic amo et amabo te,
> Solum quia rex meus es
> Et solum quia Deus es.

The Latin poem, in a Cologne book *Coeleste Palmetum* (1669), is a version of a Spanish sonnet, but there seems to be no valid evidence for the tradition which ascribes the poem to St. Francis Xavier. This tradition goes back to a belief in the seventeenth century that a Portuguese version of the sonnet, which was current in India, had been composed by Xavier, whose spirit it reflects. But an examination of the literary data disproves this. The problem was first handled critically by Foulché Delbose in the *Revue Hispanique* (vol. ii, pp. 120–45, 1895). The Jesuit scholar F. X. Drebitka, in a monograph on *Hymnus Francisci Faludi* (Budapest, 1899), corrected him in some details, but agreed with his main conclusions. And subsequent research has upon the whole confirmed critics in declining to associate Xavier with any form of the hymn.

SONG 67 (ST. MATTHIAS), by Orlando Gibbons, was set to a hymn for St. Matthias's Day. See note on Hymn 195.

FIRST MODE MELODY is the first of the nine tunes by Tallis in Parker's Psalter. See under Hymn 250.

434 LOVED WITH EVERLASTING LOVE

Mr. G. W. Robinson's hymn is from *Hymns of Consecration and Faith* (1890).

TICHFIELD is from Formby and Lambert's *Collection of Catholic Hymns for the use of Choirs and Congregations* (1853), where it has no name but is assigned to John Richardson.

435 COME, THOU FOUNT OF EVERY BLESSING

Written by Robert Robinson probably about 1758, during the author's ministry in Norfolk, and published in *A Collection of Hymns used by the Church of Christ in Angel-Alley, Bishopsgate* (1759). Text as in Madan's *Psalms and Hymns* (1760). The hymn is as truly autobiographical as any of John Newton's, for Robinson's youth had been wild and reckless. Six years before the hymn was written, a sermon on St. Matthew iii. 7 by George Whitefield made an ineffaceable impression on him, and after a lengthened period of deep spiritual concern light and peace came to him.

In the original, between verses 1 and 2:

> Teach me some melodious sonnet
>   Sung by flaming tongues above.
> Praise the mount: I'm fixed upon it,
>   Mount of God's unchanging love.
> Here I raise my Ebenezer,
>   Hither by Thy help I'm come,
> And I hope by Thy good pleasure
>   Safely to arrive at home.

In which, as Dr. Rendel Harris says, 'all the rhymes may be challenged, and all the reasons are unchallengeable.'

Robinson was a man who passed through many changes of thought

and feeling. One well-known anecdote tells that, while travelling in
a stage-coach he was asked his opinion of this hymn by a lady fellow-
passenger personally unknown to him. He waived the subject, but
she returned to it with great persistence, expressing her own great
admiration of the hymn. 'She observed that the gentleman was
strongly agitated, but as he was dressed in coloured clothes, did not
suspect the cause. . . . At length, entirely overcome by the power of
his feelings, he burst into tears and said, "Madam, I am the poor
unhappy man who composed that hymn many years ago; and I would
give a thousand worlds, if I had them, to enjoy the feelings I then
had." ' (Belcher's *Historical Sketches of Hymns*).

SHARON (HALTON HOLGATE), by Dr. Boyce, is set to Psalm iv in
Melodies for the Psalms of David, according to the version of C. Smart
(1765).

MORIAH is probably an adaptation of the same original as underlies
'Gwalia' (384).

436 IT IS A THING MOST WONDERFUL

Dr. How's hymn first appeared in *Children's Hymns* (S.P.C.K.,
1873). Only verses 1, 2, 6, and 7 are given in the present book.

SARRATT, by G. C. E. Ryley, from *Church Bells* (1904), was composed for the translation of a Christmas carol by Luther.

SOLOTHURN, as in *The English Hymnal* (1906).

437 SAVIOUR, TEACH ME, DAY BY DAY

From Miss Leeson's *Hymns and Scenes of Childhood* (1842), where
it had four eight-line stanzas; here the second half of verses 1 and 2
and the first half of ver. 3, have been omitted.

ST. BENEDICT was composed by Sir John Stainer for this hymn,
in the first edition of *The Church Hymnary*.

438 THE KING OF LOVE MY SHEPHERD IS

Written for *Hymns Ancient and Modern* (Appendix, 1868). Next
to the Scottish version of the 23rd psalm ('The Lord's my Shepherd,
I'll not want.'), Sir Henry Baker's is the best known and most popular. On his death-bed (Feb. 12, 1877) the author repeated the third
verse of this hymn.

DOMINUS REGIT ME was composed for this hymn by Dr. Dykes, in
Hymns Ancient and Modern (Appendix, 1868), and both hymn and
tune were sung at his funeral on Jan. 28, 1876.

DUNAHA is an Irish air, arranged by Professor Macalister. The
melody in modern times has been set to a hymn by John Hore,
whose birthplace was Dunaha.

439 SOMETIMES A LIGHT SURPRISES

'This brilliant lyric,' as Palgrave calls it (in *The Treasury of Sacred
Song*, p. 353), was contributed by Cowper to the *Olney Hymns*, under

the title of 'Joy and Peace in Believing'. It was read to McCheyne (see Hymn 582) on his death-bed, and was the last thing he heard and seemed to understand. The allusion in ver. 4 is to Habbakuk iii. 17.

BENTLEY was the tune composed by Dr. Hullah for this hymn, in *Psalms and Hymns for Divine Worship* (1867).

440 HAPPY ARE THEY, THEY THAT LOVE GOD

Charles Coffin's original Latin hymn occurs in the Paris Breviary (1736) as the Hymn for Tuesdays at Vespers. This version from *The Yattendon Hymnal* is a very free rendering of verses 1–3 of the original; verses 4 and 5 are by the translator, and ver. 4 of Coffin's hymn is left untranslated. For the original and another translation see the historical edition of *Hymns Ancient and Modern* (1904, No. 444).

BINCHESTER, by Dr. Croft, is set to Psalm xcvi in *The Divine Companion* (2nd edition, published by Henry Playford in 1709).

441 MY GOD, I THANK THEE, WHO HAST MADE.

From Miss Procter's *Legends and Lyrics* (1858). The following verse, which was originally the fifth, is omitted:

> I thank Thee, Lord, that Thou hast kept
> The best in store:
> We have enough, yet not too much
> To long for more,—
> A yearning for a deeper peace
> Not known before.

OLDOWN was composed by Dr. Basil Harwood for this hymn in *The Public School Hymn-book* (1919).

WENTWORTH was composed for it by F. C. Maker in *The Bristol Tune Book* (2nd series, 1876).

442 IN HEAVENLY LOVE ABIDING

First published in *Hymns and Meditations by A. L. W.* (1850). Miss Waring's other two hymns in *The Church Hymnary* are 446 and 548.

NYLAND is a Finnish folk melody named from the Finnish province of Nyland.

443 LIKE A RIVER GLORIOUS

Miss Havergal's hymn appeared first in her *Loyal Responses* (1878).

LIKE A RIVER was the tune composed by Dr. Mountain, for this hymn, in *Hymns of Consecration and Faith*.

444 PEACE, PERFECT PEACE, IN THIS DARK WORLD OF SIN

Dr. Bickersteth's hymn was published in *Songs in the House of Pilgrimage* (1875). It was written in August of that year, and was suggested by a sermon on Isaiah xxvi. 3 preached by Canon Gibbon, Vicar of Harrogate, where Dr. Bickersteth was spending his summer holiday. That afternoon he was visiting an aged relative, Archdeacon Hill of Liverpool, then on his death-bed; sitting beside him, he wrote the hymn in a few minutes and read it to his dying friend.

The hymn has acquired many associations, two of which may be mentioned. It was one of the hymns sung at Professor Robertson Smith's funeral at Keig in Aberdeenshire on April 4, 1894. Also, it was on the lips of Bishop Hannington during his last difficult journey through Masai-land in July 1885. 'All the way during that march to Taita,' says Mr. E. C. Dawson (*James Hannington*, p. 333), 'his letters reveal him to us, till we seem to see him as he strides ahead with that springy step of his, arms swinging, eyes ever on the alert to notice anything new or remarkable—now a snatch of song, now a word of encouragement . . . the very life and soul of his company; while ever and anon his emphatic voice would be raised in the notes of some old familiar tune, and the wilderness would ring to the sound of a Christian hymn—

> Peace, perfect peace, the future all unknown?
> Jesus we know, and He is on the throne.'

The tune PAX TECUM was composed for this hymn by Mr. Caldbeck, who sent it to Dr. Bickersteth. The latter included it in *The Hymnal Companion to the Book of Common Prayer* (2nd edition, 1877), of which he was the editor. The tune was arranged in its present form by Dr. Charles Vincent (q.v.).

SONG 46 is another (see on 195) of Orlando Gibbons's melodies; it is the first half of the tune set to a hymn for Christmas Day.

445 SPEAK, I PRAY THEE, GENTLE JESUS!

'This hymn by William Williams in its Welsh form is DCCIX in *Gloria in Excelsis*, Part I, printed at Llandovery by Rees Thomas. The occasion of its composition appears to be the despondency of the sisters and brethren in some of the Societies in church meetings which the author had special skill in conducting, above all, in drawing forth from the members their religious experiences' (Note by Mr. Abraham Morris).

LLANGAN is from *Llyfr Tonau Cynulleidfaol* (1859).

446 MY HEART IS RESTING, O MY GOD

Appeared, like 442, in the 3rd edition of *Hymns and Meditations by A. L. W.* (1852). It is based on Lamentations iii. 24: 'The Lord is my portion, saith my soul: therefore will I hope in Him.' Miss War-ing's original had eight stanzas.

PENTATONE is from *A Students' Hymnal* (University of Wales, 1923). It was composed by Sir Walford Davies for the hymn 'It came upon the midnight clear.'

447 COME, WE THAT LOVE THE LORD

Watts's hymn, entitled 'Heavenly Joy on Earth', appeared in *Hymns and Sacred Songs* (1707). The present hymn reproduces verses 1, 3, 6, 8, 9, and 10 of the original ten. The second verse was

> The sorrows of the mind
> > Be banished from the place!
> Religion never was designed
> > To make our pleasures less.

The only alteration introduced is in verse 2, where the third and fourth lines used to read

> But fav'rites of the heavenly King
> > May (or, should) speak their joys abroad.

MOUNT EPHRAIM, by B. Milgrove, is from *Sixteen Hymns as they are sung at the Right Honourable the Countess of Huntingdon's Chapel in Bath* (1769). (See reference in Mrs. Gaskell's *Cousin Phillis*, Part I.)

448 ALL MY HOPE ON GOD IS FOUNDED

From the Bremen A *und* Ω. *Joachimi Neandri Glaub-und-Liebes-übung* (1680) with the heading 'Grace after meat'. As in the case of the other renderings from *The Yattendon Hymnal*, this cannot be called a translation; the original is merely used for suggestion.

In his *Glaub-und Liebesübung* (Bremen, 1680), Joachim Neander notes MEINE HOFFNUNG as a melody already known, but it has not been found in any earlier collection. The present form is that used by Bach in one of his Church Cantatas.

GROESWEN, by J. Ambrose Lloyd, is from *Llyfr Tonau Cynull-eidfaol* (1859).

449 MY GOD, IS ANY HOUR SO SWEET

Miss Elliott's hymn is in her *Hours of Sorrow* (1836). The text is unaltered, save for the change of 'here' to 'there' in verse 5.

The first part of AMBERG seems founded on the melody of the chorale, 'Was mein Gott will', which is used by Bach in several of his Cantatas. That melody is again derived in part from a tune in a collection of secular songs, published at Paris in 1529. As for the remainder of the tune, the original source has not been discovered. Probably the present arrangement was made by T. L. Hately for *The Church of Scotland Hymn Tune Book* (1862), where it first appears as at present.

450 COME, MY SOUL, THY SUIT PREPARE

Five out of the seven verses of a hymn contributed by Newton to the *Olney Hymns*, and based on 1 Kings iii. 5: 'Ask what I shall give thee.' The closing stanza in the original was:

> Shew me what I have to do;
> Every hour my strength renew;
> Let me live a life of faith;
> Let me die Thy people's death.

Mr. Spurgeon used to employ this hymn effectively in public worship; he had a verse or two of it chanted very softly before the main prayer of the service.

The tune RAVENNA, in *Vollständige Sammlung . . . Choralmelodien . . . Herausgegeben von Christmann und Knecht* (Stuttgart, 1799), is set to the hymn 'Ohne Rast und unverweilt'. The melody is exactly the same as the present tune, with the exception of the second note of line 3, which in the original is flattened (F♮ in the present key).

451 APPROACH, MY SOUL, THE MERCY-SEAT

From the *Olney Hymns*, one verse being omitted. Newton's hymns in general are characterized by a certain stark simplicity, directness, and manly sincerity. 'He had the generosity of a large heart, grateful for his conversion to piety and happiness; and hence, doubtless, a singular gift in winning his hearers' (F. T. Palgrave).

SPOHR is an adaptation from the solo and chorus ('Though all thy friends forsake thee') in *Calvary (Des Heilands letzte Stunden): An Oratorio by Louis Spohr. First performed at Cassel on Good Friday* (1835).

STRACATHRO, by Charles Hutcheson, is from *Christian Vespers* (Glasgow, 1832).

452 PRESENT WITH THE TWO OR THREE

Miss Freer's hymn was written in 1868, and published in *Hymns for the Use of the Churches* (Catholic Apostolic) in 1871.

TYHOLLAND is an adaptation from what is believed to be a fourteenth-century carol. In Spangenberg's *Gesangbuch* (Eisleben, 1568) it is set to a hymn, 'Wir wollen alle fröhlich sein'. With slight variations, it is found in many later German books.

WESTON, by S. S. Wesley, is set, in *The European Psalmist* (1872), where it first occurs, to the hymn, 'Lord, in this Thy mercy's day'.

453 O KING OF MERCY, FROM THY THRONE ON HIGH

From Mr. Birks's *The Companion Psalter* (1874), a version of Psalm lxxx.

COENA DOMINI was composed by Sir Arthur Sullivan for the Communion hymn 'Draw nigh and take the Body of the Lord' in *Church Hymns with Tunes* (1874).

454 O GOD, THOU ART THE FATHER

From *Offices for the Commemoration of St. Columba*, June 9,1897, in *St. Columba, a Record and a Tribute* (1897, p. 88). A free version of part of the Latin original 'In Te, Christe', which comes from the hymn-book of the ancient Scoto-Irish Church, published by the Celtic Archaeological Society. It occurs also in Colgan's *Trias Thaumaturga*. No doubt is entertained by scholars that it was composed by Columba.

As the objection was raised that though his most famous hymn (the 'Altus') nobly praised God for His works of Creation, it gave too feeble expression to the work of Redemption, Columba, confessing that the objection was just, composed another, supplying the deficiency, and beginning 'In Te, Christe credentium miserearis omnium'. It consists of two parts, the first describing what Christ is to believers, the second what Christ has done to mankind.

DURROW is an Irish folk-song melody, connected with a County Limerick sea-song, 'Captain Thomson'.

455 O HELP US, LORD; EACH HOUR OF NEED

Published in Heber's *Hymns* (1827). For the second Sunday in Lent, and based on the Gospel for that day, St. Matthew xv. 21 (The Syro-Phoenician Woman).

ABBEY is one of the twelve Common Tunes in *The CL Psalms of David*, &c. (A. Hart, Edinburgh, 1615).

456 MY SPIRIT LONGS FOR THEE

From Dr. Byrom's *Miscellaneous Poems* (1773), entitled 'The desponding Soul's Wish'. There is a second Part, entitled 'The Answer', as follows:

Cheer up, desponding soul,
    Thy longing pleased I see;
'Tis part of that great whole,
    Wherewith I longed for thee:

Wherewith I longed for thee,
    And left my Father's throne;
From death to set thee free,
    To claim thee for my own:

To claim thee for my own,
    I suffered on the Cross:
Oh were my love but known,
    No soul could fear its loss:

No soul could fear its loss,
    But filled with love divine,
Would die on its own cross,
    And rise for ever mine.

LAWES comes from *A Paraphrase upon the Divine Poems*, by George Sandys (1638). This, the second edition of Sandys's metrical version of the Psalms, contains a number of tunes by Henry Lawes, in two parts, Treble and Bass. The present is the tune set to Psalm xxxii. The tunes are anonymous in the 1638 edition, but those of later date give Henry Lawes as the composer.

FINGAL is a tune arranged from an Irish traditional air in a publication by the Irish Gaelic League.

457 O FOR A CLOSER WALK WITH GOD

Written by Cowper on Dec. 9, 1769, during the serious illness of the poet's dear friend Mrs. Unwin. In a letter written the following day, referring to this illness, Cowper writes, 'She is the chief of blessings I have met with in my journey since the Lord was pleased to call me. . . . Her illness has been a sharp trial to me. Oh, that it may have a sanctified effect, that I may rejoice to surrender up to the Lord my dearest comforts, the moment He may require them. . . . I began to compose the verses yesterday morning before daybreak but fell asleep at the end of the first two lines: when I awaked again, the third and fourth were whispered to my heart in a way which I have often experienced.' The whole hymn follows.

It was first published in Conyers's *Collection of Psalms and Hymns* (1772) and afterwards included in the *Olney Hymns* under the title of 'Walking with God' (Genesis v. 24: 'Enoch walked with God'). Cowper once told Mr. Greatheed that when he was expected to pray in public, 'his mind was always greatly agitated for some hours preceding'. But Andrew Fuller, who was at Olney in 1776, declared that he knew 'a person who heard him pray frequently at these meetings, and I have heard him say "of all the men that I ever heard pray, no one equalled Mr. Cowper" ' (T. Wright, *Life of Cowper*, p. 176).

Dr. John Ker narrates in his *Letters* (p. 320) that on a visit to Olney in 1880 he heard from the owner of the garden and summerhouse in which the *Olney Hymns* were written, a tradition about the composition of this hymn. 'The windows of an old shoemaker's cottage, now in ruins, looked into it, and the old man at his work used to hum the tune of "Ludlow". Cowper was taken with it, and wrote the hymn . . . to suit it, and walked up and down often to hear it sung.'

CHESHIRE is set to Psalm cxlvi in *The Whole Booke of Psalmes with their wonted Tunes, as they are song in Churches, composed into foure parts. . . . Compiled by sondry authors* (London, Thomas Est, 1592). It is one of several tunes 'newly added in this booke', and named Chesshire Tune.

MARTYRDOM was composed in the end of the eighteenth century and first printed on single slips for the use of music classes. The original form of the melody is in *common* time, as in the present book. Its first appearance in *triple* time seems to have been in R. A.

Smith's *Sacred Music sung in St. George's Church, Edinburgh* (1825). There it is designated 'Old Scottish Melody', and the harmony is stated to be 'by Mr. Smith'. It also appeared in *The Seraph, a selection of Psalms and Hymns*, edited by J. Robertson, and published in Glasgow in 1827. There also it is in triple time, and a foot-note states that 'the above tune "Fenwick" or "Martyrdom", and by some called "Drumclog", was composed by Mr. Hugh Wilson, a native of Fenwick'.

The publication of the tune by R. A. Smith seems to have been the occasion of a legal dispute as to its ownership, but abundant evidence was produced to show that Wilson was without doubt the composer. Many years ago a writer in *The Psalmodist* said, 'I well remember the day it ("Martyrdom") was first sung in St. George's, Edinburgh, for Dr. Thomson then said to me, "O man! I could not sing for weeping".'

458 O LIGHT THAT KNEW NO DAWN

A cento from Gregory Nazianzen's Hymn to Christ (printed in Daniel's *Thesaurus Hymnologicus*, iii, pp. 5 f.), as translated in Dr. Brownlie's *Hymns of the Greek Church* (1900). The third verse was recast by Dr. Brownlie for the present collection.

HAREWOOD, by S. S. Wesley, was originally set to the hymn, 'Christ is our corner-stone', in *Hymns Ancient and Modern* (Appendix, 1868).

459 THOU HIDDEN LOVE OF GOD, WHOSE HEIGHT

Tersteegen's poem in ten stanzas appeared in his *Geistliches Blumengärtlein* (1729), entitled 'The longing of the Soul quietly to maintain the secret drawings of the Love of God'.

Wesley's long translation appeared in *Psalms and Hymns* (1738). It was written two years previously during his stay in America at Savannah, and reflects vividly the state of his mind in the time of unrest before his conversion. Wesley was a close student of St. Augustine's *Confessions*, and many allusions to passages in them occur in his hymns. In ver. 1, lines 5 and 6 are an unmistakable quotation from the famous passage, 'Thou hast made us for Thyself, O Lord, and our heart is restless until it repose in Thee'. Curiously enough, there is no allusion to this in Tersteegen's original.

O. W. Holmes once declared that this was the greatest hymn in the English language, and Emerson agreed.

In ver. 2, line 4, Wesley substituted 'Seem fixed' for his original 'Be fixed'.

VATER UNSER, in *Geistliche Lieder* (Leipsic, 1539) is set to Luther's version of the Lord's Prayer, 'Vater unser im Himmelreich'. In the *Anglo-Genevan Psalter* (1558) it is set to a similar English version of the Lord's Prayer by Dr. Richard Coxe. This version and tune were included in many of the later English and Scottish Psalters. In the *Anglo-Genevan Psalter* (1561) the tune is set to Kethe's version of Psalm cxii. This adaptation appears also in the complete English and Scottish Psalters, 1562 and 1564, and was continued in most later editions. Hence the tune came to be known as Old 112th. It was a favourite tune of John Wesley. He once said to some Yorkshire friends, 'If you want to hear pure psalmody you must go to Fulneck and hear the Moravians sing'—naming a hymn set to this tune.

The original air of ST. PETERSBURG is in a Mass composed by Bortnianski in 1822. It is found as a hymn tune in a Choralbuch published at Leipzig in 1825. In this book, which was edited by I. H. Tscherlitzky, an organist in St. Petersburg, the tune is set to the hymn 'Ich bete an die Macht der Liebe', as follows:

460 DEAR MASTER, IN WHOSE LIFE I SEE

Originally appeared in *The Monthly Calendar* of Trinity Church, Glasgow, and afterwards in *Hymns of Faith and Life* (1896). In the latter collection it is anonymous; in the former Dr. Hunter's name is attached to the hymn. The compilers have altered 'long' to 'would' in ver. 1 (line 2) and 'poor' to 'weak' in ver. 2 (line 2).

PSALM 86 was composed or adapted by L. Bourgeois in the *French Psalter*, 1543 or 1544. In the *Anglo-Geneven Psalter* (1561) the tune was set to Kethe's version of Psalm lxx, and both psalm and tune were included in the complete *Scottish Psalter* of 1564. From the latter the present arrangement has been made by J. S. Anderson.

461 ONE THING I OF THE LORD DESIRE

First appeared in *Thoughts and Fancies for Sunday Evenings* by W. C. Smith (1887), then in *The Home and School Hymnal* (1892).

KILDROSTAN was composed by Dr. Evans for this hymn in the present collection.

462 JESUS, MEEK AND GENTLE

Mr. Prynne's hymn was published in *The Hymnal suited for the Services of the Church* (1858), and composed two years earlier. The author writes, 'This hymn is commonly thought to have been written for children, but it was not, however, specially written for them'. . . .

ST. CONSTANTINE was composed by Dr. W. H. Monk for this hymn in *Hymns Ancient and Modern* (1861).

463 MY SOUL, THERE IS A COUNTRY

From Vaughan's *Silex Scintillans* ('Sparks from the Flint'), 1650, entitled 'Peace'.

Dr. John Brown in his Essay on Vaughan (*Horae Subsecivae*, 1st series, p. 304) says, 'Vaughan's religion is deep, lively, personal, tender, kindly, impassioned, temperate, central. His religion grows up, effloresces into the ideas and forms of poetry as naturally, as noiselessly, as beautifully as the life of the unseen seed finds its way up into the "bright consummate flower".'

The tune CHERRY TREE CAROL is from *The English Carol Book* (1913). It is the traditional melody of a carol beginning, 'Joseph was an old man', and embodying a legend about Joseph, Mary, and a cherry tree, the carol which was sung by Amyas Leigh at Smerwick Fort, in *Westward Ho!* ch. ix.

464 MAKE ME A CAPTIVE, LORD

From Dr. Matheson's *Sacred Songs* (1890), written that year at Row, Dumbartonshire. Entitled 'Christian Freedom', 'Paul, the prisoner of Jesus Christ' (Ephesians iii. 1).

LEOMINSTER, from *The Journal of Part Music* (vol. ii, 1862), was composed for this hymn. The present arrangement is by Sir A. Sullivan, and appeared in *Church Hymns with Tunes* (1874), where, however, the tune is not acknowledged to be Martins, but is stated to be an old melody.

LLANLLYFNI is from *Gemau Mawl* (D. Jenkins, 1890). Though the composition of it is attributed to the Rev. John Jones of Talysarn, it is really by David Jenkins, who based the tune on the remarkable intonations of Mr. Jones's voice in preaching. See Biographical Note.

465 BLESSÈD JESUS, HIGH IN GLORY

Contributed anonymously by the Rev. John Macleod, D.D., of Govan Parish, to *The Scottish Hymnal* (1884).

BUGAIL ISRAEL (Shepherd of Israel) is from *Supplement to Tunes, Chants, and Anthems*, ed. D. Jenkins, 1894.

466 O GRANT US LIGHT, THAT WE MAY KNOW

From Mr. Tuttiett's *Germs of Thought on the Sunday Services* (1864). One stanza is omitted, and 'dread' changed to 'dead' in verse 3.

O GRANT US LIGHT is from *Hymns and Tunes of the Presbyterian Church of Wales* (1900).

467 O FOR A HEART TO PRAISE MY GOD

From *Hymns and Sacred Poems* (1742), and based on Psalm li. 10, 'Make me a clean heart O God, and renew a right spirit within me' (Prayer Book version). Wesley wrote eight stanzas, and in the first (line 4), 'So freely spilt for me'; also 'dear' for 'great' (in ver. 2), and 'dearest' for 'gracious' (in ver. 5).

ST. ETHELDREDA is dated 1860 in *Psalms and Hymns for Public Worship, with appropriate Tunes*, edited by James Turle (1863), but it does not appear to have been published before 1863.

468 JESUS, SAVIOUR EVER MILD

From *The People's Hymnal* (1867), edited by Dr. Littledale himself; then in *Hymns Ancient and Modern* (1875).

The tune *Tres Magi de Gentibus* is from the Andernach *Catholische Geistliche Gesänge* (1608).

469 JESUS, FROM THY THRONE ON HIGH

From Mr. Pollock's Litany for Children, in *The Gospeller* (1871).

The tune LEBBAEUS is from *Church Hymns with Tunes* (1874), where it is anonymous, but marked in the Index as arranged by the editor, Sir A. Sullivan. The actual source of the melody is unknown. It appeared with a different second line in *Children's Worship* (1879), edited by Dr. Henry Allon).

470 O LAMB OF GOD, STILL KEEP ME

Mr. Deck's hymn is from *Psalms and Hymns and Spiritual Songs* (1842), a Plymouth Brethren collection. It appears in his *Hymns and Sacred Poems*, the first edition of which was published in 1876 at Melbourne, Australia. The previous edition of *The Church Hymnary* included another hymn of Mr. Deck's, beginning

> Lord Jesus, are we one with Thee?
> O height! O depth of love!
> Once slain for us upon the tree,
> We're one with Thee above.

CHENIES was composed for the hymn 'From Greenland's icy mountains', and first published in leaflet form about 1855. It was then included in *The Village Church Tune Book*, compiled by the Rev. T. Richard Matthews (1859).

KILMOREY is from *Llyfr Tonau Cynulleidfaol, Ail Attodiad* (1890).

471 O THOU WHO CAMEST FROM ABOVE

Wesley's hymn, as in *Short Hymns on Select Passages of Scripture* (1762), is based upon Leviticus vi. 13: 'The fire shall ever be burning upon the altar, it shall never go out'. He told Samuel Bradburn, when they were together in Yorkshire during 1781, that 'his experience might always be found in the first two verses of this hymn' (Telford's

The Methodist Hymnbook Illustrated, p. 332). Exception has been taken sometimes to 'inextinguishable' in ver. 2 as being too long and cumbrous a word for congregational singing, and the line has been occasionally altered, e.g. in the *Annotated Hymnal Companion* (3rd edition, 1890) to 'Unquench'd, undimmed in darkest days.'

This was the favourite hymn of Dr. W. F. Moulton, the New Testament scholar who was headmaster of the Leys School at Cambridge; it was sung at his funeral on Feb. 9, 1898.

AFFECTION is a tune from Greenwood's *Psalmody* (Halifax, 1838).

HYMNUS EUCHARISTICUS, from a MS. by the composer, Benjamin Rogers, in the Library of Christ Church, Oxford, is there set to a hymn beginning, 'Te Deum Patrem colimus'. It is sung on Mayday morning from the tower of Magdalen College, Oxford.

472 FOR THEE, MY GOD, FOR THEE ALONE

Like 251, from Mr. Burns's book, *The Evening Hymn* (1857), a small volume of prayers and hymns, consisting of an original hymn and an original prayer for every evening of the month.

BRISTOL is one of the tunes contributed by S. Wesley to Vincent Novello's *The Psalmist* (Part iv, 1842).

473 O GOD, THOU ART MY GOD ALONE

From *Songs of Zion* (1822), based by Montgomery on Psalm lxiii.

The tune WAINWRIGHT comes from *A Collection of Hymns, with appropriate Symphonies and Accompaniments, as originally composed for the Children of the Liverpool Blue Coat Hospital* (c. 1790). There it is set to the hymn 'My God, and is Thy table spread', and named 'Newmarket'. The original form of the tune is as follows:

474 O FOR A FAITH THAT WILL NOT SHRINK

Mr. Bathurst's hymn is from *Psalms and Hymns for Public and Private Use*, where it was entitled 'The Power of Faith' (St. Luke xvii. 5). The text is unaltered, except that in ver. 5 (line 3) he wrote 'e'en here'. The last line of ver. 2 about faith that 'Can lean upon its God' recalls a noble line in one of Watts's hymns (on Titus ii. 10–13):

> Religion bears our spirits up,
> While we expect that blessed hope,
> The bright appearance of the Lord—
> *And faith stands leaning on His word.*

ST. LEONARD, by Henry Smart, is from *Psalms and Hymns for Divine Worship* (1867).

475 NEARER, MY GOD, TO THEE

Written by Mrs. Adams in November 1840, and first published in *Hymns and Anthems* (1841), compiled by the Rev. W. J. Fox, of whose congregation in South Place Chapel, Finsbury (Unitarian) she was a member. It is based on Genesis xxviii. 10–22, Jacob at Bethel.

It was commonly reported at the time, though some doubt has since been cast on the story, that the ship's band on board the *Titanic* played one of the tunes of this hymn, when the vessel went down after collision with an iceberg in the Atlantic, Sunday, April 14, 1912. Mr. W. T. Stead was among the 1,635 passengers who were lost on this, its maiden voyage across the Atlantic.

LIVERPOOL, by John Roberts, is from *Llyfr Tonau Cynulleidfaol* (1859).

NENTHORN was composed by T. L. Hately for this hymn, in *The Church of Scotland Hymn Tune Book* (1865).

PROPIOR DEO was composed for it by Sir Arthur Sullivan, in *The Hymnary* (1872).

476 SAVIOUR, BLESSÈD SAVIOUR

Prebendary Thring's hymn was written in 1862, under the text of Philippians iii. 14 ('I press towards the mark for the prize of the high calling of God in Christ Jesus', and entitled 'The Goal'. In *Hymns Congregational and Others* (1866), the title was 'Pressing onwards'. The complete text has ten stanzas, from which our cento takes 1, 4, 7, 9, and 10. One of the stanzas omitted has these good lines—

> Dark and ever darker
> Was the wintry past,
> Now a ray of gladness
> O'er our path is cast;
> Every day that passeth,
> Every hour that flies,
> Tells of love unfeignèd,
> Love that never dies.

WARUM SIND DER THRÄNEN, by J. A. P. Schulz, is from *Lieder im Volkston* (Berlin, 1785).

477 BE THOU MY VISION, O LORD OF MY HEART

Miss Byrne translated the old Irish poem into prose, which was then versified by Miss Eleanor Hull.

SLANE is an Irish traditional air, from Joyce's *Old Irish Folk Music and Songs*. It is the melody of a song, 'With my love on the road'.

478 BLEST ARE THE PURE IN HEART

Verses 1 and 3 are by Keble, from *The Christian Year* ('The Purification'), where, however, ver. 3 (line 3) reads, 'for His cradle and His throne'. Verses 2 and 4 are from *The New Mitre Hymnbook*

(1836), composed either by Rev. W. J. Hall, the editor, or by his co-editor, Edward Osler. Keble authorized the text as it stands.

SWABIA comes from *Davids Harpffen Spiel, In hundert und funffzig Psalmen, Auch dreyhundert zwey und vierzig Lieder Melodien . . . Aufgesetzt von Johann Martin Spiess . . .* (Heidelberg, 1745). There it is set to the hymn 'Ach wachet! wachet auf!'.

The present arrangement of the melody is by the Rev. W. H. Havergal, and appears in his *Old Church Psalmody* (1847).

479 LOVE DIVINE, ALL LOVES EXCELLING

From *Hymns for those that seek and those that have Redemption in the Blood of Christ* (1747), where Wesley wrote 'loves' in the first line. One stanza is omitted as usual, but the only other change is the customary alteration of 'sinless' into 'spotless' (ver. 3, line 2).

HYFRYDOL, by R. H. Prichard, is from *Halelwiah Drachefn* (edited by Griffith Roberts, 1855).

480 THERE IS A CITY BRIGHT

Every year, on New Year's Sunday, Mrs. Deck's husband held a children's service in his church, St. Stephen's, Hull, when each child was given a motto-card with a printed text and also a hymn specially written for the occasion. 'There is a city bright' was one of these hymns. The first verse was composed by Miss Amy Deck—afterwards Mrs. O. F. Walton, the well-known authoress. Her mother, Mrs. Deck, wrote the other verses, and the entire hymn is now credited to her. Mrs. Walton wrote her story *Christie's Old Organ* with the view of illustrating the words of the hymn. This information was given by Mrs. Walton herself to Dr. Millar Patrick.

The tune CITY BRIGHT, by J. S. Tyler, was composed for this hymn, in *Songs of Love and Mercy* (1876), a book issued by the Children's Special Service Mission, with which the composer was connected.

481 FATHER OF PEACE, AND GOD OF LOVE

A composite hymn, of which verse 1 is by Doddridge, verses 2 and 3 as in the revised edition of *The Scottish Paraphrases* (1781), based on Doddridge, and ver. 4 by William Cameron (see on 483). It is a paraphrase of Hebrews xiii. 20, 21.

The tune CAITHNESS, from *The Psalmes of David, &c.* (Edinburgh, Hart's heirs, 1635), is one of the thirty-one Common Tunes appearing in this edition of the Scottish Psalter.

The source of ST. PAUL is less certain. So far as has yet been ascertained, the earliest book containing it is a small collection printed by James Chalmers in Aberdeen in 1749. The only copy at present known lacks the title-page, but the date is ascertained from the names of the provost and bailies of Aberdeen, to whom the work is dedicated. Here the tune bears its present name, and is in two parts, tenor and bass, as follows:

The A, fourth note of line 2 in the bass, is a misprint for C, and is duly noted in the preface as a 'fault of the engraver'.

The title-page of the third edition of this work (dated 1753) bears that the tunes are 'collected by Andrew Tait, Organist'. As Tait was organist of St. Paul's Episcopal Church, it is possible that he was the composer of the tune.

The tune is included in Bremner's collection issued in Edinburgh in 1756, under the name 'Aberdeen or St. Paul'.

482 WALK IN THE LIGHT: SO SHALT THOU KNOW

From Barton's *Devotional Verses* (1826), with the text 1 John i. 7.

The author, 'the Quaker Poet', puts into melodious verse the characteristic Quaker doctrine of the 'Inner Light'.

NOX PRAECESSIT is from *The Christian Hymnal. Five hundred Hymns for the Church and Home* (1873). It was composed for the hymn 'Bride of the Lamb! awake, awake'; but in the same book it is also set to the present hymn, and a note states that it was adapted to that hymn by the composer.

483 BEHOLD THE AMAZING GIFT OF LOVE

The original of this is a hymn of six verses in short metre, by Watts (published 1709), beginning,

> Behold what wondrous grace
> The Father hath bestowed
> On sinners of a mortal race,
> To call them Sons of God.

In the Draft of *The Scottish Paraphrases* (1745), this hymn was extensively revised, and, as may be seen by comparing it with the original, greatly improved by the compilers in a common metre of five verses. The present familiar form (as in the edition of 1781) is by William Cameron, minister of Kirknewton, Midlothian, who with little original poetical gift himself had an almost infallible knack in improving the verses of other writers. Compare Hymns 481 and especially 223, which, as Dr. Johnson said of Dryden, Cameron 'found brick and left marble'.

NEWINGTON is from *Ten Church Pieces for the Organ, with four anthems in score, composed for the use of the Church of Nayland in Suffolk, by William Jones* (1789). The tune appears at the end of this work set to Psalm xxiii, and called 'St. Stephen's Tune'. Under the name 'Stephen's' it appears in Knott's *Sacred Harmony* (Aberdeen, 1815).

ST. STEPHEN (ABRIDGE) is from *A Collection of Psalm Tunes in Three Parts . . . by Isaac Smith (c.* 1770). The original name of the tune is 'Abridge', by which it continues to be known in England. In *Sacred Harmony for the Use of St. George's Church, Edinburgh* (1820), it appears under the name 'St. Stephen's', and with the following form of the last line—

This was adopted in some later books published in Scotland, but the present form is in accordance with the original.

484 GRACIOUS SPIRIT, HOLY GHOST

In Bishop Wordsworth's *The Holy Year* (1862), under Quinquagesima, for which day the Epistle is 1 Corinthians xiii.

The original had, between verses 5 and 6,

> Faith will vanish into sight:
> Hope be emptied in delight:
> Love in heaven will shine more bright;
> Therefore give us love.

Also, after ver. 6, it had

> From the overshadowing
> Of Thy gold and silver wing,
> Shed on us who to Thee sing,
> Holy, heavenly love.

CHARITY was composed for this hymn, in *Hymns Ancient and Modern* (Appendix, 1868).

ST. AMBROSE, from *The Congregational Psalmist* (1858), is possibly based on the 8th Gregorian Tone.

485 O BROTHER MAN, FOLD TO THY HEART THY BROTHER

From Whittier's poem 'Worship' (*Poems*, p. 154) in fifteen stanzas, beginning

> The Pagan's myths through marble lips are spoken,
> And ghosts of old Beliefs still flit and moan
> Round fane and altar overthrown and broken,
> O'er tree-grown barrow and gray ring of stone.

The text 'Pure religion and undefiled', &c. (St. James i. 27) is prefixed to the poem. Verses 1, 3, and 4 of the hymn are the last three stanzas of the poem, ver. 2 being the eleventh.

INTERCESSOR, by Sir Hubert Parry, in *Hymns Ancient and Modern* (New Edition, 1904), was composed for the hymn, 'O word of pity', Hymn 97 in the present book.

486 OUR FATHER, THY DEAR NAME DOTH SHOW

Mr. Richards's hymn is, like 491, taken from *A Missionary Hymnbook* (S.P.C.K., 1922).

OLD 22ND was set to Psalm xvi in the *Anglo-Genevan Psalter*, 1561, and in other sixteenth-century Psalters, but in Day's harmonized edition (1563), and in Este's and Allison's Psalters, it is set to Psalm xxii, though it soon dropped out of use in England.

487 O GOD OF MERCY, GOD OF MIGHT

Written in 1877 and published by Mr. Thring in his *Collection* (1880). It appeared also in his *Church of England Hymnbook*, as an offertory hymn, under the text St. Luke x. 36, 37: 'Which now of these three was neighbour unto him that fell among the thieves?'

HOYLAKE, by A. O. Roberts, is from *Hymns and Tunes of the Presbyterian Church of Wales* (1900).

ELMHURST, by Edwin Drewett, was composed for this hymn, in *The Congregational Church Hymnal* (1887).

488 BELOVÈD, LET US LOVE: LOVE IS OF GOD

Dr. Bonar's hymn, as it appeared first in the Supplement to the Baptist *Psalms and Hymns* of 1880 (edited by the Rev. J. T. Wigner), had in ver. 4 (line 1) 'in love is light', and in ver. 5 (line 2) 'Shall we be with that God'.

Sir John Stainer composed GRANDPONT for this hymn, in the first edition of *The Church Hymnary*.

489 ETERNAL RULER OF THE CEASELESS ROUND

Written by Mr. Chadwick for the graduating class of the Divinity School, Cambridge, Massachusetts, June 19, 1864, shortly before the author's ordination to the Second Unitarian Church, Boston. 'These lines of peace and goodwill are especially significant as coming at a time so full of hate and slaughter' (Reeves, *The Hymn as Literature*, p. 309), for the date is a few weeks after General Grant's desperate battle against Lee in the Wilderness. 'The smoke of battle hung over the mighty hosts for six days, while the North remained in a state of suspense bordering on agony; but Grant wrote to the Government at Washington, "I propose to fight it out on this line, if it takes all summer".'

As printed in *The Treasury of American Sacred Song*, the fifth line of the third verse has 'Thy children' instead of 'the children'.

SONG 1, by Orlando Gibbons (see on Hymn 195), was set to a paraphrase of the Song in Exodus xv.

490 BLEST BE THE TIE THAT BINDS

Published in Dr. Fawcett's *Hymns adapted to the circumstances of Public Worship and Private Devotion* (1782). These were mostly composed to be sung after sermons. The story has often been told that in 1772 Fawcett had been called to Carter's Lane Church, London, from Wainsgate, a very small church, near Hebden Bridge in the West Riding of Yorkshire, where the annual stipend had never exceeded £25. He had a large family and decided to accept the call. His furniture was already packed for removal when the tears and entreaties of his people prevailed upon him to remain with them. The hymn is said to have been written shortly afterwards, and though there is no direct evidence of the connexion, internal evidence may be taken as supporting the truth of the story.

The text has been considerably altered, especially in verses 3 and 5, in order to avoid certain awkward expressions in the original. Thus, as the verses appear in Dr. Rippon's *Selection of Hymns*, ver. 3 begins

> When we asunder part,
> It gives us inward pain,
> But we shall still be join'd in heart,
> And hope to meet again.

The hymn is often sung at the close of church-meetings in America, the custom being that those who sing join hands.

DONCASTER (BETHLEHEM), by S. Wesley, was originally set to Psalms xxxi and li (part 2) in J. B. Sale's *Psalms and Hymns for the Service of the Church* (1837).

491 ALMIGHTY FATHER, WHO DOST GIVE

Bishop Masterman's hymn appeared in *A Missionary Hymnbook* (S.P.C.K., 1922).

FINNART, by K. G. Finlay, is set to the hymn in that book.

PLAISTOW is from *Hymns, &c. used at the Magdalen Chapel* (*c.* 1760).

492 O GOD OUR FATHER, THRONED ON HIGH

Mr. Coster wrote this by request for *The Fellowship Hymnbook*.

ERMUNTRE DICH, by J. Schop, is set, in triple time, to a hymn beginning with these words, in *Himmlische Lieder* (Lüneburg, 1641). The present arrangement is Bach's in his *Christmas Oratorio*.

493 FATHER OF MEN, IN WHOM ARE ONE

Professor Shuttleworth's hymn appeared first in *The Church Monthly* (1898), thereafter in the Appendix to *Church Hymns*, compiled by the author for use in his church, St. Nicholas, Cole Abbey, London, and then in the 1903 edition of *Church Hymns*.

DELHI, by Dr. E. F. Rimbault, composed in 1857, appeared in Dr. Peter Maurice's *Choral Harmony with Supplement* (1858).

LLANGOEDMOR is from *Y Gwyliedydd* (1826).

494 FAIR WAVED THE GOLDEN CORN

From the Rev. J. Hampden Gurney's *Psalms and Hymns for Public Worship Selected for some of the Churches of Marylebone* (1851).

HOLYROOD is anonymous in the English Presbyterian Church's *Psalms and Hymns for Divine Worship* (1867), published by James Nisbet & Co. The composer, James Watson (q.v.) was a partner in that firm. The harmony is by Dr. Rimbault.

495 SAVIOUR, WHILE MY HEART IS TENDER

Mr. Burton's hymn is from his *One Hundred Original Hymns for the Young* (1850).

ARUNDEL, by Dr. Dykes, is from *The Congregational Hymn and Tune Book* (1862).

SHIPSTON, from *The English Hymnal*, is as arranged by Miss L. E. Broadwood from the air of a Warwickshire ballad called 'Bedlam City'.

496 O LOVE, WHO FORMEDST ME TO WEAR

Scheffler's hymn is from *Heilige Seelenlust* (Breslau, 1657). There were originally seven verses, of which those in the present version correspond to 1–3, 6–7. It was entitled, 'She (i.e. the soul) surrenders herself to the Everlasting Love'. Miss Winkworth's translation appeared in *Lyra Germanica* (2nd series, 1858).

SOUTH CERNEY was written by Sir W. H. Hadow for the hymn, 'Thou hidden Love of God', in *The English Hymnal*.

497 JUST AS I AM, THINE OWN TO BE

Contributed by Miss Farningham to *The Voice of Praise* in 1887 (Sunday School Union of London). There are two additional verses in the original:

ver. 5.   With many dreams of fame and gold,
           Success and joy to make me bold,
           But dearer still my faith to hold,
               For my whole life I come.

ver. 6.   And for Thy sake to win renown,
           And then to take the victor's crown,
           And at Thy feet to cast it down,
               O Master, Lord, I come.

SAFFRON WALDEN, by A. H. Brown, appeared in *The Hymnal Companion* (1890).

498 LORD, IN THE FULNESS OF MY MIGHT

Written by Mr. Gill in 1855, and published in *The Golden Chain of Praise* (1869), with the heading 'Early Love. "How good it is to close with Christ betimes!" Oliver Cromwell.' The hymn begins 'With sin I would not make abode,' and the verses here are a selection from the original eight stanzas.

UNIVERSITY is from *A Collection of Psalms and Hymn Tunes* (Cambridge, 1794); as this book was edited by Dr. Randall, Professor of Music in the University, the tune has been ascribed to him, although it is anonymous. In a contemporary Cambridge tune-book, to which Dr. Randall contributed, the tune is assigned to Dr. Collignon, Professor of Anatomy in the University.

499 O HAPPY DAY, THAT FIXED MY CHOICE

The text as in the edition of Doddridge's *Hymns*, published in 1819 by his great-grandson, John Doddridge Humphreys. It is entitled, 'Rejoicing in our Covenant engagements to God' (2 Chronicles xv. 15: 'And all Judah rejoiced at the oath', &c.).

HEATON NORRIS, by J. Grimshaw, is from *Twenty-Four Hymns in four parts* (*c.* 1810).

500 JESUS CALLS US! O'ER THE TUMULT

Mrs. Alexander's hymn, as it appeared first in the S.P.C.K. *Hymns* of 1852. Based on St. Matthew iv. 18, 19.

ST. ANDREW was composed for this hymn by E. H. Thorne, in *Hymns Ancient and Modern* (1875).

501 'TAKE UP THY CROSS', THE SAVIOUR SAID

From Mr. Everest's *Visions of Death, and other Poems* (1833), published when he was nineteen years old. In the course of transmission and use among hymn-books, the original has been much altered. The present text reproduces the original, except that in ver. 4 Mr. Everest wrote 'And calmly sin's wild deluge brave', and l. 4, 'It points to glory o'er the grave', and in ver. 5, line 1, 'follow on'.

HESPERUS, by Henry Baker, originally called 'Whitburn', is from *A Hymnal for use in the English Church, with accompanying Tunes* (1866. Edited by the Hon. and Rev. J. Grey). It was originally set to the hymn 'Sun of my soul'.

BRESLAU, in *As hymnodus sacer. Zwölff Geistliche anmuhtige und theils newe Gesänge. . . .* (Leipzig, 1652), was set, in the following form, to the hymn 'Herr Jesu Christ, meins Lebens Licht'.

Later German books show variations in every line. The present form of the melody is that adopted by Mendelssohn in the oratorio *St. Paul*.

502 JESUS, I MY CROSS HAVE TAKEN

Lyte's hymn appeared in *Sacred Poetry* (1824), under the text 'Lo, we have left all, and followed Thee' (St. Mark x. 28). It was signed 'G.', but was acknowledged as Lyte's in his *Poems chiefly religious* (1833). Two stanzas are omitted, the second and the third. Lyte wrote in ver. 3 'What a Saviour'.

BETHANY, by Henry Smart, is from *Psalms and Hymns for Divine Worship* (1867). It was composed for 'Jesus, I my cross have taken' Hence its alternative name, 'Crucifer'.

TANYCASTELL, by the Rev. John Jones, is from *Jeduthun* (Bangor, 1860).

503 ALMIGHTY FATHER OF ALL THINGS THAT BE

Canon Dugmore's hymn, as in *Hymns of Adoration for Church Use* (1900), was composed for the opening of a small Industrial Exhibition in the author's parish, Parkstone, near Poole, Dorset. Text as in *Hymns Ancient and Modern* (1904), modified from the original for general use as a hymn.

CHILTON FOLIAT, by Sir G. C. Martin, comes from *The Westminster Abbey Hymn Book* (1897).

504 THINE FOR EVER! GOD OF LOVE

'Written', says Mrs. Maude in a note in Julian's *Dictionary of Hymnology*, 'in 1847 for my class in the Girl's Sunday School of St. Thomas's Church, Newport, Isle of Wight, and published in 1848 at the beginning of a little book called *Twelve Letters on Confirmation, by a Sunday School Teacher*.' These letters were written week by week during the author's enforced absence from her class, and the lines of the hymn occurred almost impromptu at the close of one of them. They remained buried for about ten years, were then discovered, and found a place without the author's knowledge in *Hymns Ancient and Modern*.

This was the hymn in which Archbishop Benson joined at his last communion in Hawarden Church on Oct. 11, 1890, and it was sung over his grave in Canterbury Cathedral, on Oct. 16.

SAVANNAH is from the *Collection of Tunes as they are sung at the Foundery* (1742), which was compiled by John Wesley.

505 TO-DAY I ARISE
506 I BIND UNTO MYSELF TO-DAY

The famous *Lorica* or 'Breastplate' of St. Patrick (also known as 'The Deer's Cry' from the legend that is mentioned below), inseparably connected with one of the greatest stories in the history of Christian Missions. For full details see the *Life of St. Patrick* by Dr. J. B. Bury. In the year A.D. 432, when Patrick landed in Ireland to 'sow the Faith', he made his way to Tara, the capital of Meath, where the 'High King' of Ireland, Leary, held his court among the vassal-kings of the land. It was the time of the triennial convention of those petty rulers, and the Christian festival of Easter was also drawing near. Patrick and his company, halting at the Hill of Slane beside the Boyne Water some ten miles from Tara, and in full view of it, celebrated the Eve of the Feast by lighting a great fire. That same night in Tara Leary and his chieftains also kept festival, but the royal edict had gone forth that no one on pain of death should kindle a fire either in Tara or anywhere on the surrounding plain till the King himself fired the beacon which had been piled up close beside the palace. As he went out to light it, far away to the north was seen the gleam of fire on the Hill of Slane. Leary summoned his Druids and demanded what this could mean. They replied 'King, unless this fire which you see be quenched this very night, it will never be quenched, and the kindler of it will overcome us all and seduce all the folk of our realm'. Greatly angered, the King replied, 'It shall not be: but we will go to see the issue of the matter, and we will put to death those who do such sin against our kingdom.' Thus saying, he gave orders for his chariots to be yoked, and wheeling them *widdershins*—contrary to the course of the sun—in order to counteract all spells, accompanied by two of his chief Druids he drove headlong over the plain to the Boyne. They drew rein before they came within the circle of the light of Patrick's fire, lest he should cast his spell upon them. But he, when he was summoned and saw their array, lifted up his voice in the 20th Psalm from the Vulgate, 'Some trust in chariots, and some in horses, but we will remember the name of the Lord our God', and then in the words of the *Lorica* in Irish. Legend tells that soldiers whom Leary had set in ambush imagined that Patrick and his companions were wild deer, and the words they heard as they lay in wait for them, were known henceforth as 'The Deer's Cry'.

There is no reason to doubt that the words of the *Lorica* are very ancient. In its complete form (see Bury, or Kuno Meyer's *Ancient Irish Poetry*, p. 25) it is at once an incantation, a war-song, and a creed. The 'Crafty wiles of demon crew' were as real to Patrick as the foemen without and the lusts within, but he summoned to his help a Power mightier still, and in that Strength the 'Day of Tara', as it is called in the old Irish records, was won. Mrs. Alexander's version, which has won great popularity partly through Sir Charles Villiers Stanford's setting of it to old Irish melodies, is a paraphrase and expansion of the original, and the lines with which four of the verses open, 'I bind unto myself to-day', rest upon a mistranslation of the Irish. The version, 'To-day I arise', by Professor Macalister which appears here for the first time, is a closer translation, and gives a more accurate idea of the picturesque abruptness and nervous vigour of the original.

LORICA PATRICII is an Irish folk-song melody, arranged by Professor Macalister.

ST. PATRICK is from Dr. George Petrie's *Irish Melodies* (arranged by Sir C. V. Stanford): it is said to be an old Irish setting of 'Jesu dulcis memoria'.

CLONMACNOISE is a traditional Irish melody, harmonized by Sir Richard R. Terry.

507 I'M NOT ASHAMED TO OWN MY LORD

The original by Watts, in his *Hymns and Sacred Songs* (1709) was retained in the 1745 Draft of *The Scottish Paraphrases*, except that Watts wrote, in ver. 1 (lines 3 and 4),

> Maintain the honour of His word
> The glory of His cross.

In the 1781 issue, the final improvements were made on ver. 2,

> Jesus my God! I know His name,
> His name is all my trust,

ver. 3.

> Firm as His throne His promise stands
> And He can well secure,

and ver. 4.   Then will He own my worthless name.

On Mar. 7, 1897, when Professor Henry Drummond was on his deathbed, his friend Dr. Hugh Barbour played several hymn tunes to him without gaining any response. 'Then he tried the old Scots melody of "Martyrdom" to which Drummond beat time with his hand, and joined in the words, "I'm not ashamed to own my Lord". When the hymn was done, he said, "There's nothing to beat that, Hugh".'

For LANCASTER see on Hymn 116.

JACKSON appears first in *Twelve Psalm Tunes and Eighteen Double and Single Chants . . . composed for Four voices* (1780), where it is set to Psalm xlvii. In Dr. Miller's collection, issued in 1800, the tune is called 'Byzantium', and it still bears this name in English collections.

508 O JESUS, I HAVE PROMISED

Originally printed as a leaflet by the S.P.C.K. in 1868, 'A Hymn for the newly confirmed'. It was written by Mr. Bode on the occasion of the confirmation of his daughter and two sons.

WOLVERCOTE was composed by W. H. Ferguson for this hymn, in *The Public School Hymnbook*, where it was given anonymously.

DAY OF REST, by J. W. Elliott, appeared in *Church Hymns with Tunes* (1874), as the tune for 'O day of rest and gladness'. But in *Hymns Ancient and Modern* (edition of 1875) it was set to the present words.

509 JESUS, MASTER, WHOSE I AM

Written by Miss Havergal in December 1865 for her nephew the Rev. J. H. Shaw; printed as one of a series of leaflets by Messrs. Parlane, Paisley; and then published in *The Ministry of Song* (1869), with the text, 'Whose I am, and whom I serve' (Acts xxvii. 23). The complete hymn, in two parts, had six stanzas.

HEATHLANDS, by Henry Smart, was originally set, in *Psalms and Hymns for Divine Worship* (1867), to the hymn, 'God of mercy, God of grace'.

510 TEACH ME, O LORD, TO FOLLOW HIM WHO TROD

Mr. Lambert's hymn appeared in *Psalms and Hymns* (Welsh Calvinistic Methodist) for 1870, also in the revised edition (1892) of that work. On one occasion when a plebiscite was taken by the monthly magazine of the Welsh Presbyterian Church as to the two hundred best hymns in that book, this hymn was one of those that received the largest number of votes.

FARLEY CASTLE was originally set to Psalm lxxii in *A Paraphrase on the Divine Poems*, by George Sandys (1638). See note under Hymn 456.

511 TEACH ME, MY GOD AND KING

Herbert's poem 'The Elixir', from *The Temple* (1633). 'Archbishop Leighton ... has a remark which appears tacitly to refer to this poem, and explains its title. "Whatsoever be the matter of [human actions] the spiritual mind hath that alchemy indeed of turning base metals into gold, earthly employments into heavenly." *Tincture* may refer to the *Elixir* regarded as a cleansing or transmuting liquid. But the more obvious sense will be, "if coloured or tinged with this thought, *For God's Sake*" ' (Note in *The Treasury of Sacred Song*, by F. T. Palgrave). John Wesley with his literary sense saw the fine qualities of Herbert's poem and its possibilities as a hymn, but unfortunately he was unable to resist the temptation to make emendations. The results were disastrous, e.g. in his version of verses 3 and 4.

> All may of Thee partake;
>   Nothing so mean can be,
> But draws when acted for Thy sake,
>   Greatness and worth from Thee.
>
> If done to obey Thy laws,
>   Even servile labour shines;
> Hallow'd all toil, if this the cause,
>   The meanest work divine.

An awful warning to all who tinker at poetry!

SANDYS, from *Christmas Carols Ancient and Modern ... by William Sandys* (1833), is a traditional air, set originally to the words, 'This day a child is born'.

512 TAKE MY LIFE, AND LET IT BE

Written by Miss Havergal at Astley House, Feb. 4, 1874, after an interesting experience in answer to her prayer 'Lord, give me all in this house!' 'It was nearly midnight. I was too happy to sleep, and passed most of the night in praise and renewal of my own consecration; and these little couplets formed themselves, and chimed in my heart one after another till they finished with "Ever, only, all for Thee!" ' Published in her *Loyal Responses* (1878).

Dr. Hopkins originally set CULFORD to the hymn, 'Songs of praise the angels sang', in *The Temple Church Choral Service* (1867) of which he was the editor.

PATMOS appeared in Havergal's *Psalmody* (1871), from an unpublished manuscript dated 1869.

513 O LORD AND MASTER OF US ALL

From Whittier's poem 'Our Master' in *The Panorama and other Poems* (1856), from which the hymn 'Immortal Love, for ever full' (Hymn 141 in the present book) is also taken.

WETHERBY, by S. S. Wesley, appeared first in *The European Psalmist* (1872).

514 THROUGH GOOD REPORT AND EVIL, LORD

From the third series of Dr. Bonar's *Hymns of Faith and Hope* (1866). The fourth and seventh stanzas are omitted.

ST. LEONARD, by H. S. Irons, appears in print for the first time in *The English Hymnal* (1916), where it is set to 'The radiant morn hath passed away'.

515 THOUGH LOWLY HERE OUR LOT MAY BE

Written by Mr. Gaskell sometime before 1860, when it appeared in Miss Courtald's *Psalms, Hymns, and Anthems*.

BUDE, by S. S. Wesley, appeared in *The European Psalmist* (1872).

516 WE ARE BUT LITTLE CHILDREN WEAK

Contributed to *The Church School Hymnbook* (1850), which was edited by Dr. W. F. Hook, Vicar of Leeds, and afterwards Dean of Chichester. 'The hymn', Miss Alexander explained, 'was written exclusively for very poor children at a crowded city Sunday School.' It was afterwards altered by the author for use in a mixed congregation. In the original ver. 1 was,

> We are but little children poor
> And born in very low estate.

Between verses 1 and 2, these stanzas originally lay:

> We know the Holy Innocents
> Laid down for Him their infant life,
> And martyrs brave and faithful saints
> Have stood for Him in fire and strife.

We wear the cross they wore of old,
  Our lips have learned like vows to make,
We need not die; we cannot fight,—
  What may we do for Jesus' sake?

The reference to the Holy Innocents explained l. 3 of ver. 4 in the original—

A death to die for Jesus' sake,
  A weary war to wage with sin.

Finally the first version of ver. 5 was,

With smiles of peace and looks of love
  We may light up our dwellings dim,
Bid kind good humour brighten there,
  And consecrate our homes to Him.

ALSTONE was composed by C. E. Willing for this hymn, in *Hymns Ancient and Modern* (Appendix, 1868).

517 FIGHT THE GOOD FIGHT

From Dr. Monsell's *Hymns of Love and Praise* (1863); written for the nineteenth Sunday after Trinity. The epistle for the day is Ephesians iv. 17.

PENTECOST, by William Boyd, was first set to this hymn in *Church Hymns* (1874). It was composed in 1864 for the hymn 'Veni Creator', and appeared in *Thirty-Two Hymn Tunes, composed by members of the University of Oxford* (1868).

DUKE STREET appears first in *A Select Collection of Psalm and Hymn Tunes . . . By the late Henry Boyd, Teacher of Psalmody* (Glasgow, 1793). The composer, John Hatton, died in 1793, but the tune does not seem to have appeared in any collection prior to the above. It is there headed 'Addison's 19th Psalm', no composer's name being given. In *Euphonia*, a collection of tunes, edited by W. Dixon, and published in Liverpool about 1805, it is found under its present name, and attributed to John Hatton.

518 A CHARGE TO KEEP I HAVE

From Wesley's *Short Hymns on Select Passages of Scripture* (1762). The text at the head of this hymn is Leviticus viii. 35: 'Therefore shall ye abide at the door of the tabernacle of the congregation day and night seven days—and keep the charge of the Lord that ye die not.' 'The genius of Methodism is almost embodied in these lines . . .' (Telford). In the original verse 4 (lines 3 and 4) is

Assured if I my trust betray,
  I shall for ever die.

The change made shows the difference in standpoint between our century and his, and, though needful, weakens the intensity of the hymn.

BOWDEN is from *The European Psalmist* (1872), as arranged by S. S. Wesley.

519 WHO IS ON THE LORD'S SIDE?

Written by Miss Havergal on Oct. 13, 1877, and published next year in her *Loyal Responses*. It is based upon the text, 1 Chronicles xii. 18.

ARMAGEDDON was originally set, in *The Church Psalter and Hymn Book*, by the Rev. W. Mercer (Appendix, 1872), to the hymn 'Onward! Christian soldiers'. The tune seems to be an adaptation by Sir J. Goss from the following melody, which appears in Part III of Layriz's *Kern des deutschen Kirchengesangs* (1853), set to the hymn 'Wenn ich Ihn nur habe', and ascribed to Luise Reichardt.

520 WORKMAN OF GOD! O LOSE NOT HEART

A selection from Faber's poem, 'The Right must win', beginning,

Oh it is hard to work for God,
To rise and take His part
Upon this battlefield of earth
And not sometimes lose heart.

The verses have been rearranged, those chosen being 10, 11, 2, 7, 13, and 18 of the original poem.

The tune MARTYRS is one of the twelve Common Tunes in *The CL Psalmes of David* (Edinburgh, A. Hart, 1615). Its first appearance in England seems to be in *Ravenscroft's Psalter* (1621), where it is classed among 'Scottish Tunes', and is in triple time. Playford and other English editors follow Ravenscroft in this respect. In the 1615 edition, the tune is in minims throughout with the exception of the first and last notes of each line. In the subsequent Scottish editions, including that of 1635, the semibreves are introduced as at present in the first and last lines. In all the old books, both Scottish and English, the tune is in the Dorian mode as in the present book, but many editors have introduced changes into the tune in order to force it into the modern minor mode.

Burns refers to this tune in 'The Cottar's Saturday Night' as 'plaintive "Martyrs", worthy of the name'. There is a tradition, adopted by Sir Walter Scott in *Old Mortality*, that the Covenanters entered the battle of Drumclog, on June 1, 1679, singing the 76th Psalm to this tune. Dr. Alexander Smellie, also accepting the tradition, thus describes the scene in his *The Men of the Covenant :* 'Down the face of the slope the Covenanters advanced, sing-

ing the familiar verses of one of the Scottish metrical psalms, the
seventy-sixth, to the fine old tune, as tradition relates, of *Martyrs*.
They were kindling words which rang out in the resonant bass of
two hundred and forty strong-throated and strong-souled men—

> In Judah's land God is well known,
>   His name's in Israel great;
> In Salem is His tabernacle,
>   In Sion is His seat.
> There arrows of the bow He brake,
>   The shield, the sword, the war,
> More glorious Thou than hills of prey,
>   More excellent art far.
>
> Those that were stout of heart are spoiled,
>   They slept their sleep outright;
> And none of those their hands did find,
>   That were the men of might.

The battle was half-won which could be introduced by a song
so confident and unafraid. . . . The suddenness of the attack was
decisive. 'Over hill and moor King Charles's troopers fled, followed
by those who had achieved a success so amazing over "the shield,
the sword, the war".'

LONDON NEW is from one of the thirty-one Common Tunes found
in *The Psalmes of David, &c.* (Edinburgh, Hart's heirs, 1635).

The tune is there named 'Newton', and the melody is the same as
the present, with the exception of line 3, which reads thus—

This form is found in the collections of Bruce (1726), Bremner
(1756), and many other Scottish books, down to about 1820; principally in the books issued in the *east* and *north* of Scotland. The present form of the melody seems to have appeared first in Playford's
Psalms (1671), and is that found in all English books, and also in
Moore (1762), Holden (1766), and other books published in the *west*
of Scotland. It is the form found in R. A. Smith's *Collection* (1825),
and since that date has become universal. Another variation in the
melody is the substitution at the fourth note of line 2 of either the
sixth or the fourth of the scale for the fifth. This peculiarity is
found in the *Supplement to the New Version of the Psalms* (1708);
in some editions of Playford; in Chalmers's *Collection* (Aberdeen,
1748 or 1749); and in one or two other books published in the *north*
of Scotland.

521 BELIEVING FATHERS OFT HAVE TOLD

Written in a steamer on Lake Como during a day's excursion in
the spring of 1889, for use by the Church of Scotland Young Men's

Guild, of which Dr. Charteris was the founder. He wrote to a friend, 'The Guild Hymn, poor as it is, is in sympathy with young men choosing to stand on Christ's side in the life-long battle.' It was published in *The Guild Magazine* for August 1889, and first sung (to Dr. Peace's music) at the Guild Conference at Dundee the same year.

GUILD was composed by Dr. Peace for the hymn, and first printed in 1889 on a single sheet for use at Guild meetings. In its original form the tune is set in Key F for male voices in three parts, first and second tenor and bass; it was afterwards arranged by the composer for mixed voices in its present form, and published in *Life and Work* for January 1890.

522 HE LIVETH LONG WHO LIVETH WELL

From the second series (1861) of Dr. Bonar's *Hymns of Faith and Hope*. The following three stanzas have been omitted:

> Waste not thy being; back to Him
> Who freely gave it, freely give,
> Else is that being like a dream,
> 'Tis but to *be* and not to *live*.

> Be wise, and use thy wisdom well;
> Who wisdom *speaks*, must *live* it too;
> He is the wisest who can tell
> How first he *lived*, then *spoke*, the true.

> Sow truth, if thou the truth wouldst reap:
> Who sows the false shall reap the vain;
> Erect and sound thy conscience keep,
> From hollow words and deeds refrain.

HOPE, by H. J. Irons, is from *The Hymnal Companion* (1870).

523 CHRISTIAN, SEEK NOT YET REPOSE

From Miss Elliott's *Morning and Evening Hymns for a Week* (1836), privately printed for sale on behalf of a benevolent institution in Brighton. This hymn is appointed for Wednesday, the text being 'Watch and pray, that ye enter not into temptation' (St. Matthew xxvi. 41).

VIGILATE, by Dr. W. H. Monk, was the tune composed for it, in *Hymns Ancient and Modern* (Appendix, 1868).

ST. APOLLOS has been written for it by A. P. Morgan.

524 JESUS, LORD OF LIFE AND GLORY

Mr. Cummins's hymn appeared in *Lyra Evangelica* (1839, 1849). One stanza is omitted.

ST. RAPHAEL, by Dr. E. J. Hopkins, is from *The Congregational Hymn and Tune Book* (1862), where it is called 'St. Giles'. Its present name was given it in the composer's *Temple Church Choral Service* (1867).

AD PERENNIS FONTEM, from *The English Hymnal*, is one of the tunes referred to in the note on Hymn 4.

525 IN THE HOUR OF TRIAL

Written on Oct. 13, 1834, and published in Montgomery's *Original Hymns* (1853). It is based on St. Luke xxii. 32: 'I have prayed for thee, that thy faith fail not.'

DUN ALUINN is from a folk-song melody in $\frac{6}{4}$ time, noted in Co. Clare, Ireland, and adapted by 'The Irish Guild of the Church'.

ST. MARY MAGDALENE, by Dr. Dykes, was the tune composed for this hymn, in *The Congregational Hymn and Tune Book* (1862).

526 A SAFE STRONGHOLD OUR GOD IS STILL

The greatest hymn of the greatest man in the greatest period in German history. Its first appearance was in Klug's *Gesangbuch* (Wittenberg, 1529). Formerly it was believed that Luther had written it either at or immediately before his appearance before the Diet at Worms, April 16, 1521. From this conjecture the step was easy to Heine's picturesque statement that he sang it as he entered the town, ver. 3 being practically the same as the message which he had sent to Spalatin two days before, 'Though there were as many devils in Worms as there are tiles on the roofs, nevertheless I will go there'. Carlyle in his article on 'Luther's Psalm' (*Fraser's Magazine*, 1831), in which this translation appears for the first time, seemingly accepted this tradition, but there is no valid evidence for dating the hymn much, if at all, before its publication. Of thirty-seven hymns which Luther wrote, twenty-one were published in 1524. Had 'Ein' feste Burg' been composed before that date it would most probably have been published in this first collection. If we are to seek for any definite occasion in Luther's life in connexion with which the hymn was written, the most appropriate would be either the time of the persecution which broke out in Southern Germany in 1527 when the Bavarian pastor Leonard Kaiser was burned at the stake, or the Diet of Speyer in 1529 when the Evangelical party, on April 19, made their famous Protest that 'in matters relating to the honour of God and the Salvation of our souls, every man must stand alone before God and give account for himself'.

The hymn is, of course, a paraphrase of the forty-sixth Psalm. Set to its magnificent tune it soon spread over Germany. It was sung by the army of Gustavus Adolphus before the battle of Leipzig, Sept. 17, 1631, and at practically every time of crisis in the nation's history. The first translation of the hymn into English was by Coverdale in 1539 ('Our God is a defence and towre'), and there is another in *Lyra Davidica* (1708, cp. Hymn 114). But the hymn was little known or used in the English-speaking world till the middle of last century. Since then some sixty-five translations have been made, of which Carlyle's (in the article above mentioned) is the best known. There are two or three inaccuracies in it. In ver. 2 Dr. Gaskell's version, as in *The Church Hymnary* (1st edition),

> Of Sabaoth the Lord,
> Sole God to be adored,
> 'Tis He must win the battle,

is nearer to the original. Also ver. 3, line 9, is, more literally and picturesquely, 'One little word shall fell him', and ver. 4 is more closely rendered in *Christian Singers of Germany*:

> Still shall they leave that word its might,
> And yet no thanks shall merit,
> Still is He with us in the fight,
> By His good gifts and spirit.
> E'en should they take our life
> Goods, honour, children, wife,
> Though all of these were gone,
> Yet nothing have they won.
> God's kingdom ours abideth.

Notwithstanding these defects, Carlyle's translation as a whole is easily the best. Of it, even as of the original, his own words hold true: 'There is something in it like the sound of Alpine avalanches or the first murmur of earthquakes: in the very vastness of which dissonance a higher unison is revealed to us.'

In 1897 Dr. Bernhard Pick published a monograph on *Dr. Martin Luther's Hymn of the Reformation*, in which he was able to print no fewer than eighty translations of it into fifty-three languages. He notes how many of the Huguenots 'in the time of their bloody persecutions between 1560 and 1572 died joyfully as martyrs with this hymn upon their lips', and how 'Through Meyerbeer's opera, "The Huguenots", this hymn with its tune has even been introduced on the stage'.

In ver. 3 (line 8) 'for why' means 'because', as in Hymn 228.

The tune EIN' FESTE BURG is first to be found in the 1535 edition of Klug's work. There, as in *Kirchè Gesenge* (Nuremberg, 1531), the melody appears as follows:

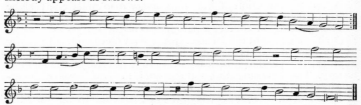

527 GOD IS MY STRONG SALVATION

From Montgomery's *Songs of Zion* (1822): a version of Psalm xxvii.

For the tune CHRISTUS DER IST MEIN LEBEN (BREMEN), see on Hymn 368.

528 I FEEL THE WINDS OF GOD TO-DAY

'The writer of this hymn . . . wrote it in 1907, when long service in certain work was met by seemingly continuous failure. "If then", the writer said, "quitting the labour at the oar, we humbly believe that God's Spirit still leads us aright, we shall pass the point of danger and helplessness. Some little act of kindness may be as the upturned sail which that spirit waits to fill, in spite of past and future." ' (Note in *The Story of our Hymns* [*Fellowship Hymnbook*] by F. J. Gillman.) See further under 'Adams, Jessie'.

Ver. 3 has been added to the original version. 'The end of the hymn as written by the author read—

> Though dim my path and future way,
> Hopeless I cannot drift,

but the Pilot lines, which are so great an improvement, were due to Mr. Gillman in his welcome and accomplished editing.' (Note by the author.)

For the tune PETERSHAM see on Hymn 398.

YATTENDON is from the source mentioned under Hymn 166. The last section of this adaptation is by H. E. Wooldridge, as in *The Yattendon Hymnal* (1899).

529 COURAGE, BROTHER! DO NOT STUMBLE

This hymn appeared in January 1857 in *The Edinburgh Christian Magazine*, of which Dr. Norman Macleod was for some years editor.

YN Y GLYN has been already published in separate form.

NORMAN was set to the hymn in *The Scottish Hymnal* (1885). It had been already set to other hymns in J. F. Dole's *Vierstimmiges Choralbuch* (Leipzig, 1785) and in Werner's *Choralbuch* (1815).

530 THE SON OF GOD GOES FORTH TO WAR

As in Heber's *Hymns* (1827). Written for St. Stephen's Day, to which ver. 2 specially refers.

ST. ANNE is by William Croft (see on Hymn 601). The present arrangement by Sir Arthur Sullivan was written for Brown-Borthwick's *Supplemental Hymn and Tune Book* (third edition, 1869).

OLD 44TH in the Anglo-Genevan Psalter (1556) was set to Psalm xliv, and so remained in the subsequent English and Scottish Psalters.

531 O GOD OF TRUTH, WHOSE LIVING WORD

This, the only hymn Thomas Hughes ever wrote, was given by him to the Hon. Mrs. Norton for insertion in *Lays of the Sanctuary*, published in 1859, three years after *Tom Brown's Schooldays* had appeared. The text, after the first two verses, has been considerably altered. The original runs thus:

3. Ah! would we join that blest array
   And follow in the might
   Of Him the Faithful and the True,
   In raiment clean and white!

4. *We* fight for truth, *we* fight for God,
   Poor slaves of lies and sin!
   He who would fight for Thee on earth
   Must first be true within.

5. Then, God of Truth, for whom we long,
   Thou who wilt hear our prayer,
   Do Thine own battle in our hearts,
   And slay the falsehood there.

6. Still smite! still burn! till naught is left
   But God's own truth and love;
   Then, Lord, as morning dew come down,
   Rest on us from above.

7. Yea, come! Then, tried as in the fire,
   From every lie set free,
   Thy perfect truth shall dwell in us,
   And we shall live in Thee.

BLACKBOURN is anonymous in Ralph Harrison's *Sacred Harmony* (vol. i, 1784), but is believed to have been composed by J. Fish, a Lancashire musician. See Dr. John Brown's *Jeems the Doorkeeper*.

NORTHUMBERLAND, by Henry Smart, comes from *Psalms and Hymns for Divine Worship* (1867).

532 STAND UP! STAND UP FOR JESUS!

Dr. Duffield wrote, 'I caught the inspiration from the dying words of the Rev. Dudley Atkins Tyng, rector of the Epiphany Church, Philadelphia, who died about 1854. His last words were, "Tell them to stand up for Jesus". As he had been much persecuted in those pro-slavery days for his persistent course in pleading the cause of the oppressed, it was thought that these words had a peculiar significance in his mind.' Dr. Duffield preached the funeral sermon from Ephesians vi. 14 to an immense concourse of people and repeated the hymn which he had just composed, as his closing exhortation.

MORNING LIGHT appeared in *The Odeon: A Collection of Secular Melodies, designed for adult singing schools and for social music parties, by G. J. Webb and Lowell Mason* (Boston, 1837). There it is set to a song beginning "Tis dawn, the lark is singing'. Its first appearance as a hymn-tune was in *The Wesleyan Psalmist* (1842).

533 MUCH IN SORROW, OFT IN WOE

The first appearance of this hymn is in Collyer's *Hymns partly collected and partly original* (1812). The first two verses and lines 1 and 2 of verse 3 were written by Kirke White on the back of a mathematical paper, when he was at Cambridge. In the original lines 3 and 4 of ver. 1 ran,

> Fight the fight, and worn with strife
> Steep with tears the bread of life.

The alteration as in the present version was made by Rev. E. Bickersteth, father of Bishop Bickersteth, in his *Christian Psalmody* (1833).

The rest of the hymn was written by Miss Fuller-Maitland, and published in *Hymns for Private Devotion* (1827), edited by the authoress's mother Mrs. Bethia Fuller-Maitland. It is often stated that Miss Fuller-Maitland was only fourteen years of age when she wrote those verses, but she was certainly eighteen when they were published.

UNIVERSITY COLLEGE, by Dr. Gauntlett, appeared in *The Church Hymn and Tune Book, edited by W. J. Blew and H. J. Gauntlett* (1852).

534 SOLDIERS OF CHRIST! ARISE

From Wesley's *Hymns and Sacred Poems* (1749), where it was entitled 'The Whole Armour of God'. The original hymn is in three parts, of four double verses each; verses 1–3 and 6 are from Part I, verse 4 from Part II, and verse 5 from Part III. In verse 6 'complete' replaces 'entire' in the original. One little known verse of the original deserves citation, for the sake of its picturesque vigour:

> But, above all, lay hold
> On faith's victorious shield,
> Armed with that adamant and gold
> Be sure to win the field.
> If faith surround your heart,
> Satan shall be subdued,
> Repelled his every dart,
> And quenched with Jesu's blood.

ST. ETHELWALD, by Dr. W. H. Monk, was composed for this hymn, in *Hymns Ancient and Modern* (1861).

FROM STRENGTH TO STRENGTH, by Dr. E. W. Naylor, was composed for it, and appeared in *The Public School Hymn Book* (1919).

535 ONWARD! CHRISTIAN SOLDIERS

Written in 1864 as a processional hymn for the school children of Horbury Bridge near Wakefield, Yorkshire, where Mr. Baring-Gould was curate in charge of a mission. The occasion of the famous hymn being written was a school-feast where the children had to march with banners flying, from one village to another. It was published in the autumn of the same year in *The Church Times* (October 15) as a 'Hymn for Procession with Cross and Banners'. Originally it was written to be sung to a tune arranged from the slow movement in Haydn's Symphony in D, No. 15, but it derived a great part of its popularity from Sullivan's tune 'St. Gertrude', which has practically superseded all other settings. From time to time Mr. Baring-Gould was persuaded by hymn-book compilers to make sundry irritating verbal alterations and to add special verses, all of which are happily forgotten, the text as it stands being that known throughout the English-speaking world. By this hymn, rather than by his novels or miscellaneous works, the author's memory will be kept fresh.

ST. GERTRUDE, composed for this hymn by Sir Arthur Sullivan, appeared in *The Hymnary* (1872). The tune was written for the above book, but appeared first in *The Musical Times* for December 1871.

536 SAY NOT, 'THE STRUGGLE NOUGHT AVAILETH'

From A. H. Clough's *Poems*, at the end of which it is always put (as 'Crossing the Bar' is in Tennyson's works), but dated 1849. ' Nothing can be more perfect in form or stronger or surer in matter . . . the note of certainty without which the poet, whatever else he may have, can have no message for mankind.' T. H. Ward in *The English Poets* (vol. iii, p. 591).

The tune GRACE DIEU, by S. S. Wesley, is from *The European Psalmist* (1872).

537 MARCH ON, MY SOUL, WITH STRENGTH

See under Mr. Wright's name, in the Biographical Notes. His hymn appeared in *The Y. M. C. A. Hymnal* (n.d.).

CHRISTCHURCH, by Dr. Steggall, is from *Hymns for the Church of England* (1865).

538 BRIGHTLY GLEAMS OUR BANNER

Mr. Potter's hymn first appeared in *The Holy Family Hymns* (1860). It was then drastically revised in order to eliminate Roman elements, with the result that verse 1 and parts of verse 2 were all that remained of the original. This text appeared in *Hymns Ancient and Modern*, where it retains its place. In its turn it was further revised for *Church Hymns* (1871), principally in verse 1, and a new verse, 'Pattern of our childhood', added, incorporating a few words of the original, with the result as seen in the present text.

VEXILLUM, by Henry Smart, was composed for this hymn, in *Hymns Ancient and Modern* (Appendix, 1868).

539 MY GOD AND FATHER, WHILE I STRAY

The hymn first appeared in Miss Elliott's *The Invalid's Hymn-book* (1835); it was reprinted with slight variations, in her *Hours of Sorrow* (1836) and in *Psalms and Hymns* edited by her brother, the Rev. H. V. Elliott, of St. Mary's, Brighton. One verse is omitted.

WIMBLEDON was composed by Dr. Wesley for this hymn, in *A Selection of Psalms and Hymns arranged for the Public Services of the Church of England, edited by the Rev. Charles Kemble and S. S. Wesley* (1864).

540 WHATE'ER MY GOD ORDAINS IS RIGHT

Rodigast's hymn, which appeared in *Das Hannoverische Gesang-buch* (1676), was written in 1675 at Jena for his sick friend Severus Gastorius, precentor there. It was the favourite hymn of King Frederick William III of Prussia, husband of the famous and beloved Queen Louise.

Miss Winkworth's version appeared in *The Chorale-Book for England* (1863). For congregational purposes the compilers have made a slight alteration in ver. 2, where the original text had,

> I know He will not leave me;
> And take, content.

The tune WAS GOTT THUT (BADEN) was composed by Gastorius himself, after his recovery. It appeared in the *Auserlesenes Wein-marisches Gesangbuch* . . . (Weimar, 1681), where, in the following form, it is set to the hymn by S. Rodigast:

541 IF THOU BUT SUFFER GOD TO GUIDE THEE

From Neumark's *Musikalisch-poetischer Lustwald* (1657). But it was composed at Kiel in 1641 with the heading 'A Song of Comfort. God will care for and help every one in His own time. Cast thy burden on the Lord and He shall sustain thee' (Psalm lv. 22). Neumark's chequered life supplies an interesting commentary on the hymn. We read of him as a young student being robbed by highwaymen near Magdeburg, left almost destitute and with no prospect of earning a living. At last he unexpectedly received an appointment as tutor in the family of a judge in Kiel, 'which good fortune', as he says, 'coming suddenly and as if fallen from heaven, greatly rejoiced me, and on that very day I composed to the honour of my beloved Lord the hymn, well known here and there, "Wer nur den lieben Gott lässt walten", and had certainly cause enough to thank the Divine compassion for such unlooked-for grace shown to me.'

In the original there are seven verses of which the three following are between verses 3 and 4:

> He knows the time for joy, and truly
>   Will send it when He sees it meet,
> When he has tried and purged thee throughly,
>   And finds thee free from all deceit,
> He comes to thee all unaware
> And makes thee own His loving care.

> Nor think amid the heat of trial
>   That God hath cast thee off unheard,
> That he whose hopes meet no denial
>   Must surely be of God preferred;
> Time passes, and much change doth bring,
> And sets a bound to everything.

> All are alike before the Highest,
>   'Tis easy to our God, we know,
> To raise thee up though low thou liest,
>   To make the rich man poor and low,
> True wonders still by Him are wrought,
> Who setteth up, and brings to nought.

Miss Winkworth's translation as in *The Chorale-book for England* (1863).

This form of NEUMARK is that adopted by Mendelssohn in the oratorio of *St. Paul*. The air was originally set to the hymn in Neumark's *Fortgepflanzter Musikalisch-poetischer Lustwald* (Jena, 1657).

542 O LET HIM WHOSE SORROW

In Oswald's *Letzte Mittheilungen* (1826), entitled 'An exhortation to Tranquillity to the Suffering, Psalm l. 15'.

Translated in Miss Cox's *Sacred Hymns from the German* (1841). This hymn was sung on Thursday, May 11, 1882, at the funeral, in Edensor Churchyard, Chatsworth, of Lord Frederick Cavendish, Chief Secretary for Ireland, who had been murdered in the Phoenix Park, Dublin, on the previous Saturday.

Miss Cox sanctioned the present form of ver. 4 (line 1), where she had written, 'When in grief you languish'.

WEM IN LEIDENSTAGEN, by F. Filitz, is from the same source as CAPETOWN (282).

543 O LORD, HOW HAPPY SHOULD WE BE

Published posthumously in Mr. Anstice's *Hymns* (1836) and included in Miss C. M. Yonge's *Child's Christian Year* (1841), for the fifteenth Sunday after Trinity, suggested doubtless by the Gospel for the day (St. Matthew vi. 24), and with the text prefixed 'Casting all your care upon Him, for He careth for you' (1 Peter v. 7). One stanza is omitted. 'These hymns were all dictated to Mr. Anstice's wife during the last few weeks of his life, and were composed just at the period of the day (the afternoon) when he most felt the oppression of his illness—all his brighter morning hours being given to pupils up to the very day of his death, Feb. 29, 1836' (Miller, in *Singers and Songs of the Church*, p. 495).

The original was in five stanzas, and read in ver. 3 (line 2) 'fallen nature's' and in ver. 4 (line 2) 'lesson'.

PSALM 6 was composed or arranged by L. Bourgeois for the French Psalter (1542). In the Anglo-Genevan Psalter (1561) it was set to Kethe's version of Psalm lxxxv, and was included in the complete Scottish Psalter (1564). The present adaptation from the last is by J. S. Anderson.

MAGDALEN COLLEGE, by Dr. W. Hayes, is from *Sixteen Psalms set to music for the use of Magdalen College Chapel in Oxford* (1774), where it is set to Merrick's version of Psalm cxxii.

544 LONG DID I TOIL, AND KNEW NO EARTHLY REST

In Lyte's *Poems chiefly Religious* (1833) this appears under the title of 'My Beloved is mine, and I am His'; Lyte adds 'Imitated from Quarles'. The compilers have omitted two stanzas and altered the fourth line of ver. 3 from 'And sweetly on His people's darkness shine' (as had already been done in the author's *Miscellaneous Poems*, 1870).

TABERNACLE, by Edward Arthur, has been already published in separate form.

545 O CHRIST, MY GOD, WHO SEEST THE UNSEEN

From Miss Rossetti's *Songs for Strangers and Pilgrims*, and her *Time Flies: A Reading Diary* (1885), where the verses are dated June 4.

SONG 24, by Orlando Gibbons, was set to a paraphrase of Lam. i. See on Hymn 195.

546 COMMIT THOU ALL THY GRIEFS

547 PUT THOU THY TRUST IN GOD

Paul Gerhardt's great hymn, 'Befiehl du deine Wege', appeared in the Frankfurt edition of J. Crüger's *Praxis Pietatis Melica* (1646), and soon acquired a wide popularity in the Church. Wesley's spirited rendering is in his *Hymns and Sacred Poems* (1739); it has been abbreviated here and divided into two separate hymns. The first stanza of 547 comes from some other hand, however. For a more literal rendering of the German in the metre of the original, see *Life of Principal Cairns*, by A. R. MacEwen, p. 340.

NARENZA is the adaptation of a melody found in *Catholische Kir-*

chen Gesäng (Cologne, 1619), where it is set, in triple time, to the hymn 'Ave Maria klare, du liechter Morgenstern'. In Töpler's *Alte Choral-Melodien* (1832) it appears as follows:

From this the present tune was arranged by the Rev. W. H. Havergal and published in his *Old Church Psalmody* (1847).

SONG 20, by Orlando Gibbons, was set to a metrical version of Isaiah xii (see on Hymn 195).

ICH HALTE TREULICH STILL is believed to be an original melody by Bach, as found in Schemelli's *Musicalisches Gesangbuch* (Leipzig, 1736).

548 FATHER, I KNOW THAT ALL MY LIFE

Like 442 and 445, from Miss Waring's *Hymns and Meditations* (1850), under the text 'My times are in Thy hand' (Psalm xxxi. 15). It was written at Clifton in 1846, four years after Miss Waring had left the Society of Friends and joined the Church of England.

MORWELLHAM, by Dr. Steggall, is from *The Hymnal Companion* (3rd edition, 1890), where it is set to this hymn.

549 LORD, IT BELONGS NOT TO MY CARE

In his *Poetical Fragments* (1681), where it first appeared, this hymn was entitled by Baxter, 'Heart Employment with God and itself: The Concordant Discord of a Broken-hearted Heart.' It was dated 'London, at the Door of Eternity: Richard Baxter, Aug. 7, 1681'. A later edition alters the title to 'The Covenant and Confidence of Faith', with the note, 'This covenant my dear wife in her former sickness subscribed with a cheerful will'. The poem begins, 'My whole though broken heart, O Lord', and in ver. 2 (line 4) Baxter originally wrote, 'That shall have the same pay'.

Of Baxter, George Macdonald remarks (in *England's Antiphon*), 'one of the purest and wisest and devoutest of men—and no mean poet either. His command of metrical form is somewhat remarkable. He has not much melody, but he keeps good time in a variety of measures.' The present hymn was a favourite of two close friends, great men of science and devout Christians, James Clerk Maxwell and Alexander Crum Brown.

ST. HUGH, by Dr. Hopkins, comes from *The Congregational Hymn* and *Tune Book* (1862), where it was set to the hymn, 'There is a fountain filled with blood'.

SIDON, by Dr. Crotch, probably appeared first in Halkett's *National Psalmist* (circa 1841).

550 GREAT GOD! AND WILT THOU CONDESCEND

This hymn, like 655, is from Ann and Jane Taylor's *Hymns for Infant Minds* (1810), and was entitled 'Our Father which art in heaven'.

HERONGATE is an English traditional air arranged by Dr. R. Vaughan Williams from a folk melody sung in Essex to a ballad about a deserted maiden, called 'Died for love'.

HOLLEY appeared in the *Boston Academy Collection*, edited by Lowell Mason (1835).

551 MY TIMES ARE IN THY HAND

From W. Freeman Lloyd's *Hymns for the Poor of the Flock* (1838). For FRANCONIA see under Hymn 190.

In Riley's *Parochial Harmony* (1762), ST. EDMUND is marked as a new tune by Mr. Edmund Gilding. Here it is slightly simplified from the original.

552 JESUS IS OUR SHEPHERD

Canon Stowell's hymn is from *A Selection of Psalms and Hymns Suited to the Services of the Church of England* (12th Edition, 1864). It was written in 1849 for Sunday School Anniversary Services at Christ Church, Salford, of which Canon Stowell was rector. He was the author of a hymn once very popular which began:

> From every stormy wind that blows,
> From every swelling tide of woes,
> There is a calm, a sure retreat;
> 'Tis found beneath the mercy-seat.

GOSHEN is adapted from a song by Miss Davis, entitled 'Childhood's Happy Hours'. It appeared, set to this hymn, in *The Bible Class Magazine* (1860).

553 THY WAY, NOT MINE, O LORD

From Dr. Bonar's *Hymns of Faith and Life* (1857). Two stanzas are omitted.

LEUCHARS was composed by T. L. Hately for the second version of Psalm cxliii. It appeared in *Scottish Psalmody* (1858).

554 SAVIOUR, LIKE A SHEPHERD LEAD US

Published anonymously in Miss D. A. Thrupp's *Hymns for the Young* (1836). Perhaps it was written by H. F. Lyte. The original has 'tenderest' instead of 'tender' in ver. 1 (line 2), 'Keep Thy flock' in ver. 2 (line 3), and 'Hear young children' in ver. 2 (line 6), as well as 'Let us early' in ver. 3 (line 6).

COLLAUDEMUS, a French carol melody, as in *The English Hymnal* (1906). See note on Hymn 4.

555 HOLD THOU MY HANDS!

First published by Mr. Canton in *Good Words* (May, 1893); thereafter in *The Invisible Playmate* (1894). He wrote it to the air of 'Phoebe's Song' in Sullivan's opera, 'The Yeomen of the Guard', as appears from this account by himself. 'When I went to bed late last night, the words "Hold Thou my hands" kept floating about in my mind, and then there grew on me the most perplexing half-recollection of a lovely air. I could not remember it quite, but it simply haunted me. Then somehow these words seemed to grow into it and out of it. . . . Well, it was from "The Yeomen of the Guard".'

The tune MISERERE MEI comes from *Seven Sobs of a Sorrowful Soule for Sinne, &c. by William Hunnis* (1583). The book contains some Poetical Meditations, under the title of 'The Widow's Mite', and a tune is set to these, of which the present is an adaptation, as in *The English Hymnal*.

556 BE STILL, MY SOUL: THE LORD IS ON THY SIDE

Katharina von Schlegel's German hymn, which appeared in six stanzas in the *Neue Sammlung Geistlicher Lieder* (Wernigerode, 1752), was adequately translated in Miss Borthwick's *Hymns from the Land of Luther* (2nd series, 1855). One stanza, the last, is here omitted.

FINLANDIA is extracted from Sibelius's Symphonic Poem entitled *Finlandia*.

ST. HELEN was composed by W. Hately for this hymn, in *The Scottish Hymnal* (1871).

557 HE THAT IS DOWN NEEDS FEAR NO FALL

This is the setting of Bunyan's song. 'Now as they were going along and talking they espied a boy feeding his father's sheep. The boy was in very mean clothes, but of a fresh and well-favoured countenance, and as he sat by himself he sung. Hark, said Mr. Greatheart, to what the Shepherd's boy saith. So they hearkened and he said. . . .' (Here the boy sings this hymn.)

'Then said their Guide, Do you hear him? I will dare to say this boy lives a merrier life, and wears more of that herb called Heartsease in his bosom than he that is clad in silk and velvet' (*The Pilgrim's Progress*).

The tune ST. HUGH, as in *The English Hymnal*, has been arranged by Miss L. E. Broadwood from the air sung to an English ballad on the legend of St. Hugh of Lincoln.

558 WHO FATHOMS THE ETERNAL THOUGHT

From Whittier's poem, *The Eternal Goodness* (1865), twenty-two verses, of which this hymn is verses 4, 11, 15–17, 19–20. The first three verses run:

> O friends with whom my feet have trod
> The quiet aisles of prayer,
> Glad witness to your zeal for God
> And love of man I bear.

> I trace your line of argument,
> Your logic linked and strong,
> I weigh as one who dreads dissent
> And fears a doubt as wrong.

> But still my human hands are weak
> To hold your iron creeds,
> Against the words ye bid me speak
> My heart within me pleads.

John Bright had a great admiration for Whittier and once described *The Eternal Goodness* as a 'poem which is worth a crowd of sermons which are spoken from the pulpits of our sects and churches, which I do not wish to undervalue'.

Broomfield's ST. KILDA was published on single slips, about 1850. For SONG 67 see on Hymn 433.

559 'TWIXT GLEAMS OF JOY AND CLOUDS OF DOUBT

Written by Principal Shairp in 1871, and published in *Glen Desseray and other Poems* (1888).

ST. SYLVESTER is from *Christmas Carols, New and Old* (edited by Bramley and Stainer).

THIRD MODE MELODY is the third of the nine tunes by Tallis in Parker's Psalter. See note on Hymn 250.

560 A SOVEREIGN PROTECTOR I HAVE

Toplady's hymn was published in *The Gospel Magazine* (December, 1774), entitled 'A chamber hymn' and signed 'Minimus'. It was written at Fen Ottery, near Exeter, and is quoted by Toplady in his diary for Jan. 1, 1768. The first verse of his original runs:

> What though my frail eyelids refuse
> Continual watching to keep,
> And, punctual, as midnight renews,
> Demand the refreshment of sleep:
> A Sovereign Protector I have, &c.

The first two lines of ver. 2 in the original run:

> Beneficent Hearer of pray'r,
> Thou Feeder and Guardian of thine.

TREWEN comes from *Gemau Mawl* (edited by D. Jenkins, 1890).

561 YOUR HARPS, YE TREMBLING SAINTS

Toplady's hymn was printed in *The Gospel Magazine* for February 1772, under the title of 'Weak Believers Encouraged'. It was composed at Broad Hembury, near Honiton. Here as elsewhere 'Toplady's note is ever clearest in face of threatened trouble' (T. Wright, *Life of Toplady*, p. 101). Sixteen stanzas in the original, of which the following are memorable:

> The time of Love will come,
> When thou shalt clearly see,
> Not only that He shed His blood,
> But that it flowed for thee.

> Tarry His leisure, then,
> Although He seem to stay;
> A moment's intercourse with Him
> Thy grief will overpay.

BUCER appeared in *Cantica Laudis, edited by Lowell Mason and G. J. Webb* (1850). The tune is said by these editors to be an adaptation from Robert Schumann, but although it was submitted for identification to Madame Schumann and other experts, nothing has been found among Schumann's compositions from which it could have been derived.

562 O GOD OF BETHEL! BY WHOSE HAND

This paraphrase of Genesis xxviii. 20–22 is founded on a hymn by Dr. Philip Doddridge entitled 'Jacob's Vow' (written Jan. 16, 1736), beginning

> O God of Bethel, by whose Hand
> Thine Israel still is fed.

The compilers of the Paraphrases (1745 Edition) took this hymn, altering only, in ver. 4, line 1, 'Shield' to 'Wings'. This version remains unaltered in the 1751 Edition, but in the final (1781) form extensive alterations and improvements were made, due for the most part perhaps to John Logan, who, earlier in the same year, had published the whole hymn (beginning, 'O God of Abraham') as his own composition. Thus 'Israel' was altered to 'people' (ver. 1): verses 2 and 3, and lines 1 and 2 of ver. 4 are by Logan, whilst ver. 5 is wholly by the compilers. It rarely happens that such a strangely composite production should result in a hymn of such great excellence, which holds a place in the affections of all Scotsmen second only to 'The Lord's my Shepherd, I'll not want'.

SALZBURG is an adaptation of J. M. Haydn's air in a movement of a Mass composed 'for the use of country choirs'. The movement is printed in the Rev. C. I. Latrobe's *Selection of Sacred Music*. It is in 6–8 time, beginning thus—

For FRENCH see note on Hymn 227.

563 LEAD US, HEAVENLY FATHER, LEAD US

From Mr. Edmeston's *Sacred Lyrics* (1823), where it is headed, 'Hymn written for the Children of the London Orphan Asylum.'

CORINTH comes from (see on Hymn 55) *An Essay on the Church Plain Chant* (1782). It occurs in the second part of the work, entitled 'Part Second, containing several Anthems, Litanies, Proses, and Hymns, as they are sung in the Public Chapels at London'. There it is headed 'The Hymn at Benediction', the words being 'Tantum ergo sacramentum', &c. To this, as to nearly all the music in the volume, no composer's name is attached, but many of the pieces are certainly by Samuel Webbe, and it is highly probable that he was the editor of the work. In his Mass in A, printed in *A Collection of Modern Church Music* (1791), and again in *A Collection of Masses . . . for the use of Small Choirs* (1792), this setting of the 'Tantum ergo' forms the closing number; and it is again included in *A Collection of Motetts or Antiphons . . . By S. Webbe* (1792). In the last volume many of the pieces are distinguished by having the name 'Webbe' printed at the close, the inference being that those not so marked are not his composition. As the present is one of those *without* his name, it remains a doubtful point, whether it is an original composition by Webbe, or a melody of older date arranged by him.

564 GUIDE ME, O THOU GREAT JEHOVAH

Written in Welsh and published by Williams in his first book of hymns, *Alleluia* (1745). The first verse in the English translation, possibly by Peter Williams of Caermarthen, the commentator, was published in *Hymns on Various Subjects* (1771). Verses 2 and 3 were translated either by William Williams himself, or by his son the Rev. John Williams, afterwards the first Principal of Trevecca College. The hymn was published as a leaflet in 1772 with the title, 'A favourite hymn sung by Lady Huntingdon's Young Collegians. Printed by the desire of many Christian friends. Lord, give it Thy blessing!' The 'Collegians' referred to were those of Trevecca.

Originally ver. 1 (line 6) was, 'Feed me till I want no more,' and ver. 3 (line 3), 'Death of deaths, and hell's destruction'. The latter echoes Hosea xiii. 14. One stanza, at the end, is omitted; there are five in the Welsh original.

MANNHEIM is from the source mentioned in the note on Hymn 282. The present form of the melody appeared in *Congregational Church*

Music (1853), and is much altered from the original, which is as under:

CAERSALEM, by R. Edwards, appeared in Parry's *Peroriaeth Hyfryd* (1873).

565 FATHER, LEAD ME DAY BY DAY

Published by Mr. Hopps in *Hymns, Chants, and Anthems for Public Worship* (1877).

The following lines, between verses 4 and 5, are omitted:

> When my work seems hard and dry,
>   May I press on cheerily:
> Help me patiently to bear
>   Pain and hardship, toil and care.
>
> May I see the good and bright,
>   When they pass before my sight:
> May I hear the heavenly voice,
>   When the pure and wise rejoice.

LYNE, in *Hymns, &c., used at the Magdalen Chapel* (*c.* 1760), was originally set to the hymn, 'Let us with a gladsome mind.'

566 LEAD US, O FATHER, IN THE PATHS OF PEACE

Mr. Burleigh's hymn is from C. D. Cleveland's *Lyra Sacra Americana* (1868), where, however, ver. 3 (line 3) reads 'shadows of a moral night'.

LONGWOOD was composed by Sir Joseph Barnby for the hymn, 'Saviour, again to Thy dear name we raise,' in *The Hymnary* (1872).

567 JESUS, STILL LEAD ON

A cento made by Christian Gregor in 1778 from two hymns by Zinzendorf, the first beginning 'Seelen-bräutigam, O du Gottes-lamm', composed in 1778 at Utrecht, the second beginning

Glanz der Ewigkeit, Gott und Herr der Zeit,

composed in May 1721 at Berlin. Verses 1 and 4 are from the former, verses 2 and 3 from the latter. Zinzendorf's hymns are both in the first person singular, but Gregor altered this throughout to adapt them for general use. The translation by Miss Borthwick appeared first in *The Free Church Magazine* (1846) and was repeated in her *Hymns from the Land of Luther* (1854). Zinzendorf's hymns have the defects of Moravian piety; they are 'often disfigured by excess in the application of the language and imagery of human affection to Divine Objects. . . . But one hymn, at least, of Zinzendorf's may be mentioned with unqualified praise, as uniting the merits of force, simplicity, and brevity—*Jesu geh' voran*' (Lord Selborne).

The tune SEELENBRÄUTIGAM, from the Darmstadt *Geistreiches Gesangbuch* (1698), is so called because it was there set to Drese's hymn, 'Seelenbräutigam, Jesu Gottes Lamm.' Zahn holds that Drese composed the tune as well. The melody is altered in later German books, and both melody and rhythm vary in English books. The present form of the air is almost exactly that of the original.

568 LEAD, KINDLY LIGHT

These verses are marked by Newman as having been composed 'at sea, June 16, 1833'. They were published in *The British Magazine* (February, 1834), then in *Lyra Apostolica* (1836). In the early summer of 1833 Newman was on a voyage home, from Sicily to Marseilles. He had left Rome with the presentiment which is expressed in his words to Wiseman, 'We have work to do in England.' This presentiment was deepened, when he fell ill of a fever in Sicily. 'My servant thought I was dying, and begged for my last directions. I gave them as he wished, but I said, "I shall not die". I repeated "I shall not die, for I have not sinned against light". . . . I was aching to get home; yet for want of a vessel, I was kept at Palermo for three weeks. . . . At last I got off in an orange-boat bound for Marseilles.' In the first (1864) edition of the *Apologia* he continues, 'We were becalmed a whole week in the Straits of Bonifacio. Then it was that I wrote the lines, "Lead, kindly Light", which have since become well known.' But in the later editions, from 1873 onwards, the passage runs, 'Then it was that I wrote the lines, "Lead, kindly Light," which have since become well known. We were becalmed a whole week in the straits of Bonifacio.' This seems to hint that the verses may have been composed before the vessel reached the straits of Bonifacio.

The lines are an outburst of tense, personal emotion. As Newman himself said, they are 'not a hymn, nor are they suitable for singing; and it is that which at once surprises and gratifies me, and makes me thankful that, in spite of their having no claim to be a hymn, they have made their way into so many collections'. Froude, in his *Short Studies* (vol. iv, p. 127), declares that this is 'the most popular hymn in the language. All of us, Catholic, Protestant, or such as can see their way to no positive creed at all, can here meet on common ground and join in a common prayer.'

The meaning of the two last lines has been much discussed. In 1879, Newman told a correspondent that he was 'not bound to remember his own meaning'. Most people probably take the 'angel faces' to mean faces of departed friends, but in an article contributed to *The Catholic World* (New York, January, 1913) the Rev. James Mearns, after a close study of Newman's writings at this period, concludes that he must have been thinking of guardian angels who would smile on him again after he had played the man in the coming struggle. Mr. Mearns also argues that 'kindly Light' originally meant the Inward Light of conscience, 'kindly' being used in the Elizabethan sense of 'implanted, innate'. These interpretations, even if correct, do not affect the power of the hymn to encourage and comfort Christians who put their own interpretation on this masterpiece of religious poetry.

BONIFACIO was composed by Dr. Evans for the hymn.

PATMOS, by Dr. S. S. Wesley, appeared in *The European Psalmist* (1872).

LUX BENIGNA was specially written by Dr. Dykes for the hymn, and appeared in *Psalms and Hymns for the Church, School, and Home, edited by the Rev. D. T. Barry, B.A. With accompanying Tunes from the Parish Tune Book* (1867). Here it is called 'St. Oswald'. It is set in the key of G, and contains slight differences in the harmony as compared with the present arrangement, which appeared in *Hymns Ancient and Modern, Appendix* (1868). It was doubtless revised by the composer of that work.

In the *Life* of the composer it is stated that 'Dr. Dykes's friends remember his telling them that the tune to "Lead, kindly Light" came into his head while walking through the Strand in London'. The Rev. George Huntington relates the following incident: 'I had been paying Cardinal Newman a visit. . . . I happened to mention his well-known hymn "Lead, kindly Light". . . . I ventured to say, "It must be a great pleasure to you to know that you have written a hymn treasured wherever English-speaking Christians are to be found; and where are they not to be found?" He was silent for some moments, and then said with emotion, "Yes, deeply thankful, and more than thankful"; then, after another pause, "But you see it is not the hymn, but the tune, that has gained the popularity! The tune is Dykes's, and Dr. Dykes was a great master." '

SANDON appeared in *The Church and Home Metrical Psalter and Hymnal* (1860), which Mr. Purday himself edited. He wrote the tune for these words.

569 LEAD, HOLY SHEPHERD, LEAD US

One of the earliest known Christian hymns, appended to a treatise By Clement, called *The Tutor*, with the title 'Hymn of the Saviour

Christ'. It is a succession of epithets of Christ, and Mrs. Charles, whose translation may be read in her *Christian Life in Song* (p. 54), says of it: 'It is a catalogue of Scriptural figures, rather than an outburst of glowing adoration. . . . Through all the images here so quaintly interwoven—like a stained window, of which the eye loses the design in the complication of colours—we may surely trace, as in quaint old letters on a scroll winding through all the mosaic of tints, "Christ all in all".'

The original begins, in Dr. W. L. Alexander's version:

> Bridle of colts untamed, Over our will presiding,
> Wing of unwandering birds Our flight securely guiding,
> Rudder of youth unbending, Firm against adverse shock,
> Shepherd with wisdom tending Lambs of the royal flock.

The present hymn is rather a paraphrase than a translation. It was written by Dr. MacGill for *The Presbyterian Hymnal* (1876), of the United Presbyterian Church, of which he was Foreign Mission Secretary.

MAMRE comes from the *Hauschoralbuch* (Gütersloh, 1844).

570 O LORD, I SING THY PRAISES

From Mr. Macbean's *Songs and Hymns of the Gael* (1900), like Hymn 53. He gives this account of it: 'The Gaelic-speaking people of the Highlands of Scotland long considered that the Old Testament psalms were the only compositions worthy of a place in public worship, although excellent hymns may be found among the Latin and the Gaelic verses of Columba and other bards. In more modern times Dugald Buchanan of Rannoch, and Peter Grant of Strathspey, composed sacred songs that glow with the devotional poetic genius of the Gael; Grant spent a long life of happy service among his own clan: he was a voluminous writer of sweet verses, and the stanzas here printed are from a much longer composition, which he named simply "A Hymn of Praise".

'The tune KILLIN is in the rousing Dorian mode, following in this a strong tendency observed in Highland folk-songs.'

571 THE GOD OF ABRAHAM PRAISE

Written probably in 1770, immediately after Olivers had heard Leoni (Meyer Lyon), a chorister in the Great Synagogue, Duke's Place, London, sing the *Yigdal* or Hebrew confession of Faith at the Evening Service there. Olivers showed the hymn to a friend, saying, 'Look at this—I have rendered it from the Hebrew, giving it as far as I could a Christian character, and I have called on Leoni the Jew who has given me a Synagogue Melody to suit it. Here is the tune, and it is to be called LEONI.' The original hymn is in three parts of four verses each, of which the present hymn represents verses 1, 2, 4, 7, and 12. It was published first as a tract with the title 'A

Hymn to the God of Abraham'. This passed through eight editions and then appeared in Wesley's *Pocket Hymnbook for the use of Christians of all Denominations* (1785).

When Henry Martyn was waiting for the ship that was to take him to the East, on July 29, 1805, he wrote in his Diary, 'I was much engaged at intervals in learning the hymn, "The God of Abraham praise": as often as I could use the language of it with any truth, my mind was a little at ease. There was something peculiarly solemn and affecting to me in this hymn and particularly at this time. The truth of the sentiments I knew well enough. But, alas, I felt that the state of mind expressed in it was above mine at the time, and I felt loath to forsake all on earth.' Martyn was distressed over his separation from Miss Lydia Grenfell.

Few hymns are so biblical as this. In the original almost every line is furnished with a reference to some chapter and verse of Scripture. Thus, in ver. 3, line 1 = Gen. xxii. 16, 17: Heb. vi. 13, line 2 = Rom. iv. 20, 21, lines 3 and 4 = Exodus xix. 4, line 5 = John xvii. 24, line 6 = Exod. xv. 2, and lines 7–8 = Psalm cxlv. 1, cxlvi. 2.

572 FAR OFF I SEE THE GOAL

Written by Mr. Roberts for the present collection. It appeared first in a small booklet, 'Programme of United Service of Praise, June 29, 1925, held in connexion with the meetings of the Presbyterian Alliance, Cardiff.' The hymn was written at the request of the Rev. S. O. Morgan, for the famous Welsh tune MOAB, which is found in *Llyfr Tonau Cynulleidfaol* (*Ychwanegiad*, 1870), and is declared by Sir Henry Hadow to be one of the greatest tunes in the world.

573 WHEN FROM EGYPT'S HOUSE OF BONDAGE

From *Sunshine and Shadow* (1873), a collection of Miss Threlfall's poems. But she wrote 'to Thee', not 'with Thee', in verse 3 (line 6).

WILDERSMOUTH was contributed by Dr. Hopkins to *The Temple Church Choral Service* (Supplement, 1877).

574 CHILDREN OF THE HEAVENLY KING

From Cennick's *Sacred Hymns for the Children of God in the Days of their Pilgrimage* (1742), under the title of 'Encouragement to Praise'. Five out of the original twelve stanzas.

DA CHRISTUS GEBOREN WAR is probably an old melody arranged by Doles. It occurs in his *Vierstimmiges Choralbuch* (Leipzig, 1785).

INNOCENTS is called an 'Ancient Litany' in *The Parish Choir* (vol. iii, no. 59, November 1850), where it appears for the first time. In a manuscript collection of tunes by Mr. Joseph Smith of Halesowen, Birmingham, there is one bearing a somewhat close resemblance to 'Innocents', but it has not been clearly proved that this is the original of the tune.

575 THE WORLD LOOKS VERY BEAUTIFUL

Probably composed about 1860; Miss Warner originally wrote 'and lay' in verse 3 (line 4).

PORTHKERRY was written for this hymn, and for the present collection.

576 WHO WOULD TRUE VALOUR SEE

Bunyan's song, like Hymn 557, is from *The Pilgrim's Progress* (Part II). The passage in which it occurs is as follows:

'Greatheart; *And did none of these things discourage you?*

Valiant-for-Truth; No. They seemed but as so many Nothings to me.

Great. *How came that about?*

Val. Why, I still believed what Mr. *Tell-true* had said, and that carried me beyond them all.

Great. *Then, this was your victory, even your Faith.*

Val. It was so, I believed and therefore came out, got into the Way, fought all that set themselves against me, and by believing am come to this Place.

> *Who would true Valour see,*
> *Let him come hither',* &c.

In his sketch of Bunyan, contributed to the 'English Men of Letters' series, Froude observes: 'Though the Globe Theatre was in the opinion of Nonconformists "the heart of Satan's empire", Bunyan must yet have known something of Shakespeare. In the second part of the *Pilgrim's Progress*, we find:

> Who would true valour see,
> Let him come hither:
> One here will constant be,
> Come wind, come weather.

The resemblance to the Song in *As You Like It* is too near to be accidental:

> Who doth ambition shun,
> And loves to live i' the sun,
> Seeking the food he eats
> And pleased with what he gets,
> Come hither, come hither, come hither:
> Here shall he see
> No enemy
> But Winter and rough weather.'

A garbled version of Valiant-for-Truth's Song, presumably by the Editorial Committee of the book, beginning:

> He who would valiant be
> 'Gainst all disaster,
> Let him in constancy
> Follow the Master, &c.,

appeared in the *English Hymnal* (1906), and, owing largely to the tune set to it by Dr. Vaughan Williams, has gained a considerable amount of popularity. The compilers of *The Church Hymnary* have felt that, notwithstanding its ruggedness and occasional quaintness of expression, Bunyan's original is so infinitely superior to any modern version, that it deserves to be sung exactly as it was written.

MONKSGATE is arranged, as in *The English Hymnal*, by Dr. R. Vaughan Williams from the melody of a Sussex folk-song.

LEITHEAD was written by Mr. Pritchard for the words in the present collection.

577 O HAPPY BAND OF PILGRIMS

From Dr. Neale's *Hymns of the Eastern Church* (1862). This, like Hymn 391, 'Art thou weary,' is not, strictly speaking, a translation from any single Greek hymn, but rather suggested by the Canon on SS. Chrysanthus and Daria (March 19). It was accordingly, by Dr. Neale's wish, put in an appendix to the rest of the book. The original title is 'The Pilgrims of Jesus'.

KNECHT is marked as a new tune in Christmann and Knecht's *Vollständige Sammlung . . . Choralmelodien* (Stuttgart, 1799).

578 WHITHER, PILGRIMS, ARE YOU GOING?

Appeared anonymously in *The Golden Chain* (1861). It is ascribed (in Julian's *Dictionary*, 1497) to Mrs. van Alstyne, but Mr. Hubert P. Main says that she did not write hymns till 1864. After that date, the number of them is to be reckoned literally by thousands, written under a baffling succession of *noms de plume*, which makes the tracing of her hymns a matter of great difficulty.

PILGRIM BAND was composed by Sir John Stainer for this hymn, in the first edition of *The Church Hymnary*.

579 'FORWARD!' BE OUR WATCHWORD

Written by Dean Alford at the request of the Rev. J. G. Wood, the eminent naturalist, as a Processional Hymn for the Tenth Festival (June 6, 1871) of the Canterbury Diocesan Choral Union, of which Mr. Wood was Precentor. The text upon which the hymn was written was Exodus xiv. 15: 'Speak unto the Children of Israel that they go forward,' the idea of which is very skilfully developed in the eight verses of the original. Dean Alford was at first averse to the idea of there being any procession at all, but, says Mr. Wood's son and biographer: 'By dint of much perseverance my father carried his point, and then incontinently followed up his victory by suggesting that the Dean himself should write a processional hymn for the occasion and compose the music also! The Dean, at first, was a little overcome by the audacity of the proposal, but finally consented; and shortly afterwards my father received a very admirable hymn with the Dean's compliments. This, however, good as it was, was by no means the kind of hymn which he wanted; and so he wrote off again to the Dean, pointing out that the hymn, while excellent in its way, was not at all adapted to be sung upon the march. Would he kindly go into his Cathedral, walk slowly along the course which the procession would take, and compose another hymn as he did so? The good old Dean was not in the least offended by the unhesitating rejection of his work, and did as he was bid; and the result was the grand hymn beginning "Forward be our watchword." . . . The manuscript reached my father with a humorous little note to the effect that the Dean had written the hymn and put it into its hat and boots; and that my father might add the coat and trousers for himself. On looking at the music, he found, accordingly, that only the treble and bass had been supplied by the composer: and fearing to employ his own imperfect knowledge of harmony in the attempt to supply the omission, he put the matter into the hands of Mrs. J. Worthington Bliss (Miss Lindsay), who kindly added what was necessary' (*Life of Rev. J. G. Wood*, pp. 47, 48). Dean Alford's tune may be found in the first edition of *Church Praise*, but is now superseded by SMART, which was composed by Henry Smart for the hymn in *The Hymnary* (1872).

580 HARK, HARK, MY SOUL! ANGELIC SONGS ARE SWELLING

In Faber's *Oratory Hymns* (1854), entitled 'The Pilgrims of the Night'. The original of ver. 4, line 3, was, 'All journeys end in welcomes to the weary', and of ver. 5, lines 3 and 4,

> While we toil on and soothe ourselves with weeping,
> Till life's long night shall break in endless love.

Of this hymn, Canon Ellerton said: 'We inquire in vain into the meaning of the "Pilgrims of the Night": congregations are carried away by the rhythm and the musical ring of the lines.'

PILGRIMS was the tune Henry Smart composed for it, in *Hymns Ancient and Modern* (Appendix, 1868).

581 THE SANDS OF TIME ARE SINKING

First published by Mrs. Cousins in *The Christian Treasury* (December 1857), and afterwards issued separately as 'Last Words of Samuel Rutherford', in nineteen stanzas of which the present hymn is verses 1, 5, 14, 12, and 10. Two of the other stanzas have become famous, referring to Rutherford's former parish of Anwoth:

> Fair Anwoth by the Solway,
> To me thou still art dear,
> E'en on the verge of heaven
> I drop for thee a tear.

Oh! if one soul from Anwoth
  Meet me at God's right hand,
My heaven will be two heavens
  In Immanuel's land!

The little birds of Anwoth,
  I used to count them blest,
Now, beside happier altars
  I go to build my nest:
O'er these there broods no silence,
  No graves around them stand,
For glory, deathless, dwelleth
  In Immanuel's land.

The whole poem is a beautiful and skilfully constructed mosaic of passages from Rutherford's *Letters and Dying Sayings.* The daughter of the gifted authoress tells how her mother fitted the pattern of her verses line by line as she sat at her sewing in the manse of Irvine, where her husband was at that time minister of the Free Church. It was the last hymn given out by Mr. Spurgeon, at the short service in his rooms at Mentone, on Jan. 17, 1892, the service which proved to be his last.

The tune, now called RUTHERFORD, by Chrétien Urhan, comes from *Chants Chrétiens* (Paris, 1834), where it is set to the hymn 'Éternel, O mon Dieu, j'implore ta clémence', as follows:

The present arrangement appears in *Psalms and Hymns for Divine Worship* (1867), and was made for that work by Dr. E. F. Rimbault.

582 WHEN THIS PASSING WORLD IS DONE

From nine stanzas contributed by McCheyne to *The Scottish Christian Herald* (May 20, 1837). One of the omitted stanzas is:

Oft I walk beneath the cloud,
Dark as midnight's gloomy shroud;
But when fear is at its height,
Jesus comes, and all is light.

Blessèd Jesus! bid me show
Doubting saints how much I owe.

The hymn was headed, 'I am debtor.'

Sir Arthur Sullivan's tune MOUNT ZION was set to 'Rock of Ages', when it first appeared in *Psalms and Hymns for Divine Worship* (1867).

583 FOR EVER WITH THE LORD

From Montgomery's *A Poet's Portfolio* (1835), in two parts of nine and thirteen four-lined stanzas, with the heading, 'At home in heaven. 1st Thessalonians iv. 17.' The process of abbreviating it for purposes of worship was begun by Montgomery himself. Some of the verses omitted are of high poetic quality, e.g.

> In darkness as in light,
> Hidden alike from view,
> I sleep, I wake within His sight
> Who looks existence through.

> Yet clouds will intervene,
> And all my prospect flies;
> Like Noah's dove I flit between
> Rough seas and stormy skies.

> Anon the clouds depart,
> The winds and waters cease;
> While sweetly o'er my gladdened heart
> Expands the bow of peace.

MONTGOMERY was composed for this hymn, in *The Choral Advocate* (1852).

OLD 25TH is set in the Anglo-Genevan Psalter (1558) to Psalm xxv, and is invariably linked to that psalm throughout the later psalters.

584 WHEN THE DAY OF TOIL IS DONE

Written by Canon Ellerton on Jan. 25, 1870, and published the same year in the Rev. R. Brown-Borthwick's *Sixteen Hymns with Tunes*, and in *Church Hymns* (1871). It was first used as a funeral hymn, and (like 332) was sung at the author's own funeral at Torquay, June 20, 1893.

IRENE was composed by C. C. Scholefield for the hymn, in *Church Hymns with Tunes* (1874).

585 DAYS AND MOMENTS QUICKLY FLYING

The first two stanzas, as in Caswall's *Masque of Mary* (1858) and *Hymns and Poems*, except that he wrote, in ver. 1,

> Soon will you and I be lying
> Each within our narrow bed.

They are the first and third verses of a poem in four stanzas, called 'The Swiftness of Time'. Verses 3–6 are as in *Church Hymns* (1871). The hymn has many forms in hymn-books.

ST. SYLVESTER was composed for the hymn by Dr. Dykes, in *The Congregational Hymn and Tune Book* (1862).

586 SOONER OR LATER, YET AT LAST

From Miss Rossetti's *Called to be Saints* (1881, p. 295), a selection made from the original nineteen stanzas.

ULTIMA was composed by Dr. Moffatt for this hymn.

OLD 18TH was the tune set to Psalm xviii in Sternhold's version in the English Psalter of 1561 and subsequent editions.

587 THERE IS A HAPPY LAND

Mr. Young's hymn appeared in Bateman and Gall's *Sacred Song Book* (1843), which was for many years in successive editions *the* hymn-book for Sunday-School use in Scotland. 'Many years ago', writes Mr. Young in the Preface to his *Poems*, 'I was spending an evening with a family of friends, and the lady of the house played several musical compositions of great beauty. Among these was a sweet and tender air which charmed me exceedingly. On asking the name of it, I was told it was an Indian air called "Happy Land". It immediately occurred to me that such a melody could not fail to be popular in Sunday Schools if wedded to appropriate words. And accordingly I wrote the little hymn which . . . was sung daily in my classes in Niddry Street School (Edinburgh); and on a later visit by Mr. James Gall he was so delighted with the music and hymn that he noted down the simple air, had it harmonized, set to the words, and published in his "Sacred Songs".'

The melody of the tune HAPPY LAND is found in a book edited by R. A. Smith (about the year 1827), *Select Melodies with appropriate Words*. The song to which it is there set is called 'The Dancing Girl', and it begins, 'I have come from a happy land where care is unknown.'

588 SUNSET AND EVENING STAR

First published in Tennyson's *Demeter and other Poems*. His son writes: ' "Crossing the Bar" was written in my father's eighty-first year, on a day in October (1889) when we came from Aldworth to Farringford. Before reaching Farringford he had the moaning of the bar in his mind, and after dinner he showed me this poem written out. I said: "That is the crown of your life's work". He answered: "It came in a moment". He explained the "Pilot" as "That Divine and Unseen Who is always guiding us". . . . A few days before my father's death (1892), he said to me, "Mind, you put *Crossing the Bar* at the end of all editions of my poems".'

'Crossing the Bar', to Sir Frederick Bridge's music, was sung at Tennyson's funeral in Westminster Abbey.

Sir Joseph Barnby's tune CROSSING THE BAR was composed for the words, in *The Home and School Hymnal* (1892).

589 WHEN ON MY DAY OF LIFE THE NIGHT IS FALL-ING

Written in 1882 in Whittier's seventy-sixth year, and published in *The Bay of Seven Islands* (1883).

'On his last Sunday before leaving' Edinburgh, on his voyage to Australia, October 1906—'a day of peculiar sacredness in which the family had been present at a special celebration of the Communion in Roseburn Church, of which Dr. Rainy was an elder —when in the evening some hymns were being sung, he asked his eldest daughter to sing Whittier's hymn beginning, "When on my day of life the night is falling". . . . When his daughter had sung this hymn, he requested it to be sung to him again' (*Life of Principal Rainy*, by Dr. Carnegie Simpson, vol. ii, p. 498).

GIFFORD was composed by Mr. Pritchard for this hymn.

590 THERE IS NO NIGHT IN HEAVEN

Mr. Knollis's hymn is from *Lays of the Sanctuary* (1859), where it was entitled 'The One Family: Thoughts for the Feast of St. Michael and All Angels' (September 29). Ver. 5 was added by Canon Ellerton.

ST. OLAVE (ST. GEORGE) comes from *The Church Hymn and Tune Book* (1852), edited by W. J. Blew and Dr. Gauntlett himself.

591 EVERY MORNING THE RED SUN

First published in Mrs. Alexander's *Hymns for Little Children* (1848); it was written to illustrate 'and the life everlasting' in the Apostles' Creed (Hymn 724).

ETERNITY, by Miss L. J. Hutton, is a tune from *Twenty Hymns for Children* (1880).

592 THERE IS A LAND OF PURE DELIGHT

From Watts's *Hymns and Spiritual Songs* (1707 and 1709) with the heading, 'A prospect of Heaven makes death easy'. Probably written during a visit to Southampton in the summer of 1706. 'According to tradition it came upon him one summer day while he was gazing across the gulf-river, Southampton Water; and the pleasant meadows near Netley are said to have suggested the "sweet fields beyond the swelling flood" ' (T. Wright, *Life of Isaac Watts*, p. 70). It is only three-quarters of a mile across to the New Forest by the ferry, and the *swelling flood* answers to the river.

It is a sad curiosity of Dr. B. H. Kennedy's *Hymnologia Christiana* (1863) that that excellent classical scholar actually omitted this hymn because 'although the two first stanzas are good, and the two next not bad, the fifth and sixth, in which lie the pith of the subject, are so poorly and so incorrectly worded, that they effectually spoil the entire hymn'!

MENDIP, from *The English Hymnal*, is arranged by Cecil J. Sharp from the air of an old ballad called 'The Miller's Apprentice, or, The Oxford Tragedy', familiar in Somerset and elsewhere.

BEATITUDO, by Dr. Dykes, was composed for 'How bright these glorious spirits shine', in *Hymns Ancient and Modern* (1875).

593 THERE'S A FRIEND FOR LITTLE CHILDREN

Written by Mr. Midlane on Feb. 27, 1859, and published in *Good News for the Little Ones* (December 1859) under the heading 'Above the Bright Blue Sky'.

In ver. 3 (lines 7 and 8) the original had,

> On all who've found His favour
> And loved His name below.

Dr. Joseph Parker on meeting the author said to him 'I would rather have written that hymn than have preached the most eloquent sermon, for your audience is the whole world' (Note in the Canadian *Book of Common Praise*).

Sir John Stainer wrote IN MEMORIAM for this hymn in the following circumstances: The committee engaged on the music of *Hymns Ancient and Modern* (1875) were meeting at the Langham Hotel, London, and when this hymn came up for consideration it was found that though they had several tunes before them, none was considered satisfactory. It was suggested that a new tune might be written by one of the committee, and Sir Henry Baker proposed that Sir John Stainer should retire to his (Sir Henry's) bedroom, and try what he could do. Sir John complied with the suggestion, and in a very short time returned with the present tune, which was at once adopted.

594 THERE IS A BLESSED HOME

Written by Sir H. W. Baker for *Hymns Ancient and Modern* (1861).

ANNUE CHRISTE comes from *Nouvelle Méthode du Plain-Chant* by La Feillée (edition of F. D. Aynes, Lyons, 1808).

595 JERUSALEM, MY HAPPY HOME

This is a selection from a hymn of twenty-six verses (given in full in the *English Hymnal*) from a MS. probably of the late sixteenth or early seventeenth century preserved in the British Museum with the title: 'A Song made by F. B. P. To the tune of Diana.' There is no certainty as to who F. B. P. was. One conjecture is that the letters stand for 'Francis Baker, Presbyter,' supposed to be a secular priest imprisoned in the Tower of London. In recent Roman Catholic hymn-books, e.g., *The Westminster Hymnal*, it is positively stated that the hymn is by Father Laurence Anderton, *alias* John Brerely, S.J., a priest of the time of Charles I; but this is quite uncertain. (For the tune 'Diana', see an interesting note in *The Musical Times*, March 1922, p. 201, by Sir R. R. Terry, with a conjectural restoration of the melody from the bass part which has been recently discovered.) In all probability the hymn is of Roman Catholic origin, and is in substance a fairly close rendering of a long passage in a book of meditations by St. Augustine, much read and frequently translated in the sixteenth century.

A hymn beginning

> O mother dear, Jerusalem,
> When shall I come to thee?

became very popular in Scotland in the seventeenth century. It has many close resemblances to F. B. P.'s hymn, and Dr. Neale characteristically says: 'It (F. B. P.'s hymn) was most impudently appropriated to himself and mixed up with a quantity of his own rubbish by one Dickson, a Covenanter' (Dr. Neale should have remembered his own travesty of *The Pilgrim's Progress*: see Brown's *Life of Bunyan*, p. 476). David Dickson's (1583–1662) hymn, however, which is given in full in Dr. Bonar's *The New Jerusalem*, is above carping criticism, and is in all probability derived from another translation of St. Augustine by Dr. W. Prid, entitled *The Glasse of Vaine Glorie* (1585), to which verses from F. B. P. have been added. A still later and shorter form is that in the *Eckington Collection* (1795). This is the well-known hymn beginning

> Jerusalem my happy home,
> Name ever dear to me!
> When shall my labours have an end
> In joy and peace and thee?

This has often been attributed to James Montgomery, but is almost certainly the work of Joseph Bromehead, the editor of the collection. Of Dickson's version—and the words are even more descriptive of F. B. P.'s poem—Dr. Bonar says: 'It offers us neither polish nor ornament . . . but the ploughman at his plough, the weaver at his loom, the traveller on his journey, the school-boy loitering along, the children round the hearth, the hunted martyr in his hiding-place, have all chanted the rude old melody, and found utterance through it to the home-sick longing of their souls' (Preface to *The New Jerusalem*, p. xxxviii).

THIS ENDRIS NYGHT comes from a manuscript of the fifteenth century, where it is set to the old English carol beginning, 'Thys endris nyght I saw a syght'.

596 FROM HEAVENLY JERUSALEM'S TOWERS

By David Charles. 'It is now difficult to ascertain the circumstances of the composition of this powerful hymn as we have it in the vernacular, unless it be the shadow of the author's last years, when his bodily frame was struck down by paralysis but his intellect was unimpaired. His soul rebelled at the enforced inactivity placed upon him, and the hymn in a measure sings of a more promising day when his frailties would be explained to him' (Note by Mr. Abraham Morris).

CRUGYBAR is from *Moliant Seion* (1883).

597 BRIEF LIFE IS HERE OUR PORTION
598 FOR THEE, O DEAR, DEAR COUNTRY
599 JERUSALEM THE GOLDEN

These are selections from a long poem of almost three thousand lines, entitled 'De Contemptu Mundi'. The greater part of this consists of a savage satire on the wickedness of the times (the middle of the twelfth century), of which, as Bernard, a Cluny monk, saw it, there was little good to be said. Of England then, during the reign of King Stephen, the Anglo-Saxon Chronicler writes: 'Never was there more misery and never acted heathens worse. . . . The earth bare no corn, you might as well have tilled the sea, for the land was all ruined by such deeds, and it was said openly that Christ and His Saints slept.'

'As a contrast to the misery and pollution of earth the poem opens with a description of the peace and glory of heaven of such rare beauty as not easily to be matched by any medieval composition on the same subject' (J. M. Neale). Of the poem as a whole Dr. S. M. Jackson says, ' It is not a rhapsody on heaven: rather is it hot with the fires of hell'; and further, 'At times it is not adapted for family reading, as the author himself confesses' (*Source of Jerusalem the Golden*, 1910, Introduction, p. 9). The original is written in the so-called 'Leonine' rhythm: technically, 'Dactylic hexameter with tailed rhymes,' as in the lines quoted below. This metre has been excellently imitated by Gerald Moultrie in his translation of the poem in *Lyra Mystica* (1865):

Here we have many fears, this is the vale of tears, the land of sorrow;

Tears are there none at all in that celestial hall on life's bright morrow.

Bernard himself says, 'Unless the Spirit of wisdom and understanding had flowed in upon me, I could not have put together so long a work in so difficult a metre.'

Dr. Neale's translation, though its metrical form differs so greatly from that of the original, is a wonderfully close and vivid rendering of Bernard's poem. No translation is quite able to reproduce the effect of the rhyming, chiming Latin original in its terse suggestiveness. Thus verses 1–2 of 597 echo

> Hic breve vivitur, hic breve plangitur, hic breve fletur;
> Non breve vivere, non breve plangere retribuetur,
> O retributio! stat brevis actio, vita perennis;
> O retributio! coelica mansio stat lue plenis.

Verses 5–6 similarly reproduce

> Spe modo vivitur, et Syon angitur a Babylone;
> Nunc tribulatio, tunc recreatio, sceptra, coronae.
> Qui modo creditur, ipse videbitur, atque scietur:
> Ipse videntibus, atque scientibus, attribuetur.

Still, it is fair to say that otherwise Dr. Neale's version now and then surpasses the Latin. It appeared in a slim little volume of forty-eight pages (price 8*d*.), *The Rhythm of Bernard de Morlaix, Monk of Cluny, on the Celestial Country* (1858). 'A new hymn which has won such a place in the affections of Christian people, as has "Jerusalem the Golden", is so priceless an acquisition that I must needs rejoice to have been the first to recall from oblivion the poem that yielded it.' (So Archbishop Trench in his *Sacred Latin Poetry*, p. 307—a volume which is still the most scholarly and catholic short anthology of Latin hymns.)

In 599 the second line of ver. 2, 'Conjubilant with song', has been sometimes changed to 'All jubilant with song'; but the former reproduces the original

> Sunt Syon atria conjubilantia, martyre plena,
> Cive micantia, Principe stantia, luce serena.

There is nothing in the Latin corresponding to the last eight lines of each of these three hymns; this climax was added in the 1861 edition of *Hymns Ancient and Modern*.

599 was sung over Dr. Pusey's grave, when he was buried at Oxford on Sept. 18, 1880.

The first tune to 597 is ST. ALPHEGE, contributed by Dr. Gauntlett to *The Church Hymn and Tune Book* (1852): JABEZ is a Welsh melody from *Caniadau y Cyssegr*, ed. by John Roberts (Henllan), 1839.

598 is set to MEIRIONYDD, a tune by William Lloyd; the original air is found in a manuscript book of tunes formerly in possession of Mr. Lloyd, where it is called 'Berth'. The present form shows some alterations from the original melody.

599 is set to EWING, which in 1853 was published on a single sheet, as the music for the section beginning 'For thee, O dear, dear country'. The tune was originally in triple time as follows:

etc.

It appears in this form under the name 'St. Bedes' in *A Manual of Psalm and Hymn Tunes . . . edited by the Hon. and Rev. J. Grey* (1857).

The first appearance of the tune in the present form was probably in *Hymns Ancient and Modern* (1861), where it was set to the present words. Colonel Ewing himself never liked it in common time; of this form of it he said, 'It now seems to me a good deal like a polka.' But, writing in 1861, Dr. Neale said: 'I have so often been asked to what tune the words of Bernard may be sung, that I may here mention that of Mr. Ewing, the earliest written, the best known, and with children the most popular; no small proof in my estimation of the goodness of church music.'

600 AROUND THE THRONE OF GOD IN HEAVEN

Published in Mrs. Shepherd's *Hymns Adapted to the Comprehension of Young Minds* (1836). Two years later Robert Moffat rendered it into the Bechuana language for his congregation at Kuruman. One verse is omitted here, and the third line of ver. 3 has been as usual corrected from the original 'Bathed in that precious purple flood'. Since its publication in Curwen's *Tune Book to the Hymns and Chants for Sunday Schools* (1842), the tune GLORY has never been divorced from the words of this hymn.

601 O GOD, OUR HELP IN AGES PAST

Perhaps the greatest hymn in the English language. It appeared in Watts's *The Psalms of David* (1719), entitled 'Man frail and God eternal'. The alteration of Watts's original first line, 'Our God, our help' to 'O God, our help', was made by John Wesley in 1737. According to Mr. Thomas Wright (*Life of Isaac Watts*), the hymn was written about the year 1714, shortly before the death of Queen Anne, in a time of great national anxiety (cp. the closing chapters of *Esmond*). Three verses are omitted.

Charlotte Brontë uses the hymn effectively in the twenty-fourth chapter of *Shirley*.

ST. ANNE appears in *A Supplement to the New Version of Psalms by Dr. Brady and Mr. Tate. . . . The Sixth Edition, corrected and much enlarged . . .* (1708). Here the tune, with its present name, is set to the new version of Psalm xlii, in two parts, treble and bass, as follows:

It is marked in the Index as a new tune. No composers' names are given in the above work, but it is generally believed that Dr. Croft was concerned in its production, and the present tune has been almost universally attributed to him. It is found with his name attached to it in *Melodies Proper to be sung to any of ye versions of the Psalms of David*, edited by Philip Hart, and published about 1720; and also in *An Introduction to Psalmody*, by John Church, published in 1723. Both of these editors were contemporaries of Croft, and Church was master of the choristers of Westminster Abbey while Croft was organist there.

602 STILL ON THE HOMEWARD JOURNEY

Miss Borthwick's hymn is from Dr. W. F. Stevenson's *Hymns for Church and Home* (1873).

WELLESLEY was composed by Sir George Elvey for the hymn, 'O Jesus, I have promised'. It appeared in *The Children's Hymnbook* (1881).

603 HEAVENLY FATHER, THOU HAST BROUGHT US

Published in *The Home Hymn-book* (1885), of which Mrs. Hawkins was editor. It was originally written for the golden wedding of Mr. and Mrs. Lewis, her father and mother. The third verse in the original has been omitted in order to make the hymn suitable for anniversaries generally, but even without this special verse the hymn becomes much more interesting when the circumstances in which it was written are kept in mind. This verse ran:

> Father, all Thy gifts are precious,
>   But we thank Thee most for this,
> That so many years of toiling
>   Have been soothed by wedded bliss;
> Since our hearts were first united
>   Life has not been free from care,
> But our burdens were the lighter
>   When each bore an equal share.

For the tune, see on Hymn 502.

604 FOR THY MERCY AND THY GRACE

Contributed by Mr. Downton to *The Church of England Magazine* (1843); it was written in 1841, and entitled 'A Hymn for the Commencement of the year'. Two stanzas are omitted. As printed in his *Hymns and Verses* (1873), the last line of the first verse is

Father, and Redeemer, hear.

SONG 13 (see on 195) was set to a metrical paraphrase of a portion of the Song of Solomon.

605 AT THY FEET, OUR GOD AND FATHER

Mr. Burns's hymn appeared in *Psalms and Hymns for Divine Worship* (1867), an English Presbyterian collection, where it was a New Year's hymn under the text 'O Thou that hearest prayer, unto Thee shall all flesh come' (Psalm lxv. 2).

For the tune, see Hymn 2.

606 FATHER, LET ME DEDICATE

This piece by Mr. Tuttiett is from his *Germs of Thought on the Sunday Special Services* (1864). It appears in several collections with considerable variations in the text. The form here given is the original, with the exception of ver. 1, line 2, which, as the author wrote it, is 'All this year to Thee'.

ST. IGNATIUS was composed for this hymn, by Sir Joseph Barnby, in *The Hymnary* (1872).

607 GREAT GOD, WE SING THAT MIGHTY HAND

From the posthumous edition of Doddridge's *Hymns Founded on various Texts in the Holy Scriptures* (1755), where it is headed 'Help obtained from God, Acts xxvi. 22. For the New Year'. The last line of ver. 1 as it stands is an improvement upon 'And mercy crowns it, till it close'; and the final line of the hymn had to be altered from 'To better worlds shall raise our dust'.

For the tune, see Hymn 253.

608 THE GLORY OF THE SPRING HOW SWEET

Composed by Mr. Gill 'on the Whitsunday of 1867, a day of singular loveliness', and published in *The Golden Chain of Praise Hymns* (1869), where it is entitled, 'The Divine Renewer'. The texts are Psalm civ. 30 ('Thou renewest the face of the earth') and Ephesians iv. 23 ('Be renewed in the spirit of your mind').

KING'S LANGLEY is a traditional English melody, from *The English Hymnal* (1906), as arranged by Miss L. E. Broadwood from a Hertfordshire May-day Carol.

609 ALL IS BRIGHT AND CHEERFUL ROUND US

From Dr. Neale's *Hymns for Children* (1846, third series), for St. Philip and St. James (May 1). The original opening was 'All is bright and gay around us'. One stanza is omitted.

ADRIAN, by Sir Robert Stewart, appeared in *The Church of England Hymnal* (1895).

EVERTON, by Henry Smart, is taken from *Psalms and Hymns for Divine Worship* (1867).

610 FOR ALL THY LOVE AND GOODNESS, SO BOUNTIFUL AND FREE

This hymn was originally written by Miss Frances How in 1848 and published in a book of poems by her, entitled *April Verses*. When *Church Hymns* was being published (1871 edition), the verses were re-written by the authoress's brother Dr. Walsham How, one of the editors, and included in the collection.

NEW GRANGE has been composed by Professor Macalister for this hymn and this collection.

611 LORD, IN THY NAME THY SERVANTS PLEAD

Written by Keble at Malvern, Aug. 4, 1856, and published anonymously in Lord Nelson's *The Salisbury Hymn Book* (1857) with a doxology which is here omitted. In the original the third line of ver. 2 ran, 'And still, now spring has on us smiled'.

GORDON, by Henry Smart, is from the same source as 'Everton' (609).

612 THE SUMMER DAYS ARE COME AGAIN

This hymn was originally intended by Mr. Longfellow to be sung in the open air, and considerable changes have been made in the text in order to make it suitable for ordinary church services. The original has three eight-line verses, each beginning 'The sweet June days are come again'. The present hymn consists of verses 2 and 3. The last four lines in the original are,

> We know who giveth all our good,
> And 'neath the arches dim
> And ancient pillars of the wood,
> We lift our grateful hymn.

FOREST GREEN as in *The English Hymnal*, arranged by Dr. R. Vaughan Williams from a folk-song called *The Ploughboy's Dream*.

613 SUMMER SUNS ARE GLOWING

Written by Dr. How for *Church Hymns* (1871).

RUTH, by Samuel Smith, was privately printed in 1865, and in *Church Hymns* (1874) it was set to the present hymn.

614 NOW SING WE A SONG FOR THE HARVEST

Arranged by Mr. Chadwick and the Rev. William Channing Gannett from a poem beginning 'Come, list to a song for the harvest', written for a Harvest Thanksgiving Service in 1871.

ST. SULIEN was written by Edward Arthur for this hymn and for the present collection.

615 LORD OF THE HARVEST, ONCE AGAIN

Like 543, from Anstice's posthumous *Hymns*. In the original, between verses 2 and 3, these lines lay:

> Nor vainly of Thy Word we ask
> A lesson from the reaper's task;
> So shall Thine angels issue forth:
> The tares be burnt; the just of earth,
> Playthings of sun and storm no more,
> Be gather'd to their Father's store.

For the tune, see on Hymn 172.

616 TO THEE, O LORD, OUR HEARTS WE RAISE

Mr. Dix's hymn is from *Hymns for the Service of the Church* (St. Raphael's, Bristol, 1864). In the original ver. 2 line 3 runs 'Upon Thine altar, Lord, we lay', but the text as in the present version was approved by Mr. Dix.

GOLDEN SHEAVES was composed by Sir Arthur Sullivan for this hymn, in *Church Hymns with Tunes* (1874).

617 FOUNTAIN OF MERCY, GOD OF LOVE

From Mrs. Flowerdew's *Poems on Moral and Religious Subjects*.

NATIVITY is from *The Metrical Psalter* (1855), in the appendix. Mr. Lahee arranged the music of this book.

618 WE PLOUGH THE FIELDS, AND SCATTER

The 'Peasants' Song' in *Paul Erdmann's Feast*, a Sketch by Matthias Claudius (Hamburg, 1783). This is a picture, charming in its simplicity and piety, of a North German harvest-thanksgiving in the farm-house of Paul Erdmann. 'They sang the Peasants' Song as here follows. I don't know what sort of effect the song has when it is read ; but I know well what that was when the peasants sang it. The music, they said, was Italian. I have here set it down as well as I could catch it. Let any one improve it, or make another one.'

The song is in seventeen four-line verses with a refrain to each. In 1800 a collection of melodies for Public Schools appeared in Hanover with the famous tune by Schulz and an arrangement of verses 3–10 of Claudius's Song of which only the chorus sung by the peasants is altered to suit the melody. Ever since this happy re-arrangement, the hymn has had an extraordinary popularity in schools and song-books for children throughout Germany. The original air, as in Claudius's Sketch, has passed completely out of use, and the words as recast are found in the 'Geistliche Lieder' supplement in most modern German hymn-books. Miss Campbell's translation appeared first in Rev. C. S. Bere's *A Garland of Songs* (1861). Though not very literal, it admirably preserves the spirit and picturesqueness of the original.

Text unaltered, except in ver. 3 (lines 5–8) :

> No gifts have we to offer
> For all Thy love imparts,
> But that which Thou desirest,
> Our humble, thankful hearts.

WIR PFLÜGEN (DRESDEN), in *Lieder für Volkschulen* (Hanover, 1800), is set to the third stanza of this hymn. Its earliest appearance in England seems to have been in *The Bible Class Magazine* (November 1854), where it is set to another translation of the German hymn.

619 COME, YE THANKFUL PEOPLE, COME

First published in Dean Alford's *Psalms and Hymns* (1844). He made considerable changes in this original version which may be read in Lord Selborne's *The Book of Praise*. The hymn as here printed is his final revision, with two minor differences in ver. 4 which originally had l. 2, 'To thy final harvest-home,' and l. 6, 'In Thy presence to abide'.

For the tune, see Hymn 118.

620 PRAISE, O PRAISE OUR GOD AND KING

Sir Henry Baker's hymn, as in *Hymns Ancient and Modern* (1861), of which he was editor, is founded on Milton's version of Psalm cxxxvi (see Hymn 11).

For the tune, see Hymn 38.

621 THE YEAR IS SWIFTLY WANING

Like Hymn 613, written by Dr. How for *Church Hymns* (1871).

For the tune, see Hymn 270.

622 WINTER REIGNETH O'ER THE LAND

Also written by Dr. How for *Church Hymns* (1871).

CLARENCE was composed for the hymn, part of it being adapted by Sir Arthur Sullivan from one of his own compositions.

623 'TIS WINTER NOW ; THE FALLEN SNOW

From Mr. Longfellow's *Hymns of the Spirit* (1864).

BRYNTEG, by J. Ambrose Lloyd, is from *The Congregational Hymn and Tune Book* (1862).

DANBY, as in *The English Hymnal*, is arranged by Dr. R. Vaughan Williams from a traditional ballad air, 'Lord Bateman'.

624 GOD BE WITH YOU TILL WE MEET AGAIN

Written in 1882 as a Christian Good-Bye, it was called forth by no person or occasion, but was deliberately composed as a Christian hymn on the basis of the etymology of 'Good-bye', which is 'God be with you' (note by Dr. Rankin).

It was first sung in the First Congregational Church in Washington of which the author was minister. The first verse was set to music written by Mr. W. G. Tomer (the well-known tune in *Sacred Songs and Solos*), and thereafter Dr. Rankin wrote the rest of the hymn (in eight stanzas), which soon obtained great popularity in the United States. The refrain, which greatly weakens the hymn, is here omitted.

RANDOLPH is a tune from *The English Hymnal*, composed for this hymn by Dr. Vaughan Williams.

625 O LORD, BE WITH US WHEN WE SAIL

Written in 1865 and contributed to *The Sarum Hymnal* (1868), of which—along with Lord Nelson (grandnephew of the great Lord Nelson) and Rev. J. R. Woodford—Canon Dayman was editor.

FARRANT is an air adapted from the anthem 'Lord, for Thy tender mercies' sake,' usually attributed to Richard Farrant, but by some writers to John Hilton, by others to William Mundy.

626 ETERNAL FATHER, STRONG TO SAVE

The text of Mr. Whiting's hymn varies greatly, there being three different versions. That which is given here is the revision by the compilers of *Hymns Ancient and Modern* in 1861. The hymn was written in 1860, and the first verse of the original was,

> O Thou who bidd'st the ocean deep
> Its own appointed limits keep,
> Thou, who didst bind the restless wave,
> Eternal Father strong to save,
> O hear us when we cry to Thee,
> For all in peril on the sea.

According to Mr. F. A. Jones (*Famous Hymns and their Authors*, pp. 223–4), the hymn is known in the French Navy, for a translation appears in the *Nouveau Libre Cantique* (the hymnal in use on the French men-of-war), with the tender and beautiful refrain—

> Vois nos pleurs, entends nos sanglots,
> Pour ceux en péril sur les flots.

MELITA was composed by Dr. Dykes for this hymn, in *Hymns Ancient and Modern* (1861).

627 STAR OF PEACE TO WANDERERS WEARY

Written by Mrs. Simpson in 1830, and published in *The Seaman's Devotional Assistant* (New York).

STAR OF PEACE was composed for this hymn, in *The National Psalmist* (Boston, Mass., 1848), a work edited by Lowell Mason and G. J. Webb.

628 WHOM OCEANS PART, O LORD, UNITE

'This hymn', says Mr. Elvet Lewis, 'was written for a Colonial Missionary Society Anniversary in London. But during the war the overseas soldiers got hold of it. They, as well as our home soldiers, arranged to sing it, after they separated, at a certain hour, wherever they would be, and so it came to be sung by many all over the vast war-area.'

For the tune, see Hymn 472.

629 HOLY FATHER, IN THY MERCY

Written at Cheltenham by Miss Stevenson on the day when her invalid brother sailed for South Africa in 1869. It was privately printed, and came into the hands of an officer on H.M.S. *Bacchante*, the ship on which King George and his brother made their voyage round the world in 1881–2. There it was used in public worship. A copy was sent home by the royal princes to their mother, and it was also sung by the Royal Family at home during the cruise. Finally, after being included in the (1889) supplement to *Hymns Ancient and Modern*, it won fresh popularity during the Great War.

The original had in ver. 1 (line 3),

> Keep our loved ones, now far absent.

MINTO, Dr. Monk's tune, was set to the hymn, 'Art thou weary', in *The Church of England Hymnal* (1895). The tune was in MS. at Dr. Monk's death, and was supplied by Mrs. Monk to Dr. Mann, the editor of the book. It was given its name in compliment to the late Rev. Alexander Galloway (q.v.), of Minto, Roxburghshire.

630 FATHER, WHO ART ALONE

Contributed by E. J. to *The Home Hymn Book* (1885).

When the first *Church Hymnary* was published the authoress desired to be known only by her initials. Now her name is freely known as Edith Jones.

RALEIGH, by Dr. E. Prout, is from *The Congregational Church Hymnal* (1887).

631 GOD SAVE OUR GRACIOUS KING

From *Harmonia Anglicana* (about 1743). In the original the first line is,

> God save our lord the king!

Ver. 2 ran,

> O Lord our God, arise,
> Scatter his enemies
>   And make them fall!
> Confound their politics,
> Frustrate their knavish tricks,
> On him our hopes we fix.
>   O, save us all.

Ver. 3, from *The Gentleman's Magazine* (October 1745), which is the first dated copy of the National Anthem, was as follows:

> Thy choicest gifts in store
> On George be pleased to pour;
> Long may he reign!
> May he defend our laws,
> And ever give us cause
> To say with heart and voice
> God save the King!

The whole history alike of the words and music is very obscure, and no certainty has yet been reached as to author and composer.

The air of the National Anthem is alleged, on rather inadequate grounds, to have been sung by Henry Carey about 1740, when it certainly appeared in *Thesaurus Musicus*, as later in *The Gentleman's Magazine* (1745). But in neither of these publications was the authorship of words or music attributed to Carey, and it was not till 1795 that his son George S. Carey claimed the authorship for his father. Dr. Arne, who arranged the anthem for performance in 1745, stated that 'it was a received opinion that it was written for the Catholic Chapel of James II'. On various grounds it is probable that this is the case, but although resemblances to the melody have been traced in various old English airs, its actual source is still undiscovered.

632 GOD BLESS OUR NATIVE LAND

The original hymn in three stanzas was published by Mr. Hickson in *The Singing Master* (1836), where the first verse ran,

> God bless our native land;
> May Heaven's protecting hand
> Still guard our shore!
> May peace her power extend,
> Foe be transformed to friend,
> And Britain's rights depend
> On war no more.

A fourth stanza was added in the second (1837) edition. But the hymn has been current in several forms, more or less dependent on Mr. Hickson's text. The present text is as in *The Public School Hymnbook*.

There is a similar American hymn, slightly earlier in origin, and also what seems to be a German original or predecessor of all such hymns in English, viz. Siegfried August Mahlmann's (1771–1826) patriotic song for Saxony. It begins,

> Gott segne Sachsenland,
> Wo fest die Treue stand

In Sturm und Nacht!
Ew'ge Gerechtigkeit,
Hoch über'm Meer der Zeit,
Die jedem Sturm 'gebeut,
Schütz' uns mit Macht!

Some account of this is printed in the New York *Outlook* (July 9, 1910) by Rev. James Mearns.

For the tune, see Hymn 364.

633 LORD, WHILE FOR ALL MANKIND WE PRAY

Dr. Wreford's hymn was contributed to Beard's *Collection of Hymns for Public and Private Worship* (1837), having been originally composed about the time of Queen Victoria's accession to the throne.

ST. LAWRENCE, in *Devotional Music Original and Selected, arranged mostly in Four parts, by R. A. Smith* (1810), was set to the twenty-fourth of *The Scottish Paraphrases*, 'Ye heavens, send forth your song of praise!', and marked as 'composed for this work'.

634 PRAISE TO OUR GOD, WHOSE BOUNTEOUS HAND

Written by Canon Ellerton in 1870 for *Church Hymns*.

AGINCOURT SONG is a fifteenth-century English melody, from the song on the battle of Agincourt, of which the first verse runs—

Owre Kynge went forth to Normandy, with grace and might of
    chyvalry;
Ther God for hym wrought mervelusly, wherfore Englonde may
    calle and cry:
       Deo gracias !

'The victory of Agincourt gave rise to a large number of minstrel pieces. Many of these were suppressed, for the King—to quote from the old Chronicler,—"seemed little to regard such vaine pompes and shewes as were in triumphant sort devised for his welcoming home from so prosperous a tournie, insomuch that he would not suffer his helmet to be carried with him, whereby might have appeared to the people the blows and dints that were to be seen in the same—neither would he suffer to be made and sung by minstrels of his glorious victorie, for that he would wholly have the praise and thanks altogether given to God." Happily this song escaped the censorship.' (From *A Book of British Song*, edited by Cecil J. Sharp, 1902.)

Though it 'has all the characteristic harshness of the earlier portion of the century', Stanford and Forsyth say in their *History of Music*, 'the tune itself . . . is a wonderful thing, greatly instinct with the mediaeval lust of battle. Its frantic cry of thanks to God at the end is worth all the commentaries on Agincourt that have ever been printed. Shakespeare himself tells us less.'

LLEDROD is a Welsh melody from *Llyfr Tonau Cynulleidfaol* (1859).

635 TO THEE, OUR GOD, WE FLY

Dr. How's lines were first published in *Church Hymns* (1871).

BEVAN was composed by Sir John Goss in 1853 for *Choral Harmony: A collection of tunes in short score, for four voices, a companion to Metrical Versions of Psalms and Hymns, by the Rev. Peter Maurice* (1854).

636 JUDGE ETERNAL, THRONED IN SPLENDOUR

Published in July 1902 in *The Commonwealth*, which Dr. Scott Holland edited.

PICARDY, as in *The English Hymnal*, is one of the melodies referred to in the note on Hymn 4. It is a carol, probably of the seventeenth century, with the title 'Romancero', from Tiersot's *Mélodies* (Paris, 1887).

637 GOD OF OUR FATHERS, KNOWN OF OLD

Mr. Kipling's poem appeared in *The Times* of July 17, 1897, and as 'Recessional' in *The Five Nations* (1903). Verses 2 and 3 have special reference to the Procession and to the Naval Review on 26 June which were such notable parts of the celebrations of the Diamond Jubilee of Queen Victoria in 1897.

RECESSIONAL, by Dr. Charles Wood, was composed for the words, in *The Public School Hymnbook* (1919).

FOLKINGHAM is described as a new tune, and is set to a metrical version of the Lord's Prayer, in *A Supplement to the New Version of the Psalms* (sixth edition, much enlarged, 1708).

638 O GOD OF EARTH AND ALTAR

Contributed by Mr. Chesterton to *The English Hymnal* (1906).

MONTAGUE was composed by Dr. A. F. Barnes for this collection.

639 THESE THINGS SHALL BE: A LOFTIER RACE

A selection of verses from a poem by John Addington Symonds entitled 'A Vista' in *New and Old: a volume of Verse* (1880). The poem, which has fifteen stanzas, begins,

> Sad heart, what will the future bring
>   To happier men when we are gone?
> What golden days shall dawn for them
>   Transcending all we gaze upon?
>
> Will our long strife be laid at rest?
>   The warfare of our blind desires
> Be merged in a perpetual peace,
>   And love illume but harmless fires?
>
> Shall faith released from forms that chain
>   And freeze the spirit while we pray,
> Expect with calm and ardent eyes
>   The morning of death's brighter day?
>
> These things shall be: &c.

The selection was made and the verses first used as a hymn about thirty years ago, sung at public meetings and summer festivals—not at first at religious services. They were included in *The Fellowship Hymn-Book* (1909), and during the war came into common use, owing to their inclusion in the S.P.C.K. collection *In hoc Signo*. The League of Nations Union has printed them in its fly-sheet of hymns. 'They were probably thrown off hurriedly during some moment of deep longing—a longing for the betterment of the people which was always with him, and which his study of Whitman and his own later life among a prosperous and democratic people helped so very much to foster' (Note by Mrs. Vaughan, the poet's daughter). The poem closes with the following verse:

> These things—they are no dream—shall be
> For happier men when we are gone:
> Those golden days for them shall dawn
> Transcending aught we gaze upon.

'Unarmed' has been suggested as a better word than 'inarmed' (verse 3, line 2), but the latter term means 'arm in arm'.

DOVERSDALE appears in Dr. Edward Miller's *Sacred Music*, where it is called 'Stonefield', and marked in the Index as a 'new tune never before published'.

640 AND DID THOSE FEET IN ANCIENT TIME

A lyric from *Milton* (1804), one of Blake's mad, mystical rhapsodies, the text subjoined being 'Would God that all the Lord's people were prophets!' (Num. xi. 29). Sir Hubert Parry's music has carried the lyric into wide popularity as a hymn of social hope and economic reconstruction. But originally it had no such outlook. 'Satanic mills', for example, have nothing to do with factories. They represent the chopping of logic and science which Blake discovered and derided in the philosophies of men like Locke and Bacon: natural science and ratiocinative philosophy were, for this prophet of intuition and imagination, anti-divine agencies. 'Jerusalem' represents the ideal life of freedom as divine. This liberty was to be built up by the unrestricted activities of the mind. 'I know of no other Christianity', said Blake, 'and of no other gospel than the liberty both of body and mind to exercise the divine arts of imagination.'

The Times, on Aug. 12, 1927, the anniversary of Blake's death, referring to 'the extraordinary popularity' of this hymn, said: 'It has become almost a second National Anthem—nay, if it be not disloyal to say so, it has come to stand for something that the National Anthem fails to express: the private loyalty to some Little England—the white and secret "Albion" of Blake's imagination—upon which public loyalty to the larger England of the National Anthem depends. . . . "Jerusalem", in fact, has become the hymn for those special occasions on which the private Englishman—the

Englishman in a minority of one—finds the need for expression, impossible in his own words, and at the same time too subtle in reference for the formal statement, adapted to all occasions, of the National Anthem.'

It was suggested by Sir Hubert Parry to Dr. Robert Bridges that he should write 'suitable simple music to Blake's stanzas—music that an audience could take up and join in'. Parry agreed, and gave the manuscript of JERUSALEM to Sir Walford Davies with the words, 'Here's a tune for you, old chap. Do what you like with it.' It was first sung at a concert in the Albert Hall. It was adopted by the Federation of Music Competition Festivals as the National Hymn of that movement, and is now almost invariably sung at these festivals.

Writing to *The Times* of August 27, 1927, Sir Walford Davies says: 'Sir Hubert Parry gave me the manuscript of this setting of Blake's "Jerusalem" one memorable morning in 1916. It may have been very late in 1915, but I do not think it was. We looked at it long together in his room at the Royal College of Music, and I recall vividly his unwonted happiness over it. One momentary act of his should perhaps be told here. He ceased to speak, and put his finger on the note D in the second stanza where the words "O clouds, unfold" break his rhythm. I do not think any word passed about it, yet he made it perfectly clear that this was the one note and one moment of the song which he treasured. . . . I copyrighted it in the composer's name and published it in 1916. We needed it for the men at that time. It is indeed good to know that Dame Millicent Fawcett needed and had asked for it for the women too. I know Dr. Bridges specifically wanted every one of us to sing it, and this is happily coming true.'

641 GOD THE OMNIPOTENT! KING WHO ORDAINEST

The first two verses are from a hymn by Henry F. Chorley, published originally in Hullah's *Part Music* (1844). Verses 3–5 are part of a hymn beginning 'God the Almighty One, wisely ordaining', which was written by Canon Ellerton on the 28th of August, 1870, four days before the battle of Sedan.

RUSSIA was composed by A. F. Lvov in 1833 for the Russian national anthem, 'God save the Tsar'.

642 GOD OF ETERNITY, LORD OF THE AGES

Composed by Dr. Merrington in 1912 for the Jubilee of St. Andrew's Presbyterian Church, Brisbane, Queensland, of which the author was then minister. He writes: 'The main thought in my heart was of thankfulness to the Giver of all good for the splendid services rendered in the Colonies of our own blood and creed, and thankfulness for the opening of Emmanuel College during that year.' Emmanuel College is the Presbyterian theological seminary in Brisbane.

Same tune as 641.

643 GREAT KING OF NATIONS, HEAR OUR PRAYER

Mr. Gurney published this in *A Collection of Hymns for Public Worship* (1838), printed for use in the Parish Church of Lutterworth, where he was then (1827–44) curate. Its title was 'Fast-Day: or Time of Public Calamity'.

OLD 137TH was the tune set to this psalm in the Anglo-Genevan Psalter of 1556, and in all the subsequent English and Scottish Psalters.

644 WHAT SERVICE SHALL WE RENDER THEE

Mr. Dodgshun's hymn was composed a few months before the outbreak of the Great War in 1914. It is included in the Supplement to *The Fellowship Hymnbook* (October 1920).

LEYDEN was composed by Jan Willem Wilms for a patriotic song 'Wir Neerlandsch Bloed', sometimes used as a National Anthem in Holland.

645 FATHER ETERNAL, RULER OF CREATION

Mr. Housman's poem was written at the request of the Rev. H. R. L. Sheppard, St. Martin-in-the-Fields, London, for the 'Life and Liberty' movement, after the War. 'Their' has been changed to 'our' in ver. 2 (line 2).

GREYFRIARS occurs only in the 1635 edition of the Scottish Psalter, where it is an alternative tune to Psalm cxxiv. Probably it was composed by Edward Miller, the musical editor of that edition. In Mainzer's *Standard Psalmody* (1845) it is entitled 'Durie's 124th', but it is a mistake to imagine that this was the tune sung by the crowd which welcomed John Durie back to Edinburgh in 1582; the one which was sung was that which is now familiar as 'Old 124th'.

646 O GOD OF LOVE, O KING OF PEACE

Written by Sir H. W. Baker for *Hymns Ancient and Modern* (1861). For the tune, see Hymn 259.

647 LAND OF OUR BIRTH, WE PLEDGE TO THEE

'The Children's Hymn' in Mr. Kipling's *Puck of Pook's Hill* (1906).

The first hymn-book to include this fine poem was *School Praise* (1907), the Hymn-Book for the Young in the Presbyterian Church of England, which was edited by the late Rev. J. M. E. Ross. *Some time editor of* "Br. Wkly"

GALILEE was composed by Dr. Armes, for the hymn 'Jesus shall reign', in *Hymns Ancient and Modern* (1875).

For TRURO see Hymn 369.

648 O HAPPY HOME, WHERE THOU ART LOVED THE DEAREST

From Spitta's *Psalter und Harfe* (Leipzig, 1833).

This hymn came into common use in Germany from its inclusion in the *Würtemberger Gesangbuch* (1842). It was written in the autumn of 1826, with the heading 'Salvation is come to this house' (St. Luke xix. 9). This version of the translation by Mrs. Findlater (in *Hymns from the Land of Luther*, 3rd Series, 1858) has been 'adopted for musical reasons, but it has not the translator's approval' (Note in *Home and School Hymnal*, p. 543).

WELWYN, by Sir Alfred Scott-Gatty, is from the *Arundel Hymns* (1902).

649 THOU GRACIOUS POWER, WHOSE MERCY LENDS

Written by Dr. Holmes in 1869 for the annual meeting of the author's College Class graduating in 1829 at Harvard University— that famous class which had among its members Chief Justice Bigelow, J. Freeman Clarke, Professor Benjamin Pierce, S. F. Smith (author of 'America'), and other well-known men. From 1855 almost till the end of his life, Dr. Holmes wrote a poem which was either read or sung by himself at the annual reunion. In a letter to Mr. J. W. Kemball, Dr. Holmes, speaking of hymns, wrote: 'It would be one of the most agreeable reflections to me if I could feel that I had left a few worthy to be remembered after me.' His hope has been realized: see Hymns 24 and 143 in the present book.

For the tune, see Hymn 275.

650 FATHER, OUR CHILDREN KEEP

From Dr. Bonar's *Hymns of Faith and Hope* (3rd Series, 1866), under the title 'Prayer for the Children'.

PRO NOSTRIS LIBERIS was composed for this hymn and the present collection.

651 FORTH IN THY NAME, O LORD, I GO

From Wesley's *Hymns and Sacred Poems* (1749), with the title 'For Believers before Work'.

Ver. 2, line 4, originally ran, 'And prove Thy acceptable will.' Between verses 2 and 3 this lay:

> Preserve me from my calling's snare,
> And hide my simple heart above,
> Above the thorns of choking care,
> The gilded baits of worldly love.

Curiously enough, this verse has been omitted from the Methodist collections, but is included in the *English Hymnal*.

SONG 34 (ANGELS' SONG), by Orlando Gibbons (see on Hymn 195), was set to the song beginning 'Thus angels sung, and thus sing we'. The melody stands as follows:

It is also set to another song in six-line form by the addition of two lines as follows:

The form of the tune, in triple time throughout, seems to have been introduced early in the eighteenth century, and is the form usually found in both English and Scottish collections down to a comparatively recent date.

652 LORD OF LIFE AND KING OF GLORY

Written by Miss Burke in December 1903, printed the following February in *The Treasury* (headed 'Prize Hymn for a Mothers' Union Service'), and thereafter included in *The English Hymnal* (1906).

CALVARY, by S. Stanley, was originally set to the hymn, 'Hark the voice of love and mercy,' in *Twenty-four Tunes* (*c.* 1800).

653 THE MORNING BRIGHT

Written, about the end of 1845, as a morning hymn for Dr. Summers's infant daughter. The hymn was written on the back of a letter on board a river steamer in Alabama, U.S.A., and published anonymously in *The Southern Christian Advocate*, of which Dr. Summers was editor. It is based on the text, 'Whether we wake or sleep, we should live together with Him' (1 Thess. v. 10).

Sir Joseph Barnby's tune SPRING-TIDE HOUR appeared in *The Methodist Sunday School Tune Book* (1881). It was set to the present hymn in *The Home and School Hymnal* (1892), of which the composer was musical editor.

654 JESUS, TENDER SHEPHERD, HEAR ME

Composed for Mrs. Duncan's infant children in 1839 (the year before her own death), and published in her *Memoir* (1841). The first evening prayer that thousands of little children learn.

EVENING PRAYER was composed by Sir John Stainer for this hymn, in the first edition of *The Church Hymnary*.

655 LORD, I WOULD OWN THY TENDER CARE

Like 550, from *Hymns for Infant Minds*, which Miss Taylor and her sister published when the former was twenty-five years old.

NEWBURY, from *The English Hymnal*, is a traditional air arranged by Miss Arkwright from an old Christmas carol beginning, 'There is six good days set in a week.'

656 BE PRESENT AT OUR TABLE, LORD

From Cennick's *Sacred Hymns for the Children of God in the Days of their Pilgrimage* (1741). Originally the third line ran,

> Thy creatures bless, and grant that we.

For the tune see Hymn 229.

657 AWAY IN A MANGER, NO CRIB FOR A BED

In many hymn-books this charming lyric is ascribed to Martin Luther (see on 56). But there is nothing corresponding to it in any of his hymns or in his other writings.

The tune CRADLE SONG was composed for the hymn by W. J. Kirkpatrick, in an American book towards the end of last century; but the exact date and title of this work cannot be ascertained.

658 CHILDREN OF JERUSALEM

This hymn is, like Hymn 93, based on St. Matthew xxi. 15. It must have been composed before 1842, the year of Mr. Henley's death, but it is first found in C. H. Bateman's *Sacred Song Book for Children* (1843), in this form.

The tune CHILDREN OF JERUSALEM appeared in John Curwen's *Tune Book to the Hymns and Chaunts for Sunday Schools*. This book has no date, but the British Museum Catalogue gives 1842. The hymn and tune also appeared in *The Juvenile Harmonist: a Selection of Tunes and Pieces for Children*, arranged by Thomas Clark of Canterbury (1843).

659 WHEN MOTHERS OF SALEM

Mr. Hutchings's hymn was written for the Anniversary Service of St. Paul's Chapel Sunday School, Wigan, April 1850, and published in a revised form in the *Juvenile Missionary Magazine* (June 1850).

ATHLONE appeared in *The Methodist Sunday School Hymnal* (1911), and was composed by R. N. Quaile for the hymn.

The tune commonly associated with the hymn is that of the famous German drinking song 'Crambambuli', published in Methfessel's *Lieder- und Commersbuch* (1818). The association is unfortunate, and as it makes children conceive of Jesus as *shrieking* the tender words of the refrain, it is well that a new association should be created.

660 JESUS LOVES ME! THIS I KNOW

Miss Warner's hymn (see 575) appeared in her *Say and Seal* (1859).

Mr. Bradbury's tune was composed for the hymn, in *The Golden Chain* (1861).

661 LORD, A LITTLE BAND AND LOWLY

Published in Curwen's *Child's own Hymn Book* (1846).

Mrs. Shelly wrote: 'At a Sunday School meeting in Manchester the Rev. John Curwen one evening gave a lecture on singing. He sang a very pretty and simple tune, to which he said he had no suitable words, and wished that some one would write a hymn to it. I wrote these verses and gave them to him after the close of the meeting.'

The tune ROUSSEAU is adapted from an air in Rousseau's opera 'Le Devin du Village', performed for the first time in 1752:

It is set to the present hymn in *Sacred Melodies for Children* (1843), edited by the Rev. C. H. Bateman.

662 GENTLE JESUS, MEEK AND MILD

From Wesley's *Hymns and Sacred Poems* (1742), along with five others for children reprinted in his *Hymns for Children* (1763). The present hymn is made up of two of those five, ver. 1 from Hymn 72, and verses 2–5 from Hymn 73, the whole of which may be read in Ward's *English Poets* (vol. iii, p. 264).

The tune GENTLE JESUS was composed by Martin Shaw for the hymn, in *Additional Tunes and Settings in use at St. Mary's, Primrose Hill* (1915).

SIMPLICITY, by Sir John Stainer, was composed for it, in the first edition of *The Church Hymnary*.

663 DO NO SINFUL ACTION

From Mrs. Alexander's *Hymns for Little Children* (1848), counselling them to 'renounce the devil and all his works'.

GLENFINLAS appeared in *Songs of Praise* (1925), set to 'Summer suns are glowing'.

664 GOD IS ALWAYS NEAR ME

No date can be assigned to this hymn of Mr. Bliss (1838–76), but it appeared first in *The Charm* for 1871, with this tune ST. CYRIL which he himself composed.

Q 2

665 JESUS, HOLY, UNDEFILED

From *Hymns for Infant Children, by A., C., and E.* (1852). 'E.' is Mrs. Shapcote (then Miss Steward), 'C.' her sister Eleanor Steward, and 'A.' their aunt, Mary Steward. This is by 'E.'

FERRIER was composed by Dr. Dykes for this hymn, in *Accompanying Tunes to the Hymns for Infant Children* (1862).

666 JESUS, HIGH IN GLORY

This hymn appeared in *The Sunday School Harmonist* (1847) of the Methodist Episcopal Church. Originally it had six verses. In the first verse Miss McKeever wrote 'Infants' praises hear' (the hymn is called an 'Infant Hymn'), in the second 'eternal King', and in the fourth 'Then, when Jesus calls us' and 'We would gladly answer'.

GOTT EIN VATER is a tune from *The English Hymnal*, but the title and date of the work in which Silcher's melody first appeared are not ascertained.

667 JESUS, FRIEND OF LITTLE CHILDREN

Composed in May 1882 at 24 Chalmers Street, Edinburgh, at the request of the Psalms and Hymns Committee of the Baptist Union, who published Mr. Mathams's hymn in their *Psalms and Hymns for School and Home*. Since then it has appeared in a large number of hymn-books for children throughout Britain, the United States, and the Colonies. It has been translated into Welsh, and is also a great favourite with the native children on the Congo, the Gold Coast, and the West Coast of Africa. A selection only of the verses is here given.

In *The English Hymnal*, the tune CUTTLE MILLS, by W. Griffith, is set to 'Art thou weary?'

668 LOVING SHEPHERD OF THY SHEEP

From Miss Leeson's *Hymns and Scenes of Childhood: or, A Sponsor's Gift* (1842), where three stanzas of eight lines each were headed with the text 'My sheep hear my voice, and I know them and they follow me' (St. John x. 27).

Considerable changes have been made from the original text of this hymn, which had, e. g.:—

ver. 1, line 2, 'Keep Thy lamb in safety keep;' ver. 2, line 1, 'Loving Saviour Thou didst give,' line 3, 'I would praise Thee every day,' line 4, 'Gladly all Thy will obey;' ver. 3, line 2, 'Teach Thy lamb Thy voice to hear,' line 3, 'Suffer not my steps to stray;' ver. 4, line 1, 'Where Thou leadest I would go,' line 3, 'Then before my Father's throne,' line 4, 'I shall know as I am known.'

BATTISHILL goes back to *Twelve Hymns; the Words by the Rev. Charles Wesley, M.A., late student at Christ Church, Oxford; set to music by Jonathan Battishill* (1765). The present tune is a much altered and abridged version of the original, which is set to the hymn 'Jesus, Lord, we look to Thee', as follows:

669 IF I COME TO JESUS

From Mrs. van Alstyne's *Silver Spray* (1868).

WOODBROOK appeared in *The School Hymnal Tune Book* (1887), which was edited by Mr. Adcock himself.

670 O WHAT CAN LITTLE HANDS DO

This appeared in *The Church Missionary Juvenile Instructor* (May 1862), signed 'Farin', and afterwards was included in *Daily Meditations for Children* (1868) by Mrs. Hinsdale. But she writes that she is not the author of the hymn. The last stanza is omitted.

CHILD SERVICE was composed by H. Elliot Button for this hymn, and sung at a Sunday School Festival in 1886; then published in *The Bristol Tune Book* (3rd series, 1891).

671 JESUS BIDS US SHINE

Miss Warner's hymn appeared in *The Little Corporal* (Chicago), but anonymously.

LUMETTO was written by Edward Arthur for this hymn.

672 GO FORTH TO LIFE, O CHILD OF EARTH

From Mr. Longfellow's *Hymns of the Spirit* (1864).

ST. BARTHOLOMEW is a tune headed 'By Mr. Henry Duncalf, organist of St. Barth.', in Riley's *Parochial Harmony* (1762).

673 GOD, WHO CREATED ME

From Canon Beeching's *In a Garden, and other poems* (1895).

ORISONS was written by Dr. Evans for this hymn in the present collection.

674 LOOKING UPWARD EVERY DAY

From Mrs. Carey Brock's *The Children's Hymn Book* (1881); written by Miss Butler for the confirmation of her niece and god-daughter.

EXCELSIOR was composed by Josiah Booth for this hymn, in *The Congregational Church Hymnal* (1887).

675 O JESUS, STRONG AND PURE AND TRUE

Written by Dr. How for the jubilee of Marlborough College in 1893. It appeared in *Hymns for the Use of Rugby School* (1896).

ST. FULBERT comes from *The Church Hymn and Tune Book, edited by W. J. Blew and H. J. Gauntlett* (1852), where it was set to the hymn 'Now Christ, our Passover, is slain'. The original name of the tune is 'St. Leofred'.

676 PRAISE TO OUR GOD, WHO WITH LOVE NEVER SWERVING

Written by Dr. Gray in 1893, and published in *The Bradfield College Supplement to Hymns Ancient and Modern* (1895), afterwards in *The Public School Hymn Book*.

BEDE is from the *Church Psalter and Hymn Book* (1864), where Sir John Goss adapted it to 'Brightest and best of the sons of the morning.'

677 LORD, BEHOLD US WITH THY BLESSING

678 LORD, DISMISS US WITH THY BLESSING

From *Psalms and Hymns for the Use of the Chapel of Rugby School* (1843), appointed respectively for the first and the last Sundays of the half-year.

For the tune LEWES see Hymn 65.

DISMISSAL, in Flood's *Harmonist* (1845), was composed for Hymn 299 in the present *Church Hymnary*.

679 REVIVE THY WORK, O LORD

Mr. Midlane's hymn, in *The Evangelist's Hymnbook* (1860) had the chorus added by Mrs. van Alstyne. The fifth verse, line 2, originally was 'Give Pentecostal showers'—which is more in keeping with the rest of the hymn.

CAMBERWELL is from *The European Psalmist* (1872), where Dr. S. S. Wesley harmonized an air whose source cannot be traced. Dr. Evans has re-harmonized it for this edition.

DOANE was the tune composed for the hymn in *Sacred Songs and Solos* (1883).

680 WE HAVE HEARD A JOYFUL SOUND

Miss Owens wrote this hymn for the mission anniversary of a Sunday School in Baltimore. It was adapted to the chorus of 'Vive le Roi' in Meyerbeer's opera *Les Huguenots* (see on Hymn 526). The sixth line of ver. 2 originally was 'Highest hills and deepest caves!'

LIMPSFIELD was composed by Josiah Booth for this hymn in the first edition of *The Church Hymnary*.

681 RESCUE THE PERISHING, CARE FOR THE DYING

From W. H. Doane's *Songs of Devotion* (1870). 'Fanny Crosby (Mrs. van Alstyne) returned one day from a visit to a mission in one of the worst districts in New York City, where she had heard about the needs of the lost and the perishing. Her sympathies were aroused to help the lowly and neglected, and the cry of her heart went forth in this hymn, which has become a battle-cry for the great army of Christian workers throughout the world' (Ira D. Sankey in *My Life and Sacred Songs*, p. 194).

The original had, in ver. 3, line 3, 'a loving heart.'

COMFORT, by C. A. Garratt, was set to this hymn in the *Hymnal of the Presbyterian Church in Canada* (1881).

682 TELL ME THE OLD, OLD STORY

Published as a leaflet in 1867, entitled 'The Story wanted'. It was composed, Miss Hankey said, on Jan. 29, 1866, 'when I was weak and weary after an illness, and especially realizing what most of us realize that simple thoughts in simple words are all that we can bear in sickness.' The authoress particularly objected to the hymn being printed in any other form than that in which she wrote it, i. e. in four-line verses, each verse complete in itself without any refrain.

REMEMBRANCE was the tune composed by Josiah Booth for the hymn in the first edition of *The Church Hymnary*.

683 I WILL SING THE WONDROUS STORY

Dr. Rowley writes: 'I was the minister of the First Baptist Church of North Adams, Massachusetts, at the time the hymn was written in 1886, as nearly as I can remember. The Church and the community were experiencing a period of unusual interest in religious matters, and I was assisted by a remarkable young singer by the name of Peter Bilhorn. One night after the close of a service he said: "Why don't you write a hymn for me to set to music".' During the night these most unpretentious and wholly unworthy verses came to me. Some years ago, as I was going down a London street one night about eleven o'clock, I discovered ahead of me a group of Salvation Army people holding a service, and as I got nearer to them it occurred to me that the hymn they were singing was very familiar. Then it dawned upon me that it was this one about which we are writing.'

The text of the hymn when it was included in *Sacred Songs and Solos* was altered, but the author never sanctioned these changes, and the present version, with the exception of the last line, is as in the original manuscript.

For the tune HYFRYDOL see note on Hymn 479. Bilhorn's tune may be found in *Sacred Songs and Solos*.

684 TO-DAY THY MERCY CALLS US

From Mr. Allen's *Hymns of the Christian Life* (1862) and *Church Hymns* (1871). One stanza is omitted, and the first person singular ('calls me') is changed as usual to the plural.

PENLAN is from *Gemau Mawl, Ail Attodiad* (1910).

685 THERE WERE NINETY AND NINE THAT SAFELY LAY

First published in *The Children's Hour* (1868), of which Miss M. Horsburgh, a cousin of Miss Elizabeth Clephane, was then editor. Myth has been busy about the circumstances in which this hymn was written, and it is not easy to ascertain the facts of the case. The following account is given in *Memories of the Past*, by the Rev. James Dodds, Dunbar. 'Miss Clephane was a regular contributor to *The Children's Hour*, and being on one occasion reminded by Miss Horsburgh that she had sent nothing for the next number, after some solicitation, she agreed to try her hand at a poetical composition. Saying that she had often thought of writing something on the Parable of the Lost Sheep, she retired to a corner of the room and began to write. In a very short time she handed to Miss Horsburgh a copy of the hymn which duly appeared in print as it now stands.' The words afterwards appeared in *The Family Treasury*, a monthly magazine very widely read at that time in religious circles of Scotland, and were copied into other periodicals. One of these, *The Christian Age* (May 13, 1874), fell into Mr. Sankey's hands. He was greatly struck by the verses, and being asked by Mr. Moody a few days afterwards at the close of an address in the Free Church Assembly Hall, Edinburgh, on the Lost Sheep, if he had any solo appropriate to sing, put the words before him on the organ, composing the music as he sang. (See an interesting account in his *My Life and Sacred Songs*, pp. 247–50.) Miss Clephane had died five years before this time. Her hymn had attracted very little notice, and it was at Melrose that her two surviving sisters heard Mr. Sankey sing the now well-known words and recognized them as her composition.

The first tune is by I. D. Sankey, as in *Sacred Songs and Solos* (1874). The present arrangement is by Dr. Evans.

BRYANT, by Dr. W. G. Alcock, has been here adapted to the words from the previous edition of *The Church Hymnary*, where it was set to the hymn, 'O north, with all thy vales of green.'

686 TO-DAY THE SAVIOUR CALLS

This appeared in *Spiritual Songs for Social Worship, adapted to the use of Families and Private Circles in Seasons of Revival* (1831). The first sketch of the hymn by Rev. Samuel F. Smith was submitted to Dr. Thomas Hastings, the editor of the above book, and was retouched by him.

Mr. Sankey tells that he was singing this hymn in a crowded meeting on Sunday evening, Oct. 8, 1871, in Farwell Hall, Chicago, at the very time when the great fire broke out which laid the city in ruins. 'By the time I had reached the third verse' (here omitted)—

> To-day the Saviour calls:
> For refuge fly:
> The storm of justice falls,
> And death is nigh.—

my voice was drowned by the loud noise of the fire engines rushing past the hall, and tolling of bells, among which we could hear, ever and anon, the deep sullen tones of the great city bell in the steeple of the Old Court House close at hand, ringing out a general alarm. Tremendous confusion was heard in the streets, and Mr. Moody decided to close the meeting at once. . . . After a few moments we separated and did not meet again for more than two months' (*My Life and Sacred Songs*, p. 8).

NAIN is from *Spiritual Songs for Social Worship . . . by T. Hastings and Lowell Mason* (1833).

687 LORD, I HEAR OF SHOWERS OF BLESSING

Written by Mrs. Codner in the summer of 1860 at Weston-super-Mare, on hearing of the news of the Revival in Ireland, and headed 'Bless me, even me also, O my Father (Gen. xxvii. 34).' The hymn was especially written for some young friends of Mrs. Codner's, on whom she was desirous of pressing an appeal that they should share in the blessing of which they had heard. 'I had no thought of sending it beyond the limits of my own circle, but passing it on to one and another it became a word of power, and I then published it (1861) as a leaflet.' In the original the closing (7th verse) runs:

> Pass me not! Thy lost one bringing:
> Bind my heart, O Lord, to Thee.
> While the streams of life are springing,
> Blessing others, O bless me—Even me.

RHEIDOL is from *Llyfr Tonau Cynulleidfaol* (1859).

688 COME, YE DISCONSOLATE, WHERE'ER YE LANGUISH

In Moore's *Sacred Songs* (1816) there appears a hymn of three verses beginning:

> Come, ye disconsolate, where'er you languish,
> Come, at God's altar fervently kneel.

In Hastings's and Mason's *Spiritual Songs for Social Worship*

(1832) the poem appears with one or two minor alterations in verses 1 and 2, and in place of Moore's third verse:

Go, ask the infidel what boon he brings us,
    What charm for aching hearts he can reveal,
Sweet as that heavenly promise Hope sings us—
    Earth hath no sorrow that God cannot heal,

the present ver. 3 is substituted. The alterations and the new verse were most probably the work of the editor, Dr. Thomas Hastings, and the hymn gains very greatly in the process.

ALMA REDEMPTORIS, by S. Webbe, is slightly altered, as in *The Scottish Mission Hymnbook* (1912), from the original in *A Collection of Motetts* (1792).

689 I HEAR THY WELCOME VOICE

'The words and music of this beautiful hymn were first published in a monthly, entitled "Guide to Holiness", a copy of which was sent to me in England in 1873. I immediately adopted it and had it published in "Sacred Songs and Solos". It proved to be one of the most helpful of the Revival hymns and was often used as an invitation hymn in England and America' (I. D. Sankey, *My Life and Sacred Songs*, p. 116).

690 THOU WHO DIDST ON CALVARY BLEED

From Mr. Burns's collection of hymns and prayers called *The Evening Hymn* (1857), where it was headed 'Out of the Depths'.

ST. AGATHA, by F. Southgate, was composed for the hymn 'Lord of mercy and of might', in *Favourite Hymn Tunes . . . used at St. Botolph's Church, Northfleet, London* (1873).

691 BENEATH THE CROSS OF JESUS

In *The Family Treasury* (1872, p. 398) two short poems appeared under the singular title, 'Breathings on the Border'. Of these the first is the hymn from which these verses have been selected. The poems were printed anonymously, with the editorial note that they expressed 'the experience, hopes and longings of a young Christian lately released'. Afterwards Miss Clephane's authorship was acknowledged (see note on Hymn 685). In ver. 2 'holy' has been changed to 'exiled' before 'patriarch'.

ST. CHRISTOPHER was composed by F. C. Maker for this hymn in *The Bristol Tune Book* (Supplement, 1881).

692 THERE IS A FOUNTAIN FILLED WITH BLOOD

Cowper wrote this probably in 1771; it was published in Conyers's *Collection of Psalms and Hymns* (1772), then in the *Olney Hymns*. Few hymns have aroused keener controversy, owing in the main to the imagery of the first verse, which is a Christian expansion or application of Zechariah xiii. 1. Attempts have been made to improve it, but they have proved disastrous failures, not excepting James Montgomery's version—

> From Calvary's Cross a fountain flows
> Of water and of blood,
> More healing than Bethesda's pool,
> Or famed Siloam's flood.

The hymn must be taken as Cowper wrote it, or not at all. Mrs. Oliphant, in her 'Golden Treasury' edition of *Cowper's Poems* (p. xxi) cannot believe 'it is often used by any congregation of worshipping people in these days'. But Professor Saintsbury declares that 'no finical or Philistine dislike of the phraseology ought to blind any lover of poetry to the wonderful tranced adoration of the movement of "There is a fountain filled with blood" ' (*History of English Prosody*, vol. ii, p. 533).

EVAN was originally a setting by Mr. Havergal, published in 1847, of Burns's poem, 'O Thou dread power, who reign'st above.' The melody is as follows:

Dr. Lowell Mason arranged the 1st, 2nd, 7th, and 8th lines as a psalm tune, and published it in the *New Carmina Sacra* (1850) under the name 'Eva', with the initial 'H.' as composer. Mr. Havergal did not approve of this, and in 1870 he rearranged the tune, and wrote thus regarding it: 'As the American arrangement was a sad estrangement, I have reconstructed the tune after a more correct form.' This is the form of the melody adopted here.

693 MAN OF SORROWS! WONDROUS NAME

This hymn by P. P. Bliss, as it appeared first in *The International Lessons Monthly* (1875), began 'Man of sorrows! what a name'. It echoes Isaiah liii. 3.

The tune is also by P. P. Bliss, as in *Sacred Songs and Solos* (1883).

694 I LAY MY SINS ON JESUS

First published in Dr. Bonar's *Songs for the Wilderness* (1844), where it is entitled 'The Fulness of Jesus'. It had been written about ten years earlier, when he was assistant in St. John's Church, Leith, 'in a desire to provide something which children could sing and appreciate in divine worship.' Probably this was the first hymn he ever wrote. He used to say of it modestly that it might be good gospel but that it was not good poetry.

The tune MUNICH, from the *Meiningen Gesangbuch* (1693), was there set to the hymn, 'O Gott, du frommer Gott.' The melody varies greatly in different books, but the present form is that adopted by Mendelssohn in the *Elijah* ('Cast thy burden upon the Lord').

695 I AM TRUSTING THEE, LORD JESUS

Written by Miss Havergal in September 1874 at Ormont Dessous, Vaud, Switzerland, and published in her *Loyal Responses* (1878), headed 'Trusting Jesus'.

'This was Miss Havergal's own favourite among her hymns, and was found in her pocket Bible after her death' (John Telford).

ST. HELEN'S was composed by Sir Robert Stewart for 'Art thou weary?' in the Irish *Church Hymnal* (1874).

696 JESUS, I WILL TRUST THEE

Mrs. Walker's hymn appeared in her husband's *Psalms and Hymns for Public and Social Worship* (Appendix of 1864).

URSWICKE, by Sir George Elvey, appeared first in *The Children's Hymnbook*, which Mrs. Carey Brock edited in 1881.

697 MY HOPE IS BUILT ON NOTHING LESS

Mr. Mote's hymn was composed probably about 1834, and published in *Hymns of Praise. A new Selection of Gospel Hymns combining all the excellencies of our Spiritual Poets, with many Originals* (1836). The hymn is entitled 'The immutable Basis of a Sinner's Hope'. In the original, the first verse begins 'Nor earth nor hell my soul can move', the present first verse being the second.

' "I went astray from my youth", said the author of this hymn. "My Sundays were spent on the streets in play. So ignorant was I that I did not know there was a God." Mote was a cabinet-maker by trade, and was converted under the preaching of the Rev. John Hyatt. The refrain came into his mind one morning as he was walking up Holborn Hill on his way to work. Four stanzas were completed that day, and two more on the following Sunday' (I. D. Sankey, *My Life and Sacred Songs*, p. 260).

TYNEMOUTH (ST. CATHERINE) is from Hemy's *Crown of Jesus Music* (1864).

698 I AM NOT SKILLED TO UNDERSTAND

From Miss Greenwell's *Songs of Salvation* (1873).

ACH GOTT UND HERR appears here in the form arranged by Bach in his *Choralgesänge*. It came out in the *Neu Leipziger Gesangbuch* of

1682, slightly altered from an air already published in a book issued at Freiburg (1655).

699 O CHRIST, IN THEE MY SOUL HATH FOUND

The authorship remains unknown. A favourite hymn of Gilmour of Mongolia; also of Professor Henry Drummond, if one may judge from the frequency with which he used to give it out at meetings for university students in the Oddfellows' Hall, Edinburgh, 1885-9.

Mr. McGranahan's tune, NONE BUT CHRIST, was composed for the hymn, in *Sacred Songs and Solos* (1883).

700 I NEED THEE EVERY HOUR

Written by Mrs. Hawks in April 1872, and published in Dr. Robert Lowry's *Royal Diadem* (1873). It first appeared in a small collection of Gospel Songs prepared for the National Baptist Sunday School Association which met at Cincinnati in November 1872, and was sung there. The refrain was added by Dr. Lowry.

The tune I NEED THEE, also by Dr. Lowry, is from *The Royal Diadem* (1873).

701 WHAT A FRIEND WE HAVE IN JESUS

From H. L. Hastings's *Social Hymns, Original and Selected* (1865). According to Dr. A. W. Mahon (*Canadian Hymns and Hymn-writers*, 1908), it is undoubtedly the most popular Canadian contribution to the hymnody of the Church. Mr. Scriven wrote the hymn near Port Hope in Canada, but its authorship remained a secret. 'A neighbour sitting up with him in his [last] illness happened upon a manuscript copy of "What a Friend we have in Jesus". Reading it with great delight, and questioning Mr. Scriven about it, he said that he had composed it for his mother, to comfort her in a time of special sorrow, not intending that any one else should see it. Some time later, when another neighbour asked him if it was true that he composed the hymn, his reply was, "The Lord and I did it between us" ' (Ira D. Sankey in *My Life and Sacred Songs*, p. 279).

EBENEZER, by T. J. Williams, is a tune from *Llawlyfr Moliant* (1890).

This tune is known by the alternative name of 'Ton y Botel', and the picturesque legend is widely credited that it was so named because it was found in a bottle washed ashore in a storm on the Welsh coast. The story, however, is entirely without foundation.

CONVERSE, by Dr. C. C. Converse, was composed for the hymn, in *Silver Wings* (1870).

702 THROUGH THE LOVE OF GOD OUR SAVIOUR

In *Hymns intended to help the Communion of Saints* (1847), Miss Peters's hymn has (in ver. 2, line 5) 'still to God confiding'.

NUTFIELD, by Dr. W. H. Monk, appeared in *Hymns Ancient and Modern* (1861), set to 'God that madest earth and heaven'.

703 A DEBTOR TO MERCY ALONE

Toplady contributed this hymn to *The Gospel Magazine* (May 1771). It is here restored to use, after a period of curious neglect in many modern hymn-books. The allusion, in the opening lines of ver. 3, is to Isaiah xlix. 16. The text is unaltered.

'One of the most noticeable characteristics of a hymn by Toplady', says Mr. Thomas Wright in his *Life of Toplady* (p. 100), 'is the forcefulness, the arresting power of the opening line. There is no waiting: you are under his spell in a moment.' This is illustrated by the previous hymns from his pen in this collection (i.e. 413, 560, 561).

LLANGRISTIOLUS, by Dr. Joseph Parry, is from *Llyfr Tonau Cynulleidfaol* (*Ychwanegiad*, ed. J. Roberts, 1870).

704 YIELD NOT TO TEMPTATION

Written by Dr. Palmer in 1868 and published in *The National Sunday School Teachers' Magazine* of the same year. Dr. Palmer wrote (as quoted by Mr. Sankey): 'This song was an inspiration. I was at work on the dry subject of "Theory" when the complete idea flashed upon me, and I laid aside the theoretical work, and hurriedly penned both words and music as fast as I could write them. I submitted them to the criticism of a friend afterwards and some changes were made in the third stanza, but the first two are exactly as they came to me. . . . I am reverently thankful it has been a power for good.'

The original text has been improved at two places: in the first line, Dr. Palmer wrote 'for weakness is sin'; and in ver. 3 (line 3) 'the Saviour'.

FORTITUDE was the tune composed for the hymn by Dr. Palmer himself, in *Sabbath School Songs* (1868).

705 I'VE FOUND A FRIEND! O SUCH A FRIEND

Mr. Small's hymn appeared in *The Revival Hymn Book* (2nd series, 1863) and later in the author's *Psalms and Sacred Songs* (1866).

HIS FOR EVER was composed by Sir Joseph Barnby for the hymn, in the third edition (1890) of *The Hymnal Companion to the Book of Common Prayer*.

706 JESUS, SAVIOUR, PILOT ME

Dr. Hopper's hymn appeared in *The Sailor's Magazine* (New York, 1871), but it was first used in public at an anniversary service of the Seamen's Friend Society held in the Broadway Tabernacle, New York, on May 10, 1880.

The tune VOLLER WUNDER comes from *Geistliche Andacht-Lieder Herrn Paul Gerhard . . . gesetzt von J. G. Ebeling* (Berlin, 1666, 1667).

707 SAFE IN THE ARMS OF JESUS

Written by Mrs. van Alstyne on April 30, 1868, at the request of Mr. W. H. Doane, to be sung to his well-known tune REFUGE, both being published first in *Songs of Devotion for Christian Associations* (1870).

When the fatal attack was made on Bishop Hannington (see on Hymn 444), he was overheard singing this hymn as he was dragged off by the savages.

Dr. John Hall of New York said at a convention of Sunday Schools that this hymn had given more peace and satisfaction to mothers who had lost children, than any other he had ever known.

In ver. 1 (line 8) the original had 'jasper', not 'crystal'.

708 NOW TO HIM WHO LOVED US

From Samuel M. Waring's *Sacred Melodies* (1826), where it was followed by a second verse. Indeed only the first two and the fourth lines belong to Mr. Waring, for he originally finished the verse thus:

> Oped His heart's pure fount to lave us,
> Gave His life that we might live,
> Give we glory;
> His be glory,
> By whose death, whose life, we live.

For the tune see Hymn 134.

709 PRAISE GOD FROM WHOM ALL BLESSINGS FLOW

The closing verse of Ken's Hymns (256, 291).
For the tune see Hymn 229.

710 NOW TO THE KING OF HEAVEN

A combination of lines from Doddridge's *Hymns* (ed. Humphreys, n. 52) and Watts's version of Psalm cxlviii. 9.

ST. JOHN appears in the third volume (1851) of *The Parish Choir*, but there is no information about its source or composer, and it has not yet been traced to any earlier collection.

711 TO HIM WHO SITS UPON THE THRONE

The original closing verse of Watts's hymn, under Paraphrase lxv, as recast by William Cameron (see note on 223).
For the tune see Hymn 131.

712 GLORY BE TO THE FATHER

This was commonly known as the Lesser Doxology, the Larger being the 'Gloria in Excelsis' (Hymn 717). The English is not an exact rendering of the Latin but is ancient and adequate. The original of the first clause goes back to the ante-Nicene period, and the second clause was added probably by the sixth century. 'Though the Latin name of it, *Gloria Patri*, be retained in our nation from the Roman Church,' says Isaac Watts in his *Hymns and Spiritual Songs*, 'and though there may be some excess of superstitious honour paid to the words of it, which may have wrought some unhappy pre-judice in weaker Christians, yet I believe it still to be one of the parts of Christian worship.' Unfortunately many of Watts's predecessors in the seventeenth century were weaker Christians who were strong enough to induce the Scottish Church to drop this hymn of praise. In the Scottish Church it was sung in its usual place after the psalm, from 1595 to about 1643, when some sympathizers with the English Brownists, a sect of the Independents, began to give up using the Lord's Prayer and the *Gloria Patri* and the practice of the minister kneeling for private devotion when he entered the pulpit, these being acts of worship which English puritans of the narrower type disliked. The General Assembly of 1642 denounced this spirit of innovation; the 'laudable practices' were commended to Presbyteries. Robert Baillie showed in detail the scriptural character of the *Gloria Patri*, and retorted to those who said it was part of the English Liturgy and the Roman Massbook, that 'this proves it not to be any worse than the Lord's Prayer and the Belief [the Creed] which are both in these evil books too!' Old Mr. David Calderwood, the learned historian, was equally eager in support of the *Gloria* as a devout act of praise. According to one tradition he exclaimed in the Assembly, 'Let that alone, for I hope to sing it in glory'. Nevertheless the formula was dropped from the *Directory for Public Worship*, out of a well-meant but misguided policy of consideration for the narrower English puritans. The general result of this deference was a decline of worship into slovenliness and irreverence, from which it took the Church of Scotland about two centuries to recover.

713 HOLY, HOLY, HOLY, LORD GOD ALMIGHTY

The Ter Sanctus or Trisagion is an early Christian reproduction of a Jewish synagogue doxology, based on Isaiah vi. 3. The Greek original in the early liturgies varies slightly. The English form is that which was printed in the Communion Service of *The Book of Common Prayer*.

714 THE BENEDICTUS (St. Luke i. 68–79), in two forms—first the text of the Authorized Version, second the text as in *The Great Bible* of 1539, from which it passed into *The Book of Common Prayer*.

715 THE MAGNIFICAT (St. Luke i. 46–55), similarly in its two forms. In the Eastern Church it is sung at morning service; but in the West it 'has been sung at Vespers since the time of St. Benet, who probably gave it that position' (*A New History of the Book of Common Prayer*, Proctor and Frere, p. 402).

716 THE NUNC DIMITTIS (St. Luke ii. 29–32), similarly in its two forms. It has been used as a canticle from early times, at evening worship.

717 GLORY BE TO GOD ON HIGH

The 'Gloria in excelsis' (see on 712) is an early hymn of the Greek Church for morning worship; its present form is first found among the psalms and canticles at the end of the famous Codex Alexandrinus, but it goes back to an earlier date than the fifth century. The version here printed is from *The Book of Common Prayer*, where it comes in the Communion Service. It is a rendering of the Latin translation.

718 THE 'TE DEUM LAUDAMUS' is here printed as in *The Book of Common Prayer*, where it forms part of the Morning Service, as indeed the original hymn has done ever since the sixth century. The original is a Latin composition, not later than the fifth century, which has undergone a number of changes in the course of transmission. Some critics to-day accept the tradition that Niceta, the Bishop of Rumesiana (392–414), was its author. 'We assume', says Dr. A. E. Burn in his *Introduction to the Creeds* (p. 275), 'that Niceta sent or brought it to Italy, possibly in time to be sung by St. Ambrose and St. Augustine in 386 or in the last decade of the century.' An examination of its contents shows that it draws upon the Apostles' Creed (724), the 'Gloria in Excelsis' (717), and the Psalms (e.g. xxviii. 9, xxxi. 1, xxxiii. 22, cxxiii. 3, cxlv. 2). It is a splendid illustration of the truth that a real confession of faith ought to be sung, and as such it has been on the lips of the Church ever since it was composed. Luther, who ranked it only third to the Apostles' Creed and the Nicene Creed, enthusiastically praised it as 'a fine symbol or confession, not only for confessing the right faith but also for praising and thanking God withal'.

Its use, not only for great occasions like a coronation but for the celebration of victories in war, is noted by Shakespeare in the fourth Act (scene 8) of *King Henry the Fifth*, where, following Holinshed, he makes the English monarch exclaim, in the hour of triumph,

> Do we all holy rites:
> Let there be sung 'Non nobis' and 'Te Deum'.

An interesting slip in the English version is worth noting. The original Latin text of ver. 21 had 'munerari' i.e. 'Cause them to be rewarded with Thy saints'. But in the fifteenth century (about 1491) 'munerari' came to be written occasionally as 'numerari' (i.e. 'Cause them to be numbered with Thy saints', and this happened to be the form adopted in the final ecclesiastical English version.

The structure of the hymn is simple: first (1–13) the praise of the

Trinity, then the praise of the Redeemer (14–21), and finally praise and prayer, mainly petitions drawn from the Psalms (22–9).

719 THE 'BENEDICITE', in its original form, is part of the Greek version of the Old Testament, being the song of the three men in the fiery furnace, which the Septuagint translators inserted between verses 23 and 24 of the third chapter of the book of Daniel. It thus became known to the early Church, and ere long was used as a canticle in morning worship. From the Latin it was rendered into English, and in its present form it is an alternative to the Te Deum in the morning service of *The Book of Common Prayer*.

720 THE TEN COMMANDMENTS, as in the Authorized Version of Exodus xx. 1–17.

721 THE COMMANDMENTS OF THE LORD JESUS, as in the Authorized Version of St. Matthew xxii. 37–39, St. Mark xii. 29–31, and St. John xiii. 34.

722 THE BEATITUDES, as in the Authorized Version of St. Matthew v. 3–10.

723 THE LORD'S PRAYER in two forms, the first being that of the Authorized Version of St. Matthew vi. 9–13, the second being that taken over from *The Great Bible* of 1539 into *The Book of Common Prayer*. Of the few sound features in *The Directory for Public Worship* (which was taken over by the Church of Scotland, in the seventeenth century, from the English Puritans), one was the admission that 'because the Prayer which Christ taught His disciples is not only a pattern of prayer but itself a most comprehensive prayer, we recommend it to be used in the prayers of the Church'.

724 THE APOSTLES' CREED, as in *The Book of Common Prayer*. The original reached its present form by the middle of the eighth century, but its earliest form is to be traced as early as the fourth century. In Scotland it remained part of the Church's heritage after the Reformation; even in the seventeenth century, when the Church felt obliged to take over the *Directory for Public Worship*, the Westminster Confession of Faith, and the Catechisms, from the English Puritans (see on Hymn 712),the Catechisms had the Apostles' Creed as well as the Ten Commandments appended to them, the reason being that this Creed 'is a brief sum of the Christian faith, agreeable to the Word of God and anciently received in the Churches of Christ'. But its exclusion from the *Directory* checked for generations the use of it in catechizing, in congregational praise, and at the sacrament of baptism; it was one of the omissions in the *Directory*

which, together with its provisos, sadly impoverished the worship of the Scottish Church till the revival of worship came in the nineteenth century. The Apostles' Creed 'to the common mind of Christendom stands as, next to Holy Writ, the most venerable bond of unity and symbol of harmonious faith. . . . Short of the supreme confession of Simon Peter, which the Lord Himself accepted, no document exists which can rival it as the Creed of Creeds' (Professor W. A. Curtis, *History of Creeds and Confessions of Faith*, pp. 63, 64).

In the first edition of *The Church Hymnary*, a note was appended to 'descended into hell', indicating that this meant 'continued in the state of the dead, and under the power of death till the third day'.

725 THE NICENE CREED

As the Apostles' Creed was originally and strictly the confession at baptism, so the so-called Nicene Creed was the confession of faith made by the communicant. It is here printed as in the Communion service of *The Book of Common Prayer*. It is Cranmer's rendering of the original, which was probably the creed of the Church of Jerusalem, as modified and sanctioned by the famous Council of Nicaea in A.D. 325. As in the later Latin form of the original, the plural has been changed into the singular ('I believe'); some other improvements were also made in the edition which thus became authoritative for the Western Church (see on 718). The Council gathered on May 20, and closed on August 25.

726 From the English Authorized Version of Ecclesiasticus xliv. 1–15 (verse 3 being divided into the present verses 3 and 4). The Greek title means that it is 'praise of the fathers', but, as Dr. Edersheim remarks, this magnificent piece of religious prose is 'rather praise of God in them and for them'. It enters specially into all commemoration services, when the duty and joy are felt of remembering those in the past to whose sacrifices and services we owe our present heritage of faith and freedom.

727 From the Authorized Version of Numbers vi. 24–6.

728 AMEN was taken over from the Jewish church as a liturgical expression. It is common to Judaism, Christianity, and Islam, always as a response. The congregation sing or repeat Amen, at the close of prayer offered by the minister, and conclude their own praise by this deliberate affirmation 'So be it!' The word pledges the worshipping people to what they have heard or uttered, and is thus, or ought to be, a solemn and heartfelt avowal of their faith. It is like signing one's name to a document, not a thing to be done casually. Yet in many congregations the 'Amen' is left, at the end of the prayers and the benediction, to the minister, or, if it is used, it is

uttered with an offhand air, so that it sounds like an anticlimax, whereas it should gather up the full heart of the people. As Sir Walford Davies observes, in his preface to *A Students' Hymnal* (p. xi), 'An Amen cannot be too good. It is music's chance to embody the great Christian affirmative. In singing an Amen it is well to pretend you may never sing another, and put everything into it, recalling St. Paul's great saying: "In Him was Yea".' This applies also to the utterance of Amen, even without a musical accompaniment, at the close of the prayers.

BIOGRAPHICAL AND HISTORICAL NOTES ON AUTHORS, COMPOSERS, SOURCES, ETC.

ABÉLARD, PIERRE (Le Pallet, 1079–1142, St. Marcel), renowned alike for his philosophical ability and his romantic story, was the son of a noble Breton house, and became a Lecturer in the Cathedral School at Notre Dame, Paris, where he had many distinguished pupils and exercised great influence. Here began, too, his passionate attachment to Héloïse, niece of a Canon named Fulbert. The pair fled to Brittany, where a son was born, and they were privately married. In view of the disclosure and catastrophe which followed, Abélard entered the Abbey of St. Denis as a monk, while Héloïse took the veil. Abélard's fame as a teacher increased, and in spite of official condemnation of his doctrines, the hermitage he built himself at Nogent became a noted theological school, which he called the Paraclete. On his taking charge of the Abbey of St. Gildas, the Paraclete was made a religious house for women under the charge of Héloïse. Finally, at the instance of Bernard of Clairvaux, Abélard was found guilty of heresy by a council at Sens and by the Pope. He died on his way to defend himself at Rome, and was buried by Héloïse. Their ashes are now in the Père-Lachaise Cemetery in Paris.

As a hymn-writer he was little known until last century, when several of his poems were discovered in the Vatican, and a number of others in the Royal Library at Brussels.

224. *O what their joy and their glory must be.*

ADAMS, JESSIE (Ipswich, 1863–   ), is a member of the Society of Friends, and leader of the local Adult School at Frimley, where she resides. She is an ardent advocate of the most advanced progressive causes. She has written many hymns and verses, which, however, have not been published in a collected form.

528. *I feel the winds of God to-day.*

ADAMS, SARAH FLOWER, *née* SARAH FULLER FLOWER (Harlow, Essex, 1805–48, London) was the second daughter of Benjamin Flower, editor of *The Cambridge Intelligencer*, and, later, of *The Political Review*. For an alleged breach of privilege in criticizing the political action of the Bishop of Llandaff, he was imprisoned in Newgate. There a schoolmistress of South Molton, Devon, one of his ardent political disciples, sought him to tender her sympathy. They were married on his release. Their two daughters were both gifted; the elder, Eliza, in music, Sarah in letters. The latter had an ambition towards the drama, but her small stature disqualified her for the stage. She contributed largely in verse and prose to *The Repository*, a periodical edited by the Rev. William Johnson Fox, her minister at South Place Religious Society, Finsbury, a prominent journalist, man of letters, orator, reformer, and philanthropist of his time; in his later years he was M.P. for Oldham. In 1840–1 he published, for use in his church, a collection of *Hymns and Anthems, the Words chiefly from Holy Scripture and the Writings of the Poets*. The music was edited by Eliza Flower, who contributed 63 of the 150 tunes, and adapted and arranged others; while Sarah contributed 13 hymns, one of which was 'Nearer, my God, to Thee'. In 1834 she married William Bridges Adams, an engineer and inventor, who was then a contributor of political articles of an advanced type to *The Repository*. Afterwards, he established large and prosperous railway-carriage works at Bow. In 1841 Mrs. Adams published *Vivia Perpetua*, a dramatic poem in five acts; and in 1845 *The Flock at the Fountain*, a catechism for children, with hymns interspersed. She had striking features, and abundant intellectual force. Leigh Hunt called her 'rare mistress of thought and tears'. Browning was her friend, and spoke of her in later life as 'a very remarkable person'. The original of his *Pauline* was her sister Eliza, whom the youthful Browning thought 'the incarnation of a poet's dreams'. Eliza died of consumption in 1847; Sarah, herself of a delicate constitution, contracted the same disease while nursing her, and died the following year. When she was buried near Harlow, her hymn, 'He sendeth sun, He sendeth shower', the only one, besides ' Nearer, my God, to Thee', which has come much into use, was sung over her grave.

 475. *Nearer, my God, to Thee.*
 303. *Part in peace; Christ's life was peace.*

ADCOCK, JOHN (Loughborough, 1838–1919, Nottingham) became at sixteen years of age, usher in a school, choirmaster of the local chapel, and conductor of a choral society, at Spalding. In 1858 he entered a music-seller's business, of which he became manager, at Nottingham. There he was for twenty-one years choirmaster of Castle Gate Congregational Church, and for sixteen, conductor of the Nottingham Sacred Harmonic Society. He compiled *The School Hymnal Tune Book*, to which he contributed a number of tunes.

 669. WOODBROOK.

ADDISON, JOSEPH (Milston, Wiltshire, 1672–1719, London), son of Lancelot Addison, Rector of Milston and afterwards Dean of Lichfield, was educated at Charterhouse (where he had as fellow-pupil his friend Richard Steele) and at Queen's College and Magdalen, Oxford. Intended for the Church, he turned instead to literature and politics, attached himself to the Whig interest, and found a patron in Charles Montague, afterwards Lord Halifax. His early literary efforts included an address to Dryden, a translation of part of Virgil's *Georgics*, and an account of the greatest English poets. In 1699 his political friends secured for him a pension with a view to foreign travel, and he visited France, Italy, Austria, Germany, and Holland. The death of William III seemed to threaten his prospects, but in the following reign a laudatory poem on Marlborough's victory at Blenheim brought him preferment to various successive offices of state. His release from public life on the fall of the Godolphin Ministry in 1710 gave him leisure for the composition of the Essays on which his fame mainly rests. Most of these were contributed to the *Tatler*, the *Spectator*, and the *Guardian*, in all of which he collaborated with his friend Steele. The best of his work is in the *Spectator*. Those years saw also the production of his tragedy *Cato*, which, mainly for political reasons, was successful beyond its deserts. The accession of George I brought Addison again into favour and office. In 1716 he married Charlotte, Countess of Warwick, but the marriage does not seem to have been a happy one, and his last years were further clouded by controversy and illness. John Wesley said that at a time when profligacy was flagrant and sobriety and religion were regarded as synonymous with Puritanism and hypocrisy, 'God raised up Mr. Addison and his associates to lash the prevailing vices and ridiculous and profane customs of the country, and to show the excellence of Christ and Christian institutions.' His hymns were all contributed to the *Spectator*.

> 10. *The spacious firmament on high.*
> 26. *When all Thy mercies, O my God.*

AHLE, JOHANN RUDOLPH (Mühlhausen, Thuringia, 1625–73, Mühlhausen), was educated at the Universities of Göttingen and Erfurt. In 1646 he was appointed Cantor at St. Andreas's Church, and director of the musical school, at Erfurt. Soon he became known as one of the most radical reformers of church music in his time. In 1649 he accepted the lucrative post of organist of St. Blasius's Church, Mühlhausen. He became a man of such public weight that he was elected to the Town Council in 1655, and was made Burgomaster in 1661. He published *Compendium pro tonellis*, a treatise on singing; *Geistliche Dialogen*; *Thüringischen Lust-Gartens*; *Neue Geistliche Chorstücke*; *Neuverfaste Chor-Musik* (motets), &c. He cultivated the simple style of the chorale, avoiding polyphonic counterpoint. His tunes were long popular, and are still much used in Thuringia.

> 203, 307. LIEBSTER JESU.

AINGER, ARTHUR CAMPBELL, M.A. (Blackheath, 1841–1919, Eton), son of a vicar of Hampstead and Prebendary of St. Paul's, was educated on the foundation at Eton, and at Trinity College, Cambridge, where he won a first class in the Classical Tripos, 1864. From that year till 1901 he was an assistant master at Eton; his whole life was dedicated to the interests of the school. Described as 'one of the most distinguished and useful of Eton masters, a man of clear head, controlling character, wide accomplishments, a fine and *habile* scholar of the old school, with a remarkable memory, an incisive speaker, a good critic, fertile in suggestion, complete in execution', he is said to have 'preserved admirable and friendly discipline by means of a dry and ready irony, which was never harsh or unamiable. He set no punishments, and his justice, courtesy, and unruffled good humour won the respect and admiration of the boys.' He had a facile and fertile pen, and published the spirited and beautiful *Carmen Etonense*, and the well-known *Vale*, both set to music by Sir Joseph Barnby; *Eton Songs*; a section on Fives in *The Badminton Library*; a volume of *Memories of Eton Sixty Years Ago* (1917); and, with H. G. Winkle, M.A., an *English-Latin Verse Dictionary*. Hymns by him appear in several standard hymnals.

380. God is working His purpose out.

ALBERT, HEINRICH (Lobenstein, Voigtland, 1604–51, Königsberg), attended the Gymnasium at Gera, and afterwards became a pupil of his distinguished uncle Heinrich Schütz at Dresden, later also of Stobäus. At the desire of his parents he abandoned the study of music, and went to Leipzig to study law. Thence he set out with an embassy for Warsaw, but on the way was taken prisoner by the Swedes, and was not able to return until 1628, after suffering many hardships. The profession of law had little interest for him, and in 1632 he was glad to abandon it on his appointment to the organistship of the cathedral of Königsberg. His chief work was a collection of arias in eight volumes, to many of which he wrote the words. The preface contains an exposition by him of the principles of music.

145. GODESBERG.

ALCOCK, JOHN, Mus.Doc. (London, 1718–1806, Lichfield), was trained as a chorister, from seven years of age, in St. Paul's Cathedral, and was a pupil of John Stanley, the celebrated blind organist of St. Andrew's, Holborn, and of the Temple Church. He was organist of St. Andrew's, Plymouth, and of St. Lawrence's, Reading, before becoming, in 1749, master of the choristers, lay vicar, and organist of Lichfield Cathedral. His salary as organist there was only £4 per annum. He complained bitterly of the neglect of the cathedral services; all the time he was there, he said, there was not a book in the organ loft fit for use, but what he bought or wrote himself. Owing to the damp condition of the cathedral he contracted rheumatism, which compelled him to resign his offices, except that of lay-vicar, which he retained, while he acted as organist at Sutton Coldfield (1761–6) and St. Editha's, Tamworth (1766–90). He published *Six Lessons for the Harpsichord*; *Twelve Songs*; *Six Concertos*; *A Collection of Psalms, Hymns and Anthems*; *Six and Twenty Select Anthems*; *Divine Harmony, a Collection of Fifty-five Double and Single Chants*; *The Harmony of Sion* (a collection of Psalms); *Harmonia Festi* (Canons, Glees, and Catches).

717. CHANT IN B FLAT

ALCOCK, WALTER GALPIN, M.V.O., Mus.Doc. (Edenbridge, Kent, 1864–), studied at the National Training School for Music under Sullivan, Stainer, and J. F. Barnett. He was assistant organist at the Parish Church, Twickenham, 1873; organist there, 1879; organist at Quebec Chapel, now the Church of the Annunciation, Portman Square, 1887–95; at Holy Trinity, Sloane Square, 1895–1902: assistant organist, Westminster Abbey, 1896–1916; organist of the Chapels Royal, 1902–16; and has been organist and choirmaster of Salisbury Cathedral since 1917. He was for a time professor of the organ at the Royal College of Music. He officiated at the organ at the coronations of King Edward VII and King George. He has published a large quantity of organ and church music, an excellent *Organ Tutor*, and articles in the musical press.

685. BRYANT.

ALDERSON, ELIZA SIBBALD, *née* DYKES (Hull, 1818–89, Heath, near Wakefield, Yorkshire), was a sister of Dr. J. B. Dykes (q.v.). She had an unusual gift for painting and languages, and a talent for versification, of which, however, the total published fruit was twelve hymns. These were partly written at Kirkthorpe, where her husband, the Rev. W. T. Alderson, was *locum tenens* for a time, and partly at Wakefield, where he held the chaplaincy to the West Riding House of Correction from 1832 to 1876. The last years of her life were passed under much suffering. She was buried at Kirkthorpe.

103. *And now, beloved Lord, Thy soul resigning.*

ALEXANDER, CECIL FRANCES, *née* HUMPHREYS (Miltoun House, County Tyrone, 1823–95, The Palace, Londonderry), the daughter of Major Humphreys, was 'a pearl among women', of great attractiveness in spite of her short sight and excessive shyness. She was loved and sought in marriage by the two most brilliant men in the Irish Church, Professor Archer Butler and the Rev. William Alexander, who, after a stormy youth at Oxford, was then a curate in Londonderry. The latter won her, and they were united in what proved a perfect marriage. He was himself a poet, as well as a preacher of rare charm and oratorical power. They set up their home in an obscure little Donegal parish, then passed to Fahan and to Camus. In 1867 Dr. Alexander's great gifts were recognized by his appointment to the bishopric of Derry and Raphoe; in 1896 he was elected Archbishop of Armagh and Primate of all Ireland. Before her marriage Miss Humphreys published *Verses from Holy Scripture*, and *Hymns for Little Children*, based on the Church Catechism. The latter book (1848) was at once recognized to be of singular excellence; it 'created a new school and became its model'. Over 100 editions of it were published, and the profits were devoted by the authoress to the support of a Londonderry school for deaf mutes. Among her later books were *Moral Songs*; *Narrative Hymns*; *Legend of the Golden Prayer*; *Verses for Holy Seasons*; *Hymns Descriptive and Devotional*; *Poems on Subjects in the Old Testament*. The best of her work was collected by her husband, after her death, in a single volume, *Poems by Cecil Frances Alexander*. The best known of her longer poems, *The Burial of Moses*, was declared by Lord Houghton to be the finest sacred lyric in the language, and Tennyson avowed that he wished he had written it himself. Of her hymns Stopford Brooke said, 'Charmingly simple and tender, clear in dogma, and of poetical beauty, combining the plainness of Watts with the feeling for and with children of the Taylor sisters, and uniting with both the liturgical associations of the English Prayer Book, they remain unequalled and unapproachable.'

18. *All things bright and beautiful.*
663. *Do no sinful action.*
591. *Every morning the red sun.*
101. *His are the thousand sparkling rills.*
506. *I bind unto myself to-day.*
500. *Jesus calls us! O'er the tumult.*
69. *Once in royal David's city.*
185 *Spirit of God, that moved of old.*
130 *The golden gates are lifted up.*
105 *There is a green hill far away.*
516 *We are but little children weak.*

ALEXANDER, JAMES WADDELL, D.D. (Hopewell, Louisa County, Virginia, 1804–59, Sweetsprings, Virginia), was of Scottish descent. He was educated at New Jersey College and Princeton Theological Seminary. After pastorates in Charlotte County, Virginia, and Trenton, New Jersey, he occupied for twelve years the Chair of Belles Lettres and Rhetoric in New Jersey College. After a period of service in the ministry of Duane Street Presbyterian Church, New York, he returned to Princeton as Professor of Ecclesiastical History and Church Government. Finally, in 1851, he returned to the ministry, in Fifth Avenue Presbyterian Church, New York. He was a distinguished pulpit orator, and a ripe scholar. He contributed much to *The Princeton Quarterly Review*, and wrote more than thirty books for the American Sunday School Union alone. He was deeply interested in hymnology, and at one time contemplated the issue of a small hymn-book, to contain none but unaltered hymns, about 250. His own contributions to hymnody were translations, which were collected and published under the title, *The Breaking Crucible, and Other Translations.*

107. *O sacred Head, sore wounded.*

ALFORD, HENRY, D.D. (London, 1810–71, Canterbury), was son of the rector of Aston Sandford. Educated at the Grammar School, Ilminster, and Trinity College, Cambridge, he served as curate to his father at Winkfield, Wilts, also at Ampton; became vicar of Wymeswold, Leicestershire, then incumbent of Quebec Chapel, London, and, finally, in 1857, Dean of Canterbury. He was a Fellow of his college, and Hulsean Lecturer. *The Contemporary Review* was started and for some time edited by him. Among his works were an edition of Homer; a volume of *English Descriptive Poetry*; *A Dissuasive against Rome*; a volume on *The Queen's English*; and various volumes of sermons. He wrote much poetry also, was greatly interested in hymnology, and himself wrote and translated many hymns, including a series for Sundays and Holy Days throughout the year. These were published in *Psalms and Hymns* (1844), *The Year of Praise* (1867), *Poetical Works* (1868), and other volumes. His *magnum opus* was his *Greek Testament*, which marked a great advance in the progress of New Testament scholarship in this country, and took its place as the standard critical commentary of the later nineteenth century. He was a member of the New Testament Revision Company. A strenuous worker, never idle, at the end of a hard day's work he would stand up, as at the end of a meal, and thank God for what he had received. He was catholic-spirited, a supporter of the Evangelical Alliance, and throughout his life maintained cordial relations with Nonconformists. All his life he cherished a desire, never to be fulfilled, to visit the Holy Land. This unrealized longing suggested the beautiful inscription on his tombstone—'Deversorium viatoris proficiscentis Hierosolymam'—'the inn of a pilgrim travelling to Jerusalem'.

> 619. *Come, ye thankful people, come.*
> 579. *'Forward!' be our watchword.*
> 221. *Ten thousand times ten thousand.*

ALLEN, OSWALD (Kirkby Lonsdale, Westmorland, 1816–78, Kirkby Lonsdale), was the son of a successful banker. From boyhood his health was impaired: he suffered all his life from a diseased spine, and was educated at home. A measure of recovery led to his beginning business in Glasgow, on the Stock Exchange, but a recurrence of his constitutional malady obliged him to abandon it. Returning to his native place (the 'Lowton' of *Jane Eyre*), he joined in 1848 the staff of the bank of the Lancaster Banking Company there, and ultimately became manager. While confined to the house during the severe winter of 1859–60, he found congenial occupation in completing his *Hymns of the Christian Life*, 148 hymns (1861). When the little book was published, the Bank staff, it is said, viewed this proceeding on the part of one of their officials with no little perturbation. The family was Sandemanian (Glasite) in its religious affiliation. Oswald's great-uncle, James Allen, who was a hymn-writer also, was a prominent and active member of that denomination.

684. *To-day Thy mercy calls us.*

ALSTYNE, FRANCES JANE VAN, *née* CROSBY, best known as Fanny Crosby (South-East, Putnam County, New York, 1820–1915, Bridgeport, Connecticut), lost her eyesight when six weeks old through the ignorant application of a warm poultice to her eyes. She was educated at the New York (City) Institute for the Blind, and afterwards was a teacher there until, in 1858, she married Alexander van Alstyne, a blind musician. She was a member of the Methodist Episcopal Church. Her first verses were published when she was eight years old, and as she continued writing with unfaltering facility until her death in her eighty-fifth year, she produced a vast quantity of verse. Till middle life she wrote songs, principally of a highly sentimental cast; some of them, like *The Hazel Dell* and *Rosalie the Prairie Flower*, had an enormous popularity. Thereafter she devoted herself to writing hymns. One New York firm salaried her to supply them with three hymns a week all the year round, and she was able to meet the contract. She is said to have written for two firms alone 5,959 hymns, and she wrote about 1,500 more for W. H. Doane, Robert Lowry, Philip Phillips, Ira D. Sankey, and other editors of evangelistic collections—nearly 8,000 in all. She published under 216 *noms de plume* as well as under her own maiden and married names. About sixty of her hymns are in use.

669. *If I come to Jesus.*
681. *Rescue the perishing.*
707. *Safe in the arms of Jesus.*

ALTENBURG, JOHANN MICHAEL (Alach, *c.* 1584–*c.* 1640, Erfurt), pastor and musician, was educated at Erfurt, and spent most of his life in the neighbourhood of that town. He was successively pastor of various charges, mostly at or near Erfurt, during the troublous times of the Thirty Years War. Altenburg was a good musician and composed tunes as well as hymns.

217. *Fear not, thou faithful Christian flock.*

ST. AMBROSE (Trèves, 340–97, Milan), the greatest bishop in his day of the Western Church, was the son of a prefect of Gaul. He studied law, and was early appointed governor of the district of Northern Italy in which is situated the city of Milan. In the conflict between Catholics and Arians he displayed such courage and wisdom that on the death of the Bishop of Milan in 374 he was elected bishop by acclamation, and, though only a catechumen, was baptized and consecrated forthwith. As bishop he showed himself at once gentle and firm. He was no respecter of persons, as was seen in his long and victorious conflict with the Arian Empress, Justina, and in his refusal to allow the Emperor Theodosius to enter the church till he had done penance for the massacre at Thessalonica. Ambrose was renowned for his piety and eloquence, of which we have strong testimony from his great pupil Augustine. His writings and sermons, while not free from the allegorising tendency of his day, made a powerful and popular appeal. Ambrose's greatest service to the Church was the improvement he effected in its musical services. He seems to have been the first to introduce in the West the practice of antiphonal singing, besides being himself a hymn-writer of distinction. Grimm calls him 'the Father of Church Song'. There is no foundation for the belief (at one time widely accepted) that he was the author or part-author of the *Te Deum*.

4. *O Trinity, O blessèd Light.*

ANCHORS, WILLIAM (early eighteenth century), published *A Choice Collection of Psalm-Tunes, Hymns, and Anthems* in 1720.

148. (WALSALL)

ANDERNACH is a little town in the district of Coblenz on the Rhine, once a Roman fortress, afterwards a residence of the Merovingian kings, which gave its name to a Gesangbuch produced there in 1608 by the Guild of St. Cecilia, under the title *Catholische Geistliche Gesänge*. This book represented a departure from the plainsong type of tune in favour of others of a more popular kind. It contained Latin hymns with German translations, and original German hymns also.

230. ANDERNACH.
420. JESU, DULCIS MEMORIA.
468. TRES MAGI DE GENTIBUS.

ANDERSON, JAMES SMITH, Mus. Bac. (Crail, Fife, 1853–), received his musical education in Edinburgh under Sir George (then Mr.) Martin, and subsequently in Glasgow under Dr. A. L. Peace. He received the degree of Mus. Bac., Oxon., in 1878, and became F.R.C.O. in the same year. As organist and choirmaster he served in succession Nicolson Square Wesleyan Chapel, Abbey Parish Church, St. Thomas's Episcopal Church, and St. Andrew's Parish Church, all in Edinburgh. He has contributed to many hymnals, and revised the harmonies of *The Blackburn Tune Book* and *The Presbyterian Hymnal for the Young* (United Presbyterian). As representing the Society of Organists of Edinburgh, Mr. Anderson acted as an associate member of the Revision Committee which prepared the present *Church Hymnary*, of the Music Sub-Committee, and of the committee of experts who edited the music.

81. ES IST EIN ROS' ENTSPRUNGEN (arr.).	543. PSALM 6 (arr.).
141. FINGAL.	97. PSALM 80 ,,
645. GREYFRIARS (arr.)	460. PSALM 86 ,,
586. OLD 18TH ,,	104. SHILOH ,,

ANSTICE, JOSEPH, M.A. (Madeley Wood, Shropshire, 1808–36, Torquay), was educated by his uncle at Enmore Rectory, Bridgwater, at Westminster School, and at Christ Church, Oxford. He gained the Newdigate Prize in 1828 for a poem on *Richard Coeur de Lion*, and a Double First Class two years later. During his Oxford days, according to Lord Morley, he was the friend who influenced Gladstone most and in the deepest things. Gladstone in 1830 describes him as 'a very clever man, and more than a clever man, a man of excellent principle, and of perfect self-command and of great industry. I bless and praise God for his presence here' (Morley's *Life of Gladstone*, i, p. 55). Again (*Diary*, Mar. 2, 1836): 'Read to my deep sorrow of Anstice's death on Monday. His friends, his young widow, the world can spare him ill; so says at least the flesh' (p. 134). At the age of twenty-two Anstice was appointed Professor of Classical Literature at King's College, London. Within three years his health failed, and he died at the age of 28. He had published his English Prize Essay on *The Influence of the Roman Conquest upon Literature and the Arts at Rome*; and *Selections from the Choice Poetry of the Greek Dramatic Writers, translated into English Verse*. His fifty-two hymns were printed for private circulation—*Hymns by the Late Joseph Anstice, M.A.* (Bridgwater, 1836).

> 615. *Lord of the harvest, once again.*
> 543. *O Lord, how happy should we be.*

AQUINAS, THOMAS (Aquino, 1227–74, Fossa Nuova), was the son of a Count of Aquino and was closely related to several of the reigning families of Europe. At an early age and in spite of family opposition, he joined the Dominican order, and studied under Albertus Magnus at Cologne and afterwards at Paris, where at the Pope's request he defended his Order with great success in its controversy with the University on liberty of teaching. His life was one of extraordinary industry, his public service and tedious journeys on behalf of his Order being only equalled by his immense literary activity. He refused all ecclesiastical preferments and rewards. Summoned by the Pope to attend the Council of Lyons on the differences between the Greek and Latin Churches, he died before reaching the Council. Thomas's philosophy aims at gathering together all known science into a single system, a condensed summary of which is given in his

Summa Theologiae, still the standard theological text-book of the Roman Church. Though his hymns are not numerous, several of those which he wrote on the Lord's Supper are of great merit.

319. *Thee we adore, O hidden Saviour, Thee.*

ARMES, PHILIP, Mus. Doc. (Norwich, 1836–1908, Durham), was trained as a chorister at Norwich and Rochester Cathedrals. In the latter he was solo boy, and at the end of his service as such was presented with a grand pianoforte by the Dean and Chapter as a mark of the exceptional value of his work. He became organist of St. Andrew's, Wells Street, London, in 1857 ; of Chichester Cathedral in 1861 ; and of Durham Cathedral in 1862. In addition to his Oxford doctorate, he held the same honour and also the M.A. degree from Durham University, in which he was Professor of Music from 1897. He was much honoured and beloved in the Cathedral city. His published works include an oratorio, *Hezekiah*; two Church oratorios, *St. John the Evangelist*, and *St. Barnabas*; services, anthems, hymn-tunes, organ music; a five-part madrigal, &c.

647. GALILEE.

ARMITAGE, ELLA SOPHIA, *née* BULLEY, M.A. (Liverpool, 1841–), is a granddaughter of the Rev. Thomas Raffles, D.D., LL.D., of Liverpool, long one of the most distinguished figures of English Nonconformity. She was one of the first students of Miss Clough at Newnham College. In 1874, she married the Rev. Elkanah Armitage, M.A., afterwards Professor in the (Congregational) Yorkshire United College, Bradford. She served on the School Boards of Rotherham and Bradford, and on the West Riding Education Committee: also as an assistant commissioner to the Royal Commission on Secondary Education. For a time she was Lecturer on English History in the former Women's Department of Manchester University. Her degree was conferred on her, *honoris causâ*, by that University, for her work in archaeology. She says, 'I believe I was intended by nature for an archaeologist, but life has made me a hymn-writer, and I shall be content to be known as such when my archaeology is forgotten.' Her publications include *The Childhood of the English Nation*; *The Connection of England and Scotland*; *A Key to English Antiquities*; *The Education of the Christian Home*; *An Introduction to English Antiquities*; *The Early Norman Castles of the British Isles*; and a Service of Song entitled *The Garden of the Lord*, in which there are sixteen of her hymns.

355. *O Lord of life, and love, and power.*

ARMSTRONG, JOHN, D.D. (Bishop Wearmouth, 1813–56, Grahamstown, South Africa), came of an ancient Border stock. He was educated at Charterhouse and Lincoln College, Oxford. Ordained in 1837, he served as curate at Alford, Gloucestershire; Wotton-Fitzpaine, Dorset; and Clifton. In 1841 he became a priest-vicar of the Cathedral, and rector of St. Paul's parish, Exeter, and in 1845 exchanged to Tidenham, a parish between the Severn and the Wye. While there he did much literary work, and originated and helped to organize the Church Penitentiary Association for the reclamation of fallen women. In 1853 he accepted the bishopric of Grahamstown, South Africa. Pulmonary disease, however, had already laid hold of him, and the strain of organizing a new diocese, and of travelling in difficult conditions over its vast distances, quickly wore out his strength; he died of 'over-work and over-anxiety' within two years of his arrival. He published *The Pastor in the Closet*; *Sermons for the Christian Seasons*; *Parochial Sermons*; and a volume of his *Notes in South Africa* was issued after his death.

334. *O Thou who makest souls to shine.*

ARTHUR, EDWARD (Resolven, 1874–   ), is a musician well known under another name in Wales.

427. BODLONDEB.	303. PAX VOBISCUM.
192. LLANSAMLET.	614. ST. SULIEN.
17. LUCERNA LAUDONIAE.	544. TABERNACLE.
671. LUMETTO.	218. ST. KENTIGERN.

ATTWOOD, THOMAS (London, 1765–1838, Chelsea), was the son of a trumpeter, viola player, and coal merchant. As a chorister in the Chapel Royal, he came under the notice of the Prince of Wales, afterwards George IV, and was sent abroad by him to study, first in Italy, then in Vienna under Mozart, one of whose favourite pupils he became. In 1796 he was appointed organist of St. Paul's Cathedral and composer to the Chapel Royal; in 1841, organist of George IV's private chapel at Brighton; in 1823, one of the first professors of the Royal Academy of Music on its foundation; and in 1836, organist of the Chapel Royal. In early life he was much engaged in dramatic composition, and did not till comparatively late begin to write Church music. In this, however, he showed marked originality, and in many respects may be called 'the father of modern church music'. He was one of the first musicians in this country to recognize the genius of Mendelssohn, who dedicated to him his three Preludes and Fugues for the organ. He wrote many songs and glees, one song, *The Soldier's Dream*, long retaining its popularity; many sonatas; and services, anthems, chants. A volume of his church compositions, containing four services, eight anthems, and nine chants, was published about fifteen years after his death. He was a man of singularly lovable character, of sincere religious spirit, and of rare musical gifts.

183. ATTWOOD (VENI CREATOR).   713. SANCTUS.

Biographical and Historical Notes

AUBER, HARRIET (London, 1773–1862, Hoddesdon), was one of the daughters of James Auber, whose grandfather, Pierre Auber (Aubert), of Ecquetat in Normandy, came to England in 1685, as a Huguenot refugee after the Revocation of the Edict of Nantes. Most of her life was spent in the quiet villages of Broxbourne and Hoddesdon, Hertfordshire. In *The Spirit of the Psalms* (1829), she endeavoured to put 'elegance' and 'poetic language' into versions of certain selected psalms, hoping that these would displace from use the often far from poetic versions of Sternhold and Hopkins. Some of them did find their way into hymn-books in England and America; Mr. Spurgeon in particular made considerable use of them in his Metropolitan Tabernacle collection. Miss Auber's volume included also a selection of hymns of literary quality, by various writers; and among a number of contributions from her own pen was the one exquisite lyric by which her name survives. She had written much poetry before the issue of this volume, and she wrote much after it, but such was her modesty that even her own relatives were not permitted to see it. Her spirit was one of singular beauty and attractiveness. A dear friend, Miss Mary Jane Mackenzie, authoress of *Lectures on the Parables*, *Lectures on the Miracles*, and other religious books, lived with her for many years, and the memory of the two saintly ladies was long cherished with veneration and affection in Hoddesdon and its neighbourhood.

180. *Our blest Redeemer, ere He breathed.*

BACH, JOHANN SEBASTIAN (Eisenach, 1685–1750, Leipzig), belonged to the most musical family ever known. They were of peasant stock, and Bach himself was an embodiment of the simple personal and domestic virtues and the deep religious sentiment most characteristic of his race. He was trained in the choir schools of Ohrdruf and Lüneburg, and held official positions at Arnstadt, Mülhausen, Weimar, and Anhalt Cöthen, before he settled finally in Leipzig as cantor of the famous Thomas School and director of music in the Thomas and Nicholas Churches. His name is held by many to be the greatest of all in the history of music, whether sacred or secular. With the exception of opera, he handled every type of musical form with unequalled mastery. He was the greatest organist, not only of his own time, but of all time; both as a player and as a composer for that instrument, he 'stands at the summit of human achievement'. His lofty genius was wholly consecrated to the service of God in the Church that held his heart, and what Palestrina was to the Roman Church, Bach became to Protestantism. He had immense physical and mental energy, and poured out works that were prodigal not only in quantity, but in fertility of ideas, variety of sentiment, and inimitable perfection. He left many vocal works, including motets, masses, about 200 cantatas (verse anthems), and two great *Passions*, the St. Matthew and the St. John. He reharmonized the old German chorales, many of which he embodied in his *Passions*. A collection of over 370 of them was subsequently published. 'In Bach's hands the music of the period marked its climax of expression, the chorale was idealized to the highest pitch, the combination of orchestra, chorus, and solo voices in the *Passions*, the *B Minor Mass*, and the *Church Cantatas*, became pillars of the house of musical art for all time.' Schumann said of him, 'To him music owes almost as great a debt as a religion owes its Founder.'

278. ACH BLEIB BEI UNS (arr.).
698. ACH GOTT UND HERR (arr.).
129. ALLE MENSCHEN MÜSSEN STERBEN (SCHÖNBERG) (arr.).
304. DAS NEUGEBORNE KINDELEIN (arr.).
89. DAS WALT' GOTT VATER (arr.).
241. EISENACH (arr.).
492. ERMUNTRE DICH (arr.).
271. GOTTLOB ES GEHT (arr.).
254. HERR JESU CHRIST (arr.).
216. HERZLIEBSTER JESU (arr.).
547. ICH HALTE TREULICH STILL.
284. INNSBRUCK (arr.).
64. LIEBSTER IMMANUEL (arr.).
203, 307. LIEBSTER JESU (arr.).
413. NICHT SO TRAURIG.
417. NUN KOMM, DER HEIDEN HEILAND (arr.).
107. PASSION CHORALE (arr.).
459. VATER UNSER (arr.).
56. VOM HIMMEL HOCH (arr.).
285. ZUM FRIEDEN (arr.).

BAKER, HENRY, Mus. Bac. (Nuneham, Oxfordshire, 1835–1910, Wimbledon), son of the Rev. James Baker, rector of Nuneham Courtney, and afterwards Chancellor of the Diocese of Durham, was educated at Winchester and as a civil engineer at Cooper's Hill. For many years he was employed in his profession on railway work in India. Music was always a passion with him, and under encouragement from Dr. Dykes, he proceeded in 1867 to his musical degree at Exeter College, Oxford. He wrote several tunes for Horder's *Worship Song*.

501. HESPERUS.

BAKER, Sir HENRY WILLIAMS, Bart., M.A. (London, 1821–77, Monkland), was the son of Vice-Admiral Sir Henry Loraine Baker, Bart., and was educated at Trinity College, Cambridge. Ordained in 1844, he became vicar of Monkland, near Leominster, in 1851. In 1859 he succeeded to the baronetcy. He was the chief promoter of *Hymns Ancient and Modern*, and from the first, for twenty years, was chairman and acknowledged leader of the Committee responsible for the preparation and development of that epoch-making book. He was an able editor, skilled in the selection of men to carry out his ideas, and firm in dealing with them. He exercised his editorial right of altering contributions freely—so freely that one contributor who smarted under his changes said sarcastically that H. A. and M. should be taken to mean, 'Hymns asked for and mutilated'. Many of his alterations, however, have been generally approved. The immense popularity of the book was a tribute to his accurate diagnosis of the needs of the Anglican Church and the masterly skill with which he provided for them. He contributed translations from the Latin, and many original hymns, some of which are among the most cherished of the devotional treasures of the Church. As a High Churchman, he held the doctrine of the celibacy of the clergy, and died unmarried. He published *Family Prayers for the Use of those who have to work hard*, and a *Daily Text Book* for the same class.

316. *I am not worthy, holy Lord.*
199. *Lord, Thy word abideth.*
646. *O God of love, O King of peace.*
102. *O perfect life of love.*
620. *Praise, O praise our God and King.*
438. *The King of Love my Shepherd is.*
594. *There is a blessed home.*
236. *We love the place, O God.*

391. STEPHANOS.

BARING-GOULD, SABINE, M.A. (Exeter, 1834–1924, Lew Trenchard), in early life lived much in Germany and France, was educated at Clare College, Cambridge, and ordained in 1861. He became curate of Horbury, with special charge of the mission at Horbury Bridge, in 1864; two years later, perpetual curate of Dalton, near Thirsk; in 1871, rector of East Mersea, Colchester; and in 1881, having in the meanwhile succeeded his father in the estate of Lew Trenchard, Devon, he exercised his privilege as squire and patron by presenting himself to the living there as rector. He was a man of an extraordinary range of interests, and of inexhaustible versatility and industry. He was said to have more works attached to his name in the British Museum catalogue than any other writer of his time. He wrote a long series of *The Lives of the Saints*; *A Study of St. Paul*; *The Origin and Development of Religious Belief*; books of travel in Iceland, Brittany, and Southern France; works on Germany and its Church; histories of the Caesars and Napoleon Bonaparte; popular books on antiquarian subjects, such as *The Book of Were-Wolves* and *Curious Myths of the Middle Ages*; and a very large number of novels, many of which, such as *Mehalah, John Herring, Richard Cable Lightshipman, Mrs. Curgenven of Curgenven*, enjoyed a large degree of popularity. He was a keen collector of folk-songs, of which he edited two valuable collections, *Songs of the West* and *A Garland of Country Song*.

288. *Now the day is over.*
535. *Onward! Christian soldiers.*
214. *Through the night of doubt and sorrow* (tr.).

258. EUDOXIA.

BARNBY, Sir JOSEPH (York, 1838–96, London), became a chorister in York Minster, and was an organist and choirmaster at twelve years of age. After studying at the R.A.M., he served as organist at St. Michael's, Queenhithe; St. James the Less, Westminster; St. Andrew's, Wells Street, where his choir reached a degree of efficiency second to none in London; and at St. Anne's, Soho, where he established annual recitals of Bach's Passion Music (St. Matthew and St. John). From 1875 to 1892, he was precentor and director of musical instruction at Eton College. From 1861 to 1876, he was musical adviser to Novello, Ewer & Co., who in 1867 established for him what became known as Barnby's Choir. Later, he conducted the Royal Choral Society. In 1892 he became Principal of the Guildhall School of Music, and was knighted. His published work includes an oratorio, *Rebekah*, part songs, vocal solos, a series of *Eton Songs*, many services and anthems, and 246 hymn-tunes, which were published in one volume after his death. He edited five hymn-books, of which the most notable was *The Hymnary* (1872) an advanced High Anglican collection which, from the importance of its music, was often spoken of as 'Barnby's Hymnary'. The only Presbyterian one was *The Home and School Hymnal* of the Free Church of Scotland (1893). He had outstanding gifts as a choirmaster, and did a great work in popularizing music; but he was primarily a church musician, 'before and beyond everything a servant of those great and solemn rites in which, faithfully carried out, there is more than enough to satisfy the most craving soul'.

128. CANTATE DOMINO.	327. O PERFECT LOVE.
216. CLOISTERS.	430. ST. CHRYSOSTOM.
588. CROSSING THE BAR.	606. ST. IGNATIUS.
705. HIS FOR EVER.	559. ST. SYLVESTER.
167. LAUDES DOMINI.	653. SPRINGTIDE HOUR.
566. LONGWOOD.	

BARNES, ARCHIE FAIRBAIRN, B.A., Mus. Doc., F.R.C.O., M.C. (Bristol, 1878–   ), was educated at Bristol Grammar School, the Royal College of Music (exhibitioner), and Keble College, Oxford (Scholar). He joined the Army in 1914, and served with the British Expeditionary Force in France, was awarded the Military Cross in 1916, and was wounded and captured in 1918. In 1920 he transferred from his regiment, the 2/5th Gloucesters, to the Army Educational Corps. For some time he was headmaster of the Queen Victoria School, Dunblane. He is now senior music master at Bishop's Stortford College. He has published nursery rhymes, songs, &c.

373. DUNBLANE CATHEDRAL.
638. MONTAGUE.

BARTHÉLÉMON, FRANÇOIS HIPPOLYTE (Bordeaux, 1741–1808, London), was the son of a French Government officer in the colonial department, and an Irish lady of a wealthy Queen's County family. Entering the army, he became an officer in Berwick's Regiment in the Irish Brigade. Here, however, he made the acquaintance of the Earl of Kellie, a musical enthusiast, who induced him to leave the army and adopt music as his profession. He came to England in 1765, and became one of the most distinguished violinists of his time. In that year he was appointed leader of the band at the opera, and in 1770, at Marylebone Gardens. He wrote much music for the theatre and the public gardens, but little for the Church. An acquaintance with the Rev. Jacob Duché, the refugee rector of Christ Church, Philadelphia, who became chaplain to the Female Orphan Asylum in 1782, and who is reputed to have edited the 1785 and 1789 editions of Riley's *Psalms and Hymns* for the chapel of that Asylum, led to his composing the one tune by which he is known. The first Mrs. Barthélémon attended Duché's ministry. Though remaining a clergyman of the Church of England, Duché preached the doctrines of the New Church (Swedenborgian), and Barthélémon himself ultimately embraced and died in that faith. His latter years were clouded by much misfortune; his daughter records that he died paralytic and broken-hearted. His works include much music for dramatic pieces, quartettes for stringed instruments, and preludes for the organ.

256. MORNING HYMN.

BARTON, BERNARD (Carlisle, 1784–1849, Woodbridge), was educated at a Quaker school at Ipswich, his parents being members of the Society of Friends, as he himself was also all his life. He was apprenticed at fourteen to a shop-keeper at Halstead, Essex, and subsequently carried on business for a time with his brother, as a coal and corn merchant, at Woodbridge, Suffolk. There he formed a friendship with Edward Fitzgerald, the translator of *The Rubaiyat of Omar Khayyam* and author of the famous *Letters*, who married his daughter. The death of his wife after a year of wedded happiness led to his going for a short time to Liverpool, where he acted as a tutor; but he returned to Woodbridge and became a clerk in a bank, which he served with exemplary faithfulness for forty years. 'So punctual and methodical was he that as he returned from the office each midday, the housewives knew it was the correct time to put their potatoes into water as he passed their doors, and they liked to watch him as, meeting a friend, he stopped to offer a pinch of snuff or tell a good story from Boswell.' He was a fascinating conversationalist, and a man of great sweetness of nature. Many distinguished men gave him their friendship, notably Charles Lamb and Byron; and he had interesting correspondence with Lord Jeffrey, Scott, Southey, and the Ettrick Shepherd. In 1841, on the recommendation of Sir Robert Peel, he was given a State pension of £100 a year. He published eight volumes of verse in his lifetime—*Metrical Effusions*; *Poems by an Amateur*, &c.; and a selection of his *Poems and Letters*, with a Memoir, was published by his daughter after his death.

> 207. *Lamp of our feet, whereby we trace.*
> 482. *Walk in the light; so shalt thou know.*

BARTON, WILLIAM (*c.* 1597–1678, Leicester), vicar of Mayfield, Staffordshire, and afterwards of St. Martin's, Leicester, was a friend of Richard Baxter and has been described as 'a conforming Puritan'. At Baxter's suggestion, he composed four metrical renderings of the *Te Deum*. He was keenly alive to the defects of the Sternhold and Hopkins Version of the Psalms, and himself essayed to produce a better, in *The Book of Psalms in Metre*, 1644. When, in 1646, the Westminster Assembly of Divines, in their desire to secure uniformity in worship throughout the kingdom, recommended for adoption, as the authorized metrical Psalter, Francis Rous's version, the House of Lords favoured Barton's in preference to it, and submitted his third edition (1646) to the Assembly for approval. They declined to countenance it, and Rous's version was ordered by the House of Commons, 'it and none other, . . . to be sung in all the churches and chapels within the kingdom.' The Scots, however, were dissatisfied with it, and in 1647 their Assembly appointed four persons to revise it, enjoining them to compare with it the versions of Zachary Boyd, Sir William Mure of Rowallan, and Barton, as well as the *Scottish Psalter* of 1564–5. Barton always claimed that the resultant version, the *Metrical Psalter* still in use in Scotland, was 'most-what' composed out of 'mine and Mr. Rous's'. His chief distinction was as a pioneer of modern hymnody. He issued successive 'centuries' of hymns which were finally assembled by his son in *Six Centuries of Select Hymns and Spiritual Songs, collected out of the Bible* (1688). Among the Independents his hymns as well as his psalms 'were widely introduced and used in some places for a long time. They accustomed the people to New Testament song and to a freer handling of Scripture than obtained under Psalmody. It was among the Independents that the new school of hymn writers was to arise and conquer the churches. And it was on them that Barton's influence told most, and through them that he helped to fix the type and character of the English Hymn as based upon Scripture and saturated with it.'

> 31. (COLESHILL.)

BATEMAN, CHRISTIAN HENRY (Wyke, near Halifax, 1813–89, Carlisle), was first a minister of the Moravian Church; then of Congregational churches in Edinburgh (Richmond Place), Hopton (Yorkshire), and Reading (Berkshire); then, taking orders in the Church of England, he served as curate of St. Luke's, Jersey, and chaplain to the Forces; as vicar of All Saints, Childshill, Middlesex; and finally as curate of St. John's, Penymynydd, Hawarden. His latter days were spent at Carlisle, without a charge. A hymn-book for children, edited by him, and published by Gall and Inglis (Edinburgh) under the title, *Sacred Melodies for Sabbath Schools and Families*, was for many years the book generally used in the Sunday schools of Scotland; its circulation ran into millions. After entering the Church of England, he published in London *The Children's Hymnal and Christian Year*.

177. *Come, children, join to sing.*

BATHURST, WILLIAM HILEY, M.A. (Cleve Dale, Mangotsfield, near Bristol, 1796–1877, Lydney Park), was son of the Rt. Hon. Charles Bragge, M.P. for Bristol, who assumed the name of Bathurst on succeeding to his uncle's estate of Lydney Park, Gloucestershire. Educated at Winchester and Christ Church, Oxford, where he graduated in 1818, he took Orders, and was presented by his kinsman, Earl Bathurst, to the rectory of Barwick-in-Elmet, near Leeds. During thirty-three years of ministry there he endeared himself to his parishioners by his 'eminent piety, his great simplicity of character, his tender love, and his abundant generosity'. Doctrinal difficulties arising out of the Prayer Book, and especially the baptismal and burial services, led to his resignation of the living in 1852. He then retired into private life at Darley Dale, near Matlock. In 1863 he succeeded to the family estate. He was a singularly shy and reserved man, 'and had the peculiarity of becoming utterly silent if one asked him the most trivial question'. He published *A Translation of the Georgics of Virgil* (1849); *Metrical Musings*; and *Psalms and Hymns for Public and Private Use* (Leeds, 1830).

474. *O for a faith that will not shrink.*

BATTISHILL, JONATHAN (London, 1738–1801, Islington), a chorister of St. Paul's, became deputy to Dr. Boyce as organist of the Chapel Royal, then organist of two city churches, St. Clement, Eastcheap, and Christ Church, Newgate Street. Possessed of a fine counter-tenor voice, he was one of the vocalists engaged to sing at the private concerts given by Charles Wesley to exhibit the precocious talent of his two marvellous boys, Charles and Samuel. For a time he was conductor (harpsichord player) at Covent Garden Theatre, and wrote much music for theatrical and concert platform use; but subsequently he composed almost exclusively for the Church. 'If he has left us too little in the way of ecclesiastical composition, it is all excellent, for it was love and true emotion which prompted him to write.' His memory was phenomenal. He could play through faultlessly a piece which he had read through but once, and on one occasion, though he had never seen a score of the work and had only twice heard it about thirty years before, he played through, to Dr.

Arnold, a large part of that composer's oratorio, *The Prodigal Son*, which Arnold himself had almost forgotten. He was buried near Boyce in the crypt of St. Paul's.

668. BATTISHILL.
717. CHANT IN A.

BAXTER, RICHARD (Rowton, 1615–91, London), one of the ablest as well as most devoted among the Puritan clergy, was brought up by his maternal grandfather, and educated at Wroxeter School, but never attended a University. After a short experience of Court life, his strong religious convictions led him to study divinity. Ordained to the ministry, he served successively at Bridgenorth and Kidderminster, with the latter of which his memory is chiefly associated, his popularity as a preacher being excelled only by his faithfulness as a pastor. Before long he began to distrust Episcopacy in its prevalent form, and during the Civil War he attached himself to the Parliamentary Army. With characteristic independence of spirit he rebuked Cromwell for assuming supreme power in the State, and defended the old Monarchy. For a short time after the Restoration he held the office of King's Chaplain, and took part in the abortive Savoy Conference, one result of which was his *Reformed Liturgy*. After the Act of Uniformity he was subjected to much intermittent persecution, culminating in his scandalous trial before the brutal Jeffreys in 1685. Released after a two years' imprisonment, he passed the remaining four years of his life in peace and honour.

Disposed to see some good in every form of Church government, and hating nothing so much as fanaticism, Baxter suffered, like Leighton, the reproach common to all moderate men in a time of stress. 'He grew too puritan for the Bishops and too episcopalian for the presbyterians.' Posterity, however, has reversed this judgement, and men of all parties have done honour to his name. Dean Stanley calls him 'the greatest of Protestant schoolmen'. His literary output is extraordinary in view of his desultory education, his constant ill health, and the frequent interruptions to his work. Among his 'books enough to fill a cart' (Jeffreys), the three which take first rank are *The Saints' Everlasting Rest* (1650); *The Reformed Pastor* (1656); and *The Call to the Unconverted* (1657). Of great biographical interest are his *Reliquiae*, containing a narrative of his life and times. His poetical works are of less merit.

225. *He wants not friends that hath Thy love.*
549. *Lord, it belongs not to my care.*
39. *Ye holy angels bright.*

BAYNES, ROBERT HALL, M.A. (Wellington, Somerset, 1831–95, Oxford) was educated at St. Edmund's Hall, Oxford, where he graduated in 1856. He was curate of Christ Church, Blackfriars; perpetual curate of St. Paul's, Whitechapel; vicar of Holy Trinity,

Maidstone; and vicar of St. Michael's, Coventry. In 1870 he was designated Bishop of Madagascar, but resigned the following year. In 1873 he received an honorary canonry in Worcester Cathedral, and in 1880 became vicar of Folkestone. His chief literary work was as a compiler and editor, of *Lyra Anglicana*, 1862; *English Lyrics*, 1865; *The Canterbury Hymnal*, 1864; *The Supplementary Hymnal*, 1869; *Home Songs for Quiet Hours*; *Hymns for Home Mission Services in the Church of England*, &c.

314. *Jesus, to Thy table led.*

BEECHING, HENRY CHARLES, D.D. (Bexhill, 1859–1919, Norwich), was educated at the City of London School and Balliol College, Oxford. After a curacy at Mossley Hill, Liverpool, he became rector of Yattendon, Berks, in 1885, and so continued till 1900; was Select Preacher at Oxford, Cambridge, and Dublin; Clark Lecturer in English Literature at Cambridge, 1900; Chaplain of Lincoln's Inn and Professor of Pastoral Theology, King's College, London, 1900–3; and in the latter year became Dean of Norwich. He was one of the authors of *Love in Idleness* and *Love in a Looking-Glass*; wrote *In a Garden, and Other Poems*; published, besides sermons, *Lectures on Poetry*, *Religio Laici*, *The Grace of Episcopacy*, *Pages from a Private Diary*, &c.; and edited Milton, Herbert, Vaughan, Daniel, Drayton, Tennyson's *In Memoriam*, also *Lyra Sacra* and *A Paradise of English Poetry*.

673. *God, who created me.*

BELL, JOHN MONTGOMERIE, W.S. (Edinburgh, 1837–1910, Edinburgh), son of Alexander Montgomerie Bell, Professor of Conveyancing in the University of Edinburgh, and author of *Bell's Lectures*, a well-known text-book on his subject; was educated at Edinburgh Academy and University, where he studied music as well as law. A member of the Society of Writers to the Signet, and of the firm of Bell, Bannerman and Finlay, W.S., he was also an enthusiastic botanist and a musician of much ability. He composed many fine tunes and anthems, and was a member of the Committee which prepared the first *Church Hymnary* (1898).

346. ST. GILES.

BELL, WILLIAM HENRY (St. Albans, 1873–   ), was trained as a chorister at St. Albans. Hearing that the Goss scholarship at the R.A.M. was vacant, he resolved to apply. As organ-playing was one of the chief requirements, and he was not an organist, he set to work, practised seven hours a day for a fortnight, and won the scholarship. He became Professor of Harmony at the R.A.M. in 1903; left in 1918 to take the oversight of the South African College of Music at Cape Town; and subsequently became Professor of Music and Dean of the Faculty of Music in the University there with which the College has been incorporated. He has written operas, songs, symphonies, *A Song of Greeting*, a symphonic poem, &c. In 1924 he was made a Fellow of the R.C.M., for services rendered to his art.

383. CATHCART.

BENSON, LOUIS FITZGERALD, D.D. (1855–   ), was educated at the University of Pennsylvania and trained first for the Bar. For seven years he practised law, then turned to the Church, was licensed to preach in 1886, and became minister of the Church of the Redeemer, Germantown, Philadelphia. This charge he resigned to edit the hymnals of the Presbyterian Church. He has been lecturer on Liturgics in Auburn Theological Seminary, and on Hymnology in Princeton Seminary. He edited *The Hymnal* (Presbyterian); *The Hymnal for Congregational Churches*; *The Chapel Hymnal*; *The School Hymnal*; and was joint-editor with Dr. Henry Van Dyke of *The Book of Common Worship of the Presbyterian Church in the United States*. He has also written books on *The Best Church Hymns*; *Best Hymns, a Handbook*; *The English Hymn, its Development and Use in Public Worship*. His collected *Hymns, Original and Translated*, were published in 1925.

74. *O sing a song of Bethlehem.*

BERNARD OF CLAIRVAUX, ST. (Fontaines, 1091–1153, Clairvaux), son of a knight who perished in the first crusade, entered the monastery of Citeaux when a young man, and became so noted for his ability and austerity, that he was chosen to head the band which founded the more famous Abbey of Clairvaux. In many ways he was the most influential man of his age. His preaching is universally admitted to have been of great power, and many of his sermons are preserved. About his hymns considerable uncertainty exists.

421. *Jesus! the very thought is sweet.*
422. *Jesus! the very thought of Thee.*
420. *Jesus, Thou Joy of loving hearts.*
249. *Light of the anxious heart.*
423. *O Jesus, King most wonderful.*

BERNARD OF CLUNY (twelfth century) sometimes called 'of Morlaix', erroneously, from his supposed birthplace (he was really born at Murles or Morlas), but more commonly 'of Cluny' from the great abbey of which he became a monk, is said to have been of English extraction. Of him, unlike his great contemporary Bernard of Clairvaux, practically nothing is known save his authorship of the poem *De Contemptu Mundi*, from which the well-known series of hymns undernoted is taken.

597. *Brief life is here our portion.*
598. *For thee, O dear, dear country.*
599. *Jerusalem the golden.*

Biographical and Historical Notes

BESLER, SAMUEL (1574–1625), son of the rector of the school of Brieg, Silesia, was appointed cantor of the seminary there in 1599, and in 1605, rector of the College of the Holy Spirit at Breslau. His compositions for the Church include: *Concentus ecclesiastico-domesticus* (chorales for four voices) (1608); *Citharae Davidicae psalmorum selectiorum prodromus* (1620), &c.

292. HERR GOTT VATER.

BEVAN, EMMA FRANCES, *née* SHUTTLEWORTH (Oxford, 1827–1909, Cannes), was a daughter of the Rev. Philip Nicholas Shuttleworth, Warden of New College, Oxford, afterwards Bishop of Chichester. She married Mr. R. C. L. Bevan of the Lombard Street banking firm, in 1856. Notwithstanding the strong ties that bound her to the Church of England, she joined the Plymouth Brethren. 'Turning (perhaps from the disappointments of Brethrenism) to the study of the German mystics, she produced from their writings, in a series of fascinating volumes, a catena of quotations in which the Darbyite is startled by the clearness and intensity of the echo of tones that have become familiar to his ear in such different surroundings' (W. B. Neatby). Among her publications were—*Songs of Eternal Life*, a series of translations from the German (1858); and *Songs of Praise for Christian Pilgrims* (1859).

394. *Sinners Jesus will receive.*
192. *Spirit of Grace, Thou Light of Life.*

BIANCO DA SIENA (Anciolina- ? , 1434, Venice). Little is known of his life. In 1367 he joined a religious order founded by John Columbinus of Siena, and is said to have spent the latter part of his life at Venice. His hymns (*Laudi Spirituali*) were published in 1851, and some of them have been translated into English by Dr. Littledale.

191. *Come down, O Love Divine.*

BICKERSTETH, EDWARD HENRY, D.D. (Islington, London, 1825–1906, London), was a son of the Rev. E. Bickersteth, who was the first secretary of the Church Missionary Society, then rector of Watton, Herts, a poet, and editor of *Christian Psalmody*, the best evangelical hymn-book of its time, and one which exercised a great influence in the Church of England. Edward was educated at Trinity College, Cambridge, and ordained in 1848. After holding curacies at Banningham, Norfolk, and Christ Church, Tunbridge Wells, he was, successively, rector of Hinton Martell; vicar of Christ Church, Hampstead; Dean of Gloucester; and Bishop of Exeter (1885–1900). His *Commentary on the New Testament* was widely used; he published also volumes of sermons and several volumes of poetry—*Poems* (1849); *The Two Brothers, and Other Poems* (1871); *Songs in the House of Pilgrimage*, &c. But his best work was probably as editor of *Psalms and Hymns*, based on his father's collection; and of *The Hymnal Companion to the Book of Common Prayer* (1870). Occasionally his editorial prerogative was unwisely exercised, as when he added a fourth verse to 'Lead, kindly light'; but the work as a whole was admirably done, more scrupulous respect than is usual being shown to authors' texts. This book soon practically superseded all other evangelical hymn-books, and by 1873 was used in nearly 1,500 churches.

> 370. *For My sake and the Gospel's, go.*
> 444. *Peace, perfect peace, in this dark world of sin?*
> 321. *'Till He come!' O let the words.*

BINNEY, THOMAS, D.D., LL.D. (Newcastle-on-Tyne, 1798–1874, London), served an apprenticeship to a bookseller, working from twelve to sixteen hours a day, yet finding time for reading and self-education. His father was of Scots extraction and a Presbyterian, but the son, for some unknown reason, turned to Congregationalism. Three years in the theological seminary of Coward College, Wymondley, Herts, prepared him for the ministry. As a student he showed no special promise, but his preaching powers soon made their mark in his first charges, at the New Meeting, Bedford, and St. James's Chapel, Newport, Isle of Wight. Going to London in 1829 as minister of the Weigh House Chapel, he quickly stepped into the front rank of Metropolitan preachers: by many he was regarded as the greatest of his day. He had an imposing presence and impressive oratorical gifts. A doughty controversialist, he waged unsparing argumentative warfare against the Church of England, then the home of many abuses which exposed it to attack. Besides many polemical writings, he published a book for young men—*Is it possible to make the best of both worlds?*—which was immensely popular: for the first twelve months it sold at the rate of 100 copies a day. He was a pioneer in the movement towards Nonconformist liturgical services. He edited and published a book by Charles W. Baird, D.D., of New York, on *Historical Sketches of the Liturgical Forms of the Reformed Churches*, with an introduction by himself and an appendix on the question, 'Are Dissenters to have a Liturgy?' This book and his own example in the devotional part of his services at the Weigh House Chapel, gave a great impulse to the movement towards improved services in Nonconformist churches. By a published sermon on *The Service of Song in the House of the Lord*, he gave an impetus also to the movement towards better music in such services: he was one of the first Nonconformists to introduce anthems and chanting. He was a voluminous writer of religious verse, but never imagined himself a poet. 'Did you ever write more poetry?' an admirer asked him. 'Cart-loads', was the reply. In his later years he was the Nestor of his denomination, and according to *The Spectator*, 'the great Dissenting Bishop.' Twice he filled the chair of the Congregational

Union of England and Wales. Dean Stanley took part in his funeral service.

36. *Eternal Light! Eternal Light!*

BIRKS, THOMAS RAWSON, M.A. (Staveley, Derbyshire, 1810–83, Cambridge), was the son of a tenant-farmer, and had a Nonconformist upbringing. Educated at Chesterfield, Mill Hill, and Trinity College, Cambridge, he graduated as second wrangler and became a Fellow of his College. On leaving the University he became curate at Watton to Edward Bickersteth, whose daughter he married. In 1844 he became vicar of Kelshall, Hertfordshire; in 1866 vicar of Holy Trinity, Cambridge, where he remained till 1877; Hon. Canon of Ely, 1871; and in 1872, Professor of Moral Philosophy, Cambridge. For twenty-one years he was hon. secretary to the Evangelical Alliance. He wrote largely on biblical, scientific, and prophetical subjects—*The Scripture Doctrine of Creation*; *The Philosophy of Human Responsibility*; *First Principles of Moral Science*; *Modern Utilitarianism*, &c. His hymns appeared in his father-in-law's *Christian Psalmody*, 1833, and *Companion Psalter*.

453. *O King of mercy, from Thy throne on high.*

BISHOP, JOHN (? 1665–1737, Winchester), a composer of the Purcellian school, became temporary organist and lay clerk of King's College, Cambridge, in 1687; organist of Winchester College in 1695; and in 1729, organist of Winchester Cathedral. He was buried in the cloisters of the College, where his epitaph describes him as 'Vir singulari probitate, integerrima vita, moribus innocuis, musicaeque scientiae bene peritus, qui, postquam huic Collegio per XLII. annos sedulo inserviisset, ad Caelestam Choram placide migravit, decimo nono die Decembris, anno Dom. 1737, Aetat. 72.'

6. LEICESTER.

BLAKE, WILLIAM (Carnaby Market, London, 1757–1827, Strand, London), was the son of a hosier. An engraver by training and profession, he was also a painter and poet of remarkable individuality and power. He determined early to be natural and sincere, and held himself aloof from the currents of ordinary practical life; so to the end of his days he remained untouched by the spirit of the world and kept his simplicity and almost innocence unspoiled. Thus his *Poetical Sketches*, begun at twelve and finished at twenty, struck an entirely new note in literature, by the freshness of their substance, music, and spirit. This book was published, by the help of friends, in the ordinary way. All his subsequent books were prepared and published by himself, the text being embodied in a scheme of pictorial design and illustration executed by himself on plates from which he printed the limited number of copies required by his narrow circle of admirers. His *Songs of Innocence*, dealing with the homeliest things, with an exquisite naturalness of feeling and expression, are 'the first sounding of the modern lyric, of its natural delight and sorrow'. The *Songs of Experience* are full of the trouble of the world. Blake was an ardent apostle of liberty, and a rebel against bondage in every form. His passion was to set men free from everything that imposed restraint on thought and conduct, whether in politics, religion, literature, art, or ordinary convention, so that the creative urge of personality, which he regarded as the divine in man, might express itself freely and fully. He was the unsparing enemy, therefore, of all social evils that tended to repress personality or destroy it—poverty, starvation, harlotry, the gambling passion, misery in all forms—at a time when these things stirred in few breasts the spirit of revolt; and he dreamed and sang of a new Jerusalem from which these things should be banished. It was to arise in this present scene; its spirit was to be the fellowship and love of which such evils are the antitheses and profanation, and the creative impulse towards it was to be derived from Jesus Christ, who is to be its centre and its head. Latterly, Blake lived and thought in the borderland between the world of reality and the world of dreams; he became a mystic and a seer. The prophetic books in which he tried to bring his visions into expression show a diminishing power of making the abstract symbols of language convey an intelligible meaning, but a steadily increasing power in the use of the language of pictorial imagery. One who was present at his death wrote, 'Just before he died, His countenance became fair—His eyes brighten'd, and He burst out singing of the things He saw in Heaven.'

640. *And did those feet, in ancient time.*

BLATCHFORD, Ambrose Nichols (Devonshire, 1842–1924, Bideford, Devon), was educated at Tavistock Grammar School and Manchester New College, London. In 1866 he became assistant minister at Lewin's Mead Unitarian Church, Bristol, and in 1876 succeeded to the full charge, in which he continued until he retired in 1915. He was deeply interested in education, politics, and social work, and became one of the best-known and most influential men in the city. 'He was a man of unusual vitality: as a preacher he attracted all sorts and conditions of people; and as a pastor his sympathy and strength and underlying tenderness won the hearts of very many to whom he became wise adviser and trusted friend.' He published in 1897 *Songs of Praise for School and Church* (56 hymns, a number of which are in current use).

28. *A gladsome hymn of praise we sing.*

BLISS, Philipp (P. P. Bliss) (Clearfield County, Pennsylvania, 1838–76, Ashtabula, Ohio), early in life separated the final p from his Christian name, and made his signature P. P. Bliss. He went to

Chicago in 1864 to conduct musical institutes and compose Sunday school melodies, under Dr. G. F. Root. Originally a Methodist, he became in 1871 a choir-member and Sunday school superintendent in the First Congregational Church in that city. He had a fine voice, great personal magnetism, and a remarkable faculty for writing simple Gospel hymns and wedding them to equally simple, vivacious popular melodies. In 1874 he joined the evangelist, Major D. W. Whittle, in his campaigning, conducting the music and singing solos, as Sankey did for Moody. He prepared for use in their meetings, *Gospel Songs*, the royalties on which, amounting to about £6,000, he devoted to their work. On Moody and Sankey's return from their first British evangelistic campaign, it was decided to combine their embryo *Sacred Songs and Solos* with Bliss's collection, and the joint-book was issued as *Gospel Hymns and Sacred Songs, by P. P. Bliss and I. D. Sankey*. This started a new school of hymn and hymn-tune writing. After their time the standard tended to deteriorate, and the immense pecuniary success of the original books tended to commercialize subsequent ventures and to vulgarize them. His death was tragic. He was travelling towards Chicago, when a railway bridge gave way and plunged his train into the stream below. He himself escaped, but in an endeavour to save his wife from the blazing car, he perished.

> 664. *God is always near me.*
> 693. *Man of sorrows! wondrous Name.*
> 693. MAN OF SORROWS.   664. ST. CYRIL.

BLUNT, (ABEL) GERALD (WILSON), M.A. (Chelsea, 1827–1902, Chelsea), was educated at Pembroke College, Cambridge. Ordained in 1851, he was a curate for a time at Lilleshall, Shropshire; in 1856 became rector of Crewe Green, Cheshire, and chaplain to Lord Crewe; and in 1860 accepted the living of St. Luke's, Chelsea. He was a Broad Churchman, and was associated with Maurice, Kingsley, and Dean Stanley. He was an intimate of Carlyle also.

> 347. *Here, Lord, we offer Thee all that is fairest.*

BLUNT, F. W. (1839–1921), was a solicitor in London.

> 288. LYNDHURST.

BODE, JOHN ERNEST, M.A. (London, 1816–74, Castle Camps, Cambridgeshire), was educated at Eton, Charterhouse, and Christ Church, Oxford, where he was the first winner of the Hertford Scholarship. He was a Student (Fellow) and Tutor of Christ Church for six years; then, in 1847, became rector of Westwell, Oxfordshire, and, later, of Castle Camps, Cambridgeshire. He was Bampton Lecturer in 1855, and in 1857 contested, unsuccessfully, the Chair of Poetry in Oxford, basing his claims on a volume of *Ballads from*

Herodotus, with an Introductory Poem (1853). He published also *Short Occasional Pieces*, and *Hymns from the Gospel of the Day for Each Sunday and Festivals of our Lord.*

508. *O Jesus, I have promised.*

BOGATZKY, KARL HEINRICH VON (Jankowe, near Militsch, Silesia, 1690–1774, Halle), was the son of a landowner of noble Hungarian family. He began life as a page at the court of the Duke of Weissenfels, then was sent to Breslau to train for the army. During a long illness, however, he became convinced that God had other plans for him. He came under the influence of A. H. Francke, and joined the Pietists. For refusing to enter the army his father, who had no sympathy with his religious views, disowned him. He became a student of theology, but, though he was able to speak at private gatherings, delicate health forbade his taking charge of a church. He devoted himself to religious authorship and to helping the Pietists in their charitable works. He had access to the higher ranks of society, and was instrumental in the conversion of not a few of the nobility of Bohemia, Silesia, and Saxony. Five years he spent at Saalfeld, writing much. The last twenty-eight years were spent at the Orphanage at Halle, where G. A. Francke gave him a room. Those years were shadowed by the decline of Pietism and the rise of a sceptical spirit. His *Das guldene Schatzkästlein der Kinder Gottes* (Breslau, 1718), begun in his student days at Halle, was translated into most European languages. Recast and expanded by John Berridge, as *The Golden Treasury*, it was for long a favourite book of devotion in Great Britain. He took a large part also in the production of the *Cöthen Hymns*, which played much the same part in the religious life of Germany at that time as the *Olney Hymns* did in England. For this and other collections he wrote some 400 hymns. His *Meditations and Prayers on the New Testament* appeared in seven volumes between 1755 and 1761, and his *Autobiography* in 1754.

377. *Wake, Spirit, who in times now olden.*

BOHEMIAN BRETHREN.—This body originated with the Calixtine or Utraquist section of the followers of the reformer John Hus. The chief demands of this community were for (1) the unrestricted preaching of God's word; (2) Communion in both kinds, the laity to receive the cup (calix) as well as the bread (communio sub utraque specie); (3) the apostolic poverty and moral purity of the clergy; (4) strictness of Church discipline. The Brethren separated from the Utraquists in 1467. They called themselves Jednota Bratrská, which they rendered into Latin as Unitas Fratrum. Their chief concern was to secure practical Christianity, the fulfilling of the law of Christ in daily life and conduct—whence they were sometimes called 'Fratres legis Christi'. Their spiritual leader about 1490 was Brother Lucas, who gave the body its organization and its first hymn-book and catechism. When the Reformation began, they were among the first to welcome it, and they sent ambassadors to Luther to see how far community of doctrine and discipline was possible. One of these was Michael Weisse (q.v.), whose translations from the Bohemian hymns in his *Ein New Gesengbuchlen* (1531) had a considerable influence on the early Lutheran hymnody. The history of the Brethren was much chequered by persecution from without and strife and division within. The last remnants of them found a refuge in Saxony and a new beginning (*vide* Zinzendorf) in 1725.

280. *Now God be with us, for the night is closing.*
114. (O MENSCH SIEH).

BONAR, HORATIUS, D.D. (Edinburgh, 1808–89, Edinburgh), the prince of Scottish hymn-writers, was the son of a solicitor of Excise, and was educated at the High School and the University of Edinburgh, at the latter under Chalmers. He began his ministry in the Church of Scotland as a missionary-assistant in Leith, but in 1838 was ordained at Kelso, in charge of the new North Parish there. His industry was prodigious. Throughout the Border country his influence was deeply felt, but his name quickly became more widely known through his evangelical tracts, devotional books of which he produced one almost every year, and the vast correspondence he carried on with inquirers who wrote to him for counsel. When the Disruption of the Church of Scotland took place in 1843, he entered the Free Church, and was for a time joint-editor of *The Border Watch*, a newspaper conducted in the interest of that Church. In 1855–6, a visit to Egypt and Palestine deepened greatly his interest in the Jews and in the study of prophecy, to which he had derived a strong impulse from Edward Irving. All his life his mind was much occupied with the subject of the Second Advent. This interest inspired much of his writing both in prose and in verse. Through many of his hymns 'sounds the refrain of "the solemn canticle of death" '; they are full of the spirit of home-sickness. For many years he edited *The Journal of Prophecy*. In 1866 he became minister of the Chalmers Memorial Free Church, Grange, Edinburgh, and in 1883 was elected Moderator of the General Assembly of his Church. His ministry was one of remarkable devotion. 'One said of him that he was always visiting, another that he was always preaching, another that he was always writing, another that he was always praying.' One of the most sacred memories of members of his household was that of the voice they used to hear for hours together from behind the locked door of his study, pouring out fervent prayer. A young servant in the house owed her conversion to this, for, she said, 'If *he* needs to pray so much, what will become of me if I do not pray?' He was a man of wide scholarship and culture. His mind was saturated with Scripture, and his heart possessed by a faith far broader and more generous than the Calvinistic creed to which his intellect gave assent. He loved children, and for them his first hymns were written. His lyrical gift was his constant solace and refuge, the lute with which he 'sang his sadness when sadness like a cloud begirt his way; the harp whose strings gave out his gladness when burst the sunshine of a happier day'. His hymns were thrown off in the most casual way: he seemed to attach little importance to them, and was seldom at pains to exercise the artificer's art upon them, or to refine their blemishes away; many of them, therefore, are marred by defective rhythm, inharmonious rhymes, and other obvious faults. But 'they have gone round the world, have been sung in churches of all communions, have been learned by little children, and hung as lights over the thickly closing waters of death'. The best of them rank with the classics; one or two have been claimed by exacting judges to be the best hymns ever written. Over 100 are in use in this country and America. Among Dr. Bonar's many books were— *Songs for the Wilderness; The Bible Hymn Book; Hymns Original and Selected; The Desert of Sinai; Hymns of Faith and Hope; The Land of Promise,* &c.

488. *Belovèd, let us love: love is of God.*
169. *Blessing and honour and glory and power.*
104. *By the Cross of Jesus standing.*
650. *Father, our children keep.*
  7. *Glory be to God the Father.*
356. *Go, labour on: spend and be spent.*
522. *He liveth long who liveth well.*
323. *Here, O my Lord, I see Thee face to face.*
410. *I heard the voice of Jesus say.*
694. *I lay my sins on Jesus.*
171. *Light of the world, for ever, ever shining.*
429. *Not what I am, O Lord, but what Thou art.*
514. *Through good report and evil, Lord.*
553. *Thy way, not mine, O Lord.*
255. *When the weary, seeking rest.*

BOOTH, JOSIAH (Coventry, 1852–   ), was educated at Oxford and at the R.A.M. He was organist, 1868–76, at Banbury, and 1877–1918 at Park Chapel (Congregational), Crouch End, London. He composed over 100 hymn-tunes, many of which appear in modern hymnals. He was part-editor of *The Congregational Hymnal* (1888), and Musical Adviser to the Committee responsible for *The Congregational Hymnary* (1916). He was elected A.R.A.M. in 1904.

20. BEECHWOOD.   674. EXCELSIOR.
680. LIMPSFIELD.   682. REMEMBRANCE.

BORTHWICK, JANE LAURIE (Edinburgh, 1813–97, Edinburgh), was the elder daughter of James Borthwick, manager of the North British Insurance Office, Edinburgh. Along with her sister Sarah

(Mrs. Findlater, q.v.) she published, in four series (1854, 1855, 1858, and 1862), *Hymns from the Land of Luther*, 69 of the translations being from her own pen, and 53 from Sarah's. The title of this book supplied the initials—H. L. L.—over which many of her hymns appeared in *The Family Treasury*. These were collected and published in 1857 as *Thoughts for Thoughtful Hours*. A further collection of translations, under the title *Alpine Lyrics*, consisting of a selection of the poems of Meta Heusser-Schweitzer, was published in 1875. It was while she was residing for a time in Switzerland that her attention was drawn by Baron de Diesbach to this study; but it was a suggestion of her father that she might translate for him some of the hymns of which she spoke in such high praise, that set her and her sister to the task in which they achieved so marked a success. She preferred to keep anonymity, and when Dr. Charles Rogers betrayed her identity in his *Lyra Britannica*, the disclosure sorely vexed her. She was a devoted religious and social worker. She showed deep interest in the Home and Foreign Missions of the Free Church of Scotland, to which she belonged, in the Edinburgh House of Refuge and one of the Reformatories, in the C.M.S. Mission in Singapore, and in the Moravian Mission in Labrador.

> 556. *Be still, my soul: the Lord is on thy side* (tr.).
> 567. *Jesus, still lead on* (tr.).
> 262. *Jesus, Sun of Righteousness* (tr.).

BORTNIANSKI, DMITRI STEPANOVITCH (Gloukoff, Ukraine, 1752–1825, St. Petersburg), early showed remarkable ability. Studying at Moscow, then at St. Petersburg under Galuppi, he followed that master, in 1768, to Venice, the Empress Catherine supplying the necessary funds, and he pursued his studies later in Bologna, Rome, and Naples. Returning to Russia in 1779, with his reputation as an operatic composer already made, he was appointed Director of the Empress's church choir, later called the Imperial Kapelle. He composed for it 35 sacred concertos in four parts, ten concertos for double choir, and a mass for three voices. His influence on Russian Church music was great and has been lasting. To him belongs the credit of having reduced it to a system. His works were edited by Tschaikovsky, and published in St. Petersburg in ten volumes.

459. ST. PETERSBURG.

BOURGEOIS, LOUIS (Paris, *c.* 1510– ?)—'a name come, with the slow justice of time, out of long obscurity, to high esteem'—was an adherent of Calvin, and followed him to Geneva in 1541. The Consistory appointed him Cantor in one of the churches there, and in 1545 master of the choristers in succession to Guillaume Franc. They also entrusted him with the duty of providing music for the metrical psalter, then under gradual preparation. A partial psalter

T 2

appeared in 1542. In this Bourgeois made alterations in some of the tunes hitherto in use, and replaced some of the old tunes with others quite different. He seems to have been concerned in the music of all editions of the psalter appearing within the following fifteen years. In 1547 there was printed at Lyons *Pseaulmes cinquante de David Roy ét Prophete, traduictz en vers françois par Clement Marot, et mis en musique par Loys Bourgeoys à quatre parties, à voix de contrepoinct égal consonnante au verbe. Tousiours mord envie.* This volume seems to embrace the whole of Bourgeois' work on the psalms to this date. It is not certain whether the melodies were composed by Bourgeois, or merely arranged by him in four-part harmony. The value set on his services by the Genevan authorities is shown by the fact that in the same year they voluntarily admitted him to the rights of citizenship in recognition of his high character and his gratuitous services in teaching the children. At the same time they exempted him from certain duties of citizenship, such as going on guard, in order that he might have more leisure for his special work. Shortly afterwards, however, they reduced his salary. An appeal against this decision, on the plea that it meant poverty for him, failed, even with the strong backing of Calvin, to secure him redress. Towards the end of 1551 he was thrown into prison for making unauthorized alterations on certain well-known tunes. Calvin, albeit remonstrating with him, secured his release after twenty-four hours. But other troubles followed, and finally, failing to induce his employers to allow the introduction of part-singing into public worship, he left Geneva and returned to Paris. From 1561, when he was still there, he vanishes from history. He had found in use at Geneva a Psalter with about thirty tunes; he left one with eighty-five, many of them, probably, his own. The alterations for which he was imprisoned ultimately received official sanction and passed into general use. Dr. Robert Bridges says, 'Historians who wish to give a true philosophical account of Calvin's influence at Geneva ought probably to refer a great part of it to the enthusiasm attendant on the singing of Bourgeois' melodies.' He rendered priceless service to the psalmody of the Reformed Church.

289. LES COMMANDEMENS DE DIEU.
156. OLD 134TH (ST. MICHAEL).
167. PSALM 3 (O SEIGNEUR).
543. PSALM 6.
360. PSALM 12 (DONNE SECOURS).
359. PSALM 42.
460. PSALM 86.
151. PSALM 107.
95. PSALM 110 (L'OMNIPOTENT).
318. PSALM 118 (RENDEZ À DIEU).

BOWRING, Sir JOHN, LL.D., F.R.S. (Exeter, 1792–1872, Exeter), was trained in his native town for a mercantile career. His amazing faculty for acquiring languages—he could boast ultimately that he knew 200 and could speak 100—was developed by travel abroad for commercial purposes. His friendship with Jeremy Bentham, whose works he afterwards edited, led to his becoming editor of the Radical *Westminster Review*. In 1831 business troubles led him to seek political employment, and he was given important commissions at home and abroad. Entering Parliament, he represented the Clyde Burghs, Kilmarnock, and Bolton, took an active share in the agitation for free trade, and was a frequent contributor to debate on fiscal, educational, and commercial problems. He obtained the introduction of the florin into the currency as the first step towards the establishment of the decimal system of coinage. In 1847 he was appointed consul at Canton, in 1854 plenipotentiary to China, and subsequently governor of Hong-Kong and chief superintendent of trade with China. He was then knighted. A successful vote of censure on him in the House of Commons, because of his policy, led to a General Election and to his resignation. Lord Elgin, who succeeded him, however, continued and carried out his policy. He was a strong supporter of the British Association. His works, published in thirty-six volumes, are almost forgotten, but some of his hymns survive, and, though he was a Unitarian, are in general Christian use.

    33. *God is love: His mercy brightens.*
    113. *In the Cross of Christ I glory.*

BOYCE, WILLIAM, Mus. Doc. (London, 1710–79, London), was the son of a cabinet-maker, and became a chorister of St. Paul's. In his youth his hearing became impaired, but this did not lessen the ardour of his studies. He became organist of several London churches; conductor of the Three Choirs of Gloucester, Worcester, and Hereford; Composer to the Chapel Royal; Master of the King's Band; one of the organists of the Chapel Royal. His deafness so increased that he had to give up teaching and relinquish some of his offices. He then employed himself in collecting and editing materials for the work by which he is best known, *Cathedral Music, being a Collection in score of the most valuable and useful compositions for that service by the several English masters of the last two hundred years* (1760). He published forty-six anthems, five services, eight symphonies, twelve sonatas, duets and songs, including *Heart of Oak*, and music for the theatre. An amiable man, of blameless life, and an excellent musician, he may be regarded as the last of the old English school of church composers. He was buried in a vault under the centre of the dome of St. Paul's.

    718. CHANT IN D.   435. SHARON (HALTON HOLGATE).

BOYD, WILLIAM (Montego Bay, Jamaica, 1847–), 'comes from an old Scots stock of lowland Border thieves'. He was educated at Hurstpierpoint, and Worcester College, Oxford. He began to compose at ten. At school Baring-Gould was his tutor. During the stay in Iceland which resulted in Baring-Gould's book on *Iceland, its*

Scenes and Sagas (1863), the teacher often wrote to the pupil recording tunes he had noted down on his tour. These Boyd put into the
harmonized shape in which they appear in the book. At Oxford he
was organ scholar of his College, and also played at St. Edmund Hall,
Trinity, and Pembroke. Ordained as deacon in 1877, and as priest
in 1882, he was rector of Wiggonholt-with-Greatham, Sussex,
1884–9, and vicar of All Saints, Norfolk Square, London, 1893–
1918. He retired in the latter year.

517. PENTECOST.

BRADBURY, WILLIAM BATCHELDER (York, Maine, 1816–68, Mont-
clair, New Jersey), after many struggles, owing to straitened circumstances, succeeded in getting a musical education under Lowell
Mason and G. J. Webb at Boston. He taught singing classes for a
time at Machias, Maine, and St. John's, New Brunswick; then obtained appointments as organist, first in the Baptist Church, Brooklyn, and afterwards in the Baptist Tabernacle, New York. Here he
organized singing classes for children, and juvenile musical festivals,
which exercised a wide influence. After a visit to England and Germany to study educational methods, he threw himself into the work
of organizing classes and conventions, and editing song-books, sacred
and secular. Sunday-school music was at a low ebb then; 'there had
begun to be a general adoption of street melodies of every description, from "Cocachelunk" to "We won't go home till morning".'
Though Bradbury's tunes were not of a high order, they furnished
'the barrier by which the fearful tide was stopped'. He was author
or editor of about sixty collections of popular music. His cantata
Esther for many years had a phenomenal popularity. In his later
years he carried on the business of a piano-maker. He died of a
lingering consumption.

660. JESUS LOVES ME.

BRIDGES, MATTHEW (Maldon, Essex, 1800–94, Quebec), the
younger son of John Bridges of Wallington House, Surrey, was
brought up in the Church of England. He published *Jerusalem regained, a Poem*, in 1825, and in 1828 a book on *The Roman Empire
under Constantine the Great*, being moved to this by the desire 'to
examine the real origin of certain papal superstitions, whose antiquity has been so often urged against Protestants, with no little
triumph and presumption'. Notwithstanding these early Protestant prepossessions, he entered the Roman Church in 1848. The
latter part of his life was spent in Canada. His later publications
were—*Babbicombe, or Visions of Memory, and Other Poems* (1842);
Hymns of the Heart (1847); *The Passion of Jesus* (1852); and *Popular
Ancient and Modern Histories*.

136. *Crown Him with many crowns.*

Biographical and Historical Notes

BRIDGES, ROBERT (SEYMOUR), M.A., M.B., F.R.C.P. (Isle of Thanet, 1844–), son of a Kentish squire, was educated at Eton and Corpus Christi College, Oxford (Hon. Fellow). On leaving the University he travelled on the Continent and in the East, then studied medicine at St. Bartholomew's Hospital, London. On qualifying, he became casualty physician there, and physician at the Great Northern Hospital, and also carried on general practice. He gave up practice in 1882, settled at Yattendon in Berkshire, and devoted himself to literature, in which he had already made his mark as a poet of unusual and highly distinctive gifts. He was appointed Poet Laureate in 1913. He is a scholar of great learning, both in ancient and modern letters, and a highly skilled and cultivated musician. His *Eros and Psyche* is dedicated to the celestial spirit of Henry Purcell, and in *The Christian Captives* he introduces the music of Anerio and Allegri. He has written an oratorio, which Villiers Stanford set to music. And his *Yattendon Hymnal* (q.v.) is, both in words and music, easily the most distinguished of individual contributions to modern hymnody.

See *Yattendon Hymnal, The.*

BRIGHT, WILLIAM, D.D. (Doncaster, 1824–1901, Oxford), was educated at University College, Oxford, and became a Fellow of his college. Ordained in 1848, he became theological tutor at Glenalmond College, Perthshire; Tutor of University College, Oxford; Hon. Canon of Cumbrae Cathedral, 1865–93; Canon of Christ Church, Oxford, and Regius Professor of Ecclesiastical History there, 1868. His *Ancient Collects, selected from Various Rituals* (1862), are of great value. Among his historical works were *A History of the Church from the Edict of Milan to the Council of Chalcedon* (1860); *Chapters of Early English History* (1877); he also edited *Eusebius' Ecclesiastical History* (1872); *Socrates' Ecclesiastical History;* and a *Latin Version of the Prayer Book.* His poetical works were—*Athanasius, and Other Poems, by a Fellow of a College* (1858); and *Hymns and Other Poems* (1866).

     320. *And now, O Father, mindful of the love.*
     296. *And now the wants are told that brought.*
     265. *At thy feet, O Christ, we lay.*

BROOKE, STOPFORD AUGUSTUS, LL.D. (Glendoen, Letterkenny, Donegal, 1832–1916, The Four Winds, Surrey), was educated at Kingstown, Kidderminster, and Trinity College, Dublin. On taking Orders, in London in 1857, he accepted a curacy in St. Matthew's, Marylebone; then another in St. Mary Abbott's, Kensington. From 1862 to 1865 he was chaplain to the British Embassy in Berlin. Returning to London, he took a lease of St. James's (proprietary) Chapel, York Street, then derelict, and in a short time crowded it to the doors. His *Life and Letters of F. W. Robertson* (1865) took rank at once as a classic biography, and brought him great reputation, which was enhanced by his first volume of *Sermons* (1869), and his *Theology in the English Poets*. He was now one of the foremost of London preachers, and in 1867 was appointed chaplain to the Queen. Her Majesty was eager to give him a canonry of Westminster, but his liberal views made the appointment impossible. On the expiry of the lease of St. James's Chapel, his services were transferred to Bedford Chapel, which was proprietary also, and there he ministered till his retirement in 1894. In 1880 his growing restiveness under the doctrinal standards of the Church of England moved him to resign his orders in that Church, and thenceforward he occupied an independent position, attached to no denomination, retaining in the main the Church of England service, but having close relations with the Unitarians. At this time he prepared for his congregation a collection entitled *Christian Hymns*, containing some fine compositions of his own, along with many standard hymns freely altered to suit his doctrinal position. After his retiral from the ministry, through ill-health, he preached and lectured from time to time, but for the most part devoted himself to literary work.

> 231. *All lands and peoples, all the earth.*
> 80. *It fell upon a summer day.*
> 85. *When the Lord of Love was here.*

BROOKS, PHILLIPS, D.D. (Boston, 1835–93, Boston), studied at Harvard, where he was deeply influenced by the works of Emerson and Theodore Parker. On graduating he tried teaching, in the Boston Latin School, but proved 'a conspicuous failure'. He then studied at the Episcopal Theological Seminary at Alexandria, Virginia. Ordained in 1859, he became rector of the Church of the Advent, Philadelphia; then of Holy Trinity, Philadelphia; then of the famous Trinity Church, Boston; and finally, in 1891, after refusing the office of preacher at Harvard, professorships, and the assistant bishopric of Pennsylvania, he was elected Bishop of Massachusetts. He was one of the most distinguished of modern preachers. Of great stature —six feet four inches—and massive build, sunny temperament, and optimistic outlook, he revealed great fertility and elevation of thought and rare powers of inspiration. He appealed to people of all classes and ages, and all phases of religious belief. Lord Bryce said of him, 'Few men have possessed in equal measure the power of touching what is best in men, and lifting them suddenly by sympathetic words to the elevation of high-strung feeling and purpose which they cannot reach of themselves, save under some wave of emotion due to some personal crisis in life.' And Professor A. B. Bruce said, 'Our great preachers take into the pulpit a bucket full or half full of the Word of God, and then, by the force of personal mechanism, they attempt to convey it to the congregation. But this man is just a great water-main, attached to the everlasting reservoir of God's truth and grace and love, and streams of life, by a heavenly gravitation, pour through him, to refresh every weary soul.' The remark when he died of a little friend of his (five years old), illustrates the feeling his personality inspired. Her mother took her in her arms and said tearfully, 'Bishop Brooks is gone to heaven.' 'Oh, mamma,' was the answer, 'how happy the angels will be!'

48. *O little town of Bethlehem.*

BROOMFIELD, WILLIAM ROBERT (Inverary, 1826–88, Aberdeen), was a mercantile clerk with a passion for church music. He received some musical training in Glasgow. In 1850 he settled in Aberdeen, where most of the rest of his life was spent. He was singularly amiable, but unstable and wayward, and, as he could not settle long to any sustained employment, his life was a troubled and shadowed one. Latterly he sank into extreme poverty; he died in St. Nicholas Poorhouse and was buried in a corner of the grounds there, a little company of faithful friends paying the pathetic tribute of singing ST. KILDA round his grave. A year later, his admirers had his body reinterred in the beautiful Allenvale cemetery, and erected over it a monument on which the tune is engraved to the quatrain of the fifty-first Psalm to which he loved to hear it sung:

> Do Thou with hyssop sprinkle me,
> I shall be cleansed so;
> Yea, wash Thou me, and then I shall
> Be whiter than the snow.

He produced many tunes, a few of which were popular in their day. A memorial collection of twelve was published in 1892, but only ST. KILDA survives. Two little books came from his pen—*A Manual of Harmony* and *The Principles of Ancient and Modern Music*.

558. ST. KILDA.

BROWN, ARTHUR HENRY (Brentwood, Essex, 1830–1926, Brentwood), apart from a few organ lessons, was self-taught as a musician. Before he was eleven he was organist of Brentwood Parish Church, and except for five years as organist at Romford, and another brief interval, he continued to hold that office for forty years. Coming under the influence of the Oxford Movement, he threw himself enthusiastically into the furtherance of that Church Revival, especially on its musical side. He was a pioneer in the restoration of the ancient Plain Chant, and by his *Gregorian Psalter*, and his work on the London Gregorian Association, did much to revive the use of the Gregorian Tones in Anglican worship. He published also—*The Altar Hymnal*, designed to enrich with appropriate hymns and introits the Anglican Eucharistic Service; *Metrical Litanies for Use in Church; Canticles of Holy Church; Accompanying Harmonies for the Gregorian Psalm Tones; Hymns of the Eastern Church; The Anglican Psalter;*

Divers Carols for Christmas and Other Tydes of Holy Church. He wrote about 700 hymn-tunes. Some of his carols have been very popular. He acted as organist of Sir Anthony Browne's School, Brentwood, till the end of his long life.

269. HOLY CROSS.	287. ST. ANATOLIUS.
497. SAFFRON WALDEN.	395. ST. MABYN.

BROWNE, SIMON (Shepton Mallet, Somersetshire, 1680–1722, Shepton Mallet), after studying at the Academy of Mr. Moore, Bridgewater, became Independent Minister at Portsmouth, and in 1716 pastor of the important congregation in Old Jewry, London. In 1720 he published *Hymns and Spiritual Songs*, and in 1722 a volume of sermons. The many controversies in which he was engaged, the accidental death of a highwayman at his hands, and the loss of his wife and son, may have combined to produce in him the mental delusion from which he latterly suffered, believing that he had 'no more sense than a parrot', that he was a 'mere beast', and that God had 'annihilated in him the thinking substance'. In spite of this his understanding remained otherwise unimpaired. Retiring to Shepton Mallet, he spent his time in translating classical authors, writing books for children, and compiling a dictionary. His hymns, once popular, have little favour now, with this exception:

188. *Come, gracious Spirit, heavenly Dove.*

BROWNLIE, JOHN, D.D. (Glasgow, 1859–1925, Crieff), was educated in Glasgow, at the University and the Free Church College. In 1885 he became junior minister of the Free Church, Portpatrick, Wigtownshire, to the full charge of which he succeeded in 1890. He took keen interest in education in his county, and was a governor, and for some time chairman of the governors, of Stranraer High School. His interest in hymnology bore fruit in *Hymns and Hymn-Writers of the Church Hymnary* (1899); and besides publishing many original hymns in *Hymns of our Pilgrimage Zionward; Hymns of the Pilgrim Life;* and *Pilgrim Songs*, he diligently cultivated the field of Latin and Greek hymnody. *Hymns of the Early Church; Hymns from East and West;* and *Hymns of the Greek Church* (4 series) attested his learning in this field and his gifts as a translator. A number of these translations have passed into use in modern hymn-books.

458. *O Light that knew no dawn.*

BRUCE, WILLIAM, D.D. (South Shields, 1812–82, Bridge of Allan), was the son of a United Secession minister who, after 1818, conducted the Ardoch Academy, Cardross, Dumbartonshire. He studied at Glasgow University, from which he received his doctorate in 1868, and at the Divinity Hall of his Church. In 1838 he became minister of the Cowgate United Secession Church, Edinburgh (afterwards Infirmary Street United Presbyterian Church). He was moderator of the United Presbyterian Synod in 1869. In 1870 he was appointed a member of the Hymnal Committee of his Church. He took an active share in preparing *The Presbyterian Hymnal* of 1876, and contributed two hymns to it. He published *Hebrew Odes and Other Poems* in 1874, and *Memories, a Tale, and Other Poems* in 1878. Robertson of Irvine said of him, 'I have known some men that did more, and many who dreamed more, but never any who united the doing and the dreaming as he did.'

> 204. *Holy Father, Thou hast given.*

BRYANT, WILLIAM CULLEN (Cummington, Massachusetts, 1794–1878, New York), was educated at Williams College, and in 1815 admitted to the Bar. After practising law for ten years, he gave it up for journalism and literature. He founded *The New York Review*, and for many years edited *The New York Evening Post*. His first volume was published when he was only fourteen, and *Thanatopsis, a Meditation on Death*, which made him famous, was written when he was but eighteen. Ecclesiastically, his affiliations were of unusual variety. Brought up as a Congregationalist, he afterwards was connected for a time with the Unitarians; subsequently he worshipped with the Episcopalians while in New York, and with the Presbyterians while at his country residence near Roslyn, Long Island; and finally, in 1858, while wintering in Italy, he was baptized in Naples. His biographer says that one day, after a long walk with a friend who was a Baptist minister, 'he spoke with softened heart of the new beauty that he felt in the old truth, and proposed to his friend to baptize him. With prayer, and hymn, and spiritual meditation, a little company of seven in a large upper room, as in the Christian story, partook of the Communion, and with his good grey head bowed William Cullen Bryant was baptized.' His first poetic impulse was derived from Watts's hymns. His own hymns were written at intervals during his life, many of them at the request of Dr. Ely, his Presbyterian minister. Twenty in number, they were at first privately printed in 1869.

> 340. *Look from the sphere of endless day.*

BUCK, PERCY CARTER, Mus. Doc. (West Ham, Essex, 1871–), was educated at the Guildhall School of Music and the Royal College of Music. He became organist of Worcester College, Oxford, 1891; of Wells Cathedral, 1895; of Bristol Cathedral, 1900; Musical Director of Harrow School, in succession to Eaton Faning, 1901; Professor of Music, Trinity College, Dublin, 1910–20; first Cramb Lecturer, Glasgow University, 1923; and, since 1925, King Edward VII Professor of Music, University of London. He has published three organ sonatas; several choral works and school songs; two organ manuals; *Unfigured Harmony* (1911); *Acoustics for Musicians* (1918).

> 23. GONFALON ROYAL.

BUCKOLL, HENRY JAMES, M.A. (Siddington, near Cirencester, 1803–71, Rugby), was educated at Rugby and Queen's College, Oxford. On graduating in 1826, he became an assistant master in his old school, and is believed to have been the first editor of the Rugby School *Collection of Hymns*. In 1893 he edited a *Collection* for Rugby Parish Church; in 1842 published *Hymns Translated from the German*, taken from Bunsen's *Versuch eines allgemeines Evangelischen Gesang- und Gebetsbuch* (1833); and in 1850, with Dean Goulburn, a new edition of the Rugby School *Collection*, in which fourteen of his own hymns appeared.

> 677. *Lord, behold us with Thy blessing.*
> 678. *Lord, dismiss us with Thy blessing.*

BULLOCK, WILLIAM, D.D. (Prettiwell, Apex, 1798–1874, Halifax, Nova Scotia), was educated at Christ's Hospital, then entered the Royal Navy. While serving under his brother, Admiral Frederic Bullock, on a survey of the coast of Newfoundland, he resolved to take holy orders and to become a missionary in that colony. This he did, and served there for thirty-two years under the Society for Propagating the Gospel. He became Dean of Nova Scotia, at Halifax, where he published in 1854 his *Songs of the Church*. His hymns were 'written amid the various scenes of missionary life, and are intended for the private and domestic use of Christians in new countries deprived of all public worship'.

> 236. *We love the place, O God.*

BUNYAN, JOHN (Elstow, 1628–88, London), though the son of a tinker, had a fixed residence and was sent to a village school. In spite of his own severe condemnation of his early years, there is no evidence of his being the abandoned profligate it has been the fashion to represent him. His outward life was pure and temperate, and his worst faults (if we except profane swearing) seem to have been his love for bell-ringing, dancing, and reading tales. After a short term of service with the Parliamentary Army (valuable for the military cast it gave to his works) Bunyan married a wife whose only dowry consisted of her piety and a few religious books. Shortly afterwards he passed through a period of extreme spiritual ferment and self-distrust. Neither the renouncing of his former pastimes nor a course of strict religious observance dissipated the gloom, and for a time he believed himself to have committed the unpardonable sin against the Holy Ghost. At last the clouds lifted and he found peace. Joining a religious community founded by John Gifford, a converted Royalist Major, he began to preach, and his sermons produced a powerful effect. No sooner, however, was Bunyan clear of his inward troubles than persecution assailed him from without. Immediately after the Restoration he was thrown into Bedford jail, and only fully liberated by the Indulgence of 1671, intended really for the benefit of Roman

Catholics. His days in jail were spent partly in making laces for the support of his family, and partly in writing controversial and other works; but it was during a second and shorter imprisonment in 1675 that *The Pilgrim's Progress* was begun. The book first appeared in 1678, and had for those days an extraordinary sale, 100,000 copies being sold in ten years. *The Holy War* was published in 1682, and the second part of *The Pilgrim's Progress* in 1684. In his latter years Bunyan possessed such influence among his fellow-Nonconformists that he was popularly known as 'Bishop Bunyan'. He went on circuit throughout the country, besides preaching to large congregations in London. His death was caused by a long ride in the rain after a successful attempt to reconcile a father and son. He was buried in Bunhill Fields. Bunyan's great allegory is too well known and too undisputed to require description or criticism here. Among its most enthusiastic admirers have been such critics as Macaulay and Froude, the latter of whom protests against the common fashion of calling Bunyan's verse 'doggerel'. If it does at times descend to that level, at its best it comes very near true poetry. Perhaps the two best lyrics from *The Pilgrim's Progress* are those selected for *The Church Hymnary*, depicting as they respectively do the peaceful and the martial aspects of the Christian life.

> 557. *He that is down needs fear no fall.*
> 576. *Who would true valour see.*

BUNNETT, EDWARD, Mus. Doc. (Shipdham, Norfolk, 1834–1923, Norwich), was a chorister in Norfolk Cathedral, and there was trained under Dr. Zechariah Buck, whose deputy and partner he became and continued to be from 1855 to 1877. In 1849 he sang at Norwich in the trio 'Lift thine eyes' with Jenny Lind and Miss Dolby. For many years he was organist of St. Peter Mancroft, conductor of the Norwich Musical Union, organist of the Norwich Musical Festivals, and borough organist. On celebrating his musical jubilee in 1896 he was presented by the mayor of Norwich with an address and a testimonial from his fellow citizens. He published cantatas, *Rhineland* and *Lora; De Profundis; Twenty-four Original Tunes to Favourite Hymns; Ten Christmas Carols;* anthems; part-songs; organ pieces, &c.

> 399. AGNES.

BURKE, CHRISTIAN (London, 1859–), contributed verse to various periodicals, and published a collection in 1896, under the title *The Flowering of the Almond, and Other Poems.*

> 652. *Lord of Life and King of Glory.*

BURLEIGH, WILLIAM HENRY (Woodstock, Connecticut, 1812–71, Brooklyn), was descended on his mother's side from Governor Bradford of the *Mayflower*. Brought up on a farm at Plainfield, Connecticut, he went in 1837 to Pittsburg, Pennsylvania, and was apprenticed to the printing trade. Then journalism claimed him. He published *The Christian Witness* and *The Temperance Banner*, being an enthusiastic reformer. In 1843 he became editor of *The Christian Freeman*, an abolitionist journal, at Hartford, Conn. Thereafter, he spent some years at Syracuse as editor, lecturer, and secretary of the New York State Temperance Society. His last appointment was as harbour-master of New York. In religion he was a Unitarian. His *Poems*, collected from periodicals, were published in 1841, and in an enlarged edition in the year of his death. His wife, Mrs. Celia Burleigh, who was for some time minister of the Unitarian Church at Brooklyn, Conn., wrote his *Life*, and added a number of his poems to it.

566. *Lead us, O Father, in the paths of peace.*

BURNS, JAMES DRUMMOND, M.A. (Edinburgh, 1823–64, Mentone), was educated at Heriot's Hospital, the High School, and the University, Edinburgh. He was studying Divinity under Dr. Chalmers at the University when the Disruption took place, and he followed his teacher into the Free Church in 1843. Sent in 1845 to preach at Dunblane, he broke down in his first sermon, but the congregation called him, and he was ordained there in that year. Soon, however, overwork brought on lung trouble, and for health reasons, in 1847, he took charge of the Free Church congregation at Funchal, Madeira. There his health so much improved that in 1855 he was able to undertake the care of a newly formed congregation at Hampstead. He was winsome in character, catholic in spirit, and endowed with a beautiful voice which made his preaching strangely affecting. He built up a strong congregation in Hampstead. At the Assembly of his Church in Edinburgh in 1863 he contracted a cold which settled on his lungs, and disease set in which the climate of southern France failed to arrest. He was buried at Highgate. He published *The Vision of Prophecy and Other Poems* (1854); *The Heavenly Jerusalem, or, Glimpses within the Gates;* and contributed the too brief article on *Hymns* to the eighth edition of *The Encyclopædia Britannica*. He was 'a man of genuine poetic feeling, with a vivid sense of beauty'.

605. *At Thy feet, our God and Father.*
472. *For Thee, my God, for Thee alone.*
251. *Hushed was the evening hymn.*
690. *Thou who didst on Calvary bleed.*

BURTON, JOHN (Stratford, Essex, 1803–77, Stratford), is usually called 'the younger ' to distinguish him from John Burton of Nottingham, who wrote 'Holy Bible, Book Divine', and other once popular hymns. For ten years, from his fifteenth to his twenty-fifth year, he was a great sufferer, but he regained strength and for about fifty years carried on business as a cooper and basket-maker in his native town. For twenty-seven years he taught in a Sunday School at Plaistow, near Stratford. A Congregationalist, he was a deacon in his chapel. He published *One Hundred Original Hymns for the Young* (1850); *Hymns for Little Children* (1851); *The Child Life of David; The Book of Psalms in English Verse* (1871); *Scripture Characters in Verse*, &c. He died of smallpox, having contracted the disease while visiting a poor chimney-sweeper. On his death, the papers he had been working with were burned, among them the sheets of his hymns, which he had been revising for publication.

495. Saviour, while my heart is tender.

BUTLER, MARY (MAY) (Langar, Notts., 1841–1916, Shrewsbury), was a granddaughter of Bishop Samuel Butler of Lichfield (1836–9), and daughter of Thomas Butler, M.A., rector of Langar, and Canon of Lincoln. Samuel Butler, author of *Erewhon, The Way of All Flesh*, &c., was her brother. All her life was spent at Langar, until her father retired to Shrewsbury. There she took a deep interest in social work, and founded St. Saviour's Home for girls. Many of her hymns were written for the inmates. She was gentle in spirit, and had strong musical and artistic tastes. 'Her prototype is to be met in the novels of Charlotte M. Yonge—the perfect Churchwoman; spiritual, intellectual, devoted; strong in her faithful following of duty; sweet-tempered, serene and cheerful from an active and disciplined life.' Her hymns, appearing in various hymnals, have never been collected.

674. Looking upward every day.

BUTTON, HENRY ELLIOT (Clevedon, Somerset, 1861–1925, Hampstead), was the son of a schoolmaster who was also organist of a Congregational Church. He showed an early aptitude for music; he was able to sing from the tonic sol-fa before he could read. For a short time he was in business in Bristol; then he taught in a school in Hastings. His interest in science drew him next into the experimental department of the Globe Telephone Company, but on the failure of that Company he turned to music as his profession. He was a good violinist and an excellent singer; he was alto soloist for some time in Holy Trinity, Sloane Square, and other churches, and for a period was choirmaster of St. Mary Abbott's. His chief work, however, was done in the publishing department of Novello & Co., where he served for forty years. He published a book on *System in Musical Notation*, a subject in which he was an expert. His knowledge of hymn-tunes was encyclopaedic. He edited the third series of *The Bristol Tune Book*, and a collection of the *Chorales Harmonized by J. S. Bach*. He also discovered and transcribed a number of madrigals in the British Museum. His published compositions include *Ivry*, a dramatic ballad for baritone solo, chorus, and orchestra; anthems, songs for children, &c.

670. CHILD SERVICE.

BYRD, WILLIAM (?Lincoln, 1538–1623, London), was one of the most illustrious figures of an age in which the musical glory of this country was at its height. Part of his training he received from Tallis, with whom he was associated in the sole right, granted to them by royal patent, to print music and ruled music paper—a venture which landed both in heavy loss. There is evidence that at one period Byrd was in serious financial straits. About 1563 he became organist of Lincoln Cathedral, and in 1569 a member of the Chapel Royal. After the Reformation he remained a Romanist, and though allowed to continue in office in the Chapel Royal, he was often in trouble because of his religion: it is on record that his wife was arraigned on a charge of proselytizing, and that his family were excommunicated for at least seven years. He wrote much for the Roman service. He was an organist of distinction, and one of the first of the great madrigalists, but it is his religious music that establishes his title to be accounted one of the greatest of English composers.

738. AMEN.   721. KYRIE.

BYRNE, MARY ELIZABETH, M.A. (Dublin, ?)—Maire ni Bhroin— graduated at the National University of Ireland in 1905, and is a research worker in Irish to the Board of Intermediate Education. She is an examiner to the Board in English and Irish, and in Irish to the Civil Service Commission. She was awarded the Chancellor's Gold Medal in the Royal University for a treatise on *England in the Age of Chaucer*. She has for some years been engaged in assisting the editor of the *Old and Mid-Irish Dictionary* of the Royal Irish Academy, and is also working at an edition of *Togail Troi* (The Destruction of Troy) from all unpublished sources. She has published an edition of *Airec Menman Uraird Maic Coisse* (*Anecdota*, vol. ii); and Middle Irish religious poems in *Eriù*, a journal published formerly by the School of Irish Learning in Dublin, and now by the Royal Irish Academy.

477. *Be Thou my Vision, O Lord of my heart* (tr.).

BYROM, JOHN (Kersall, near Manchester, 1692–1763, Manchester), son of a Manchester merchant of a good family, was educated at Merchant Taylors' School and Trinity College, Cambridge, of which he became a Fellow in 1714. In 1716 he travelled abroad and studied medicine at Montpellier, but never practised or took a medical degree. Until his fortunes improved by succession to the family estates, Byrom maintained himself by teaching a system of shorthand of his own invention, which attained considerable popularity. Of a mystical and romantic turn of mind, and with strong Jacobite sympathies, he was also greatly interested in philosophical and theological questions, and knew many thinkers of eminence, cherishing a special regard for William Law, whom he calls his master.

Byrom's poems were first published in 1793. He had a great facility in rhyming, and was fond of new metres.

54. *Christians, awake.*
456. *My spirit longs for Thee.*

CALDBECK, George Thomas (Waterford, 1852– ?), was educated in the National Model School, Waterford, and went to London in 1873 to be trained for Holy Orders in Islington Theological College. While a student and precentor there he composed the tune for 'Peace, perfect peace'. Through ill health he was compelled to relinquish his purpose of becoming a missionary. He returned to Ireland, and after school-mastering for some years in County Cork, embarked on independent evangelistic work. He itinerated in this connexion in Ireland, then, in 1888, transferred his operations to London, where he did much open-air preaching. His eccentric views made it difficult for him to work with others, and for twenty years he lived from hand to mouth. In 1908 he was living in a Church Army lodging-house off Edgware Road, and earning a meagre subsistence by selling Scripture text-cards from door to door. He was arrested for doing this without a licence, but was dismissed on informing the magistrate that he was the composer of the well-known hymn-tune. The newspapers described him then as of scholarly and gentlemanly appearance, but as manifestly in extreme indigence. His later history is unknown.

444. PAX TECUM.

CALKIN, John Baptiste (London, 1827–1905, London). He became organist and precentor of St. Columba's College, Navan (afterwards Rathfarnham), Ireland; organist of Woburn Chapel, London; of Camden Road Chapel; and of St. Thomas's, Camden Town. He was also a professor at the Guildhall School of Music and Croydon Conservatoire. He published many works, including services, anthems, part-songs, glees, songs, organ music, and hymn-tunes.

482. NOX PRAECESSIT.   328. RAMOTH.   361. ST. JOSEPH.

CALLCOTT, William Hutchins (Kensington, 1807–82, London), was the son of John Wall Callcott, one of the greatest of English glee composers. He studied music under his brother-in-law, William Horsley, and was organist of Ely Chapel, Holborn, and afterwards, for sixteen years, of St. Barnabas' Church, Kensington. He wrote anthems and songs.

255. INTERCESSION.

CAMERON, William, M.A. (Lochaber, 1751–1811, Kirknewton), studied at Marischal College, Aberdeen. There he became intimate with Dr. Beattie, author of *The Minstrel*. It is believed that Beattie

made his poetic talent known to the Committee which was then revising the Paraphrases. Cameron, while only a licentiate of the
Church, and engaged apparently in literary work, received the confidence of the Committee, and the chief responsibility for the actual
revision was left in his hands (see on 483). Two paraphrases were
written by him—xiv and xvii; and he revised at least thirty-
three, as well as two of the hymns which still appear along with the
Paraphrases. Not till 1786 did he receive a charge; in that year he
was presented by the Duke of Buccleuch to the parish of Kirknewton, where the rest of his years were spent. He published *Poems
on Various Subjects* (1781); *The Abuse of Civil and Religious Liberty*,
a Sermon; *Ode on Locheil's Birthday* (1796); *A Review of the French
Revolution* (1802); and a posthumous volume of *Poems on Several
Occasions* was published in 1813.

> 137. *Blest be the everlasting God.*
> 223. *How bright these glorious spirits shine!*

CAMPBELL, JANE MONTGOMERY (Paddington, London, 1817–78,
Bovey Tracey, South Devon), was a daughter of a rector of St.
James's, Paddington. She was a musical enthusiast and taught
singing to the children of her father's parish school. While residing
at Bovey Tracey she gave valuable help to the Rev. Charles S. Bere
in the compilation of his *Garland of Songs, or an English Liederkranz*
(1862), and his *Children's Chorale Book* (1869). To these she contributed a number of excellent translations. She published also *A
Handbook for Singers*, embodying the musical exercises she had
made use of in her work among London children.

> 618. *We plough the fields, and scatter* (tr.).

CAMPION, THOMAS, M.D. (Witham, Essex, *c.* 1575–1619, London),
physician, poet, dramatist, musician, was of French descent; his
father was organist in a Paris church for many years. He studied at
Cambridge and abroad, left Gray's Inn and the law for medicine, received his degree from some foreign university, and practised his
profession in London to the end of his life. But he found time to
write four masques, many fine lyrics, and much good music. In
1595 he published a small book of Latin elegiacs and epigrams; in
1602 *Observations on the Art of English Poesie*, in which he disparaged
'the childish titilation of riming' and advocated unrhymed verse; in
1606/7 the first of his masques, before James I at Whitehall; in
1610, he being now a recognized authority on music, *Two Bookes of
Ayres*, being songs with accompaniments, many of them to music
of his own; then in 1612–13, *A New Way of making foure parts in
Counterpoint, by a most familiar and infallible rule, with some other
Discourses on the Theory of Music*. His reputation as lyric poet and
musician was high in his lifetime, and, after long obscuration, has

risen again; his works are now held high in value by critics and collectors.

366. BABYLON'S STREAMS.

CANTON, WILLIAM (Isle of Chusan, off coast of China, 1845–1926, Hendon), spent the greater part of his childhood in Jamaica, where the scenery of the Blue Mountains first awoke in him the love of nature. He was educated in France, and the sight of a cromlech in a field there inspired him with a passion for antiquity. These enthusiasms gave distinction to his first book of poems, *A Lost Epic, and Other Poems*. Huxley said of one poem in that volume—'Through the Ages: a Legend of a Stone Axe'—that it was the first attempt to use the raw material of science as a subject for poetry. For many years journalism engaged Mr. Canton, as sub-editor and leader-writer on *The Glasgow Herald*, then as sub-editor of *The Contemporary Review*. He acted also as manager of Isbister & Co., publishers. The tender grace of *The Invisible Playmate; W. V., her Book and Various Verses;* and *In Memory of W.V.* revealed a writer of exquisite gifts; and the understanding of the child mind, and the rare sympathy with the child's heart there shown, found further expression in a book of *Children's Sayings;* and *A Child's Book of Saints*. He has also published *The Crusader, Poems Old and New; A Child's Book of Warriors;* and *The Story of Elizabeth of Hungary*. He spent years on the monumental centenary *History of the British and Foreign Bible Society*, in 4 volumes, and for more popular use wrote also *The Bible and the Anglo-Saxon People*, and *The Bible Story*.

555. *Hold Thou my hands.*

CAREY, HENRY (? 1692–1743, Clerkenwell), is said to have been the son of George Saville, Marquis of Halifax, and of a schoolmistress. He was 'a man of facetious temper', says Sir John Hawkins, 'a musician by profession and one of the lower order of poets'. His chief occupation was that of teaching in boarding schools and private families. He was a prolific author of burlesques, farces, ballad operas, and vivacious poems and songs, the best known being *Sally in our Alley*. His musical knowledge was slight, but he had a distinct inventive faculty, and composed successfully the music for a number of his songs. He was only incidentally a writer of church music. Gay and careless in life, he was often in difficulties, and at last, 'unable to resist the shafts of envy, and labouring under the pressure of his circumstances', he died by his own hand. The authorship of *God save the King* has been attributed to him, but without sufficient ground. He collected and published his songs in 1740—*The Musical Century, One Hundred English Ballads on various important Occasions;* and his dramatic works appeared in 1743.

172, 302, 615. SURREY.

Biographical and Historical Notes

CARLYLE, Thomas (Ecclefechan, 1795–1881, Chelsea), the second son of a stonemason who was a member of the Secession Church, was brought up in a frugal and godly household. He was educated first by his parents, then at Annan Academy and the University of Edinburgh. He began, but soon abandoned, study for the ministry of the Church of Scotland; earned a living for some years by teaching in Annan, Kirkcaldy, and Edinburgh, but concluded that 'it were better to perish than to continue schoolmastering'; tried law, with a view to the Scottish Bar, but dropped that also; and finally, after some hack-work experiments, settled down to the serious pursuit of literature. His struggles were arduous and intensified by ill health, and his remuneration was small: until well on in his life his income from his writings was never more than £400 a year. But few writers ever pursued their calling with a higher ideal or a more resolute devotion; and few ever spread for their readers a richer or more liberal banquet—in history, biography, criticism, politics, philosophy, poetry, and religion. He was a great artist, a humorist, and a poet. Passages of *Sartor Resartus* and of *The French Revolution* have been held to rank with the sublimest poetry of the age. In his view of life he was a practical mystic, profoundly religious, though detached from all the official creeds, a sworn foe of atheism and what he called 'beaver science'. Materialism also he hated, 'with its gospel of wealth and its practice of idleness', and he preached with ardour and moral passion his own gospel of veracity and hard work. Relentlessly, and with mordant wit, he satirized the follies and futilities of the age. But while powerfully destructive in his criticism, he had no constructive ideas. All he achieved was in the region of thought and imagination. There, however, his teaching was intensely stimulative. He did much to kindle other minds to moral enthusiasm and energy, and many of his ideas, which inspired his own generation, have become 'part of our subliminal possessions'. In 1865 he was elected Lord Rector of the University of Edinburgh. Disraeli, in 1874, offered him the G.C.B. or a baronetcy, with a pension, but the offer was declined. When he died, a burial in Westminster Abbey was offered, but in accordance with his own wish, his body was laid beside the ashes of his kindred in his native village.

526. *A safe stronghold our God is still* (tr.).

CASWALL, Edward, M.A. (Yately, Hampshire, 1814–78, Edgbaston, Birmingham), son of a vicar of Yately, was educated at Marlborough and Brasenose College, Oxford, where he graduated with honours in 1836. At the University he won a reputation as a humorist by a satire, *The Art of Pluck*, written in imitation of Aristotle, on the idle and frivolous habits of the students of his day. Taking orders in the Church of England, he became perpetual curate of Stratford-sub-Castle, Wilts., in 1840. He had been caught, however, in the tide, then running high, of the Tractarian Movement, and in

1847 resigned his living, repaired to Rome, and there was received by Cardinal Acton into the Roman Church. His wife was received a week later. On her death, three years afterwards, he became a priest, and joined the Oratory of St. Philip Neri at Edgbaston, under Newman, to whose writings he attributed his conversion. For twenty-eight years he lived there, occupied largely in ministering to the sick and poor, by whom he was greatly beloved. 'He was a very humble man,' said one who knew him: 'every good deed others did was wonderful to him; what he himself did was nothing.' Setting himself to translate the ancient Latin hymns in the Roman Breviaries, he enriched English hymnody by many versions second only to Neale's in their high poetic quality; some of them are classics. He published *Lyra Catholica* (197 translations of the Breviary hymns, 1849); *The Masque of Mary, and Other Poems* (1858); *A May Pageant and Other Poems* (1865); *Hymns and Other Poems* (1863). When he lay dying of heart-disease, Newman wrote of him: 'He is one of four very dear friends who were in a position to place and did place themselves and all they had at my service. . . . His wife was suddenly carried off by cholera at Torquay. The next day he made a will in my favour. It was but a sample of the devotion he has shown to me for thirty years, to me unworthy, as I may truly say.' It was fitting that the two friends should be buried, as they were, side by side, in the little country graveyard of Rednal, near Birmingham.

> 99. *At the Cross, her station keeping* (tr.).
> 585. *Days and moments, quickly flying.*
> 422. *Jesus, the very thought of Thee* (tr.).
> 433. *My God, I love Thee, not because* (tr.).
> 423. *O Jesus, King most wonderful* (tr.).
> 51. *See! in yonder manger low.*
> 272. *The sun is sinking fast* (tr.).
> 167. *When morning gilds the skies* (tr.).

CAWOOD, JOHN, M.A. (Matlock, Derbyshire, 1775–1852, Bewdley), was the son of a small farmer and had little education as a boy. But while in the service of a clergyman named Carsham at Sutton-in-Ashfield, Notts., he came under decisive religious impressions and was moved to seek holy orders. Three years' study enabled him to enter St. Edmund's Hall, Oxford, in 1797. Graduating four years later, he became curate of Ribbesford and Dowles; then perpetual curate of St. Anne's Chapel of Ease, Bewdley, Worcestershire. He was an intimate friend of the Havergals. He published two volumes of sermons characterized by Bickersteth as 'forcible, impressive, evangelical', but his seventeen hymns were not published by himself.

> 295. *Almighty God, Thy word is cast.*

CENNICK, JOHN (Reading 1718–55, London), belonged to a family of Quakers, but was brought up in the Church of England. His name (originally Cennik) proclaims him of Bohemian stock. At one time a land-surveyor at Reading, he became acquainted with the Wesleys, and was appointed by John Wesley teacher of a school for colliers' children at Kingswood, and subsequently the first lay preacher among the Methodists. Parting from the Wesleys on doctrinal grounds, he came for a time under the influence of Whitefield, but ultimately joined the Moravian brethren, in whose service he spent some time in Germany and North Ireland. Cennick's hymns are unequal, but some of them contain stanzas of real beauty.

656. *Be present at our table, Lord.*
574. *Children of the heavenly King.*
294. *Ere I sleep, for every favour.*
160. *Lo! He comes, with clouds descending* (altered by others).

CHADWICK, JOHN WHITE, M.A. (Marblehead, Massachusetts, 1840–1904, Brooklyn, New York), graduated at the Divinity School, Cambridge, Mass., in 1864, and received the M.A. degree from Harvard in 1888. He was minister of the Second Unitarian Church, Brooklyn, N.Y., from 1864. He wrote a *Life of Theodore Parker* and a *Life of William Ellery Channing;* was a frequent contributor of poems to periodicals like *Harper's Magazine;* and published *A Book of Poems* (1876); *In Nazareth Town, and Other Poems* (1883); *A Legend of Good Poets* (1885); and *A Few Verses* (1900). His preaching was notable for its excellence, and his *Sermons*, issued in successive series, 'form a noble body of ethical teaching'.

489. *Eternal Ruler of the ceaseless round.*
614. *Now sing we a song for the harvest.*

CHALMERS, JAMES (Aberdeen, *c.* 1700–64, Aberdeen), son of a Professor in Marischal College and University, was printer to the Town Council of Aberdeen and publisher of *The Aberdeen Journal*. About 1748 he compiled a *Collection of Twenty Church Tunes*, containing *Observations concerning the Tunes and manner of singing them*. This is now very scarce. See note on Hymn 481.

481. (ST. PAUL).

CHANDLER, JOHN, M.A. (Witley, Godalming, Surrey, 1806–76, Putney), was educated at Corpus Christi College, Oxford. Ordained in 1831, he succeeded his father as patron and vicar of Witley. His remarkable gifts as a translator were diligently employed on *The Hymns of the Primitive Church, now first Collected, Translated and Arranged* (1837); and *Hymns of the Church most Primitive, Collected, Translated and Arranged for Public Use* (1841)—the previous work revised and altered. He was one of the first and best of modern translators of Latin hymns. His treatment of them was free, but what was lost in literalness was more than compensated for by their poetic and doctrinal fitness for modern use. He wrote also a *Life of*

William of Wykeham and *Horae Sacrae, Prayers and Meditations from the Writings of the Divines of the Anglican Church, with Introduction* (1854); and numerous sermons and tracts.

> 37. *Above the clear blue sky.*
> 274. *As now the sun's declining rays* (tr.).
> 78. *On Jordan's banks the Baptist's cry* (tr.).

CHARLES, DAVID (Pant-dwfn, St. Clears, Carmarthen, 1762–1834, Carmarthen), was the youngest brother of the famous Rev. Thomas Charles, B.A. (Charles o'r Bala), one of the founders of the British and Foreign Bible Society, and a powerful religious and educational force in Wales. The father, a farmer, found himself unable to bear the expense of educating a second son at Oxford, though the lad was beyond his years intelligent. David was therefore apprenticed to a flax-dresser and rope-maker at Carmarthen. He came early under religious impressions, and was brought to final decision in 1777 by reading the sermons of Ralph Erskine. He was made a deacon of Water Street Church in 1788, and acted as such for twenty years. He carried on a flourishing business the while, and married the daughter of a Jewish banker at Haverfordwest. When forty-six years of age he was prevailed upon by the Church to enter the ministry, having given proof of his effectiveness as a preacher both in Welsh and in English. He was ordained in 1811. Methodism in Wales owed much to his wisdom. He was perhaps the greatest Church statesman of his time in Wales, discriminating in judgement and wise in counsel. He wrote several hymns, one of which—the one by which he is represented here—is one of the most famous and best-loved hymns in the Welsh language.

> 596. *From heavenly Jerusalem's towers.*

CHARTERIS, ARCHIBALD HAMILTON, D.D., LL.D. (Wamphray, Dumfriesshire, 1835–1908, Edinburgh), was educated at Wamphray, where his father was schoolmaster, and at the Universities of Edinburgh, Tübingen and Bonn. He was minister in succession of St. Quivox, Ayrshire; New Abbey, Kirkcudbrightshire; and Park Parish, Glasgow; was Professor of Biblical Criticism in Edinburgh University, 1868–95; Chaplain to Queen Victoria and King Edward; and Moderator of the Church of Scotland, 1892. He published a *Life of James Robertson*, a book on *The New Testament Scriptures*, and one on *Canonicity*. His greatest work was done as an ecclesiastical statesman and administrator. He had an ingenious and inventive mind, enthusiasm, practical ability, and tireless energy. He was the originator of the Christian Life and Work Committee of the Church of Scotland, and for long directed its activities; he built up in connexion with it a series of organizations such as the Young Men's Guild, with its Kalimpong Mission, the Women's Guild, the Order of

Deaconesses. He was instrumental in founding *Life and Work*, the Church of Scotland parish magazine, and was its first editor; and instituted the admirable *Guild Text Books* and *Guild Library* series. Along many lines he gave a great impulse to the life of the Church.

521. *Believing fathers oft have told.*

CHATFIELD, ALLEN WILLIAM, B.A. (Chatteris, 1808–96, Much Marcle), son of a vicar of Chatteris, was educated at Charterhouse and Trinity College, Cambridge, where he graduated in 1831 with first class classical honours. Ordained in 1832, he became vicar of Stotfold, Bedfordshire, and, in 1848, of Much Marcle, Herefordshire. His most notable work was his rendering into Greek, in various metres, of the Litany, the Te Deum, and other parts of the Anglican Church Offices. He published also *Songs and Hymns of the Earliest Christian Poets, Bishops and Others, translated into English Verse* (1876).

403. *Lord Jesus, think on me* (tr.).

CHENEZ, CHARITIE LEES DE. See DE CHENEZ.

CHESTERTON, GILBERT KEITH (Kensington, 1874–), was educated at St. Paul's School, London. He attended classes at the Slade School of Art, but, beginning to contribute art criticisms and reviews to *The Bookman* and *The Spectator*, found his way into journalism. He has been one of the most vivacious, versatile, and provocative figures in that field ever since. There is no more effective critic of other people's beliefs, but he is curiously uncritical in the exposition and defence of his own. Long a pillar of orthodoxy, he became a Roman Catholic under the influence of the ultramontane Hilaire Belloc. In the teeth of history he was persuaded that the medieval 'ages of faith' were Europe's halcyon age, and that only a return to the Roman obedience would destroy what remains of Puritanism and bring 'merrie England' back. A hater of capitalism, he was induced to believe the Roman Church to be antagonistic to the capitalistic system, and to look to the resuscitation of the medieval trade-guild system as the cure for modern industrial ills. His *Short History of England*, written in support of these fallacious prepossessions, is really a perversion of history to account for its author's adoption of the Roman creed.

638. *O God of earth and altar.*

CHETHAM, JOHN (*c.* 1700–63, Skipton), was a musician and clergyman who became master of the Clerk's School, Skipton, in 1737, and curate of Skipton two years later. *A Book of Psalmody, all set in four parts* was published by him in 1718. It was very widely adopted, ran through many editions, and continued in use for a century and a half. It is surmised that he may have himself composed some of the anonymous tunes in the first edition that are not traceable to any other source.

274. (BURFORD).   194. (WIRKSWORTH).

CHORLEY, HENRY FOTHERGILL (Blackley, Hurst, Lancashire, 1808–72, London), was intended for a commercial life, but his taste for literature made that career impossible. Mrs. Hemans and Caroline Jewsbury, who gave him their friendship, encouraged his literary ambitions, and he began to contribute to current literature with such effect that in 1833 he was given a post on the staff of *The Athenaeum*. In time he had full charge of the musical criticisms of the paper, and contributed largely to the review department also, exhibiting in his work an independent but eminently just judgement. His own work as an author had little success. He was a busy librettist and writer of verses for music, but his level was never high. His novels and dramas made no mark. His musical scholarship was ordinary. His best books were on *Music and Manners in France and Germany* (1841); *Modern German Music* (1854); *Thirty Years' Musical Recollections* (1862); *The National Music of the World* (1880).

641. God the Omnipotent!

CLARK, JEREMIAH (London, *c*. 1670–1707, London), was a chorister of the Chapel Royal under Dr. John Blow, and became organist of Winchester College (1692–5); organist of St. Paul's in 1695, and vicar choral, 1705; joint organist, with Croft, of the Chapel Royal, 1704. He probably officiated at Father Smith's magnificent organ in St. Paul's when that masterpiece of Sir Christopher Wren was opened on Dec. 2, 1697. He was a man of keen sensibility, and of a physical constitution that inclined him to melancholy. His music reflects his temperament: it shows great delicacy of feeling and is full of tenderness and pathos. Dr. Burney said that 'he was all feeling'. In a mood of despondency he took his own life. Tradition has it that the cause was a hopeless passion for a lady of a station higher than his own. Riding out into the country one day, resolved to end his life, he went into a field in which was a pond, and there tossed up a coin to decide whether he would shoot or drown himself. The coin falling edgewise, stuck so in the mud, and he returned to London with the dilemma unresolved. A short time later, however, he took the fatal step and 'shot himself with a little Screw-Pistol in the side of the head'. A contemporary poet, in an ode on his death which was intended to be touching, ended with these lines:

> Let us not, therefore, wonder at his fall,
> Since 'twas not so unnatural
> For him who lived by Canon to expire by Ball.

Clark wrote operatic music (Gay used one of his tunes in *The Beggar's Opera*), a cantata, numerous songs, and church music—anthems and psalm tunes—of much dignity and charm. Dr. Robert Bridges says, 'He seems to have been the inventor of the modern English hymn-tune, which degraded into empty flourish, "quavering and semi-quavering care away" before 1800. His tunes are beautiful, and have the plaintive grace characteristic of his music and melancholy temperament. They are the first in merit of their kind, as they were first in time; and they are truly national and popular in style, so that their neglect is to be regretted.'

137. BISHOPTHORPE.
 3. BROCKHAM (CONFIDENCE).
311. BROMLEY.

131, 711. ST. MAGNUS (NOTTINGHAM).
275, 649. UFFINGHAM.

CLARK, THOMAS (Canterbury, 1775–1859, Canterbury), was a cobbler by trade and a musician by talent. He was leader of psalmody first in the Wesleyan Church, Canterbury, then in a church which was originally anabaptist, and worshipped in the dilapidated monastery of the Blackfriars, which had been purchased for this purpose by Peter de la Pierre, a surgeon from Flanders. The congregation came to be called General Baptists, but by Clark's time they had drifted into Unitarianism; they were dissolved in 1913. Clark was a prolific composer of hymn-tunes, publishing over twenty sets of them. He reharmonized the second edition of *The Union Tune Book* for the Sunday School Union in 1842. A revision of it in 1854 contained between forty and fifty tunes by Clark. He arranged also a *Union Harmonist* in 1841.

40. CREDITON.   165. WARSAW.

CLAUDIUS, MATTHIAS (Reinfeld, near Lübeck, Holstein, 1740–1815, Hamburg), the son of a Lutheran pastor, was educated at Jena, and lived at Wandsbeck, near Hamburg. An ancestor had latinized his name Claus Paulsen into Claudius Pauli, and his descendants adopted Claudius as their surname. He studied theology with a view to the ministry, but an affection of the chest and the rationalizing influences then dominant at Jena turned him aside to law and languages. He became a journalist, and for some years edited *The Wandsbeck Messenger*. In 1776 he was appointed one of the Commissioners of Agriculture and Manufactures of Hesse Darmstadt, and, a year later, editor of the official newspaper there. During this time the influence of Goethe, with whom he was intimate, and of the free-thinking circle round him, detached him from religious belief; but a severe illness in 1777 wrought powerfully on his spirit and brought him back to faith. He renounced his position and returned to Wandsbeck to edit the *Messenger* in a Christian spirit. He had a long struggle with straitened means. In 1788 he was appointed by the Crown Prince of Denmark auditor of the Schleswig Holstein Bank at Altona. In 1815 he retired to his daughter's home at Hamburg, where he died. His fugitive pieces appeared as *Asmus omnia sua secum portans, oder Sämmtliche Werke des Wandsbecker Bothen* (1774). Examples of his work will be found in Longfellow's *Poets and Poetry of Europe.* 'None of his poems are used in the churches. They exercised, nevertheless, a great influence on the religious life of the country by their strong, primitive, and sympathetic Christian feeling.'

618. *We plough the fields, and scatter.*

CLAUSNITZER, Tobias (Thurn, near Annaberg, Saxony, 1619–84, Weiden, Upper Palatine), studied at various universities and finally at Leipzig, where he graduated in 1643. In 1644 he became a chaplain in the Swedish army. As such, he preached the thanksgiving sermon in the St. Thomas Church, Leipzig, on the accession of Queen Christina to the Swedish throne, and also the sermon at the peace celebration in General Wrangel's army at Weiden, when the Peace of Westphalia brought the Thirty Years War to an end in 1649. In that year he became first minister at Weiden. Later, he was a member of the Consistory and Inspector of the district. Three of his hymns survive.

203. *Look upon us, blessèd Lord.*

CLEMENT of alexandria (Athens? *c.* 170–*c.* 220, Palestine?), whose full name was Titus Flavius Clemens, was one of the most eminent fathers of the early Eastern Church. At first an eager student of philosophy, he was converted to Christianity probably through the influence of his teacher, the presbyter Pantaenus, whom he succeeded as head of the famous Catechetical School at Alexandria. During the persecution under Severus he retired to Palestine. Clement's three most important extant works are the *Exhortation to the Gentiles; The Tutor* (*Paedagogus*); and the *Miscellanies* (*Stromateis*).

569. *Lead, holy Shepherd, lead us.*

CLEPHANE, Elizabeth Cecilia Douglas (Edinburgh, 1830–69, Bridgend, Melrose), was a daughter of Andrew Douglas Clephane of Carslogie, Sheriff Principal of Fife and Kinross. Her mother was a member of the Douglas family, of which the Earls of Home are the heads. After the death of the father, the daughters lived first at Ormiston, East Lothian, and latterly at Bridgend, Melrose, where the Ellwyn Water joins the Tweed, and where the old bridge stood to which Scott refers in *The Abbot* and *The Monastery.* A chill in Elizabeth's youth left her with impaired health. She was gentle and retiring in disposition, and generous to a degree; she was known as 'the Sunbeam' among the poor and suffering in Melrose. The sisters spent all their income every year, giving what was not needed for their own maintenance to charity. They were devoted members of the then Free Church of Scotland. Eight of Elizabeth's hymns appeared first under the general title 'Breathings on the Border' in *The Family Treasury*, then edited by the Rev. William Arnot, a well-known Free Church minister.

> 691. *Beneath the Cross of Jesus.*
> 685. *There were ninety and nine.*

CLIFTON, JOHN CHARLES (London, 1781–1841, Hammersmith, London), studied under Richard Bellamy and Charles Wesley. For a time he engaged in business, but left it to make music his profession. As teacher and conductor he resided first in Bath, then in Dublin, and finally in London. He was a strong advocate of Logier's system. He was a pianist of distinction. In 1816 he invented an instrument called the Eidomusicon, 'which, on being fastened to the keyboard of the pianoforte, produced the notes and chords as they were struck, with a view to displaying them to the eye, and so to facilitate sight-singing, &c.' He published an opera, many glees and songs, and some educational works.

418. CLIFTON.

CLOUGH, ARTHUR HUGH (Liverpool, 1819–61, Florence), was educated at Chester, Rugby, where he was a favourite pupil of Arnold and was a brilliant student and athlete, and at Balliol College, Oxford. He won the blue ribbon of a Fellowship of Oriel, and was a member of a distinguished circle. The Oxford Movement threw over him a spell under the influence of which he was 'like a straw drawn up the draught of a chimney', but his mind was too veracious to be permanently affected by it, and when the reaction set in, it led to a gradual abandonment of the orthodox Christian creed. His spiritual parting from his dear and brilliant friend, William George Ward, is commemorated in his pathetic *Qua cursum ventus.* He felt it his duty to resign his fellowship. For some time he was Warden of University Hall, London, but in 1850 resigned and sailed to America, where his parents had been settled in his youth. He took pupils at Cambridge, Mass., wrote articles, and formed close friendships with Emerson and Charles Eliot Norton. Recalled to England in 1853 to an examinership in the Education Office, he married, and spent some years happily in official work. Then, in 1859, his health gave way. Travel in Greece, the Pyrenees, and Italy failed to restore it, and malarial fever, inducing paralysis, brought death to him in Florence, where he was buried. He was a diffident, sensitive, lovable man, with a rare humour, a deep love of Nature, a noble and sincere mind, and, in spite of his doctrinal detachment, a deep fundamental piety. His poetry reflects the spiritual conflict he passed through, and his relentless passion for reality. Carlyle called him 'a diamond sifted out of the general rubbish heap'. Matthew Arnold's *Thyrsis* was written in tribute to his memory. Lowell, who knew him, said, 'We have a foreboding that Clough, imperfect as he was in many respects, and dying before he had subdued his sensitive temperament to the sterner requirements of his art, will be thought a hundred years hence to have been the truest expression in verse of the moral and intellectual tendencies, the doubt and struggle towards settled convictions, of the period in which he lived.' His *Poems* were collected by F. T. Palgrave in 1863, and his *Poems and Prose Remains* by his widow, in 1869.

536. *Say not, 'The struggle nought availeth'.*

COCKBURN-CAMPBELL, MARGARET, LADY (? , 1808–41, Alphington, near Exeter), was the eldest daughter of Sir John Malcolm, G.C.B. She married, in 1827, Sir Alexander Thomas Cockburn-Campbell, Bart., one of the many aristocrats who were actively associated with the beginnings of Plymouth Brethrenism in England. In his zeal for a return to primitive Christian simplicity, he practised a kind of Pentecostal communism in his home, insisting that the servants should sit at table with his wife and himself. One day, coming in late to dinner, he found the meal already far advanced; the servants explained that as he was late, they could not wait, and had begun without him. His ideal did not long endure these practical difficulties. He became a resident magistrate at Albany, Western Australia, and died in 1871. Lady Cockburn-Campbell's hymns were first issued in lithograph from her manuscript, for private circulation, and some of them were included in the Plymouth Brethren's *Psalms and Hymns* (1842).

34. *Praise ye Jehovah, praise the Lord most holy.*

CODNER, ELIZABETH, *née* HARRIS (Dartmouth, 1824–1919, Croydon), married the Rev. Daniel Codner, some time a clergyman of the Church of England. She was for many years closely identified with the work carried on by the Rev. W. and Mrs. Pennefather at Mildmay, in the north of London. For some years she edited a monthly magazine named *Woman's Work*. In addition to several small books she published *Mornings at Mildmay* (addresses to women); *Among the Brambles;* and *Behind the Clouds*.

687. *Lord, I hear of showers of blessing.*

COFFIN, CHARLES (Buzancy, 1676–1749, Paris), a distinguished French ecclesiastic, succeeded Rollin the historian in 1712 as principal of the College of Dormans-Beauvais, and in 1718 was rector of the University of Paris. Most of his hymns appeared in *The Paris Breviary* of 1736, a work which was largely influenced by him. In the same year he published a hundred of his hymns as *Hymni Sacri Auctore Carolo Coffin*, with an interesting preface explanatory of their spirit and aim. The following three hymns are translations from Coffin:

> 274. *As now the sun's declining rays.*
> 440. *Happy are they, they that love God.*
> 78. *On Jordan's bank the Baptist's cry.*

COGHILL, ANNIE LOUISA, *née* WALKER (Brewood, Staffordshire, 1836–1907, Bath), went in her teens with her parents to Canada, where her brothers were railway engineers. They lived in Sania. Some time between 1860 and 1870, probably about 1863, they returned to England, where she became a governess. Later, she reviewed books, and made her home with Mrs. Oliphant for some years. In 1883 she married Harry Coghill, a wealthy merchant, and from that time till her death her home was at Coghurst Hall, near Hastings. She was a tall, striking-looking woman of stately appearance and charming manner. While in Canada she published a small collection of her verses at Montreal as *Leaves from the Backwoods* (1859). Subsequently she published six novels, *A Canadian Heroine; Against Her Will; Hollywood; Two Rival Loves; Lay Holme;* and *Mary Broom;* a small volume of *Plays for Children*, and a book of poems, *Oak and Maple*. She also edited the *Autobiography and Letters of Mrs. Oliphant*, who was her second cousin.

> 357. *Work, for the night is coming.*

COLLINS, HENRY, M.A. (Barningham, Darlington, 1827–1919, Coalville), was educated at Oxford and ordained in the Church of England in 1853. In the following year he published *Hymns for Schools and Missions* (thirty-seven hymns, of which two only were his own). In 1857 he went over to the Roman Church, and in 1860 became a Trappist monk in the monastery of Mount St. Bernard's Abbey, Coalville, North Leicester, being known thenceforth as Father Augustine (Austin). From 1882 till 1913 he was chaplain to the nuns of his own Cistercian order at Staplehill Priory, Wimborne, Dorset. His last years were spent in St. Bernard's Abbey.

> 430. *Jesus, my Lord, my God, my all.*

COLQUHOUN, FRANCES SARA, *née* FULLER MAITLAND (Shinfield Park, near Reading, 1809–77, Edinburgh), daughter of E. Fuller Maitland of Stanstead Hall and Park Place, Henley-on-Thames, married in 1834 John, son of Sir John Colquhoun, Bart. Three of her hymns were included in her mother's *Hymns for Private Devotion* (1827).

> 533. *Much in sorrow, oft in woe.*

COLUMBA, ST. (Gartan, Donegal, *c.* 521–97, Iona), the most renowned of the early Saints of Scotland, came of a notable family in Ireland. He studied at the monastic schools of Moville and

Clonard, and was also a pupil of the bard Gemman, whose influence may perhaps be traced in the Latin hymns and Celtic poems ascribed to Columba. The reason of his leaving Ireland is obscure. According to one account it originated in a dispute over what we should now call copyright, Columba having copied a psalter without permission. The quarrel led to a bloody battle, in which Columba's party was victorious. A synod, however, judged him guilty of the blood that had been shed. He was banished from Ireland, and enjoined to win as many souls from heathendom as the Christians he had caused to be slain in battle. Setting sail from Ireland, Columba and his twelve companions landed at Iona, a small island to the west of Scotland, which became the home of the little community, as well as the starting-point for a missionary campaign of extraordinary success on the mainland. That success, indeed, has commonly been over-estimated. 'All through the later Middle Ages,' says Dr. Douglas Simpson in his *The Historical Saint Columba*, 'the Roman Church writers misread or garbled the records of Celtic Christianity, ascribing to Columba and the Scotic school of Iona much of the work that was in fact performed by Ninian and Kentigern and their successors of the Brito-Pictish Church.' But Columba's share in the evangelization of Scotland was a great one. A large number of religious houses were founded throughout Scotland by him and his disciples. The *Life* of the Saint by Adamnan, though full of incredible marvels, sheds much light on his career, the account of Columba's last hours being especially graphic and touching. He tells how even the white horse employed on the farm shed tears over the approaching death of its master; how almost to the end the Saint was engaged in transcribing the Psalter, ending with the words of Psalm xxxiv. 10, 'They that seek the Lord shall not want any good thing'; and how he breathed his last in the church after raising his hand to bless the brethren. Cf. Bishop Dowden's note in *The Celtic Church in Scotland*, p. 115.

The ecclesiastical buildings of Iona (most of them of considerably later date) were made over in 1899 to the Church of Scotland by the then Duke of Argyll.

To Columba is ascribed sacred poetry both in Latin and in his native Gaelic. His hymn known as the *Altus* was translated by the late Marquis of Bute and by the late Bishop Anthony Mitchell of Aberdeen.

> 179. *Christ is the world's Redeemer.*
> 454. *O God, Thou art the Father.*

CONDER, EUSTACE ROGERS, D.D. (near St. Albans, 1820–92, Poole, Dorset), was son of Josiah Conder (q.v.). His mother was a granddaughter of Roubiliac the sculptor, a descendant of the Huguenots. He studied for the Congregational ministry at Spring Hill College, Birmingham, and graduated M.A. with the gold medal in philosophy at London University in 1844. He was minister of a Congregational church at Poole for seventeen years, and while there trained students for missionary work; then, in 1861, passed to East Parade Chapel, Leeds, to which he ministered till the year of his death. He was elected chairman of the Congregational Union of England and Wales in 1873. His published works were—*The Basis of Faith* (the Congregational Lecture for 1877); *Outlines of the Life of Christ; Sleepy Forest* (fairy tales for children); *Why are we Dissenters?;* and *Heart Chords*.

75. *Ye fair green hills of Galilee.*

CONDER, JOSIAH (Aldersgate, London, 1789–1855, St. John's Wood, London), was the son of an engraver and bookseller. At fifteen he became assistant in his father's book-store. In his seventeenth year he began a long correspondence with Ann and Jane Taylor, and he joined them and others in publishing, five years later, *The Associate Minstrels*, his own contribution to which received commendation from Southey, then Poet Laureate. He had marked literary ability and untiring industry, but his business enterprises did not prosper, and he had a constant struggle with difficulties due to straitened means. For twenty years he owned and edited *The Eclectic Review;* he edited also *The Patriot* newspaper. Among his numerous works were—*The Modern Traveller*, a compilation in thirty volumes which cost him seven years' labour; a *Dictionary of Ancient and Modern Geography;* a *Life of Bunyan; Protestant Nonconformity; Sacred Poems, Domestic Poems, Miscellaneous Poems; The Choir and the Oratory, or, Praise and Prayer; Hymns of Praise, Prayer, and Devout Meditation* (a collection of his poems and hymns personally revised, but published after his death). For the Congregational Union he edited their first official hymn-book, *The Congregational Hymn Book, A Supplement to Dr. Watts's Psalms and Hymns.* This book was much criticized and subjected to early revision, but it had great merit; eight out of every ten hymns in it are still in use in Great Britain or America. Of his own hymns, sixty-two appeared in it. One of his grandsons was Colonel Claude R. Conder, the well-known archaeologist and surveyor of Palestine.

25. *The Lord is King! lift up thy voice.*

CONVERSE, CHARLES CROZAT, LL.D. (Warren, Massachusetts, 1832–1918, Highwood, New Jersey), received a musical training in Germany, studying theory and composition at Leipzig under Richter, Hauptmann and Plaidy. On returning to America he prepared for the legal profession at Albany Law School, where he graduated in 1861. From 1875 he carried on a law practice at Erie, Pennsylvania. He was an inventor also. He endeavoured vainly to introduce the use of 'thon' as a pronoun. Rutherford College, in 1895, gave him its LL.D. degree. His later years were spent at Highwood.

His published compositions included an *American Concert Overture* (1869), based on *Hail, Columbia;* a Festouvertüre (1870); and an American National Hymn, *God for us* (1887).

701. CONVERSE.

COOKE, ROBERT (Westminster, 1768–1814, London), son of Dr. Benjamin Cooke, organist of Westminster Abbey and an eminent composer and musical theorist of his day, succeeded his father as organist of St. Martin-in-the-Fields; in 1802 succeeded Dr. Arnold as master of the choristers in Westminster Abbey. His mind became deranged, and he drowned himself in the Thames. He composed an evening service in C, anthems, and several songs and glees. He published a *Collection of Eight Glees* of his own (1805), and in 1795 a collection of his father's glees.

718. CHANT IN G.

COOPER, EDWARD, M.A. (1770–1833), was educated at Queen's College, and became a Fellow of All Souls, Oxford. He was rector of Hamstall-Ridware, 1788–1809, and of Yoxall, Staffordshire, 1809–33. He had a great reputation as a preacher, and published seven volumes of *Practical and Familiar Sermons*, which Bickersteth characterized as 'plain, sound and useful'. The Bishop of Lichfield recommended his younger clergymen to use them rather than sermons of their own, and the last Archbishop of Tuam admitted that when so pressed for time that he could not prepare fresh sermons, his habit was to read one of Cooper's and reproduce it in the pulpit. Cooper was associated with the Rev. Jonathan Stubbs and the Rev. Thomas Cotterill (q.v.) in the compilation of their *Selection of Psalms and Hymns for Public and Private Use* (1805); and he issued in 1811, for use in his own churches, *A Selection of Psalms and Hymns*.

5. *Father of heaven, whose love profound.*

CORNER, DAVID GREGOR (Hirschberg, Silesia, 1587–1648, Vienna), studied probably in Breslau, later in Prague and Gratz. In 1618 he became Pfarrer in Rötz, and later in Maulbronn. When forty years old he entered the Benedictine order. From 1638 till his death he was rector of the University of Vienna. It is not claimed that he composed any of the melodies in his *Gesangbuch* (1631); they appear to have been collected from many different sources.

395. (OMNI DIE).

COSIN, JOHN (Norwich, 1594–1672, London), was educated at Caius College, Cambridge, took holy orders, and was appointed Chaplain to the Bishop of Durham. He subsequently became prebendary of Durham, and Archdeacon of the East Riding of Yorkshire. Other preferments followed, and in 1640 he became Chancellor of the University of Cambridge and Dean of Peterborough. At this point, however, his fortunes suffered eclipse. His *Collection of Private Devotions* had already been severely criticized by the Puritans, and one of their number, whom Cosin had treated with severity, succeeded in inducing the Long Parliament to deprive him of his benefices. He retired to France and remained there till the Restoration, when he was restored to his dignities and became Bishop of Durham. During his episcopate he spent large sums on the cathedral, on the library, and on various works of charity. A man of profound liturgical knowledge, he took part in the final revision of *The Book of Common Prayer* (1662), in which is incorporated his translation of the *Veni, Creator Spiritus*.

182. *Come, Holy Ghost, our souls inspire* (tr.).

COSTER, GEORGE THOMAS (Chatham, Kent, 1835–1912, Rotherham), was trained for the Congregational ministry at New College, London, and held pastorates at Newport, near Saffron Walden, Essex; Barnstaple, Devon; Fish Street, Hull; South Norwood, London; West Cliff, Whitby; Bedford Chapel, Stroud; and Hessle, a suburb of Hull. He published *Temperance Melodies and Religious Hymns* (1868); *Pastors and People* (1869); *Lorrin and Other Poems* (1859); *The Rhyme of St. Peter's Fall* (1871); *Poems and Hymns* (1882); *Gloria Christi* (1896); *Hessle Hymns* (1901); *When the Stars Appear* (1903); and *Beams of Christ's Glory: Meditations for Each Sunday in the Year* (1905).

492. *O God our Father, throned on high.*

COTTERILL, THOMAS, M.A. (Cannock, Staffordshire, 1779–1823, Sheffield), son of a wool-stapler, was educated at the Free School, Birmingham, and St. John's College, Cambridge, of which he became a Fellow. Ordained in 1803, he became curate of Tutbury; incumbent of Lane End, Staffordshire; and, finally, perpetual curate of St. Paul's, Sheffield. He assisted the Rev. Jonathan Stubbs in editing *A Selection of Psalms and Hymns for Public and Private Use* (1805); and in 1810 published in Staffordshire the first form of his own notable collection under the same title. The important edition of this book was the 8th, issued in 1819. In the preparation of it he had the assistance of Montgomery, who said of it, 'Good Mr. Cotterill and I bestowed a great deal of labour and care on the compilation of that book; clipping, interlining, and remodelling hymns of all sorts as we thought we could correct the sentiment or improve the expression.' Thus Montgomery practised on others what, in relation to his own hymns, he condemned. This edition contained 150 psalms and 367 hymns, 50 of which were by Montgomery, and 25 by Cotterill. Hymns were not yet recognized as permissible in public worship; some bishops forbade as an irregularity the use of them within their dioceses; and many people regarded the increasing use of them with dismay. The opposition gathered to a head on Cotterill's new book.

He had tried to force it on his own congregation in Sheffield. Resistance among the anti-evangelical section of them was fomented by outside opponents of the innovation, and suit was brought against Cotterill in the Consistory Court of the see of York. On the persuasion of Archbishop Harcourt, the case was compromised, Cotterill agreeing to withdraw the book and prepare a new selection under the Primate's eye and at his expense. This was done in 1820, the number of hymns being reduced to 146, selected in the main by Cotterill; and his congregation each received a copy inscribed 'The gift of his Grace the Archbishop of York'. The suppressed book, however, 'did more than any other collection to mould the hymn-books of the next period; and nearly nine-tenths of the hymns therein, and usually in the altered form given them by Cotterill or James Montgomery . . . are still in common use in Great Britain and America'. It was on Cotterill's death that Montgomery wrote 'Friend after friend departs'; and it was said of him that he combined 'the piety of a saint, the tastes of a scholar, the aspect and demeanour of an unaffected Christian gentleman'.

366. *Great God of Abraham, hear our prayer.*

COURTEVILLE, RAPHAEL (London, ? –1772, London), was son of a chorister of the Chapel Royal who bore the same name, and was trained as one of the children of the Chapel. He became organist of St. James's, Piccadilly, in 1691, at a salary of £20, with £4 for a blower. According to the church records, he continued in that post for eighty-one years. So prolonged a tenure is not impossible, as one Charles Bridgman was organist of All Saints', Hertford, for eighty-one years, having been appointed at thirteen, and dying at ninety-five; A. H. Brown (q.v.) began his career as an organist at eleven and continued it till he died at ninety-six. There is no need to assume, therefore, as has been done, that a son of the same name must have succeeded him without the succession being noted in the church records, although the fact that there was such a son is attested by a monument in the church to his wife, who died in 1735. Courteville married a lady of considerable fortune, and appears latterly to have sat lightly to his duties. He was threatened with dismissal for neglect of them. An assistant was given him, but Courteville gave him only a quarter of the salary for doing all the work, and the authorities had to intervene and insist that he should give half. He was the reputed author of *The Gazetteer*, a paper written in defence of Sir Robert Walpole's administration, and probably for this reason received the nickname 'Court-evil'. He wrote *Memoirs of Lord Burleigh;* was associated with Purcell in composing music for D'Urfey's opera *Don Quixote;* and composed songs, sonatas for violins and flutes, and other music.

173. ST. JAMES.

COUSIN, ANNE ROSS, *née* CUNDELL (Hull, 1824–1906, Edinburgh), was the only child of David Ross Cundell, M.D., Leith, who had been in the army during the Napoleonic wars and served as assistant surgeon at Waterloo. She developed remarkable powers as a musician and linguist; she spoke German, French, and Italian with fluency, and acquired enough Greek to read the New Testament in the original. She was brought up in the Episcopal Church, but the great ecclesiastical controversy of her youth led her to become a convinced and resolute Presbyterian. She married the Rev. William Cousin, a man of deep piety and fine scholarship who had begun his ministry in the Free Church at Duns, and was then in a charge in Chelsea. Later, he ministered at Irvine and Melrose. On his retiral from the latter charge, they settled in Edinburgh, where he died in 1882. The Irvine days Mrs. Cousin called the idyllic period of her life. In 1845 she contributed verses anonymously to *The Christian Treasury*, and in 1876 published her collected verses under the title *Immanuel's Land and Other Poems*. All her hymns are songs of gratitude and praise, of love and hope, characteristic of the spirit of one whose deep evangelical piety invested with a rarer beauty a nature already gentle and full of grace. She has been called 'a Scottish Christina Rossetti, with a more pronounced theology'. In her last days she prayed,

> May our own God but grant to me
> An evening-time of mellow light;

and the prayer was answered.

> 581. *The sands of time are sinking.*

COWPER, WILLIAM (Berkhampstead, 1731–1800, East Dereham), the greatest English poet of his age, was son of a chaplain to George II, whose father was a Judge of Common Pleas, and whose elder brother became Lord Chancellor and first Earl Cowper. The poet's mother, a descendant of Dr. John Donne, died when he was six years old. Always a sensitive child, he suffered much at his first school from the tyranny of an older boy, but was happier when removed to Westminster School, where he had Churchill and Warren Hastings as school-fellows. After being articled to an attorney, under whom he worked along with Thurlow, the future Chancellor, he was called to the Bar in 1754. On his being offered, through his kinsman, Major Cowper, the post of Clerk to the Journals of the House of Lords, the dread of appearing before the House to stand an examination so affected his reason that he attempted suicide, and was never thereafter entirely free from deep melancholy, often of a religious cast. After undergoing treatment in a private asylum, he found a home at Huntingdon in the family of the Rev. Morley Unwin, whose wife became his lifelong friend and guardian. On the death of Mr. Unwin he removed with the family to Olney, where their

friend, the Rev. John Newton, was curate. Here Cowper collaborated with Newton in strenuous parochial and evangelistic work,
and also in the production of what became known as the *Olney
Hymns*. That Newton's somewhat gloomy Calvinism was not entirely a healthy influence is shown by the fact that Cowper's insanity
returned during the time of their close intercourse, and was relieved by Newton's eventual departure to a rectory in London. A
means of brightening the poet's outlook in life was afforded by the
arrival of Lady Austen, a widow who came to reside at Olney, and at
whose instigation Cowper began his greatest poem *The Task*. The
success attained by this work greatly cheered its author. A more ambitious, though not equally successful literary venture, was a translation of Homer, in which he was encouraged by another good
friend, his cousin Lady Hesketh. In spite of these and other distractions, the depression of spirits returned and never again left
him except for brief periods. With Mrs. Unwin, now an invalid, he
removed to East Dereham, in Norfolk, where she died in 1796, and
the poet's death followed in 1800. In his hymns, written under the
influence of Newton, he is scarcely seen at his best, though some of
them are touchingly beautiful, and reflect the gleams of light which
from time to time irradiated his troubled soul.

    31. *God moves in a mysterious way.*
   417. *Hark, my soul! it is the Lord.*
   247. *Jesus, where'er Thy people meet.*
   457. *O for a closer walk with God.*
   439. *Sometimes a light surprises.*
   197. *The Spirit breathes upon the word.*
   692. *There is a fountain filled with blood.*

COX, FRANCIS ELIZABETH (Oxford, 1812–97, ?), was one of the
most felicitous of translators of German hymns. She was indebted
to Baron Bunsen for guidance as to the hymns most worthy of being
translated. She published *Sacred Hymns from the German* (1841);
and *Hymns from the German* (1864).

   121. *Jesus lives! thy terrors now* (tr.).
   542. *O let him whose sorrow* (tr.).
   222. *Who are these, like stars appearing?* (tr.).

COXE, ARTHUR CLEVELAND, D.D., LL.D. (Mendham, New Jersey,
1818–96, Buffalo, New Jersey), was the son of the Rev. Samuel Han-
son Cox, D.D., LL.D., an eminent Presbyterian minister in Brooklyn. The son altered the spelling of the name, and entered the Episcopal Church. Both changes were the subject of much humorous
banter between father and son. He graduated at the University of
New York, took holy orders in 1841, became rector of St. John's,
Hartford, Connecticut; after a visit to Britain was elected rector of
Grace Church, Baltimore, and then of Calvary Church, New York.

In 1865 he was consecrated Bishop of Western New York. He was a scholar of distinction and a poet. His modesty and scrupulousness of conscience were such that he would not allow any of his hymns to appear in the hymn-book of his own Communion (though they were being included in the collections of most other denominations in Britain and America), for the sole reason that he had served for a time on the Hymnal Committee of his own Church. He published *Impressions of England* (1855); *Sermons on Doctrine and Duty* (1855); and contributed largely to periodicals.

382. *Saviour, sprinkle many nations.*

CREWDSON, JANE *née* FOX (Perran-arworthal, Cornwall, 1809–63, Summerlands, Whalley Range, Manchester), married Thomas D. Crewdson, a Manchester manufacturer, in 1836. Always delicate, she was long a confirmed invalid. 'As a constant sufferer, the spiritual life deepening, and the intellectual life retaining all its power, she became well prepared to testify as to the all-sufficiency of her Saviour's love.' Between the paroxysms of pain she composed the poems and hymns published as *Aunt Jane's Verses for Children* (1851); *Lays of the Reformation and Other Lyrics* (1860); *The Singer of Eisenach;* and *A Little While, and Other Poems* (1864).

425. *O Saviour, I have nought to plead.*
148. *There is no sorrow, Lord, too light.*

CROFT, WILLIAM, Mus. Doc. (or CROFTS, as he sometimes wrote) (Nether Eatington, now Ettington, Warwickshire, 1678–1727, Bath), was born of good family, became one of the children of the Chapel Royal under Dr. Blow; organist of St. Anne's, Soho, and gentleman extraordinary of the Chapel Royal, 1700; joint-organist of the Chapel Royal with Jeremiah Clark, 1704, and sole organist, 1707; organist of Westminster Abbey and composer to the Chapel Royal, 1708; Mus. Doc., Oxon., 1713. In earlier life he composed for the theatre and also wrote sonatas, songs, and odes; but he became absorbed in sacred music, and made for himself in this field one of the greatest names in English musical history. Many of his fine anthems are still sung; his service music is of the highest importance; the noble Burial Service of Croft and Purcell especially has never been surpassed for solemn grandeur. It is believed that his Cathedral music was one of the models of Handel's 'high sacred style' in his oratorios. But his tunes give him widest fame. They are 'of importance historically, as they are the earliest examples of the English psalm-tune as distinguished from the Genevan; they require quicker singing, and the glorious rhythmical impulse of "Hanover" and its triple measure marked at once a distinct originality'. In *Divine Harmony* he published a collection of the words of anthems with a brief historical account of English Church music; and in *Musica Sacra*, thirty anthems and a Burial Service of his own composition. His epitaph in

Westminster Abbey concludes, 'Having resided among mortals for fifty years, behaving with the utmost candour . . . he departed to the heavenly choir . . . that being near, he might add to the concert of angels his own HALLELUJAH.'

440. BINCHESTER.	9. HANOVER.
717. CHANT IN A MINOR.	530, 86. ST. MATTHEW.
39. CROFT'S 136TH.	601. ST. ANNE.

CROLY, GEORGE, LL.D. (Dublin, 1780–1860, London), was a graduate of Trinity College, Dublin. Taking orders, he ministered in Ireland till about 1810, when he repaired to London to engage in literary pursuits. In these he displayed great versatility of talent. He wrote poetry, serious and humorous, tragedies and comedies, satires and panegyrics, novels and songs, all of them well. His *Salathiel* produced a greater literary sensation on its appearance, than almost any other novel of its time. He was one of the first contributors to *Blackwood's Magazine*, edited *The Universal Review*, and wrote the leading articles of *Britannia*, a Conservative newspaper which advocated protection. He was a fierce Conservative in politics and religion, and an outspoken denouncer of what seemed to him the latitudinarian tendencies of his day. In 1835 he was presented by Lord Brougham to the united benefices of St. Bene't Sherehog and St. Stephen's, Walbrook, and in his parish was much admired and beloved. His bold utterances drew large congregations of all ranks to his church. At the request of his people, he prepared a collection of *Psalms and Hymns for Public Worship*, containing twenty-five psalms, ten of which were versions by the editor; fifty hymns, ten of which were original; and six longer pieces on Scripture subjects. Only one edition was issued, and the greater part of that was consumed by a fire, so that copies are now very scarce. Dr. Croly dropped dead while walking one day in Holborn.

195. *Spirit of God, descend upon my heart.*

CROSBIE, HOWARD AUGUSTUS, M.A. (Liverpool, 1844–1918, Lindfield, Sussex), was educated at Trinity College, Cambridge, and was ordained in 1867. He was curate of Habergham Eaves, Burnley, and of Birchin, Rusholme, Manchester; curate-in-charge of Bamber Bridge, near Preston; vicar of Milmow, near Rochdale; vicar of Trumpington, Cambridge; and vicar of Builth and perpetual curate of Llanddewi'r-Cwm, both English-speaking parishes in Wales. He was an amateur musician, and composed many tunes. In 1914 he retired to Lindfield, Sussex, where he died suddenly four years later.

375. SEFTON.

CROTCH, WILLIAM, Mus. Doc. (Norwich, 1775–1847, Taunton), was the son of a Norwich carpenter who was an enthusiast for music and built himself a small organ. On this, William was able to play at two years old. So extraordinary a prodigy he was that at three years of age he was the subject of papers at the Royal Society, and at four gave a course of daily public recitals in London. His manual dexterity was extraordinary; he was ambidextrous, and could write with either hand or with both at the same time. Sent to Cambridge to study under Randall, he there composed an oratorio, *The Captivity of Judah*, when only fourteen years old. Proceeding to Oxford in 1788 to study for holy orders, he became organist of Christ Church in 1790, B.Mus. 1794, Mus.Doc. 1797, and in the same year Professor of Music in the University, though only twenty-two years of age. Ten years later he settled in London. In 1823 he was appointed first Principal of the newly-founded R. A. M., but he was no disciplinarian, and resigned in 1832. He was a man of much learning, an artist and a theologian, as well as a musician of high accomplishment. His oratorio *Palestine*, to Heber's words, was perhaps his most notable achievement; he wrote also a number of anthems, but will be longest remembered by his chants, of which he wrote seventy-four.

717. CHANT IN D MINOR.   549. SIDON.

CRÜGER, JOHANN (Grossbriesen, near Guben, Prussia, 1598–1662, Berlin), the celebrated composer of chorales, was educated at the Jesuit College of Olmütz, and at the school of poetry at Regensburg. He travelled through Austria, Hungary, Bohemia, and arrived at Berlin in 1615. There he was tutor in the family of Colonel Christoph von Blumenthal for five years, and then he finished his theological studies at the University of Wittenberg. He became cantor of the Cathedral Church of St. Nicholas, Berlin, in 1622, and founded its celebrated choir. There he continued till his death. He wrote largely on the theory and practice of music, and both as author and composer had a great reputation in his day. He published many concertos and motets, and a collection of Magnificats; but is chiefly known now as composer of some of the most famous and favourite chorales. These appeared in his *Praxis Pietatis Melica* (1644), which appeared in countless editions, and 'constituted the main stream of Lutheran hymnody in the middle of the seventeenth century'. As a tune-writer he was of the first rank, and as an editor no less eminent. He preserved much fine material already in existence, and called other good composers to his aid.

154. CRÜGER.   29. NUN DANKET.
216. HERZLIEBSTER JESU.   351. NUN DANKET ALL (GRÄFEN-
394. JESU, MEINE ZUVERSICHT.   BERG).

CUMMINS, JOHN JAMES (Cork, 1795–1867, Buckland, Surrey), went to London from Ireland in 1864, and was a banker by profession. For many years he was a Director of the Union Bank of Australia. He was an ardent student of Hebrew and theology. For the use of his own children in preparation for Confirmation, he wrote

Seals of the Covenant opened in the Sacraments of the Church (1838), and in the following year published the hymns contained in it, as *Poetical Meditations and Hymns*. He published also (1849) *Lyra Evangelica: Hymns, Meditations, and Other Poems*.

524. *Jesus, Lord of Life and Glory.*

CUSHING, WILLIAM ORCUTT (New England States, 1823–1903), was a minister of 'the Christian Church'. He ministered to congregations of that body at Scarsburg, Auburn, Brooklyn, Buffalo, and Sparta, New York State. In his last years he joined the Wesleyan Methodist Church. He is said to have written more than 300 hymns of the 'gospel' type.

158. *When He cometh.*

DALE, REGINALD FRANCIS, M.A., Mus. Bac. (Sydenham, London, 1845–1919, Oxford), son of a Dean of Rochester, was a scholar of Queen's College, Oxford. Ordained in 1870, he was a master at Westminster School for seventeen years; then rector of Bletchingdon, Oxford, and subsequently vicar of Binsey. He spent his last years in retirement in Oxford. He was joint-author with the Rev. John Troutbeck of *A Music Primer for Schools*, and composed many hymn tunes, some of which appeared in *Twenty-Two Original Hymn Tunes, by Two Oxford Graduates* (1867), the other graduate being the Rev. H. J. Poole, composer of 'St. Lucy'.

348. ST. CATHERINE.

DAMON (or DAMAN), WILLIAM (*c.* 1540–*c.* 91), was organist of the Chapel Royal under Queen Elizabeth. The book by which he is best known, a collection of the Psalms in four parts, which he had prepared for the use of his friend John Bull, citizen and goldsmith of London, was published by John Day under the title: *The Psalmes of David in English meter, with notes of four parts set unto them by Guilielmo Damon*, 1579. The tunes used are, with one or two exceptions, those which had appeared in previous books—the Anglo-Genevan Psalter of 1556, the English of 1562, and the Scottish of 1564. There are four books, one for each part, and the harmony is simple note against note. This simple harmony was apparently not thought worthy of Damon's reputation and ability, and he withdrew it and destroyed the remaining copies, so that it is now extremely rare. He set himself to revise the harmonies, and in 1591 a second and more elaborate edition was published with this title, *The former (second) Booke of the Musicke of M. William Damon, late one of her majesties Musitions: contayning all the tunes of David's psalms as they are ordinarely soung in the Church, most excellently by him composed into 4 parts*. The work is in eight books, the first four of which have the melody in the tenor, and the second four in the Cantus.

276. (DUNDEE). 102. (SOUTHWELL).

Biographical and Historical Notes

DARBY, JOHN NELSON (London, 1800–82, Bournemouth), was educated at Westminster School and at Trinity College, Dublin, 'the academic parent of Plymouth Brethrenism'. He graduated there as classical gold medallist in 1819, and was called to the Irish Bar. Conscientious scruples restrained him from practising, and in 1825 he accepted ordination to a curacy in Wicklow. He was at that time a High Churchman. Difficulties about the scriptural basis of Church establishments led him to resign. Just then, Anthony Norris Groves was founding a sect called 'The Brethren', which rejected all ecclesiastical forms and denominational distinctions. This body Darby joined. A pamphlet by him on *The Nature and Unity of the Church of Christ* brought in many recruits of education and high social standing. Soon he became the pre-eminent figure in the movement. He travelled untiringly on missions of propagation. From the fact that the meeting of supporters in Plymouth was the first in England to be recognized as a meeting of Brethren, the adherents of the movement became known as Plymouth Brethren, though long called Darbyites in Ireland. The new society had for a time remarkable success, in the United Kingdom and on the Continent, especially in Switzerland and Germany. But it proved fatally fissiparous: its history is one of continual dissensions and disruptions. And though professedly founded on the free model of primitive Christianity, it developed the narrowest and most intolerant type of ecclesiastical despotism. Its interpretation of Scripture was largely vitiated by arbitrary ideas about unfulfilled prophecy, and in its confident expectation of the immediate return of the Saviour it was founded on a delusion. Darby 'was its guiding and energizing spirit'. Over many remarkable men, like Francis William Newman, the Cardinal's brother, he had an almost hypnotic influence. Personally of an ascetic habit, intense earnestness, total self-forgetfulness, and iron inflexibility of will, he has been compared to Ignatius Loyola. He published many books, doctrinal, controversial, devotional, practical; and edited the hymnal in general use among the Brethren. His own hymns were collected after his death and published as *Spiritual Songs*.

59. *God and Father, we adore Thee.*

DARLING, THOMAS, M.A. (London, 1816–93, London), son of George Darling, M.D., was educated at the Charterhouse and St. John's College, Cambridge. Ordained in 1839, he was incumbent for a time of Shanington, near Canterbury; then rector of St. Michael Royal and St. Martin Vintry, City of London. In 1855 he published *Hymns for the Church of England, arranged according to the Order of the Book of Common Prayer*. Of the 336 hymns in this collection twenty were by the editor, who was also responsible for some successful adaptations of hymns by other writers.

6. *O King of kings, before whose throne.*

DARWALL, JOHN, B.A. (Haughton, Staffordshire, 1731–89, Walsall), was educated at Manchester Grammar School and Brasenose College, Oxford, where he graduated in 1756. He became curate, and in 1769 vicar, of Walsall, Staffs. He wrote hymns and poetical pieces, and was an enthusiastic amateur musician. He composed a tune for each of the 150 metrical psalms. Few of these were published, but some are found in late eighteenth-century tune-books and in Dr. Mann's *Church of England Hymnal.* They were written in two parts only, treble and bass. He published two volumes of pianoforte sonatas, *A Christmas Hymn and Tune; A Charity Hymn and Tune;* and *A Hymn, to which is prefixed a biographical notice.*

135. DARWALL.

DAVIES Sir HENRY WALFORD, Mus. Doc., LL.D. (Oswestry, Shropshire, 1869–   ), became a chorister of St. George's, Windsor, in 1882; assistant organist to Sir Walter Parratt there, 1885–90; a teacher of counterpoint, Royal College of Music, 1895; conductor, London Bach Choir, 1903–7, and of the London Church Association, 1901–13; organist of the Temple Church, 1890–1919; Professor of Music, University College of Wales, Aberystwyth, from 1919; Chairman, National Council of Music, University of Wales, from 1919; Gresham Professor of Music, 1924; organist of St. George's, Windsor, and master of music to the King, 1927. He was knighted in 1922. He has been a great inspiring force as director of music in the Welsh University and schools, as adjudicator at musical festivals all over the country, and as a pioneer of community singing. His works include an oratorio, *The Temple;* cantatas, *Three Jovial Huntsmen; Everyman; Ode on Time; Five Sayings of Jesus; Song of St. Francis; Songs of a Day; Noble Numbers.* He is author of *Music and Christian Worship,* and has edited *The Fellowship Song Book, Fifty-Two Hymn Tunes,* and *Hymns of the Kingdom* and *A Students' Hymnal.*

317. AUCTOR VITAE.   446. PENTATONE.
48. CHRISTMAS CAROL.   155. VISION.
10. FIRMAMENT.

DAY (DAYE or DAIE), JOHN (Dunwich, Suffolk, 1552–84, Walden, Essex), was one of the earliest of music printers. He used as his device a sleeper awakened by one who points to the rising sun, with the punning motto, 'Arise, for it is Day'. He was a zealous supporter of the reformed religion, and suffered imprisonment for his loyalty to it; for a time also he had to live abroad. 'There are very few of our earlier printers to whom both literature and typography are more deeply indebted.' (Dibdin.) He printed the first edition of what is known as *Queen Elizabeth's Prayer Book;* the first edition of *Foxe's Book of Martyrs;* the first Church music book in English, *Certaine Notes set forth in foure and three parts to be song;* Archbishop Parker's translation of the Psalms, the first by one person of the whole Psalter

315

in English metre; in 1562, the first edition of the complete Metrical Psalter known as the Old Version, with the old proper tunes; and in 1563, *The Whole Psalmes, in foure partes, which may be sung to all musical instruments,* Tallis being a contributor—probably the earliest psalter in which the proper tunes were harmonized.

355. (OLD 81ST).   8. (ST. FLAVIAN).

DAYMAN, EDWARD ARTHUR, B.D. (Padstow, Cornwall, 1807–90, Shillingstone), son of John Dayman of Mambury, North Devon, was educated at Tiverton and Exeter College, Oxford. He took a first class in graduation, and became a Fellow and tutor of his college, a University Examiner, and Senior Proctor of the University. Ordained in 1835, he became in 1842 rector of Shillingstone Okeford, Dorset; Rural Dean, 1849; Proctor in Convocation, 1852; Prebendary of Bitton in Salisbury Cathedral, 1862. His chief work was a *Dictionary of Mediaeval Latin.* He published also *Modern Infidelity* (1861); *An Essay on Inspiration* (1864). Jointly with Earl Nelson and Canon (afterwards Bishop) Woodford (q.v.), he edited *The Sarum Hymnal* (1868); and, with Canon Rich-Jones, *Statuta et Consuetudines Ecclesiae Cathedralis Sarisburiensis* (1883). Many of the translations in *The Sarum Hymnal* are his, and seven original hymns by him are in *The Hymnary* (1872).

625. *O Lord, be with us when we sail.*

DEARMER, PERCY, D.D. (London, 1867–   ), was educated at Westminster School, abroad, and at Christ Church, Oxford. He served as curate in St. Anne's, Lambeth; St. John's, Great Marlborough Street; Berkeley Chapel, Mayfair; St. Mark's, Marylebone Road; then, from 1901 to 1915, was vicar of St. Mary the Virgin, Primrose Hill. He was secretary of the London branch of the Christian Social Union, and chairman of the League of Arts. After much service abroad during the war, he became in 1919 Professor of Ecclesiastical Art in King's College, London. Many books have come from his pen, e.g., *The Parson's Hand Book; The Sanctuary; Body and Soul; Highways and Byways in Normandy; The English Carol Book* (with Martin Shaw); *The Art of Public Worship; The Power of the Spirit; The Church at Prayer and the World Outside.* He was secretary of the Committee that prepared *The English Hymnal,* and acted as editor of that epoch-making book; he edited also *Songs of Praise* (1925), with the co-operation, in the music, of Dr. R. Vaughan Williams and Martin Shaw (q.v.).

263. *Father, we praise Thee, now the night is over* (tr.).
349. *Father, who on man dost shower.*

DE CHENEZ, CHARITIE LEES, *née* SMITH (Bloomfield, Merrion, County Dublin, 1841–   ), was the daughter of the Rev. Sidney Smith, D.D., rector of Aghalurcher, Co. Fermanagh, and subsequently of Drumragh, Co. Tyrone, Ireland. She married in 1869 Arthur E. Bancroft, and by a second marriage became Mrs. de Chenez. Her hymns were published in Dr. Charles Rogers's *Lyra Britannica*, Bishop Ryle's *Spiritual Songs*, M'Ilwaine's *Lyra Hibernica Sacra*, and in various periodicals. Under the title *Within the Veil* they were collected and published in 1867.

396. *The King of Glory standeth.*

DECK, JAMES GEORGE (Bury St. Edmunds, 1802–84, Motueka, near Nelson, New Zealand), was educated for the Army, and was an officer in the Indian service at Bangalore. Retiring in 1835 owing to the failure of his health, he joined the Plymouth Brethren, and in 1843 took charge of a congregation of that body at Wellington, Somerset. Afterwards, for a time, he lived at Weymouth, but in 1852 he emigrated to New Zealand. His hymns are for the most part disqualified for common use by the doctrine as to the Second Advent which inspires them, though some have found their way into many hymn-books. They were published in *Hymns for the Poor of the Flock* (1837–8); *Psalms and Hymns* (1842); *The Wellington Hymn-Book* (1857); *Hymns and Spiritual Songs* (1860); *Hymns and Sacred Poems* (Melbourne, 1876).

470. *O Lamb of God, still keep me.*

DECK, MARY ANN SANDERSON, *née* GIBSON (Hull, 1813–1902, Wolverhampton), lived nearly all her life in Hull. In 1845 she married the Rev. John Deck, brother of James G. Deck (q.v.). Her husband was vicar of St. Stephen's, Hull, a large working-class parish of 13,000 inhabitants, and she led a very busy life, working hard in Sunday School, mothers' meeting, a men's night-school, and countless other things. When seventy years old she lost her sight gradually and became totally blind, but taught herself to read the Braille type, and gradually got the whole Bible in this form. Her years of blindness were spent at Wolverhampton in the home of her daughter, Mrs. O. F. Walton, authoress of *Christie's Old Organ* and other stories. 'She took the keenest interest in everything to the end, and was bright and happy and full of love for her Saviour.'

480. *There is a city bright.*

DENNY, Sir EDWARD, Bart. (Tralee Castle, 1796–1889, ?   ), succeeded his father as 4th baronet in 1831. Nearly the whole town of Tralee belonged to him. His rental income was about £13,000 a year, but he lived for the most part in a cottage at Islington, devoting his time to a study of the prophetical books, and giving his means liberally to the poor and to religious causes. He was a considerate and popular landlord; the rents on his estate were fixed at so fair a figure that he was almost alone in escaping reductions by the Land Commissioners. In other ways, though he took no part in public affairs, he proved himself a man whose religion made him both just and generous in dealing with his fellow-men. With others of the Kerry gentry of his time, he joined the Plymouth Brethren, and was for many years a prominent and honoured figure in that body in London. Though many of his hymns are so coloured by the peculiar millenarian doctrines of his sect—on which he wrote numerous tracts and broadsheets—as to be unsuitable for general use, others have added a distinct enrichment to the Churches' treasury of praise. His *Hymns and Poems* (1839; second edition, 1848) contained his published work.

> 381. *Light of the lonely pilgrim's heart.*
> 87. *What grace, O Lord, and beauty shone.*

DIX, LEOPOLD L. (Dublin, 1861–   ), was educated at a private school and at Trinity College, Dublin. He is a solicitor by profession, but a musician also. He composed numerous arrangements of Irish and other tunes for *The Irish Hymnal* of the Irish Episcopal Church, and has published: *Quintet from, and Introduction to the 3rd Act of The Meistersingers (Wagner), arranged for String Orchestra; 17 Hymn Tunes;* songs, piano pieces, &c.

> 456. FINGAL (arr.).

DIX, WILLIAM CHATTERTON (Bristol, 1837–98, Clifton), was the son of William John Dix, a Bristol surgeon, who wrote *The Life of Chatterton* the poet, a book of *Pen Pictures of Popular English Preachers* and other works. He was educated at the Grammar School, Bristol, for a mercantile career, and became manager of a marine insurance company in Glasgow. Few modern writers have shown so signal a gift as his for the difficult art of hymn-writing. His original hymns are found in all modern hymn-books. They were published in *Hymns of Love and Joy* (1861); *Altar Songs, Verses on the Holy Eucharist* (1867); *A Vision of All Saints* (1871); *Seekers of a City* (1878). He wrote also felicitous renderings in metrical form of Littledale's translations from the Greek in his *Offices of the Holy Eastern Church;* and of Rodwell's translations of Abyssinian hymns. Some of his carols, such as *The Manger Throne*, have been very popular.

> 138. *Alleluia! sing to Jesus.*
> 63. *As with gladness men of old.*
> 390. *'Come unto Me, ye weary.'*
> 616. *To Thee, O Lord, our hearts we raise.*

DOANE, GEORGE WASHINGTON, D.D., LL.D. (Trenton, New Jersey, 1799–1859, Burlington, New Jersey), was educated at Union College, Schenectady, New York, and ordained in the Episcopal Church in 1821. After a time as assistant minister of Trinity Church, New York, he became, in 1824, Professor of Belles Lettres in Trinity

College, Hartford, Connecticut; in 1828, rector of Trinity Church,
Boston; and in 1832, Bishop of New Jersey. Under his administration the Church in his diocese made great progress in all directions.
He was closely in sympathy with the Tractarian movement in England. His life was chequered by many and severe trials, but his
'exceptional talents, learning, and force of character made him one
of the great prelates of his time'. He edited in 1834 the first American reprint of Keble's *Christian Year*, and published his own *Songs
by the Way* in 1824. His *Collected Works* were issued in four volumes
the year after his death.

> 383. *Fling out the banner! let it float.*
> 173. *Thou art the Way: to Thee alone.*

DOANE, WILLIAM HOWARD, Mus. Doc. (Preston, New London
County, Connecticut, 1832–1916, Cincinnati), was the principal of a
firm of manufacturers of wood-working machinery in Cincinnati,
Ohio, and for many years superintendent of the Sunday School of the
Baptist Church there of which he was a member. A musical en-
thusiast, he acted as conductor of the Norwich (Conn.) Harmonic
Society, published thirty-five collections of music for Church and
Sunday School, and himself composed numerous hymn-tunes,
anthems, and cantatas. The degree of Mus. Doc. was conferred on
him by Denison University, Ohio, in 1875.

> 679. DOANE.
> 707. REFUGE.

DOBREE, HENRIETTA OCTAVIA DE LISLE (?   1831–94,   ?   ),
was originally a member of the Church of England, and during that
time she contributed five hymns over the initials E. O. D. to Mrs.
Carey Brock's *Children's Hymn Book* (1881). She afterwards joined
the Church of Rome.

> 328. *Safely, safely gathered in.*

DODDRIDGE, PHILIP, D.D. (London, 1702–51, Lisbon), was the
son of a London merchant. His paternal grandfather was a clergyman
ejected from his living under the Act of Uniformity, and his mother's
father a Lutheran pastor, who fled from Bohemia to England to
escape persecution. Philip was the youngest of a family of twenty,
most of whom died young. He showed early promise, and is said
to have learned the Old Testament history from pictures on Dutch
tiles before he could read. Declining an offer from the Duchess of
Bedford to educate him for the Church of England, he studied under
Jennings for the dissenting ministry, and succeeded his preceptor
at Kibworth in 1723. In 1729 he accepted a charge at Northampton,
which included the care of a seminary. There he remained for
twenty-two years, educating pupils both for the ministry and for
other professions. In 1751, worn down by consumption, he vainly

sought health by a voyage to Lisbon, where he died. Doddridge wrote many theological works, the most notable being *The Rise and Progress of Religion in the Soul*, which went through many editions and was translated into a number of languages. He was a man of great learning, as also of a broad and catholic spirit. His letters breathe a quiet content and a playful wit, and have been compared to Cowper's. He is best remembered, however, by his hymns, first published soon after his death by his friend Orton, and since re-edited. Three of *The Scottish Paraphrases*, No. ii, 'O God of Bethel' (Hymn 562), No. xxxix, 'Hark, the glad sound' (Hymn 40), and No. lx, 'Father of peace, and God of love' (Hymn 481), owe their original form to him.

> 156. *Ye servants of the Lord.*
> 311. *My God, and is Thy table spread?*
> 345. *Fountain of good, to own Thy love.*
> 499. *O happy day, that fixed my choice.*
> 607. *Great God, we sing Thy mighty hand.*
> 710. *Now to the King of heaven* (Watts and Doddridge).

DODGSHUN, ERNEST, M.A. (Leeds, 1876–), was educated at Cambridge, where he graduated in the History Tripos. Brought up in the Congregational Church, he was attracted by the Society of Friends, which he joined in 1908. After some years in business he retired, and devoted himself to the furtherance of the Adult School movement, of which he is honorary secretary, and to work on behalf of Foreign Missions. He has visited mission fields in South Africa, and is a member of the Boards of the London Missionary Society and the Friends' Foreign Mission Association.

> 644. *What service shall we render thee?*

DOLES, JOHANN FRIEDRICH (Steinbach, Franconia, 1715–97, Leipzig), was a pupil of J. S. Bach at the Thomas Schule, Leipzig. After fourteen years as cantor at Freiburg, he became director of the Thomas Schule himself. He was an admirable teacher, and enjoyed a great reputation among musicians of his time. He was not of the spirit of his great master, however: 'he wrote in a sentimental quasi-operatic style', Fuller-Maitland says, 'and the high standard of Bach's time was lost and lowered during his tenure of office'. Among his publications were: *The Forty-Sixth Psalm* set to music; *Melodien zu Gellerts Geistlichen Oden*, for four voices, with accompaniment; *Vierstimmiges Choralbuch, oder harmonische melodien Sammlung für Kirchen* (1785).

> 574. DA CHRISTUS GEBOREN WAR.   529. (NORMAN).

DOUGALL, NEIL (Greenock, 1776–1862, Greenock), was the son of a wright, who was impressed into national service and died in Ceylon when Neil was four years old. The boy went to school till he was fifteen, then took to a seafaring life. Three years later, an accident during the firing of a salute in celebration of Lord Howe's great victory over the French on 'the glorious first of June' off Ushant, deprived him of his right arm and his eyesight. After some study of music he took up the teaching of singing. For forty-five years he conducted successful singing-classes, and for sixty gave an annual concert in Greenock. He published a small volume of poems in 1854, and wrote about a hundred psalm and hymn tunes.

400. KILMARNOCK.

DOWLAND, or DOULAND, JOHN, Mus. Bac. (Westminster, 1562–1626, London), graduated with Thomas Morley in 1588. There is evidence that he was of Irish parentage. Dr. Grattan Flood holds that the family name originally was Dolan or O'Dolan. He was a celebrated lutenist and 'a touring virtuoso'; he made a musical tour through Germany, France, and Italy, about 1585, and acquired a great reputation in these countries; his works were printed all over the Continent, and his success there was greater than in his own country. In 1598 he was appointed lutenist to the King of Denmark, and was liberally treated by him. His salary of 500 dalers was as much as a minister of state at that time received. But he had in an extreme degree an artist's habit of prodigality and carelessness in his expenditure, and, the king's patience with his embarrassments becoming exhausted, he returned to England, dismissed, in 1606. Six years later he received the only appointment he seems to have held in this country, as one of the King's Musicians for the Lutes. Both in composition and in performance his music was characterized by a rare grace and tenderness; hence the lines in which Richard Barnfield immortalized him:

> Dowland to thee is deare, whose heavenly touch
> Upon the Lute, doeth ravish humaine sense.

He published three *Bookes of Songs or Ayres*, and a fourth collection under the title *A Pilgrim's Solace*, all with accompaniments for lute and viol da gamba. He harmonized some of the tunes in *Este's Psalter*, and contributed also to Sir William Leighton's *The Teares or Lamentations of a Sorrowful Soule*.

229. OLD 100th (Faux-bourdon).

DOWNTON, HENRY, M.A. (Pulverbatch, Shropshire, 1818–85, Hopton), was son of the sub-librarian of Trinity College, Cambridge, where he graduated in 1840. Ordained in 1843, he became curate of Bembridge, Isle of Wight, and later, of Holy Trinity, Cambridge; perpetual curate of St. John's, Chatham; and in 1857, English chaplain at Geneva. Returning to this country in 1873, he became rector of Hopton Suffolk. He translated Naville's *Lectures on Modern Atheism* (1865); and his familiarity with the hymnody of the Swiss and French Churches enabled him to render a number of their hymns effectively into English. They are included in his *Hymns and Verses, Original and Translated* (1873).

> 604. *For Thy mercy and Thy grace.*
> 378. *Lord, her watch Thy Church is keeping.*

DRAPER, WILLIAM HENRY, M.A. (Kenilworth, 1855–   ), was educated at Keble College, Oxford. Ordained in 1880, he acted as curate of St. Mary's, Shrewsbury; vicar of Alfreton; vicar of the Abbey Church, Shrewsbury; rector of Adel, Leeds; rural dean of Shrewsbury; and since 1919 has been Master of the Temple, London. He has published *Hymns for Holy Week*, translations from hymns of the Greek Church; *The Victoria Book of Hymns* (1897); *The Way of the Cross;* translated Petrarch's *Secretum* (1911); and edited *Seven Spiritual Songs by Thomas Campion* (1919), and *Hymns for Tunes by Orlando Gibbons* (1925).

> 13. *All creatures of our God and King* (tr.).

DRESE, ADAM (Thuringia, 1620–1701, Arnstadt), was sent by Duke Wilhelm IV of Weimar to Warsaw, to study under the celebrated *Kapellmeister* Marco Sacchi, and on his return was appointed chapelmaster to the Duke. On the latter's death in 1662, Duke Bernhard took Drese with him to Jena, appointed him his secretary, and in 1672 town mayor. On this Duke's death he lost employment and fell into poverty. The writings of the Pietists, especially of Spener, 'the father of Pietism', and Luther on Romans, produced profound spiritual impressions on him at this time. He burned all the operas he had written up till then, and held prayer meetings in his house, which became a meeting-place for the Pietists of the district. His hymns were sung at these meetings before they appeared in print. Later, he became musical director at Arnstadt, and there remained till his death. His operas are now unknown even by name. A collection of instrumental music by him survives.

> 567. SEELENBRÄUTIGAM (ARNSTADT).

DREWETT, EDWIN (London, 1850–1924, Tunbridge Wells), studied at the Royal Academy, and for many years was organist of Harecourt Congregational Chapel, London. Later, from 1893 to 1905 he officiated at the German Lutheran Church, Dalton; from 1905 till the outbreak of the Great War in 1914, at the German Embassy Church, Brompton; and from 1917 till his death, at King Charles the Martyr, Tunbridge Wells.

> 487. ELMHURST.

DRUMMOND, WILLIAM, of Hawthornden (Hawthornden, 1585–1649, Hawthornden), a renowned Scottish poet, contemporary and friend of some of the great Elizabethans, was son of Sir John Drummond, gentleman-usher to King James VI. He graduated at Edinburgh, studied civil law in France, and succeeded his father in 1610 as laird of Hawthornden, near Edinburgh, an ideal poet's home, where he spent most of his life. Well read in classical and modern literature, he had also a turn for mechanics, and patented a number of inventions. Throughout his life he was a strong royalist, bitterly resented having to sign the Covenant under compulsion, and felt Charles I's death so keenly that it hastened his own. He wrote verses on the visits of James and Charles to Scotland, and on the death of Prince Henry. His prose works include a *History of the Five Jameses* and *The Cypress Grave*, a meditation on death.

4. *O Trinity, O blessèd Light!*

DRYDEN, JOHN (Aldwinkle, Northamptonshire, 1631–1700, London), poet and chief literary figure of the Restoration era, came from an old north country family, which took the parliamentary side in the Civil War. The first verses to bring Dryden fame were his *Heroic Stanzas* on the death of Cromwell. Yet he soon afterwards welcomed the royal exile in *Astrœa Redux*, and in 1670 was made poet laureate. For a number of years after the Restoration his work consisted mainly of plays, many of them coarse even for that not too refined age. His true genius, however, lay in his use of the heroic couplet for purposes of satire, as shown in *Absalom and Achitophel* and elsewhere. On the accession of James II he became a Roman Catholic, and remained constant to this faith at the Revolution, sacrificing thereby all his emoluments. During his later years he produced translations of Juvenal, Virgil, Boccaccio, and other poets. In addition to his translation of the *Veni, Creator Spiritus*, he is now believed to have been translator of a number of other Latin hymns, which appeared (after his death) in *The Primer or Office of the B. V. Mary, in English*, 1706.

184. *Creator Spirit! by whose aid* (tr.).

DUFFIELD, GEORGE, jun., D.D. (Carlisle, Pennsylvania, 1818–88, Detroit), son of Dr. Duffield of Detroit, was educated at Yale and Union Seminary, New York, for the Presbyterian ministry. Ordained in 1840, he held charges at Brooklyn; Bloomfield, New Jersey; Philadelphia; Adrian, Michigan; Galesburg, Illinois; Saginaw City, Michigan; Ann Arbor and Lansing, Michigan. His later years were spent at Bloomfield, N. J., with his son, the Rev. Samuel Willoughby Duffield (1843–87), who was a hymn-writer also, a distinguished hymnologist, and author of *English Hymns: their Authors and History* (1886), and *Latin Hymn Writers and their Hymns* (published posthumously, 1889).

532. *Stand up! stand up for Jesus!*

Biographical and Historical Notes

DUGMORE, ERNEST EDWARD, M.A. (Bayswater, 1843–1925, Salisbury), a son of William Dugmore, K.C., was educated at Bruce Castle School and by private tutors, and at Wadham College, Oxford. He became curate of St. Peter's, Vauxhall; vicar of Parkstone, Dorset; canon of Sarum and prebendary of Gillingham Major, 1900; and in 1910 resigned his living to become Warden of the College of Missioners, Salisbury, where he became also Succentor of the Cathedral and Vicar of the Close. While at Parkstone, he edited a weekly paper, *The Parkstone Reminder*, for thirty years. His published works were—*From the Mountains of the East; Gospel Idylls, and Other Sacred Verses; Some Principles of the Holy Catholic Church; Hymns of Adoration; Sunday Readings on the Collects.*

503. *Almighty Father of all things that be.*

DUNCALF, HENRY (eighteenth century), was organist of St. Bartholomew's, London.

672. ST. BARTHOLOMEW.

DUNCAN, MARY, *née* LUNDIE (Kelso, 1814–40, Cleish, Kinross-shire), was the daughter of the Rev. Robert Lundie, parish minister of Kelso. Her younger sister became the wife of Horatius Bonar. She went to school in London, and early showed a talent for verse. In 1836 she married the Rev. William Wallace Duncan, minister of Cleish. He was the son of the Rev. Henry Duncan, D.D., of Ruthwell, the inventor of the Savings Bank. He went out of the Church of Scotland at the Disruption, and became Free Church minister in Peebles, where he died in 1864. Mrs. Duncan was a rare spirit, amiable, accomplished, and beautiful. Those who knew her saw marked resemblance in her features to the portraits of Madame Guyon. Unhappily, a chill contracted at the end of 1839 developed into a fever that carried her off. Her hymns, written for her own children between July and December 1839, were published in a *Memoir* by her mother in 1841, and in the following year were issued separately—twenty-three in number—as *Rhymes for my Children.*

654. *Jesus, tender Shepherd, hear me.*

DWIGHT, TIMOTHY, D.D., LL.D. (Northampton, Massachusetts, 1752–1817, New Haven), was the son of a graduate of Yale and of the third daughter of Jonathan Edwards. Graduating at Yale in 1769, he remained there as tutor for six years. After a period of service as chaplain in the U.S. Army, he was minister at Fairfield, Connecticut, where he conducted at the same time, successfully, an academy, to augment his meagre stipend. In 1795 he was appointed President of Yale College, which rose to great renown under his rule, and simultaneously held the Chair of Theology. He became 'unquestionably the most conspicuous man in New England, filling a larger space in the public eye, and exerting a greater influence than any other individual'. He had great erudition and wide interests; he did memorable work as an educationist; and in American hymnology he is one of the early outstanding figures. At the request of the General Association of the Presbyterian Churches of Connecticut, and with the concurrence of the General Assembly, he undertook in 1797 a revision of Dr. Watts's *Psalms and Hymns*, with a view to 'accommodating it' to America. This revision met with great favour, and was used in the Presbyterian and Congregational Churches of Connecticut for over thirty years. A revised edition contained thirty-three hymns of his own. He published three poems also— *The Conquest of Canaan*, an epic in seven books (1785); *Greenfield Hill*, a poem in seven parts (1794); *The Triumph of Infidelity* (1788). All this work was done in spite of a failure of sight, due to overstrain caused by eager study in the early morning by candle-light, and aggravated by the effects of smallpox, with which, according to the barbarous practice of the time, he had been deliberately inoculated. This eye-trouble 'rendered it impossible for him, during forty years, to read consecutively for fifteen minutes out of the twenty-four hours; whilst the pain behind the eyeballs and in the frontal region of the brain was agonizing'.

210. *I love Thy Kingdom, Lord.*

DUPUIS, Thomas Sanders, Mus. Doc. (London, 1733–96, London), of Huguenot parentage, was educated as a chorister of the Chapel Royal under Bernard Gates, and was an organ pupil of John Travers. About 1773 he became organist of Charlotte Street (now St. Peter's) Chapel, near Buckingham Palace, and in 1779 succeeded Boyce as organist and composer to the Chapel Royal. He had few equals as an organist in his time. Haydn, on one of his visits to London, was so much delighted with Dupuis's improvisation of a fugue at one of the Chapel Royal services that when he met him afterwards he gave him two kisses to express his gratification. A selection of his Cathedral music was published after his death. He issued three sets of *Double and Single Chants*. His death was brought about by an overdose of opium.

715. CHANT IN A.

DYKES, John Bacchus, M.A., Mus. Doc. (Hull, 1823–76, St. Leonard's-on-Sea), was son of a banker, and grandson of a well-known evangelical clergyman, in Hull. 'Bacchus' was the Christian name of his maternal grandfather. John's talent for music developed early; he played the organ in his father's church at the age of ten. Educated at Wakefield, to which the family home had been removed, and at St. Catharine's College, Cambridge, he helped as an under-graduate, along with William Thomson, afterwards Lord Kelvin, to found the University Musical Society. Thomson played second horn in the orchestra, and at the early concerts Dykes's contributions of humorous songs were among the most popular features. This type of singing he abandoned after taking orders in 1847. In that year he was licensed to the curacy of Malton, but two years later proceeded to Durham to be a minor canon, and, soon after, precentor in the Cathedral there. In 1861 Durham University conferred on him his doctorate, and a year later, he became vicar of St. Oswald's in the same city. During the fourteen years of his ministry in that parish his singularly engaging personality and pastoral devotion won him great influence; but his high-churchmanship involved him in prolonged and trying disputes with his low-church bishop. Dykes needed two curates for the work of his parish; the bishop refused to license them unless a pledge was given that they would not be required to wear coloured stoles, or have anything to do with the burning of incense, which Dykes had no desire to introduce, or turn their backs to the congregation during the celebration of Communion, except when 'ordering the bread'. Dykes refused to give such a pledge, and appealed to the Court of Queen's Bench for a mandamus requiring the bishop to issue his licence without any such special declaration. He lost his case, and with the entire care of a heavy parish thrown on his hands, his health gave way under the strain; he was stricken with a general atrophy. On his death, a memorial fund of £10,000 was contributed by admirers of his tunes for the benefit of his family. He published various sermons and writings on liturgics, wrote several services and a number of anthems which are much in use; but his reputation rests on his hymn-tunes, of which he wrote about 300.

221.	ALFORD.	301.	PAX DEI.
19.	ALMSGIVING.	330.	REQUIESCAT.
495.	ARUNDEL.	5.	RIVAULX.
592.	BEATITUDO.	83.	ST. AËLRED.
390.	COME UNTO ME.	422.	ST. AGNES, DURHAM.
438.	DOMINUS REGIT ME.	417.	ST. BEES.
201.	ELVET.	96.	ST. CROSS.
665.	FERRIER.	180.	ST. CUTHBERT.
32.	GERONTIUS.	525.	ST. MARY MAGDALENE.
414.	HOLLINGSIDE.	214.	ST. OSWALD.
568.	LUX BENIGNA.	585.	ST. SYLVESTER.
626.	MELITA.	339.	THANKSGIVING.
1.	NICÆA.	410.	VOX DILECTI.

E., B.—This author is unknown.

699. *O Christ, in Thee my soul hath found.*

EBELING, JOHANN GEORG (Lüneburg, 1637–76, Stettin), in 1662 succeeded Johann Crüger as Cantor of St. Nicholas Church, Berlin, and as director of music at the College of St. Nicholas there. In 1668 he became professor of music at the College of St. Charles

(Carolinen Gymnasium), Stettin. He published *Archaeologiae Orphicae, sive antiquitates musicae* (1675); *Pauli Gerhardi Geistliche Andachten, bestehend in 120 Liedern mit 6 Singstimmen, 2 violinen und general-bass* (1666–7). Some of his chorales are high in favour still.

41. BONN.   706. VOLLER WUNDER.

EDDIS, EDWARD WILTON (Islington, London, 1825–1905, Toronto, Canada), was a minister (elder) of the Catholic Apostolic Church, the religious communion founded by Edward Irving. He compiled for it, in 1864, *Hymns for the Use of the Churches*, nineteen of which, and two translations, were his own. To the second edition he contributed forty new hymns and one translation. Prior to 1865 he published *The Time of the End, and Other Hymns*.

315. *Thou standest at the altar.*

EDMESTON, JAMES (Wapping, London, 1791–1867, Homerton, Surrey), was an eminent London architect and surveyor. Among the pupils trained by him was Sir G. Gilbert Scott. Though a grandson of the Rev. Samuel Brewer, minister of an Independent chapel in Stepney, he joined the Church of England early in life, and was latterly churchwarden of St. Barnabas' Church, Homerton. An ardent lover of children, he was a constant visitor and loyal friend of the London Orphan Asylum, and he found there the inspiration of many of his children's hymns. His *Cottage Minstrel* was written in successful response to an advertisement offering a prize of £20 for fifty simple hymns suitable for cottage meetings. The offerer of the prize was Thomas Thompson of Poundsford Park, father of Mrs. Luke (q.v.). Edmeston wrote over 2,000 hymns, many of which he published in *Sacred Lyrics, Infant Breathings*, and numerous other works. It was his practice to write a hymn every Sunday and read it at family worship.

563. *Lead us, heavenly Father, lead us.*
285. *Saviour, breathe an evening blessing.*

EDWARDS, LEWIS, D.D. (Pwllcenawon, near Penllwyn, Cardiganshire, 1809–87, Bala), was educated at schools at Aberystwyth and Llangeitho, and the Universities of London and Edinburgh. He opened a school at Aberystwyth in 1827, became head-master at Llangeitho in the following year, and entered London University in 1830. Lack of means forced him to return to Wales with his course still incomplete, and for a short time he acted as pastor at Laugharne, Carmarthenshire, then proceeded to Edinburgh University in 1833. Graduating there in 1836, he opened in Bala, in 1837, with the assistance of his brother-in-law, David Charles (afterwards D.D.), son of Thomas Charles of Bala, a school for young preachers, which was adopted a year later by the Connexion as a Theological College. He was a versatile and voluminous writer

327

on social, political, educational, and theological subjects. His *Doctrine of the Atonement* is deemed a classic by his countrymen. In conjunction with the Rev. Roger Edwards of Mold, father of Principal Ellis Edwards of Bala, he started in 1845 a quarterly magazine entitled *Y Traethodydd* (The Essayist), which did much to change the trend of thought in the best minds of the Principality. His own contributions, literary and theological, have been republished in two large volumes which rank high in Welsh literature. Edinburgh University honoured him with the D.D. degree in 1865. He was a great preacher as well as writer and teacher. His Church gave him every possible honour, and he was recognized everywhere as one of the greatest uplifting influences in his country in his time.

596. *From heavenly Jerusalem's towers* (tr.).

EDWARDS, ROBERT (Mostyn, Flintshire, 1797–1862, Liverpool), went to Liverpool as a young man and became a carter in the employ of the Bridgewater Trustees, who managed the canal system between Liverpool, Manchester, and Runcorn. Later in life, he was promoted to the position of superintendent of the carting department. He was passionately fond of music, and for many years was precentor in Bedford Street Calvinistic Methodist Chapel, the congregation now worshipping in Princes Road. On his retirement in 1859 a thousand people assembled to do him honour, and special tribute was paid to the great work he had done in teaching the young. He was a very modest man, and though he composed tunes, took no steps to make them known. During his absence from Bedford Street Chapel on one occasion, owing to illness, some one discovered the tune *Caersalem* in his desk; the choir practised it, and sang it as a surprise for him on his return. But for this, it might never have been known.

564. CAERSALEM.

ELLERTON, JOHN, M.A. (London, 1826–93, Torquay), was educated at King William's College, Isle of Man, and at Trinity College, Cambridge. At the University he was deeply influenced by Frederick Denison Maurice, but he did not identify himself with any party in the Church; he combined in himself the best characteristics of all three schools, 'the subjective piety of the Evangelical, the objective adoration of the High, the intellectual freedom of the Broad'. Ordained in 1850, he served as curate at Easebourne, Midhurst, Sussex; and at St. Nicholas, then the parish church of Brighton, for the children of which his first hymns were composed. In 1860 he became vicar of Crewe Green and domestic chaplain to Lord Crewe. While there he took a deep interest in the welfare of the artisans of Crewe, was vice-president of the Mechanics' Institution, reorganized its educational work, and himself conducted classes in English and Scripture History. He also organized one of the first choral associations of the Midlands, which met for many years at Nantwich. In 1872 he became rector of the secluded parish of Hinstock, Shropshire, and in 1876 of the suburban charge of Barnes, Surrey. The heavy burden of this large and populous parish broke him down, but after a year abroad, he was able in 1885 to accept the quiet charge of White Roding, Essex. His work as a hymnologist was of the first importance. 'He was chief compiler and editor of two important hymn-books, *Church Hymns* and *The Children's Hymn Book*, and joint-compiler of the last edition of that great hymnal which, above all others, is dearest to the heart of the English Church, *Hymns Ancient and Modern*. He edited or assisted in editing *Hymns for Schools and Bible Classes, The Temperance Hymn Book, The London Mission Hymn Book*. His advice was sought in the compiling of the last edition of the admirable *Hymnal Companion to the Book of Common Prayer;* in fact, it is no exaggeration to say that his hand may be traced and his voice heard in every hymn-book of importance during the last thirty years before his death; 'while no less than eighty-six hymns, original or translated, proceeded from his own pen'. His admirable *Notes and Illustrations of Church Hymns* appeared in the folio edition in 1881. His own hymns were published in 1888 as *Hymns, Original and Translated*. He took no copyright in his hymns, holding that if they were 'counted worthy to contribute to Christ's praise in the congregation, one ought to feel very thankful and humble'. His mind was so steeped in hymns, which had been his lifelong study and delight, that on his death-bed, while he lay half-conscious, they flowed almost unceasingly from his lips. While lying disabled by his last illness he was nominated to a prebendal stall in St. Alban's Cathedral Church, and for the last year of his life received the honorary address of 'Canon' Ellerton; but he was never installed.

237. *Again the morn of gladness.*
271. *Before the day draws near its ending.*
242. *Behold us, Lord, a little space.*
332. *God of the living, in whose eyes.*
641. *God the Omnipotent! King, who ordainest.*
330. *Now the labourer's task is o'er.*
326. *O Father, all creating.*
360. *O Son of God, our Captain of salvation.*
290. *Our day of praise is done.*
634. *Praise to our God, whose bounteous hand.*
301. *Saviour, again to Thy dear Name we raise.*
336. *Shine Thou upon us, Lord.*
289. *The day Thou gavest, Lord, is ended.*
267. *This is the day of light.*
100. *Throned upon the awful Tree.*
115. *'Welcome, happy morning!'—age to age shall say* (tr.)
584. *When the day of toil is done.*

ELLIOTT, CHARLOTTE (Clapham, 1789–1871, Brighton), was a granddaughter of the Rev. Henry Venn, a divine notable in his day as the author of a book long valued on *The Whole Duty of Man*, and sister-in-law of Julia Anne Elliott (q.v.). In her youth she wrote humorous poems, but a grave illness in 1821 which made her permanently an invalid made serious impressions on her which were deepened in the following year by the influence of César Malan, the evangelist, of Geneva. He asked her if she was a Christian; she resented the question. He said that he would pray that she might give her heart to Christ and become a worker for Him. This worked on her mind, and finally she asked him how she might find Christ. 'Come to Him just as you are,' was the answer, and she was soon at peace in Him. She corresponded with Malan for forty years, and kept the anniversary of their first meeting as the birthday of her soul. From that time she gave up secular pursuits, and devoted her life to religion. All her work was done under great physical disability; for fifty years she was a martyr to pain and helpless weakness. 'My heavenly Father knows, and He alone,' she wrote, 'what it is, day after day, and hour after hour, to fight against bodily feelings of almost overpowering weakness and languor and exhaustion, to resolve, as He enables me to do, not to yield to the slothfulness, the depression, the irritability, such a body causes me to long to indulge, but to rise every morning determined on taking this for my motto, "If any man will come after Me, let him deny himself, take up his cross daily, and follow Me".' Her hymns appeared in *Psalms and Hymns*, edited by her brother, the Rev. Henry Venn Elliott of Brighton (1835–9); and in her own *Hours of Sorrow cheered and comforted* (1836); *Hymns for a Week* (1839); *The Invalid's Hymn Book* (1834–41); and *Thoughts in Verse on Sacred Subjects* (1869). She lived with her father for thirty-two years at Clapham; the later years were spent at Torquay and Brighton.

> 523. *Christian, seek not yet repose.*
> 411. *Just as I am, without one plea.*
> 539. *My God and Father, while I stray.*
> 449. *My God, is any hour so sweet?*
> 408. *There is a holy sacrifice.*

ELLIOTT, EMILY ELIZABETH STEELE (Brighton, 1836–97, Mildmay, London), was a daughter of the Rev. Edward Bishop Elliott, of St. Mark's, Brighton, a brother of Charlotte Elliott, and author of *Horae Apocalypticae*. She was much interested in the mission work carried on at Mildmay Park. For six years she edited *The Church Missionary Juvenile Instructor*. She published *Hymns of Consecration* (1873), and *Chimes for Daily Service*.

> 68. *There came a little Child to earth.*
> 67. *Thou didst leave Thy throne.*

ELLIOTT, JAMES WILLIAM (Warwick, 1833–1915, London), was trained as a chorister in Leamington Parish Church. He was suc-cessively organist in Leamington Chapel; to the Earl of Wilton at Heaton Hall; in the Parish Church, Banbury; St. Mary Bolton's, Brompton; All Saints', St. John's Wood; St. Mark's, Hamilton Terrace, where he served for thirty-six years. His settings of *Nursery Rhymes* have long been the delight of children, and his *Hybrias the Cretan* has for half a century been in the front rank of English songs. His compositions include two operettas, anthems, and many hymn-tunes. He took an active part in the preparation of the musical edition of *Church Hymns*, 1874.

> 25. CHURCH TRIUMPHANT.   508. DAY OF REST.
> 231. GLORIA IN EXCELSIS.

ELLIOTT, JULIA ANNE, *née* MARSHALL (? –1841, Brighton), daughter of John Marshall of Hallsteads, Ullswater, on a visit to Brighton with her father, attended the ministry of the Rev. Henry Venn Elliott, brother of Charlotte Elliott, and founder and vicar of St. Mary's Church in that town. Acquaintance ripened into affec-tion, and Mr. Elliott and she were married in 1833. She had a per-sonality of great charm; she was affectionate, gentle, imaginative, devout. When, in 1835, her husband published *Psalms and Hymns for Public, Private and Social Worship*, a book which had a marked influence on subsequent collections, eleven hymns from her pen ap-peared in it, at first anonymously, but in later editions over her initials. Her death shortly after the birth of her fifth child was a cause of profound grief to her husband's congregation, by whom she was much beloved.

> 266. *Hail, thou bright and sacred morn.*

ELLIS, WILLIAM, Mus. Bac. (Durham, 1868–), was of Wesleyan parentage. His passion for church music and organs developed early. He began to play in a village chapel at nine years of age. At fourteen, he became, 'with immense pride', organist of Old Elvet Wesleyan Church, Durham, and at once began to study under Dr. Philip Armes, the learned and beloved organist of Durham Cathe-dral, whose pupil he was for over ten years. In 1887 he became or-ganist of St. Nicholas Church, Durham; in 1894, transferred to the Parish Church of Richmond, Yorkshire, where he acted also as pri-vate choirmaster to the Marquis of Zetland at Aske; and in 1903 re-turned to Durham to be assistant to his old master, being appointed the first official sub-organist at the Cathedral. In 1918 he became organist and master of the choristers at Newcastle Cathedral. He be-came F.R.C.O. in 1891, and Mus. Bac. (Durham) in 1893. He is an honorary member of University College, Durham.

> 159. ST. HILD.

ELVEY, Sir GEORGE JOB, Mus. Doc. (Canterbury, 1816–93, Windlesham, Surrey), was baptized in the Presbyterian Chapel, Canterbury (now destroyed), where a congregation worshipped which had been formed by the union, in 1713, of a Presbyterian congregation and a Congregational. He was educated as a chorister in the Cathedral. From 1835 to 1882 he was organist and master of the boys at St. George's Chapel, Windsor, and as such had charge of the music in connexion with many events of importance in the Royal House. He was knighted in 1871. Much sacred music was composed by him, oratorios, *The Resurrection, The Ascension, Mount Carmel;* a festival march, &c.; and he contributed tunes to *Hymns Ancient and Modern* and other collections. He was buried outside of the west front of St. George's Chapel.

136. DIADEMATA.	118, 619. ST. GEORGE'S, WINDSOR.
147. ELVEY.	696. URSWICKE.
204. ILLUMINATIO.	602. WELLESLEY.

ELVEY, STEPHEN, Mus. Doc. (Canterbury, 1805–60, Oxford), was elder brother of Sir George. He was trained as a chorister in Canterbury Cathedral under Highmore Skeats. He became organist of New College, Oxford, in 1830, and was Choragus of the University from 1848 till his death. His works were few, chiefly services and anthems. He edited *The Psalter, or Canticles and Psalms Pointed for Chanting, upon a new Principle.*

713. SANCTUS.

ESTE (EST, EASTE, EAST), THOMAS (1540?–1608?), a famous printer and music publisher, appeared first as a music printer in 1587, with *Sonnettes and Songs made into musick of fyve parts. By William Burd.* This is supposed to be identical with the undated edition of Byrd's *Psalmes, Sonets, and Songs of Sadness and Pietie,* 1588. In the latter year, Este's *Musica Transalpina,* a collection of Italian madrigals, laid the foundation of the splendid school of English madrigalists. In 1591 he printed the new edition of Damon's *Psalmes,* published by William Swayne. In the edition of the psalter printed by Este in 1592 the tunes were harmonized by ten eminent composers of the time, including Richard Allison, Giles Farnaby, John Douland, John Farmer, and George Kirbye. This psalter is probably the earliest example in which the parts are printed on opposite pages instead of in separate books.

457. (CHESHIRE). 181, 385. (WINCHESTER).

ETT, KASPAR (near Landsberg, 1788–1847, Munich), was a distinguished Bavarian musician who from 1816 onwards was organist of the Michaeliskirche, Munich. He made a special study of church music from the sixteenth to the eighteenth century, and made large collections of it, which went on his death to the Munich Library. He

published in 1840 *Cantica Sacra*, in which were numerous compositions of his own, after antique models.

164. ORIEL.

EVANS, DAVID, Mus. Doc. (Resolven, Glamorganshire, 1874–),
was educated at Arnold College, Swansea, and University College,
Cardiff, and graduated at Oxford. For a time he was organist and
choirmaster of Jewin Street Welsh Presbyterian Church, London.
Since 1903 he has been Professor of Music at University College,
Cardiff; he is now the senior Professor of the University of Wales.
At Cardiff he has organized a large department of music, in which
all branches of the art are taught. He is a leading adjudicator at the
National Eisteddfod, where his compositions constantly appear as
test pieces or as concert items. In spreading enthusiasm for congregational singing he has done a great work in the Principality. He
is a leading conductor of the great psalmody festivals of which Ieuan
Gwyllt was the pioneer, and which have deeply influenced the religious life of Wales; no one has done more than Dr. Evans to develop this inspiring form of communal worship. His splendid collection of standard tunes, published as *Moliant Cenedl*, reflects his
just discrimination and catholicity of taste,and has greatly influenced
and enriched subsequent hymn collections. His editorship of *Y Cerdd-
or*, a literary journal devoted to the cause of music in Wales, has
made a deep and lasting impression upon the life of the Principality.
He has been a prolific composer of choral and orchestral works, the
best known of which are *The Coming of Arthur*, a cantata for chorus
and orchestra; *Llawenhewch yn yr Ior* (Rejoice in the Lord); *Deffro
mae'n ddydd*, a Welsh choral ballad; *Bro bugeiliaid*, a children's cantata. He has written a large number of anthems, services, hymn-
tunes, songs, &c. He was one of the representatives of Wales on the
Joint Revision Committee of *The Church Hymnary*, and also chairman of the sub-committee of experts responsible for the editorship
of the music.

568. BONIFACIO.	461. KILDROSTAN.
146. CHARTERHOUSE.	127. KIRKLAND.
391. FRONDEG.	247. LLANDAF.
298. HENLLAN.	393. NEUADD WEN.
321. HINTON-MARTELL.	673. ORISONS.
424. INNELLAN.	529. YN Y GLYN.

EVANS, DAVID EMLYN (Penralltwen, Newcastle Emlyn, Cardigan,
1843–1913, Cemmaes, Montgomeryshire), was an amateur composer of great distinction. He won seventy Eisteddfod prizes. He
composed cantatas, glees, anthems, songs. He was a trusted adjudicator at Eisteddfodau. For over thirty years he was joint-editor of
a musical monthly *Y Cerddor*, published at Wrexham (1880–1913),
and he was musical editor of the Welsh Congregational *Caniedydd*

(1895), and of the Welsh Wesleyan *Llyfr Tonau*. The traditional airs collected by Nicholas Bennett and published as *Alawon fy Ngwlad* (1896) were harmonized by him. He was in the front rank of musical critics, and greatly influenced Welsh music by his weekly articles in the press. He wrote a text-book on *Harmony*.

294. CWMDU.   560. TREWEN.

EVEREST, CHARLES WILLIAM, M.A. (East Windsor, Connecticut, 1814–77, Waterbury, Conn.), graduated at Trinity College, Hartford, in 1838, was ordained in 1842, and for thirty-one years thereafter was rector of the Episcopal Church, Hampden, near New Haven. During that time he also managed successfully an important school. He was agent also for a number of years of the Society for the Increase of the Ministry. He published *Visions of Death, and Other Poems*, in 1833.

501. '*Take up thy cross,*' the Saviour said.

EWING, ALEXANDER (Old Machar, Aberdeen, 1830–95, Taunton), was the son of Alexander Ewing, M.D., lecturer on surgery at Marischal College, Aberdeen. He studied law at that College with a view to becoming a Writer to the Signet, but, having little inclination in that direction, he was allowed to abandon that aim and to go to Heidelberg to study German and music. He was a skilled musician, playing well on violin, 'cello, and cornet. He was closely identified with the Haydn Society of Aberdeen, and the Harmonic Choir, which made a speciality of madrigal and anthem singing, under the leadership of William Carnie. One evening, after the practice of this choir, he approached Carnie, told him that he had tried his hand at writing a hymn-tune, and, offering copies of the voice-parts, asked that the choir should sing it over. This was done, and his one tune was launched on its long and honourable career. Ewing left Aberdeen about 1853, joined the Army Commissariat Department in 1855, on the outbreak of the Crimean War, and attained the rank of lieutenant-colonel. He subsequently served in South Australia and China. Returning to England in 1867, he married Juliana Horatia Gatty, daughter of the Rev. Alfred Gatty, D.D., vicar of Ecclesfield, and of Margaret Gatty, authoress of *Parables fom Nature*. Mrs. Ewing's own books for children—*Jackanapes, The Story of a Short Life, Jan of the Windmill*, &c.—are widely known and loved. Retiring to Taunton in 1883, Mrs. Ewing died in 1885, and her husband ten years later.

599. EWING.

FABER, FREDERICK WILLIAM, D.D. (Calverley, Yorkshire, 1814–63, London), was educated at Shrewsbury, Harrow, and Balliol and University Colleges, Oxford. He was elected a Fellow of University in 1837. Descended from Huguenot stock, one of his ancestors having fled from France to England on the Revocation of the Edict of Nantes, he was brought up in the strictest school of Calvinism. In 1838 he published a work on *The Ancient Things of the Church of England*, in which he vindicated the Church of England as against the Roman Church, described the denomination of 'the Archbishop of Rome' as unscriptural, declared that the Romanists had added falsehood to the sacraments, and as to the Church of Rome prayed, 'God have mercy on her!' At Oxford, however, the potent influence of Newman drew him far towards the other extreme. Travels on the Continent accelerated this tendency. He took orders in the Church of England, and was for three years rector of Elton, Huntingdonshire. There by his preaching and influence he effected a moral reformation; but he also introduced auricular confession, penance, and other advanced ritualistic practices, and finally went the whole way to which these practices pointed, abjured Protestantism, and entered the Roman fold. He formed in Birmingham, with eight other young men, a community called 'Brothers of the Will of God', otherwise known as 'the Wilfridians', he himself having been re-baptized under the name of Wilfrid. In 1848, however, he and his companions joined the Oratory of St. Philip Neri, under Newman, and in the following year, he established in London a branch of that order, which developed into the present Brompton Oratory. There the rest of his years were spent. The Pope, in 1854, made him a D.D. He wrote many devotional and theological books, but is best known by his hymns, of which he wrote 150, corresponding to the number of the Psalms. They were intended primarily for devotional reading, to supply Roman Catholics with an equivalent to the Protestant hymns of Cowper, Newton, and Wesley, the influence of which he knew by personal experience. Most of them are too deeply saturated with Roman doctrine, or too sensuous, or too familiar, for ordinary use; but others are profoundly evangelical. Faber himself was a man of great personal charm, a preacher with a golden voice and every gift of persuasive eloquence, and an ardent and powerful propagandist of the extremest tenets of the Roman faith.

> 580. *Hark, hark, my soul! angelic songs are swelling.*
>   27. *My God, how wonderful Thou art!*
>   96. *O come and mourn with me awhile.*
> 302. *O Saviour, bless us ere we go.*
> 395. *Souls of men, why will ye scatter?*
> 520. *Workman of God! O lose not heart.*

FALCONER, HUGH, D.D. (Granton, Edinburgh, 1859–   ), was educated at the University and New College, Edinburgh. Ordained to the Free Church ministry at Juniper Green in 1882, he passed ten years later to the Presbyterian Church of England, and ministered at Jesmond, Newcastle-on-Tyne; Notting Hill, London; Fisher Street, Carlisle, retiring in 1923. He was Moderator of the Presbyterian

Church of England in 1919. His publications include *The Maid of Shulam; The Unfinished Symphony; Merrie Carlisle* (verse and prose).

59. *God and Father, we adore Thee.*

FARMER, JOHN (Nottingham, 1836–1901, Oxford), studied at Leipzig Conservatorium and at Coburg under Andreas Späth. For a time he taught music at Zürich; from 1862 to 1885 was music-master at Harrow School; and from the latter year was organist of Balliol College, Oxford. He conducted a musical society in Oxford. He was a brilliant improvisatore on the piano, and an admirable teacher, with a notable power of inspiring others with his own musical enthusiasms. He wrote an oratorio, *Christ and His Soldiers;* a fairy opera, *Cinderella;* a comic cantata; two septets, &c. His name will live longest probably in connexion with his fine collection of *Harrow Songs*, his settings of selections from R. F. Murray's *Scarlet Gown* for St. Andrews University, and such popular song-books as his *Gaudeamus*, for schools, and *Dulce Domum*, for children.

43. IN THE FIELD.

FARNINGHAM, MARIANNE. *See* HEARN, MARIANNE.

FARRANT, RICHARD (*c.* 1530–80), was a gentleman of the Chapel Royal during the reigns of Edward VI, Mary, and Elizabeth, with an interval of five years (1564–9), during which he was master of the choristers in St. George's Chapel, Windsor, and probably joint organist with the famous John Merbecke, whose *Book of Common Praier Noted* (1550) is one of the great landmarks in English Church music. Farrant is best remembered by his beautiful Service in G minor, and by two delightful anthems, 'Call to remembrance' and 'Hide not Thou Thy face'. The exquisite little anthem, 'Lord, for Thy tender mercies' sake', from which the tune that bears his name is taken, is only doubtfully ascribed to him. From internal evidence it is believed to be a production of a later time, and it is by some attributed with confidence to William Mundy, by others to John Hilton, organist of St. Margaret's, Westminster, from 1638–57.

716. CHANT IN F.   625. FARRANT.

FARRAR, FREDERIC WILLIAM, D.D., F.R.S. (Bombay, 1831–1903, Canterbury), the son of a missionary in India who afterwards became rector of Sidcup, was educated at King William's College, Isle of Man; King's College, London; and Trinity College, Cambridge, where he graduated with first class classical honours. Ordained in 1854, he became an assistant master, first at Marlborough College, then at Harrow; and in 1871 head-master of Marlborough. Five years later he was appointed a canon of Westminster and rector of St. Margaret's, the House of Commons Church. Both in the Abbey and in St. Margaret's his eloquence attracted immense congregations. He was deeply interested in social questions, and was a powerful advocate of temperance. Honours came to him—as Select Preacher at Cambridge; Hulsean Lecturer there; Chaplain to the Queen; Archdeacon of Westminster. But a series of sermons in the Abbey, in 1877, on *Eternal Hope*, aroused such controversy and made him so much the object of criticism and suspicion of doctrinal unsoundness, that the further preferment due to his eminence was long delayed. In 1895, however, he was appointed Dean of Canterbury. He had a great reputation as writer and preacher, and was probably the best known of Church of England clergymen in his later years. His industry was indefatigable, and his scholarship, eloquence, and versatility found unceasing expression in a flow of books of the most various kinds from his pen.

43. *In the field with their flocks abiding.*

FARRER, JOHN DOWNING (Lowestoft, 1829–1919, Boscombe, Hants), was a member of an old Lowestoft family. On retiring from business he lived for a time in Norwich, then returned to Lowestoft. In both places he took much interest in religious work, particularly the Church Colonial and Continental Society and the Mission to Seamen. He was chiefly instrumental in the erection of a Seamen's Institute at the latter place; the iron building first erected for it was humorously known as 'Farrer's Cathedral'. Though he could play no instrument, he was a keen amateur musician, and composed many hymn-tunes, of which a collection was published in 1885 under the title, *The Lowestoft Supplemental Tune Book.* His later years were spent at Boscombe.

238. NEW CALABAR.

FAWCETT, JOHN (Wennington, Lancashire, 1789–1867, Bolton), was a shoemaker who left his trade to follow the profession of music at Bolton-le-Moors. He published *A New set of Sacred Music, in three parts*, in 1830, and followed it with five collections of psalm and hymn-tunes under the titles, *Miriam's Timbrel; Melodia Divina; Harp of Zion; The Cherub Lute; Voice of Devotion.* He also produced *Music for Thousands, or, The Vocalist's Manual;* an oratorio, *Paradise;* and much other music. Melling is about a mile and a half from Fawcett's birthplace.

11. MELLING.

FAWCETT, JOHN, D.D. (Lidget Green near Bradford, 1740–1817, Hebden Bridge), was deeply impressed at the age of sixteen by the preaching of Whitefield, and a few years later joined the Baptist Church at Bradford. He became Baptist Minister at Wainsgate, and afterwards at Hebden Bridge, both near Halifax. He also opened a school at his residence in that neighbourhood. Invited to become pastor of Carter's Lane Chapel in London, he was induced to remain in Yorkshire by the affectionate regard of his people. An invitation to become President of the Baptist Academy at Bristol was also declined. Besides a number of books on practical religion, and a devotional commentary on Holy Scripture, he published a number of hymns, many of which have found an abiding place in Baptist and Congregational hymn-books.

490. *Blest be the tie that binds.*
299. *Lord, dismiss us with Thy blessing.*

FEILLÉE, FRANÇOIS DE LA (*floruit c.* 1750), was a priest attached to the choir of Chartres Cathedral. He wrote an abridgement of the Roman Antiphonary, and a book on plain-song which won wide celebrity, *Méthode pour apprendre les règles du plain-chant et de la psalmodie* (1745). This work was largely used by Helmore and others who led the way to the revival in the Anglican Church of the ancient psalm-tones which it had abandoned, not after the Reformation, but in the seventeenth century.

594. (ANNUE CHRISTE.)   263. (CHRISTE SANCTORUM.)
224. (O QUANTA QUALIA.)

FELTON, WILLIAM, M.A. (?   1715–69, Hereford), took holy orders, but was chiefly interested in Church music. He became vicar-choral and sub-chanter of Hereford Cathedral, 1741; custos of the vicars-choral, 1769; vicar of Norton Canon, 1751–69. He was one of the stewards for the Three Choirs Festival at Hereford in 1744, and at Gloucester in 1745. He was distinguished as a composer for and performer on the organ and the harpsichord; he published lessons and three sets of concertos for these instruments. His *Gavot* was long highly popular. He was buried in the vestibule to the Lady Chapel of Hereford Cathedral.

716. CHANT IN C MINOR.

FERGUSON, WILLIAM HAROLD, M.A. (Leeds, 1874–   ), was educated first as a chorister of Magdalen College, then at Keble College, and at Cuddesdon College, Oxford. Ordained in 1902, he became assistant master at St. Edward's School, Oxford, then at Bilton Grange, Rugby; next spent eleven years as assistant master, organist and chaplain at Lancing College, and thereafter eleven as Warden of St. Edward's School, Oxford. Since 1925, he has been Warden of Radley College, Berkshire. He was a member of the Headmasters' Conference which was responsible for the preparation of *The Public School Hymn Book*, and with Geoffrey Shaw, was co-editor of the music of it.

178. CUDDESDON.   139. LADYWELL.   508. WOLVERCOTE.

FILITZ (or FIELITZ), FRIEDRICH, Ph.D. (Arnstadt, Thuringia, 1804–76, Munich), resided in Berlin, 1843–7, and for the rest of his life in Munich. He edited *Vierstimmiges Choralbuch zu Kirchen- und*

Hausgebrauch; a book of four-part tunes for the *Allgemeine Gesang-und Gebetbuch* of von Bunsen, who was his friend; and collaborated with Erk in bringing out a collection of the chorales of the most distinguished masters of the sixteenth and seventeenth centuries. Later his views seem to have changed, for he published in 1853 a book *Ueber einige Interessen der älteren Kirchenmusik*, in which he asserted the superiority of Roman Catholic over Protestant music in the qualities that touch the heart.

282. CAPETOWN.   564. MANNHEIM
542. WEM IN LEIDENSTAGEN (FILITZ).

FINDLATER, SARAH, *née* BORTHWICK (Edinburgh, 1823–1907, Torquay), was the younger daughter of James Borthwick, manager of the North British Insurance Office, Edinburgh, and sister of Jane Borthwick (q.v.). She married the Rev. Eric Findlater, minister of the Free Church of Scotland at Lochearnhead. With her sister she published *Hymns from the Land of Luther*, fifty-three of the 122 translations being from her pen. Her daughters are the gifted novelists, Jane H. and Mary Findlater, authoresses of *Crossriggs*, *Penny Monypenny*, &c. The former writes of her: 'She was a woman of great individuality, almost eccentric in many ways, and with a curious simplicity of nature. She never had and *never wanted* any of the things that most people prize most. The only use she had for money was to give it away, and she used to say to us when we complained of the restrictions of poverty, "It is the lightest of all trials". Her home life with my father was almost idyllically happy, in the small manse at Lochearnhead, where there never was enough of money, yet where my parents exercised unceasing hospitality—almost foolish hospitality. They were both great readers, and used to read aloud to each other for hours. My mother was an excellent linguist, and her German translations were a great pleasure to her. That simple little hymn of hers which begins "O happy home", is really an epitome of her home life with my father—they were so single-eyed in their longing to serve God: it came first with them always. I often wonder if there *are* such simply "good" men and women now. No doubt they were not altogether enlightened in their methods, but the sincerity of their purpose was amazing.'

648. *O happy home, where Thou art loved the dearest* (tr.).

FINK, GOTTFRIED WILHELM (Sulza on the Ilm, Thuringia, 1783–1846, Halle), was educated as a chorister of the college of Naumburg, and at Leipzig, where he studied theology for five years. In 1810 he began the publication of arrangements of German popular songs and hymns, by which his name is best known. From 1812 until 1827 he conducted a school at Leipzig. During that time he published sermons and a book of *Devotions*. From 1827 to 1841 he was editor of *The Musical Gazette* of Leipzig, and acquired a considerable reputation as a critic. He was a strong conservative, however, narrow in his views and superficial in his knowledge, and in these respects little qualified for the Professorship of Music at Leipzig, to which he was appointed in 1842. Besides his copious writings in the *Allg. Mus. Zeitung*, from 1808 onwards, he wrote numerous pamphlets, contributed to Ersch and Gruber's *Conversations-Lexicon* and Schilling's *Lexicon der Tonkunst*, and published *Musikalischer Hausschatz der Deutschen* (1843), and *Die Deutsche Liedertafel* (1846).

42. EVANGEL.

FINLAY, KENNETH GEORGE (Aberdeen, 1882–   ), son of the late Prof. D. W. Finlay, Aberdeen University, was educated at Gordon's College, Aberdeen, and Merchiston Castle School, Edinburgh. He is a Member of the Institute of Naval Architects. An amateur musician, he has contributed tunes to *The Missionary Hymn Book* (S.P.C.K.) and other collections, and has in recent years published various compositions, mainly Scottish part-songs and choral arrangements.

491. FINNART.   663. GLENFINLAS.   358. HELENSBURGH.

FLETCHER, FRANK, M.A. (Atherton, Manchester, 1870–   ), was educated at Rossall School and Balliol College, Oxford. At the University he had a brilliant career, capturing the Craven, Ireland, and Derby Scholarships. He was assistant master at Rugby, 1894–1903; master of Marlborough College, 1903–11; and has been headmaster of the Charterhouse, Godalming, since 1911. He is a layman, and when he was appointed to Marlborough there was no precedent for the election of a lay headmaster by any of the great public boarding-schools.

146. *O Son of Man, our Hero strong and tender*.

FLOWERDEW, ALICE (?   1759–1830, Whitton, Ipswich), was the wife of Daniel Flowerdew, at one time a Government official in Jamaica. After his death in 1801, she kept a boarding-house for young ladies in Islington, and while there, was a member of the General Baptist congregation meeting at that time in Worship Street, and now in Bethnal Green Road. During this time most of her hymns were written. After a time she removed her school to Bury St. Edmunds, and finally to Ipswich. In 1803 she published *Poems on Moral and Religious Subjects*. She said of her poems, 'They were written at different periods of my life, some, indeed, at a very early age, and others under the severe pressure of misfortune, when my pen had frequently to give that relief which could not be derived from other employments.'

617. *Fountain of mercy, God of love*.

FORTUNATUS, Venantius Honorius Clementianus (*c.* 530–609), was a native of Italy, though he spent most of his time in Gaul He lived through the time of the Lombard invasion of Italy, and has been called 'one of the last who, amid the advancing tide of barbarism, retained anything of the old classic culture'. He studied at Milan and Ravenna with the object of excelling as a rhetorician and poet, after which he travelled in various parts of France, courted by many persons of distinction for the charm of his society and the elegance of his verses. Eventually he attached himself to Queen Radegundis, who had left her husband, Clothaire II, the Frankish king, to found the nunnery of Ste. Croix at Poitiers. Under her influence he took holy orders and was afterwards elected Bishop of Poitiers. The poetry of Fortunatus is very unequal, but the best of it ranks among the finest medieval Latin hymns. His hymns included here are :

 108. *Sing, my tongue, how glorious battle.*
 115. *'Welcome happy morning!'—age to age shall say.*

FOSTER, Frederick William (Bedford, 1760–1835, Ockbrook, near Derby), was educated at Fulneck, Yorkshire, the educational centre of the Moravian Brotherhood, and at the Moravian College at Barby, near Magdeburg. In 1781 he became assistant master at Fulneck, and later, minister and provincial superintendent. He edited the 1808 *Supplement to the Moravian Hymnbook*, and the 1826 edition of the *Hymnbook* itself. Besides translating from the German, he was the author of a number of hymns in these books and in the edition of 1789. Much of the anonymous translation work in these editions is probably also due to him. His work was generally of a traditional or secondary character, that of the compiler and adaptor of existing thoughts and phrases, rather than that of the original poet.

 234. *God reveals His presence* (tr.).

FOSTER, Myles Birket (London, 1851–1922, London), was a son of Birket Foster, the well-known artist. He studied at the R.A.M. under Sullivan and Prout, and after serving as organist of St. James's, Marylebone, and St. George's, Campden Hill, began in 1880 a memorable tenure of the directorship of music at the Foundling Hospital. Latterly, he was choirmaster of St. Alban's, Holborn. For many years he was editor to Boosey & Co., music publishers. From 1888 he was an examiner for Trinity College, part of the time in Australia and South Africa. He wrote the symphony, *Isle of Arran*, overtures, a string quartet, a piano trio, children's cantatas, services and anthems; a book on *Anthems and Anthem Composers*, and a *History of the Philharmonic Society*.

 85. SALVATOR.

FOUNDLING HOSPITAL COLLECTION. This Hospital was founded by Captain Coram in 1738 and began three years later. Singing was cultivated among the children, and the services at which they sang drew crowds to hear them. Hymns and anthems were written specially for them. In 1774 was issued *Psalms, Hymns and Anthems of the Foundling Hospital.* From additional hymns appended to this collection in 1809, the undernoted hymn was taken. Handel took a warm interest in this Hospital and its music; he has been called its second founder. In 1749 he arranged a concert in aid of the fund for finishing the chapel. Tickets were sold at half a guinea, and over 1,000 people attended. On the completion of the chapel he presented an organ for it, which he opened in 1750. For his munificence he was enrolled as a governor and guardian. Thereafter he gave an annual recital of *The Messiah* in the chapel. The proceeds brought a net gain of £7,000 to the Hospital.

35. Praise the Lord! ye heavens, adore Him.

FRANCIS OF ASSISI, ST. (Assisi, 1182–1226, Assisi), son of an Italian trader, spent a youth of self-indulgence and gaiety. A severe illness at the age of twenty-five changed his view of life, and awoke in him an earnest spirit of self-sacrifice for the good of others. With a few friends he formed at his cell outside the city an order of men sworn to poverty and the renunciation of all worldly goods, and sent them two and two to preach the gospel and relieve distress. The order spread with extraordinary rapidity, and received the sanction of the Pope. An order for women (named 'Poor Clares' from the founder Clara, a pupil of Francis) and a 'third order' of persons of both sexes who were not obliged to forsake social position or worldly employments, were also established. Francis has been well called of all Saints the most blameless and gentle—emphatically a Saint of the people. Many miraculous tales have been told of him, notably the story of his receiving on Monte Averno the sacred stigmata or wounds of the Saviour in his hands, feet, and side. A delightful feature in his character was his love for birds, beasts, and flowers, and indeed for all the powers of Nature. His hymns are among the earliest metrical works in Italian. 'In him the troubadour inspiration, dying out in its original seat, was transmuted into a spiritual minstrelsy'. The best is his 'Hymn of the Creation':

13. All creatures of our God and King.

FRANCK, JOHANN (Guben, Brandenburg, 1618–77, Guben), the son of an advocate, was educated at Guben, Cottbus, Stettin, and Thorn, and then at Königsberg, the only university not disorganized by the shattering effects of the Thirty Years War. There he was greatly influenced by Simon Dach, Professor of Poetry. After some experience of travel, he settled as an advocate in his native town, where he became a councillor, in 1651 burgomaster, and in

1671 deputy from the town to the Landtag of Lower Lusatia. He was a notable poet in his day. To a modern taste his secular poetry seems diffuse and artificial, but his·hymns are on a much higher level—simple, earnest in spirit, and compact and massive in form. He marks the transition from the objective form of church song prevalent till his time, to the more individual and mystical type: his leading idea is the union of the soul with its Saviour. His 110 hymns were published at Guben in 1674 under the title *Geistliche Sion*.

324. Deck thyself, my soul, with gladness.

FRANCK, JOHANN WOLFGANG, M.D. (? 1641–88), practised his profession of medicine and composed music in Hamburg. He wrote a number of *Geistliche Lieder*, chiefly settings of Heinrich Elmenhorst's hymns. Little of his life is known, but it is believed that he repaired to Spain in 1688, and there met his death by poisoning.

176. KOMM, SEELE.

FREER, FANNY (? 1801–91, ?), was a member of the Catholic Apostolic (Irvingite) Church, and a contributor to its *Hymns for the Use of the Churches* (1871) and other collections.

452. Present with the two or three.

FREYLINGHAUSEN, JOHANN ANASTASIUS (Gandersheim, Brunswick, 1670–1739, Halle), son of the burgomaster of Gandersheim, studied at Jena, but, attracted by the preaching of A. H. Francke and J. J. Breithaupt, the Pietist leaders, removed to Erfurt, and then followed them to Halle. There he became colleague to Francke, first in the Glaucha Church, then in St. Ulrich's. Marrying Francke's daughter, he assisted his father-in-law, who was the organizing genius of Pietism, as director of the Paedagogium and the Orphanage in Halle, and in 1727 succeeded him in that office as well as in full charge of St. Ulrich's. Under him these institutions reached their highest prosperity. He was a singularly modest and humble man, and a persuasive preacher. Francke said that while his own sermons were like a heavy shower which waters the ground but quickly passes off, Freylinghausen's were like the continuous gentle rain which sinks deep. He has been called the Charles Wesley of the Pietistic movement; his hymns are the most poetical of all produced by that school. The two hymn-books he published were sources from which later editors drew liberally—*Geist-reiches Gesangbuch den Kern alter und neuer Lieder . . . in sich haltend*, &c. (1704); and *Neues Geist-reiches Gesangbuch* (1704). The latter contained 815 hymns and 154 melodies; the former 683 hymns and 173 melodies, and in its complete edition (1741) 1,581 hymns. Freylinghausen was a musician also: he is said to have composed twenty-two melodies. His books drew less than half their tunes from the standard sources. The new tunes were of a warmer and less grave type than the old chorales, to suit the personal feeling which animated the new type of hymn.

377. (DIR, DIR JEHOVAH.)   ´ 262. (MORGENGLANZ DER EWIGKEIT.)
170. (LÜBECK); (BONN (FESTUS).)   112. (PRESSBURG.)

GALLOWAY, ALEXANDER, B.D. (Tillicoultry, 1847–1926, Strathaven), was educated at Kinross and at Edinburgh University. After assistantships at Bowden, Lasswade, and St. Mary's, Partick, he was ordained in 1878 to the parish of Milton of Balgonie, Fifeshire. Two years later he was translated to the parish of Minto, Roxburghshire, where the rest of his ministry was spent. Mr. Galloway was an expert in the subject of Church music; he lectured on it to the Divinity students of the Universities of Scotland in 1912–14. He was one of the compilers of *The Scottish Hymnal* (1885); *The Scottish Anthem Book* (1898); *The Church Hymnary* (1898); *The Scottish Mission Hymn Book* (1912); and of the present *Church Hymnary*; a member also of the Music Sub-committee of the compilers of this book. He assisted in the selection of *Hymns Ancient and Modern* (1889).

219. PSALM 84 (JERVAULX ABBEY) (arr.).

GARDINER, WILLIAM (Leicester, 1770–1853, Leicester), was a stocking manufacturer whose business took him much to the Continent. Both at home and abroad he made acquaintance with musicians of all ranks and with their music. In his youth he published songs and duets of his own composition over the *nom de plume* of 'W. G. Leicester'. His *Sacred Melodies* (1815), in six volumes, containing tunes by the best masters, adapted to English words, was intended to displace Sternhold and Hopkins, and Tate and Brady, from general use. It did good service in drawing attention to many fine compositions. He compiled an oratorio, *Judah*, on a novel principle, adapting English words to music selected mainly from Haydn, Mozart, and Beethoven, the connecting passages consisting of music of his own. He offered Beethoven 100 guineas to write an overture to it, and, receiving no reply, concluded that his letter had gone astray. He published also *The Music of Nature; Music and Friends, or, Pleasant Recollections of a Dilettante*, &c.

309. BELMONT.   109. WALTON.

GARRATT, CHARLES A. (?   ), was born in England, but spent most of his life in America. He was organist for a time of Immanuel Church, Milwaukee. Later, he went to Canada, and followed his profession chiefly in the cities of Brantford and Hamilton, Ontario. In the latter town he was organist of the Central Presbyterian Church.

681. COMFORT.

GASKELL, WILLIAM, M.A. (Latchford, near Warrington, 1805–84, Manchester), was the husband of a famous wife, Mrs. Gaskell, the beautiful and gifted authoress of *Cranford, Mary Barton, Sylvia's Lovers*, and other well-known works of fiction, and the biographer of Charlotte Brontë. It was he who urged her to begin to write, to distract her mind from the grief caused by the death of her little son. He was himself an influential and distinguished figure in his time. He studied at Glasgow University and Manchester College, York. Becoming a Unitarian minister, his one and only charge was Cross Street Chapel, Manchester. He became Professor of English History and Literature in Manchester New College, and his denomination conferred its highest honours upon him. In the public life of Manchester he bore a very active and honourable part, especially in the promotion of education and culture. At Owen's College and a Working Men's College he conducted classes with much acceptance and success. He published sermons, tracts, memoirs, lectures on the Lancashire dialect, &c., and a number of hymns which were contributed to the Rev. Dr. J. R. Beard's collection of Hymns by Unitarians. His domestic life with his brilliant wife was very beautiful. The house in which she died in Holybourne, Hampshire, had been purchased by her with the profits of her last book, as a surprise gift to him; and the memorial to her in Cross Street Chapel bears testimony not only to her genius, but to the 'tenderness and fidelity' of the wife and mother who had adorned the minister's home.

515. *Though lowly here our lot may be.*

GASTORIUS, SEVERUS, was, about 1675, Cantor in Jena. Nothing is known of his life except that during a time of sickness his friend Rodigast wrote for him the hymn 'Whate'er my God ordains is right', and Gastorius himself wrote the melody for it.

540. WAS GOTT THUT (BADEN).

GAUNTLETT, HENRY JOHN, Mus. Doc. (Wellington, Shropshire, 1805–76, Kensington), became, at the age of nine, organist of his father's Church at Olney, Buckinghamshire. His father destined him for the law, and articled him to a solicitor. This profession he followed till 1844, when he gave it up to devote himself to music. He was organist in turn of St. Olave's, Southwark; Christ Church, Newgate Street; Union Chapel (Dr. Allon's), Islington; and St. Bartholomew the Less, Smithfield. The Archbishop of Canterbury conferred on him the degree of Mus. Doc., he being the first recipient of such a degree from that source for two hundred years. Mendelssohn said of him, 'His literary attainments, his knowledge of the history of music, his acquaintance with acoustical laws, his marvellous memory, his philosophical turn of mind, as well as his practical experience, rendered him one of the most remarkable professors of the age.' He edited many hymn-books and composed thousands of tunes. The facility with which he wrote tunes was phenomenal. 'St. Alphege', for instance, was written at his dinner-table while a messenger waited for it, to take the place of another that could not be found. He published in 1844 the first *Gregorian Hymnal*, followed by a *Gregorian Psalter* and a *Bible Psalter*. He was much in demand for editing the music of hymn-books. His contribution to the reform of Church music and the promotion of hymnody was inestimably great. 'The assimilation of the compass of the old English G. organ to that of the organ long in use in Germany, and the introduction into England of the Orchestral Bass, and consequent adoption of an extended pedal organ, were in no small degree due to Dr. Gauntlett. . . . In 1851 he also took out a patent for applying electric or magnetic action to the organ.'

168. HOUGHTON.	484. ST. AMBROSE.
69. IRBY.	675. ST. FULBERT.
102. NEWLAND.	590. ST. OLAVE (ST. GEORGE).
121. ST. ALBINUS.	64. SPRINGFIELD.
597. ST. ALPHEGE.	134, 708. TRIUMPH.
	533. UNIVERSITY COLLEGE.

GELLERT,CHRISTIAN FÜRCHTEGOTT (Haynichen,Saxony,1715–69, Leipzig), son of a country clergyman who was also a poet, studied at Meissen and Leipzig with some thought of the Church, but experiment proved him too timid for the preacher's calling. He took a degree in the faculty of Belles Lettres, and became first a lecturer on poetry and eloquence, and then professor of philosophy, in Leipzig University. His lectures were much favoured by students because of their charm of style as well as their substance and high moral tone. 'The reverence and affection which Gellert received from all the young men was extraordinary. His lecture-room was always crowded to the utmost; and Gellert's beautiful soul, purity of will, his admonitions, warnings and entreaties, delivered in a somewhat hollow and sad voice, produced a deep impression.' He co-operated with some friends in a periodical called *Bremer Beiträge*, in which his *Tales and Fables*, long popular in Germany, first appeared. He composed comedies, wrote *Consolations for Valetudinarians* out of his own experience of poor health and melancholy; *Didactic Poems; Moral Poems; Letters;* and, in 1757, *Spiritual Odes and Songs*, which were welcomed with an enthusiasm only less than that which greeted Luther's hymns on their first appearance. He was deeply religious, impoverished himself by his generosity, and was much beloved. All classes of the people sang his hymns and the highest in the land paid him visits of respect. He died in prayer, and his biographer says, 'Perhaps no grave has ever been watered with so many and such sincere tears.'

121. Jesus lives! thy terrors now.

GERHARDT, PAUL (Gräfenhainichen, Saxony, 1607–76, Lübben, Saxe-Merseburg), son of a burgomaster of his native town, spent most of his life amid the distractions and disasters of the Thirty Years War. He studied at Wittenberg for the Lutheran ministry, but was a man of forty-five before he received his first ecclesiastical appointment, to the pastorate of a small village called Mittenwalde. Before that, he had been tutor in the household of Andreas Berthold, a Chancery advocate in Berlin, whose daughter he married. From Mittenwalde his hymns began to attract attention, and were quickly adopted into the hymn-books of Brandenburg and Saxony. They had already made him famous when, in 1657, he was called as third 'dia-conus' of St. Nicholas Church, Berlin. There he acquired great influence, as the favourite preacher of the city and a personality universally honoured and beloved. In 1664 the Great Elector, Friedrich Wilhelm I, in his efforts to make peace between the Lutheran and Reformed Churches in his country, issued an edict restricting freedom of speech on points of disputation between these Churches. Gerhardt, an uncompromising Lutheran, was one of the Berlin clergy who refused obedience. He was in consequence deposed from office and interdicted from performing any function of his office even in private. On the petition of the citizens of Berlin, the Elector absolved him from the obligation of subscription to the edict, but implied a condition that, without signing, he should hold himself bound by its terms. Gerhardt refused to be so bound, and his exclusion from office was made absolute. For more than a year he was without employment, and great hardship and domestic sorrow befell him at this time. In 1668, he was appointed archdeacon of Lübben, and the closing years of his life were spent there, in much unhappiness, however, through family affliction and the detraction and unkindness he suffered at the hands of a rude and unsympathetic people. The inscription on his portrait at Lübben describes him as 'Theologus in cribro Satanae versatus' (a divine sifted in Satan's sieve). His hymns appeared in Crüger's *Geistliche Kirchenmelodien* (1649), and *Praxis Pietatis Melica* (1656). After Luther he was the typical poet of the Lutheran Church, and the first hymn-writer of Germany. His hymns, which mark the transition from the objective to the subjective in hymn-writing, are the pure and spontaneous utterance of a fervent and beautiful faith.

    41. *All my heart this night rejoices.*
  546. *Commit thou all thy griefs.*
  432. *Jesus, Thy boundless love to me.*
  107. *O Sacred Head, sore wounded.*
  547. *Put thou thy trust in God.*
  284. *The duteous day now closeth.*

GIARDINI, FELICE (Turin, Piedmont, 1716–96, Moscow), was trained as a chorister in Milan Cathedral. In 1750 he made his first appearance as a violinist in this country, and took London by storm. He became leader at the Italian Opera in London, and, later, impresario. Most of his life was spent in England, but, having gone to Naples in the train of Sir William Hamilton, British Ambassador to the Sardinian Court, he found on his return, after an absence of five years, that he had lost his place in public appreciation, and was glad of such modest employment as that of playing the viola in quartets. Russia, to which he betook himself in hope of better fortune, proved as cold to him as London, and in Moscow he sank under poverty, disappointment, and distress. 'Biographers describe him as capricious and splenetic, as speaking well of few and quarrelling with many. But for all that, he was a great artist, and the precursor in English musical history, of a long and illustrious line.'

364, 632. MOSCOW.

GIBBONS, ORLANDO, Mus. Doc. (Cambridge, 1583–1625, Canterbury), was a son of one of the Cambridge Waits, and belonged to a family of musicians. He joined the choir of King's College, Cambridge, in 1596; became organist of the Chapel Royal, London, 1604; King's musician for the virginals, 1619; organist, Westminster Abbey, 1623. He was one of the greatest of the polyphonic writers; his madrigals are masterpieces in that kind of composition. Of one of his virginal pieces it is said that it is 'so masterly in design, so finely invented, and so splendidly carried out, that we meet with nothing at all comparable to it until the time of Bach'. Of his anthems Dr. T. L. Southgate says, 'Gibbons, as it were, stood at the parting of the ways. Brought up with the strains of Tallis, Byrd, Merbecke, and other worthies of the old school, ringing in his ears, he perceived that another world of music was opening; emotion and expression were destined to take the place of orderly, though cold, counterpoint. This new feeling is reflected in his music, sacred and secular. On this foundation Gibbons built up a series of noble anthems different from anything that had appeared before his time. It is exalted music that flows along with a stately melody, grand in its sonorous harmony, and impressive in its religious solemnity.' He wrote the tunes for Wither's *Hymns and Songs of the Church* (1623). These beautiful tunes, some of which were long kept in use in mutilated forms, and others dropped from use altogether, are returning now to the favour which is their due. Commanded by Charles I to attend him to Canterbury Cathedral on the occasion of his marriage with Henrietta Maria of France, Gibbons was seized with apoplexy and died there; he is buried in the Cathedral, where his epitaph describes him as 'a man of integrity, whose manner of life and sweetness of temper vy'd with that of his art'.

728. AMEN.	195. SONG 22.
489. SONG 1.	545. SONG 24.
604. SONG 13.	651. SONG 34 (ANGELS' SONG).
428. SONG 18.	444. SONG 46.
546. SONG 20.	433, 558. SONG 67 (ST. MATTHIAS).

GILBERT, ANN, *née* TAYLOR (London, 1782–1866, Nottingham), was one of the Taylors of Ongar, a literary dynasty of note in their time. Her father, Isaac Taylor the first, was by profession an engraver, but turned to the ministry of the Congregational Church, and published a score of volumes. Her brother Isaac was the well-known author of *The Natural History of Enthusiasm; A Physical Theory of Another Life; Ultimate Civilization*, &c.; and his son, Isaac also, a canon of York, made a wide reputation by his *Words and Places; The Alphabet; Etruscan Researches*, &c. Ann and her younger sister Jane (q.v.) were contributors to a volume of *Original Poems for Infant Minds, by Several Young Persons* (1805); and they collaborated alone in *Hymns for the Nursery* (1806); *Hymns for Infant Minds* (1809); and *Original Hymns for Sunday Schools* (1812). The collaboration ceased in 1813, when Ann married the Rev. Joseph Gilbert, Classical and Mathematical Tutor at the Congregational College, Masborough, Rotherham, and subsequently minister at Hull and Nottingham. Her own publications were—*Hymns for Sunday School Anniversaries; Hymns for Infant Schools; The Wedding among the Flowers*. The *Hymns for Infant Minds* broke new ground by endeavouring to give natural expression to the thoughts of little children, instead of imposing adult ideas upon them. They were very popular in their day, for this reason, both in Great Britain and in America, and were translated into German and Dutch.

550. *Great God! and wilt Thou condescend?*

GILBERT, WALTER BOND, Mus. Doc. (Exeter, 1829–1910, Oxford), was a pupil of S. S. Wesley and Sir Henry Bishop. He was organist of Topsham Parish Church, Devonshire; Bideford; Tunbridge, Maidstone; Lee, Kent; Boston, Lincolnshire; and Trinity Chapel, New York. For this last church he wrote about sixty anthems. He was the first organist in New York to introduce the works of English composers. He edited the music of *The Episcopal Hymnal* of the United States. Both Toronto and Oxford Universities gave him their doctorate. His works included two oratorios, *St. John* (1857), and *The Restoration of Israel*; services, &c.

235. MAIDSTONE.   389. THANKSGIVING.

GILDING, EDMUND (?   –1782 London), was organist of St. Martin's, Ludgate, and St. Edmund-the-King when he contributed to Riley's *Parochial Harmony* in 1762; also, at one time, of St. Giles's, Cripplegate. Subsequently, he was organist of the Parish Clerks' Company (*c.* 1765).

551. ST. EDMUND.

GILL, THOMAS HORNBLOWER (Birmingham, 1819–1906, Grove Park, Kent), belonged to a Presbyterian (Unitarian) family. One of his ancestors was assistant to Richard Baxter at Kidderminster.

Educated at King Edward's School, Birmingham, he would have proceeded to Oxford, had not his hereditary Unitarianism, although abandoned by him, made it impossible for him to comply with the condition of admission which then required subscription to the XXXIX Articles of the Church of England. He studied alone, principally in history and theology. 'Delight in the divine songs of Watts was his earliest intellectual enjoyment, and in after years the contrast between their native force and fulness and their shrunken and dwindled presentation in the mutilated version in Unitarian hymn-books, began that estrangement from his hereditary faith which gradually became complete.' R. W. Dale, in compiling his hymn-book for Carr's Lane, drew largely on Gill's work, regarding him as the first of living hymn-writers. He published *The Fortunes of Faith* (1841); *The Anniversaries* (1858); and *The Golden Chain of Praise: Hymns* (1869), which Dale found 'a very mine of wealth'. Gill's latter years were spent at Blackheath. He associated himself with the Evangelical section of the Church of England, was a vigorous opponent of ritualism, and devoted himself to the promotion of Protestant, and especially Puritan, views and movements, 'as a national power and a spiritual principle'.

> 498. *Lord, in the fulness of my might.*
> 608. *The glory of the spring how sweet!*
> 211. *We come unto our fathers' God.*

GIORNOVICHI, GIOVANNI MARIE (Palermo, 1745–1804, St. Petersburg), was a distinguished violinist. On his first appearance in Paris, in 1770, he took that city by storm: for ten years he enjoyed a vogue there that was unexampled. But he was a man of fast tastes and capricious humour, and his vanity and quarrelsomeness involved him in frequent trouble. In one dispute, he struck the Chevalier de Saint Georges, his rival on the violin, and one of the best swordsmen in Europe. The Chevalier restrained himself, saying, 'I love his talent too much to fight with him.' Graver things compromising his honour finally obliged him to leave Paris, and he went successively to Prussia, Vienna, Warsaw, St. Petersburg, Stockholm, and London. Scotland he visited in 1797. His irregular habits continued, and his arrogance frequently embroiled him with his fellow artists. Finally his failure to accept a challenge from J. B. Cramer, whom he had insulted, obliged him to quit London. For several years he lived in Hamburg, musically unemployed, but making a living by playing billiards. Death came to him at St. Petersburg while playing this game.

223. ST. ASAPH.

GLADDEN, WASHINGTON, D.D., LL.D. (Pottsgrove, Pennsylvania, 1836–1918, Columbus, Ohio), was educated at Williams College, and ordained to the ministry in the Congregational Communion in 1860. He ministered to congregations in Brooklyn, New

York; Morrisania, New York State; North Adams, Massachusetts; and Columbus, Ohio, his last pastorate continuing from 1882 till his death. He wrote largely in periodicals, mainly on civic and social subjects, in which he was profoundly interested.

339. *O Master, let me walk with Thee.*

GLADSTONE, WILLIAM HENRY (Hawarden, 1840–91, London), was the eldest son of the Rt. Hon. William Ewart Gladstone. He was educated at Eton and Christ Church, Oxford. In 1875 he was vested in the ownership of the Hawarden estate, long hereditary in his mother's family, and redeemed from embarrassment by his father's fortune. For twenty years he sat in the House of Commons, representing Chester city for three years, Whitby for twelve, and Eastern Worcestershire for five. He was a fine Greek and Latin scholar, a good singer, and a musician of no mean order, well versed in musical history, and with an especial interest in the rich treasures of Anglican Church music. He was himself an accomplished organist. Of a hymn-book which he compiled, Sir Walter Parratt said, 'It is the only one I know in which there are no bad tunes.' His compositions include chants, anthems, introits, organ voluntaries, and ten hymn-tunes. 'Not deeply concerned in ordinary politics, he was a man of many virtues and some admirable gifts; . . . I have seen letters of his to his father marked by a rare delicacy of feeling and true power of expression' (*Morley's Life of Gladstone*).

325. ERSKINE.   III. HAMMERSMITH.   24. OMBERSLEY.

GOLDSMITH, EDMUND WILLIAM (Duntisbourne Rouse, Gloucestershire, 1860–   ), was educated at King's School, Canterbury, and, as organist-scholar, at the Royal Agricultural College, Cirencester; was a pupil for a time of Dr. C. Harford Lloyd, and studied music at Leipzig also. He served as organist at the Memorial Chapel, Highnam, Glos.; St. Edward's School, Oxford (music-master also); St. Nicholas' Collegiate Church, Galway; St. Mary-le-Tower, Ipswich; Allahabad Cathedral, India; St. Mary's, Primrose Hill, Hampstead; St. Augustine's with St. Faith's, London. He is now plain-chant instructor to a community of religious at Paignton, Devon. He is a plain-chant enthusiast. He has adapted, and, in collaboration with G. R. Woodward and Maurice Bell, edited *Fourteen Ancient Faux bourdons on the Magnificat* for the Plain-song and Medieval Music Society; *Thirty Communions* (plain-chant); and was co-editor with the Rev. H. V. Hughes, of *The Plain-song Evening Psalter*. He had also to do with the musical preparation of *The English Hymnal* under Dr. Vaughan Williams.

124. O FILII ET FILIAE (arr.).

GOOCH, FREDERICK (*c.* 1858). About this composer nothing is known.

246. BAGINTON.

GOSS, Sir John, Mus. Doc. (Fareham, Hants, 1800–80, Brixton Rise, London), was the son of the organist of Fareham. He was trained as one of the children of the Chapel Royal, and as a pupil of Thomas Attwood. In 1838 he succeeded Attwood, of whom, to the last, he could not speak without emotion, as organist of St. Paul's. He sang for a time in opera, but left it early to devote his powers to church music. He was made one of the composers of the Chapel Royal in 1856, was knighted in 1872, and made Mus. Doc. by Cambridge in 1876. He had a remarkable talent for melody and for purity and symmetry of vocal treatment, and deep devotional feeling characterized all his work. Among his anthems, the best known are 'Christ our Passover' and 'O Saviour of the world'. Of the latter it has been said that 'it is the most natural, purely written, and impressive anthem in the whole range of musical literature. For depth of expression it has been not inaptly compared to the last vocal production of Mozart, the motet "Ave verum Corpus".' 'It is said that he never began the writing of an anthem without asking a blessing upon his work. He meant every anthem of his to be what an anthem should be—a sermon in music. Many of the compositions in his sketch-book are prefixed with the letters I.N.D.A., the initial letters of *In Nomine Domini. Amen.*' Sir John Stainer said that the chief features of his character were humility, genuine religious feeling, and a strong love of home and home-ties. There is a cenotaph to his memory in the crypt of St. Paul's. He edited *Parochial Psalmody* (1826); *Chants, Ancient and Modern* (1841); the music of Mercer's *Church Psalter and Hymn Book* (1856); and wrote (1833) *An Introduction to Harmony and Thorough Bass.*

519. ARMAGEDDON (arr.).	51. HUMILITY.
676. BEDE (arr.).	21. PRAISE, MY SOUL.
635. BEVAN.	200. ROTHLEY.
715. CHANT IN E.	117. WATERSTOCK.
267. FAREHAM.	

GRACE, Harvey (Romsey, 1874–   ), studied under Dr. Madeley Richardson at Southwark Cathedral. He is now editor of *The Musical Times*, having succeeded Dr. W. G. McNaught in that position in 1916. He has published *The Complete Organist* (1921); *French Organ Music, Past and Present* (1919); *The Organ Works of Bach* (1922); organ pieces, songs, part-songs, &c. 'His organ music has a strong style, free from sentimentality, without dispensing with poetic sensitiveness.'

9. HANOVER (Faux bourdon).

GRANT, Peter (Ballentua, Strathspey, 1783–1867, Grantown-on-Spey), came of a farming stock. He himself was brought up to work on the soil, and at twenty-three took over the working of the croft on which he was born. He was self-educated under great disadvantages. At twelve he could read but a little English. Gaelic, however, he could read well, and the Gaelic poems of Dugald Buchanan brought him an intellectual awakening. These poems and Alleine's *Call to the Unconverted* were his constant companions while tending cattle or shepherding on the slopes of the Grampians. In his nineteenth year he was converted, and joined the little Baptist congregation in Grantown, three miles from his home. He became an acceptable preacher, and for sixty years was very successful in attracting and arresting large congregations. Grieved by the practice, at wakes and weddings, of singing silly and often lewd songs to the traditional airs of the people, he set himself to compose spiritual songs which, sung by himself after his week-night services, became so noted that he was induced to publish a collection of them in his twenty-sixth year; and he had the satisfaction of seeing them supplant the immoral ballads of the people. This collection of hymns circulated widely, and made the name of 'Padruig Grannd nan oran' (Peter Grant of the Songs), a household word in the Highlands and Islands of Scotland. A writer in 1867 said, 'His spiritual hymns are to this day to be met with in almost every family in the Highlands, and may be heard issuing in sweet strains from the mouths of old and young in many a green grove and on many a hillside.' While still working his farm, he became minister of the congregation at Grantown, and so continued for forty-one years; but he ultimately combined with his congregational work the duties of a travelling agent of the Baptist Home Mission, and in that service travelled great distances on foot, preaching every night, and enduring much hardship. His preaching was of a high order, poetical, evangelical, convincing. 'May I ask where you were educated?' an astonished officer who heard him at Strathpeffer asked him. The characteristic answer was 'Between the stilts of the plough'.

570. *O Lord, I sing Thy praises.*

GRANT, Sir ROBERT (Bengal, 1779–1838, Dalpoorie, Western India), was a son of Charles Grant, sometime M.P. for Inverness, Director of the East India Company, and Indian philanthropist. Educated at Magdalen College, Oxford, of which he became a Fellow, he was called to the Bar in 1807, and became King's Serjeant in the Court of the Duchy of Lancaster and one of the commissioners in bankruptcy. Entering Parliament, in 1808, he represented in succession the Elgin Burghs, Inverness Burghs, Norwich, and Finsbury. In 1831 he was made a Privy Councillor. In 1833 he carried through the Commons a Bill for the emancipation of the Jews. He was made Judge Advocate General in 1832, and Governor of Bombay in 1834, being knighted on this occasion. As a memorial of his governorship, a medical college was erected, bearing his name. His hymns were contributed to *The Christian Observer*, and to H. V. Elliott's *Psalms and Hymns* (1835). His brother, Lord Glenelg, collected and published twelve of them in 1839.

9. *O worship the King, all glorious above.*

GRAY, HERBERT BRANSTON, D.D.(Layton House,Putney, London, 1851–   ), was educated at Winchester and Queen's College, Oxford. Ordained in 1877, he became assistant master at Westminster, 1875; headmaster, Routh Grammar School, 1878; headmaster of Bradfield College, Berkshire, 1880, and warden in the following year. From this post he retired in 1910. He was secretary to the Royal Commission on Taxation in British Columbia, 1911; official lecturer, Imperial Institute, 1915; and since 1918 has been vicar of St. Mary's, Bury St. Edmunds. Among his published works are—*Modern Laodiceans* (1883); *Men of Like Passions* (1894); *The Public Schools and the Empire* (1913); *Eclipse or Empire?* (1916); *America at School and at Work* (1918).

676. *Praise to our God, who with love never swerving.*

GREEN, JAMES (*c.* 1690–*c.* 1750), was an organist in Hull, who edited *A Book of Psalm Tunes, with variety of Anthems in four parts*. Appearing in 1724, this book passed through numerous editions, the eighth of which became *A Book of Psalmody, containing Chanting Tunes for the Canticles and the reading Psalms, with Eighteen Anthems and a variety of Psalm Tunes in four parts* (1734). Green composed many hymn-tunes. Latterly he lived in London and acquired fame as a bell-ringer; he had a belfry of his own on the top of his house.

94. (CROWLE.)

GREENAWAY, ADA RUNDALL (Trivandrum, India, 1861–   ), daughter of General Thomas Greenaway of the Indian Army (Madras Staff Corps), was brought to England as a child and has lived in Guildford ever since. She edited *Songs of Dawn* for Messrs. Mowbray, and writes occasional verses for their Christmas and Easter publications. She has published *A Bunch of Pansies*, a collection of her verses; a booklet for children, *The Story of a Father's Love*; and short manuals for children, *Follow Me* and *Afterwards*, for Lent and Easter. The last edition of *Hymns Ancient and Modern* contains six of her hymns.

97. *O word of pity, for our pardon pleading.*

GREENWELL, DORA (Greenwell Ford, Lanchester, Durham, 1821–82, London), was the daughter of a country gentleman, a D.L. of his county, who fell into embarrassed circumstances through no fault of his own, and was obliged to sell the family estate when Dora was twenty-seven years old. On the break-up of the home she went to live with her brothers, both clergymen of the Church of England, one at Ovingham, Northumberland, and the other at Golbourne, Lancashire, helping them in their parish work. One of her brothers, afterwards Canon Greenwell, was a famous archaeologist, also the inventor of the fly well known to all anglers, called 'Greenwell's Glory'. From 1854 to 1872 her home was with her widowed mother under the shadow of the cathedral at Durham. Her later years were spent at Torquay, Clifton, and London, and were full of labours of chivalry and love, in passionate opposition to vivisection, and in promotion of such causes as the proper care of idiots and imbecile children. Her health was always fragile, but her intellectual activity was unceasing. An accident in 1881 broke her delicate constitution and brought about her death. Her poetical works included *Carmina Crucis* (1869); *Songs of Salvation* (1873); *The Soul's Legend* (1873); *Camera Obscura* (1876). Of her prose works—*A Present Heaven; The Covenant of Life and Peace; Two Friends; Essays; Liber Humanitatis; The Life of John Woolman; The Life of Lacordaire; Colloquia Crucis; The Patience of Hope*—some, such as the last two, are of a quality to give them rank with the classics of the devotional life. Whittier classed *The Patience of Hope* with the writings of à Kempis, Fénelon, Woolman, and Tauler. Her great subject was the atonement of Christ. She took as her device Martin Luther's symbol of the heart set against a black Cross, but with both heart and Cross placed in the midst of a white rose, to signify the joy and peace and consolation faith in the Cross bestows. Her creed was that firmly grasped Cross, and was summed up in the legend 'Et teneo et teneor' (I both hold and am held). This device appears on the title-pages of her books.

698. *I am not skilled to understand.*

GREENWOOD, JOHN (*floruit c.* 1790–*c.* 1840), was a musician and teacher in Leeds. He published *A Selection of Antient and Modern Psalm Tunes* (Leeds, 1825); *Modulus Sanctus, a Collection of Sacred Music* (Leeds, 1828); and *Psalmody harmonised in score, with accompaniment for organ and pianoforte* (Halifax, 1838).

471. (AFFECTION.)

GREGORY, ST. (Rome, 540–604, Rome), surnamed the Great (Pope Gregory I), came of a Roman family distinguished alike for public service and piety. At a comparatively early age he became praetor of the city of Rome, but renounced his position, devoted his fortune to religious uses, and embraced the monastic life. The incident that suggested to him the conversion of England has often been related. Inquiring as to some fair-haired youths in the slave-market at Rome, he was told they were Angles. 'Not Angles but Angels' was his reply. 'From what country come they?' 'From Deira.' 'Then,' he said, 'they must be plucked *de ira*, from the wrath of God. And who is their King?' 'Aella.' 'Then shall Alleluia be sung in that kingdom.' Three or four years later, when Gregory became Bishop of Rome, he sent Augustine on his mission to England. Gregory's services to the Church were many. His missionaries reached all parts of the known world. He combated heresy in Lombardy, Africa, and Spain, and made his influence felt as far as Ireland. With his zeal he combined tenderness to a degree unusual in that age, and was noted for his gentle manner of dealing with Jews, infidels, heretics, and slaves. Equally valuable was his work in connexion with the liturgy and music of the Church. He founded a school at Rome for singers, and is especially remembered for the reform in ecclesiastical music which made obligatory throughout the Western Church the use of the system of plain-chant which is identified with his name.

263. Father, we praise Thee, now the night is over.

GREGORIAN TONES:

716. IST, 4TH ENDING.   718. 8TH, IST ENDING.
714. 3RD, 2ND ENDING.   712. PARISIAN TONE.
715. 7TH, IST ENDING.   716. TONUS PEREGRINUS.

GREGORY NAZIANZEN, ST. (Arizanzus Cappadocia, 325?–390? Arizanzus), one of the three great Cappadocians (the other two being Basil the Great and his brother Gregory of Nyssa), studied at Alexandria and at Athens. His life was changeful and unsettled, and he seems to have constantly wavered between the impulse toward active organizing work and the desire for religious contemplation and asceticism. His first bishopric was that of Sasima, which he seems to have found an uncongenial sphere. At Constantinople, where he vigorously defended the Catholic faith against heresy, his influence was such that the Emperor Theodosius made him Patriarch, an appointment, however, which he did not hold long. He retired to Nazianzen and thence to Arizanz, where he died. His discourses on the Divinity of the Word gained him the title of 'Theologos'. In his retirement he devoted himself to the writing of sacred poetry.

458. O Light that knew no dawn.

GREITER, MATTHÄUS (*c.* 1500–52), was originally a monk and singer in Strasburg Minster, but in 1524 became a Protestant and devoted his musical powers to the service of the Lutheran Church. In 1528 he was appointed assistant pastor of St. Martin's Church, and, later, of St. Stephen's. In 1548 he founded a choir school. Four years later he died, it is said, of the plague. Before his death he recanted and returned to the Roman Church; 'he who inspired the heroism of the Huguenots, was not a hero' himself. This refers to the tune by him which, sung to Psalm 68, 'Que Dieu se monstre seulement,' became 'Le Psaume de Batailles' of the Reformation in France. He was an accomplished musician, as several extant settings of German songs show. He contributed seven psalm-lieder to the *Strassburger Kirchenamt* (1525), and is credited with six of the chorale melodies. Four of these tunes were used in the early *French Psalter* published at Strasburg in 1539, and all these were transferred to the *French Genevan Psalter* in 1542.

217. PSALM 36 (68).

GRIFFITH, WILLIAM, Mus. Bac. (Syresham, South Northampton-shire, 1867–), was educated at Magdalen College School, Brackley, and qualified as a pharmacist in 1888. For a time he was in business in Lancashire, but in 1894 he took the degree of Mus. Bac. at Durham, and, in the following year, gave up business and adopted a musical career. He acted as organist in several English churches, but accepted in 1901 a post in King Street United Free Church, Kilmarnock, and has since then resided in Scotland. He has published anthems, songs, part-songs, hymn-tunes in various collections, &c.

667. CUTTLE MILLS.

GRIGG, ? . This composer is frequently identified with the Rev. Joseph Grigg, the hymn-writer; but this is purely assumption. No details of his life survive. Three tunes by him appeared in *A Selection of Psalm and Hymn Tunes arranged by John Rippon, D.D.* (*c.* 1795). In that book no Christian name is given.

57. TIVERTON.

GRIMSHAW, JOHN (d. 1819), organist and composer, wrote *Twenty-four Hymns in four parts*, 1810.

499. HEATON NORRIS.

GRUBER, FRANZ (Hochburg, Upper Austria, 1787–1863, Hallein, near Salzburg), was a member of the Roman Catholic Church. In 1818 he was schoolmaster and organist at Arnsdorf, near Oberndorf, where Joseph Mohr, the writer of the words 'Stille Nacht', was priest—about twelve miles down the Salzach from Salzburg. Hallein, where he died, is about the same distance up the river from that town.

49. STILLE NACHT.

GURNEY, DOROTHY FRANCES, *née* BLOMFIELD (London, 1858–), is a granddaughter of Bishop Blomfield, of Chester and London. Her father, the Rev. Frederick George Blomfield, was rector of St. Andrew's Undershaft, London. She married Mr. Gerald Gurney, whose father, the Rev. Archer Gurney, was a hymn-writer of merit. She and her husband were in 1919 received into the Roman Church at Farnborough Abbey. She has published two volumes of *Poems*, and *A Little Book of Quiet*. The best known of her poems is 'God's Garden', the last lines of which are often quoted :

> The kiss of the sun for pardon,
> The song of the birds for mirth:
> One is nearer God's heart in a garden
> Than anywhere else on earth.

327. *O perfect Love, all human thought transcending*.

GURNEY, JOHN HAMPDEN, M.A. (London, 1802–62, London), son of Sir John Gurney, a baron of the Court of Exchequer, was educated at Trinity College, Cambridge, and after some study of law, turned to the Church. He became curate of Wiclif's old parish of Lutterworth, and was chaplain of the poor-law Union there. He was a man of position and wealth, and many tempting invitations were given him to go elsewhere, but he remained there for seventeen years. In 1847 he became rector of St. Mary's, Bryanstone Square, Marylebone, London, and in 1857, a prebendary of St. Paul's. He took a deep interest in the Religious Tract Society and the S. P.C.K. Two collections of hymns were made by him—one for Lutterworth in 1838, the other for Marylebone in 1851. From his own contributions to these, several have passed into common use.

> 494. *Fair waved the golden corn.*
> 643. *Great King of nations, hear our prayer.*
> 90. *Lord, as to Thy dear Cross we flee.*
> 72. *We saw Thee not when Thou didst come.*

GWYLLT, IEUAN.   *See* ROBERTS, JOHN.

HADOW, SIR WILLIAM HENRY, C.B.E., Mus.D., LL.D. (Ebrington, Gloucestershire, 1859–   ), was educated at Worcester College, Oxford, of which he became a Fellow and Dean. For a time he was an examiner for degrees. His musical training was obtained at Darmstadt and under Dr. C. H. Lloyd. From 1909 to 1919 he was Principal of Armstrong College, Newcastle-on-Tyne; from 1916 to 1919 Vice-Chancellor of Durham University; and since 1919 he has been Vice-Chancellor of the University of Sheffield. He is one of the ablest of lecturers on music, and his contributions to musical criticism rank with the best. He edited *The Oxford History of Music*, and contributed to it the section on *The Viennese Period*; and besides numerous contributions to periodicals on non-musical subjects, has published *Studies of Modern Music* (2 series); a work on *Sonata-Form; A Croatian Composer* (J. Haydn); and *British Music, a Report on the Carnegie United Kingdom Trust*. Of music he has published a cantata, *The Soul's Pilgrimage*; incidental music to Robert Bridges' *Demeter*; song albums, a string quartet, a pianoforte sonata, violin sonatas, &c.; and a collection of *Songs of the British Isles*.

496. SOUTH CERNEY.

HANBY, BENJAMIN RUSSELL (? , 1833–67, ?), was co-editor with George Frederick Root of *Chapel Gems* (1866), all the pieces in which were taken from a musical quarterly they had edited. Root, in his autobiography, *The Story of a Musical Life*, referring to the period between 1861 and 1865, says of him, 'There came to us in those days a very interesting and talented man by the name of Hanby. He was educated for the ministry, but was so strongly inclined to music that he decided to try to make that his life's work. He had already written "Darling Nelly Gray". . . . He was also the author of "Old Shady", which is famous still. He wrote while with us some beautiful Sunday-School songs, some of which are in use yet. But he died almost at the commencement of his career.'

77. LOWLINESS.

HANDEL, GEORGE FREDERICK, originally Georg Friedrich Händel (Halle, 1685–1759, London), was son of the surgeon to Duke Augustus of Saxony. His extraordinary musical gifts early made themselves apparent, but the father, intending him for the legal profession, tried to repress them. Ultimately, through the intervention of the Duke of Saxe-Weissenfels, the boy was allowed to follow the bent of his genius and to take lessons from Zachau, organist of the Cathedral. In 1702 he entered the University of Halle, but in the following year repaired to Hamburg, joined the band of the theatre as a violinist, and in 1705, produced his first opera, *Almira*. In 1707 he went to Italy, and during some years there won many triumphs. Returning to Germany, he became chapelmaster to the Elector of Hanover, afterwards George I of Great Britain and Ireland. A first visit to England in 1710 made this country so attractive to him that in 1713 he returned to it finally and made it his home. For nearly thirty years his genius, which was essentially dramatic, was concentrated almost wholly on operatic composition. During one interval he was chapelmaster to the magnificent Duke of Chandos, who lived in almost royal splendour at Cannons, nine miles from London. Here Handel laid the foundation of his future fame, by composing for the Duke's private chapel, in which daily cathedral service was maintained, the two Te Deums and the anthems known as the Chandos Te Deums and Anthems, and by writing, in 1720, his first oratorio *Esther*. *Acis and Galatea* was also produced at Cannons. The next twenty years were a period of great strain ; a long operatic war waged between him and his rival Buononcini and the factions supporting them ended in the bankruptcy of both in 1737. Paralysis induced by this blow partially disabled him, yet subsequently he discharged all his obligations. The catastrophe was the starting-point of the work which won him his lasting fame. Except for a few airs, his operas are forgotten, but his oratorios produced, except *Esther*, after the disaster, have enduring vitality.

They gave full scope to all his ripened powers. They were intended at first for stage production, as sacred dramas, but the public performance of them as such was prohibited. Their dramatic quality, however, did not depend upon their being acted; it was inherent in the music. After *The Messiah*, composed in twenty-four days, swept Dublin with enthusiasm on its first performance there in 1741, the greatness of his genius was fully realized; from that time till blindness befell him in 1753, he lived happily in the sunshine of popular favour. His productiveness was inexhaustible. He wrote over forty operas, seven English oratorios, three English serenatas, four odes, besides Psalms, Te Deums, and other minor works. Most of his instrumental works were for the organ, in the playing of which he was a master, and for the harpsichord, his favourite instrument. His generosity was unbounded; he was the 'second founder of the Founling Hospital, and one of the original founders of the Royal Society of Musicians', 'He died as he lived, a good Christian, with a true sense of his duty to God and man, and in perfect charity to all the world'. He was buried in the Poets' Corner of Westminster Abbey. The under-noted tune is not an arrangement from any of his works, but one of three tunes—'Cannons' and 'Brunswick' being the others—which he wrote out of friendship for the Wesleys; this one for the hymn to which it is here set.

135. GOPSAL.

HANKEY, Arabella Catherine (Clapham, 1834–1911, London), always known as Kate Hankey, was a daughter of Thomas Hankey, senior partner in the banking firm of that name, and a member of the little band of Evangelicals known as the Clapham Sect. While still girls in the schoolroom, she and her sister began teaching in a Sunday School at Croydon, where their home then was. At eighteen she started a Bible Class in London for girl assistants at the big shops in the West End. The class was never a large one, but she devoted immense pains and time to it, and her influence through it was lasting; some of its members kept in touch with her all her life, and five met at her funeral, fifty years after the class had ceased. A later class for girls of her own social standing had similar results; several members of both classes became devoted religious workers. The one great adventure of her life was a visit to South Africa to nurse and bring home an invalid brother, at a time when travel up-country could be accomplished only in bullock-wagons; this inspired in her a keen interest in missions, to which she devoted the proceeds of her writings. She published a volume of *Bible Class Teachings*, a booklet on *Confirmation*, and a collection of her hymns under the title of *The Old, Old Story, and Other Verses*. Her later years were spent in hospital visiting and other good works.

682. *Tell me the old, old story.*

HARRISON, RALPH (Chinley, Derbyshire, 1748–1810, Manchester), was a member of a family notable in the history of nonconformity, and son of a Presbyterian (Unitarian) minister. Educated at Warrington Academy, he became assistant minister of the Presbyterian Chapel, Shrewsbury, 1769; and minister of Cross Street Chapel, Manchester, 1771. While ministering in the latter charge, he carried on a school, in which he gained such repute as a teacher of ancient languages that when Manchester Academy was established in 1786, he was appointed classical tutor in it. He published *Institutes of English Grammar*, geographical manuals, &c.; and after endeavouring in vain to induce others to undertake the task, compiled *Sacred Harmony* (2 vols., 1784–91), a collection of psalm tunes, ancient and modern, for use in the Manchester district. Included in it were some tunes of his own composition.

   531. (BLACKBOURN).   388. WARRINGTON.

HART, JOSEPH (London, 1712–68, London). Little is known of his early life, save that he was religiously brought up and fairly well educated. After passing through much spiritual perturbation for a long period of years, he owed his conversion to hearing a sermon on Rev. iii. 10 at the Moravian Chapel in Fetter Lane, London. From 1760 till 1768 he preached regularly at Jewin Street Chapel, where he gathered a large congregation. He was buried in Bunhill fields, and it is said that 20,000 people gathered to listen to his funeral sermon. Hart was a strong Calvinist, and one of his publications is a criticism of a sermon by John Wesley. He is better remembered for his hymns, which are for the most part of the evangelistic type.

   190. *Come, Holy Spirit, come.*
   393. *Come, ye sinners, poor and wretched.*

HARTSOUGH, LEWIS (Ithaca, New York, 1828–72, Mount Vernon, Iowa), was a minister of the Methodist Episcopal Church. After holding charges at Utica and elsewhere, he was compelled by ill-health to retire to the Rocky Mountains. There he organized the Utah Mission, and became its first superintendent. He wrote many hymns and several tunes, and edited the music edition of *The Revivalist* (*c.* 1868), which had a great circulation.

   689. *I hear Thy welcome voice.*
   689. WELCOME VOICE.

HARWOOD, BASIL, M.A., Mus. Doc. (Woodhouse, Olveston, Gloucestershire, 1859–), was educated at Charterhouse and Trinity College, Oxford. He held posts successively as organist of Trinity College, Oxford; St. Barnabas, Pimlico; Ely Cathedral; Christ Church Cathedral, Oxford; as precentor of Keble College; as conductor of the Oxford Orchestral Association and of the Oxford Bach Choir;

and as Choragus of the University of Oxford. He was musical editor of *The Oxford Hymn Book* (1908). His published works include anthems, hymn-tunes, church services, organ works; a cantata, *Song on May Day Morning*; and a motet, *Jesus, Thy boundless love to me.*

380. ALVESTON.	143. O AMOR QUAM EXSTATICUS (arr.).
330. HAZEL.	441. OLDOWN.
15. LUCKINGTON.	215. THORNBURY.

HASLOCH, MARY (Kentish Town, 1816–92, Brighton), was a daughter of the Rev. John Hasloch, minister of Kentish Town Congregational Chapel. She was a fine pianist and had exceptional musical aptitude, as well as a gift of writing easy melodious verse. She wrote many hymns of the same type as Frances Havergal's, but could never be persuaded to publish. Most of her life was spent in Walsall and Leamington. She became a devoted member of the Church of England, and was active in parish work, particularly among friendless and fallen girls.

343. Christian, work for Jesus.

HASSLER, HANS LEO (Nuremberg, 1564–1612, Frankfurt), came of a musical family in the Joachimsthal, and studied at Venice under Andrea Gabrieli, organist of St. Mark's. In 1585 he was given a home in the house of the Fuggers, the great merchant princes and art patrons of Augsburg. He was appointed musical director there in 1600, but a year later accepted the post of organist in the Frauenkirche in Nuremberg. In 1608 he entered the service of the Elector of Saxony. Accompanying that prince to the Diet at Frankfurt in 1612, he died there. His works included *XXIV Canzonetti a 4 voci; Cantiones Sacrae de praecipuis festis totius anni, 4, 5, 8, et plurium vocum; Concentus ecclesiasticae; Madrigali; Cantiones novae; Sacri Concentus* for 5 to 12 voices; 4-part Psalms and Songs; and 5 collections of German and Latin secular songs. Many of his chorales were published in the Hizler (Strassburg) *Chorale Book.* He was the most eminent organist of his day.

107. PASSION CHORALE.

HASTINGS, THOMAS, Mus. Doc. (Washington, Lichfield Co., Connecticut, 1784–1872, New York), spent his childhood at Clinton, Oneida Co., New York, where educational opportunities were small. He qualified himself, however, to be a teacher of music. Dissatisfied with the condition of Church music, he set himself to reform it, by lectures and writings, by establishing singing classes for congregations and schools for the young, and by training choirs for leadership. In 1816 he began the publication of a long series of tunebooks, and in 1823, in Utica, started a religious journal in which he specially advocated the cause of congregational praise. Called to New York to assume charge of twelve church choirs, he spent forty fruitful years there, teaching, training choirs, composing, compiling, publishing, writing hymns for tunes and tunes for hymns. He wrote over 600 hymns, and edited many books, such as *The Christian Psalmist* (1834); *Church Melodies* (1858); *Devotional Hymns and Poems* (1850); he collaborated with Lowell Mason in *Spiritual Songs for Social Worship* (1832). Though his tunes are now disused, he did valuable service in his day in stemming the tide of deteriorating influences in American hymnody, and maintaining the ideal of devoutness in church praise.

688. *Come, ye disconsolate, where'er ye languish.*

HATCH, EDWIN, D.D. (Derby, 1835–89, Oxford), was educated at King Edward's School, Birmingham, and Pembroke College, Oxford. At the University he was closely associated with Burne Jones, William Morris, and Swinburne. By the time he took his degree he was already contributing largely to reviews and magazines on a wide range of subjects. His parents were nonconformists, but he took orders in the Church of England and for a time worked in an east-end parish in London. In 1859 he accepted an appointment as Professor of Classics in Trinity College, Quebec; this post was relinquished later for the rectorship of Quebec High School. Returning to Oxford in 1867, he became Vice-Principal of St. Mary's Hall; in 1880, Bampton and Grinfield Lecturer; in 1883, rector of Purleigh, Essex; in 1884, University Reader in Ecclesiastical History; in 1888, Hibbert Lecturer. A man of great learning, original mind, and force of character, he won a European reputation by work of rare independence and thoroughness in historical research; in this field he was acknowledged a master. Harnack translated his Bampton Lectures into German and said of him: 'In his learning that of England's great old theologians, Ussher and Pearson, lived to me again. He was a glorious man, whose loss I shall never cease to mourn.' Profound as his learning was, his published sermons show that his piety was as simple and unaffected as a child's.

194. *Breathe on me, Breath of God.*

HATELY, THOMAS LEGERWOOD (Greenlaw, Berwickshire, 1815–67, Edinburgh), was by trade a printer, employed by the great firms of Ballantyne and Constable, Edinburgh. As a boy, he carried proofs to Sir Walter Scott in Castle Street, and on occasion had to wait so long that he fell asleep. Of Constable's he became manager. His passion for music, in which he was self-taught, brought him under the influence of R.A. Smith (q.v.), and led to his becoming precentor in North Leith, and then in St. Mary's Parish Church, one of the musical 'prizes' of the city then. He was one of the few precentors who 'came out' at the Disruption, and to him was given the honour after the first day, of leading the singing at the historic first General Assembly of the Free Church of Scotland, at Tanfield in 1843. In D. O. Hill's picture of that Assembly Hately is given a prominent place. Subsequently, he became official precentor of the Free Church Assembly, and of the Free High Church. In 1850 the Assembly sent him forth on a mission of musical instruction, over the country, among the churches, and from that time he devoted himself entirely to the stimulation of interest in church music, by training teachers and conducting classes, which sometimes ran into many hundreds (900 in Greenock) of members. Psalmody was then in a very backward condition. The number of tunes in use was small; the 'lining' of them—a practice imported from England after the Westminster Assembly—made the singing of them intolerably tedious; Rowland Hill said satirically that 'the Scotch took so long to sing the 100th Psalm, that one could travel from Edinburgh to London by the old conveyance, before it was finished'. The introduction of florid tunes, with 'repeats', had not improved the situation, though they were popular. The work of Hately did much to raise the standard of psalmody and to develop congregational singing. He edited many books—*Free Church Psalmody* (1844); *Gaelic Psalm Tunes* (old) taken down by him; *National Psalmody; Scottish Psalmody* (1854), &c.; and wrote over forty psalm tunes, of which some—Knox, Zwingle, Glencairn, Huntingtower, e.g.—were for long extremely popular.

553. LEUCHARS. 475. NENTHORN.

HATELY, WALTER (Edinburgh, 1843–1907, Edinburgh), son of T. L. Hately (q.v.), was educated at the High School, Edinburgh, and studied music at Leipzig Conservatorium, under Plaidy, Moscheles, Reinecke, Hauptmann, Richter, and Dreyschoek, and afterwards with Schulhoff at Dresden. From 1865 he taught music in Edinburgh, holding numerous official positions. He succeeded his father as precentor of the Free High Church in 1867, and was choirmaster of Free St. George's Church from 1885 to 1890. His duties as an examiner for the Incorporated Society of Musicians took him frequently to England. He acted as editor of the Church of Scotland *Psalm and Hymn Tune Book* of 1868, and also selected and arranged the music for H. W. Smith's *Hymns of Life and Human Encouragement* (Edinburgh, 1872). Of original work he published some admirable songs, five *Child Lyrics*, a *Nocturne*, and various pianoforte pieces.

556. ST. HELEN.

HATTON, JOHN (Warrington, ? –1793, St. Helen's), resided in St. Helen's, in the township of Windle, in a street whose name he gave to the one tune by which his name is known. His funeral sermon was preached in the Presbyterian Chapel, St. Helen's.

517. DUKE STREET.

HAVERGAL, FRANCES RIDLEY (Astley, 1836–79, Caswall Bay, near Swansea), was the youngest child of the Rev. W. H. Havergal (q.v.), the pioneer of reform in metrical psalmody. From her early years she evinced unusual gifts: she began to write verses at the age of seven, and her poems were soon admitted to *Good Words* and other religious periodicals. Her health was delicate, and systematic study had to be discouraged in her childhood; later, she studied for a time at Düsseldorf. In early life her religion was much shadowed by fear and a morbid sense of the vanity of human life, but about the age of fourteen the shadows lifted, and from that time her life was full of the joy of loving and serving Christ. Her favourite name for Him was Master, because, she said, 'it implies rule and submission, and this is what love craves. Men may feel differently, but a true woman's submission is inseparable from deep love'. Her poetic gift was limited in its range, but within her compass she sang of the life of faith and consecration with a melodiousness which endears her hymns to many. Her devotional books and religious verses, revealing a singularly sympathetic and attractive spirit, drew to her a large amount of correspondence from people who made her their confidante and sought her counsel. The time and thought and labour so required of her told on her frail constitution and so wore her spirit out sometimes that she said she hoped 'the angels would have orders to let her alone a bit when she first got to heaven'. So far as her strength allowed, she threw herself energetically into religious and philanthropic work; she wrote incessantly, and composed music also. Her collected *Poetical Works* were published in 1884. A volume of *Memorials* of her, which includes a partial *Autobiography*, disclosed a remarkable Christian character, exhibiting all the beauty, freshness and charm of that life of complete and happy consecration which was the chief subject of her song.

375. *God of heaven, hear our singing.*
133. *Golden harps are sounding.*
695. *I am trusting Thee, Lord Jesus.*
509. *Jesus, Master, whose I am.*
443. *Like a river glorious.*
338. *Lord, speak to me, that I may speak.*
512. *Take my life, and let it be.* — Mason
157. *Thou art coming, O my Saviour.*
519. *Who is on the Lord's side?*

133. HERMAS.

HAVERGAL, WILLIAM HENRY, M.A. (High Wycombe, Buckinghamshire, 1793–1870, Leamington), was educated at the Merchant Taylors' School and St. Edmund Hall, Oxford. Ordained in 1816, he served two curacies in Gloucestershire, and, in 1829, became rector of Astley, near Bewdley. A carriage accident, in which he sustained concussion of the brain and had his eyesight permanently

injured, compelled him to resign his living. He devoted his enforced leisure to the pursuit of the study of music, and began publishing anthems and services. Church music was then at a low ebb
in England; he set himself the task of securing some reform. He
reprinted *Ravenscroft's Psalter* in 1844, and in 1847 issued his best-
known work, *Old Church Psalmody*. In these works he drew attention to the classical school of English ecclesiastical music, and did
much to purify metrical psalmody. The latter book was the parent
of many other collections that succeeded it. In 1842 he was able to
resume clerical duty, as rector of St. Nicholas, Worcester, and in
1845 he received an honorary canonry in the Cathedral there. Impaired health compelled him to accept in 1860 the quiet living of
Shareshill, near Wolverhampton, and in 1867 he resigned, and withdrew into retirement at Leamington. Lowell Mason, in 1852, described the musical service in Havergal's church as excellent in all
particulars, and far in advance of anything that he heard in England.
Havergal wrote about a hundred hymns, published about fifty
musical works, and issued also two volumes of *Sermons on Historical
Subjects from the Old and New Testaments* (1853); *A History of the
Old Hundredth Psalm Tune, with Specimens* (1854); *A Hundred Psalm
and Hymn Tunes* (1859), of his own composition; and *Fireside Music*,
a collection of songs, rounds, carols, &c.

692. EVAN.	512. PATMOS.
546. NARENZA (arr.).	478. SWABIA (arr.).

HAWEIS, THOMAS, LL.B., M.D. (Truro, 1734–1820, Bath), studied
medicine for a time, but eventually resolved to study for Holy Orders,
and went to Christ Church, Oxford, subsequently to Magdalen. He
held the curacy of St. Mary Magdalen's Church at Oxford, and was
at one time assistant to Martin Madan at the Lock Hospital, London.
Later he became rector of All Saints, Aldwinkle, Northamptonshire,
and chaplain to Lady Huntingdon's chapel at Bath. He published a
collection of hymns entitled *Carmina Christo, or Hymns to the
Saviour*, a collection which was a companion to the *Select Collection
of Hymns* compiled by the Countess of Huntingdon for use in the
chapels of her Connexion, and was often bound up with it. Haweis
became manager of Lady Huntingdon's chapels. He was the most
musical of her chaplains and composed tunes published after her
death as *Original Music suited to the various metres*.

306. *Our children, Lord, in faith and prayer*.
32, 209. RICHMOND.

HAWKINS, HESTER PERIAM, *née* LEWIS, F.R.A.S., wife of Joshua
Hawkins, Bedford, published in 1885 *The Home Hymn Book, a
Manual of Sacred Song for the Family Circle*, in which, over her
initials, she included seven hymns of her own. She has also published *The A B C Guide to Astronomy; Stella Maitland, or, Love and*

the Stars; *Astronomy for Busy People*; and has edited *The Home and Empire Hymn Book*, &c.

603. *Heavenly Father, Thou hast brought us.*

HAWKS, ANNIE SHERWOOD (Hoosick, New York, 1835–1918, Binnington, Vermont), resided for many years in Brooklyn. Her hymns were contributed to various popular Sunday-school hymn-books. A member of the Baptist Church in Brooklyn of which Dr. Robert Lowry (q.v.), the hymn-writer and composer of tunes, was minister, she was encouraged by him to write hymns, and he himself set music to some of them.

700. *I need Thee every hour.*

HAYDN, FRANZ JOSEPH (Rohrau, Lower Austria, 1732–1809, Gumpendorf, near Vienna), was the son of a wheelwright. In later life he cited his own life as 'an example that after all something can be made of nothing'; he had no advantages. At eight he was taken into the Cantorei of St. Stephen's, the cathedral church of Vienna. When his voice broke, after ten years' faithful service, he was cast out penniless, and for eight years waged a dire struggle with poverty. Some of his works became known, however; Glück recognized his genius, and certain aristocratic patrons gave him his opportunity. For thirty years he was chapelmaster to Prince Anton Paul Esterhazy, with a private band at his service every day in the year. The works he now composed spread his fame over Europe. In 1791 he visited this country, and was received with unbounded enthusiasm. Oxford gave him its Mus. Doc. degree, and he returned home laden with honours. On a second visit in 1794 he was lionized more than ever. He always ascribed his fame in his own country to the enthusiasm of his recognition here. Though sixty-five on his return home, he started, with the inspiration of youth, upon his most important works, the oratorios *The Creation* and *The Seasons*. The inspiration of the oratorios was derived from what he had heard of Handel's oratorios at the Westminster Abbey commemoration and elsewhere. He was a deeply religious man, regarding his talent as a trust given him by God. Every one of his scores, great and small, is prefaced by the words 'In nomine Domini' (In the name of the Lord), and closed by the ascription 'Laus Deo' (Praise to God). Religion to him was a wholly cheerful thing. 'When I think of God', he said, 'my heart dances within me, and my music has to dance too.' There is therefore not a melancholy strain in all his works. The grace and inexhaustible freshness of his melodies give his work a charm that never fails. 'The invention of a fine melody', he said, 'is a work of genius.' In this respect his genius was of the highest. He invented the symphony and the string quartet, and has been called the father of modern instrumental music; he was a master of orchestration. As a man he was universally loved and honoured. He left about 120 symphonies, 83 instrumental quartets, 44 sonatas, 22 operas, 4 oratorios, and many other works.

206. AUSTRIAN HYMN.

HAYDN, JOHANN MICHAEL (Rohrau, Lower Austria, 1737–1806, Salzburg), a younger brother of Franz Joseph, was trained as a chorister at St. Stephen's, Vienna. He had a pure soprano voice of unusual compass. He learned to play both violin and organ, but had no formal training in composition. For a time he lived in Hungary, where his first compositions were published. He became Kapellmeister first at Grosswardein to the bishop, Count Firmian; then, in 1762, at Salzburg, to Archbishop Sigismund of that diocese. He was organist also to the churches of the Holy Trinity and St. Peter in Salzburg. He was a warm-hearted, devout man, with distinguished gifts of his own, but his fame suffered some obscuration through the lustre of his brother's. His modesty, too, was extreme, and few of his works were published. He wrote 114 Graduals, a *Mass in D minor*, a *Lauda Sion, Tenebrae in E♭*, &c.

562. SALZBURG.

HAYES, WILLIAM, Mus. Doc. (Gloucester, 1706–77, Oxford), was trained as a chorister in Gloucester Cathedral, and served as organist in St. Mary's, Shrewsbury; Worcester Cathedral; and Magdalen College, Oxford, where he remained for forty-three years up till his death. In 1741 he was appointed Professor of Music in the University. It is doubtful whether he ever delivered any lectures during his occupancy of the Chair, but he was active in other ways. He published *Twelve Ariettas or Ballads and Two Cantatas* in 1735; a setting of Collins's *Ode on the Passions; Circe, a Masque;* many anthems, which are still popular with choirs; *Sixteen Metrical Psalms selected from Merrick's Version*, set to music for use in Magdalen College Chapel; and other vocal and instrumental music. He was succeeded in the professorship by his son Philip, who was supposed to be the largest man in England, in bulk and humour 'a complete representative of Shakespeare's fat knight Sir John Falstaff', but who was one of the best extemporary performers of his age. Father and son collected a curious and valuable library of music by early English composers.

543. MAGDALEN COLLEGE.   431. NEW 113TH.

HAYNE, LEIGHTON GEORGE, Mus. Doc. (St. David's Hill, Exeter, 1836–83, Bradfield), son of the Rev. Richard Hayne, D.D., rector of Mistley, Essex, was educated at Eton and Queen's College, Oxford. He took holy orders in 1861. In 1863 he was appointed Coryphaeus (conductor of the chorus) of the University, and public examiner in the School of Music. For three years from 1868 he was succentor and organist of Eton College ; then, in 1871, became rector of Mistley and vicar of Bradfield, Essex. A large five-manual organ he had built in the music-room at Eton was subsequently divided between his churches of Mistley and Bradfield. He wrote many hymn-tunes and, with the Rev. H. W. Sargeant, edited *The Merton Tune Book.*

193. BUCKLAND.   386. ST. ANSELM (arr.).   152. ST. CECILIA.

HEARN, MARIANNE, *nom de plume* MARIANNE FARNINGHAM (Farningham, Kent, 1834–1909, Barmouth), received but a slender education, being early orphaned, and having the care of younger children thrown upon her hands when she herself was little more than a child. She resided for a time in Bristol, taught a primary school in Gravesend, then also at Northampton, where she settled in 1865. She began early to contribute to periodicals, and received from the first much encouragement from her minister at Eynsford, Kent, the Rev. J. Whittemore, who was an influential journalist as well. From the start of *The Christian World* newspaper by James Clarke & Co., she was a member of its staff and a regular and popular contributor. She also edited *The Sunday School Times.* Her scattered verses were collected in *Lays and Lyrics of the Blessed Life; Poems; Morning and Evening Hymns for a Week; Songs of Sunshine; Leaves from Elim; Harvest Gleanings and Gathered Fragments;* and, posthumously, *Songs of Joy and Faith.* She published an autobiography, *A Working Woman's Life.*

497. *Just as I am, Thine own to be.*

HEBER, REGINALD, D.D. (Malpas, Cheshire, 1783–1826, Trichinopoly, India), was a scion of an ancient Yorkshire family. His father inherited the estate of Hodnet, Shropshire, and as lord of the manor presented himself to the living as rector of Hodnet. Educated at the Grammar School, Whitchurch, privately at Neasden, near Willesden, and at Brasenose College, Oxford, Reginald showed brilliant gifts. By a poem on *Palestine* he won the Newdigate prize, and when the poem was publicly delivered, it was hailed with extraordinary enthusiasm. Heber read it to Sir Walter Scott before the public recitation, and on Scott remarking that it made no reference to the fact that no tools were used in the building of the Temple, he retired for a few minutes to the corner of the room, then came back with the famous lines—

> No hammer fell, no ponderous axes rung;
> Like some tall palm the mystic fabric sprung.
> Majestic silence!

Having won a fellowship of All Souls, he devoted two years to travel in Eastern Europe. Taking orders in 1807, he became rector of the family living at Hodnet, where he proved an excellent parish priest. In 1812 he was appointed a prebendary of St. Asaph; in 1815 was Bampton Lecturer, on *The Personality and Office of the Comforter;* in 1822 became preacher at Lincoln's Inn; and in the same year was offered the bishopric of Calcutta. Twice he refused this office, then, against the advice of his friends, accepted. The see of Calcutta at that time included the whole of British India. It demanded incessant travel and unremitting strain. Heber proved an ideal bishop, energetic, tactful, wise, and lovable; but in three years the burden broke him: at Trichinopoly he died suddenly in his bath, of apoplexy. His influence did much to popularize the use of hymns in England. In 1811 he began the publication of his own hymns in *The Christian Observer,* and with the help of Dean Milman he made the first attempt to provide a set of hymns adapted to the requirements of the Christian Year. These were published in 1827 as *Hymns written and adapted to the Weekly Church Service of the Year.*

318. *Bread of the world, in mercy broken.*
 64. *Brightest and best of the sons of the morning.*
309. *By cool Siloam's shady rill.*
371. *From Greenland's icy mountains.*
293. *God, that madest earth and heaven.*
  1. *Holy, holy, holy, Lord God Almighty.*
159. *Lord of mercy and of might.*
530. *The Son of God goes forth to war.*

HEILIGE SEELENLUST. See SCHEFFLER, JOHANN, and JOSEPH, GEORG.

277. (ANGELUS). 208. (HELFER MEINER ARMEN SEELE).
 38. (CULBACH). 300. (KEINE SCHÖNHEIT HAT DIE WELT).

HELMORE, THOMAS (Kidderminster, 1811–90, London), was educated at Magdalen Hall, Oxford; became curate of St. Michael's and priest-vicar of the Cathedral, Lichfield, 1840; Vice-Principal and Precentor of St. Mark's College, Chelsea, 1842; Master of the Choristers of the Chapel Royal, 1846; and one of the priests-in-ordinary there, 1847. He was one of the pioneers of the revival of the use of the Gregorian Tones in Anglican services. He translated Fétis's *Treatise on Choir and Chorus Singing;* composed music for some of Neale's translations of *Hymns of the Eastern Church;* and published as author or editor—*The Psalter Noted; The Canticles Noted; A Manual of Plain Song; A Brief Directory of Plain Song; The Hymnal Noted; Carols for Christmas; Carols for Easter; St. Mark's College Chaunt Book; The Canticles Accented; A Catechism of Music,* &c.

149. VENI IMMANUEL (arr.).

HEMY, HENRI FREDERICK (Newcastle-on-Tyne, 1818–1888, Hartlepool), was organist of St. Andrew's Roman Catholic Church, Newcastle-on-Tyne, and latterly a professor of music at Tynemouth, and of singing and pianoforte at St. Cuthbert's College, Durham. He compiled in four parts (1864) *Crown of Jesus Music*, which had much popularity in Roman Catholic churches. His *Royal Modern Tutor for the Pianoforte* (1858) was for many years much used by teachers.

697. TYNEMOUTH (ST. CATHERINE).

HENLEY, JOHN (Torquay, 1800–42, Weymouth), entered the Wesleyan ministry in 1824. He was singularly successful in every circuit in which he served. His spirituality and devotion made a deep impression everywhere. When he joined his last circuit in Manchester his health was already impaired; yet he wore himself out in extra labours in visiting and relieving the suffering poor in his neighbourhood. 'For several years he professed to live in the enjoyment of perfect love, and none who knew his walk . . . would be disposed to question the truth of his profession, so apparent were his heavenly-mindedness and entire consecration to his Saviour.'

658. Children of Jerusalem.

HENSLEY, LEWIS, M.A. (London, 1824–1905, near Great Ryburgh, Norfolk), was educated at Trinity College, Cambridge, where, in 1846, he was Senior Wrangler and Smith's Prizeman. For six years he was a Fellow and Tutor of Trinity. Ordained in 1851, he held the curacy of Upton-with-Chalvey, Bucks; then was vicar, in succession, of St. Ippolyts-with-Great Wymondley, and of Hitchin, both in Hertfordshire. For a time he was Rural Dean, and latterly an hon. canon of St. Albans. He died suddenly in a railway train. He published *Hymns for the Sundays after Trinity* (1864); and *Hymns for the Minor Sundays from Advent to Whitsuntide* (1867).

152. Thy Kingdom come, O God.

HERBERT, GEORGE (Montgomery, 1593–1632, Bemerton), belonged to an old English family, and was the younger brother of the soldier-philosopher Lord Herbert of Cherbury. Educated at Westminster and at Trinity College, Cambridge, he numbered among his friends the poets Wotton and Donne, and was esteemed by Bacon. As a young courtier he enjoyed the favour of James I, but in the following reign took holy orders and on April 26, 1630, became rector of Bemerton in Wiltshire, where he spent the remaining three years of his life in the faithful discharge of his duties. His principal work is *The Temple*, singularly attractive in its mingling of the devotional spirit with homely imagery and quaint humour. The same qualities are seen in the hymns by which he is represented here. Love and loyalty to his Mother Church of England are apparent in all his works, as also in his *Life* by a kindred spirit, Izaak Walton. Herbert was a musician, and sang his hymns to the lute or viol.

15. Let all the world in every corner sing.
511. Teach me, my God and King.

HERBERT, PETRUS (d. 1571, Eibenschütz). The place and date of Herbert's birth have not been ascertained. He lived at Fulnek in Moravia, and belonged to the Unity of what were known as the Bohemian Brethren, from which afterwards sprang the Moravian Church. By the Unity Herbert was entrusted with missions to Calvin, the Duke of Würtemberg, the Emperor Maximilian, and other important persons. He helped to compile the Brethren's enlarged hymn-book or *Kirchengeseng* (1566), contributed to it about 90 hymns, some of which are translations from the Bohemian.

> 280. *Now God be with us, for the night is closing.*

HERBST, MARTIN (Rothenbach, 1654–81, Eisleben), attended St. Lorenz School at Nürnberg, studied philosophy and theology at Altdorf, and studied at Jena also. In 1680 he became rector of the Gymnasium at Eisleben, and also pastor of the Church of St. Andreas there, but the plague carried him off in the following year. Zahn attributes four chorales to him, printed with the initials M.H.

> 79. AUS DER TIEFE (HEINLEIN).

HEWLETT, THOMAS, Mus. Bac. (Oxford, 1845–74, Edinburgh), was a pupil of Dr. L. G. Hayne. He took his degree at the early age of fourteen. From 1865 to 1871 he was organist of the Duke of Buccleuch's private chapel at Dalkeith Palace, and for eighteen months (1868–9) of St. Peter's Church, Lutton Place, Edinburgh, holding both posts together. Subsequently, for brief periods, he officiated in St. Mary's Roman Catholic Church, and in Newington Parish Church, Edinburgh. Over his grave in Newington Cemetery the Edinburgh Choral Union erected a monument to his memory, 'in acknowledgement of his musical talent and his great ability as organist of that Society'.

> 429. DALKEITH.

HEWS, GEORGE (Massachusetts, 1806–73, Boston), was, from about 1830, a tenor soloist, teacher of music, organist, and manufacturer of pianos in Boston. He was a prominent figure in the Handel and Haydn Societies of that city.

> 550. HOLLEY.

HICKSON, WILLIAM EDWARD (London, 1803–70, Fairseat, Sevenoaks, Kent), was a boot manufacturer at Smithfield, but retired from business at thirty-seven, to devote himself to literary and philanthropic pursuits. He was ardently desirous of promoting musical culture among the people, and to this end published *The Singing-Master: containing Instructions for teaching Singing in Schools and Families;* and, *The Use of Singing as a Part of the Moral Discipline of Schools.* He was himself a composer of some merit. He acted as a member of the

Royal Commission to inquire into the condition of the hand-loom weavers in Great Britain, and after exhaustive personal inquiries, in addition to signing the general findings of the Commission, published a separate report of great value. Another of his interests was the cause of national education, in which he was a pioneer. He embodied the results of his own close investigation of national school systems in Holland, Belgium, and North Germany, in a book on *Dutch and German Schools*. Others of his publications were: *Part Singing;* and *Time and Faith: an Enquiry into the Data of Ecclesiastical History*. He also edited *The Westminster Review*.

632. *God bless our native land.*

HILES, HENRY, Mus. Doc. (Shrewsbury, 1826–1904, Worthing), was organist at Shrewsbury; Bury; Bishopwearmouth; St.Michael's, Wood Street, and the Blind Asylum, Manchester; Bowden; St. Paul's, Manchester. In 1876 he became lecturer on harmony and composition in Owen's College, Manchester, and in 1879 at Victoria University; in 1893, a professor in Manchester College of Music. He conducted several music societies, and was editor and proprietor of the short-lived *Quarterly Musical Review*. He wrote oratorios, cantatas, anthems, services, and much miscellaneous music; and also a *Grammar of Music*, and works on *Harmony of Sounds; First Lessons in Singing; Part-Writing, or Modern Counterpoint; Harmony, Choral or Contrapuntal*, &c.

718. CHANT IN B FLAT.

HIMMEL, FRIEDRICH HEINRICH (Treuenbriezen, Brandenburg, 1765–1814, Berlin), was intended for the Church, and studied theology at Halle; but his masterly skill as a pianist made King Friedrich Wilhelm II take an interest in him and send him to Italy to study. On his return in 1792 he was appointed court composer at Berlin, and in 1795 court director of music. He was held in high honour as a composer. For his opera *Alessandro* the Russian Emperor gave him 6,000 roubles. His songs were very popular. His masterpiece was an opera *Fanchon*, to a libretto by Kotzebue. He produced, besides operas, an oratorio, *Isacco*, sonatas, a mass, psalms, a *Vater unser*, motets, &c. He visited England in 1801. After 1806 he retired to Pyrmont, and then to Cassel.

352. HIMMEL.

HINTZE, JAKOB (Bernau, Brandenburg, 1622–1702, Berlin), became in 1666 court-musician to the Elector of Brandenburg at Berlin. After Crüger's death, he undertook to edit the twelfth and succeeding editions of the *Praxis Pietatis Melica;* he added a collection of new melodies as an appendix.

129. ALLE MENSCHEN MÜSSEN STERBEN (SCHÖNBERG).

Biographical and Historical Notes

HOLLAND, HENRY SCOTT, D.D., D.Litt. (Underdown, Ledbury, 1847–1918, Oxford), was educated at Eton and Balliol College, Oxford. He became senior Student (Fellow) of Christ Church, and also tutor there. He was ordained in 1872, was Select Preacher at Oxford, 1879–1880, and again, 1894–96; Censor of Christ Church, 1882–4; Honorary Canon of Truro, 1883; Canon of St. Paul's, 1884, and Precentor there, 1886 to 1910; Romanes Lecturer, Oxford, 1908; Professor of Divinity, Oxford, 1910–18. He was one of the founders and most ardent supporters of the Christian Social Union, being passionately interested in social questions, and from 1896, when it was founded, to the end of his life, he edited *The Commonwealth*, the organ of the Union. Into this journal he poured his soul, in a stream of stimulating articles, selections from which, re-published, form five of his books. A lover of music, he did much to raise the musical quality of the services in St. Paul's. He was part-editor of *The English Hymnal* and of *The New Cathedral Psalter*. Among his published works were—*Creed and Character; Logic and Life; Christ or Ecclesiastes; On Behalf of Belief; God's City; Vital Values; A Bundle of Memories*. His memorial in Christ Church Cathedral bears the inscription, 'Invisibilem tanquam videns Deum, Regnum Ejus coeleste fide inconcussâ, spe vividâ, caritate hilari, nunquam non in terrâ praestruebat.' (As beholding God Invisible, he was unceasingly founding on earth His Heavenly Kingdom, in unshaken faith, lively hope, joyous love.)

636. *Judge Eternal, throned in splendour.*

HOLMES, OLIVER WENDELL, M.D., LL.D., D.C.L. (Cambridge, Massachusetts, 1809–94, Boston), son of the Rev. Abiel Holmes, D.D., First Congregational Church, Cambridge, was educated at Phillips Academy, New Hampshire, and at Harvard, where he graduated in Arts and Medicine; he studied in Europe also. In 1838 he was appointed Professor of Anatomy and Physiology in Dartmouth College, and in 1847 accepted the Chair of Anatomy at Harvard, where he continued to teach with high distinction till 1882. A constant contributor to periodical literature, he was the chief founder of *The Atlantic Monthly*, and it was largely his contributions that won it international fame. Essayist, novelist, poet, wit, humorist, humanist, and the raciest of talkers, he became one of the best-known and best-loved men on both sides of the ocean. *The Autocrat of the Breakfast Table; The Professor at the Breakfast Table; The Poet at the Breakfast Table;* and *Over the Teacups* contain his most characteristic writings, the many-sided expression of his brilliant mind and engaging personality. His poetry was mostly of the occasional order, verses thrown off to mark special events. To his broad mind and tender heart the harsh doctrine of orthodoxy in his youth was intolerable, and he ranged himself with the Unitarians; but his sympathies were evangelical. He 'believed more than some and less than others', and liked 'those who believed more, better than those who believed less'. In his later years he fell back for spiritual comfort on the great evangelical hymns, finding in them a strength and satisfying substance which the hymns of his own communion failed to supply.

> 24. *Lord of all being, throned afar.*
> 143. *O Love Divine! that stooped to share.*
> 649. *Thou gracious Power, whose mercy lends.*

HOLST, GUSTAV (THEODORE) (Cheltenham, 1874–   ), of English blood on his mother's side, was of Swedish extraction on his father's; his great-grandfather came to England about 1808. He was originally intended for a career as a pianist, but symptoms of neuritis led to a change of intention, and at the age of seventeen he became organist at Wyck Rissington, Gloucestershire. Educated subsequently at the Royal College of Music, London, he served for five years as trombonist in the Scottish Orchestra, and later in the Carl Rosa Opera Company. This was a fortunate experience, for he is pre-eminently an orchestral composer. In 1903 he became a music master in London and Reading, and in 1919 a teacher of composition in the Royal College of Music; he is a great teacher as well as composer. In 1918 he went, under the education scheme of the Y.M.C.A., to Salonika, Constantinople, and Asia Minor, as musical organizer in army camps. He visited America in 1923, and was Cramb Lecturer in the University of Glasgow, 1925. In faith he is a theosophist. His genius ripened slowly, but he is now one of the most markworthy of composers. His works include *The Planets*, a mammoth suite for full orchestra; *The Hymn of Jesus* (2 choruses and semi-chorus); *Ode to Death*, to Walt Whitman's words; an *Ave Maria* for female chorus; a splendid *Hymn to the Unknown;* five operas; *Songs of the West; A Somerset Rhapsody*, &c.

50. CRANHAM.   180. ESSEX.

HOOD, EDWIN PAXTON (London, 1820–85, Paris), was the son of an able seaman and a domestic servant, both of whom died before he was seven years old. He had scanty education, but made much of his opportunities, and, beginning about twenty to lecture on peace and temperance, he discovered gifts of oratory and popular presentation which led him, in 1852, into the Congregational ministry. He held charges at North Nibley, Islington, Brighton, Islington again, Cavendish Street, Manchester, where he had to resign because of acute political differences with his congregation, he being a strong and outspoken Liberal; and finally, Falcon Square Church, Aldersgate Street, London. For some time he edited *The Eclectic and Congregational Review*. He was in great demand as a popular lecturer, and many books of a popular kind came from his pen. Having sprung from the people, he had many philanthropic interests. To the Hospital for Incurables in particular he devoted unstinting thought and care.

81. *God, who hath made the daisies.*

HOPKINS, EDWARD JOHN, Mus. Doc. (Westminster, 1818–1901, London), 'one of the last and certainly the greatest representative of the old school of English Church musicians', was trained as a child of the Chapel Royal, played services in Westminster Abbey before he was sixteen, and at that age was appointed organist of Mitcham Parish Church. Thereafter he was organist successively of St. Peter's, Islington; St. Luke's, Berwick Street; and (1843–98) the Temple Church. At the Temple he raised the musical service to a high pitch of excellence. He wrote a great deal of Church music of very fine quality—services, anthems, hymn-tunes, organ pieces. 'His music is characterized by chaste melody, by a subtle unobtrusiveness in its rich harmonies, by the purity of its vocal part-writing—how wonderfully melodious and grateful to sing are his inner parts—and above all, his music is hallowed with a devotional fervour which lifts it into a region not far removed from the perfection of sanctified art.' Along with Dr. E. F. Rimbault, he wrote a standard work on *The Organ: its History and Construction.* As musical editor of hymn-books he enjoyed a great reputation. In addition to his own *Temple Choral Service Book*, he edited hymnals for the Wesleyan and the Congregational Churches, the Free Church of Scotland, and the Presbyterian Churches of England and Canada. His degree was conferred on him by the Archbishop of Canterbury in 1882.

37. CHILDREN'S VOICES.	549. ST. HUGH.
363. CHRISTMAS MORN.	524. ST. RAPHAEL.
512. CULFORD.	293. TEMPLE.
301. ELLERS.	573. WILDERSMOUTH.

HOPPER, EDWARD, D.D. (New York, 1818–88, New York), studied at the University and Union Theological Seminary, New York. He was a Presbyterian, and held pastoral charges at Greenville, New York; Sag Harbour on Long Island; and the Church of Sea and Land, New York, where he had many sailors in his congregation. He received his degree from Lafayette College in 1871. His hymns were issued anonymously. He was found to have died in his study in the act of writing lines on Heaven.

706. *Jesus, Saviour, pilot me.*

HOPPS, JOHN PAGE (London, 1834–1912, Shepperton), was educated at the Baptist College, Leicester, but after a two-years' ministry at Hugglescote and Ibstock, Leicestershire, he became colleague to George Dawson, who had also begun as a Baptist minister, but had broken loose from credal restrictions and exercised in the

Church of the Saviour, Birmingham, what was called a 'free' but was virtually a Unitarian ministry. From that time Hopps identified himself with Unitarian views. Between 1860 and 1876, he ministered to congregations of that belief at Sheffield, Dukinfield, and Glasgow; from 1876 to 1892 to the Great Meeting, Leicester; and from 1905 to 1909, to a congregation worshipping first at Little Portland Street Chapel, and then at University Hall, London. He was a vigorous controversialist, in numerous books, pamphlets, and addresses. From 1863 he edited a monthly magazine entitled *The Truthseeker*. He retained much of the evangelical spirit in which he had been trained, and this is evident in many of his hymns. He edited *Hymns for Public Worship in the Home* (1858); *Hymns of Faith and Progress* (1865); *Hymns for Public Worship* (1873); *Hymns, Chants, and Anthems for Public Worship* (1877); *The Children's Hymn Book* (1879); *The Young People's Book of Hymns* (1881); and *Hymns for Special Services*.

> 565. *Father, lead me day by day.*

HORNE, CHARLES SILVESTER, M.A. (Cuckfield, Sussex, 1865–1914, Toronto), son of a Congregational minister who became editor of a local newspaper at Newport, Shropshire, and partner in a printing and bookselling business, was educated at Newport Grammar School, the University of Glasgow, and Mansfield College, Oxford, where he was one of the first small band of students with whom the College was opened in 1886. His reputation as a preacher of unusual power led to his being called, nearly two years before his theological course was finished, to the conspicuous pulpit of Allen Street Church, Kensington. Ordained there in 1889, he fulfilled an influential ministry until, in 1903, he accepted an invitation to take charge of a great institutional church which was being organized in Whitefield's Chapel, Tottenham Court Road. There he spent eleven strenuous and fruitful years. He was chairman of the Congregational Union in 1909; entered Parliament as M.P. for Ipswich in 1910; was elected President of the National Brotherhood Council in 1913; and delivered the Yale Lectures on Preaching in 1914. Soon afterwards, as a vessel on which he had sailed from Niagara was entering Toronto harbour, he fell dead on the deck at his wife's feet. His enthusiastic public spirit and zeal in all good causes, his burning interest in the social problem, and his strong yet winsome personality, made him an admired and beloved leader in his own denomination, and, far beyond it, a power for righteousness.

> 212. *For the might of Thine arm we bless Thee, our God, our fathers' God.*

HORSLEY, WILLIAM, Mus. Bac. (London, 1774–1858, London), was in youth articled to a pianist and composer from whom he received little instruction and much ill-usage. In 1794 he became organist of Ely Chapel, Holborn; in 1802, organist of the Asylum for Female Orphans, in succession to W. H. Callcott, whose daughter he married; in 1812, organist of Belgrave Chapel; and in 1838, organist of the Charterhouse. He was an intimate friend of Mendelssohn. He published five collections of glees, which give him a foremost place among glee-composers; many songs, sonatas, &c.; two collections of psalm and hymn tunes; and some works on theory. He was one of the founders of the Philharmonic Society.

26. BELGRAVE. 105. HORSLEY.

HOSMER, FREDERICK LUCIAN, D.D. (Framingham, Massachusetts, 1840–   ), is descended from James Hosmer of Hawkhurst, Kent, one of the first settlers at Concord in 1635. Educated at Harvard, he entered the Unitarian ministry in 1872, and held charges at Northboro, Mass.; Quincy, Illinois; Cleveland, Ohio; St. Louis; and Berkeley, California, where he now lives in retirement. He was lecturer on hymnody at Harvard in 1908. He has published *The Way of Life; Prayers and Responsive Services for Sunday Schools;* along with W. C. Gannet and J. Vilas Blake, *Unity Hymns and Carols,* 'in which both theology and liturgics were frankly uprooted from a Christian basis and replanted' in another soil; and also with W. C. Gannett, *The Thought of God in Hymns and Poems,* a source-book for subsequent hymn-book editors, containing fifty-six hymns by himself.

331. *O Lord of life, where'er they be.*
153. *'Thy Kingdom come!'—on bended knee.*

HOUSMAN, LAURENCE (Bromsgrove, 1865–   ), is a brother of A. E. Housman, the lyric poet, author of *A Shropshire Lad.* He is an artist, widely known by his imaginative and masterly work as a book illustrator; a poet also, in an ornate and mystical style which is in striking contrast to the severe simplicity and directness of his brother's work. His prose is no less distinguished. He has written many books—religious plays; poems, such as *Green Arras, Mendicant Rhymes, Spikenard;* allegorical tales, like *All Fellows; The Blue Moon;* several notable novels; and, at first anonymously, *An Englishwoman's Love-Letters.* 'Laurence Housman has the heart of compassion for the little ones of the earth, the dumb and the helpless, that ought to be, but is not always, an essential part of the poetry. His is the true Franciscan spirit.'

645. *Father Eternal, Ruler of creation.*

HOW, WILLIAM WALSHAM, D.D. (Shrewsbury, 1823–97, Dhulough Lodge, Leenane, County Mayo, Ireland), son of William Wybergh How, solicitor, was educated at Shrewsbury School and Wadham College, Oxford, and was ordained in 1846. After curacies at Kidderminster and Holy Cross, Shrewsbury, he became rector of

Whittington, 1851; rural dean of Oswestry, 1853; hon. canon of St. Asaph, 1860; rector of St. Andrew's Undershaft, and Bishop Suffragan, titularly of Bedford, but really of East London, 1879; and Bishop of Wakefield, 1888. He was totally without ambition in the worldly sense, declined the offer of the see of Manchester without even mentioning it to his wife, and, later, refused also one of the most distinguished posts in the Anglican Church, the bishopric of Durham, with an income more than double what he then had. He was an unceasing worker, not wasting even odd minutes, and following a rigid method. His broad sympathies and large and genial humanity as well as his apostolic zeal attracted all classes. In London he was known as 'the poor man's bishop', 'the people's bishop', 'the omnibus bishop'. He was a master of the pastoral art, and characteristically had engraved on his pastoral staff a saying of St. Bernard, which was often on his lips, *Pasce verbo, pasce vita* (Feed with the word, feed with the life). In 1854 he collaborated with the Rev. Thomas Baker Morrell in editing a collection of *Psalms and Hymns;* and in 1871 was joint-editor of the S.P.C.K. *Church Hymns*, long the most formidable rival of *Hymns Ancient and Modern*. Its less high type of sacramental doctrine and less assertive churchmanship won favour for it among that large section of the Church of England which the High Church movement had not captured. In 1886 a collected edition of his *Poems and Hymns* was issued. Modern hymnody owes to him some of its richest treasures.

76. *Behold a little Child.*
342. *Bowed low in supplication.*
70. *Come, praise your Lord and Saviour.*
220. *For all the saints who from their labours rest.*
610. *For all Thy love and goodness.*
436. *It is a thing most wonderful.*
62. *'Jesus!' Name of wondrous love.*
238. *Lord, this day Thy children meet.*
675. *O Jesus, strong and pure and true.*
397. *O Jesus, Thou art standing.*
198. *O word of God Incarnate.*
117. *On wings of living light.*
341. *Soldiers of the Cross, arise!*
613. *Summer suns are glowing.*
621. *The year is swiftly waning.*
635. *To Thee, our God, we fly.*
346. *We give Thee but Thine own.*
73. *Who is this, so weak and helpless?*
622. *Winter reigneth o'er the land.*

HOWARD, SAMUEL, Mus. Doc. (London, 1710–82, London), was a chorister of the Chapel Royal under Croft; became organist of St. Clement Danes and of St. Bride's, Fleet Street. He wrote for the theatre and gardens as well as the Church, and composed many songs highly popular in their day.

101. ISLEWORTH.   116, 507. LANCASTER.   403. ST. BRIDE.

HOWE, JULIA WARD, *née* WARD (New York, 1819–1910, Middletown, R. I.), an American poetess and philanthropist, married in 1848 Samuel Gridley Howe, a remarkable man who in his young manhood took part in the Greek War of Independence, and wrote *Historical Sketches of the Greek Revolution*, and who afterwards devoted his life in America to philanthropic causes, especially that of the welfare of the blind, the dumb, and the insane. Whittier, in his poem, 'The Hero', celebrates him as a modern Bayard,

> Walking his round of duty
> Serenely day by day,
> With the strong man's hand of labour
> And childhood's heart of play.

Mrs. Howe was like-minded, passionately interested all her life in social reform. She was an eager advocate of women's suffrage and international peace. As long ago as 1870 she proposed that the women of the world should organize to end war. She was an influential figure on public platforms and often preached in Unitarian and other pulpits. She published three volumes of verse—*Passion Flowers* (1854), *Words for the Hour* (1856), and *Later Lyrics* (1866); and also books on *Sex in Education; Modern Society;* and *Margaret Fuller*.

155. *Mine eyes have seen the glory of the coming of the Lord.*

HOWELLS, WILLIAM, M.B., C.M. (Carmarthen, 1855–   ), is the youngest son of the Rev. William Howells, Principal of Trevecca College from 1865 to 1887, one of the best English preachers Wales ever produced, and a masterly translator of Welsh hymns into English. He studied medicine at the University of Glasgow, where he graduated in 1881. After thirty-nine years of medical service in Scarborough, South Wales, and Liverpool, he retired to Tenby, where he now resides. For sixteen years he was honorary medical attendant of Trevecca Theological College, and for eight years of Brecon Memorial Theological College. Dr. Howells has inherited the gift of his father and of his grand-uncle, the Rev. William Howells of Long Acre Episcopal Church, London, both of whom were effective English versifiers and translators of Welsh hymns; in similar work he has found the solace of a busy professional life.

384. *Onward march, all-conquering Jesus* (tr.).

HUDSON, ROBERT (London, 1732–1815, Eton), was a vocalist and composer. He began his career as a tenor singer at the Gardens of Marylebone and Ranelagh, but his life-work was done in the Church.

He was for a short time assistant organist of St. Mildred's, Bread Street, London; then became vicar-choral of St. Paul's Cathedral; Gentleman of the Chapel Royal; almoner and master of the children of St. Paul's; and music-master of Christ's Hospital. He published services, anthems, hymns, and glees, and edited *The Myrtle, a Collection of New English Songs* (1767).

257. ST. OLAVE.

HUGHES, THOMAS, M.A., Q.C. (Donington Priory, Newbury, Berkshire, 1823–96, Brighton), the son of a country squire, was educated at Rugby under Dr. Arnold, and at Oriel College, Oxford. He went to the Bar in 1848, became a Q.C. in 1869, and a County Court Judge in 1882. For some years he sat in Parliament as a Liberal, first for Lambeth, then for Frome. He was keenly interested in the condition of the poor, and joined Kingsley and Maurice in the movement for the improvement of social conditions which was known as Christian Socialism. In 1870 he went to the United States on a lecturing tour, and ten years later was chiefly instrumental in founding a colony, settled mainly by Englishmen, at Rugby, Morgan County, Tennessee. His famous *Tom Brown's Schooldays* (1856), first published anonymously, was largely a transcript of his own experience and impressions at Rugby under Arnold's great headmastership. It remains the best picture in literature of English public-school life.

531. *O God of truth, whose living word.*

HULL, ELEANOR HENRIETTA (?), was the founder, and since its beginning in 1899 has been the hon. secretary, of the Irish Text Society; she is also a former President of the Irish Literary Society of London, and a member of the Council of the Folklore Society. She studied Old and Middle Irish under Drs. Holgar Pedersen, Kuno Meyer, Standish Hayes O'Grady, and R. Flower. She has published *The Cuchullin Saga in Irish Literature* (1898, in the Grimm Library); *Pagan and Early Christian Ireland; A Text-Book of Irish Literature* (2 vols., 1906–7); *The Poem Book of the Gael* (1912); two books for young people on the Story of Cuchullin and the Saga Tales of the British Isles, from Norse and Icelandic sources; and *A History of Ireland*, which throws fresh light on the social life of the Irish people.

477. *Be Thou my Vision, O Lord of my heart.*

HULLAH, JOHN PYKE, LL.D. (Worcester, 1812–84, London), went early in life to London, and studied under W. Horsley. Later, in Paris, he studied methods of vocal instruction, thus preparing for the great work of his life. He became, in 1837, organist of Croydon Parish Church, and in 1840, instructor of students in the Training College, Battersea. From this time onwards he gained extraordinary popularity as a teacher of vocal music on a system based on Wilhems' of Paris. He was opposed to the tonic sol-fa system. In twenty years, 25,000 persons passed through his classes, and great choirs were trained by him. In 1844 he became Professor of Vocal Music in King's College, London, and also at Queen's and Bedford Colleges; in 1858, organist of the Charterhouse; in 1872, inspector in music of Training Schools. The University of Edinburgh conferred on him in 1876 its doctorate of laws. Louis N. Parker, the dramatist, a student under him, describes his charming individuality. 'First, he was good to look at; always exquisitely groomed; the perfect type of the Pall Mall clubman; always bland, always smiling. . . . Full of old saws and modern instances, he was the first who drew our attention to the fact that music had a history, and he was indefatigable in his efforts to enlarge our knowledge of the art.' Hullah, in 1836, composed music for an opera, *The Village Coquettes*, to the libretto of Dickens. Of his songs, 'The Three Fishers', 'The Storm', and 'O that We Two were Maying', won great popularity. Among his works were Grammars of Vocal Music, Harmony, and Counterpoint: *A History of Modern Music* (1862); *Music in the House* (1877). He edited *The Book of Praise Hymnal*, *The Whole Book of Psalms*, *with Chants*, &c.

439. BENTLEY.

HUNTER, JOHN, D.D. (Aberdeen, 1848–1917, London), was brought up in the Church of Scotland. He left school at thirteen, and was apprenticed to a draper. Under the influence of the Revival of 1859–61, his soul took fire with the passion for divine things, and he felt that his life-work must be the ministry. The Scottish Church was barred to him by the long training required for it, and an opportunity of going to Nottingham Congregational Institute was welcomed. There and at Spring Hill College, Birmingham, he spent five years in preparation for the Congregational ministry. Starting with a somewhat crude but intense evangelical faith, he passed at college through an intellectual rebirth which led him to diverge from the teaching in which he had been trained, chiefly in laying dominant emphasis on the Fatherhood of God, in adopting universalist ideas of future destiny, and in treating religious truth in a broader and more liberal way than was at that time common. In 1871 he became minister of the large and influential congregation of Salem Chapel, York; passed in 1882 to Wycliffe Chapel, Hull; and in 1887 entered upon a powerful ministry in Trinity Church, Glasgow. In 1901 he was persuaded to undertake the pastorate of the almost derelict Weigh House Church, London, but his work there was a disheartening fight against odds, and three years later he accepted a call to return to his Glasgow congregation. A breakdown in health led to his resignation in 1913. Retiring to London, he was able to conduct one service a Sunday in the Æolian Hall, in response to the appeals of a group of affectionate friends, until health finally failed him in 1917. He had an intense desire to raise the standard of public worship, and his pioneer book of *Devotional Services for Public Worship*, by example, inspiration, and suggestion, did much to accomplish this in all the non-episcopal Churches. His *Hymns of Faith and Life* aroused much adverse criticism by the alterations he made, to suit his own ideas, in classic hymns.

460. Dear Master, in whose life I see.

HURST, WILLIAM (Leicester, 1849–), is a business man in Coalville, Leicester, who has been a life-long lover of music. He has given his leisure to musical study, and has made it his pleasure to deputize for organists at need.

316. LEICESTER.

HUTCHESON, CHARLES (Glasgow, 1792–1860, Glasgow), was a Glasgow merchant, and a member of St. George's Parish Church there. Possessing a fine voice and much refinement of taste, he took deep interest in music generally and psalmody in particular, and was an amateur composer. He was one of the founders of the Glasgow Dilettanti Society. He published *Christian Vespers* (Glasgow, 1832), containing hymn-tunes harmonized in three and four parts, with an introductory essay on church music.

451. STRACATHRO.

HUTCHINGS, WILLIAM MEDLEN (Devonport, 1827–76, ?), was for a time a printer and publisher in London. He was a Congregationalist.

659. When mothers of Salem.

HUTTON, LAURA JOSEPHINE (Spridlington, Lincolnshire, 1852–88, Spridlington), was the devoted fellow-worker of her brother Canon Vernon Woolaston Hutton, vicar of Sneinton, Nottingham, and prebendary of Lincoln Cathedral. On his retirement from Sneinton, she went with him to live at Lincoln, and after his death lived at Spridlington rectory, where her brother-in-law was incumbent. After a serious illness she began to write tunes for Mrs. Alexander's *Hymns for Children*, and issued some in 1880 for private circulation. She also edited her brother's *Corn of Wheat*, a book of devotion.

591. ETERNITY.

INGELOW, JEAN (Boston, Lincolnshire, 1820–97, Kensington), was the daughter of a Boston banker; her mother was of Aberdeenshire stock. She lived in the fen country or at Ipswich till about 1863, when she settled in London. Her first venture in verse was *A Rhyming Chronicle of Incidents and Feelings* (1850), published anonymously; but it was not till the first series of her *Poems* was issued in 1860 that her powers attracted notice. In this book she displayed her characteristic qualities—a feeling for Nature and a marked power of description, simplicity, pathos, and both depth and truth of religious feeling. Her poem in this volume on *The High Tide on the Coast of Lincolnshire*, 1571, is one of the best of modern ballads. Her most ambitious poem, *A Story of Doom*, recounts in flowing blank verse the Biblical story of Noah. She wrote successful novels and charming fairy stories also.

144. *And didst Thou love the race that loved not Thee?*

INGEMANN, BERNHARD SEVERIN (Thorkildstrup, Island of Falster, Denmark, 1789–1862, Sorö), son of a Lutheran pastor, was a Danish poet of eminence. He was intended for the legal profession, but forsook law for letters, and became Lector of Danish Language and Literature at the Academy of Sorö, Zealand. In his youth he took part in the defence of Copenhagen against the British. This made him passionate in his patriotism, and a study of the national history, reinforced by the influence of Scott, moved him to write a series of historical romances in prose and poetry—*Valdemar den Store og hans Mænd*, *Valdemar Sojr*, &c.—which have been the most prized books of Danish youth for generations. His stories for children made him almost as much a children's favourite as Hans Andersen. His hymns and songs are sung in every Danish home, and his morning and evening songs in particular are said to have sung the Christian faith into the hearts of many children. On his seventieth birthday the children of Denmark presented him with a beautiful golden horn, ornamented with figures from his poetry. Subscriptions were limited to a halfpenny, and every child in the land contributed, to show gratitude to the man who, next to Hans Andersen, had done most to delight their childhood. In 1825 he published a collection of *High-Mass Hymns*, one for each festival. His collected works were issued in thirty-four volumes in 1851.

214. *Through the night of doubt and sorrow.*

IRELAND, JOHN (Bowden, Cheshire, 1879–   ), came of a Fife family. His father, Alexander Ireland, was for many years editor of *The Manchester Examiner*, and was widely known as the author of *The Booklover's Enchiridion* and other works, and as an intimate friend of Carlyle, Emerson, and Leigh Hunt. John was educated at Leeds Grammar School and the R.C.M., where he was a pupil of Stanford. A severe critic of his own work, he was slow to publish, but as successive works have appeared he has moved steadily forward to a place in the front rank of younger composers. His works include *The Songs of a Wayfarer; The Island Spell; The Forgotten Rite; The Tritons;* a *Pianoforte Sonata in E; London Pieces;*

a Symphonic Rhapsody, Mai Dun; shorter works for the pianoforte; songs, such as a setting of Masefield's *Sea Fever*, &c.

76. LOVE UNKNOWN.

IRONS, HERBERT STEPHEN (Canterbury, 1834–1905, Nottingham), was a chorister in Canterbury Cathedral, of which his father was a lay vicar. He was a nephew of Sir George and of Dr. Stephen Elvey, and was a pupil of the latter at Oxford. He became organist and precentor of St. Columba's College, Rathfarnham; organist and master of the choristers, Southwell Minster; assistant organist, Chester Cathedral; and organist of St. Andrew's, Nottingham. He was organist and accompanist also to the Sacred Harmonic Society in Nottingham.

522. HOPE.	272. ST. COLUMBA.
418. SOUTHWELL.	514. ST. LEONARD.

ISAAK, HEINRICH (*c.* 1460–*c.* 1527), may have been a Netherlander, but more probably was born in Germany. He went to Italy, became organist and chapelmaster of the Church of San Giovanni, Florence; was organist of the Medici Chapel, 1477–93, and musicmaster to the children of Lorenzo the Magnificent. After the death of his patron in 1492 he appears to have remained for some years in Italy, where he enjoyed a great reputation. He was in Vienna in 1496, and from 1497 to 1515 was chapelmaster to the Emperor Maximilian I at Innsbruck. He returned, on his retiral with an annual pension of 150 florins, to Italy, but failed to secure a renewal of favour, notwithstanding a recommendation to Duke Ercole of Ferrara. The last trace history gives of him is at San Lorenzo Maggiore in Rome, 'old, and sick, and without means'. He composed twenty-three masses, motets, chorales, and songs.

284. INNSBRUCK.

JACKSON, THOMAS (? 1715–81, Newark), was organist of St. Mary's, Newark-on-Trent, and master of the song-school there. He composed *Twelve Psalm Tunes and Eighteen Double and Single Chants . . . composed for four voices* (1780).

507. JACKSON.

JACKSON, WILLIAM (Masham, Yorkshire, 1815–66, Bradford), known as Jackson of Masham to distinguish him from Jackson of Exeter, composer of 'Jackson's Te Deum', was self-taught in music. For a time he was a tallow-chandler in Masham, but the passion for music was in his blood; he built organs, learned to play almost every instrument, mastered harmony and counterpoint by studying books, and became an organist in his native town. In 1840 he won the first prize for a glee, *Sisters of the Sea*, in a competition organized by the Huddersfield Glee Club. In 1852 he began business as a music-seller in Bradford, acting at the same time as organist, first of St. John's Church, then of Horton Chapel. He was also conductor of the Bradford (male voice) Choral Union, and chorus-master of the Bradford Festivals of 1853, '56, and '59. He wrote two oratorios, *The Deliverance of Israel from Babylon*, and *Isaiah;* two cantatas, *The Year*, and *The Praise of Music;* and church services, anthems, &c. He harmonized *The Bradford Tune Book* (with Samuel Smith) and *Congregational Psalmody* (1863), and published *A Manual of Singing*.

283. EVENING HYMN.

JEBOULT, HAROLD ARTHUR (Taunton, 1871–1925, Taunton), a pupil of Dr. Albert Ham (now organist of Toronto Cathedral), was organist and choirmaster of Holy Trinity Church, Taunton, from 1889 to 1897, and from 1897 till his death, of St. Mary Magdalene, in the same town. He published settings of the Canticles, part songs, numerous organ pieces, and a book on *Somerset Composers, Musicians, and Music*, in the Somerset Folk Series.

426. ST. MARY MAGDALENE.

JENKINS, DAVID, Mus. Bac. (Trecastell, Brecon, 1849–1915, Aberystwyth), was at first self-taught, but, later, studied under Dr. Joseph Parry, and graduated at Cambridge, 1878. Appointed in 1899 Lecturer in Music (Professor a few years afterwards) and head of the new Department of Music in the University College of Wales, Aberystwyth, he held that post till his death. For many years he acted as precentor to the English Presbyterian Church at Aberystwyth. He was for long a prominent figure at the National and other Eisteddfodau, first as a competitor, and later as adjudicator and as composer, 'more of his works having been performed at the National Eisteddfod concerts than any other Welsh composer's'. He had high ideals of congregational singing and did much to raise congregational taste in worship-song. Among his published compositions were: cantatas (*A Psalm of Life, Llyn y Morwynion*); oratorios (*David and Saul, Dewi Sant, Job*); an opera (*The Enchanted Isle*), songs, part-songs, anthems, and hymn-tunes (*Gemau Mawl*).

684. PENLAN.   464. LLANLLYFNI (arr.).

JENKINS, WILLIAM VAUGHAN (Bristol, 1868–1920, Bitton), was educated at Bristol Grammar School, and became a chartered accountant. He became a communicant under Dr. Richard Glover, and, later, was a member of Dr. Arnold Thomas's congregation, in connexion with which he took an active part in mission work. He was deeply interested in music, and was an experienced choir leader. In his later years he worked with the vicars of Bitton and Oldham Common, in the district in which he resided. He was a leader in the Adult School Movement in Bristol district, and a member of the

National Council. He was one of the compilers of *The Fellowship Hymn Book* and of the *Supplement* to it, and contributed two hymns. A collection of his writings, under the title *Grave and Gay*, was published after his death.

325. *O God of Love, to Thee we bow.*

JENNER, HENRY LASCELLES, D.D., LL.B., (Chislehurst, Kent, 1820–98, Preston-next-Wingham), son of the Right Hon. Sir Herbert Jenner (afterwards Jenner-Fust), Dean of the Arches, was educated at Harrow and Trinity Hall, Cambridge. Ordained in 1843, he was curate successively at Chevening, Kent; St. Columb, Cornwall; Antony, Cornwall; Leigh, Essex; Brasted, Kent. He became vicar of Preston-next-Wingham, near Sandwich, Kent, in 1854; was consecrated first Bishop of Dunedin, New Zealand, 1866; but in 1870 returned to his living at Preston, and resigned his bishopric in the following year. He was one of the Cambridge group who revived interest in ecclesiology, ancient hymnology, plainsong, &c.

236. QUAM DILECTA.

JONES, EDITH. Of this author no details are available.

630. *Father, who art alone.*

JOHN, ST., OF DAMASCUS (eighth century), Greek theologian and hymn-writer of the Eastern Church, was born at Damascus, and educated by a learned Italian monk named Cosmas. He and his foster-brother Cosmas the younger (also a hymn-writer and styled the 'Methodist'), retired to the Monastery of St. Sabas near Jerusalem. John was ordained priest late in life, and died at a very advanced age. His theological works include treatises in defence of the orthodox faith, and orations in favour of image-worship, which had been condemned by the Emperor Leo (the Isaurian). His fame as a hymn-writer mainly rests on his 'canons'. The canon, in Greek hymnology, was a series of odes, usually eight, sometimes nine, threaded on an acrostic written at the opening of the first of them, and usually founded on one of the canticles of Holy Scripture. John wrote a number of these and arranged them to music, the best known being the Easter canon or 'Golden Canon' from which the following hymn is taken.

123. *The day of resurrection.*

JOHNSON, SAMUEL, M.A. (Salem, Massachusetts, 1822–82, North Andover, Mass.), studied at Harvard and Cambridge Divinity School. He collaborated with Samuel Longfellow (q.v.) in producing *A Book of Hymns* (1846), and *Hymns of the Spirit* (1864). His contributions to these were less numerous than Longfellow's but not less meritorious. His radical theology made him unwilling to submit to any credal fetters, and in 1853 he formed a Free Church at Lynn, Mass.; there he remained till 1870. He was never connected with any denomination, but associated mainly with Unitarians. He was a man of charming modesty and deep spirituality. An active reformer, he took a manly and effective part in the anti-slavery movement. He was an ardent student, especially of oriental subjects, in which he was deeply learned. His chief work was one embodying great research, on *Oriental Religions, and their Relation to Universal Religion*. Besides many essays on religious, moral, political, and aesthetic subjects, he published a treatise on *The Worship of Jesus, in its Past and Present Aspects* (1868).

> 209. *City of God, how broad and far.*

JONES, GRIFFITH HUGH (GUTYN ARFON), (Ty Du, Llanberis, 1849–1919, Rhiwddolion), was brought up under the ministry of the Rev. John Roberts (Ieuan Gwyllt) at Capel Goch, Llanberis, his father being precentor in the church of that famous founder of the hymn-festival and writer of hymn-tunes. At the age of twenty he became a teacher in Rhiwddolion Elementary School, on the hills between Bettws-y-Coed and Dolwyddelen, and there he laboured for fifty years. He wrote poems, tunes, and anthems. An enthusiastic musician from his youth, he was appointed precentor at Capel Goch as assistant to his father at the age of 13, and in his manhood toiled indefatigably in Arvon, holding musical classes in various centres, walking many miles over the mountains each winter to train country choirs, conduct brass bands, and adjudicate at Eisteddfodau. A short biography of him, with a collection of his poetic and musical compositions, was published by his son, Owen Arfon Jones of Conway.

> 161. LLEF.

JONES, JOHN (TALYSARN) (Tan-y-castell, Dolwyddelen, Carnarvonshire, 1797–1857, Talysarn), received no schooling, but learned to read at home, and had some teaching in music from a local harper. Owing to his father's death, he began work as a quarryman at an early age, and became manager and latterly part-proprietor of a quarry at Tal-y-sarn. He had considerable natural gifts, and used them to such good effect in preaching on Sundays in various parts of the country that pressure was brought to bear on him to devote himself entirely to the work of the ministry. In 1829 he was ordained by the Welsh Calvinistic Methodist (Presbyterian) Church, and gave up his trade. He was a powerful pulpit force, a very independent thinker, and more than any one else was instrumental in breaking the tyranny of the hyper-Calvinists. Endowed with a strong deep voice of unusual compass, and a personality of almost formidable strength, he was one of the most remarkable orators the Welsh pulpit has produced. His open-air congregations often ran into many thousands. He had musical gifts also, and composed a number of hymn-tunes which are still commonly sung in Wales.

464. LLANLLYFNI.   502. TAN-Y-CASTELL.

JONES, WILLIAM (Lowick, Northamptonshire, 1726–1800, Hollingbourne), was educated at the Charterhouse and University College, Oxford. He became vicar of Bethersden, Kent, 1764; and, in succession, rector of Pluckley, Kent; rector of Paston, Northants; then perpetual curate of Nayland, Suffolk, from which he came to be known as Jones of Nayland; and, two years before his death, rector of Hollingbourne, Kent. A man of great and various accomplishment, he published many theological (High Church), philosophical and scientific works. A musician also of great ability, he published *A Treatise on the Art of Music* (1784); and *Ten Church Pieces for the Organ, with Four Anthems in Score* (1789). He established *The British Critic* in 1793.

483. NEWINGTON.

JOSEPH, ST. (known as the Hymnographer), (Sicily, *c.* 800–883, ?), spent most of his life in the East. He embraced the monastic life at Thessalonica, and went thence to Constantinople, but during the iconoclastic persecution fled to Rome, was captured by pirates, and remained for many years a slave in Crete. Returning to Constantinople he established a monastery, and by the favour of the Empress Theodora was made keeper of the sacred vessels in the Great Church of that city. He was more than once banished owing to his defence of image-worship. A voluminous hymn-writer, he is reported to have composed as many as a thousand canons.

377. *O happy band of pilgrims.*

JOSEPH, or JOSEPHI, GEORG (*c.* 1657), was a musician in the service of the Prince Bishop of Breslau. He edited the music of Scheffler's *Heilige Seelenlust, oder Geistliche Hirtenlieder der in ihren Jesum verliebten Psyche*, three books (Breslau, 1657). Of 123 tunes in these books, 107 are by Joseph; of 32 in a fourth book, subsequently published, 30 were his; and of 50 in a fifth book, 48 were by him—185 in all. Doubtless many of these were adaptations from secular melodies.

277. ANGELUS.   301. KEINE SCHÖNHEIT HAT DIE WELT.

JOWETT, JOSEPH (?   1784–1856,   ?), was the rector of Silk Willoughby, Lincolnshire. He compiled *Lyra Sacra, Select Extracts from the Cathedral Music of the Church of England, for 1, 2, 3, and 4 voices* (London, 1825); and *A Manual of Parochial*

Psalmody, containing 142 Psalm and Hymn Tunes, by various authors (London, 1832).

233. KERRY.   294. THANET.

KEBLE, JOHN, M.A. (Fairford, 1792–1866, Bournemouth), was first educated by his father, the vicar of Coln St. Aldywn, entered Corpus Christi College, Oxford, at fourteen, and after a career of great brilliance, won, at nineteen, the coveted distinction of a fellowship of Oriel. He spent nine years at Oxford as tutor and examiner, but having no ambition beyond that of being a faithful parish priest, left Oxford in 1823, and spent the next thirteen years as a curate in Gloucestershire, practically without remuneration, in order to be with his father in his declining years. The influence of his rare and saintly spirit remained strong in Oxford long after he had left it. In 1827, with diffidence, and only at the instance of friends to whom he had from time to time shown them, he published anonymously the poems of *The Christian Year, or, Thoughts in Verse for the Sundays and Holy Days throughout the Year*. His own plan had been 'to go on improving the series all his life, and leave it to come out, if judged useful, only when he should be fairly out of the way'. The book at once stirred deep interest by the purity and delicacy of its poetic feeling and its apostolic spirituality; and when the Tractarian Movement made Keble known and attracted people to his ideals, it won the hearts of the educated and refined as no other book of sacred poetry has ever done. After he became vicar of Hursley, near Winchester, in 1833, the profits from the book enabled him to rebuild the parish church, and his friends, to show their veneration and love for him, filled all its windows with stained glass. In 1833 he was appointed Professor of Poetry at Oxford, and his published *Prelections on Poetry*, delivered from that Chair, are remarkable alike for their literary judgements and their exquisite Latinity. The year 1833 also saw the Oxford Movement begin. A sermon of Keble's on National Apostasy was its real inspiration. He became one of its triumvirate of leaders, the others being Newman and Pusey. Some of the most important of the *Tracts for the Times* were written by him, inculcating 'deep submission to authority, implicit reverence for Catholic tradition, firm belief in the divine prerogative of the priesthood, the real nature of the sacraments, and the danger of independent speculation'. The Anglican Church had an invincible hold on Keble, and he remained steadfastly loyal to it when Newman and others left it for Rome. A second volume of poems, *Lyra Innocentium* (1846), was too deeply tinctured by his High Church ideas to make the same universal appeal as the first. His *Psalter, or Psalms of David in English Verse* found little favour. He wrote a *Life of Bishop Wilson*, author of the *Sacra Privata;* edited *Hooker's* Works; and his *Letters of Spiritual Counsel*, published after his death, are justly prized. His *Miscellaneous Poems*, including forty-five hymns contributed to *Lyra Apostolica,* and twelve volumes of parochial sermons, were also issued posthumously.

> 478. *Blest are the pure in heart.*
> 310. *Gracious Saviour, gentle Shepherd.*
> 281. *Hail, gladdening Light.*
> 611. *Lord, in Thy Name Thy servants plead.*
> 259. *O timely happy, timely wise.*
> 292. *Sun of my soul, Thou Saviour dear.*
>   8. *There is a book, who runs may read.*
> 181. *When God of old came down from heaven.*

KELLY, THOMAS (Kellyville, Athy, Queen's County, Ireland, 1769–1854, Dublin), the son of an Irish judge, was educated at Trinity College, Dublin, and intended for the Bar. Coming, however, under strong evangelical influences, through reading the works of Romaine, which deeply influenced Newman also, he resolved to devote his life to religious work, and was episcopally ordained in 1792. He was an intimate of Walter Shirley, and his sympathies were wholly with the evangelical movement. The Archbishop of Dublin (Dr. Fowler), disapproving of his 'methodistical' activities, inhibited him and Rowland Hill from preaching in his diocese. Thereupon Kelly embarked upon an independent course, seceded from the Episcopal Church, founded a new sect, now extinct, and, being a man of means, built places of worship at Athy, Portarlington, Wexford, and other places. He was a magnetic preacher, a man of great and various learning, and of large and humble mind. His abounding liberality made him beloved of the poor of Dublin, and indeed of the whole country during the year of famine. One man is said to have cheered his wife in a time of great trouble by saying, 'Hould up, Bridget, bedad; there's always Misther Kelly to pull us out of the bog afther we've sunk for the last time.' He was the fast friend of every worthy beneficent and religious cause. His *Hymns on Various Passages of Scripture* (1804) went through several editions, with increasing numbers of hymns included until the 1853 edition contained 765. His musical knowledge and skill enabled him to publish in 1815 a companion volume containing tunes composed by himself, suited to every kind of metre in the hymnal; some of them are original and attractive. Nearly 140 of his hymns are still in common use.

> 134. *Look, ye saints! the sight is glorious.*
> 298. *Of Thy love some gracious token.*
> 131. *The Head that once was crowned with thorns.*
> 120. *The Lord is risen indeed.*
> 109. *We sing the praise of Him who died.*

KEN, THOMAS (Little Berkhampstead, Herts., 1637–1711, Longleat, Somersetshire), belonged to a Somersetshire family. His maternal grandfather was the poet John Chalkhill, a friend of Spenser, and his step-sister Anne married Izaak Walton. Educated at Winchester and New College, Oxford, he displayed among other gifts an early aptitude for music. He held several livings, among them that of Brighstone (Brixton), Isle of Wight, where the hymns by which he is best known were written. Returning to Winchester in 1666 as a Fellow of the College, he prepared his *Manual of Prayers* for the scholars there. Ken was noted throughout his life for strength of conviction and fidelity to conscience. Appointed in 1679 chaplain to the Princess Mary at the Hague, he incurred her husband's displeasure through his outspokenness, and returned to England. Holding a similar post at the Court of Charles II, his firm refusal to give the use of his house to Nell Gwynne, the King's mistress, is said to have moved the lax but good-natured monarch to appoint him Bishop of Bath and Wells. In the following reign, true to his colours, he was one of the seven bishops sent to the Tower for refusing to read the Declaration; while at the Revolution he was deprived of his see for failure to take the oath of allegiance to the new Sovereign. He was given a home by his friend Lord Weymouth at Longleat, where he spent the remainder of his days. Macaulay's estimate of him is not undeserved—'His moral character seems to approach, as near as human infirmity permits, to the ideal perfection of Christian virtue.' His *Hymns and Poems for the Holy Days and Festivals of the Church* were much prized by Keble, who was probably indebted to them for the idea of his *Christian Year*.

> 291. *All praise to Thee, my God, this night.*
> 256. *Awake, my soul, and with the sun.*

KENNEDY, BENJAMIN HALL, D.D., LL.D. (Summerhill, Birmingham, 1804–89, Torquay), was educated at King Edward's School, Birmingham; at Shrewsbury School, where Darwin was a fellow-pupil, and where he won the Porson Prize for iambics at Cambridge, the only schoolboy who ever did so; and at St. John's College, Cambridge. He had a career of extraordinary brilliance, and became a Fellow and classical lecturer of his college. Ordained in 1829, he taught for a time at Harrow, then, in 1836, entered upon his great head-mastership at Shrewsbury, during which he raised the school to a fame without parallel for classical scholarship. He taught and inspired some of the greatest of English masters of classical learning, like H. A. J. Munro and J. E. B. Mayor. He was created a D.D. in 1836 by royal mandate; in 1843 became a prebendary of Lichfield; and in 1861 Select Preacher at Cambridge. In 1866 he accepted the living of West Felton, near Oswestry; in 1867 the Professorship of Greek at Cambridge, with a canonry of Ely, where he came to be greatly beloved. From 1870 to 1880 he was a member of the New Testament Revision Company. In 1880 he had the unique honour of being elected to an ordinary fellowship of St. John's for the second time, after fifty-eight years. He was a man of brilliant scholarship and vast and accurate learning, a telling speaker, and 'an original Latin poet'. In addition to many works of classical learning, he published *The Psalter, or Psalms of David in English Verse; Between Whiles, or Wayside Amusements of a Working Life; Occasional Sermons*, &c.

192. *Spirit of Grace, Thou Light of life* (tr.).

KETHE, WILLIAM, is said to have been a native of Scotland, but neither the place nor the date of his birth is known. During the Marian persecution of 1555–8 he lived in exile in Frankfort and Geneva, and was afterwards employed as an envoy from Geneva to the other English-speaking congregations on the Continent. When the English exiles left Geneva in 1559, Kethe may have been one of the few left behind to 'finish the Bible and the psalms both in metre and prose'. He was chaplain to the forces under the Earl of Warwick in 1563 and again in 1569, and for some time held the living of Childe Okeford in Dorsetshire. He died probably about the end of the century. Kethe is described as 'no unready rhymer', and is the author of some popular religious ballads. Twenty-five of his psalm versions are included in the Anglo-Genevan Psalter of 1561, and all of these were adopted in the Scottish Psalter of 1564–5. The only one transferred to the later Scottish Psalter of 1650 is the well-known version of Psalm c.

229. *All people that on earth do dwell.*

KING, ROBERT, Mus. Bac. (*Floruit* 1684–1711), graduated at St. Catharine's College, Cambridge, in 1696. He was a member of the band of William and Mary, and also of Queen Anne. At Christmas, 1689, a licence was granted him to establish a concert. Otherwise, apart from the fact that he was still living in 1711, nothing is known of him except from his works. Many of his songs appear in *Choice Ayres, Songs and Dialogues* (1684); *Comes Amoris* (1687–93); *The Banquet of Music* (1688–92); *The Gentleman's Journal* (1692–4); and *Thesaurus Musicus* (1695–6). A collection of twenty-four songs by him, engraven on copper, was published under the title, *Songs for One, Two, and Three Voices, composed to a Thorough Bass for ye Organ or Harpsichord.*

432. DAVID'S HARP.

KINGSLEY, CHARLES, M.A. (Holne Vicarage, Devonshire, 1819–75, Eversley, Hampshire), son of a country gentleman who became vicar of Clovelly, Devonshire, and rector of St. Luke's, Chelsea, was educated at Clifton, where he saw the Bristol Riots, which made on his sensitive nature an ineffaceable impression; at Helston, under Derwent Coleridge; at King's College, London, and Magdalene College, Cambridge. Ordained in 1842, he became curate of Eversley, on the borders of Windsor Forest, and in 1844 rector. He was a chivalrous friend of the poor. A friendship with F. D. Maurice intensified and gave direction to his social sympathies; he joined the circle, including Stanley, J. A. Froude, and Tom Hughes, which endeavoured to turn the Socialist movement, then beginning, into a Christian direction. In none but the loosest sense was any of them a socialist, but when Kingsley published his two social novels, *Yeast* and *Alton Locke*, violent prejudice was aroused against his supposed sympathy with revolutionary ideas, and the Bishop of London inhibited him from preaching within his diocese. He proved the prejudice groundless, and in 1859 was appointed chaplain to the Queen; in 1860, Professor of Modern History at Cambridge; in 1869, a canon of Chester; and in 1873, a canon of Westminster. Of his copious published works, his two chief historical novels, *Hypatia* and *Westward Ho*, are brilliant achievements, full of energetic movement, vivacity, and zest; his songs give him a place among the true poets, by their directness, simplicity, and emotional quality; and his descriptions of nature, in vivid and graphic prose, rank him high among nature-writers. He was no historian, however; nor was he a controversialist; his encounter with Newman, which evoked the overwhelming rejoinder of the *Apologia pro Vita sua*, proved him no match in dialectic for that potent antagonist. His judgement was ill-balanced; he was swayed by imagination and emotion. But he was a courageous idealist, 'a joyous knight-errant of God, thirsting for labour and strife'. Andrew Lang, describing him as 'this really great and noble and manly and blundering genius', says, 'The truth is that we should read Kingsley; we must not criticize him. We must accept him and be glad of him, as we accept a windy, sunny autumn day—beautiful and blusterous—to be enjoyed and struggled with. He did his best, the best he knew, and it is all on the side of manliness, courage, kindness.'

351. *From Thee all skill and science flow.*

KIPLING, RUDYARD (Bombay, 1865–   ), son of John Lockwood Kipling, C.I.E., was educated at the United Services College, Westward Ho, North Devon, and became a journalist in India. He was assistant editor of *The Civil and Military Gazette* and of *The Pioneer*, Allahabad, from 1882 to 1889. In these papers the first stories were published which, issued at Allahabad in shilling volumes—*Soldiers Three; Wee Willie Winkie; In Black and White*, &c.—announced that a new star of magnitude and brilliance was rising. Republished in this country, they made 'the man from nowhere' famous. They revealed a born story-teller, with a style of his own, a distinctive humour and power of character-drawing, working in fields in which he had no competitor, as an interpreter of India to the West and of the common soldier to the Empire that employed him. Since then he has published many books that have placed him in the first rank of living writers—*Plain Tales from the Hills; Life's Handicap; The Day's Work; Kim; Captains Courageous*, &c.; *From Sea to Sea*, embodying his observations during his early years of travel and residence in the United States; *The Jungle Books; Just-So Stories; Puck of Pook's Hill; Rewards and Fairies*, which have made him beloved of all children. It is in his verse that he reaches his highest level. He is the unofficial Poet Laureate of the Empire, a passionate patriot, an extoller of the virile virtues of clean living and manly duty and cheerfulness and stoic endurance, and in his highest moments, as in *Recessional* and *The Children's Song*, a singer of the faith that has made Britain great.

> 637. *God of our fathers, known of old.*
> 647. *Land of our birth, we pledge to thee.*

KIRBYE, GEORGE (? *c.* 1560–1634, Bury St. Edmunds), was probably a native of Bury St. Edmunds, where his life was spent. As he was, after John Farmer, the chief contributor of settings of tunes to Este's *Whole Book of Psalms*, published in 1592, and as Este in his preface says that he 'intreated the help' of such musicians as he knew to be 'expert in the Arte', the fact that his reputation was then already made suggests that he must have been born about 1560. He appears to have been for a time music-master in the household of Sir Robert Jermyn of Rushbrook, Bury St. Edmunds, and in his later years is believed to have been a churchwarden of St. Mary's Church in that town. He published in 1597 *The First Set of English Madrigals, to 4, 5 and 6 voyces*, and a madrigal by him, for six voices, entitled *Bright Phoebus*, appeared in *The Triumphs of Oriana* in 1601. He was one of the best madrigal-writers of his time.

> 385. WINCHESTER (Faux-bourdon).

KIRKLAND, PATRICK MILLER (Hamilton, 1857–   ), studied at Glasgow University and at the Theological Hall of the United Presbyterian Church, in Edinburgh. For a time he was assistant to the Rev. John Edmond, D.D., of Highbury, London. Appointed minister-in-charge at West Kirby in the Presbytery of Liverpool, in 1885, he was ordained there in 1887, and ministered continuously to the same charge until his retiral in 1927.

> 127. *Jesus, Lord, Redeemer.*

KIRKPATRICK, WILLIAM JAMES (Duncannon, Pennsylvania, 1838–1921, Germantown, Philadelphia), was educated at the common schools and studied music while learning his trade of carpenter at Philadelphia. He associated himself there with the Methodist Episcopal Church. In 1858 he began his editorial work by assisting A. S. Jenks in collecting materials of camp-meeting songs for *Devotional Melodies*. He engaged in business, but his active interest in Church and Sunday-School work led him to begin the composition of Gospel songs. Some forty-seven books were compiled by him in conjunction with J. R. Sweney, and after his colleague's death he published some forty more. The aggregate sales of these books ran into millions. For his own and other collections he composed many tunes.

657. CRADLE SONG.

KNAPP, ALBERT (Tübingen, 1798–1864, Stuttgart), graduated at the University of his native city, and studied theology at the Theological College there and at the Seminary at Maulbronn. In 1820 he became Lutheran pastor at Feuerbach, then at Gaisburg, both near Stuttgart, in the neighbourhood of which his life was spent. In 1825 he became diaconus at Sulz on the Neckar, and pastor of Holzhausen; in 1831, archidiaconus at Kuchheim-unter-Teck; in 1836, diaconus of the Hospitalkirche, Stuttgart; in the following year, archidiaconus of the Stiftskirche there; and finally Stadtspfarrer at St. Leonhard's Church, there also. A lyric poet, he takes very high rank as a hymn-writer, and he was a great hymnologist also. His *Christoterpe*, an annual which he issued from 1833 to 1853, contained many hymns by himself and others. The *Evangelischer Liederschatz* which he compiled was the most elaborate and comprehensive German hymn collection of modern times. The first edition (1837) contained 3,590 hymns, and the third contained 3,130.

308. O Father, Thou who hast created all.

KNAPP, WILLIAM (Wareham, 1698–1768, Poole), is said to have been the son of a German. He is referred to as ' a country psalm-singer', and is believed to have been organist both at Wareham and at Poole. He was certainly an accomplished musician, for the tune by which he is known is one of the best congregational tunes ever written. In 1738 he published *A Sett of New Psalms and Anthems in four parts . . . and an Introduction to Psalmody after a plain and familiar manner;* and in 1753 *New Church Melody, a sett of Anthems, Psalms and Hymns, in four parts, with an Imploration wrote by Charles I. during his captivity in Carisbrooke Castle.* For thirty-nine years he was parish clerk of St. James's, Poole. His occupancy of this office led to his being referred to, along with the sexton of that parish, in *An Ejaculation* by one H. Price of Poole, in *The London Magazine* for 1742:

> From pounce and paper, ink and pen,
>   Save me, O Lord, I pray;
> From Pope and Swift and such-like men,
>   And Cibber's annual lay;
> From doctors' bills and lawyers' fees,
>   From ague, gout and trap;
> And what is ten times worse than these,
>   George Savage and Will Knapp.

253, 607. WAREHAM.

KNECHT, Justin Heinrich (Biberach, Swabia, 1752–1817, Biberach), studied under Krämer, organist in his native town, and at the college of the convent of Esslingen, learning to play flute, oboe, cor, trumpet, and violin, as well as the organ. He was recalled to Biberach to undertake the Professorship of Belles Lettres, but in 1792 relinquished it to undertake the more congenial duty of director of music for the town. In 1807 he removed to Stuttgart, to conduct the court and theatre orchestra there; but that position demanded qualifications higher than he possessed, and the consequent intrigues against him made it so uncomfortable that after ten years he was glad to return to his old post at Biberach. As an organist he had no rival but Vogler, but his compositions are commonplace. He wrote many theoretic works and books on instruction, but his most valuable production was the *Würtemberg Choralbuch*, which he edited along with J. F. Christmann, and to which he contributed ninety-seven tunes of his own composition.

577. KNECHT.   450. RAVENNA.

KNOLLIS, Francis Minden, D.D. (Penn, Bucks., 1815–63, Bournemouth), studied at Magdalen College, Oxford. Ordained in 1838, he was for a time a Fellow of his college; then rector of Congerstone, Leicestershire; then, from 1856, incumbent of Fitzhead, Taunton, a charge of which the gross income was £90 per annum; during this time he was also chaplain to Lord Ribblesdale. His published works were—*A Wreath for the Altar; A Garland for the School, or, Sacred Verses for Sunday Scholars* (1854); and *Lays for the Sanctuary and Other Poems* (1867).

590. *There is no night in heaven.*

KOCHER, Conrad, Ph.D. (Ditzingen, Würtemberg, 1786–1872, Stuttgart), was intended for the teaching profession, and at seventeen went as a tutor to St. Petersburg; but the impression made on him by hearing there the music of Haydn and Mozart determined him to devote himself to a musical career. After studying in the Russian capital, he returned to Germany and published compositions of such promise that means were found by the publisher Cotta to enable him to proceed to Italy. What he learned there, particularly of the work of Palestrina, made him an enthusiast for church choral music. On his return to Germany, he set himself to improve church music by popularizing choral singing. From 1827 to 1865 he was organist of the Stiftskirche, Stuttgart, and a school of sacred song (Gesangvereins Liederkranz) founded by him in that city started a movement which spread throughout Würtemberg. In 1852 Tübingen University gave him his degree. He published a large collection of chorales under the title *Zionsharfe* (1854–5); an oratorio, *Der Tod Abels;* several operas, sonatas, &c.

63. DIX.

397

KÖNIG, JOHANN BALTHASAR (1691–1758), was director of the music in several churches in Frankfurt-am-Main. He is best known as editor of the most comprehensive chorale-book of the eighteenth century, *Harmonischer Lieder Schatz, oder Allgemeines evangelisches Choralbuch* (Frankfurt, 1738). This collection contains 1,940 tunes, including those to the French Protestant psalms. In these, however, the original variety of rhythm is destroyed, and the reduction of the tunes to uniformity of pattern by making their notes of equal length seriously qualifies the value of the work.

190, 551. FRANCONIA.

LAHEE, HENRY (Chelsea, 1826–1912, London), after studying under Sterndale Bennett, Sir John Goss, and Cipriani Potter, became organist of Holy Trinity Church, Brompton, where he remained from 1847 till 1874. Thereafter he resided at Croydon. For years he was a successful pianist and concert-giver. He produced several cantatas, and numerous madrigals, glees, and part-songs which proved very popular. Several anthems also were written by him, and while at Brompton he compiled *One Hundred Hymn Tunes*, for use along with a collection of hymns edited by the Rev. W. J. Irons, D.D.

617. NATIVITY.

LAMB, JAMES (Perth, 1835–1904, Old Kilpatrick), studied music during his Arts course at Edinburgh University. He became a minister of the United Presbyterian Church at Old Kilpatrick, Dumbartonshire, in 1867, and spent the rest of his life there. He was clerk to the committee that prepared *The Presbyterian Hymnal* and *The Presbyterian Psalter* for the United Presbyterian Church, and also a member of the music committee of the first *Church Hymnary* (1898).

362. INVERMAY.

LAMBERT, N. Of this writer nothing is known.

510. *Teach me, O Lord, to follow Him who trod.*

LAMPE, JOHANN FRIEDRICH (Saxony, 1703–51, Edinburgh), came to England at twenty-one years of age, as a bassoon player at the opera. He composed much operatic music and many single songs. He was a member of the band that performed Handel's operas. At first he was a Deist, but he came under the influence of the Wesleys, particularly of Charles, who often wrote of him with affection and composed a hymn on his death. In a hymn by Charles 'For a Musician', this verse, evidently intended for Lampe, occurs :

> With Tubal's wretched sons no more
> I prostitute my sacred powers,
>   To please the fiends beneath;
> Or modulate the wanton lay,
> Or smooth with music's hand the way
>   To everlasting death.

398

Many tunes which were long in use among the Methodists were composed by Lampe, in a florid style which commended them to the taste of that period notwithstanding abundant grace-notes, shakes, and broken time. In 1748-9 he spent some time in Dublin, and in 1750 accepted an engagement in the Theatre Royal, Edinburgh. There, a year later, he died, and was buried in the Canongate Churchyard. He set to music Charles Wesley's *Hymns on the Great Festivals* (1746). J. A. Fuller Maitland says of him that 'in spite of his satirical vein . . . he managed to endear himself to the best musicians of his time'.

225. KENT.

LANGRAN, JAMES, Mus. Bac. (London, 1835-1909, London), was a pupil of J. B. Calkin and Sir J. F. Bridge. He was organist of St. Michael's, Wood Green; Holy Trinity, Tottenham; and All Hallows (the Parish Church), Tottenham, where he was also for many years instructor of St. Katherine's Training College. He published a Morning and an Evening Service, contributed tunes to *Hymns Ancient and Modern*, and acted as musical editor of *The New Mitre Hymnal*.

2, 378, 605. DEERHURST.   323. ST. AGNES.

LATHBURY, MARY ARTEMISIA (Manchester, Ontario County, New York, 1841-1913, New York), was the daughter of a local preacher of the Methodist Episcopal Church, and two of her brothers were ministers of that communion. Art was her profession, but she contributed verses frequently to religious periodicals for children and young people, and herself for a time occupied an editorial chair. She was much interested in the Chautauqua movement, and was long known as 'the laureate of Chautauqua'. She was foundress also of the Look-up Legion, in Methodist Sunday-Schools, based on the rules which form the motto of the 'Harry Wadsworth Club' in Edward Everett Hale's *Ten Times one is Ten*—'Look up, and not down; Look forward, and not back; Look out, and not in; And lend a hand'; to which Hale added, 'In His Name'.

202. *Break Thou the bread of life.*

LAUFENBURG, HEINRICH VON (Laufenburg, Aargan, Switzerland, *c.* 1400-*c.* 1458, Strasburg), was a prolific writer and one of the fathers of German vernacular hymnody. He held office in churches both in that country and subsequently at Freiling in Baden. In 1445 he entered the monastery of the Knights of St. John at Strasburg. Many of his hymns were modelled upon popular songs and sung to their tunes. A number are in honour of the Virgin, but the under-noted hymn is a cradle song addressed to Christ.

304. *Lord Jesus Christ, our Lord most dear.*

Biographical and Historical Notes

LAWES, HENRY (Dinton, Wiltshire, 1596–1662, London), was a pupil of John Coperario, famous as a composer for the lute and the viol. He became an epistler of the Chapel Royal, then one of the gentlemen, and later, clerk of the cheque there. He composed the music for Milton's *Comus* when it was first represented, at Ludlow Castle, in 1634. Milton was thenceforward his friend, and addressed a sonnet to him beginning, 'Harry, whose tuneful and well-measured song', though Dr. Bridges holds that 'his talent in this department of music does not justify Milton's sonnet, nor his prophecy—

> To after age thou shalt be writ the man
> That with smooth air couldst humour best our tongue!'

He composed the Christmas songs in Herrick's *Hesperides*. Along with his brother William, he published a collection of *Choice Psalms* in 1648, just at the end of the Civil War. During the Protectorate he lost all his appointments, but was reinstated in them at the Restoration. He was the first musician to use bars in his music to mark the place of the accent and the rhythmical division of the melody. He did much to introduce into music a closer association with the words to which it was set, and to end the craze for Italian music that prevailed in his time. In the preface to the first volume of his *Ayres and Dialogues for one, two, and three voices*, 'he censures the partiality of the age for songs sung in a language which the hearers do not understand, and, in ridicule of it, speaks of a song of his own composition, printed at the end of the book, which was nothing more than an index of the initial words of some old Italian songs or madrigals. He says, with some sly degree of humour, that this index, which he had set to a varied air, and when read together was a strange medley of nonsense, passed with a great part of the world as an Italian song.' Lawes was buried in the cloisters of Westminster Abbey.

510. FARLEY CASTLE.   456. LAWES (PSALM 32).
297. WHITEHALL.   726. CHANT IN B FLAT.

LEESON, JANE ELIZA (London, 1807–82, London), was for many years a well-known figure in the Catholic Apostolic Church, to the hymn-book of which she contributed nine hymns and translations. Some of her hymns were produced as 'prophetical utterances', supposedly under the prompting of the Holy Spirit, at public services. A former member of the same Communion who heard her produce one such hymn at a service in Bishopsgate Church records that 'it was delivered slowly, with short pauses between the verses, a pause three times as long as any one would ordinarily make in reading'. He adds, 'I have not known any one with a similar gift; but I have heard of an improvisatore who far surpassed Miss Leeson. She only exercised her gift at long intervals, and could choose her own time and her own subject. He improvised very frequently, much more rapidly, and on any subject chosen for him by others.' Late in life, Miss Leeson entered the Roman communion. She published several books of hymns specially for children— *Infant Hymnings; Hymns and Scenes of Childhood; The Child's Book of Ballads; Songs of Christian Chivalry; Paraphrases and Hymns for Congregational Singing*, mostly re-written from the Scottish *Psalms and Paraphrases*.

> 310. *Gracious Saviour, gentle Shepherd.*
> 668. *Loving Shepherd of Thy sheep.*
> 437. *Saviour, teach me day by day.*

LEGGE, ALFRED (Cambridge, 1843–1919, Ashford, Kent), entered the choir of Trinity College, Cambridge, at the age of nine, studied under Drs. T. A. Walmisley and J. L. Hopkins, and became assistant organist of the College. Later, he served as organist at St. Clement's, Cambridge; Wickham, Berks; All Saints, Cambridge; and the Parish Church, Ashford, Kent. He held this last appointment for over fifty years. Among his pupils were the present Queen Marie of Roumania and the Grand Duchess Cyril of Russia, daughters of the late Duke of Edinburgh.

> 174. THEODORA.

LEWIS, EVELINE MARTHA, *née* GRIFFITHS, M.A., J.P. (Liverpool, 1871–), was educated at Caldecote Towers, Bushey Heath, and University College, Cardiff; she graduated at the University of London. Engaging in the teaching profession, she became the first headmistress of Newtown County Girls' School. In 1895 she was married to Hugh Lewis, Glan Hafren, Newtown, Montgomeryshire, who was also on the Commission of the Peace for that county.

> 226. *O blest communion with the saints at rest* (tr.).

LEWIS, HOWELL ELVET, M.A. (Conwil Elvet, Carnarvonshire, 1860–), was educated at the Presbyterian College, Carmarthen. Entering the Congregational ministry, he held charges at Buckley, Hull, Llanelly, and Harecourt, Canonbury, before becoming minister of his present charge, the Welsh Tabernacle, King's Cross, London. He has been called to the Chair of the Congregational Union of England and Wales. A poet, he received the bardic crown at the National Eisteddfod of Wales in 1888, and the chair as Arch-Druid, 1924–7. His degree was conferred on him *honoris causâ*, by the University of Wales. He has published *Sweet Singers of Wales; My Christ and Other Poems; The Gates of Life; By the River Chebar; Songs of Victory; The Life of Dr. Herber Evans; The Life of Howell Harris;* besides several Welsh books in verse and prose.

> 337. *Lord of light, whose Name outshineth.*
> 628. *Whom oceans part, O Lord, unite.*

LEWIS, RICHARD MORRIS (Brechfa, Carmarthenshire, 1849–1918, Swansea), came of a good stock of yeoman farmers and freeholders, and was educated at local schools and Llandovery College. In his student days he was profoundly influenced by the teaching of Carlyle and Emerson. Entering the Civil Service, he rose to the headship of the Inland Revenue at Swansea. He was a Presbyterian, connected with Argyle Church, Swansea. Reserved in disposition, he was known to his friends as a brilliant conversationalist and a formidable opponent in argument. Some fine songs by him were set to music by Professor David Jenkins (q.v.) of Aberystwyth. By many he is regarded as the best translator of hymns from the vernacular into English.

445. *Speak, I pray Thee, gentle Jesus* (tr.).

LEY, HENRY GEORGE, Mus. Doc. (Chagford, Devon, 1887–), was trained as a chorister at St. George's Chapel, Windsor, as a music scholar at Uppingham, at the Royal College of Music, and as an organ scholar at Keble College, Oxford. He was precentor of Radley College; organist of Christ Church Cathedral, Oxford; Choragus of the University, Oxford, and professor of the organ at the Royal College of Music, London. He is now organist of Eton College. He is one of the best of modern organists. He has published much organ music, songs, part-songs, &c.

331. VULPIUS (arr.).

LITTLEDALE, RICHARD FREDERICK, LL.D., D.C.L. (Dublin, 1833–90, London), was educated at Trinity College, Dublin, where he received the LL.D. degree in 1862, and in the same year received the Oxford D.C.L. *comitatis causâ*. He served as curate at St. Matthew's, Thorpe Hamlet, Norfolk, and St. Mary the Virgin, Crown Street, Soho. Chronic ill-health obliged him to devote himself mainly to literary work. He was an earnest and zealous High Churchman; he is said to have heard more confessions than any priest in the Church of England except Dr. Pusey. His learning was of vast range; he seemed to forget nothing he had ever read. This made him a formidable controversialist. His books and pamphlets in support of Anglicanism and against Romanism exhibit his great ability and polemical powers. His *Plain Reasons for not joining the Church of Rome* had a great circulation, and did much to stay the Romeward movement among English High Churchmen. He was one of the most learned of liturgiologists and a notable translator of hymns— from Greek, Latin, Syriac, German, Italian, Danish, and Swedish. He was joint-editor of *The Priest's Prayer-Book* (1864) and *The People's Hymnal* (1867). He contributed to the Rev. Orby Shipley's *Lyrae*, and published in 1863 *Carols for Christmas and Other Seasons*.

191. *Come down, O Love Divine* (tr.).
468. *Jesus, Saviour ever mild.*

LLOYD, JOHN AMBROSE (Mold, Flintshire, 1815–74, Liverpool), though in the main self-taught, became one of the best-known and most influential musicians of his time. He founded the Welsh Choral Union of Liverpool, and often acted as adjudicator at the National Eisteddfodau. He composed many hymn-tunes and published two collections of them—the first, *Casgliad o Donau*, in 1843; the second, *Aberth Moliant*, in 1873. His cantata, *The Prayer of Habakkuk*, was the first work of its kind published in Wales. His part-song, *Blodeuyn Olef*, is regarded as a Welsh classic.

183. ABERGELE.	73. HENRYD.
623. BRYNTEG.	390. WHITFORD.
448. GROESWEN.	

LLOYD, JOHN AMBROSE, jun. (Liverpool, 1840–1914, Bootle), son of the above, was educated at Liverpool Institute, and followed a commercial career in Liverpool and Chester. He was an amateur musician.

470. KILMOREY.

LLOYD, JOHN MORGAN, Mus. Bac. (Pentre, Glamorganshire, 1880–), was educated at Pengam Grammar School and University College, Cardiff, and received his degree from Trinity College, Dublin. He is Lecturer in Music and assistant to the Professor of Music in University College, Cardiff; he lectures on music also under Glamorgan County Council. As an adjudicator at leading competitive musical festivals he is well known in Wales. As organist and choirmaster he has served Trinity Presbyterian Church, Barry, and Cathedral Road Presbyterian Church, Cardiff. He has published anthems, songs, part-songs, &c. He was one of the musical representatives of Wales on the Committee which prepared the present *Church Hymnary*.

727. BENEDICTION.	68. NADOLIG.
408. COLWINSTONE.	575. PORTHKERRY.
650. PRO NOSTRIS LIBERIS.	

LLOYD, WILLIAM (Rhos Goch, Llaniestyn, Carnarvon, 1786–1852, Rhos Goch), was self-educated. Travelling often in England, being probably a cattle-dealing farmer, he took the opportunity to hear English congregations sing, and profited by all he heard. He had a fine voice, and was far in advance of his time in knowledge of music and ability to sing, especially the major tunes. Many people resorted to his house for teaching, and he travelled through the parishes and districts of Lleyn to hold singing meetings and to conduct music classes.

598. MEIRIONYDD.

LLOYD, WILLIAM FREEMAN (Uley, Gloucestershire, 1791–1853, Stanley Hall, Gloucestershire), was led by his interest in Sunday-

School work to become, in 1810, one of the secretaries of the Sunday School Union. He was connected also with the Religious Tract Society. *The Sunday School Teachers' Magazine* owed its origin to him. For many years he conducted *The Child's Companion* and *The Weekly Visitor*. Besides doing much work in compilation and revision, he wrote much himself—useful books for Sunday Schools, and a volume of verse, *Thoughts in Rhyme* (1853).

551. *My times are in Thy hand.*

LOCK HOSPITAL COLLECTION.—The Lock Hospital was founded in 1746 by Martin Madan (q.v.), who was its chaplain. In 1760 he published for it a collection of *Psalms and Hymns extracted from various Authors*, and in 1769 supplemented it by the issue of *A Collection of Psalm and Hymn Tunes*, many of the tunes in which came into general use. Madan himself was a musician, but his own tunes have not survived. Giardini's *Moscow*, Lockhart's *Carlisle*, and the under-noted tune first appeared in this collection.

160. HELMSLEY.

LOCKHART, CHARLES (London, 1745–1815, London), was blind from infancy. He became, however, a notable musician, excelling especially in the training of children's choirs. He was organist in succession of the Lock Hospital, where he was associated with Martin Madan; St. Katherine Cree; St. Mary's, Lambeth; Orange Street Chapel; then of the Lock Hospital again. His earliest tunes were published in 1791 on separate sheets at 3*d.* each. He issued also *A Set of Hymn-Tunes and Anthems for Three Voices* (1810); an *Epithalamium, or Nuptial Ode* (1770); and many songs.

344. CARLISLE.

LOGAN, JOHN (Soutra, 1748–88, London), son of a farmer who belonged to the Burgher section of the Secession Church, was educated at Musselburgh school and at Edinburgh University, where he resolved to enter the ministry of the Church of Scotland. In Edinburgh he made the acquaintance of Lord Elibank, who gave him access to his library, and of Dr. Hugh Blair, on whose recommendation he was for a time tutor to Sir John Sinclair, afterwards the compiler of *The Statistical Account of Scotland.* Licensed to preach by the Presbytery of Haddington, he was appointed in 1771 minister of the second charge of the parish of South Leith. The appointment being disputed, he was not ordained till 1773. In 1775 he was made one of the General Assembly's Committee on the paraphrases, and to him and William Cameron (then only a licentiate) most of the work seems to have been left. About 1780 he was an unsuccessful candidate for the Professorship of Civil History, and in 1783 he produced the tragedy of *Runnamede*, which proved a failure. The publication of this play, and still more the intemperate habits into which the author had unfortunately fallen, rendered it likely that proceedings might be taken against him in the Church courts. Anticipating these he resigned his charge and went to live in London, where for the last two years of his life he was engaged in literary work. Two volumes of his sermons were published in 1790–1. Logan's name became prominent in the controversy as to his authorship of certain poems, claimed also on behalf of his fellow-student Michael Bruce. Logan admittedly published in 1770 a posthumous volume of Bruce's poems, containing some (unspecified) which he said were by other authors. Eleven years afterwards he published a volume of poems bearing his own name, including some of those in the former book, among them the well-known *Ode to the Cuckoo*. The law courts decided against his claim to be owner of these poems and hymns, holding that they were the work of Michael Bruce. The controversy on the subject still arouses keen partisanship; the fact that instructed opinion is so acutely divided suggests that a final solution is scarcely possible.

See Gt. Hymns 161

562. *O God of Bethel! by whose hand.*

LÖHR, GEORGE AUGUSTUS (Norwich, 1821–97, Leicester), after training as a chorister at Magdalen College, Oxford, returned to Norwich to assist the distinguished Dr. Zechariah Buck in the Cathedral there. From 1845, for forty years, he was organist and for the most part of that period choirmaster also, in St. Margaret's Church, Leicester, the choir of which became famous under him. He was a pioneer of choral services in Leicester.

90. ST. FRANCES.

LONGFELLOW, SAMUEL, M.A. (Portland, Maine, 1819–92, Portland), was a younger brother of Henry Wadsworth Longfellow. He was educated at Harvard for the Unitarian ministry, and served congregations at Fall River, Mass.; Brooklyn; and Germantown, Pennsylvania. He resigned this last charge to write his brother's *Life* (1886), and spent the remaining years of his life quietly at Cambridge, Mass. He was gentle and retiring in spirit, yet strong in feeling and fearless in utterance where he conceived principle to be concerned. While yet a student of divinity he and his fellow-student Samuel Johnson (q.v.), to provide a young pastor with a better hymn-book than any then available, published *A Book of Hymns* (1846). While it was in preparation one of the editors remarked to some one that they had some difficulty about a title. 'Why,' was the answer, in witty allusion to the Christian name of both compilers, 'you might call it *The Sam Book*.' Both editors were radicals in theology, and their book was a landmark in Unitarian hymnody. It had a literary quality and charm of freshness unusual in hymn-books at that time. Two years later a revised edition was issued. In 1853 Longfellow collaborated with Col. T. W. Higginson in editing

Thalatta: A Book for the Seaside, some of the contents being original.
In 1859 he published *Vespers,* and a book of *Hymns and Tunes* primarily for use in Sunday Schools and the home-circle; and then, in
1864, again in collaboration with Samuel Johnson, produced *Hymns
of the Spirit,* prepared while in Europe, to take the place of the *Book
of Hymns.* This collection took an extreme theistic position. The
editors refused admission to many of the standard hymns, declining
to alter evangelical hymns to suit their dogmatic requirements.
They aimed at excluding all hymns 'which attributed a peculiar
quality and special authority to Christianity, and recognized a super-
natural element in the personality of Jesus'. A volume of Longfellow's *Sermons and Essays* was published, and a collection of his
Hymns and Verses after his death.

> 275. *Again, as evening's shadow falls.*
> 672. *Go forth to life, O child of earth.*
> 193. *Holy Spirit, Truth Divine.*
> 612. *The summer days are come again.*
> 623. *'Tis winter now; the fallen snow.*

LORD, EMILY BRYANT (New Jersey, 1839–86, Buffalo, N.J.), was
a school teacher in Buffalo for twenty-eight years. She was a member
of Central Presbyterian Church, of which her cousin, Dr. John C.
Lord, was minister, and was a devoted Christian and lover of justice.

> 350. *Maker of earth and sea and sky.*

LÖWENSTERN, MATTHÄUS APELLES VON (Neustadt, 1594–1648,
Breslau), was the son of a saddler. His musical proficiency and his
business ability were alike recognized by the various princes under
whom he successively served, by the Duke of Münsterberg, under
whom he became Staatsrath (privy councillor) at Oels, and by the
Emperor Ferdinand II and his son Ferdinand III, who ennobled
him. Löwenstern wrote about thirty hymns, of unequal merit,
originally accompanied with melodies by himself.

> 216. *Lord of our life, and God of our salvation.*

LOWRY, ROBERT, D.D. (Philadelphia, Pennsylvania, 1826–99,
Plainfield, New Jersey), was educated at Lewisburgh University,
Pennsylvania, and became Professor of Rhetoric there after a few
years in the Baptist ministry. When he resigned the chair in 1875 the
University gave him his doctorate. In the following year he resumed
the work of the ministry at Plainfield. He wrote many tunes and
edited several popular collections of hymns.

> 700. I NEED THEE.

LOWRY, SOMERSET CORRY (Dublin, 1855–), was educated at
Repton and Trinity Hall, Cambridge; ordained 1879, and, after two

curacies, was vicar of North Holmwood; St. Augustine's, Bournemouth; Wonston; and St. Bartholomew's, Southsea. He is now retired and living at Bournemouth. He has published several devotional books, about sixty hymns in various books and periodicals, and a collection of *Hymns and Spiritual Songs* (Longmans).

359. *Son of God, Eternal Saviour.*

LUKE, JEMIMA, *née* THOMPSON (Islington, 1813–1906, Isle of Wight), was the daughter of Thomas Thompson of Poundsford Park, one of the founders of the British and Foreign Sailors' Society, and a friend of every good cause. He was the offerer of the prize of £20 for fifty simple hymns for cottage meetings, which was won by James Edmeston (q.v.). In early life Miss Thompson intended to become a missionary in India. A serious illness made that impossible. She was an earnest advocate of Foreign Missions all her life. For a time she edited a missionary magazine for children, to which Edmeston contributed 'Little travellers Zionward'. In 1843 she married the Rev. Samuel Luke, who was a Congregational minister in Clifton. She published *The Female Jesuit; The Broad Road and the Narrow Way*, &c.

82. *I think when I read that sweet story of old.*

LUTHER, MARTIN (Eisleben, 1483–1546, Eisleben), by his personality and influence the greatest force in the Reformation of the sixteenth century, was the son of a miner at Eisleben. His education, attended with considerable hardship, was mainly at Magdeburg, Eisenach, and the University of Erfurt, where he took his Master's degree in 1505. Embracing the religious life after a study of the Scriptures, he entered the Augustinian Convent at Erfurt, where he spent three years, being ordained priest in 1507. A visit to Rome in 1511 opened his eyes to the corruptions of the Church, and his opposition to these reached a climax when the Dominican friar Tetzel appeared at Wittenberg selling indulgences. Luther's theses denouncing these and denying the Pope's right to forgive sins were nailed to the Church door at Wittenberg, an event which may be called the beginning of the Reformation. Luther was summoned to Rome to answer for his theses, but his University and the Elector of Saxony refused to let him go. His treatise *The Babylonian Captivity of the Church* provoked a papal bull directed against him, which he promptly and publicly burned at Wittenberg. His books were condemned and he was summoned in 1521 before the Diet of Worms, where he insisted on appearing, and refused to retract his doctrines. On his way home he was captured by the friendly Elector who feared for his life, and lodged for a year in the Wartburg, where he translated the Scriptures and wrote various works. He returned to Wittenberg in 1522, his presence being necessary in view of disorders. The latter part of his public life, embracing his controversies with Erasmus, with Henry VIII, and with the Swiss divines, and the part he played in the peasants' war, presents something of an anticlimax. Yet his strong intellect, immense energy, broad sympathies, and loving heart combined to render him one of the greatest spiritual forces in Christian history. He married in 1525 Katharina von Bora, formerly a nun. Their domestic life was happy, and Luther was a kind husband and father. Popular hymns furnished him with one of the most effective means of propagating the Reformed Faith. Thirty-seven hymns were written by himself. Tradition has credited him also with the composition of a number of original chorales. Exact proof of his authorship is lacking; he himself never advanced any claim to have composed a single air. He was an accomplished amateur musician, however, had a fine voice as a boy, and became an expert player on the flute and the lute. All his life he studied music diligently, with a passionate love of the art, in the practice of which he found his dearest recreation; and, while a monk, he gave special study to the polyphonic master-works of the Roman Church. In music he recognized one of the most potent means at his command for the development of a more popular form of worship. 'I am strongly persuaded,' he wrote, 'that after theology, there is no art that can be placed on a level with music; for besides theology, music is the only art capable of affording peace and joy of the heart, like that induced by the study of the science of divinity. A proof of this is that the devil, the originator of sorrowful anxieties and restless troubles, flees before the sound of music almost as much as before the Word of God.' In preparing melodies for the reformed worship, he found what would serve his purpose in old hymns and chants of the Latin Church, in the tunes of pre-reformation vernacular sacred songs, and in secular folk-songs. Many of the melodies have been traced to their sources. Others have not, and some of these have been attributed to him. Of his ability to write them there can be no doubt; but whether he wrote them or not, nothing can rob him of the credit of having adapted the borrowed material he employed in so masterly a fashion as to make the resultant tunes magnificently effective for their immediate purpose; some of them are immortal.

> 56. *From heaven above to earth I come.*
> 407. *From depths of woe I raise to Thee.*
> 526. *A safe stronghold our God is still.*
> 526. EIN' FESTE BURG.   56. VOM HIMMEL HOCH (?).

LUTTEROTH, ASCAN HENRI THÉODORE (Leipzig, 1802–89, Paris), though of German birth, was educated in France, and eventually naturalized there. He was a journalist and philanthropist. He edited the periodical *Le Semeur*. In the great evangelical movement in the Swiss Church, known as the *Réveil*, he took a very active part.

The collection of hymns which he made with his wife's assistance and published in Paris in 1834 under the title *Chants Chrétiens*, was for long, in its various editions, the most popular hymn-book of the Reformed Church. He himself contributed largely to it, both words and music. The definitive edition (1855) contained, among its 200 pieces, 44 by Lutteroth and 3 by his wife. Those of the latter were indexed simply as by Madame H. L., and Lutteroth's own as by Heinrich Roth, and it is under the latter name that the tune *Bryntirion* appears in British collections. The music of the *Chants Chrétiens* was much admired.

310. BRYNTIRION.

LVOV, ALEXIS FEODOROVITCH (Reval, 1799–1871, Kovno), was trained for the army, in which he rose to high rank and imperial favour; he was adjutant to the Tsar Nicholas I. In 1836, however, he left the army to become his father's successor as head of the Imperial Choir at Petrograd. *The Russian National Anthem* was written in 1833. In addition he wrote three operas, a violin concerto, violin fantasias, a *Stabat Mater*, and other church music. He edited a large collection of old Russian ritual chants, besides writing an essay on their rhythm.

641. RUSSIA.

LYNCH, THOMAS TOKE (Dunmow, Essex, 1818–71, London), after a time as usher in a school, took charge of a moribund congregation at Highgate Independent Church. It did not prosper, and he resigned and began to minister to a small congregation of inquiring spirits, first in Mortimer Street, and then in Grafton Street, Fitzroy Square (1849–52). Ill-health, from which he constantly suffered, obliged him to desist from preaching for some years. He resumed in 1860 in Gower Street, until Mornington Church, an iron building, was ready for him; there he continued till his death. His personal appearance was peculiar, and his preaching far from popular, but he gathered round him by the individuality, freshness and spirituality of his pulpit work a congregation of thoughtful and devoted people. In 1855 he published *The Rivulet: Hymns for Heart and Voice*, a title chosen because 'Christian poetry is indeed a river of the water of life, and to this river my rivulet brings its contribution'. Round this modest little book a fierce controversy arose which split Congregationalism into opposing parties and agitated other Nonconformist Churches in England. Thomas Binney, Baldwin Brown, and Newman Hall defended Lynch stoutly. Spurgeon among others unsparingly denounced him for 'negative theology' and 'a non-doctrine scheme'. The poet met the storm with admirable temper. 'The air will be all the clearer for this storm,' he said. 'We must conquer our foes by suffering them to crucify us, rather than by threatening them with crucifixion.' This was no mere form of speech; the controversy undermined his already feeble health, laid him aside for a year, and doubtless hastened his death. He was a man of gentle and sensitive spirit. A musician as well as a poet, he composed tunes (published after his death) to 25 of his hymns, and was heard singing one of them in a low voice to 'Guide me, O Thou great Jehovah' while he lay on the brink of death. His last words were, 'Now I am going to begin to live'.

> 354. *Dismiss me not Thy service, Lord.*
> 187. *Gracious Spirit, dwell with me.*
> 398. *The Lord is rich and merciful.*

LYRA DAVIDICA, a little book published anonymously in 1708, contained for the most part translations from Latin and 'the High German', with some original pieces. The intention of the compiler was to commend a freer type of tune than the solid psalm-tunes then almost exclusively in use. It marks the introduction of the florid tunes which, in the period then opening, acquired a great but transient popularity.

> 119. *Jesus Christ is risen to-day.*
> 119. (EASTER HYMN).

LYTE, HENRY FRANCIS, M.A. (Ednam, near Kelso, 1793–1847, Nice), son of Captain Thomas Lyte, was educated at Portora, the Royal School of Enniskillen, and at Trinity College, Dublin, where he won the prize for an English poem three times. He first intended to follow the medical profession, but took holy orders and became curate of Taghmon, near Wexford, in 1815. Two years later he removed to Marazion, Cornwall. There he underwent a change of heart through attending the death-bed of a neighbouring clergyman who was in need of spiritual guidance; the two friends sought light together and found it in Christ. Lyte's whole view of life was altered, and his preaching had a new vitality from that day. He took charge of the children of the friend who shared that experience with him, although, 'jostled from one curacy to another,' he was little able to bear the burden. After serving curacies at Lymington, Hampshire, Charlton, Devonshire, and Dittisham, he was appointed in 1823 perpetual curate of Lower Brixham, Devon, a fishing village newly constituted a parish. The toils and anxieties of his work there, among sailors and fisher folk who were not able to understand his rare and tender spirit, undermined his never robust health. He sought restoration on the Continent, in vain. While he lay dying at Nice the last consolations of the Church were desired. His servant, going in search of an Anglican clergyman for the purpose, brought one who proved to be Henry Edward Manning, then Archdeacon of Chichester, afterwards the well-known Roman

Cardinal. Lyte died pointing upward and saying, 'Peace, joy!' His works were—*Tales on the Lord's Prayer in Verse* (1826); *Poems, chiefly Religious* (1833); *The Spirit of the Psalms* (1834); and an edition, with a Memoir, of *The Poems of Henry Vaughan*.

286. *Abide with me: fast falls the eventide.*
379. *God of mercy, God of grace.*
502. *Jesus, I my cross have taken.*
544. *Long did I toil, and knew no earthly rest.*
368. *O that the Lord's salvation.*
235. *Pleasant are Thy courts above.*
 21. *Praise, my soul, the King of heaven.*
 16. *Praise the Lord, His glories show.*
239. *Sweet is the solemn voice that calls.*

MACALISTER, ROBERT ALEXANDER STEWART, A.R.C.O., F.S.A., Litt.D., LL.D (Dublin, 1870–), was educated at Rathmines School, in Germany (private study), and at Cambridge University. He became Director of Excavations to the Palestine Exploration Fund in 1900, so continued till 1909, and resumed work in 1923–4. On the latter expedition he and his party discovered part of the walls and fortifications of the most ancient Jerusalem, the Jebusite fortress called Millo, which retained its independence until King David stormed it and set up his kingdom in Zion. This had been one of the missing links in the historical reconstruction of Jerusalem, and the discovery settled the site of the city of David as on the eastern hill. He is now Professor of Celtic Archaeology in University College, Dublin. He has published: *Studies in Irish Epigraphy; Excavations in Palestine* (with Dr. F. J. Bliss); *The Vision of Merlino; Bible Side-Lights from the Mount of Gezer; Two Irish Arthurian Romances; A History of the Excavation of Gezer; The Philistines, their History and Civilization; A Grammar of the Nuri Language; Muiredach, Abbot of Monasterboice, his Life and Surroundings; The History and Antiquities of Inis Cealtra; Leabhar Gabhala* (with Prof. John MacNeill); *Temair Bug, a Study of the Remains and Traditions of Tara; The Life of Ciaran of Clonmacnoise; A Text-Book of European Archaeology; Ireland in Pre-Celtic Times; A Century of Excavation in Palestine;* and, with J. Garrow Duncan, *Excavations on the Hill of Ophel, Jerusalem* (1923–5). Dr. Macalister is organist and choirmaster of Adelaide Road Presbyterian Church, Dublin, and was throughout a member of the Revision Committee and the Music Sub-Committee of the present *Church Hymnary.*

203. *Look upon us, blessed Lord* (tr.).
505. *To-day I arise* (tr.).

438. DUNAHA (arr.).	92. OBER AMMERGAU (arr.).
505. LORICA PATRICII (arr.).	15. ST. DARERCA.
610. NEW GRANGE.	144. TEMPLE BRYAN.

MACBEAN, LACHLAN (Tigh-na-coille, Kiltarlity, Inverness-shire, 1853–) at fifteen years of age went to Inverness to follow a business career, but his literary proclivities drew him into journalism, first, in 1876, on the staff of *The Highlander*, and in 1877, on that of *The Fifeshire Advertiser* at Kirkcaldy. Of the latter and its associated newspapers he has long been editor. He has edited the *Kirkcaldy Burgh Records*, written *The Story of Pet Marjorie*, and published many books on subjects connected with the Scottish Highlands. His *Lessons on Gaelic* passed through many editions. His translations of Dugald Buchanan's *Spiritual Songs* in the metres of the originals are remarkable of their kind, and his *Songs and Hymns of the Gael*, also in the measures of the originals, and with their traditional tunes, have had a deserved popularity, and did much to prepare the way for the present vogue of Gaelic songs. Mr. Macbean has been one of the most ardent and effective pioneers of the Gaelic movement of to-day.

> 53. *Child in the manger* (tr.).
> 570. *O Lord, I sing Thy praises* (tr.).

McCHEYNE, ROBERT MURRAY (Edinburgh, 1813–43 Dundee), was the youngest son of Adam McCheyne, W.S. At the age of four he knew the letters of the Greek alphabet, and was able to sing and recite fluently. After education at the High School and the University of Edinburgh, he was licensed as a preacher by the Presbytery of Annan in 1835. Becoming assistant to the Rev. John Bonar of Larbert and Dunipace, he wore himself out by his strenuous labours and the intensity of spirit he threw into them. His fame as a preacher spread, and in 1836 he was called to the heavy charge of St. Peter's *quoad sacra* Church, Dundee, which had a congregation of 1,100 hearers. Within two years his health broke down under the fervour and devotion of his preaching and pastoral fidelity, and he had to give up his work for a time. Sent in 1839 to Palestine as a member of a committee of inquiry into the possibility of missionary work among the Jews, he and his friend and biographer Andrew A. Bonar published an account of the expedition on their return. He resumed his ministry in that year, but, regardless of the proved need of husbanding his strength, he threw himself also into evangelistic missions, in the north of England, in London, and in Aberdeenshire. The keen sword of his ardent spirit quickly wore the frail scabbard of his body out; on returning from his mission in Aberdeenshire, he was seized with sudden illness and died. His zeal for the Evangel consumed him. His spirituality exercised a powerful influence, and his great ministry in Dundee has become a legend. He was an accomplished Hebrew scholar, and, having a refined musical taste, was one of the first ministers in Scotland to try to improve congregational praise. His hymns appeared in *Songs of Zion to cheer and guide Pilgrims on their way to the New Jerusalem*

(Dundee, 1843). The *Memoir and Remains* by the Rev. Andrew A. Bonar, D.D., is one of Scotland's religious classics.

582. *When this passing world is done.*

MACDONALD, GEORGE, LL.D. (Huntly, Aberdeenshire, 1824–1905, Sagamore, Ashtead, Surrey), the son of a farmer, was educated at King's College, Aberdeen, and Highbury (Congregational) College, London. The only charge he served as a minister was at Arundel, Sussex; his spiritual and intellectual independence displeased his congregation, and they made his position so unhappy that when they proposed to reduce his meagre stipend because of his alleged lack of doctrine, he resigned, and turned to literature as a career. He still preached, but as a layman, and without payment. His relations with Nonconformist churches remained cordial, but a friendship with F. D. Maurice led to his becoming a member of the Church of England. He settled in Hammersmith, and devoted himself to writing novels, mystical and historical romances, literary and religious essays, and poetry, all reflecting the spiritual fervour and intellectual sincerity of the man. A long succession of novels won him wide popularity; those that portray Scots life and character —such as *David Elginbrod, Robert Falconer*, and *Alec Forbes of Howglen*—have abiding value. The religious teaching inwoven through them 'did much to weaken the influence of the traditional Calvinism of Scotland'. As a poet he was deficient in self-criticism, but his delicate imagination and spiritual suggestiveness give him a place of true distinction among the poets of this country. His poems, appearing in various volumes—*Within and Without; The Disciple, and Other Poems; Exotics; A Threefold Cord*, &c.—were published in a collected form in 1896. For some time he was editor of *Good Words for the Young*, and his stories for children—*At the Back of the North Wind; The Princess and the Goblin*, &c.—are unrivalled among modern fairy-tales. Most of his hymns were contributed to *Hymns and Sacred Songs for Sunday Schools and School Worship*, edited by his brother and the Rev. G. B. Bubier, and published in Manchester in 1855.

264. *O Lord of life, Thy quickening voice.*

MACDONALD, MARY, *née* MACDOUGALL (Ardtun, near Bunessan, Mull, 1817–*c.*1890, Mull)—known to Highlanders as 'Mairi Dhughallaich, bean Neill Dhomhnullaich, a bha ann an Ard Tunna'—came of a talented family, her brother and a nephew having also written Gaelic poems that were much admired. The fact that her brother spent his life in Tiree has led to the belief that she was a native of that island, but she lived all her days in Mull. She married Neill MacDonald, a crofter at Cnocan there. She had no English education, but was deeply versed in the Scriptures. She composed several Gaelic songs and hymns of great beauty, and residents in the island vividly remember her singing them while busy at her spinning-wheel. She wrote also a satirical poem on tobacco, of which she thought her husband smoked too much. She was deeply religious, and a member of the Baptist communion.

53. *Child in the manger.*

MACDUFF, JOHN ROSS, D.D. (Bonhard, Scone, Perthshire, 1818–95, Chislehurst), was educated at the High School and the University, Edinburgh. Ordained in 1842 to the parish of Kettins, Forfarshire, he was translated in 1849 to St. Madoes, Perthshire, and in 1855 to Sandyford Parish, Glasgow. Later, he declined an offer of appointment by the Crown to the Cathedral Church of Glasgow. In Sandyford his ministry was singularly fruitful. Dr. George Matheson was at that time a boy in the congregation, and he afterwards said, 'Dr. Macduff gave me my first sense of literary beauty, my first experience of oratory, my first idea of sanctity, my first real conviction of the beauty of Christianity'. The Universities of Edinburgh, Glasgow, and New York gave him their doctorate. In 1871 he resigned his charge to devote himself to literary work, and spent the rest of his years at Chislehurst, Kent. His books of devotion and of practical religion had enormous circulations: *The Faithful Promiser* and *Morning and Night Watches* alone reached almost a million copies. He was a strong advocate of pre-millennial views. For some years he was a member of the Hymnal Committee of the Church of Scotland, and his own thirty-one hymns were published in his *Altar Stones* (1853), and, with other poems, in *The Gates of Praise* (1876).

163. *Christ is coming! let creation.*

MACFARREN, Sir GEORGE ALEXANDER, Mus. Doc. (London, 1813–87, London), in 1829 entered the R.A.M., and in 1834 became one of its professors. His first work was dramatic; with a series of operas he had marked success. A gradual failure of his sight, ending in total blindness, in no way arrested his industry or impaired his spirit. He continued teaching and lecturing, and dictated his compositions to an amanuensis. A remarkable memory served him well. In 1875 he became Principal of the R.A.M., and Professor of Music in Cambridge University, and fulfilled the duties of both posts with high distinction. He received the degree of Mus. Doc. in 1876, and knighthood in 1883. Besides operas, cantatas and oratorios, and much other vocal and instrumental music, he wrote theoretical works on Harmony, Counterpoint, &c., and edited collections of songs. His erudition was great, and his energy and productiveness under heavy disabilities present a rare example of courage and devotion.

718. CHANT IN A FLAT.

Biographical and Historical Notes

MACFARREN, WALTER CECIL (London, 1826–1905, London), was a brother of Sir George Macfarren. He was trained as a chorister at Westminster Abbey and at the Royal Academy of Music. He became a Professor at the Academy and conductor of its concerts. For many years he was director and treasurer of the Philharmonic Society. He wrote a symphony, overtures to several plays, a piano concerto, violin sonatas, a cantata for women's voices, songs, &c., and *Musical Memories*, a book of genial autobiography.

265. BARMOUTH.

MACGILL, HAMILTON MONTGOMERIE, D.D. (Catrine, Ayrshire, 1807–80, Paris), studied at Glasgow University and the Theological Hall of the United Secession Church. He became in 1837 colleague-minister of Duke Street congregation, Glasgow, and in 1840, with a portion of it, formed a new church in Montrose Street. In 1858 he resigned on his appointment to the Home Mission Secretaryship of the United Presbyterian Church. He had edited the *Juvenile Missionary Magazine* of his Church previously; now he assumed the editorship of *The Missionary Record* also. In 1868 he was made Foreign Mission Secretary. He was a member of the Committee which compiled for his denomination *The Presbyterian Hymnal*, (1876), to which he contributed 5 translations from the Latin and 1 from the Greek. His scholarly *Songs of the Christian Creed and Life* (1876) contained 6 translations from the Greek, 68 from the Latin, and 27 from English into Latin verse, the original texts being given in every case.

569. *Lead, holy Shepherd, lead us* (tr.).

McGRANAHAN, JAMES (near Adamsville, Pennsylvania, 1840–1907, Kinsman, Ohio), acquired his education for the most part at the public schools. He had an inborn love of music. G. J. Webb, Philipp Bliss and others encouraged and helped him to equip himself for the service in which he afterwards engaged. He had some training under Carlo Bassini and Dr. William Mason, New York, and G. F. Root, Chicago. On the death of Bliss in 1876, his evangelistic work was continued by McGranahan, who associated himself later, as singer, with Major D. W. Whittle, in missions both in America and in Great Britain. This co-operation lasted for eleven years. He was co-editor, with Ira D. Sankey and George Coles Stebbins, of *Gospel Hymns* (Nos. 3 to 6). Among his other publications were *The Male Chorus Book; Songs of the Gospel;* and *The Gospel Male Choir*.

699. NONE BUT CHRIST.

MACGREGOR, DUNCAN (Fort Augustus, 1854–1923, Inveral-lochy), son of a schoolmaster who was a notable Gaelic scholar, was educated at the parish school, Dunnichen, Forfarshire, and the University of Aberdeen. After periods of service as a missionary at Drumoak and Kincardine O'Neil, Aberdeenshire, in the North Isles, Orkney, and at Gardenstown, Banffshire, he was ordained in 1881 at Inverallochy, an Aberdeenshire fishing village, where the rest of his life was spent. He was a man of fine gifts, too little recognized, a good scholar and a kindly man. He had great learning in liturgiology, and was the leading authority on the worship of the early Scottish Church. Among his published works were—*The Scald, or, The Northern Balladmonger; Clouds and Sunlight* (Poems); *General Principles of Early Scottish Worship; Columba: a Record and a Tribute; The Gospel of the Scots*, a Lecture delivered in St. Paul's Cathedral, London; and contributions to the Proceedings of learned societies on *The Celtic Inheritance of the Church of Scotland, Internal Furnishings of an Early Scottish Church, An Ancient Gaelic Treatise on the Symbolism of the Eucharist*, &c.

> 179. *Christ is the world's Redeemer* (tr.).
> 454. *O God, Thou art the Father* (tr.).

M'KEEVER, HARRIET BURN (Philadelphia, Pennsylvania, 1807–86, Chester, Pennsylvania), was educated at Philadelphia, and for more than thirty-six years taught in a successful girls' school there. She was a Protestant Episcopalian of the evangelical school, and devoted much of her time to religious work. For thirty years she was instructor of the Infant Sunday School in St. Andrew's Church. She wrote many hymns, and late in life became a prolific writer of books for the young. A history of all religions, on which she worked much in her last years, was never published.

> 666. *Jesus, high in glory*.

MACLAGAN, WILLIAM DALRYMPLE, D.D. (Edinburgh, 1826–1910, London), was a son of David Maclagan, M.D., Edinburgh, and a brother of Sir Douglas Maclagan, M.D., LL.D., Professor of Medical Jurisprudence in the University of Edinburgh, and long an honoured elder of the Church of Scotland, as another brother, Dr. Philip Maclagan, was of the Presbyterian Church of England at Berwick-on-Tweed. William attended law classes at Edinburgh University, but joined the army and served in India. Invalided home, he abandoned the army as a career, but drew his modest pension as a lieutenant to the end of his life. After studying at St. Peter's College, Cambridge, he was ordained in 1856. He served in the curacies of St. Saviour's, Paddington, and St. Stephen's, Marylebone; then as secretary to the London Diocesan Church Building Society. After a time as curate of Enfield, he became rector of Newington; vicar of Kensington; prebendary of Reculverland in St. Paul's Cathedral; in 1878 Bishop of Lichfield; and from 1891 till 1908, when he resigned, Archbishop of York. As such, he crowned Queen Alexandra at the coronation of King Edward VII.

He started the Poor Benefices Fund, and established at York a Training College for the Clergy. A broad-minded churchman, he discouraged advanced ritual in his diocese. His busy life of organizing and administrative work gave him little leisure for writing, but he wrote a number of excellent hymns and tunes.

> 98. *Lord, when Thy Kingdom comes, remember me.*
> 219. *The saints of God! their conflict past.*
> 340. LICHFIELD.

MACLEOD, John, D.D. (Morven, Argyllshire, 1840–98, Govan), a cousin of Dr. Norman Macleod, was educated at the University of Glasgow. Ordained in the Church of Scotland in 1861, at Newton-on-Ayr, he was translated in the following year to Duns, and in 1875 to the great parish of Govan. There, to meet the spiritual needs of an immense and rapidly growing population, he was the moving spirit in an heroic scheme of Church Extension, involving the building of several daughter churches and the erection of a great new mother-church for the parish. He was an ardent advocate of reform in the ordering of public worship. He aimed especially at making the prayers of the sanctuary more congregational by the introduction of responses, at the restoration of the Communion to its right place as the central and distinctive act of Christian worship, and at the observance of the redemptive commemorations of the Christian Year. These ideals he tried to realize in his own church, and to foster throughout the Church of Scotland. He was one of the founders of the Scottish Church Society, which had this for its chief aim. In 1896 he was appointed convener of the Assembly's Committee on Legislation and Church Reform. His manifold and apostolic labours left little opportunity for authorship: apart from papers contributed to the Conferences of the Scottish Church Society, one of them an elaborate treatise on *The Holy Sacrament of Baptism*, he published little except for local use. After his death a collection of his *Poems and Hymns* (1902) was issued, and a volume on *The Gospel in the Institution of the Lord's Supper* (1907).

> 465. *Blessèd Jesus, high in glory.*

MACLEOD, Norman, D.D. (Campbeltown, Argyllshire, 1812–72, Glasgow), was educated at Campbeltown, Morven, Campsie, Glasgow University, and Edinburgh University, where he studied theology under Chalmers. After three years of tutoring and continental travel he was ordained in 1838 to the parish of Loudoun, Ayrshire. At once his remarkable preaching powers were revealed; in a short time his church was crowded. At the Disruption he remained in the Church of Scotland, and was offered many attractive parishes. He elected to go to Dalkeith (1843). In 1849 he became editor of *The Edinburgh Christian Instructor*. He was translated to the Barony Parish, Glasgow, in 1851, and there fulfilled a ministry which has had few parallels for great and various and far-reaching influence. He was one of the founders of the Evangelical Alliance. The first penny savings bank in Glasgow was founded by him, and he was a leader in many schemes for ameliorating the condition of the people. In 1857 he was appointed Chaplain to the Queen. In 1860 *Good Words* was established under his editorship, and for its pages he wrote many stories and sketches, sermons and verses, afterwards published in book form. In 1865 he was the storm-centre of a fierce controversy on the Sabbath Question, he taking a liberal view, the defence of which, by a clergyman especially, required uncommon courage in those days. A visit to India in 1867, as Convener of the India Mission Committee of his Church, by the fatigues it involved left his health impaired, but he was able to act as Moderator of Assembly in 1869. He was one of the greatest of Scottish churchmen, a man of rare breadth and catholicity of spirit, an earnest philanthropist, an eloquent and moving preacher, and a warm-hearted, manly Christian. His published works included *The Earnest Student; Daily Meditations; The Old Lieutenant; Parish Papers; Wee Davie; The Starling; Reminiscences of a Highland Parish; Peeps at the Far East.*

529. *Courage, brother! do not stumble.*

MACNICOL, NICOL, D.Litt. (Lochranza, Arran, 1870–   ), studied at Glasgow University, where he had a brilliant career, and graduated with honours in classics and philosophy; and at the Free Church College, Glasgow. He was from 1895 till 1927 a distinguished missionary of the United Free Church of Scotland, in Poona, India. An Indian scholar of the highest standing, he has contributed largely to *The International Review of Missions*, and has published books on *Indian Theism; Psalms of Maratha Saints; Tom Dobson, a Champion of the Outcastes;* and *The Making of Modern India*. He is now Secretary of the National Christian Council of India.

406. *One who is all unfit to count* (tr.).

MADAN, MARTIN (Hertingfordbury, 1726–90, Epsom), son of a Colonel of the same name, and cousin, through his mother, of the poet Cowper, was educated at Westminster School and Christ Church, Oxford, and called to the Bar in 1748. Sent (according to one story) by his fellow members of a convivial club to hear and ridicule the preaching of John Wesley, he became instead deeply impressed, and shortly afterwards took orders. His preaching as chaplain to the Lock Hospital was so popular that a new chapel had to be opened for him. In 1780, however, he raised a storm by the publication of a book called *Thelyphthora*, in which he advocated polygamy, defending it by Old Testament examples. A shoal of rejoinders and refutations followed (including *Anti-Thelyphthora* by his cousin the poet), and Madan resigned his charge and retired into private life at Epsom. Madan is not known to have written any hymns himself, but he had great skill in adapting and piecing together the work of others. In 1760 he published a miscellaneous collection of hymns by various authors, which he reissued with an appendix in 1763. The collection, many of the hymns in which were retouched by Madan, attained great popularity, and it is in this form that many of the great hymns of the eighteenth century are still in use.

160. *Lo! he comes, with clouds descending.*

MAGDALEN CHAPEL HYMNS.—During the eighteenth century congregational singing had fallen into degenerate ways. The tedious practice of reading the lines before they were sung, the organist's practice of inserting interludes, usually irrelevant, between the lines, and the slow *tempo* at which the tunes were sung, reduced psalmody to a deplorable condition. One of the factors in bringing about reform was the singing of the inmates of certain great charitable foundations established in the first half of the century—the Magdalen Hospital, the Foundling Hospital (q.v.), the Female Orphan Asylum (*vide* W. Riley), the Lock Hospital (q.v.), and others. These institutions vied with each other in their choral singing, which won great celebrity; crowds flocked to hear it, and foreign musicians, Handel among them, were enraptured by it. Five *Sets* of *Psalms and Hymns* with Tunes were issued for the Magdalen Hospital, and these were published together in *A Companion to the Magdalen Chapel.*

565. (LYNE).   491. (PLAISTOW).

MAINZER, JOSEPH, Ph.D. (Trèves, 1801–51, Manchester), was the son of a butcher. He was educated in the Maîtrise of Trèves Cathedral. For a time he worked in the coal mines at Saarbruck with a view to becoming an engineer, but changing his mind, entered the Church, was ordained to the priesthood in 1826, and became an abbé. His intromissions with politics, however, obliged him to leave Germany. He settled first in Brussels, then in Paris, where he conducted workmen's classes for music and singing, and did work in musical journalism. In 1839 he came to England. Hullah had just started his singing crusade in London, and Mainzer began work on the same lines in the north. He lived in Edinburgh from 1842 to 1847, and in 1844 competed unsuccessfully for the Chair of Music in the University. He also toured the country, lecturing and teaching. He was an adept in the advertising art, and loved to be himself in the limelight: he was 'a queer mixture of charlatan and apostle'. He had great receptions in many places; was banqueted at the Burns Monument in Alloway on the occasion of his visit to Ayr, and sang a number of Burns's songs in German and to German music; and on his visit to Loch Lomond was attended by a kind of triumphal procession of people from the Vale of Leven. But the popular favour he courted successfully was deserved. He was an enthusiastic and skilful teacher, and really taught the multitude to sing. Finally he settled in Manchester. He published *Singing for the Million*, and in 1842 started a periodical, *Mainzer's Musical Times and Singing Circular*. This was devoted at first to advertising his movements and doings, but, taken over in 1844 by Alfred Novello, it developed into the present *Musical Times*.

333, 367. MAINZER.

MAIR, WILLIAM, D.D. (Savoch, Aberdeenshire, 1830–1920, Edinburgh), was educated at the Grammar School and Marischal College and University, Aberdeen. Thereafter, for seven years, he was disabled by ill-health. When able to assume a charge, he was ordained, in 1861, to the parish of Lochgelly. In 1865 he accepted the charge of Ardoch, Perthshire, and in 1869 that of Earlston, Berwickshire, where he remained till his retiral from the active ministry, in 1913. He was an ideal parish minister, but early made his mark also as a learned ecclesiastical jurist, and in his later years as an ecclesiastical statesman. His *Digest of Laws and Decisions Ecclesiastical and Civil, relating to the Constitution, Practice, and Affairs of the Church of Scotland* (1887) is the standard authority on its subject. He published also *The Truth about the Church of Scotland* (1891); *Jurisdiction in Matters Ecclesiastical* (1896); *Speaking* (1900); *My Young Communicant* (1906); *My Life* (1911); and many pamphlets on various phases of the Scottish Church question. The honour in which he was universally held was marked by his election as Moderator of the General Assembly in 1896. He was an ardent apostle of the cause of the reunion of the Presbyterian Churches of Scotland.

108. *Sing, my tongue, how glorious battle* (tr.).

MAKER, FREDERICK CHARLES (Bristol, 1844–1927, Bristol), spent his whole life in Bristol. Trained as a chorister in the Cathedral there, he became organist of Milk Street Methodist Free Church, of Clifton Downs Congregational Church, and from 1882, for about thirty years, of Redland Park Congregational Church. He contributed tunes to *The Bristol Tune Book* and other collections, and besides a collection of original hymn-tunes, published anthems, cantatas, and piano pieces, many of which have had considerable popularity.

691. ST. CHRISTOPHER.   441. WENTWORTH.

MANN, ARTHUR HENRY, Mus. Doc. (Norwich, 1850–   ), was trained as a chorister at the Cathedral of his native city, by Dr. Zechariah Buck, to whom he occasionally acted as assistant. He was organist successively of St. Peter's, Wolverhampton; Tettenhall Parish Church; Beverley Minster; King's College, Cambridge. He is also organist to the University of Cambridge, and music-master of the Leys School there. He is an honorary M.A. of the University, and a Fellow of King's College. He has composed much church and organ music, and edited Tallis's famous motet for forty voices. He was musical editor of *The Church of England Hymnal*.

71. ANGELS' STORY.   268. BERNO.   171. WILTON.

MANSFIELD, PURCELL JAMES (Torquay, 1889–), son of Dr. Orlando A. Mansfield, sometime Professor of Music in Wilson College, Chambersburg, and Gainesville College, U.S.A., became organist of the Park Parish Church, Glasgow, 1910; of Paisley Abbey and the Clark Town Hall, Paisley, 1919; and is now organist of Pollokshields Parish Church, Glasgow. He has published an opera, *The Hawaiian Maid; Five Concert Overtures* for the organ; and many other choral and orchestral works. He is a well-known recitalist. He was musical editor of the 1927 edition of *The British Students' Song Book*.

400. KILMARNOCK (Faux-bourdon).

MANT, RICHARD, D.D. (Southampton, 1776–1848, Ballymoney, Co. Antrim), was educated at Winchester and Trinity College, Oxford. He became a Fellow of Oriel. After his ordination in 1802 he travelled for a time, then became curate of Buriton, Hants; of Crawley; then of his father's parish in Southampton. In 1810 he was appointed vicar of Coggeshall, Essex; in 1811, Bampton Lecturer; in 1815, rector of St. Botolph's, Bishopgate, London, and in 1818 rector also of East Horsley, Surrey, these two livings being held simultaneously. In 1820 he was appointed Bishop of Killaloe and Kilfenoragh; in 1823 was translated to the see of Down and Connor; and in 1833 the see of Dromore was united with the latter diocese under him. He was a stalwart champion of the interests of his Church, whose history—*The History of the Church in Ireland*—he wrote (1840). Many other works came from his unresting pen. Most of his hymns appeared in *Scripture Narratives* (1831); and in *Ancient Hymns from the Roman Breviary, with Original Hymns* (1837).

2. *Round the Lord in glory seated.*

MARCKANT, JOHN (sixteenth century), incumbent of Clacton Magna (1559) and Shopland (1563–8). Little is known of him, save as author of a few hymns and other poems. He contributed four psalms (118, 131, 132, 135) to Sternhold and Hopkins's version of the Psalter. In this also appears the under-noted hymn known as 'The Lamentation',

401. *O Lord, turn not away Thy face.*

MARRIOTT, JOHN, M.A. (Cottesbach, near Lutterworth, 1780–1825, Broadclyst, near Exeter), was educated at Rugby and Christ Church, Oxford. When his elder brother told the Dean of Christ Church that he had a younger brother coming up, the old man, who was something of a character, answered, 'Glad of it. Like the breed.' John's career at college was a brilliant one. Ordained in 1804, he spent four years at Dalkeith Palace as tutor to Lord George Scott, elder brother of the 5th Duke of Buccleuch. He was also domestic chaplain to the 4th Duke, who, on the death of Lord George in 1808, presented him to the living of Church Lawford, Warwickshire. Ill-health, however, made residence there impossible. He had to live in Devonshire, where he served several curacies—St. James's, Exeter; St. Lawrence, Exeter; and Broadclyst. In 1824 he was attacked by ossification of the brain. He was a good evangelical preacher, and a man of great personal charm. While at Dalkeith he became intimate with Sir Walter Scott, who dedicated to him the second canto of *Marmion*. Marriott had previously contributed three ballads to the 3rd edition of Scott's *Minstrelsy of the Scottish Border*, and to these the dedication makes allusion—

Marriott, thy harp, on Isis strung,
To many a Border theme has rung.

Modesty would not allow him to publish his hymns in his lifetime—he would not permit 'Thou whose almighty word' even to be copied by his friends; but they were made public after his death. His son, Charles Marriott, was 'The Man of Saintly Life' whom Dean Burgon described in his *Twelve Good Men*. See also Dean Church's *The Oxford Movement*.

364. *Thou whose almighty word.*

MARTIN, Sir GEORGE CLEMENT, M.V.O., Mus. Doc. (Lambourne, Berkshire, 1844–1916, London), gave no evidence as a boy of musical gifts; he was sixteen before he could play a note. His awakening came through Sir Herbert Oakeley's playing of Bach's fugues on the parish church organ during a visit to the squire. Martin was deeply moved; Bach kindled the spark of a real genius. Three months later the novice in music had so far advanced as to be able to play the service in the village church. To obtain lessons from Stainer, then organist of Magdalen College, Oxford, he rode twenty-two miles weekly into Oxford; he proved a brilliant pupil. His first post was as organist to the Duke of Buccleuch at Dalkeith Palace, where a daily cathedral service was maintained. During part of his time there he was organist also of St. Peter's, Lutton Place, Edinburgh. In 1874, Stainer, then organist of St. Paul's Cathedral, called him to London to be master of song under him, and ultimately Martin succeeded his teacher as organist of the Cathedral. He was appointed Professor of the Organ at the R.C.M. in 1883, and at the

R.A.M. also in 1895. He was a resourceful organizer, and showed masterly skill in the management of the imposing State ceremonials held in the Cathedral. In connexion with the celebration of Queen Victoria's Diamond Jubilee in 1897 he was knighted. A special anthem which he composed for the occasion was sung outside of the western entrance to the Cathedral, the bell 'Great Paul' forming part of the orchestra. His skill as a choir trainer was unique. His primer on *The Art of Training Choir Boys* is the standard work on the subject. Of shy and retiring disposition, he yet had a strong character, and during his reign at the metropolitan cathedral the world-wide reputation of its musical services was kept at its height.

503. CHILTON FOLIAT. 110. ISRAEL.

MARTIN, GEORGE WILLIAM (London, 1828–81, London), was a chorister of St. Paul's Cathedral under William Hawes. He became Professor of Music in the Normal College for Army Schoolmasters, music-master in St. John's Training College, Battersea, and organist of Christ Church there. He composed many glees, madrigals, and part-songs, and edited cheap arrangements of the popular oratorios, also *The Journal of Part Music*, 1861–2. He had an aptitude for training choirs of school children. The concerts of the Metropolitan Schools Choral Society and the National Choral Society under his baton had a high reputation. He did much to popularize good music. Unhappily, he fell into intemperate habits, and sank so low that he died from illness brought on by exposure and want, in Bolingbroke House Hospital, Wandsworth, and was buried by the parish. He had evidently been homeless for some time, and had drunk the cup of misery to the dregs. But for one friend who had stood by him in his last illness, his identity would have been unknown.

464. LEOMINSTER.

MASON, LOWELL, Mus. Doc. (Medfield, Massachusetts, 1792–1872, Orange, New Jersey), became a bank clerk at Savannah. There he conducted the choir of a Presbyterian Church and compiled his first collection of church tunes. He offered the copyright to various publishers, stipulating only for a few copies of the book for his own use, but unavailingly. In the end the Boston Handel and Haydn Society took responsibility for it, giving Mason an interest in it. The venture was so successful that he settled in Boston and began his life-work of musical education and culture. He became organist of Dr. Lyman Beecher's church, founded in 1832 the Boston Academy of Music, instituted conventions of music teachers, and by lectures and other propaganda did much to extend interest in music and to raise its standard in the United States. Two books of tunes associated with his name—*The Sabbath Hymn and Tune Book* (1859), and *The Hallelujah*—were widely popular and had great influence on both sides of the Atlantic. Many manuals and collections of sacred music were published by him. His own compositions won enormous popularity. As a reformer of church music he rendered a service which was of high value at that time. *The New York Musical Review* was edited and published by him. He had a keen intellect and boundless enthusiasm, and was a magnetic teacher.

727. THE LORD BLESS THEE (arr.).

357. DILIGENCE.   686. NAIN.
371. HEBER.   415. OLIVET.
           627. STAR OF PEACE.

MASSIE, RICHARD (Chester, 1800–87, Pulford Hall), came of an ancient Cheshire family, and was son of the Rev. R. Massie of Coddington, sometime rector of St. Bride's, Chester, and of Eccleston. A man of wealth and leisure, with two estates—Pulford Hall, Coddington, Cheshire, and another near Wrexham, Denbighshire—he devoted himself to literature. He published a translation of *Martin Luther's Spiritual Songs* (1854); *Lyra Domestica* (2 series), a translation of Spitta's *Psalter und Harfe;* and contributed many similar translations to various collections. He was somewhat eccentric. He is remembered as wearing a red wig and a tall beaver hat. At one time he had been lame, and he always carried a crutch even after he no longer had need of it. He was interested in gardening, and had a noted rock garden, which was a rare thing in those days. He and his mother and sisters are remembered as remarkable for their quiet spirituality and saintliness.

407. *From depths of woe I raise to Thee* (tr.).

MASTERMAN, JOHN HOWARD BERTRAM, D.D. (Tunbridge Wells, 1867–), was educated at Weymouth College and St. John's College, Cambridge, of which he became a lecturer after a brilliant graduation. He has held the successive posts of University Extension Lecturer; vicar of St. Aubyn's, Devonport; Principal, Midland Clergy College, Birmingham, and Warden of Queen's College there; Canon of Birmingham; Professor of History, University of Birmingham; Hulsean Lecturer, Cambridge; vicar, Canon, and Sub-Dean of St. Michael's, Coventry; rector, St. Mary-le-Bow, Cheapside, London; rector of Stoke Damarel, and, since 1923, Suffragan Bishop of Plymouth.

491. *Almighty Father, who dost give.*

MATHAMS, WALTER JOHN (London, 1851–), spent his early life at sea. He then received training for the Baptist ministry at Regent's Park College, London, held charges in Preston, Falkirk, and Birmingham, and was chaplain to the Forces in Egypt for three years, before, in 1905, he was admitted to the ministry of the Church of Scotland. He served as ordained assistant in Stronsay,

Orkney, then, from 1909 to 1919, was in charge of Mallaig mission church. In the latter year he resigned. He published numerous books—*At Jesus' Feet*, hymns and poems; *Fireside Parables; Rough Sermons; Jack Ahoy; Comrades All; Maxim Shots for Soldiers; A Bowl of Amber; The Day of the Golden Chance; Maxims for Boys*, &c.

667. *Jesus, Friend of little children.*

MATHESON, ANNIE (Blackheath, 1853–1924, London), was the daughter of the Rev. James Matheson, Congregational minister at Nottingham, from whom she inherited an enthusiasm for beauty in life and in literature. She began to write early. Her first hymn, 'Jesus, the children are calling', was composed at the age of thirteen, and, on the recommendation of Dr. George MacDonald, printed in *Good Words* as a 'Hymn by a Child'. In spite of its immaturity, it still appears in several hymnals. A true lyrical gift and an intense love of nature and sympathy with men and women secured a welcome for her verses in such magazines as *Macmillan's*, *The Spectator*, and *St. Nicholas*. She published several volumes of verse, *Love Triumphant*, *Love's Music*, &c.; some collections of essays; edited anthologies, *A Day Book for Girls*, and *Sayings from the Saints*, and the *Rose and Dragon Series* of biographies of great or heroic men and women, for schools. Her poems for children were among her happiest works. By readings in poetry which she gave in and about London, for many years, she awoke in many women the love of poetry and inspired them with new interests. She was a devoted member of the Church of England.

361. *Dear Master, what can children do?*

MATHESON, GEORGE, D.D., LL.D., F.R.S.E. (Glasgow, 1842–1906, North Berwick), was the son of a successful Glasgow merchant. From early years he suffered from impaired vision, and though his organs of sight were perfect, by his eighteenth year he was practically blind. At Glasgow Academy and University, however, he showed brilliant intellectual gifts; he was one of the most distinguished students of his time, especially in the philosophical classes, in which he was head and shoulders above his fellows. Licensed as a preacher in 1866, he became assistant to Dr. J. R. Macduff (q.v.) in Sandyford Church, Glasgow, and in 1868 became minister of the parish of Innellan, Argyllshire. Here he established a reputation as a preacher of the first rank, and began the contributions to theological and devotional literature which proved his singular powers. In 1886 he was translated to St. Bernard's Parish Church, Edinburgh, where for thirteen years he ministered to a congregation of about 2,000 members. The blending of imagination and reason in his preaching, and the breadth of his theology, made his ministry one of great and quickening influence, especially among young men. In 1874 he had made his first appearance as a scholar and scientific theologian in his *Aids to the Study of German Theology*. This was followed by *The Growth of the Spirit of Christianity; Natural Elements of Revealed Theology* (Baird Lectures); *Landmarks of New Testament Morality;* then by several essays in apologetic—*Can the Old Faith live with the New?; The Spiritual Development of St. Paul; The Distinctive Messages of the Old Religions;* and finally by books of spiritual meditation and devotion —*My Aspirations; Moments on the Mount; Voices of the Spirit; Times of Retirement; Rests by the River; Searchings in the Silence; Studies in the Portrait of Christ,* &c., in all of which he revealed a rare gift of spiritual insight and devotional suggestiveness, which gives character also to *Sacred Songs,* his one volume of verse.

> 464. *Make me a captive, Lord.*
> 424. *O Love that wilt not let me go.*

MATHEWS, BASIL JOSEPH, M.A. (Oxford, 1879–   ), was educated at Oxford High School and University. After five years as private secretary to Principal Fairbairn of Mansfield College, he was for some years on the staff of *The Christian World,* then became editorial secretary of the London Missionary Society. He was chairman and secretary of the Literature Committee of the Ministry of Information in the closing years of the Great War; then became director of the Press Bureau of the Conference of British Missionary Societies, and editor of its magazine *Outward Bound.* He is now International Literature Secretary (Boys' Work) of the World's Committee of Y.M.C.A.'s, Geneva, and editor of a new magazine, *The World's Youth.*

> 373. *Far round the world Thy children sing their song.*

MATTHEWS, TIMOTHY RICHARD (Colmworth, Bedford, 1826–1910, Tetney, Lincs.), was a son of the Rev. T. R. Matthews to whom Edward Fitzgerald refers in his *Letters.* He was educated at Bedford Grammar School and Gonville and Caius College, Cambridge, graduating in 1853. While private tutor in the family of the Rev. Lord Wriothesley Russell, canon of Windsor, he formed a friendship, maintained through life, with Dr. (afterwards Sir) G. J. Elvey. Ordained in 1853, he was curate at St. Mary's, Nottingham, until 1859, when he accepted the curacy and sole charge of North Coates, Lincolnshire, of which he became rector in 1869. In 1907 he retired and went to live with his eldest son at Tetney Vicarage, where he died. His musical works include over a hundred hymn-tunes, settings of the morning and evening services, two or three songs, and a Christmas carol. He edited *The North Coates Supplemental Tune Book,* and *The Village Organist* in its original form.

> 470. CHENIES.   67. MARGARET.
> 188. LUDBOROUGH.   343. NORTH COATES.

MAUDE, MARY FAWLER, *née* HOOPER (London, 1819–1913, Overton, Flintshire), while yet in her teens, wrote three text-books, based on the writings of Eastern travellers, on *Scripture Manners and Customs*, *Scripture Topography*, and *Scripture Natural History*. These, published by the S.P.C.K., were widely used for many years. In 1841 she married the Rev. Joseph Maude, vicar of St. Thomas's, Newport, Isle of Wight, and afterwards of Chirk, Ruabon, and an hon. canon of St. Asaph. At Chirk she conducted classes, which were crowded, for colliers, and in her widowhood, at Overton, a Sunday class for young men was her dearest interest. When, at ninety-three, she lay dying, her young men begged leave to sing outside her door her own hymn, 'Thine for ever,' and another favourite with them, 'Will your anchor hold?' Her message in farewell was, 'Tell them that it does not fail—it holds!' The memorial brass over her seat in Overton Church bears name and dates, and the lines—

> Thine for ever! oh how blest
> They who find in Thee their rest!

504. *Thine for ever! God of Love.*

MAY, CATHERINE ELIZABETH, *née* MARTIN (Lockinge Park, near Wantage, 1808–73, Totland, Isle of Wight), was the only daughter of Sir Henry William Martin, Bart. She married in 1837 the Rev. George May, who was from 1843 to 1861 vicar of Lyddington, Wiltshire.

111. *O Saviour, where shall guilty man?*

MEJER, JOHANN DAVID (*c.* 1692), was a town councillor at Ulm. He published *Geistliche Seelenfreud, oder Davidische Hauss-Capell* (Ulm, 1692).

19. ES IST KEIN TAG

MENDELSSOHN-BARTHOLDY, (JAKOB LUDWIG) FELIX (Hamburg, 1809–47, Leipzig), was the son of a Jewish banker, and grandson of the famous Jewish philosopher, Moses Mendelssohn. The family settled in his childhood in Berlin, and were baptized into the Lutheran Church, adding Bartholdy to the name on that occasion. Felix showed extraordinary musical gifts. At the age of ten he made his first appearance as a pianist, and while yet a boy composed profusely. In his youth he discovered Bach, 'the poor cantor of Leipzig,' and while a student at the University, got together a choir of sixteen voices, and on Saturday evenings practised *The Passion according to St. Matthew*. In 1829 it was performed for the first time since Bach's death, Mendelssohn conducting without a note of the music before him. Bach's influence on him was profound. His overture to *A Midsummer Night's Dream* (1826) had already given him high rank as a composer. In 1829 he visited

Great Britain for the first time, and laid the foundations of his immense popularity there. He loved 'that smoky nest', London, because of the welcome it always gave him. His visit to Scotland inspired the overture *Fingal's Cave*. In 1833 he accepted the directorship of concerts at Düsseldorf, where he invented the new form of composition for the pianoforte now familiar in the *Lieder ohne Worte*. From 1835 to 1843 he was director of the Gewandhaus concerts at Leipzig. Reluctantly, in the latter year, at the urgent request of the King of Prussia, he left Leipzig for Berlin, to be the royal Kapellmeister, and director of the musical division of the newly-founded Academy of Arts; but in 1845 he was glad to return to Leipzig, which he had found 'a paradise', to resume the directorship of the Gewandhaus concerts, and to found the Conservatorium and give his direction to it. His industry was boundless; overwork was habitual with him, and in 1847, after he had made his last visit to London to conduct his *Elijah*, the shock of the news of a beloved sister's death broke his overstrained constitution. His death threw Europe into mourning; in Leipzig it was 'as though a king were dead'. He was a man of sunny, enthusiastic, generous, lovable nature. As a pianist and organist he was in the first rank. He left great masses of compositions—two oratorios, *St. Paul* and *Elijah;* symphonies, overtures, string quartets, concertos and other pieces for the pianoforte, organ sonatas, much vocal music, secular and sacred.

407. ALLEIN GOTT IN DER HÖH SEI EHR (STETTIN) (arr.).

46. BETHLEHEM.	382. CONTEMPLATION.
501. BRESLAU (arr.).	255. INTERCESSION (in part).

MERBECKE, JOHN, or MARBECK, Mus.D. (? 1523–*c.* 1585, Windsor), was for many years organist of St. George's Chapel, Windsor, where he had been trained as a chorister. From an early age he studied the works of Calvin and embraced the principles of the Protestant Reformation. This he did not divulge, but in private he wrote annotations on the Bible and began the compilation of a Concordance to the Scriptures in English. When, in March 1542–3, commissioners descended on Windsor to make inquisition for heretical books, these writings were found in his possession. With three other citizens of Windsor he was arrested and imprisoned in the Marshalsea. When brought to trial on a charge of having copied an epistle of Calvin against the Mass, he was found guilty and condemned to death. Early editions of Foxe's *Acts and Monuments of the Church*, popularly known as *Foxe's Book of Martyrs*, describe him as having actually died a martyr's death at the stake. This is erroneous. He was pardoned, at the instance, it is said, of Gardiner, Bishop of Winchester, because of his musical talent. He did not avow his opinions till the accession of Edward VI. He then published his *Concordāce* (1550), the first complete concordance to the Scriptures in English. He escaped being made a victim of the

Marian persecution, and in the following reign published several religious works—*The Lyues of Holy Saincts; The Holie Historie of King David; The Ripping up of the Pope's Fardel; A Booke of Notes and Commonplaces*, &c. His best-known work was *The Boke of Common Praier noted* (1550). In this he carried out Cranmer's direction about Church song, that it should 'not be full of notes, but, as near as may be, for every syllable a note, so that it may be sung distinctly and devoutly'. The old Gregorian melodies were reduced to their simplest musical expression; 'all melodic flourishes were cut off, so that nothing should remain but pure musical declamation'. From these have been selected the melodies set in *The Church Hymnary* to the Sanctus (713), the Lord's Prayer (723), the Nicene Creed (725), and the responses to the Commandments (720). Specimens of his own compositions preserved by Hawkins and Burney show him to be worthy to rank with the ablest of his contemporaries.

MERCER, WILLIAM, D.D. (Barnard Castle, Durham, 1811–73, Leavy Greave, Sheffield), studied at Trinity College, Cambridge. In 1840 he became incumbent of St. George's, Sheffield. He issued in 1857 *The Church Psalter and Hymn Book, comprising the Psalter, or Psalms of David, together with the Canticles, Pointed for Chanting; Four Hundred Metrical Hymns and Six Responses to the Commandments; the whole united to appropriate Chants and Tunes, for the Use of Congregations and Families*. This was the most popular Church of England hymn-book of its time. In 1864 its annual sale was said to be 100,000. It was used in fifty-three London churches, and continued in use in St. Paul's Cathedral for ten years after *Hymns Ancient and Modern* had appeared. Its aim was to make the hymn-singing of the Church more congregational. Mercer himself contributed to it several translations and paraphrases from Latin and German. James Montgomery attended Mercer's church in his last years, and took a keen interest in the preparation of the book. Sir John Goss was the musical editor.

> 234. *God reveals His presence* (tr.).
> 55. *O come, all ye faithful* (tr.).

MERRILL, WILLIAM PIERSON, D.D. (Orange, New Jersey, 1867–), studied at Rutgers College and at Union Theological Seminary, New York. From both these foundations he received later the D.D. degree. Ordained to the Presbyterian ministry in 1890, he held charges at Philadelphia; Sixth Church, Chicago; and since 1911, the Brick Church, New York. A preacher of note, he has published several books that have wide acceptance: *Faith Building; Faith and Sight; Footings for Faith; Christian Internationalism; The Common Creed of Christians; The Freedom of the Preacher; Liberal Christianity*.

> 344. *Rise up, O men of God!*

MERRINGTON, ERNEST NORTHCROFT, Ph.D. (Newcastle, New South Wales, 1876–   ), was educated at Sydney High School, and, after five years of business experience, at Sydney University (M.A.), Edinburgh University and New College, and Harvard University, U.S.A. (Ph.D.). He was minister of the Presbyterian Church of Australia at Kiama, New South Wales, 1905–8; Haberfield, Sydney, 1908–10; St. Andrew's Church, Brisbane, Queensland, 1910–23; and, since the latter year, of the First Church of Otago, Dunedin, New Zealand. He lectured on Philosophy to the University of Sydney, 1907–9, and while in Brisbane founded Emmanuel College, under the Presbyterian Church, and from 1912 to 1923 was lecturer in Christian Philosophy and Apologetic there. During the Great War he was senior Presbyterian Chaplain of the First Australian Expeditionary Force, and served in Egypt and Gallipoli, and, later, in England, France, and Belgium. He has published *Casuistry* (1902), and *The Problem of Personality* (1916).

642. *God of Eternity, Lord of the Ages.*

MIDLANE, ALBERT (Newport, Isle of Wight, 1825–1909, Newport), was brought up by a godly mother, his father having died shortly before he was born. He was an ironmonger in business. He belonged to the sect of the Strict Brethren, and ministered regularly to a congregation of that body. He had a lifelong interest in Sunday School work, and much of his verse drew its inspiration from that source. Of his more than 500 hymns many appeared in his *Poetry addressed to Sabbath School Teachers* (1844); *Vecta Garland* (1850); *Leaves from Olivet* (1864); *Gospel Echoes* (1865); *Above the Bright Blue Sky* (1867); *Early Lispings* (1880); and in *The Bright Blue Sky Hymn Book*, and *The Mission Hall Hymn Book*.

679. *Revive Thy work, O Lord.*
593. *There's a Friend for little children.*

MILES, SARAH ELIZABETH, *née* APPLETON (Boston, Massachusetts, 1807–77, Brattleborough, Vermont), wrote most of her hymns at an early age, and they were sent to the press by her father. She married in 1833 Solomon P. Miles, head-master of the Boston High School, and afterwards principal of a private school for girls in the same city. After his death, in 1872, Mrs. Miles resided with her son at Brattleborough.

147. *Thou who didst stoop below.*

MILGROVE, BENJAMIN (Bath? 1731–1810, Bath?), was precentor and then organist of the Countess of Huntingdon's Chapel in Bath. He published *Sixteen Hymns as they are sung at the Right Honourable the Countess of Huntingdon's Chapel in Bath. Set to Music* (*c.* 1769). He wrote some of his tunes in duet form, with lines to be sung alternately by men and women, who then sat on different sides of the chapels.

11. HARTS.   447. MOUNT EPHRAIM.

MILLER, EDWARD, Mus. Doc. (Norwich, 1731–1807, Doncaster), was apprenticed to his father's trade of pavior, but ran away to be free to follow his bent towards the study of music. He became a pupil of Dr. Burney, and for a time played the German flute in Handel's orchestra. For over fifty years (1756–1807) he was organist of Doncaster Parish Church. He is described as a 'warm-hearted, simple-hearted, right-hearted man, an enthusiast in his profession, yet not undervaluing, much less despising, other pursuits'. He wrote on antiquarian subjects, and published a *History of Doncaster*. Dissatisfaction with the existing state of church music led him to publish an edition of *The Psalms of David*, with tunes, in 1790; *Psalms and Hymns set to New Music*, 1801; *Sacred Music . . . an Appendix to Dr. Watts' Psalms and Hymns*, 1802. The first of these was very popular. George III marked his approval of it by sending the editor a gift of £25. In the Isle of Man a number of enthusiastic Manx admirers subscribed to provide a barrel-organ to play Miller's tunes.

106, 312. ROCKINGHAM (COMMUNION).

MILLER, EMILY, *née* HUNTINGTON, M.A. (Brooklyn, Connecticut, 1833–1913, St. Paul, Minnesota), was a daughter of the Rev. Thomas Huntingdon, D.D. She graduated at Oberlin College in 1857, and in 1860 married Professor John E. Miller. She was Dean of women students in North-Western University, 1891–98. She edited a periodical, *The Little Corporal*, wrote numerous stories, *Captain Frith, Little Neighbours*, &c., and published in Chicago a volume of poems, *From Avalon, and Other Poems*.

71. *I love to hear the story.*

MILLER, JOHN—originally JOHANNES MUELLER (Groshennersdorf, near Herrnhut, Saxony, 1756–90, Fulneck, Yorkshire), was of Lutheran parentage, but was educated at the Moravian Grammar School, Niesky, and the Moravian Theological College, Barby, near Magdeburg. In 1781 he came to Fulneck, the educational centre of the Moravians in England, near Leeds, as assistant preacher and chaplain to the single men and boys in the Fulneck Church and School. In 1788 he married and became minister of the neighbouring congregation in Pudsey. He died of consumption. The editor of the 1789 edition of *The Moravian Hymnbook* was J. Swertner, but Miller collaborated with F. W. Foster (q.v.) in revising older translations and preparing new ones. At least twelve translations are attributed to them jointly. Miller is not known to have written any original hymns, but several translations of entire hymns and of individual stanzas are attributed to him.

234. *God reveals His presence* (tr.).

MILMAN, HENRY HART, D.D. (London, 1791–1868, Sunninghill, Ascot), was son of Sir Francis Milman, Bart., physician to the King. He was educated at Greenwich, Eton, and Brasenose College, Oxford, where he had a career of extraordinary brilliance; he won the Newdigate Prize with his *Belvidere Apollo*, 'best of Oxford prize poems,' and became a Fellow of his college. Ordained in 1816, he received in 1818 the living of St. Mary's, Reading; in 1821–31 was Professor of Poetry at Oxford; in 1827 was Bampton Lecturer; in 1835 received a canonry of Westminster, with the rectorship of St. Margaret's; and in 1849 accepted the Deanery of St. Paul's. He wrote a number of dramas, one of which, *Fazio*, was produced at Covent Garden with triumphant success, and was afterwards translated into Italian and acted with Madame Ristori in the principal part. In *Nala and Damayanti, and other Poems translated from the Sanskrit* (1834), he was one of the first interpreters of Indian thought and life to the mind of the West. He published also admirable translations of Horace, and of the *Agamemnon* and *Bacchae*. But it is as a historian that he is likely to be remembered. His *History of the Jews* aroused great commotion in 1830, because of his application of the modern historical method to his treatment of the subject. His attitude was thoroughly reverent, though critical, but the method was unfamiliar, and the storm was so fierce that the sale of the book was stopped, and the series in which it appeared came to an end. Later, it was republished after revision. His *History of Christianity from the Birth of Christ to the Abolition of Paganism in the Roman Empire* was followed by his *History of Latin Christianity to the Pontificate of Nicholas V* (1856), one of the masterpieces of English ecclesiastical history. His *Poetical Works* were collected in three volumes. His *Annals of St. Paul's Cathedral* appeared after his death. His thirteen hymns were written at the instance of his friend Heber, and appeared in *Hymns Adapted to the Weekly Church Service of the Year*, published after Heber's death, and in *Hymns for the Use of St. Margaret's, Westminster* (1837).

455. *O help us, Lord, each hour of need*.
92. *Ride on, ride on in majesty*.
329. *When our heads are bowed with woe*.

MILTON, JOHN (London, 1608–74, London), by common consent second only to Shakespeare among English poets, was the son of a scrivener of good education and some musical talent. The poet was educated at St. Paul's School, besides having for tutor a Scotsman named Thomas Young. Among his early friends was Charles Diodati, a naturalized Italian, whose death he afterwards mourned in the Latin poem *Epitaphium Damonis*. He went to Christ's College, Cambridge, which he left for a time owing to disagreement with his tutor, but returned and graduated B.A. in 1628 and M.A. in 1632. Milton's literary life falls into three well-marked periods, the first including his earlier and shorter poems, the second almost entirely occupied with controversial and political writings, and the third containing his poems on a grander scale. Much of his best work was produced at a comparatively early age. Thus his paraphrase of Psalm cxxxvi (Hymn 11) was written before he was sixteen years of age; while the *Ode on the morning of Christ's Nativity* (from which Hymn 61 is taken) was composed in 1629, *L' Allegro* and *Il Penseroso* about 1630, *Comus* in 1634, and *Lycidas* in 1637. It was shortly after an Italian tour in 1638–9, on which he met many interesting people and saw and heard much that appealed to his artistic temperament, that Milton's energies were diverted into a far different channel—the controversies leading to the Civil War and the establishment of the Commonwealth. For many years his chief writings were of a polemical character, including tractates on the reform of Church discipline, on divorce (suggested, no doubt, by an unfortunate matrimonial experience of his own), on the liberty of unlicensed printing, and other causes. Having upheld the lawfulness of the King's execution, he was appointed Secretary for foreign tongues to the Council of State, a post which he continued to fill, notwithstanding his blindness (which became total in 1652), until the eve of the Restoration. This period saw also his *Defences* against Salmasius and Morus—works of great interest, though disfigured by bitter invective. It is to the credit of the royalists that so pronounced a republican as Milton should have escaped severe punishment on the re-establishment of the monarchy. For some years he lived in close retirement, neglected by his own family and surrounded by but a few faithful friends. The publication in 1667 of *Paradise Lost* (written in 1665 but projected many years earlier) brought him favour and the admiration of even his political enemies, Dryden being reported to have said 'This man cuts us all out, and the ancients too'. In 1771 followed *Paradise Regained* and *Samson Agonistes*. In spite of the exquisite beauty of his lyrics, Milton's direct influence on hymnology has been surprisingly slight. He is the scholar's rather than the people's poet.

> 11. *Let us with a gladsome mind.*
> 61. *Ring out, ye crystal spheres.*
> 151. *The Lord will come and not be slow.*

MOFFATT, JAMES, D.D., D.Litt. (Glasgow, 1870–), was educated at the Academy, the University, and the Free Church College, Glasgow, for the ministry of the Free (now the United Free) Church of Scotland. Ordained in 1896, he held charges at Dundonald, Ayrshire, and the East Church, Broughty Ferry. He was Jowett Lecturer, London, in 1907; Yates Professor of Greek and the New Testament in Mansfield College, Oxford, 1911–15; Professor of Church History in the United Free Church College, Glasgow, 1915–27; and is now Washburn Professor of Church History in Union Theological Seminary, New York. He was a member of the Revision Committee of the present *Church Hymnary*.

586. ULTIMA.

MOHR, JOSEPH (Salzburg, 1792–1848, Wagrein), was in 1815 ordained to the priesthood of the Roman Church by the Bishop of Salzburg. He was successively assistant-priest at Ramsau and Laufen; then coadjutor at Kuchl, at Golling, Vigann, Adnet, and Authering; then vicar-substitute at Hof and at Hintersee—all in the diocese of Salzburg. In 1828 he became vicar at Hintersee, and in 1837 at Wagrein, near St. Johann.

49. *Still the night, holy the night!*

MONK, EDWIN GEORGE, Mus. Doc. (Frome, Somerset, 1819–1900, Radley, Berkshire), went early to London, studied singing under Hullah, and was a private pupil of Henry Philips and G. A. Macfarren. After acting as organist of Midsomer Norton Parish Church and of Christ Church, Frome, he was appointed first organist, precentor, and music-master of St. Columba's College, Stackallan (afterwards removed to Rathfarnham, near Dublin), the first public school in Ireland established on strictly Anglican Church principles. After three years he removed to Oxford, and conducted the University Motet and Madrigal Society. For eleven years he was organist and music-master of St. Peter's College, Radley; he conceived such a love for that village that he retired to it ultimately to spend his closing years. In 1858 he succeeded John Camidge as organist of York Minster, and remained there till 1883. During his reign he superintended the erection of the huge screen organ. For twelve years he was examiner for musical degrees at Oxford. He was a F.R.A.S.; astronomy was his hobby. He composed a setting of Milton's *Ode on the Nativity;* numerous songs, anthems, &c.; compiled the libretti for G. A. Macfarren's oratorios *St. John the Baptist, The Resurrection,* and *Joseph;* and edited *The Anglican Chant Book, The Anglican Choral Service Book, Chants for the Daily Psalms, as used in York Minster* (which had a great circulation), *Unison Chants for the Psalter, The Anglican Hymn Book* (with the Rev. R. C. Singleton), and (with Sir F. A. Gore Ouseley) *The Psalter and Canticles Pointed for Chanting.*

252. ANGEL VOICES.

MONK, MARK JAMES, Mus. Doc. (Hunmanby, Yorkshire, 1858–), received his musical training at York Minster under his uncle, Dr. E. G. Monk (q.v.), became organist of various churches in York, then in succession, of St. John's, Ladywood, Birmingham;

Ashby-de-la-Zouch Parish Church; Banbury; and Truro Cathedral (1890–1920). At Truro he was diocesan choirmaster, conductor of the Philharmonic Society; he conducted also at various festivals. His compositions include *An Elegiac Ode* for soli, five-part chorus, strings and organ; a *Festival Te Deum;* a Madrigal; organ pieces, &c. He retired in 1920 to Bournemouth.

245. CAMPFIELDS.

MONK, WILLIAM HENRY, Mus. Doc. (Brompton, 1823–89, Stoke Newington), became organist successively of Eaton Chapel, Pimlico; St. George's Chapel, Albemarle Street; Portman Chapel, Marylebone; and St. Matthias, Stoke Newington, where a voluntary choir under his direction sustained a daily choral service. Concurrently with this last appointment he held the offices of director of the choir and organist of King's College, London, and from 1874 was professor of vocal music there. He delivered lectures at the London Institution, the Edinburgh Philosophical Institution, and the Royal Institution, Manchester. In 1876 he was appointed a professor in the National Training School for Music and in Bedford College. His chief title to fame is his identification with *Hymns Ancient and Modern*, of which he was the first musical editor. The title chosen was of his suggestion. 'He had the sole musical initiative and veto on the original edition, and no other musical counsel was called in until the position of the book had been made.' In its early days it was often called 'Monk's book'. He supervised other collections of church music also, for the Church of Scotland among others. He wrote but one song to secular words; being a man of deep religious conviction and devotional feeling, he devoted his powers entirely to the enrichment and elevation of congregational worship-music. The first thing in his mind in all church music was its worship value. 'The organ was to him an instrument, not for the display of skill, but for touching the souls of men.' He published many anthems, Te Deums, Kyries, &c.; and edited *Hymns of the Church; The Holy Year; Fifty-two Simple Chants; The Book of Psalms in Metre; The Scottish Hymnal*, and a *Book of Anthems*—these three for the Church of Scotland.

248. ADSIS JESU.
157. BEVERLEY.
66. COLYTON.
178. EVELYNS.
286. EVENTIDE.
629. MINTO.
266. MORNING.
702. NUTFIELD.

462. ST. CONSTANTINE.
534. ST. ETHELWALD.
302. ST. MATTHIAS.
186, 405. ST. PHILIP.
391. STEPHANOS (arr.).
320. UNDE ET MEMORES.
122. VICTORY (arr.).
523. VIGILATE.

MONSELL, JOHN SAMUEL BEWLEY, LL.D. (St. Columb's, Derry, 1811–75, Guildford), was the son of an archdeacon of Londonderry and brother of the first Lord Emly. He was educated at Trinity College, Dublin, and ordained in 1834. He became chaplain to Bishop Mant; Chancellor of the Diocese of Connor; rector of Ramoan; then, proceeding to England, was vicar of Egham, Surrey; and rector of St. Nicholas, Guildford. Here he died of injuries caused by the fall of a stone from the roof of his church while he was watching rebuilding operations. A hymn he wrote to raise funds for this rebuilding contained a remarkable premonition of his approaching death:

> Dear body, thou and I must part;
> Thy busy head, thy throbbing heart
> Must cease to work and cease to play,
> For me at no far distant day.

He was a persuasive preacher, and a singularly devout and sunny-hearted man. Of his home at Guildford one who knew it said: 'It was quite an ideal household, full of the beauty of holiness, with genial brightness and gaiety playing like sunshine over all the troubles of life.' He held that hymns should be 'more fervent and joyous. We are too distant and reserved in our praises; we sing not as we should sing to Him and of Him who is Chief among ten thousand, the Altogether Lovely.' He published eleven volumes of poetry, including nearly 300 hymns, of which more than seventy are in use: *Hymns and Miscellaneous Poems; Parish Musings; Spiritual Songs for the Sundays and Holy Days throughout the Year; Hymns of Love and Praise for the Church's Year; The Passing Bell; Litany Hymns; The Parish Hymnal after the Order of the Book of Common Prayer; Watches by the Cross; Simon the Cyrenian; Nursery Carols;* &c.

517. *Fight the good fight with all thy might.*
335. *Lord of the living harvest.*
426. *O Thou whose mercy found me.*
174. *Rest of the weary, joy of the sad.*
 23. *Sing to the Lord a joyful song.*
232. *Worship the Lord in the beauty of holiness.*

MONTGOMERY, JAMES (Irvine, Ayrshire, 1771–1854, Sheffield), was the son of an Ulster Scot of peasant stock who qualified for the ministry of the Moravian Brotherhood, had charge for some years of a congregation in Irvine, then removed to the Moravian Settlement formed in 1746 by John Cennick at Gracehill, Ballymena, Co. Antrim; and finally went as a missionary to the West Indies, where both he and his wife died. James used playfully to say that he had 'narrowly escaped being an Irishman'. He was educated at Fulneck with a view to the ministry, but the Brethren, dissatisfied with his progress, apprenticed him to a baker. He ran away and entered a chandler's shop at Mirfield, near Wakefield. Finding that also uncongenial, he ran away again to Wath-upon-Dearne, near Rotherham. At eighteen he repaired to London and spent a year in a vain endeavour to find a publisher for his poems. In 1794 he went to Sheffield to assist a bookseller and printer named Gales on the staff of *The Sheffield Register*. Two years later, Gales had to leave the country to avoid prosecution for the liberal opinions advocated in that newspaper. Montgomery became editor, and conducted the paper, under the name of *The Sheffield Iris*, for thirty-one years. Twice he suffered fine and imprisonment in York Castle—first, for printing a song in celebration of the Fall of the Bastille; and second, for giving an account of a political riot in Sheffield. He led a busy life, editing his paper, lecturing on poetry; advocating the causes of foreign missions and the Bible Society in many parts of the country. In 1833 he received a royal pension of £200 a year. He died in sleep, and was accorded a public funeral. A statue commemorates him in Sheffield. He published *The West Indies, a Poem in honour of the Abolition of the Slave-Trade* (1807); *The World Before the Flood* (1813); *Songs of Zion* (1822); *The Pelican Island* (1828); *The Poet's Portfolio* (1835); *Original Hymns* (1853). Most of his 400 hymns were written early in life. He composed, he said, 'very slowly, and only by fits'. He 'lay in wait for his heart, to catch its highest emotions'. More than 100 of his hymns are still in use. When asked by a Whitby solicitor, 'Which of your poems will live?' his answer was, 'None, sir; nothing, except, perhaps, a few of my hymns'. Canon Ellerton declared him 'our first hymnologist; the first Englishman who collected and criticized hymns, and who made people that had lost all recollection of ancient models understand something of what a hymn meant, and what it ought to be'.

313. *According to Thy gracious word.*
 65. *Angels from the realms of glory.*
241. *Command Thy blessing from above.*
583. *For ever with the Lord.*
527. *God is my strong salvation.*
154. *Hail to the Lord's Anointed!*
389. *Hark! the song of jubilee.*
525. *In the hour of trial.*
385. *Lift up your heads, ye gates of brass.*
473. *O God, Thou art my God alone.*
386. *O Spirit of the living God.*
333. *Pour out Thy Spirit from on high.*
 38. *Songs of praise the angels sang.*
233. *Stand up and bless the Lord.*
253. *This stone to Thee in faith we lay.*

MOORE, Thomas (Manchester? *c.* 1710–*c.* 92, Glasgow), was a music teacher in Manchester about 1740–50. In the latter year he published in that city *The Psalm-Singer's Divine Companion* (2 vols.), a second edition being issued in the same year as *The Psalm-Singer's*

Compleat Tutor and Divine Companion. Going to Glasgow, he became, in 1755, precentor in Blackfriars Parish Church, and in 1756 was appointed by the magistrates teacher of the free music classes in Hutcheson's Hospital. He published in Glasgow *The Psalm-Singer's Pocket Companion, containing great variety of the best English Psalm-Tunes, suited to the different metres in the Scotch Version of the Psalms of David, set in three and four parts; likewise all the tunes that are usually sung in most parts of Scotland; with a plain and easy introduction to Musick* (1756); and *The Psalm-Singer's Delightful Pocket Companion, Containing a Plain and Easy Introduction to Psalmody, and an Introduction explaining more at large the grounds of Music in general. Illustrated with great variety of Tables, Scales, and Initial Lessons* (1761).

365. (GLASGOW).

MOORE, THOMAS (Dublin, 1779–1852, Sloperton, Devizes), was the son of a grocer and wine-merchant, and was educated at Trinity College, Dublin, where, however, he could not graduate, owing to his being a Roman Catholic. He studied law at the Middle Temple, London. In 1804 he went to Bermuda as registrar to the Admiralty Court, but, finding the duties irksome, he appointed a deputy, and returned to England. Subsequently, this deputy was guilty of serious malfeasance, which involved Moore in financial ruin and made him flee to the Continent, where he spent three years in exile. His first volume of poetry had been published as *Poems by the late Thomas Little* (1801). The next, *Odes and Epistles* (1806), was so severely reviewed by Jeffrey that Moore challenged his critic to a duel. Bow Street officers stopped the encounter just as the two diminutive antagonists were about to fire. Moore became a favourite in London society, his sparkling wit, social gifts, and musical accomplishments making him a charming figure in the most exclusive drawing-rooms. He retired, however, to a cottage near Ashbourne, Derbyshire, and there produced *National Airs; Sacred Songs and Trios; Irish Melodies;* and *Lalla Rookh,* for which he received the then immense sum of £3,000, and which had a great popularity. His later years were saddened by heavy domestic trials. He spent them in retirement in a cottage near Devizes, with a pension of £300 a year, and there collected his *Poetical Works.* He was a pioneer in the lyrical revival. Though the most versatile writer of his time, his reputation now rests entirely on a few simple sentimental lyrics. His *Sacred Songs* (1816) number thirty-two. Byron wrote his *Life.*

688. *Come, ye disconsolate, where'er ye languish.*

MORGAN, ALFRED PHILLIPS (near Builth Wells, Breconshire, 1857–   ), won choral honours at the Welsh National Eisteddfod in 1897 and 1898. He is a composer of church music, part-songs, &c. For many years he has been director of music at the Presbyterian

Church of Wales, Builth Wells, where he has brought the congregational singing to a pitch of excellence that makes it an inspiration and pattern to the churches in a wide area around. He was a member of the Welsh sub-committee in connexion with the revision of *The Church Hymnary*.

523. ST. APOLLOS.

MORISON, JOHN, D.D. (Cairnie, Aberdeenshire, 1750–98, Canisbay), studied at King's College, Aberdeen, where he graduated, and after holding several teaching appointments in Caithness, repaired to Edinburgh for further study, especially in Greek. Probably while acting as a master in Thurso school, he had become acquainted with John Logan (q.v.), then at Thurso Castle superintending the education of young Sir John Sinclair of Ulbster; and on his arrival in Edinburgh Logan introduced him to Dr. Macfarlane of the Canongate Second Charge, who was a member of the Committee of Assembly then engaged on the preparation of the Paraphrases. Under encouragement from that quarter, Morison submitted twenty-four pieces to the Committee. Seven were accepted—Paraphrases xix, xxi, xxix, xxx, which were but slightly altered; xxvii and xxviii, which were either considerably altered by Logan, or written jointly by Morison and Logan; and xxxv, which underwent a good deal of alteration. In 1779 Morison was presented to the parish of Canisbay, Caithness, and was ordained nine months later, in September 1780. At the Assembly of the following year he was appointed a member of the Committee for revising the collection of *Translations and Paraphrases* to which he had himself contributed. A number of poetical pieces by him appeared in *The Edinburgh Weekly Magazine*, over the signature of 'Musaeus'; he wrote also the account of the parish of Canisbay for Sir John Sinclair's *Statistical Account*, and collected the topographical history of Caithness for Chalmers's *Caledonia*.

400. *Come, let us to the Lord our God.*

57. *The race that long in darkness pined.*

312. *'Twas on that night when doomed to know.*

MORLEY, HENRY KILLICK (*c.* 1855–?), was for some time organist of St. Paul's Church, Herne Hill, London, but resigned in 1883 and went to America. No information as to his life there can be found.

36. NEWCASTLE.

MORRIS, ELIZA FRANCES (FANNY), *née* GOFFE (London, 1821–74, Malvern), was brought up in the country, and her love of nature drew forth her poetical talent. Her health was delicate. In 1849 she married Josiah Morris, then sub-editor of *The Malvern News*. She contributed the words to *School Harmonies*, edited by her hus-

439

band, and herself edited a *Bible Class Hymn Book*, and published *The Voice and the Reply* (1858), and *Life Lyrics*.

240. *God of pity, God of grace.*

MOTE, EDWARD (London, 1797–1874, Horsham, Sussex), was converted under the preaching of the Rev. J. Hyatt, of Tottenham Court Road Chapel, and became a Baptist minister. During the last twenty-six years of his life he ministered to a congregation at Horsham. He published several pamphlets, and, in 1836, *Hymns of Praise, a New Selection of Gospel Hymns, combining all the Excellencies of our Spiritual Poets, with many Originals*. There were 100 originals in this book.

697. *My hope is built on nothing less.*

MOUNTAIN, JAMES, D.D. (New Wortley, Leeds, 1844– 1933), was educated for the Congregational ministry at Cheshunt College, and subsequently studied at Heidelberg and Tübingen. He was ordained at Great Marlow, but had to resign owing to a breakdown in health which necessitated two years' residence in Switzerland. Coming under the influence of the Moody and Sankey revival, he devoted eight years to mission preaching in this country, and seven to an evangelistic tour round the world. He concluded a twenty years' ministry in Emmanuel Church and St. John's Free Church, Tunbridge Wells, in 1898, and since then has been active in movements for Bible Defence and the deepening of the spiritual life. He edited *Newness of Life* for several years, and now edits *The Bible Call*. He (1892) has written many hymns and tunes, and compiled the first edition of *Hymns of Consecration and Faith*. His doctorate was conferred by Ewing College, Illinois.

443. LIKE A RIVER.

MUDIE, CHARLES EDWARD (Chelsea, 1818–90, London), was the son of Scottish parents. He was for some time a bookseller, but started, when twenty-four years old, the well-known circulating library known as Mudie's Select Library. He was a Congregationalist, and for many years was a director of the London Missionary Society. His interest in home mission work was life-long, and he engaged in it actively in the neighbourhood of Vauxhall Bridge Road until failing health compelled him to resign. In 1872 he published *Stray Leaves*, a collection of verses most of which were written during a long and severe illness.

427. *I lift my heart to Thee.*

NARES, JAMES, Mus. Doc. (Stanwell, Middlesex, 1715–83, London), was a pupil of Gates, Croft, and Pepusch, and a chorister of the Chapel Royal. For a time he was assistant organist of St. George's Chapel, Windsor; then became organist of York Cathedral in 1734;

and organist and composer to the Chapel Royal, in succession to Dr. Maurice Greene, in 1756; he was also master of the children of the Chapel Royal, 1757–80. He had a passion for literature and was a man of unusual cultivation. Grove's *Dictionary of Music* in its first edition described his music as 'poor', but in the last edition this characterization was handsomely withdrawn. He published several books of lessons on the harpsichord, a *Treatise on Singing; A Collection of Catches, Canons, and Glees; The Royal Pastoral*, a *Dramatic Ode;* over fifty anthems, six organ fugues, two Services, and some melodious psalm-tunes.

715. CHANT IN A FLAT.

NAYLOR, Edward Woodall, Mus. Doc. (Scarborough, 1867–   ), son of Dr. John Naylor, organist of York Minster, was trained as a chorister under his father. After periods of service in St. Michael's, Chester Square, and St. Mary's, Kilburn, London, he became, in 1897, organist of Emmanuel College, Cambridge, of which he is now also a lecturer and hon. Fellow. He is also Lecturer in Musical History in the University. His first appearance as a composer was in 1892, in the old St. James's Hall, London, with *Merlin and the Gleam*. He has since published *The Angelus*, an opera performed at Covent Garden in 1909; *Arthur the King; Pax Dei*, a requiem; anthems, &c.; also books on historical music, *Shakespeare and Music; An Elizabethan Virginal Book; Shakespeare Music;* papers on H. Schütz and J. Handl, &c.

534. FROM STRENGTH TO STRENGTH.

NAZIANZEN, St. Gregory. *See* GREGORY.

NEALE, John Mason, D.D. (London, 1818–66, East Grinstead), was educated at Sherborne Grammar School and Trinity College, Cambridge. He became a Fellow of Downing College, and gained the Seatonian prize for a sacred poem eleven times. Though his upbringing had been strictly evangelical, he became interested in the High Church movement while at the University, and the advanced views he came to hold proved an insuperable obstacle to his preferment. In 1843 he was presented to the small living of Crawley, Sussex, but he was never instituted to the charge, owing to an attack of lung trouble compelling him to go to Madeira. There, fortunately, a remarkable library enabled him to read enormously and to store up materials for his subsequent books. In 1846 Earl de la Warr presented him to the wardenship of Sackville College, East Grinstead, a refuge for indigent old men. There, at a salary of £27 a year, the most learned hymnologist and liturgiologist of his time was allowed to remain for the rest of his life. The only preferment ever offered him was the Provostship of St. Ninian's Cathedral, Perth, but the climate was too cold to permit him to reside there. His own Church had no honours for him; even his D.D. came from America. In the face of bitter opposition he instituted a number of beneficent agencies. The sisterhood of St. Margaret's at East Grinstead, to 'minister to the bodily, and then to the spiritual needs of the sick and suffering poor, going to their homes whenever called for, living with them, sharing their discomforts, refusing no difficulty, and adapting themselves to all circumstances', developed into a great organization, with many branches at home and abroad. He founded also an orphanage, a middle-class school for girls, and at Aldershot a house for the reclamation of fallen women. This last had to be closed because of the opposition. For fourteen years Neale was inhibited by his bishop. In time he lived suspicion and misunderstanding down. He occupied himself in literary pursuits, producing *A Commentary on the Psalms, from Primitive and Mediaeval Writers* (with Dr. Littledale, q.v.); *The History of the Holy Eastern Church; The Patriarchate of Alexandria; Essays on Liturgiology and Church History*. But his chief title to remembrance and gratitude rests on his translations. He brought to light rich treasures of Greek and Latin hymns, many of which had long been buried in monasteries and cathedral libraries on the Continent and in Asia Minor. He was an excellent classical scholar and a master of medieval Latin; a true poet also, with a clear and translucent style. The best of his translations are indubitable works of genius. He published, from the Latin—*Mediaeval Hymns and Sequences; The Hymnal Noted* (94 hymns out of 105 translated from Latin are his); *Hymns, chiefly Mediaeval, on the Joys and Glories of Paradise;* and from the Greek—*Hymns of the Eastern Church*, in which he broke entirely new ground. He claimed no rights in his hymns, holding that 'a hymn, whether original or translated, ought, the moment it is published, to become the common property of Christendom, the author retaining no private right in it whatever. I suppose that no one ever sent forth a hymn without some faint hope that he might be casting his two mites into that treasury of the Church, into which the "many that were rich"—Ambrose and Hildebert, and Adam and Bernard of Cluny, and St. Bernard; yes, and Santeüil and Coffin, "cast in much". But having so cast it in, is not the claiming a vested interest in it something like "keeping back part of the price of the land?" ' On his death-bed, when he could neither write nor compose, they sang to him the hymns of Bernard of Morlaix. At his funeral they sang 'Safe home, safe home in port', his own translation of a hymn of Joseph the hymnographer. On his coffin was inscribed by his own instruction, 'J. M. Neale, miser et indigens sacerdos requiescens sub SIGNO THAU' (poor and unworthy priest resting under the sign of the Cross—'Thau' being the word in the Vulgate translation of Ezekiel ix. 4—Transi per mediam civitatem in medio Jerusalem, et signa THAU super frontes virorum). 'Of all his teachings', one who knew him wrote, 'the most edifying to my own soul was when I saw him in his last illness laying in the dust all his works and all his talents, and casting himself as a little child only on the atoning work of Jesus Christ.'

91. *All glory, laud, and honour* (tr.).
609. *All is bright and cheerful round us.*
391. *Art thou weary, art thou languid?* (tr.).
597. *Brief life is here our portion* (tr.).
207. *Christ is made the sure foundation* (tr.).
186. *Come, Thou Holy Paraclete* (tr.).
84. *Fierce was the wild billow* (tr.).
598. *For thee, O dear, dear country* (tr.).
58. *Good Christian men, rejoice.*
599. *Jerusalem the golden* (tr.).
421. *Jesus! the very thought is sweet* (tr.).
258. *Now that the daylight fills the sky* (tr.).
149. *O come, O come, Immanuel* (tr.).
577. *O happy band of pilgrims* (tr.).
124. *O sons and daughters, let us sing!* (tr.).
224. *O what their joy and their glory must be!* (tr.).
89. *O wondrous type, O vision fair* (tr.).
60. *Of the Father's love begotten* (tr.).
108. *Sing, my tongue, how glorious battle* (tr.).
287. *The day is past and over* (tr.).
123. *The day of resurrection* (tr.).
14. *The strain upraise of joy and praise* (tr.).
164. *To the Name of our Salvation* (tr.).

NEANDER, JOACHIM (Bremen, 1650–80, Bremen), whose real name was Neumann, was educated at the Pädagogium and the Gymnasium Illustre in his native city. He was careless in his youth, but was brought under religious conviction by Undereyk, minister of St. Martin's Church, whose colleague he was afterwards to become, and the conviction was deepened by certain alarming experiences he passed through at that time. He associated himself with the Pietists, and became a friend of Spener, the leader of that school. His zeal, when appointed in 1674 to the head-mastership of the Reformed Grammar School at Düsseldorf, induced him to go beyond his official duty and seek, by preaching and private religious meetings, the spiritual good of his fellow-townsmen. Opposition was provoked, and he was suspended from office and obliged to leave the town. For some months he lived in a cave near Mettman on the Rhine, which is still called Neander's cave. In 1679 he returned to Bremen as second preacher in St. Martin's. Again his faithful preaching aroused opposition. But his ministry was brief. He was seized with consumption and died the following year. He was a man of scholarship and accomplishment in poetry, letters, and music, as well as theology. He was 'the first poet of the Reformed Church in Germany'. He wrote some sixty hymns, many of which are still used in the Reformed and Lutheran Churches there, and composed tunes for them. They were collected and published in 1680 under the curious title A *und* Ω, *Joachimi Neander Glaub- und Liebes- übung*.

22. *Praise to the Lord, the Almighty, the King of creation.*
448. *All my hope on God is founded.*

234. GOTT IST GEGENWÄRTIG (ARNSBERG).
448. MEINE HOFFNUNG (?).   163, 387. NEANDER.

NEUMARK, GEORG (Langensalza, Thuringia, 1621–81, Weimar), was the son of a clothier. He was educated at the Gymnasia of Schleusingen and Gotha. On his way to Königsberg to attend the University there, the only one which the Thirty Years War had left undisorganized, he was robbed by highwaymen on the Gardelegen Heath, and stripped of all his possessions but his prayer-book and a little money sewn into his clothing. The University having been thus made impossible, he tried to find employment, but sought it in town after town in vain. His privations were severe. At last, in Kiel, he succeeded in enlisting the interest of a fellow-Thuringian who was chief pastor there, and who got him a tutorship. This sudden relief was the occasion of his composing the hymn and tune named below. In Kiel he remained till he had saved enough to enable him to matriculate at Königsberg (1643). There he studied law, and, under Simon Dach, poetry. On leaving the University he moved about, earning a precarious living as he could—to Warsaw, Thorn, Danzig, and in 1651 to Hamburg. There again he suffered great poverty through unemployment. When things were at their worst with him, a servant of the Swedish ambassador, Baron von Rosen- kranz, enlisted his master's interest on behalf of this case of suffer- ing genius, and employment was found for him. Afterwards he returned to Thuringia and was appointed court-poet, librarian and registrar to the administration of Duke Wilhelm II of Saxe-Weimar, and finally custodian of the ducal archives. In 1656 he was made secretary of the Fruit-Bearing Society, the principal German literary union of the seventeenth century. Blindness overtook him in 1681. The hymns of his prosperous years were markedly inferior to those written during his years of hardship.

541. *If thou but suffer God to guide thee.*
541. NEUMARK.

NEUMEISTER, ERDMANN (Uechteritz, near Weissenfels, 1671– 1756, Hamburg), was the son of a schoolmaster and organist. After studying and graduating at Leipzig he became a lecturer in the University there. In 1697 he was ordained assistant-minister at Bibra, and a year later became full pastor, and assistant-superintendent of Eckatsberg district. He removed to Weissenfels in 1704 to act as tutor to the Duke's only daughter, and as assistant court preacher; and shortly afterwards was promoted to be court preacher. On the death of his pupil he transferred his services to Sorau, where he was court preacher, Consistorialrath, and superintendent. In 1715 he became pastor of St. James's Church, Hamburg. An earnest and eloquent preacher, he was a strong High Lutheran, and vehemently opposed Pietism and Moravianism because of the excessive subjectivity of their teaching; he carried on a vigorous controversy against them. He was a man of wide culture. One of the first historico-critical works on German poetry was from his pen. He is reputed also to have been the originator of the cantata form of church music; he himself composed many works in that form. Hymnwriting was, from his student-days, a life-long practice. Of the 650 hymns composed by him, many are of the highest standard and remain in general German use.

394. Sinners Jesus will receive.

NEWMAN, JOHN HENRY, Cardinal, D.D. (London, 1801–90, Edgbaston), son of a banker, had Huguenot blood in him, and was brought up in the evangelical faith. His precocious and lonely boyhood was spent in a world of dreams; he was a romanticist from his youth up. Religion from the first was of the very fibre of his being. A distinguished career at Trinity College, Oxford, led to a fellowship at Oriel and the vice-presidentship of St. Alban's Hall. From 1828 to 1843 he was vicar of St. Mary the Virgin, the University Church; his preaching from its pulpit, 'like a fine strain of unearthly music,' affected Oxford profoundly by its charm and religious power. He had a rare personality, rich in genius and gift, and refined and penetrating in influence. But his mind was reactionary, irreconcilably antipathetic to modern ideals and liberalism in all its expressions. When, therefore, he set himself, with others like-minded, to lead the Church of England towards the revival of religion of which they saw its desperate need, the movement he headed turned its face resolutely to the past. It conceived the proper bulwark against the dangers of the time to be a revival of the mystical glories of the Middle Ages. But his idealization of that period was unhistorical; the glories he was fain to lead the Church back to were largely creations of a romantic imagination. A weapon was needed with which to smite the liberal movement; he sought it in a Church whose Divinely-given authority would lay under subjection the spirit of free reason in which he saw the root of modern ills. But the notes of authority seemed to him lacking in the Church of England. Driven by his own processes of reason to the conclusion that it was neither apostolic nor catholic, he came to believe that the only Church that answered those requirements was the Church of Rome. Resigning his living, he spent three years in an agony of doubt and hesitation at Littlemore; then, in 1845, he was received into the Roman Communion. His career in that Church was a monotonous record of frustration and failure. Rome was the chilliest of step-mothers to him; he was never trusted. Monsignor Talbot, at the Vatican, characterized him as 'the most dangerous man in England'—not unjustly, for his influence was disintegrating to every cause he espoused. He was obstructed in every enterprise, and was never given a position adequate to his powers; for nearly forty years he lived a secluded life at the Oratory of St. Philip Neri, Edgbaston, Birmingham. He was intensely unhappy, despite his protestations of having found the haven for his spirit. But his *Apologia pro Vita Sua*, a masterpiece of autobiography, written under intense emotion—'in tears,' he said—was at once a powerful defence of the system for which he had left Anglicanism, and a noble vindication of his own sincerity, which Kingsley had impugned. Consolation for long neglect came to him in 1879, in his elevation to the dignity of the cardinalate. This honour, and the universal veneration felt for his saintly life, made quietly happy the last ten years. But the impression his story makes is that of 'an angel who has lost his way'. He leaves the memory of a religious poet of slender but high achievement, a master of the purest and most melodious English prose, a spiritual force of almost the first magnitude, albeit misdirected and largely wasted, a great Englishman, and a great saint.

> 568. *Lead, kindly Light.*
> 249. *Light of the anxious heart* (tr.).
> 260. *Now that the daystar glimmers bright* (tr.).
> 32. *Praise to the Holiest in the height.*

NEWTON, JOHN (London, 1725–1807, London), was the son of a shipmaster. His mother, a godly and pious woman, died when he was seven years old. The boy went for some years to sea with his father, was impressed on board a man-of-war and became a midshipman in the Navy. Attempting to desert, he was flogged and degraded, and soon after took service on a slave-trading ship bound for Africa. By his own account his early sea-faring life was godless and abandoned, but in 1748 a study of Thomas à Kempis, and a night spent in fear of imminent death, combined to effect his conversion. It is remarkable that during the six following years he commanded a slave ship, and felt no scruples as to the lawfulness of his trade, though in after years he was its ardent opponent. In 1754 an illness prevented his starting on a fresh voyage, and soon afterwards he became tide-surveyor at Liverpool. His religious convictions deepening, in 1764 he took orders and accepted the curacy of Olney, where he laboured with much earnestness. The chief interest of this period for us is his intimacy with the poet Cowper, and their collaboration in the production of the *Olney Hymns* (1779), of which he wrote 280 and Cowper 68. He never, any more than St. Paul, lost his sense of amazement and gratitude at what Christ had done for him, and his hymns are never happier than when he sings of his Saviour. His autobiography, in its own way, is as vivid as *Robinson Crusoe* or *Peter Simple*, and has a passion of religious earnestness in it which one does not look for in Defoe or Marryat. In 1779 Newton became rector of St. Mary Woolnoth, London, where he remained till his death. His epitaph there, composed by himself, runs: 'John Newton clerk | once an Infidel and Libertine | A servant of slaves in Africa | was by the rich mercy of our Lord and Saviour | JESUS CHRIST | Preserved, restored, pardoned | And appointed to preach the Faith | He had long laboured to destroy.

> 451. *Approach, my soul, the mercy-seat.*
> 450. *Come, my soul, thy suit prepare.*
> 246. *Dear Shepherd of Thy people, hear.*
> 206. *Glorious things of thee are spoken.*
> 419. *How sweet the Name of Jesus sounds.*
> 300. *Now may He who from the dead.*
> 145. *One there is above all others.*
> 170. *Sweeter sounds than music knows.*
>   30. *Though troubles assail and dangers affright.*

NICOLAI, PHILIP, D.D. (Mengeringhausen, Waldeck, 1556–1608, Hamburg), was the son of a Lutheran pastor who dropped his patronymic of Rafflenböl in favour of an adaptation of his father's Christian name Nicolaus. He studied at the Universities of Erfurt and Wittenberg. Ordained at twenty to a pastorate in his native town, he passed in 1583 to Herdecke in the Ruhr, but, most of the Town Council being Roman Catholics, he found the position one of great difficulty, and finally, in 1586, on his colleague, emboldened by the Spanish invasion, reintroducing the mass, he resigned office. He was a fervid Lutheran, and a keen and often acrimonious controversialist, alike with Romanists and with leaders of the Reformed Church. For a time he ministered to a secret Lutheran congregation 'under the cross' in the Catholic stronghold of Cologne; then held pastorates at Niederwildungen and Altwildungen; was court preacher to the Dowager Countess of Waldeck and tutor to her son; and after five years of pastorate at Unna, Westphalia, was from 1601 till his death chief pastor of St. Katherine, Hamburg. During his Unna ministry a severe visitation of the plague moved him to write and publish his *Freuden-Spiegel des ewigen Lebens* (Frankfurt, 1599), in which appeared the words and melodies of the two great chorales on which Bach based two of his most beautiful Church cantatas—*Wachet auf*, and *Wie schön leuchtet uns der Morgenstern.* The latter, described by him as 'a spiritual bridal hymn of the believing soul concerning Jesus Christ, her heavenly Bridegroom', became a favourite marriage hymn in Germany. These and other chorales he harmonized himself for four voices. Nicolai was a preacher of great power, an influential churchman, and, the bitterness of his controversial writings notwithstanding, a sweet-natured and lovable man.

162. *Wake, awake, for night is flying.*

162. WACHET AUF.

NISBET, JOHN MACDONNELL (Liverpool, 1857–   ), educated in his native city, began his professional career at Selkirk in 1876, as organist of St. John's Episcopal Church and conductor of the Choral Union, and for a time was organist of Heatherlie Parish Church; in 1878 removed to Rothesay, where he was organist of New Rothesay Parish Church, teacher of pianoforte in the Academy, and conductor of Bute Choral Union; and in 1890 became organist of the East Parish Church of St. Nicholas, Aberdeen. While in the north he has been teacher of the pianoforte in the Church of Scotland College, Blairs College, and the Convent of the Sacred Heart; since 1898 has been organist of Marischal College, University of Aberdeen, and since 1907 lecturer in music, Aberdeen Training Centre. He represented the Aberdeen Society of Organists on the *Church Hymnary* Revision Committee, and was a member of the Music Sub-committee and of the committee of experts who supervised the editing of the music.

315. CARDEN PLACE.

NOEL, CAROLINE MARIA (London, 1817–77, London), was a daughter of Canon the Rev. and Hon. Gerard Thomas Noel, himself a hymn-writer, and niece of the Hon. Baptist Noel, the well-known evangelist. She wrote her first hymn at seventeen, but her muse was silent from her twentieth to her fortieth year. Then suffering moved her to sing again. The last twenty-five years of her life were overshadowed by increasing illness, and her hymns were written to convey to other sufferers the comfort with which she herself was comforted of God. They were published in two volumes, *The Name of Jesus, and Other Verses for the Sick and Lonely* (1861); and *The Name of Jesus, and Other Poems* (1878). They were written for private meditation rather than for public use. She was buried outside of the Abbey Church of Romsey, by the side of her father, a former vicar.

178. *In the Name of Jesus.*

NOTKER (Heiligau, Switzerland, 840–912, St. Gall), entered at an early age the school of the Benedictine Abbey of St. Gall, in which he spent most of his life and filled successive positions of trust, including that of 'Magister' which he held for many years. He translated some works of Aristotle and also the Psalms into Latin, and also compiled a martyrology and other works. In spite of a stammer, from which his nickname Balbulus was derived, he rendered good service to church music, especially as the practical inventor of what were known as sequences, the origin of which seems to have been as follows: The *Gradual*, or anthem before the Gospel, ended with an *Alleluia*, the last syllable of which was prolonged and sung to a musical strain of great elaboration. Lacking words, these musical ornaments were difficult to remember, and Notker, acting on a hint from a monk from Jumièges, began the practice of setting words to them. The 'sequences' thus begun became extremely popular, and developed later into rhymed compositions, such as those of Adam of St. Victor and others.

14. *The strain upraise of joy and praise.*

NOVELLO, (FRANCIS) VINCENT (London, 1781–1861, Nice), was trained as a chorister of the Sardinian Chapel, Duke Street, London, under Samuel Webbe, whose deputy he became. From 1797 to 1822 he was organist of the Portuguese Chapel, for a time also of St. Patrick's Chapel, Soho, and from 1840 to 1843 of the Roman Catholic Chapel, Moorfields. In 1811 he founded the music-publishing firm of Novello & Co. For a time he was pianist to the Italian Opera. As a member of the Philharmonic Society and founder of the Classical Harmonists Society he did much to encourage the cultivation of choral music. But his chief service to music in this country was his work in collecting and publishing anthems, kyries, and church music of all kinds, cathedral voluntaries, select organ pieces, motets, &c., as well as glees, songs, and studies in vocal counterpoint. He published *A Biographical Sketch of Henry Purcell*, a collection of Purcell's sacred works, and a series of *Madrigalian Studies*. He was a Purcell enthusiast, and to him we owe the preservation of some of that master's works, and much of the revival of his fame. In 1828, while in York, he asked permission to copy four anthems by Purcell, and his Service in G minor—all unique—in the Minster Library. He was told that the transcription would take three weeks. On his return next day he was told that five weeks' work was involved. Novello smiled and answered that he had copied the entire series the previous day. This was fortunate, for the precious originals were destroyed by fire in the following year. Novello had the pleasure of presenting transcripts to the Minster. His later days were spent at Nice. A memorial window was erected in the north transept of Westminster Abbey.

345. ALBANO.

NYBERG, HUGO (Helsingfors, Finland, 1873–   ), was educated at Helsingfors, ordained in 1898, and since 1907 has been a district minister to the deaf and dumb. He founded the Y.M.C.A. Choir in Helsingfors and is still its leader. He had no professional musical training, and has written but few tunes.

402. HELSINGFORS.

OAKELEY, FREDERICK, D.D. (Shrewsbury, 1802–80, London), son of Sir Charles Oakeley, Bart., formerly Governor of Madras, was educated privately and at Oxford, where he became a fellow of Balliol. Under the influence of his brother-in-law, William George Ward, he became deeply interested in the Tractarian Movement, and when, in 1839, he entered upon the incumbency of Margaret Chapel, London (later, All Saints, Margaret Street), he introduced an ultra-ritualistic service. With Richard Redhead as organist great attention was given to the music and the choir. A crisis was precipitated, however, by his publication of pamphlets, in the controversy about Tract XC, asserting his right 'to hold, as distinct from teaching, all Roman doctrine'. This led to his licence being withdrawn and to his suspension from clerical duty until he retracted his errors. Instead of retracting he resigned his prebendal stall at Lichfield and all appointments in the Church of England, joined Newman at Littlemore, and in the same year (1845) was received into the Church of Rome. He worked for many years among the poor in Westminster, was made a D.D., and, on the establishment of the new Roman hierarchy in 1852, a canon of Westminster. He published a preface on antiphonal chanting to Redhead's *Laudes Diurnae; Lyra Liturgica* (1865); and many works on Roman doctrine and worship.

55. *O come, all ye faithful* (tr.).

OAKELEY, Sir HERBERT STANLEY, Mus. Doc., LL.D., D.C.L. (Ealing, 1830–1903, Eastbourne), was a son of the Rev. Sir Herbert Oakeley, Bart., vicar of Ealing, and later, Dean of Bocking and Archdeacon of Colchester. He was educated at Rugby and Christ Church, Oxford; at Dresden, Leipzig, and Bonn. For a time he acted as reporter of musical festivals and concerts to *The Guardian*. In 1865 he was appointed to the Reid Chair of Music in the University of Edinburgh, with the conductorship of the Reid Concerts. As he was not a professional musician his appointment aroused much controversy. Till 1891, when he retired, he worked hard for the development of taste in Scotland for orchestral and choral music, for the reconciliation of the Scottish Church to the use of the organ in its services, and for the establishment of musical graduation in the University. He was knighted in 1876, and appointed composer to the Queen in 1881. Nine Universities gave him an honorary doctorate, as did also the Archbishop of Canterbury. He composed anthems, hymn-tunes, part-songs, &c.

292. ABENDS.   267. DOMINICA.

OAKLEY, CHARLES EDWARD, M.A., B.C.L. (? 1832–65, Rhyl, North Wales), was educated at Oxford, where he was examiner in the School of Jurisprudence, 1859–60, and for degrees in Civil Law, 1859–60; and Select Preacher, 1860 and 1862. In 1856 he became rector of Wickwar, and in 1863 rector of St. Paul's, Covent Garden. His memorial in the latter church says: 'This remarkable man, endowed with mental powers of the highest order, had cultivated every branch of knowledge and excelled in all. None could hear without admiration his brilliant and impressive eloquence, or fail to love his noble and gentle nature. . . . He bore witness not only with his lips but in his life to the power of Divine grace. . . . Although his pastoral charge over this parish lasted only for two years, yet the great work which in that short time he was enabled to effect will long be gratefully remembered by those who could appreciate the worth of his loving spirit, devotedness of life, and eminently Christian character.'

372. *Hills of the North, rejoice!*

OLIVERS, THOMAS (Tregynon, Montgomeryshire, 1725–99, London), was early left an orphan; he grew up uncared for, and had little education. He was apprenticed to a shoemaker, but for a time led a restless life, roaming about and earning a livelihood precariously as a cobbler. He chanced to hear Whitefield preach in Bristol on the text 'Is not this a brand plucked from the burning?' This changed his life. After paying the debts he had incurred in his unregenerate days he became one of Wesley's itinerant preachers, and for twenty-two years travelled far and wide in this work, through England, Scotland, and Ireland. In 1775 Wesley appointed him supervisor of the Methodist press, but removed him from that post in 1789 because 'the errata were insufferable and pieces were inserted in the magazine without his knowledge'. He spent the rest of his life in retirement in London. Wesley wrote of him to Christopher Hopper in 1762: 'I am glad you have had a free conversation with T. Olivers. There is good in him; though he is a rough stick of wood. But love can bow down the stubborn neck.' He wrote many controversial pamphlets, several hymns, and one celebrated tune 'Olivers', now known as 'Helmsley'. (See note on tune at Hymn 160.)

571. *The God of Abraham praise.*

OSWALD, HEINRICH SIEGMUND (Nimmersatt, near Liegnitz, Silesia, 1751–1834, Breslau), received his education at Schmiedeberg, Silesia, then, in 1765–6, entered the office of his brother Ferdinand, who held a public appointment. Seven years later he became secretary to the Landgrave von Prittwitz at Glatz, but illness lost him this position, and he returned to Schmiedeberg and entered the service of a merchant who sent him on business to Hamburg. Later, he tried business for himself at Breslau, but was not successful, and he took work again as a merchant's clerk. His circumstances subsequently improved; in 1790 King Friedrich Wilhelm II of Prussia appointed him a court councillor at Potsdam, and in the following year he was made a privy councillor. On the king's death he received a pension, and retired with his family to Hirschberg, and afterwards to Breslau. His years of retirement he devoted to the composition of poetical, musical, and religious works.

542. *O let him whose sorrow.*

OUSELEY, Sir FREDERICK ARTHUR GORE, Bart., M.A., Mus. Doc., LL.D. (London, 1825–89, Hereford), was the son of Sir William Gore Ouseley, Bart., a distinguished Oriental scholar who was ambassador to Persia and then at St. Petersburg. He was educated privately and at Christ Church, Oxford. He succeeded to the baronetcy in 1844; received the Mus. Doc. degree from Durham, Oxford, Cambridge, and Dublin; and was made LL.D. by Cambridge and Edinburgh. Taking holy orders in 1849, he became curate of St. Barnabas', Pimlico, and St. Paul's, Knightsbridge; precentor of Hereford Cathedral in 1855, in which year also he was appointed Professor of Music in the University of Oxford; and canon residentiary of Hereford, 1886. He had shown a remarkable gift for music from infancy; he composed when only three years old, and exhibited a marked talent for extemporizing at five; at eight he composed an opera to words by Metastasio. His wealth enabled him to amass a unique music library, and to found, build, and partly endow, on an estate of his own near Tenbury, a church and college dedicated to St. Michael and All Angels, 'as a means of promoting the Church services of the Church of England, but also to give at a moderate cost, and in some cases with considerable assistance, to those who need it, a liberal and classical education, to the sons of the clergy and other gentlemen, combined with sound Church teaching'. Of this institution he was first vicar and warden, and John Stainer first organist. Ouseley wrote valuable treatises on Harmony, Counterpoint and Musical Form and Composition, and a very large quantity of music—about 100 anthems, church services, hymn-tunes, chants and carols, two oratorios, and much organ music. He was closely associated with *Hymns Ancient and Modern*.

18. ALL THINGS BRIGHT.   279. ST. GABRIEL.   275. WOOLMER'S.

OWENS, PRISCILLA JANE (Baltimore, 1829–*c.* 1899, Baltimore), was of Scottish and Welsh descent. She was engaged in public school work at Baltimore. For fifty years she was active in Sunday-School work, and most of her hymns were written for children's services.

680. *We have heard a joyful sound.*

P. F. B. These initials represent the author of the fine poem on the heavenly Jerusalem, from which the stanzas forming Hymn 595 are taken. (See note on that hymn.)

595. *Jerusalem, my happy home.*

PALESTRINA, GIOVANNI PIERLUIGI SANTE DA (Palestrina, 1525–94, Rome), was the son of a well-to-do peasant, Pierluigi Sante. After the fashion of the time he was called 'da Palestrina' after his birthplace. He received his training in Rome, where he was powerfully influenced by the great Netherlander, Orlando di Lasso, 'the brilliant master of the North'. After some years as chapelmaster in his native town he was appointed master of the boys in the Julian Chapel. In 1555 he entered the Sistine Chapel as one of the pontifical singers, but, under a new Pope, was dismissed a few months later because he was guilty of the crime of matrimony. He then became chapelmaster of St. John Lateran, and, later, passed to the Liberian Chapel of Santa Maria Maggiore. During his time of service there he won the honour because of which he is traditionally known as 'the saviour of church music'. Grave abuses had crept into the music of the Church. Impatient of the strict form of the traditional plain-song, composers had ventured upon one liberty after another, until the most secular airs were grafted on the stately church themes, the singers were encouraged to improvise upon them as they sang, and sometimes they departed altogether from the solemn words of the service, and sang profane and even lewd words in Italian or French instead. The authorities realized the scandal of such proceedings, and at the same time became alarmed by the captivation of the populace by the religious songs of the Reformation. The Œcumenical Council of Trent, in 1552, resolved upon reform. Palestrina was asked to prepare a mass that should be free from the admixture of alien words and secular melodies, dignified in form, and comprehensible to the hearers. He had already made a profound impression by the simplicity and solemnity of his Improperia (Good Friday Lamentation) in 1560, and now he produced three six-part masses, one of which, the *Missa Papae Marcelli*, transported those who heard it by its lofty spirit and exquisite euphony. It was hailed as a miracle. Soon afterwards, Palestrina was appointed composer to the Pontifical Chapel, and in 1571 chapelmaster of St. Peter's. His noble style was established as the only one fitting for the service of the Church. His works were extraordinarily numerous and of great variety—93 masses, 179 motets, hymns, prayers, responses, madrigals, &c. 'In all the details of modal practice he was magisterial. In his association of the authentic with the plagal; his treatment of discords and cadences; his right admixture of conjunct with disjunct movement; his perfect method of evolving the harmonic from the melodic, he has remained without challenge the greatest master in the world.

122. VICTORY (adaptation).

PALMER, HORATIO RICHMOND, Mus. Doc. (Sherburne, New York, 1834–1907, Yonkers, New York), studied at Berlin and Florence, was an organist at seventeen, and became director of Rushford Academy of Music, New York, in 1857. In 1861 he settled in Chicago, and established the magazine *Concordia* in 1866. He returned to New York in 1874, and in 1884 took charge of the Church Choral Union for the improvement of church music, of which the membership rose to 4,000 singers. In 1887 he became dean of the school of music at Chautauqua. His choral collections *The Song Queen, The Song King*, and *The Song Herald* had enormous sales for many years. He wrote also *A Theory of Music* and *A Manual for Teachers*.

704. *Yield not to temptation.*
704. FORTITUDE.

PALMER, RAY, D.D. (Little Compton, Rhode Island, 1808–87, Newark, New Jersey), was the son of a judge. He spent his early life in Boston, and was for a time a 'clerk in a dry-goods store' (draper's assistant). Thereafter he studied at Phillips' Academy, Andover, and at Yale, where he graduated in 1830. He became minister of the Central Congregational Church, Bath, Maine, where the best of his hymns were written; then of the First Congregational Church, Albany, New York; then Corresponding Secretary of the American Congregational Union, with his head-quarters in New York. In 1879 he retired to Newark. He is described as 'a wise teacher and a simple-minded and devout Christian. He was a healthy, cheerful, buoyant man, loved by everybody who knew him.' More hymns are said to have been written by him than by any other American. Certainly he wrote more that are widely known and prized by all English-speaking Churches. He published *Hymns and Sacred Pieces* (1865); and *Hymns of my Holy Hours* (1867). His complete *Poetical Works* were published in 1876.

418. *Jesus, these eyes have never seen.*
420. *Jesus, Thou Joy of loving hearts* (tr.).
415. *My faith looks up to Thee.*

PARAPHRASES.—See *SCOTTISH PARAPHRASES.*

PARKER, WILLIAM HENRY (New Basford, Nottingham, 1845–   ), long the head of an Insurance Company, is a General Baptist by church affiliation. His active interest in Sunday-School work led him to write hymns for anniversaries. In 1882 he published *The Princess Alice and Other Poems*.

189. *Holy Spirit, hear us.*

PARRATT, Sir WALTER, Mus. Doc., K.C.V.O. (Huddersfield, 1841–1924, Windsor), took a service at Armitage Bridge, near Huddersfield, when only seven years old, and became organist there at eleven. At ten he played Bach's forty-eight preludes and fugues from memory, and, his legs being too short to reach the pedals from the seat, he actually played the pedals by walking on them. For a time he was in the choir school of St. Peter's Chapel, Charlotte Street, London, the church built for the notorious Dr. Dodd. He became organist of St. Paul's, Huddersfield; Witley Court (to Lord Dudley); the Parish Church, Wigan; Magdalen College, Oxford; and, in 1882, of St. George's Chapel, Windsor. He became professor of the organ at the R.C.M., 1883; was knighted in 1892; was an hon. Fellow of Magdalen; Dean of the Faculty of Music, London University, 1916–20; and Master of the King's Music. He was a renowned chess-player. His musical memory was extraordinary, and he was a remarkable player on the organ. He edited madrigals for the Bach Choir, and contributed ten articles to Grove's *Dictionary of Music;* but apart from organ pieces, anthems and songs, did not publish much music of his own. He had a strong, magnetic personality.

240. HUDDERSFIELD.

PARRY, Sir CHARLES HUBERT HASTINGS, Bart., Mus. Doc. (Bournemouth, 1848–1918, Rustington, Littlehampton), was the son of Thomas Gambier Parry, of Highnam Court, Gloucestershire, the distinguished decorative artist and inventor of the spirit-fresco process. He was educated at Twyford, near Winchester, Eton, and Exeter College, Oxford. While still at Eton, he took the Oxford Mus. Bac. degree. At the University he took a leading part, especially in music and sports. His father being opposed to his devoting himself to music, he entered Lloyd's, and continued there for three years; but the work was uncongenial and unsuccessful, and he renounced it to embark on a musical career. In 1883 he became Prof. of Composition and Lecturer in Musical History in the R.C.M., and also Choragus at Oxford; in 1894, Director of the R.C.M.; in 1898, Prof. of Music, Oxford. He was knighted in the same year, and made a baronet in 1905. He was 'a great and various human character, whose benign influence on an unknown number of people it would be difficult to over-estimate'. His interests were endless; he was squire, magistrate, author, amateur scientist, teacher, administrator, composer, organist, pianist, diarist, playgoer and critic, motorist, yachtsman, and practitioner of many games. He was a masterly writer on musical subjects; a born teacher, infectious in his enthusiasm; a stimulating lecturer, and perhaps in his time the leading intellectual force in music in this country. His books on *The Art of Music; The Eighteenth Century* in *The Oxford History of Music; Style in Musical Art; Bach;* and *College Addresses*, are of the highest quality. Of music he produced a vast amount. His choral works in particular exhibit exceptional mastery. Sir Henry Hadow says, 'There was no side of musical life in England which was not the better and nobler because he had lived.'

485. INTERCESSOR.   640. JERUSALEM.   168. LAUDATE DOMINUM.

PARRY, JOSEPH, Mus. Doc. (Merthyr Tydvil, 1841–1903, Penarth), showed marked musical gifts in childhood, but had to begin work at a puddling-furnace when only ten years old. In 1854 he emigrated to America with his family. On a return visit he won Eisteddfod prizes. A harmonized hymn-tune submitted by him at Swansea

Eisteddfod in 1865, and awarded a prize, so impressed Brinley Richards, who was one of the adjudicators, that the latter secured the raising of a fund to enable Parry to come back from the United States and enter the R.A.M. He took his Mus. Bac. degree at Cambridge in 1871, and his doctorate seven years later. In 1874 he became Professor of Music in University College, Aberystwyth, and in 1888 Lecturer in Music, University College of South Wales, Cardiff. In 1896 the Eisteddfod awarded him £600 for his services to Welsh music, upon which he exercised a great influence during thirty years. A composer of very great but unequal merit, he wrote oratorios, cantatas, operas, choral works of all kinds, and some instrumental music, as well as anthems and many scores of hymn-tunes. He was by far the most popular composer in Wales; his compositions were sung in every hamlet in the Principality. He edited the collection of Welsh songs known as *Cambrian Minstrelsie*.

424. ABERYSTWYTH.   703. LLANGRISTIOLUS.

PATRICK, ST. (? Dumbarton, *c.* 372–466, Saulpatrick), the apostle and patron saint of Ireland, is said to have come of clerical descent, his father having been a deacon and his grandfather a presbyter. At the age of sixteen he was carried off to Ireland, where he was sold as a slave and employed in feeding cattle. During his captivity he became a fervid Christian. The ship in which he ultimately escaped carried him to France, where he spent some years. But Ireland's need of the Gospel gave him no rest, and he returned, as its second bishop, to spend his life in heroic efforts to win its people for Christ. The story of his life is involved in a mass of doubtful legendary matter, but there is no doubt about his apostolic zeal and the remarkable success of his labours. By the time of his death Ireland had been to a great extent Christianized and a powerful Church was organized and in operation. Before long the Irish Church was sending missionaries abroad, and Ireland won fame throughout Western Europe as 'the Island of Saints and Scholars'.

506. *I bind unto myself to-day.*
505. *To-day I arise.*

PEACE, ALBERT LISTER, Mus. Doc. (Huddersfield, 1844–1912, Blundellsands), was a child-prodigy in music; at four or five he could name any note or chord struck on the piano. Yet he had no great education in music; he was practically self-taught. At nine years of age he was appointed organist of Holmfirth Parish Church, Yorkshire. In rapid succession thereafter he passed through the following appointments—Dewsbury Parish Church; St. Thomas's, Huddersfield; Brunswick Street Chapel, Huddersfield; Providence Place Chapel, Cleckheaton; Trinity Congregational Church, Glasgow; the University, Glasgow; St. John's Episcopal Church, Hillhead Parish Church, St. Andrew's Halls—all in Glasgow; until, in 1879, he was appointed to Glasgow Cathedral. There he remained till 1897, when he succeeded W. T. Best as organist of St. George's Hall, Liverpool, a post which he held till his death. In 1865, when he went to Glasgow, the Church of Scotland withdrew its ban on the use of the organ in public worship. Two-thirds of the organs erected in Scotland during the next quarter of a century were opened by him. He had a great reputation, and had skill and resource to justify it. 'In church worship his playing was marked by strongly marked time, and thunderous pedalling; he would often use the pedals to beat out in semistaccato style the measure, like the double bass in the orchestra.' Glasgow was proud of its leading organist. Dr. A. K. H. Boyd of St. Andrews declared that when he preached in the Cathedral, he dared not give out the hymn, 'Peace, perfect peace' lest the organist should take it as a personal compliment. For the Church of Scotland Peace edited the music of *The Scottish Hymnal* (1885); *Psalms and Paraphrases with Tunes* (1886); *The Psalter with Chants* (1888); and *The Scottish Anthem Book* (1891).

521. GUILD.   424. ST. MARGARET.

PEARSALL, ROBERT LUCAS de (Clifton, 1795–1856, Wartensee, Constance), descended from an ancient Gloucestershire family, was educated for the bar, to which he was called in 1821. After practising for four years, he forsook law for music, which he studied at Mainz and elsewhere on the Continent. Most of his life thereafter was spent in Germany, first at Carlsruhe (1830), and from 1837 at the Castle of the Wartensee on the Lake of Constance. An enthusiastic archaeologist, he turned Roman Catholic and called himself *de* Pearsall. Though little more than an amateur in music, he composed madrigals and part-songs of first-rate excellence. 'His works are no mere curiosities of a bastard archaeology, but living creations of art, full of fire, nobility, of thought, high imagination, and splendid vocal sonority.' He was a literary artist as well, and wrote the words of many of his own madrigals. The *St. Gall Gesangbuch* of 1863 was partly edited by him.

396. PEARSALL (arr.).

PENNEFATHER, WILLIAM, B.A. (Dublin, 1816–73, Muswell Hill, London), was the son of a Baron of the Irish Exchequer. Education at Westbury, near Bristol, and Trinity College, Dublin, was followed by his ordination in 1841. He was curate for a time at Ballymacugh, and vicar of Mellifont, near Drogheda. In 1848 he removed to England, where he held the incumbencies of Trinity Church, Walton, Aylesbury; Christ Church, Barnet; and St. Jude's, Mildmay Park, East London. At Barnet he began a series of conferences which he continued to hold at Mildmay, where he also established large religious and benevolent institutions which made the name of Mild-may famous. There he introduced into England the Order of Deaconesses. He was a man of saintly character; his life impressed many as it did Frances Ridley Havergal, as 'illustrating in a peculiar degree the power of holiness'. His hymns, written for his confer-ences, were collected in *Hymns, Original and Selected* (1872), and *Original Hymns and Thoughts in Verse* (1873).

248. Jesus, stand among us.

PERRONET, EDWARD (? 1726–92, Canterbury), belonged to a family of French refugees who had lived at Chateau d'Oex in Swit-zerland. His father, Vincent Perronet, Vicar of Shoreham, was greatly esteemed by the Wesleys, and was even called 'the Arch-bishop of Methodism'. Edward was on intimate terms with both John and Charles Wesley. He was John's companion on his visit to the north in 1749, and became one of his itinerant preachers. In *The Mitre*, a religious satire published in 1757, he attacked the abuses of the Church in a way which aroused Wesley's anger, and the book was suppressed. He also differed from Wesley in urging separation from the Church of England, and the grant of licence to itinerant preachers to administer the Sacraments. By 1771 he had ceased co-operation with the Wesleys, and had joined the Countess of Huntingdon's Connexion. She in turn disagreed with him owing to his violent language about the Church of England, and he ended his days as pastor of a small Independent Church at Canterbury. Unlike his saintly father, Edward Perronet was of violent temper, and impatient of control. He possessed, however, a warm devotional spirit as well as real poetic talent. Most of his hymns (published successively in several small volumes) have somewhat undeservedly passed out of use.

139. All hail the power of Jesus' Name.

PETERS, MARY, *née* BOWLY (Cirencester, 1813–56, Clifton, Glou-cestershire), was the wife of the Rev. John M'William Peters, some-time rector of Quenington, Gloucestershire, afterwards vicar of Langford, Berkshire, with charge also of the chapelry of Little Farringdon, Oxfordshire. He died in 1834. Mrs. Peters's *magnum opus* was *The World's Story, from the Creation to the Accession of Queen Victoria* (7 volumes). Her fifty-eight hymns were published in 1847 as *Hymns intended to help the Communion of Saints*. A num-ber of them had previously been contributed to the *Psalms, Hymns, and Spiritual Songs* of the Plymouth Brethren (1842).

702. Through the love of God our Saviour.

PIAE CANTIONES (1582), a valuable collection of medieval sacred and secular song, gathered and edited by Theodoricus (Didrik) Petri, son of a landed proprietor in Borgå, Finland, whose father had migrated thither from Denmark. Didrik was a student at the University of Rostock when he made the compilation, desiring to preserve for future use some of the most beautiful psalms, hymns, and school-songs of the medieval Church. The collection was published at Greifswald, then, as Finland also was, part of the Swedish kingdom. Most of the contents were doubtless of Swedo-Finnish origin, but J. M. Neale said that they were the product of various times from the tenth to the sixteenth century, and of various countries, some being from pre-Reformation German hymn-books, others, of Hussite parentage, from Bohemia and Moravia, some from Lutheran song-books, and one probably a native of southern Europe. Until late in the nineteenth century some of them continued to be sung and danced by school children at Björneborgs in Finland. The best known of all the melodies is the fourteenth century spring-carol. 'Tempus adest floridum', to which Dr. Neale wrote the famous Christmas carol, 'Good King Wenceslas'. Petri became secretary to King Sigismund in 1591, but of his later history little is known except that his last years were spent in Poland.

60. CORDE NATUS.

PIERPOINT, FOLLIOTT SANDFORD, M.A. (Bath, 1835–1917, Bath), was educated at the Grammar School, Bath, and Queens' College, Cambridge, where he graduated in 1857. For a time he was classical master at the Somersetshire College. Thereafter he lived at various places, principally at Babbicombe, on a small patrimony, and occasionally doing a little classical teaching. He contributed to *Lyra Eucharistica*, was the author of the Hymns for the Canonical Hours in *The Hymnal Noted*, and published collections of his poems— *The Chalice of Nature and Other Poems; Songs of Love;* and *Lyra Jesu.*

17. *For the beauty of the earth.*

PIGGOTT, WILLIAM CHARTER (Huddersfield, 1872–), was educated at Huddersfield College and Headingley College for the Wesleyan ministry. He entered the Congregational ministry in 1902. After serving charges at Greville Place, London, and Bunyan Meeting, Bedford, he succeeded the Rev. C. Silvester Horne at Whitefield's, Tottenham Court Road, London. He is now minister at Streatham.

218. *For those we love within the veil.*

PLUMPTRE, EDWARD HAYES, D.D. (London, 1821–91, Wells), was educated at King's College, London, and University College, Oxford. He became a Fellow of Brasenose. Ordained in 1846, he was successively Chaplain of King's College, London; assistant preacher, Lincoln's Inn; Dean of Queen's College, Oxford; Prebendary of St. Paul's, and Professor of New Testament Exegesis,

King's College, London; rector of Pluckley, Kent; vicar of Bickley, Kent; and in 1881, Dean of Wells. He was Select Preacher repeatedly at Oxford; Boyle Lecturer in 1866; and a member of the Old Testament Company of Revisers of the Bible. He wrote many excellent works—the standard *Life of Bishop Ken*, translations of Dante, Aeschylus, and Sophocles, *Biblical Studies*, and several volumes of poems.

> 172. *O Light, whose beams illumine all.*
> 86. *Thine arm, O Lord, in days of old.*
> 215. *Thy hand, O God, has guided.*

PLUNKET, WILLIAM CONYNGHAM, D.D., 4th Baron Plunket (Dublin, 1828–97, Dublin), was educated at Cheltenham and Trinity College, Dublin. Ordained in 1857, he was Precentor of St. Patrick's Cathedral, Dublin, 1869–76; succeeded to the peerage 1871; was consecrated Bishop of Meath, 1876; and from 1884 to 1897 was Archbishop of Dublin, Glendalough, and Kildare. He had been Dean of Christ Church Cathedral also from 1884 to 1887. He was the leader of the Evangelical party in the Church of Ireland, and a resolute opponent of Irish Disestablishment. He was 'an orator of remarkable power, and a patriot who commanded the unfeigned respect of all classes and creeds in Ireland'.

> 125. *Our Lord Christ hath risen.*

POLLOCK, THOMAS BENSON, M.A. (Strathallan, Isle of Man, 1836–96, Birmingham), was educated at Trinity College, Dublin, where he gained the Vice-Chancellor's prize for English verse in 1855. He began the study of medicine and walked the London hospitals, but took ordination in 1861. After curacies at St. Luke's, Leek, Staffordshire, and St. Thomas's, Stamford Hill, London, he became, in 1865, curate to his brother, the Rev. J. S. Pollock, vicar of the mission charge of St. Alban's, Bordesley, Birmingham. The district was poor, and the housing revolting, but a large congregation was gathered, and a church built which was one of the finest in the city. The living was worth only £150 a year, but the brothers maintained three assistant clergy, six lay readers, and four sisters, and raised £100,000 in twenty years for church and school work in the district. St. Alban's became the High Church stronghold of Birmingham, and 'Father' Pollock and his brother 'Father Tom' were for a time opposed and threatened with mob violence, but their devotion and self-sacrifice turned all adverse feeling into admiration and reverence. They 'lived and died for St. Alban's Mission. They gave to it their prospects, their hopes of preferment, their money, their patrimony, and their health, for the anxieties of their work and their unceasing and almost incredible exertions undoubtedly hastened the day of their departure.' After thirty years as curate, 'Father Tom' succeeded his brother as vicar, but his health was broken by the strenuous labours of the parish, and he died ten months afterwards. He was a member for a time of the Committee of *Hymns Ancient and Modern*. He specialized in the metrical litany, and published in 1870 *Metrical Litanies for Special Services and General Use*. He contributed some hymns also to *The Gospeller*, the St. Alban's parish magazine, of which he was editor.

> 469. *Jesus, from Thy throne on high.*
> 399. *Jesus, we are far away.*
> 208. *Jesus, with Thy Church abide.*
> 95. *My Lord, my Master, at Thy feet adoring* (tr.).
> 94. *Weep not for Him who onward bears.*

POOLE, CLEMENT WILLIAM (Ealing, 1828–1924, Ealing), son of a bencher of Gray's Inn, was appointed at eighteen to a junior clerkship in the Audit Office, but relinquished his appointment in the late fifties to engage in commerce, for which, however, he was not fitted. Music was his chief interest, and being deeply religious, he found happiness in serving the Church with his gifts. He acted as honorary organist of the Parish Church, Kingston-on-Thames; Christ Church, Ealing; and Holy Trinity, Ramsgate. He composed over thirty hymn-tunes, a Magnificat, several marches, &c.

> 398, 528. PETERSHAM.

POTT, FRANCIS, M.A. (Southwark, 1832–1909, Speldhurst), was educated at Brasenose College, Oxford. Ordained in 1856, he became curate of Bishopsworth, Somerset; of Ardingley, Sussex; and of Ticehurst, Sussex; and was rector of Northill, Bedfordshire, from 1866 to 1891, when he retired owing to increasing deafness, and went to live at Speldhurst, near Tunbridge Wells. He was a member of the original Committee that produced *Hymns Ancient and Modern*. In 1861 he published *Hymns fitted to the Order of Common Prayer*. His keen interest in the reform of chanting led him to publish *The Free Rhythm Psalter* (1898), but though adopted in a few places, it was too elaborate for general use. He also wrote a book on *The Te Deum*, and a pamphlet on the Athanasian Creed.

> 252. *Angel voices, ever singing.*
> 79. *Forty days and forty nights.*
> 122. *The strife is o'er, the battle done* (tr.).

POTTER, THOMAS JOSEPH (Scarborough, 1827–73, Dublin), joined the Roman Church in 1847. Becoming a priest ten years later, he occupied for many years the Chair of Pulpit Eloquence and English Literature in the Foreign Missionary College of All Hallows, Dublin. His publications included *The Spoken Word, or, The Art of Extemporary Preaching; Sacred Eloquence, or, The Theory and Practice of Preaching; The Pastor and his People; A Panegyric of St. Patrick; Legends, Lyrics, and Hymns;* and several tales.

> 538. *Brightly gleams our banner.*

PRICE, JOHN (BEULAH) (Llangammareh, Breconshire, 1857–), became a church chorister at Beulah, Breconshire, when ten years old. At twenty-two he graduated at the Tonic Sol-fa College. For nearly forty years he has been a member of the Tonic Sol-fa Composition Club. He has composed many anthems, glees, and hymn-tunes, which are widely sung throughout the Principality.

411. GWYNETH.

PRICE, TOM (Rhymney, Monmouthshire, 1857–1925, Merthyr Tydfil), went to work in the coal-pits at the age of ten. In music he was practically self-taught, though he learned much by joining different Welsh choirs. He won numerous prizes for composition, among others the 'Lady Georgina Peel' prize for a setting of one of Lord Tennyson's poems. He became a professional musician, and for eighteen years was travelling teacher under the Glamorgan County Council. He was precentor for many years at Hope Presbyterian Church, Merthyr Tydfil, and was a well-known adjudicator and conductor at Psalmody Festivals. He composed a dramatic cantata, *The Prodigal Son*, as well as tunes, anthems, and part-songs which have been widely sung throughout Wales. He was a keen student of Welsh literature, and was musical editor of *Young Wales* and *Y Solffaydd*.

465. BUGAIL ISRAEL.

PRICHARD, ROWLAND HUGH (Graienyn, near Bala, 1811–87, Holywell), spent most of his life at Bala, but in 1880 moved to Holywell Mill and was given a position as a loom-tender's assistant in the works of the Welsh Flannel Manufacturing Company. He possessed a good voice and acted as a precentor. Many good tunes composed by him appeared in Welsh periodicals of the period. *Hyfrydol* was a composition of his youth, while he was still under twenty. In 1844 he published *Cyfaill y Cantorion* (The Singer's Friend), mostly made up of his own original tunes. He subsequently brought out a booklet for the use of children.

479, 683. HYFRYDOL.

PRITCHARD, THOMAS CUTHBERTSON LEITHEAD, M.A., Mus.Bac., F.R.C.O. (Glasgow, 1885–), was educated at the University of Glasgow, and is a graduate in music of Trinity College, Dublin. He studied church music at York Minster. He has been organist and choirmaster of Fullarton Church, Irvine; St. Stephen's United Free Church, Glasgow; North United Free Church, Bearsden; Sherbrooke United Free Church, Glasgow; and, since 1913, of Belhaven United Free Church, Glasgow. He is a professor in the Athenaeum School of Music; supervisor of music in schools under the Education Authority; lecturer on church music in a school of training for organists under the Church of Scotland and the United Free Church of Scotland; and is a well-known recitalist. He has written much music, and a number of articles on musical subjects. As representing the Glasgow Society of Organists, he was an associate member of the Revision Committee which produced the present *Church Hymnary*, and a member of the Music Sub-Committee and the editorial committee of musical experts.

34. BELHAVEN.	570. KILLIN (arr.).
589. GIFFORD.	576. LEITHEAD.

PROCTER, ADELAIDE ANNE (London, 1825–64, London), was the eldest daughter of Bryan Waller Procter (Barry Cornwall), a barrister and commissioner in lunacy who had a reputation in his time as a poet and dramatist, and was an intimate friend of Charles Lamb, Leigh Hunt, and Dickens. Her first poems were sent to Dickens as editor of *Household Words*, under the name of 'Mary Berwick', and were supposed by him to be the work of a governess who had been long in the same family, and had accompanied them to Italy. He had continued publishing her contributions for nearly two years before he discovered through her mother that she was the daughter of his old friends. Two series of her poems were issued under the title *Legends and Lyrics, a Book of Verse*, in 1858 and 1862. In 1851 she entered the Roman Church, but her spirit was in the true sense catholic, and it is difficult to tell from her hymns to which communion she belonged. Some of her songs became phenomenally popular, such as *Cleansing Fires*, *The Requital*, and *The Lost Chord*. In her later years she acquired much skill in music and languages, but her chief occupation was in beneficence. Dickens paid high tribute to her enthusiasm in good works. 'Now it was the visitation of the sick that had possession of her; now it was the sheltering of the homeless; now it was the elementary teaching of the densely ignorant; now it was the raising up of those who had wandered and got trodden underfoot; now it was the wider employment of her own sex in the general business of life; now it was all these things at once. Perfectly unselfish, swift to sympathize and eager to relieve, she wrought at such designs with a flushed earnestness that disregarded season, weather, time of day or night, food, rest.' Under the strain of such labours her health broke down, and after fifteen months of suffering she died in her mother's arms, saying, 'It has come at last'.

441. *My God, I thank Thee, who hast made the earth so bright.*

PROUT, EBENEZER, B.A., Mus. Doc. (Oundle, Northamptonshire, 1835–1909, London), was the son of a Congregational minister, and at first was engaged in the teaching profession in private schools in London and at Leatherhead. In music, apart from a few pianoforte lessons as a boy, and a subsequent course under Charles Salaman, he was self-educated, but he so cultivated his talent that in 1859 he embarked on a musical career. He was organist in succession of St. Thomas's Square Chapel, Hackney; the Congregational Church,

Kentish Town; the New Tabernacle, Old Kent Road; St. Mary, Newington Butts; and Union Chapel, Islington. He held professorships at the Crystal Palace School of Art, the National Training School for Music, the Royal Academy of Music, the Guildhall School of Music, and finally, from 1895, the Professorship of Music in the University of Dublin. From that University he received his doctorate, and was the first recipient of the same degree from the University of Edinburgh. For several years he edited *The Monthly Musical Record*, and afterwards was musical critic of *The Academy*, and, later, of *The Athenaeum*. He did much public lecturing, and conducted performances of his works at the festivals and elsewhere. His musical works were many, and of high merit, but even more valuable were his numerous works on musical theory—*Instrumentation; Harmony, its Theory and Practice; Counterpoint, Strict and Free; Double Counterpoint and Canon; Fugal Analysis; Musical Form;* and *Applied Forms.*

211. LAUS SEMPITERNA.   630. RALEIGH.

PRUDENTIUS, Aurelius Clemens (348–*c.* 413), one of the best and most prolific of early Latin Christian poets, was born in the North of Spain. We know little of his life beyond what he tells us himself in an introduction to his works. From this it appears that he received a legal training, held a judicial post in two successive cities, and was afterwards promoted to an office of some dignity at the Imperial Court. In his fifty-seventh year he forsook the world, entered a monastery, and began to exercise the talent on which his fame now rests. The poetry of Prudentius belongs to the transition period when classical models had ceased to be followed, and rhyming verse had not begun. Trench is probably right in speaking of him as 'helping forward that great transformation of the Latin language which it needed to undergo' that it might be the vehicle of new truths. Centos from his works are freely used in the ancient Breviaries and Hymnaries. His best works are *Liber Cathemerinon*, or Hymns for the twelve hours of the day, and *Liber Peristephanon*, hymns of the saints who had won the martyr's crown.

60. *Of the Father's love begotten.*

PRYNNE, George Rundle, M.A. (West Looe, Cornwall, 1818–1903, Plymouth), was educated at St. Catharine's College, Cambridge, and ordained in 1841. He became curate of Tywardreath, Cornwall; then of St. Andrew's, Clifton; and after two years as vicar of Par, Cornwall, accepted the incumbency of the new parish of St. Peter's, Plymouth, of which he was vicar from 1848 until his death. He was deeply influenced by the Oxford Movement and enjoyed the friendship of Dr. Pusey. His introduction of ritualistic innovations in St. Peter's, such as confession and the daily Eucharist made 'Priest Prynne' the object, for years, of suspicion and hostile feeling, and sometimes even of mob violence. But his self-denying labours in a district of deep poverty and spiritual destitution, and his lovable and saintly character, won him, in time, peculiar affection from those who knew him, and general honour and regard. He published *A Eucharistic Manual;* a volume of sermons; in 1857, *A Hymnal suited for the Services of the Church, together with a Selection of Introits* (177 hymns increased in the 1866 edition to 433); also, in 1881, *The Soldier's Dying Vision, and Other Poems.* He was a member of the Revision Committee of *Hymns Ancient and Modern* (1875).

462. *Jesus, meek and gentle.*

PRYS, EDMUND (Maen Twrog, Merionethshire, 1541?–1624, Maen Twrog), after studying at St. John's College, Cambridge, became rector of Festiniog, with the chapelry of Maen Twrog, in 1569; the rectory of Llaneddwyn was added in 1580, with the chapelry of Llanddwywe. In 1567 he became Archdeacon of Merioneth, and chaplain to Sir Henry Sidney, Lord President of Wales, and in 1602 received the second canonry of St. Asaph. He was an accomplished composer in Welsh metres, but did not adopt them when he translated the Psalms into Welsh, his aim being to foster congregational singing. This translation, *Llyfr y Psalmau wedi eu cyfieithu, a'u cyfansoddi ar fesur cerdd, yn gymraeg*, was appended to a new issue of *The Book of Common Prayer* in Welsh, in 1621. Many of his versions are still sung in the churches of Wales.

401. ST. MARY.

PSALMODIA EVANGELICA, a Complete Set of Psalm and Hymn Tunes for Public Worship, edited by Thomas Williams, a musician of the eighteenth century about whom nothing is known, was published in 1789.

381. (BROMSGROVE).   369, 647. (TRURO).

PSALTERS, EARLY METRICAL.

I. THE FRENCH-GENEVAN PSALTER, 1539–62.

The Metrical Psalter which was adopted in the Protestant Churches of France had its beginning in a small book printed at Strasburg in 1539 under the title—*Aulcuns pseaulmes et cantiques mys en chant.* This contained metrical versions of seventeen psalms, five of which were by John Calvin, then living at Strasburg, and the remainder were attributed to the poet, Clément Marot. Calvin returned to Genèva in 1541, and he appears to have introduced this book in the worship of the church there. Early in 1542 Marot published in Paris an edition of thirty psalms versified by himself. This publication roused the ire of the Sorbonne, and Marot was obliged to fly for his life. He came to Geneva and found that his psalms were being sung there, but in a text differing to some extent from that in the edition published by himself.

Instigated by Calvin, Marot continued his work of versification and several editions of the psalter appeared, the number of psalms being gradually increased. In 1543 there was published an edition in which the versions by Calvin were dropped, being replaced by others by Marot, a number of new versions by the latter were added, and the author's correct text substituted for that which was in the Strasburg publication. In the end of 1543 Marot left Geneva for Turin, where he died in 1544.

Calvin then endeavoured to find some one to continue Marot's work and complete the psalter, but he did not succeed in this till the arrival in Geneva in 1548 of Theodore Beza. Calvin urged Beza to undertake the work, and in 1551 there appeared the first instalment of his labours, consisting of thirty-four psalms. Further additions were made in succeeding years and at last, in 1562, the complete metrical psalter was issued, containing forty-nine psalms by Marot, and a hundred and one by Beza.

From 1542 to 1557 the arranging of the music for the psalms was in the hands of Louis Bourgeois (q.v.), but it is practically impossible to determine which of the melodies were composed by him, and which were adapted by him from existing sources.

Bourgeois left Geneva in 1557, at which date sixty-two psalms remained either untranslated or unprovided with tunes. It has not been established with any certainty who then undertook the work of providing tunes, but it seems beyond doubt that all the finest melodies in the completed psalter are among those supplied by Bourgeois. As already stated the complete psalter appeared in 1562. Of the sixty-two psalms above referred to only forty are provided with tunes which had not already appeared, the remaining twenty-two repeat tunes already set to other psalms. In the complete book, the number of separate tunes is one hundred and twenty-five.

305. COMMANDMENTS.	219. PSALM 84.
289. LES COMMANDEMENS DE DIEU.	460. PSALM 86.
229, 656, 709. OLD 100TH.	151. PSALM 107.
120, 156. OLD 134TH (ST. MICHAEL).	95. PSALM 110 (L'OMNIPOTENT).
167. PSALM 3.	318. PSALM 118 (RENDEZ À DIEU).
543. PSALM 6.	342. PSALM 130.
360. PSALM 12 (DONNE SECOURS).	261. PSALM 135 (MINISTRES DE L'ÉTERNEL).
217. PSALM 36 (68).	
359. PSALM 42.	62. PSALM 136.

II. The Anglo-Genevan Psalters.

During the persecution of the Protestants in England under Queen Mary a congregation of English exiles was formed at Frankfort. Division arose in that congregation and a considerable number betook themselves to Geneva, where they formed a congregation under the ministry of John Knox. In their order of public worship they followed the example of Calvin. In 1556 there was printed at Geneva *The forme of prayers and ministration of the Sacraments, &c. used in the Englishe Congregation at Geneva; and approved by the famous and godly learned man, John Calvyn.* The second section of the book consists of fifty-one metrical psalms, each provided with a tune. The psalms are those previously published in England (without tunes) by Thomas Sternhold and John Hopkins, with the addition of seven by William Whittingham. Two of the tunes, the 128th and the 130th, are taken from the French Psalter, but nothing has been discovered as to the origin of the others. A second edition of this work containing sixty-two psalms, and with some changes in the tunes, appeared in 1558. A much enlarged edition was issued in 1561 containing eighty-seven psalms. The additional psalms are by William Kethe, and many of his versions are founded on these in the French book, then approaching completion. A considerable number of the tunes in this edition are also taken from the French; indeed in many cases Kethe seems to have written his versions specially to suit these tunes. Unfortunately the attempt was not always a success, for even when the French and English versions have the same number of syllables in the line, the scansion and accents are quite at variance.

These Anglo-Genevan Psalters were the immediate precursors of the complete metrical psalters adopted in England and Scotland, and they contain the nucleus of the later books, as regards both words and music.

| 1556. | 486. OLD 22ND. | 1556. | 643. OLD 137TH. |
| ,, | 530. OLD 44TH. | 1558. | 583. OLD 25TH. |

III. THE ENGLISH PSALTER.

The earliest edition of the Metrical Psalms with tunes, issued for use in England, is dated 1560. The only copy now existing is in the library of Christ Church College, Oxford. It is an exact reproduction of the Anglo-Genevan Psalter of 1558, with the addition of three psalms, two of these having tunes afterwards dropped. In 1561 another edition appeared. This contained all the psalms in that of the previous year, and has in addition eighteen psalms mainly by Sternhold or Hopkins. A few new tunes appeared but many of those in the earlier book are excluded, the psalms to which they were set being referred to the tunes of others. This book is entirely independent of the Anglo-Genevan edition of 1561, and it marks the beginning of the divergence between the English and Scottish Psalters. The complete English Psalter was issued in 1562, printed by John Day, the versions still required being supplied by Hopkins and other English writers, with nine by Kethe (q.v.) from the Anglo-Genevan, 1561. This complete psalter contained only forty-six tunes, which were known as the *Proper* or *Church* tunes. These tunes continue to appear in nearly all later books, and down to the present time they are still distinguished by the adjective 'Old' prefixed to the number of the Psalm to which they were originally attached. The psalters by Damon (q.v.) (1579 and 1591) and by Allison (1599) consist practically of these proper tunes in varying arrangements.

An important psalter was issued in 1592 by Thomas Este, the well-known music printer and publisher. In his 'Epistle Dedicatorie' Este says: 'In this booke the Church Tunes are carefully corrected, and other short tunes added, which are song in London, and other places of this Realme.' The tunes are harmonized in four parts, the harmony being by eminent musicians of the time whose names appear at the head of each tune. For the first time the four parts are printed at the same opening, the Cantus and Tenor (i.e. the Melody) on the left-hand page and the Altus and Bassus on the right.

The Church tunes are attached to their proper psalms and the remaining psalms are set to the short, or four line, tunes above referred to. Editions of this psalter with some slight changes were published in 1594, 1604, and 1611.

Another psalter, arranged on the same plan as that of Este, was edited by Thomas Ravenscroft, and printed in 1621 and 1633. This has the proper tunes as in the former books, and a large number of tunes under special names, many of which are still in use. In his Index Ravenscroft classes six of these as 'Scottish Tunes'. All of these are found among the 'Common Tunes' added to the Scottish Psalter in 1615. As in Este's psalter, the tunes are harmonized by various musicians whose names are given. In very many instances the arrangement is by Ravenscroft himself.

| 1561. | 586. | OLD 18TH. | 8. ST. FLAVIAN. |
| 1562. | 355. | OLD 81ST. | |

IV. The Scottish Psalter.

In Scotland at the Reformation the church service was modelled on that used in Geneva under Calvin, and his example was followed in the provision of a metrical psalter. In the *First Book of Discipline*, 1560, the 'Order of Geneva' is mentioned as being 'in use in our Churches'. In compiling their psalter the Scottish Reformers adopted in its entirety the Anglo-Genevan edition of 1561, containing eighty-seven psalms, and a considerable number of the French tunes. In 1562 the General Assembly lent to the printer Lekprevick £200 to help him in printing the psalter, and in 1564 the complete book was issued as part of the *Book of Common Order*. The psalter consisted of the eighty-seven versions referred to above, forty-two from the English Psalter of 1562, and twenty-one by two Scottish writers, Robert Pont and John Craig. The great majority of the tunes in the Anglo-Genevan Psalters were retained, several were taken from the English of 1562 and a few more from the French. Altogether the psalms are provided with one hundred and five different tunes; the Scottish Psalter being thus much richer in this respect than the corresponding English book. In subsequent years slight changes were made, and one or two additional tunes introduced, and in 1615 an entirely new feature appeared, namely, a number of those called *Common Tunes*, that is, tunes which were not attached to any particular psalm. In the edition printed by Andro Hart in 1615 these were in a group by themselves entitled 'The XII. Common Tunes, to the which all Psalmes of eight syllables in the first line, and six in the next may bee sung'. These tunes bear the following names: Olde Common, Kinges, Dukes, English, French, London, The Stilt (=York), Dumfermling, Dundie, Abbey, Glasgow, and Martyrs. Other Common Tunes appeared in later editions, and that of 1635 contains thirty-one. In all the earlier editions the melody only of the tunes is given, but in 1635 there was issued what is perhaps the most important musical edition of the Scottish Psalter. In this the tunes, both proper and common, are all given in harmony, the work of Edward Millar, who in a lengthy preface explains his reasons for undertaking this task.

In 1643, in pursuance of the design to establish uniformity in government and worship between the churches of England and Scotland, the House of Commons, with the advice of the Westminster Assembly, resolved that one version of the psalms should be adopted and authorized for use throughout the kingdom. The version decided upon was that by Francis Rous, Provost of Eton. This version was subjected to much revision by Rous himself and by a Committee of the Assembly, and finally was sent to Scotland for the consideration of the General Assembly. The Assembly appointed a committee by whom it was again very carefully revised, and in 1650 this version, as still in use, was approved and authorized by the General Assembly. Unfortunately for the cause of Church music in Scotland no tunes were provided for the psalms, and as a consequence it is probable that music in the churches was for long confined to a limited number of the common tunes known by heart to the precentors and the people.

1564.	97. PSALM 80.		1634.	353. CULROSS.
1615.	455. ABBEY.		1635.	481. CAITHNESS.
,,	295. DUNFERMLINE.		,,	645. GREYFRIARS.
,,	227, 562. FRENCH.		,,	520. LONDON NEW.
,,	520. MARTYRS.		,,	406. WIGTOWN.
1625.	246. ELGIN.			

PURDAY, CHARLES HENRY (Folkestone, 1799–1885, London), son of a bookseller, was at one time a vocalist of some note; he sang at the coronation of Queen Victoria. He became a publisher of music, and was popular as a lecturer on musical subjects. He was an ardent advocate of reform in the law relating to musical copyright. For some years he was conductor of psalmody in the Scots Church, Crown Court, Covent Garden, for which he published *Crown Court Psalmody: one hundred Psalm Tunes and Chants* (1854). He issued also *The Sacred Musical Offering* (1833); *The Church and Home Tune Book* (1857); *Copyright, a Sketch of its Rise and Progress* (1877); and a considerable number of popular songs.

568. SANDON.

PUSEY, PHILIP, D.C.L. (Pusey, Berkshire, 1799–1855, Christ Church, Oxford), was a grandson of the first Viscount Folkestone. His father gave up the family name of Bouverie for that of Pusey on inheriting the estate of the latter name. His elder brother was the famous Dr. Edward Bouverie Pusey, the Tractarian leader. Philip was educated at Eton and Christ Church, Oxford. On leaving the University he settled on his estate, and devoted himself to agriculture and the public service. On agriculture he wrote largely; he was one of the most progressive agriculturists of his time, and one of the founders of the Royal Agricultural Society. Entering Parliament, he sat for Rye, Chippenham, Cashel, and Berkshire. He was the first to introduce the term 'tenant-right' into the House of Commons. Disraeli said of him that he was 'both by his lineage, his estate, his rare accomplishments and fine abilities, one of the most distinguished county gentlemen who ever sat in the House of Commons'. His accomplishments were many. He was a connoisseur of art, a collector of prints and etchings, a copious contributor to the reviews, and one of the founders of the London Library. Among his interests was hymnology; he wished to supplant Sternhold and Hopkins's version of the Psalms by Milman's hymns. In this his famous brother opposed him.

216. *Lord of our life, and God of our salvation* (tr.).

QUAILE, ROBERT NEWTON (Rathkeale, County Limerick, Ireland, 1867–), son of the Rev. William Quaile, Irish Methodist minister, was educated at Wesley College, Dublin, and is engaged in business at Mallow, County Cork. During the trouble in Ireland in 1920 his house was burned, with all that he possessed, and he had to begin life over again. He is an amateur musician. Three of his tunes appear in *The Methodist School Hymnal*.

659. ATHLONE.   213. OLDBRIDGE.

QUARLES, JOHN (Essex, 1624–65, London), was son of the better-known Francis Quarles, essayist and poet. He was educated at Exeter College, Oxford. An ardent royalist, he took part in the defence of Oxford against the Parliamentary forces, and is said to have held a captain's commission subsequently in King Charles's service. On the downfall of the King he retired to London, and betook himself to literature for a livelihood. He published Jeremiah's Lamentations paraphrased, with *Divine Meditations* (1648); and *Divine Meditations upon Several Subjects, whereunto is annexed God's Love to Man's Unworthiness, with Several Divine Ejaculations* (1655).

> 544. *Long did I toil, and knew no earthly rest.*
> 6. *O King of kings, before whose throne.*

RAMSEY, ROBERT, Mus. Bac. (*c.* 1600–*c.* 1650), was organist of Trinity College, Cambridge, 1623–44, and Magister Choristarum, 1637–44. He composed a Morning and an Evening Service in F, two anthems, &c.

> 728. AMEN.

RANDALL, JOHN, Mus. Doc. (1715–99), was in youth a chorister of the Chapel Royal. At the age of seventeen he sang the part of Esther in Handel's oratorio of that name. He became organist of King's College, Cambridge, in 1743; Professor of Music, Cambridge University, 1755; and, later, organist also of Trinity College: all three posts he held simultaneously. In 1794 he published *A Collection of Psalm Tunes, some of which are new, and others by permission of the authors, with six Chants and Te Deums, calculated for the use of Congregations in general.* Six original tunes of his own appeared in this book. He is best known by his two double chants. He was a friend of the poet Gray, one of whose Odes he set to music.

> 65, 677. LEWES.   498. UNIVERSITY.

RANKIN, JEREMIAH EAMES, D.D., LL.D. (Thornton, New Hampshire, 1828–1904, Cleveland, Ohio), was educated at Middelburg College, Vermont, and at Andover Theological Seminary. He was minister of Congregational churches at New York; St. Alban's; Charlestown; Washington (District of Columbia), &c.; and for several years was President of Howard University, Washington. He edited *The Gospel Temperance Hymnal*, and later, *Gospel Bells;* and published *German-English Lyrics, Sacred and Secular* (1897). He was a frequent contributor to the periodical press.

> 624. *God be with you till we meet again.*

RAVENSCROFT, THOMAS, Mus. Bac. (*c.* 1582–1635), was a chorister of St. Paul's Cathedral, and became a Mus. Bac. of Cambridge when only fourteen years of age. He edited much music, but is best known by his *Whole Booke of Psalmes* (1621), a work of high importance, representing 'the last term in a long development, and the most popular, though not in all respects the best application of the English art at its heyday to the psalmody of the Church'. This book contains all the Psalms and Hymns in the Old Version, commonly known as 'Sternhold and Hopkins'. Ravenscroft adopted practically all the *proper* tunes which had appeared in previous psalters, and to those psalms that had no such tunes associated with them he set a number of four-line tunes of more recent origin. There is no evidence that any of these melodies were his own. The title bears that the tunes are 'composed into 4 parts by Sundry Authors'; which means that the musicians whose names were attached to the tunes were merely the harmonizers. Among these were such men, however, as Thomas and John Tomkins, and John Milton, the father of the poet. A large number of the settings are by Ravenscroft himself. This book became a principal source-book for all subsequent compilers of psalmody. Ravenscroft published also in his *Pammelia* the earliest collection of rounds and canons issued in Britain. The practice of naming tunes after places, though it did not originate with him, seems to have been established in England by him. A reprint of his Psalter, with an introduction by the Rev. W. H. Havergal, was published in 1845.

260. BRISTOL (Faux-bourdon).	223. GLOUCESTER.
274. DURHAM.	30. OLD 104TH.
227. FRENCH (Faux-bourdon).	296. SALISBURY.
31. ST. DAVID.	

RAWNSLEY, HARDWICKE DRUMMOND, M.A. (Shiplake-on-Thames, 1851–1920, Grasmere), son of Canon Drummond Rawnsley, vicar of Shiplake, and afterwards of Halton Holgate, a close friend of Tennyson, was educated at Uppingham under the direct guidance of his godfather, Edward Thring; and at Balliol College, Oxford, where he came under the potent influences of Jowett and Ruskin. Graduating in Natural Science in 1874, he was ordained in the following year, and spent two years as curate of St. Barnabas', Bristol, taking special charge of the Clifton College Mission there. In 1877 he became vicar of Wray, on Windermere, and in 1883 entered upon the incumbency of Crosthwaite, near Keswick—a 'post as near heaven as anything in this world can be'—and there continued for thirty-four years. In 1909 he received a canonry in Carlisle Cathedral; he was also a chaplain to the King. He was a man of ardent public spirit, a pioneer of secondary education, and a champion of public rights of access to the hills and places of interest in the Lake District. He was the founder and secretary of the National Trust for Places of Historic Interest and Natural Beauty, which has been responsible for securing for public use in perpetuity many beautiful tracts of the Lake District and other parts of the country. Among his published works were *Sonnets at the English Lakes* (he was a facile and copious sonneteer); *Ruskin and the English Lakes; The Literary Associations of the Lake District; Valete* (Poems); *The Life of Harvey Goodwin, Bishop of Carlisle; Memories of the Tennysons.* On his death, Friar's Crag, Lord's

Island, and a part of Great Wood on the shore of Derwentwater were acquired by subscribers and given to the National Trust in memory of him, 'who, greatly loving the fair things of Nature and of art, set all his love to the service of God and man'.

353. *Father, whose will is life and good.*

RAWSON, GEORGE (Leeds, 1807–89, Clifton), was educated at Manchester, and practised as a solicitor at Leeds. His church affiliation was Congregationalist, and he helped the Congregational ministers of Leeds in 1853 to compile *The Leeds Hymn Book.* He took part also in the compilation of *Psalms and Hymns for the Use of the Baptist Denomination* (1858). His own hymns were collected and published in *Hymns, Verses and Chants* (1876), and *Songs of Spiritual Thought* (1885). A shy, retiring man, of deep piety, he published his hymns at first anonymously, preferring to be known only as 'a Leeds layman', but had to consent at last to his identity being divulged. About fifty of his hymns are in present-day use.

322. *By Christ redeemed, in Christ restored.*
283. *Father in high heaven dwelling.*

REDHEAD, RICHARD (Harrow, 1820–1901, Hellingley, Sussex), became a chorister of Magdalen College, Oxford. He was organist of Margaret Chapel (subsequently All Saints' Church), Margaret Street, Cavendish Square, London, 1839–64; then, till 1894, of St. Mary Magdalene, Paddington. He was in profound sympathy with the Oxford Movement, and Canon Oakeley (q.v.) found an ardent musical coadjutor in him in transforming the services in Margaret Chapel in an advanced ritualistic direction. They edited together the first Gregorian Psalter, with the title *Laudes Diurnae.* Among his many other compositions for the Church were—*Church Music* (chants, sanctuses, responses); *Hymns for Holy Seasons; The Celebrant's Office Book; The Parish Tune Book; The Book of Common Prayer, with Ritual Song; Ancient Hymn Melodies and Other Church Tunes; The Cathedral and Church Choir Book.* These collections exercised a leading influence on the musical side in the Catholic Revival. His own tunes were so intermingled in them with older compositions that many tunes have been attributed to him which he did not write.

35.	LAUS DEO.	329.	ST. DUNSTAN.
423.	METZLER.	150.	ST. NICOLAS.
413.	PETRA.	342.	ST. VICTOR.

REED, ANDREW, D.D. (Butcher Row, St. Clement Danes, London, 1787–1862, Hackney), was the son of a watchmaker, and was trained to that trade, but made his way to Hackney College to train for the Congregational ministry. He became minister of New Road Chapel, St. George's-in-the-East, of which he was a member and in which he had been brought up; and of Wycliffe Chapel, which he built when New Road Chapel became overcrowded; here he continued from 1831 to 1861. In 1817 he published a *Hymn Book* as a supplement to Dr. Watts, and in 1842 superseded it by *The Hymn-Book prepared from Dr. Watts's Psalms and Hymns and Other Authors, with some Originals*. His own twenty-one hymns were contributed to these volumes. An ardent philanthropist and a consummate organizer, he was chiefly instrumental in founding six great benevolent institutions—the London Orphan Asylum at Lower Clapton, the Asylum for Fatherless Children, near Croydon, the Asylum for Idiots, near Reigate, the Infant Orphan Asylum at Wanstead, the Royal Hospital for Incurables, and the Eastern Counties Asylum for Idiots, at Colchester. These cost £129,320. He was an ardent supporter of missionary work at home and abroad. His summing-up of his life, written to his son, who had suggested that he should write his autobiography, is worth recording: 'I was born yesterday, I shall die to-morrow, and I must not spend to-day in telling what I have done, but in doing what I may for HIM who has done all for me. I sprang from the people, I have lived for the people—the most for the most unhappy; and the people when they know it will not suffer me to die out of loving remembrance.'

183. *Spirit Divine, attend our prayers.*

REES, JOHN THOMAS, Mus. Bac. (Ystradgynlais, 1858–   ), received the barest elements of education, and began to work underground in the mines when only nine years old. At that work he continued till he was twenty-one. In music he was self-taught, until he was enabled to study under Dr. Joseph Parry at the University College of Wales. After taking the Mus. Bac. degree of Toronto University, he definitely entered the musical profession, and has continued in it ever since. He is a Lecturer in the School of Music, University College, Aberystwyth, and is much called upon to lead festivals and to adjudicate at Eisteddfodau.

190. DOLE.

REINAGLE, ALEXANDER ROBERT (Brighton, 1799–1877, Kidlington, Oxford), son of Joseph Reinagle, who was of Austrian extraction. The father was long well known in Scotland as a distinguished violoncellist, and for a time he was leader of the orchestra in the Edinburgh Theatre. Alexander became organist of St. Peter's-in-the-East, Oxford, from 1822 to 1853. He published two books of hymn-tunes, chants, &c.; also songs without words, music for violin, 'cello, organ, &c.

419. ST. PETER.

RHODES, SARAH BETTS (Sheffield, *c.* 1830–*c.* 1890, Worksop), was of humble origin, but on her marriage to Jehoiada Alsop Rhodes, a manufacturing silversmith and an artist in his craft, he so devoted himself to educating and refining her, that she became a very clever scholar, a good hymn-writer, and a sculptor of very fair credit. On her husband's death she took over a Girls' High School at Worksop and conducted it for the remainder of her life. She was a Congregationalist.

20. *God, who made the earth.*

RICHARDS, Charles Herbert, D.D. (Meriden, New Hampshire, 1839–1925, New York), graduated at Yale University, 1860, and at Union Theological Seminary, New York. Ordained to the Congregational ministry in 1866, he was pastor of churches in the States of Vermont and Wisconsin successively, and afterwards in the city of Philadelphia. He became secretary of the Congregational Church Building Society. He edited the following hymnals: *Christian Praise* (1880); *Songs of Christian Praise* (1882); *Songs of Praise and Prayer* (1883 and 1889); *Songs of the Christian Life* (1913).

486. *Our Father, Thy dear Name doth show.*

RICHARDS, John (Isalaw) (Bangor, North Wales, 1843–1908, Bangor), was for some years at a Grammar School in Birmingham, but spent the rest of his life in his native city. Apart from a little clerical work he had no particular occupation. From early boyhood he showed a keen interest in music, and he developed an unusual melodic gift. It is said that he would get up in the night and write down with soap on the bedroom mirror, if no other writing materials were at hand, a melody or a phrase that had come to him. He composed a large number of hymn-tunes, glees and anthems, which have been much sung in the Principality during the last half-century.

2. SANCTUS.

RICHARDSON, John (Preston, 1816–79, Preston), was trained for the trade of house painting and decoration, but did not follow it after the completion of his apprenticeship. He was in youth a fine alto singer. Making music his profession, he became organist of St. Mary's Catholic Church, Liverpool, and two years later, of St. Nicholas Chapel in the same city. In the latter post he remained for twenty years. He taught music privately and at St. Edward's College; one of his pupils was W. T. Best, the distinguished organist, who paid high tribute to Richardson's teaching powers. He composed music for Collins's *Ode to the Passions*, glees, hymn-tunes, &c. In 1860 his health broke down, and, returning to Preston, he was an invalid for the rest of his days.

87. ST. BERNARD (arr.).   434. TICHFIELD.

RICHTER, Anne, *née* Rigby (Beverley, ? –1857, Lincoln), was daughter of the Rev. Robert Rigby, of St. Mary's, Beverley. She married the Rev. W. H. Richter, chaplain of the County Gaol at Kirton Lindsey, Lincolnshire, and later, rector of St. Paul's, Lincoln. She was descended from the John Bradshaw who was the first signatory of the death-warrant of Charles I. She contributed verse to various magazines, and in 1841 published *The Nun, and Other Poems*. She was a friend of Mrs. Hemans.

72. *We saw Thee not when Thou didst come.*

RIDSDALE, CHARLES JOSEPH, M.A. (Stoke Newington, London, 1840–), was educated at Gonville and Caius College, Cambridge. Ordained in 1864, he was curate of Whitstable and Seasalter, 1864–6; and perpetual curate of St. Peter's, Folkestone, 1868–1923. He published *Cantio Dominica*, a Communion Service in three parts with full accompaniment, and in four parts for children's voices; a four-part Sequence for a Dedication Festival; *Three Festal Magnificats* set to Gregorian Chants with Faux-bourdons; four *Suites de Pièces* for the pianoforte. He was musical editor of *The Children's Service Book, with accompanying music*, edited by M. Woodward; and of *The New Office Hymn Book*.

412. NONE OTHER LAMB.

RILEY, WILLIAM (*c.* 1762), was in charge of the music at the Asylum or House of Refuge for Female Orphans at Westminster Bridge, and taught psalmody also elsewhere. He strongly disapproved of the light and secular airs that were being made popular by the Methodist Revival, and was determined that the children under his tuition should be trained to the appreciation and use of a sounder type of religious music. In his *Parochial Music Corrected* (1762) he inveighs against the innovations, and says of the Methodists that 'their Tunes mostly consist of what they call Fuges, or (more properly) Imitations, and are indeed fit to be sung only by those who made them'. Under the Stuarts pious benefactors had endowed Lectureships in many of the parish churches, in order to increase the opportunities for religious instruction. To these Lectureships the parishioners might elect any clergyman whom the bishop would license, and invite him to lecture once a week at an hour when the church was not required for a regular service. Riley complained bitterly that congregations not only chose such lectures as suited their own turn of mind, but paid the clerk and organist to stay away, so that they might introduce organists of their own choice to lead and play the obnoxious new tunes. To counter the tendency he denounced, he advocated abandonment of the custom of 'lining' the psalms and hymns, increasing the *tempo* at which they were sung, taking them twice as fast, and doing away with the organ interludes which were introduced between the lines. The prevailing methods made the singing of even four verses of a psalm seem intolerably long. Riley urged that with his reforms applied, it would be possible to sing seven or eight without weariness. He published a tune-book giving old and new tunes in the pure style he favoured—*Parochial Harmony, consisting of a Collection of psalm-tunes in three and four parts* (1762); and, with words as well as tunes, *Psalms and Hymns for the Chapel of the Asylum or House of Refuge for Female Orphans* (n.d., but after 1762). To these books we owe

403. ST. BRIDE (Samuel Howard).

551. ST. EDMUND (Edmund Gilding).

RIMBAULT, EDWARD FRANCIS, Ph.D., LL.D., F.S.A. (London, 1816–76, London), studied under Samuel Wesley and Dr. Crotch, and was organist in succession of the Swiss Church, Soho; St. Peter's, Vere Street; St. John's Wood Presbyterian Church; and St. Giles-in-the-Fields. He was one of the most learned of musical antiquaries, and editor of the Motett Society. His diligence in editing and publishing music of many kinds was unceasing. He produced works on the history of the organ and the pianoforte; collections of madrigals, carols, ballads, nursery rhymes; rounds, catches and canons; anthems and services; psalm-tunes and chants; editions of Tallis's *Cathedral Service* and *Order of Daily Service;* Este's *The Whole Book of Psalms;* Merbecke's *Book of Common Prayer Noted;* selections and transcriptions for organ and pianoforte; and a large number of articles on musical and antiquarian subjects for dictionaries and periodicals. His learning brought him honorary degrees from Harvard, Stockholm, and Göttingen.

493. DELHI.

RINKART, MARTIN (Eilenburg, 1586–1649, Eilenburg), the son of a cooper, was educated at Eilenburg and at Leipzig, where he graduated. After holding various appointments in other towns, he became in 1617 Archidiaconus at Eilenburg, where he spent the rest of his life. This period was almost entirely covered by the Thirty Years War, in which the town became an asylum for fugitives from all parts, and consequently suffered much from famine and pestilence. For some time Rinkart was the only clergyman in the place, and he is said to have often read the funeral service over as many as forty persons in a day, and to have greatly strained his resources in saving others from hunger. He was also successful in dissuading a Swedish commander from imposing on the town an excessive tribute. Rinkart was poet, dramatist, and musician.

29. *Now thank we all our God.*

RIPPON, JOHN, D.D. (Tiverton, 1751–1836, London), was one of the most distinguished and influential Nonconformist ministers of his time. At the age of twenty-two he became minister of the Baptist congregation in Carter's Lane, Tooley Street (afterwards in New Park Street), London, and so continued till his death. In 1787 he

477

published *A Selection of Hymns from the best authors, intended as an Appendix to Dr. Watts's Psalms and Hymns;* and, in 1791, *A Selection of Psalms and Hymn Tunes from the Best Authors,* adapted to Watts's collection and his own. As an editor Rippon showed great discretion and taste, and his hymn-book had great popularity. As a source-book it was much drawn upon by subsequent editors. *The Comprehensive Edition,* known as *The Comprehensive Rippon,* containing 1,174 hymns in 100 metres, appeared in 1844 after his death. It was the standard book of Baptist hymnody. The enormous sales of it made Rippon comparatively wealthy.

57. (TIVERTON).

ROBERTS, ARTHUR OWEN (Liverpool, 1869–), is son of the late Eleazar Roberts, well known throughout Wales as a *littérateur* and as the pioneer of the tonic sol-fa system in that country. He has been for thirty years honorary organist of the Presbyterian Church of Wales at Hoylake, Cheshire, where he is also an elder. He acted as secretary of the Music Section of the Welsh Presbyterian Church Committee on the Revision of *The Church Hymnary,* and as a member of the Joint Revision Committee itself.

347. BLODYN.   487. HOYLAKE.

ROBERTS, JOHN (Llanaelhaiarn, South Caernarvonshire, 1731–1806, Holyhead), otherwise known as Sion Rhobert Lewis, was converted under the preaching of Howel Harris, and became an 'exhorter' in the Calvinistic Methodist Church. Settling at Holyhead (Caergybi) he was licensed by the Bishop of Bangor to keep a school. He published what was probably the first arithmetic in Welsh, as also several tracts and other religious works in that language. Among his other accomplishments was a considerable knowledge of astronomy. He is best known by his *Almanac,* first published in 1760, which continues to be issued under his name to this day. He wrote several fine hymns in Welsh, the best known being 'Braint, braint', translated as under.

226. *O blest communion with the saints at rest.*

ROBERTS, JOHN (IEUAN GWYLLT) (Tanrhiwfelen, near Aberystwyth, 1822–77, Vron, near Caernarvon), after a variety of occupations was ordained to the ministry of the Calvinistic Methodist Church in 1859, and held pastoral charges first near Merthyr, then at Capel Coch, Llanberis until 1869, when he retired. He did a great work as a reformer of congregational singing. He was the founder of the great institution known in Wales as the *Gymanfa ganu,* or singing festival, the object of which is to encourage the love for that 'blest pair of sirens, voice and verse', the hymn and the hymn-tune. These gatherings have had a great influence, educationally and religiously, on the life of Wales. 'As a musician', says G. Parry

Williams, 'he was unique; incomparable as a musical critic and instructor and an arranger of congregational hymn-tunes; and as a conductor of Sacred Music Festivals, he was in a special sense God's gift to Wales.' Ieuan Gwyllt's *Llyfr Tonau Cynulleidfaol* (Book of Congregational Tunes, 1859), the recognized tune-book of the Calvinistic Methodists, was epoch-making. He also edited the monthly musical magazine *Y Cerddor Gymreig*. His fine tunes are high in favour throughout Wales. Competent judges deem the tune *Moab* the best Welsh tune ever written.

103. ARDUDWY.	364. MALVERN (arr.).
243. BONT-NEWYDD.	572. MOAB.
475. LIVERPOOL.	687. RHEIDOL.

ROBERTS, JOHN HENRY, Mus. Bac. (Bethesda, near Bangor, 1848–1924, Liverpool), became an organist at twelve. Removing to Towyn, he started a Choral Society there. Later, he studied at the R.A.M., attaining the Associateship, took his degree at Cambridge in 1882, and for many years was organist at Castle Square Church, Caernarvon; later, also of Chatham Street Welsh Church, Liverpool. He founded in 1874 at Caernarvon, and carried on subsequently at Liverpool, the J. H. Roberts Music Publishing Company. In 1885 he carried off all the prizes for musical composition at the National Eisteddfod. He composed many hymn-tunes and anthems, and was regarded as one of the finest composers of part-songs Wales has produced. He was musical editor of tune-books used by the Calvinistic Methodists, the Welsh Baptists, and the Welsh Independents.

466. O GRANT US LIGHT.	718. CHANT IN E FLAT.

ROBERTS, LEWIS JONES, B.A. (Aberayron, Cardiganshire, 1866–), was educated at St. David's College, Lampeter, and Exeter College, Oxford. From 1894 to 1921 he was one of His Majesty's Inspectors of Schools in Wales, with headquarters successively at Aberystwyth, Rhyl, Llandudno, and Swansea. Ill-health caused his retiral in the latter year. He has been prominently associated with the National Eisteddfod for over forty years (President, Wrexham, 1910), and with the Cambrian Archaeological Association. He founded several Cymmrodorion societies in North Wales. He has published the standard book in Welsh on *Owen Glyndwr*, edited *Awelon o Hiraethog*, and contributed many articles on Welsh subjects to various books and magazines. He has been musical editor of the national magazine *Cymru*, in which a tune has appeared monthly, since it was started in 1891 by Sir Owen Edwards. Some of his musical compositions have been sung at the National Eisteddfodau and at hundreds of local festivals, and have appeared in American as well as British hymnals.

158. NESTA.

ROBERTS, ROBERT (Liverpool, 1863–), son of Welsh parents, was educated in Liverpool and entered the teaching profession. For a time he taught in Liverpool, but in 1887 was appointed head-master of Dyffryn Board (afterwards Council) School, Merioneth. There he continued until health failed him in 1917. In music he was practically self-taught. Many prizes were won by him at Eisteddfodau for hymn-tunes, a number of which appear in Welsh hymn-books of various denominations. He published in 1889 *The Cambria Song-Book* for children.

404. ALICE.

ROBERTS, ROBERT ROWLAND (Penmaenmawr, 1865–), was ordained to the ministry of the Presbyterian Church of Wales in 1891, and has held pastorates at Aberdare, Cardiff (Cathedral Road), Chester, and Cardiff (Clifton Street), where he now ministers. He has filled several denominational offices, as Moderator of the South Wales Association, vice-chairman of the South Wales Commission, &c. He delivered the Davies Lecture for 1908, on *The Supreme Experience of Christianity*, since published as a treatise on Christian Mysticism. He is an outstanding preacher in the Principality.

572. *Far off I see the goal.*

ROBERTSON, WILLIAM, M.A. (Cambuslang, 1820–64, Monzievaird, Perthshire), son of the Rev. John Robertson, D.D., Cambuslang, studied at the University of Glasgow. In 1843 he became minister of the parish of Monzievaird. His interest in hymnody and Scottish psalmody was keen. He was a member of the Hymnal Committee of the Church of Scotland in 1851, 1853, and 1857, and contributed to *Hymns for Public Worship*, issued by that Church, two hymns afterwards included in *The Scottish Hymnal* and *The Church Hymnary*.

305. *A little child the Saviour came.*

ROBINSON, GEORGE WADE (Cork, 1838–77, Southampton), was educated at Trinity College, Dublin, and New College, Hackney, London, for the Congregational ministry. He was colleague to Dr. Urwick in the ministry of York Street Chapel, Dublin, and afterwards held charges at St. John's Wood, London; Dudley; and Union Street, Brighton. He issued two volumes of verse, *Songs in God's World*, and *Loveland*.

434. *Loved with everlasting love.*

ROBINSON, JOHN (London, 1682–1762, London), was trained as a chorister of the Chapel Royal under Blow, and was organist of St. Lawrence Jewry, and St. Magnus, London Bridge, before becoming organist of Westminster Abbey in 1727, in succession to Croft. He was a successful teacher of the harpsichord, and carried the style of playing suited to that instrument into his treatment of the organ, to such an extent as to draw an indignant comment from Hawkins. Describing him as 'a very florid and elegant performer. . . insomuch that crowds resorted to hear him', he said, 'In parish churches the voluntary between the psalms was anciently a slow solemn movement, tending to compose the mind and excite sentiments of piety and devotion. Mr. Robinson introduced a different practice, calculated to display the agility of the fingers in *allegro* movements on the cornet, trumpet, sesquialtera, and other noisy stops, degrading the instrument, and instead of the full, noble harmony with which it was designed to gratify the ear, tickling it with mere airs in two parts, in fact solos for a flute and a bass.' He composed well-known chants, psalm-tunes, &c.

714. CHANT IN E FLAT.

ROBINSON, RICHARD HAYES (? 1842–92, Bournemouth), was educated at King's College, London. Ordained in 1866, he became curate of St. Paul's, Penge, and of Weston, and afterwards was incumbent of the Octagon Chapel, Bath, and of St. Germain's, Blackheath, then a proprietary chapel. He was taken ill in the train on the day of his second wedding, and died the next day. He published *Sermons on Faith and Duty*, and *The Creed and the Age*.

282. *Holy Father, cheer our way.*

ROBINSON, ROBERT (Swaffham, Norfolk, 1735–90, Showell Green, near Birmingham), son of an exciseman, born in Scotland, was educated at the Grammar Schools of Swaffham and of Scarning, Norfolk. His mother's desire was to see him a clergyman of the Church of England, but straitened means rendered this impossible, and he was for some time apprenticed to a barber in London. His dedication to a religious life he dates from 1752, when he first heard Whitefield preach, and his complete conversion from 1755. In 1758 he began preaching as a Calvinistic Methodist, but soon developed independent views. In 1759 he received adult baptism, and shortly afterwards became pastor of Stone Yard Baptist Chapel, Cambridge. His activities were many sided. While he farmed land and carried on business as a corn and coal merchant, he regularly preached twice on Sundays, besides engaging in evangelistic work during the week. Nor did he neglect his duties. His *Plea for the Divinity of our Lord* was greatly admired by Churchmen as well as Nonconformists, and he was strongly pressed to enter the ministry of the Church of England. He maintained, however, his Baptist connexion, and published a *History of Baptism and Baptists*. In his later years he seems to have inclined somewhat towards Unitarianism; so, at any rate, Unitarians claim.

435. *Come, Thou Fount of every blessing.*

RODIGAST, Samuel (Groben, near Jena, 1649–1708, Berlin), studied at Jena and graduated there in 1671. He became 'adjunct' of the philosophical faculty there, and in 1680 conrector of the Grey-friars Gymnasium, Berlin. He had a great reputation as a scholar and educationist, and was offered a professorship at Jena, and rector-ships of schools at Stade and Stralsund. He preferred Berlin, and in 1698 became full rector of the Gymnasium, a post he held till his death. He was buried in the Kloster Kirche, Berlin.

540. *Whate'er my God ordains is right.*

ROGERS, Benjamin, Mus. Doc. (Windsor, 1614–98, Salisbury), was the son of one of the singing-men in St. George's Chapel, Windsor. He became organist of Christ Church Cathedral, Dublin, but his stay there was cut short by the Irish Rebellion, which scared him out of the country. For a time he taught at Windsor; in 1660 became organist of Eton College; in 1662, lay clerk at St. George's, Windsor; in 1664, organist of Magdalen College, Oxford. He ac-commodated himself to the political changes of the time, and kept his posts when other musicians were ejected from their places and William Lawes fell in action for the Royal cause. In 1685 he was removed from his post in Magdalen College because of irregu-larities, neglect of duty and 'troublesome behaviour in chapel', where 'usually he would talk so loud in the organ-loft that he offended the company, and would not leave off, though he hath been sent to by the President not to make such a scandalous noise there'. Frequent complaints were made of him also by the lay clerks, to whom 'he used to be very cross, in not playing services as they were willing and able to sing, but out of a thwarting humour would play nothing but Canterbury Tune, wherein he minded not the honour of the College, but his own ease and laziness'. The College gave him a good pension 'to keep him from the contempt of the world. In that condition he lived in a skirt of the city of Oxon unregarded.' After his death his wife was pensioned also. He had a considerable reputation during the Restoration period. Some of his anthems are still sung, and his Service in D is used probably in every Cathedral and College Chapel in England.

471. HYMNUS EUCHARISTICUS.

ROOKER, Alfred (Tavistock, 1814–75, Beirut, Syria), son of the Rev. William Rooker, Congregational minister at Tavistock, was descended from a Dutch officer who came to England with William of Orange in 1688 and fought at the battle of the Boyne. He became a solicitor, and practised with success in Plymouth. A man of rare moral and intellectual gifts, he rose to high position in the com-munity, was mayor when King Edward VII, then Prince of Wales, opened the new Guildhall in 1874, was chairman of the School Board, and on one occasion stood, unsuccessfully, as a candidate for

Parliament. He was prominent in religious and philanthropic work. He published books on *The Literature and Literary Men of Plymouth* (1845); *The Precursors of the English Reformation* (1853); *The Bicentenary of the Bartholomew of Ejectment* (1862); *Does it answer? Slavery in America* (1864). After his death while on a tour in the Holy Land, a statue in his honour was erected in the Guildhall Square of Plymouth. His sister Elizabeth, afterwards Mrs. Edgcombe Parson, was a hymn-writer also.

244. *O be with us, gracious Father.*

ROOT, GEORGE FREDERICK, Mus. Doc. (Sheffield, Massachusetts, 1820–95, Bailey's Island, Maine), studied under G. J. Webb, and at Paris. He was organist of Winter Street and Park Street Churches, Boston, began there to conduct choral societies, and joined Lowell Mason in teaching in public schools. In 1844 he went to New York, taught voice production in Union Theological Seminary, and acted as organist of Mercer Street Presbyterian Church. From 1859 to 1871 he was a partner in the firm of Root & Cady, music publishers, Chicago. In the latter year the great fire in that city led to the dissolution of the firm, but he continued to make Chicago his head-quarters. He wrote cantatas which had for some time an extraordinary vogue, and a number of songs which had great popularity during the American Civil War—*The Battle Cry of Freedom; Just before the Battle, Mother; The Vacant Chair; Tramp, tramp, tramp, the boys are marching* (also known to the words of *God save Ireland*), &c.

158. WHEN HE COMETH.

ROSENROTH, CHRISTIAN KNORR, BARON VON (Altrauden, Silesia, 1636–89, Sulzbach, near Arnberg, Bavaria), studied at Stettin, Leipzig, and Wittenberg, and became a pastor in Silesia. Before settling there he had travelled in France, England, and Holland, and as the result of meeting distinguished scholars in Amsterdam, he devoted himself to the study of oriental languages, chemistry, and cabbalistic science. He was an ardent seeker, for a time, after the philosophers' stone, but found truth and peace in Christianity. His learning led to his being taken into the service of the Palsgrave Christian August of Sulzbach, and that prince in 1668 made him his prime minister. He was created a baron by the Emperor Leopold I. He wrote seventy hymns, in which he showed himself a mystic of the school of Scheffler; they are full of a glowing desire after inner union with God in Christ.

262. *Jesus, Sun of Righteousness.*

ROSS, WILLIAM BAIRD, Mus. Doc. (Montrose, 1871–   ), was educated in Montrose and Edinburgh. He took his bachelor's degree at Queen's College, Oxford, 1895; the Fellowship of the College of

Organists, 1898; and his doctorate in 1903. He was organist of St. Luke's, Montrose, and has for many years now been organist of Broughton Place United Free Church, Edinburgh. He is Lecturer in Church Praise in New College, Edinburgh, and for some years lectured in the United Free Church Colleges in Glasgow and Aberdeen also. He teaches pianoforte and singing in George Watson's Ladies' College, Edinburgh, and is a leading recitalist in Edinburgh. He has published a cantata, *Collins's Ode to the Passions*.

61. CARILLON.

ROSSETTI, CHRISTINA GEORGINA (London, 1830–94, London), was the youngest member of an exceptionally brilliant family. Her father, Gabriele Rossetti, was an Italian refugee who became Professor of Italian at King's College, London; Dante Gabriel Rossetti and William Michael Rossetti were her brothers. She received her education at home, in a circle of literary people and artists. Her face is well known to multitudes who know nothing of her poetry, for she sat as model to several famous artists who were friends of the family, such as Holman Hunt, Millais, and Madox Brown, as well as to her brother Gabriel; the face of the Virgin in his 'Girlhood of the Virgin' and his 'Ecce Ancilla Domini' is hers. For some time Mrs. Rossetti and her daughters kept a small day-school in North London, but unsuccessfully. Christina broke off an engagement to a man to whom she was deeply attached, because of his having become a Roman Catholic. Disappointed love, and much sorrow and suffering in her later years, intensified her deeply religious temperament. 'Her days were spent as quietly as the noiseless and secluded days of a nun within the cloister walls.' She found relief for her burdened spirit in befriending the poor children connected with the church where she worshipped, near Regent's Park. Her biographer in *The Encyclopædia Britannica* says, 'Hers was a cloistral spirit, timid, nun-like, bowed down by suffering and humility; her character was so retiring as to be almost invisible. All that we really need to know about her, save that she was a great saint, is that she was a great poet.' She published a number of devotional books in prose— *Time Flies, a Reading Diary* (1885); *Called to be Saints* (1881); *Seek and Find* (1879); *The Face of the Deep, a Devotional Commentary on the Apocalypse* (1892); and these volumes of poems—*Goblin Market, and Other Poems* (1862); *The Prince's Progress, and Other Poems* (1866); *Poems* (1875); *A Pageant, and Other Poems* (1881); and *Verses* reprinted from her devotional books (1893).

> 50. *In the bleak mid-winter.*
> 52. *Love came down at Christmas.*
> 412. *None other Lamb, none other Name.*
> 545. *O Christ my God, who seest the unseen.*
> 358. *O ye who taste that love is sweet.*
> 586. *Sooner or later, yet at last.*

ROUSSEAU, JEAN JACQUES (Geneva, 1712–78, Ermenonville), was the son of French Protestant parents, but in the formation of his character the faith and austere moral standards of his religious ancestry played little part. When he ran away at sixteen, to begin the strange career of which his *Confessions* tell the story, it was with a nature 'swept and garnished, ready for the entrance of all devils or all gods'. He tried many occupations, and failed in most, but in time revealed himself as a daring original thinker, and became one of the most powerful forces in modern literature. Many of his ideas proved seminal. His *Émile* (1762) was the source of many of the most salutary changes in the theory and art of education throughout Europe. And in politics he was the first to proclaim the principles of liberty, equality, and fraternity, which became the watchwords of the French Revolution; Lord Morley says that to estimate fully the effect of his teaching in the sphere of French ideas would be to write the history of that political upheaval. His doctrines exposed him to political persecution, and for a time he took refuge in England. He lived a forlorn, unhappy life, and 'a dense cloud of obscure misery' hangs over its end; he is believed to have died by his own hand. One of his interests was music. He had copied it for a livelihood, and dabbled in it as an art. An opera, *Le Devin du Village*, was produced at Fontainebleau in 1752, amid such applause that he was flattered into the belief that he was a great composer. But it was full of crudities and technical blunders. Its merit lay in its melodic freshness; many of his melodies have the spontaneity and *naïveté* of folk-songs. He never ceased to cultivate the art. Late in life he collected 100 of his pieces under the suggestive title, *Consolations des Misères de ma Vie*. Some of his airs proved exceedingly popular: one may still be heard daily from one of the steeples of his native Geneva; another, adapted, is the undernoted favourite hymn-tune.

661. ROUSSEAU.

ROWLEY, FRANCIS HAROLD, D.D. (Hilton, New York, 1854–   ), was educated at Rochester University and Theological Seminary, became a Baptist minister, and served charges at Titusville, Pennsylvania; North Adams, Mass.; Oak Park, Illinois; Fall River, Mass.; and First Baptist Church, Boston. He is a noted humanitarian. At present he is president of the Massachusetts Society for the Prevention of Cruelty to Animals, and of the American Humane Education Society, and is associated with much other humanitarian work. He has published *The Humane Idea*, *The Horses of Homer*, &c.

683. *I will sing the wondrous story*.

RUSSELL, ARTHUR TOZER, B.C.L. (Northampton, 1806–74, Southwick, near Brighton), was the son of the Rev. Thomas Clout, a Congregational minister who changed his name to Russell and earned some reputation by editing the works of Tyndale, Barnes, Owen, &c.

Arthur was educated at St. Saviour's School, Southwark, and the Merchant Taylors' School, London; Manchester College, York; and St. John's College, Cambridge. Ordained in 1829 by the Bishop of Lincoln, he became curate of Great Gransden, Hunts; vicar of Caxton, 1730; vicar of Whaddon, near Royston, Cambridgeshire, 1852; of St. Thomas's, Toxteth Park, Liverpool, 1866; of Wrackwardine Wood, Wellington, Shropshire, 1867; and of Southwick, Brighton, 1874. In his earlier years an extreme High Churchman, he was changed into a moderate Calvinist by a study of Augustine, and he proved one of the most effective critics both of the High Church *Tracts for the Times*, and of the Broad Church *Essays and Reviews*. He published sermons and controversial writings; *Memorials* of Thomas Fuller and Bishop Andrewes; about 1840, *Hymn Tunes, Original and Selected, from Ravenscroft and Other Musicians;* and in 1851, *Psalms and Hymns, partly Original, partly Selected, for the Use of the Church of England*. In this last collection German hymns were numerous, and the very arrangement was based on the old Lutheran hymn-books. His own hymns number about 140. One mistake he made was in adding a verse to 'Nearer, my God, to Thee', at the request of the compilers of *The Baptist Hymn-Book*, to supply what was supposed to be a missing evangelical note:

> Christ alone beareth me
>> Where Thou dost shine;
> Joint-heir He maketh me
>> Of the Divine.
> In Christ my soul shall be
> Nearest, my God, to Thee,
>> Nearest to Thee.

132. *The Lord ascendeth up on high.*

RUSSELL, WILLIAM, Mus. Bac. (London, 1777–1813, London), son of an organ-builder and organist, held posts as organist at St. Mary, Aldermanbury; Great Queen Street Chapel; Lincoln's Inn Fields; St. Ann's, Limehouse; and the Foundling Hospital. He was pianist also at Sadler's Wells and Covent Garden. He published three oratorios, a mass in C minor, numerous operas, odes, glees and songs. He composed largely for the Church also—anthems and services, and in 1809 edited *Psalms, Hymns, and Anthems for the Foundling Chapel*. He had a high reputation as organist and pianist.

718. CHANT IN F.

RYLEY, GEOFFREY CHARLES EDWARD, M.A., Mus. Bac. (Sarratt, Herts, 1866–), was educated at King's School, Canterbury, where he studied the organ under Dr. W. H. Longhurst of the Cathedral; and at Trinity College, Oxford. For three years he was organist of the College, and for two was choirmaster and music-master at The Philberds School, Maidenhead. Ordained in 1892, he was for a time second master of St. Michael's College, Tenbury; minor canon of Gloucester, and curate of St. Catherine's there; minor canon of Canterbury; rector of Stodmarsh; and became vicar of East Peckham, Hadlow, Tonbridge, in 1911. He is a Fellow of St. Michael's College, Tenbury. He has published church services, anthems, carols, hymn-tunes, songs, organ and pianoforte music.

436. SARRATT.

ST. GALL GESANGBUCH.—The Benedictine monastery of St. Gall, founded in 614 by an Irish monk of that name, became one of the most famous centres of Church song in the Middle Ages. The monks cherished and cultivated the traditions of the Roman liturgic chant, and the type of hymn called Sequence had its origin, as we know it, among them. (See Notker.) From the twelfth century the monastery declined, and in 1790 it was suppressed. Its celebrated library is intact, containing 1,158 *incunabula*, and 1725 MSS. of great value. The old hymn-book of St. Gall, revised with R. L. de Pearsall (q.v.) as part-editor, was published in 1863 under the title *Katholisches Gesangbuch zum Gebrauch bei dem öffentlichen Gottesdienste*.

396. PEARSALL.   88. WER DA WONET.

SANDYS, WILLIAM, F.S.A. (London, 1792–1874, London), was a lawyer by profession, but also a keen amateur musician and musical antiquary. He published *Christmas Carols, ancient and modern, including the most popular in the West of England, and the airs to which they are sung; also Specimens of French Provincial Carols: with an Introduction and Notes* (London, 1833); *Christmas-tide, its History, Festivities, and Carols, with their music* (London, 1852); *History of the Violin and other Instruments played on with the Bow, from the remotest times to the present; also an account of the principal makers, English and foreign* (London, 1864).

511. (SANDYS).

SANKEY, IRA DAVID (Edinburgh, Pennsylvania, 1840–1908, Brooklyn), was a member of the Methodist and afterwards of the Methodist Episcopal Church. At Newcastle, Pa., as superintendent of a large Sunday School, he began his life-work as a singer of sacred songs and solos. Dwight L. Moody, hearing him sing at an International Convention of Y.M.C.A.'s at Indianapolis, induced him to join him in his work at Chicago. In 1872 they began their famous evangelistic tours together; they remained in association in that work until 1899. The striking effectiveness of Moody's homely and direct preaching was greatly aided by Sankey's sincere and moving singing, and by the simple, sentimental hymns he popularized, with their equally simple, emotional, contagious melodies. Sankey himself said, 'I am no musician; indeed I am no singer; I was never taught to sing.' J. S. Curwen wrote of him, 'A singing-master would find faults in every measure that he sings. His style is more recitative

487

than singing; he sacrifices time unnecessarily to impulse and feeling. The effect is often jerky, intermittent, disconnected. It is speaking with a sustained voice. But his earnestness is so apparent that it covers a multitude of faults; indeed, his transparent naturalness and his fervour so fix attention upon what he is singing that we do not think of the faults. . . . Every word throbs with feeling, and in yearning, pleading phrases the large tender heart of the man is especially conspicuous.' His *Sacred Songs and Solos* (1st ed., 1873) are familiar all over the world; they are found in many languages, associated with the well-known tunes. He published also *Gospel Hymns* (1875–91); *Winnowed Songs* (1890); and *My Life and the Story of the Gospel Hymns* (1906).

685. THE NINETY AND NINE.

SCHEFFLER, JOHANN, M.D., 'Angelus Silesius' (Breslau, Silesia, 1624–77, Breslau), was the son of Lutheran parents. He studied medicine at the Universities of Breslau, Strasburg, Leyden, and Padua, where he graduated M.D. He early evinced an interest in metaphysical and theological subjects, and fell under the influence of the writings of Jacob Böhme. While in Holland he frequented the society of a company of Böhme's followers, and steeped his mind also in the writings of such mystics as Tauler and Ruysbroeck. On returning to Silesia he was made private physician to the Duke of Württemberg-Oels. His dominant interest in mysticism brought him into controversy with the clergy of the Lutheran Church at Oels. Formalists and dogmatists as they were, they not only refused him sympathy, but assailed his views bitterly, and in the end drove him into the arms of the Roman Church, into which he was received in 1653. He was then made imperial court physician to the Emperor Ferdinand III, but soon relinquished his profession, took orders, and in 1671 entered the Jesuit monastery of St. Matthias in Breslau. He adopted the name of Angelus, after Johannes ab Angelis, a Spanish mystic of the sixteenth century, usually adding to it Silesius, to indicate his country. He espoused Romanism with the extreme zeal of a proselyte, engaged in acrimonious controversy with the Lutherans, and when the Roman Catholics of Breslau for the first time since the Reformation obtained permission to celebrate the festival of Corpus Christi by a procession through the streets, Scheffler was proud to be the bearer of the monstrance containing the Host. His hymns, almost entirely free from sectarian characteristics, were for the most part included in his *Heilige Seelenlust, oder Geistliche Hirten-Lieder* (Sacred Joy of the Soul, or Spiritual Pastorals), 1657– — hymns addressed by 'Psyche, the soul, to her Beloved Jesus'. Most of these were written while he was still a Lutheran. The music of the book was edited by Georg Joseph (q.v.).

496. O Love, who formedst me to wear.
431. Thee will I love, my Strength, my Tower.

SCHEIN, JOHANN HERMANN (Grünhayn, near Zwickau, Saxony, 1586–1630, Leipzig), was the son of a Lutheran pastor. For four years he was a chorister in the chapel of the Elector of Saxony, at Dresden; then he studied theology and philosophy at Leipzig. After some years of private tutoring he was appointed music director at the court of Duke Johann Ernst of Saxe-Weimar, in 1613. Two years later he was called back to Leipzig, to the office of cantor in St. Thomas's Church and School. One of the most distinguished musicians of his time, he devoted his life to the elevation and improvement of Church music. He added largely to the literature of the chorale, and wrote much unaccompanied choral music on the Italian model. He composed many hymn-tunes, and some hymns also. He is best known by the great hymn-book he edited for the Lutheran Church, *Cantional, oder Gesangbuch Augsburgischer Confession* (Leipzig, 1627). He published also *Musica Divina*, a collection of motets for 8, 16, and 24 voices.

241. EISENACH.

SCHENCK, HEINRICH THEOBALD (Heidelbach, near Alsfeld, Hesse 1656-1727, Giessen), studied at the Paedagogium, and the University, Giessen. In 1676 he returned to his school as a teacher of the classics. In 1689 he was ordained as town preacher and definitor of the Stadtskirche in the same town. He is not known to have written any other hymn than the one by which he is represented here.

222. *Who are these, like stars appearing?*

SCHICHT, JOHANN GOTTFRIED (Reichenau, near Zittau, 1753–1823, Leipzig), succeeded Hiller in the direction of Leipzig Gewandhaus Concerts in 1785, and became organist and cantor of different churches, until he resigned all other work to devote himself entirely to the musical direction of St. Thomas's Church. He wrote many masses, motets, and books of chorales. His *Allgemeines Choralbuch* (1819) contains nearly 300 tunes written by him.

132. ASCENDIT DEUS.   103. ZU MEINEM HERRN.

SCHLEGEL, KATHARINA AMALIA DOROTHEA von (1697– ?), is said by Koch to have been the head of the Evangelical Lutheran Stift (Protestant nunnery) at Cöthen; but this is unconfirmed, no such name occurring in the records of that institution. From her extant correspondence with Count Stolberg it seems likelier that she was a lady attached to the ducal court at Cöthen. No details of her life survive.

556. *Be still, my soul: the Lord is on thy side.*

SCHMOLCK, BENJAMIN (Brauchitzchdorf, Silesia, 1672–1737, Schweidnitz), preacher, poet and hymn-writer, studied at the Gymnasium at Lauban and the University of Leipzig. In 1701 he was ordained as assistant to his father, Lutheran pastor at Brauchitzch-dorf, and in the following year was appointed diaconus of the Friedenskirche at Schweidnitz in Silesia. As a result of the terms agreed on at the Peace of Westphalia, the Lutherans were subjected to many restrictions, only one church, with three clergy, being allowed at Schweidnitz to serve a district containing thirty-six villages. Here Schmolck laboured for the rest of his life as preacher, pastor, and organizer. In his latter years he suffered much from paralysis and cataract. He is credited with the authorship of over 900 hymns, the best of which are characterized by a fervent religious spirit, and written in a clear and forcible style. They are still popular in Germany.

307. *Blessed Jesus, here we stand.*

SCHOLEFIELD, CLEMENT COTTERILL, M.A. (Edgbaston, Bir-mingham, 1839–1904, London), was educated at Pocklington, Yorkshire, and St. John's College, Cambridge. Ordained in 1867, he served curacies at Hove, near Brighton, and St. Luke's, Chelsea; was conduct (chaplain) of Eton College, 1880–90; and from 1890 to 1895 was vicar of Holy Trinity, Knightsbridge. He composed many hymn-tunes.

584. IRENE.   289. ST. CLEMENT.

SCHOLINUS, FRIEDRICH KARL LUDWIG (Magdeburg, 1772–1816, Nedlitz), was pastor at Nedlitz, in Saxony.

569. MAMRE.

SCHOP, JOHANN (Hamburg, ? –1664, Hamburg), described as 'an intelligent performer on the violin, lute, trumpet, and zinke', entered the Court orchestra at Wolfenbüttel in 1615. In 1664 he became music director at Hamburg, and 'Ratsmusikant' in 1654. He acquired great fame as a violinist. Besides much instrumental music, he wrote many hymn-tunes for the hymns of his fellow-townsman and friend Johann Rist, and others, and these came into general use in the collections of the day.

492. ERMUNTRE DICH.

SCHULZ, JOHANN ABRAHAM PETER (Lüneburg, 1747–1800, Schwedt), was the son of a baker, and was intended for the Church, but early set his heart on a musical career. An organist who taught him the clavecin told him of the wonderful music to be heard in Berlin and of the greatness of Kirnberger, then at the height of his fame, as a teacher; and at fifteen years of age he left home, without money and against his family's wishes, to beg Kirnberger to accept him as a pupil. Against all likelihood he succeeded. Later, five years of travel in France, Italy and Germany, with the Polish Princess Sapieta, formed his taste and genius. On his return he did his generous master great service by assisting him and Sulzer with the musical articles for their *General Theory of the Fine Arts*, and edited Kirnberger's *Treatise on Pure Composition*. In 1776 he became director of the French Theatre in Berlin; in 1780 director of music in the household of Prince Henry of Prussia at Reinsberg; and in 1787 went in the same capacity to the Danish Court at Copenhagen. He exercised a great influence over Danish music, but in the effort to save the music library when the royal palace was burned down, his health was shattered. On a voyage to Lisbon he was shipwrecked, and he returned to Germany in 1796, a broken man. He published several collections of German songs, sacred and secular, operas, oratorios, and instrumental music.

237, 618. WIR PFLÜGEN (DRESDEN).
476. WARUM SIND DER THRÄNEN.

SCOTT, Sir WALTER, Bart. (Edinburgh, 1771–1832, Abbotsford), was the son of a Writer to the Signet, and was educated at the High School and the University, Edinburgh. He was called to the Bar in 1792. Literature early engaged his active and fertile mind. A translation of Goethe's *Götz von Berlichingen*, in 1799, was followed in 1802 by his *Border Minstrelsy*. Appointed Sheriff of Selkirkshire in 1804, he went to live at Ashestiel, by Tweed, and there produced his metrical romances, *The Lay of the Last Minstrel; Marmion; The Lady of the Lake; The Vision of Don Roderick*. When he settled at Abbotsford in 1812 he wrote *Rokeby; The Lord of the Isles; The Bridal of Triermain*. In 1814 he broke new ground with another order of romance, in *Waverley;* thenceforward he wrote little poetry, but poured his wide knowledge, imagination, and rare powers of mind into the great succession of novels which establish his enduring fame. He was made a baronet in 1820. His books brought him wealth. But in 1826 commercial disaster overtook him, through the failure of his publisher, Constable, and the Ballantyne printing firm, in which he was a partner. The rest of his life was a heroic struggle to retrieve this misfortune and discharge his huge liabilities. The story is one of high moral grandeur. He went down gallantly fighting, writing to the last, and dying of over-work. His place as a writer of ballads and metrical romances and as a lyric poet is high, but his novels, in which he was the pioneer of a new school of romanticists and the master of them all, secure his immortality.

161. *That day of wrath, that dreadful day* (tr.).
367. *When Israel, of the Lord beloved.*

SCOTT-GATTY, Sir ALFRED, K.C.V.O. (Ecclesfield, Yorkshire, 1847–1918, London), son of the Rev. Alfred Gatty, D.D., sub-dean of York Cathedral, assumed by royal licence as an additional surname, his mother's name of Scott, she being the daughter and heir of the Rev. A. J. Scott, D.D., private secretary to Horatio, Lord

Nelson. He became a specialist in heraldry, and held office as Rouge Dragon Pursuivant of Arms; York Herald of the College of Arms; Acting Registrar of the same College; Knight of Justice of the Order of St. John of Jerusalem and Genealogist of that Order; and Garter Principal King of Arms. On his appointment to this last office in 1904 he was knighted. Early in life he showed a great love for music, and his mother, the well-known authoress of *Parables from Nature*, published his earliest musical compositions in *Aunt Judy's Magazine*, which she edited (in 1868). Subsequently he published *Little Songs for Little Voices; Musical Plays for Children; Rumpelstiltskin; The Goose Girl; The Three Bears; Plantation Songs* (4 vols.); and hundreds of popular songs, humorous and sentimental—in many instances composing both words and music.

648. WELWYN.

SCOTTISH PARAPHRASES (1781).—It is a mistake to suppose that hymns were not introduced into public worship in Scotland until the nineteenth century. The first complete Scottish Psalter was published in 1564. In an edition published by Thomas Bassandyne in 1575 there was an appendix containing five *Spiritual Songs*. These were in use until the old Scottish Psalter gave place to Rous's version in 1650. It was unfortunate that the latter contained no supplement of hymns. The General Assembly which authorized it recognized the need for such a supplement, for a recommendation was made by it to Zachary Boyd 'to translate the other Scripturall Songs in meeter' with a view to their adoption. Boyd's *Songs of the Old and New Testament in Meeter* were published in Glasgow in 1646, but there is no evidence of their having been in any way brought before the Assembly. It was not until 1741 that an effort was made to supply the lack. An overture to the Assembly in that year led to the appointment in 1742 of a committee of nineteen ministers and three elders 'to make a Collection of Translations into English Verse or Metre of Passages of the Holy Scripture, or receive in performances of that kind from any who shall transmit them'. In 1745 the Committee, enlarged, were ready with forty-five versions of several portions of Scripture. These were printed and transmitted by the Assembly to Presbyteries for their opinions and observations. Apparently a majority were unfavourable, for delaying tactics proved so successful that the whole matter lay in abeyance for twenty years. The Synod of Glasgow and Ayr revived it in 1775. In that year a Committee was again appointed, and in 1781 their work was completed. A proof of the collection they had made was handed to every member of Assembly in that year. The Assembly, after appointing certain of its members to revise it, authorized the sending of copies to Presbyteries for their opinions, and allowed the use of it meantime in congregations where the minister might find it for edification. Thus, the *Translations and Paraphrases, in Verse, of Several Passages of Sacred Scripture,* with the five hymns appended to them, passed into Scottish use. There is no evidence that the opinions of Presbyteries were ever received or considered, or that a more formal authorization was ever given by the Assembly. With tacit consent the custom arose of printing the *Paraphrases* along with the metrical version of the Psalms, and for nearly two centuries they have had an established place in Scottish Presbyterian worship. Many of them have also found their way into hymn-books all over the world.

> 483. *Behold! the amazing gift of love.*
> 365. *Behold! the mountain of the Lord.*
> 137. *Blest be the everlasting God.*
> 400. *Come, let us to the Lord our God.*
> 481. *Father of peace, and God of love.*
>   40. *Hark the glad sound! the Saviour comes.*
> 223. *How bright these glorious spirits shine!*
> 507. *I'm not ashamed to own my Lord.*
> 562. *O God of Bethel! by whose hand.*
>   57. *The race that long in darkness pined.*
> 312. *'Twas on that night when doomed to know.*
> 140. *Where high the heavenly temple stands.*
>   42. *While humble shepherds watched their flocks.*

SCRIVEN, JOSEPH (Dublin, 1820–86, Port Hope, Ontario, Canada), was a graduate of Trinity College, Dublin, who at the age of twenty-five went to Canada and settled there, at Rice Lake, and afterwards at Port Hope, Ontario. He became somewhat eccentric, lived with several families in succession and was tutor in one of them. He lived to help people who needed such assistance as he could give them, and was pointed out as 'the man who saws wood for poor widows and sick people who are unable to pay'. He would even give his coat to one who was shivering with cold. At times he became despondent. In October, 1886, he was found drowned in a water-run near Rice Lake. Whether his death was accidental or otherwise cannot be positively determined. A monument to his memory was erected in the vicinity of Rice Lake by people who had been helped by him, and by the people of the district.

> 701. *What a Friend we have in Jesus!*

SEARS, EDMUND HAMILTON, D.D. (Sandisfield, Berkshire, W., Massachusetts, 1810–76, Weston, Mass.), claimed descent from one of the Pilgrim Fathers who emigrated to America in 1630. He used to say that the first emotion of the sublime ever awakened in him was by hearing his father read 'with great gusto' Watts's version of the nineteenth Psalm. 'At the age of ten, while working in the fields, he composed two verses of poetry, writing them with chalk in his hat. When he showed them to his friends at home they refused to believe that they were his unless he wrote another stanza on the spot, which he promptly did.' He was educated at Union College, Schenectady, New York, and the Theological School, Cambridge. He ministered to Unitarian congregations at the First Church, Wayland, Mass.; Lancaster, Mass.; then returned to Wayland owing to failure of health, and devoted himself to literature. His later years were spent at Weston. His theology, though nominally Unitarian, was far removed from the orthodox type of that doctrine. It was more like Swedenborgianism. His teaching was deeply spiritual, and he always held and preached the absolute divinity of Christ. He edited *The Monthly Religious Magazine*, and published among other books, *Regeneration* (1854); *Pictures of the Olden Time* (1857); *Athanasia, or Foregleams of Immortality* (1872); *The Fourth Gospel the Heart of Christ; Sermons and Songs of the Christian Life* (1875).

47. *It came upon the midnight clear.*

SELNECKER, NICOLAUS (Hersbrück, 1532–92, Leipzig), became organist in the chapel at Nürnberg when only twelve years old. He held successively the positions of lecturer at the University of Wittenberg, Court preacher at Dresden, Professor of Theology at Jena, and pastor of St. Thomas's Church at Leipzig. His frequent movements from one part to another were largely due to the atmosphere of acute theological controversy in which he lived. Feeling between High Lutherans and those suspected of Calvinism was strong, and Selnecker, as one of the framers of the 'Formula of Concord' designed to unite Lutherans and exclude Romanists and Calvinists, did not escape the abuse that commonly assails a man of moderate views. From these troubles he sought relief in poetry and music. He helped to build up the famous Motett Choir of St. Thomas's Church at Leipzig, afterwards conducted by Johann Sebastian Bach. He loved the Psalter, wrote Latin verse, and was the author also of many German hymns.

278. *Now cheer our hearts this eventide.*

SEVEN SOBS OF A SORROWFUL SOUL FOR SINNE, comprehending those seven Psalmes of the Princelie Prophet David commonlie called Pænitentiall, framed into a form of familiar praiers and reduced into meeter by William Hunnis one of the Gentlemen of hir Majesties honourable Chapell, and maister to the children of the same. Whereunto are also annexed his Handful of Honisuckles; the Poor Widow's Mite; a Dialogue between Christ and a sinner; divers godlie and pithie ditties with a Christian Confession of and to the Trinitie, newly printed and augmented, 1583. This curious book gives the first instance of the modern use of 'Amen' at the end of hymns, and also of the use of the chorus or refrain. Hunnis's poem, 'The Widow's

Mite', e.g., consists of seven meditations, and the direction is given to sing the following four lines at the close of each of the seven:

> So shall my soul rejoice, rejoice,
>   And still for mercy cry,
> *Peccavi, peccavi,*
>   *Miserere mei.*

555. MISERERE MEI.

SHAIRP, JOHN CAMPBELL, LL.D. (Houstoun, Linlithgowshire, 1819–85, Ormsary, Argyllshire), a son of an old Scots family, was educated at Edinburgh Academy, the University of Glasgow, where he won the Snell Exhibition, and Balliol College, Oxford, where he was a member of a distinguished circle. His deeply religious mind was profoundly affected by the preaching of Newman at St. Mary's, but the Oxford Movement, while moving him on the moral and imaginative side, never won his intellect to any distinctive tenet of the High Church creed. He meditated taking orders in the Church of England, but took a mastership at Rugby on the invitation of A.C. Tait, then head-master, afterwards Archbishop of Canterbury. One of his colleagues said of him, 'Inspiration was his gift. He was like a wave of the sea; wherever he came, he brought freshness with him. Every man should be a missionary to his pupils; Shairp was a missionary to the masters.' Tait said, 'He was a most delightful presence; everybody loved him.' He spent eleven years at Rugby; acted as deputy Professor of Greek at Glasgow University, 1856; as assistant Professor of Humanity at St. Andrews, 1857–61; was appointed to the Chair of Humanity at St. Andrews in 1861, and to the Principalship of the United College of St. Salvator and St. Leonard there in 1868; concurrently he held the Professorship of Poetry at Oxford from 1877 till 1885. He was a man of remarkable force and elevation of character, 'a loyal nature and a noble mind,' humble, kindly, and of an extraordinary personal charm. A Scotsman to the core of his being, he was steeped in the romance and poetry of his native land, and he so loved its Highlands and storied Borderland that 'he seemed to regret a summer not passed in Scotland as a summer wasted'. His poems in *Kilmahoe, a Highland Pastoral, with Other Poems*, and *Glen Desseray and Other Poems*, are full of the spirit of the scenes he loved; the pastoral melancholy of the southern highlands has found no better expression than in his *The Bush aboon Traquair*. In prose he published *Studies in Poetry and Philosophy; The Poetic Interpretation of Nature; Culture and Religion; Aspects of Poetry;* and the volume on *Burns* in the *English Men of Letters* Series. 'In his looks and in his character there was a Christian chivalry, as well as a genius, which made him one of the purifying and elevating powers of his day.' Lord Chief Justice Coleridge said of him that he was 'as simple as a child, open to every tender and generous impulse, high-minded and pure-thoughted, yet full of harmless fun and playful humour, a steadfast friend, whose life was a charm to us, and whose death was "like a disenchantment".'

559. *'Twixt gleams of joy and clouds of doubt.*

SHAPCOTE, EMILY MARY, *née* STEWARD (Liverpool, 1828– ?), married in 1856 the Rev. E. G. Shapcote, who took orders in the Church of England, and after serving for a time as curate of Odiham, Hants, became a missionary under the S.P.G. in South Africa. In 1866 Mrs. Shapcote entered the Church of Rome, and her husband followed her two years later. With an aunt and a sister, she published in 1852 *Hymns for Infant Children*. Her later hymns appeared in her *Eucharistic Hours* (1886).

665. *Jesus, holy, undefiled.*

SHAW, GEOFFREY TURTON (Clapham, 1879–), was educated at St. Paul's Cathedral Choir School, Derby School, and Caius College, Cambridge, where he was Organ Scholar. From 1902 till 1910 he was music-master of Gresham's School, Holt. Since then he has been one of His Majesty's Inspectors of Music in Schools. He is also master of music at St. Mary's, Primrose Hill. At musical festivals throughout the country he is well known as an adjudicator. He has done much to raise the standard of Church music and to foster popular interest in good music. Numerous part-songs, school-songs, hymn-tunes, &c., have been published by him.

221. GRESHAM.   106. ROCKINGHAM (Faux-bourdon).
131. ST. MAGNUS (Faux-bourdon).

SHAW, MARTIN (FALLAS), (London, 1876–), son of an organist of Hampstead Parish Church and elder brother of Geoffrey Shaw, studied at the Royal College of Music. At the end of his time as a student he 'embarked upon a long period of starving along'. He conducted for Ellen Terry, and toured Europe as conductor to Isadora Duncan. In later years he has held posts as organist and director of music at St. Mary's, Primrose Hill, and St. Martin-in-the-Fields, London. He is at present master of music at the Guildhouse, London. He has composed from his childhood up, and has published many songs and much Church music, also, in collaboration with Clifford Bax, a ballad opera, *Mr. Pepys*. With Dr. R. Vaughan Williams he was musical editor of *Songs of Praise*. He edited also *The English Carol Book*. He has rendered great service in fostering community singing, and has done much to 'free English Church music from a load of sentimentality'. What Canon Scott Holland said of his *Te Deum* is characteristic of all his Church music: it possesses 'dignity, massiveness, and reserve. Everything about it is wholesome and manly, and there are no fanciful or artificial episodes.'

155. BATTLE HYMN.
463. CHERRY TREE CAROL (arr.).
662. GENTLE JESUS.
372. LITTLE CORNARD.
520. LONDON NEW (Faux Bourdon).

214. MARCHING.
32, 209. RICHMOND (Faux Bourdon).
601. ST. ANNE (Faux Bourdon).

SHELLY, MARTHA EVANS, *née* JACKSON (Stockport, Cheshire, 1812– ?), married, in 1846, J. W. Shelly of Great Yarmouth.

661. *Lord, a little band and lowly.*

SHEPHERD, ANNE, *née* HOULDITCH (Cowes, Isle of Wight, 1809–57, Blackheath, Kent), was a daughter of the Rev. Edward H. Houlditch, sometime rector of Speen, Berkshire. In 1843 she married Mr. S. Saville Shepherd. She wrote sixty-four hymns, published under the title, *Hymns adapted to the Comprehension of Young Minds*; and two religious tales, *Ellen Seymour* and *Reality*.

600. *Around the throne of God in heaven.*

SHRUBSOLE, WILLIAM (Canterbury, 1760–1806, London), was the son of a farrier at Canterbury, and was for seven years a chorister in the Cathedral there. In 1782 he was appointed organist of Bangor Cathedral, but within a year got into trouble with the Dean and Chapter because of his unconcealed sympathy with dissenters and his frequenting of 'conventicles'. This led to his being virtually dismissed from his office. Returning to London he became a teacher of music, and from 1784 till his death was organist of Spa Fields Chapel, of Lady Huntingdon's Connexion. While in Canterbury he made acquaintance with Edward Perronet (q.v.), then in charge of a Congregational chapel there, and became so true a friend to him that Perronet appointed him one of the executors of his will and bequeathed to him some property at Wandsworth, in consideration, as the will said, of 'that fine disinterested affection he has ever shown me from our first acquaintance, even when a proverb of reproach, cast off by all my relatives, disinherited unjustly, and left to sink or swim as afflictions and God's providence should appoint'. The wedding of the hymn of the one with the tune of the other perpetuates the memory of this friendship.

139. MILES LANE.

SHRUBSOLE, WILLIAM (Sheerness, Kent, 1759–1829, Highbury, London), was the son of a mast-maker in Sheerness Dockyard who was also a lay preacher. He was himself in his earlier years a shipwright in the Dockyard, and then a clerk. In 1785 he went to London and entered the Bank of England as a clerk. He rose there till he became Secretary to the Committee of the Treasury. For some years he was a member of the Church of England, but for the last twenty years of his life he was a Congregationalist, worshipping in Hoxton Academy Chapel. He was deeply and actively interested in many religious societies, notably in the London Missionary Society, of which he was a director and one of the secretaries, the Bible Society, and the Religious Tract Society. He was a lay preacher also. His hymns, about twenty in number, were contributed to various periodicals.

369. *Arm of the Lord, awake, awake.*

SHUTTLEWORTH, HENRY CARY, M.A. (Egloshayle, Cornwall, 1850–1900, London), was educated at Forest School, Walthamstow, and St. Mary Hall and Christ Church, Oxford. Ordained in 1873, he was curate of St. Barnabas, Oxford; minor canon of St. Paul's Cathedral, 1876–84; rector of St. Nicholas Cole-Abbey, London, from 1883. He was also Professor of Pastoral and Liturgical Theology, and lecturer in other subjects, in King's College, London. He was 'a red-hot ritualist', and was prominently identified with the Christian Socialist movement. G. W. E. Russell says that he was enthusiastic, buoyant, light-hearted, sanguine, and that his devotion surrounded his church and parish with a halo of romance. His published works include *The Place of Music in Public Worship*; *Hymns for Private use*. In an appendix to *Church Hymns*, compiled for use in St. Nicholas Church, several hymns of his own appeared.

493. *Father of men, in whom are one.*

SIBELIUS, JEAN (Tavastehus, Finland, 1865–   ), was a pupil of Helsingfors Music Institute, and afterwards studied also at Berlin and Vienna. From 1893 he taught in the Philharmonic Orchestra School, Helsingfors. From 1897 till 1907 he received an annual grant of 3,000 marks from the Finnish Government, to set him free to devote himself to composition. He has produced dramatic works, symphonies, symphonic poems like the famous *Finlandia*, suites, songs, &c. His genius is essentially Scandinavian; it draws its inspiration from the mournful folk-songs of the North, and from the dark and sombre landscape of the country of his birth. 'The orchestral compositions of Sibelius seem to have passed over black torrents and desolate moorlands, through pallid sunlight and grim primeval forests, and become drenched with them. The instrumentation is all wet greys and blacks, relieved only by bits of brightness, wan and elusive as the northern summer, frostily green as the polar light.' He is the poet of his people; his music has given their spirit noble utterance in the hearing of the world.

556. FINLANDIA.

SIDEBOTHAM, MARY ANN (London, 1833–1913, Isle of Wight), was an accomplished musician, and a first-rate amateur pianist and organist. She was a lifelong friend of Henry Smart. A great part of her life was spent at her brother's vicarage, St. Thomas-on-the-Bourne, Surrey, where she acted as organist. She was the musical editor of *The Children's Hymn-Book* (S.P.C.K.), edited by Mrs. Carey Brock, but never allowed her name to appear on the title-page. Several of the tunes in it are of her composition, but are mostly above the initials M.A.S. only. She composed various songs, chiefly under *noms de plume*, and arranged collections of words and music for children, e.g. *The Bird's Nest*, a collection of fifty songs, edited by Mrs. Carey Brock, with herself as musical editor and to a great extent composer.

404. *Lord, Thy mercy now entreating.*

SILAS, ÉDOUARD (Amsterdam, 1827–1909, London), studied in Paris under Bénoit and Halévy, resided thereafter for some years at Mannheim, then, in 1850, came and settled in England. He taught music, was organist of the Roman Catholic Chapel, Kingston-on-Thames, and for a time was a teacher of harmony in the Guildhall School of Music and the London Academy of Music. In 1866 he composed a mass which won the gold medal and a prize of 1,000 francs at the Assemblée générale des Catholiques en Belgique. He wrote besides, an oratorio, *Joash*, orchestral music, anthems, hymn-tunes, &c. Among frequenters of the British Museum he was well known as one of its 'characters'—a little man with remarkable features and wearing a red fez. He had a pretty wit and an endless fund of stories; his company was much enjoyed.

84. SILAS.

SILCHER, (PHILIPP) FRIEDRICH, Ph. D. (Schnaith, near Schorndorf, Würtemberg, 1789–1860, Tübingen), a pupil of his father, an organist, and of Auberlen, was trained for the teaching profession, but began early to compose, and in 1815 took a conductorship at Stuttgart. A cantata written there led to his appointment, in 1817, as organist of the University of Tübingen. This post he held till his retiral in 1860. He edited text-books on harmony and composition; *Sechs vierstimmige Hymnen; Dreistimmiges Würtemb. Choralbuch; Gesch. d. evangelisch. Kirchengesänge*; but his fame rests on his *Sammlung deutscher Volkslieder* in 12 vols., a standard collection of German songs. Many of the melodies are his own, and some of them, such as *Aennchen von Tharau, Morgen muss ich fort von hier*, and *Die Lorelei*, have an international celebrity as characteristic songs of the German people.

666. GOTT EIN VATER.

SIMPSON, JANE CROSS, *née* BELL (Glasgow, 1811–86, Glasgow), was a daughter of James Bell, advocate, and sister of Henry Glassford Bell, advocate, sheriff, and author of a noteworthy *Life of Mary*

Queen of Scots. In 1837 she married her cousin, J. B. Simpson, of Glasgow. While her brother was editor of *The Edinburgh Literary Journal*, she contributed to it over the pen-name 'Gertrude', and, later, she wrote for *The Scottish Christian Herald*. Her published works were—*The Piety of Daily Life* (1836); *April Hours* (1838); *Woman's History* (1848); *Linda, or, Beauty and Genius* (1859); *Picture Poems* (1879); *Linda, and Other Poems* (1879).

627. *Star of peace to wanderers weary.*

SIMPSON, ROBERT (Glasgow, 1790–1832, Greenock), was a weaver by trade, but of good education and keen musical taste. For a time he was choir-leader in Dr. Ralph Wardlaw's church, Albion Street Chapel (Congregational), Glasgow; but in 1823 he became precentor and session-clerk of the East Parish Church, Greenock, at a salary of £40 a year, and from that time onward he made music his profession. Never of a robust constitution, he fell a victim to one of the cholera epidemics.

313. BALLERMA (arr.).

SMALL, JAMES GRINDLAY (Edinburgh, 1817–88, Renfrew), was educated at the Royal High School and the University, Edinburgh, Dr. Chalmers being one of his professors. At the Disruption in 1843 he threw in his lot with the Free Church of Scotland, and in 1847 became minister of that Church at Bervie, near Montrose. Owing to peculiarities of voice and manner he never made a mark as a preacher, but he had the confidence of his brethren, who made him clerk of presbytery, and was generally beloved as one of the gentlest and kindest of men. He was enthusiastically interested in psalmody. In Christopher North's class at the University he had won a prize for a poem which gave the title to his first volume, *The Highlands and Other Poems* (1843). *Songs of the Vineyard in Days of Gloom and Sadness* (1846); *Hymns for Youthful Voices* (1859); and *Psalms and Sacred Songs* (1866) were his other works.

705. *I've found a Friend, O such a Friend.*

SMART, HENRY (THOMAS) (London, 1813–79, London), a nephew of Sir George Smart—organist of St. George's, Windsor, and composer of the tune WILTSHIRE—was the son of a well-known violinist. He declined the offer of a commission in the Indian Army, and, after four years' trial of law, turned aside from that profession to devote his life to music. In the main, he was self-taught. Organ-playing became his passion; as an executant and composer for this instrument he had few equals. He developed great skill also in the planning and erection of organs, and was responsible for the instruments built in some of the chief halls of the country; he superintended the construction of the one in St. Andrew's Hall, Glasgow, in every detail, though he was then quite blind. His appointments as organist were at the Parish Church, Blackburn; St. Giles', Cripplegate; St. Philip's, Regent Street; St. Luke's, Old Street; and St. Pancras, London. From 1865, his sight, always defective, failed him altogether; but an extraordinarily retentive memory stood him in good stead, and his rare skill in extempore playing had full scope. Even after becoming blind, he wrote a great deal of music. A strong advocate of congregational praise, he favoured unison singing, and the 'stately, dignified "measured beat and slow" movement of the old psalm-tunes was more to his taste' than the quicker style that was becoming popular in his time. His church music is of a high order. His complete *Service in F* is very fine: 'certain portions of the *Credo* might have been written by Beethoven'; and his anthems and hymn tunes are of great purity and excellence. He wrote also cantatas—*The Bride of Dunkerron, King René's Daughter; The Fishermaidens*; an oratorio, *Jacob*; &c. He edited the music of *The Presbyterian Hymnal* (1876) for the United Presbyterian Church.

603, 502. BETHANY (CRUCIFER).	232. MOREDUN.
718. CHANT IN G.	531. NORTHUMBERLAND.
198. CHEBAR.	580. PILGRIMS.
609. EVERTON.	7. REGENT SQUARE.
611. GORDON.	474. ST. LEONARD.
509. HEATHLANDS.	579. SMART.
123. LANCASHIRE.	169. TRISAGION.
411. MISERICORDIA.	538. VEXILLUM.

SMITH, HENRY PERCY, M.A. (1825–98), was educated at Balliol College, Oxford, graduated B.A., 1848; M.A., 1850. He became curate of Eversley, Hants, 1849, under Charles Kingsley; perpetual curate of St. Michael's, York Town, Farnborough, Surrey, 1851; vicar of Great Barnton, Suffolk, 1868; chaplain of Christ Church, Cannes, 1882 till 1895; canon of Gibraltar, 1892.

420. MARYTON.

SMITH, ISAAC (London, *c.* 1725–*c.* 1800, London), was for a time clerk (precentor) to the Alie Street Meeting-House in Goodman's Fields, London. He is said to have been the first dissenting clerk to receive for his services the munificent salary of £20 a year. 'Latterly, being in a respectable line of business, he declined that profession; but having a taste for music, he composed and published a number of Psalm-tunes which are in very general use among Dissenters, and some of them in many churches.' The 'respectable' business in which he engaged is believed to have been that of a linen-draper in Cheapside. About 1770, he published *A Collection of Psalm Tunes in Three Parts: to which are added 2 Anthems and 2 Canons*. In this ST. STEPHEN, then and still known as ABRIDGE also, first appeared, with other tunes of his which long remained popular.

483. ST. STEPHEN (ABRIDGE).

SMITH, ISAAC GREGORY, D.D. (Manchester, 1826–1920, Horsell, near Woking), a son of the Rev. Jeremiah Smith, D.D., High Master of the Manchester School, was educated at Rugby under Arnold (he was head of the school), and at Trinity College, Oxford. He gained the Hertford and Ireland Scholarships, and a Fellowship of Brasenose. He became rector of Tedston-Delamere, Herefordshire, 1854; vicar of Great Malvern, 1872; Bampton Lecturer, 1873; Prebendary of Pratum Minus in Hereford Cathedral, 1870; Rural Dean of Powick; hon. canon of Worcester, 1887; rector of Great Shefford, Lambourne, Berks., 1896. He retired to Horsell in 1904. He published books on *Monasticism*, *Psychology*, and *The Characteristics of Christian Morality* (Bampton Lectures). With his brother John George Smith, barrister, and the Rev. W. S. Raymond, he edited *A Hymn Book for the Services of the Church and for Private Reading* (1855). He published also *Fra Angelico and Other Poems*. His memorial in Malvern Priory Church describes him as 'a fine scholar, a far-seeing thinker, a heavenly-minded poet, withal the wise and loving pastor of this parish'.

114. *By Jesus' grave on either hand.*

SMITH, JOSEPH (Halesowen, 1800–73, Halesowen), spent most of his life in his native town. He was not a professional musician, but was interested in music and had an excellent alto voice. He composed a number of hymn-tunes and similar pieces, chiefly for Sunday School festivals.

574. INNOCENTS.

SMITH, ROBERT ARCHIBALD (Reading, 1780–1829, Edinburgh), was son of a Paisley weaver who had gone to Reading for employment during a time of depression of trade. He showed musical talent early, and could play the violin at ten. His father tried to make him a weaver, but as the result was indifferent workmanship and despondency that injured his health, he was allowed to give that trade up, and in 1803 he began teaching music. In 1807 he was appointed precentor (he had a fine tenor voice) and session-clerk of the Abbey Church, Paisley. A friendship with Tannahill led to his setting to music some of that poet's songs, such as *Jessie the Flower o' Dunblane*, showing that he possessed a fine vein of melody and a talent for vocal composition then without equal in Scotland. In 1820 he began to publish his great work *The Scottish Minstrel* (6 vols., 1820–4). In 1823 he went to Edinburgh to be leader of psalmody under Dr. Andrew Thomson, of 'St. George's, Edinburgh'. The next six years were very full for him, with teaching, editing collections of psalm-tunes and of songs, &c.—*The Irish Minstrel* (1825); *Flowers of Scottish Song; Sacred Harmony, for the Use of St. George's Church, Edinburgh; Sacred Music* (1825); *Edinburgh Sacred Harmony for the Use of Churches and Families* (1829);

The Sacred Harmony of the Church of Scotland (1828). He was a skilled performer on the viola and the violoncello. He 'enriched the music of Scotland with many melodies which have deservedly become national, and will probably descend in that character from generation to generation. . . . His sacred music is uniformly excellent, possessing in a high degree the simplicity of design and solemnity of effect which this species of music requires.'

   633. ST. LAWRENCE.   249. SELMA.

SMITH, SAMUEL (Eton, 1821–1917, Windsor), was the son of a lay clerk of St. George's Chapel, Windsor. At fourteen, he became a child of the Chapel Royal, St. James's, and sang at the coronation and the funeral of William IV. He became organist of Hayes Church, Middlesex; then at Eton and Egham; afterwards at Trinity Church, Windsor, and finally at the Parish Church, Windsor, where he continued for thirty-four years. He was musical instructor of Beaumont College, Old Windsor, and succeeded Sir George Elvey, whose pupil he had been, as conductor of Windsor and Eton Choral Society.

   59. NEWTON FERNS.   613. RUTH.

SMITH, SAMUEL FRANCIS, D.D. (Boston, Massachusetts, 1808–95, near Boston), graduated at Harvard in Arts, and at Andover in Theology. He entered the Baptist ministry in 1832, and in the same year became editor of the American *Baptist Missionary Magazine*. From 1834 to 1842 he was pastor of a congregation at Waterville, Maine, and Professor of Modern Languages at Waterville College. Thereafter he ministered at Newton Centre, Mass., until 1854, when he became editor to the Baptist Missionary Union. For some years he edited *The Christian Review*. With the Rev. Baron Stow, D.D., he edited *The Psalmist, a New Collection of Hymns for the Baptist Churches* (1843), the best and most widely used of American Baptist collections. He published also *Lyric Gems* (1854), and *The Rock of Ages* (1870). His fame in America rests on his hymn, *My country, 'tis of thee*, which was written for a Fourth of July celebration in 1832, to the tune of *God save the King*, and has become virtually the American National Anthem. He died while travelling near Boston.

   686. *To-day the Saviour calls.*

SMITH, WALTER CHALMERS, D.D., LL.D. (Aberdeen, 1824–1908, Kinbuck, Perthshire), was educated at the Grammar School and University, Aberdeen, and at New College, Edinburgh. Ordained in 1850 to the charge of a congregation in Chadwell Street, Islington, London, he afterwards became minister of Orwell Free Church, Milnathort; the Free Tron Church, Glasgow; and the Free High Church, Edinburgh (1876–94). He was Moderator of the Assembly of the Free Church of Scotland in its Jubilee year (1893), and in the following year he withdrew into retirement. He was a cultured, catholic-minded man. His poetry was 'the retreat of his nature from the burden of his labours'; he found relief in it, and a means of giving expression to many phases of his message which could not so fitly find utterance in his pulpit. His published works were— *The Bishop's Walk* (1860); *Olrig Grange* (1872); *Borland Hall* (1874); *Hilda among the Broken Gods* (1878); *Raban, or Life Splinters* (1881); *North Country Folk* (1883); *Kildrostan* (1884); *Hymns of Christ and the Christian Life* (1876); *Thoughts and Fancies for Sunday Evenings* (1887); *A Heretic, and Other Poems* (1891); *Poetical Works* (1902).

12. *Immortal, invisible, God only wise.*
461. *One thing I of the Lord desire.*

SMYTTAN, GEORGE HUNT, B.A. (*c.* 1822–70, Frankfort-am-Main), was son of Dr. Smyttan of the Bombay Medical Board. Educated at Corpus Christi College, Cambridge, he graduated in 1845, and was ordained in 1848. In 1850 he became rector of Hawksworth, Nottingham, but resigned in 1859. He died suddenly abroad and friendless. Being unknown, he was entered in the register of burials at Frankfort simply as 'Smyttan, England', and interred among the poor in an unpurchased grave, long since forgotten. He published *Thoughts in Verse for the Afflicted* (1849); *Mission Songs and Ballads* (1860); *Florum Sacra* (n.d.).

79. *Forty days and forty nights.*

SOLESMES is a village near Le Mans which acquired fame through the foundation there, in 1833, of a Benedictine monastery which became a centre for the study and execution of the old liturgical music. For the propagation of this the monks established a printing-press with special type, and their work came to be recognized as authoritative. Their official title was the Order of the Congregation of France. The passing of the French Law of Associations, however, drove them from that country. In 1901 they settled at Quarr House, near Ryde, in the Isle of Wight, where they continue to study and foster the development of plain-song.

319. ADORO TE.

SOUTHGATE, FREDERIC, B.A. (Gravesend, 1824–85, Northfleet), was educated at Ramsgate, began training for the profession of law, but turned to the Church, studied at Emmanuel College, Cambridge (B.A.), and was ordained in 1849. After a curacy at Castle Headingham, Suffolk, he became incumbent of St. Mark's, Rosherville, Kent, and subsequently of Northfleet. He published a collection of *Favourite Hymn-Tunes . . . used at St. Botolph's Church, Northfleet* (1873), and composed other church music.

690. ST. AGATHA.

SPIESS, JOHANN MARTIN (Bavaria, 1715–after 1766, Berne?), was professor of music in the Gymnasium at Heidelberg, and organist of St. Peter's Church there; and latterly was settled in Berne. He published *Davids Harpffen Spiel, In hundert und funfzig Psalmen, Auch dreyhundert zwey und vierzig Lieder Melodien*, Heydelberg, 1745; *Geistliche Liebesposaune, in 342 Liedermelodien; Geistliche Arien* (1761). 478. (SWABIA.)

SPITTA, KARL JOHANN PHILIPP, D.D. (Hanover, 1801–59, Burgdorf), began to write verse at eight years of age. He was apprenticed to a watchmaker, and his desire to enter the ministry seemed frustrated, but the death of a younger brother who was preparing for ordination led to his longing being discovered, and the way was prepared for him. He studied at the University of Göttingen, and after four years of a tutorship, was ordained in 1828 as assistant pastor at Sudwalde, near Hoya. At the University he wrote songs and secular poems, and published a number of them anonymously as a *Sangbüchlein der Liebe für Handwerksleute*. But after a spiritual change he began writing hymns in 1824, and two years later wrote to a friend, 'In the manner in which I formerly sang I sing no more. To the Lord I consecrate my life and my love, and likewise my song. His love is the one great theme of all my songs; to praise and exalt it worthily is the desire of the Christian singer. He gave to me song and melody; I give it back to Him.' In 1830 he was appointed assistant chaplain to the garrison and the prison at Hamelin on the Weser; the report that he was a Pietist and a mystic raised against him a prejudice that lost him the full chaplaincy. After a ten years' pastorate at Wechold, near Hoya, he was Lutheran superintendent at Wittingen, at Peine, and at Burgdorf, where, soon after his appointment, he died suddenly at his writing-table. His *Psalter und Harfe, Eine Sammlung christlicher Lieder zur häuslicher Erbauung* (2 series, 1833 and 1843) won in Germany a popular favour similar to that of Keble's *Christian Year* in this country. Richard Massie (q.v.) published an excellent version of both series in English. Spitta's son, Johann August Philipp, was the author of the great biography of Bach.

> 648. *O happy home, where Thou art loved the dearest.*

SPOHR, LUDWIG (Brunswick, 1784–1859, Cassel), was the son of a physician who afterwards became judge of appeals at Seesen. He early showed his talent; his aptitude for the violin became evident at five years of age, when he obtained his first instrument. The Duke of Brunswick took an interest in him, appointed him to a post in the court orchestra in 1799, and in 1802 placed him under the tuition of Franz Eck, with whom he toured Europe and visited St. Petersburg, where for a time he held an appointment as solo violinist in the Imperial Orchestra. In 1805 he was appointed concert director to the court of Saxe-Gotha, and with his wife (a brilliant musician also, who relinquished the violin in deference to his opinion that it was an instrument unbecoming for a woman, and adopted first the harp, and then the pianoforte instead), he went annually on concert tours, with brilliant success. He was then the first virtuoso in Europe. In 1816 in a public competition with the renowned Paganini he carried off the honours even from that 'first of singers on the violin'. In 1822 he was appointed director of the orchestra at the court theatre at Cassel, where he remained until pensioned off in 1857. The revenues of this state were largely derived at that time from the sale of Hessian soldiers to Great Britain. Spohr tried almost every form of musical composition, and achieved a contemporary success in them all. Few musicians have enjoyed so high a reputation in their own time. He wrote operas— *Faust, Jessonda,* &c.; oratorios, *The Last Judgment; Calvary; The Fall of Babylon;* thirty-four string quartets, violin concertos, &c. His reputation has not stood the test of time, although the grace of many of his melodies still retains its charm.

451. SPOHR.

STAINER, Sir JOHN, M.A., Mus. Doc. (London, 1840–1901, Verona), was a chorister of St. Paul's, 1847–56. During this time an anthem and several chants of his composition were sung in the services, and latterly he often acted as organist. He became organist of St. Benet and St. Peter's, Paul's Wharf, at fourteen, and two years later was appointed by Sir F. Gore Ouseley first organist of St. Michael's, Tenbury. In 1859 he matriculated at Christ Church, Oxford, and was appointed organist of Magdalen College, and then of the University. In 1872 he succeeded Sir John Goss at St. Paul's Cathedral, and carried through a great work of revival in the music of the services there. Other appointments held by him were those of Professor of the Organ, and then Principal, of the National Training School for Music; organist to the Royal Choral Society; Government Inspector of Music in Training Schools; Professor of Music in the University of Oxford. He was knighted in 1888. He wrote a book on *The Music of the Bible, A Treatise on Harmony,* and other theoretical works; an oratorio, *Gideon*; several cantatas, of which *The Crucifixion* is widely known; many service anthems, hymn-tunes, and other church music. His editorial work was extensive, among the books the music of which he supervised being the first *Church Hymnary.*

484. CHARITY.	593. IN MEMORIAM.
72. CREDO.	578. PILGRIM BAND.
728. DRESDEN AMEN (arr.).	219. REST.
654. EVENING PRAYER.	437. ST. BENEDICT.
273. GLOAMING.	281. SEBASTE.
18. GOD IN NATURE.	728. SEVENFOLD AMEN.
488. GRANDPONT.	662. SIMPLICITY.

194. VENI SPIRITUS.

Biographical and Historical Notes

STANFORD, Sir CHARLES VILLIERS, Mus. Doc. (Dublin, 1852–1924, London), early revealed musical gifts of a remarkable order, and at ten years of age heard one of his own compositions played in Dublin Theatre Royal. At Cambridge—Queen's and Trinity Colleges—he had a classical education and graduated with honours. He succeeded Dr. J. L. Hopkins as organist of Trinity College; became leader of the University Musical Society, into which he infused new life; conductor of the London Bach Choir, 1885; of the R.C.M. orchestra, 1887; of Leeds Festival, 1901; Professor of Music, Cambridge, 1887, and of composition, R.C.M., in the same year. He was a Mus. Doc. of Cambridge and Oxford, and was knighted in 1901. One of the most distinguished figures in the world of music in his time, he appeared as conductor in Berlin, Paris, Amsterdam, Brussels, and America. He did much to help in the revival of interest in folk-music; his settings of Irish airs are singularly fine. He was a prolific composer, producing seven operas, seven symphonies, two cantatas (*Phaudrig Crohoore* and *Revenge*); four *Irish Rhapsodies;* a *Stabat Mater; Songs of the Sea; Songs of the Fleet.*

506. ST. PATRICK (arr.).

STANLEY, ARTHUR PENRHYN, D.D. (Alderley, Cheshire, 1815–81, Westminster), was a nephew of the first Lord Stanley of Alderley. His father was rector of Alderley till, in 1837, he was appointed Bishop of Norwich. Arthur was educated first by his father, because of his delicate health; then at Rugby under the direct care of Dr. Arnold, whose influence permeated the whole of his life; and at Balliol, where he had an exceptionally brilliant career, gaining the Newdigate Prize for English verse, the Ireland Scholarship in Greek, first class classical honours, and the prizes for the Latin, English, and theological essays. He was elected a Fellow of University College, and was a tutor for twelve years. In 1845–6 he was Select Preacher; in 1850–2, secretary to the Oxford University Commission; in 1851 was given a canonry at Canterbury; in 1855, was appointed Regius Professor of Ecclesiastical History at Oxford, and Canon of Christ Church; and in 1863 became Dean of Westminster. His marriage in 1863 to Lady Augusta Bruce, sister of the Earl of Elgin and an intimate friend of Queen Victoria, brought him into close relation to the Court. In 1872 he took part in the Old Catholic Congress at Cologne, and in the same year was again Select Preacher at Oxford, in spite of fierce opposition because of his broad theological views. In 1875 he was elected Lord Rector of St. Andrews University. He published *Historical Memorials of Canterbury*, and *of Westminster; Sinai and Palestine; The Life of Arnold of Rugby;* and a *History of the Jewish Church*. He is said to have been the original of Arthur in Tom Hughes's *Tom Brown's Schooldays*. A singularly gentle, attractive, and fascinating personality, he was

507

universally beloved, and by his character won the homage of sceptic and believer alike, and of those who, theologically, were most implacably opposed to him. Many of his hymns were composed during his walks round Canterbury. 'The tunes were generally selected, and some indeed composed, at the weekly meeting on Sunday evenings between himself and his coadjutor, Rev. R. Hake. His first object was to initiate and develop congregational singing in the Cathedral.'

> 129. *He is gone—beyond the skies.*
> 88. *O Master, it is good to be.*

STANLEY, SAMUEL (Birmingham, 1767–1822, Birmingham), at the age of twenty, became leader of the singing at Carr's Lane Meeting House, Birmingham. The congregation was then small, but Stanley soon made its music famous. He continued with the congregation when it moved in 1818 to a larger chapel in Steelhouse Lane, and served it altogether for thirty-three years. His position in it was not then regarded as inconsistent with his keeping for a time the Crown Tavern in the town. He was an accomplished violoncellist, and as such was long a member of the orchestra of the Birmingham Theatre and the Festival Choral Society. He was a Handel enthusiast, and his opinions as to the correct mode of rendering that master's music were quoted and followed in that Society for a generation after his death. He published *Twenty-four Tunes in Four Parts; Nineteen Psalms, Hymns and Charity Hymn-Tunes; Sacred Music, comprising two new Psalm and Hymn Tunes;* and *Psalm and Hymn Tunes,* in three books. Some of his tunes, such as SHIRLAND, SIMEON, WILTON, KENT, enjoyed long and wide popularity.

> 652. CALVARY.   639. DOVERSDALE.
> 385. WARWICK.

STEGGALL, CHARLES, Mus. Doc. (London, 1826–1905, London), was educated at the Royal Academy of Music. As organist, he served Christ Church, Maida Hill; Christ Church, Lancaster Gate; and Lincoln's Inn Chapel. For half a century he was chief professor of the organ at the R.A.M., and he was said to have trained more organists than any other teacher in the country. He was one of the founders of the Royal College of Organists, and at the opening of it gave the inaugural address. The 'Bach crusade' in this country found one of its most powerful supporters in him; he was honorary secretary of the Bach Society. He composed anthems and Church music, and had a lifelong interest in hymnology. He succeeded W. H. Monk as musical editor of *Hymns Ancient and Modern*; one of his last pieces of work was to pass the proofs of the 1904 edition for the press. 'His views on plain-song were those of the experts of to-day, and his intense love of the early school of English writers from Byrd onward, would have made him, had he been still living, a prominent figure in the present Elizabethan revival.'

537. CHRISTCHURCH.   548. MORWELLHAM.
290. DAY OF PRAISE.   276. ST. AMBROSE.

STEPHEN OF MAR SABA, ST. (*c.* 725–94), was nephew of St. John of Damascus (q.v.) and belonged, like him, to the monastery of Mar Saba. This monastery is still inhabited. It stands on a lofty cliff overhanging the ravine of the Kedron, between Jerusalem and the Dead Sea, many of the cells and chapels being cut out of the solid rock. The monks have been subjected at various times to much persecution at the hands of the Persians, Moslems, and Bedouin Arabs, and the place has all the appearance of a fortress.

391. *Art thou weary, art thou languid.*

STEVENSON, ISABEL STEPHANA (Cheltenham, 1843–90, Cheltenham), daughter of an Army officer, spent the whole of an uneventful life in Cheltenham. She was a devoted member of the Church of England. For many years she was an invalid. Her one hymn was composed when her faith and affection were under the stress of a special need to find some such mode of expression; that impulse past, she never wrote verse, or published either poetry or prose again.

629. *Holy Father, in Thy mercy.*

STEWART, CHARLES HYLTON, M.A., Mus. Bac. (Chester, 1884–), son of the Rev. C. Hylton Stewart, vicar of New Brighton and canon of Chester, was educated at Magdalen College School, Oxford, and Peterhouse, Cambridge (organ scholar). He has served as assistant organist, King's College, Cambridge; organist and choirmaster, Sedbergh School; organist and choirmaster, St. Martin's, Scarborough, and Blackburn Parish Church, and, since 1916, Rochester Cathedral. He has composed an evening service in A minor, and other Church music.

718. EIGHTH GREGORIAN TONE (arr.).
422. ROCHESTER.

STEWART, Sir ROBERT PRESCOTT, Mus. Doc. (Dublin, 1825–94, Dublin), son of the librarian of the King's Inns, Dublin, was educated as a chorister of Christ Church Cathedral, and became organist there in 1844, as well as at St. Patrick's Cathedral and at Trinity College. There were no funds at St. Patrick's from which to pay an organist: so he was appointed a vicar choral in 1852, on the understanding that he should continue to play the organ as before. In 1861 he was appointed Professor of Music in Dublin University. Later, he acted also as one of the professors in the

Irish Academy of Music. In 1872 he was knighted by Earl Spencer, the Lord Lieutenant. His fine personal qualities won him universal admiration and respect. He was a man of high accomplishment, wide culture, and literary skill, and had a great reputation as an organist and extemporizer. He travelled much, lectured widely, was an authority on bagpipes of all kinds, and was the first to require candidates for musical degrees to pass a literary test. He wrote cantatas, Church services, motets, anthems; many glees and songs. He was musical editor of *The Irish Church Hymnal* of 1876.

609. ADRIAN.	210. ST. AUDOËN.
335. COELI ENARRANT.	695. ST. HELEN'S.

STOCKS, George Gilbert, Mus. Doc. (Huddersfield, 1877–), was first, from 1893, organist at Almondbury, then taught music for ten years in St. Edward's School, Oxford. Since 1912 he has been chief music master of Repton School. In *Hymns for Use in Chapel* (1924)—a supplement to *Hymns Ancient and Modern*, for use at Repton—twenty-two tunes specially written by him for unison singing were published, along with five arrangements by him and twenty-two tunes by other composers.

271. SUNSET.	48. VILLAGE.

STONE, Samuel John, M.A. (Whitmore, Staffordshire, 1839–1900, Charterhouse), was educated at Charterhouse and Pembroke College, Oxford. He was curate, first of Windsor, then of St. Paul's, Haggerston, London, a parish which, when his father became vicar of it, had an endowment only of £13 per annum, and was without church, school, or vicarage. He succeeded his father as vicar in 1874. Under their devoted labours the parish became fully equipped and a well-cultivated and fruitful field. In 1890, he accepted the rectorship of All-Hallows-on-the-Wall, London. He published *Lyra Fidelium* (1866); *The Knight of Intercession, and Other Poems* (1872); *Sonnets of the Christian Year* (1875); *Hymns* (Original and Translated) (1886); *Order of the Consecutive Church Service for Children, with Original Hymns* (1883); and his *Collected Poems and Hymns* were edited, with a Memoir, by F. G. Ellerton, after his death. He was a member of the committee of *Hymns Ancient and Modern* in the later stages of that work.

348. *O Thou, before whose presence.*
205. *The Church's one foundation.*

STOWELL, Hugh, M.A. (Douglas, Isle of Man, 1799–1865, Salford), was son of a rector of Ballaugh, near Ramsey, Isle of Man. Educated at St. Edmund's Hall, Oxford, and ordained in 1823, he served curacies at Shepscombe, Gloucestershire, and Holy Trinity, Huddersfield; then, in 1828, was appointed curate-in-charge of St. Stephen's, Salford. When Bishop Blomfield licensed him to this charge, it was with great hesitation, as the young Manxman had the reputation of being 'an extemporaneous firebrand'. But in a few weeks there was no standing-room in the church, and in 1831 a new church, Christ Church, Salford, was built for him; there he continued till his death. He was a fervid and powerful orator. 'His first words were always halting, but, when he warmed to his subject, the rush of rhetoric fairly swept his hearers off their feet. The May meeting audiences were entirely at his mercy; they wept, or laughed, or emptied their purses just as he desired.' He had an intense love for children; his enormous Sunday Schools were his especial pride. He was a public force in Manchester, and one of the leaders of the Evangelical school in the Church of England. In 1845 he was appointed hon. canon of Chester; in 1851, chaplain to the Bishop of Manchester and Rural Dean of Eccles. In 1831 he published *A Selection of Psalms and Hymns suited to the Services of the Church of England*; in 1845, *Tractarianism Tested*; in 1832, *The Pleasures of Religion, and Other Poems*; in 1826, *The Peaceful Valley*. A collection of his *Hymns* was published in 1868.

552. *Jesus is our Shepherd.*

STRONG, THOMAS BANKS, D.D., Litt. D., Mus. Doc., C.B.E. (West Brompton, London, 1861–   ), was educated at Westminster School and Christ Church, Oxford. Ordained in 1885, he was Bampton Lecturer in 1895; Dean of Christ Church, 1901–20; Vice-Chancellor of Oxford University, 1913–17; Bishop of Ripon, 1920–5; appointed Bishop of Oxford, 1925. He was one of the editors of *The Oxford Hymn Book*.

175. HEBDOMADAL.

SULLIVAN, Sir ARTHUR SEYMOUR, Mus. Doc. (London, 1842–1900, London), was the son of a player on bass brass instruments and the clarinet. He became a child of the Chapel Royal in 1854, and his first song was published in 1855. After studying at the R.A.M., and Leipzig Conservatorium, he was organist of St. Michael's, Chester Square, and St. Peter's, Onslow Gardens; musical director, Royal Aquarium, Principal of the National Training School for Music, and Professor of Composition, 1876; conductor of Glasgow Choral Union, 1875–7; of Covent Garden Promenade Concerts, 1878–9; of Leeds Festival from 1880 onwards; and of the Philharmonic Society, 1885–7. He received the Legion of Honour in 1878, and in 1883 was knighted. He wrote oratorios, *The Light of the World*, *The Prodigal Son*, &c.; a *Festival Te Deum*, to celebrate the recovery of the Prince of Wales in 1872; music for *The Tempest* and *The Merchant of Venice*; many songs, much choral and instrumental music, and church music of great excellence. But it is by his attractive music for the Savoy Operas, in which he was associated with Sir W. S. Gilbert, that he has international fame.

His hymn-tunes were mostly written between 1867 and 1874, and were contributed principally to *The Hymnary* and *Church Hymns*. Of the latter he was musical editor.

370. BISHOPGARTH.	126. LUX EOI.
622. CLARENCE (arr.).	582. MOUNT ZION.
453. COENA DOMINI.	47. NOEL (arr.).
115. FORTUNATUS.	475. PROPIOR DEO.
616. GOLDEN SHEAVES.	530. ST. ANNE (arr.).
314. LACRYMAE.	308. ST. FRANCIS.
469. LEBBAEUS (arr.).	535. ST. GERTRUDE.
464. LEOMINSTER (arr.)	75. SAINTS OF GOD.

251. SAMUEL.

SUMMERS, THOMAS OSMOND, D.D., LL.D. (near Corfe Castle, Dorsetshire, 1812–82, Nashville, Tennessee), went in 1830 to America, and was admitted to the Baltimore Conference of the Methodist Episcopal Church in 1835. He was a missionary in Texas from 1840 to 1843; removed to Tuscaloosa, Alabama, 1844; and to Charlton, South Carolina, 1846. From 1845 he was Book Editor and Secretary of the Conference of the Methodist Episcopal Church, South, when the Southern Conference seceded from the main body of the Church on the issue of slavery; he was chairman also of its Hymn-Book Committee. He edited *Songs of Zion* (1851), including in it some 'doggerel hymns' in the vain hope of displacing thereby the camp-meeting song-books which had vulgarized hymnody in the south; also *The Wesleyan Psalter* (1855). In his later years he was Professor of Systematic Theology in Vanderbilt University, Nashville, Tennessee.

653. *The morning bright.*

SWAIN, JOSEPH (Birmingham, 1761–96, Walworth), belongs to 'the golden age of Baptist hymnody', the principal figure in which was Anne Steele. He lost his parents early, and was apprenticed to an engraver. For a time he led a careless, frivolous life; then, through reading the Scriptures, his conscience was aroused, and he became a fervent Christian. He was baptized by Dr. Rippon (q.v.) in 1783. Qualifying for the Baptist ministry, he became minister of a congregation in East Street, Walworth, in 1791. He was of an emotional, poetic temperament, and his short ministry made a deep impression. The poetic gifts he had previously employed in the composition of light songs and plays he now used to give point and power to his evangelical appeals. The hymns thus composed were published in *Walworth Hymns* (1792), for the use of his congregation. In the preceding year he had published *Redemption, a Poem in Five Books.*

392. *Come, ye souls by sin afflicted.*

Biographical and Historical Notes

SWIFT, James Frederick (Manchester, 1847–   ), was educated at Liverpool, early developed an aptitude for music, and at sixteen became organist in Cranmer Wesleyan Church; subsequently he served St. Andrew's Church and St. Bride's Church, all in Liverpool. For many years he conducted three choral societies there. At present, he resides in Liscard, Cheshire. Under the pseudonym of 'Godfrey Marks' he has published over 200 songs and ballads, some of which, such as *Sailing*, *A Brave Heart*, and *Jack's Return*, won extraordinary popularity. He has also composed many hymntunes.

189. ERNSTEIN.

SYMONDS, John Addington (Bristol, 1840–93, Rome), was educated at Harrow and Balliol College, Oxford, where he achieved brilliant distinction, and became a Fellow of Magdalen. Overwork brought on a tendency to consumption, and most of his life was spent under heavy disabilities due to the constant threat of that disease. Thoughts of law as his profession had to be abandoned, and he embraced literature as his career. For a time he lived at Clifton, with intervals abroad, but at last life in this country became impossible, and he built a house at Davos Platz, in the Swiss highlands. There he threw himself into the life and interests of the people, and lived a life of great industry and productiveness. He poured out books of many kinds, entertained his friends, of whom he had a wide and distinguished circle, maintained with eagerness his intellectual interests, and was inexhaustibly bountiful and kind. His ardent spirit kept up a brave fight with hopeless ill-health until a chill contracted in Rome, where he was seeking relief after bereavement and overwork, brought it to an end. His chief works were— his great *Renaissance in Italy* (6 volumes); *Introduction to the Study of Dante; Studies of the Greek Poets; Shakespeare's Predecessors in the English Drama; Sketches in Italy and Greece; Our Life in the Swiss Highlands*; translations of the Autobiographies of Benvenuto Cellini and Count Carlo Gozzi, and of the sonnets of Michelangelo and Campanella. He was a skilful versifier, and his verse translations are masterly, but his original poems reach no high level.

639. *These things shall be; a loftier race.*

SYNESIUS (Cyrene, *c.* 375–430?), came of an illustrious family. After studying at Alexandria under the renowned Hypatia, he devoted himself to philosophy and the life of a country gentleman. When his country was attacked by Libyan nomads, he raised a corps of volunteers for the defence of Cyrene. Though he became a Christian in 401, and was consecrated Bishop of Ptolemais in response to the will of the people, there was little of the ecclesiastic in his composition. He was no ascetic, adhered to the married state, and loved sport and open-air life. He wrote a number of odes. Only one, the undernoted, has come into common use. Charles Kingsley's delightful sketch of him as 'the squire-bishop' should be read in chap. xxi of *Hypatia*.

403. *Lord Jesus, think on me.*

TALLIS, or TALLYS, THOMAS (*c.* 1510–85, Greenwich), was 'the father of English cathedral music'. Beginning, probably, as a chorister of a metropolitan choir, he became organist of Waltham Abbey. On the dissolution of the monasteries he was dismissed with 20*s.* for wages, and 20*s.* as reward. Soon afterwards, he became a gentleman of the Chapel Royal. In 1575–6, he and William Byrd obtained letters patent, according them the exclusive right to print music and ruled music-paper for twenty-one years. The first work printed under the patent was their own *Cantiones quae ab argumento Sacrae vocantur, quinque et sex partium*, containing 34 motets, 16 by Tallis, and 18 by Byrd. This is a fine example of early English musical typography, but it proved a failure financially, and Queen Elizabeth granted the two musicians compensation in various tithes and lands to the value of £30 a year. Outwardly, Tallis conformed to the changes in the forms of worship imposed by the various rulers from Henry VIII to Elizabeth, but the fact that he wrote much before the Reformation and but little for the Reformed Church indicates that his sympathies in the main were with the older faith. He was buried in the chancel of Greenwich Parish Church. 'His fame rests on the Preces, Responses, and Litany used in the Anglican choral service. Yet it is necessary to point out that he is generally underrated and misunderstood, because his simpler works are so very well known that they have obscured the most ambitious and elaborate. Tallis can only be fairly judged by his great contrapuntal works; the title of "father of English Cathedral Music" is not his most honourable title. Let Tallis be ranked as a composer of the highest science, to whom all the difficulties of counterpoint were as child's play, and who produced motets and masses almost worthy to be ranked with Palestrina's; not as a man fettered by the regulations of the Reformed worship, and forcing himself to write in a succession of solid heavy chords.' His most wonderful composition is his motet, *Spem in alium non habui*, written for forty voices, eight choirs of five parts each. This is 'probably the noblest achievement of the English nation in sacred music.'

433. FIRST MODE MELODY.	353. TALLIS.
250. FIFTH MODE MELODY	281. TALLIS' CANON.
712. GLORIA PATRI.	559. THIRD MODE MELODY.

TANS'UR, WILLIAM (Dunchurch, Warwickshire, 1706–83, St. Neots), was the son of a labourer, whose name is spelt Tanzer in the parish register. In his youth he became a teacher of psalmody, and in pursuance of this profession appears to have moved about a great deal from town to town, conducting psalmody classes; he is found for a time in Barnes, Ewell, Cambridge, Stamford, Boston, Leicester, and other parts of England. Latterly he settled in St. Neots as a bookseller and teacher of music. His classes did much to improve psalm-singing in the Church of England. An eccentric man, skilled in the art of self-advertisement, he described his first book, *A Compleat Melody, or, The Harmony of Sion* (1734), as 'the most curiosest Book that ever was published.' Some of the tunes in it, such as 'Bangor' and 'Colchester,' are believed to have been composed by him, but certainty is lacking. He published also *Heaven on Earth, or, The Beauty of Holiness* (1738); *Sacred Mirth, or, The Pious Soul's Daily Delight* (1739); *The Universal Harmony, containing the Whole Book of Psalms* (1743); *The Psalm-Singer's Jewel, or Useful Companion to the Book of Psalms* (1760); *Melodia Sacra, or, The Devout Psalmist's Musical Companion* (1771); *A New Musical Grammar, or, The Harmonical Spectator* (1746); *The Elements of Musick Displayed* (1772); *Poetical Meditations* (1740).

313. (BANGOR.)

TATE, NAHUM (Dublin, 1652–1715, London), son of an Irish clergyman, was educated at Trinity College, Dublin. Though his poetical talent did not rise above mediocrity he was, through Court influence, appointed in 1690 Poet Laureate in succession to Shadwell. He also became historiographer-royal in 1702. Tate wrote largely for the stage, besides translating and adapting other men's works. Among his efforts in this field were versions of Shakespeare's *King Lear* and *Richard II*. He also wrote, apparently with Dryden's approval and help, a continuation of that poet's *Absalom and Achitophel*. Along with Nicholas Brady, Tate produced in 1696 the 'New Version' (metrical) of the Psalms, which gradually supplanted the older version of Sternhold and Hopkins. He fell latterly into dissolute habits, and died within the precincts of the Mint, then a sanctuary for debtors.

42. While humble shepherds watched their flocks.

TAYLOR, JANE (London, 1783–1824, Ongar, Essex), was the younger daughter of Isaac Taylor, who at the time of her birth was an engraver, but later became a well-known Congregational minister at Colchester and Ongar. She was of a delicate constitution, and though of a happy and humorous spirit among her intimates, was with others diffident and reserved. She was earnestly religious all her life, yet her sensitiveness delayed her acceptance of Church membership until she was thirty-four years of age. She and her sister Ann, afterwards Mrs. Gilbert (q.v.), were taught the art of engraving by their father, but their tastes were literary, and they collaborated in the volumes of verses and hymns detailed under Mrs. Gilbert's name. The nursery rhyme, 'Twinkle, twinkle, little star' was one of Jane's contributions. Her method of writing her verses for children was, she said, to shut her eyes and 'imagine the presence of some pretty little mortal; and then endeavour to catch, as it were, the very language it would use on the subject.' Her successes she attributed to 'this imaginary little being', and her failures to her being compelled so frequently to say: 'Now you may go, dear: I shall finish this hymn by myself.' While resident at Marazion in the interest of the health of her brother Isaac, afterwards well known as the author of *The Natural History of Enthusiasm* and other books of mark and influence in their time, she published *Display, a Tale,* and began a series of contributions to *The Youth's Magazine,* which she continued regularly for seven years. These pieces in prose and verse were collected and published after her death as *The Contributions of Q. Q.* In 1825 her brother issued *A Memoir and Poetical Remains.*

655. *Lord, I would own Thy tender care.*

TAYLOR, JOHN PRENTICE (Hamilton, 1871–   ), was educated in Hamilton, and took up the profession of pharmacy, but, having a strong bent towards music, studied it at Glasgow Athenaeum and Technical College and at Birmingham Midland Institute. He was leader of praise for a time in Chapel Street United Presbyterian (now Avon Street United Free) Church, Hamilton, and was afterwards organist of Kirn Parish Church.

125. KIRN.

TENNYSON, ALFRED, Lord (Somersby, Lincolnshire, 1809–92, Aldworth), was the third son of the Rev. George Clayton Tennyson, LL.D., rector of Somersby. He was educated at Louth Grammar School, privately, and at Trinity College, Cambridge. *Poems by Two Brothers* (1827), in which his brother Charles made a first venture with him, showed a promise which *Poems, chiefly Lyrical,* in 1830, confirmed; but it was the *Poems by Alfred Tennyson,* in 1842, which placed him definitely in the first rank of poets. When he succeeded Wordsworth as Poet Laureate in 1850, that pre-eminence was everywhere regarded as his by native and indisputable right. His successive homes were at Twickenham and Farringford, Freshwater, Isle of Wight; and from 1869 onwards, he spent winter and spring at the latter, and the summer and early autumn at a second home he acquired at Aldworth, Haslemere, Surrey. A peerage was conferred on him in 1884, with the title of Baron Tennyson of Aldworth and Farringford. On his death, he was buried in Westminster Abbey. For finished and exquisite artistry he had no peer among his contemporaries. His mind moved habitually on high levels; his teaching was always of what ennobles and exalts; and though his sensitive spirit was acutely alive to the questionings and spiritual uncertainties of his age, which his work faithfully reflects, his faith in Divine goodness and guidance and in the life beyond gave comfort and strength to his generation.

> 142. *Strong Son of God, immortal Love.*
> 588. *Sunset and evening star.*

TERRY, Sir RICHARD RUNCIMAN, Mus.Doc. (Ellington, Northumberland, 1865–   ), was educated at Oxford and Cambridge (choral scholarship, King's College), held organistships at Elstow School, near Bedford, 1890; St. John's Cathedral, Antigua, West Indies, 1892; Downside Abbey, 1896; and Westminster Cathedral, 1901–24. He was knighted in 1922. At Westminster he raised choral music to a high pitch of excellence. He has specialized in the revival of the church music of the polyphonic composers of the sixteenth century; he has brought whole schools of this type of composition to light. For a time he was chairman of the *Tudor Church Music* Publications under the Carnegie Trust. He now devotes himself to writing and research work. He has published: *Downside Masses; Downside Motets; Motets Ancient and Modern; Old Rhymes with New Tunes; A Shanty Book; A Benediction Manual;* and a book on *Catholic Church Music;* has written five masses, a requiem, many motets; and edited *The Westminster Hymnal*, the official Roman Catholic Hymnal for England.

> 506. CLONMACNOISE (arr.).

TERSTEEGEN, GERHARD (Mörs, Westphalia, 1697–1769, Mühlheim), was the son of a tradesman, and was apprenticed at fifteen to an elder brother, a shopkeeper at Mühlheim. He was of delicate health and scrupulous conscience. After his conversion at sixteen he spent whole days and nights fasting and in prayer, and, resolving to devote his life entirely to God, left his brother, took up his abode in a cottage near the town, and for some years made a scanty living by weaving silk ribbons. He ate only once a day, a meagre meal, and gave what he so saved to the poor. These privations told on him, and brought on deep spiritual depression, under the darkness of which he continued for five years. When light and peace returned, he made a new covenant with God, and wrote it out with his own blood. He gave up association with the Church, but formed no sect of his own. In 1725 he took a young friend to stay with him. They worked ten hours daily at the loom, and thereafter Tersteegen spent two hours in prayer, and gave two to writing devotional books and addressing private meetings of friends on religion. So many people flocked to him for spiritual fellowship and counsel, that he had to give up weaving and devote himself entirely to an informal ministry. His house was known as 'the Pilgrims' Cottage', a retreat for men seeking the way of life. People came to him from many lands; the sick sent for him to minister to them, and when he was known to be coming people would waylay him and gather others to hear him address them. He carried on an immense correspondence, and new editions of his hymns and spiritual writings were constantly called for. At one time these exertions almost killed him. In hymnody he is the chief representative of the mystics, who attached little importance to the ordinary means of grace because they held that the soul may possess an inner light of its own, and enjoy without any mediation direct and intimate fellowship with God. He was 'a gentle, heaven-inspired soul, whose hymns are the reflection of a heavenly, happy life'. His writings include a collection of hymns, *Geistliches Blumen-Gärtlein* (1729); and a selection of his addresses, taken down in shorthand, *Geistliche Brosamen von des Herrn Tisch gefallen* (Spiritual Crumbs fallen from the Master's table).

> 234. *God reveals His presence.*
> 192. *Spirit of Grace, Thou Light of Life.*
> 459. *Thou hidden Love of God, whose height.*

TESCHNER, MELCHIOR (*c.* 1615), was Lutheran Cantor at Fraustadt, in Silesia, at the beginning of the seventeenth century, and subsequently was pastor of Oberprietschen, near Fraustadt. The chorale tune which made him famous was composed in 1613 for an acrostic hymn written during a time of pestilence by Valerius Herberger, a famous preacher, then pastor at Fraustadt.

91. ST. THEODULPH.

THEODULPH OF ORLEANS, ST. (*c.* 821) is said to have been born in Italy, where he became abbot of a monastery in Florence. Brought to France by Charlemagne in 821, he was appointed soon afterwards to the bishopric of Orleans. He fell into disfavour with the Emperor Louis (the Pious) on suspicion of conspiracy against him, and was imprisoned in a monastery at Angers. While in confinement there, according to legend, he composed the original of the undernoted hymn; on Palm Sunday, 821, he sang it at the window of his cell as the King passed the prison on his way to church, and the King was so much impressed that he ordered the bishop's release and restoration to his see. This story is probably untrue. Theodulph appears to have died in prison or very soon after his release.

91. *All glory, laud, and honour.*

THOMAS, JOHN, M.A. (Blaenanerch, Cardiganshire, 1839–1922, Llanwrtyd Wells, Breconshire), was an amateur musician of great natural gifts. He had no professional training, but thought and studied much in music and Welsh literature. His home at Llanwrtyd, where his family kept the Post Office, was a favourite resort of Welsh musicians and poets. He was a popular adjudicator and conductor of Welsh religious singing festivals, and himself composed many part-songs and anthems which won wide favour. The best known of these were *Bendigedig fyddo Arglwydd Dduw Israel*, *Jerusalem*, and *Dattod mae Rhwymau*. One of the best known figures in the religious and musical life of Wales throughout his lifetime, his services to his native country were recognized not long before the end by the University of Wales conferring on him the honorary degree of M.A.

387. BLAENCEFN.

THOMMEN, JOHANN (? –1783, Basel), was from 1738 till his death cantor at St. Peter's, Basel. He published in 1745 *Erbaulicher musicalischer Schatz*, containing 500 hymns and 257 melodies, arranged partly for three, and partly for four parts. The sources of twenty-three of the melodies are unknown.

187. (CASSEL.)

THORNE, EDWARD HENRY, Mus.Doc. (Cranborne, Dorset, 1834–1916, London), was educated at St. George's Chapel, Windsor, under Sir George Elvey, whose assistant he became at the organ at the early age of twelve. The churches he served as organist were— Henley-on-Thames Parish Church; Chichester Cathedral; St. Patrick's, Brighton; St. Peter's, Onslow Gardens, South Kensington; St. Michael's, Cornhill; and St. Anne's, Soho. At St. Anne's his enthusiasm for Bach inspired many notable recitals of that master's organ music, and special services at which the St. John Passion music attracted large attendances. It is computed that under his two predecessors and himself, these special services must have drawn to them at least 200,000 people. The doctorate of music was conferred on him by the Archbishop of Canterbury. He wrote twenty anthems, eleven services, seven books of original organ music, piano pieces, part-songs, &c.

500. ST. ANDREW.

THRELFALL, JENNETTE (Blackburn, Lancashire, 1821–80, Westminster), was the daughter of a Blackburn wine-merchant, whose marriage to her mother was disapproved by the latter's family, which was locally of good social standing. She was early left an orphan, and lived with an uncle and aunt at Blackburn, then at Leyland, and latterly with their daughter and her husband at Dean's Yard, Westminster. By an unhappy accident she was lamed and mutilated for life, and another, later, rendered her a helpless invalid. Yet she displayed a beautiful self-forgetfulness, was 'the centre of the household, the adviser and counsellor of each', a generous friend of the poor of the district, and radiated cheerfulness and courage around her. Her verses, 'thrown off' at intervals in her reading, were published in various periodicals, and were collected for publication in *Woodsorrel, or, Leaves from a Retired Home* (1856); and *Sunshine and*

Shadow (1873). A third edition of the latter contained memorial tributes by Dean Stanley and Dean Farrar.

> 93. *Hosanna, loud hosanna.*
> 573. *When from Israel's house of bondage.*

THRING, GODFREY, B.A. (Alford, Somerset, 1823–1903, Ploncks Hill, Shamleigh Green, Guildford), was a son of the rector of Alford and brother of Lord Thring and of Edward Thring, the distinguished educationist and head master of Uppingham. Educated at Shrewsbury and Balliol College, Oxford, he became curate of Stratfield-Turgis; then of Strathfieldsaye; and in 1858 succeeded his father as rector of Alford-with-Hornblotton. He was rural dean in 1867–76, and in the latter year became prebendary of East Harptree in Wells Cathedral. He resigned his living in 1893. In 1866 he published *Hymns Congregational and Others; Hymns and Verses* in 1866: and *Hymns and Sacred Lyrics* in 1874. Impressed by the fact that all the hymn-books that had obtained large circulation in the Church of England were issued by representatives of different parties in the Church, he prepared and published as a protest 'against this system of party hymn-books' which deprived congregations of the use of some of the best hymns, *A Church of England Hymn Book adapted to the daily services of the Church throughout the Year* (1880). This book set a higher literary standard than any other hymn-book of its time. An improved edition of it appeared in 1882 under the title *The Church of England Hymn Book.*

> 136. *Crown Him with many crowns* (in part).
> 83. *Fierce raged the tempest o'er the deep.*
> 66. *From the eastern mountains.*
> 269. *Hail, sacred day of earthly rest.*
> 487. *O God of mercy, God of might.*
> 476. *Saviour, blessèd Saviour.*
> 279. *The radiant morn hath passed away.*
> 352. *Thou to whom the sick and dying.*
> 200. *To Thee, O God, we render thanks.*

THRUPP, DOROTHY ANN (London, 1779–1847, London), contributed hymns to the Rev. W. Carus Wilson's *Friendly Visitor* and *Children's Friend*, and to Mrs. Herbert Mayo's *Selection of Hymns and Poetry for the use of Infant Schools and Nurseries* (3rd ed., 1846), and herself edited a volume of *Hymns for the Young* (c. 1830).

> 554. (*Saviour, like a shepherd lead us.*)

THRUPP, JOSEPH FRANCIS (London, 1827–67, Surbiton), was educated at Winchester and at Trinity College, Cambridge. He became a Fellow of his college. Ordained in 1852, he became vicar of Barrington, Cambridge, in the same year, and was Select Preacher, Cambridge University, 1865. He published a book on

Ancient Jerusalem; An Introduction to the Study and Use of the Psalms; and *Psalms and Hymns* (1853), containing twenty-eight psalms and eighteen hymns by himself.

64. EPIPHANY.

TILAK, NARAYAN VAMAN (1862–1919), was born at Karazgaon, Ratnagiri District, Bombay Presidency, his father being a government registrar. He was 'born in the purple' of Hinduism, steeped in its spirit and tradition, and proud of its history—'a typical son of his people in many of the noblest Hindu qualities—in his engrossment with religion, in his readiness to count the world well lost if only he could find a truth that would content him, in the simplicity and unworldliness of his nature'. For a time he taught school, but, becoming a Christian in 1894, he was baptized in the following year in Bombay, and for twenty-one years thereafter worked in connexion with the American Marāthi Mission at Ahmednagar, teaching, preaching, doing social work. He was a passionate patriot, and eager for the naturalization of the Christian Church in India. With this view he used his great poetic gifts to enrich the Marāthi Christian Church with an indigenous hymnody. He produced a great body of spiritual songs, simple, intense, passionate, expressive of the Indian Christian heart in its vision of Christ and its worship of God. In 1917 he renounced all means of support, to pursue a new method of evangelism, what he called 'God's Durbār', a brotherhood of the baptized and unbaptized disciples of Christ, which should become 'a real universal family, to be known as real friends of men and real patriots through whom the world gains once more a vision of the Lord Jesus Christ'. His works were: *Tilakāñchi Kavitā; Upāsanā Sangīt; Bhajan Sangraha; Abhangāñjali; Christāyan.* A *Life* of him is published by the Rev. J. C. Winslow.

406. One who is all unfit to count.

TISSERAND, JEAN (?   –1494, Paris), was a Franscican friar who lived in Paris, and seems to have been a man of some note in his day. He founded an order for penitent women, and was the author of an historical or devotional work commemorating some members of his own Order who suffered martyrdom in Morocco in 1220. He also wrote various Latin poems, the most famous of which, *O filii et filiae*, was published shortly after his death in Paris, but has only in recent times been identified as his.

124. O sons and daughters, let us sing.

TOPLADY, AUGUSTUS MONTAGUE (Farnham, 1740–78, London), son of a Major who was killed at the siege of Carthagena, was educated at Westminster School, and at Trinity College, Dublin. He describes his conversion as occurring in Ireland under the ministry of a Wesleyan lay preacher. Ordained to the ministry of the Church of

England in 1762, he was some time afterwards appointed vicar of Broadhembury, Devon. In 1775 he was preacher in a chapel of French Calvinists in Leicester Fields, London. He was a fervent and powerful preacher, and immense crowds waited upon his ministry. Always a strong Calvinist, he wrote various tractates to vindicate the Anglican Church from what he considered the reproach of Arminianism. The controversies on this subject between him and John Wesley show neither disputant at his best. It is charitable to suppose that much of Toplady's bitterness may have been due to the ill-health which carried him off at the early age of thirty-eight.

> 703. *A debtor to mercy alone.*
> 560. *A Sovereign Protector I have.*
> 413. *Rock of Ages, cleft for me.*
> 561. *Your harps, ye trembling saints.*

TROYTE, ARTHUR HENRY DYKE, born ACLAND, M.A. (Killerton, near Exeter, 1811–57, Bridehead, near Dorchester), second son of Sir Thomas Dyke Acland, Bart., of Killerton, was educated at Harrow and Christ Church, Oxford, where he graduated in 1832. He studied for the bar, and was also much engaged in scientific pursuits. In 1852 he assumed the name of Troyte. The well-known chants bearing his name were composed at the request of Bishop Hamilton of Salisbury, and first appeared in *The Salisbury Hymn Book* (1857). He composed a number of hymn-tunes besides, and wrote *Liturgia Domestica*, a book of family prayers; *The Hours; Daily Steps Towards Heaven;* and *Letters on Musical Notation* (1841).

> 14. CHANT, TROYTE, NO. 2.

TSCHIRSCH, (FRIEDRICH) WILHELM (Lichtenau, 1818–92, Gera), was a pupil of the Berlin Institute for Church Music and Academy of Fine Arts. From 1843 to 1852 he was cantor of the Church of St. Peter and St. Paul, Leignitz, and from 1852 to 1889, court director at Gera. He toured America in 1869 in the interest of various German singing societies there. He published an opera, *Meister Martin und seine Gesellen*; a cantata, *Der Herr ist Gott*; a motet, many Lieder and choral works, and a collection of songs, *Der Volksänger*.

> 666. GOTT EIN VATER (arr.).

TURLE, JAMES (Taunton, Somerset, 1802–82, Westminster), was for some years a chorister in Wells Cathedral. Coming to London at eleven, he was articled as pupil to J. J. Goss, an uncle of Sir John, but gained most of his training by his own exertions. After serving Christ Church, Blackfriars, and St. James's, Bermondsey, as organist, he became, in 1831, organist of Westminster Abbey, and there spent the next fifty-one years of his life. He acted as organist at some of the great musical festivals, notably that at Norwich in 1839, when Spohr directed the production of his own oratorio *Calvary*, and the Handel Festival in Westminster Abbey in 1834. He had an enormous hand, and could stretch on the keyboard over an octave and a half. A canon of Westminster said: 'Mr. Turle makes the organ talk to him.' Beyond some anthems, chants, and hymn-tunes, he wrote little, but he edited *The People's Music Book*, 1844, *Psalms and Hymns*, for the S.P.C.K., 1862. His hymn-tunes were collected and published in 1885.

354. FAIRFIELD.   27. WESTMINSTER.

TURTON, THOMAS, D.D. (Yorkshire, 1780–1864, Ely House, London), was educated at Catharine Hall, Cambridge, and graduated as Senior Wrangler. He became Professor of Mathematics, and subsequently of Divinity, in the University. By way of the deaneries of Peterborough and Westminster he passed on to the bishopric of Ely. His degree of D.D. was given him by royal mandate on his appointment to the Professorship of Divinity in 1827. He was a man of varied gifts. He had sound taste in the fine arts, and no mean musical ability. He was a vigorous controversialist in his own field of theology, and waged effective argumentative warfare with Lord Brougham on Natural Theology, and with Cardinal Wiseman on the doctrine of the Eucharist. He wrote many polemical tracts and pamphlets, and some music for the Church.

334. ELY.   467. ST. ETHELDREDA.

TUTTIETT, LAWRENCE (Colyton, Devonshire, 1825–97, St. Andrews), son of a surgeon in the Royal Navy, was educated at Christ's Hospital and King's College, London. He intended at first to follow the medical profession, but turned to the Church, and was ordained in 1848. In 1854 he became vicar of Lea Marston, Warwickshire. Sixteen years later, he became incumbent of the Episcopal Church, St. Andrews, where he became, he said, 'quite a Scotsman at heart'; and in 1880 he received a canonry of St. Ninian's Cathedral, Perth. His last few years were spent in retirement at Pitlochry, but he died at St. Andrews while there on a visit. His published works included —*Hymns for Churchmen* (1854); *Hymns for the Children of the Church* (1862); *Germs of Thought on the Sunday Services*. He is said to have composed much of his verse on returning from his visitation of the sick or the burial of the dead, to express the consolatory thoughts suggested to him by what he had seen or heard.

606. *Father, let me dedicate.*
466. *O grant us light, that we may know.*
176. *O Jesus, ever present.*

TWELLS, HENRY, M.A. (Ashted, Birmingham, 1823–1900, Bournemouth), was educated at King Edward's School, Birmingham, where his schoolfellows included Archbishop Benson, Bishop Lightfoot, and Bishop Westcott, and at St. Peter's College, Cambridge. Ordained in 1849, he became curate at Great Berkhampsted; sub-vicar of Stratford-on-Avon, where he was chiefly instrumental in building the new church of St. James's; master of St. Andrew's House School, Wells; head master of Godolphin School, Hammersmith. In 1870, he became rector of Baldock, Hertfordshire; in 1871, rector of Waltham-on-the-Wolds, Melton Mowbray; was Select Preacher at Cambridge, 1873–4, and was made hon. canon of Peterborough in 1884. He acted as Warden of the Society of Mission Clergy in the Diocese of Peterborough. Owing to failing health he retired to Bournemouth in 1890, but built there and partly endowed with his own means the new church of St. Augustine, and, his health improving, served it as priest-in-charge until his death. He took an active part in the preparation of *Hymns Ancient and Modern*, and was on the Committee for the *Appendix* of 1889.

277. *At even, when the sun was set.*

TYE, CHRISTOPHER, Mus.Doc. (*c.* 1508–72, Doddington?), was a native probably of East Anglia, graduated Mus. Bac., Cambridge, 1536, and Mus. Doc., 1545; and became master of the choristers, Ely Cathedral, 1541–2. In 1560 he was ordained, and presented to the living of Doddington-cum-March, in the Isle of Ely. This was long considered the richest living in England : in 1835 its value was authoritatively given as £7,306 per annum. But in Tye's time the fen country was undrained, and he cannot have enjoyed the emoluments which thorough drainage and tillage secured to his later successors. He held simultaneously the rectorship of two other livings, Newton-cum-Capella and Little Wilbraham or Wilberham Parva, near Cambridge. In a contemporary document he is described as 'a doctor of music, but not skilful at preaching'; and other records show that he was either careless or deficient in capacity for business affairs. Anthony Wood says, 'Dr. Tye was a peevish and humoursome man, especially in his latter dayes, and sometimes playing on ye Organ in ye chap. of qu. Elizab. wh. contained much musicke, but little delight to the ear, she would send ye verger to tell him he play'd out of Tune: whereupon he sent word yt her eares were out of Tune.' He was a zealous adherent of the Reformed Church, but continued in the service of the Chapel Royal under Edward VI, Mary, and Elizabeth, without any apparent strain on his conscience. His place in the history of church music is of the first importance. He did more than any man to rescue it from ruin after the dissolution of the monasteries, and to give it the direct and popular character which the new conditions called for. He has been styled the 'father of the anthem'. having set the model which others followed. The work his name is most associated with appeared in 1553 with this title: *The Actes of the Apostles, translated into Englyshe Metre and dedicated to the Kynge's most excellent Maiestye by Cristopher Tye, Doctor in Musyke, and one the Gentylmen of hys grace's most honourable Chapell, with notes to eche Chapter, to synge, and also to play upon the Lute, very necessarye for studentes after theyr studye, to fyle their wyttes, and also for all Christians that cannot synge, to reade the good and Godlye storyes of the lyves of Christ hys Appostles.* To this source two well-known tunes, DUNDEE (or WINDSOR, or ETON), and WINCHESTER OLD, have been traced.

166. SOUTHWARK.   528. YATTENDON.

TYLER, JAMES SHERMAN (London, 1842–1917, London), was joint-superintendent with his brother, from its commencement in 1867, of the Children's Special Service Mission, and conducted missions for children, seaside services, &c., in many parts of the country. He was an amateur musician.

480. CITY BRIGHT.

URHAN, CHRÉTIEN (Montjoie, near Aix-la-Chapelle, 1790–1845, Belleville, near Paris), showed remarkable musical talent from his earliest years, learned without help to play the piano and several other instruments, and composed waltzes and violin variations before he reached his teens. The Empress Josephine heard him play in Aix in 1805, and carried him off to Paris to have his talent trained under the best masters. He became a brilliant player, not only on the violin, but on the five- and four-stringed viola and the *viol d'amour*. He specialized in this last instrument, which had dropped out of use; it was for him that Meyerbeer wrote the solo for that instrument in the first act of *The Huguenots*. Entering the orchestra of the Opéra Française in 1816, he became solo violinist in it. During the thirty years he played in it he is said to have never once glanced at the stage, owing to his religious scruples. He was for a long time organist in the Church of St. Vincent de Paul. Short in stature and of no personal attraction, he yet had a remarkable personality. He was eccentric, dressed like a clergyman, followed the regimen of an ascetic, taking but one meal a day, and that often of bread and radishes; but had a most kind and generous heart for the needs of others. A genuine artist, a man of wide culture, and a composer of originality.

581. RUTHERFORD.

VAUGHAN, HENRY (Skethiog, Wales, 1621–95, Skethiog), belonged to an old family of South Wales, the land of the ancient Silures (hence his self-conferred name 'The Silurist' by which he is still known). Along with his twin brother Thomas, the alchemist and Rosicrucian, he was educated at Jesus College, Oxford. Both brothers were staunch royalists, and suffered imprisonment and loss of property on account of their loyalty. At the age of twenty-four Henry published a volume of poems, including a translation from the tenth satire of Juvenal. He afterwards became a physician, and practised for some time in Wales, ultimately retiring to his native Skethiog. His religious convictions were deepened by a serious illness, and are reflected in his later writings. Various poems, prose translations, and other works appeared from time to time, some of which were published by his brother without his own consent. Vaughan's poems were practically forgotten for two centuries, till Henry Francis Lyte edited them in 1847. They were known, however, to Wordsworth, whose *Intimations of Immortality* owes something to Vaughan's *Retreat*. Apart from this his best-known poems are *The World* and *Beyond the Veil*. He belonged to the 'Metaphysical' school of which Donne is the chief representative. Herbert was his acknowledged master, but 'the great age of the Church of England finds in Vaughan, at his best, its best poetical exponent. He stops short of the almost maudlin intoxication with divinity which carried Crashaw out of the Church altogether, and he far transcends the decent piety of Herbert.' (Saintsbury.)

463. *My soul, there is a country.*

VEHE, MICHAEL, Th.D. (Biberach, near Wimpfen, ? –1559, Halle), received his degree from Heidelberg, where he was a teacher. In 1515 he was appointed regent of the Dominican house of studies there; later, he was appointed theologian and was given charge of the church at Halle, Saxony. In 1530 he was summoned to Augsburg to refute the doctrines of the Lutheran confession of faith, and in 1534 he took a prominent part in a debate against the Lutherans at Leipzig. In 1559, he was made Bishop of Halberstadt. In addition to controversial works he published a small collection of hymns, *Ein neues Gesangbüchlein* (1537).

88. (WER DA WONET.)

VETTER, DANIEL (d. 1730?), was organist of St. Nicholas Church, Leipzig. He is believed to have composed four of the melodies, though he lays claim only to one, in his *Musicalische Kirch- und Hauss-Ergötzlichkeit* (1713). No other source of them is known.

89. DAS WALT' GOTT VATER.

VINCENT, CHARLES JOHN, Mus. Doc. (Houghton-le-Spring, Durham, 1852–   ), son of an organist and composer who was also head of a music business in Sunderland, was trained as a chorister in Durham Cathedral under Dr. Armes, and at Leipzig under Reinecke, Richter, and Maas. He held posts as organist in Monkwearmouth Parish Church; the Parish Church and Kelly College, Tavistock; and Christ Church, Hampstead. As an examiner for Trinity College he visited South Africa and Australia. He founded the Vincent Music Publishing Co. (later, Schirmer & Co., and later still, Winthrop Rogers). He composed an oratorio, *Ruth*; cantatas, *Psalm 68*, *The Day of Rest*, *The Crowning of the Wheat*; songs, anthems, orchestral music: edited *The Organist and Choirmaster*; along with Sir John Stainer and Dr. D. J. Wood, the 1890 edition of *The Hymnal Companion to the Book of Common Prayer; The Chant Book Companion; The Anglican Organist; Bach's 48 Fugues in Score; A Reliquary of English Songs; Trinity College Song Books*, &c.; and wrote books on *First Principles of Music; Harmony, Diatonic and Chromatic*, &c.

444. PAX TECUM (arr.).

VINER, WILLIAM LETTON (Bath, 1790–1867, Westfield, Massachusetts), studied under Charles Wesley, was for eighteen years organist of St. Michael's, Bath, and for twenty-one of St. Mary's, Penzance; then, in 1859, he went to the United States. He composed organ music, church music, and songs, and edited *A Useful Selection from the most approved Psalms* (1846): *One Hundred Psalm and Hymn Tunes in Score* (1838), and *The Chanter's Companion* (1857).

678. DISMISSAL.

VULPIUS, MELCHIOR (Wasungen, Canton of Henneberg, Thuringia, *c.* 1560–1616, Weimar), became cantor at Weimar about 1600. He composed a number of tunes which were published in two important collections which he edited and issued in 1604 and 1609— *Ein schön geistlich Gesangbuch, &c., durch M. V. Cantorem zu Weymar*. Others were published after his death, in the *Cantional* of Gotha.

368, 527. CHRISTUS DER IST MEIN LEBEN (BREMEN).
304. DAS NEUGEBORNE KINDELEIN.   331. VULPIUS.

WAINWRIGHT, JOHN (Stockport, 1723?–68, Stockport), settled in Manchester in 1746, and was 'singing man' of the Collegiate Church, now the Cathedral, there. In 1750 he appears to have been organist of Stockport Parish Church, his famous tune to Byrom's Christmas carol having been first sung there on Christmas Day of that year, and subsequently, on the same day, by Wainwright and 'his singing men and boys', in Byrom's house in Manchester. He composed anthems and hymn tunes, and in 1766 published a *Collection of Psalm Tunes, Anthems, Hymns and Chants, for 1, 2, 3, and 4 voices*.

54. STOCKPORT.

WAINWRIGHT, RICHARD (Manchester, 1758–1825, Liverpool), younger son of John, was organist of the Collegiate Church and of St. Ann's, Manchester. In 1782, he succeeded his elder brother Robert in St. Peter's, Liverpool. For a time he officiated in St. James's, Toxteth Park Liverpool, but afterwards returned to St. Peter's. On one occasion a man who had a grudge against him seized his hand and bent several fingers back until they were dislocated.

527

They were useless from that day; yet Wainwright's skill triumphed over even such a disability, and he continued to play with remarkable effect. He wrote the well-known glee, *Life's a Bumper*, and published a *Collection of Hymns* composed for the children of the Liverpool Blue-Coat Hospital.

473. WAINWRIGHT.

WALES, UNIVERSITY OF.—The tunes given as from this source represent a co-operative enterprise in composition by a small community of minds under the leadership of Sir H. Walford Davies (q.v.). 'In two cases no less than five melodists took an essential part in a four-line tune.' The tunes appeared in *A Students' Hymnal, for Use in Schools and Colleges*, edited by Sir Walford Davies for the National Council of Music in Wales and the Welsh County Schools Association (1923).

80. CHILDHOOD.   120. QUINTA.

WALKER, MARY JANE, *née* DECK (Bury St. Edmunds, ? –1878, Cheltenham), was a sister of J. G. Deck (q.v.). She married in 1848 the Rev. Edward Walker, afterwards D.C.L., Oxon., the first rector of Cheltenham. Dr. Walker, an ardent evangelical, edited *Psalms and Hymns for Public and Social Worship* (1855), which had the merit of bringing into general knowledge and use a number of hymns by members of the then recently formed sect of Plymouth Brethren. It included over thirty by J. G. Deck, and nine by Mrs. Walker. An elder son, Edward, who became a clergyman, but died young, was an excellent organist and a composer of hymn-tunes, one of them being 'Kirkbraddan', well known in England. A younger son, John, attracted by Presbyterian ideals of worship, set up in his father's parish an iron church, long known as the Church of Scotland, although it had no affiliation with the Scottish Church, and he, the minister, never formally took Scottish orders. He, like his brother, was of a gentle, sensitive spirit, and left the memory of a saint.

696. *Jesus, I will trust Thee.*

WALMSLEY, ROBERT (Manchester, 1831–1905, Sale), was a jeweller in Sale from 1870 till his death. He was a Congregationalist, and deeply interested in Sunday School work. Many of his hymns were written for the Whit-week Festivals of the Manchester Sunday School Union. He published forty-four hymns in *Sacred Songs for Children of All Ages* (1900).

273. *The sun declines; o'er land and sea.*

WALTHER, JOHANN (Gotha, near Cola, Thuringia, 1496–1570, Torgau), was in 1524 bass singer in the choir at Torgau, when Luther, knowing his merit, summoned him to Wittenberg to assist in the preparation of the music for the services of the Lutheran

Church, and particularly for the new service for Holy Communion. He spent three weeks in Luther's house, helping to adapt the old Church music to the new use, wherever possible, and harmonizing the tunes in five parts. He was present in the Stadtkirche at Wittenberg on Oct. 29, 1525, when the new communion service, arranged by Luther and himself, was first used in German. The Elector Johann of Saxony made him his choir-master in 1526, at Dresden, and took into his pay the choir of eighteen men-singers and twelve boys, which it was his duty to direct. Four years later, on the disbandment of the Electoral Orchestra, it was reconstituted under his leadership by the town of Torgau, and in 1534 he was appointed singing-master also to the school there. In 1548 he accompanied the Elector Moritz to Dresden as his Kapellmeister. Pensioned in 1554, he retired to Torgau. He wrote a number of hymns, a few of which have been translated, but he was more notable as a composer. He published *Deutsche Messe und Ordnung Gottes-Dienst; Geystliche Gesangk Buchleyn* (Wittenberg); *Wittenbergisch deudsch geistlich Gesangbuchlein.*

417. (NUN KOMM, DER HEIDEN HEILAND.)   140, 185. (SOLDAU.)

WALTON, HERBERT FRANCIS RAINE (Thirsk, Yorkshire, 1869–   ), studied first under his father, a schoolmaster and organist of Thirsk Parish Church; then at the R.C.M. under Parratt, Parry, and Frederick Cliffe. In 1890 he became organist to the Earl of Aberdeen, and two years later at St. Mark's Church, Leeds. In 1897 he went to Glasgow as organist of Glasgow Cathedral, where in subsequent years his recitals have done much to advance musical appreciation in that city. He has published *Rhapsodic Variations*, and much other organ music.

68. CHILDREN'S SONG.

WARDLAW, RALPH, D.D. (Dalkeith, 1779–1853, Glasgow), was the son of a merchant who became a magistrate of Glasgow, and a mother who was a descendant of Ebenezer Erskine. He studied Arts in Glasgow University, then entered the Theological Hall of the Secession Church, but left it for Congregationalism. His only church was Albion Chapel, Glasgow, which he founded and built up. In 1811 he was appointed Professor of Divinity in the Congregational Theological Hall, Glasgow, an office he held for forty years. Offers of the Principalship of Hoxton Academy, of Spring Hill College, and of Lancashire Independent College, failed to draw him from Glasgow, where he was a man of outstanding mark and influence. He had a powerful mind, was a doughty controversialist on the chief problems of his time, and published a number of theological, expository, and polemical works. To displace the badly edited hymn-book then in use in 'the Tabernacles in Scotland', he published in 1803 *A Selection of Hymns for Public Worship*. Though this was an advance upon its predecessor, it also was ill-arranged and presented many hymns in a badly 'tinkered' form. It contained eleven hymns of his own, and had considerable popularity: it ran to thirteen editions.

376. *O Lord our God, arise!*

WARING, ANNA LAETITIA (Plas-y-Velin, Neath, Glamorganshire, 1820–1910, Bristol), was brought up in the Society of Friends, but was drawn by desire for the sacraments into the Church of England, and baptized in 1842 at St. Martin's, Winnall, Winchester. She began early to write hymns, and contributed to *The Sunday Magazine*. She published *Hymns and Meditations by A. L. W.* (19 hymns) in 1850, and in the tenth edition, in 1863, enlarged the number to thirty-nine; also *Days of Remembrance* (1886). She learned Hebrew to be able to study Old Testament poetry in the original, and daily read the Hebrew Psalter. A gentle spirit, yet of 'a merry, quiet humour', she was rich in friendships and abundant in good deeds. In her later years she was an assiduous visitor of the prisons in Bristol and a warm friend of the Discharged Prisoners' Aid Society. James Martineau acknowledged a 'long-standing spiritual obligation' to her.

548. *Father, I know that all my life.*
442. *In heavenly love abiding.*
446. *My heart is resting, O my God.*

WARING, SAMUEL MILLER (Alton, Hampshire, 1792–1827, Bath), like his niece, Anna Laetitia Waring (q.v.), was brought up in the Society of Friends, but left it for the Church of England. He published in 1826 *Sacred Melodies*, in which his hymns appeared.

708. *Now to Him who loved us.*

WARNER, ANNA BARTLETT (New York, 1820–1915, Highland Falls, New York), was a younger sister of Susan Warner (q.v.), and was herself a popular authoress. The sisters collaborated in several novels, *Say and Seal, Ellen Montgomery's Book-shelf*, &c.; and Anna, using the pseudonym of 'Amy Lothrop', wrote *Dollars and Cents, My Brother's Keeper*, and other stories. She edited *Hymns of the Church Militant* (1858), and published *Wayfaring Hymns, Original and Translated* (1869), and a biography of her sister.

660. *Jesus loves me! this I know.*
575. *The world looks very beautiful.*

WARNER, SUSAN (New York, 1819–85, Highland Falls, Orange County, New York), was the daughter of a lawyer of high character, who fell into undeserved misfortune. His daughters, both deeply religious, were impelled by the family difficulties to try to earn money by story-writing, and for many years, by their books, they were the breadwinners of the household. Susan's first book, *The*

Wide, Wide World, published in 1850 under the pseudonym of 'Elizabeth Wetherell', was, next to *Uncle Tom's Cabin*, the most popular of American novels. It was translated into French and German, and had an enormous sale on both sides of the Atlantic. Other stories from her pen—*Queechy*, *The Old Helmet*, *The Hills of the Shatemuc*, *Melbourne House*, *Daisy*, and many more, though critics had little to say in their favour and much to say about their 'sentimental piety and didactic emotionalism', were welcomed because of their simplicity and religious tone, by a very large public. She wrote definitely religious books also, going over the Bible story for children, and illustrating it from manners and customs of Biblical times, and from geography and records of travel—*The Law and the Testimony*, *The Kingdom of Judah*, *The Walls of Jerusalem*, *Standard Bearers of the Old Testament*, &c. She was buried at West Point, where she had conducted a Bible Class for the cadets of the U.S. Military Academy, and opposite Constitution Island, in the Hudson River, where the home had been in which most of her books were written.

671. *Jesus bids us shine*.

WATSON, JAMES (Glasgow 1816–80, London), went to London in youth, but returned to Scotland in 1838, and in 1844 became joint-editor with Dr. Horatius Bonar of *The Border Watch*, now *The Border Advertiser*, a weekly newspaper founded in the interest of the Free Church of Scotland. In 1845 he became a partner in the publishing firm of James Nisbet & Co. As principal partner of this firm in 1867, he assumed the entire risk of publishing *Psalms and Hymns for Divine Worship* for the Presbyterian Church of England. He was also largely responsible for the editing of that book. He served as a member of the first London School Board, 1870.

494. HOLYROOD.

WATT, LAUCHLAN MACLEAN, D.D., F.R.S.E., F.S.A. (Grantown, Inverness-shire, 1867–   ), comes of an Isle of Skye stock. He was educated at Edinburgh University, where he graduated in Arts and Divinity, and after mission work and social study in Edinburgh and the Highlands, entered the Church of Scotland ministry in 1896, and was ordained in the following year at Turriff, Aberdeenshire. He was translated to Alloa and Tullibody in 1901; to St. Stephen's, Edinburgh, in 1911; and to Glasgow Cathedral in 1923. In 1907 he accompanied the King of Denmark to Iceland, as special correspondent of *The Times*, *The Scotsman*, and *The Manchester Guardian*. He was in France with the Expeditionary Force, 1914–15, and acted as chaplain to the Forces in France and Flanders, 1916–17. He has published *God's Altar Stairs; In Love's Garden; The Grey Mother; The Communion Table; By Still Waters; The Tryst* (poems); *Edragil, 1745, a Story of the Jacobite Rising; The House of Sands; Gates* of Prayer; Green Meadows; Scottish Life and Poetry; Hills of Home; The Saviour of the World; In the Land of War; The Soldier's Friend; &c.   He was a member of the Committee for the Revision of *The Church Hymnary*.

> 112. *Dark the day on Calvary's Cross.*
> 402. *O Thou, my Judge and King.*

WATTS, ISAAC (Southampton, 1674–1748, Stoke Newington), was the son of an Independent who kept a boarding-house at Southampton, and who suffered imprisonment for his convictions. Isaac was offered an education at one of the universities with a view to ordination in the Church of England, but refused, and entered an Independent Academy. For six years he was tutor in the family of Sir John Hartopp (where his assiduity in study was such as to undermine his constitution), and in 1702 he became pastor of the distinguished Independent congregation in Mark Lane, London. Not long afterwards his health began to fail, and Mr. Samuel Price was appointed his assistant and afterwards his co-pastor. From 1712 till his death, thirty-six years afterwards, he lived the quiet life of a semi-invalid as the guest of Sir Thomas Abney and afterwards of his widow, devoting his time to the production of theological and lyrical works. His *Logic* was for long a text-book at Oxford. In 1728 he received the degree of D.D. from Edinburgh. Upon this Dr. Johnson, who, though no friend to Nonconformity, includes him in his *Lives of the Poets*, remarks, 'Academical honours would have more value if they were always bestowed with equal judgement.' His tolerant spirit, his liberal views, and above all his deservedly popular hymns, did much to sweeten relations between Anglicans and Dissenters. Watts wrote about 600 hymns and versions, an extraordinary number of which are still in common use. Judged by his best hymns, he takes rank with the greatest of English hymn-writers.

> 230. *Before Jehovah's awful throne.*
> 116. *Blest morning, whose first dawning rays.*
> 297. *Come, dearest Lord, descend and dwell.*
> 175. *Come, let us join our cheerful songs.*   T. 617
> 447. *Come, we that love the Lord.*
> 228. *From all that dwell below the skies.*
> 388. *Jesus shall reign where'er the sun.*
> 165. *Join all the glorious names.*
> 710. *Now to the King of Heaven* (partly by Doddridge).
> 601. *O God, our help in ages past.*
> 592. *There is a land of pure delight.*
> 711. *To Him who sits upon the throne.*
> 106. *When I survey the wondrous Cross.*

Watts is also the originator of a number of *The Scottish Paraphrases*, though in most cases these have been more or less altered by other hands. Of the paraphrases which owe their first form to him the following are in *The Church Hymnary*:

> 483. *Behold the amazing gift of love* (Par. 63).
> 137. *Blest be the everlasting God* (Par. 61).
> 223. *How bright these glorious spirits shine* (Par. 66).
> 507. *I'm not ashamed to own my Lord* (Par. 54).

WEALE, or WHEALL, WILLIAM, Mus. Bac. (*c*. 1690–1727), was organist of St. Paul's, Bedford, from about 1715. The bells of that church, for over a hundred years, rang out his tune 'Bedford'. He received his degree from Cambridge University in 1719.

242. BEDFORD.

WEBB, GEORGE JAMES (Rushmore Lodge, near Salisbury, Wilts., 1803–87, Orange, New Jersey), was intended for the ministry, but chose music as his profession. He became organist of a church in Falmouth, but in 1830 emigrated to the United States. There he quickly took a leading position as a music teacher and as a leader in musical progress. For forty years he was organist of the Old South Church in Boston. Along with Lowell Mason, he acted as Professor in the Boston Academy of Music for many years. In 1870 he left Boston for Orange, New Jersey, and six years later removed to New York, but he settled again in Orange in 1885. A Swedenborgian in religion, he did important work for the Church of the New Jerusalem in arranging its musical service. He published a work on *Vocal Technics*, was part author of another on *Voice Culture*, and, with Lowell Mason and others, edited about a score of volumes of sacred and secular music.

532. MORNING LIGHT.

WEBBE, SAMUEL (England, 1740–1816, London), was the son of a Government official in Minorca, but was not born there, as most books of reference say. His father died early and left his family unprovided for. Samuel was apprenticed at eleven to a cabinet-maker, but on completing his apprenticeship forsook that calling to copy music and earn enough to obtain music lessons. He received his first instruction from Barbaudt, organist of the Bavarian Chapel, London. With great difficulty, he acquired a considerable knowledge of several foreign languages also at this time. He became a prolific composer of unaccompanied vocal music, was secretary to the Catch Club and librarian to the Glee Club, for which he wrote his celebrated glee, *Glorious Apollo*. He is in the first rank of glee writers. In religion a Roman Catholic, he was organist of the chapel of the Sardinian Embassy in London, and wrote much religious music—masses, motets, and many hymn-tunes which are among the most valuable contributions of the Roman Church in this country to modern hymnody; some of them rank with the best loved of all hymn melodies.

Webbe as a man was greatly beloved. He died in Gray's Inn and was buried in Old St. Pancras churchyard.

688. ALMA REDEMPTORIS. 259, 646. MELCOMBE.
186. VENI, SANCTE SPIRITUS.

WEBBE, SAMUEL, Jun. (London, 1770–1843, Hammersmith), son of the preceding, studied under his father and Clementi. He became organist successively of the Unitarian Church, Paradise Street, Liverpool; the Spanish Ambassador's Chapel, London; St. Nicholas Church, and St. Patrick's Roman Catholic Chapel, Liverpool. He was a composer of glees of considerable merit, songs, motets, madrigals, &c. He published a *Collection of Psalm Tunes, interspersed with Airs adapted as such, for four voices,* in 1808; *Convito Armonico* (4 vols.), a collection of madrigals, glees, canons, catches, &c.; *Harmony epitomized, or Elements of Thoroughbass,* &c.

32, 208. RICHMOND (adapted).

WEIMAR, GEORG PETER (Stotternheim, Saxe-Weimar, 1734–1800, Erfurt), was devoted to music in his earliest youth. In 1752 he entered the Gymnasium at Erfurt. For a time he was cantor at Zerbst; in 1763 became cantor of the Kaufmannskirche, Erfurt, and in 1774 music director at the Gymnasium there. He composed songs, motets, cantatas. His *Choral-Melodienbuch* was published after his death, in 1803. It included five melodies of his own.

428. ALLGÜTIGER, MEIN PREISGESANG.

WEISSE (or WEISS), MICHAEL (Neisse, Silesia, *c.* 1480–1534, Landskron, Bohemia), became a priest, and for a time was a monk at Breslau. Luther's writings moved him deeply, and with two other monks he left the convent and took refuge in the Bohemian Brethren's house at Leutomischl, Bohemia. He joined the Brethren in 1531, and became their preacher at Landskron, and at Fulnek, Moravia. He became a man of great influence among them, a member of their council, and editor of their first hymn-book in German, *Ein Neu Gesengbuchlen* (1531). This book contained 155 hymns, most, if not all, of which were either translations by him from Bohemian into German or originals by himself. Mr. Mearns, in Julian's *Dictionary of Hymnology,* says, 'Many of his hymns possess considerable merit. The style is flowing and musical, the religious tone is earnest and manly, but yet tender and truly devout, and the best of them are distinguished by a certain charming simplicity of thought and expression.'

199. (RAVENSHAW.)

WESLEY, CHARLES (Epworth, 1707–88, London), brother of the great John Wesley, and himself perhaps the greatest hymn-writer of any age, was the youngest son of Samuel and Susannah Wesley. He was educated at Westminster School and at Christ Church

Oxford, where he graduated in 1729 and became a college tutor. In the same year he became one of the band known as the 'Oxford Methodists'. In 1735, having been ordained, he went with his brother John to Georgia as secretary to General Oglethorpe, but came back after a few months' stay. Not long afterwards he came, as did John, under the influence of Peter Böhler and other Moravians, and 'found rest to his soul' in 1738. His work after this was mainly identified with that of his brother, to whom he proved of invaluable service. In 1756 he gave up itinerating and settled in Bristol, and in 1771 removed to London. Charles was even less of a separatist than John, disapproved of the latter's ordinations, and declared that he had lived and would die in the communion of the Church of England. It was as a hymn-writer that Charles Wesley rendered of far the greatest service to religion. With him every public event, every personal experience, found readiest and fittest expression in a hymn. He is said to have written as many as 6,500 hymns. The great mass of them will be forgotten, but a very large number are of high quality, and the best of them rank with the finest hymns in the language. Two of his sons, Charles and Samuel, and also Samuel Sebastian, son of the latter of these, attained high distinction as musicians.

518. *A charge to keep I have.*
110. *And can it be that I should gain.*
317. *Author of life divine.*
118. *Christ the Lord is risen to-day.*
261. *Christ, whose glory fills the skies.*
196. *Come, Holy Ghost, our hearts inspire.*
416. *Come, O Thou Traveller unknown.*
150. *Come, Thou long expected Jesus.*
651. *Forth in Thy Name, O Lord, I go.*
662. *Gentle Jesus, meek and mild.*
 46. *Hark! the herald angels sing.*
414. *Jesus, Lover of my soul.*
227. *Let saints on earth in concert sing* (in part).
160. *Lo, He comes, with clouds descending* (in part).
479. *Love Divine, all loves excelling.*
467. *O for a heart to praise my God.*
166. *O for a thousand tongues to sing.*
409. *O Jesus, full of pardoning grace.*
428. *O Love Divine, how sweet thou art.*
471. *O Thou who camest from above.*
128. *Our Lord is risen from the dead.*
135. *Rejoice, the Lord is King.*
534. *Soldiers of Christ! arise.*
168. *Ye servants of God, your Master proclaim.*

WESLEY, CHARLES (Bristol, 1757–1834, London), was a son of the Rev. Charles Wesley, the hymn-writer. Like his brother Samuel (q.v.) he showed a precocious musical talent; before he was three years old, he was able to play a tune on the harpsichord 'readily and in just time', and 'always put a true bass to it', although he had to be strapped into the chair while doing it. His father was unwilling that he should follow his natural bent and become a musician, and refused an opportunity of having him trained as one of the children of the Chapel Royal. Partly, perhaps, because he missed that early training, his early promise never came to the expected brilliant fulfilment. He proved a good practical organist in several London churches, and finally in Marylebone Parish Church. His compositions made no great mark in their time, and they are now for the most part forgotten.

264. EPWORTH.

WESLEY, JOHN (Epworth, 1703–91, London), founder of Methodism, and incomparably the greatest religious force of the eighteenth century, was a son of the Rev. Samuel Wesley, rector of Epworth in Lincolnshire, and his wife Susannah, a woman of deep piety and great force of character. Educated at Charterhouse and Christ Church, Oxford, he became in 1726 Fellow of Lincoln and Greek Lecturer, and later acted for a time as curate to his father. In 1735 he undertook a mission to Georgia under the Society for the Propagation of the Gospel. There he published the first hymnbook issued in America. Conscious, however, of failure in his mission, he returned to England in 1738. It was at a meeting in Aldersgate Street in May of that year that he felt his heart 'strangely warmed', and experienced the great spiritual change which made him a fervent evangelist. Thenceforward he devoted himself to the work of itinerant evangelism, and, since many of the clergy closed their pulpits against him, took to preaching in the open air. He was no dissenter, however, loved order and good music, and never refused an invitation to preach in church. His marvellous activity is recorded in his famous *Journal*. Riding up and down the country on horseback he is said to have covered 250,000 miles, to have preached some 40,000 sermons, and to have sometimes addressed as many as 30,000 people at one time. Nor was his literary activity less astonishing. During his ministry he translated large portions of the classics, wrote many grammars, dictionaries and histories, edited the works of Bunyan, Baxter, and other religious writers, and brought out a 'Christian Library' of fifty volumes for the use of his itinerant preachers. If he did little in the way of original hymn composition, his fine taste is shown in his translations from the German, and also in the emendations he made—nearly all of these improvements—on the hymns of his brother Charles and of Isaac Watts.

> 230. *Before Jehovah's awful throne* (in part).
> 546. *Commit thou all thy griefs* (tr.).

432. *Jesus, Thy boundless love to me* (tr.).
547. *Put thou thy trust in God* (tr.).
431. *Thee will I love, my Strength, my Tower* (tr.).
459. *Thou hidden Love of God, whose height* (tr.).

WESLEY, SAMUEL (Bristol, 1766–1837, London), was a younger son of Charles Wesley, the hymn-writer. Very early he gave proof of extraordinary powers. He learned to read before he was five years old by poring over Handel's *Samson*, and soon after, without instruction, learned how to write. Before he was eight, he composed an oratorio, *Ruth*, which was a really musicianly work and as such was commended by Dr. Boyce. He became a fine classical scholar, a first-rate performer on the violin, the piano, and the harpsichord; but his chief delight was in the organ, on which he was recognized to be the most masterly performer of his time. In extempore playing, which was his forte, he had no rival. His influence dominated ecclesiastical music at the beginning of the nineteenth century. In 1784 he fell under the influence of the Roman Church, and there is evidence that he joined it, or was regarded as having joined it. This he denied in later life, declaring that the Gregorian music of the Roman Church seduced him to its chapels, but that its tenets never had any influence over his mind. He was more at home in composing for the Roman than for the Anglican service; of some of his music for the Roman ritual it is said that 'nothing by any other Englishman since the days of Byrd is so full of that sort of dim, introspective, tender austerity that marks the great masterpieces of the old Catholic composers'. He wrote four masses and many shorter works for that Church, several Anglican anthems and services, and many glees, songs, symphonies, concertos, &c. His masterpieces are vocal. In 1787, an accident to his head, which he refused to allow to be treated by trephining, left a portion of his skull pressing on his brain, and the result was recurring periods of despondency and high nervous irritability, during which he was disabled for the pursuit of his profession. In 1811 he conducted the Birmingham Festival, and in 1824 was organist of Camden Chapel, now Camden Town Parish Church. He was enthusiastic in propagating interest in Bach's works among English musicians. Indisputably, he was the greatest English organist of his time, and one of the great geniuses in music of his country.

472, 628. BRISTOL.   490. DONCASTER.
 714. CHANT IN G. 239. HIERAPOLIS.

WESLEY, SAMUEL SEBASTIAN, Mus. Doc. (London, 1810–76, Gloucester), 'the Anglican composer *par excellence*,' was a son of Samuel Wesley, and was named after his father and his father's idol, Bach. He was one of the children of the Chapel Royal, and became an organist at sixteen. He served five parish churches, including that of Leeds, and four cathedrals—Hereford, Exeter,

Winchester, and Gloucester. While at Gloucester he conducted the Three Choirs Festival. In 1844 he was a candidate for the Professorship of Music in Edinburgh University, but Sir Henry Bishop was preferred to him. He had a strongly marked individuality, and was regarded as something of a character. His passion for angling was insatiable; it is said that he accepted or rejected posts that were offered him according to the fishing advantages of the district, and that he almost surrendered his distinguished position at Leeds for Tavistock, because of the attractions of the river Tavy. One of his assistants recorded that once Wesley, while driving with him to open an organ somewhere, could not resist the apparently fine fishing condition of a river they had to cross; he sent the assistant on to open the instrument, instructing him to say that he himself was unavoidably detained. His quarrels with his deans and chapters were notorious. They arose invariably from his outspoken demands for reform. The choral establishments of the cathedrals were miserably inadequate, and church music generally had sunk to a low ebb; the first exponent of church music and organ playing in this country, and the finest extempore player of his time, never had the opportunity he deserved to give full scope to his powers. Yet he did great work. He 'made a new departure in English service music. Without deserting the stately massiveness of the best of the earlier styles, he introduced some of the freshest and newest forms of modulation and harmonic progression, and movements that were at that time as novel as they were beautiful.' His *Service in E* is one of the finest in English church music. In 1872 he published *The European Psalmist*, a collection of 733 hymn tunes, of which 130 were his own. He was a 'great Englishman. In that word lies perhaps the secret of much of his appeal. He was above all English. In his downrightness, his humours (using the word in its old sense), his blend of kindliness and wrongheadedness, and his love of outdoor life, no less than in his music, he bore the stamp of the country that produced him.' His great work for the music of his time received very inadequate recognition, as his sensitive nature felt acutely, but in 1873 he was granted a Civil List Pension of £100 per annum.

138. ALLELUIA.	322. MEMORIA.
392. ASHBURTON.	374. MORNING.
205. AURELIA.	256. MORNING HYMN (arr.).
518. BOWDEN (harm.).	568. PATMOS.
515. BUDE.	416. PENIEL.
197. CASTLEFORD (arr.).	289. RADFORD.
719. CHANT IN D.	257. ST. OLAVE (arr.).
332, 350. COLCHESTER.	452. WESTON.
536. GRACE DIEU.	513. WETHERBY.
458. HAREWOOD.	539. WIMBLEDON.
336. HAWARDEN.	338. WINSCOTT.

Biographical and Historical Notes

WESLEY'S *FOUNDERY COLLECTION*.—The first meeting-house erected for Wesley's followers in London was built on the site of a disused Government iron-foundry for the casting of cannon, near Upper Moorfield, in the City, in 1739. The Methodist revival was then producing its own type of tune, to suit the new hymnody which was coming into use. A collection of the new tunes was published in 1742 under the title, *A Collection of Tunes Set to Music as they are commonly sung at the Foundery*. Over forty tunes were included. Of these only a few were of the old psalm-tune order, and these appeared only because the Wesleys had written new hymns for them. The others were intended to furnish a supplement to the psalm-tunes already in common use.

504. SAVANNAH.

WESTBROOK, Benjamin Vine, F.R.C.O. (Greenwich, 1859–), was trained as a chorister in St. Paul's, Greenwich, and has been organist of Holy Trinity and Christ Church, Greenwich, and of St. George's, Perry Hill, London, where he is still. He was for some time active in connexion with the London Gregorian Association, and on several occasions conducted their choir in St. Paul's Cathedral. He has published works on *Piano Technique* and on *Singing Technique*, and orchestral and church music.

716. CHANT IN E.

WESTLAKE, Frederick (Romsey, 1840–98, London), was a pupil, and from 1863 a professor, at the R.A.M. A brilliant pianist, he played in public with success until teaching absorbed all his time. He published a mass; an *O Salutaris*; a *Kyrie and Gloria* with orchestra; a *duo concertante* for piano and 'cello: a set of nine *Episodes*; songs and part-songs, *Lyra Studentium*, &c.; and completed Sterndale Bennett's edition of *Bach's 48 Preludes and Fugues*.

355. ST. URSULA.

WHATELY, Richard, D.D. (London, 1787–1863, Dublin), was so delicate as a child that he was not expected to live. His precocity in calculation and reasoning was extraordinary. He had a brilliant career at Oxford, and became Fellow of Oriel at a time when Copleston, Thomas Arnold, and Keble were already, and Newman and Pusey were about to be, Fellows there. In 1822, after six years as a College tutor, he accepted the living of Halesworth, Suffolk; in 1825 returned to Oxford as Principal of St. Alban's Hall; in 1829 became Professor of Political Economy; and in 1831 was appointed Archbishop of Dublin. There was bitter opposition to this appointment, but he justified it by his consecrated zeal and ability as an administrator. He rendered great service also to elementary education in Ireland, and as chairman of a Royal Commission on the Condition of the Irish Poor. In 1832 he founded a Chair of Political Economy in Trinity College, Dublin. His mind worked powerfully within its limitations. He had no ear for music, and no sense of artistic or natural beauty, had little speculative faculty, and little care for theology; but 'his acute intellect enlightened every subject that he touched, and his powers of exposition and illustration have hardly ever been surpassed'. He was of the Broad Church school, and an opponent alike of Calvinism, evangelicalism, and the Oxford Movement. Newman, however, declared in his *Apologia* that it was Whately who taught him to think and reason. And his courage, devotion to duty, generosity, and high ability, won him the respect of men of every school. Among his writings were *The Elements of Logic; The Elements of Rhetoric; Historic Doubts relative to Napoleon Bonaparte*, a characteristic illustration of his humour and argumentative power, reducing to absurdity Hume's contention that no amount of evidence can establish a miracle; *Peculiarities of the Christian Religion; Difficulties of the Writings of the Apostle Paul; Thoughts on the Sabbath; Christian Evidences; The Kingdom of Christ Delineated.*

293. *God, that madest earth and heaven.*

WHITE, HENRY KIRKE (Nottingham, 1783–1806, Cambridge), was a son of a butcher; his mother conducted a successful boarding school for girls. He was baptized in Castle Gate Congregational Chapel, Nottingham. At fourteen he left school and was put to a stocking-frame to learn the business of a hosier. He disliked it so much that he was removed to an attorney's office, with a view to the legal profession. In that also he would have been unhappy, for his master-passion was for literature; he found time while at law to study Latin, Greek, Italian, Spanish, Portuguese, and some of the sciences as well. At seventeen, he published *Clifton Grove and Other Poems*. He had been of a sceptical turn of mind, but about this time Scott's *Force of Truth* decisively changed his attitude, and he became an earnest Christian. (See his poem 'The Star of Bethlehem'—'Once on the stormy seas I rode'—and Dr. John Brown's effective use of it at the end of 'Jeems the Doorkeeper). He now desired to become a minister. His employer released him from his articles, and with the help of Charles Simeon of Cambridge, Henry Martyn, and others, the way was opened for him to St. John's College, Cambridge. There he won such distinction that the highest honours seemed to be within his grasp, when overstrain broke his health, and consumption seized him; but his mind was worn out and would have been permanently injured, his doctors believed, had death not taken him. Southey published his *Remains* with a Memoir: Byron paid tribute to him; his death made a profound impression in England and

America. Though it has been said that 'he possessed the poetical temperament in a higher measure than any other English poet who has prematurely died, except Chatterton, Keats, and perhaps Michael Bruce', his work was quite immature, and but for the pathos of his story, would probably by now have been forgotten.

533. *Much in sorrow, oft in woe.*

WHITING, William (Kensington, 1825–78, Winchester), was educated at Clapham and Winchester, and was for over twenty years master of the Winchester College Choristers' School. His *Rural Thoughts and Other Poems* (1851) contained no hymns. The solitary hymn by which he is represented in hymnody is the highly-valued

626. *Eternal Father, strong to save.*

WHITMORE, Lady Lucy Elizabeth Georgina (1792–1840), was the only daughter of Orlando Bridgeman, 2nd Baron and 1st Earl of Bradford. She married in 1810 William Wolryche Whitmore, of Dodmaston, Shropshire. She published *Family Prayers for Every Day of the Week.*

243. *Father, again in Jesus' Name we meet.*

WHITTIER, John Greenleaf (Haverhill, Massachusetts, 1807–92, Hampton Falls, New Hampshire), began life as a farm boy and a slipper-maker. A copy of Burns's poems, bought from a Scots pedlar, whose singing of the Ayrshire poet's songs, in a rich voice, threw the lad into raptures, first awoke his lyrical genius, and led him to experiment in verse himself. His sister sent some of his verses to a newspaper edited by William Lloyd Garrison, who was so much struck by their quality that he sought young Whittier out. The friendship thus begun led the lad to enter the journalistic profession. He became, like Garrison, an ardent abolitionist, and used his pen powerfully in the anti-slavery crusade. In 1828 he became editor of *The American Manufacturer*; in 1830, of *The New England Review*; in 1836, of *The Pennsylvania Freeman*; he was also for some time corresponding editor of *The National Era.* He was a member of the Society of Friends, and to the last wore the distinctive garb of the Quakers and used their mode of speech. He made his home, in 1840, at Amesbury, Mass., but his last years were spent at Oak Knoll, Danvers. 'I am not really a hymn-writer,' he said, 'for the good reason that I know nothing of music. Only a very few of my pieces were written for singing. A good hymn is the best use to which poetry can be devoted, but I do not claim that I have succeeded in composing one.' He said also that two hundred years of silence had taken all the 'sing' out of the Quakers. None the less, over fifty hymns by him are found in modern hymn-books, most of them being centos from his poems. Phoebe Cary wrote of him in her memorial verses:

> But not thy strains with courage rife,
>   Nor holiest hymns, shall rank above
> The rhythmic beauty of thy life,
>   Itself a canticle of love.

254. *All things are Thine; no gifts have we.*
245. *Dear Lord and Father of mankind.*
141. *Immortal Love, for ever full.*
485. *O brother man, fold to thy heart thy brother.*
513. *O Lord and Master of us all.*
589. *When on my day of life the night is falling.*
558. *Who fathoms the eternal thought.*

WILKES, JOHN BERNARD (1785–1869), was organist at Monkland, near Leominster, the parish of Sir H. W. Baker, about 1860, at the time when *Hymns Ancient and Modern* was about to make its first appearance, and was thus associated with the first edition of that famous book. Later, he became organist of St. David's, Merthyr Tydvil, and then of Llandaff Cathedral. In 1865 he retired to London.

38, 620. MONKLAND (arr.).

WILLCOX, MARY JANE, *née* COOLEY (Tolland, Connecticut, 1835–1919, Chicago), was educated at the Hartford Female Seminary, founded by Miss Katherine Beecher, sister of Henry Ward Beecher and of Mrs. Beecher Stowe. She married the Rev. Giles Buckingham Willcox, afterwards D.D., and for forty years Professor of Pastoral Theology in Chicago Theological Seminary. She wrote many poems, some hymns, and for many years contributed a missionary column weekly to one of the denominational papers. For many years she was one of the corresponding secretaries of the Women's Board of Missions of the Interior, of the Congregational Church in the United States, and helped in its editorial work.

374. *Once again, dear Lord, we pray.*

WILLIAMS, AARON (London, 1731–76, London), was a music engraver and publisher of psalmody, a music teacher also, and he acted as clerk to the Scots Church, London Wall. He compiled and published *The Universal Psalmodist, containing* (1) *a Complete Introduction to Psalmody* . . . (2) *a choice and valuable Collection of Tunes* (4th edition, 1770); *New Universal Psalmodist* (1770); *Harmonia Coelestis, or, the Harmony of Heaven imitated, a Collection of scarce and much-esteemed anthems* (6th edition, 1775); *Psalmody in Miniature,* 1778; *Royal Harmony, or the Beauties of Church Music* (1780).

376. (HAMPTON.)

Biographical and Historical Notes

WILLIAMS, BENJAMIN (Wyddfyd, Great Orme, Llandudno, 1838–1918, Llandudno), received only an elementary education at the local British School, became a carpenter by trade, and later, a builder. His early taste for music was acquired through the medium of the tonic sol-fa system, and while still in his teens he became a successful teacher of this method; he continued teaching until a few years before his death. His enthusiasm for music led him on to choral conducting. Under his leadership the Llandudno Philharmonic Society gave many of the chief choral works of the great composers. For fifty-seven years he was precentor of the Welsh Presbyterian Church, Llandudno, and for most of that time was an elder also. His services to music throughout his life were entirely voluntary. A number of hymn-tunes were composed by him.

28. DEGANWY (adapted).

WILLIAMS, ISAAC, B.D. (Cwmcynfelin, Cardiganshire, 1802–65, Stinchcombe), was the son of a Chancery barrister at Lincoln's Inn. He was educated at Harrow and Trinity College, Oxford. The Oriel College circle influenced him deeply; Keble he called 'his spiritual father'. Ordained, he became curate at Windrush; Fellow and tutor of Trinity; Newman's curate at St. Mary's; and curate to Thomas Keble at Bisley. His candidature for the Oxford Chair of Poetry in succession to Keble was bitterly opposed because of his association with the Tractarian Movement and his friendship with Newman. His relation with Newman, indeed, 'had long been a curious mixture of the most affectionate attachment and intimacy, with growing distrust and sense of divergence'; but his deep implication in the Tractarian Movement was incontestable: he was the author of the notorious Tract LXXX, *On Reserve in Communicating Religious Knowledge*, which, next to Tract XC, was far the most obnoxious to the opponents of the Movement. The odium aroused against him led to a man who was no poet being preferred to him for the Chair. His disappointment was so acute that he withdrew from Oxford and public life. He removed to Stinchcombe in 1848, and lived there till a decline carried him off. Though modest, retiring, and sensitive, he was one of the most convinced and resolute of the Tractarian leaders. In addition to sermons, he published *The Cathedral; Thoughts on Past Years; Hymns translated from the Parisian Breviary; Hymns on the Catechism; The Baptistery; The Altar; Ancient Hymns for Children*. Like other leaders of the Oxford Movement, he disapproved of the use of metrical hymns, apart from the Psalter, in the services of the Church, and his hymns were designedly made rough to prevent such a use of them. His translations, however, from the Parisian Breviary set John Chandler (q.v.) to prepare the versions which gave those hymns a place in English hymnody. Canon Ellerton says that Williams 'impressed his friends

543

and companions with the mark of sanctity more than any of his contemporaries, except John Keble'.

405. *Lord, in this Thy mercy's day.*

WILLIAMS, PETER (Laugharne, Carmarthenshire, 1722–96, Carmarthen), one of the most prominent figures in the Methodist Revival in Wales, was educated at Carmarthen Grammar School, and while there, converted under the preaching of George Whitefield. Ordained by the Bishop of St. David's, he held several curacies, but the fervency of his preaching was not acceptable, and he was eventually compelled to leave the Established Church and throw in his lot with the Revivalists. He travelled much and suffered great persecution. He was an eloquent preacher, and did great service by his *Expository Bible*. His connexion with hymnody is slight, the first stanza only of the undernoted hymn being doubtfully attributed to his translation of one of Williams of Pantecelyn's hymns.

564. *Guide me, O Thou great Jehovah* (tr.).

WILLIAMS, RALPH VAUGHAN, Mus. Doc. (Down Ampney, near Cirencester, 1872–   ), was educated at Trinity College, Cambridge, where he graduated in Arts and Music, and at the Royal College of Music under Stanford, Parry, and Charles Wood; also at Paris and Berlin. He was organist of South Lambeth Church, 1896–9; Extension Lecturer for Oxford University; Professor of Composition, Royal College of Music, London. He joined the R.A.M.C. as a private at the outbreak of the European War in 1914, and later held a commission in the artillery. He did not develop early; practically all his music dates after his thirtieth year. He has done work of great value in collecting and editing for publication folk-songs and carols, chiefly in East Anglia and Herefordshire; and folk-song music and old English music from the Tudor period to Purcell has deeply influenced his own composition. His gift of melodic invention is marked, his style is severe and noble, and his work as a whole is of great originality and beauty. 'Time will place him high for his choral and orchestral works alone.' His works include *Towards the Unknown Region* (to Walt Whitman's words); *Willow Wood; A London Symphony; A Sea Symphony; Mystical Songs; A Pastoral Symphony; Songs of Travel; In the Fen Country; The Wasps* (overture); *Harnham Down*; beautiful rhapsodies on folk melodies; attractive songs, like *On Wenlock Edge* and *Linden Lea*. He was musical editor of *The English Hymnal*, and, with Martin Shaw, of *Songs of Praise*.

191. DOWN AMPNEY.   624. RANDOLPH.
243. MAGDA.   220. SINE NOMINE.

WILLIAMS, ROBERT (Mynydd Ithel, Llanfechell, Anglesey, *c.* 1781–1821, Mynydd Ithel), was born blind, but became a skilled basketmaker, so earning his living. He sang well and was an able musician. 'He had a quick ear to take in all the notes, and if he heard a tune once, he could then write it out without a single mistake.'

16, 119. LLANFAIR.

WILLIAMS, THOMAS, (HAFRENYDD) (Llanidloes, 1807–94, Llanidloes, Montgomery), was a self-taught musician. In 1845 he published the *Salmydd Cenedlaethol*, a book of tunes, anthems, and sacred choruses, selected from the works of Handel, Haydn, Mozart, and other masters, and set to Welsh words. In 1852 appeared *Ceinion Cerddoriaeth Gôrawl ac Eglwysig*, containing anthems, tunes, and chants by Bach, Mendelssohn, Beethoven, Croft, Wesley, &c.; and in 1860 *Y Gemau Cerddorol*, a small collection of sacred works. These books did useful service. He also published a few literary works.

65. LLANDINAM.

WILLIAMS, THOMAS JOHN (Ynysmeudwy, Swansea Valley, Glamorganshire, 1869–   ), studied music composition under Professor David Evans of Cardiff. He was organist and choirmaster of Zion Church, Llanelly, 1903–13; and of Calfaria Church, Llanelly, from 1913 to the present. He has written a large number of hymn-tunes and a few anthems.

701. EBENEZER.

WILLIAMS, WILLIAM (Cefn-y-coed, 1717–91, Pantecelyn, near Llandovery), the chief hymn-writer of Wales and one of her greatest poets, was the son of a well-to-do farmer. He received a good education, and was sent to Llwynllwyd Academy (later, the Presbyterian College) Carmarthen, to be trained for the medical profession. But in 1738, on his way home from Llwynllwyd, he heard Howel Harris preaching in Talgarth Churchyard, and came under spiritual influences that changed his life. He decided to enter the ministry, prepared for holy orders, and was ordained by the Bishop of St. David's and licensed to the curacy of Llanwrtyd, Breconshire. There he spent about three years. Being refused priest's orders, however, because of his evangelical views, he withdrew from the Established Church and threw himself into the evangelistic work led by the Rev. David Rowlands and Howel Harris. In his preaching itineraries throughout Wales he travelled on an average 3,000 miles every year for fifty years. He composed over 800 hymns in Welsh and over 100 in English, and in addition wrote two long poems, *Theomemphus*, and *Golwg ar Deyrnas Crist* (A View of the Kingdom of Christ), several prose treatises and numerous elegies. 'What Paul Gerhardt has been to Germany, what Isaac Watts has been to England, that and more has William Williams been to the little Principality of Wales. His hymns have both stirred and soothed a whole nation for more than a hundred years; they have helped to fashion a nation's character and to deepen a nation's piety' (Elvet Lewis).

> 564. *Guide me, O Thou great Jehovah.*
> 387. *O'er those gloomy hills of darkness.*
> 384. *Onward march, all-conquering Jesus.*
> 445. *Speak, I pray Thee, gentle Jesus!*

WILLING, CHRISTOPHER EDWIN (Devon, 1830–1904, London), was the son of a chorister of Westminster Abbey and the Chapel Royal, and himself became a chorister in the Abbey under James Turle, whose pupil and deputy he became. He held office as organist of Blackheath Parish Church; the Foundling Hospital; St. Paul's, Covent Garden; and All Saints, Margaret Street. He acted also as organist and sub-conductor of the Sacred Harmonic Society, *maestro al piano*, under Sir Michael Costa, at Her Majesty's Theatre, and chorus master at the Covent Garden Opera. For over twenty years he conducted the triennial festivals of the St. Albans Choral Union. He compiled the hymnal and psalter used at the Foundling Hospital, and raised the music there to a high pitch of excellence.

> 516. ALSTONE.

WILMS, JAN WILLEM (Witzhelden, Sondershausen, 1772–1847, Amsterdam), was the son of an organist. After training by his father, he settled, in 1791, in Amsterdam as a teacher of music. From 1824 he was organist of the Baptist Church there. He gained a great reputation as a virtuoso, composer, and conductor. He wrote symphonies, concertos, string quartets, violin and flute sonatas, &c., but his fame rests on his tune for one of the national hymns of Holland.

> 644. LEYDEN.

WILSON, DAVID FREDERICK RUDDELL, M.A. (Tyholland, 1871–), was ordained in 1895 in the Church of Ireland (Episcopal), served as curate, St. Anne's, Belfast, 1898–9; was Succentor and Master of the Choir School, St. Patrick's Cathedral, Dublin, 1899–1916; rector of Drumcondra, 1914, and of Donnybrook, 1917; and is canon and precentor of St. Patrick's. He is an authority on Church music, and was general editor of *The Irish Hymnal* and of *The Irish Chant-book*.

> 452. TYHOLLAND (arr.).

WILSON, HUGH (Fenwick, Ayrshire, 1766–1824, Duntocher), was the son of a shoemaker, and was apprenticed to his father's trade. In his spare time he was a diligent student of mathematics and kindred subjects, and qualified himself to add to his income by teaching others. A favourite pastime was the making of sundials. Occasionally he led the psalmody in the Secession Church. Removing about the end of the eighteenth century to Pollokshaws, he held positions of responsibility in certain mills there, and afterwards at

Duntocher, he being a skilled draughtsman and calculator. While at Duntocher, he acted as a manager in the Secession Church, and was one of the two founders of the first Sunday School there. He composed many psalm tunes, but only two—MARTYRDOM and CAROLINE—appear to have been published. The latter long since fell out of use, but MARTYRDOM, or FENWICK, as it was first called, has a place in modern hymnody.

457. MARTYRDOM.

WINKWORTH, CATHERINE (London, 1829–78, Monnetier, Savoy), was a daughter of Henry Winkworth of Alderley Edge, Cheshire, and spent most of her life in the neighbourhood of Manchester. She was the best of our translators from the German. Her *Lyra Germanica* (two series, 1855 and 1858) ranks with the devotional classics of the nineteenth century. She published also *The Chorale Book for England* (translations with music, 1863), and *Christian Singers of Germany* (1869). Dr. Martineau said her translations have 'not quite the fire of John Wesley's versions of Moravian hymns, or the wonderful fusion and reproduction of thought which may be found in Coleridge. But, if less flowing, they are more conscientious than either, and obtain a result as poetical as severe exactitude admits, being only a little short of "native music".' During her later years, which she spent at Clifton, Bristol, she took an active interest in the Clifton Association for the Higher Education of Women, and in kindred societies. Bishop Percival of Hereford, then head master of Clifton College, said of her, 'She was a person of remarkable intellectual and social gifts and very unusual attainments; but what specially distinguished her was her combination of rare ability and great knowledge with a certain tender and sympathetic refinement which constitutes the special charm of the womanly character.'

41. *All my heart this night rejoices* (tr.).
307. *Blessed Jesus, here we stand* (tr.).
324. *Deck thyself, my soul, with gladness* (tr.).
56. *From heaven above to earth I come* (tr.).
541. *If thou but suffer God to guide thee* (tr.).
304. *Lord, Jesus Christ, our Lord most dear* (tr.).
280. *Now God be with us, for the night is closing* (tr.).
29. *Now thank we all our God* (tr.).
308. *O Father, Thou who hast created all* (tr.).
496. *O Love, who formedst me to wear* (tr.).
22. *Praise to the Lord, the Almighty, the King of creation* (tr.).
162. *Wake, awake! for the night is flying* (tr.).
377. *Wake, Spirit, who in times now olden* (tr.).
540. *Whate'er my God ordains is right* (tr.).

WISE, MICHAEL (Wiltshire, probably Salisbury, 1648–87, Salisbury), in 1663 became a lay clerk and alto singer in St. George's

Chapel, Windsor; in 1668, organist of Salisbury Cathedral; in 1675/6 a gentleman of the Chapel Royal and counter-tenor singer there; was given the right to play the organ in any church visited by Charles II during his royal progresses; and in 1686/7 was appointed almoner and master of the choristers in St. Paul's Cathedral. He was a troublesome man, of hasty and uncertain temper. On one occasion, at a service at which the King was present, Wise, 'thinking the sermon, probably, somewhat long and dry, struck up a voluntary in the middle of it, which greatly displeased His Majesty'. During his term of office in Salisbury he was fined and admonished for absences and irregular attendance, and an apology from him is recorded in the Chapter books for speaking 'rashly and inconsiderately to the reproach and dishonour of the Dean and Chapter'. He was a man of humour also. When asked in Charles II's reign to sign a petition of which he did not approve, he answered, 'No, gentlemen, that's not my business; but I'll set a tune to't an you please.' His hot temper cost him 'his life. Visiting his wife in Salisbury, he had a dispute with her, in the heat of which he rushed out into the street, and when, the hour being late, he was challenged by a watchman, he quarrelled with him also, and in the altercation received a blow on the head from the man's bill, which killed him. He was buried near the west door of the Cathedral. He was a consummate musician, combining with mastery of the technique of his art a lively imagination, dramatic power, and a gift of melody. His church compositions are 'among the glories of our cathedral music', and it is said of some of his anthems that they 'are as fresh as if newly given from the brain of the most tender and expressive among modern musicians'.

98, 202. CONGLETON.

WITT (or WITTE), CHRISTIAN FRIEDRICH (Altenburg, *c.* 1660–1716, Gotha), was court organist, and, later, Kapellmeister, at Gotha. He composed a number of hymn-tunes, which appeared in his *Psalmodia Sacra* (Gotha, 1715).

113. STUTTGART.

WOOD, CHARLES, Mus. Doc. (Armagh, 1866–1926, Cambridge), studied at Armagh, the Royal College of Music, London, and Cambridge, where he became a Fellow of Gonville and Caius College. He became Professor of Harmony at the R.C.M. in 1888; assistant to Villiers Stanford as conductor of the Cambridge University Musical Society, 1888–94; University Lecturer in Harmony and Counterpoint, 1897. He published *Patrick Sarsfield* (symphonic variations); choral works, *Ode to the West Wind; Milton's Ode on Time; Dirge for Two Veterans; Swinburne's Ode on Music; Song of the Tempest, Ballad of Dundee*; many part-songs, solo songs (e.g. *Ethiopia*

548

saluting the colours), and church music. His compositions show great originality. In his treatment of *Irish Folk Songs* he excelled.

637. RECESSIONAL.

WOODBURY, ISAAC BAKER (Beverley, Massachusetts, 1819–58, Columbia, South Carolina), learned the trade of blacksmith, but educated himself, learned the violin, and devoted himself to music. In 1839 he was a member of a travelling glee-club in New England, and, later (in 1849), after some study abroad, settled in New York as a teacher of music and editor of *The Musical Review* and *The Musical Pioneer*. He frequently visited England. Various collections of religious music were published by him—*Liber Musicus, Cythera, The New Lute of Zion*, &c.—and many secular collections. He died at Columbia while on his way to the south in quest of health.

583. MONTGOMERY.

WOODFORD, JAMES RUSSELL, D.D. (Henley-on-Thames, 1820–1885, Ely), was educated at the Merchant Taylors' School, London, and Pembroke College, Cambridge. Ordained in 1843, he was second master for a time in Bishop's College, Bristol, and curate of St. John the Baptist Church in that city. He became incumbent of St. Saviour's, Coalpit Heath, and of St. Mark's, Easton, Bristol; rector of Kempsford, Gloucestershire; vicar of Leeds; honorary chaplain to the Queen; several times Select Preacher at Oxford; and in 1873, Bishop of Ely. His published works included sermons, *Lectures on the Creed; Hymns arranged for the Sundays and Holy Days of the Church of England* (1852 and 1855). He was joint-editor of *The Parish Hymn Book* (1863 and 1875). His original hymns and translations from the Latin appeared in these books.

319. *Thee we adore, O hidden Saviour, Thee* (tr.).

WOODWARD, RICHARD, Mus. Doc. (Dublin, 1744–77, Dublin), son of a vicar-choral of Christ Church and St. Patrick's Cathedrals, himself became vicar-choral of St. Patrick's in 1772; organist of Christ Church, 1765; and was also master of the choristers of both cathedrals. He published in 1771, *Cathedral Music, consisting of one Compleat Service, Seven Anthems, Several Chants, and Veni Creator Spiritus, in Score*. He issued a collection of songs, catches, and canons also.

715. CHANT IN B FLAT.   718. CHANT IN D.

WOOLDRIDGE, HARRY ELLIS (Winchester, 1845–1917, London), was from 1895 Professor of Fine Art at Oxford University, and was an antiquarian musical expert who specialized in old polyphonic music. He published *The English Metrical Psalter* (1890), edited an enlarged edition of *Chappell's Music of the Olden Time* (1893), and wrote volumes 1 and 2 of *The Oxford History of Music*. He was editor also of examples of English harmony prior to 1500; of three volumes of *Purcell's Church Music*; and, with Robert Bridges, of *The Yattendon Hymnal* (1899).

528. YATTENDON (in part).

WORDSWORTH, CHRISTOPHER, D.D. (Lambeth, 1807–85, Harewood), was a nephew of the poet Wordsworth, and youngest son of Christopher Wordsworth, in 1807 rector of Lambeth, and afterwards Master of Trinity College, Cambridge. Educated at Winchester and Trinity College, he had an extraordinarily brilliant career, graduating as Senior Classic and Senior Optime in the Mathematical Tripos. He showed distinguished prowess in athletics also, and used to tell with glee how, at a cricket match between Harrow and Winchester, he 'caught-out Manning'. He became Fellow and Classical Lecturer in his College, and in 1836, Public Orator of the University. At Harrow, as head master, while still under thirty, he began in 1836 a great moral reform. In 1844 he was given a canonry at Westminster; in 1848–9 was Hulsean Lecturer at Cambridge; in 1850 began a nineteen-years' ministry in the quiet country parish of Stanford-in-the-Vale-cum-Goosey, Berkshire, where he proved a model parish priest; and in 1868 was appointed Bishop of Lincoln. He was unceasingly diligent as a writer, publishing sermons, addresses, a *Commentary* on the whole Bible, an enormous undertaking for one man; books on *Athens and Attica*, *Pompeian Inscriptions*, &c.; and in 1862, *The Holy Year*, hymns for every season and for every phase of each season in the Christian Year. He held it to be 'the first duty of a hymn to teach sound doctrine, and thus to save souls'. This didactic purpose, and the wide range of subjects on which he wrote, many of them not well adapted for poetic treatment, made much of his work of little value; but the best of his hymns are of high quality. Canon Ellerton says of him that he was 'a most holy, humble, loving, self-denying man. And the man is reflected in his verse. To read one of his best hymns is like looking into a plain face, without one striking feature, but with an irresistible charm of honesty, intelligence, and affection.'

213. *Father of all, from land and sea.*
484. *Gracious Spirit, Holy Ghost.*
126. *Hallelujah, hallelujah.*
268. *O day of rest and gladness.*
19. *O Lord of heaven and earth and sea.*

WOTHERSPOON, ARTHUR WELLESLEY, M.A. (Kilspindie, Perthshire, 1853–   ), son of the Rev. W. L. Wotherspoon, D.D., was educated at Perth Academy and St. Andrews University. On being licensed as a probationer of the Church of Scotland, he acted as assistant at Moulin, Beith, Toward, and Hamilton. In 1883 he was

ordained to the parish of Oatlands, Glasgow, of which he was the
first minister. He has been an active member, and in 1910 was
president, of the Scottish Church Society; he has contributed a
number of papers to the proceedings of that Society and to those
of the Ecclesiological Society. He acted as sub-editor of *The Scottish
Mission Hymn Book* (1912), to which he contributed three hymns
and two tunes.

108. *Sing my tongue, how glorious battle* (tr.).

WREFORD, JOHN REYNELL, D.D. (Barnstaple, 1800–81, Bristol),
was educated at Manchester College, York, for the Unitarian
ministry. He became colleague-minister of the New Meeting, Birmingham, in 1826, but was compelled to resign in 1831 because of
failure of voice. He then withdrew from the ministry and opened
a school at Edgbaston. The later years of his life were spent in
retirement at Bristol. He wrote *A Sketch of the History of Presbyterian Nonconformity in Birmingham* (the Unitarian variety), and
several volumes of devotional verse. In 1837 he contributed fifty-
five hymns to the Rev. J. R. Beard's *Collection of Hymns for Public
and Private Worship*, which was designed 'as a protest against hymn-
tinkering, and as a novel effort to reconstruct Unitarian Hymnody
out of materials exclusively Unitarian'. It rejected all Trinitarian
and evangelical hymns, and thus sacrificed all the great hymns of the
Church, Beard refusing to adapt them to Unitarian use. Even among
Unitarians the book had no success.

633. *Lord, while for all mankind we pray.*

WRIGHT, WILLIAM (Lockerbie, Dumfriesshire, 1859–1924, Belfast), was brought up in the Free Church of Scotland, of which he
became an elder at the age of twenty-four. Trained as a pharmacist
in Lockerbie, Worthing, and Glasgow, he carried on business as such
in his native town until invited to join the secretariat of the Scottish
Y.M.C.A. After some years spent in this work, he was asked to
transfer his service to Ireland, as National Secretary of the Y.M.C.A.
there. In that office he did notable work during twenty-four years.
For his management of the Red Triangle work in the camps and
barracks of Ireland during the Great War he received from the
Government the decoration of M.B.E.

537. *March on, my soul, with strength.*

XAVIER, ST. FRANCIS. See FRANCIS XAVIER, ST.

YATTENDON HYMNAL, The (Clarendon Press, 1899), was the
work of Dr. Robert Bridges (q.v.), Poet Laureate. After he settled
in the Berkshire village of Yattendon, he took charge of the congregational singing in the parish church. With a view to reviving
certain old church tunes—'masterpieces', which 'are, without ques-

tion, of an excellence which sets them above either the enhancement or ruin of Time'—set to hymns worthy of them, he published this *Hymnal* in sumptuous form, containing 100 hymns, with the music, largely from the *Genevan Psalter*, arranged in four parts for unaccompanied singing. Of these hymns, no fewer than forty-four were of his own workmanship as author, translator, or adaptor. The adaptations were made to suit the tunes. 'Where the hymn has to be translated from a foreign language, some reconstruction is generally inevitable, and it can follow no better aim than that of mutual enforcement of words and music. And the words owe a courtesy to the music; for if a balance be struck between the words and music of hymns, it will be found to be heavily in favour of the musicians, whose fine work has been unscrupulously altered and reduced to dullness by English compilers, with the object of conforming it in rhythm to words that are unworthy of any music whatever.' Dr. Percy Dearmer regards Bridges's hymns as 'the advance-guard of a movement which will lead the Englishman of the future to read hymn-books for the poetry that is in them'.

448. *All my hope on God is founded* (tr.).
250. *Enter Thy courts, Thou Word of life.*
217. *Fear not, thou faithful Christian flock* (tr.).
440. *Happy are they, they that love God* (tr.).
278. *Now cheer our hearts* (tr.).
248. *The duteous day now closeth* (tr.).

YOAKLEY, JOHN (Portsmouth, Ohio, 1860–   ), son of an organist of the Episcopal Church, whose father was a native of Yorkshire, is himself a member of the American Guild of Organists, and has been organist of the Church of the Advent, Walnut Hills, Cincinnati, and of Christ Church (Episcopal), Cincinnati. He has been organist also of the A.A. Scottish Rite, and still continues his interest in its music. He has composed anthems and other church music.

202. ALL SOULS.

YOUNG, ANDREW (Edinburgh, 1807–89, Edinburgh), studied arts and theology at Edinburgh University. He made teaching his profession, was for ten years head master of Niddry Street School, Edinburgh, and then, from 1840 to 1853, head English master of the Madras College, a secondary school, St. Andrews. After his retiral to Edinburgh, he was for over thirty years an honoured elder and superintendent of the Sunday School in Greenside Parish Church, and abounded in good works besides. In Christopher North's class, as a student, he had gained prizes for poems on 'Parthia' and 'The Scottish Highlands'. The latter gave the title to a volume he published in 1876, *The Scottish Highlands, and Other Poems*.

587. *There is a happy land.*

ZINZENDORF, NICOLAUS LUDWIG, Count von Zinzendorf und Pottendorf (Dresden, 1700–60, Herrnhut), was the son of one of the principal ministers of State in Saxony. The family was noble, wealthy, and religious. He had Spener as godfather and Francke for tutor, and was brought up in a Pietist circle. He came early under religious impressions, and while at school founded the Order of the Mustard Seed, the members of which bound themselves to the service of Christ and the conversion of the heathen. He studied at the Universities of Halle and Wittenberg. During a subsequent period of travel, he saw at Düsseldorf, a picture of the Saviour crowned with thorns, over which was the inscription, 'This have I done for thee; what doest thou for Me?' From that time the service of Christ was the passion of his heart. From 1721 to 1732 he was Aulic Counsellor to the Elector of Saxony. In 1722 he began to settle on a corner of his estate of Berthelsdorf in Saxony the persecuted descendants of the Moravian Brethren, and founded the great Moravian settlement of Herrnhut. Five years later, he went himself to live there. To equip himself better for his work he went incognito to Stralsund, passed the necessary examinations, and was ordained. But he was not allowed to return for ten years; he was exiled on a charge of spreading false doctrine. He spent those years in journeying and preaching, from St. Petersburg to the West Indies. He planted missions in America, and founded settlements of the Brethren in Germany, Holland, England, and Scotland. Four years were spent in this country, organizing his followers. His later years were spent at Herrnhut, where, having been consecrated as bishop at Berlin in 1737, he occupied the chief place. He devoted the whole of his fortune to the work, was almost reduced to bankruptcy, and died poor. By the time of his death he had succeeded in welding the conflicting elements he found among the Brethren into a unified organization, with common worship, a kind of 'militia Christi, based not on monastic, but on family life'; and they carried their missionary work into many lands. Zinzendorf wrote over 2,000 hymns, many of them of no merit, some of them fantastic to the point of irreverence. They were contained in his *Deutsche Gedichte* (1735) and other collections.

567. Jesus, still lead on.

A CALENDAR OF THE HYMNARY

Some dates specially connected with the origin or use of the hymns and tunes, as mentioned in the Notes. The numbers refer to the numbers of the hymns, not to the pages of this book.

b. = born.   d. = died.

JANUARY

1. 560; b. A. H. Clough, D. Jenkins, Henry Lawes (baptized); d. Samuel Smith.
2. d. Edward Caswall, E. Perronet, J. E. Rankin.
3. b. Alexander Ewing; d. E. G. Monk, R. A. Smith.
4.
5. d. M. L. Duncan, T. R. Matthews.
6. b. John Fawcett (299, 490).
7. b. W. E. Hickson, Peter Williams; d. W. B. Bradbury, J. S. Edmeston, Anne Shepherd, Thomas Turton.
8. b. Lowell Mason.
9. b. William Jackson.
10. d. A. W. Chatfield.
11. b. C. H. Purday; d. Timothy Dwight, C. W. Everest, R. F. Littledale, William Williams.
12. d. Dean Alford.
13. John Darwall (baptized), W. Shrubsole (the composer) (baptized).
14. d. E. H. Sears.
15. d. John Cosin.
16. 562; b. W. B. Bradbury.
17. 221, 581.
18. b. John Fawcett, W. H. Havergal; d. W. Shrubsole (the composer).
19. b. H. S. Irons; d. H. Twells.
20. b. J. H. Schein; d. Harriet Auber.
21. b. Edward Mote; d. M. Claudius.
22. b. Lucy E. G. Whitmore; d. J. B. Dykes (see on 221).
23. 333; b. Albert Midlane; d. Charles Kingsley.
24. b. J. M. Neale.
25. 584; b. E. H. Bickersteth, Harvey Grace; d. Mary L. Duncan, R. H. Prichard.
26. b. A. L. Peace.
27. b. H. S. Holland.
28. 438; b. Sabine Baring Gould; d. Joseph Barnby, G. Wade Robinson, John Wainwright (buried).
29. 326, 682; b. Walter Hately; d. F. Oakeley.
30. b. Ann Gilbert; d. F. Southgate.
31. b. Bernard Barton.

FEBRUARY

1. b. Richard Whateley; d. E. H. Plumptre.
2. 326; d. Jemima Luke, Palestrina (122), A. A. Procter.
3. b. W. H. Doane, Mendelssohn.
4. 512; d. Carlyle, E. J. Hopkins.

554

5. b. Tobias Clausnitzer, W. Pennefather; d. J. W. Elliott.
6. d. William Jones.
7. 593; d. H. B. McKeever, W. Boyce.
8. d. J. F. Doles.
9. 471; b. E. W. Naylor; d. Charles Lockhart.
10. 183; b. T. H. Gill, Dean Milman, Walter Parratt; d. James Nares.
11. b. Washington Gladden; d. T. Haweis, J. G. Small, W. Williams.
12. 206, 419; b. W. H. Burleigh, H. Downton, Richard Mant; d. Fanny van Alstyne, J. M. Altenburg, H. W. Baker, J. A. Freylinghausen, B. Schmolck.
13. 107; b. J. W. Elliott.
14.
15. d. H. F. Chorley, Adam Drese. 'Olney Hymns' published (1779).
16. 288; b. C. Urhan; d. J. G. Schicht.
17. d. John Jones.
18. b. J. Drummond Burns, A. Galloway; d. J. Grimshaw, Martin Luther, W. Sandys.
19. b. C. E. May; d. Bernard Barton, E. C. Clephane, Samuel Johnson.
20. 407.
21. b. J. H. Newman; d. H. J. Gauntlett, John Hullah.
22. b. S. F. Adams.
23. b. John E. Bode, G. F. Handel; d. J. Crüger, G. C. Martin.
24. b. Samuel Wesley; d. Thomas Binney.
25. b. R. Hudson, Thomas Turton, F. Westlake; d. Andrew Reed.
26. d. Edward Cooper, Thomas Moore (688).
27. 593; b. Percy Dearmer, C. H. H. Parry, H. F. R. Walton.
28. b. L. G. Hayne, S. E. Miles, C. E. Willing.
29. 543; d. Joseph Anstice.

MARCH

1. b. E. Prout, Richard Redhead, John Thomas; Thomas Campion (buried), d. W. H. Monk.
2. b. G. A. Macfarren, J. S. B. Monsell; d. W. B. Gilbert, John Wesley.
3. b. Ella S. Armitage, d. L. G. Hayne.
4. b. W. H. Parker.
5. b. James Turle.
6. d. William Bright.
7. 507; d. Thomas Aquinas.
8. b. G. W. Martin; d. J. H. Gurney.
9. b. Martin Shaw.
10. b. R. H. Baynes, J. B. Dykes, H. M. MacGill.
11. d. Mary Hasloch, R. Massie.
12. b. Paul Gerhardt, R. Lowry; d. R. H. Baynes, C. Kocher, St. Gregory the Great.
13. b. J. W. Alexander.
14. b. R. L. de Pearsall; d. A. L. Peace.
15. 233; b. W. Gardiner.
16. b. J. B. Calkin, F. Filitz, Fanny Freer, T. Hewlett, M. J. Monk, W. H. Monk, G. Neumark; d. William Bullock.
17. b. Jean Ingelow; d. H. Scott Holland, Lucy E. G. Whittemore.
18. b. J. Cawood, Charlotte Elliott, John Henley, Robert Walmsley; d. E. S. Alderson, S. A. Brooke, W. H. Burleigh, W. H. Monk, John Randall.

19. 577; d. Ken.
20. 107; b. A. T. Russell; d. C. Wordsworth.
21. 256; b. J. S. Bach, S. C. Lowry, Joseph Parry, H. Kirke White.
22. d. W. E. Hickson, T. L. Hately.
23. b. H. Twells.
24. b. Fanny van Alstyne, J. Threlfall; d. Thomas Attwood, R. P. Stewart.
25. b. Godfrey Thring; d. R. M. McCheyne, G. Rawson, J. Walther.
26.
27. b. Michael Bruce, Josiah Booth, G. J. Elvey, George Matheson; d. C. H. H. Parry, Walter Parratt.
28. b. S. E. Miles.
29. d. Dora Greenwell, Keble, Ray Palmer, G. R. Prynne, S. Rodigast, C. Villiers Stanford, Charles Wesley.
30.
31. b. James Chalmers, J. D. Farrer, F. J. Haydn, J. H. Roberts; d. John Marriott, John Stainer.

APRIL

1. b. A. Rooker; d. W. C. Plunket.
2.
3. b. George Herbert; d. Ambrose of Milan, Heber, Tersteegen.
4. 329, 444.
5. 360; b. E. R. Conder, L. Spohr.
6. b. E. H. Sears; d. B. H. Kennedy, Balbulus Notker, F. A. G. Ouseley, A. R. Reinagle.
7. b. William Bruce, Xavier.
8.
9. b. Jane L. Borthwick, J. Crüger; d. J. S. B. Monsell.
10. b. C. M. Noel, H. T. Schenk; d. T. Hewlett.
11. b. John Alcock, Basil Harwood, H. Lahee; d. M. A. Löwenstern, H. T. Schenk.
12. 1; b. F. de Giardini; d. Jane Taylor.
13. d. Handel, John Richardson.
14. 154, 475; b. H. Elvet Lewis, John Wainwright (baptized); d. J. Swain.
15. 106; d. Henry Baker, J. B. Calkin, William Jackson.
16. 526; d. G. W. Martin.
17.
18.
19. 526; James Nares (baptized); d. W. H. Havergal, J. A. Symonds, S. S. Wesley.
20. b. M. A. von Löwenstern.
21. b. W. B. Gilbert, Heber; d. Abélard.
22. b. H. B. Gray; d. W. F. Lloyd.
23. b. J. F. Doles, G. A. Löhr, Martin Rinkart, A. Young; d. H. A. Crosbie, C. H. Purday, Henry Vaughan.
24. d. A. H. Charteris.
25. b. A. Scott Gatty, Keble, S. J. Stone; d. Cowper.
26. b. Mary L. Duncan, H. R. Palmer; see under 'George Herbert'.
27. d. G. W. Doane, Richard Redhead.
28. 338.
29. d. J. N. Darby, H. Lahee.
30. 707; b. J. R. Woodford; d. J. R. Macduff, J. Montgomery, W. Pennefather, John Robinson.

A Calendar of the Hymnary

MAY

1. 609; b. Addison; d. Dryden, Isaac Williams; see on 471 (second tune).
2. d. John Henley, Martin Madan, Cowper (buried).
3. b. A. H. D. Troyte, d. W. Whiting.
4. d. H. R. Palmer.
5. 'Ludborough' (see on 188).
6.
7. b. Thomas Helmore.
8. d. Baron von Rosenroth.
9. 407; b. E. H. Thorne; d. Tobias Clausnitzer, T. T. Lynch, Zinzendorf St. Gregory Nazianzen.
10. b. A. C. Coxe; d. J. Goss.
11. 542.
12. 364; b. E. Neumeister, J. A. Rothe.
13. 685; b. A. S. Sullivan; d. Joseph Jowett.
14. b. Timothy Dwight, W. L. Viner; d. Thomas Kelly.
15. b. H. C. Beeching; d. Thomas Hastings.
16. b. A. H. Mann; d. John Armstrong, E. H. Bickersteth.
17.
18. d. Dryden.
19.
20. 582, 725; b. L. Hensley.
21. 166; b. R. M. McCheyne, Joseph Parry; d. W. M. Hutchings, Laurence Tuttiett.
22. d. A. L. Waring.
23. 110; b. J. R. Macduff; d. C. Wesley ('Epworth').
24. 432; d. Joseph Hart, N. Selnecker.
25. b. A. F. Lvov; d. S. Webbe.
26. b. Zinzendorf.
27. b. H. W. Baker, G. W. Doane, C. W. Everest; d. F. S. Colquhoun.
28. 32; b. J. M. Bell, A. S. Hawks, B. S. Ingemann, Thomas Moore (688), T. B. Pollock; d. Zinzendorf.
29.
30. d. Thomas Clark.
31. d. F. J. Haydn, Joachim Neander.

JUNE

1. b. J. Franck, Lyte.
2.
3. 241; b. W. H. Gladstone, Norman Macleod, C. Steggall; d. F. R. Havergal, H. M. MacGill.
4. 386, 545.
5. b. George Rawson; d. Orlando Gibbons.
6. 424, 579; b. John Stainer; d. H. J. Buckoll.
7. b. C. W. Poole; d. Paul Gerhardt, C. Steggall.
8. d. J. M. Bell, H. Downton, F. H. Himmel, H. L. Hassler, J. Langran, R. Robinson.
9. 454; b. T. J. Potter; d. R. Robinson, William Robertson.
10. b. James Watson; d. J. A. P. Schultz, R. Courteville (buried).
11. d. W. Gaskell.
12. 153; b. Charles Kingsley; d. W. C. Bryant, W. Horsley, E. P. Hood John Morison.
13. b. E. F. Rimbault.

14. b. W. C. Dix, J. Ambrose Lloyd.
15. 347; b. Charles Wood; d. John Ellerton.
16. 568; b. John Chandler; d. Norman Macleod.
17. b. John Wesley; d. Addison, J. Chalmers, L. J. Hutton, J. C. Simpson.
18. b. E. C. Clephane, S. Longfellow, W. D. Maclagan, R. Massie; d. J. Franck, Albert Knapp.
19. 489; b. F. K. L. Scholinus; d. A. H. D. Troyte.
20. 301; b. F. S. Colquhoun.
21. 358; b. C. L. de Chenez; Benjamin Rogers (buried).
22. b. C. C. Scholefield.
23.
24. b. G. J. Webb.
25. b. Philip Pusey.
26. 637; b. E. Bunnett, Philip Doddridge.
27. Stephen Elvey, b. John Hullah, F. Silcher.
28. 572; b. H. Albert, F. W. Faber, Rousseau, John Wesley; d. James Turle.
29. d. H. S. Irons.
30. b. J. S. Anderson, E. J. Hopkins, H. S. Oswald.

JULY

1. d. John Chandler, John Fawcett.
2. d. Washington Gladden, Mary Hasloch, Mary J. Walker, J. R. Wreford.
3. d. Rousseau.
4. b. A. C. Ainger, C. F. Gellert; d. W. Byrd, John Cennick.
5. b. W. Crotch, T. T. Lynch; d. Michael Bruce.
6. d. E. R. Conder, George Duffield, Thomas Helmore, George Hews, Henry Smart.
7.
8. d. G. Neumark.
9. b Philipp Bliss, H. J. Gauntlett; d. Robert Grant, Philip Pusey, J. Scheffler.
10.
11. b. E. A. Dayman; d. Alexander Ewing.
12.
13. b. Thomas Kelly; d. Samuel Howard.
14. b. Matthew Bridges, John Hunter; 'Llanfair' composed (16).
15. b. Edward Caswall, William Robertson, C. K. von Rosenroth.
16.
17. 637; b. L. J. Hutton, Isaac Watts; d. T. S. Dupuis, John Farmer.
18. b. Laurence Housman; d. Georg Neumark, Dean Stanley.
19. d. S. Besler.
20. d. F. H. Barthélémon, Jean Ingelow.
21. b. Priscilla J. Owens; d. T. R. Birks.
22. b. L. F. Benson, H. S. Oakeley.
23. b. John Burton; d. John Day.
24. b. A. H. Brown, William Gaskell, John Newton; d. W. L. Viner.
25. b. Albert Knapp; d. John Fawcett, J. F. Lampe.
26.
27. b. F. H. Barthélémon; d. William Hayes.
28. d. J. S. Bach.
29. 571; d. Mary Peters.

30. b. William Jones, J. C. Shairp; d. M. F. Maude.
31. d. J. W. Alexander, Horatius Bonar.

AUGUST

1. b. Karl J. P. Spitta; d. L. Hensley.
2.
3.
4. 611.
5. d. W. H. Callcott, E. E. S. Elliott, R. L. de Pearsall.
6. b. E. H. Plumptre, Tennyson; d. J. M. Neale, G. F. Root.
7. 549; b. F. W. Farrar; Melchior Vulpius (buried).
8. b. H. E. Button, Peter Williams.
9. 26; b. C. H. Bateman, Dryden; d. Vincent Novello.
10. b. Mary A. Lathbury, P. Nicolai; d. J. M. Haydn, W. W. How.
11. d. Lowell Mason, J. H. Newman, Toplady.
12. b. Joseph Barnby, F. A. G. Ouseley; d. William Blake, Nahum Tate.
13. b. John Ireland; d. S. F. Adams, Robert Cooke, Ira D. Sankey.
14. b. S. S. Wesley; d. S. F. Adams, William Croft, Hugh Wilson.
15. b. P. Armes, Matthias Claudius, J. H. Gurney, Sir Walter Scott.
16. b. E. S. Alderson, John Farmer.
17. b. George Croly.
18. d. E. Neumeister.
19. b. Jemima Luke.
20. d. A. Galloway, Richard Wainwright.
21. b. Heber, A. R. Reinagle; d. Thomas Darling, W. Mercer.
22. b. John Armstrong, W. H. Cummings, E. Silas; d. Robert Cooke.
23. 10; b. G. R. Prynne; d. William Shrubsole (369); William Croft (buried).
24. d. L. Bourgeois, M. Wise.
25. 725; d. F. M. Knollis, G. A. Löhr.
26. 39; b. W. C. Plunket.
27.
28. 182, 641; b. W. H. Bathurst, W. M. Hutchings, W. C. Macfarren, H. B. McKeever, I. D. Sankey; d. F. Silcher, George Matheson.
29. b. Oliver Wendell Holmes, Samuel Smith; d. Mary Peters; John Chetham (buried).
30. b. G. F. Root.
31. b. John Adcock, Lewis Hartsough; d. T. J. Potter.

SEPTEMBER.

1. d. James Watson.
2.
3.
4. 240, 286; b. Edwin Hatch; William Weale (buried).
5. b. F. Oakeley.
6. b. Vincent Novello, H. Walford Davies.
7. b. Bogatzky; d. Whittier.
8. d. H. S. Oswald.
9. b. H. J. Buckoll; d. W. C. Dix.
10. b. J. Edmeston, Ralph Harrison; d. C. C. S. Scholefield.
11. b. G. C. Martin, Anne Shepherd.
12. b. R. F. Dale, George Duffield; d. C. E. May, Edward Miller.
13. b. Catherine Winkworth; d. Godfrey Thring.

14. b. J. M. Haydn, R. F. Littledale; d. Jane Crewdson, J. Ambrose Lloyd.
15. d. C. E. Oakley.
16. 'Newcastle' written (see on 36); 167.
17. 526; b. Josiah Conder.
18. 599; b. C. Burke; d. H. L. Jenner, George Macdonald, J. C. Shairp.
19. b. Charles Vincent; d. W. D. Maclagan, S. M. Waring.
20. 259; d. W. C. Smith.
21. b. H. A. Crosbie, D. Emlyn Evans, Gustav Holst; d. Sir Walter Scott.
22. d. Charlotte Elliott.
23. b. Jane Taylor; d. Alice Flowerdew.
24. d. Dean Milman.
25. b. E. F. Bevan.
26. b. T. L. Hately, H. D. Rawnsley; d. John Byrom, F. W. Faber, E. F. Rimbault, W. Knapp (buried).
27. b. Robert Robinson.
28. b. W. H. Callcott, H. D. Rawnsley; d. Karl J. P. Spitta.
29. 590; b. J. G. Schicht.
30. b. J. H. Knecht, C. Villiers Stanford.

OCTOBER

1. d. Neil Dougall.
2. b. Edward Denny, A. W. Chatfield; d. Oswald Allen.
3. d. S. Longfellow.
4. b. Harriet Auber, D. F. Gurney; d. Henry Carey, St. Francis of Assisi.
5. b. J. A. Symonds.
6. b. R. Robinson, W. Russell; d. Heinrich Albert, J. Ernest Bode, M. Bridges, Stephen Elvey, F. K. L. Scholinus, Tennyson.
7. 115; b. Dean Alford, C. C. Converse, F. S. Pierpoint, F. Southgate; d. Oliver Wendell Holmes, C. H. H. Parry, G. J. Webb.
8. 686; d. Hugh Stowell, R. Whateley.
9.
10. b. Samuel Johnson.
11. 504; b. T. O. Summers; d. Samuel Wesley.
12. b. A. R. Greenaway, R. Vaughan Williams; d. C. F. Alexander, Edward Miller.
13. 519, 525.
14. b. W. R. Broomfield, R. F. Littledale.
15. 535; b. Thomas Hastings.
16. 504; b. Samuel Wesley; d. W. R. Broomfield.
17. b. John Bowring.
18. b. Charles E. Mudie.
19. b. J. W. Chadwick, S. Rodigast; d. H. Kirke White.
20. b. Thomas Hughes, H. C. Shuttleworth, J. S. Tyler.
21. b. Joseph Mainzer, Samuel F. Smith; d. Henry Lawes.
22. 375; b. E. H. Miller, Katharina von Schlegel; d. L. Spohr.
23. b. I. B. Woodbury.
24. b. E. Paxton Hood; d. H. C. Shuttleworth, J. R. Woodford.
25. b. M. F. Maude.
26. b. Henry Smart; d. Philip Doddridge, P. Nicolai, H. S. Oakeley, I. B. Woodbury.
27. b. William Canton.

28. b. D. S. Bortnianski; d. Charles E. Mudie.
29.
30. b. W. J. Mathams, A. A. Procter, C. Wordsworth; d. E. A. Dayman, Robert Walmsley.
31. d. G. A. Macfarren.

NOVEMBER.

1. b. W. Whiting.
2. d. Richard Mant, C. Urhan.
3. b. W. C. Bryant; d. Julia A. Elliott.
4. b. T. R. Matthews, Montgomery, Robert Simpson, Toplady; d. R. Harrison, Mendelssohn.
5. b. T. S. Dupuis; d. R. H. Robinson.
6. 217; b. J. P. Hopps, B. H. Kennedy.
7. d. J. Cawood.
8. d. Milton.
9.
10. b. J. Langran, Martin Luther; d. Edwin Hatch, Joseph Mainzer.
11. d. Thomas Jackson.
12. b. Richard Baxter, H. F. Hemy, Ray Palmer, J. C. Simpson.
13. d. A. H. Clough, E. Mote.
14. b. Stopford A. Brooke, F. M. Knollis, Geoffrey T. Shaw.
15. b. Cowper, W. Horsley; d. William Bruce, Jane M. Campbell.
16. b. R. A. Smith; d. W. Gardiner.
17. 414; b. J. Lamb; d. W. Cameron.
18. b. J. N. Darby; d. J. C. Clifton, A. T. Russell.
19. d. S. J. Stone.
20. b. F. H. Himmel; d. Lyte, M. Greiter.
21. b. William Shrubsole (369); d. G. M. Giornovichi, W. Russell.
22. 211; d. John Bowring, Arthur S. Sullivan, Richard Woodward.
23. 113; b. Thomas Attwood; d. J. Cummins, T. Tallis.
24. d. George Croly, J. H. Schein.
25. 292; b. Tersteegen; d. W. H. Bathurst, R. Lowry, Isaac Watts, S. Webbe, junr.
26. b. Cowper; d. Henrietta Dobree.
27. b. Andrew Reed; d. J. Drummond Burns.
28. d. William Blake, J. E. Rankin.
29. b. M. B. Foster.
30. b. John Cosin; d. Richard Farrant, Jennette Threlfall, Andrew Young.

DECEMBER

1. d. Jeremiah Clark, J. H. Knecht, C. E. Willing.
2. 157; b. J. A. Freylinghausen, Hugh Wilson (baptized).
3. b. W. Hurst, Hugh Stowell; d. Xavier.
4. 351; b. Carlyle, Thomas Cotterill; d. Drummond of Hawthornden, John of Damascus, Joseph Mohr.
5. b. C. G. Rossetti, N. Selnecker, W. C. Smith.
6. b. Dora Greenwell; d. William Felton.
7. b. Thomas Williams; d. C. M. Noel, St. Ambrose.
8. b. J. Sibelius; d. Richard Baxter, F. Filitz, M. Rinkart.
9. 457; b. Neil Dougall, Milton; d. G. J. Elvey.
10. b. George Macdonald; d. J. Battishill.

O O

11. b. Joseph Mohr, John Thomas, C. Wesley ('Epworth'), J. R. Wreford; d. J. W. Chadwick.
12. b. J. Cennick, Isaac Williams, William Hayes (baptized).
13. b. A. H. Charteris, Drummond of Hawthornden, W. W. How, E. G. Monk, Dean Stanley; d. C. F. Gellert.
14. b. William Bright, F. R. Havergal, John Richardson.
15. b. S. Besler, H. F. Chorley; d. T. B. Pollock.
16. b. J. Ellerton, C. Kocher, R. P. Stewart; d. Thomas Williams.
17. 149; b. M. Farningham, Whittier; d. F. de Giardini, R. Wardlaw.
18. b. Charles Wesley; d. John Darwall, M. B. Foster.
19. b. Horatius Bonar; d. John Bishop, Robert Hudson.
20. d. Ann Gilbert.
21. b. I. G. Smith, B. Schmolck; d. John Newton.
22. b. W. F. Lloyd, R. Wardlaw, John Bishop (buried).
23.
24. 49, 65; b. J. R. Ahle; d. W. H. Doane.
24–27. 34.
25.
26. d. E. H. Thorne.
27. b. John Goss, W. H. Hadow; d. Josiah Conder.
28. 40; b. J. F. Swift; d. John Logan, A. F. Lvov.
29. b. Charles Wesley, W. G. Alcock, Francis Pott; d. T. Cotterill, W. Crotch, J. Lamb, C. G. Rossetti.
30. b. Rudyard Kipling, William Croft (baptized); d. Philipp Bliss.
31. b. W. O. Cushing, Henry Hiles.

This calendar may be supplemented with a chronological outline, in brief, first of the hymns and then of their music.

I

i. If we take the psalm-versions, the paraphrases, and the canticles as representing the Church down to the first century A. D., the remaining hymns and hymn-writers (so far as they can be dated at all) may be classified as follows by centuries. A century is, no doubt, a rough-and-ready division of time. Still, it is convenient. And this survey will show that almost every century has been drawn upon for contributions to *The Church Hymnary*.

ii. Clement of Alexandria.

iv. St. Ambrose, St. Gregory Nazianzen, Prudentius; 3 (718), 281, 717, 725.

v. St. Patrick, Synesius of Cyrene.

vi. St. Columba, Fortunatus, St. Gregory the Great; 207, 287 (?) 712.

viii. St. John of Damascus, St. Stephen of Mar Saba (?); 84 (?) 258 (260), 727.

ix. Joseph the Hymnographer, Balbulus Notker (?), St. Theodulph of Orleans; 182 (184).

xii. Abélard, St. Bernard of Clairvaux (?), Bernard of Cluny.

xiii. St. Thomas Aquinas, St. Francis of Assisi; 99, 161, 186.

xv. Bianco da Siena, H. von Laufenburg, Jean Tisserand; 45 (?), 89, 164.

xvi. Xavier (?), Petrus Herbert, William Kethe, Martin Luther, John Marckant, Nicolai, F. B. P. (?), N. Selnecker.

xvii. Altenburg, R. Baxter, Bunyan, Clausnitzer, John Cosin, Drummond of Hawthornden, Dryden, Johann Franck, Paul Gerhardt, George

Herbert, Ken, M.A. von Löwenstern, Milton, Joachim Neander, G. Neumark, Quarles, M. Rinkart, S. Rodigast, C. K. von Rosenroth, Johann Scheffler, H. T. Schenck, B. Schmolk, Nahum Tate, Henry Vaughan; 122.

xviii. Addison, Bogatzky, Jacques Bridaine, Simon Browne, Michael Bruce, John Byrom, William Cameron, Cennick, M. Claudius, Coffin, Cowper, Doddridge, John Fawcett, Gellert, Joseph Hart, Thomas Hāweis, John Logan, Martin Madan, Montgomery, John Morison, E. Neumeister, John Newton, T. Olivers, H. S. Oswald, E. Perronet, John Roberts, R. Robinson, K. von Schlegel, W. Shrubsole, Joseph Swain, Tersteegen, Toplady, Watts, the Wesleys, Peter Williams, William Williams, Zinzendorf; 55, 119, 631, &c.

xix and xx. Most of the other hymns and hymn-writers fall within these two centuries.

II

A glance at the critical notes upon the music of the hymns will show that in many cases it is impossible to trace a melody to its original date and source. The Gregorian Tones represent the most ancient music in the book. They were in use in the early centuries of the Christian Church, and are by some believed to have been derived from music used in the Temple at Jerusalem. There is a legend that the *Tonus Peregrinus* was sung by our Lord and His Disciples at the Last Supper. A number of the traditional airs which have passed into the service of the Church, both from sacred and secular sources, come from the Middle Ages; some go back to the fourteenth century, or even earlier. Thus CORDE NATUS seems to be not later than the thirteenth century. *Christ ist erstanden* belongs to that century. *Agincourt Song* is of the fifteenth. But most of the tunes may be provisionally, if approximately, assigned to five centuries, to the sixteenth, when the revival of religion took place in Europe, to the seventeenth, to the eighteenth—Frederic Harrison declared that 'music is the art of the eighteenth century, the art in which it stands supreme in the ages'—, to the nineteenth, and to the twentieth. The following classification is not complete, but it will serve to indicate the proportions of the contribution made by each of these centuries to *The Church Hymnary* upon the musical side.

xvi. The *Anglo-Genevan Psalter*, S. Besler, L. Bourgeois, W. Byrd, T. Campion, *Damon's Psalmes*, John Dowland, *The English Psalter*, *Este's Psalter*, Farrant, *The French Psalter*, the *Geistliche Lieder*, M. Greiter, H. L. Hassler, H. Isaak, Martin Luther, Merbecke, Philipp Nicolai, Palestrina, Tallis, Christopher Tye, M. Vulpius: the tunes mentioned on Hymn 4, MISERERE MEI, MORAVIA, NUN FREUT EUCH, NUN KOMM, O MENSCH SIEH, PRAETORIUS, RAVENSHAW, *The Scottish Psalter*, SOLDAU, WER DA WONET.

xvii. Ahle, Albert, Jeremiah Clark, William Croft, Johann Crüger, Adam Drese, J. Ebeling, J. W. Franck, Gastorius, Orlando Gibbons, *Heilige Seelenlust*, Martin Herbst, J. Hintze, G. Joseph, G. Kirbye, J. D. Mejer, Joachim Neander, G. Neumark, R. Ramsey, Thomas Ravenscroft, Benjamin Rogers, J. H. Schein, Schop, Melchior Teschner, Michael Wise, C. F. Witt: tunes like ACH GOTT UND HERR, ALL SAINTS, ANDERNACH, BRESLAU, COLESHILL, CRASSELIUS, HERR JESU CHRIST, JESU DULCIS MEMORIA, LASST UNS ERFREUEN, LIEBSTER IMMANUEL, LOBE DEN HERRN, MUNICH, NARENZA, NOMEN DOMINI, OMNI DIE, ST. MARY, TRES MAGI DE GENTIBUS, WAS GOTT THUT, ZURICH.

A Calendar of the Hymnary

xviii. John Alcock, J. S. Bach, F. H. Barthélémon, J. Battishill, John Bishop, Bortnianski, William Boyce, Henry Carey, Robert Cooke, Raphael Courteville, W. Crotch, John Darwall, J. F. Doles, H. Duncalf, T. S. Dupuis, W. Felton, *Freylinghausen's Gesangbuch*, F. de Giardini, G. M. Giornovichi, Grigg, Handel, R. Harrison, J. Hatton, T. Haweis, F. J. Haydn, J. M. Haydn, W. Hayes, S. Howard, R. Hudson, T. Jackson, W. Jones, W. Knapp, J. H. Knecht, J. F. Lampe, H. Lawes, C. Lockhart, B. Milgrove, E. Miller, J. Nares, J. Randall, J. Robinson, Rousseau, W. Russell, J. G. Schicht, Scholinus, J. A. P. Schultz, W. Shrubsole, I. Smith, S. Stanley, D. Vetter, J. Wainwright, R. Wainwright, W. Weale, S. Webbe, S. Webbe, junr., G. P. Weimar, C. Wesley, Samuel Wesley, R. Woodward: with tunes like AMOR DEI, BANGOR, BROMSGROVE, BURFORD, CASSEL, CASTLEFORD, CORINTH, CROWLE, DAVID'S HARP, EASTER HYMN, FOLKINGHAM, FRANCONIA, GLASGOW, HAMPTON, HELMSLEY, HURSLEY (PASCAL), IRISH, MARTYRDOM, PLAISTOW, STUTTGART, SWABIA, TIVERTON, TRURO.

xix and xx. Most of the other hymn tunes and composers fall within these two centuries.

INDEX I. THE FIRST LINES OF HYMNS IN OTHER LANGUAGES

The numbers in this index are the numbers of the hymns.

Index I. First Lines of Hymns in other Languages

INDEX II. SCRIPTURE TEXTS

Sometimes, where the reference is only to a passage of the hymn, this is noted as follows; e.g. '626.3' means that the Scripture text, opposite to which these figures are printed, is echoed in the third verse of Hymn 626.

567

Index II. Scripture Texts

INDEX III. SUBJECTS

Christ, Friendship of 145, 147, 174, 416, 463, 486, 489, 544, 593, 605, 667, 701, 705.

—, Humanity of 67, 69, 71–7, 79, 87, 101–2, 140, 144, 146–7, 200, 277, 304–5, 309, 329, 360.

—, Humiliation of 67, 69, 72–3, 75–7, 79, 94–114, 147, 178, 478.

—, Incarnation of (v. Incarnation).

—, Life and example of 67–93, 141, 478, 510, 513–14, 528, 549, 659, 662, 694.

—, Love of 87, 102, 106, 136, 141, 143–6, 148, 154, 359, 396–7, 406, 410–12, 414, 416–17, 422, 424–30, 432–7, 463, 479, 496, 581, 660, 682–3, 685, 691–2.

— Man of Sorrows 693

—, Praise of 32, 60, 62, 70–1, 74, 77, 91, 93, 107–9, 116, 119, 133, 136, 139, 154, 164–79, 281, 379, 388, 419–23, 430, 435, 476, 535, 574, 587, 594, 598, 692–3.

—, Priesthood of 132, 140, 157, 165, 217, 315.

—, Resurrection of 115–27, 237, 266, 268, 481.

—, Saving power of 680–707, and references at 707.

—, Seven words from the Cross 97–103.

—, Stilling the tempest 83–4, 396, 625–6, 706.

—, Sufferings and death of (v. Lord's Supper) 32, 73, 94–114, 329, 413, 433, 690, 692, 698.

—, Sympathy and intercession of 86, 97, 102, 140–8, 277, 315, 329, 352, 410, 556, 701.

—, Temptation of 79.

—, The Good Physician 86, 141, 277, 352–3.

—, Transfiguration of 88–9.

—, Victory of (v. Christ, Resurrection of; Ascension and Exaltation of; Coming in power) 73, 108, 179, 372, 384–5, 388–9, 519, 532, 535.

Christmas (v. Christ, Birth of).

Church, The 198, 205–27, 635.

—, Dedication of a 254.

—, Laying foundation-stone of a 253.

Church Militant 216, 217, 385, 526, 530, 533–5.

— Overseas, The 642.

— Triumphant 218–24, 227.

— Unity of, The 205, 209, 213–15.

— Workers (v. Service of the Kingdom, Missions).

Close of Worship 295–303, 624.

Colonies, The 642.

Comfort in bereavement (v. Bereavement, Comfort in).

Coming of the Kingdom (v. Kingdom, Coming of).

Commandments, The Ten 720.

— of Christ 721.

Commemoration 676.

Communion, The (v. Lord's Supper).

Communion, First (v. Consecration and Discipleship) 241, 492, 606, 673.

— of Saints 39, 205–27, 237, 493.

Condescension, The divine 20, 316, 406, 436, 550.

Confession (v. Penitence).

— of Christ 505–7.

Confidence (v. Trust).

Conflict and Victory (v. Soldiers of Christ) 79, 403, 523–38.

Consecration and Discipleship 63, 87, 90, 106, 156, 241–2, 245, 492, 494–522, 606, 647, 673.

— of Children (v. Baptism) 494–5, 497.

Courage 212, 217, 490, 501, 517, 520, 527, 529, 533, 537, 574, 576.

Creation (v. Nature).

Creeds 724–5.

Cross (v. Christ, Sufferings and Death of) 90, 131, 160, 179, 272, 274, 313–14, 381–3, 385, 413, 424, 451, 492, 503, 535, 551, 577, 598, 606, 628, 642, 645, 683, 690–1, 696.

—, The Christian's 90, 304, 475, 501–2, 530, 537, 556, 606.

DAILY Work 242, 259, 287, 302, 357, 493, 648, 651.

Day, The Lord's 237–8, 266–9, 289–90.

Death 84, 107, 120–1, 125, 137, 147, 282, 284–6, 291–4, 328–32,

413, 415, 438, 440, 549, 556, 558, 564, 570, 572–3, 582–600, 607, 622.

Death and Resurrection 137, 218–27, 286, 328–32, 582, 585–600, 622.

Dedication of a Church 239, 246, 247, 254.

— of Church Workers 335–9.

— of an Organ 16, 252.

Departed, The 39, 218–27, 321, 328–32, 587, 590–600, 602–3.

Dies Irae 161.

Discipleship (v. Consecration and Discipleship).

Dismission 295–303, 624.

Doxologies 7, 29³, 34–5, 116⁶, 126³, 179⁴, 207⁴, 228, 252⁴, 708–13.

EASTER 115–27, 237, 481.

Everlasting Life 137, 218–27, 284, 328, 330–2, 480, 582–4, 587–600.

Evening Hymn, Child's 288, 294, 654.

— Worship 4, 127, 271–94, 301–2.

Exaltation (v. Christ, Ascension and Exaltation of).

FACING the World 672.

Faith (v. Trust; Penitence and Faith) 72, 112, 137, 142, 213, 251, 261, 398, 418, 455, 472, 474, 502, 520, 536–7, 546–7, 567, 580, 592, 702.

Family Life 648–50.

Farewell 624.

Fatherland (v. National Hymns).

Flowers 17–20, 347, 543, 609–10, 618.

Flower Service 347.

Following Christ 90, 176, 245, 500–2, 510, 513–15, 521, 530–1, 567–9, 574–5, 591, 668.

Forgiveness (v. The Gospel Call) 5, 97, 104, 240, 245, 283, 291, 302, 342, 407, 409, 411, 415, 476, 563, 589, 684, 695.

Foundation-stone, Laying the 253.

Friend, The Children's 593, 667.

GLORIA in excelsis 717.

Gospel Call, The 390–8, 410, 684, 686, 689.

Gospel Story, The 71, 77, 107, 163, 370–1, 375, 682–3.

Grace before meat 656.

Gratitude to God (v. Love and Gratitude: Mercies, Praise for) 6, 9, 11, 17–19, 21–3, 26, 28–9, 32, 170, 299, 345, 441, 603–5, 607, 614–20, 634, 642, 649, 655, 676.

Guidance 26, 29, 30, 227, 273, 414–15, 541, 546, 548, 553–4, 556–7, 562–70, 590, 603–4, 666, 668–9, 695.

Guild Hymn 521.

HARVEST 494, 614–20.

Heaven 68, 137, 218–27, 286, 328, 330–2, 463, 480, 578–600, 602, 605, 609–10, 616, 648, 650, 654, 660–1, 665–6, 669.

Help 455, 460, 487, 492–3, 604, 643, 704.

Holiness (v. The Holy Spirit) 36, 319, 334, 457–9, 461, 465, 467–9, 471–2, 478–82, 490, 513, 604, 663.

—, God's 1–3, 36, 713.

Holy Scriptures 196–204.

— Spirit, The 180–96, 203, 244, 248, 305, 333, 336, 377, 386, 405, 457, 484, 589, 608, 673.

Home 326, 440, 623, 648–50.

— and School 648–78.

Hospital 3, 351–3.

Humility 76, 106, 191, 316, 406, 467, 478.

IMITATION of Christ (v. Following Christ) 69–71, 75–6, 80, 85, 87–8, 90, 662.

Incarnation (v. Christ, Life and Example of) 40–66, 657.

Infirmaries 351–3.

Intercession 276, 302, 320, 342, 347, 355, 374, 452, 626–33, 650, 657, 659.

International 632, 639, 645–6.

JACOB wrestling 416.

Jerusalem, The heavenly 224, 583, 595–9.

Joy (v. Peace and Joy) 41, 58, 123, 131, 135, 149, 166, 193, 324,

INDEX IV. TUNES

Where the name of a tune appears in alphabetical order in brackets, the tune is indexed elsewhere under another name.

INDEX V. FIRST LINES OF HYMNS

Brackets indicate that the first line in some collections begins thus.

PRINTED IN ENGLAND AT THE
UNIVERSITY PRESS, OXFORD
BY JOHN JOHNSON
PRINTER TO THE UNIVERSITY

HANDBOOK TO
THE CHURCH HYMNARY
SUPPLEMENT

HANDBOOK TO
THE CHURCH HYMNARY
SUPPLEMENT

EDITED BY

The Rev. MILLAR PATRICK
D.D.

OXFORD UNIVERSITY PRESS
LONDON : HUMPHREY MILFORD
1935

OXFORD
UNIVERSITY PRESS
AMEN HOUSE, E.C. 4
London Edinburgh Glasgow
New York Toronto Melbourne
Capetown Bombay Calcutta
Madras Shanghai
HUMPHREY MILFORD
PUBLISHER TO THE
UNIVERSITY

PRINTED IN GREAT BRITAIN

CONTENTS

PRINCIPAL AUTHORITIES CONSULTED
(Additional)

Nelle, Wilhelm, *Schlüssel zum Evangelischen Gesangbuch für Rheinland und Westfalen* (1924).

Raby, F. J. E., *A History of Christian-Latin Poetry from the beginning to the close of the Middle Ages* (1927).

Jones, J. Edmund, *The Book of Common Praise* (Canada), *Annotated Edition* (1909).

Dearmer, Percy, and Jacob, Archibald, *Songs of Praise Discussed* (1933).

Lightwood, James T., *The Music of the Methodist Hymn Book* (1935).

PREFACE

THE publication of the *Handbook* was hastened in 1927 in order that it might synchronize with the appearance of *The Revised Church Hymnary*. Its value, its sponsors felt, would to some extent depend upon its being available at once upon the publication of the book on which it was a commentary. A price had to be paid, however, for the advantages of this immediacy of issue: there was no opportunity for a final deliberate and comprehensive survey of the material, with a view to eliminating errors and supplying deficiencies.

The *errata*, considering the large amount of historical detail involved, have been found to be extraordinarily few; but it is right that they should be corrected. Omissions have been more numerous, and though none of them is serious, it is desirable that they should be made good. Additional material has been gathering also in the intervening years. It has been thought worth while, therefore, to issue a Supplement to the *Handbook*, presenting all the *corrigenda* and *addenda* that have been found to be required.

It has been deemed opportune, at the same time, to offer annotations, similar to those on the hymn-tunes, on those tunes in *The Scottish Psalter 1929, Metrical Version*, which were not included in the *Hymnary*. To have dealt in the same way with the chants in the *Prose Version* would have demanded an amount of research out of all proportion to any value or even interest in the result, and it has not been thought necessary to attempt such a task. Biographical notes, however, on the composers represented in both versions who have not already received attention in the *Handbook*, have been thought likely to prove welcome.

The preparation of all this material fell naturally to the present editor. It was on his initiative that the *Handbook* was undertaken; he was chairman of the group of collaborators who assembled the material; and in the end the editorship itself devolved on him when Dr. Moffatt, called to New York, was obliged to relinquish an uncompleted task.

Preface

Various obligations must gratefully be expressed: to the late James Love's *Scottish Church Music*, the pioneer book of this kind; to the work of the late William Cowan, that admirable scholar, whose invincible modesty and inflexible austerity of style concealed an accomplishment, in the field of the music of psalmody and hymnody, as wide in its range as it was unassailable in its accuracy; to Miss Anne G. Gilchrist, learned alike in folk-song and in the history of church tunes, for a number of interesting identifications of sources and for other invaluable assistance; to Mr. James T. Lightwood, editor of *The Choir* and author of *Hymn Tunes and their Story*, for much friendly suggestion; to Mr. Humphrey Milford, of the Oxford University Press, who, having received willing permission for Canon Dearmer to draw *ad libitum* upon the contents of the *Handbook* for *Songs of Praise Discussed* (1933), has reciprocated the courtesy by allowing the use of such extracts from the latter book as are useful for the present purpose; to Miss Helen Waddell, the Rev. F. Luke Wiseman, Sir Richard Terry, Mr. J. A. Fuller-Maitland, for permission to use the quotations which are specifically acknowledged in their places; to *The Musical Times*, *The Choir*, and the other sources of help detailed in the *Handbook*; to Professor R. A. S. Macalister; and, last but not least, to the Rev. William T. Cairns, D.D., for placing his numerous notes at the editor's disposal, and for unfailing encouragement and help.

EDINBURGH,
May, 1935.

SUPPLEMENTARY NOTES ON HYMNS AND TUNES

INTRODUCTIONS.—To the Third Introduction (The Story of the Revision) the initials M.P.—W.T.C. should be appended.

10 THE SPACIOUS FIRMAMENT ON HIGH

Thackeray's comment on this hymn, in the lecture on Congreve and Addison in *The English Humourists*, deserves quotation: 'When this man looks from the world, whose weaknesses he describes so benevolently, up to the Heaven which shines over us all, I can hardly fancy a human face lighted up with a more serene rapture: a human intellect thrilling with a purer love and adoration than Joseph Addison's. Listen to him: from your childhood you have known the verses: but who can hear their sacred music without love and awe? . . . It seems to me those verses shine like the stars. They shine out of a great deep calm. When he turns to Heaven, a Sabbath comes over that man's mind: and his face lights up from it with a glory of thanks and prayer.'

The tune FIRMAMENT is one of four tunes composed by Sir Walford Davies for the London Church Choir Association for their Festival in St. Paul's in 1908.

11 LET US WITH A GLADSOME MIND

In the Countess of Huntingdon's chapel at Bath, for which Milgrove wrote HARTS, the men and women sat apart on different sides of the building. This facilitated the carrying out of the anti-phonal arrangement of the second part of the tune (see the *Hand-book* note) and the instruction given with it: 'The Men that sing the Air must rest where 'tis written the Women to sing this part alone, and begin where the word Altogether is written.'

MELLING in its original form, as set to 'Children of the heavenly King', has the first three lines exactly as in the *Hymnary*, but then proceeds as follows, line 4 being repeated:

12 IMMORTAL, INVISIBLE, GOD ONLY WISE

This hymn had been published seventeen years before it was set to music. The credit of being the first to introduce it into church use belongs to W. Garrett Horder, who included it in his *Congregational Hymns* in 1884.

The tune JOANNA, known also as ST. DENIO, though it has been ascribed to John Roberts of Henllan, is a Welsh traditional secular melody, belonging to a song about the cuckoo, 'Y Gog Lwydlas,' or 'Y Gwcw', and another, 'Can Mlynedd i 'Nawr' (A hundred years from now). The tune has many relatives in English folk-song, one of which is also called 'The Cuckoo'. The *Welsh Folk-Song Journal* prints an early form which appears in the Jenkins Keri MSS. (written about the end of the eighteenth or beginning of the nineteenth century) as 'Rowlands' or 'Can Mlynedd i 'Nawr':

See the *Welsh Folk-Song Journal*, vol. i, pt. iii (1911), pp. 125-8, for variants and notes.

JOANNA as a hymn-tune, first printed as such in 1839, used to be sung, like 'Crug-y-bar' (H. 596), in this form, lengthening the second beat of the bar thus:

(See *Canadiau y Cyssegr*, Denbigh, 1878.)

This apparently syncopated form is a mannerism which seems to have been due to the singing, in Welsh chapels, of triple-time tunes in very slow time, with a pause on the third note of each short phrase.

13 ALL CREATURES OF OUR GOD AND KING

Ozanam, in *Les Poètes Franciscains*, tells how Francis had spent forty nights in his vigils, and had an ecstasy, at the conclusion of which he desired Brother Leo to take a pen and to write, upon which he chanted the Canticle of the Sun. After he had thus improvised, he charged Brother Pacifico, who in the world had been a poet, to reduce the words into a rhythm more exact, and commanded that the brethren should learn them by heart in order to recite them every day.

The original hymn consisted of verses 1 to 4. Verse 5 was occasioned by a quarrel between the Bishop of Assisi and the magistrates. 'The bishop', says Ozanam, 'had put the town under an interdict, and the magistrates in their turn had outlawed the bishop and forbidden all intercourse with him and his.' Francis was deeply affected by this quarrel; and finding that nobody stepped in to interfere, he himself took up his newly-found weapon. He added another verse to the canticle, and 'commanded his disciples to go boldly and seek the great people of the town, and beg them to meet at the bishop's palace.' The name of Francis was so potent that the surprised and reluctant burghers obeyed, not knowing what communication might be about to be made to them. . . . But when the song, with its new verse, fell on their ears, their hearts smote them. 'At the sound of these words, to which God seemed to have lent a gentle strength, the adversaries repented and embraced, and asked each other's pardon.'

Another verse was added to the song a little later, when Francis, weak and suffering, worn out by his great labours and suffering from many bodily afflictions, his eyes so worn that he could scarcely see, his strength reduced by perpetual attacks of fever, after a temporary rally, had a vision from which he learned that in two years his sufferings should be over, and he should enter into eternal rest. Then once more in the joy of his heart he sent for Brother Leo, and added to the song . . . the following and final verse: 'Praised be my Lord by our sister the death of the body' (verses 6 and 7 in Dr. Draper's paraphrase).

'The poem of St. Francis', says Ozanam, 'is very short, and yet all his soul is to be found there—his fraternal friendship for the creatures, the charity which impels a man so humble and gentle to interfere in public quarrels, and that infinite love which, after having sought God in Nature, and served Him in the person of suffering humanity, desires nothing more than to find Him in death. . . . It is nothing but a cry; but it is the cry of a new-born poetry, destined to grow and make itself heard through the whole earth.'

Mrs. Oliphant, from whose *Francis of Assisi* these passages are taken, remarks that 'these quaint and unskilled rhymes' (of the *Cantico del Sole* or *Cantico delle Creature*) 'were the first beginning of vernacular poetry in Italy. . . . It was the faltering tones of the first essay, the hesitating, broken speech of a beginner who is doubtful how far his words will serve him or whether the language is equal to the call he is making upon it.'

Dr. Draper's paraphrase was written for a school-children's Whitsuntide Festival at Leeds, he being then rector of Adel, a few miles away; the precise year is forgotten.

15 LET ALL THE WORLD IN EVERY CORNER SING

Herbert did not write his hymns for congregational singing. Even this one was meant for reading. Yet the fact that he entitled it 'Antiphon' shows that he felt that it ought to be sung; he intended a chorus to sing, 'Let all the world in every corner sing, My God and King!'

17 FOR THE BEAUTY OF THE EARTH

Much objection has been taken to the phrase 'Christ, our God' in the refrain. In some hymn-books it is altered to 'Father, unto Thee'. Mr. Pierpoint answered a correspondent who raised this objection, thus: 'Pliny in his letter to the Emperor said that Christians, when meeting for worship, sang a hymn to Christ as God. As the only public service of the Church was the daily Eucharist, I addressed my hymn to "Christ, our God".'

20 GOD, WHO MADE THE EARTH

First printed in *The Methodist Sunday-School Hymn Book* (1879).

23 SING TO THE LORD A JOYFUL SONG

GONFALON ROYAL was so named because it was written for the hymn 'Vexilla regis prodeunt' ('The royal banners forward go'). A gonfalon is a banner with streamers. Dr. Buck wrote the tune for use in Harrow School, where he was Director of Music.

26 WHEN ALL THY MERCIES, O MY GOD

This hymn comes at the close of an essay on 'Gratitude' in *The Spectator* for August 9, 1712. The subject was congenial to the mind of Addison, of whom Macaulay, in his essay on 'The Life and Writings of Addison', remarks: 'The piety of Addison was of a singularly cheerful character. The feeling which predominates in all his devotional writings is gratitude. . . . On that goodness to which he ascribed all the happiness of his life he relied in the hour of death with the love that casteth out fear.'

Addison, earlier in the essay which the hymn concluded, commented on the curious failure of Christian poets to celebrate adequately the praise of Almighty God. There are few hymns of pure adoration, and every hymn-book shows that the number of great objective hymns to God is very limited. Addison says: 'Most of the works of the pagan poets were either direct hymns to their deities, or tended indirectly to the celebration of their respective attributes and perfections. . . . One would wonder that more of our Christian poets have not turned their thoughts this way, especially if we consider, that our idea of the Supreme Being is not only infinitely more great and noble than what could possibly enter into the heart of an heathen, but filled with everything that can raise the imagination, and give an opportunity for the sublimest thoughts and conceptions.'

31 GOD MOVES IN A MYSTERIOUS WAY

'The tune COLESHILL', says J. A. Fuller-Maitland, 'is nothing more than our English WINDSOR (DUNDEE) translated into the Pentatonic scale.' The musical editor of *Songs of Praise Discussed* says of it: 'It is a magnificent tune, and, in its present version, possibly the greatest of all psalm-tunes.'

Another old form of it is to be found in the MS. psalm-book (1709) of Nicholas Reay, curate of Cumwhitton, near Carlisle, 1711–18. It is there called 'Boulton Tune':

Another traditional variant was used by a 'whole race of sextons' in another Cumberland village to the verse 'Thou turnest man, O Lord, to dust' (from Tate and Brady's Psalm xc. v. 3), sung unaccompanied from the lych-gate to the church:

(See *Transactions*, N.S. xxvi, pp. 334–6, of the Cumberland and Westmorland Antiquarian and Archaeological Society.)

36 ETERNAL LIGHT! ETERNAL LIGHT!

NEWCASTLE was not written by H. K. Morley, but by Henry L. Morley. Mr. Edwin Moss, one of the editors of *The London Tune Book* (1875), for which the tune was written and in which it first appeared, wrote as follows in 1905 to the Rev. Carey Bonner: 'The tune . . . was written by Henry L. Morley at my request. I named it "Newcastle", that being Dr. Binney's birthplace. I knew Mr. Morley by repute as an able musician and an excellent organist. My acquaintance was not a personal one. I have made frequent attempts to obtain information respecting him, but without result. Possibly Mr. Killick Morley (if alive) could help you.' There were thus two Henry Morleys, with different middle names. About neither does much that is definite seem now to be known.

38 SONGS OF PRAISE THE ANGELS SANG

The tune MONKLAND is first found in *Hymn Tunes of the United Brethren* (1824), edited by John Lees, in which the alto and tenor parts are printed on separate staves. Lees was organist of a congregation of the United Brethren (Moravians) at Leominster. This is three miles from Monkland, where John Wilkes was organist, who arranged the tune for the use of Sir Henry Baker, his vicar, in *Hymns Ancient and Modern*, in 1861.

In Lees's book no indication of sources is given, but nearly all his tunes are German chorales. The supposition that MONKLAND might have been derived from a chorale also was confirmed by Dr. W. H. Grattan Flood, who found the source of it in J. A. Freylinghausen's *Geistreiches Gesangbuch* (Hamburg, 1704), in the tune 'Fahre fort'. This tune, which Zahn treats of in his monumental *Die Melodien* (p. 4791), is as follows:

It is obvious that this tune, halved, is transmuted into MONKLAND as it is given in Lees's book:

Note should be taken also of the similarity between FAHRE FORT and LÜBECK (Hymn 170), which was composed by Freylinghausen.

44 LITTLE CHILDREN, WAKE AND LISTEN

In *School Worship* (Congregational Union, 1926) this hymn is credited to Samuel Smith (1771–1835), but authority for this has not been obtainable.

CHARTRES is certainly not later than the middle of the fifteenth century. See *Oxford Book of Carols*, p. 189.

45 THE FIRST NOWELL THE ANGEL DID SAY

The tune is believed to have originally been the treble part (above the melody) of a tune by Jeremiah Clark to 'An Hymn for Christmas Day', which is an elaborated form of ST. MAGNUS. See *Folk-Song Journal*, vol. v, pp. 240–2.

46 HARK! THE HERALD ANGELS SING

Charles Wesley wrote:

> Hark, how all the welkin rings,
> 'Glory to the King of kings!'

This is much closer to the words of Scripture: 'And suddenly there was with the angel [the 'herald angel'] a multitude of the heavenly host, praising God.' The 1904 edition of *Hymns Ancient and Modern* restored 'welkin', but the outcry against it was one of the causes of the non-success of that notable edition.

47 IT CAME UPON THE MIDNIGHT CLEAR

Though it appeared in December, 1850, this hymn had been written in the latter part of the previous year, a time of extra-ordinary unrest throughout the world, caused by the aftermath of revolution in France and Germany and of the Chartist movement in Great Britain, and in America the passing of the Fugitive Slave Law, and the great 'forty-niner' gold rush to California. The reflection of these occurrences may be traced in vv. 3–5. The American Civil War followed within ten years.

The first half of NOEL is an old English carol-tune, of which various traditional versions are known, which were sung to 'Righteous Joseph', to 'Dives and Lazarus', and to the Sussex carol:

> A glorious angel from Heaven came
> Unto the Virgin Maid,
> Strange news and tidings of great joy
> The humble Mary had.

52 LOVE CAME DOWN AT CHRISTMAS

First appeared in *Time Flies: a Reading Diary* (1885), where the last line, altered in the last edition, was, 'Love the universal sign.'

53 CHILD IN THE MANGER

Between vv. 1 and 2 the original has:

> Monarchs have tender
> Delicate children,
> Nourished in splendour,
> Proud and gay;
> Death soon shall banish
> Honour and beauty,
> Pleasure shall vanish,
> Forms decay.
>
> *But* the most holy . . .

In the *Hymnary* version this contrast is lost.

54 CHRISTIANS, AWAKE, SALUTE THE HAPPY MORN

Byrom asked his daughter one day what she would like for a Christmas present. She answered, 'Please write me a poem.' When she came down to breakfast on Christmas Day, 1749, she found on her plate a sheet with this hymn on it, headed, 'Christmas Day for Dolly.' The original MS. is preserved in the Chetham Library, Manchester. Considerable changes, all improvements, were made on the first draft by the author before he published the hymn in his *Poems, &c.* 1773.

The form in which the tune is given in John Wainwright's own *Collection* is in two parts, soprano and bass, with the bass figured; but at the words 'Of God Incarnate and the Virgin's Son' the music is in four parts and headed 'Chorus'. This probably accounts for the West Riding custom of repeating the last strain of the tune as a chorus.

55 O COME, ALL YE FAITHFUL

In the Preface (p. x) to *The Hundred Best Latin Hymns* Prof. J. S. Phillimore said: 'It is not impossible that we have in it the remains of a medieval Christmas Sequence from some manuscript that was lost in the ravaging of libraries at the Reformation.' This, however, is conjecture.

58 GOOD CHRISTIAN MEN, REJOICE

A *patois* carol, perhaps of the fourteenth century, from *Carols for Christmastide*, by Rev. Thomas Helmore and Rev. J. M. Neale. In the Preface to the first edition (1853) Neale said: 'It will be sufficient to observe that, scattered over the whole of medieval Europe, there were a certain number of these compositions—the ground-work of words and music being the same; but certain national peculiarities, in the course of ages, finding their way into both. They belong, exclusively, to no one portion of the Western Church—though one carol might be more popular here, and another there. They were generally in Latin—often had a vernacular translation—and were sometimes composed in a *patois* of the two.'

60 OF THE FATHER'S LOVE BEGOTTEN

In an article on Prudentius in *The Church Quarterly Review* for July 1928, Dr. Alex. Nairne, Regius Professor of Divinity, Cambridge, says: 'The fact is that Prudentius is not a writer of hymns. He is called so, for he is popularly known through hymn-books. Extracts were made from his long poems and were put into Latin breviaries. The very ancient Spanish or Mozarabic Breviary has many of these, and sometimes considerable liberties have been taken with the text. These hymns, more or less faithfully representing him, have been made out of Prudentius. But at their best they spoil him. The length, the elbow-room, as of an out-door landscape, are characteristic. What he wrote were poems, to be read—not always aloud—in the study, the garden, on the mountain or by the river; a prayer-book, but a poet's—a book of meditations, not of Church offices.'

63 AS WITH GLADNESS MEN OF OLD

Chatterton Dix wrote this while lying ill, on the Epiphany, *c.* 1858, after reading the Gospel for the day.

64 BRIGHTEST AND BEST OF THE SONS OF THE MORNING

Heber wrote this hymn for the Scots tune 'Wandering Willie'. See Introduction, p. xxix.

65 ANGELS FROM THE REALMS OF GLORY

LLANDINAM appeared under the name ERPINGHAM in *The People's Music Book*, Pt. I, edited by James Turle and Edward Taylor (London, 1848). It was there given anonymously.

68 THERE CAME A LITTLE CHILD TO EARTH

'My simple little CHILDREN'S SONG was expressly written for the Earl (afterwards Marquess) of Aberdeen, for his children to sing on Christmas morning, 1890.' (Note by Mr. Walton in *The Book of Common Praise* of the Episcopal Church of Canada.)

70 COME, PRAISE YOUR LORD AND SAVIOUR

A version of GOSTERWOOD noted by the late Dr. Clague in the Isle of Man as a 'carval' (ballad-carol) tune is printed in W. H. Gill's *Manx National Music*, p. 87. It was also sung to the early Primitive Methodist hymn, 'Come, all ye weary travellers,' and appears as late as *c.* 1895 in the P.M. *Mission Hymnal* to 'Gospel News'. It seems to have been an old tune to which 'When the stormy winds do blow' was sung.

74 O SING A SONG OF BETHLEHEM

The melody named KINGSFOLD is a widely spread folk-tune whose proper name seems to be 'Come all you worthy Christians', from the old ballad-carol beginning thus, to which it used to be sung. The particular version called KINGSFOLD by Dr. Vaughan Williams is based on the variant noted by A. J. Hipkins in Westminster, without words, but under the name of 'Lazarus'. The 'Dives and Lazarus' carol with which it was associated is printed with Mr. Hipkins' tune in *English County Songs* (1893) edited by Miss Lucy E. Broadwood and J. A. Fuller Maitland, from which it was reproduced in *The English Hymnal* and *The Church Hymnary*, but the tune has been used also by folk-singers for other ballads of a tragic or melancholy cast. For various other versions and references see

The Folk-Song Journal, vol. ii, pp. 115–23, under the heading 'Come, all ye faithful Christians'. Dr. Vaughan Williams found one of the versions he noted at Kingsfold, Surrey, whence his name for the tune; but there is no doubt that the carol is earlier than 'Maria Martin', the Kingsfold ballad. Miss Broadwood traces a likeness between this air and the tune of the old Scottish ballad 'Gilderoy'.

76 BEHOLD A LITTLE CHILD

LOVE UNKNOWN was contributed by John Ireland to *The Public School Hymn Book* (1919).

WESLEY is founded on the undernoted melody, named 'David' in *The Wesleyan Sunday School Tune Book* (1858), where it is said to be by Handel. Apparently it was adapted from an air in Handel's opera *Sosarme*.

81 GOD WHO HATH MADE THE DAISIES

The carol-melody of ES IST EIN ROS' ENTSPRUNGEN is believed to have belonged to an older Christmas or Twelfth Night carol, used in the diocese of Trier or Trèves, the ancient Augusta Trevirorum, which claims to be the oldest town in Germany. The title ('A rose has bloomed') uses the image of a rose come forth from 'the stem of Jesse', and applies it to Mary the mother of the child.

The melody in its proper form has a tune of seven lines, and is as follows:

84 FIERCE WAS THE WILD BILLOW

'Congregations used to be puzzled by the "wail of Euroclydon" in verse 2. Who was Euroclydon? Only a learned blunder of Neale's. St. Mark does not make the mistake of calling the fierce local squalls on the lake of Galilee by this name. The "euroclydon" or "euraquilo" is indeed mentioned in Acts xxvii. 14; but it was a north-east wind from the mountains of Crete. "Euros" is the south-east wind, and "aquilo" the north wind, so that "euraquilo" was probably a sailor's name for a local "tempestuous wind" such as buffeted the ship of St. Paul off Cape Matala.'—*Songs of Praise Discussed*.

91 ALL GLORY, LAUD, AND HONOUR.

The legend that Louis the Pious, on Palm Sunday, 821, hearing Theodulph sing the original of this hymn at the window of his prison at Angers, released the bishop, restored him to his see, and ordained that thenceforth the hymn was always to be sung in processions on Palm Sunday, cannot possibly be true, since Louis was never in Angers after 818, and Theodulph almost certainly never had his see restored. Yet it is a fact that soon after the good bishop's time the hymn came into use in the Palm Sunday procession in France and England. According to the Sarum use the first four verses were to be sung before leaving the church by seven boys in a high place near the south door. In the use of York a temporary gallery was provided over the door of the church from which the boys of the choir sang the first four stanzas. After each of the first three stanzas the rest of the choir, kneeling below, sang ver. 1 as refrain. At the end of ver. 4 the boys began the refrain and the rest of the choir stood up and sang it with them. In many places the full thirty-nine verses would be none too many for the requirements, for the Hereford use provided that the procession should go to the gates of the city, and, that the gates being shut, seven choir-boys should mount to the top of the gate-house and there sing. The uses of Tours and Rouen also required it to be sung at the gate of the city.

The theory that the tune is an adaptation of the famous sixteenth-century air and dance known as 'Sellinger's Round', though the editor of *The Oxford Hymn Book* (1920) has the courage to advance it as a fact, is fantastic.

A setting of the chorale by Bach will be found in *The Church Anthem Book*.

97 O WORD OF PITY, FOR OUR PARDON PLEADING

The supposition that PSALM 80 might be of Scottish origin is now known to be untenable. The tune is found in the *Piae Cantiones* (1582) (see pp. 458–9 of *Handbook*). It made its appearance in Scotland earlier (1564). But Woodward, in his reprint of the *Piae Cantiones*, says: 'For the earliest form [of this tune] see the Hohenfurth MS. (*Graduale Altovadense* of 1410), as given in *Analecta Hymnica*, I. Anhang, No. ix, p. 92; see Zahn, No. 1576, Meister I, No. 278.' He states also that the *Piae Cantiones* air has been harmonized by fourteen musicians (amongst others) whose names he gives, from Johann Walther in 1524 to J. S. Bach, both in his 371 *Vierstimmige Choral-Gesänge* (No. 30) and in his *Organ Works*;

and that it appears in 1854 in *The Hymnal Noted*, there set to English words beginning 'In our common celebration' (Neale's translation of 'Omnes una celebremus'). 'But to accommodate the tune of "Jesus Christus nostra salus" (as in the *Piae Cantiones*) to words of a different metre, unpardonable liberties were taken with it.'

100 THRONED UPON THE AWFUL TREE

ARFON, though arranged from a Welsh melody, appears to have been derived from a French original; at any rate it is given in R. Guilmant's *Noëls* (1885) as the traditional melody to the carol 'Joseph est bien marié'; and in G. Legeay's *Noëls Anciens* (1875) to 'Un nouveau présent des Cieux', in a slightly simpler form.

The Welsh form appears, according to the Rev. James Mearns, to be taken from a folk-song *Tros y Garreg* (Over the stone), in Edward Jones's *Welsh Bards*, 1794. There seem to be two tunes of this name, 'Meribah' being an alternative title for this one, whose metre is given by W. S. Gwynn Williams (*Welsh National Music and Dance*) as 87.87 Double.

102 O PERFECT LIFE OF LOVE

The subject of the tune SOUTHWELL is identical with that of Tallis's sequence motet 'Absterge, Domine', in the *Cantiones Sacrae* (1578).

106 WHEN I SURVEY THE WONDROUS CROSS

The tune TUNBRIDGE referred to in the note on ROCKINGHAM (COMMUNION) leaves no doubt as to its being the proximate source from which Dr. Miller acknowledged having taken part of his melody; his own copy of the tune exists, with a note in his handwriting, 'would make a good Long M[etre].' See facsimile in *The Musical Times*, May 1909, p. 314.

But TUNBRIDGE appears, fairly clearly, to have been itself derived from some earlier source. The crotchets at the beginning of the bars in the 2nd, 3rd, and 4th lines are palpably split minims, showing that the tune has been adapted to fit the words—'All ye that pass by, To Jesus draw nigh'—to which it is set in the book where it is found, Aaron Williams's *Psalmody in Miniature* (1778 onwards), which Mr. J. T. Lightwood calls a 'minified form' of Williams's *Universal Psalmodist*.

Miss A. G. Gilchrist draws attention to the melody of 'The Bonie Banks of Ayr' in the *Miniature Museum of Scottish Song* (*c*. 1810), as showing in several of its phrases a remarkable resemblance to this tune.

The name ROCKINGHAM was given to the tune by Dr. Miller 'in grateful memory of the Marquis of Rockingham, his kind and zealous patron and honoured lord'. Rockingham was Prime Minister in 1765–6 and 1782; in the latter year he died.

108 SING, MY TONGUE, HOW GLORIOUS BATTLE

The relic of the true Cross referred to in the note on this hymn was set in a gold triptych enriched with enamel and inlaid with precious stones; part of it is still treasured at Poitiers in the present Convent of the Holy Cross. It is described as a small gold panel, covered with a scroll design in cloisonné enamel, and a cruciform cavity in the middle contains the wood.

Miss Helen Waddell says in her *Medieval Latin Lyrics* (pp. 301–2): 'There was no grossness in Fortunatus, and there were times when fire was laid upon his lips. . . . If he loved good cheer, he loved goodness more; and he had as absolute a vision as that older materialist and mystic, of the ladder between earth and heaven.' In her fine book on *The Wandering Scholars* also (p. 26) she says: 'Both "Vexilla Regis" and the other, "Pange lingua gloriosi", are a mystic's Dream of the Rood. It is not as the Latins took it, the symbol and the sign: to Fortunatus, it is still the tree as it grew in the forest, foredoomed to its great and terrible destiny.'

'Fortunatus was the chief representative of literature in Gaul in the sixth century,' says E. L. F. Veitch in *The Church Quarterly Review* for October, 1929. 'The man who wrote "Vexilla Regis" and "Pange lingua" had in him the gift of expression approaching the quality of creation, able to suggest things beyond perception. . . . To Fortunatus the Cross is the *spes unica* of the world, and it is in his poems on the subject and in his hymns that we realize his passionate piety, his Christian mysticism, his capacity for deep religious experience and emotion. . . . His hymns will for ever rank among the most precious possessions of the Church.'

110 AND CAN IT BE, THAT I SHOULD GAIN

F. Luke Wiseman, in his *Charles Wesley, Evangelist and Poet* (p. 76), says of this hymn: 'Note especially the last two verses in which, using the figure of his oft-quoted Galatians passage, he represents himself as "concluded"—that is, shut up, or as we might say, "locked up", for his sin, like the poor denizens of Newgate Jail he so often visited. Weaving in with this the details of the story of Peter in prison on the night before his expected execution, Wesley dramatically describes his own condition in verse—"Long my imprisoned spirit lay".'

The tune to which this hymn is set in the *Collection of Tunes, set to Music, as they are commonly Sung at the Foundery*, issued by John Wesley in 1742, for use in the old state cannon-foundry which Charles Wesley bought in 1739 as the site of the first Methodist meeting-house in London, is LAMBETH or CRUCIFIXION, by S. Akeroyd (published in *The Divine Companion*, 1722). See *The English Hymnal*, 340, and *The Methodist Hymn Book* (1933), 28 in Additional Tunes. A note in the latter book says: 'There is strong reason to believe that this is the tune sung by John Wesley on the night of his conversion, May 24, 1738.'

119 JESUS CHRIST IS RISEN TO-DAY

For another old version of EASTER HYMN, with a different distribution of the words, see *The Musical Times*, April 1904.

122 THE STRIFE IS O'ER, THE BATTLE DONE

Sir Richard Terry, in an essay on 'The Genesis of a Popular Hymn-Tune' in his *On Music's Borders*, offers strong objection to the tune VICTORY being ascribed to Palestrina. It is an adaptation from the *Gloria* of Palestrina's *Magnificat Tertii Toni* (1591), which is as follows:

Sir Richard thus criticizes Monk's treatment of 'this perfectly constructed, beautifully balanced, and delicately poised little gem, first destroying its modal character, secondly destroying its rhythm, and finally mauling its harmonies about, till *only one bar* (the thirteenth) remains as Palestrina wrote it. . . . Even when he does get his chords in the same position as Palestrina's, he alters the value of the notes. And yet "in quires and places where they sing", Doctor Monk's grotesque perversion is still quoted as an example of Palestrina's style.' Upon this Sir Richard not unreasonably pleads that in future VICTORY should bear Monk's name alone.

Probably the earliest English hymn-tune constructed from Palestrina's *Gloria Patri* is the adaptation in *The Parish Choir* (1846–51), where it is set to the hymn 'Come, Holy Ghost, our souls inspire'. As W. H. Monk was the anonymous editor of that collection, this earlier adaptation was doubtless by him also. It bears, as will be seen below, a closer relation than VICTORY to the original:

There is a reminiscence of Palestrina's melody in Dowland's 'Floodis of Teares' in Forbes's Aberdeen *Cantus* (1662). Can some echo of 'Floodis of Teares' have suggested the use of the Scottish 8.6.8.6. form of the tune PALESTRINA for penitential psalms?

123 THE DAY OF RESURRECTION

This is the first of the eight odes of *The Golden Canon* or *Queen of Canons*, by John of Damascus, which is sung in the Eastern Church after midnight on Easter morning, to set forth the fact of the resurrection, its fulfilment of the prophecies, and the benefits it has brought mankind, and to call the people to thanksgiving and praise. In the preface to his *Hymns of the Eastern Church* Neale quotes an eloquent description of a typical service in Athens on Easter morning, at which the canon was sung. The passage is given also in Julian's *Dictionary of Hymnology*, p. 62. The people assemble in the darkened church, with unlighted tapers in their hands, and while the priests chant in a half-whisper, they await the signal that Easter Day has begun. A cannon is fired when the moment comes, and on the instant the Cross is raised with the cry 'Christos anesti, Christ is risen'. The multitude take up the exultant cry, the tapers are lighted, and the dark church is filled with a blaze of light. Outside, drums beat and trumpets sound, and people, meeting, embrace and congratulate one another with beaming faces, repeating the salutation, 'Christ is risen'. In Russia in the old days even the Tsar as he left his palace on Easter morning would kiss the sentry at the gate as he gave him the salutation 'Christ is risen'.

124 O SONS AND DAUGHTERS, LET US SING

The melody O FILII ET FILIAE has been found in seventeenth- as well as eighteenth-century collections, the first so far being *Airs sur les hymnes sacrez, odes et noëls* (Paris, 1673). It is of the second mode, and is probably an adaptation of a French traditional melody.

125 OUR LORD CHRIST HATH RISEN

This hymn was specially written for the Irish *Church Hymnal* in order to make it possible to include the tune there fitted to it.

130 THE GOLDEN GATES ARE LIFTED UP

An earlier form of this hymn, 'The eternal gates lift up their heads', appeared in the S.P.C.K. *Hymns* (1852), and is still in use.

131 THE HEAD THAT ONCE WAS CROWNED WITH THORNS

In line 5 of the note, for *second* read *third* edition: see *The Musical Times*, January 1906.

135 REJOICE, THE LORD IS KING

The story of Handel's tune GOPSAL is interesting. The owner of Covent Garden theatre in the middle of the eighteenth century was John Rich, who invented the pantomime, was himself known as 'the prince of harlequins', and was the producer of *The Beggar's Opera*, of which a popular quip said that 'it made Gay rich and Rich gay'. His wife, herself an actress, was converted under Charles Wesley's preaching, and renounced the stage; when her husband insisted on her returning to it, she declared that she would only go back to bear her testimony against it. Handel taught her daughters, and it was doubtless at her request that he wrote tunes for three of Charles Wesley's hymns, her own favourites probably. The tunes were: GOPSAL, to this hymn; CANNONS (see note on the tune in Notes on Psalter Tunes in this Supplement), originally called 'The Invitation' because of its being written for the hymn 'Sinners, obey the Gospel word'; and FITZWILLIAM, then called 'Desiring to Love', because of its being set to 'O Love Divine, how sweet thou art'. The date of their composition is uncertain, but it must have been between 1749, when two of the hymns first appeared, and 1752, when Handel's eyesight was rapidly failing.

The subsequent fortunes of the tunes are uncertain. They seem to have remained in private possession, for none of them appeared in any of the books for the use of Methodists in the eighteenth century. Nor did any of them appear in print till over seventy years after Handel's death. By a remarkable coincidence they were discovered in 1826, in Handel's autograph, probably on the very slip of paper on which he had written them for Mrs. Rich, by Samuel Wesley, Charles's son, the composer. He had obtained a Grace from the University of Cambridge authorizing him to transcribe and publish any of the valuable musical MSS. in the library of the Fitzwilliam Museum, and there the treasure was found. Samuel described the style of the tunes as 'alike simple, solemn, and easy of execution to all who can sing or play a plain Psalm tune'. He believed that these 'Relicks of Piety' deserved publication, and in January, 1827, they were advertised in *The Wesleyan Methodist Magazine* as follows:

'The FITZWILLIAM MUSIC, never before published: *Three Hymns*: the words by the late Rev. Charles Wesley, A.M., of Christ Church College, Oxford; and set to music by George Frederick Handel, faithfully transcribed from his Autography in the Library of the Fitzwilliam Museum, Cambridge, by Samuel Wesley, and now very respectfully promoted to the Wesleyan Society at large. Price 1s. 6d.'

A photograph of the autograph MS. is given in the annotated edition of *The Book of Common Praise* of the Canadian Episcopal Church, and also in *The Choir* for May, 1930. From articles by Mr. J. T. Lightwood in the March and May numbers of that magazine for 1930, these particulars are taken.

In Whit-week of 1773 a new organ was opened in Walsall Parish Church. The service on the occasion closed with the 148th Psalm to a new tune by the vicar. This was the tune that bears his name, DARWALL. It had appeared three years previously in Williams's *New Universal Psalmodist*. It was for Tate and Brady's (New)

Version of the Psalter that Darwall wrote his 150 tunes, one for each psalm. A facsimile of Darwall's MS. of the present tune is given in the Historical Edition (1904) of *Hymns Ancient and Modern*, p. xcviii. This shows that the first note, as he wrote the tune, was A, thus:

144 AND DIDST THOU LOVE THE RACE THAT LOVED NOT THEE?

Miss Ingelow's poem is on 'The Love of Christ'. The credit of making the cento from it belongs to *The Congregational Church Hymnal* of 1887.

146 O SON OF MAN, OUR HERO STRONG AND TENDER

Written for Charterhouse about 1924, and used in the school for some time before it was published. The tune sung to it there is by Mr. R. S. Thatcher.

149 O COME, O COME, IMMANUEL

The Greater Antiphons, sung at Vespers from Dec. 17 each evening till Christmas Eve, began as follows:

O Sapientia, quae ex ore altissimi.
O Adonay et dux domus Israel.
O Radix Jesse qui stas in signum populorum.
O Clavis David et sceptrum domus Israel.
O Oriens, splendor lucis aeternae.
O Rex gentium et desideratus.
O Emanuel, rex et legifer noster.

It is easy to observe which five of these were selected by the unknown writer of the twelfth or thirteenth century to be woven into the Latin hymn which Neale translated. Neale's first version began, 'Draw nigh, draw nigh, Emmanuel', in his *Medieval Hymns* (1851); but two years later, in *The Hymnal Noted*, he altered this to the well-known form.

153 'THY KINGDOM COME!'—ON BENDED KNEE

Dr. Hosmer's hymn first appeared in the second series of his *The Thought of God* (1894). Its first appearance in Great Britain was in Garrett Horder's *Worship Song* (1905), *The English Hymnal* coming next in 1906.

The Dublin *Collection of Hymns and Sacred Poems* (1749) in which IRISH made its first appearance is sometimes claimed for John Wesley. He was certainly in Dublin in that year, and J. F. Lampe (q.v.) was with him; the supposition is that Lampe edited the music of the collection for him. There is nothing characteristically Irish about the tune, but neither does it exhibit the qualities of Lampe's usual work.

154 HAIL TO THE LORD'S ANOINTED

The original form of CRÜGER was as follows:

In late editions of his *Praxis Pietatis Melica* the second line runs:

Variants have been numerous, but W. H. Monk's adaptation of it for *Hymns Ancient and Modern*, with line 5 of his own composition, has greatly improved the tune and probably settled its form for use with the English language.

155 MINE EYES HAVE SEEN THE GLORY OF THE COMING OF THE LORD

This hymn was written to be sung to the tune of 'John Brown's body lies a-mouldering in the grave'. John Brown (1800–59), as became a scion of Pilgrim Fathers' stock, was a man of intense religious convictions and heroic and self-sacrificing courage. He became in boyhood a passionate abolitionist. After years of apparently useless pleading and struggle for the emancipation of the slaves, he resolved in 1859 to force the Government to take action. In October of that year, with nineteen men, he seized the Government arsenal at Harper's Ferry, Virginia, with a view to starting a widespread uprising of the slaves. The attempt failed. Brown was arrested, tried, and executed at Charlestown on Dec. 2. Before the attack on the arsenal he had said, 'If we lose our lives, it will perhaps do more for the cause than our lives would be worth in any other way.' He went to the scaffold, an observer said, 'with a radiant countenance and the step of a conqueror'. In a striking poem written before the execution Edmund Clarence Stedman warned the Virginian authorities against proceeding to extremities: 'Old Brown . . . may trouble you more than ever when you've nailed his coffin down.' So it befell. Soon after Brown's death Thoreau wrote: 'Of all the men who were my contemporaries, it seems to me that John Brown is the only one who has not died. I meet him at every turn. He is more alive than ever he was. He is not longer working in secret. He works in public in the clearest light that shines in the land.'

Brown's death aroused the conscience of the North on the subject of emancipation as nothing else had done. It helped also to consolidate the South. Victor Hugo's verdict was: 'What the South slew was not John Brown, but slavery.' A poet had written:

> Not any spot six feet by two
> Can hold a man like thee;
> John Brown shall tramp the shaking earth
> From Blue Ridge to the sea.

This prophecy also was fulfilled. Brown's name became a battle-cry among the armies of the North; they marched to the strains of the doggerel song, which enshrines his heroic memory:

> John Brown's body lies a-mouldering in the grave;
> But his soul is marching on.

One verse in particular expresses the fiery passion his death aroused:

> He captured Harper's Ferry
> With his nineteen men so true,
> And he frightened old Virginia
> Till she trembled through and through;
> They hung him for a traitor,
> Themselves a traitor-crew;
> But his soul is marching on.

Brander Matthews, in an article on 'The Songs of the War' in *The Century Magazine* of Aug. 1887, says that the genesis of both words and music of this song is obscure and involved. 'The martial hymn has been called a spontaneous generation of the uprising of the North—a self-made song, which sang itself into being of its own accord. Some have treated it as a sudden evolution from the inner consciousness of the early soldiers all aglow with free-soil enthusiasm; and these speak of it as springing, like Minerva from the head of Jove, full-armed and mature. Others have more happily likened it to Topsy, in that it never was born, it growed; and this latter theory has the support of the facts as far as they can be disentangled from a maze of fiction and legend.'

The facts appear to be that the song was put together by a quartet of men in the Twelfth Massachusetts Volunteers, and was first adopted as a marching song by that regiment; they first sang it in public as they marched down Broadway, New York, on July 24, 1861, on their way from Boston to the front. The tune which thus passed into national use in association with Brown's name was perfect for its purpose. 'There was a majestic simplicity in the rhythm like the beating of mighty hammers.' Louis Elson, in *The National Music of America* (1900), states that it was originally a hymn-tune. Though claimed by William Steffe, of Philadelphia, a popular Sunday School composer, as his own, it appears to have been a very old Methodist camp-meeting song, said to have been used in Charleston, both in coloured churches and among the firemen, long before the Civil War. The hymn belongs to the improvisatory type, and the soldiers' parody, in improvised lines (no rhymes were required) was of that type also. Elson prints a copy of the hymn-tune 'Say, brothers, will you meet us?' from an old Methodist hymnal 'of about half a century ago' (from 1900). This hymn, as 'Say, brother, will you meet me?' was brought, with its music, to this country by Mr. John Macgregor of the Temple, who asked Dr. E. J. Hopkins to make a four-part arrangement of it, which was published in 1859 for Mr. Edmund Macrory (author of *Notes on the Temple Organ*) and presented by the two Benchers to the Ragged School Shoe-black Society, for whose benefit it was sold. The hymn was sung at the Shoe-blacks' winter treat on February 8, 1859, at St. Martin's Hall. Hymn and tune are found in *Richard Weaver's Tune-Book* (c. 1861–2).

The circumstances in which Mrs. Julia Ward Howe was moved to write the present hymn to the popular air are given in the *Handbook* note, the first sentence of which, however, should read, 'written in December 1861, six months after the outbreak of the American Civil War.' A copy of the hymn, in her autograph, appeared in the article referred to in *The Century Magazine* for 1887, with a portrait of herself and a striking one of John Brown.

From this autograph it appears that Mrs. Howe wrote 'fateful' and 'through the vineyard' in v. 1, and in v. 3, 'let us die to make men free.' The two verses (3 and 4) omitted in the *Hymnary* were as follows:

I have seen Him in the watch-fires of an hundred circling camps;
They have builded Him an altar in the evening dews and damps;
I can read His righteous sentence by the dim and flaring lamps.
    His day is marching on.

I have read a fiery gospel, writ in burnished rows of steel,
'As ye deal with my contemners, so with you my grace shall deal;
Let the hero, born of woman, crush the serpent with his heel,
    Since God is marching on.'

160 LO! HE COMES, WITH CLOUDS DESCENDING

There seems to be little doubt that HELMSLEY is an adaptation of a popular eighteenth-century air, known variously as 'De'il tak' the wars that hurried Billy frae me', 'Guardian Angels', and 'Miss Catley's Hornpipe', and used by Sheridan for his song 'When sable night each drooping plant restoring', in *The Duenna*. And so the story that Olivers had heard it whistled in the street can easily be credited. See 'New Light on the Ancestry of *Helmsley*' in *The Choir*, April 1928.

161 THAT DAY OF WRATH, THAT DREADFUL DAY

The 'Dies Irae' was one of the five sequences spared in the holocaust of hymns of that type ordained by the Council of Trent. Originally it was probably an Advent hymn, but it was early taken into use for masses for the dead and for All Souls' Day.

Sir Walter Scott, writing about 1812 to Crabbe, who had been asked by the Rev. A. Brunton, Edinburgh, to 'furnish hymns which had relation to the Old or New Testament', said: 'I think these hymns which do not immediately recall the warm and exalted language of the Bible are apt to be, however elegant, rather cold and flat for purposes of devotion. You will readily believe that I do not approve of the vague and indiscriminate Scripture language which the fanatics of old, and the modern Methodists, have adopted, but merely that solemnity and peculiarity of diction which at once puts the reader on his guard as to the purpose of the poetry. To my Gothic ear, indeed, the *Stabat Mater*, the *Dies Irae*, and some of the other hymns of the Catholic Church, are more solemn and affecting than the fine classical poetry of Buchanan: the one has the gloomy dignity of a Gothic church, and reminds us instantly of the worship to which it is dedicated: the other is more like a Pagan temple, recalling to our memory the classical and fabulous deities.' (Lockhart, *Life of Scott*, vol. ii, p. 240.)

166 O FOR A THOUSAND TONGUES, TO SING

This hymn has stood first in Methodist hymn-books on both sides of the Atlantic for 150 years.

Sydney Dimond, in *The Psychology of the Methodist Revival*, says: 'In the manuscript hymn-book which was Wesley's constant companion on his evangelistic tours . . . the pages which show signs of most frequent use are those where he found

> O for a thousand tongues, to sing
> My dear Redeemer's praise.'

168 YE SERVANTS OF GOD, YOUR MASTER PROCLAIM

This hymn is No. 1 of 'Hymns to be sung in Tumult' in *Hymns for Times of Trouble and Persecution* (1744).

Parry's magnificent tune, LAUDATE DOMINUM, is an arrangement made by himself from one of his anthems, 'Hear my words, O ye people', which he composed in 1894 for the Festival of the Salisbury Diocesan Festival Association. The music was written for Sir Henry Baker's hymn 'O praise ye the Lord, praise Him in the height', which forms the concluding part of the anthem.

170 SWEETER SOUNDS THAN MUSIC KNOWS

For the tune LÜBECK see note on MONKLAND (Hymn 38) in this Supplement.

The tune from which FESTUS is derived, in Freylinghausen's *Geistreiches Gesangbuch* (Halle, 1704), set to the hymn 'O du Hüter Israels', is as follows:

FESTUS appears sometimes as L.M., sometimes as 77.77, in English tune-books about the sixties or seventies of last century. Whoever made the adaptation spoiled a magnificent tune.

172 O LIGHT, WHOSE BEAMS ILLUMINE ALL

In its original form SURREY was in two parts, treble and figured bass, the melody being as follows:

174 REST OF THE WEARY, JOY OF THE SAD

The tune FORTUNE has a remarkable history. The old Titus Andronicus ballad upon which Shakespeare is said to have founded his play was sung to it. It is mentioned in *The Merry Wives of Windsor*, and was the tune to which scores of ballads, mostly of a melancholy cast, were sung in Elizabethan days and later. It was called the 'Hanging Tune' because lamentations of criminals were sung to it for at least 200 years. In some parts of Scotland MARTYRS was used in a similar way.

FORTUNE was sung in Scotland in the sixteenth century to two of the earliest songs of the Reformation. About the year 1546 there appeared a notable book entitled *Ane Compendious Buik of Godlie Psalmes and Spirituall Sangis*, better known by the briefer name, *The Gude and Godlie Ballatis*, which leapt into widespread favour in Scotland among the middle and trading classes. The authors were three brothers Wedderburn, of Dundee. It contained not only twenty-two psalms in metre, translations into Scots of several Lutheran hymns, and spiritual meditations, but racy satires on the clergy and the Church as it then was.

Among the songs was one, 'Welcum Fortoun'—a simple love-song —which had a curious history. One theory about it is, that it was a purified form of an older and grosser song; another, that it was written by Robert Wedderburn, who was vicar of Dundee, to express his undying devotion to the lady of his heart whom his position as a priest made it impossible for him to marry. If the latter theory be correct, it would appear probable that the constancy was on one side only, for another of the ballads is entitled 'My Lufe was fals and ful of flattry', and another still, one of the finest hymns in the book, adapts 'Welcum Fortoun' to the theme of heavenly love, as though the writer's heart-ache made him turn to One whose love would never fail him.

By some unexplained fortune—trick or accident?—the first song found its way into one of the early editions of the Psalm-book, published by Bassandyne. The General Assembly of July 1568 took grave notice of the irregularity, as its records show: 'It was delaitit and found that Thomas Bassandine, Printer in Edinburgh, imprintit . . . ane psalme booke, in the end whereof was found printed ane baudie song called Welcum Fortoun, whilk book he had printed without licence of the magistrate, or reviseing of the Kirk: Therfor the haill Assemblie ordainit the said Thomas to call in againe all the said bookes that he has sauld, and keip the rest unsauld untill he . . . delete the said baudie song out of the end of the psalm booke. And farther, that he abstaine in all tyme coming from farther printing of anything without licence of the supreame magistrate, and reviseing of sick things as pertaine to religioun be some of the Kirk appointed for that purpose.'

The edict of the Assembly was so thoroughly carried out that the song in question disappeared from knowledge for 300 years. When Prof. A. F. Mitchell discovered a copy, the Assembly's description of it was found to exceed in severity. A few lines were somewhat free, according to the habit of the time, but in the main the song is accurately described by Prof. J. H. Millar (*The Literary History of Scotland*) as 'a love song of very considerable merit and unimpeachable decency'. Even so, of course, it was ludicrously out of place in the Church's authorized Psalm-book.

Two verses from the later—spiritual—song, sung to the tune FORTUNE, are as follows:

> Welcum, Lord Christ, welcum againe,
>   My joy, my comfort, and my bliss,
> That culd me saif from hellis paine,
>   Bot onlie thow nane was, and is . . .

> Was never nane to me mair kynde
>   Nor Christ; thairfore I will him pryse,
> Onlie with saule, body, and mynde,
>   My hope and traist haill in him lyes.

179 CHRIST IS THE WORLD'S REDEEMER

See Note in *Handbook* on Hymn 454. The tradition is that Columba laboured for seven years, in a dark cell without light, in penance for his famous fight against the High-king Diarmuid at Cooldrevny, on his great hymn ('or rather cosmogonical and eschatological poem', says Mr. Stephen Gaselee, 'though it was used as a hymn in Ireland'), the *Altus Prosator*, so called from its opening words, 'Altus prosator vetustus dierum et ingenitus'. (The Latin text is given by Mr. Gaselee in *The Oxford Book of Medieval Latin Verse*.) When messengers came to Iona from Pope Gregory (the Great) bearing gifts among which was a book of Hymns of the Week which Gregory himself had compiled, Columba gave them his own hymn to take back to the Pope. The latter, acknowledging it, 'said the hymn would be the best of all praises if Colum Cille had not too slightly commended the Trinity *per se*, as well as in Its creatures' (Helen Waddell, *Medieval Latin Lyrics*). Columba, admitting the justice of the criticism, made amends by composing a new hymn to the glory of the Trinity alone: *In Te, Christe, credentium miserearis omnium*. One portion of this, translated, gives us the present hymn; another is found in Hymn 454.

Of part of the *Altus* Prof. R. A. S. Macalister gives the following vigorous rendering:

> Ancient of Days, throned high in majesty,
>   The Father, Holy Spirit, Christ the Son,
> Who wast and art from all eternity
>   In everlasting glory, Three in One,
> Founder of all the worlds, we worship Thee.

> Called into being by the word of might,
>   The angels stood within Thy Holy Place,
> To do Thy will as ministers of light,
>   To bear throughout the furthest bounds of space
> The bounties of Thy goodness infinite.

Then, O Most-Highest, all-foreseeing, fast
   This earth on its foundations didst Thou build,
Yon sky, the seas, the lands upon them cast,
   With waving trees and living creatures filled,
And man, their ruler, fashioned at the last.

The Morning Stars their mighty chorus sang,
   The angels praised Thy wondrous works of power,
Throughout Heav'n's arches the tremendous clang
   Thundered and echoed in that birth-time hour,
And the great anthem thro' the universe rang.

When once again the trumpet-blast shall sound,
   When in the awful Second Advent-Day,
Stars, like ripe fruit, shall rain upon the ground,
   The sun and moon shall fail, and men shall say
'Fall on us' to the rugged cliffs around,

When by the fiery wrath of judgement-sword
   Thine enemies shall perish: but Thy grace
Hath promised us who trust Thee and Thy word,
   We in the air shall meet Thee, face to face—
So shall we be for ever with the Lord.

The original melody of MOVILLE will be found in Petrie, No. 1234, 'Scorching is this love'.

182 COME, HOLY GHOST, OUR SOULS INSPIRE

184 CREATOR SPIRIT! BY WHOSE AID

It is unfortunate that the creative idea in *Veni, Creator Spiritus* is lost in Cosin's version; Dryden's 'Creator Spirit' preserves it.

This great hymn has for a thousand years been associated with many of the most solemn offices of the Church, at coronations, consecrations, and ordinations, for example. Its use at ordination services has not been traced earlier than the eleventh century, but its use at Pentecost can be traced to the tenth. Its importance was marked in medieval times by special ceremonies designed to invest the singing of it with greater dignity, the wearing of the best vestments, the use of incense, and the ringing of bells.

The anthem-form of Attwood's tune is given in *The Church Anthem Book*.

186 COME, THOU HOLY PARACLETE

This hymn, often in medieval times called the 'Golden Sequence', is not only one of the best examples of the sequence type of hymn, but 'one of the masterpieces of sacred Latin poetry'. Julian quotes the following appreciation of it from Clichtovaeus (1516): 'Nor indeed, in my opinion, can this piece be sufficiently praised; for it is above all praise, whether by reason of its wonderful sweetness along with a most clear and flowing style, or by reason of its agreeable brevity along with wealth and profusion of ideas, especially as every line expresses one idea, or finally by reason of the elegant grace of its structure, in which things contrasted are set over against each other, and most aptly linked together. And I well believe that the author (whoever he was), when he composed this piece, had his soul transfused by a certain heavenly sweetness, by which, the Holy Spirit being its author, he uttered so much sweetness in so few words.'

Of its authorship Mr. Gaselee says, in *The Oxford Book of Medieval Latin Verse*, that 'the ascriptions to King Robert II of France and Hermannus Contractus are certainly wrong: Pope Innocent III is a possibility, but the most probable author is Cardinal Stephen Langton, Archbishop of Canterbury.'

It is a striking witness to the extent to which this sequence had come into popular use throughout the Church, that when the immense multiplication of sequence hymns created one of the problems for which the Council of Trent had to find some redress, and the extreme measure was adopted, in 1570, of sweeping almost all of them out of permitted use, only five exceptions were made. Of these, this was one, the others being the *Dies Irae*, *Stabat Mater*, *Lauda Sion*, and *Victimae Paschali*; these alone remain in the Roman Missal to this day.

190 COME, HOLY SPIRIT, COME

Hart's hymn was written on Whit-Sunday, May 29, 1757. See Thomas Wright's *Life of Joseph Hart* (p. 42).

196 COME, HOLY GHOST, OUR HEARTS INSPIRE

ST. COLUMBA is No. 1043 in the Stanford-Petrie Collection.

205 THE CHURCH'S ONE FOUNDATION

Mr. Kendrick Pyne, long organist of the Cathedral and the Town Hall, Manchester, related in some published Memorials that he was a resident pupil in Wesley's house in Winchester when AURELIA was composed. The house had a large garden attached, which being very untidily kept, was known among the local musical wits as 'Wesley's *Wilderness*', this being also the name of one of his most famous anthems. One Sunday afternoon, Wesley was playing and improvising in his drawing-room alone, when suddenly and imperatively he summoned those members of his family who were within call, to listen to an idea that had occurred to him 'in the way of a popular tune'. He then played over the present tune, which subsequently received its name from the hymn for which it was written—'Urbs Sion aurea' (Jerusalem the Golden).

206 GLORIOUS THINGS OF THEE ARE SPOKEN

The tune is founded on a Croatian melody. In English collections it first appeared in Edward Miller's *Sacred Music* (1802). It is used in Germany as the tune of 'Deutschland über alles'.

212 FOR THE MIGHT OF THINE ARM WE BLESS THEE

Mrs. Hemans' 'Hymn of the Vaudois Mountain Christians' is inspired throughout by the thought of the mountains as the defence of God's people; e.g. the first verse:

> For the strength of the Hills we bless thee,
> Our God, our Fathers' God;
> Thou hast made thy people mighty
> By the touch of the mountain sod;
> Thou hast fixed our ark of refuge
> Where the spoiler's feet ne'er trod:
> For the strength of the Hills we bless thee,
> Our God, our Fathers' God.

215 THY HAND, O GOD, HAS GUIDED

THORNBURY was composed for the Twenty-fifth Annual Festival of the London Church Choir Association in 1898, and first appeared in the Association's Festival Book of Nov. 17, 1898; thereafter it was printed in the composer's *Hymn Tunes Original and Selected* (1905).

218 FOR THOSE WE LOVE WITHIN THE VEIL

Mr. Charter Piggott's hymn was written for a Commemoration Service early in the War (1915), in his church at Streatham. It was published in *Songs of Praise* (1925), and in *Congregational School Worship* (1926).

224 O WHAT THEIR JOY AND THEIR GLORY MUST BE

A fine translation of Abélard's *O quanta qualia*, by Miss Helen Waddell, will be found in *Medieval Latin Lyrics*. Unfortunately, she adopts a metre which does not suit the lovely proper tune.

> How mighty are the Sabbaths,
> How mighty and how deep,
> That the high courts of heaven
> To everlasting keep.
> What peace unto the weary,
> What pride unto the strong,
> When God in Whom are all things
> Shall be all things to men.

Jerusalem is the city
  Of everlasting peace,
A peace that is surpassing
  And utter blessedness;
Where finds the dreamer waking
  Truth beyond dreaming far,
Nor is the heart's possessing
  Less than the heart's desire. . . .

There is an anthem setting of this hymn in *The Church Anthem Book*.

225 HE WANTS NOT FRIENDS THAT HATH THY LOVE

The original form of KENT was as follows:

226 O BLEST

The peculiar metre of BRAINT, the first line consisting of two identical monosyllables, seems to have been derived from an old Welsh carol, 'Cloch, cloch,' or 'Tincian y cloch' ('Bell, Bell,' or 'Toll, Bell'). The words of this 'carol of praise and worship' are from *Bardd a Byrddau*, by Jonathan Hughes, 1788—a writer who in many other ballads and carols in this metre strictly adhered (as other writers have not always done) to the repeated monosyllabic word for the first line. See *The Welsh Folk-Song Journal*, vol. ii (1925), pp. 247–51.

The penultimate strain of this tune has been omitted by Ieuan Gwyllt and his successors. But in the unabridged Dorian form this strain, preceding the last four bars, to which the same words are repeated, runs thus:

The curious old form, mainly major, given below from the same *Journal*, is found, with negligible variations, in several old Welsh MS. tune-books. The editor noted it from an old precentor near

Portmadoc about forty years ago. Alternative names for BRAINT are 'Trawsfynedd' and 'Union'.

227 LET SAINTS ON EARTH IN CONCERT SING

The first changes in Wesley's original (in five double verses) were made in Cotterill's *Selection of Psalms and Hymns* (1815), possibly by Montgomery, who was closely associated with Cotterill and contributed fifty hymns to his eighth edition; but the present version appeared first in Murray's *Hymnal for Use in the English Church* (1852), which is sometimes called Mosley's Hymnal, from the name of the publisher. Murray (the Rev. Francis H. Murray of Chislehurst) deserves particular remembrance as the originator of the idea of *Hymns Ancient and Modern* and as one of the most active members of the editorial committee that produced the first edition of that epoch-making book. The version of this hymn which he made is a masterpiece of editing. The first couplet is his own; the second couplet of ver. 1 and vv. 2 and 3 are all Wesley's; vv. 4 and 5 are Murray's superb emendation of the first quatrain of Wesley's third and the second quatrain of Wesley's last verse. Only at one point did Murray's fine sense fail him. Wesley wrote:

> 'Part of His host have cross'd the flood,
>   And part are crossing now.'

The plural gives the idea of *multitude*—the 'militant, embodied host'—much more finely than the singular, which is thin, and also makes the lines too sibilant.

231 ALL LANDS AND PEOPLES, ALL THE EARTH

J. W. Elliott's tune, GLORIA IN EXCELSIS, was written in 1862 for Trinity Sunday, and appeared in *Church Hymns with Tunes* (1st ed., 1874) under the heading 'Choral Festival', to a hymn beginning:

> Hark! Hark! The organ loudly peals,
>   Our thankful hearts inviting.

Elliott was practically the editor of *Church Hymns*, though Sullivan's name is on the title-page.

236 WE LOVE THE PLACE, O GOD

This hymn was written by William Bullock, then a young sailor-missionary, for the opening of a mission-chapel at Trinity Bay, Newfoundland, in 1827. Seventy years later a church replaced the chapel on the same site, and at its consecration, not only was this hymn in a revised form sung once more, but the sermon preached by its author at the opening of the chapel was read to the people.

242 BEHOLD US, LORD, A LITTLE SPACE

Canon Dearmer says of this hymn: 'It must be one of the earliest hymns in which science and art are mentioned and are recognized as part of God's work. . . . Free from the sentimentality of the period, it handles tersely and epigrammatically the modern world of business and labour, and after more than sixty years it is modern still.'

The history of the tune BEDFORD is fully discussed in the *Handbook* note on this hymn. Since the note was written, the undoubted matrix of the tune has been discovered by Miss Anne G. Gilchrist in the Proper Tune to the Hymn after Communion in Playford's Psalter of 1677. This tune, which is in three parts, Cantus, Medius, and Bassus, is as follows:

It looks as if Weale adapted this original; or it may be that both Playford and Weale adapted an earlier original in different ways. The similarity of the first line of the Playford tune to the third line of ROCKINGHAM (COMMUNION) will be noted.

244 O BE WITH US, GRACIOUS FATHER

DULCINA, with a second half different entirely from that in the MS. in the British Museum, is included in Forbes's *Cantus* to a carol, 'Of ye Birth of Christ', ver. 1 of which is as follows:

> Jurie cam to Jerussalem,
>   All the warld was taxit then;
> Blissid Marie brought to Bethlem
>   Moir than all the warld again:
> A gift so blist, so goode ye best
>   That evir was sein, was hard or done,
> A King, a Chryst, prophet a priest,
>   A Jesus God, a man a sone.

There is a setting of this carol by Sir Frederick Bridge.

246 DEAR SHEPHERD OF THY PEOPLE, HEAR
247 JESUS, WHERE'ER THY PEOPLE MEET

Newton found difficulty in attracting his people to the prayer meeting. One device he used to draw them was to provide a new hymn every Tuesday. In April, 1769, the meeting was moved 'to the great room in the Great House. It is a noble place', he wrote, 'with a parlour behind it, and holds 130 people conveniently.' It was to celebrate this move that these two hymns were written by Newton and Cowper respectively. This explains the reference in 'Thy former mercies here renew'. Another verse, now everywhere omitted, was the one quoted in the note on Hymn 247 in the *Handbook*; the last line of it should read, 'And bless us with a large increase.'

249 LIGHT OF THE ANXIOUS HEART

T. L. Hately, who was a member of R. A. Smith's choir in St. George's, Edinburgh, maintained that SELMA was of Smith's own composition. The tune, however, has considerable likeness to various airs sung to the folk-song 'I sowed the seeds of love', and probably is founded upon one of them heard traditionally by Smith. On the name, see note on MORVEN under Psalter Tunes.

250 ENTER THY COURTS, THOU WORD OF LIFE

The form of the FIFTH MODE MELODY which appears in *The Yattendon Hymnal* was discovered by Dr. Evans to be really the Faux Bourdon for the tune, and as such was set by him to ver. 2 in the *Hymnary*.

The tune itself appeared, under the name WATERBROOK, in 3/4 time, in *The Scottish Psalmody* (1854), set to Psalm xxv, 'Shew me Thy ways, O Lord', with the following note, highly characteristic of the time: 'This tasteful composition—taken from Dibdin's *Standard Tune Book*—is given as left by its distinguished author (Tallis), with the exception of a change from 2/4 to 3/4 time, in order to adapt it to congregational use.'

254 ALL THINGS ARE THINE; NO GIFT HAVE WE

HERR JESU CHRIST appeared in *Pensum Sacrum*, set to six of its
267 Latin odes, in the following form:

The tune takes its name from the hymn 'Herr Jesus Christ, dich zu uns wend', to which it was set in the *Gothäer Cantional* (1651).

261 CHRIST, WHOSE GLORY FILLS THE SKIES

In view of the fierce controversy between Toplady and the Wesleys it is of interest to note that Toplady included this hymn, without the author's name, in his *Psalms and Hymns* (1776). The belief grew up that he had written it, and was widely held until Montgomery disproved it, pointing out that the hymn was written in 1740, the year of Toplady's birth.

271 BEFORE THE DAY DRAWS NEAR ITS ENDING

Among the variants of the tune GOTTLOB, ES GEHT the last line of the form used in the published edition of Bach's *Choralgesänge* should be noted:

The original metre is 98.98.88.

274 AS NOW THE SUN'S DECLINING RAYS

There is an earlier ascription of BURFORD to Purcell than the one mentioned in the *Handbook* note—that made by Edward Miller in his *Psalms of David* (1790), where the tune is headed 'Said to be Purcell's'. See note on ST. THOMAS in the present Supplement (Psalter Tunes). Grove's *Dictionary of Music* still (1927 edition) definitely includes BURFORD among Purcell's works.

286 ABIDE WITH ME: FAST FALLS THE EVENTIDE

In the *Life of Frederick Denison Maurice*, by his son (vol. ii, p. 641), it is stated that this 'was always his favourite of all hymns: the one he was sure to select for any service that specially interested him.'

W. H. Monk's tune EVENTIDE is said to have been written in ten minutes. Judging from the frequency with which it is sung at popular gatherings such as international football matches, it is one of the best known of hymn-tunes, and has made 'Abide with me' the most popular of hymns.

288 NOW THE DAY IS OVER

The German tune which Baring-Gould heard as a child, and which, he came to believe, unconsciously suggested EUDOXIA to him, was in all probability that of a song which was very widely taught in schools about the middle of last century, *The Cricket*, by A. Weber. As noted by Miss Anne G. Gilchrist this tune is as follows:

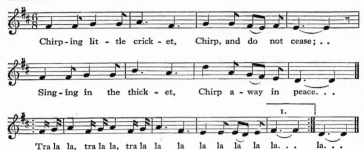

Chirp - ing lit - tle crick - et, Chirp, and do not cease; . .

Sing - ing in the thick - et, Chirp a - way in peace. . .

Tra la la, tra la la, tra la la la la la la la la la. . . la. . .

Miss Gilchrist says: 'I think we may have here the German air of which EUDOXIA is a "reminiscence"—though it does not seem to be more. The metre of Baring-Gould's verses is the same, and I think there may have been in his mind a sub-conscious association of ideas with a hazy remembrance of tune and words heard as a child, and giving an impression of night-time and peace:

> While the world is sleeping
> Chirp away in peace—

so forming the germ both of verses and tune. But a "reminiscence" is a long way from being an adaptation, and I think Baring-Gould had a right to call the tune he made for his hymn his own.'

There is, however, a children's evening hymn, No. 1356 in the *Plymouth Collection* (1856), set to this German tune, without the refrain, and very much of the same character as Baring-Gould's. It begins:

> See, the light is fading
> From the western sky;
> Day, thou art departing,
> Night is drawing nigh.

Is this an intermediate link?

289 THE DAY THOU GAVEST, LORD, IS ENDED

The proper rhythm of LES COMMANDEMENS DE DIEU, as Bourgeois wrote it, is as follows:

291 ALL PRAISE TO THEE, MY GOD, THIS NIGHT

'This is a perfect canon, in that the necessities of the form nowhere obtrude themselves, the tune being as clear and "natural" as if these necessities did not exist' (*Songs of Praise Discussed*). In the original, the tenors led, the sopranos followed, when the tune was sung in canon form, as in the full version in the *Hymnary*. Tallis was fond of this device. In his monkish days he and his fellow inmates of the cloisters used to amuse themselves in this way. To *The Black Sanctus or Monks' Hymn to Saint Satan* he set a canon in three parts, and King Henry VIII, musical enthusiast as he was, would sometimes delight in taking part.

292 SUN OF MY SOUL, THOU SAVIOUR DEAR

The significance of the opening of this famous hymn is not evident unless the first two verses of the poem are quoted, as they deserve to be, for their own beauty, as well as to furnish the background of the poet's thought. The sun has gone down, and the traveller must pursue his way without its light; but the Sun of the soul will never set.

> 'Tis gone, that bright and orbéd blaze,
> Fast fading from our wistful gaze;
> Yon mantling cloud has hid from sight
> The last faint pulse of quivering light.
>
> In darkness and in weariness
> The traveller on his way must press,
> No gleam to watch on tree or tower
> Whiling away the lonesome hour.
>
> Sun of my soul, Thou Saviour dear,
> It is not night if Thou be near. . . .

It is a tradition that it was in the rectory garden at East Leach that Keble wrote this hymn. In an article in *The Church Quarterly Review*, vol. cv, the Rev. Canon E. F. Smith, vicar of Tewkesbury, says: 'Certainly the first two verses (generally omitted when it is sung as a hymn) would fit in well with the westward aspect looking from that garden westward towards Fairford across the dark woods and winding ways.' Referring to the description of the benighted traveller in the second verse, he goes on to say: 'Such was in fact the unpleasant experience of Isaac Williams when he first went as a pupil to John Keble, and walked over from Southrop to find Dean Farm, where he lodged: it was evening when he set out with Hurrell Froude, and a thick mist came on: the night grew perfectly dark, and they wandered about (Williams tells us) the whole night till near the morning.'

The date of the Irish *Church Hymnal* in which ABENDS first appeared should be 1873.

HERR GOTT VATER is set in *Tisch Gesänge* (Breslau, 1615) to a Grace before Meat, beginning:

> Herr Gott, Vater im Himmelreich,
> Wir, deine kinder allzugleich,
> Bitten dich jetzt aus Herzensgrund:
> Speise uns auch zu dieser Stund.

This tune would perfectly suit the Grace before Meat (Hymn 656), 'Be present at our table, Lord'.

293 GOD, THAT MADEST EARTH AND HEAVEN

Heber's evening hymn of one verse was written to the Welsh air *Ar hyd y nos* (All through the night), played by a Welsh harper in the hall of a house where he was a visitor—either at Llangedwyn, near Oswestry, where he often stayed with the Hon. C. W. W. Wynn, or at Bodryddan, near Rhuddlan, the house of his father-in-law, Dean Shipley. It is set to this Welsh air in the choir-book arranged by his sister Mary (afterwards Mrs. Cholmondeley) before 1822, for use at Hodnet Church.

294 ERE I SLEEP, FOR EVERY FAVOUR

THANET first appeared in Jowett's *Musæ Solitariæ* (1823).

297 COME, DEAREST LORD, DESCEND AND DWELL

Lawes's tunes have not the attractiveness of those which Gibbons wrote for Wither's verses. His music was characterized by Hawkins (according to Dr. Johnson 'a very unclubable man') as deficient in melody and as being 'neither recitative nor air, but in so precise a medium between both that a name is wanting for it'. According to Sir Henry Hadow, however, 'it was not Lawes's object to produce melody in the proper sense of the word, but to set "words with just note and accent", to make the prosody of his text his principal care; and it was doubtless that quality which induced all the best poetical writers of his day, from Milton and Waller downwards, to desire that their verses should be set by him.' Milton's sonnet 'To Mr. H. Lawes on his Airs', from which Sir Henry quotes, has these lines:

> Harry, whose tuneful and well-measured song
>   First taught our English Music how to span
>   Words with just note and accent, not to scan
> With Midas' ears, committing short and long,
> Thy worth and skill exempts thee from the throng,
>   With praise enough for Envy to look wan;
>   To after age thou shalt be writ the man
> That with smooth air couldst humour best our tongue.
> Thou honour'st Verse, and Verse must lend her wing
>   To honour thee, the priest of Phoebus' quire,
>   That tunest their happiest lines in hymn or story.

299 LORD, DISMISS US WITH THY BLESSING

The omitted third stanza illustrates the change of thought that has taken place in hymnody since the hymn was written 150 years ago:

> So whene'er the Signal's given
> Us from Earth to call away,
> Borne on Angels' wings to Heaven,
> Glad the Summons to obey,
> May we ever
> Reign with Christ in endless Day.

309 BY COOL SILOAM'S SHADY RILL

The first two lines of this hymn have been caustically described, by one who has intimate knowledge of the conditions in present-day Jerusalem, as containing 'the maximum of mis-statement in the minimum of space'.

310 GRACIOUS SAVIOUR, GENTLE SHEPHERD

BRYNTIRION is in *Chants Chrétiens* set to Cantique 110, which begins thus:

> O Jésus, dans ta bergerie
> Introduis tes heureux troupeaux;
> Garde ton Église chérie,
> Et nous pais comme tes agneaux.
> Que tous les enfants de lumière
> Remplis de ton Esprit d'amour
> S'entr'aiment partout sur la terre
> Jusqu'au moment de ton retour.

313 ACCORDING TO THY GRACIOUS WORD

Burns's reference to BANGOR in *The Ordination* should be quoted, as illustrating both the popularity of the tune in his time, and the quality of the singing:

> Mak' haste an' turn King David owre,
> An' lilt wi' holy clangor;
> O' double verse come gie us four,
> An' skirl up the 'Bangor'.

Barthélémon's song, referred to in the *Handbook* note, seems to have travelled out to America described as 'a pathetic Scotch ballad'! There the melody became a hymn-tune, preserving its original form, save for the smoothing out of one or two dotted notes, &c. As an '8s and 7s Double' it occurs in several American hymnbooks of the 'sixties under the name of AUTUMN or BETHLEHEM, and is described as 'Spanish', from a mistaken idea that the tune as well as the words of Monk Lewis's song was taken from the

Spanish. In Dadmun's *Melodeon*, 1861, it is set to 'Glorious things of thee are spoken' as follows:

The original song begins:

> Sad and fearful is the story
> Of the Roncesvales fight,
> On those fatal plains of glory
> Perished many a gallant knight.

Durandarte, a brave knight, was slain by the Moors at Roncesvalles in Spain. Belerma was his beloved lady.

317 AUTHOR OF LIFE DIVINE

It is a curious fact that this hymn never appeared in any of the official hymn-books of Methodism from 1780 until the most recent *Methodist Hymn Book* appeared in 1933. It came into common use through its publication in the 1875 revised edition of *Hymns Ancient and Modern*.

With the opening strain of AUCTOR VITAE cf. the Pilgrim's Song in *Parsifal*.

318 BREAD OF THE WORLD, IN MERCY BROKEN

The musical editor of *Songs of Praise Discussed* says of PSALM CXVIII (RENDEZ À DIEU): 'This lovely and impressive tune is in some ways the finest of all the early psalm-tunes; it is perfectly proportioned; it begins with a phrase of remarkable expressiveness, and continues with others as significant as they are logically consistent, while the beauty of the change of rhythm in the downward scale of the fifth line is extraordinary. This is a tune which gives the true "spinal thrill"; of its kind it is unsurpassed.' All this is justly said of one of the loveliest church tunes ever written.

319 THEE WE ADORE, O HIDDEN SAVIOUR, THEE

The lines of the original in which 'Pious Pelican' occurs are as follows:

> Pie pellicane Jesu Domine,
> Me immundum munda tuo sanguine.

320 AND NOW, O FATHER, MINDFUL OF THE LOVE

In a note on this hymn, in *Songs of Praise Discussed*, the use of the words 'And now' at the beginning is criticized, and attention called to the number of hymns 'disfigured by this unnecessary commencement'. Blake is excused for beginning 'Jerusalem' with the words 'And did those feet', on the ground that that poem occurs after two paragraphs as part of the preface to his *Milton*. But a preface to Bright's hymn has to be understood. The clue to what was in his mind is given by W. H. Monk in the title he gave the tune. UNDE ET MEMORES are the opening words of the prayer in the Roman canon of the Mass which occurs after the consecration of the elements, at the elevation of the chalice: 'Unde et memores, Domine, nos servi tui sed et plebs tua sancta', &c.: 'Wherefore, O Lord, we, Thy servants, as also Thy holy people, remembering the blessed passion of the same Christ Thy Son our Lord,' &c. Bright assumes that those who sing the hymn will set it mentally in the context of all that has led up to the moment preceding participation; the 'And now' is the fitting opening for what is intended as the *aditus* to the consummating act.

324 DECK THYSELF, MY SOUL, WITH GLADNESS

Schumann wrote thus to Mendelssohn after hearing him play Bach's organ setting of SCHMÜCKE DICH—one of the most beautiful of Bach's organ chorales: 'Round the *cantus firmus* hung golden garlands of leaves, and such blissfulness was breathed from within it, that you yourself avowed that if life was bereft of all hope and faith, this one chorale could renew them for you. I was silent and went away dazed into God's acre, feeling acutely pained that I could lay no flower on his urn.' (*Musik und Musiker*, vol. i, p. 153.)

333 POUR OUT THY SPIRIT FROM ON HIGH

This hymn appeared in the year in which it was written, 1833, for J. Birchell's *Selection of Hymns*, and in the same year in Edward Bickersteth's *Christian Psalmody*.

337 LORD OF LIGHT, WHOSE NAME OUTSHINETH

The Welsh song from which LLANSANNAN is derived is 'Y Gwelltyn Glas' (The green blade). See *Journal of the Welsh Folk-Song Society*, vol. ii, p. 79.

347 HERE, LORD, WE OFFER THEE ALL THAT IS FAIREST

For a description of St. Luke's, Chelsea, for which this hymn was written, see Henry Kingsley's *The Hillyars and the Burtons*, ch. 23.

BLODYN means not 'flowers' but 'a flower'; the plural is *blodau*.

349 FATHER, WHO ON MAN DOST SHOWER

The carol QUEM PASTORES LAUDAVERE appears with the original words in *The Oxford Book of Carols* (1928). It was much used at Christmastide during the ceremonies round the crib in churches. Its widespread use is evident from the number of collections, both Roman and Protestant in which it appears, from 1555, when it was first published in F. Triller's *Ein Schlesich singebüchlein aus Göttlicher schrifft*, &c. (Breslau), downwards. In the usual form of the melody the last bar of the first three lines is syncopated thus:

♩ ♩

353 FATHER, WHOSE WILL IS LIFE AND GOOD

TALLIS is often called TALLIS'S ORDINAL because in Archbishop Parker's *The Whole Psalter translated into English Metre* (vide *Handbook* note on Hymn 250), in which it first appeared, it was set to the version of *Veni, Creator Spiritus* used in the Prayer Book Ordination service. Of the nine tunes written by Tallis for this Psalter, eight were in the eight ecclesiastical modes; the present one follows them. This instruction was printed with them: 'The tenor of these partes be for the people when they will synge alone; the other parts, put for greater queers, or such as will syng or play them privatlye.' The present tune differs from the others, however, in that it has the melody in the top part and not in the tenor.

355 O LORD OF LIFE, AND LOVE, AND POWER

The fact that this hymn was written for the opening of a new Sunday School is evident in an omitted verse, between 2 and 3:

In this new house our hands have raised
Thy service to pursue,
O may Thy name henceforth be praised
By work more pure and true.
May child and teacher evermore
Come here with earnest heart,
And those who never worked before
Stand forth and bear their part.

371 FROM GREENLAND'S ICY MOUNTAINS

The air for which Heber wrote the hymn was, ''Twas when the sea was roaring'. Mason's tune was written at the request of a lady who had just received the hymn from a friend in England; thereafter it was published as indicated in the *Handbook*.

373 FAR ROUND THE WORLD THY CHILDREN SING THEIR SONG

The hymn was written in 1909 for a Sunday School Anniversary at Bowes Park, London; the verses on Asia, Africa, and the Islands were added three years later.

374 ONCE AGAIN, DEAR LORD, WE PRAY

MORNING, No. 3, in *The European Psalmist*, was originally in 3/2 time, and was set to 'Wake and lift up thyself, my heart' (Hymn 256).

389 HARK! THE SONG OF JUBILEE

The original broadsheet on which this hymn was printed says that it was 'composed at the express desire of the London Missionary Society, with a special reference to the renunciation of Idolatry and acknowledgement of the Gospel, in the Georgian Isles of the South Seas', and sung at Spa Fields Chapel, London, May 14, 1818.

403 LORD JESUS, THINK ON ME

The extent of the liberty Chatfield allowed himself in making this 'paraphrase or amplification' of Synesius' original, is shown in the following literal prose translation of the Greek poem, made by Dr. Costley White, Head Master of Westminster School:

> Be mindful, Christ, Son of God,
> Who rulest on high, of thy servant,
> Sinful of heart, who wrote these words.
> And grant to me release from passions breeding death,
> Which are inborn in my unclean soul.
> But give me to behold, Saviour Jesus,
> Thy divine brightness, wherein appearing
> > I shall sing a song
> > To the healer of souls,
> > To the healer of limbs,
> > With the great Father
> > > And the Holy Spirit.

ST. BRIDE was originally called 'St. Bridget's' after Wren's well-known church (St. Bride's) off Fleet Street, where Dr. Howard was organist. Later, it was known simply as 'Bridget's'.

405 LORD, IN THIS THY MERCY'S DAY

HEILIGER GEIST appeared eight years before the date first indicated in the *Handbook*—1639—in D. G. Corner's *Gross Catolisch Gesangbuch* (1631), and also, later, in the same editor's *Geistliche Nachtigall der Catholischen Teütschen*, &c. (Vienna, 1648).

411 JUST AS I AM, WITHOUT ONE PLEA

Bishop Moule of Durham, a relative of Charlotte Elliott, stated that the origin of this hymn was, that at a time when the authoress's brother, the Rev. Henry Venn Elliott, of Brighton, was holding a bazaar in St. Mary's Hall there, to raise funds for the building of a school, Charlotte lay awake all night, oppressed with the feeling of uselessness and 'tossed about with many a doubt'. While every one else was out and busy with the bazaar on the following day, she lay at home, in greater misery than ever; and it was in her effort to fight her depression off that she took her pen and wrote the hymn.

After her death over a thousand letters thanking her for this hymn were found.

413 ROCK OF AGES, CLEFT FOR ME

The hymn was first published in *The Gospel Magazine*, March, 1776. Where did Toplady get his inspiration? The following passage from Dr. Brevint's *The Christian Sacrament and Sacrifice*, prefixed to John and Charles Wesley's *Hymns of the Lord's Supper* (1745), seems to give the answer: 'O Rock of Israel, Rock of Salvation, Rock struck and cleft for me, let those two streams of blood and water which once gushed out of Thy side bring down pardon and holiness into my soul; and let me thirst after them now, as if I stood upon the mountain whence sprung this water, and near the cleft of that rock, the wounds of my Lord, whence gushed this sacred blood.' This, and the current use of 'Rock of Ages' as a name for Christ in and before Toplady's day, furnish a much more probable explanation of the origin of the hymn than the widely credited legend connected with Burrington Combe in the Mendips. (See note on the hymn in the *Handbook*.)

No such originative suggestion, however, detracts from the pure inspiration of the hymn. Canon Dearmer thus expresses his reluctant admiration: 'There may be here some influence of early associations, to which we are all subject; but the intensity of religious passion has surely endued Toplady with a power beyond his normal gifts: there is such vigour of unconscious art—the violence of the opening cry, the sweeping negatives of the second and third verses, the growing exultation of the last, and the quiet return at the end, in a changed tone of gentle confidence, to the opening words. It may be questioned whether we ought to sing the hymn to-day; but it remains a notable monument of the religion which gripped our fathers.'—*Songs of Praise Discussed*, p. 337.

NICHT SO TRAURIG is from Freylinghausen's *Neues Geistreiches Gesangbuch* (1714), where it is set to Gerhardt's 'Nicht so traurig, nicht so sehr'.

414 JESUS, LOVER OF MY SOUL

This was Henry Ward Beecher's favourite hymn. He said of it: 'I would rather have written that hymn than have the fame of all the kings that ever sat on earth; it has more power in it.'

'The nearer waters roll' is borrowed from Prior, of whom the Wesleys thought highly.

HOLLINGSIDE, though not published till 1861, was probably written during Dykes's time of residence in Hollingside Cottage, 1850–3. (See *Musical Times*, October 1904.) The reharmonization of the tune has lost a neat bit of imitation in the fifth line.

ABERYSTWYTH was so named because Joseph Parry, when he composed it, was Professor of Music in University College in that town.

416 COME, O THOU TRAVELLER UNKNOWN

C. E. Vulliamy, referring to John Wesley's emotion when he gave out this hymn a fortnight after Charles's death, says: 'For the first time in a ministry of fifty years he broke down in public under the stress of a personal emotion.'

417 HARK, MY SOUL! IT IS THE LORD

NUN KOMM, DER HEIDEN HEILAND is a simplified form of the plainsong melody associated with the hymn 'Veni Redemptor Gentium'. It is found in the Erfurt *Enchiridion* of 1524 as well as in Walther's Wittenberg *Gesangbuchlein* of the same year; it occurs also in other books of that time.

420 JESUS, THOU JOY OF LOVING HEARTS
421 JESUS! THE VERY THOUGHT IS SWEET
422 JESUS, THE VERY THOUGHT OF THEE
423 O JESUS, KING MOST WONDERFUL

The *Handbook* note on these centos from 'Jesu, dulcis memoria' is in error, owing to a misunderstanding of Dom Pothier's words in the *Revue du Chant Grégorien*. These words in turn are shown by Reginald Vaux in *The Church Quarterly Review* of April, 1929, to have rested on a misquotation of Dom Guéranger's *L'Année Liturgique*. That again was based on an otherwise unsupported statement of Mabillon, who edited Bernard's works in the early eighteenth century. To make confusion worse confounded, so high an authority as Bishop W. H. Frere, in his invaluable Notes in the Historical Edition of *Hymns Ancient and Modern*, p. 357, states that Dom Pothier 'has found the hymn in MSS. of the eleventh century, ascribed to a Benedictine Abbess'. Of this discovery no trace can be found in Dom Pothier's own words.

The pungent language of Mr. Vaux on all this is thus fully justified: 'Upon the narrow and insecure foundation laid down by Mabillon . . . subsequent commentators have raised a structure that it will not support: by a seeming corroboration of his statement that is in fact probably nothing more than repetition: by additions thereto based upon inference: and even by unintentional errors that have become canonized through the eminence of the writers they have deceived, and by whom they have been quoted in good faith.'

Dogmatic statements like this—'It is not by St. Bernard. . . . While a few verses were added later, the poem itself has been found in a manuscript of the eleventh century' (*Songs of Praise Discussed*), are quite unwarranted by the facts. The one thing certain is that the picturesque figure of the eleventh century Benedictine Abbess, the supposed supplanter of St. Bernard in the authorship of the hymn, has vanished into thin air.

So good an authority as Archbishop Trench believed the attribution of the hymn to St. Bernard to be well founded. Of all the hymns so ascribed, with one exception, he said: 'If he did not write, it is not easy to guess who could have written them; and indeed they bear profoundly the stamp of his mind, being only inferior in beauty to his prose.' Dr. G. G. Coulton takes an opposite view. Bernard, he says, 'disapproved of poetry, and indeed it was one of the clauses of the *Carta Caritatis* that no Cistercian should compose verse. When Bernard wrote the Office for St. Victor's Day at the request of the Victorines of Paris, the hymns were purposely composed so that they would not scan, though they lent themselves to chanting.' (*Five Centuries of Religion*, vol. i, p. 301.) Mr. Stephen Gaselee, in *The Oxford Book of Medieval Latin Verse*, ventures upon a new suggestion, that, judging from the nationality of the best MSS. of the poem, the author may possibly be of English origin. Certainty is impossible, and in the absence of positive evidence for any theory, all that can be said is that the hymn is 'attributed to St. Bernard', and that it was ascribed to him within about a century of his death.

422 JESUS, THE VERY THOUGHT OF THEE

ROCHESTER was issued separately in sheet form by Curwen in 1924, Hylton Stewart being then organist of Rochester Cathedral. It was included in *Songs of Praise* in the following year.

424 O LOVE THAT WILT NOT LET ME GO

It was in January 1882 that the hymn appeared in *Life and Work*. In 1885 it appeared in *The Scottish Hymnal*. Dr. Matheson's memory must therefore have been at fault when he said that the hymn was composed at Innellan in June 1882, six months after its publication. Probably the year was 1881.

428 O LOVE DIVINE, HOW SWEET THOU ART

The tune ALLGÜTIGER, MEIN PREISGESANG in its original form gives the fifth line, not as a reproduction of the fourth, but thus:

432 JESUS, THY BOUNDLESS LOVE TO ME

In the *Handbook* note on this hymn 'the Mark of Brandenburg' should be 'the Westphalian county of Mark'.

434 LOVED WITH EVERLASTING LOVE

For the thought of ver. 2 cf. Henry Martyn's *Cambridge Diary*: 'Since I have known God in a saving manner, painting, poetry, and music have had charms unknown to me before; for Religion has refined my mind, and made it susceptible of impressions from the sublime and beautiful.'

436 IT IS A THING MOST WONDERFUL

SOLOTHURN is used by Beethoven as the theme for his *Variationen über ein Schweizerlied*. 'The tune, both in rhythm and general form, has several counterparts among Swiss folk songs, and, in particular, resembles strongly "Dursli und Bäbeli", which may be found in *Sammlung von Schweizer Kühreihen und Volksliedern* (1826), a large collection of such songs, while others may be found in *Lieder aus der Schweiz*, &c. (1837) and *Recueil de Chants populaires suisses* (1920). Apart from the *ranz-des-vaches*, which is of necessity formed on the harmonies of the Alpine horn, the Swiss folk-tunes are mostly of a very simple type, though often attractively gay and rhythmic; the present tune is a good specimen of a more staid kind.' (*Songs of Praise Discussed.*)

438 THE KING OF LOVE MY SHEPHERD IS

Dr. Dykes died on Jan. 22, 1876. 'He was laid to rest at St. Oswald's, Durham, amid a vast concourse of friends, to the strains of this hymn.'

DUNAHA is a small village in County Clare, near the mouth of the Shannon, where John Hore, the blacksmith-poet, was born (*floruit c.* 1780).

The hymn to which he set the tune is a song of penitence written towards the end of his life, and first published in O'Daly's *Irish Miscellany* (1876). The original name of the tune is *Muinntear na n-Déis* (People of the Decies—a tract in Co. Waterford).

446 MY HEART IS RESTING, O MY GOD

The name of the tune PENTATONE is explained by the fact that it is in the 'Caledonian' five-note scale.

454 O GOD, THOU ART THE FATHER

See note on Hymn 179.

The Limerick sea-song 'Captain Thomson' is No. 380 in Joyce.

455 O HELP US, LORD; EACH HOUR OF NEED

In many hymn-books vv. 4 and 5 are omitted, following the example of Dean Milman in his *Selection of Psalms and Hymns*

(1837), so that the remaining verses should all begin with 'O help us, Lord'. For certain uses, however, the loss of these verses weakens the hymn.

457 O FOR A CLOSER WALK WITH GOD

Strange myths have gathered round MARTYRDOM, one asserting that it is 'partly borrowed from a Covenanting melody', and another even that it was written by David Rizzio! Much more likely is the theory that it had a ballad origin. R. A. Smith described it as an 'Old Scottish Melody', and though in the lawsuit which arose upon his publication of it evidence enough was produced to show that Wilson had composed it, the possibility remained that it was suggested to Wilson's mind by a traditional tune. In *The Choir* for July, 1934, Miss Anne G. Gilchrist traces affinities between it and versions of the air of 'Helen of Kirkconnel', and affirms her belief that Smith was right in recognizing the tune as a traditional melody. Wilson was dead before Smith published the tune with the attribution of it to a traditional source; it is impossible, therefore, not to wonder whether, if he had been alive when Smith's claim was made, he would not have confirmed it. The lawsuit was concerned only with the publisher's property right. Whatever its origin, the comment on the tune in *Songs of Praise Discussed* will meet with agreement: 'The tune was certainly worth a dispute, for it would have been a credit to any composer; on the other hand, if, as it seems, R. A. Smith was responsible for re-writing it in triple time, a large part of the credit must be his, since the beauty of the melody is immensely enhanced by the change.'

463 MY SOUL, THERE IS A COUNTRY

In *The Oxford Book of Carols* (1928) there is this note on the tune CHERRY-TREE CAROL: 'The whole story of carol-music is summed up in an incident related by Baring-Gould: about 1865 he was teaching carols to mill-girls in the West Riding; and amongst them that by Dr. Gauntlett—"St. Joseph was a walking"—when they burst out with "Nay! we know one a great deal better nor yond", and lifting up their voices, they sang'—the Cherry-Tree Carol. Though it is taken from Husk's *Songs of the Nativity* (1868), therefore it had been traditional long before that; it was printed on broadsides in all parts of England.

Sandys, an early collector, barred the tune wrongly, so that it cannot be sung as he noted it, and it is doubtful whether Husk's interpretation, here followed, as in *The Oxford Book of Carols*, is what Sandys really intended. Cecil Sharp noted (also in Cornwall) a variant of the same air in triple time, and by altering the barring, Sandys's tune falls into the same measure—the usual one for Cherry-Tree Carol tunes. See *Folk-Song Journal*, vol. v, pp. 11–14.

464 MAKE ME A CAPTIVE, LORD

LEOMINSTER was composed for Dr. Bonar's 'A few more years shall roll'. Martin's own name for it was 'The Pilgrim Song'. Sir Arthur Sullivan, in *Church Hymns*, wrote a new harmony for the tune, and made slight changes in rhythm and melody, e.g. at the end of lines 2 and 4 ♩. ♩ ♩, and in line 7:

469 JESUS, FROM THY THRONE ON HIGH

LEBBAEUS appeared without any composer's name in *The St. Albans Tune Book* (1863).

471 O THOU WHO CAMEST FROM ABOVE

This hymn is taken by the Rev. F. Luke Wiseman, in his *Charles Wesley, Evangelist and Poet*, as an illustration of how scriptural language and thought is the warp and woof of the texture of Wesley's poetry. It is based on the passage in Lev. vi. 13, 'Fire shall be kept burning upon the altar continually; it shall not go out.' But in expatiating on the passage, line after line is indebted to some scriptural passage for its expression:

> O Thou who camest from above,[1]
> The pure celestial[3] fire[2] to impart,
> Kindle[2] a flame[4] of sacred love
> On the mean altar[5] of my heart.
> There let it for Thy glory[6] burn
> With inextinguishable[7] blaze,
> And trembling[8] to its source return
> In humble prayer[9] and fervent praise.
> Jesus, confirm my heart's desire[10]
> To work, and speak, and think for Thee;
> Still let me guard[11] the holy fire,
> And still stir up[12] Thy gift in me.
> Ready[13] for all Thy perfect will,[14]
> My acts of[15] faith and love repeat,
> Till death Thy endless mercies seal,[16]
> And make the sacrifice[17] complete.

[1] John iii. 31.
[2] Luke xii. 49; 2 Chron. vii. 3.
[3] 1 Kings xviii. 38; 1 Cor. xv. 40.
[4] Isaiah xliii. 2.
[5] Lev. ix. 24; Chron. xxi. 26.
[6] 2 Cor. iv. 15; viii. 19.
[7] Lev. vi. 13.
[8] Job v. 7, margin.
[9] James iv. 6–10.
[10] Rom. x. 1.
[11] Lev. vi. 13.
[12] 2 Tim. i. 6 (Greek).
[13] Titus iii. 1.
[14] Rom. xii. 2.
[15] 1 Thess. i. 3.
[16] Ephes. iv. 30.
[17] Phil. ii. 17; 2 Tim. iv. 6; Heb. xiii. 15–16.

472 FOR THEE, MY GOD, FOR THEE ALONE

BRISTOL appeared in Vincent Novello's *The Psalmist* (Part iv, 1842), but was not written for it; Wesley died in 1839.

478 BLEST ARE THE PURE IN HEART

This, on the Purification, was the earliest written of all the poems in *The Christian Year*, the first in the MS. of 1820. An anthem setting of this hymn, by Sir Walford Davies, is in *The Church Anthem Book*.

479 LOVE DIVINE, ALL LOVES EXCELLING

The Rev. F. Luke Wiseman, in his *Charles Wesley, Evangelist and Poet*, has this interesting note on this hymn: 'Without doubt his muse was set going by the "Song of Venus" from Dryden's play, *King Arthur*. Probably, however, it was not the words but Purcell's entrancing aria to which they were set which haunted his ear. At any rate, the hymn was sung to this melody. At one and the same time, therefore, our Sir Galahad rescued this captive melody from Dryden's amorous words, and the great word "Love" from its bondage to the heathen goddess, united the two, and set them free for the glorious service of their heavenly Lord. So Dryden's words,

> Fairest Isle, all Isles Excelling,
> Seat of Pleasures, and of Loves;
> Venus here will chuse her Dwelling,
> And forsake her *Cyprian* Groves.

> Cupid, from his Fav'rite Nation
> Care and Envy will Remove;
> Jealousy that poysons Passion
> And Despair that dies for Love,

are transfigured into

> Love Divine, all loves excelling, &c.'

A verse in the original of the hymn was omitted in *The Wesleyan Hymn Book* of 1780, and has been generally omitted since, to the great gain of the hymn:

> Breathe, O breathe Thy living Spirit
> Into every troubled Breast,
> Let us all in Thee inherit,
> Let us find that Second Rest.
> Take away our power of sinning,
> Alpha and Omega be;
> End of Faith as its beginning,
> Set our hearts at liberty.

The aria of Purcell referred to as inspiring the hymn appeared in *Sacred Harmony* under the name WESTMINSTER, as follows:

Love di - vine, all loves... ex - cell - ing,
Fix in us thy hum - ble dwell - ing,

Joy... of heav'n.. to earth come down;
All... thy faith - - ful mer - cies crown;

Je - su, thou.. art all... com - pas - sion,

Pure.. un - bound - ed love thou art;

Vis - it us with thy.. sal - va - tion,

En - ter ev - - 'ry trem - bling heart.

481 FATHER OF PEACE, AND GOD OF LOVE

It is interesting to note how the name—Andrew Tait—of the putative composer of ST. PAUL misled Henry Edward Dibdin, who had evidently only heard, not seen it, into a wild guess at his identity; in *The Standard Psalm Tune Book* (1850) he ascribed the tune to Nahum Tate! By the time his historical preface to the book was written, however, he had discovered that he was mistaken, for he wrote there as follows: 'This tune is not clearly traced. These are the facts connected with it. 1st.—It is not in Tate's Supplement, 1703. 2nd.—It is in William Gray's Collection of Psalm Tunes, Edinburgh, 1758. Dr. Mainzer assigns the tune to William Tate. If he had sufficient authority for so doing, the question is settled so far as Nahum Tate is concerned. It is probably of Scottish origin.'

The title of Chalmers's book, which Tait is believed to have edited, as given in the third edition, was: *A New and Correct Set of Church Tunes, viz.* [twenty-three tunes named] *with the Scale and Directions. Dedicated to the Provost, Baillies, and Permanent Members of Town Council, 'Encouragers and Promoters of useful Learning'.*

491 ALMIGHTY FATHER, WHO DOST GIVE

Bishop Masterman's hymn first appeared in *In Hoc Signo* (1916).

493 FATHER OF MEN, IN WHOM ARE ONE

Shuttleworth, a follower of Maurice and Kingsley in their Christian Socialism, wrote this hymn for the members of a club in connexion with his church of St. Nicholas Cole Abbey. It appeared in 1897 in the *Hymnal Appendix* (to *Church Hymns*) issued for use in that church, and, with music by the author, in his *Church Monthly* in the following year.

495 SAVIOUR, WHILE MY HEART IS TENDER

The ballad referred to, from which SHIPSTON is derived, is to be found in *English County Songs*, p. 71.

497 JUST AS I AM, THINE OWN TO BE

SAFFRON WALDEN was written for Charlotte Elliott's hymn 'O holy Saviour, Friend unseen'.

498 LORD, IN THE FULNESS OF MY MIGHT

The contemporary Cambridge tune-book referred to in the *Handbook* note on UNIVERSITY was Pieter Hellendaal's *A Collection of Psalms for the use of Parish Churches*, &c. (Cambridge, 1780). The fact that Randall was a contributor to this book, and that in his own *Collection of Psalm Tunes* (1754) he made no claim to the tune, makes it extremely unlikely that he was the composer.

501 'TAKE UP THY CROSS,' THE SAVIOUR SAID

The date given for *As Hymnodus Sacer* in the *Handbook* note—1652—is a misprint for 1625. BRESLAU is a recast of the folk-song 'Ich fahr dahin', from the *Locheimer Liederbuch*, *c.* 1452.

504 THINE FOR EVER! GOD OF LOVE

The year of Archbishop Benson's death was 1896.

Wesley's name for the tune here named SAVANNAH was HERRNHUT, his SAVANNAH being quite a different tune.

506 I BIND UNTO MYSELF TO-DAY

ST. PATRICK is tune No. 1048 in the complete Petrie collection.

517 FIGHT THE GOOD FIGHT

The tune PENTECOST is altered to common time in the *Students' Hymnal*. This alteration is stated to have been made with the consent of the composer, who had been grieved at the alienation of his tune from its *Veni Creator* association by its annexation to a hymn of so different a character. Since it is now so firmly welded to the present hymn, the editor of the *Students' Hymnal* evidently judged that the best thing to be done was to suit it better to these words by setting it to a more vigorous rhythm, suggesting a march-tune rather than a devotional hymn, thus:

520 WORKMAN OF GOD! O LOSE NOT HEART

It is fair to say that the tradition that MARTYRS was sung by the Covenanters at Drumclog as they marched into battle probably originated with Sir Walter Scott. There is no trustworthy anterior evidence for it. The Laird of Torfoot's *Narrative of Drumclog and Bothwell Bridge* says that the aged men who stayed behind sang a cheering psalm to the tune MARTYRS, but does not say what psalm it was; then says that the fighting men, as they were in order opposite to Claverhouse and ready to join battle, sang a part of Psalm lxxvi, but makes no mention of the tune to which they sang it. The authenticity of this *Narrative*, however, is open to the gravest doubt.

There was no conventicle at Drumclog. One had been in process at Loudoun Hill, but broke up when word came that Claverhouse was on the march. The Covenanters then moved to meet him in a better strategic position. Claverhouse in his account of the engagement says plainly that they had sent away their women and children, and that when he saw them he found that they were 'drawn up in battle, upon a most advantageous ground, to which there was no coming but through mosses and lakes'. This last detail is fairly conclusive evidence against the tradition.

The late Rev. James Mearns, of *The Dictionary of Hymnology*, an expert assayer of the value of evidence, examined all the data in this question and concluded that the psalm-singing looked like a picturesque invention. 'Sir Walter', he wrote, in a series of letters to the late William Cowan, now in the possession of the editor of this Supplement, 'makes the Covenanters sing Psalm lxxvi after they had got into their chosen battle-ground. The person who invented the story of their singing on the march probably never tried to set his best foot foremost going down a broken, boggy hillside, and sing at the same time.'

John Gibson Lockhart, in *Peter's Letters to his Kinsfolk* (vol. iii, p. 332), stated that MARTYRS was at that time, about 1819, a great favourite over the west of Scotland, and that it was usually sung in schools to the following words:

> This is the tune the Martyrs sang
> When they, condemned to die,
> Did stand all at the gallows-tree
> Their God to glorify.

Supplementary Notes on Hymns and Tunes

Peter Morris, in his description, which follows, of a Scottish sacramental Sabbath, speaks of 'the deep and thrilling harmony' of the people's untaught voices, 'when they lifted them all up together in that old tune which immemorial custom has set apart for the last psalm sung upon this sacred day—a tune which is endeared to them by the memory of those from whose attachment its designation is derived, still more than by the low and affecting swell of its own sad, composing cadences—the "plaintive *Martyrs*, worthy of the name". The quaint choral falls of this antique melody, breathed by such a multitude of old and young, diffused a kind of holy charm over the tall, whispering groves and darkening fields around—a thousand times more grand and majestic than all the gorgeous stops of an organ ever wakened in the echoing aisles of a cathedral. There was a breath of sober, enduring heroism in its long-repeated, melancholy accents—which seemed to fall like a sweet evening dew upon all the hearts that drank in the sacred murmurs.'

It is possible that the tune MARTYRS, first printed under this name in the Scottish Psalter of 1615, commemorates the martyrs of the previous century on account of its association with Psalm li, which was the psalm which the martyr George Wishart desired to be sung on the evening before his apprehension in 1546. But it will not fit the Wedderburn version, in *The Gude and Godlie Ballatis* (see note on Hymn 174 in this Supplement), quoted by Knox as the one used on that occasion, which consists of six-line stanzas followed in each verse by a refrain; nor yet does it fit Whittingham's rendering in eight eights. It will, however, fit T. Norton's D.C.M. version in the English Psalter of 1562, if the stanza be divided into two. And it is rather an interesting point that Norton's psalm is directed in the English Psalter to be sung to the tune of LAMENTATION (No. I), and that one line of LAMENTATION is almost exactly the same as the third line of MARTYRS; there are general resemblances also, suggesting that MARTYRS might have been partly constructed out of LAMENTATION reduced to the length of a 'common tune' for the 'Martyr's psalm' and altered in traditional use.

LAMENTATION, in the Aeolian mode, as in Day's Psalter, 1591, has lines 1, 6, 7, and 8 as follows:

524 JESUS, LORD OF LIFE AND GLORY

AD PERENNIS VITAE FONTEM is said to be from the *Tours Breviary*, but confirmation of this is lacking.

52

525 IN THE HOUR OF TRIAL

The original form of DÚN ÁLUINN is as follows:

526 A SAFE STRONGHOLD OUR GOD IS STILL

Dr. James Mackinnon, in his *Luther and the Reformation* (vol. iv, p. 327), refers thus to this hymn: 'In this magnificent challenge of the foe we have the thrilling manifestation of the spirit that carried him and the Reformation to triumph in the struggle with the might and majesty of Rome. It is unquestionably a masterpiece of religious emotion, into which he put, as Lucke expresses it, "the quintessence of his life".'

531 O GOD OF TRUTH, WHOSE LIVING WORD

This hymn, according to Ellerton, 'is obviously suggested by Mr. Maurice's sermon on "The Word of God conquering by Sacrifice" in his volume on *The Doctrine of Sacrifice*'.

The identity of the supposed composer of BLACKBOURN—a Lancashire musician named J. Fish—cannot be determined. This being so, there is probability in the attribution of the tune to Willem Defesch, a Dutch organist of the first half of the eighteenth century, who wrote two oratorios, *Joseph* and *Judith*, a mass, and a variety of instrumental works. The name 'Fish' is probably a corruption of this name.

533 MUCH IN SORROW, OFT IN WOE

The 'Miss Fuller-Maitland' of the *Handbook* note was Frances Sara, afterwards Mrs. John Colquhoun. The story is that her mother showed her Kirke White's fragment, expressing regret that it had not been finished. Frances took it to her room and 'presently brought it back with the 14 lines completed'. Mrs. Colquhoun included the hymn in her collected verses, *Rhymes and Chimes* (1876). Edward Bickersteth was the first to include it in a hymn-book—in his *Christian Psalmody* (1833). It was he who altered the first line to the form in which it appears in most hymnals—'Oft in danger, oft in woe'; he made numerous other changes besides.

534 SOLDIERS OF CHRIST! ARISE

'It seems likely that the words were set going by the melody. In the 1761 tune-book the hymn is set to one of Handel's stirring marches, which requires two 8-line verses for the complete recital of the tune. Altogether it is a *tour de force*.' (F. Luke Wiseman, in *Charles Wesley, Evangelist and Poet*.)

This being so, Dr. Naylor's fine tune, FROM STRENGTH TO STRENGTH, restores the hymn to the 8-line form which Wesley intended for it. The tune was composed for use in Emmanuel College Chapel, Cambridge, about 1902, and was first published in sheet form.

The march referred to is in the opera *Richard the First*. The tune may be found as JERICHO TUNE in *The Methodist Hymnbook*, 819, and also in an abridged form in *Songs of Praise*, 343, under the name MILITES. (See J. T. Lightwood's *Hymn Tunes and their Story*, p. 123.)

536 SAY NOT, 'THE STRUGGLE NOUGHT AVAILETH'

The tune GRACE DIEU, in *The European Psalmist* (1872), where it first appeared, was set to Jane Maurice's hymn 'There is a rest from sin and sorrow'.

549 LORD, IT BELONGS NOT TO MY CARE

The title Baxter gave to this hymn, misquoted in the *Handbook* note, was 'The Concordant Discord of a Broken-healed Heart'. The poem begins:

> My whole, though broken heart, O Lord!
> From henceforth shall be Thine.
> And here I do my vow record:
> This hand, these words, are mine.

The hymn begins with ver. 4 of the original:

> Now it belongs not to my care.

The Church Anthem Book contains an anthem setting of this hymn, by Sir Walford Davies.

552 JESUS IS OUR SHEPHERD

All that can be discovered about the writer of the tune from which GOSHEN was adapted is that her name was Marchel Davis, and that she lived in Dublin. The date of her song is about 1848–50.

GOSHEN is almost identical with Miss Davis's 'Happy Hours of Childhood', but a few more of the notes are dotted in the original, which is reprinted in Kidson and Moffat's *Minstrelsy of Childhood*, 1911. It is a pretty and rather wistful song, beginning:

> Happy hours of childhood,
> Soon they pass away,
> O'er the mount and wild-wood
> Joyous all the day.

Swift those laughing hours,
On light pinions borne,
Pass like summer flowers,
Never to return.

557 HE THAT IS DOWN NEEDS FEAR NO FALL

The air, 'Little Sir William'—on which ST. HUGH is based will be
found in *English County Songs*, p. 86.

559 'TWIXT GLEAMS OF JOY AND CLOUDS OF DOUBT

Of the THIRD MODE MELODY the musical editor of *Songs of
Praise Discussed* says: 'It is a remarkable tune, with a nobility and
solid grandeur which . . . place it among the greatest melodic conceptions of Tallis's genius. It is the theme of R. Vaughan Williams's
Fantasia for Strings, where the supreme beauty of the tune is given
full value.'

562 O GOD OF BETHEL! BY WHOSE HAND

This was sung at the funeral of David Livingstone, 'brought by
faithful hands over land and sea,' in Westminster Abbey, on Saturday, April 18, 1874.

568 LEAD, KINDLY LIGHT

Newman, questioned as to the precise meaning of 'kindly Light',
answered: 'There must be a statute of limitation for writers of verse,
or it would be quite tyranny if, in an art which is the expression, not
of truth, but of imagination and sentiment, one were obliged to be
ready for examination on the transient states of mind which came
upon one when home-sick, or sea-sick, or in any other way sensitive
or excited.' (*Letter to Dr. Greenhill*, Jan. 18, 1879.)

Dykes's tune LUX BENIGNA came to the composer as he walked
along the Strand—'a curious contrast to the calm Mediterranean
night which inspired the words'.

570 O LORD, I SING THY PRAISES

Of KILLIN, Miss Gilchrist says: 'It does not sound to me like a
Gaelic air, and in the absence of the 6th degree of the mode it cannot
conclusively be called Dorian. It has the Aeolian signature of B♭.
Also the Dorian mode is very rare amongst Highland airs; it is a
mode belonging to the Lowlands of Scotland and to English folk-
music.'

571 THE GOD OF ABRAHAM PRAISE

The Hebrew *Yigdal* which suggested this hymn to Olivers is a
confession of faith which is read at the opening of the morning
service every day in the Jewish ritual, but is sung to traditional

tunes on the Sabbath eve and on the evenings of the Jewish Festivals. It is believed to have been written by Daniel ben Judah Dayyan in 1404, and is founded on the thirteen creeds of Moses ben Maimon. The traditional tunes to which it is sung are many, derived from various countries.

574 CHILDREN OF THE HEAVENLY KING

The tune by Joseph Smith referred to in the *Handbook* note as the possible source of INNOCENTS is given below. Smith set his tune to a child's song called by him 'The Sun', which Miss A. G. Gilchrist found in the collected works of Ann and Jane Taylor (q.v.), under the title 'A Fine Thing'—a sort of poetic riddle (in five verses) of which Smith oddly preferred to give away the answer in his title.

> Who am I with noble face,
> Shining in a clear blue place?
> If to look at me you try,
> I shall blind your little eye.
>
> When my noble face I shew
> Over yonder mountains blue,
> All the clouds away do ride,
> And the dusky night beside. . . .

According to one supposition, Smith's tune fell into the hands of the then anonymous editor of *The Parish Choir* (1846–51), afterwards known to be W. H. Monk, and by him was adapted to a 'Hymn for Innocents' Day' (whence the name of the tune)—a translation of Prudentius's 'Salvete flores martyrum'.

In an article in *The Choir* for April 1929, Miss Gilchrist argued that Monk did not use Smith's tune, but that both drew from a common original, the tune 'Saxony', which was familiar in psalm-tune books from 1791, when it was first printed in Arnold and Callcott's *The Psalms of David for Use in Parish Churches*, down to the latter half of the nineteenth century. SAXONY was an adaptation from the air 'Non vi piacque ingiusti Dei' (One cannot please unjust gods), in Handel's opera *Siroë* (1728); it is made out of the first four bars and later selected phrases of the aria. (Cf. note under Psalter Tunes in this Supplement on 'Heriot's Tune'.)

Another link in the history of INNOCENTS may be found in the air of 'Dear is my little native vale', in *The Edinburgh Musical Miscellany* of 1793, though its precise place in the evolution is not clear. It appeared in an English collection ten years later, and may possibly have furnished the medium through which Smith received his suggestion.

576 WHO WOULD TRUE VALOUR SEE

Although Bunyan may have known Shakespeare's song in *As You Like It*—'Who doth ambition shun'—his own is written in a different metre, a ballad-measure popular in the sixteenth and seventeenth centuries, of which the best-known example to-day is 'O what a plague is love' (Phillida flouts me). See Chappell's *Popular Music* for this and other similar triple-time tunes. Bunyan's stanza is the same as that of the Shakespeare song, except that he does not double the first four lines before coming to his triplet of rhyming lines. Other contemporary songs in this dactylic metre dispense with the triplet, merely doubling the first quatrain, but their tunes are interchangeable. One of these, 'The Valiant Seaman's Happy Return to his True Love', may have helped to suggest Bunyan's opening line, following on Mr. Valiant's speech:

Who would true valour see . . .

MONKS GATE was noted as sung by a Mrs. Verrall, of Monks Gate, near Horsham, Sussex, to a traditional version of the same 'Valiant' or 'Welcome Sailor' ballad, beginning:

> Our captain calls all hands
> On board to-morrow,
> Leaving my dear to mourn
> In grief and sorrow.
> Dry up those briny tears
> And leave off weeping,
> So happy may we be
> At our next meeting.

It is not impossible that MONKS GATE is a traditional version of the very tune Bunyan had in his mind when he wrote his Pilgrim Song. The 'Valiant Seaman' ballad was directed to be sung to a triple-time tune, 'I am so deep in love: Or, Through the cool shady Woods' (Cupid's Courtesy), preserved in Chappell's *Popular Music of the Olden Time*. The ambiguous and irregular rhythm of MONKS GATE— of which there are other versions in the *Folk-Song Journal*—suggests an origin as a triple-time tune, like others belonging to Elizabethan songs in the Bunyan metre. See *Folk-Song Journal*, vol. iii, pp. 97–8. For MONKS GATE see vol. ii, p. 202.

580 HARK, HARK, MY SOUL! ANGELIC SONGS ARE SWELLING

Sullivan, whether deliberately plagiarizing or not, seems to have borrowed the last four lines of this melody for a chorus in *Patience*.

581 THE SANDS OF TIME ARE SINKING

It was the melody only for the arrangement of which E. F. Rimbault was responsible.

587 THERE IS A HAPPY LAND

The tunes of this hymn and 'Jesus loves me' (660) are both pentatonic, and because of this, our China missionaries find that they are easily learnt by the Chinese, whose attempts to sing the semitones of certain English hymn-tunes are very painful. Chinese music is pentatonic in its system, and these tunes are therefore more akin to the native gapped modes.

592 THERE IS A LAND OF PURE DELIGHT

There is some uncertainty as to the traditional localization of the 'sweet fields beyond the swelling flood' on the shores of Southampton Water. On the one hand T. Wright suggests 'the pleasant meadows near Netley', but on the other, he goes on to say: 'Few cities can boast a fairer landscape than that which greets the tourist when, standing on Southampton Pier, he looks out over the broad waters of the estuary and the swelling uplands, and ample meadows which stretch beyond, as far even as the waving masses of the New Forest.' If the meadows near Netley inspired the line, the poet must have been looking eastward, and the New Forest must be ruled out; if he was thinking of those between the estuary and the Forest, he must have been looking in the opposite direction, and Netley must be ruled out. Julian's suggestion that the Isle of Wight inspired the line can hardly be entertained, for with the fair prospects both east and west, and near at hand, before the poet's eyes, it is not likely that he would find his inspiration beyond them, in an island ten miles or more away.

595 JERUSALEM, MY HAPPY HOME

THIS ENDRIS NYGHT ('endris' meaning 'last') was the tune of a carol beginning:

> Thys endris nygth I saw a sygth,
> A ster as brygth as daye,
> And ever among a maydyn song
> By by, baby, lullay.

A facsimile of the MS. from which it was taken, both words and music, may be seen in the Historical Edition (1904) of *Hymns Ancient and Modern*, p. xxviii.

596 FROM HEAVENLY JERUSALEM'S TOWERS

CRUGYBAR, which does not seem to have appeared in print before 1883, was probably, like JOANNA (q.v.), originally in triple time; but from its use as a funeral hymn, sung at a very slow *tempo*, it has assumed its present form. 'Old Derby' is another example of this development from triple time. In the *Welsh Folk-Song Journal*, vol. ii (1919), p. 128, under the carol 'O deued Pob Cristion', the editor comments on the 'tendency among old singers to divide the lines into short phrases, prolonging the end of each phrase and giving the effect of syncopation'. The carol in question furnishes an example of this way of singing a triple-time air. CRUGYBAR belongs to a group of triple-time folk-tunes in three-bar phrases, suggesting an origin as a dance-air. It is rather like a major form of 'The pretty girl milking her cow', which appears in Ieuan Gwyllt's earlier book as 'Llanarmon'. Cf. also 'Old Derby' and 'Bethel', the latter being set to the same hymn to which CRUGYBAR belongs, in *Canadiau y Cyssegr a'r Teulu*. The original form of CRUGYBAR was probably this:

&c.

597–9 BRIEF LIFE IS HERE OUR PORTION

The metre of the original poem has been imitated also by Swinburne:

'O land, without guilt, strong city safe built in a marvellous place,
I cling to thee, ache for thee, sing to thee, wake for thee, watch for thy face.'

See *The Boyhood of Swinburne*, by Mrs. Disney Leith, p. 33.

597 BRIEF LIFE IS HERE OUR PORTION

The tune JABEZ has appeared in various forms since 1839, under the names also of 'Rhuabon', 'Deisyfiod', 'Jamaica', and 'Dewi Sant'. It is a variant of a tune in Nicholas Bennett's *Alawon fy Ngwlad* (Songs of our land) which, without any Welsh title, is called 'The Spanish Minuet'. The South Wales form most nearly resembles JABEZ, the North Wales version, given on the same page (103), being a major version.

601 O GOD, OUR HELP IN AGES PAST

F. J. Gillman, in *The Evolution of the English Hymn* (1927), p. 209, compares Watts's two masterpieces, 'O God, our help' and 'When I survey', thus:

'They both, in a superlative degree, reveal the characteristic features of his best work—its simple strength, its transparency, its hold upon the common mind, its straightforwardness, its accentual and punctuative perfection, and its faithfulness to Scripture. The first has become the great ceremonial hymn of the English nation, and if nothing else had come from his pen, it justifies its author's memorial in Westminster Abbey. The other is more personal, and has more passion.'

Dr. Jowett once asked a tea-party of Balliol and other dons to jot down a small list of the best hymns. It is said that they all returned their papers with one hymn only mentioned, 'O God, our help', each feeling that it fulfilled all the conditions of a perfect hymn.

The tune ST. ANNE no doubt gets its name from St. Anne's, Soho, where Croft was organist when it was composed. Like many other first-class tunes, TALLIS, for instance, it is not wholly original. The first line is a stock phrase which makes frequent appearances in the seventeenth and eighteenth centuries. It is the initial phrase, for example, in two tunes by Henry Lawes in Sandys's *Paraphrase upon the Psalms of David* (1637), and of the first chorus in Handel's sixth Chandos Anthem, 'O praise the Lord' (1734); it is the theme also of Bach's famous organ fugue in E♭, which has therefore, in England, come to be known as 'St. Anne's Fugue'.

605 AT THY FEET, OUR GOD AND FATHER

James Drummond Burns's hymn appeared first in 1861 in *The Family Treasury*, a religious monthly then circulating widely in Scotland, and six years later in his *Psalms and Hymns for Divine Worship*.

608 THE GLORY OF THE SPRING HOW SWEET

The English traditional May Day carol referred to in the *Handbook* note as 'The moon shines bright', is given, as sung by Mrs. Marshall, King's Langley (whence the name of the hymn-tune), in *English County Songs*, p. 108.

612 THE SUMMER DAYS ARE COME AGAIN

This hymn, dated 1859, and entitled 'Summer Rural Gathering' in *Hymns and Verses* (Houghton and Mifflin, 1894), began as follows:

> The sweet June days are come again,
>   With sun and clouds between,
> And, fed alike by sun and rain,
>   The trees grow broad and green;
> Spreads broad and green the leafy tent,
>   Upon whose grassy floor
> Our feet, too long in cities pent,
>   Their freedom find once more.

625 O LORD, BE WITH US WHEN WE SAIL

The adaptation of FARRANT as a hymn-tune was made by Dr. Edward Hodges of Bristol, who arranged it as a common metre tune and sent it to W. H. Havergal for inclusion in his *Old Church Psalmody* (1847).

626 ETERNAL FATHER, STRONG TO SAVE

Of MELITA F. G. Edwards says: 'In the last line but one of each verse the inflected note (F sharp) gives to the word "cry" a piercing and plaintive emphasis, and yet its introduction seems both natural and unrestrained.'

631 GOD SAVE OUR GRACIOUS KING

Mr. J. A. Fuller-Maitland, in his autobiographical *A Door-keeper of Music* (1929), threw light on the history of the tune. 'In editing the catches of Purcell for the Purcell Society', he wrote, 'Squire [i.e. W. Barclay Squire] and I found one written to celebrate the return of the Duke of York (James II) from virtual exile in 1680; and that the words 'God save the King' which occur in it are set to the very same four notes of the tune. The little phrase is obviously used as an allusion to something already familiar, and though the identity of the phrase does not at once strike the eye, yet when the catch was sung at a meeting of the Musical Association at which I reported the discovery, the prominence given to the four notes made it a matter of certainty that the quotation was deliberately made. Before this catch was found, the earliest date for the appearance of the tune we know was 1740 or 1743; as the MS. containing the catch, now in the British Museum, bears as a date of ownership 1681, the song is undoubtedly older than that, since it seems to be quoted in the catch as though the allusion would be recognized by those who heard it. Incidentally, the catch proves that the reference of the song was to the house of Stuart, not to that of Hanover.'

This assignment of a Stuart origin to the hymn may be supported by the line

Send him victorious,

which suggests a reference to the exiled king. In the Jacobite version, extant as engraved on the 'treason glasses' of the Jacobite period, privately used for drinking the 'king's' health, we have the line '*Soon* to reign over us', and a second verse:

> God bless the Prince of Wales,
> The true-born Prince of Wales,
> Sent us by Thee.
> Grant us one favour more,
> The king for to restore,
> As Thou hast done before
> The familie.

See *The Romance of the White Rose*, 1933, by Grant R. Francis, F.S.A.

634 PRAISE TO OUR GOD, WHOSE BOUNTEOUS HAND

The main source of our knowledge of AGINCOURT SONG is a long parchment roll in the Library of Trinity College, Cambridge. There is another MS. in the Pepys Library, Magdalene College. See J. A. Fuller-Maitland's *A Doorkeeper of Music*.

636 JUDGE ETERNAL, THRONED IN SPLENDOUR

Mr. Archibald Jacob, in his note on PICARDY in *Songs of Praise Discussed*, says that this tune is unlike other French carol tunes used in that book in this respect, that 'there is no childlike mirth or gaiety here, whether the tune be sung fast or slow. In the present instance it must be sung very slowly, when its character appears rather sombre, but at the same time dignified and ceremonious; if, however, it is sung fast, the sombreness changes to fierceness, and though it may suggest a dance, it is a dance of no amenable kind. All tunes change their character, to a certain degree, with a considerable change of speed, but the cleavage here is of a very remarkable nature, and denotes an unusual tune.'

638 O GOD OF EARTH AND ALTAR

Chesterton's hymn appeared originally in Scott Holland's monthly magazine *The Commonwealth*. Knowing nothing of music himself, and unable to tell one tune from another, he told Canon Dearmer that he assumed that AURELIA was the typical tune for hymns, and therefore wrote this hymn in that metre.

639 THESE THINGS SHALL BE

The first hymn-book to include this hymn was *The Methodist Hymn Book* of 1904. It has a place in *The League of Nations Song Book*.

640 AND DID THOSE FEET IN ANCIENT TIME

The first sentence of the first paragraph on p. 222 should read: 'It was suggested to Sir Hubert Parry by Dr. Robert Bridges.'

654 JESUS, TENDER SHEPHERD, HEAR ME

Sir John Stainer told F. G. Edwards, a former editor of *The Musical Times*, that the melody of EVENING PRAYER was founded on the opening theme of Beethoven's Andante in F.

659 WHEN MOTHERS OF SALEM

It should be said for Mr. Hutchings, who wrote this hymn, that he was probably quite unaware that the tune to which he wrote it was originally a German drinking song. The tune is to be found in a collection of social songs, *c.* 1850—W. E. Hickson's *Part Music*—to quite innocuous words beginning:

> O come, come away, from labour now reposing,
> Let busy care awhile forbear,
> O come, come away.

Come, come, our social joys renew,
And there where love and friendship grew
    Let true hearts welcome you,
      O come, come away.

This was obviously the model for at least three early Sunday-school hymns to the same tune (one of them beginning with exactly the same three lines), which are to be found in Brumby's *Gems of Sacred Poetry* (1858), in *Lancashire Sunday School Songs*, and in *The North of England Sunday School Hymnbook*. In this last collection No. 48 is 'The Sunday Scholar's Invitation':

O come, come to school, your teachers join in praises,
    On this happy Pearl of days
      O come, come away.

No. 50 is 'The Child's Welcome to Jesus'—Hutchings's hymn. In the Lancashire book 'O come, come away' is No. 15, with 'Mothers of Salem' set later in the book to the same tune. In Brumby's *Gems* the 'Come, come away' hymn, only, is printed to the tune. From this it seems probable that the *Krambambuli* tune was already in use in North of England Sunday schools when Hutchings wrote his hymn to it, that the hymns of 'Invitation' suggested 'The Child's Welcome to Jesus' for the Wigan anniversary for which it was written, and that all the 'Come, come away' versions were based on Hickson's part-song to the German tune. (For Hickson see biographical note in Handbook.)

661 LORD, A LITTLE BAND AND LOWLY

The tune ROUSSEAU is adapted from the *divertissement* (Scene VIII) in *Le Devin du Village* (The Village Sorcerer), *Intermède* in one Act, words and music by J. J. Rousseau; first played at Fontainebleau, Oct. 18, 1752; translated and adapted as *The Cunning Man* by Dr. Burney, and produced at Drury Lane in 1766.

The first vocal adaptation of it appears to have been under the title 'Melissa' to words by Charles James (1788). Mr. James T. Lightwood has recently traced this song under its proper title, 'Sweet Melissa', in the British Museum. It furnishes a valuable link between the *divertissement* air and 'Rousseau's Dream', as J. B. Cramer, with whom this name seems to have originated, published it in his *Songe de J. J. Rousseau, Air varié pour le Forte Piano, arrangé pour les petits Pianos* (Paris, vers 1812; and in England by Chappell in the same year). What Cramer meant by 'Songe' (Dream) is wholly left to the imagination.

In the British Museum copy or catalogue the date 1788 for 'Sweet Melissa' is given with a query. The writer of the words may probably be identified with the Charles James (d. 1821), major and author, who travelled through France during the Revolution (which he upheld), was imprisoned, and died at Boulogne. (See *Dictionary of*

National Biography.) In America the tune as we know it is called 'Days of Absence', from the 'thrice familiar' words set to the tune, which begin:

> Days of absence, sad and dreary,
> Cloth'd in sorrow's dark array;
> Days of absence, I am weary,
> She I love is far away.
> Hours of bliss, too quickly vanish'd,
> When will aught like you return,
> When the heavy sigh be banish'd,
> When this bosom cease to mourn?

The song is addressed to 'Antoinette', which may be the only colour for the suggestion that Rousseau wrote the words (presumably in French) as well as adapted the tune from his opera. (See *Our Familiar Songs and those who wrote them*, edited by Helen Kendrick Johnson, New York, 1889.) The tune has been known as a hymn-tune in America at least since 1838, when it appeared in *The Christian Lyre* under the name 'Greenville'. It seems never to have been known in America as 'Rousseau's Dream'. 'Sweet Melissa' is as follows:

It is possible that the following hymn-tune, known in earlier American hymn-books as 'Middleton' or 'Opal', and sung to 'Hail, Thou once-despised Jesus', is an independent offshoot from Rousseau's original air:

The first adaptation of the tune to a hymn appears to have been in Thomas Walter's *Companion to Dr. Rippon's Tunes* (1825). It afterwards appeared in *Sacred Melodies* (1843) with the name 'Rousseau' attached to it.

A remarkable resemblance may be noted between this tune and the Scots air, 'Gude e'en to you, Kimmer', in Johnson's *Museum* (No. 523).

673. GOD, WHO CREATED ME

Appeared first in *Love in a Looking-Glass* (1891).

676 PRAISE TO OUR GOD, WHO WITH LOVE NEVER SWERVING

Goss's tune BEDE is an adaptation from the duet 'Cease thy anguish, smile once more' in Handel's oratorio *Athalia*, Part Second, Scene III. Handel's melody is as follows:

679 REVIVE THY WORK, O LORD

CAMBERWELL is by Ralph Harrison. It appeared in vol. i of his *Sacred Harmony* in 1784. The name usually given to it is CAMBRIDGE.

692 THERE IS A FOUNTAIN FILLED WITH BLOOD

Dr. Lowell Mason published a shortened form of Havergal's song-melody in 1850, calling it EVA. It was afterwards named EVAN. The 3/2 form in which Mason rearranged it was as follows, in a halting metre to which as a hymn-composer he was rather addicted.

It appears thus as 'Arranged by Dr. Lowell Mason' in *The Shawm*, 1853. This was evidently the American version—also found in later American tune-books—which Havergal called 'a sad estrangement', preferring to reconstruct his tune himself, if it had to be done, in common time, as it appears in the *Church Hymnary*, except that in Havergal's own arrangement of 1870 each line begins with a semibreve.

Havergal's original air was deliberately composed for 'Burns's Prayer', in what he conceived to be the Scottish manner, and it appears as though he may have taken MARTYRDOM as his model, for his tune is rather like MARTYRDOM the wrong side up.

In the United States the tune is generally sung still in 3/2 time.

The Tonic Sol-fa Reporter of May, 1878, said that at that time the popularity of this tune in Scotland, America, and the Colonies was quite unprecedented.

703 A DEBTOR TO MERCY ALONE

C. J. Abbey, in *The English Church in the Eighteenth Century*, vol. ii, p. 523, has the following criticism: 'Toplady's hymns have many faults. His rhymes are often extremely careless. . . . He is apt to employ a variety of confused metaphors: sometimes he uses expressions which offend by their want of taste; and occasionally he does not scruple to use an Alexander Selkirk metre which is particularly disagreeable to the ear when adapted to sacred subjects. Apart from all question whether statements of peculiar dogmatic views are not prosaic and inappropriate as introduced into a hymn, what solemnity can there be in such a jingle as the following?

> A debtor to mercy alone,
>   Of covenant mercy I sing;
> Nor fear, with Thy righteousness on,
>   My person and offering to bring.'

In a little collection of about sixty hymns edited for use in the morning worship of a girls' school in Bombay which is attended by Moslems, Parsis, and Hindus, as well as Christians, this hymn, rather remarkably, is one of those included.

704 YIELD NOT TO TEMPTATION

If Dr. Palmer's hymn was written in 1868, as is stated in the *Handbook* note, and set to its tune in the same year, the latter would seem to have been merely an adaptation from the following earlier tune, which appeared in Bradbury's *Golden Chain* in 1864, and in the same editor's *New Golden Trio* in 1866, set to a hymn:

> Come, come, sing to the Saviour,
>   Love, love, beams from His eye.
> Haste, then, share in His favour,
>   Worship the Saviour on high.
>   Worship the Saviour (*bis*),
>   Worship the Saviour on high.

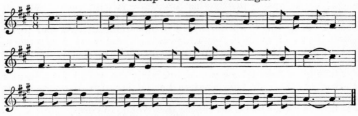

727 'Authorized' should be 'Revised'.

HISTORICAL NOTES ON THE PSALTER TUNES NOT INCLUDED IN THE REVISED CHURCH HYMNARY

ABERFELDY first appeared in *The Psalms of David, in Prose and Metre: with the whole Forme of Discipline, and Prayers, according to the Church of Scotland.* (Aberdene: Printed by Edward Raban. 1633.) It is placed there among the Common Tunes, and is named 'Montrosse Tune'. In the 1633 Psalter, printed by Andro Hart's Heirs, it is set without a name to Psalm xxi. The name it now bears appears to have been given to it by H. E. Dibdin (q.v.) in his *Standard Psalm Tune Book* (1851). In its modern form it differs slightly at some points, principally in the inner parts, from that in which it is given in those early psalters.

Like BON ACCORD (q.v.), this tune is an example of what were called 'Tunes in Reports' in the books that first printed them. The name is derived from the French *rapporter*, to carry back, and it is used to describe what musicians now would call a short fugal passage. 'It may have been understood to mean either a *carrying back*, that is, after a passage has been started by one harmonic part, taking it back to the same point and starting it anew by another; or, *carrying again*, that is, repeating the passage by the parts in succession. Or, if the term referred to echoing, answering, or what is now called Imitation, the idea is still the same.' (Dr. Neil Livingston, *The Scottish Metrical Psalter of A.D. 1635, reprinted in full from the Original Work, with Dissertations, Notes, and Facsimiles.* 1864.)

In both these tunes the melody is given to the 'Trebbles', contrary to the universal practice in those times, which is followed in every other instance in the early psalm-books, of assigning the 'Church Part' or melody to the tenors.

ARNOLD first appeared in *The Psalms of David for the Use of Parish Churches. The Music selected, adapted, and composed by Dr. Arnold . . . assisted by J. W. Callcott* (1791). It was there set to Psalm xv, and arranged so that the first two lines should be sung as a duet by first and second trebles, the same lines repeated also as a duet by tenor and bass, and the third and fourth lines sung in full chorus. It is first found in Scotland, in the form in which it is now used, in Robert Gilmour's *Psalm Singer's Assistant* (n.d., but before 1793).

ASPURG (also known as 'Kornthal') is from *Vierstimmige Gesänge der evangelischen Kirche* (Stuttgart, 1825). It is there set to the hymn 'Singt unserm Herrn ein dankvoll Lied'.

AYNHOE, though commonly attributed to Dr. Nares (q.v.), does not appear in the collections of Smart and Riley, to which he contributed. It is an altered form of a tune named HAYNOR, which Dibdin ascribed to Christopher Clark, from *Vocal Harmony* (1745), and which is found also, but without any composer's name, in Abraham Milner's *Psalm Singer's Companion* (1751).

BLOXHAM is from Aaron Williams's *New Universal Psalmodist*, (1770), where it is set to Dr. Watts's version of Psalm xxxiv. The melody there is as follows:

BON ACCORD is from the edition of the Scottish Psalter published in 1625 in Aberdeen by Edward Raban. The exact title of this edition cannot be given, as the title-page is lacking in both of the two copies which alone are known to be in existence. The date and the printer's name are given on the last page. This tune is headed 'Bon Accord for the xii. Psalm'. It is harmonized 'in Reports' like ABERFELDY (q.v.). In the same form it appears again in Hart's Edinburgh Psalter of 1635, but with some slight differences in the parts.

BREDON is from *The Church Psalter and Hymnal*, edited by the Rev. Edward Harland, M.A. (1855).

CANNONS (always spelt CANONS in Handel's time) is one of the three tunes composed by Handel out of friendship for the Wesleys. Its original title was 'The Invitation', because of its being written for the hymn 'Sinners, obey the Gospel word'. Canons was the palace, nine miles out of London, near Edgware, where 'the magnificent' Duke of Chandos lived in almost royal splendour, and where for a time Handel was his chapel-master and wrote the famous Chandos Anthems and Te Deums, as well as *Esther* and *Acis and Galatea*. See note on Hymn 135 in this Supplement.

CAROLINE first appeared in *The Seraph: A Selection of Psalm and Hymn Tunes, many of them original, for four voices* (Glasgow, 1827). This book was edited and published by John Robertson, who was a teacher of vocal and instrumental music in Glasgow, and who had previously (1814) published *A Selection of the best Psalm and Hymn Tunes, some of which are original, in four parts: adapted to the various Metres used in the Established Churches, Chapels, and Dissenting Congregations in Scotland*.

CAROLINE is one of thirteen tunes in *The Seraph* which are starred as original and 'the private property' of Robertson. It bears no composer's name, although Hugh Wilson, who wrote it, is named as composer of MARTYRDOM.

The tune in its original form had a 'repeat' for the fourth line, as below. The omission of it, while an improvement for present-day use, robs the tune of a good deal of its character, which hardly deserves the adjective 'insipid' which T. L. Hately applied to it.

Our life con-tains a . . thou - sand springs,
And dies if one be gone; Strange that a
harp of thou - sand strings Should keep in
tune so long, Should keep . . . in tune so long.

The verse set under this tune is one of the practice-rhymes of Scottish psalmody in the first half of the nineteenth century, after the precentor had acquired a 'band', to sing in parts. These verses were invented as a substitute for the sacred words to which otherwise the 'band' would rehearse its more secular tunes. These rhymes, as printed in tune-books, were of a moral rather than a religious character—such sacred words as 'God' and 'Christ' being excluded—and were composed not only to sing to long, short, and common measure, but to suit major and minor modes (one for each measure and class) and worded accordingly. They would seem to have been the amateur efforts of the precentor, whose ear in the case above (C.M., Minor Mode) did not tell him that 'long' was not a proper rhyme for 'gone'. These psalmody rhymes have been extensively parodied, but authentic examples are known that are banal enough in character. See the rhyme quoted under MARTYRS in this Supplement.

CHICHESTER is from Ravenscroft's *The Whole Booke of Psalmes . . . composed into 4 parts by sundry Authors* (1621).

COLCHESTER appeared in *A Compleat Melody; or, The Harmony of Zion. . . .* By William Tans'ur. (Preface dated September 29, 1734.) There it is set to Psalm cl, and headed 'Colchester Tune. Composed in Four Parts. W.T.' Whether the initials were intended to indicate that the tune was an original one by Tans'ur, or only that he arranged it, is uncertain.

In its original form the tune was as below:

CONSOLATION (also called EMMANUEL or IMMANUEL) is an adaptation from the theme of the Finale of a Piano Quartet of Beethoven, in E♭ major.

CORONA was written by Mrs. Raymond Barker for *Catholic Hymns. Set to Music by the Composer of Hymns of the Eastern Church* (1868). It is there set to the hymn entitled 'The Crown of Thorns', beginning 'From circlets starred with many a gem'.

COVENTRY appeared in Christopher Smart's *Translation of the Psalms of David* (1765). Poor Kit Smart had two years before this book was published been confined in a madhouse. Dr. Johnson said: 'I did not think he ought to be shut up. His infirmities were not noxious to society. He insisted on people praying with him: and I'd as lief pray with Kit Smart as any one else. Another charge was that he did not love clean linen; and I have no passion for it.' Garrick gave a performance for Smart's benefit, and, when this translation of the Psalms was published, among the names of subscribers appeared those of Gray, Cowper, Akenside, Churchill, Sterne, Smollett, and Hogarth. He was much loved, but foolish and improvident; he died in the debtors' prison of the King's Bench. Deeply religious, he wrote kneeling. His *Song to David*, composed in the asylum, Sir Edmund Gosse declared to be 'a portent of beauty and originality', and Browning, in his *Parleyings*, says it 'stations Smart on either hand with Milton and with Keats'.

CRIMOND appeared in *The Northern Psalter*, edited by William Carnie, Aberdeen, 1872. This Psalter began by the issue of a series of *Fly Leaves of Psalm and Hymn Tunes*, the first part appearing in 1859. Each number consisted of a lithographed four-paged penny sheet, containing seven tunes, old and new. The lithographing was well done, and the sheets sold in thousands. From them the *Northern Psalter* was in due time compiled. (See biographical note on David Grant.) The tune is set in that Psalter to the hymn 'I am the Way, the Truth, the Life'.

DRUMCLOG appeared in *The Sacred Harp*, published by Robert Burns in Glasgow in 1840; also in *Cameron's Selection of Sacred Music* (Glasgow, G. & J. Cameron, 1852). The preface of the latter says: 'It has been carefully compiled from *The Sacred Harp*, the property of the publishers, which has been universally pronounced *The Classic Standard of Scottish Psalmody*, not only by the entire Scottish press, but by the most eminent practical musicians. . . . Many popular tunes are inserted which were not published in *The Sacred Harp*, and several others are now issued for the first time by permission of the composers.' The tune appeared also in the 1848 and later editions of Mitchison's *Selection of Sacred Music*, which was published in 1834 and enlarged from time to time. All these books give the tune as by Matthew Wilson (q.v.). The tune was a great favourite in the west of Scotland, especially to the 23rd Psalm, until the issue of official Psalters and hymn-books, in which it was not included, led to its falling out of use.

Readers of William Black's novel, *A Daughter of Heth*, will remember the description in chapter xxi, of how Coquette, the heroine of the story, played this tune on board the *Caroline* in Oban Bay. She played first 'the clear, and sweet, and melancholy cadence of Mendelssohn's gondola song. The empty silence of the bay seemed to grow full of this rich and harmonious music. . . . But suddenly she changed the key, and with sharp and powerful chords struck out the proud and ringing melody of "Drumclog". The old Scotch psalm-tune stirred the Whaup, as a trumpet might stir the heart of a dragoon. He rose to his feet, and drew a long breath, as if the plaintive gondola-music had been stifling him.

' "What a grand tune that Drumclog is," he said. "It means business. I dare say the old troopers sang it with their teeth set hard, and their hands on their musket-barrels." '

Later in the story, in chapter xlix, there is a description of Coquette playing the tune in Airlie Manse (supposed to be Stevenston Manse, Ayrshire): 'She seldom opened the piano, and when she did, Drumclog was no longer a martial air, but a plaintive wail of grief.'

Black evidently supposed that the name of the tune implied some historical connexion with the Covenanters; in such wise do accepted traditions arise. By some it has been suggested that the tune in his mind was another, which also has been supposed to be connected with

71

the Covenanters (it has been described as 'partly borrowed from an old Covenanting melody'), with equally little foundation—the tune MARTYRDOM, which appeared in *The Seraph* in 1827 as 'Drum-clog'. It was also known as 'Fenwick', from the parish in which Hugh Wilson composed it, about the end of the eighteenth century. But these names for it were forgotten, and it was universally known as MARTYRDOM, by the mid-nineteenth century. And that is the time about which the events of Black's story are supposed to have taken place. He is not likely to have mistaken the tune.

Black was born in Glasgow in 1841, and did not settle in London till 1864. *A Daughter of Heth* was published in 1871. Its period is round about the 'fifties: 'not earlier than 1855, not later than 1869, probably about 1860', says the Rev. James Mearns in an interesting article in *The Choir*, from which the facts here detailed are taken. At that time there were no official tune-books. Precentors used such Glasgow tune-books as those named above, or manuscript copies of tunes that were in use. The books most likely to have been in use in the churches with which Black was familiar were these; it may reasonably be concluded therefore that this was the tune that was in his mind.

DUKE'S TUNE appeared in *The CL Psalmes of David*, the edition of the first Scottish Psalter published in Edinburgh by Andro Hart in 1615. This was one of the first set published of what were called *Common Tunes*, that is, tunes not attached to any particular psalm, but usable with any psalm in common metre. In this Psalter they were grouped together under the title, 'The XII Common Tunes, to the which all Psalmes of eight syllables in the first line, and sixe in the next may be sung'. (See article in *Handbook* on Early Metrical Psalters.) This tune is so obviously a piece of cobblery that its disuse is not surprising. Of its twenty-eight notes the first five are identical with 'Tallis', and four of its second section and the last thirteen with 'Winchester'.

EATINGTON is from the third edition of Playford's *The Divine Companion; or, David's Harp New Tun'd* (1709), where it bears no name. It is set there to Psalm cxvi, 'I love the Lord because he heard'. It is the third of a group headed thus: 'This Hymn and the following Three Psalms sett by Docter Crofts'. The original was in two parts, and in the key of B♭. In the same book a tune by Jeremiah Clark appears to 'A Morning Hymn. Awake, my soul', the first line of which is exactly the same as the first line of this tune. The similarity will also be remarked between this tune and lines 1 and 3 of Clark's 'St. Magnus'. Eatington (now Ettington) was Croft's birthplace.

EDEN is from W. H. Havergal's *A Hundred Psalm and Hymn Tunes* (1859). It had been composed, however, in 1845, and must have found its way in manuscript across the Atlantic shortly afterwards, for Lowell Mason was using it there, under the name 'St. Nicholas', in April, 1847. In April of that year he wrote thus to Havergal about it: 'I have lately introduced into my choir, and sing with admirable effect, your tune "St. Nicholas". The effect of it was truly magnificent. . . . I have never heard anything come nearer to my *beau ideal* of Choral Music than did the singing of this tune on a fine Sabbath morning, in a Church filled with people. It made a deep impression.' (Havergal's *Psalmody and Century of Chants*, 1870.) The present setting is not Havergal's.

EFFINGHAM is clearly a derivative from 'Crasselius' (q.v., in *Handbook*): *Musicalisch Hand-Buch der Geistlichen Melodien à Cant. et Bass.* (Hamburg, 1690.)

EGHAM is attributed to Dr. William Turner (q.v.) by Dibdin in his *Standard Psalm Tune Book* (1852), and, doubtless on this authority, by Dr. E. J. Hopkins in *The Temple Tune Book, Division I*, but in neither case is there any indication of the source. It is not found in any of the collections to which Turner himself is known to have contributed.

FELIX is founded on a phrase in the chorus 'He stirreth up the Jews' in Mendelssohn's unfinished oratorio *Christus* (Op. 97, Posthumous Works, No. 26), first performed at the Birmingham Musical Festival, 1852. The phrase is as follows:

The tune first appeared under the name BALTIC, in Lowell Mason's *The Hallelujah* (1854), and may be assumed to be his composition.

GENEVA is a modification, of a kind too long customary in Scotland, of PSALM XLII (see Hymn 359 in R.C.H., and note thereon in the *Handbook*), which was composed or adapted by Louis Bourgeois, for Psalm xlii in the Genevan French Psalter of 1551. The Scottish Psalter of 1564, following the Anglo-Genevan Psalter of 1561, set it to Psalm xxvii. It is included in the present Psalter in this form because it has still a measure of use among those who sing the first version of Psalm cxxxvi. Now that the noble original tune is again available, GENEVA will doubtless gradually be disused.

GLENLUCE is No. XX of the Common Tunes in the Scottish Psalter of 1635.

HARINGTON was originally written as a glee for three voices under the title 'Retirement', to words of which the first of three verses is as follows:

> Beneath the silent rural cell
> Of innocence and peace,
> With sage retirement let me dwell
> And taste each home-felt bliss.

The original form of the music was this:

HEREFORD (also called Tranmere, Christchurch, or Psalm xlvii) is from *Sixteen Psalms selected from the Rev. Mr. Merrick's New Version. Set to Music by W. Hayes* (1774), where it is set to the version of Psalm xlvii: 'Arise, ye people, clap the hand'. Hayes says that it is to be played 'on the swelling organ'. In its original form lines 5 and 6 of the tune are as follows:

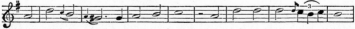

The Rev. James Merrick, M.A. (1720–69), a Fellow of Trinity

College, Oxford, published at Reading in 1765 *The Psalms of David Translated or Paraphrased in English Verse*. Curiously, only a few of his versions were divided into stanzas. In 1797 the Rev. W. D. Tattersall repaired the omission by publishing Merrick's work 'Divided into stanzas for parochial Use, and paraphrased in such language as will be intelligible to every capacity . . . with a suitable Collect to each Psalm from the Works of Archbishop Parker'. Merrick had vainly tried to obtain the royal sanction for his book; Tattersall was more fortunate: his book, under sanction of the King, was introduced into Weymouth Parish Church in 1804. Both in the Church of England and among Nonconformists a number of Merrick's paraphrases, which Dr. Julian stigmatized as 'weak and verbose', were long in use, and some, chiefly in the form of centos, survived into modern hymn-books. From the newer collections they have disappeared.

HERIOT'S TUNE takes its name from George Heriot's Hospital, Edinburgh. Its first traceable appearance was in *A New Collection of Vocal Music, containing Church Tunes, Anthems, and Songs, for the use of the several Hospitals of this City. By Andrew Lawrie, Teacher of these Hospitals and Writing Master* (Edinburgh, 1780). Lawrie in his Preface says: 'Besides Church tunes I have brought into this collection the several tunes and anthems usually sung on George Heriot's day [the first Monday in June], to which I have added more: and after that, a good number of songs . . . which persons of the chastest ear and strictest character may hear without being offended; and would to God that none but inoffensive songs, such as these, were ever heard in any company; and that all indecent and licentious songs were hissed and banished from mankind, as being more infectious and hurtful than the plague.'

In this volume there are three 'George Heriot's Tunes', one of them being the present one.

A successor to this book was published in *A Collection of Vocal Music, containing Church Tunes, Anthems, and Songs, for the use of the several Hospitals of this City* (Edinburgh, 1807). The editor of this book was Alexander McDonald (q.v.), then joint music-master with his father in the Hospitals. He also gives three so-called 'George Heriot's Tunes'. One is the tune named 'Saxony', which was an adaptation of an air in Handel's opera *Siroë* (1728), and which, from the time of its introduction into Scotland in 1820 in Dr. Andrew Thomson's *Sacred Harmony*, remained in high favour in Scotland for half a century. (See note on INNOCENTS under Hymn 574 in this Supplement.) A second is apparently an amateur's production with its last line taken straight from the tune MANCHESTER. The third is the present tune, which, as it alone appears in both the books here mentioned, appears to be the only one with any claim to be traditional. Its origin is unknown.

HERMON has the 'plaintive grace' which characterizes most of Jeremiah Clark's tunes, reflecting the subdued melancholic strain in his spirit. It does not suggest the triumphant joy of Eastertide, yet it first appeared in Henry Playford's *The Divine Companion; or, David's Harp New Tun'd* (1708), set to *A Hymn for Easter Day*, which began:

> If angels sung a Saviour's birth
> On that auspicious morn,
> We well may imitate their mirth
> Now He again is born.

Playford gives the second half of the tune, which is unnamed by him, in this form:

HOWARD, though attributed to Dr. Samuel Howard in Scotland during the last hundred years and more, was not composed by him. The name doubtless gave rise to the mistake. Its first known appearance was in John Wilson's *A Selection of Psalm Tunes, Sanctuses, Doxologies, &c., for the use of the Congregation of St. Mary's Church, Edinburgh* (1825). There no composer's name is given. In books published in 1840 and 1854 it is ascribed to Sir John Andrew Stevenson (q.v.), but with what reason does not appear. In the *Wesleyan Tune Book* of 1877 it is called DUBLIN, ascribed to Stevenson, and printed 'by permission of H. H. Bemrose'. This ascription is repeated in *The Methodist Hymn-Book* of 1933, but Mr. Lightwood, in his *The Music of the Methodist Hymn-Book*, says that it 'lacks corroboration'.

HUDDERSFIELD is one of thirty-three tunes contributed by Martin Madan (q.v. in *Handbook*) to *A Collection of Psalm and Hymn Tunes never Published before. Edited by Martin Madan.* (1769). In this book, known as the *Lock Collection* (q.v. in *Handbook*) it bears its present name, and is set to the hymn beginning:

> My hiding-place, my refuge, tower,
> And shield art Thou, O God.

In its original form the second half of the tune is as follows:

Historical Notes on the Psalter Tunes

ICONIUM, though traditionally attributed to Dr. James Nares (q.v. in *Handbook*), is not found in any collection to which he is known to have contributed, nor in any collection earlier than 1843. In that year it appeared in *The Sacred Harmony of St. Andrew's Church, Edinburgh, in four vocal parts, with Accompaniment for the Organ or Pianoforte* (1843). Intended as a supplement to R. A. Smith's collections, which were then in very general use, this book contains forty-six tunes, two of which bear the name of Adam Ramage, who had been precentor of the church since 1838 and remained so after the Disruption. Several of the tunes are by John Thomson, Professor of Music in Edinburgh University, who was a son of Dr. Andrew Thomson (q.v.).

INVOCATION is from *Sacred Music . . . sung in St. George's Church, Edinburgh. Edited by R. A. Smith* (Edinburgh, 1825). It was composed for the psalm with which it is inseparably associated —Psalm xliii, vv. 3 to 5. This psalm has from time immemorial been used in the approach to Holy Communion. It has its fixed place there in the Roman Mass, and doubtless its use at the beginning of the Scottish Communion Service is an unrealized inheritance from pre-Reformation days.

This ancientry of use might suggest the propriety of wedding the psalm to a tune in the great tradition which goes back to the Reformation period. There is no more Scottish tune than MARTYRS, for example; it has come down from 1615, and would be singularly appropriate in character and spirit to this psalm. But though INVOCATION has held the field for no more than a century, and is a survival from a time when repeating tunes had a vogue which they have long since lost, it still holds a place in the affections of Scottish people from which it is not likely soon to be driven.

KILSYTH is an adaptation from the chorale *Allein zu Dir Herr Jesu Christ*, which, according to *The Chorale Book for England* (1865), was published first as a broadside at Nürnberg in 1541, and afterwards in *Geistliche Lieder*, Second Part (Leipzig, 1545). The original tune was as follows, but see also Bach's splendid version of it in Dr. Sanford Terry's *J. S. Bach's Four-Part Chorales*.

KING'S NORTON by Jeremiah Clark is from Playford's *The Divine Companion; or, David's Harp New Tun'd, &c.* (1708), where it is set to 'An Hymn for Good-Fryday' beginning, 'No songs of Tryumph now be sung'. It is a tune of much attraction, like all that Clark wrote, but the difficulty with which it confronts the average singer in lines 3 and 4 will probably limit its use. 'The whole melody', says Mr. Archibald Jacob in *Songs of Praise Discussed*, 'is reminiscent of many of this composer's small pieces for the harpsichord.'

LANGHOLM is from *The Psalms of David, for the Use of Parish Churches* (1791), edited by Dr. Arnold and Dr. Callcott. There, under the name 'Lancaster', it is set to Psalm xc.

LAWES (PSALM XLVIII) is from *A Paraphrase upon the Psalmes of David. By G[eorge] S[andys]. Set to new Tunes for private Devotion. And a thorow Base, for Voice or Instrument. By Henry Lawes* (1637). Sandys (1577–1643) was son of an Archbishop of York, a Gentleman of the Privy Chamber to Charles I, Treasurer for a time to the colony of Virginia, and a poet, according to Dryden, 'ingenious and learned, the best versifier of a former age'. A few of his versions are found still in modern hymn-books. On Lawes's tunes see note on Hymn 297 in this Supplement.

LINCOLN is from Ravenscroft's *The Whole Booke of Psalmes* (1621), where it is set to Psalms vii and lvi, and described as an 'English' tune, without the composer's name. It is typical of the uninteresting, rather dull music for which too many of Ravenscroft's unnamed composers were responsible.

LIVERPOOL first appeared in *Divine Harmony; being a Collection in Score of Psalms and Anthems, composed by the most eminent masters . . . Selected and . . . Revised by R. Langdon* (1774), where it bears no name, and is set to Psalm viii. It received its name from Ralph Harrison in the second volume of his *Sacred Harmony, or, a Collection of Psalm Tunes, Ancient & Modern* (vol. i, 1784; vol. ii, 1791). Robert Wainwright, who composed it, a Manchester man, died in 1782 in Liverpool, where he was for the last seven years of his life organist of the church which later became the cathedral; hence Harrison's choice of names for this tune and the next. The first form of the melody was this:

MANCHESTER first appeared in Richard Langdon's book, named above as the source of LIVERPOOL; it was set to Psalm ciii. Harrison gave it its name in the second volume of his *Sacred Harmony*. As Wainwright wrote it, it ran thus:

MANCHESTER was christened CHARMOUTH in America when it first appeared there in 1798, and many books in this country have given the tune under that name.

MELROSE is from *The Psalmes of David in Prose and Meeter. With their whole Tunes in foure or mo parts, and some Psalmes in Reports. Whereunto is added many godly Prayers, and an exact Kalendar for xxv. yeeres to come. Printed at Edinburgh by the Heires of Andrew Hart, Anno Dom. 1635.* This was by far the most important of all the editions of the first Scottish Metrical Psalter. It is the only one in which the Proper Tunes, printed at the head of the psalms, are harmonized throughout; it contains also thirty-one Common Tunes, of which the present one is No. 24; and it gives, in addition, eight tunes harmonized 'in reports', as described under ABERFELDY. The usefulness of this edition was of brief duration, for it went out of use only fifteen years after publication, owing to the present *Psalter in Metre*, authorized for use in 1650, substituting for the old text, which had been in use since 1564, a new one which was metrically unsuitable for most of the old tunes.

MILTON is American. Lowell Mason published it under the name 'Kinlock', in 1854, in his *The Hallelujah*, and it quickly found favour in Scotland.

As an illustration of a phase of Scottish Church life and character that has now almost entirely vanished, it may be recorded that to many of a past generation in the north of Scotland this tune was known as *Kitty's Retreat*. 'Kitty' was one of those stalwarts who were always ready to lift up a standard of testimony against anything in the nature of what they considered to be innovations in public worship. Whenever the precentor in the church which she attended gave out MILTON with its broken rhythm, it was a fearful joy among the younger portion of the congregation to see her rise in her place—fifty years ago in the North people sat during the singing, as they do in Germany to-day—and at once make for the door, scattering hats and umbrellas and anything else that happened to impede her progress out of church.

MORVEN appeared in *The Edinburgh Sacred Harmony, for the Use of Churches and Families, consisting of Psalm and Hymn Tunes, Doxologies, Thanksgivings, and Dismissions*, a work issued in parts, at quarterly intervals, by R. A. Smith (q.v.). About ten parts were published; it was not completed when Smith died. This tune appeared set to Psalm cxlii in No. vi, and was described as an 'Ancient Scottish Melody' as SELMA also was; but T. L. Hately (q.v.), who was a member of Smith's choir in St. George's, Edinburgh, held that Smith composed them both.

There is not much room for doubt that this tune, like SELMA and MARTYRDOM (q.v.), is of folk-ballad origin. R. A. Smith was no doubt wise in his day in not announcing the sources of any of the three by name, though their associations were harmless enough. MORVEN suggests one of the numberless tunes sung to 'Barbara Allen', and it has the characteristic rising cadence at the end of the second line found in many of them. It is here set below a 'Barbara Allen' tune, after its reduction (or reversion) to folk-rhythm, for comparison. The 'Barbara Allen' tune (hexatonic) is from Sussex, as noted in 1906 by Miss A. G. Gilchrist.

MORVEN (pentatonic), in folk-ballad rhythm:

The latter is quite as like the former as many 'Barbara Allen' variants are to each other. Numerous traditional Scottish tunes in the same metrical form belong to such ballads as 'The Dowie Dens of Yarrow' and 'Geordie', so it is uncertain to what particular ballad R. A. Smith may have heard MORVEN, in its original form, sung.

The name MORVEN is sometimes, but mistakenly, understood to be taken from the beautiful district so named in Argyll. Like SELMA, it is derived from Macpherson's *Ossian*, in which Selma is the capital of the country called Morven. 'I beheld thy towers, O Selma, the oaks of thy shadowed wall.' It is sometimes stated also that Morven is an anglicized form of 'Mor Bean, signifying the hill country or highlands'. Dr. Neil Ross of Laggan, the Celtic scholar, thus dismisses that idea: 'The district in Argyll known as Morven is in Gaelic Marairne. Mór-bheinn would mean a big mountain, if that form were used; but it is not so used. As a rule in Gaelic the adjective comes after the noun, except occasionally in poetic usage. The ordinary form is Beinn-mhór, which is anglicized in Benmore in Mull and Benmore in Assynt. We may dismiss the hill etymology for Morven.

'The simple fact is that Macpherson, like Dickens, had a faculty for coining new names. Neither Morven nor Selma occurs in the genuine Ossianic remnants. The names were pure inventions of Macpherson. In his day, a century and a half ago, his *Ossian* was taken for the real article, and his fine-sounding names were popular. It is not surprising that even psalm-tunes composed in that period should be called by such lovely, mystical but mythical names. They are poetic merely.'

NEWARK appeared anonymously in Nathaniel Gawthorn's *Harmonia Perfecta: a Compleat Collection of Psalm Tunes in Four Parts . . . Taken from the Most Eminent Masters, chiefly from Mr. Ravenscroft* (1730).

NORWICH is from *The Whole Booke of Psalmes . . . Composed into four parts by sundry Authors . . . Newly corrected and enlarged by Tho. Ravenscroft* (1621), where it is set to Psalms v, lv, and cii, the harmony being by John Milton, father of the poet. It is named there 'Norwich tune', and is classed among English Tunes in the index. The last line of the original runs thus:

OLD 29TH is from what is popularly known as *John Knox's Genevan Service Book* (1556), so called because it was used by Knox while he was a minister of the congregation of Marian exiles at Geneva from 1556 to 1559. The full title is *The Forme of Prayers and Ministration of the Sacraments, &c., used in the Englishe Congregation at Geneva . . . Geneva, 1556.* It originated really at Frankfort, where it was drawn up for a similar congregation of exiles, but not found acceptable to them and never used. Because the Genevan congregation adopted it, it was known as the Order of Geneva. In its completed form it was adopted by the Church of Scotland in 1564 as its *Book of Common Order*. The first part was liturgical. The second contained metrical versions of the psalms with the following title, *One and Fiftie Psalmes of David in Englishe Metre, whereof 37 were made by Thomas Sternholde and the rest by others, &c.* The 'others' were John Hopkins, whose name is associated with Sternhold's in connexion with the first English Metrical Psalter, and William Whittingham, who married Calvin's sister, and in later life became

Dean of Durham. Each was responsible for seven of the additions to Sternhold's thirty-seven.

Each of the fifty-one is furnished with a tune. The present one is that set to Psalm xxix. Who the musicians were who contributed these tunes, and who was responsible for the selection and arrangement of them, there is no means of knowing; but both English and Scottish musicians were among the most devoted adherents of the Reformation, and possibly some of these among the exiles in Geneva supplied the music. The fact that this tune was retained in all subsequent Scottish editions, but appeared in none of the English, suggests the possibility that it came from a Scottish composer.

OLD 68TH is from John Day's *Whole Booke of Psalmes, collected into Englysh metre by T. Starnhold, I. Hopkins, and others: conferred with the Ebrue, with apt notes to synge thē withal: Faithfully perused and alowed according to the ordre appointed in the Quenes maiesties Iniunctions. Imprinted at Lōdon by Iohn Day, dwelling ouer Aldersgate . . . An. 1562.* This is important as the first complete edition of the English Metrical Psalter.

With the first two lines of the tune in the original, as follows, compare those of OLD 100TH:

The seventh line also varies from the present form, thus:

In the rare 1562 (English) Psalter Psalm c is not given in Kethe's now familiar version, but in another, anonymous, which begins 'In God the Lorde be glad and lyght'. No tune is given with it, but a marginal direction says: 'Sing this as the lxvii'. This is a misprint for 'lxviii'. The tune given with lxviii is the present one. Major G. A. Crawford, an unrivalled authority on Reformation psalmody, remarked: 'It was a not uncommon practice of the old writers to construct new tunes by adding different terminations to the same fragment of older melody. The strain with which the "Old Hundredth" commences seems to have been very popular from this point of view.'

OLD 124TH appeared first in the book which gave us OLD 100TH, *Pseaumes octante trois de David, mis en rime francoise. A savoir quarante neuf par Clement Marot, . . . Et trente quatre par Theodore de Besze. . . . A Geneve, 1551.* The psalm to which this tune is set and which gives it its name was one of the thirty-four by Beza.

The English version of the words was by William Whittingham, who, as will be seen from a comparison of the first verses, closely followed his original. Thus Beza:

> Or peut bien dire Israel maintenant,
> Si le Seigneur pour nous n'eust point esté,
> Si le Seigneur nostre droit n'eust porté,
> Quand tout le monde a grand' fureur venant,
> Pour nous meurtrir dessus nous s'est jetté.

Here is Whittingham's translation:

> Now Israel may say and that truely,
> If that the Lord had not our cause maintaind,
> If that the Lord had not our right sustaind,
> When all the world against us furiouslie
> Made their uproares, and said wee should all die.

Not only in these last two lines, but at many other points, the Scottish revisers who produced our present version in 1650 greatly strengthened Whittingham's version.

The glorious tune, one of the dearest of all to Scottish hearts, differed from the present form. Here is the tune as it originally stood:

In *The English Hymnal* the tune is set to two sets of verses, written *ad hoc* to make the tune available; one is by the late Canon T. A. Lacey, and the other, a version of a hymn of Prudentius, by Canon Percy Dearmer. In *Songs of Praise* a better, but still unsatisfactory set is provided in Clifford Bax's 'Turn back, O Man, forswear thy foolish ways'. This was written by him in 1916 for Gustav Holst, who wished to use the tune for a motet, which, as now published, has become widely known through the wireless. The first verse runs:

> Turn back, O Man, forswear thy foolish ways.
> Old now is Earth, and none may count her days,
>   Yet thou, her child, whose head is crowned with flame,
>   Still wilt not hear thine inner God proclaim—
> 'Turn back, O Man, forswear thy foolish ways.'

In *Farewell, my Muse* (1932), in which Bax published his verses, he says, 'The regular structure of these verses and the large number of long monosyllables were necessitated by the form of the music.' Scotland is fortunate in having the perfect words provided for the great tune in Whittingham's rugged version of the Psalm, to which it is so closely wedded that to sing it to anything else seems to the Scotsman little short of profanation, for the association has remained unbroken since the Reformation. This fact is remarkable, for though the Scottish Reformers were deeply indebted to the Church of Geneva as regards both the words and the music of their first metrical Psalter, this is the solitary instance in which the same psalm and tune have remained inseparable in the Churches of Calvin and Knox.

Several historic episodes in which psalm and tune together played a part deserve to be recorded.

One is Genevan. It relates to one of the last attempts made by the Dukes of Savoy to reconquer the town of Geneva and crush the Protestant movement. It took place in 1602, and is known as the *Escalade*. The attack was repulsed by the bravery of the citizens. As soon as the enemy was driven off and peace was restored, Beza, then eighty years of age, returned thanks for the victory, and gave out this psalm to be sung to this melody (in Geneva singing in harmony was forbidden). Ever since, the same rite has been observed each year on the 12th of November, the anniversary of the deliverance; and on a monument erected to commemorate it, one of the reliefs represents the aged Reformer at the door of the cathedral, giving out the psalm. This episode is vividly portrayed in Stanley Weyman's novel *The Long Night*.

The second incident is Scottish. John Durie, one of the ministers of Edinburgh, was banished from the city in June, 1582, 'for his plean speitches against the Duc [of Lennox] and proceedings of the Court'. In the August following he was allowed to return. The description of his triumphal entry into the city, as given by Calderwood, has often been quoted; here is the account of it by James Melvill in his *Diary*, upon which Calderwood drew in writing his *History*: 'Jhone Durie gat leiue to ga ham to his awin flok of Edinbruche, at whase retourning there was a grait concurs of the haill town, wha met him at the Nather Bow; and, going upe the streit, with bear heads and loud voices, sang to the prais of God, and testifeing of grait joy and consolation, the 124th Psalm, "Now Israel may say, and that trewlie," &c., till heavin and erthe resoundit. This noyes, when the Duc, being in the town, hard, and ludgit in the Hiegat, luiked out and saw, he raue his berde for anger, and hasted him af the town.'

Nine years later the tables were turned. James VI, who had consented to Durie's exile under Lennox's influence, after his escape from Bothwell's attempt on his life, went to 'the Great Kirk of Edinburgh' on December 28, 1591. Patrick Galloway preached the sermon 'and declared the King was come to give publict thanks to God for the same', and the 124th Psalm was sung.

Still another incident may be mentioned. When the two great branches of the divided Church of Scotland were united in October 1929, as the two processions marched, one upwards from the Mound, the other downwards by the Lawnmarket, to meet and coalesce at the top of Bank Street, on their way to St. Giles', the watching crowds who lined the streets spontaneously broke into singing, chiefly of Psalm cxxxiii, 'Behold, how good a thing it is', and of Psalm cxxiv.

ORLINGTON was for many years the fixed tune to the 23rd Psalm in some parts of Scotland. It appeared in 1854 in *The Sacred Psaltery, in four vocal parts, consisting principally of Original Psalm and Hymn Tunes*, the editor of which was John Campbell (q.v.). Its kinship with WILTSHIRE is obvious.

PALESTRINA is usually stated to be an adaptation from the *Gloria Patri* of the *Magnificat Tertii Toni* in Palestrina's *Magnificat Octo Tonorum* (1591). W. H. Monk's tune VICTORY, to 'The strife is o'er, the battle done', is derived from the same source, but, like this one, *longo intervallo*—at so long an interval indeed that it is no more than the initiatory suggestion that can be ascribed to Palestrina. See the note in this Supplement on the tune VICTORY, Hymn 122.

The present tune seems to have been published first in *The Parish Choir* in 1851, but in a metre of six lines of eight syllables each. The Common Metre form of it was made by T. L. Hately (q.v.), who published it in *The Church of Scotland Hymn Tune Book* of 1862, of which he was the musical editor.

PETERBOROUGH was composed by Sir John Goss in 1864, and published in the same year in *The Church Psalter and Hymn Book*, edited by the Rev. William Mercer (q.v. in *Handbook*). In the first *Church Hymnary* it was set to 'The spacious firmament on high'.

PHILIPPI was composed in 1835 by Samuel Wesley for *The Psalmist, a Collection of Psalm and Hymn Tunes*.

POTSDAM is an adaptation from the subject of the *Fugue in E* in Bach's *Forty-eight Preludes and Fugues*.

Dr. Greenhouse Allt, of St. Giles', Edinburgh, permits this interesting quotation from a work of his on 'the typical rhythm of the "Canzon alla francesce":

'So Gabrieli, "Canzon ariosa" (1596). Froberger transforms it thus:

while Kerl (*c.* 1625–90), "Canzona V", thus

produces, as is well known, the composition adapted by Handel in *Israel in Egypt* as "Egypt was glad when they departed". In the major it is, of course, one of the oldest themes in the world, and finds its apotheosis in Bach's *Wohltemperirte Klavier* in the fugue (vol. ii, No. xxxiii) called by Samuel Wesley "The Saints in Glory",

PRAGUE appeared in *The Hymn Tunes of the Church of the Brethren. . . . Arranged for Four Voices in Score, by John Lees* (1824). Nearly all the tunes in this Moravian book are German chorales or derivatives from chorales. L. R. West was a minister of that Church, and the name given to this tune suggests that it also may have had a German origin.

ST. ANDREW appeared in *The New Harmony of Sion . . . by W. Tans'ur. Book II* (1764), where it is set to Psalm cl, and headed 'Barby Tune, composed in four parts, W.T.' The initials may mean no more than that the harmony was by Tans'ur.

ST. GEORGE appeared in *Ein Christlicher Abentreien, vom Leben und ampt Johannis des Tauffers . . . N.H. 1554.* This was a tract of seven leaves. Herman was a poet as well as a composer, and here he set the tune to a hymn of his own, 'Kommt her ihr liebsten Schwesterlein'. The melody is as follows:

In his collection of hymns entitled *Die Sontags Evangelia uber das gantze Jar, in Gesenge verfasset* (1560), he set the tune to his hymn 'Lobt Gott, ihr Christen, allzugleich', and with that hymn it has remained associated in Germany ever since. It has undergone various modifications both in German and English books. Bach gives it in four different forms in his arrangements of the Chorales.

See especially his treatment of it in Cantata 151, *Süsser Trost, mein Jesus kommt,* and the Wedding Cantata, *Dem Gerechten muss das Licht.*

ST. GEORGE'S, EDINBURGH appeared in *Sacred Harmony, for the use of St. George's Church, Edinburgh* (1820), which was prepared by Dr. Andrew Thomson (q.v.), minister of the church, with the assistance of R. A. Smith, who had not yet at that time become, as he did three years later, precentor of St. George's. The tune is inseparably associated in Scotland with Psalm xxiv, vv. 7–10. This psalm was customarily sung at Communion in many places in Scotland, while minister and elders were bringing the elements into the church in solemn procession before the administration of the ordinance began; and it was for this stately ceremonial act, which corresponds to the Great Entrance in the Eastern rite, that Dr. Thomson composed the tune. When the 35th Paraphrase came into use and displaced the psalm at this point, the custom arose of using the psalm as the first act of worship in the post-Communion service, a much less appropriate place for it.

ST. GREGORY is from *A Collection of Psalm Tunes interspersed with Airs, . . . set for four voices, for the use of Choirs and Families . . . and dedicated to S. Webbe, sen., by his son, S. Webbe, jun.* (1808). Webbe was at that time organist of a Unitarian church in Liverpool. Wainwright, who composed it, had died there twenty-six years before. The tune therefore is likely to have been known locally, and may have been printed in some ephemeral form, before Webbe published it.

It appeared also in *Euphonia, containing Sixty-two Psalm and Hymn Tunes . . . Harmonised, Arranged and Composed . . . by W. Dixon.* This book is undated, but it must have been published between 1805 and 1808.

ST. MIRREN is from *Sacred Music . . . sung in St. George's Church, Edinburgh, edited by R. A. Smith* (1825), the source from which 'Invocation' and 'Selma' were also derived. The name was given in homage to Paisley, Smith's father having been a Paisley weaver, and he himself precentor in the Abbey Church, 1807–23. Mirren here is not, as generally supposed, the Scots phonetic spelling of the name Marion, but the name of the Celtic saint Mirin, or Mirinus, a pupil of St. Comgall, abbot of Bangor, and a contemporary of St. Columba, whom he must have known, and of Columbanus. Leaving Ireland in 580, he became a missionary in the west and south-west of Scotland; his name lingers in Ayrshire, Dumbarton, and the Stewartry of Kirkcudbright, and it is a household word in Paisley, where, 'full of miracles and holiness, he slept in the Lord'. When the monks from Wenloc came to Paisley 600 years after his death, they found his memory green. In their charters and the bulls of the Popes they called him 'the glorious confessor St. Mirin'.

ST. NEOT appeared as WORKSOP TUNE in *A Collection of Choice Psalm-Tunes in Three and Four Parts; with New and Easie Psalm-Tunes, Hymns, Anthems, and Spiritual Songs. . . . Third edition, 1715.* This was edited by John and James Green. No trace can be found of the first two editions of the book. James Green was an organist in Hull in 1724, when he published, under his own name only, the fifth edition, the earliest known, of *A Book of Psalmody, containing Chanting Tunes, with eighteen Anthems, and Variety of Psalm-Tunes in Four Parts.*

The tune, under the name WORKSOP, is found in many collections of the eighteenth century. Green gives the melody in this form:

ST. NICHOLAS is from *The Spiritual Man's Companion: Or, The Pious Christian's Recreation. Containing . . . a Set of Psalm-Tunes, in One, Two, Three, and Four Parts, as they are sung in England and Scotland, &c. The Fifth Edition, with large Additions, never before Printed, by Israel Holdroyd, Philo-Musicae* (1753). The tune is there set to Psalm cxix, Second Part, Old Version, and headed ST. NICHOLAS'S TUNE. No composer's name is given. The form of the melody is this:

In Riley's *Parochial Music Corrected* (1762) it is given thus:

Later books exhibit various slight differences in the form of the melody, especially in the close of line 1 and in line 4. The earliest appearance of the tune in Scotland appears to have been in *The Rudiments of Music: To which is added, A Collection of the best Church Tunes, Hymns, Canons, and Anthems. By James Thomson, Philo-Musicae* (Edinburgh, 1778). The present form, so far as can be traced, appeared first in *Scottish Psalmody*, 1854, where it is said to have been 'arranged by Herr Dürrner'.

ST. SEPULCHRE appeared first in *The Congregational Hymn and Tune Book*, edited by the Rev. R. R. Chope (1862), where it was set to the hymn 'Lord Jesu! when we stand afar'. It had been composed, however, in 1836, when the composer's father was organist of St. Sepulchre's Church, London. Cooper himself became organist there seven years later. The tune is sometimes known as 'St. Agnes'.

ST. THOMAS (C.M.) is from *A Collection of Tunes suited to the several Metres commonly used in Public Worship, set in Four Parts . . . by C. Ashworth.* This book is undated, but it must have been published about 1760, as the third edition, printed from the same plates, is dated 1766. In both the name given is 'Walney Tune'. The form of it is as follows:

Its first appearance in Scotland, so far as is known, was in Thomas Moore's *The Psalm Singer's Delightful Companion* (Glasgow, 1762), where it is in the present form and bears its present name.

In some old collections it is ascribed to Purcell, but such random and groundless ascriptions were then common, HANOVER, for instance, being attributed to Handel, ST. STEPHEN to Battishill, WALTON, under the horrific name of 'Necropolis', to Beethoven, J. F. Lampe's KENT to Green, and not ST. THOMAS only, but STROUDWATER, WALSALL, and BURFORD to Purcell.

ST. THOMAS (S.M.) appeared in *The New Universal Psalmodist* published by Aaron Williams in 1770, where it is named ST. THOMAS's and set to Psalm xlviii, 'Great is the Lord our God'. Williams (1731–76) was a music engraver and publisher, a teacher of music also, and clerk (leader of praise) in the Scots Church, London Wall. He published a number of important collections of psalmody. The one named had a great popularity, for the first edition appeared in 1763, and the fourth and fifth (from the latter the present tune was taken) in 1770. In the fourth edition another tune also called

'St. Thomas's' appears, which bears no resemblance to this one. In the original form of the present tune the second line begins thus:

and the third ends:

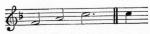

SERENITY appeared in Cornelius Bryan's *A Collection of the most esteemed Psalm Tunes, Ancient and Modern, Selected and Harmonised for Four Voices, and interspersed with a few original Compositions* (*c.* 1830). No name is there given to it. The second line had this difference:

SHEFFIELD appeared first in William Mather's *Sacred Music, consisting of Twenty-six Psalm and Hymn Tunes . . . composed in an Easy Style for the Children of Charity Schools, by William Mather, Organist of St. Paul's and St. James's Churches, Sheffield, &c.* This book bears no date, but it must have appeared about 1800, for the tune appears also in *Dr. Watts's Psalms and Hymns, set to new music . . . composed by Edward Miller . . . to which is added a copious Appendix containing the most favourite tunes now used in different Congregations* (1802). Curiously, in the latter book it is marked in the index as a 'new tune, never before printed'. Mather called it 'Lively', and set it to Psalm xxiii, 'My Shepherd is the living Lord'. Miller (the famous Doncaster organist who adapted TUNBRIDGE as ROCKINGHAM) named it SHEFFIELD and set it to Mrs. Elizabeth Rowe's hymn, 'Begin the high celestial strain'.

SOLOMON is adapted from the solo 'What though I trace each herb and flower' in Handel's oratorio *Solomon*, composed in 1748. In the form in which the tune is usually given the first strain is closely similar to that of TALLIS. In the present arrangement this likeness is minimized by reversion to Handel's original, which is as follows:

The rest follows the original, note for note, and as much of the accompaniment as could be incorporated has been retained.

STOCKTON was originally named 'Elizabeth', but was given its present name while still in manuscript. It was sung in the parish churches of Stockton and Wakefield, and was popular in both, for years before it was published. The change of name took place about 1820, but there was no publication until the tune was included in *Hymns Ancient and Modern* (1861), with alterations by Dr. J. B. Dykes, which were not improvements, thus:

The present form reverts to Wright's original.

STROUDWATER, named from the river on which Stroud stands in Gloucestershire, appeared in *A Book of Psalmody, containing some easy instructions for young beginners; to which is added a select number of Psalm-tunes, Hymns, and Anthems. Collected, Printed, Taught, and Sold by Matthew Wilkins of Great Milton, near Thame in Oxfordshire* (c. 1730). Wilkins was a butcher at Great Milton, and evidently a musical enthusiast. His book went into at least a second edition (c. 1735). He names the tune 'Stroudwater New Tune' to distinguish it from a 'Stroudwater Old Tune', entirely different, which also he includes. The former was set to Psalm cxlvi, the latter to Psalm xl. The third line has a slight difference from the familiar form:

The tune has evidently become disused in the country of its origin, for the musical editor of *Songs of Praise Discussed* (1933) says of it, 'It is an excellent tune, and should rapidly become popular'.

UXBRIDGE is from *The Standard Psalm Tune Book . . . Arranged for 4 voices with an organ accompaniment, by Henry Edward Dibdin* [q.v.] . . . (1851). According to the loose habit which then prevailed of ascribing tunes to distinguished composers without any proof that the ascription was justified, Dibdin headed this tune 'Ascribed to Purcell'. His book is 'notoriously untrustworthy as regards the source and authorship of tunes'; but most books of the period stand in the same condemnation.

WILTSHIRE was long better known in Scotland as 'New St. Ann', and doubtless it was this that led to its being for a time currently ascribed to Dr. Croft. It appeared in *Divine Amusement: Being a Selection of the most admired Psalms, Hymns, and Anthems used at St. James's Chapel . . .* (c. 1795). Smart was at that time organist of the chapel. He set the tune to Psalm xlviii. The original form is given with a figured bass, as below, and there is a note at the beginning of the volume to this effect: 'For the accommodation of those who do not understand Thorough Bass, it is explained in Small Notes, which may be Played or Omitted at Pleasure.' Observe how a misreading of these small notes led to a modification of the tune at the beginning of the second line.

From this it will be seen that at the beginning of the second line the small notes have been incorporated into the tune, and the notes of the original melody have been transferred to the alto part. This change was sanctioned by the composer, for he himself adopted it when he included the tune in his own *Collection of Sacred Music* in 1863; he also gave his approval to the present form when it was included by Dr. Andrew Henderson of Paisley in his *Church Melodies* in 1856. The tune has been subjected to many changes in different collections.

WITTENBERG, also known as 'Reading' and as 'Spires', is also, in some of the old tune-books, called '*Serva nos, Domine*', from the Latin of the first words of Luther's hymn, 'Erhalt uns, Herr, bei deinem Wort', to which the tune was originally set in Klug's *Gesang-buch* (1543). A close translation of it by Robert Wisdome used to be printed at the end of the Old (English) Version of the Psalms. The first verse ran thus:

> Preserve us, Lord, by Thy deare word;
> From Turk and Pope defend us, Lord,
> Both which would thrust out of His throne
> Our Lord Christ Jesus, Thy dear Son.

In Klug the hymn is headed in characteristic fashion, 'A children's Song, to be sung against the two Arch-enemies of Christ and His holy Church, the Pope and the Turk.' Hence the tune came to be known as 'the Pope and Turk tune', popular opinion having apparently decided that the Pope was the worse enemy of the two!

It is printed by Klug in the old notation, and is believed to be based on a plainsong melody. In several versions the second last note is sharp, but it is natural in the original, and this gives support to the belief that originally the tune was plainsong.

Hymn and tune were exceedingly popular in England. In the older collections they were never omitted, and they continued to appear in most till the close of the eighteenth century; they appeared as late as 1832 (in J. Bickersteth's *Psalms and Hymns*).

In *Daye's Psalter* (1563) the tune appears both in its simple form and with an elaborate harmonization. Two earlier settings (1563 and 1592) may be seen in the Historical Edition of *Hymns Ancient and Modern* (1904).

YORK was one of the twelve Common Tunes in *The CL Psalmes of David, in Prose and Meeter, with their whole Usuall Tunes*, published by Andro Hart in Edinburgh in 1615. It is there named 'The Stilt', doubtless because the somewhat awkward movement of the first and third phrases suggests the swinging difficult gait of a man walking on stilts. 'St. David' is another Stilt. Robert Bridges says: 'The best stilts are beautiful, and together with their active vigour they show an unexpected plaintiveness in fetching their long intervals.'

These Common Tunes were a new departure in Scottish psalmody. Till then each psalm was given its 'proper' tune; but a concession had to be made to the average person's difficulty in mastering many tunes, and this was done by introducing Common Tunes without any special psalm being specified to be sung to them, so that they might be used for any psalm versified in common metre.

In Ravenscroft's *Whole Book of Psalms* (1621) the tune appears four times, with three different harmonizations, two of them by John Milton, father of the poet. One of these is the arrangement used in the present Psalter. This association of the name Milton with the tune led many compilers to assume that the poet composed it; thus in many old collections it is definitely assigned to him. No countenance to such an idea is given by Ravenscroft, who classes it as a 'Northern Tune', and 'proper for joyful ditties'! It was he who abandoned the Scots name and called it 'Yorke'.

For a long time, next to OLD 100TH, it was the most popular tune in England; in some places, at the time of the decadence, it was almost the only tune known. So late as 1762 a writer says that he has heard YORK sung fifteen times in one week in the same church. Sir John Hawkins says that it was sung as a lullaby by 'half the nurses in England', and he adds, 'the chimes of many country churches have played it six or eight times in four-and-twenty hours from time immemorial.' In Scotland it had an equal favour. When the number of tunes in use there sank to twelve, and in the Highlands to five, YORK was one of the number retained in use.

It is possible that the tune may have originated in a church chime. The first and third strains, which are identical, suggest a 'change' in a six-bell chime; they are in fact part of a tune known in Cornwall as 'Stratton Church Chimes'. This tune was contributed to *English County Songs*, edited by L. E. Broadwood and J. A. Fuller-Maitland (1893), together with old rhymes locally sung to it, one being:

> They bored a hole in Oliver's nose
> And put therein a ring,
> And drew him round about the town
> For murdering Charles our king.

There is some evidence for believing that this rhyme from the days of Cavaliers and Roundheads is a late edition of an earlier one in which the Jew is the 'guy' exhibited as an object of hatred.

The Stratton tune, given below, does not appear to have been founded on YORK as we know it, because on the same chimes YORK itself could have been played except for one note—the raised fourth which marks the modulation to the dominant at the end of the second strain, for which another could easily have been substituted. (Did Hawkins hear this sharpened note on the country church chimes of which he speaks?) The same six-bell chime would seem also to have belonged to Osney Abbey, Oxfordshire, long ago destroyed, for 'The Bells of Osney' is the alternative name for 'Turn again, Whittington', which is composed on the same six notes of the scale. The bells of Osney were famous in olden times.

As for YORK's earlier name 'The Stilt', the tendency of most church choirs to accent the higher notes of the tune, which fall on the second and fourth beats of its natural rhythm, accounts for most of its awkwardness. If it were written in $\frac{4}{4}$ time, with the natural accent on the first and third beats only—as in the verse set to Stratton chimes—its 'stilted' character would disappear. It would benefit at the same time by fewer changes of harmony, so that, as 'proper for joyful ditties', it could be sung less slowly and more rhythmically, like the joyful chiming of bells.

BIOGRAPHICAL NOTES

ADDITIONS AND CORRECTIONS

ABÉLARD, PIERRE. In line 5 of the *Handbook* note 'buried by Héloïse' should read 'buried beside Héloïse'.

ALCOCK, WALTER GALPIN, Mus.Doc., b. 1861, was knighted, 1933.

ALDRICH, HENRY, D.D. (Westminster, 1647–1710, Oxford), was one of the most remarkable figures in academic England in his time. Educated at Westminster School and Christ Church, Oxford, he became rector of Wem, Shropshire; tutor in Christ Church, canon in 1681, Dean in 1689; Vice-Chancellor of the University, 1692–5. He was the first amateur of his day. 'Divinity, classics, architecture, logic, polemics, and music engaged his attention in turn, and in all he did well.' His *Artis Logicae Rudimenta* was used as a text-book at Oxford till within living memory. The monuments of his architectural ability, in three sides of Peckwater Quadrangle in Christ Church, the Chapel of Trinity College, and All Saints' Church, High Street, Oxford, suggest that the admiration it evoked was aroused less by the merit of his achievement than by wonderment that a man skilled in so many other things could in an art remote from his other interests do so well. He was one of the first members of the Philosophical Society, the forerunner of the Royal Society, and was active in Church affairs, acting for a time as Prolocutor of Canterbury Convocation. In music he showed no originality, but a skill remarkable in a man so many-sided. He is best known by his *Smoaking Catch* (he was himself an inveterate smoker), so arranged that the four men singing it are given time to take puffs at the rests provided for the purpose. Of this catch and another—*Hark, the bonny Christ Church Bells*—Henry Davey says that they are the only two catches of the Restoration period endurable at the present day. Another, long well known, was *Great Tom is cast*. The Dean wrote many anthems, and his *Service in G* is still heard in cathedrals. He was an attractive personality. 'The suavity of his manners, the hilarity of his conversation, the variety and excellence of his talents, in conjunction with a fine person, conciliated and attached all committed to his superintendence, to such a degree that his last surviving disciples of the first rank have been unable to speak recollectedly of their intercourse with him, without the tenderest indications of affection to his memory.'

98. CHANT IN A.

ARMITAGE, Ella Sophia (d. 1931, Middlesbrough), was one of the five original students of Miss Clough at the beginning of Newnham College. She had an intimate knowledge of seven languages, in addition to a fair acquaintance with classical and New Testament Greek. Principal Griffith Jones of Bradford says of her that she was 'a personality of rich gifts and rare attainments; of beautiful piety; sympathetic, generously kind, and nobly hospitable. . . . She always reminded me of what Henry Ward Beecher said of his Aunt Esther, that "she was a woman so beautiful in spirit and so modest in temper that when she went to heaven she would spend ages wondering how she got there, and the angels would be wondering how it was that she had not been there from all eternity".'

ARNOLD, Samuel, Mus.Doc. (London, 1740–1802, Westminster), was educated at the Chapel Royal under Bernard Gates and Nares. In 1763 he was appointed composer to Covent Garden Theatre. In 1769 he became owner of Marylebone Gardens, where he produced burlettas, operas, and entertainments of a dramatic kind, two of which were written by Chatterton. The speculation was financially a failure; before he withdrew he had lost £10,000. Oxford gave him his Mus.Doc. degree in 1773. In 1783 he succeeded Nares as organist and composer to the Chapel Royal; in 1784 was sub-director of the Handel Commemoration; from 1789 was conductor of the Academy of Ancient Music; and in 1798 became organist of Westminster Abbey. He wrote many songs for Vauxhall Gardens, glees, forty-three operas, after-pieces, and burlettas or pantomimes, many of which contained melodies which should not be allowed to die, four oratorios, and many anthems. He also edited *Cathedral Music* in four volumes, a continuation of Boyce; *Psalms of David for Parish Churches* (along with J. W. Callcott); and *The Works of Handel* in thirty-six volumes, at the request of George III; this last he was unable to complete because of want of patronage. His epitaph in the Abbey is as follows:

> Here lies of genius, probity, and worth
> All that belongs to nature and to earth.
> The hand that freely felt and warmly gave,
> The heart that pity stretched to help and save,
> The form that late a glowing spirit warmed,
> Whose science tutor'd and whose talents charmed,
> Whose spirit fled to Him who spirit gave,
> Now smiles triumphant o'er the feeble grave
> That could not chain it here, and joins to raise
> With Heaven's own choir the song of prayer and praise.
> Oh Shade revered! Our nation's loss and pride,
> For mute was harmony when ARNOLD died.

25. ARNOLD.   23. CHANT IN B♭.
79. LANGHOLM.

Biographical Notes

AYLWARD, THEODORE (?, 1730–1801, London), was organist of Oxford Chapel, London, c. 1760; St. Lawrence Jewry, 1762; St. Michael, Cornhill, 1768; in 1769 received the prize medal from the Catch Club for his glee *A Cruel Fate*; in 1771 became Professor of Music in Gresham College; and in 1788 organist and master of the choristers, St. George's Chapel, Windsor; he was also private organist to Queen Charlotte. He composed glees, songs, and musical dramas. On his tombstone in St. George's this epitaph, by Hayley, is engraved:

> Aylward, adieu! my pleasing gentle friend,
> Regret and honour on thy grave attend.
> Thy rapid hand harmonious skill possest,
> And moral harmony enriched thy breast,
> For heaven most freely to thy life assign'd
> Benevolence, the music of the mind;
> Mild as thy nature all thy mortal scene,
> Thy death was easy, and thy life serene.

119–113. CHANT IN D♭.

BATHURST, WILLIAM HENRY. To his publications add *The Roman Antiquities of Lydney Park* (pub. posthumously, 1879).

BAXTER, RICHARD. Probably few nowadays would be inclined to take Johnson's heroic and incautious advice to Boswell: 'I asked him what works of Richard Baxter's I should read. He said, "Read any of them; they are all good."' There is humour now in this recommendation, for the standard edition of Baxter's *Practical Works* is in no fewer than twenty-three large octavo volumes.

BEETHOVEN, LUDWIG VAN (Bonn, 1770–1827, Vienna), was of Flemish ancestry, but was himself wholly German, son and grandson of musicians at the court of the Elector of Cologne. His childhood was extremely unhappy. At 8 he played at a concert, and at 12 published nine variations on a march by Dressler. In 1784 he became second court organist; in 1785 composed three piano and string quartets; in 1787 visited Vienna and met Mozart; in 1792 met Haydn at Bonn and dedicated a cantata to him. When he settled in Vienna in 1792 he was already one of the finest pianoforte players of the day. His first pianoforte concerto was published in 1795. In 1798 he began to grow deaf, and the deafness grew until in 1822 he had to be turned round, when conducting, to realize that the audience was applauding; for the last few years he could not conduct conversations except in writing. He was slow to publish, but when he began, the eight years ending with 1802 saw the production of 92 compositions, including his only oratorio *The Mount of Olives* and two symphonies. He was a prodigious worker, and took endless pains with what he wrote: there is scarcely a bar of his music of which it may not be said that it was re-written a dozen times. His brain teemed with ideas. His sketch-books were crammed with notes for symphonies. If he had carried out all the symphonies he had begun, there would have been fifty more. He was a mighty genius. This was recognized in his lifetime, and he was appreciated and honoured. His name will always be associated with the symphony; his nine symphonies are his greatest as well as his most representative works.

43. CONSOLATION.

BEXFIELD, WILLIAM RICHARD, Mus.Doc. (Norwich, 1824–53, London), was trained under Dr. Buck in Norwich Cathedral. As a boy he had a voice of remarkable sweetness and sang with rare charm. He became organist at Boston, Lincolnshire, in 1846, and two years later, of St. Helen's, Bishopsgate, London, the parish in which Byrd, Wilbye, Sir Thomas Gresham, and other notable musicians had lived. In 1848 he received from Oxford the Mus. Doc. degree. He wrote an oratorio, *Israel Restored*, which was performed in 1851 at the Norwich Musical Festival.

137 (*2*). CHANT IN c♯.

BLUNT, FREDERIC WILLIAM (Mayfair, London, 1839–1921, London), was educated at East Sheen, London, and at Rugby; was articled to his father as a solicitor and practised as such in London till he retired in 1918; was fond of music and sang a great deal in his younger days. He is believed to have written only one other tune, now lost. LYNDHURST appeared anonymously in *Church Praise*, first edition, 1882.

BOOTH, JOSIAH, d. London, 1930.

BORTHWICK, JANE LAURIE. Add to hymn under this name: 602. 'Still on the homeward journey'.

BOYD, WILLIAM, d. London, 1928. For some time before his death he was blind. While he was vicar of All Saints, Norfolk Square, he had three organists who were destined to reach high eminence—E. C. Bairstow, Hamilton Harty, and William Wolstenholme.

BRIDGES, ROBERT (SEYMOUR), d. Boar's Hill, Oxford, 1930.

BROOMFIELD, WILLIAM ROBERT. The statement in the *Handbook* that Broomfield was buried in a corner of the poorhouse grounds is inaccurate. His funeral took place on Friday, October 19, 1888, from the Hospital of St. Nicholas Poorhouse to St. Peter's Cemetery, Aberdeen. Before the coffin was taken out of the room the party of mourners sang part of Psalm li to his tune ST. KILDA.

Biographical Notes

BROWNE, SIMON (d. 1732), wrote the exposition of 1 Corinthians in Matthew Henry's *Commentary*. The inscription on the tablet to his memory in Shepton Mallet Unitarian Chapel is as follows: 'Near this Place lies the Remains / of Mr. Simon Browne, Minister of / the Gospel A Native of this Town / but known throughout the Nation by his Writings / Portsmouth and London enjoyed his / Ministry And when Nature was op/prest with so strange a Disorder that / He thought himself less than man / he attacked the boldest Infidels of the / age and tryumphed in the cause of / God. He dy'd A.D. 1732. Aet. 52.'

BRYAN, CORNELIUS (Bristol, *c.* 1775–1840, Bristol), was organist of St. Mark's (the Mayor's) Chapel, Bristol; later, also of St. Mary Redcliffe, holding both appointments at the same time. While conducting an operetta *Lundy*, of his own composition, in the Theatre Royal, Bristol, he fell through a trapdoor which had not been properly fastened, and so injured his spine that he died a few days later. About 1840 he published *A Collection of the most esteemed Psalm Tunes, Ancient and Modern, Selected and Harmonised for Four Voices, and interspersed with a few original Compositions*; he published also some organ pieces.

174. SERENITY.

BUCK, PERCY CARTER, Mus.Doc., was Musical Director of Harrow School, 1901–27, and is now Musical Adviser to the London County Council.

BUNNETT, EDWARD, Mus.Doc. Norfolk Cathedral should, of course, be Norwich.

BYRD, WILLIAM (b. 1543), became a cathedral organist, at Lincoln, at the age of twenty. It was in 1570 that he became a member of the Chapel Royal. About 1593 he became a country gentleman at Stondon Place, Essex, and during the latter part of his life realized his ambition of founding a county family. Tallis and he, in gratitude for the privilege given them by the Queen, dedicated to her their joint work, *Cantiones Sacrae*. His contemporaries had no doubt about his greatness; 'a Father of Musicke' was a title they more than once bestowed on him, and one calls him 'ye inimitable'. He wrote excellent Latin, was a man of sound sense and excellent culture, and exercised an enormous influence in his lifetime. He was the father of the madrigalists and the virginal composers, and by far the greatest musical pioneer this country has ever known. His birth-year is variously given, but as his will in 1622 states that he was then in his 80th year, 1543 is taken to be correct.

BYRNE, MARY ELIZABETH (Dublin, 1881–1931, Dublin), was educated at the Dominican Convent in Eccles Street, Dublin. At

99

the Royal University she graduated as M.A. with first-class honours in Modern Literature, and gained a studentship. For some years she worked at the Catalogue of the Royal Irish Academy, the 3rd fasciculus of which (1928) was compiled by her. An edition of *Tain Bo Fraich*, largely her work, is soon to appear. Her chief employment was on the *Dictionary of the Irish Language*, but her part of the work is not yet (1935) published.

BYROM, JOHN, was in every way a remarkable man. 'Extremely tall, he wore a peculiar slouched hat, from under which peered a face at once benignant and inquisitive.' He was the chief inventor of modern shorthand (his *Universal English Shorthand* was published in 1767); and it was owing to his having taught the Wesleys this form of rapid writing that Charles was able to dash his hymns down in shorthand as they came into his mind. He was made an F.R.S. in 1724.

He was a wit; some of his epigrams are not likely to be forgotten. When the Pretender marched into England in the '45, Byrom came out on his side, but afterwards covered himself by the famous lines (cf. *Redgauntlet*, ch. vii):

> God bless the King!—I mean the Faith's Defender!
> God bless—no harm in blessing—the Pretender:
> Who that Pretender is, and who that King,
> God bless us all!—is quite another thing.

He was also the inventor of Tweedledum and Tweedledee, in connexion with the extraordinary rivalry of Bononcini and Handel (1726–34), and the operatic war between them which rent society into opposing factions, was fomented by a copious flow of scurrilous pamphlets and poems, and was even taken up by the two political parties. It was when Handel revived his English Pastoral, with additions from his early Italian work, *Aci, Galatea e Polifemo*, and Bononcini produced a rival serenata, that Byrom wrote:

> Some say, compar'd to Bononcini,
> That Mynheer Handel's but a ninny;
> Others aver that he to Handel
> Is scarcely fit to hold a candle.
> Strange all this difference should be
> 'Twixt Tweedledum and Tweedledee.

Byrom was withal a man of rare piety. F. T. Palgrave, in *The Treasury of Sacred Song* (p. 349), says of him that he was 'one of the many men of strong feeling in whom faith burned "like a hidden flame" through the eighteenth century'.

CAMIDGE, JOHN, Mus.Doc. (York, 1790–1859, York), son of Matthew Camidge (q.v.) and grandson of John the elder, took his Mus.Doc. degree in 1829, and was appointed organist of York

Minster in 1842, after performing the duties for many years on behalf of his father. In 1848, while playing the evening service, he was stricken with paralysis, and never played again. His duties were then taken by his son, Thomas Simpson Camidge. In 1828 he published a volume of cathedral music of his own composition.

The record of the Camidge family in music was remarkable. At the farewell service for the Rt. Rev. Charles E. Camidge, D.D., after his consecration as Bishop of Bathurst, in York Minster in October, 1887, the music included compositions by five generations of the Camidge family, relatives of the Bishop. These were—John the first, Matthew, John the second, Dr. T. S. Camidge, and his son, John the third, organist of Beverley Minster.

116. CHANT (D) IN E.

CAMIDGE, MATTHEW (York, 1758–1844, York), son of John the elder, was educated at the Chapel Royal under Dr. Nares, returned to York as assistant to his father, and in 1799 succeeded him as organist of the Minster. He resigned in 1842. He published sonatas, marches for the pianoforte, a collection of *Tunes adapted to Sandys's Version of the Psalms* (York, 1789), and *A Method of Instruction in Music, by Questions and Answers*.

22–23. CHANT (D) IN E.

22–1, 51. CHANT (D) IN e.

CAMPBELL, JOHN (Paisley, 1807–60, Glasgow), a merchant in Glasgow, was an amateur in music and an organist. He was one of the first members of Glasgow Choral Union. 'He had the misfortune to flourish at a time when our psalmody was sadly blemished by florid divisions and repeating lines, and naturally he followed the same bad pattern in most of his tunes.' He published: *The Sacred Psaltery in four vocal parts, consisting principally of original psalm and hymn tunes* (Glasgow, 1854)—nearly fifty tunes, and his anthem *Rejoice in the Lord*, which was long popular in the West of Scotland. He edited also *Campbell's Selection of Anthems and Doxologies, with a separate piano accompaniment* (Glasgow, 1848); also Hamilton's collection of *Anthems, Choruses, Sanctuses*, &c., with another anthem, *I will sing of the mercies of the Lord*, six anthems by R. A. Smith, and several of Handel's choruses.

93. ORLINGTON.

CAREY, HENRY. The story about his birth is described by Sir John Squire as an exploded myth.

CHIPP, EDMUND THOMAS (London, 1823–86, Nice), son of T. P. Chipp, well known as the player of the 'Tower Drums', was one of Dr. William Hawes' choristers at the Chapel Royal. As a violinist he was a member of the Queen's private band and of other orchestras.

As organist he held office in Albany Chapel, Regent's Park, 1843–6; St. Mary-at-Hill, Eastcheap, 1852; the Royal Panopticon, Leicester Square, in succession to W. T. Best, 1855; Holy Trinity, Paddington, 1856; St. George's Church and the Ulster Hall, Belfast, 1862; Kinnaird Hall, Dundee, and St.Paul's Episcopal Church, Edinburgh, 1866; and in the same year organist and magister choristarum, Ely Cathedral. He took his Mus.Doc. degree at Cambridge in 1860. His works included an oratorio, *Job*; *Naomi, a Sacred Idyl*; and much church music.

6. CHANT IN f.

COCKBURN, ROBERT WILLIAM, LL.B., W.S. (Edinburgh, 1879–   ), was educated at Merchiston Castle School and the University, Edinburgh; at the latter he took the degrees of M.A. and LL.B. Since 1904 he has practised as a Writer to the Signet. He has always been interested as an amateur in the theory and practice of music, and since boyhood has deputized for over seventy church organists. He has been an elder in North Morningside Church, Edinburgh, since 1917, and is also Preses of the congregation. He is a member of the Committee on Public Worship and Aids to Devotion of the Church of Scotland, and was one of the revisers of the music of the Scottish Psalter, 1928–9.

13. Appendix 13. OLD 100TH.
Arrangements of 38, 128, and 182.

CONDER, JOSIAH, married a grand-daughter of Roubiliac, the famous sculptor, and the hereditary geographical, literary, and artistic ability of the family was seen in two of their grandsons, Colonel Claude R. Conder, R.E., author, archaeologist, and surveyor of Palestine, and Charles Conder, the well-known artist.

COOKE, BENJAMIN, Mus.Doc. (London, 1734–93, Westminster), became in his ninth year a pupil of Dr. Pepusch, and in three years' time was able to take the place of John Robinson at the organ in Westminster Abbey. In 1752 he succeeded Pepusch as conductor of the Academy of Ancient Music, and in 1757 became master of the choristers, Westminster Abbey; in 1757 lay vicar there; in 1762 organist in succession to Robinson; and in 1782 organist also of St. Martin's-in-the-Fields. He had the Mus.Doc. degree from both Cambridge and Oxford. His fine Service in G was composed for the reopening of the Abbey organ. He composed much church music besides, anthems, chants, and psalm and hymn tunes; and in addition, many fine glees, canons, &c. A collection of his glees was published in his lifetime, and after his death a second collection appeared under the editorship of his son Robert. The epitaph on his tomb in the Abbey says: 'His professional knowledge, talents and skill were profound, pleasing, and various: in his works they are recorded, and within these walls their power has been felt and understood. The simplicity of his manners, the integrity of his heart, and the innocency of his life have numbered him among those who kept the commandments of God, and the faith of their Saviour Jesus Christ.' Then follows his AMEN, a masterly canon, three in one, by double augmentation, which he intended to be sung at the close of Byrd's 'Non nobis'.

73–*18*. CHANT (D) IN a.
32. CHANT (D) IN B♭.

COOPER, GEORGE (Lambeth, 1820–76, London), was son of the assistant organist at St. Paul's. At the age of eleven he deputized for his father. Attwood delighted in hearing him extemporize. Before he was fourteen he was organist of St. Benet, Paul's Wharf. He succeeded his father in the assistant organistship of St. Paul's; in 1836 became organist of St. Ann and St. Agnes; in 1843 followed his father at St. Sepulchre's and was singing-master and organist to Christ's Hospital as well; in 1856 was appointed organist of the Chapel Royal. 'It is as a performer on and arranger for the organ that he will be long remembered. . . . As a player of Bach he was simply unsurpassed.' He published an *Organist's Assistant*, a series of arrangements; an *Organist's Manual. . . . Select Movements from the most eminent composers*; part-songs, &c.

15. ST. SEPULCHRE.

CORFE, JOSEPH (Salisbury, 1740–1820, Salisbury), after training as a chorister in Salisbury Cathedral, became a gentleman of the Chapel Royal in 1783; sang in the Handel Commemoration in 1784; and was organist and master of the choristers in Salisbury from 1792 till 1804, when he resigned in favour of his son, Arthur Thomas Corfe. He died suddenly while kneeling in prayer at his bedside, and was buried in the Cathedral cloisters. He was author of a book on *Harmony and Thorough Bass*, and published a volume of cathedral music, containing a Morning and an Evening Service in B flat, and eleven anthems.

*8. CHANT (D) IN C.

COTTERILL, THOMAS. Lane End, Staffordshire, is now Longton.

CUMMINGS, WILLIAM HAYMAN, Mus.Doc. (Sidbury, Devon, 1831–1915, London), was trained as a chorister in St. Paul's and the Temple Church; sang as alto in the London performance of *Elijah*, 1847; became organist of Waltham Abbey, 1847; tenor singer in the Temple Church and Westminster Abbey; then a leading concert tenor, identified with the tenor parts in Bach's Passion music, &c.; professor of singing in the Royal College for the Blind, Norwood; also at the Royal Academy of Music, 1879–96; Principal of the Guildhall School of Music, 1896–1911. He was one of the founders of the Purcell Society and edited 3 volumes of its publications. His works included a cantata *The Fairy Ring*, a biographical dictionary, a *Primer of the Rudiments of Music*, and a Life of Purcell. He had a remarkable musical library, and was a keen musical antiquary.

46 (Hymnary). BETHLEHEM (adaptation).

CUMMINS, JOHN JAMES, went to London, not in 1864 but in 1834.

DARLING, THOMAS. Shanington should be Thanington.

DAVIES, Sir HENRY WALFORD, C.V.O., O.B.E., resigned the organistship of St. George's, Windsor, in 1932. He was appointed Master of the King's Musick, 1934, and in the same year was made a freeman of Oswestry, his native town. He was joint-editor of *The Church Anthem Book* (1933).

103. CHANT (D) IN C.

DECK, JAMES GEORGE (b. 1807), served the East India Company in the 14th Madras Native Infantry.

DIBDIN, HENRY EDWARD (Sadler's Wells, 1813–66, Edinburgh), grandson of Charles Dibdin, the composer of popular songs, was a clever harpist, and as such played at Covent Garden when Paganini made his last appearance there, in 1832. In the following year he went to Edinburgh, where he was organist of Trinity Chapel and became a teacher of music. Though he composed a few psalm tunes and pieces for organ and pianoforte, he is best known as compiler of *The Standard Psalm Tune Book*, described as 'the largest and most authentic collection of psalm tunes ever published, the contents being mainly derived from ancient psalters'; also of *The Praise Book* (1865). Dibdin had a somewhat uncritical mind: his attributions of tunes to composers are frequently ludicrously astray. See note on ST. PAUL in this Supplement.

*138. UXBRIDGE.

DIX, LEOPOLD L. The hymn-book to which he contributed his arrangements was *The Church Hymnal* of the Irish Episcopal Church, 1919.

DRAPER, WILLIAM HENRY, D.D., d. 1933.

DUNCALF, HENRY, was organist in 1752 of St. Bartholomew-the-Little-by-the-Exchange, a church destroyed in 1841, and at the same time of St. Mary-at-Hill, which still stands.

DYKES, JOHN BACCHUS. Lord Kelvin, in his later years, spoke of his debt to 'the incomparable John Dykes'. Dykes wrote tunes for all who applied to him, not grudgingly or of necessity, and frequently refused payment for them. The last tune he wrote was for *The Congregational Hymn Book*.

ELLIS, WILLIAM, Mus.Doc. (Cantuar.) 1929.

FALCONER, HUGH, D.D., d. Moffat, 1931.

FELTON, WILLIAM. His *Gavot* was often set to the words, 'Farewell, Manchester, noble town, farewell'. The inscription on the memorial tablet in the cloisters of Hereford Cathedral is as follows: 'Gul. Felton, A.M. / hujusque ecclesiae succentor / Collegii Vicariorum Choralium / Custos / Frederico Walliae Principi a sacris / vir animose justus / multiplici doctrina eruditus / Rerum musicarum peritissimus / Obiit sexto die Decembris A.D. MDCCLXIX. Aetatis LIV.'

42, 43. CHANT IN E♭.
91. CHANT IN G.

FINLAY, KENNETH GEORGE, in 1928 resolved to devote himself altogether to music, and after a year at the Royal College of Music and another at the Teachers' Training College, Jordanhill, Glasgow, was appointed in 1930 a teacher of class singing at Irvine, under the Ayrshire County Council. He has published papers dealing with Safety of Life at Sea in the *Transactions* of the Institute of Naval Architects; hymn-tunes in many collections, a cantata *The Saviour's Birth* (1928), and many unaccompanied choral works and educational part-songs.

FITZHERBERT, WILLIAM (?, 1713–97, St. Paul's College, London), was in 1744 elected to the fourth minor canonry, which carried with it the title of Epistolar, in St. Paul's Cathedral. In 1746 he was appointed one of the priests of the Chapel Royal, and in 1776 Sub-Dean of the Cathedral. From 1751 to 1778 he was a minor canon also of St. Peter's, Westminster. He became rector of Hadlow, Kent, in 1753; of Horndon-on-the-Hill, Essex, in 1756. He held the latter cure till 1771, and then passed to St. Gregory by St. Paul, London. On his Double Chant in F, Dr. Crotch once composed a very clever fugue. The second half of the chant is believed not to be Fitzherbert's, but to have been added, not improbably by Dr. Philip Hayes (q.v.), 'who was somewhat fond of adding his own effusions to those of other people'.

50. CHANT (D) IN F.

FLINTOFT, LUKE (Worcester, 1678–1727, London), graduated at Queens' College, Cambridge, in 1700, took holy orders, and became priest-vicar, Lincoln Cathedral, in 1704; passed to a similar office in Worcester Cathedral in 1714; became a gentleman of the Chapel Royal, 1715; reader in Whitehall Chapel, 1719; minor canon of Westminster Abbey, 1719. The chapter books of the Abbey record in 1725 that fifteen guineas were to be paid towards his release from prison, where he was confined for debt. He was buried in the south cloister of the Abbey. He is commonly credited with the invention of the double chant, the beautiful chant in G minor associated with his name being the earliest example known. This composition, however, was not original with him. He adapted it from a psalm-tune published in Allison's Psalter (1599), and subsequently in Playford's *Whole Booke of Psalms* (1677). Dr. Crotch printed the chant in his Collection of 1842, as 'from a harmony by Flintoft'. It first appeared in 1769, in *Fifty Double and Single Chaunts, being the most favourite as performed at St. Paul's, Westminster, and most of the cathedrals in England*, which is thought to be the first regular collection of chants made in this country.

90. CHANT (D) IN g.

FOSTER, JOHN (Staines, 1827–1915, Hampstead), was a pupil of Sir George Elvey at St. George's Chapel, Windsor; became organist of St. Andrew's, Wells Street, London, and established there the cathedral type of service; and in 1856 was appointed a lay vicar of Westminster Abbey. He was conductor of the Civil Services Musical Society and of other similar organizations. He had a fine tenor voice, and became a gentleman of the Chapel Royal. He published a *Gloria in Excelsis* to match and complete Orlando Gibbons's Service in F (1852); *Psalms and Hymns adapted to the Church of England* (1865); *Tunes for the Psalms and Hymns* (1864); *The Choral Harmonist* (1872).

39. CHANT IN E.   *41*. CHANT IN E.
40. CHANT IN f♯.

FOSTER, FREDERICK WILLIAM, was born at Bradford, not Bedford.

FRECH, JOHANN GEORG (Stuttgart, 1790–1864, Esslingen), was son of a watch-maker and organ-seller, and was educated at Stuttgart. At first he showed no inclination towards music, but later, a taste for singing and organ-playing developed and became a passion. In 1806 he became a teacher in the village school at Degerloch, near Stuttgart, and while there studied harmony, composition, violin, flute, and 'cello. In 1811 he became master in a model school erected at Esslingen for Protestant teachers; and in 1820 organist and director of the music of the principal church in Stuttgart. There he had to direct the music of the pupils of the seminary. In 1832 the Government appointed him inspector of the organs in the arrondissement of the Necker; and in the following year he was called to the direction of the music-school at Esslingen, where he remained till 1845. With Kocher and Silcher he edited a *Book of Chorales for Four Voices*. He also published a German Mass for Four Voices, cantatas, a grand opera *Montezuma*, and instrumental music.

26. ASPURG.

FUSSELL, PETER (?, 1750–1802, Winchester), was a pupil of James Kent at Winchester, and succeeded him there in 1774 in the double office of organist of the Cathedral and the College. He taught a number of musicians who subsequently made their mark, among them Charles Dibdin, sen. His Service in A was once popular, and he composed other church music which was appreciated in its day. He was buried in the north transept of the Cathedral.

128. CHANT IN G.

GARRATT, CHARLES A., according to an article by C. E. Miller, composer of WALDRONS, in *Musical Opinion*, Sept. 1933, on 'Some Organists I have known', was a pupil of Thomas Badsmore, organist at Lichfield (1833–81), and was himself teaching in London 1870–1, being then organist of St. Peter's, Croydon. He died at Toronto, in what year cannot now be discovered.

GAUNTLETT, HENRY JOHN, Mus.Doc. In his early childhood at Olney there was only a village band, in the west gallery of the church, to lead the singing. The vicar urged the parishioners to buy an organ and promised to supply an organist. His purpose was that his two girls, Arabella, aged 13, and Lydia, aged 10, should play the hymns, chants, and voluntaries, arranged as duets, as he was afraid that one child would not be able to produce sufficient effect in the large church. But Henry, aged 9, solemnly informed his father that 'it was not fitting for girls to take such a prominent part in the service of the sanctuary, and that if his mother would teach him to play, he would be ready to take the service by the time the organ was built'. Six months later he was as good as his word. Thomas Wright of Olney had this from Miss Gauntlett.

GAWTHORN, NATHANIEL, was clerk, that is, conductor of psalmody, at the Friday lecture in Eastcheap, early in the eighteenth century. In 1730 he published a collection of psalm-tunes in four parts, with some hymn-tunes and anthems, and an Introduction to Psalmody, under the title *Harmonia Perfecta, a complete collection of psalm tunes in four parts, fitted to all the various measures now in use, taken from all the most eminent masters.*

*91. NEWARK.

GIBBONS, CHRISTOPHER, Mus.Doc. (Westminster, 1615–76, Westminster), was the second son of Orlando, by whose genius he was overshadowed. He was not ten years old when his father died, and for a time he was in the care of his uncle Edward Gibbons, who was organist of Exeter Cathedral. There he came to know Matthew Locke, with whom he afterwards collaborated in the music for Shirley's masque *Cupid and Death* (1638), one of the most elaborate of such compositions. He became one of the children of the Chapel Royal. From 1638 till the Rebellion in 1644 he was organist of

Winchester Cathedral. 'When the dean and prebends fled', on the outbreak of the Civil War, 'he accompanied them and served in one of the garrisons' on the Royalist side. During the Commonwealth he earned his living by teaching the organ and playing the virginal. At the Restoration he was one of the few organists of the Chapel Royal at the time of Charles I's death who came forward to claim their posts. 'Modern illustrations of the Seven Sleepers,' says Hullah, 'they woke up in a world for whose ways they had no preparation—old-fashioned people, learned in Canon and believing in the ecclesiastical modes, called upon to furnish material for the Chapel and Chamber Royal.' Evelyn in his *Diary* indicates how complete the change was: 'Instead of ye antient, grave and solemn wind music accompanying ye organ, was introduc'd a concert of 24 violins between every pause, after ye French fantastical light way, better suiting a tavern, or a play-house, than a church.' Gibbons, however, was a great favourite of the King. According to Wood, he was 'a grand debauchee. He would often sleep at Morning Prayers when he was to play the organ.' In 1660 he was appointed organist to the Chapel Royal and private organist to the King; in the same year, organist of Westminster Abbey; and in 1663, at the express request of the King, received the Mus.Doc. degree from Oxford. He wrote a large number of string fantasias and some anthems.

23. CHANT IN G.

GOOCH, FREDERICK, D.C.L. (?, 1804–87, Baginton), son of the Rev. John Gooch, Archdeacon of Sudbury and rector of Benacre, became a Fellow of All Souls, Oxford, and for fifty-four years was rector of Baginton, a small village about two miles south of Coventry and three north-east of Kenilworth. His interest in music is evident from the fact that his name appears in the list of subscribers to S. S. Wesley's *European Psalmist* (1872). 'Old inhabitants of Baginton still speak of Dr. Gooch's fondness for and skill in matters musical.'

GOODENOUGH, ROBERT PHILIP (Ealing, 1776–1826, ?), second son of Samuel Goodenough, D.C.L. (Dean of Rochester, 1802, Bishop of Carlisle, 1808–27, a noted botanist in his day), was educated at Westminster School, of which his younger brother afterwards (1819–28) was headmaster, and at Christ Church, Oxford; B.A. 1796, M.A. 1799; married a daughter of Dr. William Markham, Archbishop of York, who preferred him in 1805 to the Prebend of Fenton in York Minster, and in 1806 to the rectory of Carlton-in-Lindrick, Notts. He is an example of the shameless pluralism that prevailed in the Church in those days, for on the same day on which he was inducted to his living in Nottinghamshire, he was installed in the Prebend of Hallaughton in the Collegiate Church (later Cathedral) of Southwell; in 1811 his father appointed him to the second Prebend in Carlisle Cathedral; in the same year he was given a similar stall in Ripon Minster; and in 1819 the Chapter of South-well appointed him Rector of Beelsby, near Grimsby. After the evil fashion of the time he retained all these preferments till his death. It is probable that he never visited Beelsby except to be inducted to the living. He composed at least four double chants: in A and G (J. St. B. Joule's *Collection of Chants*); in F minor and in F (*The Cathedral Psalter*).

74–12. CHANT (D) IN F.

GOODSON, RICHARD, Mus.Bac. (?, 1655–1718?), was a well-known figure in the musical life of Oxford in his day. Trained as a chorister in St. Paul's Cathedral, he became organist of New College, Oxford, and Choragus, or superintendent of the music students' practice, in 1682, and in 1691 organist of Christ Church and Professor of Music in the University. In the professorship his son succeeded him in 1718. His chants are in a florid style. See Cowper's essay *The Village to the Town*.

15. CHANT IN C.

GRACE, HARVEY, Mus.Doc. (Cantuar.), has since 1931 been organist and director of the choir in Chichester Cathedral. He has published, in addition to the works named in the *Handbook*: *Ludwig van Beethoven*; *The Organ Works of Rheinberger*; *A Musician at Large*; *A Handbook for Choralists*.

GRANT, DAVID (Aberdeen, 1833–93, London), was a tobac-conist in Union Street, Aberdeen. He had keen musical interest, and skill as well, for he scored parts for instrumental bands, and arranged tunes for *The Northern Psalter*. 'Here', he said one day to William Carnie, then editing that Psalter in parts, 'here, pit that in your bookie'—giving him the MS. of a new long-metre tune. 'What shall we call it?' 'Anything you like.' 'Well, seeing you deal so successfully in the weed, what do you say to naming it after the introducer of that article?' 'Good,' and so *Raleigh* the tune became. Grant was a well-read man and an interesting conversationalist, Carnie says in his *Reminiscences*. He was a member of the Footdee (pronounced Fittie in Aberdeen) church and choir. A song sung by his friends there contained this verse:

> Then if our frien' should ever dee
>   And seek the unkent valley, O,
> His epitaph it read shall be
>   From Bon Accord to Callao;
> Auld Fittie bell shall mournfu' ring
> While o'er his grave our heads we hing,
> And softly, slowly, sadly sing
>   Sweet Crimond and then Raleigh, O.

47. CRIMOND.

GRAY, ALAN (York, 1855–   ), was educated at St. Peter's School, York, and Trinity College, Cambridge. At first he intended to follow law, and took the degrees of LL.B. and LL.M.; but after studying under Dr. E. G. Monk, he devoted himself to music. He was musical director of Wellington College from 1883 until in 1892 he succeeded Stanford as organist of his old college and as conductor of the Cambridge Musical Society. He resigned in 1912. He has produced cantatas, *The Widow of Zarephath*, *Arethusa*, *The Legend of the Rock Buoy Bell*, *The Vision of Belshazzar*, *A Song of Redemption*; also *Odysseus in Phaeacia*; *An Easter Ode*; a Festival Te Deum; and compositions for the organ. He has acted as one of the editors of the Purcell Society. In 1926 he published *A Book of Descants*, from which the following are taken:

51. *DUNDEE.	85. *MARTYRDOM.	114. *ST. MAGNUS.
164. *FRANCONIA.	12. *MELCOMBE.	115. *ST. MARY.
61. *FRENCH.	13. *OLD HUNDREDTH.	144. *WILTSHIRE.
	82. *LONDON NEW.	105. *ST. FLAVIAN.

GRAY, HERBERT BRANSTON, D.D., was headmaster of Louth, not Routh, Grammar School. He died in 1929.

GREGORY NAZIANZEN retired to Nazianzus, then to Arizanz.

GRIFFITH, WILLIAM, d. Leicester, 1929.

GRIMSHAW, JOHN, was a Manchester musician. His *Twenty-four Hymns* was dedicated to the rector of St. John's, Manchester; so it is probable that he was organist at that church.

GURNEY, DOROTHY FRANCES, d. London, 1932.

HARINGTON, HENRY, M.D. (Kelston, Somersetshire, 1727–1816, Bath), son of Henry Harington of Kelston, who inherited that estate in 1726, was educated at Queen's College, Oxford, first with a view to holy orders, then for the medical profession; B.A., M.A., M.D. Settling as a physician at Wells in 1753, he moved in 1771 to Bath, where he became one of the best-known public figures; in 1793 he was alderman and mayor, serving in these offices with high credit. He had some poetic talent; he wrote a legend of the Cheddar Cliffs, entitled 'The Witch of Wokey', which subsequently found a place in Percy's *Reliques*. He had great charm of manner, which, according to a Bath historian, did his patients as much good as his medicines. J. T. Lightwood, in *The Music of the Methodist Hymn-Book*, says: 'For many years the good doctor was a conspicuous figure in the streets of Bath, recognized everywhere by his well-defined features and his eccentric old-fashioned garb. Tall, thin, and with an inclination to stoop as he walked, he looked older than his age warranted. He wore the triangular hat and the powdered full-bottomed wig of an earlier period; the whole of his

suit—his court dress, deep-pocketed waistcoat, and knee-breeches—
were all cut from the same sombre-hued cloth, and when he went
out walking he invariably held his handkerchief to his mouth as
a perpetual preventive against chills.' His leisure was largely devoted
to musical pursuits; he founded the Harmonic Society of Bath, and
was honoured with the title of its 'composer and physician'. He
published three books of glees, and a sacred dirge for Passion Week.
He was buried at Kelston, but there is a cenotaph to his memory in
Bath Abbey, with an organ and a passage from his dirge, 'Eloi,
Eloi, lama sabachthani', engraved upon it with this inscription:
'Dr. Harington / Medicus solers et fidelis / Poeta lepidus / Musicus
sciens et peritus / Magistratus gravis justus acer / Erga suos
amantissimus / Erga omnes comis et benevolus.'

66. HARINGTON.

HARRISON, RALPH, published the two volumes of his *Sacred
Harmony* in 1784 and 1791.

HART, JOSEPH, published the first edition of his *Hymns* in 1759.
Dr. Johnson, in his *Prayers and Meditations*, writes: 'On Easter
Day, 22nd April, 1764, I went to church (St. Clement Danes).
I gave a shilling: and seeing a poor girl at the Sacrament in a bed-
gown, gave her privately a crown, though I saw Hart's *Hymns* in
her hand.'

HARTSOUGH, LEWIS, died at Mount Vernon, Indiana, in 1919.
The year given in the *Handbook* for his death (1872) was the year
of the composition of his hymn and tune.

HATCH, EDWIN, was Professor of Classics in Trinity College,
Toronto (not Quebec).

HAYES, PHILIP, Mus.Doc. (Shrewsbury, 1738–97, London), was
probably educated by his father, Dr. William Hayes (q.v.). He
took his Mus.Bac. degree in 1763, became one of the gentlemen of
the Chapel Royal in 1769; organist of New College, Oxford, 1776;
of Magdalen, 1777; of St. John's, 1790. He was 'a monopolist of
organs', for he held these three posts simultaneously, and was,
besides, organist of St. Mary's Church, and from 1777, when he
succeeded his father, Professor of Music in the University. He
was extremely corpulent, and supposed to be the hugest man in
England; 'Phil Chaise' was his nickname. 'In good humour and
appearance he was a complete representation of Shakespeare's fat
knight, Sir John Falstaff.' A relative thus summed up his character:
'Very fond of works of *vertu*: a lazy dog, fond of good living, in fact,
a gourmand: fine temper, good-looking handsome man.' A lazy
man, however, he cannot have been, judging by the number of the
positions he filled, the large number of services and anthems he

wrote, and his many transcriptions in score of earlier works. He wrote *Prophecy*, an oratorio (still in MS.); an Ode for St. Cecilia's Day; *Telemachus*, a masque; eight anthems, &c. He edited also *Harmonia Wiccamica*. He died in London, where he had gone to attend the Chapel Royal, and was buried in St. Paul's.

81. CHANT IN A.   *117*. CHANT IN C.
81–11. CHANT IN a.   *119–81*. CHANT IN E♭.

HENLEY, PHOCION (Wootton Abbots, Wilts., 1728–98, London), when at Oxford spent much of his time in the cultivation of music in company with his friend William Jones, afterwards of Nayland, the composer of the tune ST. STEPHEN. In 1759 he became rector of St. Andrew-by-the-Wardrobe with St. Anne's, Blackfriars. In conjunction with Thomas Sharp he published *Divine Harmony: being a Collection of Psalm and Hymn Tunes in score*, 2 vols. (1798). He also composed chants and anthems, and a set of six hymns entitled *The Cure of Saul*.

29. CHANT (D) IN E♭.

HERMAN, NICOLAUS—also HEERMANN—(*c.* 1485–1561), was cantor of Joachimsthal, a place that grew up in a night when silver began to be mined there in 1556. The silver obtained was so famous that the German word *thaler* is taken from the last syllable of the name of the town. Herman was a poet and scholar as well as a musician; his verse has much the same kind of *naïveté* as that of Hans Sachs. He became cantor in 1518. In 1559 he spoke of himself as an old man, and in 1560 said he had not many more years to live; whence it has been inferred that he was then about 75 years of age. A number of chorales are extant of which he wrote both words and music. In the municipal library at Joachimsthal there is a folio containing all his songs.

108. ST. GEORGE.

HEYWOOD, JOHN (Birmingham, 1841– ?), studied at the R.A.M.; became organist of St. Jude's, Birmingham, in 1863; of St. Mary's, Aston Brook, and of the Plainsong Choir in Holy Trinity, Bordesley, in 1864; of St. Margaret's, Ward End, in 1865; and of St. Paul's, Balsall Heath, in 1856. He acted as organizing choirmaster of the Church Choral Association for the Archdeaconry of Coventry from 1871 to 1895, and in the latter year became chief inspector for the same Archdeaconry. For some time he was on the staff of *The Choir and Saturday Musical Review* and of *The Monthly Musical Record*. He composed chants, hymn-tunes, songs, anthems; and edited *The Anglican Psalter Noted* (1864) and *The Choral Office of Matins and Evensong* (1876).

101. CHANT IN E♭.

Biographical Notes

HILES, HENRY, Mus Doc. (Shrewsbury, 1826–1904, Worthing), was organist successively at Shrewsbury, Bury, Bishop Wearmouth; St. Michael's, Wood Street, and the Blind Asylum, Manchester; Bowden; St. Paul's, Manchester. In 1876 he became Lecturer in Harmony and Composition in Owens College, Manchester, and three years later in the Victoria University; and in 1893 a professor at Manchester College of Music. He was owner and editor of *The Quarterly Musical Review*. His works included oratorios, cantatas, anthems; a *Grammar of Music* (1879); and a book on *Harmony of Sounds* (1871).

24–7. CHANT IN A.   30. CHANT IN A♭.
                    76. CHANT IN B♭.

HINDLE, JOHN (Westminster, 1761–96, London), matriculated at Oxford in 1791 and took his Mus.Bac. degree. He became a lay vicar of Westminster Abbey. He was chiefly a song-writer, publishing a *Collection of Songs for 1 and 2 Voices* (1790), and a *Set of Glees for 3, 4, and 5 Voices*, in the same year.

86. CHANT IN G.

HOLDROYD, ISRAEL (*fl.* first half of eighteenth century), used the pseudonym *Philo-Musicae*. He published *The Spiritual Man's Companion, or the Pious Christian's Recreation, containing an historical Account of Music, &c.*; *Grounds of Music and Composition in all branches, ... Psalm and Hymn Tunes* (2nd edition, 1733); *Chants and Anthems* (1733), and other works.

119. *ST. NICHOLAS.

HOLST, GUSTAV, died in 1934, and was buried in Chichester Cathedral, immediately under the memorial tablet to Weelkes, who, with Purcell, among English composers, stood highest in his admiration. The music at his funeral included his own 'Turn back, O Man' and 'This have I done'; Weelkes's 'Let Thy merciful ears'; and Vaughan Williams's Mass in G minor, and 'Let us now praise famous men'.

HOSMER, FREDERICK LUCIAN, D.D., d. Berkeley, California, in 1929.

HULL, ELEANOR HENRIETTA, D.Litt. (b. 1860), is daughter of Edward Hull, LL.D., the eminent geologist. She was long on the staff of *The Literary World*, contributed to Hastings's *Encyclopaedia of Religion and Ethics*; was one of the founders of the Irish Text Society, and for some time was secretary of the Royal Asiatic Society; is a member of the Council of the Folklore Society, and editor of the *Lives of the Celtic Saints* series, &c.

HUMPHREYS, PELHAM—Humphrey also, or Humfrey (he spelt his name all three ways)—(?, 1647–74, Windsor), was a chorister of the Chapel Royal under Captain Henry Cook, 1660–4, then was sent abroad by Charles II to pursue his studies, which he did chiefly in Paris under Lully. He was appointed in 1665 musician for the lute in the royal band; in 1666 a gentleman of the Chapel Royal; in 1672 master of the choristers. He was also 'composer in ordinary for the violins to His Majesty'. In 1667 Pepys records in his Diary: 'Home, and there find, as I expected . . . little Pelham Humphreys, lately returned from France, and is an absolute Monsieur, as full of form and confidence and vanity, and disparages everything and everybody's skill but his own. But to hear how he laughs at the King's music here . . . that they cannot keep time or tune nor understand anything . . . and that he and the King are mighty great.' He imported into church music the lighter style he learned from Lully, and introduced the instrumental symphonies which so delighted the King. He began early to compose, five of his anthems appearing in Clifford's *Divine Service and Anthems* in 1664, while he was still one of the Children of the Chapel Royal. At the same stage, along with Blow and Turner (q.v.), fellow choristers, he helped to compose what is known as the Club Anthem, which they intended to be a memorial of their friendship. Several fine anthems by him are in Boyce's *Cathedral Music*. Many of his songs remain. He is said to have written the words for many of the songs set by other composers of his time, and to have had 'as fanciful a wit as he had a delicate hand with the lute'. He sang 'tenner' also. He was a man of such great and various ability that his early death was a heavy loss to music. In a less pleasure-loving age doubtless his life would not have ended so soon. As it was, his work was of great importance, showing marked originality and charm. He introduced many new and beautiful effects into his compositions. Boyce says that he was the first of our ecclesiastical composers who had 'the least idea of musical pathos in expression of the words'. 'In his grave', says Sir W. H. Hadow, 'as in that of a greater musician than he, were buried "a rich possession and still fairer hopes".'

150. CHANT IN C.

HURST, WILLIAM, d. Coalville, 1934. His last composition was a tune to 'How sweet the name of Jesus sounds', written the day before his death. At his own request it was sung at his funeral.

IRELAND, JOHN, Mus.Doc. (Dunelm.).

JONES, EDITH (Lower Norwood, 1849–1929, Croydon).

JONES, JOHN (?, 1728–96, London), became organist of the Temple Church in 1749; of Charterhouse, in succession to Dr. Pepusch, in 1752; and of St. Paul's Cathedral in 1755. He held all three offices simultaneously. He was one of the directors of the Handel Commemoration in 1784. He was buried in the Charterhouse. He published several sets of harpsichord lessons, and in 1785 *Sixty Chants, Single and Double*. The *English Musical Gazette* of January 1819 said of him: 'Jones . . . appears not to have been worthy of his situation, for he was not capable of doing the duty for a length of time after the appointment; and as he could not play from score, he employed himself in arranging the Anthems in two lines. The same book is now in use at the Cathedral.' Of his well-known Double Chant in D, Haydn, who noted it down and in doing so improved it, said: 'A week before Whitsuntide I heard 4,000 children sing in St. Paul's Cathedral. . . . No music for a long time affected me so much as this innocent and reverential strain.' Not all his chants, however, were of this quality. The majority of them 'are florid and undevotional, "streams of crotchets", as Dr. Crotch would have said, also dotted quavers being freely used in the prevailing taste of the late Georgian period'.

73. CHANT (D) IN A.

JOSEPH, or JOSEPHI, GEORG. Add to the tunes noted as from *Heilige Seelenlust*:

38. CULBACH.

JOWETT, JOSEPH, published also *Musae Solitariae*, 2 vols. (1823), as 'a help to devotion, in the closet or the domestic circle', all the melodies being of his own composition. He also published *Verses on Various Occasions for Friends*, short poems, chiefly on musical subjects, printed for private circulation.

KEBLE, JOHN, is generally supposed to have been merely gentle, quiet, meek. As a fact, says Canon E. F. Smith of Tewkesbury, he was meek only in the sense in which Moses was meek. His 'meekness, which was almost a passion, veiled the inflexibility of a soldier sworn to hold the fort. In all emergencies his judgement turned instinctively to the course that was most daring and most dangerous. It was natural to him to take the line that would demand the severest strain. . . .

'It is Keble who most fully represents the peculiar *ethos* of the English Church.'—*Church Quarterly Review*.

It is curious to reflect, when the enormous popularity of *The Christian Year* is considered, that Parker, the well-known Church publisher, refused to give £60 for it when it was offered him, and indeed declined to publish it at all. The sale of it was prohibited in 1866 by the 'Dublin Commission for Discountenancing Vice', whose action, strangely, was approved by Archbishop Trench, himself a poet of no mean order.

KELWAY, THOMAS (Chichester, ?–1749, Chichester), was trained as a chorister in Chichester Cathedral, where he was probably a pupil of John Reading, whom he succeeded as lay vicar and organist, first 'on probation', in 1720, then properly 'sworn', in 1733. Seven services and nine anthems by him are contained in a MS. in Chichester Cathedral. Three of the services have been published—in B minor, A minor, and G minor; and of these J. S. Bumpus says, 'It may be confidently said that they are in use in every cathedral in England.' The burial-place of Kelway in the south aisle of the Cathedral was long lost to knowledge. When it was discovered and the stone replaced in 1846, Charles Crocker, the Bishop's verger—a remarkable man who published a volume of creditable poems—wrote the following sonnet:

> Kelway! thy memory, fresh as vernal day
>> In many a heart's most secret holiest cell,
>> Where love of sacred song delights to dwell,
> Lives, and shall live while music holds her sway
> Within these hallowed walls where, day by day,
>> Year after year, he plied the wondrous art
>> Which bids the spirit from its prison start
> And soar awhile to happier realms away.
> His strains full oft still fall upon the ear
>> Of those who tread yon aisle, while at their feet
> His name and record of his hope appear.
>> Peace to his ashes—be his slumbers sweet,
> Till that glad morn when he shall wake to hear
> The angel choir in nightless heaven's bright sphere.

76, 113. CHANT IN D.   *28.* CHANT IN G.

77. CHANT IN g.

KEN, THOMAS. To the hymns under his name add—257: 'All praise to Thee who safe hast kept'.

KNAPP, WILLIAM. His portrait hangs in the vestry of Wareham Church.

LAMPE, JOHANN FRIEDRICH, was bassoonist in Covent Garden Theatre, the wife of the proprietor of which was a convert of Charles Wesley. (See note on GOPSAL in this Supplement.) Charles thought highly of him and of his tunes; he published a volume of 24 of his own hymns set to Lampe's music. In *Sacred Melody* about 20 tunes are from Lampe's hand, chiefly set to 'peculiar metres'. They are for the most part florid and lively. With the exception of KENT they are rarely heard now. See note on IRISH, Hymn 153, in this Supplement; also *The Music of the Methodist Hymn-Book*, pp. 275–7.

LANGDON, RICHARD (Exeter, *c.* 1729–1803, Exeter), was grandson of a priest-vicar of Exeter Cathedral. In 1753 he became organist and sub-chanter there, and was succeeded in 1777 by

William Jackson, composer of the setting of the Te Deum known as Jackson in F. In that year Langdon became organist of Ely Cathedral; in the following year of Bristol Cathedral; and in 1782 of the Cathedral of Armagh, where he remained till 1794, when he resigned and was succeeded by Dr. John Clarke, afterwards Clarke-Whitfeld. He published *Twelve Glees* (1770); two books of songs, &c.; and *Divine Harmony, a Collection, in Score, of Psalms and Anthems* (1774), in which the Double Chant in F, usually attributed to him, appeared anonymously.

37. CHANT (D) IN F.

LEE, WILLIAM (?, –1754, ?), was organist of Southwell Cathedral from 1718 till his death.

93. CHANT IN G.

LEMON, JOHN (Truro, 1754–1814, Polvellen, near Looe), was an officer in the Horse Guards, attaining the rank of lieutenant-colonel. He became M.P. for West Looe in 1784, but applied for the Chiltern Hundreds in the same year. From 1786 to 1790 he was M.P. for Saltash, and subsequently for Truro, in four successive Parliaments, until his death. He was colonel of the Cornish Miners, and in 1804 a Lord Commissioner of the Admiralty.

19. CHANT (D) IN G.

LEY, HENRY GEORGE, M.A., Mus.Doc., was precentor of St. Peter's College, Radley, 1916–17; organist of Christ Church Cathedral, Oxford, 1919–26; Choragus of the University of Oxford, 1923–6; and is now precentor and musical instructor, Eton College, professor of the organ, Royal College of Music, and president of the Royal College of Organists. He was joint editor of *The Oxford Psalter* and *The Church Anthem Book*.

LITTLEDALE, RICHARD FREDERICK, LL.D., D.C.L. In *The English Reformers* (1933) this is said of him: 'Behind his Dublin eloquence and his inimitable Dublin wit, was a profound spirituality which brought to his confessional as many penitents as came to Pusey himself; behind them too were a powerful brain, an extraordinarily retentive memory, and great learning.'

LLOYD, JOHN MORGAN, Mus.Doc., Dublin.

LONGFELLOW, SAMUEL. It was in connexion with the beginning of his ministry at Fall River in 1848 that H. W. Longfellow wrote the beautiful 'Hymn for my Brother's Ordination', beginning:

> Christ to the young man said, 'Yet one thing more;
>   If thou wouldst perfect be,
> Sell all thou hast and give it to the poor,
>   And come and follow me.'

ΓEROTH, Ascan Henri Théodore, contributed only seven to the definitive edition of *Chants Chrétiens*.

MACALISTER, Robert Alexander Stewart. In the note on him *Temair Bug* should be *Temair Breg*. Prof. Macalister was organist of Adelaide Road Presbyterian Church, Dublin, 1920–7.

MACBEAN, Lachlan, d. 1931, Kirkcaldy.

McDONALD, Alexander (Edinburgh, *c.* 1770–?), was precentor of Old Greyfriars Church, Edinburgh, from 1803 till 1817. He succeeded one John Neil, who was dismissed by the Town Council from his office as 'uptaker o' the Psalm' because the Kirk Session made complaint that 'he had last Sunday fallen asleep in the desk during the time of the forenoon service, and was with great difficulty wakened, and could not sing the Psalm till the minister was obliged to give out the Psalm a second time'. McDonald also had to be dismissed after fourteen years' service for not attending to his duties. From 1807 to 1810 he was joint music master with Archibald McDonald, presumably his father, at George Heriot's Hospital, Edinburgh. He edited and published in 1807 *A Collection of Vocal Music, containing Church Tunes, Anthems, and Songs, for the Use of the several Hospitals of the City*; and is believed to have edited also *The Notation of Music Simplified* (Glasgow, 1826).

68. HERIOT'S TUNE.

MACNICOL, Nicol, D.Litt., D.D., has now retired from missionary work in India. He was Wilde Lecturer in Natural and Comparative Religion in the University of Oxford, 1932–4, and holds a lectureship in Hartford Seminary, U.S.A., 1934–5. To his other books add: *What Jesus means for Men*; *India in the Dark Wood*; *The Living Religions of the Indian People*.

MANN, Arthur Henry, d. 1929, Cambridge.

MASTERMAN, John Henry Bertram, d. 1933, Stoke Damerel.

MATHAMS, Walter John, d. 1931, Swanage.

MATHER, William (?, 1756–1808, Sheffield), was organist of St. Paul's and St. James's, Sheffield.

In 1806 he issued from his own house in 11 Norfolk Row *Sacred Music*, containing 26 tunes and 6 anthems. Some of his tunes had previously appeared in other publications, but as they were not always correctly printed he published this book in order that mistakes might be rectified.

His son John (Sheffield, 1781–1850, Edinburgh), after serving for a time as organist of Sheffield Parish Church, removed to Edinburgh, about 1810, and thereafter was one of the most prominent musicians in that city. He composed *Hail to the Chief*, a glee, songs, &c.

126. SHEFFIELD.

MATTHEWS, SAMUEL, Mus.Bac. (?, 1796–1832, Cambridge), was trained as a chorister in Westminster Abbey under Robert Cooke. Afterwards he was a lay clerk of Winchester Cathedral. In 1822 he was appointed organist of Trinity and St. John's Colleges, Cambridge, in succession to William Beale, the distinguished madrigal writer. William Glover, in his *Memoirs of a Cambridge Chorister*, says that he was 'a kindly man in private, but a regular martinet during official hours'. He composed a Service in D, and published four anthems from the works of Haydn, Mozart, and others.

84. CHANT (D) IN E.

MILTON, JOHN (Milton, near Halton and Thame, Oxfordshire, c. 1563–1646/7, London), son of a well-to-do yeoman of Stanton St. John, near Oxford, was 'cast out by his father, a bigoted Roman Catholic, for abjuring the Roman tenets'. He is believed to have been, before this, at Christ Church, Oxford. Going to London to seek his fortune, he was apprenticed to a member of the Scriveners' Company in 1595, and in 1599 or 1600 was admitted to the freedom of the Company. Thirty-four years later he was elected Master of the Company, but did not accept office. In his house in Bread Street in the City his poet son grew up in an atmosphere of music. Masson in his *Life* of the poet suggests that the father practised music professionally, but that is unlikely, in view of the eminence to which he rose in his profession and the considerable fortune he made in it. He was able to retire about 1632 to Horton, Bucks.; later, he lived at Reading, and in 1643 returned to London to live with his son in the Barbican. There he died, and was buried in St. Giles', Cripplegate. A madrigal by him—*Fair Oriana in the Morn*—appeared in *The Triumphes of Oriana*, and several of his songs for three voices are in Leighton's *Teares and Lamentacions*. He is said to have composed an *In Nomine* of forty parts, for which, according to his grandson Edward Phillips, on the authority of the poet, he was rewarded with a gold medal and chain by a Polish Prince to whom he presented it. For Ravenscroft's *Whole Booke of Psalmes* (1625) he harmonized two tunes, *Norwich* and *York*, the latter in two versions. His anthems have been reprinted by G. E. P. Arkwright. Milton pays tribute to his father's musical gifts in his poem *Ad Patrem*.

146.* YORK.

MONK, MARK JAMES, Mus.Doc., d. 1929, Blackheath.

MOORE, THOMAS. The last sentence of this note should read: He wrote the *Life of Byron*.

MORLEY, HENRY KILLICK. This note is inaccurate. The writer of the tune NEWCASTLE was Henry L. Morley, about whom little is known beyond the fact that he wrote another tune, named CHARLTON, for the same book, *The London Tune Book*, in which NEWCASTLE appeared. See note on Hymn 36.

MORLEY, WILLIAM, Mus.Bac. (d. 1731), was admitted a gentleman of the Chapel Royal, 1715. He composed some songs, but is now known only by his double chant in D minor, printed in Boyce's Collection. It is by some supposed to be the oldest double chant in existence.

77. CHANT (D) IN D MINOR.

MORNINGTON, EARL OF, Mus.Doc. (Dangan, Ireland, 1735–81, Kensington)—Garrett Colley Wellesley (Wesley)—was a born musician: with very little help he learned to play the organ and the violin and to compose. When he consulted Th. Rosengrave and Geminiani about further study, they informed him that he already knew all they could teach him. After graduating M.A. in Dublin, 1757, he founded in that year the Academy of Music, an amateur society in which ladies for the first time sang in the chorus. In 1764 he took his Mus.Doc. degree, and became Professor of Music in Dublin University. In 1758 he succeeded his father as Baron Mornington, and in 1760 was created Viscount Wellesley and Earl of Mornington. He was the father of the Duke of Wellington and the Marquis Wellesley. He excelled as a composer of glees. A complete collection of his glees and madrigals was edited by Sir Henry Bishop in 1846.

18. CHANT (D) IN D.

MOUNTAIN, JAMES, D.D., d. 1933, Tunbridge Wells.

NAYLOR, EDWARD WOODALL, Mus.Doc., d. 1934, Cambridge. He became Lecturer in Musical History in the University of Cambridge, in 1926. Besides the books mentioned, he wrote *The Poets and Music* (1928).

NEALE, JOHN MASON. These facts about this remarkable man may be added. At Sackville College, in spite of his troubles and derisory salary, he was 'supremely happy, with his pensioners, his five children, his books, his dreams, and the great Sussex Downs'. He is said to have been able to read, write, and think in twenty-one different languages. The Ancient section of *Hymns Ancient and Modern* was entirely his work. For some time he earned enough to pay for his children's governess by acting as a leader-writer for *The Morning Chronicle*.

NISBET, JOHN MACDONNELL, d. 1935, Aberdeen.

NOVELLO, VINCENT. Cf. Lamb's *Essays of Elia—A Chapter on Ears*, where Lamb speaks of 'my good Catholic friend Nov——;

who, by the aid of a capital organ, himself the most finished of players, converts his drawing-room into a chapel, his week-days into Sundays, and these into minor heavens'. This was Novello, who was a friend of all the Lamb group. His biography was written by his daughter.

OAKELEY, FREDERICK, D.D. Dean Church, in *The Oxford Movement*, says: 'Mr. Oakeley was perhaps the first to realize the capacities of the Anglican ritual for impressive devotional use, and his services, in spite of the disadvantages of the time and also of his chapel, are still remembered by some as having realized for them, in a way never since surpassed, the secrets and the consolations of the worship of the Church. Mr. Oakeley without much learning was master of a facile and elegant pen. He was a man who followed a trusted leader with chivalrous boldness, and was not afraid of strengthening his statements.'

OAKELEY, Sir HERBERT STANLEY, Mus.Doc. His father was Dean of Barking, not Bocking.

78. CHANT (Q) IN F.

PATRICK, ST. The birthplace is uncertain. On the whole, Abergavenny has most of the probabilities in its favour.

PURCELL, DANIEL (*c.* 1660–1717), younger brother of Henry, became organist of Magdalen College, Oxford, 1688–95, then settled in London. After Henry's death he was in great demand for the kind of work in which Henry excelled, the composition of music for plays; of this, a great deal survives. He was organist of St. Andrew's, Holborn, 1713–17. He published *The Psalmes set full for the Organ or Harpsichord as they are Plaid in Churches and Chappels in the manner given out; as also with their Interludes of great Variety*. One of the 'givings-out' and one of the interludes may be seen in *The Musical Times* for 1905.

4. CHANT IN G.

PURCELL, HENRY (?, 1658–95, London), son of a gentleman of the Chapel Royal and Master of the Choristers of Westminster Abbey, was trained as a choir-boy in the Chapel Royal, and studied under Cooke, Blow, and Humfrey, from whom he learned the new French style which Humfrey acquired from Lully. In 1679 he became organist of the Abbey, Blow resigning, it is said, in his favour. He is by many regarded as the greatest of English musicians. He touched the music of his age at every point, and in every department left great works; the large amount of music written by him in his short life is equalled by its variety. He wrote odes, incidental music for plays, *Dido and Aeneas*, 'the only perfect English opera ever written, and the only opera of the seventeenth century that is performed nowadays for the sheer pleasure it gives as opera', and a great mass of anthems and services, the greatest religious music of his time; also songs, duets, catches, music for organ, strings, harpsichord, &c. Even now a vast quantity remains in manuscript. At the end of his short life he was master of every branch of musical technique. His gift of melody has been excelled, some think, only by Mozart. It was from his work that Handel imbibed that English quality which distinguishes it. None of his church music was published in his lifetime, and until Vincent Novello began editing it in 1828, not more than a dozen of his anthems were known to exist in print.

> 7, *130*. CHANT IN a.
> *80*. CHANT (D) IN c.
> *38*, *55*. CHANT (D) IN f.

PURCELL, THOMAS (d. 1682), uncle of the great Henry Purcell, was appointed a gentleman of the Chapel Royal, 1660; copyist and lay vicar of Westminster Abbey, 1661; Composer in Ordinary for the Violins to the King, along with Pelham Humfrey; and Musician in Ordinary for the Lute and Voice, in succession to Henry Lawes, 1662; Master of the King's Band of Music, in conjunction with Humfrey, 1672. He composed several chants.

> *102*. CHANT IN g.
> *102–12*. CHANT IN G.
> *131*. CHANT IN G.

PYE, KELLOW JOHN, Mus.Bac. (Exeter, 1812–1901, Exmouth), entered the R.A.M. immediately upon its foundation, and took the first pianoforte lesson ever given within its walls, from Cipriani Potter; he studied there also under Crotch, and remained for six years. In 1830 he returned to Exeter and acquired a great reputation in the south-west of England as a music teacher. In 1832 he was awarded the Gresham medal for his full anthem 'Turn Thee again, O Lord'. In 1842 he took the Oxford Mus.Bac. degree. In 1853 he abandoned music as a profession and entered as a partner a wine merchant's business in London. In his new position, however, he was able to render great service to musical education and culture in the capital. He joined the directorate of the R.A.M., and was chairman of the committee of management; the executive of the National Training School of Music; the Committee of the Bach Choir; the Council of the R.C.M.; the Madrigal Society; the Mendelssohn Scholarship Foundation, &c. He published *Four Full Anthems, Three Short Full Anthems*, &c.

> *104*. CHANT (D) IN E.

RAYMOND-BARKER, ELIZABETH (Leicester, 1829–1916, Hayward's Heath), daughter of William Hacket of Ayleston Hall, Leicester, married in 1853 the Rev. Frederic Mills Raymond-Barker,

M.A., of Oriel College, Oxford. She entered the Roman Church in 1867, when she took the additional names of Mary Agnes. At the request of J. M. Neale she composed tunes to his *Hymns of the Eastern Church* (1864–68); the first series (1864) contains six hymns, which she set to music at Bisley, Gloucestershire, in 1863. Her tune *Damascus*, set to Neale's hymn 'Those eternal bowers', was familiar in the 1899 edition of *The Church Hymnary*. Neale seems to have admired her work greatly. Of her setting to 'Safe home, safe home in port' he says: 'One feels that the anonymous writer of such a plaintive yet soothing melody, must have been one—to quote Abp. Trench's words with regard to the author of *Veni, Sancte Spiritus*—acquainted with great sorrow, but also with great consolation.'

44. CORONA.

RIDSDALE, CHARLES JOSEPH, d. 1929.

ROBERTS, LEWIS JONES, d. Aberayron, 1931.

RUSSELL, WILLIAM (London, 1777–1813, London), was deputy for his father as organist of St. Mary Aldermanbury, 1789–93; organist, Great Queen Street, Lincoln's Inn Fields, 1793–8, the chapel being sold to the Methodists in the latter year; organist of St. Ann's, Limehouse, 1798, and of the Foundling Hospital Chapel, 1801; pianist and composer at Sadler's Wells from 1800 for about four years. He had a high reputation as organist and pianist. He composed three oratorios, a Mass in C minor, glees, songs, spectacles, and pantomimes. In 1809 he published *Psalms, Hymns and Anthems for the Foundling Chapel*.

136. CHANT IN C.	*107.* CHANT (D) IN E.
122. CHANT IN G.	*9, 10.* CHANT (D) IN G.

RYLEY, GEOFFREY CHARLES EDWARD, vacated the living of Hadlow, Tonbridge, 1929, to become Domestic Chaplain to the Bishop of Rochester.

SAVAGE, WILLIAM (?, 1720–89, London), was a pupil of Dr. Pepusch. He became organist of Finchley Parish Church, and in 1744 one of the gentlemen of the Chapel Royal. In 1748 he became almoner, vicar-choral, and Master of the Boys (choristers) in St. Paul's Cathedral. In that office, it is on record, 'he does not appear to have preserved the amiable qualities of his predecessor (Charles King). As was his name, so was his nature, for we find that in 1773 it was deemed expedient to remove him, on account, it is said, of the great harshness with which he treated the boys committed to his charge.' He was a fine bass vocalist, and a capable organist. He published chants and other church music, but his reputation survives only by his single Chant in C.

129. CHANT IN C.

Biographical Notes

SCOTT-GATTY, Sir ALFRED. Among his hundreds of popular songs the best known in Scotland is 'Rothesay Bay', the words by Mrs. Craik.

SEVEN SOBS OF A SORROWFUL SOUL.—For William Hunnis's chequered career see *The Dictionary of National Biography.*.

SHAW, GEOFFREY, Mus.Doc. (Cantuar.).

SHAW, MARTIN, Mus.Doc. (Cantuar.), edited, in addition to the works mentioned, *The English Carol Book*, and, jointly with R. Vaughan Williams, *The Oxford Book of Carols* (1928); in 1929 he published his autobiography under the title *Up till Now*.

SILAS, ÉDOUARD. J. A. Fuller-Maitland relates in *A Door-keeper of Music*, that when, as musical critic of *The Times* he was searching for some one to deputize for him, 'Many were the oddities among those who tried their hands at helping me; one, highly recommended, expressed the opinion that there was only one really great composer then living, in the person of a certain Édouard Silas, whose name may be read in the annals of the Philharmonic Society.'

SMART, Sir GEORGE THOMAS, Mus.Doc. (London 1776–1867, London), was educated under Ayrton, Dupuis, and Arnold; organist, St. James's Chapel, Hampstead Road; taught singing and harpsichord; knighted in 1811 by the Lord Lieutenant of Ireland for successful conducting of concerts in Dublin; was conductor of the Philharmonic Society's concerts for many years; one of the organists of the Chapel Royal, 1822; succeeded Attwood as composer to the Chapel Royal, 1838. He united great administrative ability with a genius for conducting, and for a long period of years was in great demand all over the country for conducting festivals; he introduced Mendelssohn's *St. Paul* to this country at Liverpool. He gave lessons in singing till he was over eighty, instructing among others Sontag and Jenny Lind in the traditional manner of singing Handel's songs. He edited Orlando Gibbons's madrigals for the Musical Antiquarian Society, and the *Dettingen Te Deum* for the Handel Society; and composed anthems, chants, psalm-tunes, &c. See *Leaves from the Journal of Sir George Smart*, published in 1907.

144. WILTSHIRE.

SMITH, JOHN STAFFORD (Gloucester, 1750–1836, London), son of an organist of Gloucester Cathedral, was taught by his father, then by Boyce, then as a chorister of the Chapel Royal under Nares. He was a distinguished organist, tenor singer, composer, and musical antiquary. In 1784 he became a gentleman of the Chapel Royal; 1785, lay vicar of Westminster Abbey; 1790, organist of Gloucester Musical Festival; 1802, one of the organists of the Chapel Royal in succession to Arnold; 1805, master of the choristers there.

His training of the boys was of a happy-go-lucky description. John Goss, who was one of them, having saved enough of his pocket-money to buy a copy of Handel's Organ Concertos, encountered Smith while carrying it under his arm. 'What is that you are carrying?' 'Only Handel's Organ Concertos, sir; I thought I'd like to learn to play them.' 'Oh, and pray, sir, did you come here to learn to play, or sing?' 'To sing, sir.' Whereupon the master seized the book, and hit the boy over the head with it. Goss never saw it again. Smith used to take Goss with him occasionally on his walks, and would unbend to him, telling him stories of his experiences and the people he had met. On returning home, 'he impressed his teaching on the skin of his pupil by a mild castigation. By this means his dignity as a master was maintained, he consoled himself for having unbent his mind to a junior, and felt that he had justified his position as a senior, according to the rule then prevalent with parents and guardians.' Smith was in the front rank of glee composers; he published five collections of glees alone. His chief publications were: *A Collection of English Songs, in score, for three and four voices, composed about the year 1500. Taken from MSS. of the same age* (this contains the Agincourt Song); *Musica Antiqua*, a collection of old music from the twelfth to the eighteenth century; he also assisted Sir John Hawkins, as Hawkins acknowledged in his Preface, in preparing his *History of Music*, by reducing ancient compositions to modern notation, and by lending MSS. from his remarkable library. After his death, this library was auctioned by a man who knew nothing of its value and had done nothing to let connoisseurs know of what it consisted, and most of its treasures were lost. In 1793 Smith published *Twelve Chants composed for the Use of the Choir Service of the Church of England*, and also a volume of anthems.

89–1. CHANT (D) IN G.
89–38. CHANT (D) IN g.

SMITH, SAMUEL FRANCIS, D.D., was an ardent advocate of foreign missions, would himself have become a foreign missionary if circumstances had not prevented him, and wrote eighteen missionary hymns. He wrote also two books on missions, *Missionary Sketches* and *Rambles in Missionary Fields*, the latter recording impressions of a visit to the missions of India, Ceylon, and Burma.

STANLEY, R. H. Of this composer nothing has been discovered.

40. CHANT IN A.

STEVENSON, Sir JOHN ANDREW, Mus.Doc. (Dublin, 1761–1833, Headfort House), was son of a violinist in the State Band, Dublin; chorister, Christ Church Cathedral, Dublin, 1771; in choir of St. Patrick's, 1775–80; vicar choral of St. Patrick's, 1783, and of

Christ Church, 1800. In 1791 he received the Mus.Doc. degree from Dublin University; in 1803 was knighted by the Lord Lieutenant, Lord Hardwicke; and in 1814 was appointed first organist and musical director of Dublin Castle Chapel. He died while on a visit to the Marchioness of Headfort. He composed a good deal for the stage; wrote an oratorio *Thanksgiving*, which was performed at the Dublin Musical Festival of 1831; published many glees, songs, canzonets, also (1825) a collection of services and anthems; but is best known by his symphonies and accompaniments to Moore's *Irish Melodies*. See note in this Supplement on HOWARD.

STEWART, CHARLES HYLTON, d. 1932, Windsor, two months after taking up duty as organist of St. George's Chapel there. He was organist of Chester Cathedral 1930–2.

STRONG, THOMAS BANKS, D.D., &c., Bishop of Oxford, is now G.B.E., Chancellor of the Order of the Garter and Clerk of the Closet; Visitor of Cuddesdon, Bradley, Radley, and Dorchester, and Warden of Ripon Hall, Oxford.

SWIFT, JAMES FREDERICK, d. 1931.

TATE, NAHUM. Southey, quoting from Oldys, says of Tate: 'He was a good-natured fuddling companion, and his latter days were spent in the Mint as a refuge from his creditors.'

THOMSON, ANDREW MITCHELL, D.D. (Sanquhar, 1778–1831, Edinburgh), was educated at the University of Edinburgh, was for a brief time schoolmaster at Markinch, Fife, and in 1802 was licensed by the Presbytery of Kelso and ordained at Sprouston. He was translated to the East Church, Perth, in 1808, and to New Greyfriars, Edinburgh, in 1810. In the following year he graduated as M.A. in the University there. Because of his outstanding pulpit gifts he was presented by the Town Council in 1814 to the newly erected church and parish of St. George's in the New Town of the city. Lord Cockburn, in his *Memorials of his Time*, referring to the poverty of town councils then, says: 'It was necessary to fill churches, for the sake of the seat rents; and churches could only be filled by putting in ministers for whom congregations would pay. This business principle operated seriously in Edinburgh, where the magistrates had laid out large sums in building and repairing kirks. This brought Andrew Thomson into this city; which was the opening of his career. His Whig reputation was so odious, that it rather seemed at one time as if civic beggary would be preferred to it; and most vehemently was his entrance into our untroubled fold opposed. But, after as much plotting as if it had been for the Popedom, he got in, and in a few years rewarded his electors by drawing about £1,800 a year for them; a fact which, of itself, loosened all the city churches from the dead sea in which they were standing.' In ideas and enter-prise he was far ahead of his time. An enthusiastic musical amateur, he set himself to improve the psalmody of his church, and in 1823 did a great service to congregational singing generally by inducing R. A. Smith (q.v.) to come from Paisley to be his precentor. He encouraged Smith in every way. They had already collaborated in the compilation of *Sacred Harmony, Part I, for the Use of St. George's Church, Edinburgh* (1820), to which Thomson himself contributed *Redemption* and *St. George's, Edinburgh*, and eleven other tunes now forgotten. They again collaborated in *Sacred Music, consisting of Tunes, Sanctuses, Doxologies, Thanksgivings, &c., Sung in St. George's Church, Edinburgh* (1825). Thomson was a leading public figure in Edinburgh. He wrote copiously besides, publishing many books of sermons and lectures. For twenty years he edited *The Edinburgh Christian Instructor* (30 vols.), and he wrote forty-three articles in *The Edinburgh Encyclopaedia*, of which he was part proprietor. He died suddenly within a few steps of his own door, when returning from a Presbytery meeting. His son John became Professor of Music in the University of Edinburgh.

190. ST. GEORGE'S, EDINBURGH.

TOMLINSON, ——. Of this composer nothing has been dis-covered.

16. CHANT IN G.

TOPLADY, AUGUSTUS MONTAGUE. That there was little to choose between the Wesleys and Toplady as disputants is shown by the fact that John Wesley, irritated by the torrent of scurrilous pamphlets from his opponent's pen, wrote : 'Mr. Augustus Toplady I know well ; but I do not fight with chimney-sweepers' ; and Toplady wrote : 'Mr. Wesley and his subalterns are in general so excessively scurrilous and abusive, that contending with them resembles fighting with chimney-sweepers, or bathing in a mud pool.' Yet this same virulent controversialist, when he lay dying at the age of thirty-eight, answered a friend who suggested that he might recover, by saying, 'No, no. I shall die. For no mortal could endure such manifesta-tions of God's glory as I have done, and live.'

TRAVERS, JOHN (?, 1703–58, London), was trained as a chorister of St. George's, Windsor, under John Goldwin, and on leaving was enabled by the generosity of Henry Godolphin, Dean of St. Paul's and Provost of Eton College, to become an articled pupil of Dr. Maurice Greene. He was assisted in his studies also by Dr. Pepusch (chapelmaster to the 'magnificent' Duke of Chandos, and afterwards (1737–52) organist of the Charterhouse ; possessor of a remarkable library, a learned theorist, and one of the first to study English medieval music). About 1725 he became organist of St. Paul's, Covent Garden, and concurrently of Fulham Church ; in

1732, of the Chapel Royal. He copied, Burney says, Pepusch's 'correct, dry, and fanciless style'. Pepusch left him half of his fine musical library. Travers published *Eighteen Canzonets for two, and three, Voices*, the words chiefly from the posthumous works of Matthew Prior; *XII Voluntaries for the organ or harpsichord;* and *The Whole Book of Psalms for one, two, three, four, and five Voices, with a Thorough Bass for the Harpsichord*. 'Few pieces of liturgical music are so frequently drawn upon in our Cathedrals as "Travers in F".'

125. CHANT IN E.

TRENT, ——. Of this composer no particulars have been found.

25. CHANT (D) IN A♭.

TUCKER, WILLIAM—also TUCKERE and TUCKERS—(?, 1678, Westminster), was in holy orders, a gentleman of the Chapel Royal, and (1660) a minor canon and precentor of Westminster Abbey. His name appears many times in the accounts of payments to the royal musicians. It is surmised that he may have been a son of Edmund Tucker (*fl.* late sixteenth and early seventeenth century), who was organist of Salisbury Cathedral. Some of Edmund's works are believed to be among those attributed to William, which consisted of anthems, church services—a *Whole Service in F*, and an *Evening Service in F*.

124. CHANT IN A.

TURNER, WILLIAM, Mus.Doc. (Oxford, 1651–1739/40, Westminster), son of the cook at Pembroke College, Oxford, was trained as a chorister of Christ Church there, and afterwards at the Chapel Royal, where he had as fellow pupils John Blow and Pelham Humphreys (q.v.). The three friends collaborated during their time there in the composition of the Club Anthem. 'They agreed', Boyce says, 'each to set different verses, and to connect and form them into a regular performance; to remain as a memorial of their fraternal esteem and friendship.' Turner's contribution was a bass solo in the middle. He had a fine counter-tenor voice, and sang for a time in Lincoln Cathedral. Becoming a gentleman of the Chapel Royal in 1669, he served as such under seven kings and queens successively, 'and in the former part of his life his voice . . . recommended him to much favour'. He was also a vicar-choral of St. Paul's, and a lay vicar of Westminster Abbey. He received his Mus. Doc. degree from Cambridge in 1696. He composed songs and catches, many of which were popular in their day, operas, and a large quantity of church music, services and anthems. He also edited *Ravenscroft's Psalm Tunes* (1728). He died within four days of his wife, and they are buried together in the cloisters of the Abbey. On his tombstone there is engraved on an open book the canon set to the words of the Psalm in his Gamut Service. The inscription concludes: 'His own musical compositions, especially his church musick, are a far nobler monument to his memory than any other that can be raised for him.'

163. EGHAM.
112. CHANT IN A.
27. CHANT IN D.

VINCENT, CHARLES JOHN, Mus.Doc., d. 1934.

WAINWRIGHT, ROBERT, Mus.Doc. (Stockport, 1748–82, Liverpool), was the eldest son of John Wainwright (q.v.). He gained the Mus.Doc. degree at Oxford, 1774, a *Te Deum* of his composition being performed at the graduation. He succeeded his father as organist of the Collegiate Church, Manchester, 1768, and in 1775 was appointed organist of St. Peter's (afterwards the cathedral), Liverpool. He composed an oratorio, *The Fall of Egypt*, anthems, services, &c. The rapidity of his execution on the organ was remarkable. Edward Miller, in his *History of Doncaster*, relates that on the erection of a new organ in Doncaster Church by Snetzler, Wainwright was a candidate for the post of organist. Among his six competitors was no less a person than F. W. Herschel, afterwards famous as Sir William Herschel, the astronomer, but then making his way as a musician in this country, having lately come from Germany. Wainwright had to play second before the judges, and Herschel third. 'Wainwright's execution was so rapid that old Snetzler ran about exclaiming, "Te tevil, te tevil, he run over te key like one cat; he will not give my piphes room for to shpeak!" During this performance Miller said to Herschel, "What chance have you to follow this man?" He replied, "I don't know, but I am sure fingers will not do." In due time he ascended the gallery, and drew from the organ such a full volume of slow solemn harmony as Miller could by no means account for. After a short extempore effusion of this character, he finished with the Old Hundredth tune, which he played better than his opponent had done. "Ay, ay!" cried Snetzler, "tish is very goot, very goot inteet; I vill luff tish man, for he gives my piphes room for to shpeak." Herschel being afterwards asked by Miller by what means he had produced so uncommon an effect, answered, "I told you fingers would not do"; and taking two pieces of lead from his waistcoat pocket, he said, "One of these I placed on the lowest key of the organ, the other on the octave above; thus, by accommodating the harmony, I gained the power of four hands instead of two." Herschel was thereupon appointed, but soon afterwards entered upon other pursuits, and the musician has been long forgotten in the astronomer.'

81. LIVERPOOL.
83. MANCHESTER.
109. ST. GREGORY.

WALMISLEY, THOMAS ATTWOOD (London, 1814–56, Hastings), son of Thomas Forbes Walmisley, organist of the Female Orphan Asylum and of St. Martin's-in-the-Fields, studied under his godfather Attwood; became a brilliant pianist; organist of Croydon Church, 1830; of Trinity and St. John's Colleges, Cambridge, 1833; Mus.Bac. the same year; entered Corpus Christi College, where he distinguished himself in mathematics; while still in residence for the B.A. degree became Professor of Music in succession to Clarke-Whitfeld, 1836; B.A. two years later; M.A. 1841; Mus.Doc. 1848. In general culture as well as musical scholarship he was far ahead of most musicians of his time; he was also one of the first organists of his day. He was much overworked, as his Sunday engagements in Cambridge show: 7.15, St. John's College; 8, Trinity; 9.30, King's; 10.30, St. Mary's Church; 2, University Service, St. Mary's; 3.15, King's; 5, St. John's; 6.15, Trinity. He was highly strung and sensitive. Once he asked Mendelssohn, with whom he was on terms of friendship, to consider a symphony he had written. Mendelssohn, on learning that it was a first attempt, declined, saying, 'Let us see first what number 12 will be like'. Walmisley was so discouraged that he gave up orchestral writing altogether. He published *Cathedral Music*, a collection of anthems and services; a collection of chants; choral hymns in four parts; and a volume of his anthems and services was edited by his father after his death. 'The desire to be free from the burning current of his thoughts, which led he knew not whither,' led to his indulging unduly in sedatives to soothe his too active brain, and an overdose of one of these lethal remedies caused his death. He was buried in the beautiful churchyard of Fairlight. On the tablet to his memory in the ante-chapel of Trinity College, this phrase from the quartet of his noble anthem 'If the Lord Himself' is engraved: 'The snare is broken, and we are delivered.'

35. CHANT (D) IN F.
87. CHANT IN G.

WALTON, HERBERT FRANCIS RAINE, d. 1929, Glasgow.

WARING, ANNA LAETITIA, b. 1823.

WATT, LAUCHLAN MACLEAN, D.D., LL.D., was Moderator of the General Assembly of the Church of Scotland, 1933, and resigned the charge of Glasgow Cathedral, 1934.

WELDON, JOHN (Chichester, 1676–1736, London), received his education first as a chorister of Eton College, then as a pupil of Henry Purcell. His appointments were: 1694–1701, organist of New College, Oxford; 1701, gentleman extraordinary of the Chapel Royal; 1708, organist of the Chapel Royal in succession to Blow; 1715, second composer there. He was very popular as an organist, and held office in St. Bride's, Fleet Street, and St. Martin-in-the-Fields, concurrently with his other appointment. He received his appointment to the latter church out of compliment to George I, who had been elected churchwarden of this parish, in which he lived, but who tired of his duty in two months and presented the church with, as solatium for his withdrawal, an organ costing £1,500. Weldon wrote three books of songs, music for four operas, many anthems, and in particular published *Divine Harmony: Six Select Anthems for a Voice alone, with a Thorow Bass for the Organ, Harpsichord, or Arch-Lute.* In this book there is a picture of the interior of St. James's Chapel with service going on, in which the violists, lutenists, and 'Hoboy players' are shown playing left-handed. 'John Weldon wrote some exceedingly beautiful music for the Church, in which deep religious sentiment seems to have been his motive power. If it does not indicate a very masterly or comprehensive genius, it is distinguished by smooth harmony and a vocal elegance in its phrases which remains unimpaired even at the present day' (J. S. Bumpus, *History of English Cathedral Music*).

79. CHANT IN g.

WEST, LEWIS RENATUS (London, 1753–1826, Tytherton, Wiltshire), belonged to the United Brethren (Moravians), and for a time was a master in their school at Fulneck, Leeds. After a brief time as tutor and assistant preacher at Bedford, he settled in Dublin in 1784 as assistant minister, with special charge of the young men of the Moravian congregation. He was ordained as deacon in 1785, and after leaving Dublin was minister in succession of congregations in Gracehill, Ireland, Mirfield, Bath, Bristol, and Tytherton, where he died. He was buried in the Moravian burial-ground there. He was a keen musician.

169. PRAGUE.

WHITE, HENRY KIRKE. The first line of his poem on 'The Star of Bethlehem' should read: 'Once on the raging seas I rode'.

WILLIAMS, ISAAC, was curate at the Gloucestershire Bisley. Dean Church said of him that 'he had the true poetic gift, though his power of expression was often not equal to what he wanted to say'. See also note on Hymn 292.

WILLIAMS, THOMAS. See in this Supplement note on LLANDINAM under Hymn 65.

WILSON, DAVID FREDERICK RUDDELL, was general editor of *The Church Hymnal* of the Episcopal Church of Ireland, and of *The Irish Chant-book*.

WILSON, JOHN (Edinburgh, 1800–49, Quebec), was early apprenticed to a firm of printers in Edinburgh, and later became proof-reader to Ballantyne, the printer of the *Waverley Novels*. He studied music under John Mather (*vide* William Mather) and Benjamin Gleadhill, and was a member of the choir of Duddingston Church under the ministry of John Thomson, the landscape-painter. He had a very fine tenor voice, and when he became precentor of Roxburgh Place Relief Church his singing and fine taste drew crowds to the church. In 1825 he passed to the precentorship of St. Mary's Parish Church, and edited in the same year *A Selection of Psalm Tunes, Sanctuses, Doxologies, &c.*, for the use of that congregation. Soon afterwards he devoted himself entirely to the study and teaching of music. In 1830 he resigned his post in St. Mary's and took to the stage. His first appearance in opera was in *Guy Mannering*, in Edinburgh. Later, he appeared at Covent Garden and Drury Lane. Finally, he became famous as an exponent of Scottish song, and as such sang before Queen Victoria at Taymouth Castle in 1842. While on tour he died at Quebec. When David Kennedy, another renowned Scots vocalist and erstwhile precentor, visited that city many years afterwards, he restored Wilson's tomb and left a sum of money for its proper preservation.

70. HOWARD (Wilson's *Collection*, 1825).

WILSON, MATTHEW (*c.* 1812–56, Glasgow), in an advertisement in *The Glasgow Herald* for Aug. 28, 1835, described himself as Conductor of the Music in St. Enoch's Church, and as teacher of the piano, singing, and musical composition. One of his pupils has left it on record that he was a good player and teacher, but that it was evident that he had difficulty in making ends meet. Apparently music alone did not suffice to provide a living for him, for he is known to have been for a time a 'traveller' for a tea merchant in the city. He was much in demand as accompanist at free-and-easy concerts in the city. Latterly he seems to have been in deep waters, for in the Glasgow Directory his name does not appear in the lists of teachers of music between 1850 and the year of his death. Another of his tunes appeared under the name 'Union Street' in *The Sacred Harp* of 1840, in which 'Drumclog' is found. He was best known as composer of popular songs, five of which (Nos. 8, 10, 13, 14, 21) are in *The Lyric Gems of Scotland* (Glasgow, 1856), all to words by William Cameron. Some of these, notably *Morag's Faery Glen*, had great popularity in their day.

49. DRUMCLOG.

WOODWARD, GEORGE. Of this composer's identity nothing has been determined.

114. CHANT IN B♭.

WOODWARD, RICHARD, Mus.Doc. (Dublin, 1744–77, Dublin), son of a vicar choral of Christ Church and St. Patrick's Cathedrals,

Dublin, was a chorister of the former and became organist in 1765; vicar choral in St. Patrick's, 1772. In 1771 he published a folio volume of his church music—one complete service, seven anthems, several chants, and a *Veni Creator Spiritus*. He published also a collection of songs, catches, and canons such as were popular in those days. For the most part his anthems are forgotten, but certain of his chants, notably the double one in D, are still in use. One of his canons, 'Let the words of my mouth', is engraved on his tomb in Christ Church Cathedral.

145. CHANT (D) IN A♭.

61–121. CHANT IN C.   *21.* CHANT (D) IN D.

WRIGHT, THOMAS (Stockton-on-Tees, 1763–1829, Wycliffe Keeley, near Barnard Castle), son of Robert Wright, organist in Stockton Church, 1766–97, and grandson of Thomas Wright the elder, who was the first organist of Stockton, *c.* 1758–60; was organist at Sedgefield, nine miles from Stockton, 1785–97, and soon acquired a high reputation as a teacher of piano, violin, and organ, and as an extemporizer on the organ; succeeded his father in Stockton Church, 1797, and continued there till 1817, when he resigned. After a period at Kirkleathen, near Redcar, he returned to Stockton and resumed teaching. He was in great demand as a music-teacher in the county of Durham and the North Riding of Yorkshire, and it was while fulfilling a professional service at Wycliffe Keeley that he was seized with fatal illness and died in the rectory there. He composed *Rusticity*, an operetta; a simple anthem, several songs, and a Concerto for piano and harpsichord, notable as being the first music to contain metronome marks to indicate speed value. He had a remarkable inventive gift, and produced a simple pocket metronome, an organ attachment to a square pianoforte, and other ingenious devices.

132. STOCKTON.

YATTENDON HYMNAL.—Last line. For 248 read 284.

PRINTED IN
GREAT BRITAIN
AT THE
UNIVERSITY PRESS
OXFORD
BY
JOHN JOHNSON
PRINTER
TO THE
UNIVERSITY

Communion in both kinds /272
Mar-Saba Mnastery p.509